Open Economy Macroeconomics in Developing Countries

Open Economy Macroeconomics in Developing Countries

Carlos A. Végh

The MIT Press
Cambridge, Massachusetts
London, England

MIT Press books may be purchased at special quantity discounts for business or sales promotional use. For information, please email special_sales@mitpress.mit.edu or write to Special Sales Department, The MIT Press, 55 Hayward Street, Cambridge, MA 02142.

This book was set in Syntax and Times New Roman by Westchester Book Group. Printed and bound in the United States of America.

Library of Congress Cataloging-in-Publication Data

Végh Gramont, Carlos A., 1958–
Open economy macroeconomics in developing countries / Carlos A. Végh.
pages cm
Includes bibliographical references and index.
ISBN 978-0-262-01890-6 (hbk. : alk. paper)
1. Fiscal policy—Developing countries. 2. Monetary policy—Developing countries. I. Title.
HJ1620.V44 2013
339.509172'4—dc23

2012046601

10 9 8 7 6 5 4 3 2 1

Contents

Preface

This book grew out of a desire to understand the fascinating world of macroeconomics in emerging markets and developing economies. When should emerging markets borrow? How do imperfect capital markets affect borrowing decisions? Why are boom–bust cycles in economic activity so frequent? How do relative prices adjust to different shocks? How do prices respond to a devaluation? What are the effects of terms of trade shocks? What are the macroeconomic consequences of capital inflows? What policy tools should be deployed to deal with them? What determines the optimal exchange rate regime? Why do emerging markets typically pursue procyclical fiscal policy? How long should a Central Bank defend the domestic currency by raising interest rates? At what cost? What can explain the simultaneous occurrence of banking and balance-of-payments crises? These are just some of the many questions that inspired this book and that, paradoxically, have also become relevant for many industrial countries in this post–Lehman world.

Methodologically, this book was driven by the belief that the world is too complicated to understand without the guiding hand of theoretical models, and that complicated models, as Milton Friedman once put it, are as "helpful" as a map with a one to one scale. A map is helpful precisely because, by abstracting from literally thousands of irrelevant details, it clearly brings out the big picture. We see no trees, just the forest. A map is thus the best example of how powerful a simple model can be.

The same should be true of economic models. The only point of writing down a model is to simplify reality and focus on what the researcher believes is the essence of the problem at hand. Unfortunately, as the field of international finance has increasingly relied (over-relied?) on quantitative methods, it has done so at the expense of teaching graduate students how to think in terms of simple models and truly grasp the conceptual foundations of open economy macroeconomics. There is no doubt that calibrated models have become an essential tool of the trade. They provide us with the luxury (for a social science) of having a small laboratory in which to evaluate the quantitative effects of different policies or transmission channels in a variety of models. In the best hands (and there are certainly many in the profession), this methodological tool is powerful and extremely helpful. Unfortunately, giving graduate students such a powerful tool without teaching them in depth the underlying theoretical models is like giving a child an

AK-47. The probability of a disastrous outcome is high. At best, they will use the AK-47 to kill a fly and, at worst, they will shoot indiscriminately with no specific target in mind. I often see bright graduate students who can solve the most intricate and complicated model on the computer but are, alas, incapable of answering even basic questions about the underlying model, the mechanisms involved, or the lessons to be learned from the exercise. A bright mind is indeed a terrible thing to waste.

In this spirit, this book takes the basic small open economy model and shows how it can be easily extended to answer most of the relevant macroeconomic questions in emerging markets. Frictions into the basic model are introduced only as needed to answer new questions. Every friction plays a role in understanding a certain question. We never complicate a model to make it "more realistic," which, to my mind, makes no methodological sense. By construction, a model is "unrealistic," and that is precisely why it is helpful. Assumptions need to be judged not on their "realism" but on their role in addressing a certain issue. For instance, it is obvious that a cash-in-advance constraint is an "unrealistic" assumption for an emerging economy because the implied zero interest rate elasticity violates any available estimate. But if the interest rate elasticity plays no role in understanding the question being asked and the cash-in-advance constraint greatly simplifies the model, then it makes sense to adopt such an assumption. In other words, assumptions cannot be judged in a vacuum; they should be judged in the context of the question being asked. In contrast, a cash-in-advance constraint would be a terrible assumption if we are trying to understand the role of the interest rate elasticity in generating an overshooting of the nominal exchange rate in response to an increase in money growth.

This is not, of course, the first graduate textbook that attempts to develop a rigorous analytical apparatus to understand relevant issues in open economy macroeconomics and international finance. Obstfeld and Rogoff's (1996) monumental work is rightly viewed as the gold standard in the field. Like Obstfeld and Rogoff, this book uses the basic small open economy paradigm as the starting point of our investigative journey. But the path that we follow quickly takes us into different territory since our aim is to use extensions/modifications of the basic model to understand emerging markets macroeconomics, rather than providing an exhaustive review of the foundations of international finance. Furthermore, and particularly in the monetary and exchange rate area, this book develops new paradigms to address certain issues of interest. This book should therefore be viewed as using the theoretical tools of international finance, as presented in Obstfeld and Rogoff, extending them as needed in several important directions, and then applying them to emerging markets' macroeconomics.

Nor is this book the first to cover a wide array of macroeconomic issues pertaining to developing countries. Agenor and Montiel's (1999) comprehensive review of development macroeconomics should rightly remain the main reference in this area. I choose to focus on a narrower set of issues—having to do mostly with monetary, fiscal, and exchange rate policy—reflecting my judgement of what policy issues are important and the desire to go as deep as possible into those issues within a unified conceptual framework.

Over the long gestation of the book, I have accumulated substantial debts:

• My greatest intellectual debt is clearly to Guillermo Calvo. Guillermo's influence throughout this book will be obvious to anybody who is familiar with his work. Guillermo was the intellectual leader of a young group of researchers (which I was fortunate to be part of, and also included Pablo Guidotti, Enrique Mendoza, and Carmen Reinhart) at the IMF's Research Department in the late 1980s and early 1990s. Through joint papers and innumerable conversations, he left his imprint on all of us. In my view, Guillermo's mind is the best example of what economic thinking should be all about. His instinct to identify relevant issues is uncanny. He will then strip down all irrelevant details and focus on the main point at the expense of everything else (and certainly make no apologies for it!). I learned from Guillermo that simplicity is something to strive for. As I often tell my students, complicating a model is easy, the tough part is to simplify it.

• My advisors and teachers at Chicago—Jacob Frenkel, Michael Mussa, Joshua Aizenman, and Bob Lucas—irremediably shaped my thinking on many of the issues touched in the book. Once at the IMF's Research Department, Mohsin Khan provided a stimulating research environment and Stanley Fischer became an inexhaustible source of support and wisdom and first put me in contact with Elizabeth Murry at MIT Press.

• Many parts of this book draw on, and were greatly influenced by, joint work that I have carried over the years with Michael Bordo, Guillermo Calvo, Sebastian Edwards, Stanley Fischer, Jose de Gregorio, Pablo Guidotti, Graciela Kaminsky, Anton Korinek, Amartya Lahiri, Sergio Rebelo, Carmen Reinhart, Ratna Sahay, Agustin Roitman, Ernesto Talvi, and Rajesh Singh.

• During my years at UCLA and the University of Maryland I have been extremely fortunate to have had many bright, insightful, and loyal students, many of whom have played a critical role in bringing this book to fruition. Their generosity—in terms of time and effort—has been nothing short of remarkable. They have really been my main source of inspiration—particularly at times when the light at the end of the tunnel was nowhere to be seen. With his boundless enthusiasm, Pablo Lopez Murphy (now at the IMF) was instrumental in convincing me to write this book and helped me plan and write some of the earlier chapters at UCLA. Once in Maryland, Guillermo Vuletin (now at Colby College) spent countless hours helping me with the empirics and MATLAB codes for later chapters. Once Guillermo left, Agustin Roitman (now at the IMF) took over and, until the very end, spent an inordinate amount of time and effort helping me with models for later chapters, MATLAB codes, and countless other tasks. Rajesh Singh (from UCLA and now at Iowa State University) provided extremely valuable comments and suggestions on every single chapter, helped me with many derivations and models in the book, and, until the very end, was a constant source of help. In the final stretch, Igor Zuccardi read carefully every chapter, rechecked all the derivations, and helped me improve models and exercises, Daniel Hernaiz and Maria Belen Sbrancia graciously endured my constant requests for updating data and revising boxes, and Hyunsoo Joo read tirelessly through many "final" drafts, helping me clean the final version.

- The time-consuming and difficult task of preparing the boxes for the book was handled deftly by Daniel Hernaiz, Fernando Im, Rong Qiang, Maria Belen Sbrancia, Agustin Roitman, and Guillermo Tolosa. Juliana Araujo, Carlos Garcia, Pablo Lopez Murphy, Nicolas Magud, and Jorge Restrepo were also kind enough to prepare boxes in areas of their expertise.
- Over the years many other students at UCLA, Maryland, and elsewhere provided very helpful comments and, by asking the right questions, helped me in claryfing my ideas and improving the exposition. While, unfortunately, they are too numerous to mention, I would like to single out Gustavo Adler, Ari Aisen, Laura Alfaro, Francisco Arizala, Julien Bengui, Javier Bianchi, Marcelo Catena, Sebastian Claro, Pablo Federico, Eduardo Ganapolsky, Inci Gumus, Ho Chi Pui, Fabio Kanzcuk, Ruy Lama, Eduardo Olaberria, Alvaro Riascos, and Yossi Yakhim.
- Anton Korinek, my colleague at Maryland, went way beyond the call of duty helping me with some of the models for chapter 17. Ed Buffie generously commented on many of the early chapters. Leonardo Auernheimer, Jorge Baldrich, Anton Korinek, Alessandro Rebucci, and Ratna Sahay provided very helpful comments on various chapters.
- The IMF's Research Department graciously provided me with the dataset used in the October 2007 World Economic Outlook chapter on capital inflows.
- At MIT Press, I found extremely supportive and, above all, infinitely patient acquiring editors in Elizabeth Murry, Jane MacDonald, and Emily Taber. Manuscript editor Dana Andrus ably guided me through the editing process.
- In addition to his encouragement over the years, my father, Alejandro, has always been an inspiring example of clear economic thinking in the real world.
- My wife, Ratna, my stepdaughter, Maansi, and my mother, Susan, were a constant source of support, strength, and encouragement throughout the process and, in the final stretch, did not complain about the endless number of evenings and weekends that I spent in my home office trying to finalize the book.

To all of them, my deepest thanks.

Introduction

The book is divided into four parts. The first two parts (Real building blocks and Monetary building blocks) develop the main theoretical models, while part III (Macroeconomic policy) and part IV (Applications) use these models to address important policy issues.

Part I: Real Building Blocks

Chapter 1 develops from first principles the standard intertemporal small open economy model, which serves as the backbone for all subsequent chapters. It derives the key proposition that in the presence of perfect capital mobility, households are able to smooth consumption over time regardless of the path of output. This is a major departure from closed economy models, in which consumption would fully reflect the variability of the aggregate endowment. The main policy implication of the basic model is that an open economy should adjust to permanent negative shocks but "finance" (through foreign borrowing) temporary negative shocks. This simple lesson is, of course, often ignored by countries in a futile attempt to finance permanent negative shocks and, in the process, build unsustainable levels of foreign debt.

Chapters 2, 3, and 4 analyze departures from the frictionless world of chapter 1 that prevent full consumption smoothing over time. Chapter 2 introduces frictions in international capital markets. In the extreme case of financial autarky, a temporary negative endowment shock will lead to higher domestic real interest rates. Intuitively, since the economy is unable to borrow from abroad as in chapter 1, higher real interest rates are needed to induce households to reduce consumption. The economy thus completely loses the ability to smooth consumption over time. Given that, in practice, most economies will lie somewhere in between the perfect capital mobility world of chapter 1 and financial autarky, our simple model would predict that negative output shocks should lead to some combination of trade deficits and higher real interest rates. In contrast, positive output shocks should lead to trade surpluses and lower real interest rates.

If the endowment path is uncertain, a natural friction in capital markets is the assumption that asset markets are incomplete, in the sense that no state-contingent claims are available. In this scenario, an open economy also loses some of the ability to smooth consumption over time, as well as across states of nature, which renders consumption procyclical (i.e., consumption is high in good times and low in bad times). Complete markets would, of course, recover the full consumption-smoothing result, an important theoretical proposition but not relevant in practice. A second major friction in international capital markets is the presence of sovereign risk. Countries' inability to commit to full repayment of their external debt limits their capacity to borrow against temporary negative shocks.

Chapter 3 studies departures from perfect consumption smoothing that stem from the presence of intertemporal distortions. Intertemporal distortions are policy-induced fluctuations in intertemporal relative prices that induce households to choose nonconstant paths of consumption. In practice, they could arise from temporary increases in taxes (import tariffs being a prime example) or from temporary changes in monetary policy. Chapter 3 focuses on the case of a temporary trade liberalization (i.e., a temporary reduction in import tariffs) and shows how such a policy will generate a socially inefficient consumption boom as households take advantage of temporarily cheaper prices. In and of itself, this theoretical result would be a prescription for policy inaction since no trade liberalization at all would always be preferable to any liberalization that has even a small probability to be reversed in the future. This situation changes if we allow for the trade liberalization to have wealth effects (e.g., through increases in productivity). In this case there is a trade-off between the wealth effect and the intertemporal distortion. The longer the policy is in place, the more likely that the wealth effect will dominate and hence that the policy will be welfare-improving. One could add many bells and whistles to this kind of model (as has been the case in the literature), but this tension between intertemporal distortions and wealth effects will remain at the core of the model.

Chapter 4 closes the first part of the book by introducing nontradable goods in the model of chapter 1. Nontradable goods imply a major departure from chapter 1 because consumption of nontradables cannot be smoothed out over time. As a result fluctuations in the endowment of nontradables will require changes in the relative price of nontradables in terms of tradables, which in turn may affect the consumption of tradable goods. While socially efficient, this departure from consumption smoothing has important implications for the dynamics of the model. The presence of nontradable goods also changes fundamentally how the economy adjusts to shocks. Consider a temporary increase in the demand for both tradable and nontradable goods. Since the small open economy faces an infinitely elastic supply of tradable goods, the higher demand will translate into a higher trade deficit. In contrast, the supply of nontradables is completely inelastic, and hence the higher demand will be reflected in an increase in the relative price of nontradable goods (a real appreciation). In other words, a temporarily higher aggregate demand will be reflected in higher consumption of tradable goods, a trade deficit, foreign borrowing, and a real appreciation. When the demand shock is reversed, consumption of tradables plummets, the trade balance goes into surplus, capital flows out, and there is a sharp real depreciation. This cyclical pattern has characterized innumerable boom–bust cycles in emerging economies. Again, one could add many bells and whistles to this basic model (as has been the case in the literature) but, at its core, it is the difference between the supply elasticity of tradables and nontradables that is responsible for the real appreciation–real depreciation cycles (which, in practice, cause costly sectoral reallocations).

Part II: Monetary Building Blocks

Part II of the book opens with chapter 5, which introduces money into the model of chapter 1. To focus exclusively on monetary phenomena (as opposed to focusing on the *interaction* between monetary and real phenomena), the chapter introduces money in such a way that money is a "veil" in the sense that changes in the money supply (under flexible exchange rates) or exchange rate (under predetermined exchange rates) do not affect real variables. In this context, we analyze how the economy responds to temporary changes in money demand. Despite a common misperception to the effect that exchange rate regimes are somehow irrelevant under flexible prices, we see how the economy's response critically depends on the exchange rate regime. Consider an anticipated fall in real money demand at time T. Under predetermined exchange rates, the rate of inflation remains firmly anchored by the (unchanged) rate of devaluation and the fall in real money demand at time T is accommodated by the public exchanging nominal money balances for foreign bonds at the Central Bank. Under flexible exchange rates, however, the anticipated fall in real money demand requires that the inflation rate increases *before* time T so as to gradually erode real money balances before the shock actually occurs, which in turn calls for the nominal interest rate to increase over time before time T. The behavior of inflation and interest rates is thus fundamentally different across exchange rate regimes. In particular, inflation and interest rates are more variable under flexible than under predetermined exchange rates.

As already mentioned, money is a veil in chapter 5 and hence monetary and exchange rate policy have no real effects. The following three chapters introduce frictions in the model of chapter 5 that will imply that monetary/exchange rate policy will have real effects. Chapter 6 assumes away the existence of interest-bearing bonds, which can be construed as limited capital mobility. In such a world, changes in either the level or the rate of change of the nominal exchange rate have real effects. By reducing real money balances, a devaluation (i.e., an increase in the level of the nominal exchange rate) leads to a fall in consumption, a trade surplus, and hence a gain in international reserves. By the same token, by reducing the nominal money supply, a reduction in the level of domestic credit would also increase international reserves at the Central Bank. This is the essential mechanism behind the so-called monetary approach to the balance of payments, which was at the core of all financial programming done at the IMF when most of the world operated under predetermined exchange rates. The Fund would set a target for the increase in international reserves and, using essentially this kind of model, back up the change in domestic credit needed to accomplish such a goal. This mechanism remains valid today, of course, for any country operating under predetermined exchange rates (including exchange rate bands) or under flexible exchange rate regimes that include regular intervention by the Central Bank.

By introducing endogenous labor allocation across production sectors, chapter 6 also tackles the important question of what are the effects of a nominal devaluation on prices. The chapter shows that even though prices are fully flexible, prices of nontradable goods respond only sluggishly to the devaluation. The reason is that households reduce consumption to rebuild real money balances and the excess supply of nontradables causes their relative price to fall. This real depreciation requires prices of nontradables to rise less than prices of tradables (which increase, of course, by the extent of the devaluation).

Chapter 7 introduces a key friction in the model of chapter 5 whereby temporary changes in nominal interest rates have real effects. Specifically, money is introduced through a cash-in-advance constraint that requires money to be used to purchase the consumption good. As a result the opportunity cost of holding money (i.e., the nominal interest rate) becomes part of the "effective" price of consumption. Temporary changes in the nominal interest rate will thus lead to a nonconstant path of the effective price of consumption, which, through the mechanism highlighted in chapter 3, will induce temporary changes in consumption. This simple model thus provides a plausible explanation whereby monetary/exchange rate policy changes lead to boom–bust cycles in consumption (and hence real exchange rates in the presence of nontradable goods for the reasons highlighted in chapter 4).

Chapter 8 closes part II of the book by introducing sticky prices into the model of chapter 5, by far the most popular friction when it comes to generating nonneutralities of monetary/exchange rate policy. In such a Mundell–Fleming model in modern clothes, an increase in the money supply leads to (1) higher consumption and—since output is demand-determined—higher output, (2) increases in both the nominal and real exchange rate (i.e., a nominal and real depreciation) thus explaining the high co-movement found in the data, and (3) the possibility of an overshooting of the nominal exchange rate on impact (the idea that the nominal exchange rate will rise by more in the short run than in the long run). While in the literature sticky-prices models come in many varieties of colors and flavors, these essential channels will always be present and are thus worthy of careful understanding. We then develop a sticky-wages model that allows us to illustrate the notion of how a negative productivity shock may lead to involuntary unemployment and how a devaluation could help the economy move immediately to what would be its flexible price equilibrium. This is the best-case scenario for a devaluation often heard in policy circles, the most famous being Rudi Dornbusch's call for a devaluation in Mexico in 1994. Needless to say, the model does not incorporate other factors such as policy credibility, which are ignored at the policy makers' peril as the disastrous consequences of such a devaluation made abundantly clear.

Parts III and IV put to use the theoretical tools developed in parts I and II to a variety of important macroeconomic issues relevant for emerging markets. While the coverage is not intended to be exhaustive, it reflects my views of what issues are important from a conceptual point of view and/or what issues lend themselves to be analyzed with the tools developed in parts I and II.

Part III: Macroeconomic Policy

Reflecting the traditional emphasis of open economy macroeconomics, part II of the book has carried out the discussion of monetary/exchange rate policy in the context of two main nominal anchors: the money supply and the nominal exchange rate. In recent times, however, the nominal interest rate has clearly become the policy instrument of choice around the world. This shift has reflected, first, a disenchantment with the money supply as a nominal anchor given the often unpredictable behavior of real money demand and, second, the disastrous consequences of many exchange rate pegs that, despite auspicious and highly touted beginnings, have ended in costly balance of payments and financial crises (topics discussed in part IV).

Chapter 9 is devoted entirely to study the use of a nominal interest rate as the main policy instrument. A key theme of the chapter is the fact that care is needed when it comes to specifying interest rate policy because, in the simplest monetary model, an interest rate peg leads to price level indeterminacy. We take the view that this is a problem with the theory and not with the real world. The problem lies in that, in the simplest model, monetary policy is not fully specified if just the nominal interest rate is set by the monetary authority. We discuss several ways in which we can fully specify monetary policy so as to generate a model that we can use to think about the effects of interest rate policy on the economy. We show that, interestingly enough, just assuming sticky prices does not get rid of the fundamental indeterminacy mentioned above; it just becomes a higher order indeterminacy in the sense that there is nothing tying down the initial level of the inflation rate and there is thus a multiplicity of equilibrium paths. Assuming a Taylor-type rule gets rid of this higher order indeterminacy and provides us with an extremely tractable model in which to study, for instance, how the economy reacts to a reduction in the inflation target, in the spirit of the so-called inflation-targeting regimes seen in many countries around the world.

Up to this point, the book has dealt with positive, as opposed to normative, analysis. Chapter 10 focuses on how fiscal and monetary policy *should* be conducted. As a benchmark, the chapter first presents a model in which it is optimal to smooth consumption tax rates over time. This is, of course, not surprising given the intuition developed in chapter 3 regarding the social inefficiency of introducing intertemporal distortions. Deviations from this paradigm are then studied. Notably—and in line with the intuition developed in chapter 2—in the presence of uncertainty and incomplete markets, it is no longer possible to smooth tax rates over time. We show how in this case optimal tax rates will co-move negatively with consumption, falling in good times and increasing in bad times, which is consistent with the evidence of tax rate procyclicality observed in emerging markets. Market incompleteness could also rationalize the observed procyclicality of government spending in emerging markets compared to the acyclicality or countercyclicality found in industrial countries. An additional—and perhaps complementary—explanation is the presence of political pressures to increase public spending in good times. Turning to optimal monetary policy, we show an example where the Friedman rule (i.e., setting the nominal interest rate to zero) is optimal and show how collection costs could explain optimal and possibly time-varying deviations from the Friedman rule.

Chapter 11 turns to a perennial question in open economy macroeconomics: Which exchange rate regime is better? We first show how, in the cash-in-advance world of chapter 7, flexible exchange rates completely insulate the economy from nominal foreign shocks, such as changes in foreign inflation. In contrast, predetermined exchange rates have the upper hand when it comes to real shocks. This example clearly contradicts the popular notion that holds that in the absence of sticky prices, the exchange rate regime is irrelevant. Following chapter 8, the chapter then introduces sticky prices and identifies the conditions needed for the famous Mundell–Fleming dictum to hold: predetermined exchange rates are better in dealing with monetary shocks while flexible exchange rates are better in dealing with real shocks. Intuitively, the endogeneity of the money supply under predetermined exchange rates allows for quick and efficient adjustments to monetary shocks. In contrast, real shocks typically require a change in relative prices that is more easily effected under flexible exchange rates through changes in the nominal exchange rate.

While sticky prices are the most popular friction, one could argue that asset market frictions are equally, if not more, prevalent in emerging countries. Modeling asset market frictions as asset market segmentation (i.e., a fraction of the households does not have access to asset markets), chapter 11 shows that the Mundell–Fleming dictum is turned on its head: predetermined exchange rates are now better in dealing with real shocks while flexible exchange rates are better when it comes to nominal shocks. The intuition is simply that changes in real money balances required by monetary shocks are more easily accommodated through changes in the nominal exchange rate whereas, by keeping purchasing power constant across periods, predetermined exchange rates allow some risk sharing over time in response to real shocks.

Chapter 12 closes part III by looking at the controversial role of "real anchors." The expression "real anchors" refers to policy makers' attempt to target a certain level of a real variable. For example, policy makers may try to set a more depreciated level of the currency in real terms (i.e., a higher real exchange rate) in an attempt to improve the trade balance. This practice is fraught with dangers because, by forgoing a nominal anchor, policy makers run the risk of nominal instability given that there is nothing to anchor down the public's expectations about future prices or the level of the nominal exchange rate. We first look at real exchange rate targeting in the context of the cash-in-advance model of chapter 7 and conclude that policy makers can only set a temporarily higher level of the real exchange rate but at the cost of higher inflation and/or higher domestic real interest rates. Higher inflation and/or higher domestic real interest rates are needed to curtail demand for nontradable goods, which leads to a fall in their relative price. We then switch our attention to purchasing power parity (PPP) rules, which typically devalue the domestic currency in an attempt to keep a roughly constant real exchange rate. These PPP rules can lead to nominal indeterminacies in a flexible prices world or more inflation in response to shocks that require a real appreciation in a world with sticky inflation.

Another real anchor that has been observed—notably in Chile—is the real interest rate. We show that a "pure" real interest rate target leaves the inflation rate undetermined and hence should lead to nominal instability. However, when changes in the real interest rate are set according to the deviation of the actual inflation rate from an inflation target, the economy is well behaved as long as the inflation target is fully credible. Finally, we see how threshold rules, whereby policy makers announce changes in policy conditional on certain outcomes (e.g., raising import tariffs if the trade deficit reaches certain threshold), can lead to multiple equilibria and trigger the precise outcomes that they are purported to avoid!

Part IV: Applications

The last part of the book uses many of the theoretical tools developed in earlier chapters to analyze in detail some important policy issues. Chapter 13 looks at inflation stabilization programs. High inflation (relative to industrial countries) has been a chronic problem of developing countries for more than fifty years. After many failed attempts, most emerging markets seem to have finally conquered the scourge of high inflation, but the problem occasionally resurfaces (Argentina and Venezuela immediately come to mind), and policy makers, keenly aware of how sensitive markets' expectations are to renewed inflation, keep it under close watch. While inflation stabilization plans in industrial countries typically entail output costs, the real effects of such programs in emerging markets seem to depend on which nominal anchor is used. Under predetermined exchange rates, the economy initially experiences a consumption and output boom, trade deficits, and real appreciation followed by a later bust. Under flexible exchange rates, there seems to be an initial recession, in line with the experience of industrial countries. Put differently, the choice appears to be between recession now (under flexible exchange rates) versus recession later (under predetermined exchange rates). The chapter develops several explanations for the boom–bust cycle under predetermined exchange rates, including lack of policy credibility (which introduces intertemporal distortions as in chapters 3 and 7) and inflation inertia.

Chapter 14 deals with a recurrent theme for emerging markets: how to deal with the macroeconomic effects of capital inflows. While capital inflows undoubtedly boost long-term growth by providing much needed financing for many investment opportunities that may otherwise remain unexploited, they entail short-term macroeconomic dislocations in the form of an overheated economy, a real appreciation of the currency, and trade/current account deficits. In particular, countries often fear the negative effects of a real appreciation on the domestic manufacturing industry. We develop a version of our sticky-prices model of chapter 8 to replicate most of the macroeconomic effects of capital inflows observed in the data as the response to a temporary reduction in world real interests rates or a temporary increase in domestic aggregate demand. We conclude that while a real appreciation will occur regardless of the shock and the exchange rate regime in place, the bulk of the initial real appreciation occurs through higher nontradables inflation under predetermined exchange rates and through a fall in the nominal exchange rate under flexible exchange rates. Hence, by adopting more flexible exchange rate regimes, emerging countries could avoid, if not the real appreciation, some of the inflationary consequences of capital inflows. We then analyze some common policy responses to episodes of capital inflows: foreign exchange market intervention and fiscal tightening. While both policies can help in alleviating the initial real appreciation, they come at the cost of higher inflation in the former case and output costs in the latter. As usual, there is no free lunch. The same is true of taxes on short-term capital inflows that may, at best, shift the composition of flows toward longer horizons but at the cost of a myriad of inefficiencies and rent-seeking activities and making credit more expensive for small and medium-sized firms.

Chapter 15 focuses on "dollarization," which refers to the phenomenon of a foreign currency replacing the domestic currency as a store of value, unit of account, and medium of exchange. Dollarization is a widespread phenomenon not only in Latin America but also in countries such as Egypt, Israel, Lebanon, Poland, and Turkey. We reserve the term "currency substitution" for the case in which a foreign currency is used only as a medium of exchange. To model currency substitution, we introduce a foreign currency in our benchmark monetary model of chapter 5. In such a model, a fall in domestic inflation reduces the ratio of foreign to domestic currency. In practice, however, currency substitution has not come down substantially as a response to lower inflation, a puzzle referred to as "hysteresis." We show that introducing a fixed cost of switching among currencies creates an inaction band within which currency substitution remains constant even if inflation falls.

A typical concern raised in dollarized economies is that monetary policy can lose the ability to determine nominal quantities because it cannot control the relevant monetary aggregate, which includes the domestic value of foreign currency. We show an example—perfect substitution between the two currencies—where the exchange rate is indeed indeterminate. While admittedly extreme, this result calls attention to the fact that the nominal exchange rate is likely to become extremely volatile in economies with high currency substitution operating under flexible exchange rates. The chapter closes by developing a stochastic portfolio model to illustrate the critical difference between asset substitution (i.e., holding foreign currency as store of value) and currency substitution. In such a model, the optimal share of foreign currency denominated assets (i.e., the sum of foreign currency and foreign-currency bonds) will depend on real, as opposed to nominal, returns. A reduction in inflation would thus not lead to any change in the level of asset substitution even if currency substitution falls. Since what we really measure in practice is asset substitution, this suggests that the hysteresis puzzle mentioned above is no puzzle after all and simply reflects an incorrect interpretation of the empirical evidence.

Chapter 16 turns our attention to balance-of-payments crises, an unfortunately common occurrence in emerging markets with the collapse of the Argentinean Convertibility plan in 2001 being perhaps the most spectacular example in recent times. In this context, the unsustainability of a predetermined exchange rate regime reflects the monetary authority's need to monetize an underlying fiscal deficit. The public refuses to keep these money balances and exchanges them for foreign assets at the Central Bank window. When the Central Bank runs out of international reserves, it is forced to give up the peg and float the currency. We add to the traditional model the possibility of defending the peg by raising interest rates to increase the demand for interest-bearing domestic-currency assets. In the context of a chapter 7 type model, we show how we would expect the balance-of-payments crisis to be preceded by a consumption boom, real appreciation, and trade deficits, followed by a drastic fall in consumption and real depreciation, a boom–bust cycle reminiscent of the one characterized in chapter 4. Finally, we let the monetary authority choose optimally the time of abandonment once it becomes known that the regime is unsustainable. Unless there are costs of abandonment, it is optimal to give up the peg right away, which clearly suggests that prolonging the agony, as most often happens in practice, is an exercise in futility.

Perhaps fittingly, chapter 17 closes the book by analyzing financial crises, the latest addition to an already filled catalog of cataclysms that can affect not only emerging markets but industrial countries as well. We begin by illustrating the extremely high levels of leverage—defined as the ratio of assets to net worth—observed in the run up to Lehman Brothers' fall in September 2008. Leverage reached levels of 30 in several major financial institutions. The temptation to become highly leveraged is perhaps almost irresistible because a financial institution that is operating with a leverage ratio of 30 may make an excess return of 29 times the spread between the return on the asset and the borrowing rate. We use some simple arithmetic to show that if leverage is, for example, 30, a fall in asset prices of just 3 percent will wipe out net worth completely, which suggests that many financial empires resembled more a house of cards. We then put some content into the concept of leverage by developing a simple model that shows how a higher tolerance for risk, lower uncertainty, and more productive investment opportunities lead to an increase in the optimal level of leverage. While this model cannot explain "excess leverage" (i.e., leverage beyond that explained by fundamentals), it could explain some of the increase in leverage in the early 2000s.

We then illustrate the potential amplification of shocks due to financial frictions and how the development of a shadow banking system could have led to higher housing prices by raising the liquidity associated with the underlying asset. We also provide a rationale for a low interest rate policy in response to the collapse of asset prices. In terms of how the financial crisis propagated, we offer a theoretical rationale for the observed decoupling–recoupling cycle whereby emerging countries first seemed immune to the crisis in the United States but were later affected. We close the chapter by developing a model to explain the simultaneous occurrence of banking and balance of payments crises (the so-called twin crises).[1]

1. All chapters contain a set of exercises that is an integral part of the discussion. Answer keys are available at the book's website.

1 The Basic Intertemporal Model

1.1 Introduction

What is the fundamental difference between a closed and an open economy? Consider first a pure exchange economy (i.e., an economy with perishable goods and no production). A closed economy (i.e., an economy that does not trade in goods and assets with the rest of the world) is forced to consume its own endowment. Consumption will thus be high in times of plenty and low in times of distress. Even though it would be socially desirable, the closed economy has no means of saving in "sunny days" to support higher consumption in "rainy days." In contrast, an open economy can borrow from the rest of the world during bad times and repay in good times. In other words, an open economy can engage in *intertemporal trade*. By borrowing and lending from the rest of the world, an open economy can completely sever the link between today's consumption and today's endowment. In particular, despite a fluctuating endowment path, it may choose to fully smooth consumption. The ability of an open economy to engage in intertemporal trade is thus at the core of modern open economy macroeconomics.

Consider now a production economy. The ability to invest provides a closed economy with some ability for transferring resources over time. However, the closed economy is constrained to invest only what it saves. Hence, to take advantage of a profitable investment opportunity, the closed economy is forced to save by reducing consumption. In contrast, by running current account imbalances (i.e., by borrowing from or lending to the rest of the world), an open economy may choose to invest more or less than what it saves. This allows the open economy to, once again, sever all ties between today's consumption (i.e., saving decisions) and investment. An open economy can thus borrow from abroad to finance a profitable investment opportunity without the need to reduce current consumption to generate domestic savings.

Given the central role of the current account in open economy macroeconomics, it comes as no surprise that the analysis of the determinants of the current account constitutes the core of open economy macroeconomics. In the early days of open economy macroeconomics, current account determination was essentially viewed as a static (i.e., one period) problem and limited to the determination of the trade balance. The emphasis was thus put on relative prices as the key determinant of a country's trade balance.[1] However, as Sachs (1981, p. 212) aptly put it, "[a] one-period theory of the current account that describes a static balance of import and exports makes as much sense as a one-period theory of saving and investment." Saving is, by definition, an intertemporal decision whereby an agent is willing to sacrifice consumption today for greater future consumption. Investment is, of course, just the other side of the coin. A static analysis is thus fundamentally flawed.[2]

Since saving and investment are *intertemporal* choices, the natural conceptual framework to analyze them is in the context of an intertemporal model (i.e., a multi-period model). As a result intertemporal models of the current account (pioneered by Sachs 1981) constitute the foundation of modern open economy macroeconomics. Intertemporal models have further proved to be much more than a natural and elegant apparatus and have delivered results that critically depend on the intertemporal dimension of the analysis. The more relevant example is the very different reaction of the current account to permanent and temporary shocks, which a static model would completely miss.

If anything, current account determination is even more critical for developing countries because they typically face larger shocks, which implies that they should rely more on current account imbalances to smooth consumption over time. It is only natural therefore that our journey into the macroeconomic world of developing countries should start by a detailed analysis of the modern intertemporal approach to the current account. Methodologically, as well, this model provides the foundation for the rest of the book.

To isolate the basic ideas, section 1.2 abstracts from investment and develops the basic intertemporal model in the context of an endowment economy. Section 1.3 then derives the central result of this chapter: consumers choose to keep consumption flat over time regardless of the path of output. To achieve perfect consumption smoothing, consumers borrow in bad times and lend in good times. The trade balance thus acts as a shock absorber, improving in good times and worsening in bad times. The critical assumptions behind this result are perfect capital mobility and no intertemporal distortions, both of which will be relaxed in subsequent chapters. Section 1.4 then turns to the economy's response to unanticipated and negative output shocks. If the output shock is permanent, the economy adjusts immediately by reducing consumption. If the shock is temporary, however, the economy runs a current account deficit (i.e., borrows from abroad) during bad times to keep consumption constant over time. In other words, *the economy adjusts to permanent negative shocks but finances temporary ones*. Since there are no distortions in this economy, such response is socially optimal. Hence, from a normative point of view, the model yields the key policy dictum that an open economy should adjust to a permanent negative shock (i.e., reduce consumption) but finance a temporary one (i.e., borrow from abroad). This provides

1. Obstfeld (1987) offers an insightful account of the evolution of ideas in international finance.

2. Interestingly, while the analysis of an individual's saving and investment decisions in a closed economy was rightly casted in an intertemporal context by Irving Fisher in 1930, it took the economics profession roughly fifty years to take the seemingly obvious step of extending Fisher's analysis to an open economy.

a theoretical rationale for efforts aimed at ensuring that developing countries have access to external finance during bad times—either through well-functioning international capital markets or through multilateral financial organizations such as the International Monetary Fund.

A key prediction of the basic model is thus that the trade balance and the current account are procyclical; in other words, they improve in good times and worsen in bad times. In practice, however, the trade balance behaves countercyclically (it worsens in good times and improves in bad times). This stylized fact provides the main motivation for introducing investment into the model in section 1.5. After all, we expect investment to increase in good times and fall in bad times. Since the current account is the difference between saving and investment, changes in investment should, all else equal, lead to countercyclical changes in the trade balance and current account. The cyclical behavior of the external accounts should thus depend on the relative strength of the saving and investment effects. The results in section 1.5 make clear this intuition by showing that the response of the current account to, say, a positive productivity shock depends on the duration of the shock. The longer the shock, the smaller is the saving effect and the more likely that the investment effect will dominate, leading to a deterioration in the current account (countercyclical external accounts). The model can thus be made consistent with the stylized facts.

1.2 The Model

Consider a small open economy inhabited by a large number of identical consumers. There is no uncertainty and consumers are blessed with perfect foresight. There is only one (tradable and nonstorable) good. Since the economy is small in goods markets, it takes the price of the tradable good as given by the rest of the world. The economy receives an exogenous amount of the good at each point in time (i.e., there is no production). Capital mobility is perfect in the sense that consumers can borrow/lend in international capital markets as much as they wish—subject to a solvency constraint to be discussed below—at an exogenously given real interest rate, r_t. We will assume that r_t is constant over time at the value r.

1.2.1 Consumer's Problem

Preferences

The consumer's lifetime utility as of time $t = 0$, U_0, is represented by

$$U_0 = \int_0^T u(c_t)e^{-\beta t}dt, \tag{1.1}$$

where c_t is consumption at time t, $\beta(> 0)$ is the subjective discount rate, and $u(.)$ is the instantaneous utility function, which is continuously differentiable, strictly increasing, and strictly concave.[3] The parameter $T(>0)$ denotes the individual's life span.[4] In addition, to ensure an interior optimum, we assume that $u(.)$ satisfies

$$\lim_{c_t \to 0} u'(c_t) = \infty. \tag{1.2}$$

An important assumption behind expression (1.1) is that instantaneous utility depends only on c_t and discounting is exponential. Such a formulation of lifetime utility is not only more tractable than alternative specifications—where today's utility may depend on past or future consumption and/or other types of discounting are assumed—but also exhibits a key property known as time consistency. Time consistency implies that the consumer's tastes remain unchanged over time, and hence plans formulated at time 0 (which are the plans that will be characterized below) would be chosen again if the consumer reoptimized later on.[5]

Flow Budget Constraint

Let b_t denote net foreign assets denominated in terms of the tradable good held by the consumer at time t.[6] The consumer's flow budget constraint is thus given by

$$\dot{b}_t = rb_t + y_t - c_t, \tag{1.3}$$

where y_t denotes the endowment flow received by the consumer at time t. Equation (1.3) says that the consumer will accumulate net foreign assets to the extent that his/her total income (interest receipts and endowment) exceeds his/her consumption. Notice that the stock of net foreign assets, b_t, is a predetermined variable in the sense that, barring some exogenous change, it is a continuous function of time.[7] The consumer is born with some net foreign assets (b_0).

Basic Formulation

The consumer's maximization problem can be formally stated as

$$\max_{c_t,\, t\in[0,T]} \int_0^T u(c_t)e^{-\beta t}dt$$

3. To keep notation as compact as possible, we will use the notation x_t to indicate that variable x is a function of time. In other words, x_t should be read as $x(t)$.

4. We have assumed a finite horizon to highlight some subtle issues involved in the infinite horizon formulation, which will be our main setup throughout this book.

5. Exercises 1 and 2 at the end of this chapter ask the reader to verify, in the context of a discrete version of this model, that the preferences in the text are indeed time consistent and show how alternative discounting methods (exercise 1) and non–time separability (exercise 2) may generate time inconsistent preferences. (See Calvo 1996 for a detailed analysis of time inconsistency and the proof that, in the continuous time setting of this chapter, preferences are time consistent.)

6. In our framework with one agent and one asset, there is really no difference between net and gross assets.

7. By exogenous change, we mean, for instance, a foreign grant. A foreign grant would discretely change the consumer's *stock* of net foreign assets. Barring such events, the stock of net foreign assets must be a continuous function of time because it can only change as a result of saving or dissaving (which are *flows*). This is the reason why the evolution over time of predetermined variables is usually characterized by some accumulation equation such as (1.3).

subject to

$$\dot{b}_t = rb_t + y_t - c_t,$$

$$b_T \geq 0, \tag{1.4}$$

$$b_0 \text{ given.}$$

Condition (1.4) is typically referred to as a "no–Ponzi games condition" and requires that the consumer not "die" with positive debt.[8] In addition, since the instantaneous utility function is strictly increasing in consumption (i.e., there is no satiation point), it will never be optimal for the individual to "die" with assets because increasing consumption at some point in time would always lead to higher lifetime utility. In other words, at an optimum, $b_T \leq 0$. Combining this condition with the constraint, given by (1.4), that the consumer not "die" with positive debt yields the condition

$$b_T = 0. \tag{1.5}$$

Hence, in solving the basic problem, we can use condition (1.5) instead of (1.4).

As it stands, this problem cannot be solved using standard calculus techniques. Standard calculus techniques deal with problems aimed at finding maxima or minima of functions of a real variable. This problem instead requires maximizing a functional; that is, a quantity that depends on a function rather than on real numbers. The branches of mathematics that study the maximization or minimization of quantities that depend on functions are referred to as the calculus of variations and optimal control (e.g., see Reed 1998).[9]

The way we will proceed here is to transform this problem into one that can be solved with standard Lagrange multiplier techniques. To this end, we will reformulate this maximization problem subject to an uncountable number of constraints (i.e., flow constraints at each point of time) into a maximization problem subject to one constraint (i.e., an intertemporal constraint).[10]

Intertemporal Budget Constraint

To derive the consumer's intertemporal budget constraint, rewrite equation (1.3) as

$$\left(\dot{b}_t - rb_t\right) e^{-rt} = (y_t - c_t)\, e^{-rt}.$$

8. After Charles Ponzi (1882–1949), an Italian swindler who ran well-known scams in Boston by paying off early investors with money coming from subsequent investors.

9. Optimal control is a generalization of calculus of variations that enables us to deal with corner solutions. However, for the problems that are analyzed in this book one can consider them "perfect substitutes." We will use optimal control techniques starting in chapter 6.

10. Throughout this book we will proceed in this way whenever it is straightforward to use the flow constraint to derive the intertemporal constraint.

Integrating forward, we obtain

$$\int_0^T (\dot{b}_t - rb_t)e^{-rt}dt = \int_0^T (y_t - c_t)e^{-rt}dt. \tag{1.6}$$

The left-hand side of equation (1.6) can be solved to yield

$$\int_0^T (\dot{b}_t - rb_t)e^{-rt}dt = \int_0^T \frac{d\left(b_t e^{-rt}\right)}{dt}dt = e^{-rT}b_T - b_0. \tag{1.7}$$

Substituting (1.7) into (1.6), we have

$$e^{-rT}b_T - b_0 = \int_0^T (y_t - c_t)e^{-rt}dt. \tag{1.8}$$

Taking into account condition (1.5), we can rewrite the consumer's intertemporal budget constraint (1.8) as

$$b_0 + \int_0^T y_t e^{-rt}dt = \int_0^T c_t e^{-rt}dt. \tag{1.9}$$

This intertemporal constraint is highly intuitive as it simply says that the present discounted value of consumption (right-hand side, RHS) must be equal to the consumer's wealth (left-hand side, LHS), given by the initial stock of net foreign assets plus the present discounted value of his/her endowment.

Alternative Formulation

The consumer's problem can then be restated as choosing a path for c_t, $t \in [0, T]$, to maximize (1.1) subject to (1.9). We can study this problem by means of standard Lagrange-multiplier techniques. The Lagrangian is given by

$$\mathcal{L} = \int_0^T u(c_t)e^{-\beta t}dt + \lambda\left(b_0 + \int_0^T y_t e^{-rt}dt - \int_0^T c_t e^{-rt}dt\right),$$

where λ is the Lagrange multiplier.

It can be shown that the first-order condition with respect to c_t is given by[11]

$$u'(c_t)e^{-\beta t} = \lambda e^{-rt}. \tag{1.10}$$

11. Appendix 1.7.1 at the end of this chapter shows how to obtain this first-order condition using (1) a discrete time approximation referred to as "pointwise optimization" or (2) "perturbation" methods. The term "pointwise optimization" captures the idea that, intuitively, the consumer is choosing optimal consumption at each point in time. In practice, pointwise optimization allows us to "ignore" the integral when differentiating. Notice that we are choosing consumption at each (uncountable) point of time, so this first-order condition holds for any c_t, $t \in [0, T]$.

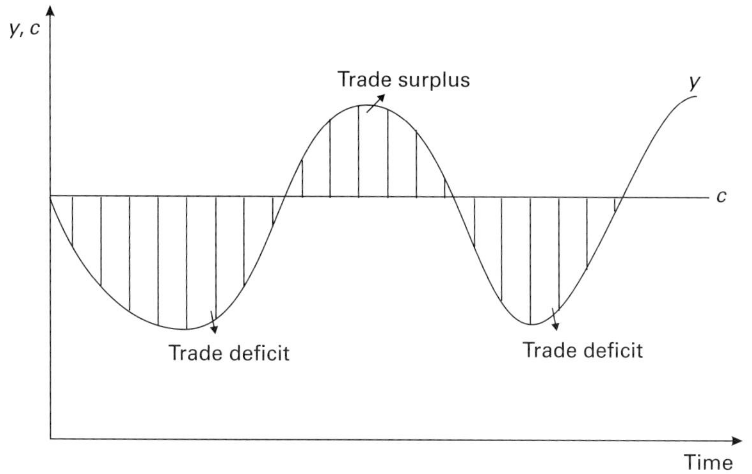

Figure 1.1
Perfect foresight paths

As is the case in standard constrained optimization, the derivative of the Lagrangian with respect to the Lagrange multiplier yields back the intertemporal budget constraint (1.9).

Assuming $\beta = r$, first-order condition (1.10) implies that

$$u'(c_t) = \lambda. \tag{1.11}$$

At an optimum the consumer equates his/her marginal utility of consumption to the marginal utility of wealth (the Lagrange multiplier). This simple condition constitutes the whole foundation of the modern intertemporal approach to open economy macroeconomics. Since λ is some fixed number and we have not imposed any restrictions on the path of output, condition (1.11) delivers the strong implication that the path of consumption will be flat over time regardless of the path of output. In other words, anticipated output fluctuations have no effect on consumption (see figure 1.1). As discussed in more detail below, this perfect consumption-smoothing outcome is the result of a preference for consumption smoothing (as a consequence of a strictly concave utility function) combined with perfect access to capital markets that allows consumers to borrow in bad times and lend in good times at a constant real interest rate.[12]

We should make two important observations about the assumption $\beta = r$ (which are, of course, valid for the infinite-horizon formulation below).[13] First, if r were still constant over time but different from β (i.e., $\beta \neq r$), there would be consumption tilting, in the sense that the path

12. Appendix 1.7.2 verifies that the consumption path identified by first-order condition (1.11) is indeed a maximum.

13. As shown in exercise 3 at the end of the chapter, the assumption $\beta = r$ also implies that the system has a zero root (or unit root in the discrete-time version). The interpretation and numerical implications of a unit root are discussed in chapter 2 (box 2.4).

of consumption would be either increasing or decreasing over time (see exercise 4 at the end of this chapter). From a conceptual point of view, however, such consumption dynamics are uninteresting because they are unrelated to the behavior of any driving force in the model. In other words, there is little we can learn from these cases. In addition—as also illustrated in exercise 4—in an infinite-horizon setting, an optimal consumption plan may not even exist if $\beta \neq r$.

Second, we could have a fluctuating world real interest rate over time. As illustrated in exercise 5 at the end of this chapter, whenever $r_t > \beta$, consumption would be increasing, reflecting the fact that households discount utility at a lower rate than the market discounts resources. The converse is true whenever $r_t < \beta$. These fluctuations in consumption are optimal since they reflect fluctuations in the world real interest rate. Quantitatively, however, fluctuations in consumption as a response to fluctuating real interest rates seem to be small.[14] For real interest rates to matter quantitatively, one would need to introduce a different channel through which they can have real effects such as affecting the effective cost of labor for firms (Neumeyer and Perri 2005).

1.2.2 Infinite-Horizon Formulation

The most attractive formulation of our basic problem relies on an infinite horizon since it avoids an arbitrary cutoff point at T. There are, however, some mathematical subtleties involved in the infinite-horizon formulation.[15] Consider first the extension of preferences to an infinite horizon. Lifetime utility now becomes

$$U_0 = \int_0^{\infty} u(c_t)e^{-\beta t}dt. \tag{1.12}$$

Notice that (1.12) involves an improper integral that might or might not converge. Clearly, if the integral did not converge for some consumption paths, we would not be able to rank them.[16]

As in the finite-horizon case, we can formally state the maximization problem as

$$\max_{c_t,\, t\in[0,\infty)} \int_0^{\infty} u(c_t)e^{-\beta t}dt$$

14. See, for instance, Mendoza (1991) and Correia, Neves, and Rebelo (1995).

15. See Calvo (1996) for an insightful discussion.

16. The simplest way of ensuring that this integral converges is to assume that the instantaneous utility function is bounded from above (i.e., that there is satiation). In such a case, however, we would need to ensure that the parameters of the problem are such that the satiation point is not reached so that we can apply the arguments below regarding the transversality condition. In general, we would need to check whether this integral converges to ensure that the problem is well-defined. Exercise 4 at the end of the chapter shows that for a CES utility function, this integral always converges in the case of $r = \beta$ and derives sufficient conditions for convergence in the case of $r \neq \beta$. See Chakravarty (1962) and Chiang (1992, ch. 5) for a detailed discussion.

subject to

$$\dot{b}_t = rb_t + y_t - c_t,$$

$$\lim_{t \longrightarrow \infty} e^{-rt} b_t \geq 0, \tag{1.13}$$

b_0 given.

With an infinite horizon, the no-Ponzi games condition takes the form specified in (1.13). In other words, the present discounted value of net foreign assets "at the end of the consumer's life" should be nonnegative (i.e., net debt should be nonpositive). We should make three related observations on this point. First, to establish a complete analogy between the finite- and infinite-horizon cases, we can think of the no-Ponzi games condition for the finite-horizon case as $e^{-rT} b_T \geq 0$. Since $e^{-rT} > 0$, this condition reduces to $b_T \geq 0$, as stated in (1.4). Second, stating the no-Ponzi games condition in the infinite-horizon case as

$$\lim_{t \longrightarrow \infty} b_t \geq 0 \tag{1.14}$$

would be incorrect. In particular, note that asymptotic debt (i.e., $\lim_{t \longrightarrow \infty} b_t < 0$) is consistent with (1.13).[17] Equation (1.13) only imposes a constraint on the growth rate of debt (i.e., debt could grow at a rate which is less than r).

As in the finite-horizon case, the nonsatiation assumption ensures that the consumer will never want to "die" with a positive level of assets. Formally, optimality requires that

$$\lim_{t \longrightarrow \infty} e^{-rt} b_t \leq 0. \tag{1.15}$$

The combination of the no–Ponzi games condition—given by (1.13)—and optimality condition (1.15) implies the condition

$$\lim_{t \longrightarrow \infty} e^{-rt} b_t = 0, \tag{1.16}$$

typically referred to as the transversality condition.

How is the derivation of the intertemporal constraint affected by the switch to an infinite horizon? By following the same series of steps as above and using the transversality condition (1.16), we obtain[18]

$$b_0 + \int_0^{\infty} y_t e^{-rt} dt = \int_0^{\infty} c_t e^{-rt} dt, \tag{1.17}$$

17. It might seem counterintuitive that the consumer is allowed to "die" with debt. The key, however, is to realize that servicing debt up to infinity is like repaying the principal (see the example discussed in note 23 below).

18. It should also be remarked that (1.17) is a meaningful budget constraint only if the present discounted value of output is finite, which implies that output cannot grow at a rate equal to or higher than r.

which is, of course, the infinite-horizon counterpart of the intertemporal constraint for the finite case, given by (1.9).

As in the finite-horizon case, we can restate this maximization problem in terms of a familiar Lagrangian:

$$\mathcal{L} = \int_0^\infty u(c_t)e^{-\beta t}dt + \lambda\left(b_0 + \int_0^\infty y_t e^{-rt}dt - \int_0^\infty c_t e^{-rt}dt\right).$$

The first-order condition in an infinite-horizon framework continues to be given by (1.11). From now on, we will work with the infinite-horizon model.

1.2.3 Interpretation of the Lagrange Multiplier

Since first-order condition (1.11) is the foundation of small open macroeconomics, it is worth taking a brief detour to offer an insightful interpretation of the Lagrange multiplier λ. This interpretation will shed light on the fact that the Lagrange multiplier will always be constant along a perfect foresight path even if exogenous variables—such as the endowment in this chapter—fluctuate over time, but may change in response to unanticipated changes.

The idea is to think of λ/r as an asset price and of λ as a dividend. To this effect, multiply both sides of equation (1.11) by e^{-rt} and integrate forward to obtain

$$\frac{\lambda}{r} = \int_0^\infty u'(c_t)e^{-rt}dt.$$

The term λ/r can then be interpreted as the (relative) price of an asset that would offer the consumer a "dividend" of $u'(c_t)$ at every point in time. The variable λ would correspond to the annuity value of the present discounted value of dividends. If c_t were constant over time and equal to c, then λ would correspond to the dividend itself (i.e., $\lambda = u'(c)$). This is completely analogous to, say, a stock price that reflects the present discounted value of a stream of dividends. As we know from basic finance theory, a stock price will not change in response to anticipated changes in the factors driving dividends because such information is already incorporated in the price. But a stock price may change in response to "news," that is, unanticipated events that change the future path of dividends. In the same vein, the multiplier λ will *not* change in response to anticipated fluctuations in output, since the path of consumption—and hence the path of marginal utilities—already incorporates such information. In other words, anticipated changes in output do not affect "permanent income," as defined below. In contrast, the multiplier may change in response to *unanticipated* changes in output because those changes represent "news" and will change permanent income. We should keep this interpretation in mind as we solve this basic model under different scenarios.

1.2.4 Equilibrium Conditions

Since consumers are the only agent in this economy (i.e., there are no firms or government), the flow constraint (1.3) and the intertemporal constraint (1.17) are also the economy's aggregate constraints. We now take a brief detour into balance of payments accounting.

Let the trade balance, TB_t, be given by net exports of goods and services and the income balance, IB_t, by net factor payments from abroad. Then, by definition,

$$TB_t \equiv y_t - c_t, \tag{1.18}$$

$$IB_t \equiv rb_t. \tag{1.19}$$

Also, by definition, the current account is given by

$$CA_t \equiv TB_t + IB_t. \tag{1.20}$$

In light of (1.18) and (1.19), expression (1.3) becomes $\dot{b}_t = IB_t + TB_t$. Hence, from (1.20),

$$\dot{b}_t = CA_t. \tag{1.21}$$

The economy's accumulation of net foreign assets is thus given by the current account balance. In other words, if the economy is running a current account surplus, double-entry bookkeeping ensures that it must be accumulating claims against the rest of the world. If we define the capital account balance, KA_t, in the standard way (whereby acquiring claims against the rest of the world implies a negative capital account balance), we have

$$KA_t \equiv -\dot{b}_t. \tag{1.22}$$

Hence, from (1.21),

$$CA_t + KA_t = 0,$$

which is the fundamental identity of balance of payments accounting. A deficit in the current account, for example, must be necessarily financed by a capital account surplus (i.e., by borrowing from the rest of the world).

Alternatively, we can express the current account balance as being equal to saving. To this effect, define saving, S_t, as

$$S_t \equiv rb_t + y_t - c_t. \tag{1.23}$$

Then, from the definition of the current account balance (equation 1.20) and using (1.18) and (1.19), it follows that

$$CA_t = S_t. \tag{1.24}$$

Finally, notice that using the definition of the trade balance, given by (1.18), we can rewrite the intertemporal constraint (1.17) as

$$\int_0^\infty TB_t e^{-rt} dt = -b_0,$$

which says that the present discounted value of the trade balances must equal the economy's initial net *foreign debt*. We thus see that basic accounting requires that an indebted economy run, on average, trade surpluses in order to repay the debt over time.

1.3 Solution of the Model

1.3.1 General Solution

We have already mentioned that first-order condition (1.11) implies that consumption will be constant along a perfect foresight path (at a level denoted by c).[19] From (1.17) it follows that

$$c = r\left(b_0 + \int_0^\infty y_t e^{-rt} dt\right). \tag{1.25}$$

Consumption equals "permanent income," defined as the annuity value of the present discounted value of available resources. The best way to think about permanent income is as the level of constant consumption that can be maintained forever. This idea is, of course, hardly new and dates back to Friedman's (1957) seminal contribution on the permanent income hypothesis. In essence, Friedman argued that current consumption should not depend on *current* income as Keynes had argued but rather on long-term expected income (which he called "permanent income").[20] Hence, as a model of consumption behavior, the modern approach to open economy macroeconomics can be viewed as just an elegant and rigorous exposition of Friedman's pioneering work. As in the finite-horizon case, figure 1.1 illustrates the fact that consumption remains flat over time even if the endowment fluctuates over time.

What will be the path of the trade balance along a perfect foresight equilibrium path? Taking into account (1.25), we write the trade balance (1.18) as

$$TB_t = y_t - c.$$

19. Throughout the book—and unless otherwise noted—we will drop time subscripts to denote constant values of variables.

20. Of course, if liquidity and/or borrowing constraints were present, then consumption would depend (at least partly) on current income. The same is true for a small open economy faced with incomplete markets, as analyzed in chapter 2.

It follows that in "good times" (i.e., when y_t is high), the economy will run trade surpluses, while in "bad times" (i.e., when y_t is low) the economy will run trade deficits (figure 1.1). Intuitively, the trade balance acts as a shock absorber and allows the economy to sustain a flat path of consumption when faced with a fluctuating path of output.

The current account path along a perfect foresight equilibrium path is given by

$$CA_t = rb_t + y_t - c.$$

It is clear that when output switches from high to low, the current account balance worsens since consumption is flat and b_t is a predetermined variable. Hence, in bad times, the economy increases its borrowing from the rest of the world. The opposite is true in good times.

It should be pointed out that the perfect consumption smoothing result captured in equation (1.25) is just a useful conceptual benchmark and should not be viewed as the key empirical prediction of the modern intertemporal approach to the current account. A casual glance at the data, of course, clearly indicates that consumption is not flat over time (or, more generally, constant along a trend). However, far from being an empirical rejection of this approach, such observation simply suggests that the many frictions examined in subsequent chapters that imply departures from perfect consumption smoothing are pervasive in the real world. Depending on the type of friction, deviations from consumption smoothing may be efficient (i.e., socially optimal) or inefficient (i.e., socially suboptimal):

• *Inefficient deviations* The most prominent frictions that lead to a nonconstant path of consumption are imperfections in capital markets (chapter 2) and distortions in intertemporal prices stemming from policy actions or noncredible policies (chapter 3). The first friction makes it impossible for consumers to borrow as much as they would like during bad times, while the second induces consumers *not* to choose a constant path of consumption to begin with. In both cases, this is a suboptimal outcome from a social point of view because a planner would choose a constant path of consumption.

• *Efficient deviations* The main sources of optimal deviations from consumption smoothing are (1) fluctuating real interest rates, (2) a second argument in the utility function (e.g., labor/leisure or nontradable goods), and (3) fluctuations in the terms of trade. As examined in exercise 5 at the end of the chapter, fluctuating real interest rates will induce consumption tilting. Shocks to labor productivity will induce a nonconstant path of consumption in a model in which the marginal utility of consumption depends on labor, as analyzed in exercise 6 at the end of this chapter. The same is true of shocks to the endowment of nontradable goods in a model where the marginal utility of consumption of tradables depends on consumption of nontradables (chapter 4). Fluctuations in the terms of trade will affect intertemporal relative prices and lead to a nonconstant consumption path (chapter 3).

1.3.2 Stationary Equilibrium

Finally—and for further reference—let us characterize a stationary equilibrium.[21] Typically, though not always, if exogenous variables are constant over time, so will endogenous variables.[22] In any event, stationarity of an equilibrium is a feature that we need to prove; it would be wrong to simply assume it.

In this case suppose that the endowment path is given by

$$y_t = y^H, \qquad t \geq 0. \tag{1.26}$$

Since we have already derived a general solution for the model (i.e., a solution valid for any path of output), we can rewrite (1.25), taking into account (1.26), as

$$c = rb_0 + y^H. \tag{1.27}$$

Substituting (1.27) into (1.18), and taking into account (1.26), yields

$$TB_t = -rb_0. \tag{1.28}$$

The stationary trade balance can therefore be positive, zero, or negative depending on the initial level of net foreign assets.[23]

We now show that, in a stationary equilibrium, the current account will always be zero. Substituting (1.26) and (1.27) into (1.3), we obtain

$$\dot{b}_t = rb_t - rb_0.$$

Evaluating this equation at $t = 0$, we obtain $\dot{b}_0 = 0$. It follows that

$$b_t = b_0$$

for all $t \geq 0$. Since net foreign assets are constant over time, the current account is always zero along a stationary equilibrium.

Finally, notice that the value of the Lagrange multiplier in this stationary equilibrium follows from (1.11) and (1.27):

21. We will purposely use the expression "stationary equilibrium," as opposed to "steady state," to refer to an equilibrium along which both exogenous and endogenous variables are constant over time. We will reserve the expression "steady state" for models that have intrinsic dynamics and hence where endogenous variables converge to the steady state independently of initial conditions. We will not encounter such models, however, until chapter 6.

22. Examples where this is not so include the case $\beta \neq r$ analyzed in exercise 4 at the end of this chapter and the balance of payments crises models studied in chapter 16.

23. A stationary equilibrium offers an interesting example of the no–Ponzi game condition $\lim_{t\to\infty} b_t e^{-rt} \geq 0$. Suppose $b_0 < 0$. Then the trade balance will be constant over time and equal to $-rb_0 > 0$. Clearly, in the limit the initial debt (b_0) is paid in full because the present discounted value of the trade surpluses is $-b_0$. The no–Ponzi games condition is then satisfied. Interestingly, however, the value of the debt is $b_t = b_0 < 0$ for all $t \in [0, \infty)$. This illustrates how a condition such as (1.14) can be too restrictive.

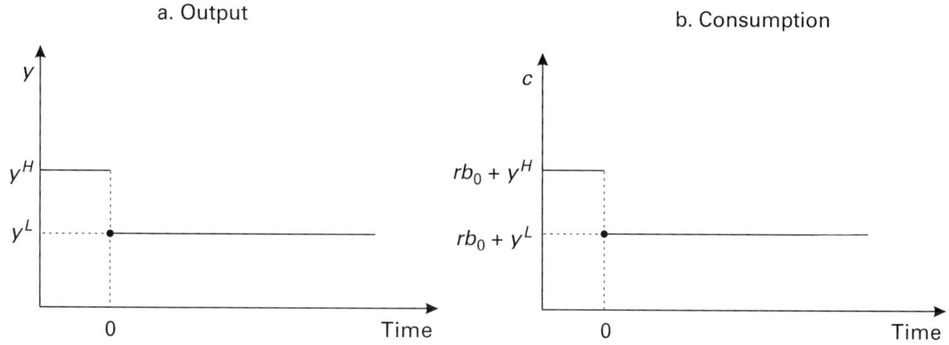

Figure 1.2
Permanent fall in output

$$\lambda = u'(rb_0 + y^H).$$

The value of the multiplier is thus determined by the level of permanent income.

1.4 Unanticipated Shocks

To gain further insights into how a small open economy reacts to output shocks, we will study the effects of unexpected changes in the path of output that take place at time 0.[24]

1.4.1 Permanent Fall in Output

Suppose that an instant before time 0 the economy is in the stationary equilibrium characterized in section 1.3.2. At time 0 there is an unanticipated and permanent fall in output from y^H to y^L, where $y^L < y^H$ (see figure 1.2, panel a). Since there has been an unanticipated shock, the individual will reoptimize immediately. The first-order condition will now be given by

$$u'(c_t) = \tilde{\lambda},$$

where $\tilde{\lambda}$ is the multiplier corresponding to the new intertemporal constraint (recall that the Lagrange multiplier may change in response to unanticipated shocks as any asset price would). Since consumption will be constant along the new perfect foresight path, we can use (1.17) with $y_t = y^L$ to conclude that the new level of consumption is given by (see figure 1.2, panel b)

24. A legitimate question that the reader may ask is how to think about *unanticipated* shocks in *perfect foresight* models, since, when taken at face value, it would seem a contradiction in terms. Strictly speaking, this is true and a "purist" would probably reject such an intellectual experiment. However, an unanticipated shock should be viewed as an approximation to a stochastic world in which the shock had such a small probability of occurring that, for all intents and purposes, it did not affect the initial stationary equilibrium.

$$c = rb_0 + y^L.$$

Since consumption falls one to one with output, the trade balance and the current account do not change. Hence an unanticipated and permanent fall in output leads to a *pari passu* fall in consumption and has no impact on the current account. The economy fully adjusts to the lower output level.

Finally, notice that the Lagrange multiplier is now higher (reflecting the lower wealth) as its value is given by

$$\tilde{\lambda} = u'(rb_0 + y^L).$$

We conclude that the economy adjusts immediately to a permanent negative shock. Since there are no distortions in this economy, this response is socially optimal. This result underlies the standard policy prescription that says that, however painful, an economy has no choice but to adjust to any long-lasting negative shock.

1.4.2 Temporary Fall in Output

Suppose now that an instant before time 0 the economy is in the stationary equilibrium characterized above and that at time $t = 0$ there is an unanticipated and temporary fall in output. Formally, the path of output for $t \geq 0$ is given by

$$y_t = y^L, \qquad 0 \leq t < T,$$
$$y_t = y^H, \qquad t \geq T,$$

for some $T > 0$ (see figure 1.3, panel a).

Since there has been an unanticipated shock, the consumer immediately reoptimizes at $t = 0$. The problem he/she faces is formally the same as before, with his/her intertemporal constraint now given by

$$b_0 + \int_0^T y^L e^{-rt} dt + \int_T^\infty y^H e^{-rt} dt = \int_0^\infty c_t e^{-rt} dt. \tag{1.29}$$

The consumer thus maximizes (1.12) subject to the intertemporal constraint (1.29). As before, the corresponding first-order condition implies that consumption will be flat along the new perfect foresight equilibrium path. Hence, from (1.29), it follows that

$$c = rb_0 + y^L(1 - e^{-rT}) + y^H e^{-rT}. \tag{1.30}$$

Consumption falls by the same amount as permanent income (see figure 1.3, panel b). Permanent income has fallen from $rb_0 + y^H$ before the shock to $rb_0 + y^L(1 - e^{-rT}) + y^H e^{-rT}$ after the shock. The larger is T, the bigger will be the fall in permanent income and hence the bigger the

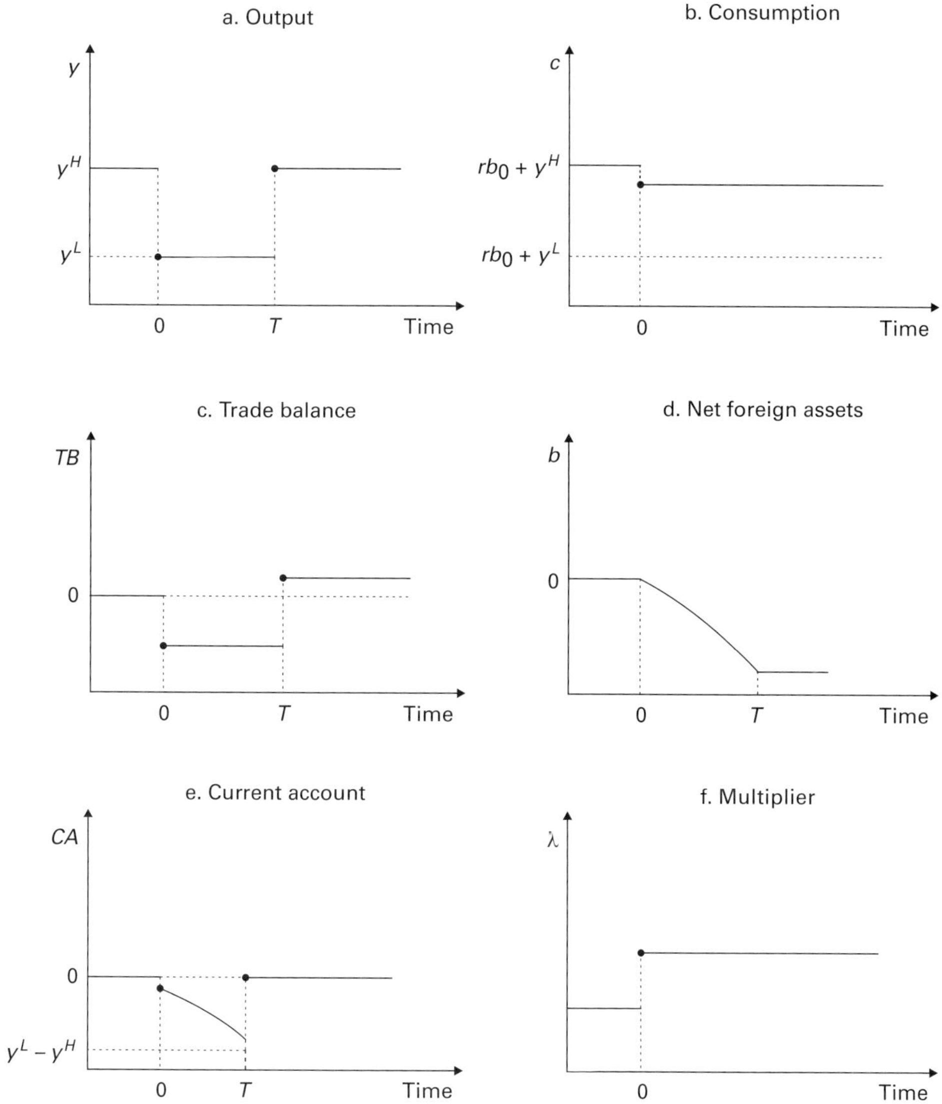

Figure 1.3
Temporary fall in output

fall in consumption. For a small value of T, consumption will fall by very little. For a very large value of T (i.e., $T \longrightarrow \infty$), consumption will fall by almost the same amount as it would fall if the shock were permanent.[25]

Using (1.30), we can derive the path of the trade balance (see figure 1.3, panel c):

$$TB_t = y^L - c = -rb_0 - (y^H - y^L)e^{-rT} < -rb_0, \qquad 0 \leq t < T,$$
$$TB_t = y^H - c = -rb_0 + (y^H - y^L)(1 - e^{-rT}) > -rb_0, \qquad t \geq T.$$

To fix ideas, let $b_0 = 0$. Then, in order to keep the path of consumption flat after $t = 0$, the economy runs a trade deficit while output is low and a trade surplus when output goes back to its initial level (see figure 1.3, panel c).

What about saving at $t = 0$? Recalling (1.23), we know that $S_0 = rb_0 + y^L - c$. Hence, using (1.30), we obtain

$$S_0 = -(y^H - y^L)e^{-rT} < 0. \tag{1.31}$$

Saving is, of course, negative as households dissave to smooth consumption over time. Furthermore S_0 is an increasing function of T: the longer is the duration of the shock, the smaller is the dissaving carried out by households on impact. The model thus predicts a positive comovement of saving and output which, by and large, is consistent with the evidence as discussed in box 1.1.

To derive the current account path, we will first derive the path of net foreign assets. To this effect, rewrite flow constraint (1.3) as

$$\dot{b}_t = rb_t + y^L - c, \qquad t < T, \tag{1.32}$$

$$\dot{b}_t = rb_t + y^H - c, \qquad t \geq T. \tag{1.33}$$

These are first-order differential equations with constant term $y^L - c$ and $y^H - c$, respectively. The general solution for each of these first-order differential equations takes the form, respectively,

$$b_t = b_0 e^{rt} + \frac{y^L - c}{r}(e^{rt} - 1), \qquad t < T,$$

$$b_t = b_T e^{r(t-T)} + \frac{y^H - c}{r}\left[e^{r(t-T)} - 1\right], \qquad t \geq T.$$

Taking into account that c is given by expression (1.30), we obtain

$$b_t = b_0 - e^{-r(T-t)}(1 - e^{-rt})\frac{(y^H - y^L)}{r}, \qquad t < T, \tag{1.34}$$

25. Since consumption falls, the multiplier rises at $t = 0$, as illustrated in figure 1.3, panel f.

Box 1.1
Is saving procyclical?

Our model predicts that in response to an unanticipated and temporary increase (fall) in output, there should be a positive comovement between output and saving as households save (dissave) in order to smooth consumption over time. In a stochastic version of our model, this comovement would translate into a positive correlation between saving and output.[a] That is, saving should be procyclical.

What do the data say? Table 1.1 reports correlations between the cyclical components of saving and GDP for 22 developing and 18 industrial countries for the period 1970 to 2010 (sample dictated

Table 1.1
Correlation between GDP and saving (in real terms)

Developing countries		Industrial countries	
Algeria	0.26	Austria	0.84
Argentina	0.81	Belgium	0.77
Bolivia	0.33	Canada	0.82
Colombia	0.73	Denmark	0.81
Dominican Republic	−0.20	Finland	0.88
Honduras	0.11	France	0.92
Hungary	0.29	Germany	0.83
Iceland	0.69	Greece	0.76
Indonesia	0.83	Ireland	0.88
Israel	0.70	Italy	0.72
Kenya	0.15	Japan	0.91
Malaysia	0.64	Netherlands	0.82
Mexico	0.78	New Zealand	0.84
Paraguay	0.26	Norway	0.56
Peru	0.48	Portugal	0.74
Singapore	−0.18	Sweden	0.88
South Africa	0.21	Switzerland	0.58
Thailand	0.93	United States	0.72
Trinidad and Tobago	0.20		
Tunisia	0.59		
Turkey	0.76		
Uruguay	0.72		
Average	0.46	Average	0.79

Source: Word Development Indicators (World Bank).
Note: Based on annual data, 1970 to 2010.

a. As will become clear in chapter 2, a stochastic version of our basic model (with an uncertain endowment path) with incomplete markets will generate correlations that match exactly the comovements predicted by unanticipated temporary shocks in this chapter's model. The reason is that in both cases the shocks generate wealth effects.

Box 1.1
(continued)

by data availability).[b] Series were detrended using the HP filter.[c] The average correlation is positive in both group of countries (in fact the correlation is negative in only two out of the 40 countries, both developing). Further, the average correlation is smaller in developing (0.46) than in industrial countries (0.79).

Lane and Tornell (1998) have argued that saving rates in Latin America tend to be lower than in industrial countries—and even countercyclical in some instances—and have proposed a political-economy explanation whereby, in response to a positive shock, pressure groups fight for the newly available resources, leading to higher spending than is socially optimal and resulting in a lower, and possibly negative, saving rate.

While Lane and Tornell's story may well be valid, our simple model can rationalize a negative comovement between saving and output. Think of an unanticipated output shock that raises today's endowment but increases it even more in the future. Households will dissave to smooth consumption because today's endowment is lower than in the future. Hence today's comovement between saving and output will be negative.[d] Our model can also rationalize a smaller comovement in developing than in industrial countries. To see this, think of a temporary and positive shock. Then equation (1.31) would become $S_0 = (y^H - y^L)e^{-rT} > 0$. It follows that the larger is T, the smaller is the response of saving. Hence, to the extent that shocks in developing countries have a higher permanent component—as argued by Aguiar and Gopinath (2007)—our model could explain a lower correlation in developing countries.

In sum, by and large, the evidence clearly indicates that saving is procyclical, as predicted by our basic model. Other features of the data—such as a lower correlation in developing countries and occasionally negative correlations—are also consistent with our model.

b. The sample period varies from country to country. We require ten consecutive annual observations for a country to be included in the sample.
c. The smoothing parameter used was 100, which is the standard value for annual data.
d. This is in fact the case analyzed in figure 1.4 (once we introduce investment into our model). Output increases in period 0 while saving falls.

$$b_t = b_0 - (1 - e^{-rT})\frac{(y^H - y^L)}{r}, \qquad t \geq T, \tag{1.35}$$

where we have evaluated the first expression at $t = T$ to get rid of b_T in the second equation.

Several remarks are in order. First, as a check on our solution, we can evaluate the RHS of the first equation at $t = 0$ to verify that $b_t = b_0$ at that point. Second, we can check that b_t is continuous at $t = T$ (though not differentiable, as becomes clear below) by evaluating both expressions at $t = T$ and noting that the values coincide. Third, the level of net foreign assets for $t \geq T$ is constant since the economy is, once again, in a stationary equilibrium. Figure 1.3, panel d, illustrates the path of net foreign assets.

To derive the path of the current account, we simply differentiate equations (1.34) and (1.35) with respect to time to obtain (see figure 1.3, panel e):

$$\dot{b}_t = -e^{-r(T-t)}(y^H - y^L) < 0, \qquad t < T,$$

$$\dot{b}_t = 0, \qquad t \geq T.$$

At $t = 0$, the current account jumps into a deficit reflecting the deterioration in the trade balance. Further, differentiating again with respect to time, we have

$$\ddot{b}_t = -re^{-r(T-t)}(y^H - y^L) < 0,$$

$$\dddot{b}_t = -r^2 e^{-r(T-t)}(y^H - y^L) < 0.$$

The current account thus falls over time at an increasing rate (in absolute value), reflecting the fact that while the trade balance is constant over time, interest receipts fall over time (and/or debt repayments increase over time). At time T the current account deficit disappears as output increases and the trade balance improves.

The key message that follows from the analysis of unanticipated negative shocks is that the economy "adjusts" to permanent shocks but "finances" temporary shocks. Since there are no distortions and the economy is thus always operating in a first-best equilibrium, such responses are socially optimal. If market frictions prevent international capital markets from providing financing to developing countries in bad times, this result provides a rationale for the existence of multilateral financial organizations, such as the IMF, that may provide financing in bad times.

1.5 Adding Investment to the Basic Model

The model just examined assumed that the economy was endowed with an exogenous output stream. Since there was no investment, the current account was identically equal to saving. In that context we analyzed how a temporary fall in the endowment leads to lower saving and hence to a current account deficit. The model thus predicts that the trade balance behaves procyclically (i.e., the trade balance improves in good times and worsens in bad times). The evidence, however, suggests precisely the opposite (see box 1.2): the trade balance is countercyclical (i.e., it worsens in good times and improves in bad times). A missing ingredient in our model might be investment. After all, our intuition tells us that a temporary fall in productivity should lead to both lower saving (based on the consumption smoothing motive studied above) and lower investment (since productivity is temporarily lower). So it would seem that the effect of a temporary fall in productivity on the current account would depend on the relative strength of both effects. In particular, if the investment effect dominates (i.e., if the fall in investment is larger than the fall in saving), there may be an improvement in the current account. In the case of a temporary improvement in productivity, if the positive investment effect dominates the positive effect on saving, there will be a worsening in the current account. This section will formalize this intuition

Box 1.2
Confronting the model with the data

How does our basic model fare in practice? A highly popular method of confronting the model with the data—which is the hallmark of the real business cycle approach—is to compare the correlations generated by a stochastic version of our basic model with investment to the correlations actually observed in the data.[a] In particular, think of the impact effect of a temporary increase in productivity (figure 1.7) as capturing the relevant comovements. Assume that the investment effect dominates. Then our model would predict the following comovements (translated into correlations):

- A positive correlation between consumption and output.
- A positive correlation between investment and output.
- A negative correlation between the trade balance and output.

Table 1.2 shows the contemporaneous correlations with output of consumption, investment, and net exports (computed using the cyclical components obtained with the Hodrick–Prescott filter) for 13 emerging markets and 13 developed countries that can be regarded as "small open economies."

Table 1.2
Business cycle correlations

Emerging markets	ρ(c,y)	ρ(y,I)	ρ(NX/y,y)
Argentina	0.90	0.96	−0.70
Brazil	0.41	0.62	0.01
Ecuador	0.73	0.89	−0.79
Israel	0.45	0.49	0.12
Korea	0.85	0.78	−0.61
Malaysia	0.76	0.86	−0.74
Mexico	0.92	0.91	−0.74
Peru	0.78	0.85	−0.24
Philippines	0.59	0.76	−0.41
Slovak Republic	0.42	0.46	−0.44
South Africa	0.72	0.75	−0.54
Thailand	0.92	0.91	−0.83
Turkey	0.89	0.83	−0.69
Mean	**0.72**	**0.77**	**−0.51**

a. The real business cycle approach was pioneered by Finn Kydland (a Norwegian economist born in 1943) and Edward Prescott (an American economist born in 1940) in a 1982 *Econometrica* paper. They were awarded the 2004 Nobel Prize in Economics partly because of this contribution. While originally conceived as a theory of the business cycle—arguing that productivity shocks could be the source of business cycles—it has become much more influential as a methodological tool. For an excellent survey of the real business cycle literature, see King and Rebelo (2000). Open economy versions of the standard real business cycle model may be found in, for example, Aguiar and Gopinath (2007), Correia, Neves, and Rebelo (1995), and Mendoza (1991).

Box 1.2
(continued)

Table 1.2
(continued)

Small industrial countries	ρ(c,y)	ρ(y,I)	ρ(NX/y,y)
Australia	0.48	0.80	−0.43
Austria	0.74	0.75	0.10
Belgium	0.67	0.62	−0.04
Canada	0.88	0.77	−0.20
Denmark	0.36	0.51	−0.08
Finland	0.84	0.88	−0.45
Netherlands	0.72	0.70	−0.19
New Zealand	0.76	0.82	−0.26
Norway	0.63	0.00	0.11
Portugal	0.75	0.70	−0.11
Spain	0.83	0.83	−0.60
Sweden	0.35	0.68	0.01
Switzerland	0.58	0.69	−0.03
Mean	**0.66**	**0.67**	**−0.17**

Source: Aguiar and Gopinath (2007).
Note: Based on quarterly data; see Aguiar and Gopinath (2007) for data sources and sample periods. NX denotes net exports and ρ denotes correlation. Other variables as defined in text.

The data indicate that the correlation between consumption and output is, on average, 0.72 for emerging markets and 0.66 for industrial countries (and positive for every single country). The average correlation between investment and output is 0.77 for emerging countries and 0.67 for industrial countries (and, again, positive for every single country). The average correlation between net exports (a proxy for the trade balance) and output is −0.51 for emerging markets (and negative for 11 of the 13 countries in the sample) and −0.17 for industrial countries (and negative for 10 out of the 13 countries in the sample). We can conclude that at least based on this metric, the now standard intertemporal model of the current account works remarkably well in terms of describing the cyclical behavior of the main macroeconomic aggregates—consumption, investment, and trade balance (net exports).

As analyzed in the text, whether the trade balance turns negative in response to an increase in productivity will critically depend on the length of the shock: the longer is the duration of the shock, the more likely that the investment effect will dominate and that the trade balance will become negative. Aguiar and Gopinath (2007) show empirically that the "permanent" component of shocks in emerging markets is larger than in industrial countries. In terms of our model, if the temporary increase in productivity lasts longer, then the negative response of the trade balance will be larger (in absolute value) because the saving effect is smaller. This would be consistent with the larger correlation (in absolute value) for emerging markets than in industrial countries indicated in table 1.2.[b]

b. Similarly Aguiar and Gopinath (2007) show, in the context of a stochastic model, that more persistent shocks are critical in generating a larger correlation (in absolute value) for emerging markets.

by introducing investment into our basic model and showing how the relative strength of both effects depends on the duration of the shock.

While our basic model was formulated in continuous time, it will prove convenient at this point to switch to discrete time. The reason is that sticking with continuous time would require adding adjustment costs to the model (otherwise, investment might be "infinite" at any point in time and the current account would not be well-defined).[26] The introduction of adjustment costs would greatly complicate the analytical solution of the model without adding any additional insights. In contrast, discrete time introduces a natural one-period lag in the adjustment of the capital stock to its new equilibrium, which implies that investment is well-defined without having to add adjustment costs.

1.5.1 Household's Problem

Technology

Denote by k_t the stock of capital in period t. Output in period t is thus given by

$$y_t = A_t f(k_t), \tag{1.36}$$

where A_t (> 0) is a productivity parameter and $f(k_t)$ is a strictly increasing and strictly concave function:

$$f'(k_t) > 0,$$

$$f''(k_t) < 0.$$

We assume that the capital stock does not depreciate. Hence, by definition, investment (I_t) is given by the increase in the stock of capital:

$$I_t \equiv k_{t+1} - k_t. \tag{1.37}$$

By assumption, the choice variable in period t is k_{t+1}; that is, households choose in period t the capital stock at the beginning of period $t+1$. There is thus a one-period adjustment in the stock of capital. In addition we assume that investment can be negative (i.e., households can "eat" part of their capital stock if they so desire).

Budget Constraints

For simplicity, we assume that the household also carries production activities.[27] Let b_t denote net foreign assets held by households in period t. The household's flow constraint is given by

$$b_{t+1} = (1+r)b_t + y_t - c_t - (k_{t+1} - k_t). \tag{1.38}$$

26. By "infinite" investment, we mean a discontinuity in the path of the capital stock.

27. Exercise 7 at the end of this chapter shows how this economy can be decentralized. In a decentralized setup, households would own both the capital stock and the firms and would rent the capital stock to firms. Firms would rent capital, produce, and return profits to households.

Except for the investment term, this flow constraint is the discrete-time counterpart of flow constraint (1.3). In addition to consumption, resources are now also used for investment purposes.

By iterating forward and imposing the condition

$$\lim_{t\to\infty}\frac{b_t}{(1+r)^{t-1}}=0,$$

we can derive the intertemporal constraint

$$(1+r)b_0+\sum_{t=0}^{\infty}\left(\frac{1}{1+r}\right)^t y_t=\sum_{t=0}^{\infty}\left(\frac{1}{1+r}\right)^t[c_t+(k_{t+1}-k_t)], \tag{1.39}$$

where b_0 and k_0 are exogenously given. Again, and except for the investment term, this intertemporal constraint is the discrete time counterpart of equation (1.17).

Utility Maximization

The household's lifetime utility is given by

$$\sum_{t=0}^{\infty}\beta^t u(c_t), \tag{1.40}$$

where $\beta(>0)$ is now the discount factor and $u(c_t)$ is strictly increasing, strictly concave, and satisfies condition (1.2).[28]

The household thus chooses $\{c_t, k_{t+1}\}_{t=0}^{\infty}$ to maximize (1.40) subject to the intertemporal constraint (1.39). In terms of the Lagrangian, the maximization problem can be stated as (after using equation 1.36 to substitute out for output)

$$\mathcal{L}=\sum_{t=0}^{\infty}\beta^t u(c_t)+\lambda\left\{(1+r)b_0+\sum_{t=0}^{\infty}\left(\frac{1}{1+r}\right)^t A_t f(k_t)\right.$$
$$\left.-\sum_{t=0}^{\infty}\left(\frac{1}{1+r}\right)^t[c_t+(k_{t+1}-k_t)]\right\}.$$

The first-order conditions are given by

$$\beta^t u'(c_t)=\lambda\left(\frac{1}{1+r}\right)^t, \tag{1.41}$$

28. Notice that, even though we are using the same notation, β here stands for the discount *factor*, which, by definition, equals $1/(1 + \text{discount rate})$. In the continuous-time formulation it refers to the discount *rate*.

$$A_{t+1}f'(k_{t+1}) = r, \tag{1.42}$$

for $t = 0, 1, 2, \ldots$.[29]

Assuming, for the same reasons discussed for the continuous time case, that $\beta(1+r) = 1$, we can express first-order condition (1.41) as

$$u'(c_t) = \lambda. \tag{1.43}$$

As in our previous model without investment (recall equation 1.11), condition (1.43) implies that along a perfect foresight equilibrium path, consumption will be flat regardless of the path of output (and hence of the path of A_t). Figure 1.1 thus remains valid for this model with investment. This result was to be expected since perfect access to international capital markets allows consumption decisions to be independent of production decisions (see Fisher 1930).

Equation (1.42) determines the optimal level of the capital stock. This arbitrage condition says that at the margin the return on a unit of capital—given by the LHS—should be equal to the return on net foreign assets, r. If this were not true, it would be profitable for households to readjust their portfolio between bonds and capital. It is worth emphasizing that condition (1.42) does *not* hold for k_0 since the initial capital stock is given and is thus not a choice variable.

1.5.2 Equilibrium Conditions

Since, as before, the households are the only agent in this economy, the constraints discussed above also apply to the economy as a whole. In particular, using (1.37), we can rewrite equation (1.38) as follows:

$$b_{t+1} - b_t = rb_t + y_t - c_t - I_t. \tag{1.44}$$

To write this equation in terms of familiar balance of payments accounting, define the current account balance as the change in net foreign assets:

$$CA_t \equiv b_{t+1} - b_t. \tag{1.45}$$

Combining (1.44) and (1.45) obtains

$$CA_t = rb_t + y_t - c_t - I_t. \tag{1.46}$$

As before, there are two useful ways of rewriting the current account balance. First, define the trade balance as

$$TB_t \equiv y_t - c_t - I_t. \tag{1.47}$$

29. Of course, the derivative of the Lagrangian with respect to λ yields back the intertemporal constraint (1.39), which is technically part of the first-order conditions.

Then, using this definition and recalling (1.19), rewrite the current account balance as the sum of the income and trade balances:

$$CA_t = IB_t + TB_t. \tag{1.48}$$

Alternatively, the current account could be expressed as the difference between saving and investment. To this effect, use the definition of saving provided in (1.23) to rewrite (1.46) as

$$CA_t = S_t - I_t. \tag{1.49}$$

1.5.3 Perfect Foresight Equilibrium for a Stationary Economy

Let us characterize a perfect foresight equilibrium path for a constant value of A_t (i.e., let $A_t = A$ for all $t = 0, 1, \ldots$). First-order condition (1.42) then determines a constant level of the capital stock, k, implicitly defined by

$$Af'(k) = r. \tag{1.50}$$

We assume $k_0 = k$. In other words, the economy starts with its desired capital stock and hence does not need to invest. (The case of $k_0 < k$ is addressed below.) Investment is thus zero in every period. In light of equation (1.36), the constant level of output will be given by

$$y = Af(k). \tag{1.51}$$

We know from condition (1.43) that consumption will be constant over time. Hence, since investment is always zero, it follows from the intertemporal constraint (1.39) that[30]

$$c = rb_0 + Af(k). \tag{1.52}$$

We have enough information to compute saving in period 0. Since $y_0 = y$ and $c_0 = c$, it follows from (1.23) that

$$S_0 = rb_0 + y - c. \tag{1.53}$$

Using (1.51) and (1.52), it follows that $S_0 = 0$. To compute saving in subsequent periods, we will first need to derive the path of net foreign assets.

Using (1.47), (1.51), and (1.52), the trade balance in period 0 is given by

$$TB_0 = -rb_0.$$

Recall from (1.49) that the current account is the difference between saving and investment. Since both saving and investment are zero in period 0, the current account is also zero in period 0. By

30. In deriving (1.52), recall that the sum of an infinite geometric progression is equal to $a/(1 - x)$, where a is the first term and x is the common multiplier (equal to $1/(1 + r)$ in this case).

(1.45), this implies that $b_1 = b_0$. We can now compute saving in period 1 and check that it will be zero as well. Hence the current account will also be zero in period 1 and $b_2 = b_1$. Proceeding in this way, it should be clear that the current account is always zero and hence the path of net foreign assets is constant over time. This implies that the trade balance is also constant over time and equal to $-rb_0$.

1.5.4 Unanticipated and Permanent Increase in Productivity

Suppose that in $t = -1$ the economy is in the stationary equilibrium described in section 1.5.3. In $t = 0$, there is an unanticipated and permanent increase in the productivity parameter from A to A^H, where $A^H > A$ (figure 1.4, panel a).[31] Since there has been an unanticipated shock, households reoptimize. The first-order conditions are still given by (1.42) and (1.43), with the multiplier possibly taking a different value as discussed above for the continuous-time case.

Since the capital stock in period $t = 0$ (k_0) was chosen in period $t = -1$, it cannot respond to the change in A. In other words, households take as given $k_0 (= k)$ in their reoptimization. From period 1 onward, however, the capital stock is higher (figure 1.4, panel b) and implicitly given by the condition

$$A^H f'(k^H) = r, \qquad t = 1, 2, \ldots, \tag{1.54}$$

where k^H denotes the new and higher stationary value of the capital stock.

Given the path of k_t depicted in figure 1.4, panel b, the path of investment is given by (figure 1.4, panel c)

$$I_0 = k^H - k > 0, \tag{1.55}$$

$$I_t = 0, \qquad t = 1, 2, \ldots.$$

What happens to output? (Figure 1.4, panel d illustrates the path of output.) In period $t = 0$, output is higher than in period $t = -1$ because, even though the capital stock has yet to change, the productivity of the existing capital stock has increased. In period 1, output increases further because the capital stock has now adjusted to its new and higher level. From period 1 onward, output is constant again. Formally,

$$y_0 = A^H f(k) > y_{-1}, \tag{1.56}$$

$$y_t = A^H f(k^H) > y_0, \qquad t = 1, 2, \ldots. \tag{1.57}$$

Let us now turn our attention to the consumption path (figure 1.4, panel d). As before, first-order condition (1.43) indicates that consumption will be constant along the new perfect foresight

31. In figures 1.4, 1.6, and 1.7 we draw lines connecting discrete data points for visual illustration.

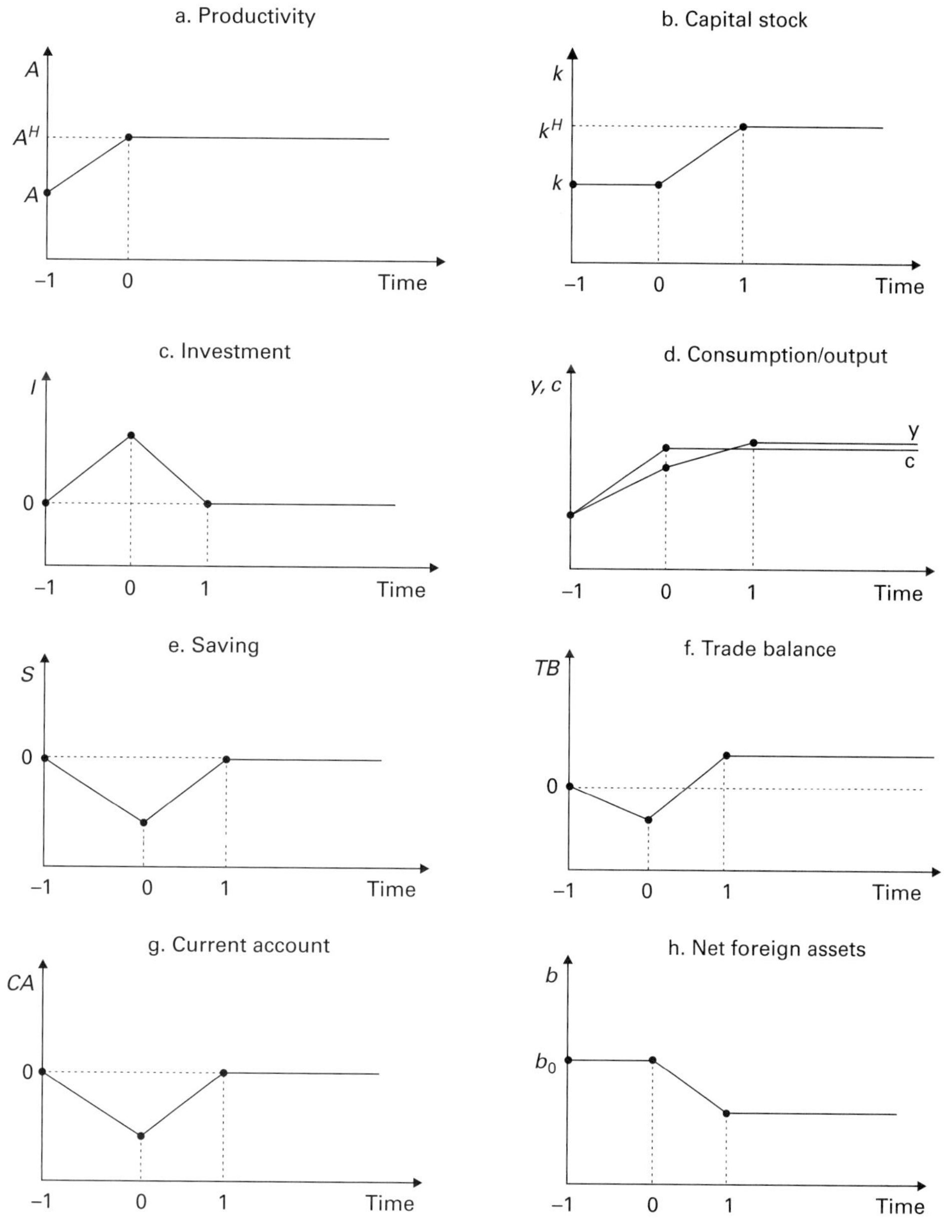

Figure 1.4
Permanent increase in productivity

equilibrium. To find out the level of consumption, we solve from the intertemporal constraint (1.39), taking into account the paths of the capital stock and output just derived to obtain

$$c = rb_0 + A^H f(k) + \frac{r}{1+r} \underbrace{\left[\frac{A^H[f(k^H) - f(k)]}{r} - (k^H - k) \right]}_{\text{Net present value of investment}}. \tag{1.58}$$

In an economy with a fixed capital stock (equal to k), the new (and higher) level of consumption would be given by the first two terms on the RHS. This would correspond to an unanticipated and permanent increase in the endowment in our first model. This economy, however, will have a higher capital stock from period 1 onward as a result of the investment carried out in period 0. The term in square brackets captures the net present value (as of period 0) of undertaking such an investment. (This term is multiplied by $r/(1+r)$ because households consume the annuity value of this net present value.[32]) What are the costs and benefits of this investment project? The cost—which is incurred in period 0—is, of course, the investment undertaken in period 0, given by $k^H - k$. The benefits consist of higher output from period 1 onward. The present discounted value (as of period 0) of this *additional* output is given by $A^H[f(k^H) - f(k)]/r$. The term in square brackets thus denotes the net benefits (i.e., the net present value) of this investment project.

Clearly, we should expect that the net present value of this investment will be positive (otherwise, it would not be undertaken). We thus want to show that

$$\frac{A^H[f(k^H) - f(k)]}{r} > k^H - k.$$

Rearranging terms, we can write this inequality as

$$\frac{A^H[f(k^H) - f(k)]}{k^H - k} > r.$$

Using the marginal condition for the capital stock—given by (1.54)—we get

$$\underbrace{\frac{A^H[f(k^H) - f(k)]}{k^H - k}}_{\text{Average return}} > \underbrace{A^H f'(k^H)}_{\text{Return on the marginal unit}},$$

which holds given the strict concavity of $f(.)$. Intuitively, the LHS of this inequality captures the "average" return on the investment, whereas the RHS captures the return on the last unit (the

32. Notice that, in discrete time, the annuity value (or permanent component) of some stock is $r/(1+r)$ times the stock.

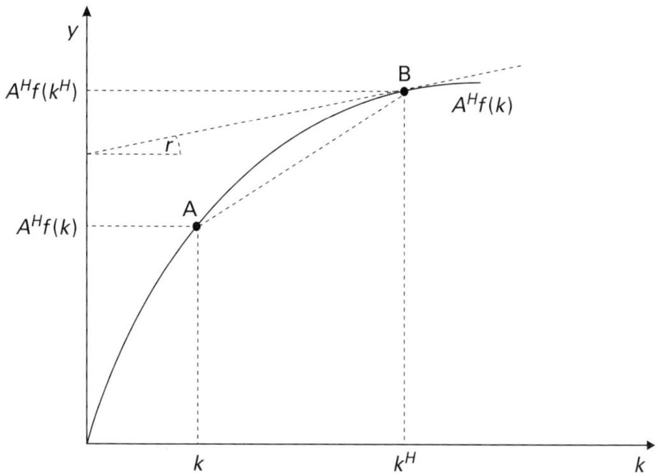

Figure 1.5
Production and investment

marginal unit). By strict concavity, all the units of capital that precede the marginal unit (i.e., the "inframarginal" units) have a higher return than the marginal unit. Figure 1.5—which depicts the production function given by (1.36)—provides a graphical illustration of this idea. Point A represents production in period 0 (i.e., with a capital stock of k), whereas point B represents production in period 1 (and subsequent periods, with a capital stock of k^H). The average return on the new capital ($k^H - k$) is given by the slope of the line connecting points A and B. The marginal return on the last unit of capital, r, is captured by the slope of the line tangent to the production function at point B. Clearly, all units of capital below k^H have a marginal return (given by the slope of the production function) higher than r.

Since, as we have just shown, the net present value of investment is positive, we infer from equation (1.58) that consumption is higher than before the shock. In fact, and as illustrated in figure 1.4, panel d, consumption rises by more than output in period 0 since output increases only by the direct effect of the higher productivity whereas consumption also rises by the permanent component of the net present value of investment.

Since consumption rises in anticipation of the higher output in period 1, saving will be negative (figure 1.4, panel e). From (1.23) and (1.58),

$$S_0 = -\frac{r}{1+r}\underbrace{\left[\frac{A^H[f(k^H) - f(k)]}{r} - (k^H - k)\right]}_{+} < 0. \tag{1.59}$$

Not surprisingly, the term in square brackets is the net present value of investment which—as shown above—is positive. The dissaving in period 0 is thus equal to the permanent income component of this net present value of investment.[33]

What will be the trade balance in period 0? The trade balance will reflect not only the dissaving of period 0—as in the basic model without investment—but also the investment carried out in period 0. Formally, from (1.47) and (1.55) and the fact that $c_0 = c$, the trade balance in period 0 is given by

$$TB_0 = y_0 - c - (k^H - k).$$

Using (1.56) and (1.58) and rearranging terms, we can rewrite this expression as

$$TB_0 = -rb_0 - \underbrace{\frac{r}{1+r}\left[\frac{A^H[f(k^H) - f(k)]}{r} - (k^H - k)\right]}_{\text{Consumption smoothing effect}} - \underbrace{(k^H - k)}_{\text{Investment effect}} < -rb_0.$$

This expression makes clear our intuition by highlighting the role of the consumption-smoothing motive and the investment effect. Assuming, to fix ideas, that initial net foreign assets are zero (i.e., $b_0 = 0$), the trade balance will be negative in period 0 (figure 1.4, panel f).

If $b_0 = 0$, the present discounted value of the path of the trade balance must add up to zero. Hence the economy will be running trade surpluses from period 1 onward to repay the external debt incurred in period 0. Formally, using (1.47), (1.55), and (1.58), it follows that

$$TB_t = -rb_0 + \frac{r}{1+r}\left\{A^H[f(k^H) - f(k)] + (k^H - k)\right\} > -rb_0, \qquad t = 1, 2, \ldots,$$

which is positive for $b_0 = 0$ (figure 1.4, panel f).

What will be the path of the current account? Clearly, the current account will be negative in period 0 reflecting negative saving (recall equation 1.59) and positive investment (panel g). Formally, from (1.49),

$$CA_0 = \underset{-}{S_0} - \underset{+}{I_0} < 0. \tag{1.60}$$

Since in period 1 the economy becomes stationary, the current account should be zero from period 1 onward. To check this, we first need to derive an explicit expression for the current account in period 0. Substituting (1.55) and (1.59) in equation (1.60) and rearranging terms, we obtain

$$CA_0 = -\frac{1}{1+r}\left\{A^H[f(k^H) - f(k)] + (k^H - k)\right\} < 0.$$

33. While it should be intuitively clear that saving from period 1 onward is zero, a formal proof must wait until we derive the path of net foreign assets.

Since, from (1.45), $b_1 = b_0 + CA_0$, then

$$b_1 = b_0 - \frac{1}{1+r}\left\{A^H[f(k^H) - f(k)] + (k^H - k)\right\} < b_0. \tag{1.61}$$

Net foreign assets thus decline as a result of the current account deficit in period 0 (figure 1.4, panel h). We can now compute saving in period 1. From (1.23), (1.57), and the fact that $c_1 = c$, we have

$$S_1 = rb_1 + A^H f(k^H) - c.$$

Using (1.58) and (1.61), we can easily verify that $S_1 = 0$. Since investment in period 1 is zero, the current account in period 1 will be zero as well and net foreign assets remain constant (i.e., $b_2 = b_1$). Hence saving and the current account will also be zero in all subsequent periods.

We can conclude that in the presence of investment, *a permanent increase in productivity leads to a trade and current account deficit.* The current account deficit results from both negative saving and positive investment. This contrasts sharply with the case studied in section 1.4.1 where a permanent increase in output would leave both the trade and current account balances unchanged.

Finally, it is worth commenting further on the behavior of saving. It may come as somewhat of a surprise that saving falls in response to a *permanent* increase in productivity. As stressed above, however, this happens because the rise in productivity leads to an *anticipated* increase in output from period 1 onward. Saving would also fall in the basic model if the endowment was expected to be higher from some date T onward. Interestingly enough, if the increase in productivity were small (i.e., infinitesimal), saving would not change (see exercise 8 at the end of this chapter), which is consistent with our intuition for the case of a permanent change in the endowment. In that case the net output effect of the increase in investment is zero, and hence there is no reason to dissave in anticipation of higher future output. The current account still goes into deficit, of course, due to the rise in investment.

1.5.5 Unanticipated One-Period Increase in Productivity

We have just seen that a permanent rise in productivity leads to a current account deficit by reducing saving and increasing investment (figure 1.4). (And even if the increase in productivity were small, the rise in investment would generate a current account deficit.) We will now analyze the case of a temporary (one-period) rise in productivity that yields exactly the opposite result (i.e., a current account surplus). This case is the exact analogue to the temporary change in output studied in section 1.4.2 above.

Suppose that in $t = -1$ the economy is in the stationary equilibrium described in section 1.5.3. In period 0, A rises from A to A^H, where $A^H > A$, and then goes back to its initial level in period 1 (figure 1.6, panel a). Given that an unanticipated shock has taken place, households reoptimize in

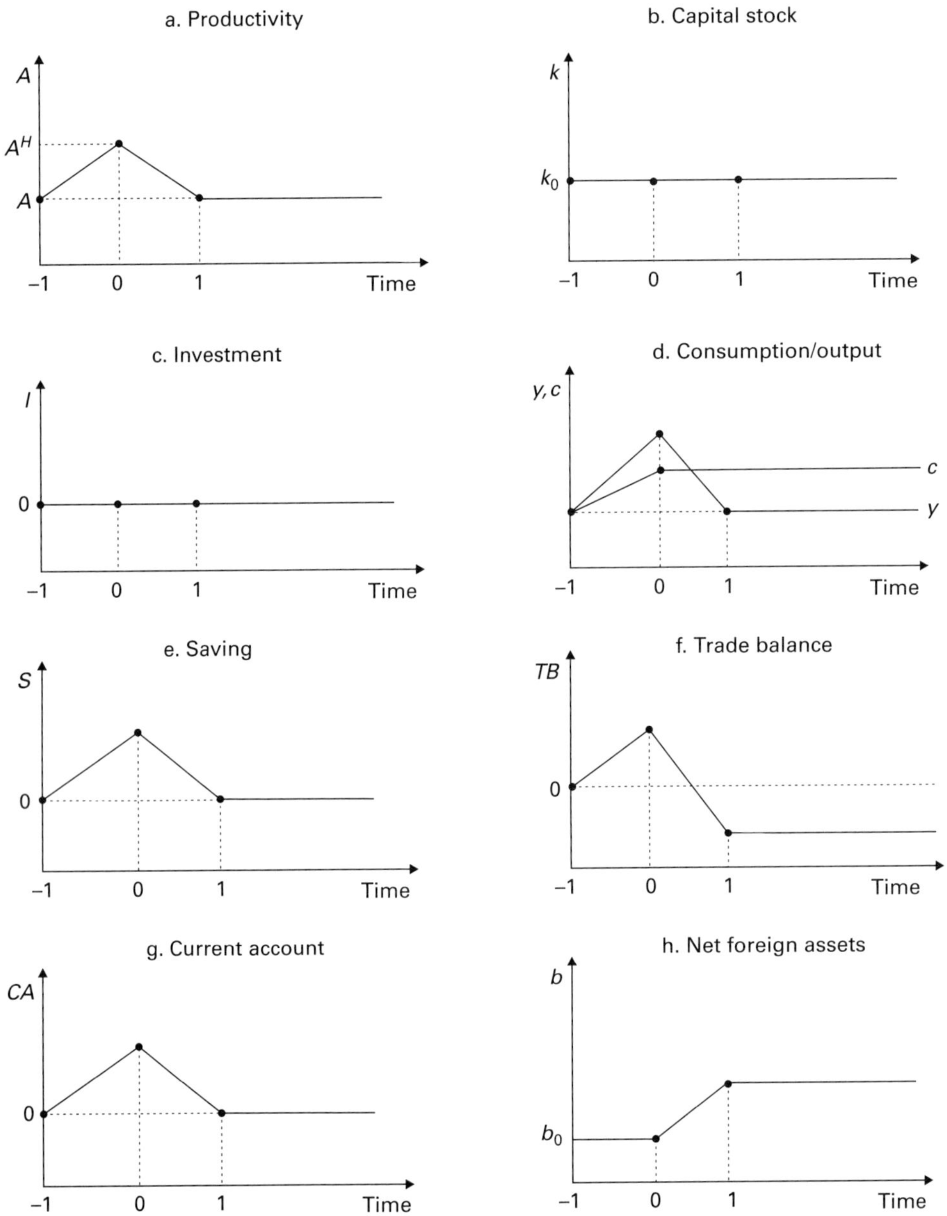

Figure 1.6
One-period increase in productivity

$t = 0$, taking k_0 as given. The first-order conditions are still given by (1.42) and (1.43). Since the increase in productivity lasts for only one period, the capital stock does not change (figure 1.6, panel b). Hence investment remains zero (figure 1.6, panel c). Given that productivity is higher in period 0, output is also higher in period 0 and then falls back to its initial level in period 1 (figure 1.6, panel d).

As (1.43) makes clear, consumers spread out the temporary increase in output over time by choosing a constant level of consumption from period 0 onward (figure 1.6, panel d). To compute this new level of consumption, we solve from (1.39), taking into account the new path of output, to obtain

$$c = rb_0 + Af(k) + \underbrace{\frac{r}{1+r}f(k)(A^H - A)}_{\text{Consumption-smoothing effect}}. \tag{1.62}$$

The third term on the RHS captures the consumption-smoothing effect. The additional output brought about by this one-period increase in productivity is $f(k)(A^H - A)$. Households spread out this gain over time by consuming the annuity value. As a result we expect saving to be positive in period 0 (panel e). Indeed, from (1.23) and (1.62), it follows that

$$S_0 = \frac{f(k)(A^H - A)}{1+r} > 0. \tag{1.63}$$

What happens to the trade balance? Since investment remains zero, $y_0 = A^H f(k)$, and $c_0 = c$, it follows from (1.47) that

$$TB_0 = A^H f(k) - c. \tag{1.64}$$

Substituting (1.62) into (1.64) yields

$$TB_0 = -rb_0 + \frac{f(k)(A^H - A)}{1+r} > -rb_0. \tag{1.65}$$

As expected, the trade balance improves in period 0. (If $b_0 = 0$, then the economy runs a trade surplus in period 0 as illustrated in figure 1.6, panel f.) From period 1 onward, the trade balance will fall below its pre-shock level. To show this, notice that

$$TB_t = Af(k) - c, \qquad t = 1, 2, \ldots. \tag{1.66}$$

Substituting (1.62) into the last expression yields

$$TB_t = -rb_0 + \frac{rf(k)(A - A^H)}{1+r} < -rb_0, \qquad t = 1, 2, \ldots.$$

Hence, if $b_0 = 0$, the economy runs a trade deficit from period 1 onward.

What about the current account? Clearly, this economy will run a current account surplus in period 0 since, as we have seen, saving is positive and investment is zero (see figure 1.6, panel g). Formally, using (1.49) and (1.63), we can write

$$CA_0 = \frac{f(k)(A^H - A)}{1+r} > 0. \tag{1.67}$$

Since there is a current account surplus in period 0, net foreign assets in period 1 will be higher (figure 1.6, panel h). Using the value obtained for b_1, it can be verified that saving from period 1 onward is zero, as illustrated in figure 1.6, panel e. Hence the current account is also zero from period 1 onward.

In sum, an unanticipated one-period rise in productivity leads to a trade and current account surplus. Since in this case there is no change in investment, this experiment is analogous (though with the opposite sign) to the temporary fall in endowment analyzed in section 1.4.2 and illustrated in figure 1.3.

1.5.6 Unanticipated and Temporary Rise in Productivity

Thus far we have seen two extreme cases, as captured in figures 1.4 and 1.6. In the first case (figure 1.4), a permanent rise in productivity leads to a current account deficit (fall in saving and increase in investment). In the second case (figure 1.6), a one-period rise in productivity leads to a current account surplus (positive saving and no change in investment). These two extreme examples thus illustrate the proposition that a positive productivity shock may lead to either a current account deficit or a current account surplus. For positive productivity shocks of more than one period, we would conjecture that there will be both a rise in saving (and, eventually, for a large enough horizon a fall in saving) and a rise in investment and that the relative strength of these two effects will depend on the duration of the shock. The longer is the duration of the shock, the smaller will be the saving effect in period 0, and hence the more likely that the shock will lead to a current account deficit in period 0.

To verify this conjecture, we now study an unanticipated and temporary rise in productivity that lasts for T periods. Since we have already analyzed the case $T = 1$ in section 1.5.5, we will examine the case where $T \geq 2$. Once again, suppose that as of $t = -1$, the economy is in the stationary equilibrium described above, with the capital stock given by k. In period 0, A increases from A to A^H for T periods (i.e., A is higher from period 0 up to, and including, period $T-1$) and then goes back to its initial level in period T (figure 1.7, panel a). In response to the unanticipated shock, households reoptimize, taking as given $k_0(= k)$. The first-order conditions continue to be given by (1.42) and (1.43).

Let us begin by deriving the path of the capital stock, illustrated in figure 1.7, panel b. The capital stock in period 0 is given by k. From period 1 onward, the path of the stock of capital follows from condition (1.42):

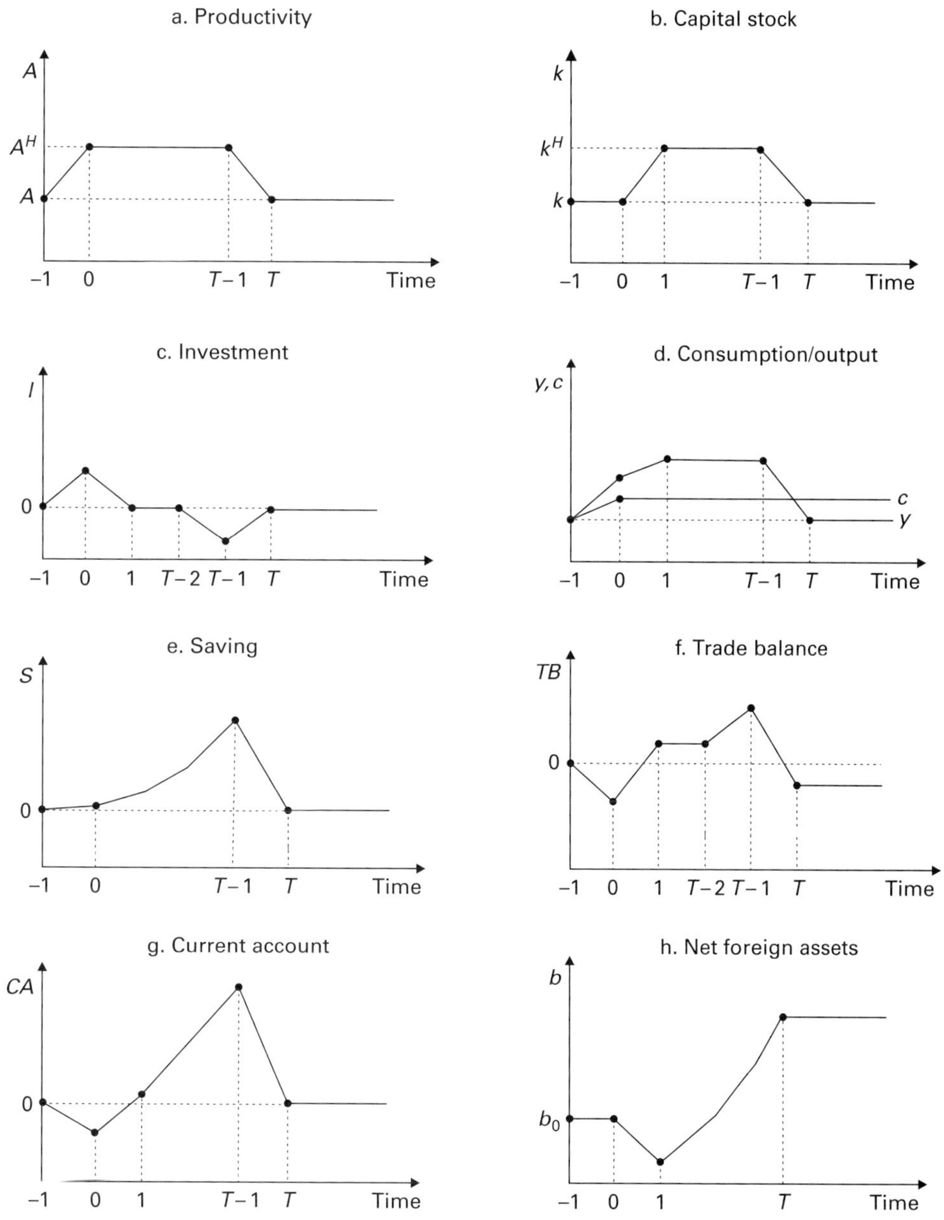

Figure 1.7
Temporary increase in productivity

$$A^H f'(k^H) = r, \qquad t = 1, 2, \ldots, T-1, \tag{1.68}$$

$$Af'(k) = r, \qquad t = T, T+1, \ldots. \tag{1.69}$$

Hence the capital stock is higher from period 1 until and including period $T-1$ (and denoted by k^H) and then falls back to its pre-shock level. It is worth noting that the rise in the capital stock in period 1 does *not* depend on the duration of the shock, T.

The path of investment, illustrated in figure 1.7, panel c, follows immediately from the path of the capital stock. Investment is positive in period 0 as the economy increases its capital stock and negative in period $T-1$ as the economy disinvests in anticipation of the productivity fall in period T.

Let us now derive the path of output, illustrated in figure 1.7, panel d. From (1.36) and the path of capital just derived, it follows that

$$\begin{aligned} y_0 &= A^H f(k) > y_{-1}, \\ y_t &= A^H f(k^H) > y_0, \qquad t = 1, 2, \ldots, T-1, \\ y_t &= Af(k) = y_{-1}, \qquad t = T, \ldots. \end{aligned} \tag{1.70}$$

Output thus rises in period 0, increases further in period $t = 1$, and then remains at that higher level up to, and including, period $T-1$. In period T, output returns to its pre-shock level.

To compute the change in consumption, it will be useful to proceed in steps and first compute the present discounted value of output (denoted by $PDV(y)$) and net output (i.e., output net of investment). Using (1.70), we can write the present discounted value of output as

$$PDV(y) = A^H f(k) + \sum_{t=1}^{T-1} \left(\frac{1}{1+r}\right)^t A^H f(k^H) + \sum_{t=T}^{\infty} \left(\frac{1}{1+r}\right)^t Af(k). \tag{1.71}$$

By applying the formula for a geometric progression, we simplify this expression to[34]

$$PDV(y) = A^H f(k) + \left[1 - \left(\frac{1}{1+r}\right)^{T-1}\right] \frac{A^H f(k^H)}{r} + \left(\frac{1}{1+r}\right)^{T-1} \frac{Af(k)}{r}. \tag{1.72}$$

34. To derive the equation below, recall that the sum for a geometric progression, S_n, is

$$S_n = \frac{a(1-x^n)}{1-x},$$

where a is the first term, n is the number of terms, and x is the common multiplier.

To compute the present discounted value of net output (i.e., output net of investment), we must subtract from the present discounted value of output, given by (1.72), the investment that takes place at time 0 and the disinvestment that takes place at $T-1$:

$$PDV(\text{net output}) = PDV(y) - (k_1 - k_0) - \left(\frac{1}{1+r}\right)^{T-1}(k_T - k_{T-1}). \tag{1.73}$$

Using (1.72) and taking into account that $k_0 = k_T = k$ and $k_1 = k_{T-1} = k^H$, we can rewrite this expression as

$$PDV(\text{net output}) = \underbrace{\left(\frac{1+r}{r}\right)Af(k)}_{\text{PDV of output with no shock}} + \underbrace{\left(\frac{1+r}{r}\right)\left[1-\left(\frac{1}{1+r}\right)^{T}\right]f(k)(A^H - A)}_{\text{PDV of direct effect}}$$
$$+ \underbrace{\left[1-\left(\frac{1}{1+r}\right)^{T-1}\right]\left[\frac{A^H f(k^H) - A^H f(k)}{r} - (k^H - k)\right]}_{\text{NPV of investment}}. \tag{1.74}$$

As indicated, the present discounted value of net output can be broken down into three components. The first tells us what the PDV of output would have been in the absence of the shock. The second captures the PDV of the direct effect on output of the increase in productivity.[35] The third component—which is by now familiar to us—captures the net present value of the investment carried out by this economy (now adjusted by the fact that the project only lasts for $T-1$ periods). As expected, the PDV of net output is higher the larger is T, since the higher productivity will last for a longer period of time.

Let us now turn to consumption. Once again, consumption will be constant along the new perfect foresight equilibrium path. From (1.39) and (1.74), it follows that

$$c = rb_0 + Af(k) + \left[1-\left(\frac{1}{1+r}\right)^{T}\right]f(k)(A^H - A)$$
$$+ \frac{r}{1+r}\left[1-\left(\frac{1}{1+r}\right)^{T-1}\right]\left[\frac{A^H f(k^H) - A^H f(k)}{r} - (k^H - k)\right]. \tag{1.75}$$

As is clear from (1.74), the new level of consumption is simply interest income plus the permanent component of the PDV value of net output. As expected, consumption is an increasing function of T.

35. By direct effect, we mean the increase in the level of output in the absence of any new investment.

What happens to saving in period 0? From (1.23) and (1.75), it follows that

$$S_0 = \underbrace{\left(\frac{1}{1+r}\right)^T f(k)(A^H - A)}_{+}$$
$$\underbrace{-\frac{r}{1+r}\left[1-\left(\frac{1}{1+r}\right)^{T-1}\right]\left[\frac{A^H[f(k^H)-f(k)]}{r} - (k^H - k)\right]}_{-} \gtreqless 0. \tag{1.76}$$

As we should have expected based on the two extreme cases studied above—illustrated in figures 1.4 and 1.6—saving in period 0 has two components (which go in opposite directions). The first component (which is positive, as indicated below the equation) reflects the saving induced by the temporarily higher output in period 0 (this is the effect that we saw when we studied a one-period increase in output; recall equation 1.63). This effect becomes smaller as T increases because the shock becomes "more permanent." In the extreme case of a permanent shock ($T \longrightarrow \infty$), this effect vanishes. The second component (which is negative, as indicated below the equation) reflects the dissaving induced by the future increase in output (this is the effect that we saw when we studied a permanent increase in productivity; recall equation 1.59). This dissaving becomes larger as T increases simply because the net present value of the investment increases (as the higher capital stock is in place for a longer time). Whether saving is positive or negative in period 0 will depend on the strength of these two effects (see box 1.3).[36] Whatever saving is in period 0, however, we have established that saving is a decreasing function of T.

Box 1.3
The Feldstein–Horioka puzzle

In a widely cited 1980 paper in the *Economic Journal*, Martin Feldstein and Charles Horioka documented a puzzle regarding saving and investment in open economies.[a] They argued that if perfect capital mobility prevailed, investors should invest in those countries with the highest marginal productivity of capital until marginal productivities of capital are equalized across countries. Since there is no need to finance domestic investment with domestic saving, we should expect a very low or no correlation between saving and investment in any particular country. Feldstein and Horioka presented data for OECD countries that showed, contrary to our theoretical expectations, saving and investment to be highly correlated. Table 1.3 supports this stylized fact by presenting saving–investment correlations for 10 developing and 14 industrial countries. The average correlation is positive for

a. The Felstein–Horioka paper spanned a large literature; see Coakleya, Kulasib, and Smith (1998) for a survey.

36. As discussed in box 1.3, the fact that saving could be positive provides a potential explanation for the so-called Feldstein–Horioka puzzle.

Box 1.3
(continued)

Table 1.3
Correlation between saving and investment (in real terms)

Developing countries		Industrial countries	
Argentina	0.92	Austria	0.80
Bolivia	0.08	Belgium	0.83
Colombia	0.85	Canada	0.87
Honduras	0.10	Denmark	0.78
Mexico	0.59	Finland	0.85
Paraguay	0.26	France	0.93
Peru	0.65	Germany	0.80
Turkey	0.68	Italy	0.66
Uruguay	0.88	Japan	0.91
Venezuela	0.56	Netherlands	0.81
		New Zealand	0.78
		Sweden	0.87
		Switzerland	0.67
		United States	0.85
Average	0.56	Average	0.81

Source: World Development Indicators (World Bank).
Note: Based on annual data, 1970 to 2010. Investment is the sum of gross capital formation and (when available) change in inventories.

both groups of countries (0.56 for developing countries and 0.81 for industrial countries) and is positive for every single country. Feldstein and Horioka argued that the explanation for such a puzzle was that the assumption of very high capital mobility was unrealistic and that, by and large, capital mobility—particularly of the kind that would support long-term investment—was limited at best.

While the facts themselves are uncontroversial, Feldstein and Horioka's take on this puzzle as reflecting limited capital mobility is much more debatable. Our simple model with investment is in fact able to solve this puzzle, at least qualitatively speaking. Indeed, as analyzed in section 1.5.6, our model predicts that in response to an unanticipated and positive increase in productivity, saving may actually increase. This is the case illustrated in figure 1.7, where we can see that both investment and saving increase at time 0. Intuitively, by increasing output, a positive and temporary productivity shock induces households to save in order to spread the benefits of the higher level of output over time. Quantitatively, calibrated versions of our basic model such as Mendoza's (1991) are also consistent with a positive saving–investment correlation even in the presence of perfect capital mobility. In fact, for a version of the model with adjustment costs calibrated for Canada, Mendoza (1991) reports a saving–investment correlation of around 0.5 to 0.6, which is consistent with table 1.3. We can conclude that in terms of our model the Feldstein–Horioka puzzle is actually no puzzle at all!

The fact that saving at $t = 0$ may be positive or negative is also telling us that consumption at $t = 0$ could be higher or lower than output at $t = 0$. To see this, consider the case where $b_0 = 0$, and hence $S_0 = y_0 - c$. If saving is positive (as assumed in figure 1.7, panel e), then $c < y_0$ (panel d).

What will happen to the trade balance in period 0? Using (1.47) and (1.75), we can write

$$TB_0 = -rb_0 + \underbrace{\left(\frac{1}{1+r}\right)^T f(k)(A^H - A)}_{A}$$
$$\underbrace{- \left[1 - \left(\frac{1}{1+r}\right)^{T-1}\right] \frac{r}{1+r} \left[\frac{A^H[f(k^H) - f(k)]}{r} - (k^H - k)\right]}_{B}$$
$$- \underbrace{(k^H - k)}_{\text{Investment effect}}.$$

In a model without investment, we would only have term A above, which, as was explained, is positive. The trade balance would therefore behave procyclically (i.e., improving in the case of a temporary increase in productivity). Once investment enters into the picture, however, we have two additional effects that go in the opposite direction and could therefore induce the trade balance to behave countercyclically. The second effect—term B—captures the dissaving induced by anticipated future higher output. The third is the investment effect. The behavior of the trade balance in period 0 will thus depend on the strength of these three effects. If the last two effects dominate—as figure 1.7, panel f, assumes—then the trade balance worsens on impact (i.e., it moves countercyclically), which is consistent with the data (see box 1.2).[37]

From period 1 up to, and including, period $T - 2$, the trade balance will improve relative to its pre-shock level. In period $T - 1$, the trade balance improves further reflecting that period's negative investment. From period T onward, there is a trade deficit.[38]

What about the current account? Using (1.49), we can write

$$CA_0 = S_0 - I_0 \gtreqless 0. \tag{1.77}$$

The sign of the current account is ambiguous because saving could be either positive or negative and investment is, of course, positive. Figure 1.7, panel g, assumes that the current account goes into deficit in period 0. To compute the entire path of the current account, we need to keep track of the path of net foreign assets, as the latter influences saving through the returns on net

37. As exercise 8 at the end of this chapter makes clear, if the change in productivity were small, then the second effect would not be present and the effect on the trade balance (and hence current account) would capture the tension between the first (consumption smoothing) and third (investment) effects. Panel f assumes that $b_0 = 0$.

38. See appendix 1.7.3 for the formal derivation of the paths of the trade balance, saving, and current account.

foreign assets. While straightforward, the algebra is somewhat tedious and is left for appendix 1.7.3. Intuitively, as the trade balance moves into surplus in period 1, so does the current account balance. It then continues to improve over time because, while the trade balance remains constant up to, and including, period $T-2$, returns on assets keep accumulating. In period $T-1$, the current account surplus is further fed by the disinvestment. In period T, the current account balance falls to zero as the economy becomes stationary thereafter. Figure 1.7, panel h, illustrates the corresponding path of net foreign assets.

In sum, we have shown that once investment is brought into the picture, a temporary shock can lead to a countercyclical response of the trade and current account balances. In the experiment just analyzed, a temporary increase in productivity can lead to either a current account surplus or a current account deficit. It is worth noting that in the event where the investment effect dominates, the current account goes into deficit for only one period because it only takes one period for the capital stock to increase. If there were adjustment costs and investment took longer to adjust to its new value, the current account deficit could also last for more than one period.

1.5.7 A Numerical Example

To fix ideas, let us compute a numerical example to illustrate the impact response (i.e., the response in $t=0$) of the current account to a temporary increase in productivity. As equation (1.77) indicates, the response of the current account will depend on the relative strength of the saving and investment effects. While the investment effect does not depend on the length of the shock, T, the saving effect will be smaller the larger is T. In fact we know that for large enough values of T, the investment effect will prevail because saving eventually becomes negative as well. We also know that for $T=1$, there is no investment effect and therefore the current account goes into surplus. But what happens for intermediate values of T?

Suppose that the production function takes the Cobb–Douglas form

$$f(k)=k^{\alpha}. \tag{1.78}$$

Assume the following parameterization:

$$A=0.1,$$

$$A^H=0.11,$$

$$\alpha=0.1,$$

$$r=0.3.$$

Figure 1.8 illustrates the corresponding results using equation (1.63) for $T=1$, equation (1.76) for $T\geq 2$, and equation (1.77). Panel a depicts the impact response of saving and investment as a function of T, and panel b illustrates the impact response of the current account. For $T=1$, there

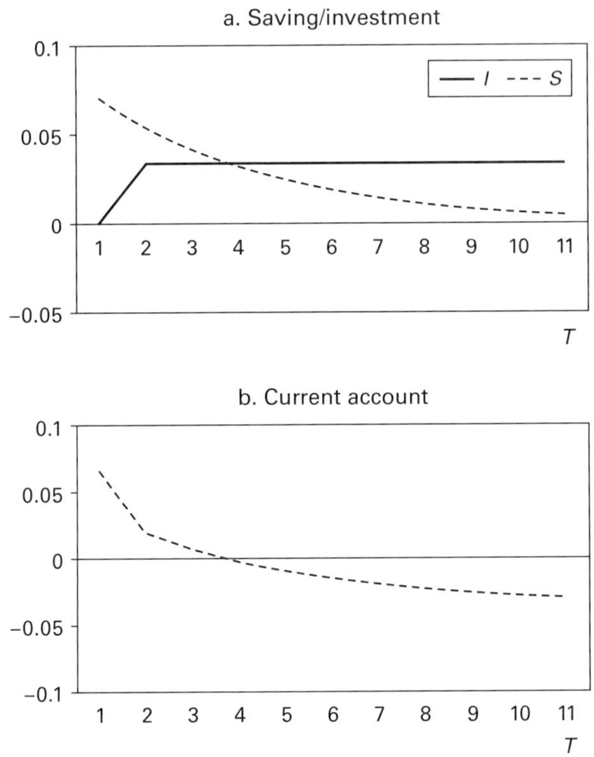

Figure 1.8
Saving, investment, and current account

is no investment effect, and hence the current account must necessarily be in surplus in $t = 0$. As proved analytically, saving is a decreasing function of T. For $T \geq 2$, investment does not depend on T. For this particular parameterization the saving effect dominates until the duration of the shock becomes $T = 4$. For any shock lasting more than four periods, the investment effect dominates and a temporary increase in productivity leads to a current account deficit.[39]

1.6 Final Remarks

This chapter has shown how, in a world with no frictions and a constant world real interest rate, a small open economy will achieve perfect consumption smoothing even when output fluctuates

39. Due to the absence of adjustment costs, the value of r must be rather large for the investment effect not to always dominate the saving effect. For $r = 0.1$, for example, the investment effect dominates already for $T = 2$, so the current account is in deficit for any $T \geq 2$. Exercise 9 at the end of the chapter asks you to take T as given and plot the current account as a function of time for different parameterizations.

over time.[40] As a benchmark this is perhaps the most important result of modern open economy macroeconomics. In practice, however, many countries face a variety of frictions that will imply substantial (and welfare-reducing) departures from this first-best world. In the next chapter, for example, we will analyze how imperfections in international capital markets may critically affect the economy's ability to achieve consumption smoothing over time. In chapter 3, we will see how policy-induced intertemporal distortions lead the private sector to choose nonflat (and socially suboptimal) consumption paths.

1.7 Appendixes

1.7.1 Pointwise Optimization

This appendix formally derives the first-order condition (1.10). We will show this in two alternative ways: (1) partition method and (2) perturbation method.

Partition Method

For convenience, let us restate the consumer's problem as

$$\max_{\{c_t\}} \int_0^T u(c_t)e^{-\beta t}dt$$

subject to

$$\int_0^T c_t e^{-rt}dt = K,$$

where

$$K \equiv b_0 + \int_0^T y_t e^{-rt}dt.$$

We proceed by dividing the interval $[0, T]$ into N equal subintervals, each of length Δ:

$$\Delta = \frac{T}{N}.$$

40. An online appendix develops a discrete-time version of our basic endowment model and solves it for permanent and temporary shocks using MATLAB. While, in practice, one would not use numerical methods to solve such a simple model, it proves illuminating for pedagogical purposes to solve numerically exactly the same model that one has been able to solve analytically. Such an exercise will also prove extremely useful for the analysis of chapters 13, 14, and 15 where monetary versions of this model will be used to derive various results numerically.

Let $t_0, t_1, \dots, t_N$ denote the beginning and endpoints of these intervals:

$$t_0 = 0, \quad t_1 = \Delta, \quad t_2 = 2\Delta, \dots, \quad t_N = N\Delta = T. \tag{1.79}$$

The original consumer's problem can then be approximated as

$$\max_{\{c_{t_1},\dots,c_{t_N}\}} \; u(c_{t_1})e^{-\beta t_1}(t_1 - t_0) + u(c_{t_2})e^{-\beta t_2}(t_2 - t_1) + .. + \; u(c_{t_N})e^{-\beta t_N}(t_N - t_{N-1})$$

subject to

$$c_{t_1}e^{-rt_1}(t_1 - t_0) + c_{t_2}e^{-rt_2}(t_2 - t_1) + .. + \; c_{t_N}e^{-rt_N}(t_N - t_{N-1}) = K.$$

Using (1.79), we can restate this problem more compactly as

$$\max_{\{c_{t_1},\dots,c_{t_N}\}} \sum_{i=1}^{N} u(c_{t_i})e^{-\beta t_i}\Delta$$

subject to

$$\sum_{i=1}^{N} c_{t_i}e^{-rt_i}\Delta = K.$$

The corresponding Lagrangian reads as

$$\mathcal{L} = \sum_{i=1}^{N} u(c_{t_i})e^{-\beta t_i}\Delta + \lambda\left[K - \sum_{i=1}^{N} c_{t_i}e^{-rt_i}\Delta\right].$$

The first-order conditions for this problems are given by

$$u'(c_{t_i})e^{-\beta t_i} = \lambda e^{-rt_i} \qquad \text{for all } i = 1, \dots, N.$$

These first-order conditions are valid for any size of the subintervals. In particular, they are valid for an infinitesimal subinterval. Since as Δ tends to zero, the values of $t_i, i = 1, \dots, N$ become arbitrarily close to each other, we can write

$$u'(c_t)e^{-\beta t} = \lambda e^{-rt} \qquad \text{for all } t \in [0, T]$$

as the first-order condition when the problem is formulated in continuous time.

Perturbation Method

To illustrate the logic behind this method, we first look at a simple case. Let $f(x)$ be a function that maps numbers from the real line to numbers in the real line. Consider the problem of choosing x so as to maximize $f(x)$. We will show that

$$f'(x^*) = 0$$

is a necessary condition for x^* to be a local maximum.

If x^* is a local interior maximum then, by definition,

$$f(x^*) \geq f(x^* + \Delta x), \tag{1.80}$$

where $\Delta x (\equiv x - x^*)$ represents a "perturbation." For a small Δx around x^*,

$$f(x^* + \Delta x) = f(x) \simeq f(x^*) + f'(x^*)\Delta x. \tag{1.81}$$

Substituting $f(x^* + \Delta x) = f(x^*) + f'(x^*)\Delta x$ into (1.80) we obtain the fundamental inequality

$$f'(x^*)\Delta x \leq 0. \tag{1.82}$$

For condition (1.82) to hold for any arbitrary Δx, it must be the case that

$$f'(x^*) = 0. \tag{1.83}$$

We now turn to the problem at hand. Let $\int_0^T f(x(t))dt$ be a functional that maps functions from a set of eligible functions to numbers in the real line.[41] Consider the problem of choosing the function $x(t)$ so as to maximize $\int_0^T f(x(t))dt$. In such a problem, if $x^*(t)$ is a local interior maximum, then, by definition,

$$\int_0^T f(x^*(t))dt \geq \int_0^T f(x^*(t) + \varepsilon h(t))dt, \tag{1.84}$$

where ε is an arbitrary real number and $h(t)$ is any arbitrary function in the opportunity set. The term $\varepsilon h(t)$ represents a "perturbation." We will derive a necessary condition for $x^*(t)$ to be a local maximum of the objective functional.

Note that

$$\int_0^T f(x(t))dt = \int_0^T f(x^*(t) + \varepsilon h(t))dt = F(\varepsilon). \tag{1.85}$$

Thus we now have a mapping from numbers in the real line into numbers in the real line. By construction, $F(\varepsilon)$ must be maximized when $\varepsilon = 0$. From (1.83) we know that a necessary condition for a local interior maximum is

$$F'(0) = 0.$$

41. A functional should not be confused with a function. A functional maps a function into a real number, whereas a function maps a number (or, more generally, a vector) into a real number.

We use Leibniz's rule to differentiate (1.85),[42]

$$F'(0) = \int_0^T f'(x^*(t))h(t)dt = 0. \tag{1.86}$$

For condition (1.86) to hold for any arbitrary $h(t)$, it must be the case that

$$f'(x^*(t)) = 0 \tag{1.87}$$

for any value of $t \in [0, T]$.

1.7.2 Proof That Solution Is a Maximum[43]

We now show that a consumption path characterized by first-order condition (1.10) and intertemporal constraint (1.9) characterizes a maximum. Since $u(c)$ is strictly concave, then for any two points, c^1 and c^2, $c^1 \neq c^2$, it must be true that

$$u(c^2) - u(c^1) < u'(c^1)(c^2 - c^1).$$

Let path c_t^1 satisfy first-order condition (1.10) and intertemporal constraint (1.9). Let path c_t^2 satisfy intertemporal constraint (1.9). Then

$$\begin{aligned}\int_0^T \left[u(c_t^2) - u(c_t^1)\right] e^{-\beta t} dt &\leq \int_0^T u'(c_t^1)(c_t^2 - c_t^1)e^{-\beta t} dt \\ &= \lambda \int_0^T (c_t^2 - c_t^1)e^{-rt} dt = 0,\end{aligned}$$

where we have used first-order condition (1.10), and the right-most equality follows from the fact that, by assumption, both paths satisfy intertemporal constraint (1.9). Hence path c_t^1 is indeed a maximum.

42. In its more general formulation, Leibniz's rule states that if we have a function, $F(t)$, defined as

$$F(t) = \int_{g(t)}^{x(t)} f(s,t)ds,$$

then its derivative is given by

$$F'(t) = f(x(t),t)x'(t) - f(g(t),t)g'(t) + \int_{g(t)}^{x(t)} \frac{\partial f(s,t)}{\partial t} ds.$$

43. We follow Calvo (1996).

1.7.3 Derivation of Trade Balance and Current Account Paths

This appendix computes the path of the current account for the case of an unanticipated and temporary rise in productivity. We follow an iterative procedure that consists in first computing the change in the current account in $t = 0$, then computing the resulting change in net foreign assets (which allows us to compute the change in the current account in $t = 1$), and then repeating the same steps for all subsequent time periods.

Path of the Trade Balance

Since $I_t = 0$ for $t = 1, 2, \ldots, T-2$, the trade balance for $t = 1, 2, \ldots, T-2$ is given by

$$TB_t = y_t - c_t, \qquad t = 1, 2, \ldots, T-2.$$

Using (1.70) and (1.75), we obtain

$$\begin{aligned} TB_t|_{t=1,2,\ldots,T-2} &= -rb_0 + \frac{r}{1+r} A^H \left[f(k^H) - f(k)\right] + \left(\frac{1}{1+r}\right)^T \left[A^H f(k^H) - Af(k)\right] \\ &\quad + \frac{r}{1+r}\left[1 - \left(\frac{1}{1+r}\right)^{T-1}\right](k^H - k) \\ &> -rb_0. \end{aligned}$$

Hence, for $b_0 = 0$, the trade balance goes into surplus in $t = 1$. For $t = T-1$, we need to add the disinvestment effect to the expression above:

$$\begin{aligned} TB_{T-1} &= -rb_0 + \frac{r}{1+r} A^H \left[f(k^H) - f(k)\right] + \left(\frac{1}{1+r}\right)^T \left[A^H f(k^H) - Af(k)\right] \\ &\quad + \frac{r}{1+r}\left[1 - \left(\frac{1}{1+r}\right)^{T-1}\right](k^H - k) - (k_T - k_{T-1}) \\ &> TB_t|_{t=1,2,\ldots,T-2}\,. \end{aligned}$$

Since investment is negative in $T-1$, the trade balance will be larger in $T-1$ than in $T-2$.

What about T? Intuitively, it is clear that there should be a deficit (for $b_0 = 0$). Output is the same as before the shock, but we have a higher level of consumption. Indeed, using (1.70) and (1.75), we obtain

$$\begin{aligned} TB_T = -rb_0 - \Bigg\{ &\left[1 - \left(\frac{1}{1+r}\right)^T\right] f(k)(A^H - A) \\ &+ \frac{r}{1+r}\left[1 - \left(\frac{1}{1+r}\right)^{T-1}\right]\left[\frac{A^H f(k^H) - A^H f(k)}{r} - (k^H - k)\right]\Bigg\} < -rb_0. \end{aligned}$$

Path of Saving

By definition, saving in period 1 is given by

$$S_1 = rb_1 + A^H f(k^H) - c.$$

Adding and subtracting $rb_0 + A^H f(k)$ and noting that $S_0 = rb_0 + A^H f(k) - c$ and $b_1 - b_0 = S_0 - I_0$, we can rewrite this expression as

$$S_1 = (1+r)S_0 + r\left[A^H\left(\frac{f(k^H) - f(k)}{r}\right) - I_0\right] > S_0. \tag{1.88}$$

Saving in $t = 1$ is thus bigger than in $t = 0$. Proceeding in a similar way, it is easy to check that for periods $t = 2$ through $t = T - 1$ saving can be written recursively as

$$S_t = (1+r)S_{t-1}, \qquad t = 2, \ldots, T-1. \tag{1.89}$$

Saving thus keeps increasing over time up to (and including) period $T - 1$. By the same token, saving in period T is given by

$$S_T = (1+r)S_{T-1} - rI_{T-1} - \left[A^H f(k^H) - Af(k)\right].$$

To show that $S_T = 0$, we use (1.89) repeatedly to express S_T as a function of S_0:

$$S_T = (1+r)^T S_0 + (1+r)^{T-1} r\left[A^H\left(\frac{f(k^H) - f(k)}{r}\right) - I_0\right]$$
$$- rI_{T-1} - \left[A^H f(k^H) - Af(k)\right].$$

From the expression for c given by (1.75) and the fact that $S_0 = rb_0 + A^H f(k) - c$, it follows that $S_T = 0$.

Path of the Current Account

We have already shown in the text that the current account in period 0 could take any sign. In period 1, investment is zero and therefore $CA_1 = S_1$. Hence, from (1.88),

$$CA_1 = S_1 = (1+r)S_0 + r\left[A^H\left(\frac{f(k^H) - f(k)}{r}\right) - I_0\right] > CA_0.$$

The current account balance in $t = 1$ is larger than in $t = 0$ because $S_1 > S_0$, and there is no investment. Since investment remains zero up to and including period $T - 2$, it follows that

$$CA_t = S_t, \qquad t = 2, \ldots, T-2.$$

Given that we have already established that saving increases up to and including $T - 2$, the current account balance also increases over time. In period $T - 1$ the current account is given by

$$CA_{T-1} = S_{T-1} - I_{T-1} > CA_{T-2},$$

where the inequality follows from the fact that $S_{T-1} > S_{T-2}$ and $I_{T-1} < 0$. In sum, while the level of the current account balance in period 0 is ambiguous, its level keeps increasing over time up to and including period $T-1$. In period T the current account is zero, since, as shown above, saving in T is zero and investment is also zero.

Exercises

1. (Time inconsistency: The role of discounting) This exercise takes as given the time separability of preferences and illustrates the role of hyperbolic discounting in generating time inconsistency. To this end, the exercise first asks you to verify that time-separable preferences with exponential discounting (i.e., the preferences used in the text) are time consistent. It then asks you to work out an example in which the introduction of hyperbolic discounting renders preferences time inconsistent.[44]

a. (Exponential consumer) Suppose that the preferences of the "exponential" consumer are given by

$$U_0(c_0, c_1, \ldots) = \sum_{t=0}^{\infty} \delta^t \log(c_t), \tag{1.90}$$

where c_t is consumption in period t, $\delta \in (0, 1)$, and the subscript 0 on the lifetime utility function indicates that the consumption path is being evaluated as of time $t = 0$. Assume $\delta(1 + r) = 1$. The flow constraint for period t is given by

$$b_{t+1} = (1 + r)b_t + y - c_t,$$

where y is the constant endowment, r is the exogenously given world real interest rate, and b_t are net foreign assets held between period t and period $t+1$. Iterating forward the flow constraint and imposing the condition that

$$\lim_{t \to \infty} \frac{b_{t+1}}{(1 + r)^t} = 0$$

yields the following intertemporal constraint:

$$\sum_{t=0}^{\infty} \left(\frac{1}{1 + r}\right)^t c_t = (1 + r)\left(b_0 + \frac{y}{r}\right). \tag{1.91}$$

44. See Backus, Routledge, and Zin (2005) for a detailed discussion on the role of preferences in generating time-inconsistency problems. See also the discussion in Calvo (1996).

In this context:

i. Define the discount factor at time t (a measure of the degree of the consumer's impatience) as the marginal rate of substitution between consumption at two consecutive dates for a constant consumption path, c:

$$\text{Discount factor}_t \equiv MRS^t_{t,t+1} = \left.\frac{\partial U_t(c_0, c_1, \ldots)/\partial c_{t+1}}{\partial U_t(c_0, c_1, \ldots)/\partial c_t}\right|_{c_0=c_1=\ldots=c}.$$

Suppose that the consumer is standing at time t. Compute the discount factor for consumption between $t+1$ and $t+2$ (i.e., compute $MRS^t_{t+1,t+2}$). Next suppose that the consumer is standing at $t+1$. Recompute the discount factor for consumption between $t+1$ and $t+2$ (i.e., compute $MRS^{t+1}_{t+1,t+2}$). Verify that $MRS^t_{t+1,t+2} = MRS^{t+1}_{t+1,t+2}$.

ii. Denote by c^0_t, $t = 0, 1, \ldots$, the optimal consumption path chosen at $t = 0$. Compute reduced forms for c^0_t, $t = 0, 1, \ldots$.

iii. Denote by c^1_t, $t = 1, 2, \ldots$, the optimal consumption path chosen at $t = 1$. Verify that the optimal consumption path chosen at $t = 1$ is time consistent (i.e., coincides with the path chosen at $t = 0$). (Hint: Compute reduced forms for c^1_t, $t = 1, 2, \ldots$, and check that $c^0_1 = c^1_1$, $c^0_2 = c^1_2$, etc.)

b. (Hyperbolic consumer) Suppose now that preferences are of the "quasi-hyperbolic" type (e.g., Backus, Routledge, and Zin 2005):

$$U_0(c_0, c_1, \ldots) = \log(c_0) + \rho \sum_{t=1}^{\infty} \delta^t \log(c_t), \tag{1.92}$$

where $\rho \in (0, 1)$. Assume $\delta(1+r) = 1$.
In this context:

i. Suppose that the consumer is standing at time t. Compute the discount factor for consumption between $t+1$ and $t+2$ (i.e., compute $MRS^t_{t+1,t+2}$). Next suppose that the consumer is standing at $t+1$. Recompute the discount factor for consumption between $t+1$ and $t+2$ (i.e., compute $MRS^{t+1}_{t+1,t+2}$). Verify that $MRS^t_{t+1,t+2} > MRS^{t+1}_{t+1,t+2}$. Notice that this implies that the consumer is more patient about consuming between tomorrow and the day after tomorrow from the standpoint of today than from the standpoint of tomorrow. In this sense, the consumer is more impatient in the "short run" than in the "long run," which is the defining characteristic of hyperbolic discounting.

ii. Compute reduced forms for c^0_t, $t = 0, 1, \ldots$.

iii. Compute reduced forms for c^1_t, $t = 1, 2, \ldots$. Assume, for simplicity, that $b_0 = 0$. Show that the optimal consumption path chosen at $t = 1$ is time inconsistent (i.e., does not coincide with the path chosen at $t = 0$). (Hint: Compute reduced-forms for c^j_1, $j = 0, 1, \ldots$, and verify that $c^1_1 > c^0_1$.) Explain intuitively the source of the time inconsistency.

2. (Time inconsistency: The role of non–time separability) This exercise—which complements the previous one—takes as given the presence of exponential discounting and illustrates the role of non–time separability in generating time inconsistency.

a. (Past consumption affects today's utility) Let preferences be given by

$$U_0(c_0, c_1, \ldots) = \log(c_0) + \sum_{t=1}^{\infty} \delta^t[\log(c_t) + \alpha \log(c_{t-1})].$$

The sign of α defines the type of preferences. Naturally, if $\alpha = 0$, then these are the standard time-separable preferences. If $\alpha < 0$, then there is habit persistence in the sense that higher consumption in period $t-1$ decreases utility in t (capturing the idea that consumers get used or "addicted" to that level of consumption). If $\alpha > 0$, then there is durability of consumption goods in the sense that higher consumption at $t-1$ increases utility at t.[45] The intertemporal constraint remains given by (1.91). (Assume $\delta(1+r) = 1$.)

In this context:

i. Compute reduced forms for c_t^0, $t = 0, 1, \ldots$.

ii. Compute reduced forms for c_t^1, $t = 0, 1, \ldots$. Verify that the optimal consumption path chosen at $t = 1$ is time consistent.

b. (Future consumption yields utility) Let preferences be given by

$$U_0(c_0, c_1, \ldots) = \sum_{t=0}^{\infty} \delta^t[\log(c_t) + \log(c_{t+1})].$$

In this case the consumer derives utility not only from today's consumption but also from next period's consumption. Assume $\delta(1+r) = 1$.

i. Compute reduced forms for c_t^0, $t = 0, 1, \ldots$.

ii. Compute reduced forms for c_t^1, $t = 0, 1, \ldots$. Assume, for simplicity, that $b_0 = 0$. Show that the optimal consumption path chosen at $t = 1$ is time inconsistent. Explain intuitively the source of time inconsistency.

3. (Roots of the system) Consider the infinite-horizon model of section 1.2.2 with logarithmic preferences. In this context:

a. Show that the dynamic system associated with this model has roots $r - \beta$ and r. (If $r = \beta$, then the roots are zero and r.)

45. Habit persistence has been used extensively in the finance literature as a possible explanation for the equity-premium puzzle (see Constantinides 1990). In the area of development macroeconomics, habit persistence has been used by Uribe (2002) to explain some of the stylized facts associated with exchange rate based stabilization, which we will study in chapter 13.

b. Consider a discrete-time version of the model. Show that for the $(1+r)\beta = 1$ case, the roots are 1 and $1+r$.

4. (Consumption tilting) This exercise analyzes consumption tilting (i.e., optimal consumption plans when β is not necessarily equal to r) in both the finite- and infinite-horizon settings.

Let the instantaneous utility function be given by

$$u(c_t) = \frac{c_t^{1-(1/\sigma)} - 1}{1-(1/\sigma)}, \tag{1.93}$$

where $\sigma > 0$ denotes the intertemporal rate of substitution in consumption.

a. (Finite horizon) Consider the finite-horizon problem analyzed in the text where the consumer maximizes (1.1) (with the instantaneous utility function given by equation 1.93) subject to (1.9). In this context:

i. Derive the first-order conditions for the consumer's problem, and show how the rate of growth of consumption depends on the relation between β and r.

ii. Derive a closed form solution for c_t.

b. (Infinite horizon; based on Calvo 1996) In an infinite-horizon setting, the existence of a well-defined optimal consumption path when r is different from β cannot be taken for granted. (By well-defined optimal consumption path, we mean a consumption path whose present discounted value is finite.)

Consider the basic infinite-horizon model described in the text, in which the consumer maximizes (1.12) (with the instantaneous utility function given by equation 1.93) subject to (1.17). For simplicity, let the endowment stream be constant over time and equal to y and $b_0 = 0$. In this context:

i. Derive a condition involving r, β, and σ that guarantees the existence of a well-defined optimal consumption path. In particular, show that $\sigma \leq 1$ is a *sufficient* condition for existence. (Hint: Solve for the optimal consumption path, write the intertemporal budget constraint in terms of c_0, and establish the condition for the integral to converge.)

ii. Illustrate the fact that $\sigma \leq 1$ is not a *necessary* condition to guarantee the existence of a well-defined optimal consumption path by considering the case where $\sigma = 1.5$. What is the condition involving r and β for which existence is guaranteed?

iii. Restrict your attention to cases where a well-defined optimal consumption path exists. Show that: (1) If $r = \beta$, $c_t = y$ for all $t \geq 0$, (2) if $r > \beta$, $c_0 < y$ and consumption increases over time, and (3) if $r < \beta$, $c_0 > y$ and consumption falls over time.

iv. Check that the same condition that you derived in part i above guarantees that the utility functional (1.12), with $u(c)$ given by (1.93), converges.

5. (Fluctuating real interest rate) Suppose that in the infinite-horizon model analyzed in section 1.2.2 the world real interest rate fluctuates over time. In particular, to fix ideas, assume that the time path of the real interest rate is given by

$$r_t = \begin{cases} r^H & \text{for } 0 \leqslant t \leqslant T, \\ r^L & \text{for } t > T, \end{cases}$$

where $r^H > \beta$ and $r^L < \beta$. Assume logarithmic preferences.

In this context, derive a reduced-form solution for the path of consumption.

6. (Adding labor supply to the basic model) This exercise adds labor supply to the basic infinite-horizon model of section 1.2.2. Production is thus endogenous. Specifically, consider the economy of section 1.2.2 with the following modifications (same notation is used).

Households

Let preferences be given by

$$\int_0^\infty \log[c_t - \phi(\ell_t^s)^\upsilon]e^{-\beta t}dt,$$

where ℓ^s is labor supply and $\phi(> 0)$ and $\upsilon(> 1)$ are positive parameters. This class of preferences—referred to in the literature as GHH preferences after the paper by Greenwood, Hercowitz, and Huffman (1988)—generates a labor supply function that depends only on the real wage. In other words, there is no wealth effect on leisure. The household's flow constraint is given by

$$\dot{b}_t = rb_t + w_t\ell_t^s - c_t + \Omega_t,$$

where w_t is the real wage and Ω_t are the profits from firms (i.e., households own the firms). The corresponding intertemporal constraint is given by

$$b_0 + \int_0^\infty \left(w_t\ell_t^s + \Omega_t\right) e^{-rt}dt = \int_0^\infty c_t e^{-rt}dt.$$

Firms

Firms face a static problem. Production is given by

$$y_t = \Psi_t\left(\ell_t^d\right)^\alpha, \qquad \alpha < 1,$$

where ℓ_t^d is labor demand and Ψ_t is a productivity parameter.

In the context of this model:

a. Solve the household's maximization problem. Using the first-order conditions, derive a labor supply function (i.e., express ℓ_t^s as a function of w_t).

b. Solve for the firms' problem.

c. After imposing labor market equilibrium (i.e., $\ell_t^s = \ell_t^d$), solve for a perfect foresight path along which Ψ_t is at some high value between time 0 and time T and low afterward.

d. What key difference do you notice in the behavior of consumption relative to the model of section 1.2.2? Show that if the labor supply elasticity is small (as is the case in practice), then, from a quantitative viewpoint, the behavior of consumption in response to a fluctuating path of Ψ_t will not differ significantly from the behavior of consumption in response to a fluctuating endowment path in the model of section 1.2.2.[46]

7. (Decentralized economy) This exercise asks you to check that the centralized production economy analyzed in section 1.5 can be decentralized. Suppose that there are two agents in the economy: consumers and firms. Consumers own both the capital stock and the firms. There is a market for physical capital in which consumers rent the capital stock to firms at a rate r_t^k. Firms produce the good using the capital stock and give back profits to consumers. Preferences and technology are the same as in the text.

a. Write down the consumer's flow constraint, and then derive the consumer's intertemporal constraint. Derive the consumer's first-order conditions.

b. Write down the firm's flow constraint, and derive the first-order condition.

c. Show that the optimality conditions characterizing consumption and the capital stock are the same as in the centralized economy.

d. Derive aggregate constraints (both the flow constraint, or current account, and the intertemporal constraint) and show that they correspond exactly to those for the centralized economy (equations 1.38 and 1.39).

8. (Small changes in productivity) This exercise asks you to revisit some of the experiments performed in the text for the model with investment for the case where the change in productivity is small (i.e., the change is given by dA). This exercise will shed light on the reaction of saving to changes in productivity.

Consider the model with investment described in section 1.5. In this context:

a. Analyze the effects of a (small) unanticipated and permanent increase in A. (In other words, assume that A changes by dA.) In particular, show that there will be no change in saving.

b. Analyze the effects of a (small) unanticipated and temporary increase in A that lasts for $T (\geq 2)$ periods. Derive a reduced form for the change in the current account in period 0, and show how it depends on T.

46. In practice, however, total labor hours fluctuate considerably over the business cycle due to entry and exit from the labor force (the extensive margin), as opposed to changes in hours worked by existing agents (the intensive margin). To generate the observed comovement between total labor hours and the cycle at an aggregate level, one needs to incorporate this "extensive margin" into the model (see King and Rebelo 2000 for a detailed discussion).

9. (Numerical example) Consider the model with investment of section 1.5 and focus on a temporary increase in productivity that lasts for four periods (i.e., $T = 4$). Using any computer program that you feel comfortable with (Excel, Matlab, Mathematica), solve the model numerically and generate the following pictures:

a. Plot as a function of *time* output, investment, consumption, saving, trade balance, and current account for the case where the current account initially worsens.

b. Plot as a function of *time* output, investment, consumption, saving, trade balance, and current account for the case where the current account initially improves.

Provide some intuition regarding the paths of the different variables in each of the two cases. (Note that these are *not* the plots presented in figure 1.8. Those plots depict the response in $t = 0$ of saving, investment, and the current account as a function of the duration of the shock, T. Here you are asked to take T as given and plot the path of the variables over time.)

References

Aguiar, Mark, and Gita Gopinath. 2007. Emerging market business cycles: The cycle is the trend. *Journal of Political Economy* 115: 69–102.

Backus, David K., Bryan R. Routledge, and Stanley E. Zin. 2005. Exotic preferences for macroeconomists. *NBER Macroeconomics Annual* 19: 319–414.

Calvo, Guillermo A. 1996. The basic intertemporal model. Lecture notes. University of Maryland, College Park, MD.

Chakravarty, Sukhamoy. 1962. The existence of an optimum savings program. *Econometrica* 30 (1): 178–87.

Chiang, Alpha C. 1992. *Elements of Dynamic Optimization*. New York: McGraw-Hill.

Coakleya, Jerry, Farida Kulasib, and Ron Smith. 1998. The Feldstein–Horioka puzzle and capital mobility: A review. *International Journal of Finance and Economics* 3 (2): 169–88.

Constantinides, George M. 1990. Habit formation: A resolution of the equity premium puzzle. *Journal of Political Economy* 98 (3): 519–43.

Correla, Isabel, Joao Neves, and Sergio Rebelo. 1995. Business cycles in a small open economy. *European Economic Review* 39 (6): 1089–1113.

Feldstein, Martin, and Charles Horioka. 1980. Domestic saving and international capital flows. *Economic Journal* 90 (358): 314–29.

Fisher, Irving. 1930. *The Theory of Interest*. New York: Macmillan.

Friedman, Milton. 1957. *Theory of the Consumption Function*. Princeton University Press.

Greenwood, Jeremy, Zvi Hercowitz, and Gregory W. Huffman. 1988. Investment, capacity utilization and the business cycle. *American Economic Review* 78: 402–17.

King, Robert G., and Sergio T. Rebelo. 2000. Resuscitating real business cycles. In John Taylor and Michael Woodford, eds., *Handbook of Macroeconomics*. Amsterdam: North Holland, 927–1007.

Kydland, Finn E., and Edward C. Prescott. 1982. Time to build and aggregate fluctuations. *Econometrica* 50 (6): 1345–70.

Lane, Philip R., and Aaron Tornell. 1998. Why aren't savings rates in Latin America procyclical? *Journal of Development Economics* 57 (1): 185–99.

Mendoza, Enrique. 1991. Real business cycles in a small open economy. *American Economic Review* 81: 797–818.

Neumeyer, Pablo A., and Fabrizio Perri. 2005. Business cycles in emerging markets: The role of interest rates. *Journal of Monetary Economics* 52: 345–80.

Obstfeld, Maurice. 1987. International finance. In John Eatwell, Murray Milgate, and Peter Newman, eds., *The New Palgrave: A Dictionary of Economics*. New York: Stockton Press.

Reed, Michael. 1998. *Fundamental Ideas of Analysis*. New York: Wiley.

Sachs, Jeffrey D. 1981. The current account and macroeconomic adjustment in the 1970s. *Brookings Papers on Economic Activity* 12 (1): 201–82.

Uribe, Martin. 2002. The price-consumption puzzle of currency pegs. *Journal of Monetary Economics* 49 (3): 533–69.

2 Capital Market Imperfections

2.1 Introduction

The basic model analyzed in chapter 1 yields the key result that along a perfect foresight equilibrium path, a small open economy will smooth out consumption over time regardless of the output path. Three key assumptions underlie this result. First, the economy has perfect access to international capital markets (i.e., it can borrow from/lend to the rest of the world at a given and constant real interest rate). Second, the output path is known with certainty. Third, the country is able to precommit to repaying its debt. How would that result change if these assumptions were relaxed?

This chapter analyzes the consequences of relaxing each of the three assumptions. Section 2.2 addresses the case of financial autarky in a two-period model in which the economy has no financial links to the rest of the world. While extreme, this scenario provides a useful illustration of economies with severe restrictions on capital flows. As one would expect, a single-good economy in financial autarky behaves exactly as a closed economy and is forced to consume its endowment every period.[1] Since, in bad times, the economy cannot borrow from abroad, the domestic real interest rate will have to be higher to induce households to curtail consumption. The real interest rate—rather than the trade balance as in chapter 1—thus becomes the key adjusting variable. In practice, of course, developing countries' access to international capital markets generally falls somewhere in between the extreme cases of perfect capital mobility—analyzed in chapter 1—and financial autarky. In such cases a temporarily lower level of output will lead to both trade deficits and higher real interest rates.

Section 2.3 introduces uncertainty into the model of section 2.2 by assuming that period 2 output is a stochastic variable. In the presence of uncertainty, the menu of financial claims available to the economy becomes critical. If the economy has access to only a risk-free asset instead of a complete set of state contingent claims (i.e., asset markets are incomplete), then the economy will

1. If there were two goods, then trade in goods could still occur with the rest of the world but the trade balance must be zero.

be unable to smooth consumption over time. There will be a positive correlation between output and consumption. In contrast, if asset markets are complete, the economy will be able to fully smooth out consumption over time by buying state-contingent claims. Since developing countries have access to a more limited menu of financial instruments than industrial countries, the model predicts that the correlation between output and consumption should be higher in developing countries than in industrial countries. In terms of welfare, incomplete markets impose social costs by preventing the economy from smoothing consumption. These costs will be larger the higher is the variability of output.

Finally, section 2.4 relaxes the assumption that the economy can precommit to repaying its foreign debt. We capture in this way the presence of *sovereign risk*, which refers to the fact that since sovereign countries are not subject to standard bankruptcy laws as would be individuals or corporations within a country, international creditors face more risk than domestic lenders. We show that the presence of sovereign risk leads to the emergence of credit ceilings, beyond which foreign lenders will not be willing to lend at any interest rate. Hence, faced with a temporarily lower level of output, the economy may not be able to borrow as much as it would need to keep consumption constant over time, and domestic real interest rates will need to rise to induce lower consumption. While providing some key insights, this benchmark model of sovereign risk with no uncertainty exhibits two unattractive features: (1) the supply of funds is flat until the credit ceiling is reached and (2) we never observe default in equilibrium. By introducing uncertainty regarding period 2 output, the model generates an upward-sloping supply of funds and default in equilibrium.

The punchline of this chapter is that imperfections in international capital markets will severely limit the ability of a small open economy to smooth consumption over time. From a positive point of view, the inability to fully smooth consumption introduces a positive correlation between output and consumption, which is consistent with the empirical evidence. From a normative point of view, we conclude that such imperfections in capital markets are socially costly, which justifies efforts to improve developing countries' access to external financing in bad times.

On the methodological front, this chapter introduces a two-period version of the basic model developed in chapter 1. As will become clear below, this two-period model is particularly tractable for examining issues related to imperfect access to capital markets and uncertainty.

2.2 Financial Autarky

Consider a small open economy inhabited by a large number of identical individuals who live for two periods and are blessed with perfect foresight. There exists only one (tradable and nonstorable) good. The consumer receives an endowment of the good in every period. We depart from the basic model of chapter 1 by assuming that while the consumer perceives him/herself as being able to borrow as much as he/she wants at a constant real interest rate (subject, of course, to his/her intertemporal constraint), the economy as a whole cannot borrow from the rest of the world (financial autarky).

2.2.1 Consumer's Problem

Budget Constraints

Let b_i^d, $i = 1, 2$, stand for the level of net *domestic* assets at the end of period i. These domestic bonds are denominated in terms of the tradable good and have a face value of unity. The flow budget constraint for period 1 is thus given by[2]

$$b_1^d = y_1 - c_1. \tag{2.1}$$

As in chapter 1, we constrain the consumer not to "die" with outstanding debt (i.e., we impose the condition that $b_2^d \geq 0$). In addition, given a strictly increasing utility function, it would not be optimal to "die" with a positive level of assets (which implies that $b_2^d \leq 0$). Hence net domestic assets at the end of period 2 must be zero (i.e., $b_2^d = 0$). In period 2 the consumer gets interest payments on his/her bond holdings. The flow budget constraint for period 2 is thus

$$c_2 = (1 + \rho)b_1^d + y_2, \tag{2.2}$$

where ρ is the *domestic* real interest rate. Given that the domestic bond is nontradable, ρ may differ from the international real interest rate, r, as will become clear below.

Combining (2.1) and (2.2) yields the consumer's intertemporal budget constraint:

$$y_1 + \frac{1}{1+\rho} y_2 = c_1 + \frac{1}{1+\rho} c_2. \tag{2.3}$$

Utility Maximization

The lifetime utility of the representative household (W) is given by

$$W = u(c_1) + \beta u(c_2), \tag{2.4}$$

where c_i, $i = 1, 2$, denotes consumption in period i and β ($1 > \beta > 0$) is the discount factor.[3]

The consumer's problem consists in choosing c_1 and c_2 to maximize lifetime utility, given by (2.4), subject to the intertemporal budget constraint, given by (2.3), taking as given ρ, y_1 and y_2. We can set up the following Lagrangian:

$$\mathcal{L} = u(c_1) + \beta u(c_2) + \lambda \left(y_1 + \frac{1}{1+\rho} y_2 - c_1 - \frac{1}{1+\rho} c_2 \right).$$

2. We assume, for simplicity, that initial bonds are zero.

3. The discount factor, β, is, by definition, equal to $1/(1+\delta)$, where δ is the rate of time preference (or discount rate). The higher the rate of time preference (i.e., the higher the rate at which the future is discounted), the smaller is the discount factor.

The first-order conditions are given by

$$u'(c_1) = \lambda, \tag{2.5}$$

$$\beta u'(c_2) = \frac{\lambda}{1+\rho}. \tag{2.6}$$

Combining (2.5) and (2.6) yields:

$$u'(c_1) = \beta(1+\rho)u'(c_2), \tag{2.7}$$

which is the Euler equation.

To establish the appropriate analogy with the basic model of chapter 1, notice that if the economy has full access to international capital markets, then $\rho = r$, which, given the assumption that $\beta(1+r) = 1$, implies that

$$u'(c_1) = u'(c_2). \tag{2.8}$$

We are thus back to the world of chapter 1, where the consumption path is flat regardless of the output path.

2.2.2 Equilibrium Conditions

Bond Market Equilibrium

Since the economy is closed in bond markets, the aggregate stock of domestic bonds circulating in the economy at the end of period 1 must be equal to zero. Formally,

$$b_1^d = 0. \tag{2.9}$$

Given that the aggregate stock of bonds is zero, the domestic real interest rate, ρ, will need to adjust to clear the bond market. Unlike the economy of chapter 1, which faces a completely elastic supply of foreign funds at a constant real interest rate, this economy faces a completely vertical supply of foreign funds (at zero).

Aggregate Constraints

To obtain the flow constraints for the economy as a whole, substitute the bond market equilibrium (2.9) into the household's flow constraints (2.1) and (2.2) to obtain

$$c_1 = y_1, \tag{2.10}$$

$$c_2 = y_2. \tag{2.11}$$

The trade balance in this economy ($TB_t \equiv y_t - c_t$) is therefore always equal to zero. The same is true of the current account.

2.2.3 Solution of the Model

The model has three endogenous variables: c_1, c_2, and ρ. From (2.10) and (2.11), it follows immediately that, in equilibrium, the economy must consume its endowment in every period. This is to be expected, since, due to financial autarky, the economy cannot run a trade imbalance.

To determine ρ, substitute (2.10) and (2.11) into (2.7) to obtain

$$1+\rho = \frac{u'(y_1)}{\beta u'(y_2)}. \tag{2.12}$$

Equation (2.12) makes clear that in financial autarky the domestic real interest rate is solely determined by the path of output (as would be the case in a closed economy).

2.2.4 Stationary Equilibrium

As a benchmark, suppose that the output path is flat; that is, $y_1 = y_2 = y$. It then follows from (2.10) and (2.11) that $c_1 = c_2 = y$. From (2.12) it follows that $1 + \rho = 1/\beta$. This is, of course, the same equilibrium involving full consumption smoothing that would obtain in the basic model of chapter 1 under perfect capital mobility. The reason is simply that faced with a constant path of output, households have no incentive to save or dissave. Hence being shut off from international capital markets is not a binding constraint.

2.2.5 Nonstationary Equilibrium

Suppose now that output is lower in the first period; that is, $y_1 < y_2$. From (2.10) and (2.11), it follows that $c_1 = y_1 < c_2 = y_2$. Since $c_1 < c_2$, it follows from (2.12) that $1 + \rho > 1/\beta$. Under our maintained assumption that $\beta(1 + r) = 1$, this implies that $\rho > r$. In other words, the domestic real interest rate is higher than the international one.

Intuitively, faced with a lower output in the first period, individual consumers would like to dissave (i.e., to sell bonds) in order to smooth consumption over time. Since the aggregate supply of bonds is zero, however, this excess supply of bonds must lead to a fall in their price (i.e., an increase in ρ).[4] In equilibrium the price of bonds must fall (i.e., the domestic real interest rate must rise) up to the point at which consumers are content with consuming the available endowment. In other words, the high domestic real interest rate reflects the scarcity of goods in period 1 relative to period 2.

It should be intuitively clear that financial autarky is costly, since welfare would be higher if the economy were able to smooth consumption over time. To show this formally, notice that

4. Notice that the price in period 1 of a bond that pays one unit of output in period 2 is $1/(1+\rho)$. There is thus an inverse relationship between the price of the bond and the domestic real interest rate.

under perfect capital mobility, consumption would be constant over time (i.e., $c_1 = c_2 = c$) and given by

$$c = \frac{1+r}{2+r}\left(y_1 + \frac{y_2}{1+r}\right). \tag{2.13}$$

Welfare under perfect capital mobility would thus be higher than under financial autarky if

$$\underbrace{u(c) + \beta u(c)}_{\text{Welfare under perfect capital mobility}} > \underbrace{u(y_1) + \beta u(y_2)}_{\text{Welfare under financial autarky}}. \tag{2.14}$$

Rewrite this inequality as

$$u(c) > \frac{1}{1+\beta}u(y_1) + \frac{\beta}{1+\beta}u(y_2). \tag{2.15}$$

Since, by assumption, $\beta(1+r) = 1$, it follows from (2.13) that $c = [1/(1+\beta)]y_1 + [\beta/(1+\beta)]y_2$. Hence, by strict concavity of $u(.)$, inequality (2.15) holds for any pair of values $y_1 \neq y_2$.

Figure 2.1 provides a graphical illustration of the welfare costs of financial autarky for the case at hand ($y_1 < y_2$). The left-hand side of inequality (2.15) is given by point A while the right-hand side is given by point B. Clearly, welfare at point A is higher than welfare at point B. In addition the figure provides a graphical demonstration of the fact that a mean-preserving spread of the output distribution (from (y_1, y_2) to $(\tilde{y}_1, \tilde{y}_2)$) reduces welfare from point B to point C. Hence the more variable is output, the higher the costs of financial autarky.

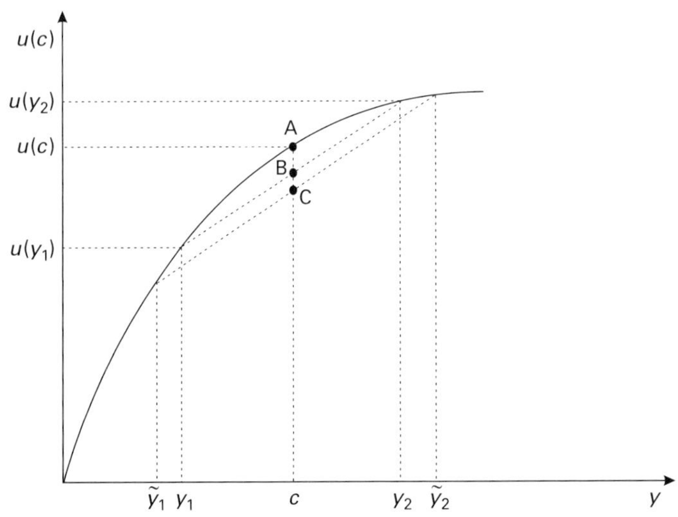

Figure 2.1
Welfare costs of financial autarky

2.2.6 Intermediate Cases

We have just seen that in the presence of financial autarky, a temporarily lower level of output will lead to reduced consumption, a higher real interest rate, and, of course, no change in the trade balance. In the previous chapter we saw that in the presence of perfect capital mobility, a temporarily lower level of output along a perfect foresight equilibrium path results in a deficit in the trade balance but no change in consumption. In reality the world lies somewhere in between these two extremes (and, of course, the degree of capital mobility varies from country to country). Hence, based on the analysis of these two extreme cases, our model predicts that, in practice, a temporarily lower level of output should be reflected in a combination of lower consumption, a higher trade deficit, and a higher domestic real interest rate. In particular, the more open the capital account, the more a temporarily lower level of output should be reflected in a larger current account deficit, whereas the more closed the capital account, the more the shock should be reflected in a higher domestic real interest rate and lower consumption.

2.3 Uncertain Output Path

As mentioned in the introduction, a second key assumption of the basic model of chapter 1 is that the output path is known with certainty. In other words, because households know exactly the present discounted value of their resources, they can keep consumption smooth by borrowing today while having the certainty that they will have the resources to repay their creditors tomorrow. But suppose that households did not know for sure what their future endowment will be. How would they decide whether to save or dissave? This section addresses this important question.

Consider the following modification of the two-period model presented in section 2.2. The first-period endowment is y_1 with certainty. The second-period endowment, however, is stochastic:

$$y_2 = \begin{cases} y_2^H & \text{with probability } p, \\ y_2^L & \text{with probability } 1-p, \end{cases} \tag{2.16}$$

where $y_2^H > y_2^L$.[5] Furthermore—and to capture a situation where the economy is going through rough times in period 1 relative to period 2—suppose that the expected value of y_2 is higher than y_1. Formally,

$$E\{y_2\} = py_2^H + (1-p)y_2^L > y_1. \tag{2.17}$$

5. Appendix 2.6 develops an infinite horizon version of this stochastic model and shows that the basic insights remain valid.

Clearly, in a perfect-foresight version of this setup where consumers are endowed with the average level of output in period 2, they would borrow in the first period (i.e., run a current account deficit) to fully smooth consumption over time, as analyzed in chapter 1.

We will first study the case of incomplete markets and then the case of complete markets.

2.3.1 Incomplete Capital Markets

Consider the following financial environment. This small economy can borrow from/lend to the rest of the world at a constant world real interest rate, r, as in chapter 1. However, it has no access to contingent debt; in other words, it cannot borrow contingent on the realization of output in the second period. In this sense, markets are incomplete.[6]

Box 2.1
How incomplete are markets?

When thinking about whether or not a small open economy faces complete markets, it proves insightful to first review the evidence on market completeness at the household level. If households within a financially sophisticated market, such as the United States, do not face complete markets, we would think that, if anything, countries would face even more market incompleteness because of international credit market imperfections stemming principally from the lack of contract enforcement at a transnational level. The question is then whether households can insure themselves against idiosyncratic shocks—such as illness, loss of job, and other shocks to income—through stock and security markets, borrowing and lending in credit markets, unemployment insurance, and help from family and/or community members.

While there are different econometric methods to test for full insurance, the basic strategy remains the same: reject the complete markets (full insurance) hypothesis if one can find idiosyncratic shocks that affect the marginal utility of consumption, after controlling for aggregate shocks. A common problem with tests for full insurance is the potential endogeneity of right-hand variables. Most studies attempt to address this problem by finding idiosyncratic variables that are genuinely exogenous, rather than choice variables for the household. Others, like Ham and Jacobs (2000), address the endogeneity problem using instrumental variables technique. Table 2.1 offers a summary of some of the most influential studies. While some of the evidence is mixed, it is fair to conclude that, by and large, available studies suggest that households in the United States are not able to fully insure against idiosyncratic shocks.

At an international level, complete markets would imply that domestic consumption should be very highly correlated with world consumption, rather than with domestic output. An extreme version of this idea can be illustrated in a two-country version of our two period model analyzed in exercise 5. Given the simple stochastic structure, the model predicts that consumption across countries should be perfectly correlated, whereas in the absence of world uncertainty, the correlation between domestic consumption and domestic output should be zero. As table 2.2 details, however, empirical studies

6. See Blanchard and Fischer (1989, ch. 6) for a detailed analysis of consumption under uncertainty. As box 2.1 documents, market incompleteness seems to be the rule in the actual world. While market incompleteness is just assumed in this chapter, it could be derived endogenously from enforcement constraints (e.g., see Kehoe and Perri 2002).

Box 2.1
(continued)

Table 2.1
Studies on market completeness based on household data

Author(s)	Dataset	Methodology	Main results
Cochrane (1991)	Panel Study of Income Dynamics, 1980–1983	Full consumption insurance implies that consumption growth should be independent of idiosyncratic shocks to households. Idiosyncratic shocks are captured by involuntary job loss (sickness, strike, move).	Full insurance rejected for long illness and involuntary job loss, but not for spells of unemployment, loss of work due to strike, or involuntary move.
Mace (1991)	Consumer Expenditure Survey, 1980–1983	Risk sharing implies that individual consumption varies positively with aggregate consumption only and not with individual income or changes in employment status. For specific preferences, changes in consumption or growth rates of consumption, net of preference shocks, should be equalized across individuals.	Once the change in aggregate consumption is accounted for, the change in household income does not help explain the change in household consumption. Results for the growth rate specification, however, reject full insurance.
Hayashi, Altonji, and Kotlikoff (1996)	Panel Study of Income Dynamics, 1968–1981 1985–1987	Full risk sharing implies that one-year consumption changes are uncorrelated with the wage rate at all leads and lags. This is tested by examining the correlation of long term and one-year changes in consumption and the wage rate.	Both intra- and interfamily risk sharing rejected, but not self-insurance.
Attanasio and Davis (1996)	Consumption Expenditure Survey and the Current Population Survey, 1980–1990	Examines the impact of systematic, publicly observable shifts in the hourly wage structure on the distribution of household consumption.	Relative wage movements among men had large impact on the distribution of household consumption, thus rejecting the hypothesis of consumption insurance.
Ham and Jacobs (2000)	Panel Study of Income Dynamics, 1974–1987	To avoid potential endogeneity problems, authors use current unemployment rates in the household head's industry and the head's occupation separately as instruments for idiosyncratic shock.	Strong rejection of full insurance hypothesis. Households not insured against changes in unemployment rate associated with the household head's occupation.

tend to reject the hypotheses that domestic and foreign consumption are highly correlated and/or that domestic consumption is less correlated with domestic output.

We thus conclude that, by and large, studies based on both household data and country data tend to reject the hypothesis of complete markets. However, some studies do find that, as one would expect, markets are less incomplete within a country than across countries (Kose, Prasad, and Terrones 2009).

Box 2.1
(continued)

Table 2.2
International evidence on market incompleteness

Author(s)	Dataset	Methodology	Main results
Atkeson and Bayoumi (1993)	US, 1963–1986 6 members of OECD, 1970–1987	Consumers should try to construct asset portfolios generating income that is negatively correlated with regional income.	Full insurance rejected in both panels. Despite opportunities available for consumers to smooth regional risks, a large fraction of consumers do not seem to privately insulate their consumption from regional conditions.
Crucini (1999)	US, 1972–1990 Canada, 1973–1991 G-7, 1970–1987	Imperfect risk sharing implies that after controlling for common income shocks, consumption should move together more closely across individuals that engage in more risk sharing.	Much more risk sharing is found across Canadian provinces and US states than across G7 countries.
Obstfeld (1994)	7 largest industrial countries, 1950–1988	In an integrated world asset market with representative national agents, the ex post difference between two countries' intertemporal marginal rates of substitution in consumption should be uncorrelated with any random shock that is insurable.	In the postwar period there is an increasing comovement between domestic and world consumption growth, but the correlation between them remains far below expected, even in a world of unrestricted international asset trade.
Kose, Prasad, and Terrones (2009)	69 countries, 1960–2004	Financial integration predicts countries' consumption growth to be more correlated with world output than with country's output growth.	For most countries the correlation between domestic consumption and output is higher than between domestic consumption and world output. The gap between the two measures is much larger for emerging markets and other developing countries than for industrial countries.

Budget Constraints

Let us begin by looking at the first period flow constraint. Assume that initial net foreign assets are zero. Then, since there is no uncertainty in period 1,

$$b_1 = y_1 - c_1. \tag{2.18}$$

The second-period flow constraint will depend on the realization of output. Let c_2^H and c_2^L denote second-period consumption in the high-output state of nature and low-output state of nature, respectively. Then, since the budget constraint must hold in every state of nature,

$$c_2^H = (1+r)b_1 + y_2^H, \tag{2.19}$$

$$c_2^L = (1+r)b_1 + y_2^L. \tag{2.20}$$

Combining equations (2.18), (2.19), and (2.20), we obtain an intertemporal budget constraint for each of the two possible output paths:

$$y_1 + \frac{1}{1+r} y_2^H = c_1 + \frac{1}{1+r} c_2^H, \tag{2.21}$$

$$y_1 + \frac{1}{1+r} y_2^L = c_1 + \frac{1}{1+r} c_2^L. \tag{2.22}$$

Utility Maximization

As is standard, we will assume that consumers maximize expected lifetime utility, given by

$$W = u(c_1) + \beta E\{u(c_2)\}. \tag{2.23}$$

Taking into account the distribution of output (given by equation 2.16), we can rewrite (2.23) as

$$W = u(c_1) + \beta[pu(c_2^H) + (1-p)u(c_2^L)]. \tag{2.24}$$

The consumer's problem consists in choosing c_1, c_2^H, c_2^L to maximize (2.24) subject to (2.21) and (2.22). In terms of the Lagrangian,

$$\begin{aligned}\mathcal{L} = {} & u(c_1) + \beta[pu(c_2^H) + (1-p)u(c_2^L)] \\ & + \lambda^H \left(y_1 + \frac{1}{1+r} y_2^H - c_1 - \frac{1}{1+r} c_2^H \right) \\ & + \lambda^L \left(y_1 + \frac{1}{1+r} y_2^L - c_1 - \frac{1}{1+r} c_2^L \right).\end{aligned} \tag{2.25}$$

The first-order conditions with respect to c_1, c_2^H, and c_2^L are given by, respectively,

$$u'(c_1) = \lambda^H + \lambda^L,$$

$$\beta p u'(c_2^H) = \frac{\lambda^H}{1+r},$$

$$\beta(1-p)u'(c_2^L) = \frac{\lambda^L}{1+r}.$$

Combining these three equations (and imposing the condition that $\beta(1+r) = 1$), we get

$$u'(c_1) = pu'(c_2^H) + (1-p)u'(c_2^L), \tag{2.26}$$

which can be rewritten as

$$u'(c_1) = E\{u'(c_2)\}. \tag{2.27}$$

This is the stochastic Euler equation (i.e., the counterpart of equation 2.8).

2.3.2 Equilibrium

The solution of the model will critically depend on the sign of $u'''(c)$.[7] Two pieces of information will be important in the derivations below.

First, notice that $u'(c)$ is linear, strictly convex, or strictly concave depending on whether $u'''(c) = 0$, $u'''(c) > 0$, or $u'''(c) < 0$, respectively. It follows that

$$pu'(c_2^H) + (1-p)u'(c_2^L) = u'[pc_2^H + (1-p)c_2^L], \quad \text{if } u'''(c) = 0, \tag{2.28}$$

$$pu'(c_2^H) + (1-p)u'(c_2^L) > u'[pc_2^H + (1-p)c_2^L], \quad \text{if } u'''(c) > 0, \tag{2.29}$$

$$pu'(c_2^H) + (1-p)u'(c_2^L) < u'[pc_2^H + (1-p)c_2^L], \quad \text{if } u'''(c) < 0. \tag{2.30}$$

Second, notice that by multiplying (2.21) by p and (2.22) by $1-p$, we can derive an intertemporal constraint in expected values:[8]

$$c_1 + \frac{E\{c_2\}}{1+r} = y_1 + \frac{E\{y_2\}}{1+r}. \tag{2.31}$$

7. We should note that the tight link to be established below between the sign of the third derivative and the existence of precautionary savings in this two-period model does not necessarily hold in models with longer but finite horizon (with time-varying degrees of risk aversion) or infinite horizon (see Huggett and Ospina 2001 and Roitman 2011).

8. A general point is in order. Since the intertemporal constraint must hold for *each* state of nature, it will always hold in expected value. The reverse, however, is *not* true. It would therefore be incorrect to solve a model with uncertainty using an intertemporal constraint that holds only in expected value.

We now consider each case individually.

Case 1 (Certainty equivalence) $u'''(c) = 0$. This case corresponds to quadratic preferences. Using (2.28), we can rewrite the Euler equation (2.26) as

$$u'(c_1) = u'[pc_2^H + (1-p)c_2^L],$$

or, equivalently,

$$u'(c_1) = u'(E\{c_2\}).$$

Since $u'(c)$ is a strictly decreasing function (recall that $u''(c) < 0$), it follows that

$$c_1 = E\{c_2\}. \tag{2.32}$$

In an expected value sense the economy therefore smooths consumption over time.[9] As will become clear below, however, c_1 will differ from actual period-2 consumption and hence the economy will not be able to smooth actual consumption over time, which will negatively affect welfare.

To compute a reduced form for consumption, combine the Euler equation for the quadratic case (equation 2.32) with the intertemporal constraint in expected value (equation 2.31) to obtain

$$c_1 = \frac{1+r}{2+r}\left[y_1 + \frac{E\{y_2\}}{1+r}\right]. \tag{2.33}$$

With quadratic preferences, certainty equivalence holds in the sense that consumption in the first period is the same as it would have been if consumers had been endowed in the second period with the average value of y_2.[10] This implies that with quadratic preferences, consumption in period 1 does not depend on the variance of output in period 2.

To derive the current account balance in period 1 (which, given the assumption of zero initial net foreign assets, is the same as the trade balance), combine (2.18) and (2.33) to obtain

$$b_1 = \frac{1}{2+r}[y_1 - E\{y_2\}] < 0.$$

As expected, the economy runs a current account deficit. The current account deficit is in fact the same as it would have been if second period's output were $E\{y_2\}$. Substituting this expression for the current account into (2.19) and (2.20), we obtain reduced-form expressions for c_2^H and c_2^L:

9. This is Robert Hall's (1978) celebrated result that under quadratic utility and $\beta(1+r) = 1$, consumption follows a random walk. In other words, the best predictor of tomorrow's consumption is today's consumption since, under rational expectations, news about permanent income are unforecastable.

10. Appendix 2.6 shows that the same result obtains in an infinite-horizon version of this model.

$$c_2^H = y_2^H + \frac{1+r}{2+r}\left[y_1 - E\{y_2\}\right] < y_2^H, \tag{2.34}$$

$$c_2^L = y_2^L + \frac{1+r}{2+r}\left[y_1 - E\{y_2\}\right] < y_2^L. \tag{2.35}$$

Two observations are worth making. First, consumption in period 2 will always be lower than output because of the need to repay the debt incurred in period 1. Second, consumption in period 2 depends on the actual realization of output, which implies that $c_2^H > c_2^L$.[11] Incomplete markets thus introduce a positive correlation between period 2 consumption and output. In fact, as should be obvious from (2.34) and (2.35) and is formally checked in exercise 1 at the end of this chapter, there is a perfect correlation between consumption and output in the second period.

Finally, notice that the fact that the economy is not able to smooth actual consumption over time has negative welfare consequences (compared to the certainty case). To show this, notice that in the certainty case, period-1 consumption would be given by c_1 (i.e., the same as in the quadratic case) while period-2 consumption would be given by $E\{c_2\}$. Hence we would like to show that

$$\underbrace{u(c_1) + \beta u(E\{c_2\})}_{\text{Welfare under certainty}} > \underbrace{u(c_1) + \beta\left[pu(c_2^H) + (1-p)u(c_2^L)\right]}_{\text{Welfare under uncertainty}},$$

which, given that first-period utility is the same, simplifies to

$$u(E\{c_2\}) > pu(c_2^H) + (1-p)u(c_2^L).$$

This inequality holds in light of the strict concavity of $u()$. Suitably relabeled in an obvious way, figure 2.1 would in fact apply to this case as well with point A denoting period-2 utility under certainty and point B denoting period-2 utility under uncertainty.

It is also easy to show that the more variable is output, the higher are the welfare costs. To see this, consider a mean-preserving spread of output; that is, suppose that the possible realizations of output are $\tilde{y}_2^H (> y_2^H)$ and $\tilde{y}_2^L (< y_2^L)$ but the expected value is the same. By analogy with (2.34) and (2.35), we know that in this case second-period consumption would be given by

$$\tilde{c}_2^H = \tilde{y}_2^H + \frac{1+r}{2+r}\left[y_1 - E\{y_2\}\right], \tag{2.36}$$

$$\tilde{c}_2^L = \tilde{y}_2^L + \frac{1+r}{2+r}\left[y_1 - E\{y_2\}\right]. \tag{2.37}$$

11. This illustrates the general point that, under incomplete markets, consumers are unable to equalize consumption across states of nature. This would also be true, of course, in a closed economy with idiosyncratic risk and is, in fact, at the core of empirical tests of market incompleteness at the household level (see box 2.1).

Then, by strict concavity of $u(.)$,

$$pu(\tilde{c}_2^H) + (1-p)u(\tilde{c}_2^L) < pu(c_2^H) + (1-p)u(c_2^L).$$

In terms of figure 2.1, period-2 utility for the mean-preserving spread would correspond to point C. Hence welfare is lower than before (point B).

Case 2 (Precautionary savings) $u'''(c) > 0$. Using (2.29), we can rewrite the Euler equation (2.26) as

$$u'(c_1) > u'[pc_2^H + (1-p)c_2^L].$$

It follows that

$$c_1 < E\{c_2\}. \tag{2.38}$$

Unlike the previous case, consumers do *not* smooth consumption in an expected value sense. From (2.31) and (2.38), it follows that

$$c_1 < \frac{1+r}{2+r}\left[y_1 + \frac{E\{y_2\}}{1+r}\right].$$

Consumption is thus lower than it would be in the certainty (or certainty equivalence) case. In other words, the economy engages in *precautionary savings*. The uncertainty regarding second-period output induces consumers to be more prudent and dissave less than they would otherwise. Hence the current account deficit will be smaller than in the quadratic case.[12] As before, the presence of uncertainty prevents consumers from achieving full consumption smoothing and introduces a positive correlation between output and consumption in period 2.

Two important observations are worth making at this point. First, it is important to distinguish between the concepts of "risk aversion" and "prudence" (see Kimball 1990). Risk aversion refers to the fact that consumers dislike uncertainty, while prudence refers to the idea that consumers are prepared to save in anticipation of an uncertain outcome. The degree of risk aversion is measured by the concavity of $u(.)$, whereas the degree of prudence is measured by the convexity of $u'(c)$ or, equivalently, the concavity of $-u'(c)$.

Second, standard preferences—such as constant relative (or absolute) risk aversion—are characterized by $u'''(.) > 0$ and will therefore exhibit precautionary savings. Exercise 2 at the end of this chapter examines the case where preferences exhibit constant absolute risk aversion and period-2 output follows a normal distribution. In this case we can compute a reduced-form for consumption in period 1. As one might expect, period-1 consumption is lower the higher is the

12. It may be even possible that the introduction of uncertainty induces consumers to *save* in the first period (i.e., run a current account surplus) even if $y_1 < E\{y_2\}$. You should check that this is indeed a possibility by constructing numerical examples using, say, a constant relative risk aversion function.

variance of period-2 output. Greater uncertainty thus makes consumers more prudent and leads to more precautionary savings.

Intuitively, recall the stochastic Euler equation—given by (2.27)—and notice that $u'''(c) > 0$ implies that the marginal utility of consumption is a *convex* function. Hence a mean-preserving spread—which, by construction, leaves expected consumption in period 2 unchanged—increases the corresponding expected marginal utility in period 2 and induces consumers to decrease consumption in period 1 (i.e., induces consumers to choose a steeper consumption path in an expected value sense). Finally, welfare is strictly decreasing in the variance of output.[13] Exercise 3 at the end of the chapter asks you to show numerically that the same results follow for the case of constant relative risk aversion.

Case 3 (Dissavings) $u'''(c) < 0$. Using (2.30), we can rewrite the Euler equation (2.26) as

$$u'(c_1) < u'[pc_2^H + (1-p)c_2^L].$$

It follows that

$$c_1 > E\{c_2\}. \tag{2.39}$$

In this case consumers are "imprudent" in the sense that they choose to dissave more than they would otherwise and will in fact consume more in period 1 than in the certainty case. Therefore the current account deficit in period 1 will be higher than in the certainty case. It is still the case that consumption is not smooth over time and that this is costly from a welfare point of view.

While utility functions that exhibit a negative third derivative are much less common in economic theory, an example would be the following:

$$u(c) = ac - bc^3, \quad c < \sqrt{\frac{a}{3b}}.$$

As can be easily checked, $u'(c) > 0$, $u''(c) < 0$, and $u'''(c) < 0$.[14] This consumer is thus risk averse but *imprudent*, which illustrates the fact that risk aversion does not necessarily imply prudence. Exercise 4 at the end of the chapter asks you to compute first-period consumption and welfare as a function of a mean-preserving spread in the distribution of second-period output. As expected, c_1 increases due to the fact that the consumer is imprudent, but welfare decreases since the consumer is still risk averse. Intuitively, recall once again the stochastic Euler equation—given by (2.27)—and notice that the marginal utility of consumption is now a concave function. Hence

13. See Jacobs, Pallage, and Robe (2005) for an empirical estimation of the welfare costs of incomplete markets using state-level data for the United States.

14. See Roitman (2011) for a detailed analysis of precautionary saving for this class of preferences.

a mean-preserving spread will *reduce* the expected marginal utility of period-2 consumption and thus induce consumers to increase c_1.

2.3.3 Complete Capital Markets

Suppose now that there are complete asset markets in the sense that households can buy contingent claims in international capital markets. In other words, households may buy a claim that promises to pay one unit of output in the good state of nature for the price (as of period 1) $q^H/(1+r)$ and a claim that promises to pay a unit of output in the bad state of nature for the price $q^L/(1+r)$. In addition there exists (as before) a risk-free asset that promises to pay one unit of output regardless of the state of nature, which can be acquired at the price $1/(1+r)$.[15]

Budget Constraints

Assume that initial net foreign assets are zero. Denote by b_1^j, $j = H, L$, the number of claims purchased in period 1 that promise to pay one unit of output in the second period in state of nature j. The flow budget constraint for period 1 is thus

$$\frac{q^H}{1+r}b_1^H + \frac{q^L}{1+r}b_1^L = y_1 - c_1. \tag{2.40}$$

As in the incomplete markets case, the second-period flow budget constraint will depend on the realization of output. We continue to use c_2^H and c_2^L to denote second-period consumption in the high-output state of nature and low-output state of nature, respectively. Then

$$c_2^H = b_1^H + y_2^H, \tag{2.41}$$

$$c_2^L = b_1^L + y_2^L. \tag{2.42}$$

Substituting (2.41) and (2.42) into (2.40), we obtain

$$y_1 + \underbrace{\frac{q^H y_2^H + q^L y_2^L}{1+r}}_{\text{Value of claims that can be sold}} = c_1 + \underbrace{\frac{q^H c_2^H + q^L c_2^L}{1+r}}_{\text{Value of claims that can be bought}}. \tag{2.43}$$

As indicated, the second term on the LHS captures the value of all the claims on output that can be sold, whereas the second term on the RHS denotes the value of all claims on consumption that need to be bought.

15. Notice, however, that as far as the consumer is concerned, the risk-free asset is redundant because it can be replicated with contingent claims (see below). For simplicity the consumer's problem below assumes that consumers only purchase contingent claims.

Utility Maximization

Consumers choose c_1, c_2^H, c_2^L to maximize (2.24) subject to (2.43). In terms of the Lagrangian:

$$\mathcal{L} = u(c_1) + \beta[pu(c_2^H) + (1-p)u(c_2^L)]$$
$$+ \lambda\left(y_1 + \frac{q^H y_2^H + q^L y_2^L}{1+r} - c_1 - \frac{q^H c_2^H + q^L c_2^L}{1+r}\right).$$

The first-order conditions with respect to c_1, c_2^H, and c_2^L are given by, respectively,

$$u'(c_1) = \lambda, \tag{2.44}$$

$$\beta p u'(c_2^H) = \lambda \frac{q^H}{1+r}, \tag{2.45}$$

$$\beta(1-p)u'(c_2^L) = \lambda \frac{q^L}{1+r}. \tag{2.46}$$

Combining (2.45) and (2.46), we obtain

$$\frac{pu'(c_2^H)}{(1-p)u'(c_2^L)} = \frac{q^H}{q^L}, \tag{2.47}$$

which says that the consumer equates the marginal rate of substitution across states of nature to the relative price of the corresponding contingent claims. If prices are actuarially fair, it will be the case that[16]

$$\frac{q^H}{q^L} = \frac{p}{1-p}. \tag{2.48}$$

Substituting (2.48) into (2.47), it follows that $c_2^H = c_2^L$. Hence, under actuarially fair prices, the consumer equates period-2 consumption across states of nature.

To show that consumption will be smoothed across time, we need to derive an arbitrage condition between a riskless bond and the price of contingent claims. Notice that a riskless bond that pays one unit of output in period 2 can be bought in period 1 by the price $1/(1+r)$. The same outcome can be achieved by buying one unit of b^H at the price $q^H/(1+r)$ and one unit of b^L at the price $q^L/(1+r)$. Since these are just two different ways of receiving one unit of output in period 2, they should have the same period-1 price:

$$\frac{1}{1+r} = \frac{q^H}{1+r} + \frac{q^L}{1+r},$$

16. Actuarially fair prices means that the market is offering a fair gamble (i.e., a gamble with zero expected value at the prevailing market prices). See Hirshleifer and Riley (1992) for a detailed analysis.

which implies that $q^H + q^L = 1$.[17] Combining the latter with (2.48) and the first-order conditions (2.44), (2.45), and (2.46), we obtain (recalling that $\beta(1+r) = 1$)

$$c_1 = c_2^H = c_2^L.$$

We conclude that *with complete markets, consumption is fully smoothed* even when the output path is uncertain. Hence—and in contrast to the incomplete markets case—the correlation between period-2 output and consumption will be zero. Complete markets thus allow the economy to fully smooth consumption regardless of the path of output as in chapter 1.[18]

2.4 No Precommitment

The basic model of chapter 1 assumes that if a country has borrowed during bad times, it will repay its debt in good times. In other words, the model assumes that the country can precommit itself to repaying its debt. This is quite a strong assumption since casual observation suggests that sovereign countries often default on their external debt. It follows that in practice precommitment mechanisms are, at best, tenuous and countries tend to default if they find it convenient to do so.

2.4.1 Implications of No Precommitment

The best way of understanding the implications of no precommitment is to first consider the two-period model discussed above under perfect capital mobility and precommitment. In this case the representative consumer chooses c_1 and c_2 to maximize (2.4) subject to the following intertemporal constraint:

$$y_1 + \frac{1}{1+r} y_2 = c_1 + \frac{1}{1+r} c_2. \tag{2.49}$$

It immediately follows from the first-order conditions that $c_1 = c_2$. Let us denote this constant level of consumption by c (i.e., $c_1 = c_2 = c$). From (2.49), this implies that

$$c = \frac{1+r}{2+r} \left(y_1 + \frac{1}{1+r} y_2 \right). \tag{2.50}$$

17. This arbitrage condition could be explicitly derived from the consumer's problem by allowing him/her to also purchase a riskless bond in period 1.

18. As exercise 5 at the end of the chapter shows, in a two-country model the assumption of complete markets would imply perfect correlation between consumption growth rates in both countries. In particular, this correlation should be higher than the correlation between consumption and domestic output. This prediction is at the core of most empirical tests of market completeness (see box 2.1).

Suppose, again, that $y_1 < y_2$. How much does this economy borrow in period 1? Substituting (2.50) into the flow constraint for period 1 (given by $b_1 = y_1 - c$) and solving for b_1, we obtain

$$b_1 = \frac{y_1 - y_2}{2 + r} < 0. \tag{2.51}$$

Let d_1 denote net debt (i.e., $d_1 \equiv -b_1$). Then

$$d_1 = -\left(\frac{y_1 - y_2}{2 + r}\right) > 0.$$

Under precommitment, the economy pays $(1 + r)d_1$ in period 2. Consumption in period 2 is thus $y_2 - (1 + r)d_1 < y_2$. In the absence of precommitment, however, the economy would be clearly better off by not repaying its debt and instead consuming the entire second-period endowment. But, of course, rational creditors would anticipate this and not lend to this economy in period 1 to begin with. Hence, in the absence of precommitment, this economy would not be able to borrow at all in period 1. The economy would thus be in a state of financial autarky and forced to consume its endowment in every period (as in section 2.2).

2.4.2 Cost of Default

The example just examined assumes that there are no costs associated with defaulting. In practice, however, there will be some costs stemming from possible sanctions that creditors may impose (see box 2.2). For simplicity, suppose that there is some exogenous cost of defaulting in the second period. Formally, this cost is a fraction $\phi \in [0, 1)$ of y_2.[19] We assume that the country will repay its debt only if it is in its own benefit to do so. Formally, the country will repay its debt in period 2 if and only if consumption under no default (LHS in the expression below) is higher than consumption under default (RHS):

$$y_2 - (1 + r)d_1 \geq (1 - \phi)y_2.$$

Simplifying this no-default condition, we obtain

$$d_1 \leq \frac{\phi y_2}{1 + r}, \tag{2.52}$$

which says that if debt is higher than $\phi y_2/(1 + r)$, then the consumer will choose to default. Since creditors, however, internalize the debtor country's incentives to default, they will not lend over and above $\phi y_2/(1+r)$. Hence this no-default condition effectively imposes an upper bound on the feasible amount of borrowing in the first period. In other words—and as illustrated in figure 2.2, where r^s denotes the interest rate charged by creditors—the country faces a completely elastic

19. This fraction ϕ is intended to capture various costs associated with default in practice, as discussed in box 2.2. See Bulow and Roggof (1989), Eaton and Gersovitz (1981), Sachs (1984), and Sachs and Cohen (1982).

Box 2.2
How costly is to default?

Since, unlike private debt, sovereign debt repayment is not enforceable, there must be costs associated with default for countries to have an incentive to repay their debts. Empirically, four types of default costs have been identified in the literature (table 2.3 summarizes the main empirical findings associated with each type of default cost):

Table 2.3
Costs of default

Author(s)	Dataset	Default cost	Main results
English (1996)	US states/ 19th century	Reputational/ borrowing	Since foreign creditors could not impose trade embargoes on US states, states paid back their debt exclusively for reputational reasons and not because of the threat of sanctions.
Reinhart et al. (2003)	53 Countries/ 1979–2000	Reputational/ borrowing	A history of default is associated with lower ratings assigned by the Institutional Investor.
Borensztein and Panizza (2008)	83 Countries/ 1972–2000	Reputational/ borrowing	Default episodes do not have a long-term impact on credit ratings; only recent defaults correlate with current credit ratings.
Ozler (1993)	64 Countries/ 1968–1981	Reputational/ borrowing	Recent defaults influence spreads, but the size of premium attached to previous defaults fades with time.
Dell' Ariccia et al. (2002)	Russian crisis/54 countries	Reputational/ borrowing	Defaults have long-lasting effects. Countries involved in Brady exchange faced higher borrowing costs in the late 1990s.
Flandreau and Zumer (2004)	16 Countries/ 1880–1914	Reputational/ borrowing	Default is associated with a jump in spreads of about 90 basis points in the year that follows the end of a default episode. Effects on spread, however, declines rapidly over time.
Borensztein and Panizza (2008)	31 Countries/ 1997–2004	Reputational/ borrowing	Significant effect of up to 400 basis points in the year following default. Subsequent effects are smaller and not statistically significant.
Gelos, Sahay, and Sandleris (2011)	143 Developing countries/ 1980–2000	Reputational/ borrowing	Probability of market access not influenced by a country's frequency of defaults. If resolved quickly, a default does not reduce significantly the probability of tapping the markets.
Rose (2005)	200 Countries/ 1948–1997	International Trade	Paris Club debt renegotiations are associated with a decline in bilateral trade that lasts for 15 years and amounts to around 8 percent per year.
Borensztein and Panizza (2006)	Industry-level data/ 1980–2000	International Trade	Sovereign defaults are costly for export-oriented industries, but effect tends to be short-lived.
Borensztein and Panizza (2008)	149 Countries/ 1975–2000	Domestic banking system	Controlling for banking crises, defaults do not appear to have an effect on industries that depend more on external finance.
Borensztein and Panizza (2008)	19 Countries/ 1980–2003	Political cost	On average, ruling governments in countries that defaulted face a 16 percent reduction in electoral support. In 50 percent of the cases there was a change in the executive head either in the year of the default or in the following year (more than twice the probability in normal times).

Box 2.2
(continued)

- *Reputational/borrowing costs* Costs that countries suffer due to loss of access to capital markets (Eaton and Gersovitz 1981). While, in practice, countries that default are certainly not excluded from international capital markets forever, they face higher borrowing costs once they regain access.[a]
- *International trade costs* Costs that countries suffer due to various disruptions to international trade. There are two main channels involved: (1) direct import sanctions or restrictions, and (2) damage to exporters' creditworthiness. While the evidence for direct trade sanctions is rare, there is some evidence in favor of the second. When a country is in a situation of external financing distress, it often resorts to exchange controls or capital outflow restrictions, which affect the repayment capacity of all private debtors, especially export-linked credits (Ozler 1993; Borensztein and Panizza 2006).
- *Domestic banking sector costs* Since banks in emerging markets hold a significant amount of government bonds, a sovereign default (which, on occasions, may also include a default on domestic debt) will likely weaken banks' balance sheets and perhaps even cause a bank run (Borensztein and Panizza 2008).
- *Political costs* A weakened economy and, possibly, a banking system in crisis does not bode well for the survival in power of the incumbent party and policy makers (Borensztein and Panizza 2008).

Naturally, defaulting affects a country's rate of growth through the channels above and possibly others. Available estimates (Sturzenegger and Zettelmeyer 2006; Borensztein and Panizza 2008) suggest that in the year of default, growth falls between 0.5 and 2 percent.

a. Gelos, Sahay, and Sandleris (2011) document that the average exclusion from international credit markets following a default was four years in the 1980s but declined to two years in the 1990s.

supply of funds from abroad at a constant interest rate r until $d_1 = \phi y_2/(1+r)$, at which point the supply of funds becomes vertical. If $\phi = 0$, then this upper bound is zero (no lending from the rest of the world). At the other extreme, for high enough values of ϕ, this constraint will not bind and perfect smoothing will obtain. In this sense, *high costs of default are beneficial as a precommitment device.*

Formally, the maximization problem gets simplified by the fact that we know that in equilibrium we will never observe default (which implies that condition 2.52 will hold) and that, as a result, the intertemporal constraint (2.49) will also hold. Hence the consumer's maximization problem consists in choosing c_1 and c_2 to maximize (2.4) subject to the intertemporal constraint (2.49) and the no-default condition (2.52). Since d_1 would show up in the Lagrangian through the no-default condition, it proves convenient to re-state the maximization problem in terms of d_1. To this effect, use the flow constraints

$$c_1 = y_1 + d_1, \tag{2.53}$$

$$c_2 = y_2 - (1+r)d_1, \tag{2.54}$$

to write the Lagrangian as follows:

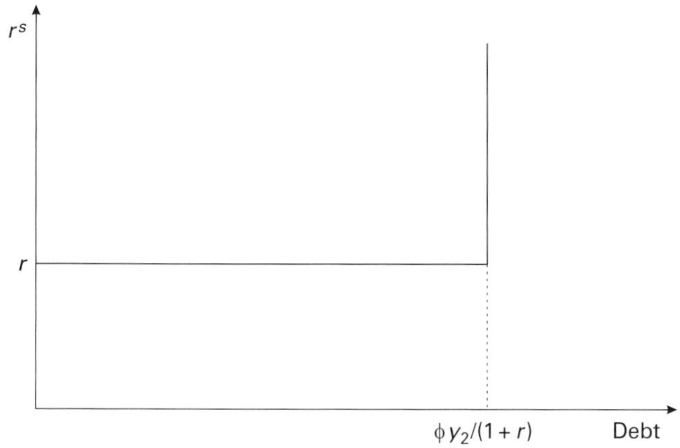

Figure 2.2
Supply of funds

$$\mathcal{L} = u(y_1 + d_1) + \beta u[y_2 - (1+r)d_1] + \chi \left(\frac{\phi y_2}{1+r} - d_1 \right),$$

where χ is the multiplier associated with constraint (2.52). Using (2.53) and (2.54), the Kuhn–Tucker conditions for d_1 and χ can be written as

$$u'(c_1) = u'(c_2) + \chi,$$

$$\frac{\phi y_2}{1+r} - d_1 \geqslant 0, \quad \chi \left(\frac{\phi y_2}{1+r} - d_1 \right) = 0. \tag{2.55}$$

There are two possible solutions for this problem depending on what would be the level of borrowing for the unconstrained case (i.e., the case where condition 2.52 is not present).

Nonbinding Constraint

Suppose that y_1 and y_2 are such that the unconstrained problem calls for a level of first-period borrowing that satisfies condition (2.52). Then, by construction, constraint (2.52) does not bind and $\chi = 0$. Hence from (2.55),

$$u'(c_1) = u'(c_2),$$

and full consumption smoothing would obtain.

Binding Constraint

Suppose that y_1 and y_2 are such that the unconstrained problem calls for a level of first-period borrowing that does not satisfy condition (2.52). In other words, the fluctuations in endowment are such that the economy would like to borrow in the first period more than what international creditors are willing to lend. Then condition (2.52) is binding, which implies that $\chi > 0$. Hence from (2.55),

$$u'(c_1) > u'(c_2),$$

which implies that $c_1 < c_2$. In fact, from (2.53) and (2.54), consumption will be given by

$$c_1 = y_1 + d_1^{\max}, \tag{2.56}$$

$$c_2 = y_2 - (1 + r)d_1^{\max}, \tag{2.57}$$

where $d_1^{\max} (= \phi y_2/(1 + r))$ is the maximum amount of borrowing. Hence the consumer cannot smooth consumption over time and is forced to consume less in bad times than in good times.[20] This simple example thus illustrates the idea that sovereign risk may severely limit the ability of a small open economy to smooth out consumption over time by imposing constraints on its ability to borrow during bad times. Furthermore the more output fluctuates (i.e., the larger the difference between y_1 and y_2), the more likely it is that the no-default condition will bind and hence that sovereign risk will prevent the economy from achieving full consumption smoothing. Since output fluctuations are much more pronounced in developing than in industrial countries, sovereign risk is particularly relevant for the former.[21]

2.4.3 Default Risk under Uncertainty

The certainty model just analyzed delivers quite insightful, but somewhat extreme, implications. First, the supply of funds is kinked (recall figure 2.2) but nowhere upward sloping. Second, while the threat of default generates a debt ceiling, there will never be default in equilibrium. We will now see how introducing uncertainty into the model (i.e., an uncertain level of period-2 output)—along the lines Sachs and Cohen (1982)—generates both an upward-sloping supply of funds and default in equilibrium.[22]

Supply of International Credit

Suppose that period-2 output (y_2) is a random variable drawn from a uniform distribution with support $[0, y_2^H]$. The probability density function is thus given by

20. Notice that for the same reasons as in section 2.2, the domestic real interest rate will be higher than the international one. In fact the domestic real interest rate will be given by an equation such as (2.12) with c_1 and c_2 given by (2.56) and (2.57).

21. According to figures reported in Talvi and Végh (2005), output in developing countries is more than twice as volatile as in OECD countries.

22. See Sachs and Cohen (1982) for a three-period version of this model, which enables them to study the issue of rescheduling.

$$f(y_2) = \begin{cases} \frac{1}{y_2^H}, & 0 \leq y_2 \leq y_2^H, \\ 0, & \text{otherwise.} \end{cases} \tag{2.58}$$

The corresponding cumulative distribution function, given by $F(\alpha) = \int_{-\infty}^{\alpha} f(y_2)dy_2$, is thus

$$F(\alpha) = \begin{cases} 0, & \alpha \leq 0, \\ \frac{\alpha}{y_2^H}, & 0 < \alpha < y_2^H, \\ 1, & \alpha \geq y_2^H. \end{cases} \tag{2.59}$$

Denote by r^s the real interest rate charged by creditors. As before, we assume that in the second period the country will repay its debt only if the cost of repaying (given by $d_1(1 + r^s)$) is smaller than the cost of not repaying (given by ϕy_2). Hence the default decision is given by

Default if $\quad y_2 \leq y_2^*$,

No default if $\quad y_2 > y_2^*$,

where

$$y_2^* \equiv \frac{d_1(1 + r^s)}{\phi} \tag{2.60}$$

is the default threshold. The country will thus choose to default for low values of period-2 output (i.e., it chooses to default in bad times) and choose to repay for high values of period-2 output (i.e., it chooses not to default in good times).

What is the probability that a country will default? Denote the probability of default by π. Then, using (2.60), write

$$\pi = \Pr\left(y_2 < y_2^*\right) = F\left[\frac{d_1(1 + r^s)}{\phi}\right]. \tag{2.61}$$

For a given value of r^s, the probability of default depends on the level of debt. On the one hand, for "high" levels of debt (i.e., $d_1(1 + r^s)/\phi \geq y_2^H$), the economy will *always* default because the benefits of doing so outweigh the costs for any possible realization of output.[23] On the other hand, if the economy is a creditor (i.e., $d_1 \leq 0$), the economy will obviously never default. For intermediate levels of debt (i.e., $0 < d_1(1 + r^s)/\phi < y_2^H$), the probability of default is an increasing function of the debt level because the higher the level of debt, the more likely that the realization of output will be such that the economy will find it in its advantage to default. For this intermediate range we can use (2.59) to express the probability of default as

23. Of course, in *equilibrium*, we will never observe levels of debt such that $d_1(1 + r^s)/\phi > y_2^H$. Since the country would default with probability one, lenders will never lend the country this amount of funds to begin with.

$$\pi = \frac{(1+r^s)d_1}{\phi y_2^H}. \tag{2.62}$$

How does the probability of default vary with the level of debt? To answer this question, suppose that international lenders are risk neutral and that their opportunity cost of funds is r. Then

$$1 + r = (1 - \pi)(1 + r^s). \tag{2.63}$$

Now solve for $1 + r^s$ from (2.63), substitute the resulting expression into (2.62), and differentiate with respect to π and d_1 to obtain

$$\frac{d\pi}{dd_1} = \frac{1+r}{\phi y_2^H(1-2\pi)}. \tag{2.64}$$

As will become clear below, at an optimum $d\pi/dd_1$ will always be positive. Intuitively, r^s is an increasing function of d_1. Hence both the direct effect of additional debt and the indirect effect (through a higher r^s) increase the probability of default.

We will now derive an explicit functional form for the supply of funds; that is, the interest rate at which creditors will be willing to lend a given amount of funds. Using (2.62), we can rewrite equation (2.63) as

$$r^s = \frac{1+r}{1-(1+r^s)d_1/\phi y_2^H} - 1. \tag{2.65}$$

This equation implicitly defines r^s as a function of d_1. In fact we can solve (2.65) explicitly to obtain[24]

$$r^s = \begin{cases} r, & d_1 \le 0, \\ \frac{2(1+r)d_1^{\max}}{d_1}\left(1 - \sqrt{1 - \frac{d_1}{d_1^{\max}}}\right) - 1, & 0 < d_1 \le d_1^{\max}, \end{cases} \tag{2.66}$$

where

$$d_1^{\max} \equiv \frac{\phi y_2^H}{4(1+r)}$$

is the maximum level of debt that can be sustained by international markets.[25] Beyond this level of debt, international lenders cannot be compensated for the risk that they would be taking. Furthermore r^s is an increasing function of d_1:

24. Equation (2.65) leads to a quadratic equation in $1 + r^s$. There are thus two values of r^s corresponding to a single value of d_1. The economically sensible solution is the smaller value of r^s.

25. Naturally, equation (2.65) holds for $d_1 \ge 0$. For $d_1 < 0$, it follows from (2.59) and (2.60) that $F(y_2^*) = 0$, and hence, from (2.66), $r^s = r$.

$$\frac{dr^s}{dd_1} = \frac{(1+r)d_1^{\max}}{d_1^2\sqrt{1-\frac{d_1}{d_1^{\max}}}}\left(2-\frac{d_1}{d_1^{\max}}-2\sqrt{1-\frac{d_1}{d_1^{\max}}}\right) > 0, \qquad 0 < d_1 \le d_1^{\max}.$$

What is the maximum interest rate charged by creditors? To find out, evaluate (2.66) at $d_1 = d_1^{\max}$ to obtain

$$r^s\big|_{d_1=d_1^{\max}} = 1 + 2r. \tag{2.67}$$

While the model is certainly not geared to offer quantitative predictions, it is still interesting to point out that it generates a substantial premium over the risk-free international real interest rate. Indeed equation (2.67) says that if, say, r is 3 percent, the maximum interest rate will be 106 percent!

Figure 2.3 illustrates the upward-sloping supply of funds just derived. Intuitively, for a given ϕ, the real interest rate faced by this small open economy, r^s, is an increasing function of the level of indebtedness (d_1), reflecting the fact that the higher the level of debt the more likely that the economy will default.[26] Figure 2.3 thus offers a simple and insightful rationalization of an upward-sloping supply of funds and suggests that developing countries may pay a substantial premium for their international loans due to the implicit default risk.

Demand for International Credit

The demand for credit comes from the consumer's side. To simplify the analysis, we will assume that preferences are linear. Lifetime utility (W) is thus given by

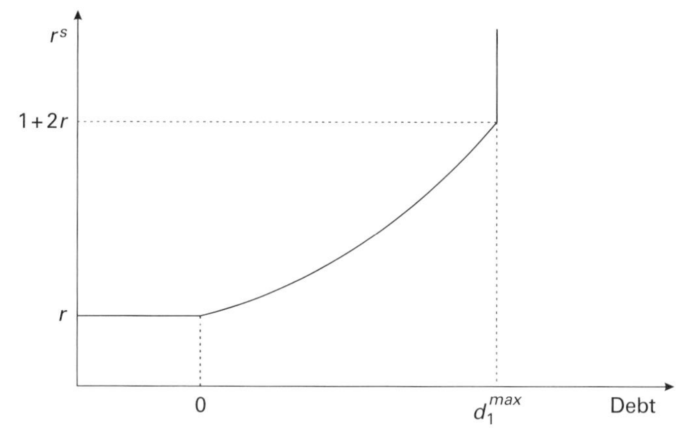

Figure 2.3
Upward-sloping supply of funds

26. In practice—and as discussed in box 2.3—other factors may also affect the risk premium paid by emerging countries.

Box 2.3
What explains the risk premium in practice?

While, in our simple model, the level of indebtedness is the main determinant of the risk premium, in practice, there are a host of variables that appear to influence it.[a] As summarized in table 2.4, the main determinants identified in the empirical literature are as follows:

• *Solvency and liquidity variables* The main measures of solvency include the level of debt, the budget deficit, debt service, and the export to GDP ratio. Liquidity is normally measured by the amount of foreign currency reserves held by a country, typically as a proportion of international trade

Table 2.4
Studies explaining sovereign risk premium

Author(s)	Dataset	Determinants	Main results
Edwards (1986)	26 countries/ 1976–1980	Solvency	Risk premium is positively related to debt-to-GDP ratio.
Min (1998)	11 countries/ 1991–1995	Solvency/liquidity /macroeconomic fundamentals	Increases in debt-to-GDP ratio and inflation rate raise spread. Increases in net foreign assets and improvements in terms of trade lower spread.
Caceres et al. (2010)	Euro area / mid-2005–2010	Solvency	Swap spreads tighten when public debt (in percentage of GDP) rises or budget balance deteriorates.
Akitoby and Stratmann (2006)	32 countries/ 1994–2003	Macroeconomic fundamentals	Reduction in public expenditure is a more powerful tool for reducing spreads than increases in revenues.
Hallerberg and Wolff (2006)	12 EU members/ 1993–2005	Solvency/fiscal institutions	An increase in the deficit of 1 percent of GDP increases the spread by 1.5 to 4 basis points. Countries that have institutions better suited to solving deficit biases pay lower risk premia for current deficits.
Caceres et al. (2010)	Euro area / mid-2005–2010	External factors	When global risk aversion is on the rise, spreads between AAA-rated countries and lower rated ones tend to widen significantly. Contagion always negative for government bonds. When probability of a credit squeeze in a country rises, swap spreads tighten. High-debt, lower rated countries more sensitive to market conditions.
Hartelius et al. (2010)	33 emerging countries/ 1991–2007	External factors	An increase of one percent in the expected US policy rate over the next three-month window increases spreads by about 5 percent. The VIX is used as proxy for investors' attitude toward risk. An increase of the VIX by one standard deviation increases spreads by about 30 percent.

a. In practice, the risk premium is typically computed as the spread between the interest rate that a country must pay on its debt relative to US debt of comparable maturity.

Box 2.3
(continued)

or, more recently, short-term debt (the so-called Guidotti–Greenspan rule).[b] Studies generally find that a higher debt to GDP ratio and lower liquidity increase spreads (Edwards 1986 and Caceres et al 2010).

• *Macroeconomic fundamentals* These are variables that have an impact on the long-term solvency of a country, such as the inflation rate, public expenditure, and terms of trade. In general, better fundamentals in the form of lower inflation, lower public expenditures, and better terms of trade are associated with lower spreads (Min 1998; Akitoby and Stratmann 2006).

• *Fiscal institutions* Sounder fiscal institutions are associated with a lower risk premium. Furthermore fiscal imbalances matter less for risk premium in countries with better institutions (Hallerberg and Wolff 2006).

• *External factors: global risk aversion, contagion, and international liquidity* Investors' attitude toward risk appears to explain movements of the emerging market bond spread in recent years. For advanced economies, higher global risk aversion generally lowers spreads due to flight-to-quality reasons.[c] Contagion, in contrast, is always negative for government bonds (i.e., leads to higher spreads). Finally, higher (lower) international liquidity, measured by low (high) US interest rates, leads to lower (higher) spreads in emerging markets (see Caceres et al. 2010; Hartelius et al. 2010).

There is evidence of substantial comovement in sovereign bond spreads over time, indicating that spreads do not only capture country specific information but also reflect spillover or contagion from regional and/or global forces. McGuire and Schrijvers (2003) and Ciarlone et al. (2007) find that common factors account for one-third of the total variation. Common factors include (1) the level of short- and long-term interest rates in advanced economies (mainly United States), as a measure of global liquidity conditions; (2) their volatility, as a measure of the uncertainty about the path of monetary policy in advanced economies (Arora and Cerisola 2001); and (3) the yield spread between low- and high-rating corporate bonds or US long-term bonds, as a measure of international investors' appetite for risk (Hartelius et al. 2010).

b. The Guidotti–Greenspan rule states that reserves should equal short-term debt (one year or less maturity), implying a ratio of reserves-to-short term debt of 1.
c. When global risk aversion increases, capital flows away from risky assets and toward advanced countries' government securities.

$$W = c_1 + \frac{1}{1+\delta} E\{c_2\}, \tag{2.68}$$

where $\delta(> 0)$ is the discount rate. To introduce a motive for borrowing in this linear case, we will assume $\delta > r$. Since future utility is discounted at a higher rate than the risk-free world real interest rate, the economy would prefer to consume all of its endowment in the first period rather than in the second.

Denote by c_2^D and c_2^{ND} the levels of consumption in period 2 in the event of default (D) and nondefault (ND), respectively. It follows that (assuming that net initial assets are zero)

$$c_1 = y_1 + d_1, \tag{2.69}$$

$$c_2^D = (1 - \phi)y_2, \tag{2.70}$$

$$c_2^{ND} = y_2 - (1 + r^s)d_1. \tag{2.71}$$

We will now express lifetime utility—given by (2.68)—as a function of d_1, which we will view as the planner's choice variable. To this effect, notice that, by the law of iterated expectations, we can write

$$E\{c_2\} = E_X\{E\{c_2|X\}\},$$

where X is the random variable that takes the value D with probability π and ND with probability $1 - \pi$. Hence

$$E\{c_2\} = \pi E\{c_2^D\} + (1 - \pi)E\{c_2^{ND}\}. \tag{2.72}$$

Substituting equation (2.72) into (2.68), we obtain

$$W = c_1 + \frac{\pi}{1+\delta}E\{c_2^D\} + \frac{1-\pi}{1+\delta}E\{c_2^{ND}\}. \tag{2.73}$$

Now take conditional expectations of (2.70) and (2.71), substitute the resulting expressions and (2.69) into (2.72), and use (2.63) to obtain

$$W = y_1 + \frac{1}{1+\delta}E\{y_2\} + \frac{\delta - r}{1+\delta}d_1 - \frac{\pi}{1+\delta}\phi E\{y_2|D\}. \tag{2.74}$$

Given that preferences are linear, the planner cares only about expected values, as captured by the first two terms on the RHS of (2.74).[27] The third term on the RHS of (2.74) captures the benefits of bringing forward consumption given that second period utility is discounted at a higher rate than the risk-free real interest rate. The last term captures the loss of resources that the economy suffers if it defaults. Notice that the expected output loss in case of default is $\phi E\{y_2|D\}$. Since the economy defaults with probability π, the expected resource loss in terms of period-1 utility is $\pi\phi E\{y_2|D\}/(1+\delta)$.

To proceed further, notice that conditional on the economy having defaulted, y_2 varies uniformly between 0 and y_2^*. By the same token, conditional on the economy not having defaulted, output varies uniformly between y_2^* and y_2^H. Hence

27. Notice that in the standard model with $\delta = r$ and no sovereign risk ($\pi = 0$), then $W = y_1 + \beta E\{y_2\}$ where $\beta = 1/(1+\delta)$.

$$E\{y_2|D\} = \frac{y_2^*}{2} = \frac{\pi y_2^H}{2}, \tag{2.75}$$

$$E\{y_2|ND\} = \frac{y_2^* + y_2^H}{2} = \frac{(1+\pi)y_2^H}{2}, \tag{2.76}$$

where the right-most expressions follows from the fact that, from (2.60) and (2.62), $\pi = y_2^*/y_2^H$.

Substituting (2.75) into (2.74), we obtain

$$W = y_1 + \frac{1}{1+\delta}E\{y_2\} + \frac{\delta - r}{1+\delta}d_1 - \frac{\phi\pi^2 y_2^H}{2(1+\delta)}. \tag{2.77}$$

The planner's problem consists in choosing d_1 to maximize (2.77). The first-order condition is given by

$$\delta - r = \phi\pi y_2^H \frac{d\pi}{dd_1}. \tag{2.78}$$

The LHS of this expression captures the marginal benefit of borrowing to increase period's 1 consumption (net of the risk-free real interest rate). Since the rate of time preference, δ, is greater than the risk-free real interest rate, r, the marginal benefit of borrowing is constant and positive. The RHS captures the marginal cost of borrowing.[28] Recall, from the last term on the RHS of (2.74), that the cost of borrowing is given by the expected output loss in case of default. Borrowing an additional unit increases the marginal cost of borrowing on two accounts. First, for a given loss $\phi E\{y_2|D\}$, an additional unit of borrowing increases the probability of default by $d\pi/dd_1$ and hence raises the marginal cost of borrowing by $\phi E\{y_2|D\}(d\pi/dd_1)$. Second, for a given probability of default, an additional unit of borrowing increases the expected loss in case of default by $\phi\,[d(E\{y_2|D\})/d\pi)]\,(d\pi/dd_1)$. Since default occurs with probability π, the marginal cost of borrowing increases by $\pi\phi\,[d(E\{y_2|D\})/d\pi)]\,(d\pi/dd_1)$. Recalling (2.75), these two effects add up to the RHS of equation (2.78).

We can now compute reduced forms for the equilibrium values of π, d_1, and r^s. Using (2.63), (2.62), (2.64), and (2.78), we obtain

$$\pi = \frac{\delta - r}{1 + 2\delta - r}, \tag{2.79}$$

$$d_1 = \frac{\phi y_2^H (1+\delta)(\delta - r)}{(1+r)(1+2\delta - r)^2}, \tag{2.80}$$

28. Notice that since $\delta > r$, $(d\pi/dd_1) > 0$ in equilibrium.

$$r^s = \frac{1+r}{1+\delta}(1+2\delta-r)-1. \tag{2.81}$$

Several features of the equilibrium solution are worth noting. First, as (2.79) makes clear, the probability of default is independent of the cost of default, ϕ. The reason is that although, for a given level of borrowing, a higher ϕ makes it more costly to default (and hence decreases the probability of default, as follows from equation 2.62), it also increases the amount that the economy may borrow (thus increasing the probability of default). In equilibrium, these two effects cancel each other out.[29] Second, π, d_1, and r^s are all increasing functions of δ. Hence, an economy with a higher δ (i.e., a more "impatient" economy) will borrow more, pay a higher real interest rate, and face a higher probability of default.

Even though the probability of default does not depend on ϕ, it can be checked that welfare is an increasing function of ϕ. Substituting (2.79) and (2.80) into (2.77), we obtain

$$W = y_1 + \frac{1}{1+\delta}E\{y_2\} + \phi\frac{y_2^H(\delta-r)^2}{2(1+2\delta-r)(1+r)(1+\delta)}.$$

Welfare is thus a linear function of ϕ. Hence higher costs of default are welfare improving for this economy as the benefits of more borrowing outweigh the resulting increase in the expected cost of default. It is worth noticing, however, that even for $\phi = 1$ (which means that all of period-2 endowment would be lost in case of default), this economy cannot replicate the first-best equilibrium (i.e., the equilibrium that would obtain under no sovereign risk). To see this, notice that if there were no sovereign risk (and complete markets), this economy would want to consume all of its endowment (in a present-value sense) in period 1. Borrowing would thus be given by

$$d_1|_{\text{no sovereign risk}} = \frac{E\{y_2\}}{1+r}.$$

With sovereign risk, we see from (2.80) that the maximum borrowing would obtain for very large values of δ and be given by (noting that $E\{y_2\} = y_2^H/2$)

$$d_1^{\max} = \frac{\phi}{2}\frac{E\{y_2\}}{1+r}.$$

Hence, even for $\phi = 1$, this economy would be borrowing just half of the amount it would borrow under perfect capital markets. It is thus clear from (2.77) that welfare under sovereign risk (even for $\phi = 1$) is lower than welfare under no sovereign risk. Sovereign risk thus imposes welfare costs to this economy even under very high costs of default.

Finally, notice that this model generates the possibility of default as an equilibrium outcome. The economy borrows in the first period an amount given by (2.80) at the interest rate given by (2.81). In the second period the economy will default for any realization of y_2 such that the

29. This need not be the case, of course, in more general models; see Sachs and Cohen (1982) for some examples.

cost of defaulting (ϕy_2) is lower than the cost of repaying $(1 + r^s)d_1$. Hence bad times (i.e., low realizations of y_2) will be associated with more defaults.

Upward-Sloping Supply of Funds

Assuming some ad hoc upward sloping supply of funds is common in the literature.[30] Typically it is just assumed that the real interest rate charged by creditors is an increasing function of the level of debt:

$$r^s = r + f(d), \tag{2.82}$$

where $f'(d) > 0$. This should be viewed as an approximation to an endogenously-derived supply of funds, such as the one depicted in figure 2.3. A key implicit assumption behind (2.82) is that the economy is operating on the upward portion of the "true" supply of funds (i.e., the one depicted in figure 2.3).

As exercise 6 at the end of this chapter illustrates, an upward-sloping supply of funds has important consequences for the optimal choice of borrowing by a small open economy. First, the economy will choose *not* to smooth consumption. Specifically, if $y_1 < y_2$, the economy will borrow in the first period but still consume less than in the second period. Given the imperfection in international capital markets, it is in fact socially optimal not to smooth consumption over time since more borrowing increases the cost of funds. Second, a planner would choose to borrow less than the private sector would. In other words, the social marginal cost of borrowing is higher than the private marginal cost. Intuitively, the country is a monopsonist in world capital markets as its borrowing affects the interest rate charged by creditors. The planner fully internalizes this monopsony power and equates the marginal benefit of borrowing with the *marginal* social cost of borrowing. Individual consumers, however, equate the marginal benefit of borrowing with the *average* social cost of borrowing. It would thus be optimal for the government to impose a tax on foreign borrowing that would reduce private borrowing to the socially optimal level. This is an example of a "second-best" policy, wherein an existing distortion (i.e., the upward-sloping supply of funds) makes it optimal to introduce a second distortion (i.e., a tax on foreign borrowing).

Exercise 6 thus provides a strong theoretical case for a so-called Tobin tax—so named after Tobin's (1978) celebrated article advocating throwing some sand in the wheels of excessively efficient international financial markets.[31] Even from a theoretical point of view, however, the argument is weaker than it appears for two reasons. First, our simple model does not take into account well-known microeconomic distortions introduced by taxes on foreign borrowing such as misallocation of resources and rent-seeking activities.[32] Second, even in the simple example examined in exercise 6, the first-best policy would be to address the initial distortion (i.e., to

30. Bardhan (1967) was a precursor.

31. See also Harberger (1986). Of course, there may be other factors calling for controls of capital inflows, such as real exchange rate appreciation and asset prices bubbles that may render economies more prone to financial crisis; see Ostry et al. (2010) and chapter 14.

32. See De Gregorio, Edwards, and Valdes (2000) for an examination of the practical effectiveness of capital controls.

address the imperfections in capital markets that give rise to the upward-sloping supply of funds) and ensure that the country faces an infinitely elastic supply of funds. Unfortunately, while there have been many proposals involving some sort of international bankruptcy law that would deal with problems of sovereign risk, there has been little progress in addressing the tremendous practical problems of effectively implementing such a proposal.

2.5 Final Remarks

This chapter has examined the implications of relaxing the main three assumptions of the basic model presented in chapter 1: (1) full access to international capital markets, (2) no uncertainty in the output path, and (3) the ability to precommit to repaying outstanding debts. We have seen that relaxing each of these assumptions may fundamentally alter the economy's ability to smooth consumption over time. In all three cases the economy is unable to smooth consumption over time as in the first-best world of chapter 1. These restrictions have therefore important welfare consequences that will be particularly severe for countries facing high output variability and limited access to international financing in bad times.

2.6 Appendix: Closed Form Solution for Consumption in an Infinite-Horizon Stochastic Model

This appendix derives a closed form solution for consumption in an infinite horizon version of the two-period stochastic model of section 2.3. Let preferences be given by

$$E_0\left\{\sum_{t=0}^{\infty}\beta^t u(c_t)\right\}. \tag{2.83}$$

The flow budget constraint takes the form

$$b_{t+1} = (1+r)\,b_t + y_t - c_t. \tag{2.84}$$

Imposing the transversality condition

$$\lim_{t\longrightarrow\infty}\left(\frac{1}{1+r}\right)^t b_t = 0,$$

we can derive the intertemporal constraint

$$(1+r)\,b_0 + \sum_{t=0}^{\infty}\left(\frac{1}{1+r}\right)^t y_t = \sum_{t=0}^{\infty}\left(\frac{1}{1+r}\right)^t c_t. \tag{2.85}$$

Notice that this lifetime constraint must hold for *every* possible history of output shocks.

To derive the first-order condition, substitute the flow constraint (2.84) into (2.83) and differentiate with respect to b_{t+1} to obtain (assuming that $\beta(1+r)=1$)

$$u'(c_t) = E\left\{u'(c_{t+1})\right\}. \tag{2.86}$$

As Hall (1978) has emphasized, marginal utility follows a random walk. Furthermore, if preferences are quadratic, consumption will follow a random walk. To see this, rewrite optimality condition (2.86) under quadratic preferences as

$$c_t = E\{c_{t+1}\}. \tag{2.87}$$

This implies that

$$c_0 = E\{c_1\} = E\{c_2\} = \ldots. \tag{2.88}$$

Since the intertemporal constraint holds for every history of shocks, it also holds in expectations:

$$(1+r)\,b_0 + \sum_{t=0}^{\infty}\left(\frac{1}{1+r}\right)^t E_0\{y_t\} = \sum_{t=0}^{\infty}\left(\frac{1}{1+r}\right)^t E_0\{c_t\}. \tag{2.89}$$

Using (2.88), we can rewrite this last expression as

$$c_0 = \frac{r}{1+r}\left[(1+r)\,b_0 + \sum_{t=0}^{\infty}\left(\frac{1}{1+r}\right)^t E_0\{y_t\}\right]. \tag{2.90}$$

As discussed in the text, certainty equivalence holds in the sense that households decide today's consumption as though the future realizations of output were given by their expected values.

To see the permanent income hypothesis in action, suppose that output follows a random walk process

$$y_t = y_{t-1} + \varepsilon_t,$$

where ε_t is an i.i.d. shock with mean zero. Then

$$y_0 = E_0\{y_1\} = E_0\{y_2\} = \ldots.$$

Using this in (2.90), we obtain

$$c_0 = rb_0 + y_0.$$

Intuitively, since output is a random walk, any shock to output is permanent. Consumers therefore adjust consumption one to one with higher output. Notice that this is exactly the result that we obtained in our perfect foresight model.[33]

33. See Obstfeld and Rogoff (1996) for further analysis of this infinite-horizon stochastic model.

Box 2.4
To close or not to close the small open economy model?

As exercise 3 at the end of chapter 1 made clear, our basic perfect-foresight, small open economy model in continuous time has roots equal to r and $r - \beta$. If $r = \beta$, the roots are r and 0. This would correspond, in a discrete-time model and under the assumption that $\beta(1+r) = 1$, to the system having roots $1 + r$ and 1. In other words, under the assumption that $\beta(1 + r) = 1$, our basic small open economy model has a unit root. Intuitively, this simply means that if permanent income increases by one unit, the permanent level of consumption also increases by one unit, a natural and logical implication of the permanent income hypothesis. On occasions, researchers speak of consumption depending on initial conditions because if, say, the initial level of assets were to change exogenously, the permanent level of consumption would change by the permanent income component of the change in the stock of assets, again a very logical implication. Under perfect foresight, having a unit root therefore presents no formal problem and is in fact the natural outcome of Friedman's permanent income hypothesis. We should have been shocked if this had not been the result!

What happens when we introduce uncertainty? If the horizon is finite, uncertainty introduces no problems whatsoever. In infinite-horizon problems, things become trickier. Theoretically, however, very little changes. As appendix 2.6 shows, the marginal utility of consumption follows a random walk (the stochastic equivalent of a unit root), and under quadratic preferences, consumption itself follows a random walk. In fact we can compute a reduced form for consumption that exactly replicates our perfect foresight counterpart. Further, specifying a particular stochastic process for output, we can perform all of our main experiments such as analyzing how consumption and the current account respond to different shocks. In this sense, our random walk result is no different from some of the more popular models in macroeconomics that yield the prediction that the main variable of interest—for instance, aggregate consumption or stock prices—should follow a random walk. In sum, the nonstationary of the consumption process is a fundamental feature of the standard (stochastic) small open economy model and is just the counterpart of the unit root in the perfect foresight version of the model. In fact, if the computer had never been invented (and hence quantitative considerations had not become paramount), we would probably be dealing only with these nonstationary models in open economy macroeconomics.

Computers, however, are here to stay, and influenced by a paper of Schmitt-Grohé and Uribe (2003), open economy researchers often refer to the need to "close" a small open economy model. By "closing" they mean getting rid of the unit root by introducing some friction—such as an upward-sloping supply of funds, Uzawa preferences, or cost of adjustments in the stock of net foreign assets—which transforms the unit root into a stable root and renders the model stationary. Since, as argued above, there is nothing wrong with the nonstationary model, and hence there is no formal *need* to "close" a stochastic small open economy model, why may we *choose* to do so? The "problem" is that a nonstationary model has no well-defined second moments. (Recall that the variance of a random walk is infinite.) In other words, nonstationary models do not have a well-behaved stationary stochastic distribution. If our only objective is to solve a small open economy model quantitatively and compute impulse responses (i.e., responses of the endogenous variables to a single shock), we do not need to get rid of the unit root. This is equivalent to studying the response of our perfect foresight economy in chapter 1 to a temporary shock. More typically, however, researchers who solve models with the computer following the real business cycle methodology seek to compute second moments to capture variances and covariances of the main endogenous variables and compare them with the

Box 2.4
(continued)

> second moments in the data. Since variances/covariances would not be well defined in the presence of a unit root, the need arises to get rid of this unit root by "closing" the model.
>
> While "closing" small open economy models is therefore necessary for the purposes of computing variances and covariances, it does come at the cost of blurring some important conceptual foundations. Consider, for instance, Uzawa preferences that force consumption to remain the same across steady states. This implies that even if your wealth increases by one unit, your steady-state consumption would remain unchanged, a clear violation of the permanent income hypothesis! You would be forced to consume a lot during the transition in order to go back to the same steady-state consumption.

As discussed in box 2.4, however, nonstationary stochastic models do not have well-behaved stochastic distributions. As a result researchers often introduce frictions into the model to get rid of nonstationarity.

Exercises

1. (Correlation between output and consumption) Consider the certainty equivalence case discussed in section 2.3.2. Check that the correlation between c_2 and y_2 is one.

2. (Reduced forms for consumption and welfare under CARA utility) Consider the incomplete markets case analyzed in section 2.3.1 with the following two modifications. First, assume that preferences are given by the constant absolute risk aversion function (CARA):

$$u(c) = -\frac{1}{\alpha}e^{-\alpha c}. \tag{2.91}$$

Second, instead of the Bernoulli distribution for period 2's output specified in (2.16), suppose that

$$y_2 = y_1 + \varepsilon, \quad \varepsilon \sim N(0, \sigma^2).$$

In this context:

a. Show that the coefficient of absolute risk aversion is equal to α. (Recall that the Arrow–Pratt measure of absolute risk aversion is given by $-u''/u'$.)

b. Following Kimball (1990), show that the coefficient of absolute prudence (defined as $-u'''/u''$) is equal to α.

c. Derive reduced-form solutions for c_1 and c_2. In particular, how does a higher σ^2 affect c_1 and c_2? (Hint: Recall that if $x \sim N(E\{x\}, \sigma_x^2)$, then $E\{e^x\} = e^{E\{x\}+\sigma_x^2/2}$.)

d. Compute the correlation coefficient between c_2 and y_2.

e. Show that welfare is a decreasing function of σ^2.

3. (Numerical example of incomplete markets model with CRRA preferences) Consider the incomplete markets model analyzed in section 2.3.1 with constant relative risk aversion (CRRA) preferences of the form

$$u(c) = \frac{c^{1-\theta} - 1}{1 - \theta}$$

where θ is the coefficient of constant relative risk aversion. In this context:

a. Show that the coefficient of relative risk aversion is equal to θ. (Recall that the Arrow–Pratt measure of relative risk aversion is given by $-cu''/u'$.)

b. Following Kimball (1990), show that the coefficient of relative prudence (defined as $-cu'''/u''$) is equal to $1 + \theta$.

c. Plot c_1, c_2^H, c_2^L, current account, and expected utility as a function of the coefficient of risk aversion.

d. Plot the same variables as a function of a mean-preserving spread in the output distribution.

4. (Numerical example of incomplete markets model with imprudent preferences) Consider the incomplete markets model analyzed in section 2.3.1 with the following preferences:

$$u(c) = 10c - \frac{1}{5}c^3$$

for $c < \sqrt{50/3}$.

In this context:

a. Show that these preferences exhibit risk aversion and *imprudence.*

b. Plot c_1, c_2^H, c_2^L, current account, and expected utility as a function of the coefficient of risk aversion.

5. (A two-country world with complete markets) Consider a two-country (domestic and foreign) version of our small open economy model with complete markets analyzed in section 2.3.3. Suppose that preferences are logarithmic and that countries have the same discount factor. We will use star superscripts to denote the foreign country variables. Since this is a two-country model, the following world output constraints will hold:

$$c_1 + c_1^* = y_1 + y_1^* \equiv y_1^W,$$
$$c_2^A + c_2^{A*} = y_2^A + y_2^{A*} \equiv y_2^{AW},$$
$$c_2^B + c_2^{B*} = y_2^B + y_2^{B*} \equiv y_2^{BW},$$

where a superscript W denotes world quantities. Notice that we have re-labeled states "high" and "low" as A and B, respectively. (The reason is that if, for instance, there is no aggregate uncertainty, then when domestic output is high, foreign output will be low and vice versa.)

In this context:

a. Derive first-order conditions and show that the ratio of consumption across states of nature is the same at home and abroad.

b. Derive reduced forms for q^A and q^B.

c. Derive a reduced-form solution for the world real interest rate.

d. Show that consumption as a proportion of world output is constant across time and states of nature in both countries.

e. Show that corr $(c_2, c_2^*) = 1$.

f. Show that, if there is no world uncertainty (i.e., $y_2^{AW} = y_2^{BW}$), c_2 is uncorrelated with domestic output.

6. (An ad hoc upward-sloping supply of funds) Let preferences be given by

$$W = \log(c_1) + \beta \log(c_2), \tag{92}$$

where $\beta(\equiv 1/(1+\delta))$ is the discount factor and δ is the discount rate. Assume $\beta(1+r) = 1$, where r is the world real interest rate.
The flow constraints are given by:

$$c_1 = d_1, \tag{2.93}$$

$$c_2 = y_2 - (1+r^s)d_1, \tag{2.94}$$

where d_1 is net external debt and $y_2 > 0$ is second period's output (notice that, for simplicity, we have assumed that output in the first period is zero).
The economy faces an upward sloping supply of funds of the form:

$$r^s = r + f(d_1), \qquad f(0) = 0,\ f'(d_1) > 0, \tag{2.95}$$

where r^s is the real interest rate charged to the country.
In this context:

a. Solve the planner's problem. Show that the planner will choose not to smooth consumption over time.

b. Solve the consumer's problem (i.e., the free-market solution). Show that relative to the planner's solution, the market solution implies that consumption in the first period is too high relative to the second period.

c. Consider a linear version of this model (i.e., linear preferences and linear supply of funds):

$$W = c_1 + \frac{c_2}{1+\delta}, \tag{2.96}$$

$$f(d_1) = \alpha d_1. \tag{2.97}$$

Assume $\delta > r$. In this context:

i. Derive a reduced-form solution for the equilibrium values of d_1 and r^S for both the planner's problem and the market problem.

ii. Provide a graphical illustration of how the equilibrium values of d_1 and r^S are determined and interpret the results intuitively. (Hint: Think of the country as a monopsonist in world capital markets and proceed as in the textbook analysis of a monopsonist in factor markets).

iii. Show that by imposing a borrowing tax rate (which increases linearly with the amount of borrowing), the government can implement the planner's solution.

References

Akitoby, Bernardin, and Thomas Stratmann. 2006. Fiscal policy and financial markets. IMF Working Paper 06/16. International Monetary Fund, Washington, DC.

Arora, Vivek, and Martín Cerisola. 2001. How does U.S. monetary policy influence sovereign spreads in emerging markets? *IMF Staff Papers* 48 (3): 474–98.

Atkeson, Andrew, and Tamim Bayoumi. 1993. Do private capital markets insure regional risk? Evidence from the United States and Europe. *Open Economies Review* 4 (3): 303–324.

Attanasio, Orazio, and Steven J. Davis. 1996. Relative wage movements and the distribution of consumption. *Journal of Political Economy* 104 (6): 1227–62

Bardhan, Pranab. 1967. Optimum foreign borrowing. In Karl Shell, ed., *Essays on the Theory of Optimal Economic Growth*. Cambridge: MIT Press.

Blanchard, Olivier, and Stanley Fischer. 1989. *Lectures on Macroeconomics*. Cambridge: MIT Press.

Borensztein, Eduardo, and Ugo Panizza. 2006. Do sovereign defaults hurt exporters? IDB Working Paper 553. Inter-American Development Bank, Washington, DC.

Borensztein, Eduardo, and Ugo Panizza. 2008. The costs of sovereign default. IMF Working Paper 08/238. International Monetary Fund, Washington, DC.

Bulow, Jeremy, and Kenneth Rogoff. 1989. Sovereign debt: Is to forgive to forget? *American Economic Review* 79 (1): 43–50.

Caceres, Carlos, Vincenzo Guzzo, and Miguel Segoviano. 2010. Sovereign spreads: Global risk aversion, contagion or fundamentals? IMF Working Paper 10/120. International Monetary Fund, Washington, DC.

Ciarlone, Alessio, Paolo Piselli, and Giorgio Trebeschi. 2007. Emerging markets spreads and global financial conditions. Temi di discussione (Economic working papers) 637. Bank of Italy.

Cochrane, John H. 1991. A simple test of consumption insurance. *Journal of Political Economy* 99 (5): 957–76.

Crucini, Mario J. 1999. On international and national dimensions of risk sharing. *Review of Economics and Statistics* 81 (1): 73–84.

De Gregorio, Jose, Sebastian Edwards, and Rodrigo O. Valdes. 2000. Controls on capital inflows: Do they work? *Journal of Development Economics* 63 (1): 59–83.

Dell'Ariccia, Giovanni, Isabel Schnabel, and Jeromin Zettelmeyer. 2002. Moral hazard and international crisis lending: A test. IMF Working Paper 02/181. International Monetary Fund, Washington, DC.

Eaton, Jonathan, and Mark Gersovitz. 1981. Debt with potential repudiation: Theory and estimation. *Review of Economic Studies* 48 (2): 289–309.

Edwards, Sebastian. 1986. The pricing of bonds and bank loans in international markets: An empirical analysis of developing countries' foreign borrowing. *European Economic Review* 30 (3): 565–589.

English, William B. 1996. Understanding the costs of sovereign default: American state debts in the 1840s. *American Economic Review* 86 (1): 259–75.

Flandreau, Marc, and Frederic Zumer. 2004. *Development Center Studies: The Making of Global Finance 1880–1913*. Paris: OECD Development Center Research.

Gelos, Gaston, Ratna Sahay, and Guido Sandleris. 2011. Sovereign borrowing by developing countries: What determines market access? *Journal of International Economics* 83 (2): 243–54.

Hall, Robert. 1978. Stochastic implications of the life cycle–permanent income hypothesis: Theory and evidence. *Journal of Political Economy* 86 (6): 971–87.

Hallerberg, Mark, and Guntram Wolff. 2006. Fiscal institutions, fiscal policy and sovereign risk premia. Discussion Paper Series 35. Deutsche Bundesbank.

Ham, John C., and Kris Jacobs. 2000. Testing for full insurance using exogenous information. *Journal of Business & Econometric Statistics* 18 (4): 387–97.

Harberger, Arnold. 1986. Welfare consequences of capital inflows. In Armeane Choksi and Demetris Papageorgiou, eds., *Economic Liberalization in Developing Countries*. Oxford: Blackwell, ch. 6.

Hartelius, Kristian, Kenichiro Kashiwase, and Laura Kodres. 2010. Emerging market spread compression: Is it real or is it liquidity? IMF Working Paper 08/10. International Monetary Fund, Washington, DC.

Hayashi, Fumio, Altonji Joseph, and Laurence Kotlikoff. 1996. Risk-sharing between and within families. *Econometrica* 64 (2): 261–94.

Hirshleifer, Jack, and John Riley. 1992. *The Analytics of Uncertainty and Information*. New York: Cambridge University Press.

Jacobs, Kris, Stephane Pallage, and Michel A. Robe. 2005. The welfare costs of macroeconomic fluctuations under incomplete markets: Evidence from state-level consumption data. Cahiers de recherche 0524. CIRPEE, Montreal, Canada.

Huggett, Mark, and Sandra Ospina. 2001. Aggregate precautionary savings: When is the third derivative irrelevant? *Journal of Monetary Economics* 48 (2): 373–96.

Kehoe, Patrick J., and Fabrizio Perri. 2002. International business cycles with endogenous incomplete markets. *Econometrica* 70: 907–28.

Kimball, Miles S. 1990. Precautionary saving in the small and in the large. *Econometrica* 58 (1): 53–73.

Kose, Ayhan M., Eswar S. Prasad, and Marco E. Terrones. 2009. Does financial globalization promote risk sharing? *Journal of Development Economics* 89 (2): 258–70.

Mace, Barbara J. 1991. Full insurance in the presence of aggregate uncertainty. *Journal of Political Economy* 99 (5): 928–56.

McGuire, Patrick, and Martijn A. Schrijvers. 2003. Common factors in emerging market spreads. *BIS Quarterly Review* (December): 65–78.

Min, Hong G. 1998. Determinants of emerging market bond spread: Do economic fundamentals matters? Policy Research Working Paper 1899. World Bank, Washington, DC.

Obstfeld, Maurice. 1994. Are industrial-country consumption risks globally diversified? Working Paper 4308. National Bureau of Economic Research, Cambridge, MA.

Obstfeld, Maurice, and Kenneth S. Rogoff. 1996. *Foundations of International Macroeconomics*. Cambridge: MIT Press.

Ostry, Jonathan, Atish R. Ghosh, Karl Habermeier, Marcos Chamon, Mahvash S. Qureshi, and Dennis B.S. Reinhart, 2010. Capital inflows: The role of controls. IMF Staff Position Note 10/04. International Monetary Fund, Washington, DC.

Ozler, Sule. 1993. Have commercial banks ignored history? *American Economic Review* 83 (3): 608–20.

Reinhart, Carmen M., Kenneth S. Rogoff, and Miguel A. Savastano. 2003. Debt intolerance. *Brookings Papers on Economic Activity* 34 (1): 1–74.

Roitman, Agustin. 2011. Precautionary savings in a small open economy revisited. IMF Working Paper 11/253. International Monetary Fund, Washington, DC.

Rose, Andrew K. 2005. One reason countries pay their debts: Renegotiation and international trade. *Journal of Development Economics* 77 (1): 189–206.

Sachs, Jeffrey D. 1984. *Theoretical Issues in International Borrowing*. Princeton: Princeton University Press.

Sachs, Jeffrey D., and Daniel Cohen. 1982. LDC borrowing with default risk. Working Paper 925. National Bureau of Economic Research, Cambridge, MA.

Schmitt-Grohé, Stephanie, and Martin Uribe. 2003. Closing small open economy models. *Journal of International Economics* 61 (1): 163–85.

Sturzenegger, Federico, and Jeromin Zettelmeyer. 2006. *Debt Defaults and Lessons from a Decade of Crises*. Cambridge: MIT Press.

Talvi, Ernesto, and Carlos A. Végh. 2005. Tax base variability and procyclical fiscal policy. *Journal of Development Economics* 78 (1): 156–90.

Tobin, James. 1978. A proposal for international monetary reform. *Eastern Economic Journal* 4: 153–59.

3 Intertemporal Prices

3.1 Introduction

A key feature of the basic intertemporal model presented in chapter 1 is that the relative price of consumption was constant over time, or put differently, the relative price of consumption across different points in time was always equal to one. As a result consumers chose a constant path of consumption. In practice, however, there are myriad factors that lead to a nonconstant path of intertemporal prices, ranging from temporary government policies (e.g., changes in taxes, tariffs, and monetary policy) to temporary terms of trade shocks. In all these cases, even though they could, consumers will choose not to smooth consumption over time because they will find it in their advantage to consume more when the good is relatively cheap.

When the intertemporal price of consumption varies over time due to policy actions, we will speak of *intertemporal distortions*. The distortion arises because, in a first-best world, a planner would choose to keep the relative price of consumption flat over time. The bulk of this chapter is devoted to the analysis of this key feature of intertemporal models. To provide a real-world motivation for intertemporal distortions, we will follow Calvo (1987) and study a model with two goods, exportables and importables, in which temporary import tariffs introduce intertemporal distortions. In the benchmark model of sections 3.2 and 3.3, a permanent reduction in tariffs has no impact on consumption and welfare. In contrast, a temporary reduction in tariffs leads to a temporary boom in consumption—as consumers take advantage of temporarily cheaper prices—followed by a consumption bust. This nonflat path of consumption is socially suboptimal. Hence a temporary trade liberalization is always welfare reducing.

In general, policy makers will rarely embark purposely on a temporary reform. Typically reforms turn out to be temporary because poor results coupled with waning political support force a reversal. Another intriguing source of de facto temporary reforms—suggested by Calvo (1989) and pursued in section 3.4—is lack of credibility. The basic idea is that when policy makers announce a reform (which they intend to be permanent), the public does not believe that the reform will be sustained over time (i.e., the announcement is not fully credible). In fact, if the public believes that the reform will be abandoned at some point in the future, the announcement will have the same short-run effects as a temporary reform. A temporary trade liberalization can thus be reinterpreted as arising from lack of credibility. Hence lack of credibility is socially costly because it generates an intertemporal distortion. Given the history of failed reforms in many developing countries, lack of credibility is bound to be an important source of social losses. This underscores the importance of efforts aimed at building mechanisms and institutions that may enhance policy credibility in developing countries.

Taken at face value, the policy prescription of this chapter's benchmark model would be a recipe for inaction since, at best, the welfare effects of a liberalization would be nil (when the liberalization is permanent). The model, however, abstracted from possible wealth effects. In practice, trade liberalizations are likely to generate wealth effects by, say, increasing productivity in the tradable goods sector. To capture such a scenario, section 3.5 introduces wealth effects into the benchmark model. In this case a permanent reduction in tariffs leads to higher consumption and welfare. More interesting, even a temporary tariff reduction may increase welfare if the wealth effect dominates the intertemporal distortion effect. Since the wealth effect will be larger the longer is the liberalization, a long-lasting liberalization will be welfare improving even if a short-lived one is not. Hence, from a normative point of view, the model yields the policy prescription that reforms such as trade liberalization may be worth pursuing, even if they may prove temporary, as long as they generate sizable increases in productivity.

As a second example of intertemporal distortions, section 3.6 analyzes the case where the government finances an exogenously given level of spending by resorting to a consumption tax. To fix ideas, we assume that the government must balance its budget on a period-by-period basis. In this context, permanent changes in government spending will lead to a wealth effect but no intertemporal distortions since the consumption tax rate will be constant over time. A temporary increase in government spending, however, will lead to a nonconstant path of tax rates and hence introduce an intertemporal distortion. Consumers' welfare will therefore be lower because of a wealth effect (due to higher government spending) and an intertemporal distortion (nonconstant tax rates). If lump-sum taxation were available, only the wealth effect would be present.

The source of fluctuations in intertemporal prices may, of course, be other than temporary policies. A prime example is given by fluctuations in the terms of trade (i.e., the relative price of exportables in terms of importables). Section 3.7 shows how the two-good model considered so far in the chapter can be used to analyze the effects of changes in the terms of trade on the current account. In particular, we show that whether a temporary deterioration in the terms of trade worsens the current account—the Harberger–Laursen–Metzler (HLM) effect—depends critically on the value of the intertemporal elasticity of substitution. If the intertemporal elasticity of substitution is less than one (the relevant case in practice), then the HLM effect holds. Whatever the effect on the current account—and since there are no distortions in this economy—the fluctuations in consumption that arise from fluctuations in the terms of trade are socially optimal. Intuitively, it is clearly optimal for this economy to take advantage of temporarily cheaper international prices for imports to consume more. We thus conclude that whether fluctuations in consumption due to nonconstant intertemporal prices are optimal depends on the source of the fluctuations.

3.2 The Model

Consider a small open economy inhabited by a representative, infinitely lived consumer. Following Calvo (1987), assume that there exist two (nondurable) tradable goods: an exportable good (not consumed) and an importable good. The world relative price of exportables in terms of importables (i.e., the terms of trade) is assumed constant and equal to one. The economy is endowed with exportable goods (but not importables). The government may impose tariffs on the importable good and return the proceeds to consumers in a lump-sum way.

Notice that, relative to the models of chapters 1 and 2, we have another economic agent in the model: the government. While having two goods in the model is not critical to illustrate the effects of an intertemporal distortion, it allows us to study this key notion in the context of trade liberalization policies.[1] The assumption that consumers only derive utility from consuming the importable good enables us to isolate the effects of *intertemporal distortions*. Having exportables in the utility function would also introduce *intratemporal* (or static) distortions (a concept that will be discussed only in chapter 10).

3.2.1 Consumer's Problem

The consumer's lifetime utility is given by

$$\int_0^\infty u(c_t)e^{-\beta t}dt, \tag{3.1}$$

where $\beta(>0)$ is the subjective discount rate, c_t denotes consumption of the importable good at time t, and the function $u(.)$ satisfies $u'(.)>0$ and $u''(.)<0$.

Let b_t denote net foreign assets (denominated in terms of the exportable good) held by the consumer. The consumer's flow constraint is thus

$$\dot{b}_t = rb_t + y + \tau_t - p_t c_t, \tag{3.2}$$

where y denotes the exogenous and constant endowment of the exportable good, τ_t represents lump-sum transfers from the government, and p_t denotes the *domestic* relative price of importables in terms of exportables. Since the world relative price of importables in terms of exportables is equal to one, $p_t - 1$ captures the tariff imposed by the government.

Proceeding as in chapter 1, we can integrate forward equation (3.2) and impose the transversality condition to obtain the consumer's intertemporal budget constraint:

$$b_0 + \frac{y}{r} + \int_0^\infty \tau_t e^{-rt}dt = \int_0^\infty p_t c_t e^{-rt}dt. \tag{3.3}$$

1. In other words, we could have introduced the concept of intertemporal distortions in the one-good model of chapter 1 by simply adding a consumption tax that is not constant over time (see section 3.6).

The consumer's optimization problem consists in choosing $\{c_t\}$ for all $t \in [0, \infty)$ to maximize lifetime utility (3.1), subject to (3.3), for given paths of τ_t and p_t and given values of b_0, r, and y. Setting up the Lagrangian, we have

$$\mathcal{L} = \int_0^{\infty} u(c_t)e^{-\beta t}dt + \lambda \left(b_0 + \frac{y}{r} + \int_0^{\infty} \tau_t e^{-rt}dt - \int_0^{\infty} p_t c_t e^{-rt}dt \right).$$

Assume $\beta = r$. The first-order condition with respect to c_t then takes the form

$$u'(c_t) = \lambda p_t. \tag{3.4}$$

Equation (3.4) says that at an optimum the representative consumer equates the marginal utility of consumption to the Lagrange multiplier times the relative domestic price of the good, which is a familiar condition from static consumer theory. In the current intertemporal context, however, this condition already implies a major departure from the world of chapter 1. In chapter 1, the relative price of the good was flat over time (and equal to unity in that particular case since there was only one good), which resulted in perfect consumption smoothing over time. The model of chapter 1 may in fact be viewed as a particular case of the more general model of this chapter by just setting $p_t = 1$ for all t. In this chapter, however, the relative price of the good is not necessarily constant over time. It is already apparent from equation (3.4) that a nonconstant path of the relative price of the good will translate into a nonflat path of consumption over time. Hence a preference for consumption smoothing (as reflected in a strictly concave utility function) coupled with perfect international capital mobility is not enough to obtain consumption smoothing as an implication of intertemporal optimization.

3.2.2 Government

Since we are not interested at this point in studying the effects of government spending or the effects of government debt, we abstract from these considerations by simply assuming that the government sets the tariff, $p_t - 1$, and returns the proceeds to the consumer in the form of a lump-sum transfer:

$$\tau_t = (p_t - 1)c_t. \tag{3.5}$$

By assuming that proceeds are returned to consumers, we abstract from any possible *wealth* effects associated with tariffs. This important assumption will be relaxed in section 3.5.

3.2.3 Equilibrium Conditions

In chapter 1 we only had one economic agent (the consumer). Hence the consumer's constraints were identical to the economy's constraints. Since there are now two economic agents (the consumer and the government), we need to aggregate the constraints of each individual agent to obtain the economy's constraint.

Combining the consumer's flow constraint, given by (3.2), with the government's, given by (3.5), we obtain the economy's flow constraint (i.e., the current account):

$$\dot{b}_t (\equiv CA_t) = rb_t + y - c_t. \tag{3.6}$$

By the same token, combining the consumer's intertemporal constraint, given by (3.3), and (3.5), we obtain the economy's intertemporal constraint (or resource constraint):

$$b_0 + \frac{y}{r} = \int_0^\infty c_t e^{-rt} dt. \tag{3.7}$$

It is worth stressing that the relative price of importables, p_t, does not enter the aggregate constraints. This was, of course, to be expected because a p_t higher than one represents a domestic transfer and does not imply a transfer of resources abroad.[2]

Finally, notice that, by definition, the trade balance will be given by

$$TB_t \equiv y - c_t. \tag{3.8}$$

3.2.4 Solution of the Model

We now solve for the model's perfect foresight equilibrium path. In a perfect foresight equilibrium, the time path of the four endogenous variables (c_t, b_t, τ_t, and λ) is completely characterized by equations (3.4), (3.5), (3.6), and (3.7).

Suppose that the tariff is constant over time; that is, $p_t - 1 = p^H - 1$ for all $t \geq 0$. Since p_t is constant over time, first-order condition (3.4) tells us that consumption will also be constant over time (at a level denoted by c). The resource constraint, given by (3.7), then determines the level of consumption:

$$c = rb_0 + y. \tag{3.9}$$

Notice that in equilibrium, consumption does not depend on p^H. The reason is that the level of the tariff does not affect aggregate wealth (given by $b_0 + y/r$) because of the assumption that the proceeds of the tariff are returned to the consumer as lump-sum transfers. As analyzed below (section 3.5), if the proceeds from the tariff were not returned to the consumer, there would be wealth effects and consumption would depend on the level of the tariff.

Substituting (3.9) into (3.5), we obtain the path of transfers:

$$\tau_t = (p^H - 1)(rb_0 + y).$$

2. Of course, if the terms of trade differed from one (as opposed to being one, as assumed in this section), then this would be captured in the aggregate constraints as it affects the purchasing power of the country's endowment of exports; see section 3.7.

As expected, the constant level of transfers depends on the level of the tariff: the higher is the tariff, the higher are the proceeds from the tariff and therefore the higher the level of transfers to the consumer.

Substituting (3.9) into (3.8) yields the path for the trade balance:

$$TB_t = -rb_0. \tag{3.10}$$

Substituting (3.10) into (3.6), we can see that $\dot{b}_t = rb_t - rb_0$, which implies that $b_t = b_0$ for all t. Hence

$$CA_t = 0.$$

Finally, notice that the constant value of the Lagrange multiplier follows from substituting (3.9) into (3.4) to obtain

$$\lambda = \frac{u'(rb_0 + y)}{p^H}.$$

3.3 Unanticipated Shocks

3.3.1 Permanent Fall in Tariffs

Suppose now that an instant before time 0 the economy is in the stationary equilibrium just described. At $t = 0$ there is an unanticipated and permanent fall in p_t from p^H to p^L, where $p^L < p^H$ (see figure 3.1). Since the shock is unanticipated, the consumer reoptimizes at $t = 0$. The new perfect foresight path will still be characterized by first-order condition (3.4) (with a possibly new value for the Lagrange multiplier) and the resource constraint (3.7). Proceeding as above, we conclude that consumption is still given by (3.9). Hence an unanticipated and permanent

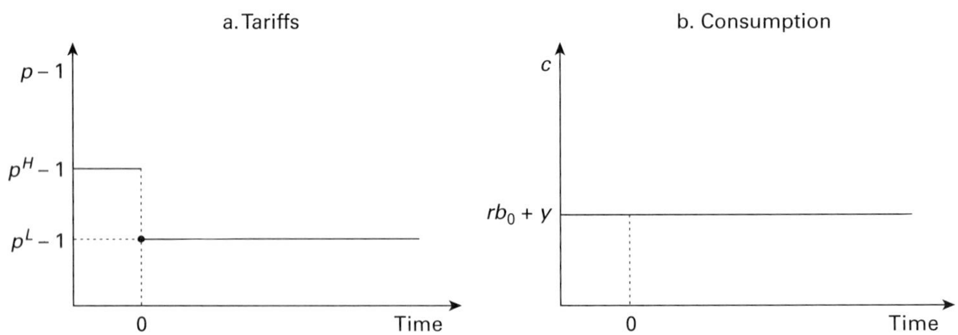

Figure 3.1
Permanent fall in tariffs

fall in tariffs leaves consumption of the importable good unchanged. The same is true, of course, of the current account.

Since consumption does not change, neither does welfare (i.e., lifetime utility). In other words, consumer's welfare is the same for any flat path of tariffs. This result should not be surprising because there is no wealth effect associated with changes in tariffs.

3.3.2 Temporary Fall in Tariffs

Solution of the Model

Suppose again that an instant before time 0 the economy is in the stationary equilibrium characterized above and that at time 0 there is an unanticipated and temporary fall in p_t from p^H to p^L, where $p^L < p^H$. Formally, the path of p_t is given by

$$p_t = \begin{cases} p^L, & 0 \leq t < T, \\ p^H, & t \geq T, \end{cases} \tag{3.11}$$

for some $T > 0$. In other words, the government lowers the tariff from time 0 until time T and then raises it back to its original level (see figure 3.2, panel a).

Again, since the shock comes as a surprise, the consumer reoptimizes at $t = 0$. The first-order condition can be written as

$$u'(c_t) = \tilde{\lambda} p^L, \qquad 0 \leq t < T, \tag{3.12}$$

$$u'(c_t) = \tilde{\lambda} p^H, \qquad t \geq T, \tag{3.13}$$

where $\tilde{\lambda}$ denotes the new value of the Lagrange multiplier. Two key implications follow immediately from (3.12) and (3.13). First, consumption will be constant in each subperiod. Formally,

$$c_t = c^1, \qquad 0 \leq t < T, \tag{3.14}$$

$$c_t = c^2, \qquad t \geq T. \tag{3.15}$$

Second, given that $u(c)$ is a strictly concave function and $p^L < p^H$, then $c^1 > c^2$. Consumption is thus higher between 0 and T than afterward (panel b).

Intuitively, since consumption is cheaper "today" than "tomorrow," rational consumers choose to consume more today than tomorrow. Put differently, faced with a lower price for today's consumption, consumers engage in *intertemporal consumption substitution* (i.e., they substitute away from the more expensive future consumption in favor of today's cheaper consumption). Notice that if today's and tomorrow's consumption are viewed as different goods, the intuition is exactly the same as in standard consumer theory: a lower relative price of good 1 in terms of 2 induces the consumer to substitute away from good 2 and toward good 1. The analogy with

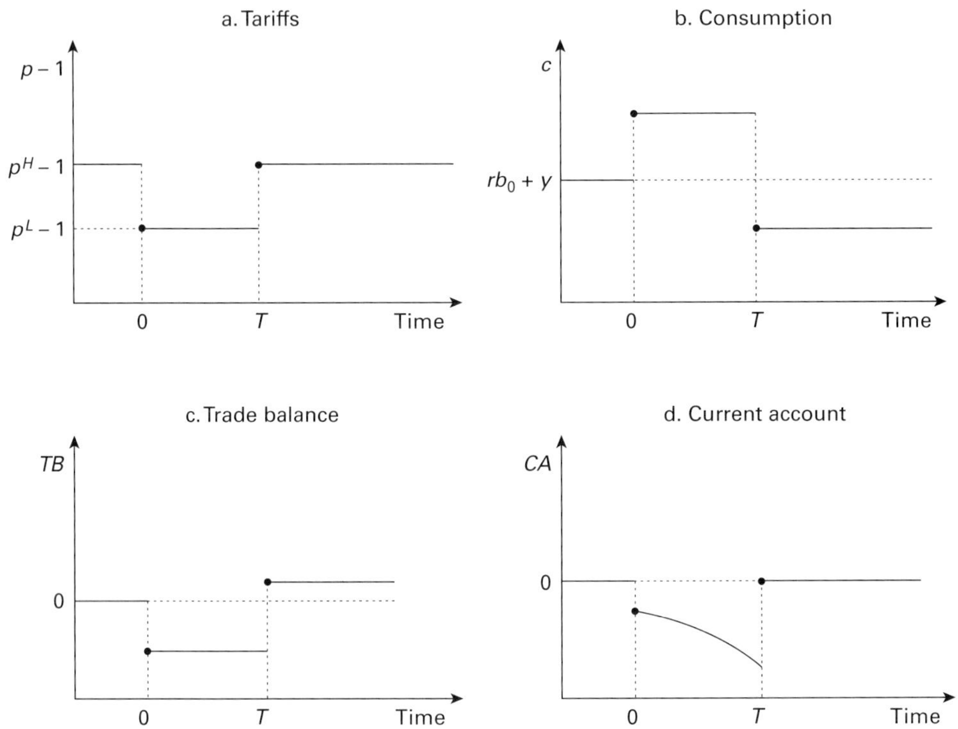

Figure 3.2
Temporary fall in tariffs

standard consumer theory becomes even more transparent if, using (3.14) and (3.15), we combine first-order conditions (3.12) and (3.13) to obtain

$$\frac{u'(c^1)}{u'(c^2)} = \frac{p^L}{p^H}, \tag{3.16}$$

which says that the marginal rate of substitution between today's and tomorrow's consumption (LHS) equals the relative price of today's consumption in terms of tomorrow's consumption (RHS).

Having solved for the time profile of consumption, we now make use of the resource constraint to solve for the level of consumption. Given that $c^1 > c^2$, it follows from (3.7) that c^1 is higher than initial permanent income and c^2 is lower than initial permanent income. The logic behind this result is that wealth in the economy (given by $b_0 + y/r$) has not been altered by the temporary fall in the tariff. Hence the present discounted value of consumption cannot change either. It should be clear that the only path of consumption consistent with an unchanged present discounted value is the one depicted in figure 3.2, panel b, as any other path with $c^1 > c^2$ would not be consistent with the resource constraint.[3]

The higher level of consumption during $[0, T)$ leads to the trade balance path shown in figure 3.2, panel c (which assumes, to fix ideas, that $b_0 = 0$ and hence that the initial trade balance is zero, as follows from equations 3.8 and 3.9). Starting from a zero trade balance, the trade balance is thus in deficit between 0 and T and goes into a surplus thereafter.

The resulting current account path is shown in figure 3.2, panel d. Since $CA_0 = rb_0 + TB_0$, the current account falls on impact in line with the deterioration of the trade balance. During $[0, T)$ the current account falls over time because the trade balance is constant but the income balance worsens over time. At $t = T$ the economy becomes stationary again (exogenous variables are constant forever), and as we saw in chapter 1, this implies that the current account is necessarily zero from that point on.

Welfare Analysis

How does a temporary liberalization affect consumer's welfare (i.e., the consumer's lifetime utility given by equation 3.1)? In this model a temporary liberalization always reduces welfare. To show this, notice that since the resources available to this economy (given by the LHS of equation 3.7) are not affected by a liberalization, the present discounted value of consumption is the same regardless of whether or not there is a liberalization. Since resources do not change, a planner would always choose the flat path of consumption given by (3.9). However, faced with a temporary liberalization, the consumer chooses a nonflat path of consumption, which yields lower utility than a flat path of consumption with the same present discounted value. We thus conclude that this policy-induced intertemporal distortion is socially costly.

To some extent, this fall in welfare may seem surprising because the economy as a whole can still afford the initial flat path of consumption (i.e., the economy's resources have not changed). So why does the consumer not choose it? Simply because, from an individual point of view, choosing a flat path of consumption is clearly suboptimal as can easily be inferred from optimality condition (3.16). In other words, if the consumer chose the same level of consumption in both periods, he/she could always be better off by reallocating spending from period 2 (when consumption is relatively more expensive) to period 1 (when consumption is relatively cheaper).

Effects of T

It is interesting to analyze how the path of endogenous variables reacts to changes in the length of the liberalization period, T. (Exercise 1 at the end of the chapter asks you to work out the formal details.) It is in fact quite intuitive to expect that when the liberalization period is shortened,

3. On the one hand, paths with c^1 higher than initial permanent income and c^2 higher than or equal to initial permanent income would imply a present discounted value of consumption higher than the economy's wealth. On the other hand, paths with c^1 equal to or lower than initial permanent income and c^2 lower than initial permanent income would imply that the economy is not consuming all of its resources, which, given that preferences exhibit nonsatiation, cannot be optimal.

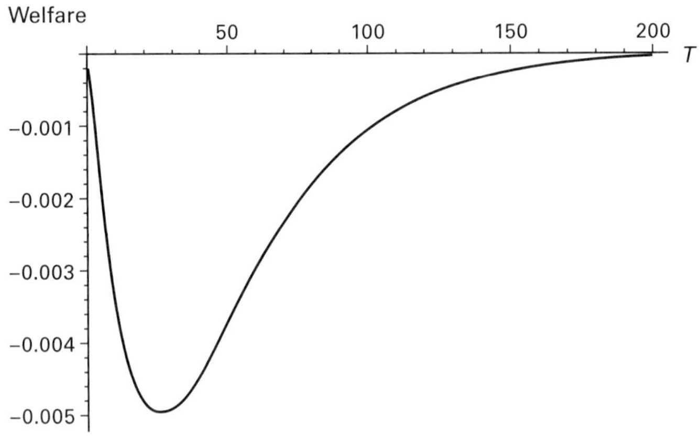

Figure 3.3
Welfare change as a function of T

consumption during the liberalization period, c^1, will increase. In other words, the shorter the liberalization period, the more consumers take advantage of cheaper relative prices per unit of time. The effects of T on welfare are less obvious because there are some trade-offs involved. Intuition suggests that a one-instant liberalization (i.e., $T \longrightarrow 0$) has no welfare costs because it is like having no liberalization at all. By the same token, a very long liberalization (i.e., $T \longrightarrow \infty$) has no welfare costs because it is like a permanent liberalization. Since we know that for any $T > 0$, the temporary liberalization is welfare-reducing, we would expect welfare to be a U-shaped function of T, as shown in exercise 1 at the end of the chapter. To illustrate this idea, figure 3.3 shows a plot of the change in welfare (i.e., relative to welfare before the liberalization) as a function of T for the CES function specified in exercise 1.[4]

Role of the Intertemporal Elasticity of Substitution

A key concept when it comes to evaluating the extent of intertemporal consumption substitution is the intertemporal elasticity of substitution (see appendix 3.9 for a formal definition). The intertemporal elasticity of substitution captures the willingness to change "today's" consumption relative to "tomorrow's" consumption in response to a change in intertemporal relative prices. The role of the intertemporal elasticity of substitution becomes more transparent if we focus on the class of constant-elasticity of substitution (CES) preferences, given by

$$u(c) = \begin{cases} \frac{c^{1-1/\sigma}-1}{1-1/\sigma}, & \sigma \neq 1, \\ \log(c), & \sigma = 1, \end{cases} \tag{3.17}$$

4. The parameter values used to obtain figure 3.3 are the following: $r = 0.03$, $p^H = 1$, $p^L = 0.4$, $\sigma = 0.3$, $b_0 = 0$, and $y = 10$.

where $\sigma > 0$ is the intertemporal elasticity of substitution.[5] For CES preferences, using equation (3.16), we can show that (see appendix 3.9)

$$\sigma = -\frac{d\log(c^1/c^2)}{d\log(p^L/p^H)}. \tag{3.18}$$

The parameter σ thus captures the consumer's willingness to substitute consumption across time for a given change in intertemporal relative prices. Hence it should be intuitively clear that for a given T and a given change in intertemporal relative prices, the higher is σ, the higher will be consumption during the liberalization period (c^1) and the lower afterward (c^2). (Exercise 1 at the end of the chapter asks you to show this formally.) In the extreme case of a consumer with Leontief preferences (which, conceptually, would correspond to the case $\sigma = 0$), consumption will not respond at all to a change in intertemporal prices and will continue to be constant over time (and given by $rb_0 + y$).[6]

Given the critical theoretical role of the intertemporal elasticity of substitution, we should wonder how large this parameter is in practice. As discussed in box 3.1, existing estimates of this

Box 3.1
How large is the intertemporal elasticity of substitution?

In our theoretical framework the intertemporal elasticity of substitution plays a key role in determining the real effects of temporary policies. To judge the practical relevance of such a channel, we need to assess the quantitative importance of this parameter. What do econometric estimates of the intertemporal elasticity of substitution show?

Early empirical studies for developing countries—along the lines of Hall (1988) for US data—suggested that the intertemporal elasticity of substitution was generally not significantly different from zero. These studies, however, were typically based on a one-good, non-monetary model. Once such restrictive assumptions were relaxed, the estimates became significantly different from zero with most estimates falling in a range of 0.2 to 0.5 (though estimates vary widely; see table 3.1). Some studies kept the one-good assumption but added money to the model. In this vein, Reinhart and Végh (1995) find elasticities to be in the 0.2 to 0.5 range for the Southern Cone countries. A different strand of the literature allowed for more than one type of good (typically incorporating nontradables goods), though this line of research has been hampered by the lack of disaggregated data. Within this class of models, Ostry and Reinhart (1992) and Ogaki, Ostry, and Reinhart (1996) found elasticities in the

5. Notice that, as shown in exercise 1 at the end of the chapter, $\log(c)$ is the limit of $\left(c^{1-1/\sigma} - 1\right)/(1 - 1/\sigma)$ as $\sigma \to 1$. Technically, however, we need to define $u(c)$ in this piecewise form because $\left(c^{1-1/\sigma} - 1\right)/(1 - 1/\sigma)$ does not exist at $\sigma = 1$. In the remainder of the book, however, it will be understood that $\left(c^{1-1/\sigma} - 1\right)/(1 - 1/\sigma)$ encompasses the logarithmic case.

6. The reader may wonder why we do not analyze how welfare changes as the intertemporal elasticity of substitution, σ, varies (as we did for the case of T). The reason is that in addition to affecting consumption, changes in the intertemporal elasticity of substitution alter the utilify function itself. This feature renders the exercise meaningless.

Box 3.1
(continued)

Table 3.1
Empirical estimates of the intertemporal elasticity of substitution

Countries	Point estimates	Dataset	Type of model	Author(s)
Argentina	0.21 (0.03)	Quarterly 1978:1–1989:2	Transactions costs model	Reinhart and Végh (1995)
	0.15 to 0.19 (0.16) (0.11)	Annual 1960–77	Hall's one good, pure consumption model	Giovannini (1985)
Brazil	−0.17 to 0.01 (0.13) (0.14)	Annual 1967–79	Hall's one good, pure consumption model	Giovannini (1985)
Chile	0.19 (0.10)	Quarterly 1976:2–1989:2	Transactions costs model	Reinhart and Végh (1995)
	1.59 (na)	Quarterly 1971:3–1981:4	Money in the utility function model	Arrau (1990)
	0.46 to 0.56 (0.15) (0.26)	Quarterly 1986:1–2002:4	Pure consumption two-good model	Duncan (2003)
Israel	0.15 to 1.32 (na) (na)	Quarterly 1970:1–1988:3	Money in the utility function model	Eckstein and Leiderman (1991)
Mexico	2.87 (na)	Quarterly 1980:1–1987:4	Money in the utility function model	Arrau (1990)
	0.07 to 0.12 (0.10) (0.12)	Annual 1965–79	Hall's one good, pure consumption model	Giovannini (1985)
Uruguay	0.53 (0.22)	Quarterly 1977:2–1989:3	Transactions costs model	Reinhart and Végh (1995)
Panel of countries*		Annual	Pure consumption	Ostry and Reinhart
Latin America (4)	0.37 to 0.43 (0.11) (0.14)	1968–87	two-good model	(1992)
Asia (5)	0.80 to 0.80 (0.20) (0.24)			
Africa (4)	0.44 to 0.45 (0.18) (0.16)			
Panel of countries*		Annual	Pure consumption	Ogaki, Ostry,
Low income (31)	0.34 (na)	1968–92	two-good model.	and Reinhart
Lower middle Income (21)	0.58 (na)		Stone-Geary	(1996)
upper middle income (15)	0.61 (na)		utility function.	
Panel of 9 South American countries	0.09 (0.07)	Annual 1973–83	Hall's one good, pure consumption	Rossi (1988)
	0.09 (0.04)	Annual 1973–81	model With liquidity constraints	Rossi (1988)

Note: The highest and lowest point estimates are reported. Standard errors are in parenthesis. An "na" denotes the standard error was not reported.
*Number of countries is in parentheses

Box 3.1
(continued)

range of 0.4 to 0.8 for various classifications of regions and income levels.[a] More recently Duncan (2003) estimates an elasticity of 0.5 for the case of Chile.

Importantly, however, research in this area for industrial countries suggests that the available estimates for developing countries could have a downward bias. In particular, Attanasio and Weber (1995) point out that aggregation of macroeconomic data can cause such a bias, showing estimates from cohort data for the United States that are significantly higher. In addition, introducing durable goods into the picture appears to increase the estimates of the intertemporal elasticity of substitution considerably. For the case of Canada, Fauvel and Samson (1991) estimate the elasticity of substitution to be in the range 1.5 to 2.3 when durable goods are included. When they are excluded, the estimates become very imprecise (i.e., not significally different from zero). For the case of the United States, Ogaki and Reinhart (1998) provide a range for the elasticity of 0.32 to 0.45 when durables are included and a negative point estimate when they are excluded.

a. Notice that, as table 3.1 indicates, Ogaki, Ostry, and Reinhart (1996) find that estimates of the intertemporal elasticity tend to be larger for higher income countries. This is consistent with results obtained for developed countries (see Beaudry and van Wincoop 1995; Cashin and McDermott 2003), which typically imply higher elasticities than for developing countries. Higher elasticities for richer countries—which is also consistent with the work of Atkeson and Ogaki (1996) for household data—could be explained by the presence of higher levels of subsistence consumption and tighter liquidity constraints for poorer households.

parameter for developing countries fall mostly in the range of 0.2 to 0.5. Since these estimates are not very large, substantial changes in intertemporal prices will be required for this channel to be quantitatively important.

Intertemporal Price Speculation

We have just argued that with Leontief preferences over time a temporary liberalization would have no welfare effects. Since estimates of the intertemporal elasticity of substitution are typically low, one might in fact conclude that, in practice, the welfare implications of a temporary liberalization would be rather small unless changes in intertemporal prices are substantially large. This result, however, critically depends on the assumption that there are no durable goods. If we allow for durable (i.e., perfectly storable) goods, we can show that even for Leontief preferences, a temporary liberalization would reduce welfare by leading to *intertemporal price speculation* (see exercise 2 at the end of the chapter). Consumers would want to purchase more durables while they are relatively cheaper. From a social point of view, however, this is not optimal because durable goods are dominated in return by foreign bonds. In other words, a planner would never choose to buy durables for storage purposes; the planner would always buy exactly the amount that will be consumed at that particular instant. Hence, once the possibility of intertemporal price speculation is taken into account, we can conclude that temporary trade liberalizations are likely to be quite costly in practice even if the intertemporal elasticity of substitution is low.[7]

3.4 Lack of Credibility

We have just analyzed the effects of both a permanent and a temporary fall in tariffs. These two experiments can in fact be seen as part of the same phenomenon by introducing credibility considerations. Specifically, suppose that at time $t = 0$ the government announces that import tariffs will be permanently reduced. If the announcement is fully credible, in the sense that the public believes that the reduction in tariffs will be indeed permanent, then there will be no real effects, as shown above.

In contrast, suppose that the announcement at $t = 0$ is not credible, in the sense that the public believes that tariffs will be raised again at time $T > 0$. Since consumers believe that the liberalization will be temporary, they will react in the same way as analyzed above (i.e., consuming more between 0 and T and running a current account deficit).[8] In other words, the temporary liberalization analyzed above may be interpreted as arising from a situation in which the announcement of a permanent reduction in tariffs was not fully credible.[9]

In this simple but illuminating interpretation, lack of credibility is equivalent to having an intertemporal distortion and is therefore socially costly.[10] Since we would expect lack of credibility to be pervasive in countries that suffer frequent policy failures, this type of distortion is likely to be an important feature. We will revisit this issue when we study the real effects of exchange rate based stabilizations in chapter 13.

It should be noted that capital controls can be welfare improving in an environment characterized by lack of credibility. To see this, consider the extreme case of full capital controls (i.e., financial autarky). In such an economy consumers will be unable to take advantage of temporarily lower prices because they cannot borrow from abroad. This is yet another example of a second-best policy: the government faces an exogenously given distortion (i.e., lack of credibility) and, by an appropriate set of taxes or regulations, is able to achieve a Pareto improvement. One should be

7. Another remarkable feature of introducing durable goods into the analysis is that even a *one-instant liberalization* (the case analyzed in exercise 2) will have (negative) welfare effects, whereas, without durable goods, a one-instant liberalization would have no welfare effects.

8. Notice that what happens at T will be independent of whether the beliefs turn out to be true. If the beliefs are correct and policy makers indeed raise tariffs at T, then the experiment exactly replicates the temporary liberalization studied above. If the beliefs are not correct and policy makers stick to the lower tariff when time T arrives, this constitutes (from the consumer's point of view) an unanticipated and permanent reduction in tariffs at time T. Consumers would then choose a flat path of consumption from T onward that would be the same as in the temporary case.

9. Exercise 3 at the end of this chapter formalizes the idea of lack of credibility by modeling it as uncertainty on the part of consumers as to whether the government will impose tariffs in the second period. The exercise makes clear that the mere expectation of a possible tariff is enough to introduce an intertemporal distortion, regardless of whether it eventually materializes.

10. In several papers, Calvo (1987, 1988, 1989) pioneered this interpretation.

careful, however, when trying to apply this result to the real world. In practice, capital controls are known to introduce myriad microeconomic distortions and rent-seeking activities that our analysis has completely abstracted from. Hence, in practice, the costs of imposing capital controls may call into question their usefulness as a second-best policy. In any event, the first-best policy would always be to attack the original distortion (i.e., to try to address the underlying causes of the lack of credibility).

3.5 Wealth Effects

We concluded above that a permanent liberalization would have no effects on welfare, whereas a temporary liberalization would always reduce welfare. From a practical point of view, these results appear counterintuitive since one could argue that there should be some static gains from trade liberalization such as higher productivity (see box 3.2). Such static gains would increase the

Box 3.2
Do trade liberalizations lead to productivity gains?

Section 3.5 shows that in the presence of wealth effects, a permanent trade liberalization is welfare improving, and even a temporary trade liberalization might lead to welfare gains if the wealth effect dominates the intertemporal distortion effect (which will always be the case for a sufficiently long liberalization). We have argued that, in practice, such wealth effects might be the result of increases in productivity brought about by reducing tariffs. Can we find these effects in the data?

In the real world, trade liberalization might affect plant-level productivity through several mechanisms:

- Trade liberalization could lead to easier access to imported intermediate inputs and more efficient capital goods, leading to productivity gains.
- A tariff reduction might lead to a drop in domestic prices, prompting less productive firms to exit the market (in the absence of investment irreversibility). Resources will thus be relocated to more efficient plants, increasing industrywide efficiency.
- Trade liberalization might induce firms to use inputs more efficiently, increase international technology diffusion, increase managerial effort, improve capacity utilization, or push domestic plants toward scale efficiency, generating within-plant productivity gains.
- A higher exposure to foreign competition is likely to reduce the market power of domestic producers, move down their average cost curves, and expand output.

If these effects are present, a trade liberalization, whether temporary or permanent, is likely to produce wealth effects through productivity gains. By and large, existing studies are consistent with this idea. Edwards (1998), for instance, analyzes empirically the relationship between openness and TFP growth in a panel of 93 countries for the period 1960 to 1990 and concludes that countries with higher levels of trade distortions have experienced lower TFP growth. The results of microeconomic studies—summarized in table 3.2—offer further support for the idea that a trade liberalization

Box 3.2
(continued)

Table 3.2
Impact of trade liberalization on productivity

Author(s)	Dataset	Methodology	Main results
Tybout, Melo, and Corbo (1991)	Chile 1974–1979 Industrial census establishment-level data	Maximum likelihood estimation	• No evidence found of improvements in productive efficiency for the manufacturing sector. • Some improvements in average efficiency levels and cross-plant efficiency dispersion in industries undergoing relative large reductions in protection. • Adverse macroeconomic shocks might have masked the effects of the trade liberalization.
MacDonald (1994)	United States 1972–1987 3- and 4-digit manufacturing industry data	Instrumental variables approach, fixed effects	• Statistically weak, small, and positive association between import shocks and productivity growth. • Import shocks have a large and statistically significant effect on next period productivity in highly concentrated industries.
Tybout and Westbrook (1995)	Mexico 1984–1990 Plant-level panel data	Panel data analysis	• Fall in average costs in most industries and gains in productivity (especially in tradables). Largest fall in average costs in more open sectors. • Minor gains in scale efficiency after liberalization, uncorrelated with increases in import competition. • Productivity gains through movements of individuals plants toward the production frontier, innovation and externalities.
Krishna and Mitra (1998)	India 1986–1993 Firm-level data	Panel data analysis, numerical simulations	• Evidence of increased foreign competition reflected in the drop of price–marginal cost markups in the post liberalization period. • Statistically weak evidence of increases in productivity growth.
Hay (2001)	Brazil 1986–1994 Data of large manufacturing firms	Panel data analysis	• Trade liberalization had negative effect on market shares of domestic producers and led to a fall in profits. • Growth in productivity due to recovery from recession, trade liberalization, and deregulation of the economy (hard to distinguish among these).
Pavcnik (2002)	Chile 1979–1986 Industrial census Establishment-level data	Panel data analysis	• Productivity improvements due to trade liberalization. • Exit of less productive plants helped reallocate market shares and resources within the economy, contributing to productivity gains. • Continuing plants in import competing sectors improved their productivity, adjusting to a more open-trade environment (within-plant productivity improvements). • Export-oriented sectors did not experience productivity gains due to trade liberalization.

Box 3.2
(continued)

Table 3.2
(continued)

Author(s)	Dataset	Methodology	Main results
Fernandes (2007)	Colombia 1977–91 Annual Colombian manufacturing census plant-level data	Panel data analysis	• Protection had a statistically significant negative effect on TFP, after controlling for plant and industry heterogeneity, RER, and cyclical effects. • Impact of tariffs is greater for larger plants and for plants in less competitive industries. • Productivity gains through increases in within-plant imports of intermediate inputs, skill intensity, machinery investments, and output reallocation from less to more efficient plants

increases productivity. In particular, plant- and firm-level evidence suggests that a trade liberalization is likely to encourage domestic firms to improve efficiency—through greater access to embodied technology in intermediate and capital goods and higher foreign competition—leading to important static and dynamic productivity gains.

economy's wealth and lead to higher welfare in the case of a permanent liberalization and perhaps even in the case of a temporary liberalization. This logic is, of course, right. The previous analysis ignored wealth effects to isolate the effects of intertemporal distortions. We now introduce wealth effects into the picture.

A simple way of introducing wealth effects is to relax the assumption that the government gives back to the consumer all proceeds from the tariff in a lump-sum way. In particular, we will now consider the other extreme case in which all tariff revenues are used by the government to finance socially unproductive public spending.

In this new setup the flow constraint of the representative consumer is given by

$$\dot{b}_t = rb_t + y - p_t c_t, \tag{3.19}$$

where the only difference with equation (3.2) is that the consumer is not receiving lump-sum transfers from the government. His/her corresponding intertemporal budget constraint is given by

$$b_0 + \frac{y}{r} = \int_0^{\infty} p_t c_t e^{-rt} dt. \tag{3.20}$$

To fix ideas, let preferences be given by the CES utility function specified in (3.17).[11] At the margin the optimal choice of consumption is then characterized by

$$c_t^{-1/\sigma} = \lambda p_t, \tag{3.21}$$

where σ is the intertemporal elasticity of substitution.

The government sets the tariff, $p_t - 1$, and, given the consumer's choice of consumption, spends all proceeds on unproductive government spending, g_t (think of the government as throwing the tariff proceeds into the ocean). The government's flow constraint is thus given by

$$g_t = (p_t - 1)c_t. \tag{3.22}$$

By definition, the trade balance is given by

$$TB_t \equiv y - c_t - g_t.$$

For further reference, note that, using (3.22), the trade balance can be rewritten as

$$TB_t \equiv y - p_t c_t. \tag{3.23}$$

To obtain the economy's current account and resource constraint, combine (3.22) with, respectively, (3.19) and (3.20) so that

$$\dot{b}_t = rb_t + y - c_t - g_t, \tag{3.24}$$

$$b_0 + \frac{y}{r} = \int_0^{\infty} (c_t + g_t)e^{-rt}dt. \tag{3.25}$$

Notice, by comparing these with (3.6) and (3.7), how government spending now constitutes an additional use of resources.

In equilibrium, the time path of the four endogenous variables of the model (c_t, b_t, g_t, and λ) is completely characterized by equations (3.20) to (3.22), and (3.24).[12]

As before, we will first solve for a perfect foresight equilibrium for a constant value of p_t; that is, $p_t = p^H$ for all $t \geq 0$. From first-order condition (3.21), we infer that consumption is constant along a perfect foresight equilibrium path (PFEP). Hence from (3.20) it follows that

$$c = \frac{rb_0 + y}{p^H}. \tag{3.26}$$

11. While the results hold for any utility function, the CES specification will prove useful when it comes to characterizing the behavior of the trade balance and the current account, as will become clear below.

12. Notice that in this particular case it is more useful to use the consumer's intertemporal constraint to solve the model than the resource constraint because of the endogeneity of g.

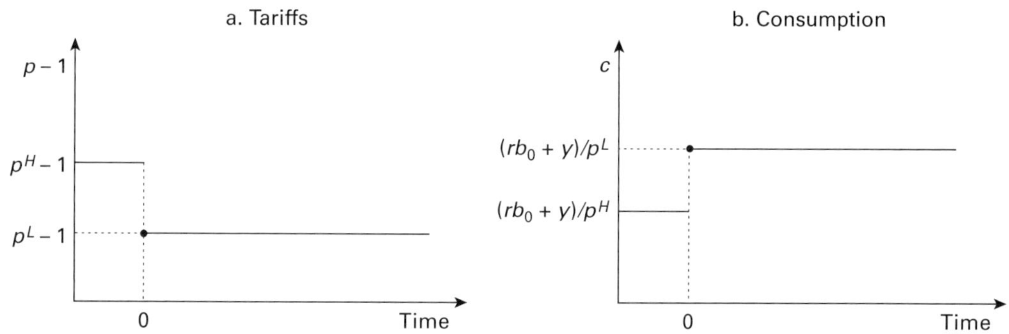

Figure 3.4
Permanent fall in tariffs (with wealth effect)

Substituting (3.26) into (3.22), it follows that the constant level of government spending is given by

$$g = \frac{p^H - 1}{p^H}(rb_0 + y). \tag{3.27}$$

To compute the trade balance, substitute (3.26) into (3.23) to obtain

$$TB_t = -rb_0. \tag{3.28}$$

Finally, from (3.19) at time 0, we know that $CA_0 = rb_0 + TB_0$. Hence from (3.28) it follows that $CA_0 = 0$. Hence $CA_t = 0$ for all $t \geq 0$.[13]

3.5.1 Permanent Fall in Tariffs

Suppose now that an instant before time 0 the economy is in the stationary equilibrium just characterized. At time 0 there is an unanticipated and permanent reduction in the tariff from $p^H - 1$ to $p^L - 1$, where $p^L < p^H$. The consumer will reoptimize immediately. Proceeding as above, it follows that the new consumption path is given by (see figure 3.4)

$$c = \frac{rb_0 + y}{p^L}.$$

We see that consumption is permanently higher as a consequence of the liberalization. The economic intuition behind the result is simply that the liberalization implies a higher wealth for the private sector. Taking the argument to the extreme, a complete liberalization (i.e., $p^L = 1$ or

13. To see this, notice that if $TB_t = -rb_0$ for all $t \geq 0$, then $b_t = b_0$.

no tariffs at all) would imply that no resources are thrown into the ocean and the private sector consumes all the resources available to this economy.

Since consumption is permanently higher, a permanent reduction in tariffs increases welfare. The contrast with the previous case where a permanent liberalization had no effects on welfare can be easily rationalized. With full rebate, the level of tariffs was irrelevant because all the proceeds were returned to consumers. With no rebate at all, the government is just wasting whatever tariff revenues it collects. Under such circumstances a reduction in tariffs means less wasteful spending and more resources available for private consumption.

3.5.2 Temporary Fall in Tariffs

Suppose, again, that an instant before time 0 the economy is in the stationary equilibrium described above. At time 0, there is an unanticipated and temporary fall in p_t from p^H to p^L, where $p^L < p^H$ (figure 3.5, panel a). Formally, the path of p_t is once again given by (3.11). The consumer re-optimizes at time 0 and the new optimal path of consumption is characterized by the first-order conditions

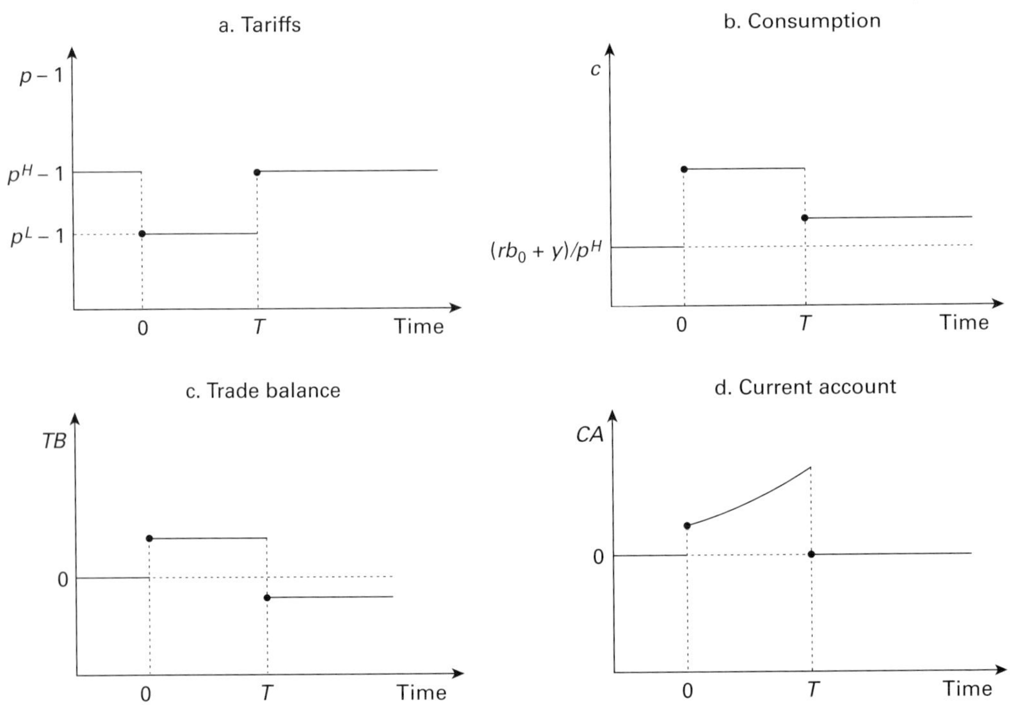

Figure 3.5
Temporary fall in tariffs (with wealth effect)

$$(c^1)^{-1/\sigma} = \tilde{\lambda} p^L, \qquad 0 \le t < T, \tag{3.29}$$

$$(c^2)^{-1/\sigma} = \tilde{\lambda} p^H, \qquad t \ge T, \tag{3.30}$$

where we have already incorporated the fact that consumption will be constant within each subperiod and equal to c^1 and c^2, respectively. Clearly, $c^1 > c^2$. Hence, as before, consumption is higher during the liberalization period as consumers take advantage of cheaper prices.

While the consumption time *profile* is the same as before, the *level* of the new path will be different. From the intertemporal constraint (3.20) it follows that c^1 must be higher than initial consumption (given by equation 3.26). If this were not the case, the new consumption path would not exhaust the available resources since p is lower during $[0, T)$ and $c^1 > c^2$. In contrast, whether c^2 will be higher than, equal to, or lower than initial consumption depends on the value of σ. To see this, rewrite the intertemporal constraint (3.20) as

$$b_0 + \frac{y}{r} = (1 - e^{-rT})\frac{p^L c^1}{r} + e^{-rT}\frac{p^H c^2}{r}. \tag{3.31}$$

Then combine (3.29), (3.30), and (3.31) to obtain

$$p^H c^2 = \frac{rb_0 + y}{\left(p^L/p^H\right)^{1-\sigma}(1 - e^{-rT}) + e^{-rT}}.$$

It follows that

$$p^H c^2 \begin{cases} = rb_0 + y, & \sigma = 1, \\ > rb_0 + y, & \sigma < 1, \\ < rb_0 + y, & \sigma > 1. \end{cases} \tag{3.32}$$

Since in the initial equilibrium (i.e., before $t = 0$), $p^H c = rb_0 + y$, it follows that

$$c^2 \begin{cases} = c, & \sigma = 1, \\ > c, & \sigma < 1, \\ < c, & \sigma > 1. \end{cases}$$

Intuitively, the different possibilities for c^2 reflect the tension between the intertemporal substitution effect and the wealth effect. While these two effects go in the same direction for c^1 (with both effects calling for higher c^1), they go in opposite direction for c^2: the intertemporal substitution effect calls for a lower c^2, while the wealth effect calls for a higher c^2. In the $\sigma < 1$ case, c^2 is higher than it is initially (figure 3.5, panel b), reflecting a weak intertemporal substitution effect due to the low intertemporal elasticity of substitution.

Whatever the value of c^2, however, (3.31) makes clear that the present discounted value of consumption will be higher. Compared to the initial equilibrium, p_t is now lower between 0 and T. Hence, for a given T and, say, a given c^2, c^1 will have to be higher to satisfy (3.31). It follows that the resources available to the private sector have increased as a result of temporarily lower tariffs.

What is the effect on the trade balance? From (3.23) we see that the path of the trade balance depends on the path of expenditure. Since the present discounted value of $p_t c_t$ does not change (i.e., it remains equal to $b_0 + y/r$, as equation 3.20 makes clear), expression (3.32) provides us with all the information we need. For the logarithmic case, the path of expenditure is flat over time. Hence the trade balance is flat over time and equal to its initial value, $-rb_0$. For the more relevant case $\sigma < 1$, expenditure after T is higher than before T. The trade balance thus follows the path depicted in figure 3.5, panel c, improving at $t = 0$ and worsening at $t = T$. For $\sigma > 1$, the opposite would be true.

The behavior of the current account mirrors that of the trade balance. In the logarithmic case, there is no change in the current account. In the $\sigma < 1$ case, the current account improves at $t = 0$ and worsens at time T (figure 3.5, panel d).

How does this temporary liberalization affect welfare? Clearly, for $\sigma = 1$ and $\sigma < 1$ welfare increases because $c^2 \geq c$ and, of course, $c^1 > c^2$. In other words, consumption is always equal or greater than before the shock. The case $\sigma > 1$ is less obvious because $c^2 < c$. However, as exercise 4 at the end of the chapter shows, welfare unambiguously increases as well. The intuition behind the increase in welfare in this case of no rebates is that the opportunity set is strictly larger than before the shock because the price of one of the "two goods" consumed falls, so consumers cannot be worse off. We can conclude that in this case the wealth effect always dominates the intertemporal distortion effect.

Moreover—and as also shown in exercise 4—consumer's welfare is a strictly increasing function of the length of the liberalization period, T. Intuitively, a larger T extends the period during which the good is relatively cheap, thus making consumers better off.

3.5.3 Partial Rebates

So far we have examined two extreme cases. In the full rebate case (no wealth effect), examined in section 3.3, a temporary reduction in tariffs always reduces welfare. In the case examined in this section (no rebate), the same policy always leads to higher welfare. In practice, however, the wealth effects resulting from a temporary tariff reduction will likely not be captured by either extreme, but will fall somewhere in between. To capture this—and in the process provide further insights into the strength of the intertemporal distortion effect relative to the wealth effect—exercise 5 at the end of the chapter asks you to work out the case of partial rebates, that is, cases where the government wastes some fraction ϕ of the tariff revenues and returns the rest $(1 - \phi)$ to consumers in a lump-sum fashion. Of course, as particular cases, we have the full rebate case $(\phi = 0)$ and the no rebate case $(\phi = 1)$.

Clearly, for large values of T, a temporary trade liberalization will be welfare improving as it becomes essentially a permanent liberalization with a wealth effect (even if smaller than in the no rebate case). The more illuminating result to come out of this exercise is that, as illustrated

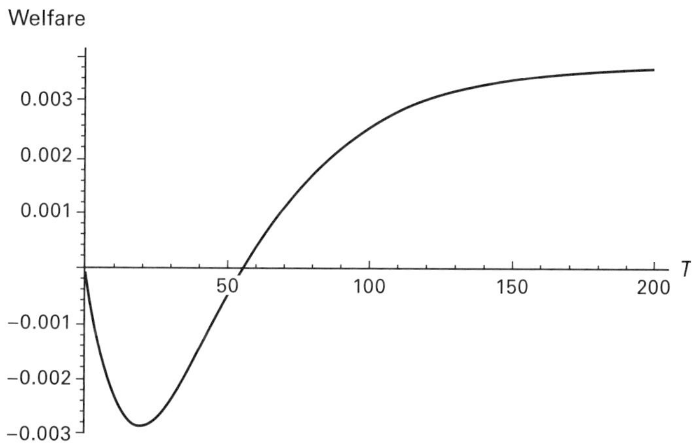

Figure 3.6
Welfare change as a function of T (with wealth effect and partial rebate)

in figure 3.6, for some parameter configurations involving low values of ϕ (i.e., a small wealth effect), a given temporary tariff liberalization may be welfare reducing for low values of T (i.e., the intertemporal distortion effect dominates) and welfare improving for large values of T (i.e., the wealth effect dominates).[14]

Needless to say, we have looked at partial rebates as a convenient—but admittedly mechanical—way of illustrating the tension between the intertemporal distortion and the wealth effects that is likely to be associated with temporary trade liberalizations. Box 3.3 discusses a richer framework that allows for wealth effects in the form of gains from trade and enables us to obtain quantitative estimates of whether the resulting wealth effects are likely to dominate the intertemporal distortion effects. The punchline is that wealth effects tend to dominate, and reducing tariffs is therefore the optimal policy even under imperfect credibility.

3.6 Distortionary Taxation

We have illustrated above how a temporary trade liberalization will impose an intertemporal distortion on the household's consumption path. As another real-world example of this phenomenon, we will now analyze a situation where the government needs to resort to distortionary taxation to finance an exogenously given level of expenditures. While we will devote chapter 10 to study optimal fiscal policy, the purpose at hand is to illustrate how a time-varying tax rate will impose an intertemporal distortion, thus leading to a welfare loss over and above the one resulting from the presence of wasteful government spending.

14. The parameter values used to obtain figure 3.6 are the following: $\phi = 0.04$, $r = 0.03$, $p^H = 1$, $p^L = 0.4$, $\sigma = 0.3$, $b_0 = 0$, and $y = 10$. See Calvo and Mendoza (1994) for a quantitative analysis of the welfare effects of temporary trade liberalization under full and no rebates.

Box 3.3
Is it optimal to reduce tariffs even in the presence of imperfect credibility?

In this chapter we have used Calvo's (1987) model as a benchmark to study the welfare effects of intertemporal distortions. As shown in sections 3.2 and 3.3, a permanent reduction in tariffs has no impact on consumption, while a temporary reduction in tariffs leads to a consumption boom-bust cycle. In the benchmark model a temporary trade liberalization is therefore always welfare reducing because it imposes an intertemporal distortion. In section 3.5 we introduced a wealth effect by assuming that tariffs proceeds are used to finance socially unproductive spending. In such a case a permanent cut in tariffs is always welfare improving, and even a temporary reduction may increase welfare if the wealth effect dominates the intertemporal distortion effect. Hence trade liberalization reforms may be worth pursuing even under incomplete credibility.

In this light, a quantitative question arises: can gains from trade be large enough to generate a post-reform increase in welfare even under imperfect credibility? To answer this question, Buffie (1999) sets up a model that allows for gains from trade, by departing from Calvo's assumption of complete specialization (output is exported, consumer goods are imported) and thus allowing for substitution in both consumption and production. He shows that the welfare implications of a temporary liberalization under imperfect credibility depend, among other factors, on the length of the liberalization period, the size of the initial tariff, and the intertemporal elasticity of substitution. The model is solved numerically allowing the key parameters in the model to take on several different values, which results in 240 different combinations.

The paper's main conclusion is that even in the presence of lack of credibility, a temporary trade liberalization may be welfare improving. The general idea is that even when gains from trade are small, losses from the intertemporal distortion are usually smaller. The optimal tariff cut is in fact on the order of 50 to 80 percent. Buffie also finds that the optimal tariff cut is always larger the higher is the initial tariff, which supports the view that relatively closed economies should liberalize more. In addition he concludes that free trade is welfare improving when the intertemporal elasticity of substitution is smaller than one, which is consistent with the discussion in the main body of the chapter.

In closing, Buffie stresses the fact that temporary liberalizations may be costly for reasons not explored in his model, such as the role of durable goods. Indeed, as discussed in section 3.3.2, the presence of durable goods can lead to intertemporal price speculation and thus result in welfare costs even when the intertemporal elasticity of substitution is equal to zero.

Consider a small open economy perfectly integrated into the world economy in both goods and capital markets. The endowment of the only (tradable and nonstorable) good is constant over time and equal to y.

3.6.1 Consumers

Let preferences be given by

$$\int_0^\infty \log(c_t)e^{-\beta t}dt, \tag{3.33}$$

where c_t is consumption of the only (nonstorable) good and β is the discount rate (equal to the world real interest rate).

The flow constraint is given by

$$\dot{b}_t = rb_t + y - (1 + \theta_t)c_t, \tag{3.34}$$

where b_t are net foreign assets, r is the world real interest rate, y is the constant endowment of the good, and θ_t is a consumption tax. Integrating forward and imposing the corresponding transversality condition, we obtain

$$b_0 + \frac{y}{r} = \int_0^\infty (1 + \theta_t)c_t e^{-rt} dt. \tag{3.35}$$

The representative consumer chooses $\{c_t\}_{t=0}^\infty$ to maximize (3.33) subject to the intertemporal constraint (3.35), taking as given the path of θ_t. The first-order condition is given by

$$\frac{1}{c_t} = \lambda(1 + \theta_t). \tag{3.36}$$

Since $1 + \theta_t$ is the price of consumption faced by the consumer, first-order condition (3.36) is exactly analogous to first-order condition (3.4) in the model with tariffs examined earlier in this chapter. Hence we can already see that fluctuations in the tax rate will induce consumers not to choose a flat path of consumption because of the desire to engage in intertemporal consumption substitution.

3.6.2 Government

The government spends on tradable goods (g_t) and must balance its budget at every point in time:

$$g_t = \theta_t c_t. \tag{3.37}$$

The level of government spending, g_t, is exogenously given. The tax rate, θ_t, will adjust so as to ensure that the budget constraint (3.37) holds.

3.6.3 Equilibrium Conditions

Substituting (3.37) into the consumer's flow constraint (3.34), we obtain the economy's flow constraint (i.e., the current account):

$$\dot{b}_t = rb_t + y - c_t - g_t.$$

By definition, the trade balance is

$$TB_t \equiv y - c_t - g_t. \tag{3.38}$$

Substituting (3.37) into the consumer's intertemporal constraint (3.35), we obtain the resource constraint:

$$b_0 + \frac{y}{r} = \int_0^\infty (c_t + g_t)e^{-rt}dt. \tag{3.39}$$

3.6.4 Initial Stationary Equilibrium

Let us characterize a PFEP for a constant path of g_t, given by g^L. If g_t is constant over time, equation (3.37) tells us that $\theta_t c_t$ will be constant over time. Also first-order condition (3.36) indicates that $c_t(1 + \theta_t)$ will be constant over time. Since $c_t(1 + \theta_t) = c_t + \theta_t c_t$ and we have already established that $\theta_t c_t$ is constant over time, it follows that c_t is constant over time. This in turn implies, from (3.37), that θ_t will be constant over time.

Having established that all endogenous variables will be constant over time, we can derive a closed-form solution for consumption from the resource constraint (3.39):

$$c = rb_0 + y - g^L. \tag{3.40}$$

From the government's flow constraint (3.37), we can derive a reduced-form for the constant value of the tax rate:

$$\theta = \frac{g^L}{rb_0 + y - g^L}. \tag{3.41}$$

Substituting (3.40) into (3.38), we obtain

$$TB_t = -rb_0.$$

3.6.5 Permanent Increase in Government Spending

Suppose that just before $t = 0$, the economy is in the stationary equilibrium described above. At $t = 0$ there is an unanticipated and permanent increase in g_t from g^L to g^H (figure 3.7, panel a). Since the shock is permanent, the same solution derived above holds for the new PFEP. Hence expression (3.40) tells us that consumption falls one to one with the increase in government spending (panel b), and equation (3.41) indicates that the consumption tax rate increases (panel c). Since the shock is permanent, there is, of course, no effect on the trade balance (panel d, which assumes that $b_0 = 0$).

We conclude that the increase in government spending has imposed a wealth effect on the economy (akin to the permanent reduction in the endowment studied in chapter 1) but no intertemporal distortion.

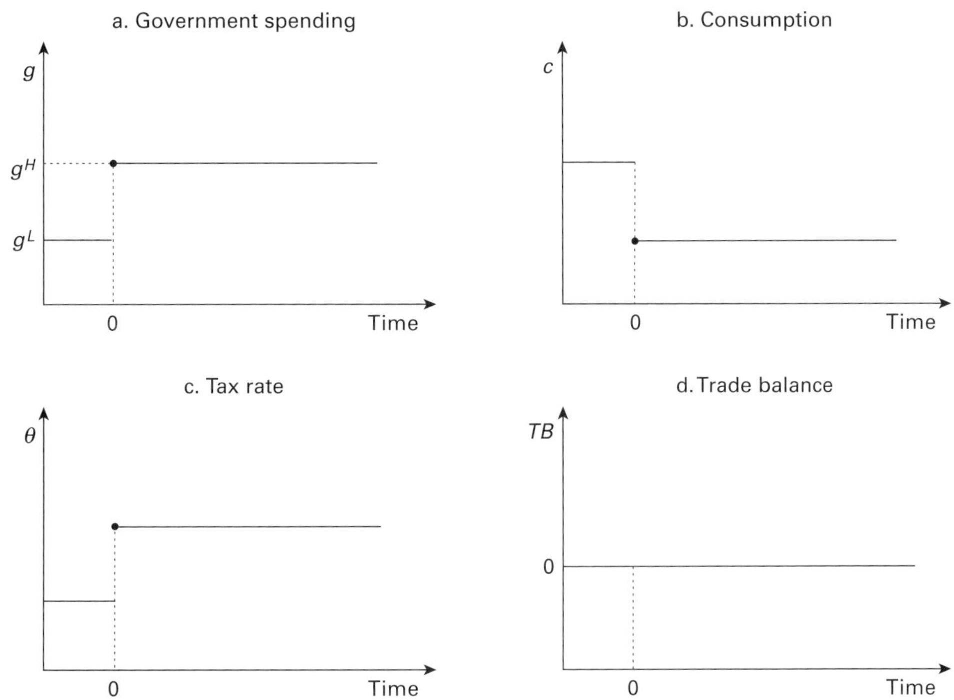

Figure 3.7
Permanent increase in government spending

3.6.6 Temporary Increase in Government Spending

Suppose now that at $t = 0$ there is an unanticipated and temporary increase in g_t. The path of g_t is then given by (figure 3.8, panel a):

$$g_t = \begin{cases} g^H, & 0 \leq t < T, \\ g^L, & t \geq T. \end{cases}$$

The consumer reoptimizes at time $t = 0$. The first-order condition can be written as

$$\frac{1}{c_t} = \tilde{\lambda}(1 + \theta_t), \tag{3.42}$$

where, once again, we have used $\tilde{\lambda}$ to call attention to the fact that the Lagrange multiplier may change at $t = 0$.

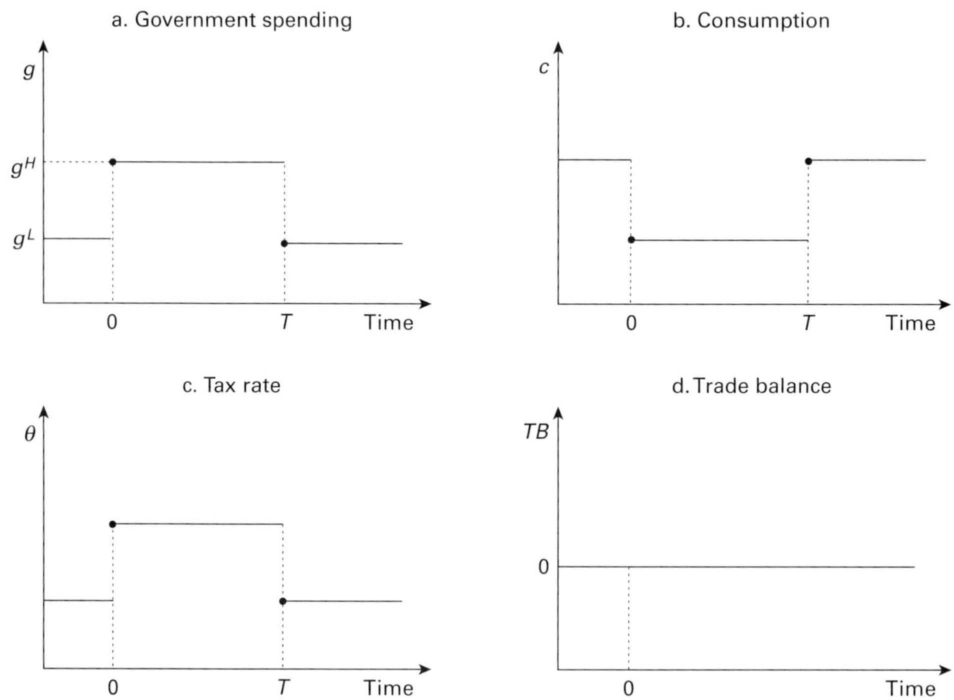

Figure 3.8
Temporary increase in government spending

As always when studying a temporary shock, we begin by establishing the change in the endogenous variables at time T.[15] Two pieces of information will be key in this instance. First, we know from the government's flow constraint (3.37) that $\theta_t c_t$ will be high during $[0, T)$ and low for $t \geq T$. In other words, $\theta_t c_t$ will fall at time T. Second, first-order condition (3.42) tells us that $c_t(1 + \theta_t)$ will be constant along the new PFEP. Combining these two pieces of information, we infer that c_t will jump up at time T. In turn the fact that c_t jumps up at time T implies, from (3.42), that θ_t jumps down.

To establish the initial jump in c_t, notice that since $c_t(1 + \theta_t)$ is constant along the new PFEP and $g_t = \theta_t c_t$, it follows that $c_t + g_t$ will be constant as well. This implies that $c_t + g_t$ cannot jump at $t = 0$ for, if it did, it would violate the economy's resource constraint. Hence c_t will fall at $t = 0$ by the same amount that g_t increases. Since g_t increases but c_t falls at $t = 0$, it follows from the government's budget constraint (3.37) that θ_t must increase. Finally, the fact that $c_t + g_t$ does not change at $t = 0$ implies that the trade balance does not change either (panel d).

15. Proceeding as above, it is easy to establish that within each subperiod, all endogenous variables are constant.

In sum, we have established that the temporary increase in government spending leads to a temporary rise in the consumption tax rate (panel c). As in the case of a temporary trade liberalization studied earlier in this chapter, this nonconstant path of the price of consumption introduces an intertemporal distortion. Consumers find it optimal to reduce consumption now compared to the future because of the temporarily higher price. However, this is clearly suboptimal from a social point of view. Indeed, as can easily be checked (see exercise 6 at the end of this chapter), if lump-sum taxation were available, consumption would fall at time 0 by the amount of the reduction in permanent income but remain flat thereafter. In other words, under lump-sum taxation, only the (negative) wealth effect of the temporary increase in government spending would affect consumers. Under distortionary taxation, however, consumers suffer an additional loss of welfare due to the nonflat consumption path.

3.7 Terms of Trade Shocks

We noted at the beginning of this chapter that the effect of intertemporal distortions could be analyzed in a one-good model (as we have done in section 3.6) but that we would use a model with importables and exportables to motivate the exercise as a trade liberalization. Another nice application of this same model with two tradable goods is to study the effects of terms of trade shocks on the current account.[16]

The link between terms of trade and the current account has its theoretical roots in Harberger (1950) and Laursen and Metzler (1950). They claimed that an improvement in a country's terms of trade would result in an increase in saving and, consequently, in an improvement of the current account. This proposition is known in the literature as the Harberger–Laursen–Metzler (HLM) effect: positive (negative) terms of trade shocks are associated with current account surpluses (deficits).

The rationale behind their analysis was essentially that an improvement in the terms of trade would result in higher "real income" because of the higher purchasing power of exports. Within a typical Keynesian model with a marginal propensity to consume less than one, an increase in real income increases savings and results in a current account improvement.

We will study the effect of terms of trade shocks on the current account using the model of section 3.2 with three modifications: (1) preferences follow the CES specification in (3.17), (2) there are no tariffs (or government), and (3) the world relative price of exportables (i.e., the terms of trade) is now given by $1/p_t$.

In this context the consumer's flow constraint becomes

$$\dot{b}_t = rb_t + y - p_t c_t,$$

16. We will revisit this question in chapter 4 in the context of a model with nontradable goods.

with the corresponding lifetime budget constraint given by

$$\int_0^\infty p_t c_t e^{-rt} dt = b_0 + \frac{y}{r}.$$

At the margin the optimal choice of consumption continues to be characterized by first-order condition (3.21). It should be apparent that this model is formally the same as the one analyzed in section 3.5. We can therefore use the results derived in that section to discuss the HLM effect.

An unanticipated and permanent improvement in the terms of trade (a fall in p_t) results in a higher "permanent income" for the consumer because each unit of exportables is now worth more in terms of importables. Hence consumption increases *pari passu* with permanent income, and there is no change in either the trade balance or the current account. Welfare, of course, increases.

An unanticipated and temporary improvement in the terms of trade leads to higher consumption on impact. In the more relevant practical case ($\sigma < 1$), both the trade balance and the current account improve. Intuitively, expenditure falls between 0 and T because of the low intertemporal elasticity of substitution. This is consistent with the original HLM effect. However, for $\sigma = 1$, the trade balance will not change, and for $\sigma > 1$, the trade balance will actually worsen on impact, as discussed in section 3.5. Further, as shown in section 3.5, a temporary improvement in the terms of trade is always welfare improving because it enlarges the economy's opportunity set.

It should be noticed that while temporary terms of trade shocks do imply a nonconstant path of the relative price of consumption (as in the preceding analysis) and hence lead to a nonconstant path of consumption, they should not be referred to as an "intertemporal distortion," since they are not policy induced and hence the economy is still operating in the first-best equilibrium. In other words, a planner would react in the same way as the consumer does.

The bottom line of the analysis is that the HLM effect is consistent with the intertemporal approach to the current account whenever the improvement in the terms of trade is temporary and the intertemporal elasticity of substitution is low. The HLM effect vanishes when the improvement in terms of trade is perceived as permanent.[17] While the empirical evidence on the HLM is somewhat mixed (see box 3.4), it is consistent with the idea that the HLM is more likely to be present in economies with small nontradable sectors (this model with no nontradable goods can be thought of as an extreme case) and face predominantly temporary shocks.

Finally, notice that the assumption that assets are denominated in terms of exportables is critical for our results. As exercise 7 at the end of the chapter makes clear, if assets were denominated in terms of importables, then the impact of an improvement in the terms of trade would be different. Specifically, a temporary improvement in the terms of trade would always lead to a current account surplus. Intuitively, if you save in terms of importables, the relevant relative price for

17. See Obstfeld (1983) and Svensson and Razin (1983) for an analysis of the HLM effect in a more general context. In a model with Uzawa preferences, Obstfeld (1982) shows that a permanent improvement in the terms of trade can be associated with a worsening in the current account (contradicting the HLM effect). See Ostry and Reinhart (1992) for an analysis of the HLM effect in a model with nontradable goods and an empirical estimation of the relevant parameters.

Box 3.4
What are the effects of terms of trade shocks on the current account?

As discussed in the text, the Harberger–Laursen–Metlzer effect holds that an improvement (deterioration) in a country's terms of trade will lead to an improvement (deterioration) in the trade balance. When the intertemporal elasticity of substitution is less than one (the relevant case in practice), our model can in fact replicate the HLM effect.

What does the empirical evidence show? Overall, the evidence is mixed (see table 3.3 for a summary of the main studies). Evidence in favor of the HLM can be found in Otto (2003) and Kent and Cashin (2003). Using a structural vector-autoregression model, Otto (2003) finds strong evidence of the HLM effect in a sample of 55 countries. Kent and Cashin (2003) find that the HLM

Table 3.3
Empirical studies on the HLM effect

Author(s)	Dataset	Methodology	Main results
Bouakez and Kano (2008)	Quarterly data Australia 1972–2001, Canada 1962–2001, and United Kingdom 1971–2001	Derive an approximate closed-form solution for the present-value representation of the current account that takes into account, in addition to the HLM effect, consumption-smoothing effects of future changes in the interest rate and exchange rate.	Terms of trade shocks do not significantly affect the current account. Extended model is rejected by the data, indicating that terms of trade shocks are not important in explaining current account movements in Australia and Canada. For United Kingdom, model is not rejected but improvement is marginal.
Kent and Cashin (2003)	128 countries 1960–99	Consumption-smoothing effect on savings and the investment effect work in opposite directions—the greater the persistence of a terms of trade shock, the more the investment effect will dominate the saving effect.	Persistence of terms of trade shocks varies across countries. The current account response is positively (negatively) related to unanticipated changes in the terms of trade for countries with predominantly temporary (permanent) terms of trade shocks.
Otto (2003)	15 small OECD and 40 developing countries 1960–1999	Uses a structural vector autoregression (SVAR) model to summarize the first and second moments of the data. Empirical evidence of a HLM effect is obtained from the SVAR model by examining the estimated response function for the trade balance following a terms of trade shock.	Strong evidence in favor of the HLM effect. The immediate effect of a positive shock to the terms of trade is an improvement in the trade balance. On average, terms of trade shocks are marginally more important in explaining fluctuations in the trade balance for developing countries than for developed countries.
Cashin and McDermott (2002)	5 OECD countries 1970–97	By comparing two commodity-exporting countries with relative small nontradables sectors with three major industrial countries, study examines how important terms of trade shocks are in affecting current account balance.	Terms of trade shocks found to be highly persistent. However, they do not have any impact on the current account balance of countries with a large nontradable sector. Only for those countries with relatively small nontradable sectors (Australia and New Zealand), there is evidence in support of the HLM effect.

Box 3.4
(continued)

effect is present when countries face predominantly temporary terms of trade shocks.[a] However, Cashin and McDermott (2002) find that terms of trade shocks do not affect the current account in countries with large nontradable sectors. Using a different empirical approach, Bouakez and Kano (2008) conclude that terms of trade shocks do not have a significant effect on the current account.

We conclude that the jury is still out regarding the empirical validity of the HLM. The evidence, however, is consistent with the idea that we are more likely to observe the HLM effect in economies that are more open to trade and face predominantly temporary terms of trade shocks.

a. It is worth noting that Kent and Cashin's (2003) findings are fully consistent with our analysis of chapter 1 in which we show that, in a model with investment, the response of the current account is related to the duration of the shock (i.e., the less persistent the shock, the more likely that the saving effect will dominate).

consumption decisions is one. Hence the consumption path will always be flat. In this context terms of trade shocks act exactly like the endowment shocks in the basic model of chapter 1. Hence an unanticipated and temporary fall in p_t (i.e., a temporary improvement in the terms of trade) leads to a current account surplus for consumption-smoothing purposes.[18]

3.8 Final Remarks

This chapter has analyzed the implications of intertemporal fluctuations in relative prices on consumption and the current account. Fluctuations in relative prices may be due to market forces (e.g., terms of trade) or policy measures (e.g., temporary tariffs or tax rates). In the latter case we refer to them as intertemporal distortions because they induce consumers to choose a socially suboptimal path of consumption. For example, a temporary reduction in tariffs leads consumers to increase consumption to take advantage of the temporarily cheaper price. In the absence of wealth effects, such a temporary reduction in tariffs will lower welfare.

Conceptually, this chapter has introduced two key effects in intertemporal models: intertemporal substitution effects and wealth effects. In some form or another, these two effects will be present in all of the models that we will study in subsequent chapters. As a preview, chapter 7 will study the real effects of a temporary reduction in the rate of devaluation (or inflation in a one-good model). Since money will be needed to buy goods, the effective price of the good will be cheaper when inflation is low than when inflation is high. A temporary reduction in the rate of devaluation will thus introduce an intertemporal distortion by making goods temporarily cheaper.

18. If households consumed both importables and exportables, then terms of trade shocks would also affect the relevant real interest rate leading to an additional channel (see Obstfeld 1983).

If, in addition, lower inflation leads to higher real money balances and thus to lower transaction costs, a lower rate of devaluation (even if temporary) will lead to a wealth effect. The welfare effects of a temporary reduction in the rate of devaluation will thus depend on the relative strength of the intertemporal substitution effect and the wealth effect.

3.9 Appendix: Intertemporal Elasticity of Substitution

This appendix defines and discusses the intertemporal elasticity of substitution. Specifically, we want to ask the following question: by how much (in proportional terms) will the ratio of consumption change in response to a change in intertemporal prices? In other words, we want to compute $d\log(c^1/c^2)/d\log(p^L/p^H)$. To this effect we can first define the intertemporal elasticity of substitution between c^1 and c^2 as

$$\sigma(c^1, c^2) \equiv -\frac{d\log(c^1/c^2)}{d\log\big(u'(c^1)/u'(c^2)\big)}. \tag{3.43}$$

This is, of course, the standard definition of an elasticity of substitution from microeconomic theory.[19] In this particular case it is a property of the utility function that describes the percentage change in the consumption ratio per percentage change in the marginal rate of substitution.

Taking into account (3.16), we can rewrite this equation as

$$\frac{d\log(c^1/c^2)}{d\log(p^L/p^H)} = -\sigma(c^1, c^2). \tag{3.44}$$

Since utility maximization implies that the marginal rate of substitution is equated to the price ratio, the elasticity of substitution can also be thought of as the percentage change in the consumption ratio per percentage change in the price ratio.

From (3.17) and (3.43), it follows that for CES utility functions,

$$\sigma(c^1, c^2) = \sigma.$$

Notice that the intertemporal elasticity of substitution defined in (3.43) involves consumption at two *different* points in time and asks how the ratio of consumption varies in response to a change in the relative intertemporal prices. A closely related (but different) concept is to ask how consumption at a *particular* point in time would change in response to a change in prices. To answer this question, totally differentiate first-order condition (3.4) to obtain

$$\frac{dc_t}{c_t} = -\eta(c_t)\frac{dp_t}{p_t}, \tag{3.45}$$

19. See, for instance, Varian (1992).

where

$$\eta(c_t) \equiv -\frac{u'(c_t)}{u''(c_t)c_t} > 0$$

denotes the (absolute value of the) elasticity of the marginal utility with respect to consumption and captures the willingness of the consumer to change consumption at a particular point in time in response to a change in prices. For the particular case of CES functions, $\eta(c_t)$ is also constant and equal to σ. In models with uncertainty, the inverse of $\eta(c_t)$ is known as the coefficient of relative risk aversion and CES functions are often referred to as constant relative risk aversion functions.

The connection between the two concepts, σ and η, is best understood by taking the limit of $\sigma(c^1, c^2)$ as c^2 becomes arbitrarily close to c^1 to obtain[20]

$$\lim_{c^2 \to c^1} \sigma(c^1, c^2) = -\frac{\lim_{c^2 \to c^1} d \log(c^1/c^2)}{\lim_{c^2 \to c^1} d \log\big(u'(c^1)/u'(c^2)\big)} = -\frac{u'(c^1)}{c^1 u''(c^1)}.$$

As expected, as c^1 and c^2 become the same, the elasticity of substitution, σ, converges to the elasticity of the marginal utility with respect to consumption, η.

Exercises

1. (Effects of changes in the liberalization period and the intertemporal elasticity of substitution) Consider again the temporary liberalization discussed in section 3.3.2 with $q \equiv p^L/p^H < 1$. Assume that preferences take the iso-elastic form given by equation (3.17), where σ is the intertemporal elasticity of substitution.

In this context:

a. Obtain a reduced form for c^1 and c^2 as a function of q, T, and σ.

b. Obtain a reduced form for the Lagrange multiplier, λ.

c. Show how c^1 and c^2 change as the liberalization period is shortened (i.e., as T becomes smaller).

d. Show how c^1 and c^2 change as the intertemporal elasticity of substitution (σ) becomes larger.

e. Consider the logarithmic case. Using L' Hôpital's rule, show first that logarithmic preferences are the limiting case of (3.17) when $\sigma \to 1$. Then derive the indirect lifetime utility as a function of q and T. Show how it varies with T.

f. Show how welfare changes in the case of (a) a one instant liberalization (i.e., $T \longrightarrow 0$) and (b) an arbitrarily long liberalization (i.e., $T \longrightarrow \infty$).

g. Plot welfare as a function of T (for reasonable parameter values) and verify that welfare has a U-shaped form.

20. To obtain the expression below, keep in mind that you need to compute the differentials before taking the limit.

2. (Durable goods and intertemporal price speculation) This exercise follows Calvo (1988). Consider the case of an individual who has Leontief preferences over time and therefore chooses a flat path of consumption (c) independently of the path of p. Suppose also that the importable good can be stored at no cost and that there is no depreciation. Based on arbitrage considerations, it should be clear that if p is constant over time, there are no incentives to accumulate stocks of the importable good because the good is dominated in rate of return by the foreign bond. Suppose instead that there is a "one-instant liberalization":

$$p_0 = 1,$$

$$p_t = p > 1, \qquad t > 0.$$

Assume that the proceeds from the tariff are given back to consumers in a lump-sum fashion.

The consumer's intertemporal budget constraint can be written as

$$Z + pc \int_{\phi}^{\infty} e^{-rt} dt = b_0 + \frac{y}{r} + \Psi, \tag{3.46}$$

where Z denotes the stock of importables accumulated at $t = 0$, y is the constant endowment of the exportable good, Ψ denotes the present discounted value of government transfers, and ϕ denotes the time at which the stock of importables, Z, is depleted. Since there is no depreciation, it follows that

$$\phi c = Z. \tag{3.47}$$

In this context:

a. Show that the intertemporal budget constraint can be written as

$$c\left(r\phi + pe^{-r\phi}\right) = r\left(b_0 + \frac{y}{r} + \Psi\right).$$

b. Find the optimal ϕ.

c. Find a reduced form for c. (Hint: Take into account that, in equilibrium, $\Psi = (p-1)c \int_{\phi}^{\infty} e^{-rt} dt$.)

d. Discuss the welfare implications of a one-instant liberalization.

3. (Lack of credibility) This exercise, which follows Engel and Kletzer (1991), deals with a formalization of the idea of lack of credibility that we discussed in section 3.4. Consider a two-period endowment economy. The economy is endowed with a constant endowment, y, of an exportable good. It consumes an importable good, c. The terms of trade are equal to one. The domestic price of importables, however, may be greater than one if a tariff is imposed. The economy can borrow/lend at a fixed rate, r. In the first period, there is no tariff (i.e., the domestic relative price of importables is equal to one). In the second period, a tariff $(p-1)$ may be imposed with probability π.

The consumer's problem is to maximize expected utility

$$E\{U\} = \log c_1 + \beta(1-\pi)\log c_2 + \beta\pi \log c_2^*,$$

where $\beta(1+r) = 1$, c_1 is consumption in period 1, c_2 is consumption in period 2 if the tariff is not imposed, and c_2^* is consumption in period 2 if the tariff is imposed.
Using the exportable good as the numéraire, the consumer's flow constraints are given by (assume $b_0 = 0$)

$$c_1 = y - b_1,$$

$$c_2 = y + (1+r)b_1,$$

$$pc_2^* = y + (1+r)b_1 + \tau^*,$$

where b_1 denotes end of period 1 (beginning of period 2) net foreign assets and τ^* denotes lump-sum transfers in case the tariff is imposed.[21] (In general equilibrium, $\tau^* = (p-1)c_2^*$.)
In this context:

a. Compute reduced forms for c_1, c_2, and c_2^*.

b. Compute consumer's welfare as a function of π.

c. Compare consumer's welfare when the tariff is $p-1$ in both periods with certainty.

d. What would you conclude about the desirability of trade reforms if you took the model at face value?

e. How could you modify the model to yield a more sensible policy prescription?

4. (Welfare in the no rebate case) Consider the model of section 3.5 with no rebates. In this context:

a. Compute a reduced form for welfare for the CES case and show that welfare increases for $\sigma > 1$.

b. Compute a reduced form for welfare for the logarithmic case.

c. Show that welfare increases if T becomes larger.

5. (Effects of changes in the liberalization period with wealth effect) Let preferences be given by

$$u(c_t) = \log c_t.$$

21. Note that we are implicitly assuming that consumers cannot insure against uncertain trade policy in period 2 (which is, of course, the natural assumption). In other words, there are incomplete markets (as defined in chapter 2).

Assume that a fraction ϕ of tariff revenues is spent on unproductive government spending, g_t, while a fraction $1-\phi$ is returned to consumers as lump-sum transfers:

$$g_t = \phi(p_t - 1)c_t,$$

$$\tau_t = (1-\phi)(p_t - 1)c_t.$$

Notice that the two cases analyzed in the text are particular cases of this more general formulation: $\phi = 0$ corresponds to the full rebate case (section 3.2) while $\phi = 1$ corresponds to the no rebate case (section 3.5).

In this context:

a. Compute a reduced form for c^1 and c^2 as a function of q, T, and ϕ.

b. Derive the indirect utility function as a function of q, T, and ϕ.

c. Plot the consumer's indirect utility function as a function of T for different values of ϕ. In particular, show that for low values of ϕ there is a welfare loss for values of T below some critical value and a welfare gain for higher values (as illustrated in figure 3.6), whereas for higher values of ϕ the temporary liberalization will always be welfare improving.

6. (Increases in government spending with lump-sum taxation) Solve for the two experiments carried out in section 3.6—a permanent and a temporary increase in government spending—assuming that the government can resort to lump-sum taxation. Explain the intuition behind the differences that may arise.

7. (HLM effect with debt in terms of importables) As a result of using exportables as the numéraire, the model developed in the text assumes that external debt is denominated in terms of the exportable good. Perhaps a more natural assumption is that debt is denominated in terms of importables since, after all, in the real world importables and foreign debt of the typical emerging market economy are denominated in US dollars.

To examine this alternative scenario, set up the model of section 3.7 in terms of importables (and with a general utility function) and study the response of the current account to both a permanent and a temporary improvement in the terms of trade. In particular, does the HLM effect hold for temporary shocks?

References

Arrau, Patricio. 1990. Intertemporal substitution in a monetary framework: Evidence from Chile and Mexico. Working Paper 549. The World Bank. Washington, DC.

Attanasio, Orazio P., and Guglielmo Weber. 1995. Is consumption growth consistent with intertemporal optimization? Evidence from the consumer expenditure survey. *Journal of Political Economy* 103 (6): 1121–57.

Atkeson, Andrew, and Masao Ogaki. 1996. Wealth-varying intertemporal elasticities of substitution: Evidence from panel and aggregate data. *Journal of Monetary Economics* 38 (3): 507–34.

Beaudry, Paul, and Eric van Wincoop. 1995. The intertemporal elasticity of substitution: An exploration using US panel of state data. *Economica* 63: 495–512.

Bouakez, Hafedh, and Takashi Kano. 2008. Terms of trade and current account fluctuations: The Harberger–Laursen–Metzler effect revisited. *Journal of Macroeconomics* 30 (1): 260–81.

Buffie, Edward. 1999. Optimal trade liberalization and the welfare costs of imperfect credibility. *Journal of International Economics* 47: 371–98.

Calvo, Guillermo A. 1987. On the costs of temporary policy. *Journal of Development Economics* 27 (1–2): 245–61.

Calvo, Guillermo A. 1988. Costly trade liberalizations: Durable goods and capital mobility. *IMF Staff Papers* 35 (3): 461–73.

Calvo, Guillermo A. 1989. Incredible reforms. In G. Calvo, R. Findlay, P. Kouri, and J. B. de Macedo, eds., *Debt, Stabilization and Development*. New York: Blackwell, 217–34.

Calvo, Guillermo A., and Enrique Mendoza. 1994. Trade reforms of uncertain duration and real uncertainty: A first approximation. IMF Working Paper 94/45. International Monetary Fund, Washington, DC.

Cashin, Paul, and John McDermott. 2002. Terms of trade shocks and the current account: Evidence from five industrial countries. *Open Economies Review* 13 (3): 219–235.

Cashin, Paul, and John McDermott. 2003. Intertemporal substitution and terms-of-trade shocks. *Review of International Economics* 11 (4): 604–18.

Duncan, Roberto. 2003. The Harberger–Laursen–Metzler effect revisited: An indirect-utility-function approach. Working Paper 250. Central Bank of Chile, Santiago.

Eckstein, Zvi, and Leonardo Leiderman. 1991. Seignorage and the welfare cost of inflation: Evidence from an intertemporal model of money and consumption. *Journal of Monetary Economics* 29: 389–410.

Edwards, Sebastian. 1998. Openness, productivity and growth: What do we really know? *Economic Journal* 108 (447): 383–98.

Engel, Charles, and Kenneth M. Kletzer. 1991. Trade policy under endogenous credibility. *Journal of Development Economics* 36 (2): 213–28.

Fauvel, Yvon, and Lucie Samson. 1991. Intertemporal substitution and durable goods: An empirical analysis. *Canadian Journal of Economics* 24 (1): 192–205.

Fernandes, Ana. 2007. Trade policy, trade volumes and plant-level productivity in Colombian manufacturing industries. *Journal of International Economics* 71 (1): 52–71.

Giovannini, Alberto. 1985. Saving and the real interest rate in LDCs. *Journal of Development Economics* 18 (2–3): 197–217.

Hall, Robert E. 1988. Intertemporal substitution in consumption. *Journal of Political Economy* 96 (2): 339–57.

Harberger, Arnold C. 1950. Currency depreciation, income, and the balance of trade. *Journal of Political Economy* 58: 47–60.

Hay, Donald. 2001. The post-1990 Brazilian trade liberalisation and the performance of large manufacturing firms: Productivity, market share and profits. *Economic Journal* 111 (473): 620–41.

Kent, Christopher J., and Paul Cashin. 2003. The response of the current account to terms of trade shocks: Persistence matters. IMF Working Paper 03/143. International Monetary Fund, Washington, DC.

Krishna, Pravin, and Devashish Mitra. 1998. Trade liberalization, market discipline and productivity growth: New evidence from India. *Journal of Development Economics* 56 (2): 447–62.

Laursen, Svend, and Lloyd A. Metzler. 1950. Flexible exchange rates and the theory of employment. *Review of Economics and Statistics* 32 (February): 281–99.

MacDonald, James. 1994. Does import competition force efficient production? *Review of Economics and Statistics* 76 (4): 721–27.

Obstfeld, Maurice. 1982. Aggregate spending and the terms of trade: Is there a Laursen–Metzler effect? *Quarterly Journal of Economics* 97 (2): 251–70.

Obstfeld, Maurice. 1983. Intertemporal price speculation and the optimal current-account deficit. *Journal of International Money and Finance* 2 (2): 135–45.

Ogaki, Masao, and Carmen M. Reinhart. 1998. Measuring intertemporal substitution: The role of durable goods. *Journal of Political Economy* 106 (5): 1078–98.

Ogaki, Masao, Jonathan Ostry, and Carmen M. Reinhart. 1996. Saving behavior in low- and middle-income developing countries: A comparison. *IMF Staff Papers* 43 (1): 38–71.

Ostry, Jonathan, and Carmen M. Reinhart, 1992. Private saving and terms of trade shocks: Evidence from developing countries. *IMF Staff Papers* 39 (3): 495–517.

Otto, Glenn. 2003. Terms of trade shocks and the balance of trade: There is a Harberger–Laursen–Metzler effect. *Journal of International Money and Finance* 22 (2): 155–84.

Pavcnik, Nina. 2002. Trade liberalization, exit, and productivity improvements: Evidence from Chilean plants. *Review of Economic Studies* 69 (1): 245–76.

Reinhart, Carmen M., and Carlos A. Végh. 1995. Nominal interest rates, consumption booms, and lack of credibility: A quantitative examination. *Journal of Development Economics* 46 (2): 357–78.

Rossi, Nicola. 1988. Government spending, the real interest rate, and the behavior of liquidity-constrained consumers in developing countries. *IMF Staff Papers* 35 (1): 104–40.

Svensson, Lars, and Assaf Razin. 1983. The terms of trade and the current account: The Harberger–Laursen–Metzler effect. *Journal of Political Economy* 91 (1): 97–125.

Tybout, James, Jaime de Melo, and Vittorio Corbo. 1991. The effects of trade reforms on scale and technical efficiency: New evidence from Chile. *Journal of International Economics* 31 (3–4): 231–50.

Tybout, James, and Daniel Westbrook. 1995. Trade liberalization and the dimensions of efficiency in Mexican manufacturing industries. *Journal of International Economics* 39 (1): 53–78.

Varian, Hal R. 1992. *Microeconomic Analysis*, 3rd ed. New York: Norton.

4 Nontradable Goods and Relative Prices

4.1 Introduction

Thus far we have only looked at models with tradable goods. In reality, however, many of the goods consumed in an open economy are nontradable. The presence of nontradable goods introduces a key relative price in the economy: the price of nontradable goods in terms of tradable goods (the inverse of what is commonly defined as the real exchange rate). This is, by far, the most important relative price in a small open economy as it provides the main adjustment mechanism to both demand and supply shocks.

The key difference between tradable and nontradable goods lies in their supply elasticity: the supply elasticity of tradable goods is in effect infinite since a small open economy can buy/sell as many tradable goods as it wants at a given world price (subject, of course, to its resource constraint). In sharp contrast, nontradable goods must be produced at home. In the case of an endowment economy, this implies that the supply elasticity is zero. As a result the adjustment to demand shocks will need to be met by a change in relative prices. Even when production is endogenous, an excess demand for nontradable goods relative to tradable goods will require an increase in their relative price to elicit a shift in productive resources from the tradable to the nontradable sector. In this case the adjustment will come about through both prices and quantities.

This supply side asymmetry between tradable and nontradable goods, and the resulting need for relative price changes, is at the core of any macroeconomic adjustment in developing countries. Consider, for instance, a typical boom–bust cycle in a developing country. During the boom, consumption of both tradable and nontradable goods is high. What is the production pattern that will meet this high demand? Since nontradables must be produced at home—whereas tradable goods can be imported—more resources will be needed in the nontradable goods sector. To entice this shift in resources, the relative price of nontradable goods must be high. The good times will thus be characterized by high consumption, trade and current account deficits, relatively low production of tradables, relatively high production of nontradables, and a high relative price of nontradable goods.

At some point, however, consumption will need to adjust to satisfy the economy's intertemporal resource constraint. Put differently, at some point the economy will need to run a trade surplus to repay the external debt incurred in the good times. To run a trade surplus, production of tradable goods must exceed consumption of tradable goods. How does this adjustment come about? It takes place via a fall in the relative price of nontradable goods (in response to an excess supply of nontradable goods at the pre-bust relative price). This fall will induce resources to shift from the nontradable goods sector to the tradable goods sector. The bad times will thus be characterized by low consumption, trade and current account surpluses, relatively high production of tradables, relatively low production of nontradables, and a low relative price of nontradable goods. Our very simple model will explain precisely this adjustment mechanism. One can add many bells and whistles to this basic adjustment mechanism but, at its core, the essential mechanism will be fully uncovered in this chapter.

The chapter proceeds as follows. Section 4.2 begins by adding nontradable goods to the endowment model studied in chapter 1. This gives us our basic model with nontradable goods, which will be the workhorse for the rest of this chapter. A key feature of the basic model with nontradable goods is that the consumption-smoothing result obtained in chapter 1 (i.e., in the absence of any friction, consumption will be flat over time regardless of the path of output) no longer holds. By affecting the marginal utility of tradable goods, a fluctuating path of consumption of nontradable goods may induce the consumer to vary consumption of tradable goods over time. In this vein, this section explores in detail how consumers react to changes in relative prices.

Section 4.3 puts our basic model to work and derives the first key message of this chapter: whether in response to supply or demand shocks, trade deficits go hand in hand with real appreciation and trade surpluses go hand in hand with real depreciation.[1] There is no sense, however, in which a real appreciation "causes" a trade deficit (or a real depreciation a trade surplus), a commonly held view among practitioners. In the model the real exchange rate and the trade balance are simply responding to some exogenous shock. The logic behind this result is as simple as it is compelling. Suppose that there is an excess demand for both tradable and nontradable goods (as a result of either a negative supply shock or a positive demand shock). On the tradable side, this excess demand is met by importing more tradable goods from abroad (a trade deficit). On the nontradable side, this cannot happen since the supply of nontradables is fixed. Hence the relative price of nontradable goods must rise to clear the market (real appreciation). In sum, a trade deficit and real appreciation (or trade surplus and real depreciation) are just two sides of the same coin and thus must necessarily go hand in hand.

Section 4.4 brings fiscal policy into the picture by introducing government spending and taxes into our basic model with nontradable goods. The rationale for doing so is that some of the most important policy questions in developing countries revolve around fiscal policy, the real exchange

1. Throughout this chapter, and following standard terminology, we will be using the expression "real exchange rate" to refer to the relative price of tradable goods (i.e., the inverse of the relative price of nontradable goods). We will do so despite the fact that, arguably, it may only make sense to use the label "real exchange rate" in a monetary model, since this label obviously follows from the idea that by deflating the nominal exchange rate by some price index one gets a real exchange rate (as discussed in chapter 6). In this context a real depreciation (appreciation) means an increase (decrease) in the real exchange rate.

rate, and trade imbalances. In particular, will a fiscal contraction cause a real depreciation? Will a fiscal expansion lead to a trade deficit? This section clarifies the conditions under which the answer to both questions is affirmative. If government spending is biased toward nontradable goods (relative to the private sector's spending patterns), then a reduction in government spending will indeed lead to a real depreciation. This section then shows how temporary increases in government spending may lead to trade deficits, thus validating the commonly held view that fiscal deficits may cause trade deficits (the so-called twin deficits hypothesis).

Up to this point in the chapter, the supply side has been kept out of the picture by assuming that the economy is endowed with some amount of tradable and nontradable goods. Section 4.5 endogeneizes production by introducing labor supply into the model. This will enable us to get a fuller picture of how the economy adjusts to different shocks. We pay particular attention to how the economy adjusts to a boom–bust cycle caused by demand shocks and the key role played by the relative price of nontradable goods in bringing about the needed adjustment.

Finally, section 4.6 tackles two important and related questions regarding the response of the real exchange rate: How does the real exchange rate respond to a terms of trade shock? How does a trade liberalization (i.e., a reduction in import tariffs) affect the real exchange rate? To answer these questions, we modify the model by distinguishing between importable and exportable goods. In this context, we find that a terms of trade improvement (i.e., a rise in the relative price of exportables in terms of importables) will always lead to an increase in the relative price of nontradable goods (real appreciation) through two effects: a wealth effect and an intertemporal substitution effect. We also show that a temporary trade liberalization (like the one studied in chapter 3) leads to an increase in the relative price of nontradable goods.

4.2 Basic Model with Nontradable Goods

Except for the addition of nontradable goods, the model is the same as the basic endowment model developed in chapter 1. Consider a small open economy inhabited by a large number of identical, infinitely lived consumers, who are blessed with perfect foresight. There exist two physical goods: a tradable and a nontradable good (both nonstorable). The tradable good is the numéraire. The endowment path of both goods is exogenously given. There is no government. Perfect capital mobility prevails in the sense that consumers can buy or sell bonds that are denominated in terms of the tradable good (the numéraire) at a constant real interest rate r.

4.2.1 Consumer's problem

The consumer's lifetime utility is given by

$$\int_0^\infty u(c_t^T, c_t^N)e^{-\beta t}dt, \tag{4.1}$$

where $\beta(>0)$ is the subjective discount rate, c_t^T and c_t^N denote consumption of tradable and nontradable goods, respectively, and the function $u(.)$ is assumed to be strictly increasing and strictly concave:[2]

$$u_{c^T} > 0, \quad u_{c^N} > 0, \quad u_{c^T c^T} < 0, \quad u_{c^T c^T} u_{c^N c^N} - u_{c^T c^N}^2 > 0.$$

In addition we will assume that both c_t^T and c_t^N are normal goods.[3] Normality for tradables and nontradables, respectively, requires that (see appendix 4.8)

$$u_{c^N} u_{c^T c^N} - u_{c^T} u_{c^N c^N} > 0, \tag{4.2}$$

$$u_{c^T} u_{c^T c^N} - u_{c^N} u_{c^T c^T} > 0. \tag{4.3}$$

Let b_t denote net foreign assets held by the consumer. The flow constraint is given by

$$\dot{b}_t = rb_t + y_t^T + p_t y_t^N - c_t^T - p_t c_t^N, \tag{4.4}$$

where y_t^T and y_t^N denote the endowment of tradable and nontradable goods in period t, respectively, and p_t is the relative price of nontradable goods in terms of tradable goods. As already mentioned, we will refer to the inverse of p_t as the real exchange rate. An increase in p_t (i.e., an increase in the relative price of nontradable goods) or, equivalently, a fall in the real exchange rate is referred to as a real appreciation. A fall in p_t or, equivalently, an increase in the real exchange rate is referred to as a real depreciation.[4]

Integrating forward (4.4) and imposing the transversality condition

$$\lim_{t \longrightarrow \infty} e^{-rt} b_t = 0,$$

we obtain the consumer's intertemporal budget constraint:

$$\int_0^\infty (c_t^T + p_t c_t^N) e^{-rt} dt = b_0 + \int_0^\infty (y_t^T + p_t y_t^N) e^{-rt} dt. \tag{4.5}$$

The consumer's problem consists in choosing $\{c_t^T, c_t^N\}_{t=0}^\infty$ to maximize lifetime utility (4.1), subject to the intertemporal constraint (4.5), for a given path of y_t^T, y_t^N, p_t, and r and a given b_0.

2. Note that taken together, the last two conditions below for strict concavity imply that $u_{c^N c^N} < 0$.

3. Recall that a normal good is one whose income effect is positive (as opposed to a so-called inferior good, whose income effect is negative). While for some individual goods normality may not hold, at an aggregate level of merely two goods—tradables and nontradables—normality is all but guaranteed.

4. We often encounter in the literature the expression "real exchange rate appreciation" or "real exchange rate depreciation." This terminology is, strictly speaking, incorrect because the real exchange rate (a ratio) can go up and down but does not "appreciate" or "depreciate." In monetary models it is the currency (an asset) that can appreciate or depreciate in either nominal or real terms. The expressions "real appreciation" and "real depreciation" thus refer to an appreciation or depreciation of the currency in real terms.

We set up the Lagrangian as

$$\mathcal{L} = \int_0^\infty u(c_t^T, c_t^N)e^{-\beta t}dt + \lambda\left[b_0 + \int_0^\infty (y_t^T + p_t y_t^N)e^{-rt}dt - \int_0^\infty (c_t^T + p_t c_t^N)e^{-rt}dt\right].$$

The corresponding first-order conditions are given by

$$e^{-\beta t}u_{c^T}(c_t^T, c_t^N) = \lambda e^{-rt}, \tag{4.6}$$

$$e^{-\beta t}u_{c^N}(c_t^T, c_t^N) = \lambda e^{-rt}p_t. \tag{4.7}$$

Assume, for the reasons discussed in chapter 1, that $\beta = r$. We can then rewrite the first-order conditions as

$$u_{c^T}(c_t^T, c_t^N) = \lambda, \tag{4.8}$$

$$u_{c^N}(c_t^T, c_t^N) = \lambda p_t. \tag{4.9}$$

Equation (4.8) says that the marginal utility from consuming tradable goods will be constant over time. This is, of course, the same result that we encountered in chapter 1. The key difference, however, is that since there was only one (tradable) good in chapter 1, a constant marginal utility implied a constant consumption path over time. This is no longer true in a model with nontradable goods. In fact it is already apparent from condition (4.8) that if consumption of nontradable goods fluctuates over time, then consumption of tradable goods will generally not be constant over time.

First-order condition (4.9) makes clear that if p_t is not constant over time, then the marginal utility from consuming nontradable goods will be affected. To see this formally, consider a small change in p_t along a perfect foresight equilibrium path (PFEP) and totally differentiate first-order conditions (4.8) and (4.9) with respect to p_t to obtain:[5]

$$\frac{dc_t^T}{dp_t} = -\lambda \frac{u_{c^T c^N}}{u_{c^T c^T}u_{c^N c^N} - u_{c^T c^N}^2} \begin{cases} = 0, & \text{if } u_{c^T c^N} = 0, \\ > 0, & \text{if } u_{c^T c^N} < 0, \\ < 0, & \text{if } u_{c^T c^N} > 0, \end{cases} \tag{4.10}$$

$$\frac{dc_t^N}{dp_t} = \lambda \frac{u_{c^T c^T}}{u_{c^T c^T}u_{c^N c^N} - u_{c^T c^N}^2} < 0, \tag{4.11}$$

5. Of course, in general equilibrium p_t will be determined endogenously as analyzed below. Here we are looking at the consumer's response to changes in p_t (i.e., partial equilibrium).

where the denominator in both expressions is positive due to the assumption of strict concavity of the utility function. Equation (4.11) says that whenever p_t is, say, low along a perfect foresight path, the consumption of nontradable goods will be high. The intuition is the same as we saw in chapter 3: a low p_t (relative to other periods) indicates that nontradable goods are relatively cheaper, which induces consumers to engage in intertemporal consumption substitution.

In turn, we can see from (4.10) that the response of c_t^T to a change in p_t depends on the sign of the cross-derivative of the utility function. In other words, the response of c_t^T to changes in p_t depends on whether c_t^T and c_t^N are Edgeworth substitutes, independent, or complements.[6] There are three possible cases:

- *Tradables and nontradables are Edgeworth independent (i.e., $u_{c^T c^N} = 0$)* In this case, changes in p_t have no effect on the path of c_t^T. We are thus back to the world of chapter 1 and consumption of tradable goods is fully smoothed over time.
- *Tradables and nontradables are Edgeworth substitutes (i.e., $u_{c^T c^N} < 0$)* In this case, additional consumption of nontradables reduces the marginal utility of consuming tradable goods and hence tradable goods consumption is lower. Hence, when p_t is relatively low along a perfect foresight path, c_t^N will be relatively high and c_t^T will be relatively low. In other words, c_t^T and c_t^N move in opposite directions.
- *Tradables and nontradables are Edgeworth complements (i.e., $u_{c^T c^N} > 0$)* In this case, additional consumption of nontradables increases the marginal utility of consuming tradable goods, and hence tradable goods consumption is higher. In other words, c_t^T and c_t^N move in the same direction.

Besides these effects of changes in the level of p_t, changes in p_t *over time* will have an impact on how consumption evolves over time. To see this formally, let us consider the case where β is not necessarily equal to r. Take logarithms and then totally differentiate first-order conditions (4.6) and (4.7) with respect to time to obtain

$$-\frac{u_{c^T c^T}}{u_{c^T}}\dot{c}_t^T - \frac{u_{c^T c^N}}{u_{c^T}}\dot{c}_t^N = r - \beta, \tag{4.12}$$

$$-\frac{u_{c^T c^N}}{u_{c^N}}\dot{c}_t^T - \frac{u_{c^N c^N}}{u_{c^N}}\dot{c}_t^N = r_t^d - \beta, \tag{4.13}$$

where

$$r_t^d \equiv r - \frac{\dot{p}_t}{p_t} \tag{4.14}$$

6. Two goods are said to be Edgeworth substitutes, independent, or complement depending on whether the cross-derivative of the utility function is negative, zero, or positive, respectively. At a microeconomic level, an example of Edgeworth complements would be coffee and sugar and of Edgeworth substitutes Coke and Pepsi.

is, by definition, the *domestic real interest rate*.[7] Naturally the LHS of equations (4.12) and (4.13) tells us how the marginal utility of tradables and nontradables, respectively, evolves over time. As equation (4.13) makes clear, the domestic real interest rate is the relevant real interest rate in determining the time profile of the marginal utility of nontradable goods, as opposed to the world real interest rate, r, which is the relevant real interest rate in determining the profile of the marginal utility of tradable goods (as reflected in equation 4.12).

To see more clearly the role of the domestic real interest rate, let us focus for a moment on the separable case; that is, suppose that $u_{c^T c^N} = 0$. In this particular case, equations (4.12) and (4.13) reduce to

$$\frac{-u_{c^T c^T}}{u_{c^T}} \dot{c}_t^T = r - \beta, \tag{4.15}$$

$$\frac{-u_{c^N c^N}}{u_{c^N}} \dot{c}_t^N = r_t^d - \beta. \tag{4.16}$$

In the separable case, then, equation (4.16) tells us that the time profile of consumption of nontradable goods is fully determined by the difference between the domestic real interest rate and the discount rate. Instead, for the case of tradable goods, the time profile is determined by the difference between the world real interest rate and the discount rate, as was the case in chapter 1. Furthermore it follows from equation (4.16)—recall the definition of r_t^d given in (4.14)—that even under our usual assumption that $r = \beta$, consumption of nontradable goods will not be constant over time if the relative price of nontradable goods is changing over time (i.e., if $\dot{p}_t$ is different from zero).[8]

What is the intuition behind the domestic real interest rate being the relevant real interest rate for nontradable goods consumption? Intuitively, suppose that you forgo one unit of nontradable consumption today. The market value of that unit (in terms of the numéraire) is p_t. Hence you can buy tradable bonds for a value of p_t. Since the return on these bonds is r, the next instant you will have a gross return of rp_t. However, if the relative price of nontradable goods has increased over time (i.e., $\dot{p}_t > 0$), you will suffer a capital loss because your tradable bond will buy fewer nontradable goods. Therefore your net return will be $rp_t - \dot{p}_t$. To obtain the rate of return, you need to divide this net return by your initial investment, p_t, which yields the rate of return $r - \dot{p}_t/p_t$.[9] Naturally, if the relative price of nontradable goods does not vary over time (i.e., if $\dot{p}_t = 0$), then from (4.14), $r_t^d = r$.

Since the real interest rates relevant for the consumption decision of tradable and nontradable goods differ, it should be intuitively clear that the real interest rate relevant for a consumption

7. As discussed below, the domestic real interest rate can be thought of as the real interest rate in terms of nontradable goods.

8. In monetary models with sticky prices (chapter 8), we will see examples where this is the case.

9. Incidentally, notice how expression (4.14) tells us that the real interest rate burden for small open economies will be particularly high in bad times. In effect, bad times are typically accompanied by real depreciation (i.e., $\dot{p}_t < 0$) which, according to (4.14), will increase the real interest rate in terms of nontradable goods.

aggregate (i.e., an average of tradable and nontradable goods) will be some average of r and r_t^d. This real interest rate is referred to in the literature as the "consumption based real interest rate." Exercise 1 at the end of this chapter asks you to derive this expression in a discrete-time counterpart of this model. The main insight to be extracted from this exercise—which should be clear from the discussion above—is that if the relative price of nontradable goods is not constant over time, then aggregate consumption will not be constant over time even if the discount factor equals $1/(1+r)$.

4.2.2 Equilibrium Conditions

Since, by definition, the economy cannot import or export nontradable goods, equilibrium in the nontradable goods market requires that the consumption of nontradable goods be equal to the supply of nontradable goods in every period:

$$c_t^N = y_t^N. \tag{4.17}$$

Substituting condition (4.17) into (4.4), we obtain the current account:

$$\dot{b}_t = rb_t + y_t^T - c_t^T. \tag{4.18}$$

Note that the presence of nontradable goods does not change the expression for the current account that we encountered in chapter 1. This should clearly be the case since, by definition, nontradable goods are not traded with the rest of the world.

Substituting condition (4.17) into (4.5) yields the economy's intertemporal constraint (i.e., the resource constraint):

$$b_0 + \int_0^\infty y_t^T e^{-rt} dt = \int_0^\infty c_t^T e^{-rt} dt. \tag{4.19}$$

4.2.3 Perfect Foresight Equilibrium

The path of consumption of nontradable goods is fully determined by the path of nontradable goods endowment, as equation (4.17) makes clear. Substitute the nontradable goods market equilibrium condition into the first-order conditions (4.8) and (4.9) to obtain

$$u_{c^T}(c_t^T, y_t^N) = \lambda, \tag{4.20}$$

$$u_{c^N}(c_t^T, y_t^N) = \lambda p_t. \tag{4.21}$$

These two conditions, together with the intertemporal constraint (4.19) and the exogenous paths of y_t^T and y_t^N, fully determine the perfect foresight paths of c_t^T and p_t and the unique value of λ.

It follows from (4.20) that the path of y_t^N will determine the time *profile* of c_t^T (as opposed to the particular level which will be determined by the intertemporal budget constraint, given by equation 4.19). If the path of y_t^N is flat over time, then the path of c_t^T will also be flat over time. In this case—and as in chapter 1—the economy will run trade surpluses when the endowment of tradables is high and trade deficits when it is low. However, if the path of y_t^N fluctuates over time, then the path of c_t^T will also fluctuate over time. Formally, differentiate equation (4.20) along a perfect foresight equilibrium path (i.e., for a given λ) to obtain

$$\frac{dc_t^T}{dy_t^N} = -\frac{u_{c^Tc^N}(c_t^T, y_t^N)}{u_{c^Tc^T}(c_t^T, y_t^N)} \begin{cases} = 0, & \text{if } u_{c^Tc^N} = 0, \\ < 0, & \text{if } u_{c^Tc^N} < 0, \\ > 0, & \text{if } u_{c^Tc^N} > 0. \end{cases} \tag{4.22}$$

It follows that whether c_t^T is high or low when the endowment of nontradables is, say, high depends on whether c_t^T and c_t^N are Edgeworth substitutes, independent, or complements.[10] Specifically, consider the following three cases regarding the behavior of the trade balance:[11]

- *Tradables and nontradables are Edgeworth independent (i.e., $u_{c^Tc^N} = 0$)* In this case, the path of y_t^N has no effect on the path of c_t^T. We are thus back to the world of chapter 1: the path of c_t^T is flat over time and the economy will run trade surpluses when the endowment of tradables is high and deficits when the endowment of tradables is low, regardless of the path of y_t^N.
- *Tradables and nontradables are Edgeworth substitutes (i.e., $u_{c^Tc^N} < 0$)* In this case, when y_t^N is relatively high along a perfect foresight path, c_t^T is relatively low. If the path of y_t^T is relatively smooth (in figure 4.1 it has been drawn as flat), then the economy will run trade surpluses when output of nontradables is high and trade deficits when output of nontradables is low, as illustrated in figure 4.1.
- *Tradables and nontradables are Edgeworth complements (i.e., $u_{c^Tc^N} > 0$)* In this case, if the path of y_t^T is flat, then the economy will run trade surpluses when y_t^N is low and deficits when y_t^N is high.

In general equilibrium—and given the exogenously given path of y_t^N—the path of p_t will adjust so as to induce the consumer to choose the existing path of consumption of nontradable goods. From equations (4.20) and (4.21) the path of p_t is given by

$$p_t = \frac{u_{c^N}(c_t^T, y_t^N)}{u_{c^T}(c_t^T, y_t^N)}. \tag{4.23}$$

10. This is, of course, the same channel studied above but in a general equilibrium context.

11. Exercise 2 at the end of this chapter asks the reader to work out a specific example with CES preferences that shows how Edgeworth substitutability/complementarity depends on the relation between the intra- and intertemporal elasticities of substitution. The relationship between these two parameters will thus determine the behavior of the trade balance along a perfect foresight path with a fluctuating path of nontradables.

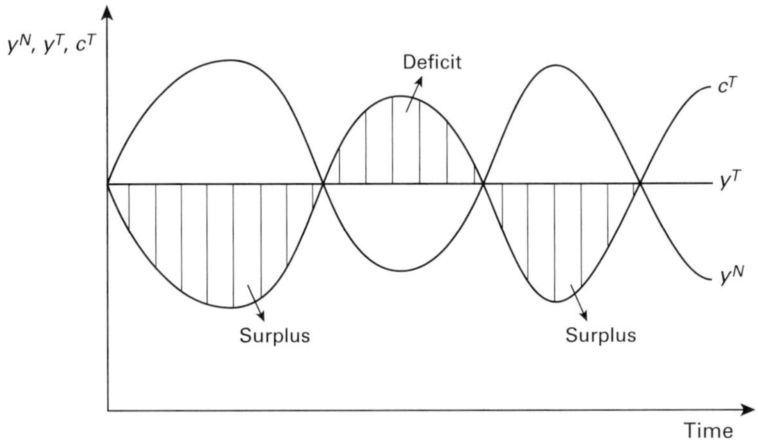

Figure 4.1
Perfect foresight paths

To figure out how fluctuations in y_t^N will affect p_t, totally differentiate (4.23) with respect to y^N and use (4.22) to obtain

$$\frac{dp_t}{dy_t^N} = \frac{1}{u_{c^T} u_{c^T c^T}} \underbrace{(u_{c^T c^T} u_{c^N c^N} - u^2_{c^T c^N})}_{+} < 0, \tag{4.24}$$

where the term in brackets is positive due to the strict concavity of the utility function. It follows that if, along a perfect foresight equilibrium, the endowment of nontradable goods increases, then the relative price of nontradable goods will fall.[12] Intuitively, at an unchanged relative price, there would be an excess supply of nontradable goods. To clear the market, the relative price needs to fall.

In sum—and relative to chapter 1—we have identified a new channel that affects an economy's desire to run trade imbalances. This channel is related to how changes in the endowment of nontradable goods affect the desire to consume tradable goods. Hence, in a general case where both the endowments of tradable and nontradable goods fluctuate over time, trade imbalances will be driven by both (1) the consumption-smoothing motive analyzed in chapter 1 and (2) the effects of fluctuations in the endowment of nontradable goods on tradable goods' consumption.

Given this new channel, a natural question that arises is the following: Could fluctuations in the supply of nontradable goods provide a possible explanation for the countercyclicality of the trade balance shown by the data? In other words—and in the world of chapter 1—could we

12. This is, of course, fully consistent with the partial equilibrium effects of p_t that we analyzed above. In other words, when y_t^N increases, p_t falls, and the consumer reacts in the way described by (4.10) and (4.11).

dispense with investment and still explain the countercyclical behavior of the trade balance? As exercise 2 at the end of this chapter makes clear, the answer is negative: under the most plausible parameterization of preferences, good times (i.e., times of high endowment of nontradable goods) will be associated with trade surpluses and bad times with trade deficits.

4.3 External Deficits and the Real Exchange Rate

An important question to ask in the presence of nontradable goods is the following: What is the relation between external imbalances (i.e., trade and current account imbalances) and the real exchange rate? In other words, will external deficits be accompanied by real appreciation? We will answer this question in the context of the basic model developed in section 4.2. But, to simplify the presentation, we will focus on the separable and logarithmic case.[13] The experiment to be carried out will be an unanticipated and temporary reduction in the endowment of both goods.

Let lifetime utility be given by

$$\int_0^\infty \left[\gamma \log(c_t^T) + (1-\gamma)\log(c_t^N)\right] e^{-\beta t} dt, \tag{4.25}$$

where $\gamma \in (0, 1)$ is a preference parameter. The flow and intertemporal constraints continue to be given by equations (4.4) and (4.5).

Under these preferences first-order conditions (4.8) and (4.9) reduce to

$$\frac{\gamma}{c_t^T} = \lambda, \tag{4.26}$$

$$\frac{1-\gamma}{c_t^N} = \lambda p_t. \tag{4.27}$$

Combining these two conditions, we obtain

$$\frac{c_t^N}{c_t^T} = \left(\frac{1-\gamma}{\gamma}\right)\frac{1}{p_t}. \tag{4.28}$$

As will become clear below, this condition can be interpreted as a demand function for nontradable goods relative to tradable goods. As in standard consumer theory, this demand function depends negatively on the relative price of nontradables, p_t.

The economy's equilibrium conditions continue to be given by equations (4.17), (4.18), and (4.19).

13. Exercise 3 at the end of the chapter shows that Edgeworth substitutability is a sufficient (though not necessary) condition for the same results to go through for a general utility function.

4.3.1 Initial Stationary Equilibrium

Suppose that the endowment of both tradables and nontradables is constant over time (i.e., $y_t^T = y^T$ and $y_t^N = y^N$). Equation (4.26) then says that c_t^T will be constant over time at a level given by (4.19):

$$c^T = rb_0 + y^T. \tag{4.29}$$

From (4.17) the equilibrium value of nontradable goods is given by the constant value of the endowment

$$c^N = y^N. \tag{4.30}$$

Combining (4.28), (4.29), and (4.30) yields the reduced form for the relative price of nontradable goods:

$$p = \left(\frac{1-\gamma}{\gamma}\right)\frac{rb_0 + y^T}{y^N}. \tag{4.31}$$

The determination of the relative price of nontradable goods, p, is best understood in terms of a familiar supply and demand diagram. Figure 4.2 depicts the supply and demand for nontradable *relative* to tradable goods. The demand function is given by (4.28), which, expressed in more familiar terms, takes the form

$$D(p) = \left(\frac{1-\gamma}{\gamma}\right)\frac{1}{p}.$$

Since there is no production in this economy, the supply function is a vertical line, given by

$$S(p) = \frac{y^N}{rb_0 + y^T}.$$

Notice that since the initial stock of net foreign assets, b_0, constitutes a claim for tradable goods on the rest of the world, it must be part of the "supply" of tradable goods. The intersection of these two curves, $D(p) = S(p)$, yields the equilibrium value of p (point A in figure 4.2).

4.3.2 Comparative Statics

Three simple experiments will help us understand how the relative price of nontradable goods is determined:

- Consider first an unanticipated and permanent increase in the supply of tradable goods. Since the change is permanent, the equilibrium discussed above remains valid (for the new value of y^T).

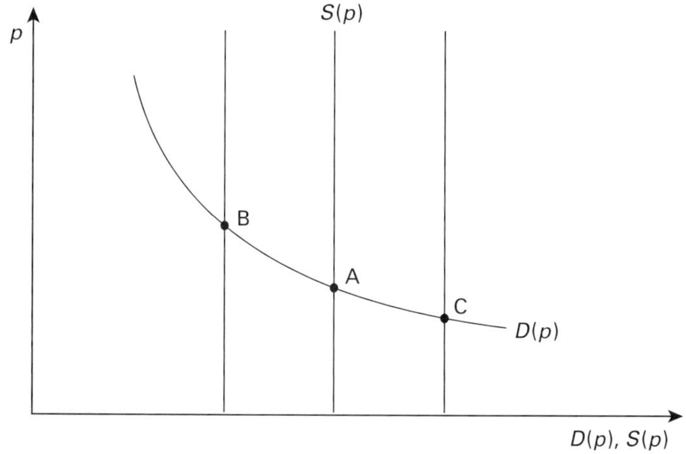

Figure 4.2
Determination of relative price of nontradable goods

As expected, consumption of tradable goods will increase one for one with the increase in y^T, as equation (4.29) makes clear. The equilibrium relative price of nontradable goods will also increase, as follows from (4.31). Intuitively—and in terms of figure 4.2—a permanent increase in y^T shows up as a leftward shift of the vertical supply schedule. At the initial value of p, there is an excess demand for nontradable goods. Hence the relative price of nontradable goods must increase to clear the market once again. In the new equilibrium (point B) the relative price is higher than initially

- Consider an unanticipated and permanent increase in the supply of nontradable goods. In terms of figure 4.2, this shock would show up as a rightward shift of the vertical supply schedule. At the initial relative price, there would be an excess supply of nontradable goods. To clear the market, p needs to fall to increase the demand for nontradables (point C).
- Finally, consider an unanticipated and permanent increase in the demand for tradable goods (i.e., an increase in γ). In terms of figure 4.2, this shock would manifest itself as a leftward shift of the demand curve (not drawn), which would lead to a lower p. Intuitively, at the initial relative price, there would be an excess supply of nontradables, which calls for a lower equilibrium relative price.[14]

Notice that in all three cases there are no external imbalances because the economy adjusts instantaneously to permanent shocks.

14. Exercise 4 at the end of the chapter illustrates a case where tradables act as an input in the production of nontradables (which are the only consumption good). Then an exogenous increase in the demand for nontradables also leads to an increase in the relative price of nontradables.

4.3.3 Temporary Fall in Supply

While the permanent shocks just studied are helpful for understanding how different shocks affect the real exchange rate, they cannot shed any light on the relation between external imbalances and the real exchange rate because permanent shocks cause the economy to jump from one stationary equilibrium to another. For these purposes we need to study temporary shocks.

Suppose that the economy is initially in the stationary equilibrium described above. Let, for simplicity, $b_0 = 0$. At $t = 0$, there is an unanticipated and temporary (equiproportional) fall in the endowment of both goods (i.e., both y_t^T and y_t^N fall but the ratio y_t^T/y_t^N remains unchanged), as depicted in figure 4.3, panel a.[15]

What happens to the endogenous variables at time T? Clearly, c_t^T remains constant at T as follows from (4.26). We also know from (4.27)—by taking into account (4.30)—that $p_t y_t^N$ remains constant at T. Hence, since y_t^N increases at time T, p_t falls at time T.

Given that the path of c_t^T is flat from time 0 onward and that the present discounted value of tradable resources has fallen, we know that c_t^T will fall at time 0 (figure 4.3, panel b). The path of c_t^N simply follows the path of y_t^N (figure 4.3, panel c).

What happens to p_t on impact? From (4.28), we know that

$$p_t = \left(\frac{1-\gamma}{\gamma}\right)\frac{c_t^T}{c_t^N}.$$

It follows that p_t will increase at time $t = 0$ because, while c_t^N falls by the same amount as y_t^N does, c_t^T falls by less (i.e., it falls by the annuity value of the fall in y_t^T). At time T, p_t falls below its initial level (figure 4.3, panel d).[16]

The path of the trade balance follows from the paths of y_t^T and c_t^T (see figure 4.3, panel e). The economy runs a trade deficit between time 0 and time T and a surplus afterward. The path of the current account follows immediately from that of the trade balance. At $t = 0$, the current account goes into deficit, and then the deficit increases over time as the economy accumulates debt and debt service increases. At $t = T$, the increase in y_t^T is such that the current account becomes balanced.

The punchline of this experiment is that trade deficits go hand in hand with real appreciation while trade surpluses go hand in hand with real depreciation. This association between trade deficits and real appreciation is intuitively clear: on impact, there is an excess demand for both goods, which leads to a trade deficit (the economy imports from abroad the desired tradable goods) and a real appreciation (the relative price of nontradable goods must increase to clear the market).

15. We study an equiproportional change to abstract from effects caused by changes in the *relative* supply of tradable and nontradable goods.

16. We know this because at time T, c_t^N has returned to its pre-shock value, while c_t^T remains below its pre-shock value.

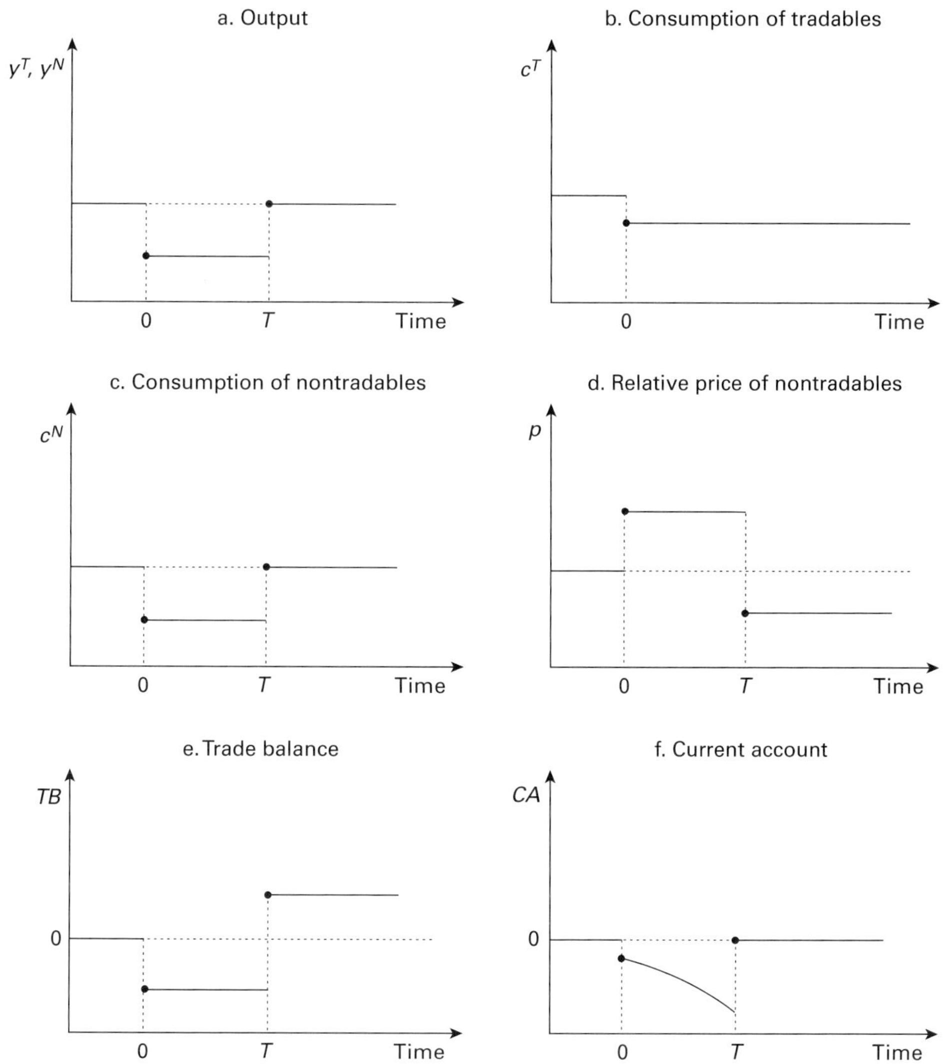

Figure 4.3
Temporary and proportional fall in output

Put differently, the excess demand for tradable goods is fully met by a quantity adjustment whereas the excess demand for nontradable goods is fully met by a relative price adjustment.

In the context of this paradigm, an important corollary is that the commonly held view that real appreciation "causes" trade deficits (or, conversely, that real depreciation "causes" trade surpluses) would be incorrect. Here trade deficits and real appreciation (or trade surpluses and real depreciation) are simply an equilibrium response to a common shock; there is no causality whatsoever.[17]

The same association between trade imbalances and the real exchange rate would emerge in response to a temporary demand shock that increases the demand for both tradable and nontradable goods. (Exercise 5 at the end of this chapter asks you to work out this case.) Intuitively, on impact, a positive demand shock increases the demand for both tradable and nontradable goods. While the excess demand for tradable goods can be met by importing goods from abroad (i.e., by running a trade deficit), the excess demand for nontradable goods must be choked off by an increase in the relative price of nontradable goods (i.e., a real appreciation).

4.4 Fiscal Policy, Trade Imbalances, and the Real Exchange Rate

Will a fiscal contraction lead to a real depreciation? Will a fiscal expansion cause a trade deficit? This section will seek to answer these key policy questions regarding the effects of fiscal policy. To this effect, we incorporate government spending into our basic model with logarithmic preferences. To isolate the effects of changes in government spending on the real exchange rate, we will assume that government spending is financed by lump-sum taxation.[18]

4.4.1 Consumers

We continue to work with the logarithmic preferences given in (4.25). As far as the consumer is concerned, the only modification of the model is that he/she is subject to lump-sum taxes, ψ_t. The flow constraint, (4.4), will now read as

$$\dot{b}_t = rb_t + y_t^T + p_t y_t^N - c_t^T - p_t c_t^N - \psi_t. \tag{4.32}$$

By the same token, the intertemporal constraint will now be given by

$$b_0 + \int_0^\infty (y_t^T + p_t y_t^N - \psi_t)e^{-rt}dt = \int_0^\infty (c_t^T + p_t c_t^N)e^{-rt}dt. \tag{4.33}$$

17. To see models where one could meaningfully argue that real appreciations "cause" trade deficits under certain circumstances, we will need to wait until chapter 8 where we will introduce sticky prices in monetary models.

18. The effects of distortionary taxation will be studied in chapter 10.

It should be clear that the introduction of lump-sum taxation does not affect the consumer's first-order conditions, which continue to be given by (4.26) and (4.27).

4.4.2 Government

Up to this point in this chapter, the government has played no role. It now comes into action. The government spends on both tradable (g_t^T) and nontradable goods (g_t^N) and finances this spending with lump-sum taxes, ψ_t. While g_t^T and g_t^N are assumed to be policy variables (i.e., they are exogenous variables), the path of ψ_t will be endogenously determined so as to satisfy the government budget constraint. To simplify the presentation, we will assume that the government has no initial debt and that it balances its budget period by period:

$$\psi_t = g_t^T + p_t g_t^N. \tag{4.34}$$

4.4.3 Equilibrium Conditions

Equilibrium in the nontradable goods sector requires that

$$c_t^N + g_t^N = y_t^N. \tag{4.35}$$

Combining the consumer's flow constraint (4.32) with the government's (4.34) and imposing (4.35), we obtain the flow constraint for the economy as a whole (i.e., the current account):

$$\dot{b}_t = rb_t + y_t^T - c_t^T - g_t^T. \tag{4.36}$$

Similarly, by substituting the government's constraint (4.34) into the consumer's intertemporal budget constraint (4.33) and imposing equilibrium in the nontradable goods market (condition 4.35), we obtain the economy's resource constraint:

$$b_0 + \int_0^\infty y_t^T e^{-rt} dt = \int_0^\infty (c_t^T + g_t^T) e^{-rt} dt. \tag{4.37}$$

4.4.4 Perfect Foresight Equilibrium

Along a perfect foresight equilibrium, consumption of tradable goods will be constant, as follows from condition (4.26). Taking into account the resource constraint (4.37), we obtain a reduced form for c^T:

$$c^T = r\left[b_0 + \int_0^\infty \left(y_t^T - g_t^T\right) e^{-rt} dt\right]. \tag{4.38}$$

The path of consumption of nontradable goods follows directly from the equilibrium in the nontradable goods market, equation (4.35):

$$c_t^N = y_t^N - g_t^N. \tag{4.39}$$

From (4.28), (4.38), and (4.39), we obtain a reduced form for p_t:

$$p_t = \left(\frac{1-\gamma}{\gamma}\right) \frac{r\left[b_0 + \int_0^\infty \left(y_t^T - g_t^T\right) e^{-rt} dt\right]}{y_t^N - g_t^N}. \tag{4.40}$$

Some important observations follow from this characterization of the perfect foresight equilibrium. First, equation (4.40) makes clear that the path of p_t depends only on the present discounted value of g_t^T, and not on the particular time path of g_t^T. The reason is that from the consumer's standpoint, he/she only cares about how much tradable resources the government is taking away from him/her in present value terms. The path of g_t^T is irrelevant because, as in chapter 1, the consumer will smooth out this negative shock over time. In contrast, the path of g_t^N will affect the relative price of nontradable goods. All else equal, when g_t^N is high (low), p_t will also be high (low). Intuitively, periods of, say, high g_t^N imply a reduced supply of nontradable goods available to the private sector. The resulting excess demand for nontradable goods must lead to an increase in their relative price.

Second, given the exogenous paths of g_t^T and g_t^N and the path of p_t determined by equation (4.40), the government's flow constraint determines the level of lump-sum taxes:

$$\psi_t = g_t^T + p_t g_t^N. \tag{4.41}$$

4.4.5 Comparative Statics

To analyze the effects of permanent changes in government spending, let us first derive the perfect foresight path corresponding to a constant path of the exogenous variables. Suppose then that $y_t^T = y^T$, $y_t^N = y^N$, $g_t^T = g^T$, and $g_t^N = g^N$. Given these constant paths, the perfect foresight equilibrium characterized by equations (4.38), (4.39), (4.40), and (4.41) reduces to (set also $b_0 = 0$):

$$c^T = y^T - g^T, \tag{4.42}$$

$$c^N = y^N - g^N, \tag{4.43}$$

$$p = \left(\frac{1-\gamma}{\gamma}\right) \frac{y^T - g^T}{y^N - g^N}, \tag{4.44}$$

$$\psi = g^T + \left(\frac{1-\gamma}{\gamma}\right)\left(\frac{y^T - g^T}{y^N - g^N}\right) g^N. \tag{4.45}$$

What will be the effects of unanticipated and permanent changes in g^T and g^N? The answer is, of course, straightforward since the new perfect foresight equilibrium will also be characterized by equations (4.42) to (4.45). A permanent increase in g^T will thus lead to a one-for-one reduction in c^T and a fall in p. To understand this result intuitively, we can resort again to figure 4.2 and think of the vertical supply schedule as depicting $(y^N - g^N)/(y^T - g^T)$. In this case an increase in g^T would imply a rightward shift of the vertical supply schedule. At the initial value of p there would be an excess supply of nontradable goods, which requires a fall in p. Similarly, an unanticipated and permanent increase in g^N leads to a one-for-one fall in c^N and a rise in p. In terms of figure 4.2, the higher g^N would lead to a leftward shift of the vertical supply schedule. Hence at the initial relative price there is an excess demand for nontradable goods, which requires an increase in the relative price, p.

In practice, however, governments normally change *total* government spending, as opposed to spending on either tradables or nontradables. What will be the effect of an increase in total government spending on the real exchange rate? To answer this question in a simple and illuminating way, suppose that the government sets an overall level of spending equal to g (expressed in terms of tradable goods) and spends in fixed proportions:

$$g^T = \alpha g, \tag{4.46}$$

$$pg^N = (1 - \alpha)g, \tag{4.47}$$

where $0 \leq \alpha \leq 1$ denotes the proportion of government spending spent on tradable goods and $1 - \alpha$ the proportion spent on nontradable goods. Substituting (4.46) and (4.47) into (4.44), it follows that

$$p = \frac{1-\gamma}{\gamma}\frac{y^T}{y^N} + \frac{g}{y^N}\left(1 - \frac{\alpha}{\gamma}\right).$$

In response to an unanticipated and permanent increase in g, the change in p will be given by

$$\frac{dp}{dg} = \frac{1 - (\alpha/\gamma)}{y^N} = \begin{cases} 0, & \alpha = \gamma, \\ < 0, & \alpha > \gamma, \\ > 0, & \alpha < \gamma. \end{cases}$$

The effect of g on p thus depends on the *composition* of government spending relative to the *composition* of private spending. To see this, notice that we can rewrite the intratemporal condition (4.28) as

$$\frac{c^T}{pc^N} = \frac{\gamma}{1-\gamma},$$

which implies that the private sector spends a fraction γ of consumption expenditures on tradables and a fraction $1 - \gamma$ on nontradables. If government spending is biased toward tradable goods (i.e., $\alpha > \gamma$), then an increase in g would lead to a lower p. If government spending is biased toward nontradable goods (i.e., $\alpha < \gamma$), then an increase in g would lead to a higher p. If the government spends in the same proportion as the private sector ($\alpha = \gamma$), then there is no change in p.

What is the intuition behind these results? When the government increases spending, it takes away those resources from the private sector. Given this fall in income, the private sector reduces the demand for tradable and nontradable goods in a proportion given by $\gamma/(1-\gamma)$. If the government, in turn, spends in the same proportion, the market for nontradable goods will clear at the initial relative price. If, in contrast, the government spends a higher fraction of these resources on nontradables (which is the case when $\alpha < \gamma$), then there will be an excess demand for nontradable goods, which will require a rise in p to clear the market. If the government spends a lower fraction on nontradables ($\alpha > \gamma$), then there will be an excess supply for nontradable goods, which will lead to a fall in the relative price.[19]

Given that, in practice, government spending is biased in favor of nontradable goods, we can conclude that there is indeed a theoretical presumption that a reduction in government spending will lead to a fall in the relative price of nontradable goods (i.e., a real depreciation). But, from a policy point of view, the question remains: Will the *quantitative* effect of a fiscal contraction on the real exchange rate be large enough to merit such an action? This is, of course, an important empirical question that has been addressed in the literature (see box 4.1). While estimates vary from study to study, the overall message is that this policy action could indeed have some significant effects on the real exchange rate.

4.4.6 Fiscal Expansions and Trade Deficits

An important policy issue is the "twin deficits" hypothesis, which refers to the idea that budget deficits and trade deficits tend to occur simultaneously because, to some extent, the former causes the latter. While in our model the budget is balanced by assumption, we can still investigate one aspect of this issue: do increases in government spending lead to trade deficits? To answer this question, we need to look at temporary changes in government spending.[20] We will first consider changes in g_t^T and then in g_t^N.

Temporary Changes in Government Spending on Tradable Goods

Suppose that the economy is initially in the stationary equilibrium characterized by equations (4.42), (4.43), and (4.44). At time 0 there is an unanticipated and temporary increase in g_t^T (figure 4.4, panel a).

19. In this case, providing intuition in terms of figure 4.2 is not very appealing because, given (4.46) and (4.47), the net supply schedule now depends on p itself.

20. Permanent changes in government spending would, of course, result in no change in the external accounts.

Box 4.1
How much does a fiscal contraction lower the relative price of nontradables?

Estimating the impact of changes in fiscal spending on the real exchange rate has proved difficult because the magnitude of the effect depends critically on variables that are difficult to quantify. Table 4.1 summarizes some of the main studies.

Two different methodologies can be found in the literature. The first one is to derive equations from a model and test them econometrically. The link between the model and the regressions, however, varies from study to study, and in some cases there is no explicit theoretical framework to accompany the econometric estimation. A second approach consists of calibrating a theoretical model by mapping observable characteristics of the economy into "deep parameters" (the real business cycle approach described in box 1.2 of chapter 1). The calibrated model shows the reaction of the variables of interest to different shocks.

The first method has been more popular and has produced a variety of results for different countries. In addition to some measure of government spending, the regressions typically incorporate various

Table 4.1
Effects of government spending on real exchange rate

Country(ies)	Point estimation[a]	Dataset	Methodology	Author(s)
8 European countries	−2.1 to −3.5	Annual 1979–1989	Panel	Froot and Rogoff (1991)
Japan	Not significant	Quarterly 1975.1–1990.3	Cointegration analysis	Rogoff (1992)
Chile	−0.8	Calibration	Calibration	Arrau et al. (1992)
Chile	−3.1	Quarterly 1982.1–1993.4	Cointegration analysis	Arellano and Larrain (1996)
12 Latin American countries	−0.3	Annual 1962–1984	Panel data, fixed effects	Edwards (1989)
9 Asian countries	Not significant	Annual 1970–1991	Error correction regressions, nonlinear least squares	Chinn (1997)
14 OECD countries	−2 to −5	Annual 1970–1985	SUR	De Gregorio and Wolf (1994)
United States and United Kingdom	Not significant	Annual 1779–1914	VAR	Kaminsky and Klein (1994)
United States	0.5	Quarterly 1973:1–2004:1	VAR	Kim and Roubini (2008)
United States, United Kingdom, Canada, and Australia	−0.3 to 0.6	Quarterly 1980:1–2006:4	VAR	Monacelli and Perotti (2010)

a. Percent response of real exchange rate to a permanent 1 percent increase in the ratio of government spending to GDP. A negative coefficient implies a real appreciation.

Box 4.1
(continued)

control variables, such as terms of trade and productivity differentials among sectors. Overall, the results tend to confirm that in Latin America and the OECD countries there is a negative impact of government spending on the real exchange rate (i.e., a contraction in government spending leads to a real depreciation). This is, of course, consistent with the result derived in the text under the assumption that government spending is more biased toward nontradable goods than private spending, as is likely to be the case in practice, given heavy government spending on health, education, and services.

In the studies conducted for Asia, however, no significant relationship has been found. Given our theoretical framework, one might conclude that Asian governments have a stronger preference for spending on tradable goods. As a matter of fact, there is some evidence that points in that direction, since the share of public investment in GDP—a component of spending intensive in tradable goods—is systematically higher in Asia than in other developing regions such as Latin America (Bouton and Sumlinski 1997). There are some studies, however, that show the opposite effect of government spending on the real exchange rate. Kim and Roubini (2008) and Monacelli and Perotti (2010) show that, in the United States, United Kingdom, Canada, and Australia, a rise in government spending leads to a real depreciation. They argue that the key failure of the standard model lies in the equilibrium behavior of private consumption. In the model a negative wealth effect causes private consumption to fall in response to a rise in government spending, whereas the opposite is true in the data.

While the second approach has been much less common in the literature, it has provided key insights on the differential effect of permanent and temporary shocks. For the case of Chile, Arrau et al. (1992) shows that a 1 percent temporary increase in government spending leads to a real appreciation of 1 percent, compared to 0.8 percent if the change is permanent. This finding is in line with our conceptual framework, as temporary changes in government spending imply a smaller permanent reduction in the consumption of tradables (and thus a higher transitory increase in the relative price of nontradables).

There are some avenues still to be explored in this empirical literature that go beyond our basic benchmark model. For instance, some authors have suggested that effects might vary with the exchange rate regime. Kaminsky and Klein (1994) provide evidence in that direction for the Gold Standard era. Other issues that need more attention are the sources of government financing and interest rate effects associated with variations in the credibility of the government.

Given first-order condition (4.26), we know that the path of c_t^T will be constant along the new perfect foresight equilibrium path and given by equation (4.38). Since the present discounted value of g_t^T has increased, the new level of c_t^T will be lower than initially (figure 4.4, panel b).

The path of consumption of nontradable goods remains flat (figure 4.4, panel c) because there has been no change in the endowment path of nontradables. As a result the relative price of nontradable goods falls on impact and remains flat thereafter (figure 4.4, panel d). Intuitively, due to the fall in the present discounted value of tradable resources available to the private sector, there is an excess demand for tradable goods relative to nontradable goods, which requires, in equilibrium, a higher relative price of tradable goods (i.e., a lower relative price of nontradable goods).

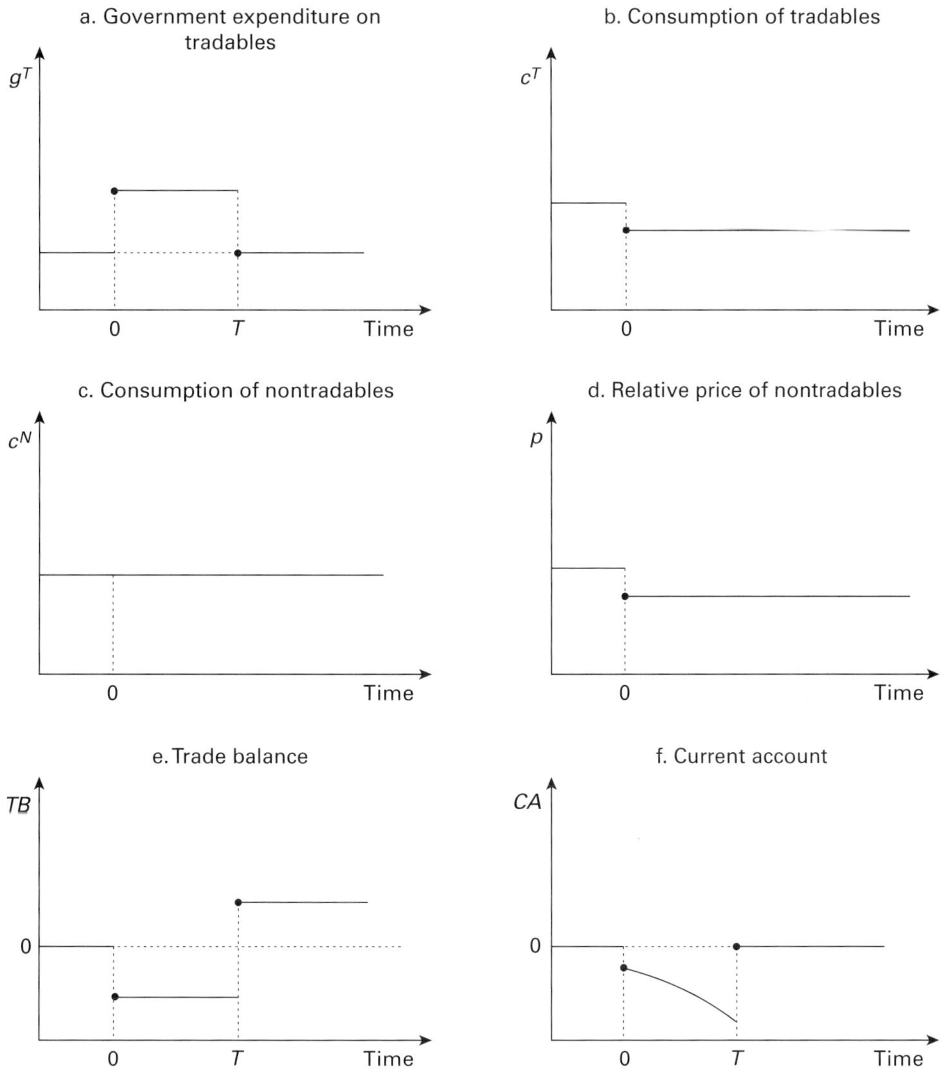

Figure 4.4
Temporary increase in government expenditure on tradable goods

What happens to the trade balance? Recall that the trade balance is given by

$$TB_t = y^T - c_t^T - g_t^T.$$

Since c_t^T falls at time 0 by less than g_t^T increases (notice from equation 4.38 that c_t^T falls only by the permanent component of the increase in g_t^T), the trade balance worsens at time 0 (figure 4.4, panel e). At time T the trade balance improves as g_t^T falls but c_t^T does not change. The corresponding path of the current account is illustrated in figure 4.4, panel f.

We thus conclude that a temporary increase in g_t^T leads indeed to a trade deficit. Intuitively, an increase in g_t^T is like a negative supply shock in chapter 1. To smooth out consumption, the consumer will run a trade deficit. Exercise 6 at the end of this chapter shows that it is straightforward to extend this result and establish a link between budget deficits and trade deficits validating the twin deficits hypothesis.

Temporary Changes in Government Spending on Nontradable Goods

Would the same association between increases in government spending and trade deficits hold if the increase in government spending were on nontradable goods? To answer this question, we need to consider the general preferences specified in equation (4.1), rather than those given by (4.25). We will further assume that tradables and nontradables are Edgeworth substitutes; that is, $u_{c^Tc^N} < 0$.[21] Under these general preferences, the consumer's first-order conditions are given by equations (4.8) and (4.9). The rest of the model remains unchanged.

Imposing the equilibrium condition in the nontradable goods markets (assuming a constant path for the endowment of nontradables, given by equation 4.35), we can rewrite the first-order conditions as

$$u_{c^T}(c_t^T, y^N - g_t^N) = \lambda, \tag{4.48}$$

$$u_{c^N}(c_t^T, y^N - g_t^N) = \lambda p_t. \tag{4.49}$$

Combining these two equations, we obtain

$$p_t = \frac{u_{c^N}(c_t^T, y^N - g_t^N)}{u_{c^T}(c_t^T, y^N - g_t^N)}. \tag{4.50}$$

Suppose that, starting from a stationary equilibrium, there is an unanticipated and temporary increase in g_t^N at time 0 (figure 4.5, panel a). Naturally, the path of c_t^N follows directly from the path of g_t^N and the nontradable goods market equilibrium, as illustrated in figure 4.5, panel b.

21. As will become clear below, the assumption of Edgeworth substitutability is the one that generates empirically plausible results.

What happens at time T? To find out, totally differentiate equation (4.48) to obtain

$$\left.\frac{dc_t^T}{dg_t^N}\right|_{t=T} = \frac{u_{c^T c^N}}{u_{c^T c^T}} > 0. \tag{4.51}$$

Notice that the sign of this expression crucially depends on the assumption that tradable and nontradable goods are Edgeworth substitutes (i.e., $u_{c^T c^N} < 0$). Hence at time T, when g_t^N falls back to its initial level, c_t^T will also fall. Since the present discounted value of tradable resources has not changed relative to the pre-shock level, we infer that c_t^T rises at $t = 0$ and then follows the path illustrated in figure 4.5, panel c.

How does p_t change at time T? Totally differentiate optimality condition (4.49) and use (4.51) to obtain

$$\left.\frac{dp_t}{dg_t^N}\right|_{t=T} = -\frac{1}{\lambda u_{c^T c^T}}\underbrace{\left(u_{c^T c^T} u_{c^N c^N} - u_{c^T c^N}^2\right)}_{+} > 0, \tag{4.52}$$

by strict concavity of the utility function.[22] Hence, when g_t^N falls at time T, p_t also falls.

How will the level of p_t at time T compare to the pre-shock level? Since we know that, at time T, g_t^N is back to its pre-shock level and c_t^T is lower, we can simply differentiate the optimality condition (4.50) with respect to c_t^T holding constant g_t^N to obtain

$$\left.\frac{dp_t}{dc_t^T}\right|_{\text{constant } g^N} = \frac{1}{u_{c^T}^2}\underbrace{\left(u_{c^T} u_{c^T c^N} - u_{c^N} u_{c^T c^T}\right)}_{+} > 0,$$

where the sign of the term in brackets follows from the assumption that c_t^N is a normal good (recall condition 4.3). Hence p_t at time T will be lower than before the shock. Intuitively, the lower level of c_t^T (compared to its pre-shock level) needs to be accommodated, in equilibrium, by a higher relative price of tradable goods (i.e., a lower p_t).

How will p_t react on impact? To figure this out, differentiate (4.50) with respect to c_t^T and g_t^N to obtain

$$\left.\frac{dp_t}{dg_t^N}\right|_{t=0} = \frac{1}{u_{c^T}^2}\left[\underbrace{\left(u_{c^N} u_{c^T c^N} - u_{c^T} u_{c^N c^N}\right)}_{+} + \underbrace{\left(u_{c^T} u_{c^N c^T} - u_{c^N} u_{c^T c^T}\right)}_{+}\underbrace{\left.\frac{dc_t^T}{dg_t^N}\right|_{t=0}}_{+}\right] > 0,$$

22. As we should have expected (and given 4.48), this expression is the same as (4.24) but with opposite sign.

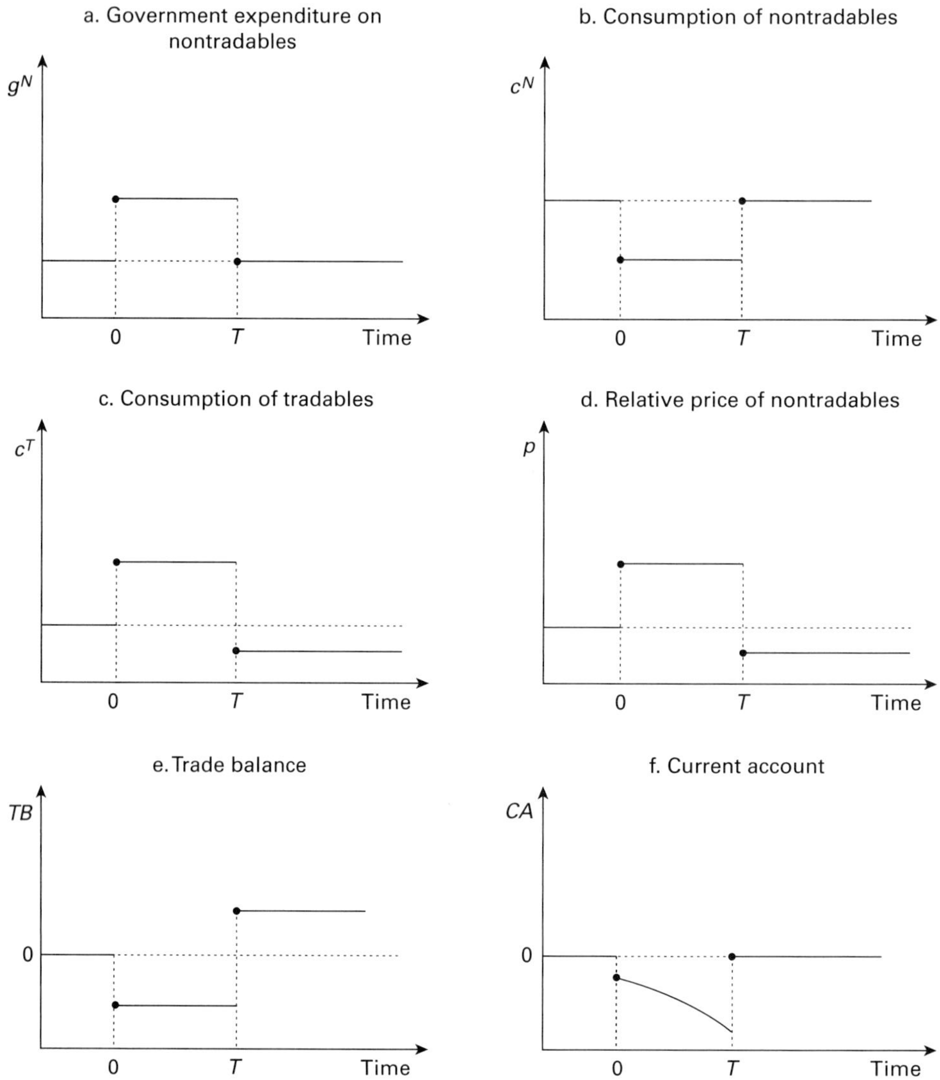

Figure 4.5
Temporary increase in government expenditure on nontradable goods

where, as indicated, the sign of the terms in brackets follows from the assumption that c_t^T and c_t^N are normal goods (recall conditions 4.2 and 4.3) and, from figure 4.5, panel c, we know that dc_t^T/dg_t^N at $t = 0$ is positive.[23] Hence, on impact, the relative price of nontradable goods will increase, as illustrated in figure 4.5, panel d. Intuitively, there are two forces acting on p_t at $t = 0$ that reinforce each other. First, the increase in g_t^N leads to a reduction in the supply of nontradable goods available to the private sector. The resulting excess demand for nontradables would lead to an increase in p_t. Second, the rise in c_t^T means that, at the pre-shock relative price, there is also an excess demand for c_t^N (to keep the marginal rate of substitution constant), which should also lead to an increase in p_t.

The path of the trade balance (figure 4.5, panel e) follows directly from that of c_t^T. The corresponding path of the current account is illustrated in figure 4.5, panel f.

We thus conclude that, provided that the consumption of tradable and nontradable goods are Edgeworth substitutes (i.e., $u_{c^Tc^N} < 0$), a temporary increase in g_t^N leads to a trade deficit.[24] The channel through which this happens is precisely the one that we studied in section 4.2 when we discussed the effects that fluctuations in the endowment of nontradable goods may have on the trade balance. Intuitively, an increase in g_t^N reduces nontradable resources available to the private sector and reduces c_t^N. If c_t^T and c_t^N are Edgeworth substitutes, then a reduction in c_t^N increases the marginal utility of consuming tradable goods, which leads to a higher c_t^T and hence to a trade deficit.

4.5 Resource Reallocation and Relative Prices

This section modifies the basic model introduced in section 4.2 by endogeneizing production. We will assume that there is one scarce factor of production (labor) that must be allocated to the production of either tradable or nontradable goods. Labor services are nontradable internationally. To simplify the exposition—and since it is not central to this section's message—we will also assume that labor supply is exogenous (i.e., leisure does not enter the utility function).

The key feature that we wish to highlight in this section is the role of the relative price of nontradable goods in guiding the allocation of the scarce factor among sectors.

4.5.1 Consumer's Problem

The lifetime utility of the representative individual is given by

$$\int_0^\infty \left[\log(c_t^T) + \log(c_t^N)\right] e^{-\beta t} dt. \tag{4.53}$$

23. Notice that we cannot use expression (4.51)—which we use to derive equation (4.52)—because expression (4.51) only holds at time T.

24. It is worth noticing, though, that the path of p_t is not dependent on the sign of the cross-derivative.

The flow constraint of the consumer is given by

$$\dot{b}_t = rb_t + y_t^T + p_t y_t^N - c_t^T - p_t c_t^N, \tag{4.54}$$

where y_t^T and y_t^N denote the production of tradable and nontradable goods, respectively.

Production takes place according to the following technologies:

$$y_t^T = Z_t^T (n_t^T)^\alpha, \qquad 0 < \alpha < 1, \tag{4.55}$$

$$y_t^N = Z_t^N n_t^N, \tag{4.56}$$

where Z_t^T and Z_t^N are productivity parameters, n_t^T and n_t^N denote the amount of labor used in each sector, and α captures decreasing returns to scale in the production of tradable goods.[25]

Finally, there is the labor supply constraint:

$$n_t = n_t^T + n_t^N, \tag{4.57}$$

where n_t is the (exogenously given) endowment of labor.

Integrating forward equation (4.54), we can write the individual's intertemporal budget constraint as

$$\int_0^\infty (c_t^T + p_t c_t^N) e^{-rt} dt = b_0 + \int_0^\infty (y_t^T + p_t y_t^N) e^{-rt} dt. \tag{4.58}$$

The consumer's problem consists in choosing $\{c_t^T, c_t^N, n_t^T, n_t^N\}$ for all $t \in [0, \infty)$ to maximize lifetime utility (4.53), subject to (4.55), (4.56), (4.57), and (4.58), for a given path of Z_t^T, Z_t^N, n_t, and a given b_0. We set up the Lagrangian as[26]

$$\begin{aligned}\mathcal{L} = &\int_0^\infty \left[\log(c_t^T) + \log(c_t^N)\right] e^{-\beta t} dt + \lambda \left\{ b_0 + \int_0^\infty \left[Z_t^T (n_t^T)^\alpha + p_t Z_t^N n_t^N\right] e^{-rt} dt \right. \\ &\left. - \int_0^\infty (c_t^T + p_t c_t^N) e^{-rt} dt \right\} + \int_0^\infty e^{-rt} \mu_t (n_t - n_t^T - n_t^N) dt.\end{aligned}$$

The first-order conditions are given by

$$\frac{1}{c_t^T} = \lambda, \tag{4.59}$$

25. To simplify the presentation, we assume that the production technology for nontradable goods is linear (in practice, the nontradable sector is indeed more labor intensive than the tradable sector). This is not critical, however, for the results derived in the text. Indeed, as exercise 7 at the end of this chapter asks you to verify, the same results would go through regardless of which sector is more labor intensive (or if they are equally intensive). As analyzed in the same exercise, labor intensity would matter, however, for the effects of an increase in the labor supply.

26. We multiply the multiplier μ_t by e^{-rt} so that μ_t is expressed in current value terms (rather than present discounted value terms). Of course, results are the same regardless of how we set up this multiplier.

$$\frac{1}{c_t^N} = \lambda p_t, \tag{4.60}$$

$$\lambda \alpha Z_t^T (n_t^T)^{\alpha-1} = \mu_t,$$

$$\lambda p_t Z_t^N = \mu_t.$$

Combining the last two conditions yields the production efficiency condition:

$$\alpha Z_t^T (n_t^T)^{\alpha-1} = p_t Z_t^N. \tag{4.61}$$

This condition says that, at an optimum, the marginal productivity of labor must be the same across the two sectors. If this were not the case, it would be optimal to reallocate labor from the low marginal productivity sector to the high marginal productivity sector.

4.5.2 Equilibrium Conditions

In equilibrium the consumption of nontradables must equal the production of nontradable goods:

$$c_t^N = y_t^N. \tag{4.62}$$

Combining equations (4.54) and (4.62) yields the economy's current account:

$$\dot{b}_t = rb_t + y_t^T - c_t^T. \tag{4.63}$$

From (4.58) and (4.62), we obtain the intertemporal constraint of the economy:

$$\int_0^\infty c_t^T e^{-rt} dt = b_0 + \int_0^\infty y_t^T e^{-rt} dt. \tag{4.64}$$

4.5.3 Perfect Foresight Equilibrium

Let us characterize a perfect foresight equilibrium for a constant path of the exogenous variables, Z_t^T, Z_t^N, and n_t, denoted by Z^T, Z^N, and n, respectively.

From equation (4.59), it is easy to establish that c_t^T will be constant over time. Taking into account equations (4.56), (4.57), (4.59), (4.60), and (4.62), write equation (4.61) as

$$\alpha(n - n_t^T) Z^T = c_t^T (n_t^T)^{1-\alpha}. \tag{4.65}$$

Since c_t^T is constant over time and the LHS of this condition is a decreasing function of n_t^T but the RHS is an increasing function of n_t^T, then n_t^T must also remain constant along a PFEP. Hence, from the labor supply constraint (4.57), n_t^N is constant over time. Production of nontradables is therefore constant and so is c_t^N. From (4.60), p_t is constant over time.

Having shown that if Z^T, Z^N, and n are constant over time, then c_t^T, c_t^N, p_t, n_t^T, and n_t^N are also constant over time, we can solve implicitly for this perfect foresight equilibrium:

$$c^T = rb_0 + Z^T(n^T)^\alpha, \tag{4.66}$$

$$c^N = Z^N n^N, \tag{4.67}$$

$$p = \frac{rb_0 + Z^T(n^T)^\alpha}{Z^N n^N}, \tag{4.68}$$

$$p = \frac{\alpha Z^T(n^T)^{\alpha-1}}{Z^N}, \tag{4.69}$$

$$n = n^T + n^N. \tag{4.70}$$

For given values of Z^T, Z^N, n, and b_0, this can be viewed as a system of five equations in five unknowns: c^T, c^N, p, n^T, and n^N.

4.5.4 Wealth Effect

To illustrate how a wealth effect leads to a reallocation of resources across sectors, suppose that an instant before time 0, the economy is in the stationary equilibrium just described with net foreign assets given by b_0^L. At time 0 there is an unanticipated and permanent increase in b_0 (e.g., a foreign grant) to b_0^H ($b_0^H > b_0^L$). Given this unanticipated event, the consumer will reoptimize. Naturally the new perfect foresight equilibrium will be characterized by the same five equations, (4.66) through (4.70), with $b_0 = b_0^H$. Hence, from a mathematical point of view, we need to do a comparative statics exercise and find out how c^T, c^N, p, n^T, and n^N respond to a higher b_0.

The best way to proceed is to substitute (4.69) and (4.70) into (4.68) to obtain n^T as a function of Z^T, Z^N, n, and b_0:

$$\alpha n(n^T)^{\alpha-1} - \alpha(n^T)^\alpha - (n^T)^\alpha - rb_0(Z^T)^{-1} = 0. \tag{4.71}$$

Totally differentiating with respect to n^T and b_0, we obtain

$$\frac{dn^T}{db_0} = -\frac{-r/Z^T}{\alpha(\alpha-1)n(n^T)^{\alpha-2} - \alpha(1+\alpha)(n^T)^{\alpha-1}} < 0. \tag{4.72}$$

It follows that in response to an increase in b_0, n^T will fall. From (4.70), it follows that n^N increases, which implies, by (4.67), that c^N increases. Given the fall in n^T, equation (4.69) indicates that p rises. The rise in p implies, by equation (4.68), that c^T not only rises but in fact rises by a higher proportion than c^N.

Intuitively, the higher b_0 implies that the economy has more tradable resources available and will therefore increase consumption of tradable goods. At an unchanged relative price, consumers will want to increase consumption of nontradable goods by the same proportion. In an endowment economy the higher demand for nontradable goods would be reflected entirely in an increase in their relative price. In this economy with endogenous production, the excess demand for nontradable goods—at the initial relative price—induces a rise in p. This rise in p brings about two effects, both of which tend to reduce the excess demand. First, the higher p increases the value of the marginal productivity of labor in the nontradable sector. This induces a reallocation of labor from the tradable to the nontradable sector. Second, the higher p chokes off some of the excess demand for nontradables. In other words, the combination of more supply and lower demand equilibrates the nontradable goods market.

This experiment has thus illustrated the key role played by the relative price of nontradable goods in bringing about a reallocation of resources across sectors that contributes to restoring equilibrium in this economy.

4.5.5 Demand Shock

We will now study a temporary demand shock (which will lead to a boom–bust cycle) to illustrate the role of relative prices in engineering the adjustment needed for this economy to repay its debt. To this end, let us modify the preferences given by (4.53) to incorporate a demand shock, γ_t:

$$\int_0^{\infty} \gamma_t[\log(c_t^T) + \log(c_t^N)]e^{-\beta t}dt. \tag{4.73}$$

The rest of the model remains the same. Under the preferences given by (4.73), the first-order conditions reduce to

$$\frac{\gamma_t}{c_t^T} = \lambda, \tag{4.74}$$

$$\frac{\gamma_t}{c_t^N} = \lambda p_t, \tag{4.75}$$

$$\alpha Z_t^T (n_t^T)^{\alpha-1} = p_t Z_t^N. \tag{4.76}$$

We will characterize a perfect foresight equilibrium path for constant paths of Z^T, Z^N, and n but for a *nonconstant* path of γ_t. Specifically, suppose that γ is high until T and low thereafter (figure 4.6, panel a). What will be the corresponding paths of c_t^T, c_t^N, p_t, n_t^T and n_t^N?

To answer this question, we need to focus on what happens at time T. From (4.74), we infer that at T, c_t^T will decrease as a result of the fall in γ (figure 4.6, panel b). From (4.65), n_t^T will then increase at time T (panel c). From (4.57), n_t^N falls at time T (panel d). Hence c_t^N also falls at time T (panel e). In turn, the rise in n_t^T implies, from condition (4.76), that p_t falls at time T (panel f). Since the output of tradable goods follows the path of n_t^T, the economy will run a trade deficit between 0 and T and a surplus after T (panel g). The corresponding current account path is illustrated in panel h.

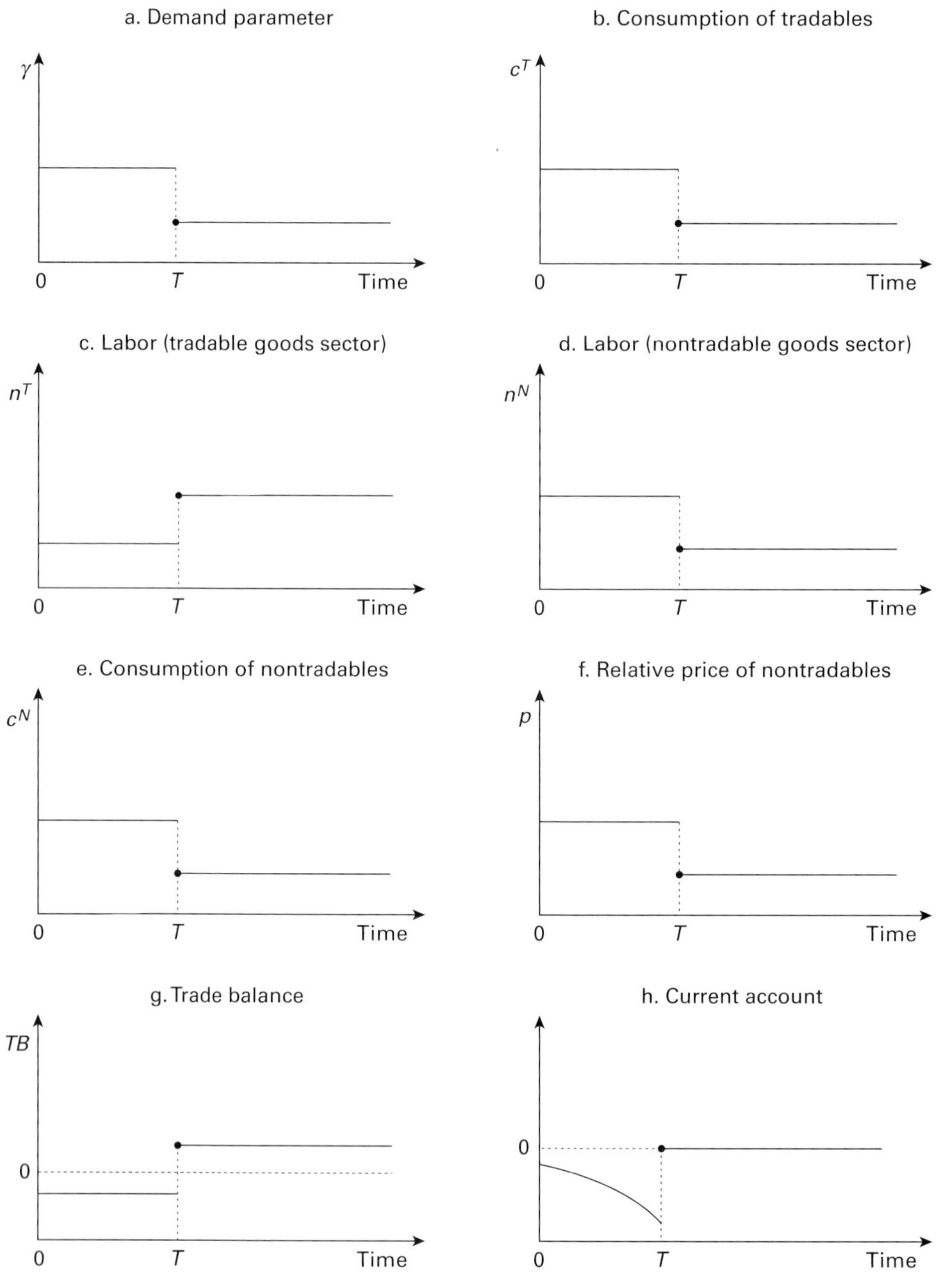

Figure 4.6
Temporary demand shock

Box 4.2
How do economies adjust in practice?

In section 4.5.5 we analyzed how a small open economy adjusts to a negative demand shock (i.e., a fall in the demand for both tradable and nontradable goods). The model predicts that in response to such a shock, (1) the trade balance improves, (2) the current account improves, and (3) the relative price of nontradables falls. What do the data show?

To abstract from other factors, it proves helpful to look at the behavior of these macroeconomic variables during crises episodes in which consumption fell substantially. Figure 4.7 illustrates the average behavior of the four variables relative to the year of the crisis for nine major crises in emerging countries: the Southern Cone "tablitas" (Argentina, Chile, and Uruguay in 1982), the Mexican 1994 crisis, the Southeast Asia 1997 crises (Indonesia, Korea, Malaysia, and Thailand), and the Turkish

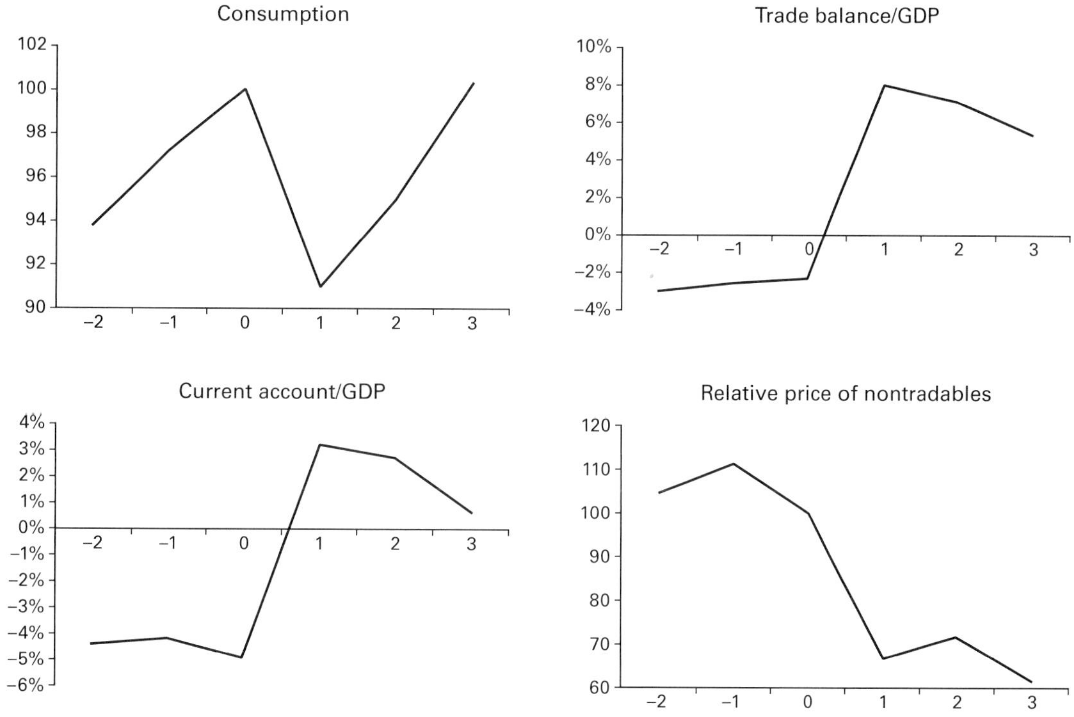

Note: Values represent unweighted averages from nine currency crises: Argentina (1982), Chile (1982), Uruguay (1982), Mexico (1994), Thailand (1997), Indonesia (1997), Korea (1997), Malaysia (1997), and Turkey (2001). Period 1 is defined as the year after the crisis or the year of the crisis if it took place before July.

Figure 4.7
Consumption, external accounts, and relative prices during crises

Box 4.2
(continued)

2001 crisis.[a] On average, consumption fell by almost 10 percent in the first year after the crisis. This dramatic fall in consumption was accompanied by a shift in the trade balance from an average deficit of 2 percent of GDP to a surplus of 8 percent of GDP and in the current account from a deficit of 5 percent to a surplus of 3 percent. In turn the relative price of nontradable goods fell on average by almost 35 percent.[b]

Table 4.2 presents three-year averages before and after the nine crises for the three main variables of interest. Looking at the individual episodes, we can get a clear sense of how dramatic the turnaround in the external accounts can be. In Thailand, for example, the shift in the trade balance was close to 15 percent of GDP and in Malaysia more than 20 percent of GDP. The fall in the relative price of nontradable may be equally dramatic, even halving in some cases (Argentina, Uruguay, and Indonesia).

In sum, while in practice the shock that triggered the fall in consumption may have differed from crisis to crisis, the sharp improvement in the external accounts and the large fall in the relative price of nontradable goods is fully consistent with the predictions of our simple model.

Table 4.2
Crises episodes: Relative price of nontradable goods, trade balance, and current account

Argentina 1982		
Variable	*Before*	*After*
p	100	49.6
TB/GDP	0.6%	3.8%
CA/GDP	−2.7%	−1.9%

Chile 1982		
Variable	*Before*	*After*
p	100	70.1
TB/GDP	−3.4%	2.1%
CA/GDP	−7.3%	−7.6%

Uruguay 1982		
Variable	*Before*	*After*
p	100	49.2
TB/GDP	−4.3%	3.8%
CA/GDP	−5.6%	−3.0%

Mexico 1994		
Variable	*Before*	*After*
p	100	77.9
TB/GDP	−4.0%	1.5%
CA/GDP	−6.5%	−1.0%

Indonesia 1997		
Variable	*Before*	*After*
p	100	53.2
TB/GDP	1.6%	14.4%
CA/GDP	−2.8%	4.5%

Korea 1997		
Variable	*Before*	*After*
p	100	73.7
TB/GDP	−1.5%	7.9%
CA/GDP	−2.6%	−7.1%

Malaysia 1997		
Variable	*Before*	*After*
p	100	71.6
TB/GDP	2.6%	25.4%
CA/GDP	−6.7%	12.8%

Thailand 1997		
Variable	*Before*	*After*
p	100	74.1
TB/GDP	−6.9%	7.7%
CA/GDP	−5.9%	10.2%

Turkey 2001		
Variable	*Before*	*After*
p	100	84.4
TB/GDP	−7.8%	−4.3%
CA/GDP	−1.5%	−0.6%

Source: All data from IFS (IMF).
Note: "Before" and "After" are three-year averages before and after the crisis. "Before" includes the year of the crisis if the crisis took place in July or later. The variable p denotes the relative price of nontradable goods; TB/GDP is the trade balance as a proportion of GDP, and CA/GDP is the current account as a proportion of GDP.

a. We selected these crises because, in all nine of them, consumption fell in the first year after the crisis. The fall in consumption ranges from 5.5 percent in Argentina 1982 to 16 percent in Malaysia 1997. (In Chapter 16, we will reinterpreted this evidence in light of balance of payments crises models.) The relative price of nontradable goods was computed as P/EP^*, with P being the domestic CPI, E the nominal exchange rate, and P^* the US CPI.
b. While outside of the scope of the model, it is interesting to notice that consumption recovers relatively quickly and by the third year after the crisis it has returned to its initial level. (Output behaves similarly.)

This experiment thus illustrates a small open economy going through a boom–bust cycle, which is typical of developing countries. In the good times consumption of both tradables and nontradables is high, the relative price of nontradable goods is high, production of tradables is low, production of nontradables is high, and there is a trade deficit. When the situation turns for the worse, consumption of both goods collapses, the relative price of nontradable goods falls, and the economy runs a trade surplus. In other words, the adjustment of the economy involves a sharp real depreciation, a collapse in consumption, and a switch in resources from the nontradable to the tradable goods sector.[27] While disaggregated data for tradables and nontradables are hard to come by, box 4.2 illustrates the adjustment in the trade balance, the current account balance, and the relative price of nontradable goods for nine episodes in emerging countries where consumption fell sharply. As argued in the box, the facts coincide exactly with the predictions of the model.

4.6 Terms of Trade and the Real Exchange Rate

Exports in many developing countries are often concentrated on some key commodities or agricultural products. Commodity prices, in particular, are extremely volatile, which results in large fluctuations in developing countries' terms of trade (i.e., the relative price of exports in terms of imports). The question of how will a change in the terms of trade affect the real exchange rate has thus been a perennial one in open economy macroeconomics. The traditional wisdom has been that a deterioration in the terms of trade will lead to a real depreciation (e.g., Edwards and van Wijnbergen 1987).

To answer this question in our theoretical framework, we need to extend the basic model with nontradable goods studied in section 4.2 to allow for both exportables and importables. We will thus study a small open economy with three nonstorable goods (exportables, importables, and nontradables). The exportable good will be the numéraire. There is a given and constant endowment path of exportables (which are not consumed) and nontradables. The economy consumes but is not endowed with importables. International bonds are denominated in terms of the exportable good.

4.6.1 Consumer's Problem

The consumer's lifetime utility is given by

$$\int_0^\infty u(c_t^I, c_t^N)e^{-\beta t}dt, \tag{4.77}$$

27. Several shocks—some of which we will see in more detail in later chapters—would lead to these same dynamics. For instance, the demand shock could be due to, say, a temporary exchange rate stabilization program along the lines of Calvo (1986) and Rebelo and Végh (1995) or to a temporary fall in international interest rates, along the lines of Edwards and Végh (1997).

where $\beta > 0$ is the subjective discount rate, and c_t^I and c_t^N denote consumption of importables and nontradable goods, respectively.

In a model with three goods, we need to be careful with the definition of the various relative prices. In the model developed in section 4.2, we denoted by p_t the relative price of nontradable goods in terms of the numéraire (tradable goods). This relative price was the relevant one for consumption decisions. In the current model, the relevant relative price for consumption decisions is the relative price of nontradable goods in terms of the importable good (denoted by p_t^I). There is, of course, another relative price: the relative price of the nontradable good in terms of the exportable (denoted by p_t^x). Since p_t^I is the only relative price that affects marginal conditions, we will use it as our measure of the (inverse of) real exchange rate.[28] We will denote by q_t the relative price of importables in terms of exportables (i.e., the inverse of the terms of trade). Then, by definition,

$$p_t^I = \frac{p_t^x}{q_t}. \tag{4.78}$$

Our main question will be: How do changes in q_t affect the relative price of nontradable goods (p_t^I)?

Let b_t denote net foreign assets held by the consumer. The flow constraint is given by

$$\dot{b}_t = rb_t + y^x + p_t^x y^N - q_t c_t^I - p_t^x c_t^N, \tag{4.79}$$

where y^x and y^N denote the constant endowments of exportable and nontradable goods, respectively. Taking into account (4.78), we can rewrite the flow constraint as

$$\dot{b}_t = rb_t + y^x + q_t p_t^I y^N - q_t c_t^I - q_t p_t^I c_t^N, \tag{4.80}$$

Integrating (4.80) forward, we obtain the intertemporal budget constraint:

$$b_0 + \int_0^\infty (y^x + q_t p_t^I y^N) e^{-rt} dt = \int_0^\infty (q_t c_t^I + q_t p_t^I c_t^N) e^{-rt} dt. \tag{4.81}$$

The consumer's problem consists in choosing paths of c_t^I and c_t^N to maximize lifetime utility (4.77), subject to (4.81), for a given path of p_t^I and q_t, and given values of y^x, y^N and b_0. The Lagrangian is given by

$$\begin{aligned}\mathcal{L} = &\int_0^\infty u(c_t^I, c_t^N) e^{-\beta t} dt \\ &+ \lambda \left[b_0 + \int_0^\infty (y^x + q_t p_t^I y^N) e^{-rt} dt - \int_0^\infty (q_t c_t^I + q_t p_t^I c_t^N) e^{-rt} dt \right].\end{aligned}$$

28. If exportables were consumed (or produced), it would make sense to define the real exchange rate in terms of some index for tradable goods (see Buffie 1999). Box 4.3 discusses the measurement of the real exchange rate in practice.

Box 4.3
How is the real exchange rate measured in practice?

From a theoretical point of view, the definition of the real exchange rate (i.e., the inverse of the relative price of nontradable goods) is rather straightforward, but the question of how to measure this concept in practice is far from trivial. The most direct and obvious way would be to compute

$$RER_1 = \frac{P^T}{P^N}, \tag{4.3a}$$

where P^T and P^N here denote price indexes of all goods classified as tradable or nontradable, respectively, from consumer price indexes or national accounts. Food, beverages, apparel, furniture, and the like, are usually considered tradable goods. Housing, health, transportation, education, and entertainment are typically viewed as nontradable goods. Such a measure, however, would represent at best an approximation to the "true" relative price, since most goods for which prices are available represent essentially a mix of tradables and nontradables. Tradable goods, on the one hand, have an important nontradable component given mainly by distribution costs.[a] Nontradable goods, on the other hand, usually include tradable goods inputs for their production.

The methodology captured in (4.3a) presents a more fundamental drawback, as should be clear from section 4.6. In theory, an increase in the price of exports should cause an appreciation of nontradable goods relative to imported goods—the well-known "Dutch disease" phenomenon. The measure (4.3a), however, might not reveal this important effect, as average tradable prices can increase and thus the relative price of nontradables decrease if the export good is important enough in the basket of tradable goods. Taking an index of import prices as a proxy for tradable prices would overcome this problem. However, reliable data for this series are rarely available. Many countries do not even compute such an index, and others merely follow the price of some relevant commodities.

To avoid this problem, the standard practice is to measure tradable goods prices using foreign prices. Under such a procedure the measured real exchange rate would be

$$RER_2 = \frac{EP^*}{P^N}, \tag{4.3b}$$

where P^* is an index of international prices multiplied by the nominal exchange rate (E) to express it in domestic currency. More specifically, P^* is often computed as a weighted average of tradable prices (proxied by the wholesale price index) among main trading partners, or even main industrial countries. In this setup nontradable prices are usually substituted by the consumer price index (CPI) for ease of computation. It can be easily shown that this is still a very good approximation to variations of the RER. Specifically, if the CPI can be expressed as

$$CPI = \alpha P^T + (1 - \alpha)P^N;$$

then the RER measure (4.3b) becomes

$$RER_2 = \frac{EP^*}{\alpha P^T + (1 - \alpha)P^N}.$$

a. See Burstein, Neves, and Rebelo (2003).

Box 4.3
(continued)

If we further assume that $EP^* = P^T$, then

$$RER_2 = \frac{1}{\alpha + (1-\alpha)(P^N/P^T)},$$

which varies inversely with P^N/P^T (as our theoretical measure does, of course).

Alternatively, measure (4.3b) is computed with P^* as the consumer price inflation of another country (typically the United States). In such a case the real exchange rate becomes a measure of relative prices of two countries, which intends to capture competitiveness.[b] Conceptually, however, factors that may affect nontradables prices in, say, the United States should have no impact whatsoever on the real exchange rate, which is a relative price in a small economy facing world markets (Harberger 2004). In other words, the concept of the real exchange rate as the ratio of prices in two countries only makes sense in two-country models, which are essentially irrelevant for developing countries.[c] As a practical matter, however, this measure is widely used since it has the advantage that the real exchange rate becomes easy to compute and exhibits a high correlation with previous definitions (see Edwards 1989). This high correlation is hardly surprising since in most cases the movement in the real exchange rate for developing countries are dominated by the behavior of domestic prices (i.e., the denominator in equation 4.3b).

b. Others, among them the IMF, have gone further and compute the real exchange rate as the relative unit labor costs. This measure is even questionable to measure competitiveness, as increase in wages can reflect increases in productivity. See Harberger (2004) for a scathing critique of IMF's measures of the real exchange rate.
c. Standard textbooks in fact define the real exchange rate as the ratio of the CPI of two countries (e.g., see Krugman and Obstfeld 2009). For a small open economy facing multiple foreign countries, such a definition clearly makes little sense.

Assuming $\beta = r$, the corresponding first-order conditions are

$$u_{c^I}(c_t^I, c_t^N) = \lambda q_t, \tag{4.82}$$

$$u_{c^N}(c_t^I, c_t^N) = \lambda q_t p_t^I. \tag{4.83}$$

Combining these two first-order conditions, we obtain

$$\frac{u_{c^N}(c_t^I, c_t^N)}{u_{c^I}(c_t^I, c_t^N)} = p_t^I. \tag{4.84}$$

Equations (4.82) and (4.83) say that, at an optimum, consumers equate the marginal utility of consuming each good to the shadow value of wealth times the relative price. Condition (4.84) says that, at an optimum, the consumer equates the marginal rate of substitution between nontradables and importables to the corresponding relative price.

4.6.2 Equilibrium Conditions

The market for nontradable goods clears:

$$c_t^N = y^N. \tag{4.85}$$

Imposing the equilibrium condition (4.85) into (4.79) yields the economy's flow constraint (i.e., the current account):

$$\dot{b}_t = rb_t + y^x - q_t c_t^I. \tag{4.86}$$

The corresponding resource constraint is given by

$$b_0 + \int_0^\infty y^x e^{-rt} dt = \int_0^\infty q_t c_t^I e^{-rt} dt. \tag{4.87}$$

4.6.3 Perfect Foresight Equilibrium

Let us characterize a perfect foresight equilibrium path for a constant path of q_t (denoted by q). It follows from (4.82) and (4.85) that consumption of importables will be constant over time. From the resource constraint (4.87), this constant level will be given by

$$c^I = \frac{rb_0 + y^x}{q}. \tag{4.88}$$

Consumption of nontradables is, of course, constant and equal to the constant endowment of nontradables. Then, from (4.84), p^I will be constant as well:

$$p^I = \frac{u_{c^N}(c^I, y^N)}{u_{c^I}(c^I, y^N)}. \tag{4.89}$$

4.6.4 Permanent Change in Terms of Trade

Suppose that starting from the stationary equilibrium just derived, there is an unanticipated and permanent improvement in the terms of trade (i.e., a fall in q_t) at $t = 0$. Since there has been an unanticipated shock, consumers reoptimize at $t = 0$. Given that q_t will still be constant along the new perfect foresight equilibrium path, equation (4.88) remains valid. Clearly, since q_t has fallen, c_t^I will be higher in the new equilibrium. The increase in c_t^I reflects the wealth effect due to the fact that the same amount of exportables now buys a larger quantity of imports.

What happens to p_t^I? To find this out, assume that the change in q_t is small. We can then use (4.88) to compute the change in the constant value of c_t^I:

$$\frac{dc^I}{dq} = -\frac{rb_0 + y^x}{q^2} < 0.$$

Totally differentiating (4.89), we obtain

$$\frac{dp^I}{dq} = \frac{dc^I}{dq}\left(\frac{u_{c^I}u_{c^Ic^N} - u_{c^N}u_{c^Ic^I}}{u_{c^I}^2}\right) < 0,$$

since the term in brackets is positive if nontradable goods are normal and $dc^I/dq < 0$. This result implies that a permanent fall in q_t leads to an increase in p_t^I (a real appreciation).

Intuitively, an improvement in the terms of trade makes the consumer wealthier. At the pre-shock relative price, the consumer would like to consume more of both importables and nontradables. Importables can be procured from the rest of the world. Nontradable goods, however, are in fixed supply. At the pre-shock relative price, there is thus an excess demand for nontradable goods that must be met by an increase in their relative price.

4.6.5 Change in Terms of Trade along a Perfect Foresight Path

Having just isolated the effect on the relative price of nontradable goods brought about by the wealth effect stemming from an improvement in the terms of trade, we now abstract from the wealth effect and study the effect arising from intertemporal consumption substitution. To this effect, consider an improvement in the terms of trade along a perfect foresight path. In other words, consider a perfect foresight path along which q_t falls at time $t = T$ (figure 4.8, panel a). What will be the effect on p_t^I?

Since λ is constant along a perfect foresight path, it follows from first-order condition (4.82) that if q_t falls at T, c_t^I will increase (figure 4.8, panel b). Intuitively—and as we saw in chapter 3—if importables become relatively cheaper at T, consumers will engage in intertemporal consumption substitution and consume more importables.

To find out what happens to p_t^I, impose the nontradable goods equilibrium condition (4.85) into (4.84) to obtain

$$\frac{u_{c^N}(c_t^I, y^N)}{u_{c^I}(c_t^I, y^N)} = p_t^I. \tag{4.90}$$

Totally differentiating this condition at time T yields

$$\left.\frac{dp_t^I}{dc_t^I}\right|_{t=T} = \left(\frac{u_{c^I}u_{c^Ic^N} - u_{c^N}u_{c^Ic^I}}{u_{c^I}^2}\right) > 0,$$

where, again, the numerator is positive due to the assumption of normality. The increase in c_t^I at time T will be accompanied by an increase in p_t^I (figure 4.8, panel c). Intuitively, at an unchanged relative price, and given the increase in consumption of importables at time T, consumers would

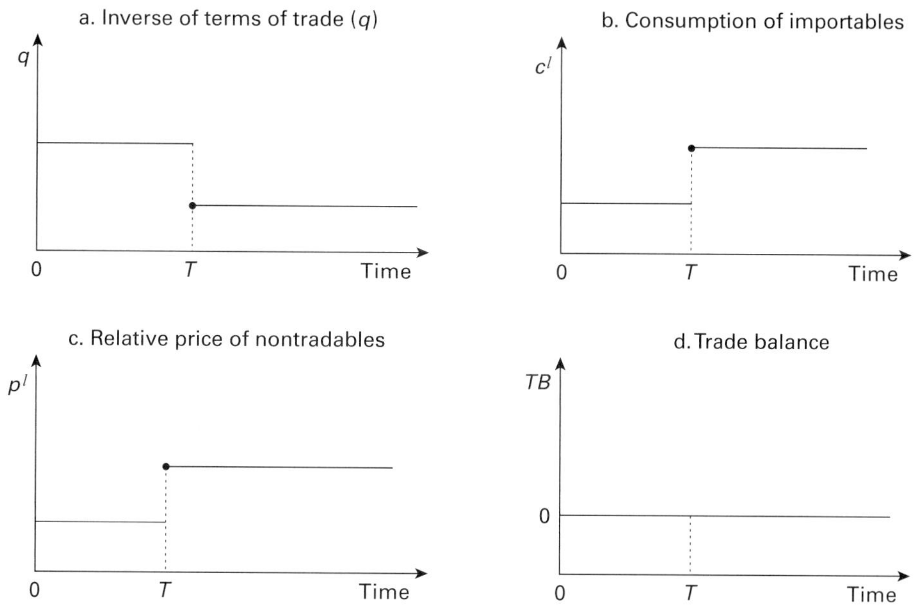

Figure 4.8
Anticipated improvement in terms of trade

like to consume more nontradables. The excess demand for nontradables leads to an increase in their relative price, p_t^I.

In general, the behavior of the trade balance and p_t^x will depend on preferences. In the case of logarithmic preferences (i.e., $u(c_t^I, c_t^N) = \log(c_t^I) + \log(c_t^N)$), it is easy to see from (4.82) that $q_t c_t^I$ is constant along a perfect foresight equilibrium path and, hence, that the trade balance (equal to $y^x - q_t c_t^I$) would also be constant over time (figure 4.8, panel d). Similarly, from (4.78), p_t^x would be constant over time since, from (4.83) and (4.85), $q_t p_t^I$ would be constant over time.

In sum, an improvement in the terms of trade along a perfect foresight path will bring about an increase in the relative price of nontradable goods in terms of importables due to the intertemporal substitution effect. Together with the results derived in the previous subsection, we conclude that both the wealth and intertemporal substitution effect associated with an improvement in the terms of trade will lead to a real appreciation. It then follows—as can be easily verified by the reader—that an unanticipated and temporary improvement in the terms of trade at time 0 will lead to an initial increase in p_t^I since both the wealth effect and the intertemporal substitution effect will increase consumption of importables.[29]

29. See Mendoza (1995) for a quantitative analysis of the effects of terms of trade shocks on the real exchange rate. In models with two tradable sectors, the relation between an improvement in the terms of trade (in particular, increases in the price of commodities such as oil) and a real appreciation that negatively affects other tradable sectors is the subject of the so-called Dutch disease phenomenon (see Corden and Neary 1982).

4.6.6 Trade Liberalizations

We can use the same three-good model just developed to consider another important question in open economy macroeconomics: How will a trade liberalization affect the real exchange rate? The conventional wisdom is that a trade liberalization will lead to a real exchange rate depreciation (see Edwards 1989, ch. 2).[30] However, as the analysis below makes clear, our simple model will lead us to expect precisely the opposite.

To reinterpret the model above as applying to a trade liberalization, assume (as in chapter 3) that the international terms of trade are equal to one and think of q_t as the tariff-inclusive relative price of importables in terms of exportables. Hence $q_t - 1$ represents the import tariff. To analyze a trade liberalization, the more natural assumption is that the government returns to consumers the tariff proceeds in a lump-sum way (as in chapter 3). We thus modify the intertemporal constraint (4.81) to read

$$b_0 + \int_0^{\infty} (y^x + q_t p_t^I y^N + \tau_t) e^{-rt} dt = \int_0^{\infty} (q_t c_t^I + q_t p_t^I c_t^N) e^{-rt} dt, \tag{4.91}$$

where τ_t denotes lump-sum transfers from the government. It should be obvious that this modification does not alter the consumer's first-order conditions, which continue to be given by (4.82), (4.83), and hence (4.84).

The government's role is to impose the tariff and to return the proceeds from the tariff in a lump-sum way. Hence

$$\tau_t = (q_t - 1) c_t^I. \tag{4.92}$$

To derive the economy's resource constraint, substitute (4.92) into (4.91)—taking into account the equilibrium condition in the nontradable goods market—to obtain

$$b_0 + \int_0^{\infty} y^x e^{-rt} dt = \int_0^{\infty} c_t^I e^{-rt} dt. \tag{4.93}$$

A comparison of (4.93) and (4.87) reveals that the critical difference with the terms of trade case is that q_t does not enter the resource constraint. This was to be expected since, by assumption, the terms of trade are equal to one.

Permanent Reduction in Tariffs

Consider a perfect foresight equilibrium path for constant paths of y_t^x, y_t^N, and q_t, denoted by y^x, y^N, and q, respectively. From the nontradable goods market equilibrium condition (4.85), the

30. The traditional argument runs as follows: a reduction in tariffs will increase consumption of importables, which leads to a trade deficit. This requires a real depreciation for equilibrium to be restored.

first-order condition (4.82), and the resource constraint (4.93), we obtain the constant value of c_t^I as

$$c^I = rb_0 + y^x. \tag{4.94}$$

From (4.90) and (4.94) we obtain the constant value of p_t^I:

$$p^I = \frac{u_{c^N}(rb_0 + y^x, y^N)}{u_{c^I}(rb_0 + y^x, y^N)}.$$

Since neither c^I nor p^I depends on q, it should be clear that an unanticipated and permanent reduction in q_t will have no effects. This was to be expected since q_t continues to be constant along the new perfect foresight equilibrium path and changes in q_t do not have wealth effects.[31]

Temporary Reduction in Tariffs

In contrast to the permanent case, an unanticipated and temporary reduction in tariffs will have real effects. From (4.82) and (4.93) it follows that c_t^I will rise at time 0 and then fall at T below its initial value (since the present discounted value of c_t^I remains unchanged).[32]

Given the intratemporal condition (4.84), the path of c_t^I fully determines the path of p_t^I. Specifically, substitute the nontradable goods equilibrium condition into (4.84) to obtain

$$p_t^I = \frac{u_{c^N}(c_t^I, y^N)}{u_{c^I}(c_t^I, y^N)}.$$

Totally differentiate at any given point in time to obtain

$$\frac{dp_t^I}{dc_t^I} = \left(\frac{u_{c^I}u_{c^I c^N} - u_{c^N}u_{c^I c^I}}{u_{c^I}^2}\right) > 0,$$

where the numerator is positive by the condition of normality. It follows that p_t^I increases on impact and falls at time T. Since c_t^I is below its initial value after time T, p_t^I is also below its initial value.

We conclude that in the context of our simple model, a temporary trade liberalization leads to an increase in the relative price of nontradable goods in terms of importables (a real appreciation).

31. Of course, if exportables were consumed, a permanent change in q_t would have real effects through consumption substitution between exportables and importables. See Edwards (1989), Edwards and van Wijnbergen (1987), and Buffie (1999) for detailed analyses.

32. This is, of course, the same result that we obtained in chapter 3 for a temporary fall in tariffs.

Intuitively, importables become cheaper, which leads to a higher consumption of importables. At the initial relative price, consumers do not wish to change the relative consumption of importables and nontradable goods and hence would demand more nontradables as well. The excess demand for nontradables leads to an increase in their relative price. Our result is the exact opposite of the conventional wisdom.[33]

4.7 Final Remarks

This chapter has introduced nontradable goods into the basic model developed in chapter 1. Once nontradable goods enter the picture, the full consumption smoothing result obtained in chapter 1 needs to be qualified since a fluctuating path of nontradable goods may lead to a nonconstant path of tradable goods consumption. The presence of nontradable goods introduces a key relative price—the relative price of nontradable goods—that plays a critical role in the adjustment of a small open economy to various shocks.

We analyzed how, in response to a temporary negative supply shock, trade and current account deficits coexist with a high relative price of nontradable goods (real appreciation) while surpluses coexist with real depreciation. There is no sense, however, in which the changes in the real exchange rate "cause" the external imbalances; they are both equilibrium responses to a common shock.

We also emphasized the role of the relative price of nontradable goods in bringing about the adjustment required when a small open economy goes from boom to bust. The fall in the relative price of nontradable goods that accompanies the shift from boom to bust is key in engineering the shift in resources from the nontradable to the tradable goods sector that will be needed to repay the external debt accumulated in the good times. We will encounter this adjustment mechanism time and time again in the rest of the book.

4.8 Appendix: Conditions for Normality

Since some of the results of this chapter depend on the assumption that c^T and c^N are normal goods, it will prove useful to derive the conditions that ensure normality.[34] To do so, consider the static problem corresponding to our dynamic problem:

$$\max_{\{c^T,c^N\}} u(c^T, c^N)$$

33. If exportables were consumed (and/or produced), substitution in both consumption and production would affect how the relevant real exchange rate (which, in such a model, would be best defined as the inverse of the relative price of nontradable goods in terms of some index of tradable goods) is affected by changes in tariffs (see Edwards 1989, Buffie 1999). In particular, Buffie (1999) shows that under the more plausible parameter configuration, a temporary liberalization will lead to a real appreciation.

34. For more details, see, for example, Silberberg and Suen (2000).

subject to

$$c^T + pc^N = y,$$

where y ($\equiv y^T + py^N$) denotes the value of the endowment. The first-order conditions are given by

$$u_{c^T}(c^T, c^N) = \lambda, \tag{4.95}$$

$$u_{c^N}(c^T, c^N) = \lambda p, \tag{4.96}$$

$$c^T + pc^N = y,$$

where λ is the Lagrange multiplier associated with the budget constraint.

Totally differentiating the system above with respect to c^T, c^N, λ, and y, we obtain (in matrix form)[35]

$$\begin{bmatrix} u_{c^Tc^T} & u_{c^Tc^N} & -1 \\ u_{c^Nc^T} & u_{c^Nc^N} & -p \\ -1 & -p & 0 \end{bmatrix} \begin{bmatrix} dc^T \\ dc^N \\ d\lambda \end{bmatrix} = \begin{bmatrix} 0 \\ 0 \\ -1 \end{bmatrix} dy.$$

Letting Δ denote the determinant associated with the 3×3 matrix above, we obtain, by Cramer's rule,

$$\frac{dc^T}{dy} = \frac{1}{\Delta} \begin{vmatrix} 0 & u_{c^Tc^N} & -1 \\ 0 & u_{c^Nc^N} & -p \\ -1 & -p & 0 \end{vmatrix} = \frac{u_{c^Tc^N}p - u_{c^Nc^N}}{\Delta},$$

$$\frac{dc^N}{dy} = \frac{1}{\Delta} \begin{vmatrix} u_{c^Tc^T} & 0 & -1 \\ u_{c^Nc^T} & 0 & -p \\ -1 & -1 & 0 \end{vmatrix} = \frac{u_{c^Nc^T} - pu_{c^Tc^T}}{\Delta},$$

where $\Delta > 0$ (by the sufficient second order conditions for a maximum). Since, from (4.95) and (4.96), we know that $p = u_{c^N}/u_{c^T}$, we can rewrite these expressions as

$$\frac{dc^T}{dy} = \frac{u_{c^N}u_{c^Tc^N} - u_{c^T}u_{c^Nc^N}}{u_{c^T}\Delta},$$

$$\frac{dc^N}{dy} = \frac{u_{c^T}u_{c^Nc^T} - u_{c^N}u_{c^Tc^T}}{u_{c^T}\Delta}.$$

35. We are implicitly assuming that y increases due to a change in y^T or y^N (and not p).

For these expressions to be positive (which implies that consumption of both goods increases in response to an increase in output), it must be the case that

$$u_{c^N} u_{c^T c^N} - u_{c^T} u_{c^N c^N} > 0,$$

$$u_{c^T} u_{c^T c^N} - u_{c^N} u_{c^T c^T} > 0,$$

which are conditions (4.2) and (4.3) in the text.

Exercises

1. (Consumption based real interest rate) This exercise derives the so-called consumption based real interest rate, an influential concept popularized by Dornbusch (1983).

a. Write a discrete-time version of the model analyzed in section 4.2 with the discount factor given by δ and preferences given by (4.98) and c_t, the consumption composite, given by

$$c_t \equiv \left(c_t^T\right)^{\alpha} \left(c_t^N\right)^{1-\alpha}. \tag{4.97}$$

b. Show that the domestic real interest rate, r_t^d, is given by $r_t^d \equiv (1+r)(p_t/p_{t+1}) - 1$. Interpret intuitively this real interest rate.

c. Show that you can combine the first-order conditions to obtain the following Euler equation for the consumption aggregate:

$$\frac{c_{t+1}}{c_t} = [\delta(1 + r_t^c)]^{\sigma},$$

where

$$r_t^c \equiv (1+r)\left(\frac{p_t}{p_{t+1}}\right)^{1-\alpha} - 1$$

is the consumption based real interest rate. Notice how, in determining the time profile for the consumption aggregate, the consumer compares the discount factor, δ, to r_t^c. Further, if the relative price of nontradable goods does not vary over time, then $r_t^c = r$. In contrast, if the relative price of nontradable goods is not constant over time, then aggregate consumption will not be constant over time even if $\delta(1+r) = 1$.

2. (Comovements between output and trade balance) This exercise uses a specific class of preferences to illustrate the effect that fluctuations in the endowment of nontradable goods have on tradable goods consumption and hence on the trade balance.

Consider the same economy analyzed in section 4.2. Let preferences be given by

$$u(c_t^T, c_t^N) = \frac{c_t^{1-1/\sigma} - 1}{1 - 1/\sigma}, \tag{4.98}$$

where c_t is a CES consumption composite defined as

$$c_t = \left[q(c_t^T)^{(\rho-1)/\rho} + (1-q)(c_t^N)^{(\rho-1)/\rho}\right]^{\rho/(\rho-1)}, \tag{4.99}$$

where $q \in (0, 1)$ is a parameter. The parameter $\sigma > 0$ is the *intertemporal* elasticity of consumption substitution. The parameter $\rho > 0$ captures the *intratemporal* elasticity of substitution between tradable and nontradable goods.

a. Recall from exercise 1 in chapter 3 that equation (4.98) becomes $\log(c_t)$ as $\sigma \to 1$. Using L'Hôpital's rule, show that (4.99) becomes $\left(c_t^T\right)^q \left(c_t^N\right)^{1-q}$ if $\rho \to 1$. (Hence, if both σ and ρ tend to 1, $u(c_t^T, c_t^N) = q\log(c_t^T) + (1-q)\log(c_t^N)$.)

b. Suppose that the endowment of tradable goods is flat over time and that the endowment of nontradable goods fluctuates over time. Show that whether the economy runs trade surpluses or deficits during periods of high nontradable endowment depends on the relation between σ and ρ. (Hint: Differentiate the marginal condition for tradable goods along a perfect foresight path.)

c. Available empirical evidence for developing countries suggests that $\rho > \sigma$ (see Ostry and Reinhart 1992).[36] What does the model predict in terms of the relation between good times (i.e., high nontradable endowment) and the trade balance? Does the sign of this comovement match the stylized facts described in box 1.2 in chapter 1?

d. Compute the cross-derivative for the CES preferences in (4.98) and show that it depends on the relation between σ and ρ. Relate this finding to the expression that you derived in part b above.

3. (External deficits and the real exchange rate) This exercise illustrates the fact that Edgeworth substitutability is a sufficient (though not necessary) condition for the association between trade deficits (trade surpluses) and real appreciation (real depreciation) derived in section 4.3 to hold for the general preferences given by equation (4.1).

Consider the model of section 4.3 with preferences given by (4.1). Assume that goods are Edgeworth substitutes. In this context, analyze the effects of a temporary and equiproportional fall in the endowment of both goods. In particular, show that trade deficits go hand in hand with real appreciation.

4. (Demand shocks in a production economy) Suppose that households consume only nontradable goods and that nontradable goods are produced using tradable goods as an input. (If it helps you, think of an economy importing candies, which are not directly consumed, wrapping them domestically, and selling them domestically for consumption.)

Specifically, consider a small open economy fully integrated into the world economy. Preferences are given by

36. Based on data for 13 developing countries, Ostry and Reinhart (1992) estimate the intratemporal elasticity of substitution between tradable and nontradable goods to be in the range 1.22 to 1.27, whereas the intertemporal elasticity is estimated to be in the range 0.38 to 0.50 (which is consistent with the evidence provided in chapter 3, box 3.1).

$$\int_0^\infty \gamma_t u(c_t^N) e^{-\beta t} dt,$$

where $u' > 0$, $u'' < 0$, c_t^N is consumption of nontradable goods, and $\gamma_t > 0$ is a parameter that captures demand shocks.

Nontradable goods are produced using tradable goods as an input:

$$y_t^N = \frac{(c_t^T)^\alpha}{\alpha}, \qquad \alpha < 1.$$

where c_t^T now denotes the amount of tradables used as an input in the production of nontradables. There is an exogenous and constant endowment of tradable goods, y^T.

a. State the household's flow and intertemporal budget constraints. (Assume that households also carry productive activities.)

b. Derive the first-order conditions.

c. Suppose that starting from an initial stationary equilibrium, there is an unanticipated and temporary increase in γ_t. Derive the time path for all endogenous variables.

5. (Demand shocks in an endowment economy) This exercise analyzes the effects of demand shocks in the endowment model developed in section 4.2. Suppose that preferences are given by

$$\int_0^\infty \left[\alpha_t^T \log(c_t^T) + \alpha_t^N \log(c_t^N)\right] e^{-\beta t} dt,$$

where $\alpha_t^T > 0$ and $\alpha_t^N > 0$ are parameters meant to capture "demand shocks" to consumption of tradables and nontradables, respectively.

a. Suppose $\alpha_t^N = 1 - \alpha_t^T$.

i. Characterize the perfect foresight equilibrium of this economy for a constant path of all exogenous variables. Does the relative price of nontradable goods depend on α_t^T?

ii. Analyze the effects of both an unanticipated and permanent increase in α^T and an unanticipated and permanent fall in α^T. Show the results both analytically and graphically (i.e., in terms of figure 4.2).

b. Suppose $\alpha_t^T = \alpha_t^N = \alpha_t$.

i. Characterize the perfect foresight equilibrium of this economy for a constant path of all exogenous variables. Does the relative price of nontradable goods depend on α_t?

ii. Show that an unanticipated and permanent increase in α_t does not affect the economy's equilibrium.

iii. Analyze the effects of an unanticipated and temporary increase in α_t. In particular, show that high demand periods will be characterized by a consumption boom, real appreciation, and trade deficits while low demand periods will be associated with low consumption, real depreciation, and trade surpluses.

6. (The twin deficits revisited) The purpose of this exercise is to show that once we allow the government to borrow/lend over time, we can establish a link between fiscal deficits and trade deficits. In other words, we will see how a temporary increase in g_t^T leads to both a primary fiscal deficit and a trade deficit.

Consider the model analyzed in section 4.4 but, for simplicity, assume that the government spends only on tradable goods. More important, relax the assumption that the government must balance its budget period by period (reflected in equation 4.34). Assume instead that the government's flow constraint takes the form

$$\dot{b}_t^G = rb_t^G + pb_t,$$

where

$$pb_t \equiv \psi - g_t^T \tag{4.100}$$

denotes the primary balance, ψ is a constant lump-sum tax (whose level will be endogenously determined), and b_t^G denotes net foreign assets held by the government. The corresponding intertemporal constraint is given by

$$b_0^G + \frac{\psi}{r} = \int_0^\infty g_t^T e^{-rt} dt,$$

which says that the present discounted value of primary balances must match the initial government debt (given by $-b_0^G$).

In this context:

a. Characterize the perfect foresight equilibrium corresponding to constant paths of y_t^T, y_t^N, and g_t^T. To simplify the exercise, assume that $b_0^G = 0$ and $pb_0 = 0$.

b. Analyze the effects of an unanticipated and temporary increase in g_t^T. Does the twin deficits hypothesis hold?

7. (Endogenous supply revisited) In the context of the model in section 4.5:

a. Consider a more general version of this model in which the production of nontradables is given by $y_t^N = Z_t^N (n_t^N)^\beta$, where β could be greater, equal, or smaller than α. Solve for the effects of an increase in b_0 and a temporary demand shock and show that the same results that we found in the text hold.

b. Analyze in the more general version the effects of an unanticipated and permanent increase in Z_t^T. Do the results depend on whether $\alpha \gtreqless \beta$? How do the results relate to the celebrated Balassa–Samuelson effect?

c. Analyze in the more general version the effects of an unanticipated and permanent increase in n_t. Do the results depend on whether $\alpha \gtreqless \beta$?

d. Suppose that production is linear in both sectors; that is, $y_t^T = Z_t^T n_t^T$ and $y_t^N = Z_t^N n_t^N$. Consider a stationary equilibrium and obtain a reduced form for all endogenous variables in the model. How is the real exchange rate determined in this model?

e. Analyze the effects of an unanticipated and temporary increase in Z_t^T in the case of linear production in both sectors.

References

Arrau, Patricio, Jorge Quiroz, and Romulo Chumacero. 1992. Ahorro fiscal y tipo de cambio real. *Cuadernos de Economia* 29 (88): 349–86.

Arellano, Soledad and Felipe Larrain. 1996. Tipo de cambio real y gasto publico: Un modelo econometrico para Chile. *Cuadernos de Economia* 33 (98): 47–76.

Bouton, Lawrence and Mariusz A. Sumlinski. 1997. Trends in private investment in developing countries: Statistics for 1970–95. Discussion Paper 31. International Financial Corporation, Washington DC.

Buffie, Edward F. 1999. Optimal trade liberalization and the welfare costs of imperfect credibility. *Journal of International Economics* 47: 371–98.

Burstein, Ariel T., Joao C. Neves, and Sergio Rebelo. 2003. Distribution costs and real exchange rate dynamics during exchange-rate-based stabilizations. *Journal of Monetary Economics* 50 (6): 1189–1214.

Calvo, Guillermo A. 1986. Temporary stabilization: Predetermined exchange rates. *Journal of Political Economy* 94 (6): 1319–29.

Chinn, Menzie. 1997. The usual suspects? Productivity and demand shocks and Asia-Pacific real exchange rates. Pacific Basin Working Papers PB 97-06. Federal Reserve Bank of San Francisco, California.

Corden W. Max, and J. Peter Neary. 1982. Booming sector and de-industrialisation in a small open economy. *Economic Journal* 92: 825–48.

De Gregorio, Jose, and Holger C. Wolf. 1994. Terms of trade, productivity, and the real exchange rate. Working Paper 4807. National Bureau of Economic Research, Cambridge, MA.

Dornbusch, Rudiger. 1983. Real interest rates, home goods, and optimal external borrowing. *Journal of Political Economy* 91 (1): 141–53.

Edwards, Sebastian. 1989. *Real Exchange Rates, Devaluation, and Adjustment.* Cambridge: MIT Press.

Edwards, Sebastian, and Sweder van Wijnbergen. 1987. Tariffs, the real exchange rate, and the terms of trade: On two popular propositions in international economics. *Oxford Economic Papers* 39: 458–64.

Edwards, Sebastian, and Carlos A. Végh. 1997. Banks and macroeconomic disturbances under predetermined exchange rates. *Journal of Monetary Economics* 40 (2): 239–78.

Froot, Kenneth, and Kenneth Rogoff. 1991. The EMS, the EMU and the transition to a common currency. *NBER Macroeconomics Annual* 4: 269–317.

Harberger, Arnold C. 2004. The real exchange rate: Issues of concept and measurement. Mimeo. University of California Los Angeles.

Kaminsky, Graciela, and Michael Klein. 1994. The real exchange rate and fiscal policy during the gold standard period: Evidence from the United States and Great Britain. Working Paper 4809. National Bureau of Economic Research, Cambridge, MA.

Kim, Soyoung, and Nouriel Roubini. 2008. Twin deficit or twin divergence? Fiscal policy, current account, and real exchange rate in the U.S. *Journal of International Economics* 74 (2): 362–83.

Krugman, Paul R., and Maurice Obsfeld. 2009. *International Economics: Theory and Policy*, 8th ed. Boston: Pearson, Addison Wesley.

Mendoza, Enrique. 1995. The terms of trade, the real exchange rate, and economic fluctuations. *International Economic Review* 36 (1): 101–37.

Monacelli, Tommaso, and Roberto Perotti. 2010. Fiscal policy, the real exchange rate and traded goods. *Economic Journal* 120 (544): 437–61.

Ostry, Jonathan, and Carmen M. Reinhart. 1992. Private saving and terms of trade shocks: Evidence from developing countries. *IMF Staff Papers* 39 (3): 495–517.

Rebelo, Sergio, and Carlos A. Végh. 1995. Real effects of exchange rate-based stabilizations: An analysis of competing theories. *NBER Macroeconomics Annual* 8: 125–74.

Rogoff, Kenneth. 1992. Traded goods consumption smoothing and the random walk behavior of the real exchange rate. Working Paper 4119. National Bureau of Economic Research, Cambridge, MA.

Silberberg, Eugene, and Wing Suen. 2000. *The Structure of Economics: A Mathematical Analysis*, 3rd ed. New York: McGraw-Hill.

5 The Basic Monetary Model

5.1 Introduction

Up to this point we have only looked at real models that have completely abstracted from monetary considerations. The second part of this book—which comprises chapters 5 through 8—looks at the foundations of monetary economics in an open economy. This chapter starts our journey into this monetary world by introducing money into the endowment economy of chapter 1. To focus exclusively on monetary phenomena (as opposed to focusing on the *interaction* between monetary and real phenomena), we introduce money in such a way that it acts as a "veil" in the sense that the economy's real variables (i.e., consumption and the external accounts) are independent of the path of monetary variables such as the money supply and the exchange rate.

In this context we look at some basic monetary experiments that will enable us to understand monetary considerations in isolation from the rest of the economy. Section 5.2 starts by defining the two basic regimes under which an open economy can operate: predetermined exchange rates and flexible exchange rates. The fundamental difference between these two regimes is that while under flexible exchange rates the monetary authority controls the path of the nominal money supply, under predetermined exchange rates the nominal money supply is *endogenously* determined. Section 5.3 then shows that monetary and exchange rate policy are both *neutral* (changes in the level of the money supply or the exchange rate do not affect the real sector) and *superneutral* (changes in the rate of growth of the money supply or the exchange rate do not affect the real sector). Section 5.4 then proceeds to show that there is a fundamental equivalence between predetermined and flexible exchange rates. Specifically, for any given path of the nominal exchange rate set by the monetary authority under predetermined exchange rates, there will be some endogenously determined path of the nominal money supply. If, under flexible exchange rates, the monetary authority set this precise path of the nominal money supply, the same equilibrium would obviously obtain.

While this fundamental equivalence is an important conceptual benchmark, it should not be taken to imply that in the real world exchange rate regimes are irrelevant. Consider, for instance, an economy operating under predetermined exchange rates. Given that the economy will be subject to myriad monetary and real shocks, the resulting equilibrium path of the nominal money supply will exhibit high variability. Such a highly variable path would not be a path that would be set by the monetary authority under flexible rates. Rather, under flexible rates, the monetary authority would choose a more stable and predictable path since, after all, the whole idea of choosing a nominal anchor is to provide a stable nominal foundation to the economy. Put differently, since, in practice, the monetary authority will choose relatively simple paths of either the nominal exchange rate or the money supply, the economy will react differently to the same shocks.

We illustrate this idea in section 5.5 by analyzing the different response of the economy to money shocks depending on the exchange rate regime. Suppose that there is a negative money demand shock that will occur with certainty sometime in the future (e.g., at time T). Under predetermined exchange rates, real money balances will only fall at the moment that the shocks hits. This fall will come about by the public buying foreign bonds from the Central Bank in exchange for domestic money. In sharp contrast, under flexible exchange rates, the private sector as a whole has no means of getting rid of unwanted money balances at time T. Further the nominal exchange rate cannot jump at time T because, if it did, there would be unbounded profit opportunities. As a result real money balances must begin to fall in anticipation of the negative shock, which requires high inflation *before* the shock. The anticipation of the negative money demand shock will have inflationary consequences under flexible exchange rates but not under predetermined exchange rates.

Until this point in the chapter money will have been introduced by entering real money balances as an argument in the utility function. While this is a convenient shortcut, it does not make explicit the trading environment that may underlie the presence of money. A more explicit framework is analyzed in section 5.6 where we switch from continuous to discrete time and introduce money via a *cash-in-advance constraint*. We adopt a formulation—originally due to Lucas (1982)—in which asset markets open before goods markets, which implies that money continues to be a veil.[1]

In sum, this chapter focuses on the simplest monetary model of a small open economy in which money is a veil in the sense that monetary/exchange rate policy does not affect the real sector. Subsequent chapters will introduce various frictions into this benchmark model that will "remove the veil" and allow monetary variables to affect the real sector.

5.2 The Basic Monetary Model

Consider a small open economy inhabited by a large number of identical, infinitely lived consumers who are endowed with perfect foresight. The economy is perfectly integrated with the rest of the world in both goods and capital markets. There is only one (tradable and nonstorable) good, whose price is given by the law of one price. The economy receives a flow endowment of the good (y_t). The international real interest rate (r) is given and constant over time.

1. As will become clear in chapter 7, alternative timing assumptions in a discrete time environment (i.e., goods markets open before asset markets) or a continuous-time formulation of a cash-in-advance model imply that temporary changes in monetary/exchange rate policy will affect the real sector.

5.2.1 Consumer's Problem

Budget Constraints

The consumer holds two assets: domestic money (M_t) and an internationally-traded bond denominated in the foreign currency (B_t^*). Nominal asset holdings are therefore

$$A_t = M_t + E_t B_t^*, \tag{5.1}$$

where E_t is the nominal exchange rate (units of domestic currency per unit of foreign currency). By the law of one price,

$$P_t = E_t P_t^*, \tag{5.2}$$

where P_t is the domestic currency price of the good and P_t^* is the foreign currency price. By differentiating equation (5.2) with respect to time, we obtain

$$\pi_t = \varepsilon_t + \pi_t^*, \tag{5.3}$$

where $\pi_t(\equiv \dot{P}_t/P_t)$ is the rate of inflation, $\varepsilon_t(\equiv \dot{E}_t/E_t)$ is the rate of change of the exchange rate, and $\pi_t^*(\equiv \dot{P}_t^*/P_t^*)$ is the foreign inflation rate.[2]

The numéraire of this economy will be the tradable good. Hence "real" variables will be defined in terms of tradable goods. Dividing (5.1) by P_t, we obtain

$$a_t = m_t + b_t, \tag{5.4}$$

where $a_t(\equiv A_t/P_t)$, $m_t(\equiv M_t/P_t)$, and $b_t(\equiv B_t^*/P_t^*)$ denote real financial assets, real money balances, and real foreign bonds, respectively.

The consumer's flow constraint in nominal terms is given by

$$\dot{A}_t = \underbrace{E_t i_t^* B_t^*}_{\text{Interest income}} + \underbrace{\dot{E}_t B_t^*}_{\text{Capital gains}} + P_t y_t + P_t \tau_t - P_t c_t, \tag{5.5}$$

where i_t^* denotes the foreign nominal interest rate, y_t is the endowment of the good, τ_t denotes real lump-sum transfers from the government and c_t denotes consumption. As indicated, the term $E_t i_t^* B_t^*$ captures interest income on the foreign bonds (in terms of domestic currency), while the term $\dot{E}_t B_t^*$ denotes capital gains on the foreign bonds.

To express the flow constraint in real terms, divide (5.5) by P_t (taking into account the law of one price) to obtain

$$\frac{\dot{A}_t}{P_t} = (i_t^* + \varepsilon_t) b_t + y_t + \tau_t - c_t. \tag{5.6}$$

2. As a matter of terminology, we will refer to ε_t as the rate of *devaluation* under predetermined exchange rates and as the rate of *depreciation* under flexible exchange rates.

Since by definition, $a_t = A_t/E_tP_t^*$, it follows that

$$\dot{a}_t = \frac{\dot{A}_t}{P_t} - (\varepsilon_t + \pi_t^*)a_t. \tag{5.7}$$

Substituting (5.6) into (5.7), taking into account (5.4), and rearranging terms yields

$$\dot{a}_t = (i_t^* - \pi_t^*)a_t + y_t + \tau_t - c_t - (i_t^* + \varepsilon_t)m_t. \tag{5.8}$$

Assuming that the Fisher equation holds in the rest of the world (i.e., $i_t^* = r + \pi_t^*$) and taking into account that perfect capital mobility implies that interest parity will hold (i.e., $i_t = i_t^* + \varepsilon_t$), we can rewrite (5.8) as

$$\dot{a}_t = ra_t + y_t + \tau_t - c_t - i_tm_t. \tag{5.9}$$

Integrating forward equation (5.9) and imposing the transversality condition $\lim_{t\to\infty} a_te^{-rt} = 0$ (for the reasons discussed in chapter 1), we finally obtain

$$a_0 + \int_0^\infty (y_t + \tau_t)e^{-rt}dt = \int_0^\infty (c_t + i_tm_t)e^{-rt}dt. \tag{5.10}$$

This lifetime constraint makes perfect sense as it says that the present discounted value of "total expenditures" (given by the RHS, and which include the opportunity cost of holding real money balances) must equal the consumer's wealth (LHS), which comprises his/her initial real financial assets (a_0) and the present discounted value of the endowment and government transfers.

Utility Maximization

The consumer's lifetime utility is given by

$$\int_0^\infty [u(c_t) + v(m_t)]e^{-\beta t}dt, \tag{5.11}$$

where $\beta(>0)$ is the subjective discount rate, and the functions $u(c_t)$ and $v(m_t)$ are strictly increasing and strictly concave in their arguments:

$$u'(c_t) > 0, \quad v'(m_t) > 0,$$
$$u''(c_t) < 0, \quad v''(m_t) < 0.$$

The rationale behind introducing money in the utility function (MIUF) is that real money balances provide liquidity services that can be thought of as proportional to the stock of real money balances. In other words, liquidity services are captured by ξm_t where, for simplicity, it is assumed that

$\xi = 1$. Hence the way to think of $v(m_t)$ is that consumers derive utility from the liquidity services provided by money.[3]

The consumer's problem consists in choosing $\{c_t, m_t\}$ for all $t \in [0, \infty)$ to maximize lifetime utility (5.11) subject to the lifetime constraint (5.10), for a given path of τ_t, i_t, and y_t, and given values of r and a_0.

Assume, as usual, that $\beta = r$. The first-order conditions are then given by

$$u'(c_t) = \lambda, \tag{5.12}$$

$$v'(m_t) = \lambda i_t. \tag{5.13}$$

Combining these two equations, we obtain

$$u'(c_t) = \frac{v'(m_t)}{i_t},$$

which implicitly defines a real money demand with standard properties:

$$m_t = L(c_t, i_t), \tag{5.14}$$

$$\frac{\partial L}{\partial c_t} = \frac{i_t u''(c_t)}{v''(m_t)} > 0, \tag{5.15}$$

$$\frac{\partial L}{\partial i_t} = \frac{u'(c_t)}{v''(m_t)} < 0. \tag{5.16}$$

Real money demand is thus increasing in consumption and decreasing in the nominal interest rate (the opportunity cost of holding money).[4]

5.2.2 Government

The government comprises the fiscal authority and the monetary authority (i.e., the Central Bank). Let H_t^* be the amount of net foreign bonds (measured in terms of foreign currency) that the government holds and $H_t (\equiv E_t H_t^*)$ denote the domestic currency value of these bonds. The government's flow constraint in nominal terms is given by[5]

3. There are two other popular ways of introducing money: via a cash-in-advance constraint (as analyzed later in this chapter and in chapter 7) or a transactions costs technology (chapter 7). All three ways have pros and cons that will be made clear as we proceed further.

4. It is worth noting that in any microfounded model of money, real money demand will depend on *consumption*, as opposed to income or output.

5. Appendix 5.8.1 breaks down the government into the monetary and the fiscal authority and shows how equation (5.17) follows from consolidating their respective nominal budget constraints.

$$\dot{H}_t = \underbrace{i_t^* E_t H_t^*}_{\text{Interest income}} + \underbrace{\dot{E}_t H_t^*}_{\text{Capital gains}} + \underbrace{\dot{M}_t}_{\text{Money printing}} - \underbrace{P_t \tau_t}_{\text{Transfers}}. \tag{5.17}$$

As indicated below the equation, the government has three sources of revenues: (1) interest income on its international reserves, (2) capital gains on its international reserves, and (3) money printing or revenues from money creation. The only government expenditure consists of lump-sum transfers.[6]

To obtain the government's flow constraint in real terms, we proceed in the same way as we did above for the consumer. Define the real value of international reserves (i.e., international reserves in terms of real "dollars") as $h_t (\equiv H_t/P_t)$. It then follows that

$$\dot{h}_t = \frac{\dot{H}_t}{P_t} - (\varepsilon_t + \pi_t^*)h_t. \tag{5.18}$$

Dividing (5.17) by P_t, substituting the resulting expression into (5.18) (and imposing the Fisher equation for the rest of the world), we obtain

$$\dot{h}_t = rh_t + \frac{\dot{M}_t}{P_t} - \tau_t. \tag{5.19}$$

It proves illuminating to write the real revenues from money creation, $\dot{M}_t/P_t$, as

$$\frac{\dot{M}_t}{P_t} = \underbrace{\dot{m}_t}_{\text{Seigniorage}} + \underbrace{(\varepsilon_t + \pi_t^*)m_t}_{\text{Inflation tax}}. \tag{5.20}$$

As indicated, real revenues from money creation can be divided into two components: (1) seigniorage, which refers to the revenues that may accrue to the government as the result of an increase in the public's *real* demand for money, and (2) the inflation tax, which refers to the revenues that may accrue to the government as a result of the public's desire to replace the loss of value of real money balances due to a positive inflation rate.[7]

Substituting equation (5.20) into equation (5.19), we obtain

$$\dot{h}_t = rh_t + \dot{m}_t + (\varepsilon_t + \pi_t^*)m_t - \tau_t. \tag{5.21}$$

Integrating forward equation (5.19) and imposing the transversality condition $\lim_{t\to\infty} h_t e^{-rt} = 0$, we obtain the government's intertemporal constraint:[8]

6. At this point we are, of course, abstracting from tax revenues from conventional taxes (i.e., taxes other than the inflation tax) and government spending.

7. We should warn the reader that in the context of public finance models of the type studied in chapter 10, the expression "inflation tax" is typically used to denote $i_t m_t$, which is what accrues to the government due to its ability to issue a non–interest-bearing liability.

8. Strictly speaking—and as discussed in appendix 5.8.2—the LHS of constraint (5.22) should include all future jumps in real money balances.

$$h_0 + \int_0^\infty \frac{\dot{M}_t}{P_t} e^{-rt} dt = \int_0^\infty \tau_t e^{-rt} dt. \tag{5.22}$$

In closing, notice that so far we have only looked at fiscal accounting and made no policy assumptions.

5.2.3 Equilibrium Conditions

The assumption of perfect capital mobility implies that the interest parity condition holds:

$$i_t = i_t^* + \varepsilon_t. \tag{5.23}$$

Let $k_t (\equiv b_t + h_t)$ denote the economy's stock of net foreign assets. Combining the consumer's flow constraint (equation 5.9) with the government's (equation 5.21) yields the economy's flow constraint:

$$\dot{k}_t = rk_t + y_t - c_t. \tag{5.24}$$

The economy accumulates net foreign assets (i.e., $\dot{k}_t > 0$) to the extent that the economy's income $(rk_t + y_t)$ exceeds the economy's consumption (c_t). To link the economy's flow constraint to standard balance of payments accounting, rewrite this equation as

$$\underbrace{\dot{h}_t}_{\Delta h} = \underbrace{-\dot{b}_t}_{KA} + \underbrace{\underbrace{r(b_t + h_t)}_{IB} + \underbrace{y_t - c_t}_{TB}}_{CA}, \tag{5.25}$$

where TB, IB, CA, KA, and Δh denote trade balance, income balance, current account, capital account, and increase in international reserves, respectively. As indicated, equation (5.25) therefore constitutes the fundamental identity of balance of payment accounting which, in words, reads as[9]

Increase in international reserves = Capital account + Current account.

In the "real" world of chapter 1, a current account deficit had to be financed by a capital account surplus (i.e., by borrowing from abroad). In contrast, a monetary economy can run a current account deficit *and* a capital account deficit (i.e., lending abroad) provided that the Central Bank is financing these two deficits by losing international reserves.

Finally, notice that integrating forward the economy's flow constraint (equation 5.24) and imposing the transversality condition $\lim_{t \to \infty} k_t e^{-rt} = 0$ yields the economy's resource constraint:[10]

9. As a matter of terminology, notice that the change in international reserves is often referred to as the "balance of payments." If the country is gaining (losing) international reserves, the balance of payments is positive (negative).

10. Alternatively, and as exercise 1 at the end of the chapter shows, equation (5.26) can be derived by combining the consumer's and the government's intertemporal constraints, given by (5.10) and (5.22), respectively.

$$k_0 + \int_0^\infty y_t e^{-rt} dt = \int_0^\infty c_t e^{-rt} dt. \tag{5.26}$$

5.2.4 Perfect Foresight Equilibrium

We now characterize the perfect foresight equilibrium paths (PFEP) of consumption and real money balances. It follows from first-order condition (5.12) that consumption will be constant (and denoted by c) along a perfect foresight equilibrium. Then, from the economy's resource constraint (5.26),

$$c = r\left(k_0 + \int_0^\infty y_t e^{-rt} dt\right). \tag{5.27}$$

Due to the separability of consumption and real money balances in the utility function, consumption is constant over time (and equal to permanent income) *regardless* of the path of the nominal variables. As in the endowment model of chapter 1, consumption will be flat over time for any path of the endowment. In periods of low (high) endowment, the economy will run trade deficits (surpluses) to smooth consumption over time. Furthermore consumption and the external accounts would respond to unanticipated endowment shocks in exactly the same way as they did in chapter 1. Hence, in this basic monetary model, money is just a "veil" in the sense that the model exhibits the "dichotomy" between the real and monetary sectors emphasized in classical monetary economics.[11]

From (5.14), real money demand along a PFEP will be given by

$$m_t = L(c, i_t). \tag{5.28}$$

Hence real money demand will be constant if the nominal interest rate is constant over time. We now turn to the determination of the nominal interest rate and other nominal variables. (In what follows we will assume that the foreign inflation rate is constant at the level π^*.)

5.2.5 Nominal Anchors

The determination of the nominal interest rate and the paths of both the nominal exchange rate and the nominal money supply will depend on the specific monetary regime adopted by the monetary authority. We will now study the determination of these variables under the two main nominal anchors: the exchange rate (predetermined exchange rates) and the money supply (flexible exchange rate).[12]

11. It is worth noticing that this dichotomy refers to the fact that the monetary sector does not influence the real sector. But real shocks, of course, may affect monetary variables.

12. In most modern economies, the Central Bank has a legal monopoly over the issuance of money. As with any monopolist, the Central Bank can either set the price (and let the quantity be market-determined) or the quantity (and let the price be market determined). The former is the case of predetermined exchange rates and the latter is the case of flexible exchange rates.

Table 5.1
Balance sheet

$E_t H_t^*$	M_t
D_t	

As a starting point, consider the Central Bank's balance sheet illustrated in table 5.1.[13] From the balance sheet, it follows that

$$E_t H_t^* + D_t = M_t, \tag{5.29}$$

where D_t denotes the stock of nominal domestic credit.[14]

To organize our thoughts regarding the *mechanics* of nominal anchors and the determination of nominal magnitudes, it is helpful to rewrite equation (5.28) as

$$\frac{M_t}{E_t P_t^*} = L(c, i_t), \tag{5.30}$$

where P_t^* is, of course, exogenously given. As will be clear below, in a stationary equilibrium, the nominal interest rate, i_t, will be determined by the rate of growth of the nominal anchor. Hence let us view i_t as having been determined already for the purposes of analyzing the determination of nominal magnitudes. We can then view equations (5.29) and (5.30) as a two-equation system with four unknowns: E_t, H_t^*, D_t, and M_t. The monetary authority can then set two of these four variables, and let the other two be determined endogenously. In addition equation (5.30) tells us that either M_t or E_t must be set by the monetary authority (but not both because, in that case, equation 5.30 would be overdetermined).

In this context—and as table 5.2 illustrates—we can define a predetermined exchange rate regime as one in which the monetary authority sets E_t and D_t and lets M_t and H_t^* be determined endogenously. Put differently, we can think of the monetary authority as setting E_t which, through equation (5.30), determines M_t. With E_t and M_t so determined and D_t being set by the monetary authority, the Central Bank's balance sheet (5.29) endogenously determines H_t^*.

13. Following common practice—and for simplicity—the balance sheet assumes that the Central Bank's net worth is zero.

14. In the context of this model—in which we do not explicitly model domestic bonds—the label "domestic credit" is somewhat of a misnomer. The label "domestic credit" is more natural when the monetary authority introduces money into the system via open market operations whereby a purchase of domestic bonds (an increase in domestic credit) increases the money supply and a sale of domestic bonds (a reduction in domestic credit) reduces the money supply. In the current model, however, money should be thought of as being introduced into the economy through a "helicopter drop" (and being retired from the system with a giant vacuum cleaner!). Hence "domestic credit" is essentially an accounting fiction that could, however, be interpreted as a non–interest-bearing obligation of the private sector and/or nonfinancial public sector vis-à-vis the monetary authority.

Table 5.2
Nominal anchors

	Predetermined	Flexible
E	Set by policy	Endogenous
H^*	Endogenous	Set by policy
D	Set by policy	Set by policy
M	Endogenous	Set by policy
Z	na	Endogenous

Note: na means "not applicable." See text for definition of variables.

To define a flexible exchange rate regime, we need an additional wrinkle. Under flexible exchange rates, the nominal exchange rate will be an endogenous variable. The Central Bank's balance sheet (5.29) would then tell us that, for given H_t^* and D_t, changes in E_t would change the money supply. For instance, an increase in the nominal exchange rate would lead the Central Bank to print more money. In practice, however, Central Banks typically do not "monetize" changes in the nominal exchange rate and simply credit/debit a non-monetary liability. To fix ideas, denote this non-monetary liability by Z_t and rewrite the balance sheet of the Central Bank as

$$E_t H_t^* + D_t = M_t + Z_t. \tag{5.31}$$

We can then view equations (5.30) and (5.31) as a system of two equations in five unknowns: E_t, H_t^*, D_t, M_t, and Z_t. The Central Bank can then set three of these five variables and let the other two be determined endogenously (see table 5.2) . Under flexible exchange rates, the Central Bank sets D_t, M_t, and H_t^* and lets E_t and Z_t be determined endogenously. In other words, we can think of the Central Bank setting M_t and the money market equilibrium (5.30) determining E_t. With M_t and E_t so determined and the Central Bank setting H_t^* and D_t, equation (5.31) determines Z_t.

Having discussed the mechanics behind predetermined and flexible exchange rates regimes, we now turn to a more detailed discussion and solve the model under both regimes.

Predetermined Exchange Rates

Under predetermined exchange rates, the monetary authority sets the path of the nominal exchange rate (E_t) and the path of the nominal stock of domestic credit (D_t). The path of international reserves (H_t^*) and the path of the nominal supply of money (M_t) will be *endogenously* determined. The idea that the nominal money supply is *endogenous* under predetermined exchange rates is critical to the understanding of this regime.

We use the term "predetermined exchange rates" rather than the more common label "fixed exchange rates" because, strictly speaking, the latter is just a particular case of the former. The key feature of a predetermined exchange rates regime is that at any given point in time, the monetary authority stands ready to buy and sell foreign exchange at a given price (i.e., at a given exchange rate). In other words, the public can go to the Central Bank and sell foreign currency (e.g., dollars) in exchange for domestic currency and vice versa. If the price at which the Central Bank sells/buys foreign exchange is constant over time, we then talk of a fixed exchange rate regime. But if that price varies over time, then we use the more general term “predetermined exchange rate.”[15]

Formally, setting the path of the nominal exchange rate implies setting the initial level, E_0, and a constant rate of growth, ε, of the nominal exchange rate.[16] Given ε, the interest parity condition (5.23) determines a constant level of the nominal interest rate, i:

$$i = i^* + \varepsilon. \tag{5.32}$$

The constancy of the nominal interest rate implies, from (5.28), that real money balances will be constant over time at a level given by

$$m = L(c, i). \tag{5.33}$$

Hence, $\dot{m}_t = 0$ for all $t \in [0, \infty)$. Since, by definition, $m_t = M_t/E_tP_t^*$, it follows that the rate of money growth, μ_t, will also be constant over time:

$$\mu = \varepsilon + \pi^*. \tag{5.34}$$

The only nominal variable yet to be determined is the initial level of the nominal money supply, M_0. Since equation (5.28) holds at time 0, we can write

$$\frac{M_0}{P_0^*E_0} = L(c, i).$$

We then solve for M_0:

$$M_0 = P_0^*E_0L(c, i). \tag{5.35}$$

Interestingly, so far we have not made use of the path of nominal domestic credit. Hence, all the endogenous variables derived above are independent of the path of nominal domestic credit. The path of nominal domestic credit will matter though in determining the path of international reserves (h_t). As indicated above, the monetary authority sets the initial level, D_0, and the (constant) rate of growth (θ) of domestic credit. To determine the resulting path of international reserves, first express the Central Bank's balance sheet in real terms:

$$h_t + d_t = m_t.$$

Then differentiate this identity and solve for $\dot{h}_t$:

$$\dot{h}_t = \dot{m}_t - \dot{d}_t. \tag{5.36}$$

15. Appendix 5.8.5 reviews the many forms that predetermined exchange rates regimes may take in practice.

16. Of course, the monetary authority could set a nonconstant path of the devaluation rate. We will study some of those cases in later chapters.

This equation says that, under predetermined exchange rates, any creation in real domestic credit in excess of changes in real money demand will result in a loss of international reserves. In other words, if $\dot{d}_t > \dot{m}_t$, then $\dot{h}_t < 0$. Intuitively, money printed by the Central Bank that is not demanded by the private sector will result in a loss of international reserves as the private sector gets rid of unwanted money balances by exchanging them for net foreign assets at the Central Bank. To gain additional insights, notice that since $d_t \equiv D_t/E_tP_t^*$,

$$\dot{d}_t = d_t(\theta - \varepsilon - \pi^*). \tag{5.37}$$

Substituting (5.37) into (5.36), we obtain

$$\dot{h}_t = \dot{m}_t - d_t(\theta - \varepsilon - \pi^*).$$

In this particular case, $\dot{m}_t = 0$ because, from (5.33), real money demand is constant. Hence we can rewrite this equation as

$$\dot{h}_t = -d_t(\theta - \varepsilon - \pi^*). \tag{5.38}$$

Given that real money demand is constant, if nominal domestic credit is growing faster than domestic inflation (i.e., if $\theta > \varepsilon + \pi^*$), then the monetary authority will be losing international reserves (i.e., $\dot{h}_t < 0$). This has been a common situation in many countries where the monetary authority is often coerced into printing money to finance the fiscal authority's spending. If this situation persists and there is some threshold below which international reserve cannot fall, the monetary authority will run out of international reserves and a balance-of-payments crisis will ensue (as analyzed in detail in chapter 16). Conversely, a situation in which $\theta < \varepsilon + \pi^*$would imply that the monetary authority accumulates international reserves without bound and so can also be ruled out. Hence, for a predetermined exchange rates regime to be sustainable over time, the rate of domestic credit growth must equal the domestic inflation rate (i.e., $\theta = \varepsilon + \pi^*$), which will be our maintained assumption.[17] From (5.37) this implies that $\dot{d}_t = 0$, and hence from (5.36),

$$\dot{h}_t = \dot{m}_t. \tag{5.39}$$

In equilibrium, changes in real money demand will be reflected in changes in international reserves.

Having established that the path of international reserves is constant over time, we need to establish their initial value, h_0. From the Central Bank's balance sheet at $t = 0$ and (5.33), it follows that

$$h_0 = L(c, i) - d_0. \tag{5.40}$$

In principle, h_0 could take any sign, since the Central Bank could have a negative asset position.

17. Strictly speaking, this is a sufficient, though not necessary, condition for a predetermined exchange rate regime to be sustainable (see appendix 5.8.3).

Finally, notice that the variable that adjusts to make the government constraint hold at any point in time is the level of transfers. From (5.21), and taking into account that h_t, ε_t, and m_t are all constant over time, it follows that

$$\tau = rh + (\varepsilon + \pi^*)m. \tag{5.41}$$

To fix ideas, consider a fixed exchange rate regime ($\varepsilon = 0$) and zero foreign inflation. Then $\tau = rh$. If $h < 0$, then the government is financing the debt service by taxing the private sector.

Flexible Exchange Rates

Under flexible exchange rates the monetary authority does not intervene in the foreign exchange market and allows the exchange rate to be determined by market forces. If the Central Bank does not intervene in the foreign exchange market, its international reserves will be constant over time.[18] For simplicity, it is typically assumed that this initial level of international reserves is zero.

If international reserves are zero, then the Central Bank's balance sheet reduces to

$$D_t = M_t.$$

Hence, under flexible exchange rates, setting the path of nominal domestic credit is equivalent to setting the path of the nominal money supply.[19] In particular, the monetary authority sets the initial level, M_0, and a constant rate of growth, μ, of the nominal money supply.

We first show that real money balances will be constant over time. To see this, notice that $\dot{m}_t/m_t = \mu - \varepsilon_t - \pi^*$, and use (5.13) and (5.23) to obtain

$$\dot{m}_t = m_t\left[r + \mu - \frac{v'(m_t)}{\lambda}\right]. \tag{5.42}$$

This is a differential equation in m_t because λ is simply some number that has been determined by (5.12) and (5.27). Linearizing this equation around the stationary value for real money balances, denoted by $\bar{m}$ and implicitly given by $r + \mu = v'(\bar{m})/\lambda$, we see that this is an unstable differential equation.[20] Formally,

$$\left.\frac{\partial \dot{m}_t}{\partial m_t}\right|_{\bar{m}} = -\frac{\bar{m}v''(\bar{m})}{\lambda} > 0.$$

18. The Central Bank could, of course, choose a nonconstant path of international reserves by appropriately intervening in the foreign exchange market. This would be the case of "dirty floating" analyzed in exercise 2 at the end of this chapter.

19. If the constant level of reserves had not been set equal to zero, then this statement would not be quite correct because changes in the nominal exchange rate would imply capital gains or losses, which would affect the nominal money supply. As already discussed, in practice Central Banks do not "monetize" capital gains or losses but instead debit a nonmonetary liability.

20. As an example, notice that if $v(m_t) = \log(m_t)$, then equation (5.42) becomes a linear differential equation given by $\dot{m}_t = (r + \mu)m_t - 1/\lambda$, which is, of course, unstable.

This implies that unless m_t is already at its stationary value at $t = 0$, it will diverge over time. Hence the only convergent equilibrium path is $m_t = \bar{m}$ for all $t \geq 0$. Intuitively, if m_t increases, the nominal interest rate must fall to accommodate this increase. By the interest parity condition, this implies a fall in the rate of depreciation (inflation); this in turn implies that real money supply will grow faster, which requires a further fall in the nominal interest rate, and so forth. Further, since $\dot{m}_t/m_t = \mu - \varepsilon_t - \pi^* = 0$, the (constant) rate of depreciation will be given by

$$\varepsilon = \mu - \pi^*. \tag{5.43}$$

From the interest parity condition (5.23) and (5.43)—and taking into account that $i^* = r + \pi^*$ —it follows that the constant level of the nominal interest rate is given by

$$i = r + \mu. \tag{5.44}$$

The only nominal variable yet to be determined is the initial level of the nominal exchange rate, E_0 (i.e., the initial price level). Since equation (5.28) holds at time 0, we can write

$$\frac{M_0}{P_0^* E_0} = L(c, i).$$

We then solve for E_0 to obtain

$$E_0 = \frac{M_0}{P_0^* L(c, i)}.$$

We have thus shown that as under predetermined exchange rates, the value of all nominal variables is perfectly well defined under flexible exchange rates.

Finally, how does the level of transfers get determined? Since international reserves are equal to zero and $\dot{m}_t = 0$, then from (5.21), the constant level of transfers is given by

$$\tau = (\varepsilon + \pi^*)m. \tag{5.45}$$

5.3 Neutrality and Superneutrality

We now proceed to show that in our basic monetary model, monetary and exchange rate policy are neutral and superneutral. By "neutral" monetary policy, we mean that an (unanticipated) and permanent change in the *level* of the money supply has no real effects.[21] It simply leads to an equi-proportional change in the exchange rate. By the same token, a neutral exchange rate policy means that a permanent devaluation has no real effects and leads to an equi-proportional change in the nominal money supply. By "superneutral" monetary or exchange rate policy, we mean

21. In this context it is always implicitly understood that "real effects" refers to real variables other than real monetary balances (which may change).

that neither changes in the rate of money growth nor in the rate of devaluation have any real effects.

Since both monetary and exchange rate policy are neutral and superneutral, changes in monetary/exchange rate policy will have no effects on the real economy. Conversely, real shocks will have the same real effects under either flexible or predetermined exchange rates regimes, as examined in exercise 3 at the end of the chapter. Hence money is a veil in this basic model in the sense that the economy's real variables are independent of the path of monetary variables.

5.3.1 Exchange Rate Policy

We will now study the effects of (1) an unanticipated and permanent devaluation (i.e., an increase in the level of the exchange rate), and (2) an unanticipated and permanent increase in the devaluation rate.

A Permanent Devaluation

Suppose that the economy is initially in the stationary perfect foresight equilibrium characterized above (for $\pi^* = 0$). For simplicity, assume that initially $\varepsilon = \theta = 0$, so that the exchange rate is initially fixed. At $t = 0$ there is an unanticipated and permanent increase in the level of the nominal exchange rate (i.e., a permanent devaluation); see figure 5.1, panel a. What will be the effects of this devaluation?

Clearly, the devaluation has no real effects since we have already shown that along a PFEP, consumption is given by (5.27) regardless of the path of the exchange rate (figure 5.1, panel b). From (5.32), we also see that the nominal interest rate will not change (figure 5.1, panel c). Hence, from (5.33), real money demand does not change either (figure 5.1, panel d). From (5.34), the same is true of the rate of money growth. From (5.35), we see that the initial level of nominal money balances will increase in the same proportion as the exchange rate.

The main action resulting from a permanent devaluation actually takes place in the Central Bank's balance sheet. Since the stock of nominal domestic credit is controlled by policy makers and hence is given at $t = 0$, the real stock of domestic credit falls at $t = 0$ and remains at that lower level thereafter (figure 5.1, panel e). We can then infer the path of international reserves from the Central Bank balance sheet ($h_t = m_t - d_t$). It follows that international reserves jump up on impact and remain constant thereafter (figure 5.1, panel f). In fact—as follows from the Central Bank's balance sheet—the change in international reserves at $t = 0$ is exactly equal to the reduction in the real stock of domestic credit:

$$\Delta h_0 = -\Delta d_0 > 0.$$

We thus conclude that *a devaluation leads to a gain in international reserves.*

What is the intuition behind the increase in international reserves at the Central Bank? The key is that while the devaluation does not affect real money demand, it reduces real money supply for

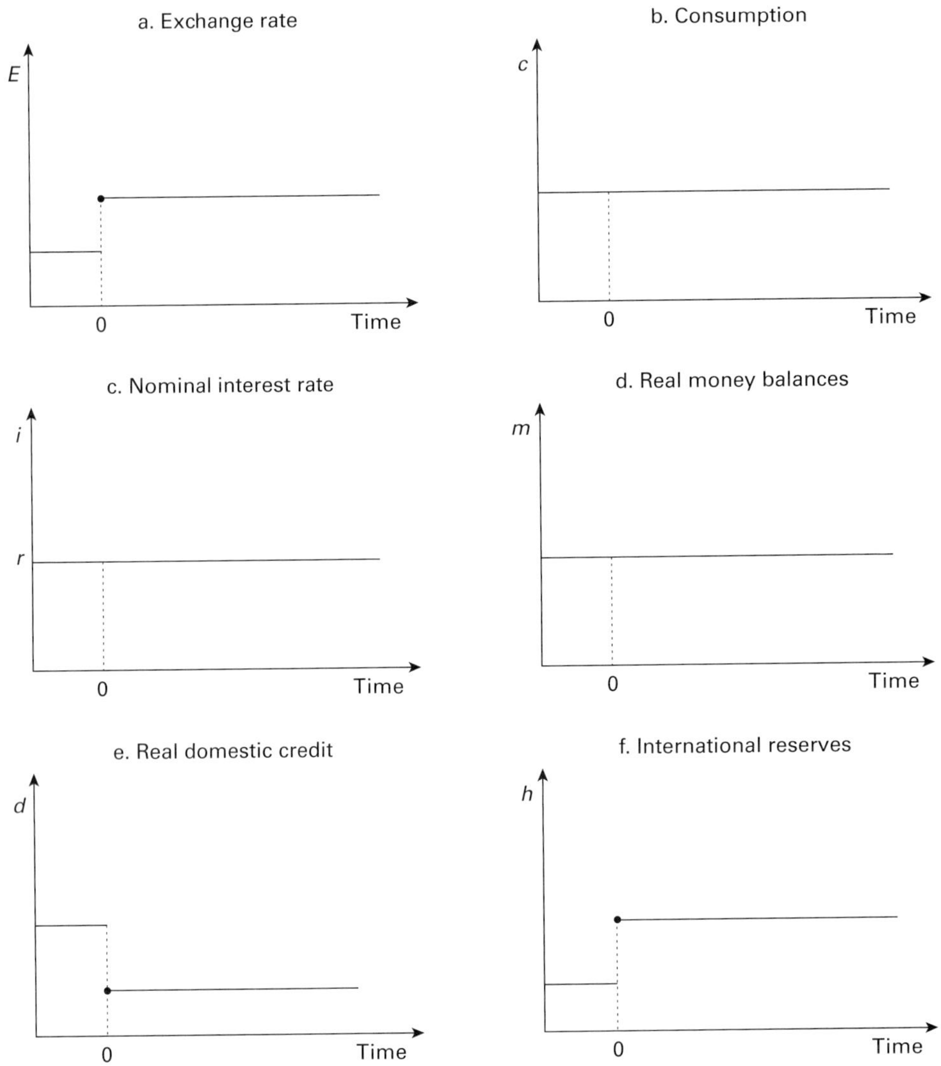

Figure 5.1
Permanent devaluation

the initial nominal money supply. In other words, at the initial money supply, there is an incipient excess demand for money. To rebuild their money balances, consumers go to the Central Bank and exchange net foreign assets for nominal money balances.[22]

The idea of an "excess money demand" leading to a gain in international reserves—which occurs instantaneously in this model with no frictions—is one of the most fundamental monetary adjustment mechanisms under predetermined exchange rates. Introducing various frictions into this basic model (e.g., assuming that there are no interest-bearing bonds as in chapter 6 or assuming that there are capital controls) will force this adjustment to take place gradually over time but will not alter its fundamental nature.[23]

A Permanent Increase in the Rate of Devaluation

Suppose now that starting from the same initial equilibrium (for $\pi^* = \varepsilon = \theta = 0$), there is an unanticipated and permanent increase in the devaluation rate (figure 5.2, panel a).[24] Once again, consumption remains constant (figure 5.2, panel b). From (5.32) we infer that the nominal interest rate increases pari passu with the devaluation rate (figure 5.2, panel c). Since the opportunity cost of holding money increases, real money demand falls at $t = 0$, as follows from (5.33) (figure 5.2, panel d).[25] The rate of money growth increases (from equation 5.34). From (5.35) the initial level of the money supply also falls. The path of real domestic credit remains unchanged (figure 5.2, panel e). Finally, since real money demand falls, we infer from (5.40) that international reserves fall at $t = 0$ (panel f).

How does this adjustment take place? In response to the increase in the opportunity cost of holding money, the consumer wants to reduce his/her real money holdings. To do so, he/she goes to the Central Bank and exchanges domestic money for foreign assets (i.e., sells domestic currency and buys foreign assets). As a result international reserves at the Central Bank fall, whereas private holdings of net foreign assets go up. For the economy as a whole, net foreign assets do not change.

Note that while a permanent devaluation leads to an *increase* in international reserves, a permanent increase in the devaluation rate results in a *fall* in international reserves. These contrasting outcomes are due to the different way in which equilibrium in the money market is affected. In the

22. An alternative interpretation, which focuses on Central Bank intervention, goes as follows. To rebuild money balances, consumers sell foreign assets. This puts downward pressure on the nominal exchange rate (the nominal price of foreign bonds). To prevent the domestic currency from appreciating, the Central Bank must step in and buy the foreign assets offered by the private sector. By so doing, the Central Bank increases the money supply until the money market is in equilibrium, at which point there are no further pressures on the nominal exchange rate.

23. By the same token, a revaluation (i.e., a fall in E_t) would lead to a loss in international reserves because, at the initial nominal money supply, there would be an excess supply of money.

24. To ensure that the predetermined exchange rate regime continues to be sustainable, we assume that θ increases by the same amount.

25. The extent to which real money demand reacts to changes in the nominal interest rate, which will determine in turn the magnitude of the ensuing effects, will depend on the interest-rate elasticity of money demand. Appendix 5.8.6 reviews the empirical estimates of this important parameter.

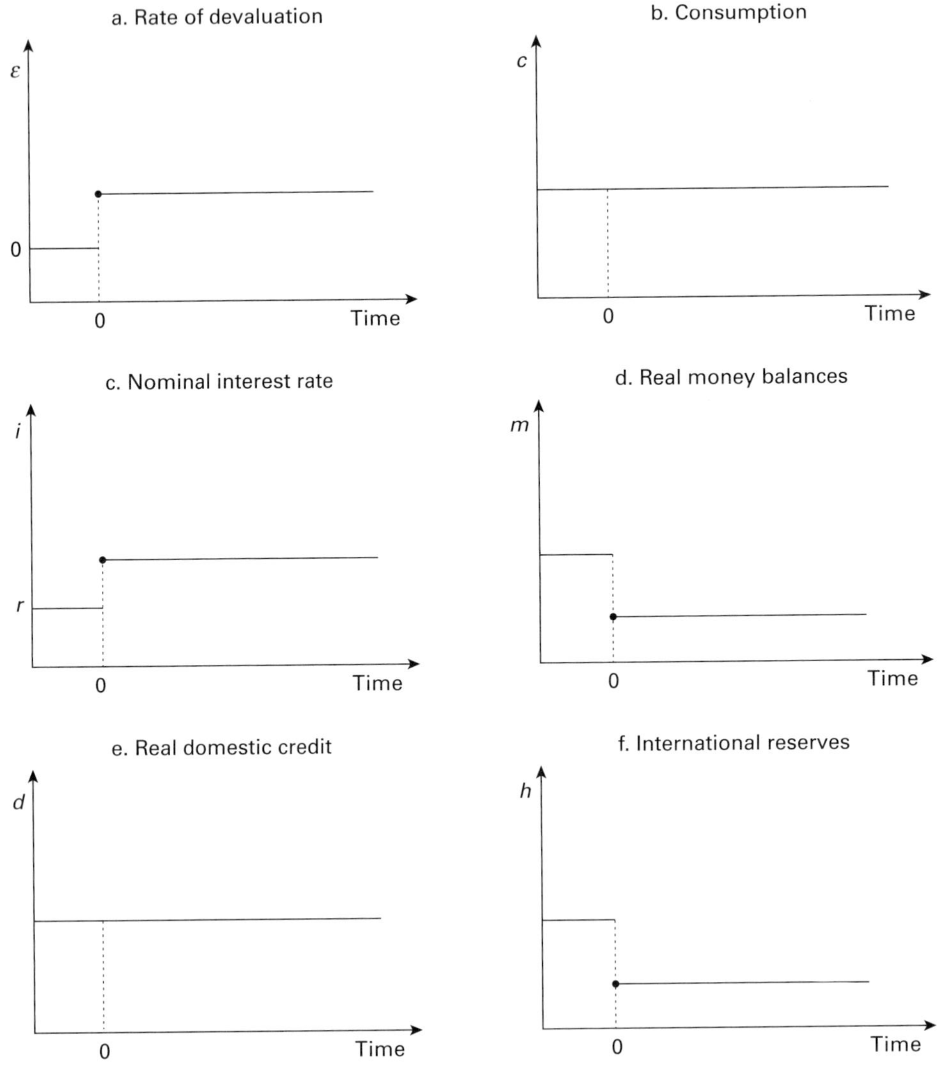

Figure 5.2
Permanent increase in devaluation rate

first case—and for the initial nominal money supply—the devaluation leads to an incipient excess real money demand that requires an upward adjustment in the nominal money supply.[26] In the second case—and for the initial nominal money supply—the increase in the rate of devaluation leads to an incipient excess real money supply that requires a fall in the nominal money supply.

5.3.2 Monetary Policy

We now turn to flexible exchange rates and examine the effects of (1) an unanticipated and permanent increase in the stock of nominal money and (2) an unanticipated and permanent increase in the rate of money growth.

Permanent Increase in Money Supply

Suppose that starting from the initial equilibrium described above (with $\mu = \pi^* = 0$), there is an unanticipated and permanent increase in the nominal money supply (figure 5.3, panel a). Consumption, of course, remains constant (figure 5.3, panel b). In the new equilibrium, real money balances must remain constant; otherwise, the path of real money balances would diverge over time (figure 5.3, panel c). The constancy of real money balances implies that on impact, the nominal exchange rate will increase by the same proportion as the nominal money supply and remain at that level thereafter (figure 5.3, panel d). The fact that $\dot{m}_t = 0$ for all t implies that the rate of depreciation continues to be equal to 0 (figure 5.3, panel e). This implies that the nominal interest rate also remains constant (figure 5.3, panel f).

We conclude that a permanent increase in the nominal money supply leads to an equiproportional increase in the nominal exchange rate, leaving unchanged all other variables.

Permanent Increase in the Rate of Money Growth

Suppose that starting from the initial equilibrium described above (with $\mu = \pi^* = 0$), there is an unanticipated and permanent increase in the rate of money growth (figure 5.4, panel a). Consumption, of course, remains unchanged (figure 5.4, panel b). Since real money balances are governed by an unstable differential equation, they must adjust immediately to their new and lower stationary value (figure 5.4, panel c). Otherwise, the path of real money balances would diverge over time. Since the nominal money supply is given at $t = 0$, we infer that the nominal exchange rate increases on impact (figure 5.4, panel d). The fact that $\dot{m}_t = 0$ for all t implies that the rate of depreciation increases on impact and remains at that level thereafter (panel e). This, in turn, implies that the nominal exchange rate jumps up at $t = 0$ and then increases at the rate of money growth from $t = 0$ onward (figure 5.4, panel d). By interest parity, the nominal interest rate increases on impact and stays constant thereafter (figure 5.4, panel f).

26. In contrast, a permanent increase in domestic credit (i.e., an increase in D_t) would lead to an incipient excess supply of money and hence a loss of international reserves, as analyzed in exercise 4 at the end of the chapter.

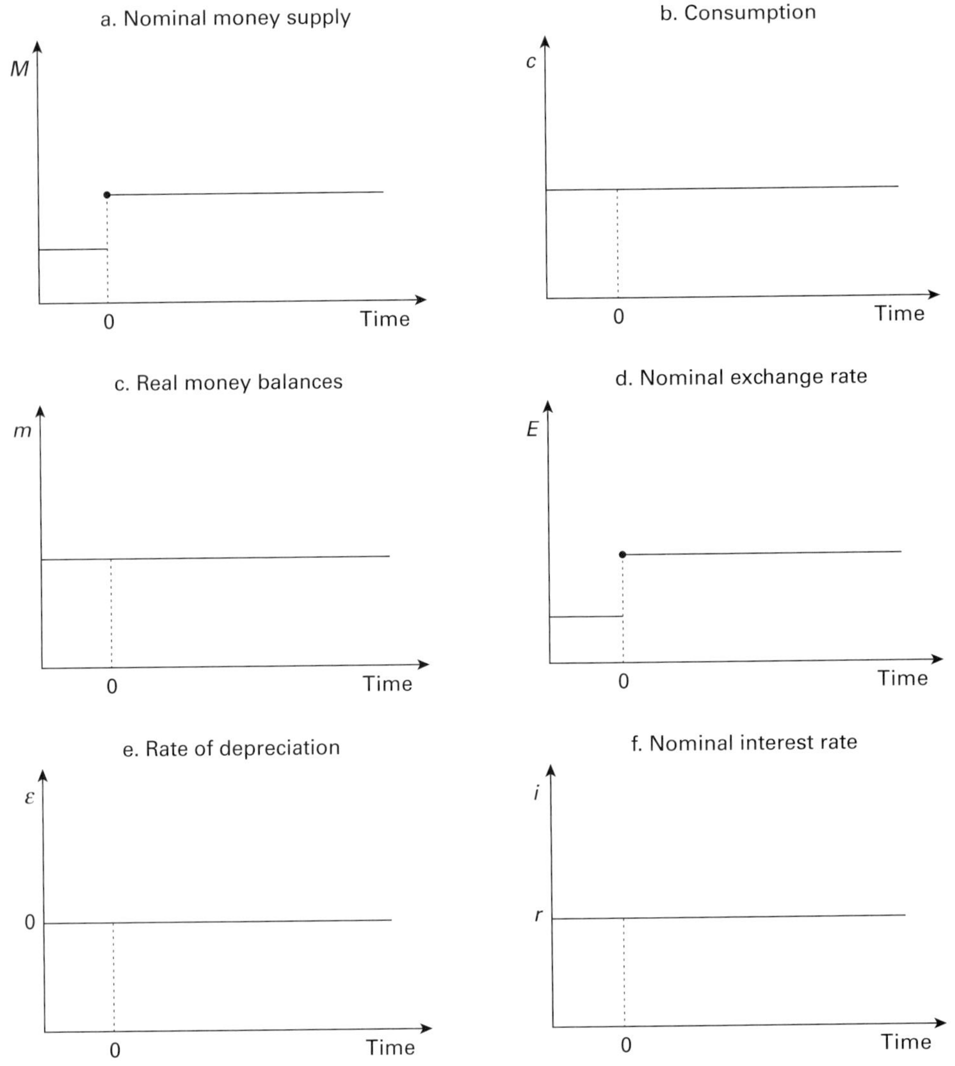

Figure 5.3
Permanent increase in nominal money supply

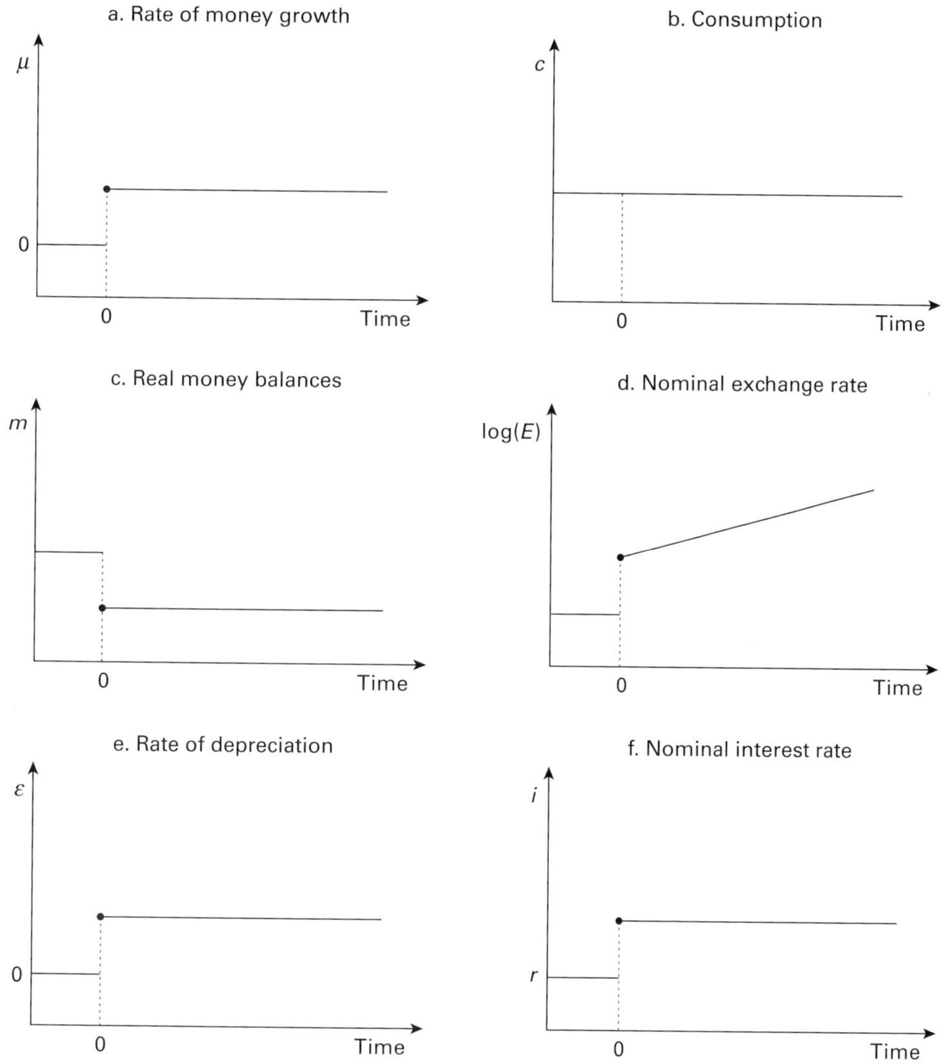

Figure 5.4
Permanent increase in rate of money growth

We conclude that a permanent increase in the rate of money growth leads to an increase in the exchange rate and a corresponding increase in the rate of depreciation and the nominal interest rate.

5.4 Equivalence Results

We will now show that there is a fundamental equivalence between predetermined and flexible exchange rates. Consider an economy operating under predetermined exchange rates. (For simplicity, assume that foreign inflation is zero.) For any given path of the exchange rate set by the monetary authority, there will be a corresponding path of the nominal money supply. If, under flexible rates, the monetary authority were to set exogenously that path of the nominal money supply, the same equilibrium paths would obtain. In fact—and unless you were able to see the movements in international reserves at the Central Bank—you would be unable to tell the two regimes apart.

We will illustrate this point by looking at two examples. First, we will assume that the economy is operating under predetermined exchange rates with a nonconstant rate of devaluation and study the implications for the path of the nominal money supply. We will then examine the opposite case: we will assume that the economy is operating under flexible exchange rates with a nonconstant path of the money growth rate and examine the implications for the path of the nominal exchange rate.[27]

5.4.1 A Nonconstant Rate of Devaluation

Suppose that the economy is operating under predetermined exchange rates. Consider the perfect foresight equilibrium corresponding to the path of the devaluation rate illustrated in figure 5.5, panel a. The rate of devaluation is constant until time T (at the level ε^H) at which time it falls to a lower level (ε^L) and stays there afterward. The corresponding path of the nominal exchange rate is illustrated in figure 5.5, panel b. By the interest parity condition (equation 5.23), the nominal interest rate is high and then low (figure 5.5, panel c). From (5.28), real money demand will be low until time T and then jump to a higher level at time T (figure 5.5, panel d). (Consumption is of course constant and independent of the path of the nominal exchange rate.) The path of the nominal money supply (figure 5.5, panel e) follows from the paths of real money balances and the nominal exchange rate. Since real money balances are constant until time T, the nominal money stock must be growing at the same rate as the nominal exchange rate (ε^H). At time T, the nominal money stock increases discretely as the public exchanges foreign assets for domestic money at the Central Bank. After time T, the nominal money supply increases at the lower rate of devaluation (ε^L). Finally, since $\dot{m}_t = 0$ for all $t \geq 0$, then $\mu_t = \varepsilon_t$. Hence μ_t is first high and then falls at time T (figure 5.5, panel f).

27. Exercise 5 at the end of the chapter looks at a third example (an anticipated increase in the money supply under flexible rates).

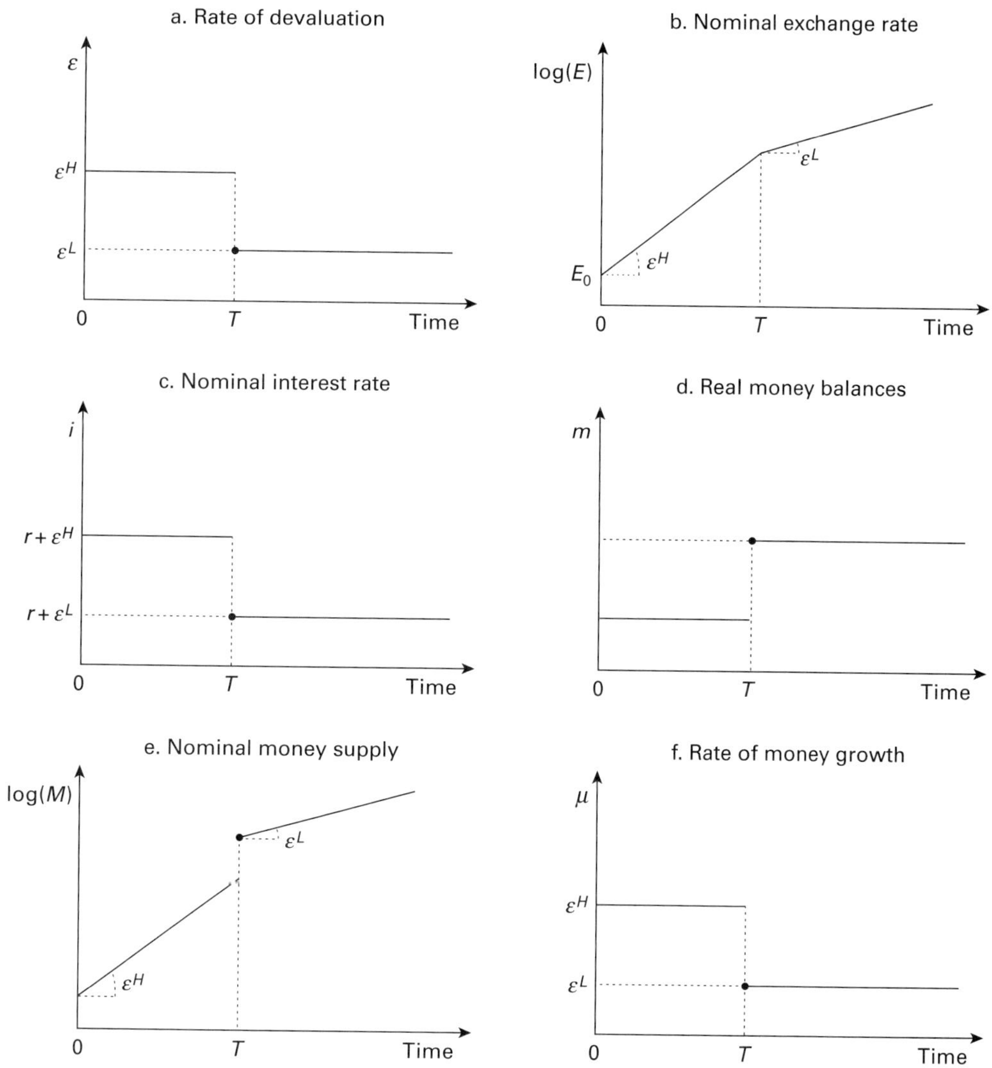

Figure 5.5
Equivalence between predetermined and flexible exchange rates I

Consider now this same economy operating under flexible exchange rates. Further suppose that the path of the nominal money supply set by the Central Bank is described by figure 5.5, panel e. In other words, the Central Bank has announced that the nominal money supply will grow at the rate ε^H until time T, increase discretely at time T, and then grow at the lower rate ε^L. We will now check that—as we should expect—the corresponding paths of the rate of depreciation, the nominal exchange rate, the nominal interest rate, and real money balances are as illustrated in figure 5.5.

Recall that under flexible exchange rates, real money balances are governed by the unstable differential equation given by (5.42). Between 0 and T, the dynamics of real money balances will be governed by the laws of motion corresponding to the stationary equilibrium given implicitly by $r+\varepsilon^H = v'(\bar{m})/\lambda$. At time T real money balances will jump since nominal money supply goes up but the nominal exchange rate does not change. By construction (recall figure 5.5, panel d), the jump in nominal money at time T is exactly the increase needed to take real money balances from their level between $[0, T)$ to their new and higher level. Hence real money balances will stay at their stationary value until time T and at that point jump to their new value. This is, of course, the same path described by figure 5.5, panel d. Having established that $\dot{m}_t = 0$ for all $t \geq 0$, it follows that the rate of depreciation is given by the rate of money growth at all points in time and thus follows the path illustrated in figure 5.5, panel a. The corresponding path of the nominal exchange rate is given by figure 5.5, panel b.

In sum, if under flexible exchange rates the monetary authority sets the path of the nominal money supply given by figure 5.5, panel e, the equilibrium paths of the rate of depreciation, the nominal exchange rate, the nominal interest rate, and real money balances would be exactly the same as under a predetermined exchange rates system in which the Central Bank sets the path of the rate of devaluation given by figure 5.5, panel a. An outside observer who can only see the six variables illustrated in figure 5.5 would *not* be able to tell if the economy is operating under predetermined exchange rates or flexible exchange rates. But, of course, if the observer could see the Central Bank's balance sheet, he/she would be able to tell by the changes in the balance sheet at time T. Under predetermined exchange rates, he/she would see the increase in the monetary base accompanied by an increase in international reserves, whereas under flexible exchange rates, he/she would see an increase in nominal domestic credit.[28]

5.4.2 A Nonconstant Path of the Money Growth Rate

Suppose now that the economy is operating under flexible exchange rates and the Central Bank sets a nonconstant rate of money growth, as illustrated in figure 5.6, panel a. The corresponding path of the nominal money supply is depicted in figure 5.6, panel b.

28. Of course, if under predetermined exchange rates, the Central Bank increased domestic credit at T by precisely the amount needed to meet the additional real money demand, our observer would not be able to tell which regime the economy is operating under even by looking at the Central Bank's balance sheet!

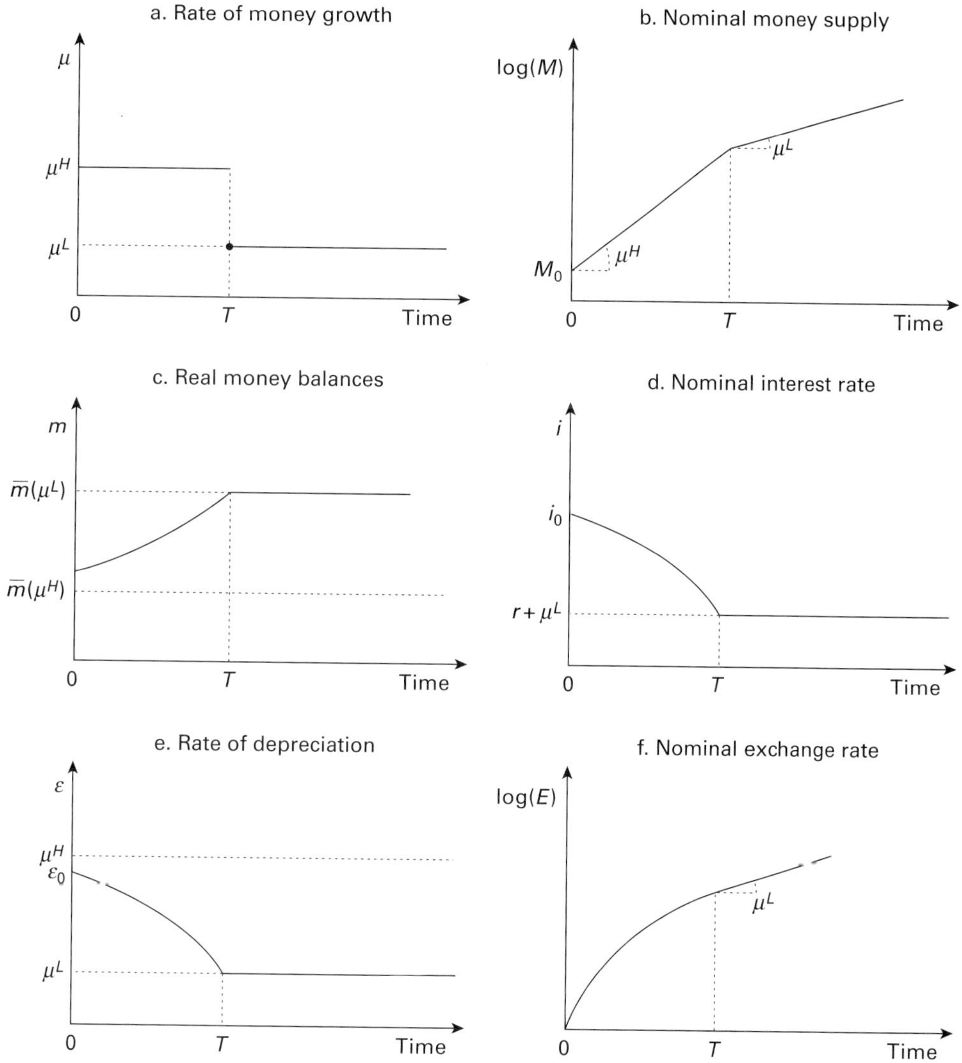

Figure 5.6
Equivalence between predetermined and flexible exchange rates II

To solve for the perfect foresight path of real money demand, we need to make the critical observation that real money balances cannot jump at T. To see this, recall that by definition, $m_t = M_t/E_tP^*_t$. The path of the nominal money supply is, by assumption, continuous at time T. The same is true of P^*_t. Furthermore, in equilibrium, the nominal exchange rate cannot jump at T. If it did, there would be infinite arbitrage opportunities that would be inconsistent with equilibrium. For example, suppose that the exchange rate is expected to increase at time T. Since the consumer knows this with certainty, he/she would get rid of all money balances just an instant before the increase in the exchange rate. Real money demand would thus fall to zero an instant before T, which is inconsistent with equilibrium (as it would lead to an infinite price level or exchange rate). Conversely, if the exchange rate is expected to fall at T, consumers would want to get rid of all net foreign assets and switch into domestic money in anticipation of infinite returns at time T. Money demand just an instant before T would be infinite, which, again, is inconsistent with equilibrium. We conclude that real money balances must be continuous at time T.

Given that real money balances cannot jump at T, we infer that m_t will have to converge in a continuous fashion to its higher stationary equilibrium. Hence m_0 will need to be above the level corresponding to the stationary equilibrium implicitly defined by $r + \mu^H = v'(\bar{m})/\lambda$ and denoted by $\bar{m}(\mu^H)$, so that it increases during the transition period (figure 5.6, panel c). Since consumption is always equal to permanent income in this model, we can infer the behavior of the nominal interest rate from the real money demand equation (5.28). The nominal interest rate will thus fall over time toward its stationary value (figure 5.6, panel d).

As for the path of the rate of depreciation, notice that

$$\frac{\dot{m}_t}{m_t} = \mu^H - \varepsilon_t > 0, \qquad t \in [0, T).$$

We infer that during the transition the rate of depreciation will be below μ^H. From the interest parity condition we also know that the rate of depreciation will be falling over time and be continuous at T (see figure 5.6, panel e). The corresponding path of the nominal exchange rate is depicted in figure 5.6, panel f.

Suppose now that the economy were operating under predetermined exchange rates and that the Central Bank set the path for the nominal exchange rate depicted in figure 5.6, panel f. In other words, the Central Bank would set a path that would involve a declining rate of devaluation over time until it converges to μ^L. From the interest parity condition (5.23), the nominal interest rate would follow the path illustrated in figure 5.6, panel d. From the real money demand equation (5.28) and the fact that consumption is constant throughout, the path of real money balances would be as illustrated in figure 5.6, panel c. The change in real money balances over time combined with the rate of devaluation would yield, by construction, the path for the rate of money growth illustrated in figure 5.6, panel a.

Once again, if an outside observer saw the behavior of the six variables in figure 5.6, he/she would be unable to tell which exchange rate regime the economy is operating under. The observer would need to see the Central Bank's balance sheet to find out the exchange rate regime. Under predetermined exchange rates, the Central Bank is gaining international reserves between time 0 and time T, whereas under flexible rates, domestic credit is increasing.[29]

5.4.3 On the Nonequivalence in Practice

Even though, as we just saw, there is a fundamental theoretical equivalence between predetermined and flexible exchange rates, it does *not* follow that exchange rate regimes are irrelevant. Far from it—and as we will see in this and subsequent chapters—the exchange rate regime is often crucial in determining the economy's response to various shocks. The reason is that in practice, policy makers set relatively simple paths for the exchange rate (under predetermined exchange rates) or the money supply (under flexible exchange rates). Given these simple paths, and the fact that economies are subject to myriad real and monetary shocks, the nominal money supply (under predetermined exchange rates) or the nominal exchange rate (under flexible exchange rates) will follow very volatile paths. For exchange rate regimes to be equivalent in practice, we would need to observe policy makers' setting, say, some simple path for the nominal exchange rate (under predetermined exchange rates) and then some other policy makers setting the corresponding, and very volatile, path for the nominal money supply (under flexible rates). Or vice versa, we would need to observe some policy makers setting simple paths for the money supply and others setting the equivalent (and possibly highly volatile) paths for the nominal exchange rate. This is not how policy makers actually operate in practice; policy makers operating under predetermined exchange rates will set some simple path for the nominal exchange rate and policy makers operating under flexible exchange rates will set simple paths for the nominal money supply. The reason is that nominal exchange rate rules or money supply rules can credibly anchor inflationary expectations only to the extent that they are simple and easy to understand by the public. As a result exchange rate regimes are not equivalent in practice. The next section provides an illustration of the economy's response to the same shock under predetermined and then flexible exchange rates. We will see, as we would expect, that the responses are quite different.

5.5 Anticipated Money Shocks

This section illustrates the practical "nonequivalence" of exchange rate regimes by analyzing how an anticipated negative shock to money demand will lead to a different dynamic response under predetermined exchange rates compared to flexible exchange rates. Under predetermined exchange rates, the inflation rate (i.e., the rate of devaluation) is controlled by policy makers and the negative demand shock will show up as a loss of reserves. In sharp contrast, under flexible exchange rates, inflation (i.e., the rate of depreciation) will increase in *anticipation* of the shock and reach its maximum right before the shock occurs (which reminds us of Sargent and Wallace's 1981 unpleasant monetarist arithmetic).

29. Again, if, under predetermined exchange rates, the Central Bank had kept on increasing domestic credit to satisfy the increasing money demand, then the two systems would behave identically in all dimensions.

To incorporate money demand shocks in our framework, we modify the preferences given in (5.11) to read as

$$\int_0^\infty [u(c_t) + \gamma_t v(m_t)]e^{-\beta t} dt, \tag{5.46}$$

where $\gamma_t (> 0)$ is a shock to the liquidity services provided by real money balances. The rest of the model remains unchanged.

While the first-order condition for consumption remains given by (5.12), the first-order condition for real money balances now reads as

$$\gamma_t v'(m_t) = \lambda i_t. \tag{5.47}$$

Combining (5.12) and (5.47) implicitly defines a real money demand of the form

$$m_t = L(c_t, i_t, \gamma_t), \tag{5.48}$$

$$\frac{\partial L}{\partial c_t} = \frac{i_t u''(c_t)}{v''(m_t)\gamma_t} > 0,$$

$$\frac{\partial L}{\partial i_t} = \frac{u'(c_t)}{\gamma_t v''(m_t)} < 0,$$

$$\frac{\partial L}{\partial \gamma_t} = -\frac{v'(m_t)}{\gamma_t v''(m_t)} > 0.$$

As expected, an increase in γ_t raises real money demand.

We will now consider a perfect foresight equilibrium path for a *nonconstant* path of the money shock parameter, γ_t. (We assume that foreign inflation is constant over time and equal to π^*.) Specifically, suppose that γ_t is constant until T, at which point it falls. In other words, there is an anticipated negative money demand shock. Formally,

$$\gamma_t = \begin{cases} \gamma^H, & 0 \leq t < T, \\ \gamma^L, & t \geq T, \end{cases} \tag{5.49}$$

where $\gamma^H > \gamma^L$.

We will now characterize the corresponding PFEP under both predetermined and flexible exchange rates.

5.5.1 Predetermined Exchange Rates

Suppose that the economy is operating under a predetermined exchange rate regime with a constant rate of devaluation given by ε. The path of the money shock parameter is given by (5.49) (figure 5.7, panel a). How will the economy behave?

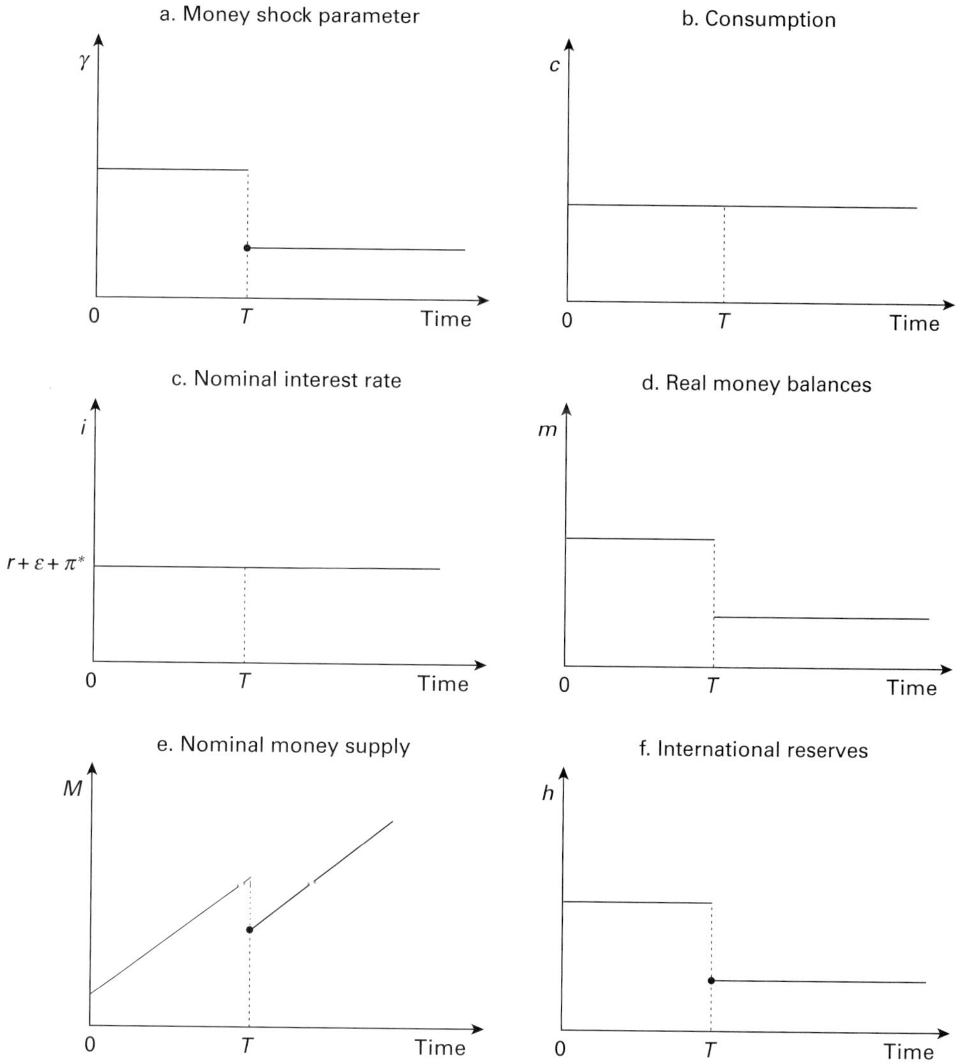

Figure 5.7
Negative money demand shock under predetermined exchange rates

We know, of course, that consumption is not affected (figure 5.7, panel b). The path of the nominal interest rate which, given the interest parity condition (5.23), is determined by the constant rate of devaluation, is also constant over time (figure 5.7, panel c). Real money balances, however, will fall at time T in response to the negative money demand shock, as follows from the real money demand (5.48) (panel d). Since both the nominal exchange rate and foreign price level are given at time T, the fall in real money balances must come through a fall in the nominal money supply (panel e). Further, since the real stock of domestic credit remains constant throughout, the fall in real money balances has as a counterpart a fall in international reserves at T (panel f).

5.5.2 Flexible Exchange Rates

Suppose now that the economy is operating under a flexible exchange rate regime with a constant rate of money growth given by μ. Again, the path of the money shock parameter is given by (5.49) (figure 5.8, panel a). How will this economy behave over time?

Under flexible exchange rates, the path of real money demand will be governed by an unstable differential equation along the lines of (5.42). Given that we now have a money demand shock in the model, it is straightforward to verify that the corresponding differential equation for real money balances is given by

$$\dot{m}_t = m_t\left[r + \mu - \frac{\gamma_t v'(m_t)}{\lambda}\right].$$

The stationary value of real money demand, $\bar{m}$, is therefore implicitly given by

$$r + \mu = \frac{\gamma_t v'(\bar{m})}{\lambda}. \tag{5.50}$$

The path of real money balances is illustrated in figure 5.8, panel c. It follows from (5.50) that at time T, the stationary value of real money balances falls (recall that λ is constant along a perfect foresight path). Further, for the same reasons argued above (i.e., both M_t and E_t are continuous functions of time at T), m_t will be continuous at time T. For the path of m_t to be continuous at time T, m_t needs to start below the stationary equilibrium corresponding to γ^H, denoted by $\bar{m}(\gamma^H)$ in the figure, fall over time, and reach the stationary equilibrium corresponding to γ^L, denoted by $\bar{m}(\gamma^L)$, at precisely time T.

Given the path of real money balances depicted in figure 5.8, panel c, we can derive the path of the rate of depreciation and hence of the nominal interest rate. Since $\dot{m}_t/m_t = \mu - \varepsilon_t - \pi^*$, it follows that

$$\varepsilon_t = \mu - \pi^* - \frac{\dot{m}_t}{m_t}. \tag{5.51}$$

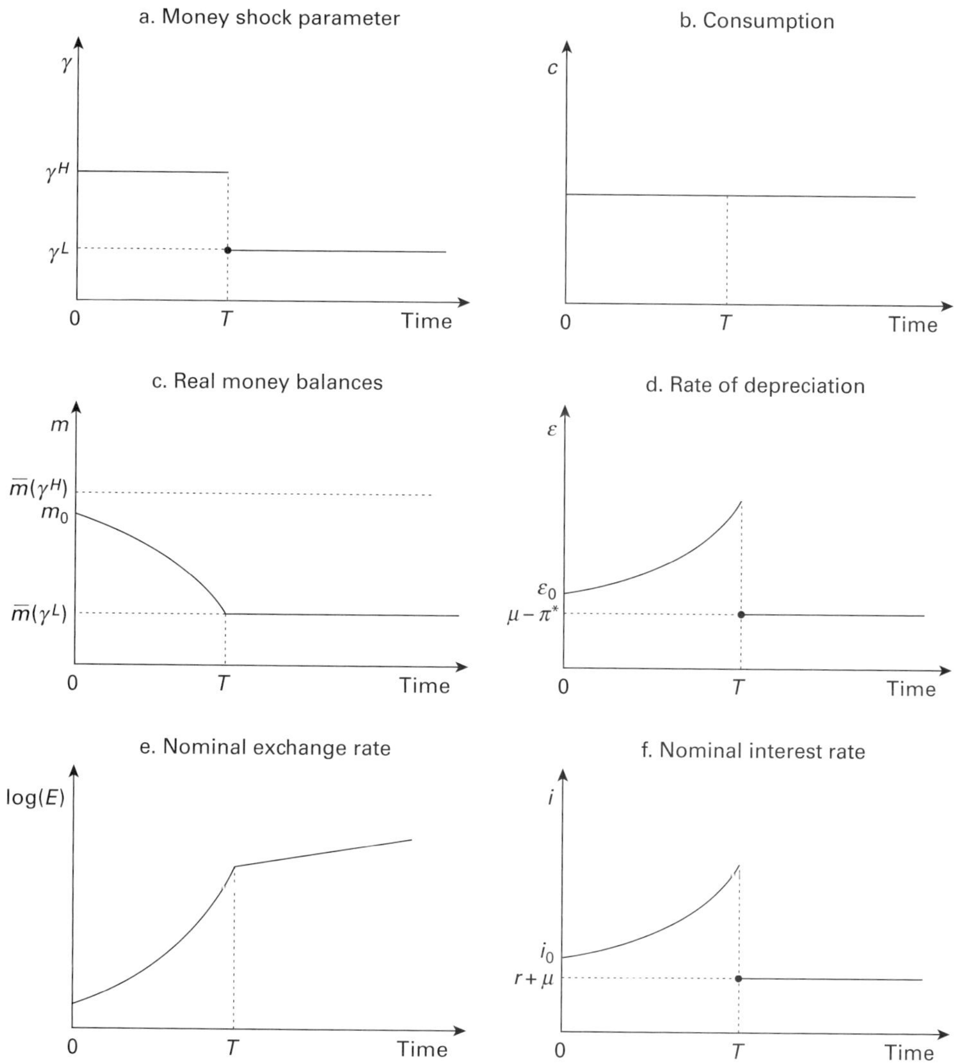

Figure 5.8
Negative money demand shock under flexible exchange rates

Four pieces of information follow from equation (5.51). First, for $t \geq T$, $\dot{m}_t = 0$ and therefore ε_t will be constant and equal to $\mu - \pi^*$. Second, for $t \in [0, T)$, the fact that $\dot{m}_t < 0$ implies that $\varepsilon_t > \mu - \pi^*$. Third, at time T, ε_t will jump down because, as figure 5.8, panel c makes clear, $\dot{m}_t$ is negative until just before T and then becomes zero at T. Fourth, to find out how ε_t behaves for $t \in [0, T)$, differentiate (5.51) with respect to time to obtain

$$\dot{\varepsilon}_t = -\frac{1}{m_t^2}(\ddot{m}_t m_t - \dot{m}_t^2) > 0,$$

where the sign follows from the fact that $\ddot{m}_t < 0$. Putting together all these pieces of information, we conclude that ε_t starts above its stationary equilibrium, increases over time, and then falls at time T (figure 5.8, panel d). Given interest parity, the path of the nominal interest rate will follow exactly the same pattern (figure 5.8, panel f).

What about the nominal exchange rate? We already know that the nominal exchange rate cannot jump at time T. Hence, given that the rate of depreciation itself increases over time until time T, the logarithm of the nominal exchange rate increases over time at an increasing rate until time T, after which it increases at a constant rate (figure 5.8, panel e).

The remarkable feature of this case is that the inflation (depreciation) rate is high (and increasing over time) *before* the negative money demand shock actually occurs. In fact an outside observer who is not aware of the forthcoming shock to money demand would be dumbfounded by the emergence of inflation when the money supply has not changed at all!

In sum—and comparing figures 5.7 and 5.8—we can see the very different response of this economy to an anticipated fall in money demand. Under predetermined exchange rates, this shock has no effect whatsoever on the inflation rate (i.e., on the rate of devaluation) or the nominal interest rate. In sharp contrast, under flexible exchange rates, the rate of inflation (i.e., depreciation) rises in anticipation of the shock, as does the nominal interest rate.[30]

5.6 Money as a Veil in a Cash-in-Advance Model

So far in this chapter we have examined monetary phenomena in a money-in-the-utility function model in which money is a veil in the sense that the real equilibrium is independent of monetary/exchange rate policy. Another popular way of introducing money into the endowment model of chapter 1 is through a cash-in-advance constraint.[31] We will now study a discrete-time formulation of a cash-in-advance model in which money is a veil and analyze how the monetary

30. Drazen and Helpman (1990) study the inflationary consequences of anticipated policies in the context of a closed economy. Exercise 6 at the end of this chapter provides yet another illustration of how the economy responds differently depending on the exchange rate regime by studying the consequences of an anticipated increase in the rate of growth of the nominal anchor.

31. See Helpman (1981) and Lucas (1982).

equilibrium is determined under both predetermined and flexible exchange rates.[32] In so doing, we will also have a chance to go over some important accounting in discrete-time terms.

5.6.1 Households

Budget Constraints

We first need to be specific about the economic environment in which households operate. Households enter period t with a certain amount of nominal cash balances, M_{t-1}, and a certain amount of nominal foreign bonds, B^*_{t-1}. Periods are divided into two subperiods. In the first subperiod, asset markets open. In the asset markets, agents receive/pay interest on the net foreign bonds they carried over from last period, buy or sell bonds in exchange for money (at the Central Bank under predetermined exchange rates or in the foreign exchange market under flexible exchange rates), and receive nominal transfers from the government, $P_t\tau_t$. Households exit the asset market with a quantity M^p_t of nominal cash balances and B^*_t of nominal bonds. Formally,

$$M^p_t + E_t B^*_t = E_t(1 + i^*_{t-1})B^*_{t-1} + M_{t-1} + P_t\tau_t, \tag{5.52}$$

where E_t and i^*_t continue to denote the nominal exchange rate and the foreign nominal interest rate, respectively.

In the second subperiod, goods markets open. Think of households as composed of two individuals: a shopper and a seller. The shopper and seller part at the beginning of the goods market subperiod and do not meet again until goods markets close.[33] Think of the seller as staying in the store selling the endowment of the good to other households' shoppers. The shopper leaves the store with nominal money balances in the amount of M^p_t and uses part or all of this money to buy goods from other stores. Since, by assumption, the shopper needs to use money acquired in the asset markets to buy goods in the goods markets, we refer to this as a cash in advance constraint.[34] Formally,

$$M^p_t \geq P_t c_t. \tag{5.53}$$

What are the households's money balances at the end of period t (denoted by M_t)? Households will have the money obtained from selling goods at the store ($P_t y_t$) and the money brought from the asset markets that was not spent on purchasing goods ($M^p_t - P_t c_t$). Formally,

32. We develop this first cash-in-advance model in the book in discrete time because, as the discussion will make clear, the economic environment underlying cash-in-advance models is more naturally suited to discrete-time. Chapter 7 will then develop a continuous-time formulation of cash-in-advance models.

33. If it helps, think of a "period" as a day. Assets markets open in the morning and close at noon. Goods markets open at noon and close at 5 pm. The shopper and the seller say good-bye at noon and do not see each other until after 5 pm.

34. The implicit assumption is that even though all households are identical, they do not consume their own endowment. Think of each household as being endowed with the same good (e.g., candy) but that candy comes in different colors. Households do not like the color of their own candy and wish to buy other households' candies.

$$M_t = M_t^p - P_t c_t + P_t y_t. \tag{5.54}$$

By substituting (5.54) into (5.52), we obtain the households' flow constraint for period t as a whole:

$$M_t + E_t B_t^* = E_t(1 + i_{t-1}^*)B_{t-1}^* + M_{t-1} + P_t \tau_t + P_t y_t - P_t c_t. \tag{5.55}$$

For the sake of comparison with the continuous-time case, we can define nominal assets as $A_t \equiv M_t + E_t B_t^*$ and, by adding and subtracting $E_{t-1}B_{t-1}^*$ on the LHS of equation (5.55), rewrite it as

$$A_t - A_{t-1} = \underbrace{E_t i_{t-1}^* B_{t-1}^*}_{\text{Interest income}} + \underbrace{(E_t - E_{t-1})B_{t-1}^*}_{\text{Capital gains}} + P_t \tau_t + P_t y_t - P_t c_t,$$

which is the discrete-time counterpart of flow constraint (5.5) in the continuous-time case.

To express the flow constraint in real terms, divide both sides of (5.55) by P_t and manipulate terms to obtain

$$m_t + b_t = \frac{E_t}{P_t} P_{t-1}^*(1 + i_{t-1}^*)b_{t-1} + \frac{P_{t-1}}{P_t} m_{t-1} + \tau_t + y_t - c_t,$$

where, by definition, $m_t \equiv M_t/P_t$ and $b_t \equiv E_t B_t^*/P_t = B_t^*/P_t^*$ denote real money balances and real bond holdings, respectively. Defining the inflation rate in period t as $1 + \pi_t = P_t/P_{t-1}$, assuming that the Fisher equation holds in the rest of the world (i.e., $1 + i_{t-1}^* = (1+r)(P_t^*/P_{t-1}^*)$), and using the law of one price (i.e., $P_t = EP_t^*$), we can rewrite the last equation as

$$m_t + b_t = (1 + r)b_{t-1} + \frac{m_{t-1}}{1 + \pi_t} + \tau_t + y_t - c_t. \tag{5.56}$$

Adding and subtracting $(1 + r)m_{t-1}$ from the RHS of the last equation and taking into account that, by definition, $a_t = m_t + b_t$, we obtain

$$a_t = (1 + r)a_{t-1} + \tau_t + y_t - c_t - \frac{i_{t-1}}{1 + \pi_t} m_{t-1}, \tag{5.57}$$

which is the discrete-time counterpart of equation (5.9).

Utility Maximization

We can set up the household's maximization problem in various ways depending on which constraints we use. It proves convenient to substitute equation (5.52) into the cash-in-advance constraint (5.53) to obtain

$$E_t(1 + i_{t-1}^*)B_{t-1}^* + M_{t-1} + P_t \tau_t - E_t B_t^* \geq P_t c_t. \tag{5.58}$$

Expressing this equation in real terms, we obtain

$$(1+r)b_{t-1}+\frac{m_{t-1}}{1+\pi_t}+\tau_t-b_t\geq c_t. \tag{5.59}$$

Households then choose $\{c_t, b_t, m_t\}_{t=0}^{\infty}$ to maximize lifetime utility subject to a sequence of flow budget constraints given by (5.56) and a sequence of *inequality* constraints given by the cash-in-advance constraints (5.59). We set up the Lagrangian as

$$\begin{aligned}\mathcal{L}&=\sum_{t=0}^{\infty}\beta^t u(c_t)\\&+\sum_{t=0}^{\infty}\beta^t\lambda_t\left[(1+r)b_{t-1}+\frac{m_{t-1}}{1+\pi_t}+\tau_t+y_t-c_t-b_t-m_t\right]\\&+\sum_{t=0}^{\infty}\beta^t\Psi_t\left[(1+r)b_{t-1}+\frac{m_{t-1}}{1+\pi_t}+\tau_t-b_t-c_t\right].\end{aligned}$$

The first-order conditions for c_t, m_t, and b_t are given, respectively, by

$$u'(c_t)=\lambda_t+\Psi_t, \tag{5.60}$$

$$-\lambda_t+\frac{\beta\lambda_{t+1}}{1+\pi_{t+1}}+\frac{\beta\Psi_{t+1}}{1+\pi_{t+1}}=0, \tag{5.61}$$

$$\beta(1+r)(\lambda_{t+1}+\Psi_{t+1})=\lambda_t+\Psi_t. \tag{5.62}$$

The first-order condition for λ_t recovers equation (5.56). The first-order condition for Ψ_t takes the form of a Kuhn–Tucker condition:

$$\begin{aligned}&(1+r)b_{t-1}+\frac{m_{t-1}}{1+\pi_t}+\tau_t-b_t\geq c_t,\qquad \Psi_t\geq 0,\\&\left[(1+r)b_{t-1}+\frac{m_{t-1}}{1+\pi_t}+\tau_t-b_t-c_t\right]\Psi_t=0.\end{aligned} \tag{5.63}$$

In words, if the cash-in-advance constraint holds as an inequality, the associated multiplier will be zero.

Given the assumption that $\beta(1+r)=1$, it follows from condition (5.62) that $\lambda_{t+1}+\Psi_{t+1}=\lambda_t+\Psi_t$ and hence, from condition (5.60), that

$$u'(c_{t+1})=u'(c_t). \tag{5.64}$$

As in the endowment economy of chapter 1, consumption will be constant along any perfect foresight path. Moreover, since we have yet to say anything about monetary/exchange rate policy, full consumption smoothing will hold regardless of the exchange rate regime in place. This proves that in this version of the cash-in-advance model, money is a veil in the sense that the real equilibrium will not depend on the path of monetary variables. Hence, in response to fluctuations in the endowment, the economy will use the trade balance as a shock absorber and keep consumption constant by borrowing in bad times (i.e., when the endowment is low) and repaying in good times (i.e., when the endowment is high).

We will now show that if the nominal interest rate is positive, the cash-in-advance constraint will bind. Taking into account that $\beta = 1/(1+r)$, we can rewrite condition (5.61) as

$$\frac{\lambda_{t+1} + \Psi_{t+1}}{1 + i_t} = \lambda_t.$$

Since $\lambda_{t+1} + \Psi_{t+1} = \lambda_t + \Psi_t$, we can further simplify this last condition to read

$$\lambda_t i_t = \Psi_t.$$

given that $\lambda_t > 0$, it follows that if $i_t > 0$, then $\Psi_t > 0$, which implies, from the slackness condition, that the cash-in-advance constraint binds. If the nominal interest rate is positive, it makes no sense for households to leave the asset markets with more money than they need to purchase goods when goods markets open. The reason is that they could have always used that money to buy bonds and receive interest rate payments at the beginning of the following period.

If instead $i_t = 0$, $\Psi_t = 0$ and the cash-in-advance constraint is nonbinding in the sense that it becomes irrelevant for the consumer's choice. In this case households will be indifferent between holding money or bonds and hence the choice of money balances is indeterminate.[35]

5.6.2 Government

As before, let H^* denote the foreign currency value of international reserves. The government's flow budget constraint in nominal terms is thus given by

$$E_t H_t^* = E_t(1 + i_{t-1}^*)H_{t-1}^* + M_t - M_{t-1} - P_t \tau_t.$$

To express it in real terms, divide both sides of this equation by P_t to obtain

$$h_t = (1+r)h_{t-1} + \frac{M_t - M_{t-1}}{P_t} - \tau_t, \tag{5.65}$$

where we have used the fact that, by definition, $h_t \equiv H_t^*/P_t^*$, from the law of one price, $P_t = E_t P_t^*$, and, from the Fisher equation in the rest of the world, $1 + i_{t-1}^* = (1+r)(P_t^*/P_{t-1}^*)$.

35. Of course, from a purely mathematical point of view, the cash-in-advance constraint could still hold as an equality even if $\Psi_t = 0$. But, from an economic point of view, this is irrelevant since money and bonds are perfect substitutes and the cash-in-advance constraint does not restrict consumers' choices.

Finally, and for further reference, notice that revenues from money creation may be expressed as

$$\frac{M_t - M_{t-1}}{P_t} = m_t - m_{t-1} + \frac{\pi_t}{1+\pi_t} m_{t-1}. \tag{5.66}$$

5.6.3 Equilibrium Conditions

Perfect capital mobility implies that the interest parity condition holds:

$$1 + i_t = (1 + i_t^*) \frac{E_{t+1}}{E_t}. \tag{5.67}$$

To obtain the economy's flow constraint, combine the consumer's flow constraint (given by equation 5.56) with the government's (given by equation 5.65)—taking into account (5.66)—to obtain

$$b_t + h_t = (1+r)(b_{t-1} + h_{t-1}) + y_t - c_t. \tag{5.68}$$

Let $k_t (\equiv b_t + h_t)$ denote the economy's total net foreign assets. Iterating forward and imposing the transversality condition $\lim_{t\to\infty} k_t / (1+r)^t = 0$ yields

$$\sum_{t=0}^{\infty} \frac{c_t}{(1+r)^t} = (1+r)(b_{-1} + h_{-1}) + \sum_{t=0}^{\infty} \frac{y_t}{(1+r)^t}. \tag{5.69}$$

Perfect Foresight Equilibrium

We have established from (5.64) that consumption is constant over time. From the resource constraint (5.69), it then follows that

$$c = \frac{r}{1+r} \left[(1+r)(b_{-1} + h_{-1}) + \sum_{t=0}^{\infty} \frac{y_t}{(1+r)^t} \right]. \tag{5.70}$$

As in the continuous-time case, the constant level of consumption is equal to permanent income.

Taking into account (5.53) and the fact that we have established that the cash-in-advance constraint will bind for a positive nominal interest rate, we infer that the constant value of consumption will determine the value of real money balances taken into the goods markets:

$$\frac{M_t^p}{P_t} = c. \tag{5.71}$$

Then, by substituting (5.71) into (5.54), we obtain

$$M_t = P_t y_t, \tag{5.72}$$

which you will recognize as a quantity theory equation with unitary velocity.

5.6.4 Predetermined Exchange Rates

Under predetermined exchange rates the Central Bank sets the path of the nominal exchange rate (i.e., $E_0, E_1, \ldots$) and the path of the stock of nominal domestic credit $(D_0, D_1, \ldots)$. Specifically—and as in the continuous-time case—suppose that the monetary authority sets E_0 and then a constant rate of devaluation. Formally,

$$\frac{E_{t+1}}{E_t} = 1 + \varepsilon, \qquad t = 0, 1, 2, \ldots.$$

Given this constant rate of devaluation, the nominal interest rate follows from the interest parity condition (5.67):

$$1 + i_t = (1 + i_t^*)(1 + \varepsilon). \tag{5.73}$$

Let us now determine the path of the price level. Let the rate of foreign inflation be constant; that is, $P_{t+1}^*/P_t^* = 1 + \pi^*$. Then, by the law of one price ($P_t = E_t P_t^*$), the initial price level is $P_0 = E_0 P_0^*$. The law of one price also determines a constant level of inflation:

$$1 + \pi = (1 + \varepsilon)\,(1 + \pi^*),$$

where $1 + \pi = P_{t+1}/P_t$.

We now turn to the path of the nominal money supply. Given the quantity theory equation (5.72), $M_0 = P_0 y_0$. The rate of growth of the nominal money supply also follows from the quantity theory equation (5.72):

$$1 + \mu_{t+1} = (1 + \pi)\,\frac{y_{t+1}}{y_t},$$

where $1 + \mu_{t+1} \equiv M_{t+1}/M_t$. Money supply growth will be higher in good times and lower in bad times because a higher (lower) endowment implies higher (lower) sales during the goods market period and hence more (less) nominal money balances carried over to next period.

To derive the path of international reserves, we start from the Central Bank's balance sheet, given by

$$h_t + \frac{D_t}{E_t P_t^*} = \frac{M_t}{E_t P_t^*}.$$

Considering the same identity for $t + 1$ and subtracting, we get

$$h_{t+1} - h_t = \frac{M_{t+1}}{E_{t+1} P_{t+1}^*} - \frac{M_t}{E_t P_t^*} - \frac{D_t}{E_t P_t^*}\left[\frac{(1 + \theta) - (1 + \varepsilon)(1 + \pi^*)}{(1 + \varepsilon)(1 + \pi^*)}\right],$$

where θ is the constant rate of domestic credit set by the Central Bank. For the same reasons discussed for the continuous-time case, we will assume that $1 + \theta = (1 + \varepsilon)(1 + \pi^*)$ to ensure that the predetermined exchange rate system is sustainable over time. Imposing that assumption, we can rewrite this last expression as

$$h_{t+1} - h_t = \frac{M_{t+1}}{E_{t+1}P^*_{t+1}} - \frac{M_t}{E_t P^*_t},$$

which is, of course, the counterpart to equation (5.39) in the continuous-time case. Changes in international reserves will solely reflect changes in real money balances. Using the quantity theory equation (5.72) and the law of one price, we can rewrite this last equation as

$$h_{t+1} - h_t = y_{t+1} - y_t.$$

Increases (decreases) in the endowment will be reflected in higher (lower) reserves through their effect on real money balances. This is a feature that is not present in the MIUF, continous-time case analyzed above because in that case fluctuations in the endowment along a perfect foresight path do not affect real money balances.[36]

This characterization of predetermined exchange rates makes clear the dichotomy between the real and monetary sectors of the economy. Specifically—and since we made no assumption on exchange/monetary policy in deriving the constant level of consumption (5.70)—exchange rate policy is both neutral and superneutral.

5.6.5 Flexible Exchange Rates

Under flexible exchange rates the Central Bank controls the path of the money supply by setting M_t, $t \geq 0$. Specifically, we assume that the monetary authority sets M_0 and then sets a constant rate of money growth:

$$M_t = (1 + \mu)M_{t-1}, \qquad t \geq 1.$$

The rate of inflation follows from the quantity theory equation, given by expression (5.72):

$$\frac{P_{t+1}}{P_t} = \frac{1 + \mu}{y_{t+1}/y_t}, \qquad t \geq 0. \tag{5.74}$$

Since the quantity theory equation holds, of course, for $t = 0$, the initial price level is determined by

$$P_0 = \frac{M_0}{y_0}.$$

36. The same would be true in the continuous-time, cash-in-advance model developed in chapter 7.

The nominal exchange rate is determined by the law of one price:

$$E_t = \frac{P_t}{P_t^*}. \tag{5.75}$$

The rate of depreciation is thus (once again, assume a constant foreign inflation rate)

$$\frac{E_{t+1}}{E_t} = \frac{P_{t+1}/P_t}{1+\pi^*}. \tag{5.76}$$

From (5.67), (5.74), and (5.76), the nominal interest rate is given by

$$1 + i_t = (1+r)\left(\frac{1+\mu}{y_{t+1}/y_t}\right), \tag{5.77}$$

where we have made use of the fact that the Fischer equation holds in the rest of the world; that is, $1 + i^* = (1+r)(1+\pi^*)$. Equation (5.77) should be compared to (5.44), which is the expression for the nominal interest rate in the continuous-time case.[37] If the endowment is constant, then the determination of the nominal interest rate is the same in both cases. But if the endowment fluctuates over time, then the nominal interest rate will fluctuate in this discrete-time, cash-in-advance formulation, but not in the continuous time case because, in the former case, equilibrium real money balances depend on output (as opposed to consumption) through the quantity theory equation (5.72).

Once again, it is easy to see that monetary policy would be both neutral and superneutral.

5.7 Final Remarks

As discussed before, in this basic monetary model, money is a "veil" in the sense that changes in monetary/exchange rate policy do not affect the path of real variables. While this model provides the natural conceptual benchmark for studying monetary economics in the open economy—and could even be a good description of the actual world in the long run or under extreme hyperinflationary conditions—it certainly does not provide us with tools to understand the possible real effects of monetary/exchange rate policy in an open economy. In essence, the main task of monetary economics in the open economy is to study departures from this benchmark in which monetary and exchange rate policy have real effects.

Subsequent chapters will thus introduce various frictions that will remove the veil and allow monetary/exchange rate policy to affect the real sector. Specifically, chapter 6 will assume that there are no interest-bearing bonds in the economy, chapter 7 will introduce money through a continuous-time cash-in-advance constraint that will establish a link between nominal interest rates and consumption, and chapter 8 will introduce sticky prices.

37. As shown in chapter 7, the same expression for the nominal interest rate holds in a continuous-time, cash-in-advance model.

5.8 Appendixes

5.8.1 Breaking Down the Government into the Monetary and the Fiscal Authority

To simplify the presentation of the basic monetary model, we considered in the text the government as a whole and did not break it down into its separate entities: the monetary authority (i.e., the Central Bank) and the fiscal authority (typically the Finance Ministry or Treasury Department). It proves illuminating, however, to consider each entity separately and see how aggregating them leads to equation (5.19) in the text.

The Monetary Authority

The Central Bank holds international reserves, prints money, lends to the fiscal authority by issuing domestic credit (think of domestic credit as loans), and transfers its profits to the fiscal authority. As in the text, let H_t^* denote the net foreign assets (measured in the foreign currency) held by the monetary authority and H_t denote the domestic currency value of these international reserves (i.e., $H_t \equiv E_t H_t^*$). The Central Bank's flow budget constraint in domestic currency terms is then given by

$$\dot{H}_t = \underbrace{i_t^* E_t H_t^* + \dot{E}_t H_t^* + i_t D_t + \dot{M}_t}_{\text{Revenues}} - \underbrace{(\dot{D}_t + P_t \tau_t^g)}_{\text{Expenditures}}. \tag{5.78}$$

The first four terms on the RHS of equation (5.78) represent sources of revenues for the Central Bank. Specifically, the first term ($i_t^* E_t H_t^*$) captures the domestic-currency value of the interest proceeds on the stock of international reserves, the second term ($\dot{E}_t H_t^*$) denotes the capital gains on the existing stock of international reserves, the third term ($i_t D_t$) captures the interest income on the stock of nominal domestic credit, and the fourth term ($\dot{M}_t$) indicates that money printing is a source of revenues for the Central Bank. The last two terms on the RHS of equation (5.78) capture the Central Bank's expenditures. The Central Bank buys domestic bonds issued by the fiscal authority ($\dot{D}_t$) and transfers to the fiscal authority whatever profits it makes ($P_t \tau_t^g$).[38]

Dividing (5.78) by P_t—and recalling that $P_t = E_t P_t^*$—we obtain

$$\frac{\dot{H}_t}{P_t} = i_t^* h_t + \varepsilon_t h_t + i_t d_t + \frac{\dot{M}_t}{P_t} - \frac{\dot{D}_t}{P_t} - \tau_t^g, \tag{5.79}$$

where $h_t \equiv H_t^* / P_t^*$.

Recall that

$$\dot{h}_t = \frac{\dot{H}_t}{P_t} - (\varepsilon_t + \pi_t^*) h_t. \tag{5.80}$$

38. Recall that following standard practice, we are assuming that the Central Bank does not accumulate/decumulate wealth (i.e., it keeps its net worth constant over time and equal to zero).

Substituting (5.79) into (5.80) (and imposing the Fisher equation for the rest of the world), we obtain

$$\dot{h}_t = rh_t + i_t d_t + \frac{\dot{M}_t}{P_t} - \frac{\dot{D}_t}{P_t} - \tau_t^g. \tag{5.81}$$

Taking into account that $\dot{M}_t/P_t = \dot{m}_t + (\varepsilon_t + \pi_t^*)m_t$ and $\dot{D}_t/P_t = \dot{d}_t + (\varepsilon_t + \pi_t^*)d_t$, we can rewrite this expression as

$$\dot{h}_t + \dot{d}_t - \dot{m}_t = rh_t + i_t d_t + (\varepsilon_t + \pi_t^*)m_t - (\varepsilon_t + \pi_t^*)d_t - \tau_t^g.$$

Since, by assumption, the Central Bank's net worth is always zero, $\dot{h}_t + \dot{d}_t - \dot{m}_t = 0$. Imposing this condition in the last expression and using the interest parity condition ($i_t = r + \pi_t^* + \varepsilon_t$), we obtain

$$\tau_t^g = rh_t + rd_t + (\varepsilon_t + \pi_t^*)m_t. \tag{5.82}$$

Intuitively, the Central Bank transfers to the fiscal authority its "profits" so as to keep its net worth zero. The Central Bank's profits consist of the real interest rate on reserves and domestic credit (first two terms on the RHS) and the inflation tax on the real money supply (last term). Further, using the Central Bank's balance sheet ($m_t = h_t + d_t$) and the interest parity condition, the last expression can be rewritten as

$$\tau_t^g = i_t m_t. \tag{5.83}$$

In this interpretation, the Central Bank makes profits because it can issue a non–interest-rate-bearing liability (i.e., money).

The Fiscal Authority

The fiscal authority (in practice, the Finance Ministry or Treasury Department) borrows from the Central Bank (i.e., sells bonds to the Central Bank), pays interest on these bonds (i.e., on the stock of domestic credit), receives a transfer of τ_t^g from the Central Bank, and makes lump-sum transfers to the private sector (τ_t).[39] The fiscal authority's flow constraint in nominal terms is thus

$$\dot{D}_t = \underbrace{i_t D_t + P_t \tau_t}_{\text{Expenditures}} - \underbrace{P_t \tau_t^g}_{\text{Revenues}}. \tag{5.84}$$

Dividing this expression by P_t, we get

$$\frac{\dot{D}_t}{P_t} = i_t d_t + \tau_t - \tau_t^g. \tag{5.85}$$

39. Needless to say, the fiscal authority would typically spend on goods (as in chapter 4), a feature that we are abstracting from in this chapter and to which we will return in later chapters.

Noting that $\dot{D}_t/P_t = \dot{d}_t + (\varepsilon_t + \pi_t^*)d_t$ and using (5.82) and interest parity, we obtain

$$\tau_t = \dot{d}_t + (\varepsilon_t + \pi_t^*)m_t + rh_t.$$

We see that if $\dot{d}_t = 0$ (our maintained assumption; see the discussion following equation 5.38), then $\tau_t = (\varepsilon_t + \pi_t^*)m_t + rh_t$. This coincides, of course, with what we derived in the text (equation 5.41 in the case of predetermined exchange rates and equation 5.45 in the case of flexible rates, in which case $h_t = 0$ for all t).

Aggregating the Monetary and the Fiscal Authority

Combining the monetary's authority nominal budget constraint—given by equation (5.78)—and the fiscal authority's nominal budget constraint—given by equation (5.84)—we obtain

$$\dot{H}_t = i_t^* E_t H_t^* + \dot{E}_t H_t^* + \dot{M}_t - P_t \tau_t, \tag{5.86}$$

which, of course, coincides with equation (5.17) in the text.

By the same token, by combining the monetary authority's flow constraint—given by (5.81)—and the fiscal authority's flow constraint—given by (5.85)—we obtain

$$\dot{h}_t = rh_t + \frac{\dot{M}_t}{P_t} - \tau_t, \tag{5.87}$$

which coincides with constraint (5.19) in the text. As a final remark, notice that we have just gone through a purely accounting exercise so that all the derivations in this appendix hold for any exchange rate regime.

5.8.2 Accounting in Basic Monetary Model with Jumps in Real Money Balances

We mentioned in the text that, strictly speaking, both the household's and the government's budget constraints should take into account the possibility of jumps in real money balances (e.g., Drazen and Helpman 1987). We develop such a formulation in this appendix.

Consumer

The consumer's flow constraint takes the form

$$\begin{aligned} b_t - b_{t^-} &= -\frac{M_t - M_{t^-}}{E_t}, \qquad \text{if } t \in J, \\ \dot{b}_t &= rb_t + y_t + \tau_t - c_t - \dot{m}_t - (\varepsilon_t + \pi_t^*)m_t \qquad \text{if } t \notin J. \end{aligned} \tag{5.88}$$

These flow constraints allow for the possibility of discrete changes in b_t and m_t at a finite set of points (which may include $t = 0$) belonging to the set J.[40] The precise points that belong to

40. A jump at $t = 0$ may occur in the case of an unanticipated shock at $t = 0$. If we are analyzing a PFEP, then by construction, there will be no jumps at $t = 0$.

set J will naturally depend on the specific problem at hand. For example, when we analyze the effects of an unanticipated and temporary shock under predetermined exchange rates, the set J will typically include two points: $t = 0$ and $t = T$. Notice also that along a perfect foresight path, the total level of financial assets, a_t, cannot change discretely at any point in time.

Integrating forward and imposing the condition $\lim_{t\to\infty} e^{-rt} b_t = 0$, we obtain the following consumer's lifetime budget constraint:

$$b_{0^-} + \int_0^\infty (y_t + \tau_t)\, e^{-rt} dt = \int_0^\infty \left[c_t + \dot{m}_t + \left(\varepsilon_t + \pi_t^*\right) m_t\right] e^{-rt} dt + \sum_{j\in J} \frac{M_j - M_{j-}}{E_j} e^{-rj}, \tag{5.89}$$

where, in general, t^- refers to the value of the variable just before time t (e.g., b_{0^-} denotes net foreign assets an instant before $t = 0$) and j are values of t that belong to set J.

This intertemporal constraint can be further simplified if we impose the condition that $\lim_{t\to\infty} e^{-rt} m_t = 0$ and use the interest parity condition ($i_t = r + \varepsilon_t + \pi_t^*$) to obtain[41]

$$b_{0^-} + \frac{M_{0^-}}{E_0} + \int_0^\infty (y_t + \tau_t)\, e^{-rt} dt = \int_0^\infty (c_t + i_t m_t) e^{-rt} dt. \tag{5.90}$$

Unless there is a discrete change in the consumer's real financial assets at $t = 0$, then $b_{0^-} + M_{0^-}/E_0 = a_0$ and this expression coincides with constraint (5.10) in the text. Even if there is a discrete change in the consumer's real financial assets at $t = 0$—which would be the case if an unanticipated devaluation occur—our assumption that the government transfers back to the consumer all proceeds ensures that the solution would be the same as in the text. Of course, if the government used the proceeds of a discrete devaluation to, say, increase spending, we would need to modify the analysis.

Government

The government's flow constraint should read as

$$\begin{aligned} h_t - h_{t^-} &= \tfrac{M_t - M_{t^-}}{E_t}, && \text{if } t \in J, \\ \dot{h}_t &= r h_t + \dot{m}_t + (\varepsilon_t + \pi_t^*) m_t - \tau_t, && \text{if } t \notin J, \end{aligned} \tag{5.91}$$

where the set J has been defined above. Under predetermined exchange rates these discrete changes will take place when consumers decide to trade net foreign assets for domestic money (and vice versa) at the Central Bank.

If we integrate forward equation (5.91), imposing the condition that $\lim_{t\to\infty} e^{-rt} h_t = 0$, we obtain the following intertemporal constraint for the government:

41. The condition on real money balances will hold in equilibrium because, at an optimum, the choice of m_t will be finite.

$$\int_0^\infty \tau_t e^{-rt} dt = h_{0^-} + \int_0^\infty \left[\dot{m}_t + \left(\varepsilon_t + \pi_t^*\right) m_t\right] e^{-rt} dt + \sum_{j \in J} \frac{M_j - M_{j-}}{E_j} e^{-rj}, \tag{5.92}$$

where h_{0^-} denotes the level of international reserves an instant before $t = 0$. Notice, for example, that a discrete fall in real money balances implies a loss of revenues for the government. This intertemporal constraint simply says that the present discounted value of transfers must be financed with the initial stock of international reserves plus the present discounted value of revenues from money creation (including discrete jumps).

This intertemporal constraint can be further simplified if we impose the condition that $\lim_{t\to\infty} e^{-rt} m_t = 0$ and use the interest parity condition ($i_t = r + \varepsilon_t + \pi_t^*$) to obtain

$$\int_0^\infty \tau_t e^{-rt} dt = h_{0^-} - \frac{M_{0^-}}{E_0} + \int_0^\infty i_t m_t e^{-rt} dt. \tag{5.93}$$

Aggregation

Combining the consumer's intertemporal constraint, given by equation (5.90), with the government's, given by equation (5.93), we obtain

$$b_{0^-} + h_{0^-} + \int_0^\infty y_t e^{-rt} dt = \int_0^\infty c_t e^{-rt} dt.$$

Unless there is a jump in the economy's net foreign assets at $t = 0$, we have $b_{0^-} + h_{0^-} = k_0$, and this intertemporal constraint coincides with expression (5.26) in the text.

5.8.3 Restrictions on the Rate of Growth of Domestic Credit

In deriving the government's intertemporal constraint—given by equation (5.22)—we imposed the condition

$$\lim_{t\to\infty} h_t e^{-rt} = 0. \tag{5.94}$$

Similarly, in deriving the economy's resource constraint—given by equation (5.26)—we imposed the condition

$$\lim_{t\to\infty} k_t e^{-rt} = 0. \tag{5.95}$$

Since $k_t = h_t + b_t$, conditions (5.94) and (5.95) imply that

$$\lim_{t\to\infty} b_t e^{-rt} = 0. \tag{5.96}$$

Further, in deriving the consumer's intertemporal constraint—given by equation (5.10)—we imposed the condition

$$\lim_{t\to\infty} (b_t + m_t)e^{-rt} = 0. \tag{5.97}$$

Conditions (5.96) and (5.97) imply that

$$\lim_{t\to\infty} m_t e^{-rt} = 0. \tag{5.98}$$

Since, from the Central Bank's balance sheet, $d_t = m_t - h_t$, conditions (5.94) and (5.98) imply that

$$\lim_{t\to\infty} d_t e^{-rt} = 0. \tag{5.99}$$

By definition, $d_t = D_t/E_t P_t^*$. Hence

$$d_t = d_0 e^{\int_0^t (\theta_s - \varepsilon_s - \pi_s^*)ds}.$$

Using the latter equation, we can rewrite (5.99) as

$$\lim_{t\to\infty} d_0 e^{\int_0^t (\theta_s - \varepsilon_s - \pi_s^* - r)ds} = 0. \tag{5.100}$$

This condition provides an upper bound on the rate of expansion of domestic credit that is consistent with the maintenance of a predetermined exchange rates regime. In the case where θ_s, ε_s, and π_s^* are constant over time and equal to θ, ε, and π^*, respectively, the condition $\theta = \varepsilon + \pi^*$, as assumed in the text, is sufficient to ensure that (5.100) holds. In general, however, all that we need for condition (5.100) to hold is that, "on average," $\theta_s - \varepsilon_s - \pi_s^* - r < 0$. In the case in which the exchange rate is fixed ($\varepsilon_t = 0$), foreign inflation is zero, and the rate of growth of domestic credit is constant at θ, then condition (5.100) holds as long as $\theta < r$.[42] Intuitively, under a fixed exchange rate, and as long as $\theta > 0$, the Central Bank is increasing its external debt (i.e., international reserves become increasingly negative) but can finance the debt service by lump-sum taxing the private sector. If, however, $\theta > r$, it is no longer possible to service the debt because the rate of growth of government's debt exceeds the real interest rate. As Obstfeld (1986) points out, if lump-sum taxation were not available, then any $\theta > 0$ is no longer feasible because it would imply ever-growing revenue needs that can only be raised by distortionary taxation.

42. This is one of Obstfeld's (1986) points: if there are no constraints on the government's external borrowing, then a fixed exchange rate regime is sustainable as long as the rate of growth of domestic credit does not exceed the world real interest rate.

5.8.4 MIUF Model in Discrete Time

This appendix develops a discrete-time version of the continuous-time MIUF model developed in the text. This will prove useful for subsequent chapters in the book. Unlike real models in which the switch from continuous to discrete time does not pose any methodological problem, in monetary models this switch is nontrivial because—as will become clear below—timing issues play a critical role.

Households' Maximization

Suppose that preferences are given by

$$\sum_{t=0}^{\infty} \beta^t \left[u(c_t) + v\left(\frac{M_t}{P_t}\right) \right]. \tag{5.101}$$

A critical issue in discrete-time monetary models is related to timing. Due to analytical tractability, the more common assumption in the literature for MIUF models—which is captured in the preferences above—is that *end-of-period* money balances enter the utility function. While this assumption may look somewhat odd, it is the most common assumption in the literature (e.g., Calvo and Leiderman 1992).[43] The intertemporal budget constraint remains given by (5.57).

Households thus choose $\{c_t, m_t, a_t\}_{t=0}^{\infty}$ to maximize lifetime utility—given by (5.101)—subject to a sequence of flow budget constraints given by (5.57). In terms of the Lagrangian,

$$\begin{aligned}\mathcal{L} = &\sum_{t=0}^{\infty} \beta^t \left[u(c_t) + v\left(\frac{M_t}{P_t}\right) \right] \\ &+ \sum_{t=0}^{\infty} \beta^t \lambda_t \left[(1+r)a_{t-1} + \tau_t + y_t - c_t - \frac{i_{t-1}}{1+\pi_t} m_{t-1} - a_t \right].\end{aligned}$$

The first-order conditions with respect to c_t, m_t, and a_t are given by, respectively,

$$u'(c_t) - \lambda_t = 0, \tag{5.102}$$

$$v'(m_t) - \lambda_{t+1}\beta \frac{i_t}{1+\pi_{t+1}} = 0, \tag{5.103}$$

$$-\lambda_t + \beta(1+r)\lambda_{t+1} = 0, \tag{5.104}$$

43. As discussed by Carlstrom and Fuerst (2001), this assumption is rather odd because it amounts to assuming that what matters for liquidity purposes is the money balances that the consumer *leaves* the grocery store with, rather than the money that he/she *enters* the store with! The more natural assumption would be that *beginning-of-period money* balances provide liquidity services, which is the focus of exercise 7 at the end of the chapter.

Notice that under our usual assumption that $\beta(1+r)=1$, the last condition reduces to

$$\lambda_{t+1}=\lambda_t.$$

The Lagrange multiplier is constant over time. Denote the constant value of the multiplier by λ (i.e., $\lambda_{t+1}=\lambda_t=\lambda$). Hence, from (5.102), it follows that

$$u'(c_t)=\lambda. \tag{5.105}$$

As expected, consumption will be constant over time.

Taking into account that (1) the Lagrange multiplier is constant, (2) $\beta(1+r)=1$, and (3) by definition, $1+i_t=(1+r)(1+\pi_{t+1})$, we can rewrite first-order condition (5.103) as

$$v'(m_t)=\lambda\frac{i_t}{1+i_t}. \tag{5.106}$$

This is the condition analogous to equation (5.13) in the continuous-time version. As equation (5.106) makes clear, the opportunity cost of holding real money balances is $i_t/(1+i_t)$. Intuitively, in period t the household uses M_t instead of purchasing interest-bearing bonds and hence forgoes i_tM_t in interest payments at the beginning of period $t+1$. The real value of these interest payments in $t+1$ is i_tM_t/P_{t+1}, which discounted to time t amounts to $i_t(M_t/P_{t+1})/(1+r)$. Multiplying and dividing by P_t and recalling that, by definition, $1+i_t=(1+r)(P_{t+1}/P_t)$, this expression can be written as $[i_t/(1+i_t)]m_t$.

Substituting (5.105) into (5.106), we obtain

$$v'(m_t)=u'(c_t)\frac{i_t}{1+i_t}, \tag{5.107}$$

which implicitly defines a real money demand with standard properties.

Perfect Foresight Equilibrium

The aggregate conditions (5.68) and (5.69) still hold in this model. We know, from equation (5.105), that consumption is constant over time. Hence, from the resource constraint,

$$c=\frac{r}{1+r}\left[(1+r)(b_{-1}+h_{-1})+\sum_{t=0}^{\infty}\frac{y_t}{(1+r)^t}\right]. \tag{5.108}$$

Predetermined Exchange Rates

We now solve the model under predetermined exchange rates. Needless to say, the same logic that applied to the continuous-time case remains valid. The monetary authority sets the path of both the nominal exchange rate and the stock of domestic credit. Formally, the monetary authority sets E_t, $t=0,1,\ldots$, and D_t, $t=0,1,\ldots$. Suppose, for simplicity, that the monetary authority sets a constant rate of devaluation. Formally,

$$\frac{E_{t+1}}{E_t} = 1 + \varepsilon.$$

Through the interest parity condition the constant rate of devaluation determines a constant nominal interest rate (assuming, of course, a constant foreign inflation rate):

$$1 + i = (1 + i^*)(1 + \varepsilon).$$

Given constant consumption and a constant nominal interest rate, real money demand will also be constant. Given a constant real money demand, the path of international reserves will be given by

$$h_{t+1} - h_t = -\frac{D_t}{E_t P_t^*}\left[\frac{(1+\theta) - (1+\varepsilon)(1+\pi^*)}{(1+\varepsilon)(1+\pi^*)}\right].$$

Imposing the condition that the predetermined exchange rate regime be sustainable over time (i.e., $1 + \theta = (1 + \varepsilon)(1 + \pi^*)$), we obtain

$$h_{t+1} = h_t.$$

International reserves will be constant over time.

Flexible Exchange Rates

We now solve the model under flexible exchange rates. Assume, for simplicity, that the monetary authority sets an initial level of the nominal money supply, M_0, and a constant rate of money growth:

$$\frac{M_{t+1}}{M_t} = 1 + \mu, \qquad t = 0, 1, \ldots. \tag{5.109}$$

We will proceed in an analogous way to the continuous-time case and derive an unstable difference equation for real money balances. To this effect, multiply and divide by P_{t+1} and P_t on the LHS of equation (5.109) to obtain

$$\frac{m_{t+1}}{m_t} = \frac{1}{P_{t+1}/P_t}(1 + \mu). \tag{5.110}$$

Using the interest parity condition and the law of one price, we can rewrite this equation as

$$\frac{m_{t+1}}{m_t} = \frac{(1 + \mu)(1 + r)}{1 + i_t}. \tag{5.111}$$

Solving for i_t from (5.106) and substituting the resulting expression into the last equation, we obtain a difference equation in m_t:

$$m_{t+1} = m_t (1+\mu)(1+r)\left[1 - \frac{v'(m_t)}{\lambda}\right]. \tag{5.112}$$

This difference equation is the analogue to the differential equation (5.42) in the continuous-time case.

The stationary state corresponding to this equation is implicitly given by (as follows from setting $m_{t+1} = m_t = \bar{m}$)

$$v'(\bar{m}) = \lambda \frac{(1+\mu)(1+r) - 1}{(1+\mu)(1+r)}.$$

By linearizing this equation around the stationary state, we can check that this is an unstable differential equation:[44]

$$\left.\frac{\partial m_{t+1}}{\partial m_t}\right|_{\bar{m}} = 1 - \bar{m}\frac{(1+\mu)(1+r)}{\lambda} v''(\bar{m}) > 1.$$

Given the instability of (5.112), m_t will need to be at its stationary state from $t = 0$ onward. Otherwise, it would diverge over time. In other words, the constant value of m_t, $t = 0, 1, \ldots$, will be implicity given by

$$v'(\bar{m}) = u'(c)\frac{(1+\mu)(1+r) - 1}{(1+\mu)(1+r)}.$$

It then follows from (5.111) that the nominal interest rate will also be constant over time and given by

$$i_t = (1+\mu)(1+r) - 1.$$

Through interest parity, the rate of depreciation will also be constant.

5.8.5 Exchange Rate Regimes in Practice

Section 5.2.5 analyzes the main characteristics of predetermined exchange rates and flexible exchange rates regimes. For conceptual clarity, we studied those regimes in their "pure" form: under predetermined exchange rates, the monetary authority controls the path of the nominal exchange rate, and under flexible exchange rates, the monetary authority does not intervene at all in the foreign exchange market. In practice, however, such "pure" forms are hard to find (particularly for flexible exchange rates), and we in fact observe a whole continuum of exchange rate regimes in between these two extremes. In addition there are exchange rate regimes that go

44. As in the continuous-time case, if $v(m_t) = \log(m_t)$, this difference equation becomes a linear difference equation given by $m_{t+1} = (1+\mu)(1+r)(m_t - 1/\lambda)$.

beyond predetermined exchange rates, such as "full dollarization" (i.e., no domestic currency). What follows is an exchange rate taxonomy—based on the degree of exchange rate flexibility and the existence of formal or informal commitments to exchange rate paths—reported in the 2008 IMF report on "De facto Classification of Exchange Rate Regimes and Monetary Policy Framework."[45]

• *No separate legal tender* Two possible cases arise: (1) the currency of another country circulates as the sole legal tender, or (2) the member belongs to a monetary or currency union in which the same legal tender is shared by the members of the union. Adopting such regimes implies the complete surrender of the monetary authorities' control over domestic monetary policy. Examples of the first type of regime are Ecuador, Panama, and El Salvador; examples of the second type are the eurozone and the Eastern Caribbean Currency Union.

• *Currency board arrangements* A monetary regime based on an explicit legislative commitment to exchange domestic currency for a specified foreign currency at a fixed exchange rate, combined with restrictions on the issuing authority to ensure the fulfillment of its legal obligation. This implies that domestic currency will be issued only against foreign exchange and that it remains fully backed by foreign assets, leaving little scope for discretionary monetary policy and eliminating traditional Central Bank functions, such as monetary control and lender of last resort. Some flexibility may still be afforded, depending on how strict the banking rules of the currency board arrangement are. Hong Kong, for instance, has had a currency board (with the exchange rate fixed at 7.8 Honk Kong dollars per US dollar) since October 17, 1983. Other examples are Estonia (until January 1, 2011, when it became the 17th member of the eurozone), Lithuania, and Djibouti.[46]

• *Conventional fixed peg arrangements* The country pegs its currency within margins of ± 1 percent or less vis-à-vis another currency; a cooperative arrangement, such as the ERM II; or a basket of currencies, where the basket is formed from the currencies of major trading or financial partners and weights reflect the geographical distribution of trade, services, or capital flows. The currency composites can also be standardized, as in the case of the Special Drawing Rights (SDR). There is no commitment to keep the parity irrevocably. The exchange rate may fluctuate within narrow margins of less than ± 1 percent around a central rate—or the maximum and minimum value of the exchange rate may remain within a narrow margin of 2 percent—for at least three months. The monetary authority maintains the fixed parity through direct intervention (i.e., via sale/purchase of foreign exchange in the market) or indirect intervention (i.e., via the use of interest rate policy, imposition of foreign exchange regulations, exercise of moral suasion that constrains foreign exchange activity, or through intervention by other public institutions).

45. The description of the different regimes is taken from the IMF report. Examples given are current as of April 30, 2011. This classification system is based on members' de facto arrangements as identified by IMF staff, which may differ from their officially announced arrangements (see the discussion below on de jure versus de facto regimes).

46. Another recent and highly publicized example of a currency board would be Argentina's Convertibility plan (1991–2001).

Flexibility of monetary policy, though limited, is greater than in exchange rate arrangements with no separate legal tender or currency boards because traditional Central Bank functions are still possible, and the monetary authority can in principle adjust the level of the exchange rate. Examples are Venezuela, Barbados, and Belize.

- *Pegged exchange rates within horizontal bands* The value of the currency is maintained within certain margins of fluctuation of more than ± 1 percent around a fixed central rate or the margin between the maximum and minimum value of the exchange rate exceeds 2 percent. As in the case of conventional fixed pegs, reference may be made to a single currency, a cooperative arrangement, or a currency composite. There is a limited degree of monetary policy discretion, depending on the band width. An example is Tonga.
- *Crawling pegs* The currency is adjusted periodically in small amounts at a fixed rate or in response to changes in selective quantitative indicators, such as past inflation differentials vis-à-vis major trading partners, and differentials between the inflation target and expected inflation in major trading partners. The rate of crawl can be set to adjust for measured inflation or other (backward-looking) indicators or set at a preannounced fixed rate and/or below the projected inflation differentials (forward looking). Maintaining a crawling peg imposes constraints on monetary policy in a manner similar to a fixed peg system. Examples are Botswana and Nicaragua.
- *Managed floating with no predetermined path for the exchange rate* The monetary authority attempts to influence the exchange rate without having a specific exchange rate path or target. Indicators for managing the exchange rate are broadly judgmental (i.e., balance-of-payments position, international reserves, parallel market developments), and adjustments may not be automatic. Intervention may be direct or indirect. Examples are Algeria, Singapore and Paraguay.
- *Independently floating* The exchange rate is determined by the market, with any official foreign exchange market intervention aimed at moderating the rate of change and preventing undue fluctuations in the exchange rate, rather than at establishing a level for it. Examples are United States, Japan, and Chile.

When it comes to quantifying the effects of different exchange rate regimes on, among other things, growth and inflation, a major issue confronting empirical researchers is whether to use de jure or de facto classifications of exchange rate regimes. Until recently most papers followed de jure classifications, typically based on the approach that the IMF followed until 1997 of asking member countries to self-declare their arrangements. More recently, however, Levy Yeyati and Sturzenegger (2005) and Reinhart and Rogoff (2004) have provided de facto classifications (like the one above by the IMF). These authors argue that de jure classifications usually fail to describe actual exchange rate regimes and that the gap between de facto (what countries actually do) and de jure (what countries say they do) classifications may be critical for understanding/quantifying a host of important issues. An example of this gap is the so-called "fear of floating" phenomenon analyzed in Calvo and Reinhart (2000), who argue that while many emerging markets claim to pursue flexible exchange rate arrangements, many in fact intervene heavily to keep the nominal exchange rate within certain ranges. Table 5.3 illustrates the gap between de jure and de facto regimes by

Table 5.3
De jure versus de facto exchange rate regimes

		RR de facto classification	
		Fixed	Flexible
IMF de jure classification	Fixed	1,363	366
	Flexible	487	303

Sources: IMF and Reinhart and Rogoff (2004).
Note: Data points are annual observations for 132 developing countries for the period 1970 to 2001.

comparing the traditional de jure IMF classification with the de facto classification provided by Reinhart and Rogoff (2004). Note that according to this table, 487 annual observations with a de jure flexible exchange rate are reclassified by Reinhart and Rogoff (2004) as a fixed exchange rate regime. Two interesting cases are China, 1994 to 1997, and Mexico, 1992 to 1994, both with a de jure flexible exchange rate regime but classified as fixed by Reinhart and Rogoff (2004).

5.8.6 What Is the Interest Rate Elasticity of Money Demand?

In our theoretical framework—and as shown in equation (5.14)—real money demand is a positive function of consumption and a negative function of the nominal interest rate. The interest rate elasticity of money demand is a particularly important parameter because it tells us the extent to which money demand will be affected by changes in interest rates.

The estimation procedure typically used in finding the empirical counterpart of expression (5.14) starts by developing an equilibrium model in discrete time similar to the one outlined in appendix 5.8.4. Given the timing assumptions of most models, the interest rate enters the money demand equation through the expression $i_t/(1+i_t)$, as is the case in the end-of-period specification captured in equation (5.107). Arrau et al. (1995) introduce money in a general equilibrium model through a transactions costs technology that takes the form

$$H(m_t, \theta_t, c_t) = \frac{1}{c_t^{1-\phi}} h\left(\frac{m_t}{c_t^{\phi}}, \theta_t\right),$$

where $H(.)$ represents transactions costs per unit of consumption (i.e., total transactions costs are $c_t H(.)$) and $h(.)$ is given by

$$h\left(\frac{m_t}{c_t^{\phi}}, \theta_t\right) = K\theta_t + \frac{1}{\alpha}\left[\frac{m_t}{c_t^{\phi}} \log\left(\frac{m_t}{c_t^{\phi}\theta_t}\right) - \frac{m_t}{c_t^{\phi}}\right],$$

where α and K are constants such that $\alpha > 0$ and K is large enough to ensure $h(.) > 0$ and $\partial h/\partial\theta_t > 0$, θ_t is a technological parameter that captures financial innovation, and ϕ is a parameter that represents the degree of scale economies in transaction (when $\phi = 1$, H is a function of the ratio m_t/c_t, which is the most common theoretical specification).

Under this functional form, and as shown in Arrau et al. (1995), the money demand equation takes the form

$$\log(m_t) = \log(\theta_t) + \phi \log(c_t) + \beta \left(\frac{i_t}{1 + i_t} \right). \tag{5.113}$$

The parameter $\beta (= -\alpha)$ is usually referred to as the interest rate semielasticity of money demand or, more generally, the opportunity cost semielasticity of money. Using M1 as their measure of money balances, Arrau et al. (1995) estimate the money demand function for a sample of ten developing countries using quarterly time series from the mid-1970s to the early 1980s. They also run regressions using i_t instead of $i_t/(1 + i_t)$ as the opportunity cost of holding money. Panel A in table 5.4 presents their estimates for β for the five countries where they find a long-run (cointegrating) relation between the dependent and independent variables. Their estimates vary between -0.5 and -3 and are, for the most part, significantly different from zero.

Reinhart and Végh (1995) develop a similar general equilibrium framework in which money also reduces transactions costs. Under certain functional forms, they derive the following money demand equation:

$$\log(m_t) = \delta + \varphi \log(\theta_t) + \phi \log(c_t) + \beta \log \left(\frac{i_t}{1 + i_t} \right), \tag{5.114}$$

where θ_t is a proxy for financial innovation and δ, φ, ϕ, and β are combinations of the primitive parameters of the transactions costs function. The authors simultaneously estimate equation (5.114) and the model's intertemporal optimality condition (the standard Euler equation) applying Hansen's (1982) generalized method of moments (GMM). Their database consists of quarterly time series for the 1970s and 1980s for Argentina, Chile, and Uruguay. Panel B in table 5.4 reports their estimates for β, which in this case corresponds to the interest rate elasticity of money and not to the semielasticity as in equation (5.113).[47] Their estimates are significantly differently from zero for all countries and not inconsistent with the findings of Arrau et al. (1995).

Some researchers have argued that many developing countries, particularly high-inflation countries, have gone through periods of interest rate controls that limit the usefulness of the interest rate when measuring the opportunity cost of holding money. Easterly, Mauro, and Schmidt-Hebbel (1995), for example, use the inflation rate, π_t, instead of the interest rate, when constructing their opportunity cost variable, estimating an equation of the form

$$\log \left(\frac{m_t}{y_t} \right) = \delta + \beta \left(\frac{\pi_t}{1 + \pi_t} \right)^{\gamma}, \tag{5.115}$$

where y_t is output and γ is a parameter that captures the possibility of a nonlinear relationship between money balances and the corresponding opportunity cost. The authors use output instead

47. It can be easily checked that the interest rate elasticity equals $i/(1 + i)$ times the semielasticity.

Table 5.4
Empirical estimates of the opportunity cost semielasticity of money

A. Country-specific regressions (Arrau et al. 1995)[a]

	Estimated β when the opportunity cost measure is:	
Country	*i*	*i*/(1 + *i*)
Argentina		−0.47
		(−2.14)
Brazil		−2.17
		(−3.50)
India	−2.83	
	(−1.98)	
Israel		−2.97
		(−13.70)
Korea	−2.97	
	(−1.14)	

B. Country-specific regressions (Reinhart and Végh 1995)[a]

Country	*Estimated β*[b]
Argentina	−0.10
	(−5.00)
Chile	−0.09
	(−2.25)
Uruguay	−0.22
	(−2.20)

C. Panel regressions (Easterly, Mauro, and Schmidt-Hebbel 1995)[a]

Specification	*Estimated β*	*Estimated γ*
Levels—linear ($\gamma = 1$)	−1.42	
	(−11.46)	
Levels—nonlinear	−1.53	1.59
	(−10.04)	(6.78)
First-differences—linear ($\gamma = 1$)	−0.74	
	(−6.53)	
First-differences—nonlinear	−0.92	2.20
	(−4.15)	(4.06)

D. Money demand in the United States (Goldfeld and Sichel 1990)[a]

Interest rate	*Estimated β*[b]
Commercial paper rate	−0.013
	(5.2)
Commercial bank passbook rate	−0.003
	(0.9)

a. *t*-values are in parenthesis.
b. Estimates correspond to the interest rate elasticity of money.

of consumption as their scale variable because this aggregate is less subject to measurement error in their particular sample of countries. Panel C reports the results of their estimations for a panel of eleven high-inflation countries using annual data for the 1960 to 1990 period, and using M1 as their money balances measure. The first two rows correspond to equation (5.115) estimated in levels, while the second two rows correspond to equation (5.115) estimated in first differences due to the difficulty of finding a cointegrating relationship in the levels specification. The authors find that the γ coefficient is positive and statistically significant in the nonlinear versions of both specifications, and therefore argue that in high-inflation countries the opportunity cost semielasticity of money is not constant but rather increases with inflation.

How large is the interest rate elasticity of money in the United States? Goldfeld and Sichel (1990) argue that until the mid-1970s the behavior of money demand in the United States was well explained by a simple partial adjustment model of the following form:

$$\log(m_t) = a_0 + a_1 \log(y_t) + a_2 \log(m_{t-1}) + a_3 \log(\pi_t) + \beta \log(i_t), \tag{5.116}$$

where a_i, $i = 0, 1, 2, 3$, are regression coefficients and β is the interest rate elasticity of money demand. Panel D shows the results of estimating (5.116) applying a Cochrane–Orcutt procedure to quarterly data for the 1952 to 1986 period, taking M1 as the relevant measure of money holdings and using two different measures of i_t: the commercial paper rate and the commercial bank passbook rate. In this case the value of the interest rate elasticity is much smaller than the semielasticity estimates for developing countries presented in panels A though C. The authors also run regressions for different time periods and different variants of equation (5.116), obtaining low interest rate elasticity estimates in almost every case. Estimates for other G7 countries summarized in Goldfeld and Sichel (1990) also point out to small numbers.

Taking into account the overall performance of their estimations, Goldfeld and Sichel (1990) suggested the need for rethinking the conventional specification, and experimented with different alternatives like estimating the money demand equation by maximum likelihood, using last day of quarter flow of funds data for M1, and amending the initial model by a buffer-stock component in the partial adjustment equation. In every instance the estimated elasticity is below 0.04. We thus conclude that the low value of the estimated interest rate elasticity of money in the United States provides some empirical support for modeling money through a cash in advance constraint. Indeed this has been the route followed by Cooley and Hansen (1989, 1995) in their seminal work introducing money in a real business cycles model.

Exercises

1. (Economy's resource constraint) Derive the economy's resource constraint—equation (5.26) in the text—by combining the consumer's intertemporal constraint, given by (5.10), and the government's intertemporal constraint, given by (5.22).

2. (Dirty floating) This exercise illustrates how one would think about "dirty floating" in the monetary model analyzed in the main section. Specifically, we analyze how the economy would respond to a positive monetary shock that would lead to an appreciation of the domestic currency and how the monetary authority (MA) might intervene to partly offset such an appreciation (perhaps because, for reasons left out of the model, it fears that a large appreciation might worsen the trade balance).

Consider the model of section 5.2 with the only modification that preferences are now given by

$$\int_0^{\infty} [u(c_t) + \alpha_t v(m_t)]e^{-\beta t} dt, \tag{5.117}$$

where α_t should be thought of as a money demand shock. In the context of this model:

a. Consider the case of flexible exchange rates (with $\mu_t = 0$). Suppose that just before $t = 0$, the economy is in a stationary equilibrium with a constant α. At $t = 0$, there is unanticipated and permanent increase in α. Solve for the nonintervention case (i.e., a "pure floating").

b. Solve for the extreme case of "full intervention" (i.e., the MA reacts in such a way that it does not let the nominal exchange rate change). Explain intuitively how this policy works.

c. Consider an "intermediate case" where the MA chooses to intervene in the foreign exchange market (but allows some of the adjustment to take place through the nominal exchange rate). In particular, derive a "policy reaction function" that would tell the MA how much to intervene as a function of the change in real money demand (which the MA must take as given) and the targeted change in the nominal exchange rate. (Hint: Think of small changes so that you can use differentiation to compute changes at $t = 0$.)

3. (Demand shocks) This exercise shows that, as one would expect, the dichotomy between the real and the monetary sectors is still valid when the path of consumption is not constant over time. To this effect, consider the following variation of the model in the text. Preferences are given by

$$\int_0^{\infty} [\alpha_t u(c_t) + v(m_t)]e^{-\beta t} dt,$$

where α_t is a preference shock. The rest of the model is unchanged. The parameter α_t can be viewed as a demand shock. Suppose that the path of α_t is as follows:

$$\alpha_t = \begin{cases} \alpha^H, & 0 \leq t < T, \\ \alpha^L, & t \geq T, \end{cases}$$

where $\alpha^H > \alpha^L$. In this context:

a. Solve for the perfect foresight equilibrium path corresponding to predetermined exchange rates.

b. Solve for the perfect foresight equilibrium path corresponding to flexible exchange rates and show that the real effects coincide with the ones you just derived for predetermined exchange rates.

4. (Increase in domestic credit) Consider the economy analyzed in section 5.3 and operating under predetermined exchange rates. Discuss the effects of an unanticipated and permanent increase in the stock of domestic credit at time 0.

5. (Equivalence between predetermined and flexible rates) Consider the economy from section 5.2 operating under flexible exchange rates. Suppose that the rate of money growth is zero (i.e., $\mu_t = 0$) and that the level of the money supply follows the path given by

$$M_t = \begin{cases} M^L, & 0 \leq t < T, \\ M^H, & t \geq T, \end{cases}$$

where $M^L < M^H$. In this context:

a. Solve for the perfect foresight equilibrium path of all relevant variables.

b. Show that if the economy were operating under predetermined exchange rates and the Central Bank set the path of the nominal exchange rate that you obtained in part a, the same equilibrium would obtain.

6. (Inflationary consequences of anticipated changes in policy) Consider the model of section 5.2. Characterize the perfect foresight equilibrium paths corresponding to the following cases:

a. Under predetermined exchange rates, suppose that the rate of devaluation is zero between 0 and T and increases to $\varepsilon > 0$ at $t = T$. Solve for the path of all relevant variables.

b. Under flexible exchange rates, suppose that the rate of money growth is zero between 0 and T and increases to $\mu > 0$ at time T. Solve for the path of all relevant variables.

How does the behavior of inflation differ? What is the intuition behind the results?

7. (MIUF with beginning-of-period money balances) Solve the discrete-time MIUF model analyzed in appendix 5.8.4 with the following preferences:

$$\sum_{t=0}^{\infty} \beta^t \left[u(c_t) + v\left(\frac{M_{t-1}}{P_t}\right) \right].$$

References

Arrau, Patricio, Jose de Gregorio, Carmen M. Reinhart, and Peter Wickham. 1995. The demand for money in developing countries: Assessing the role of financial innovation. *Journal of Development Economics* 46 (2): 317–40.

Calvo, Guillermo, and Leonardo Leiderman. 1992. Optimal inflation tax under precommitment: Theory and Evidence. *American Economic Review* 82 (1): 179–94.

Calvo, Guillermo, and Carmen M. Reinhart. 2000. Fear of floating. *Quarterly Journal of Economics* 107 (2): 379–408.

Carlstrom, Charles T., and Timothy S. Fuerst. 2001. Timing and real indeterminacy in monetary models. *Journal of Monetary Economics* 47 (2): 285–98.

Cooley, Thomas, and Gary Hansen. 1989. The inflation tax in real business cycle models. *American Economic Review* 79: 733–48.

Cooley, Thomas, and Gary Hansen. 1995. Money and the business cycle. In Thomas Cooley, ed., *Frontiers of Business Cycle Research.* Princeton: Princeton University Press, 175–221.

Drazen, Allan, and Elhanan Helpman. 1987. Stabilization with exchange rate management. *Quarterly Journal of Economics* 102 (4): 835–56.

Drazen, Allan, and Elhanan Helpman. 1990. Inflationary consequences of anticipated macroeconomic policies. *Review of Economic Studies* 57 (1): 147–64.

Easterly, William, Paolo Mauro, and Klaus Schmidt-Hebbel. 1995. Money demand and seigniorage-maximizing inflation. *Journal of Money, Credit, and Banking* 27 (2): 583–603.

Goldfeld, Stephen M., and Daniel E. Sichel. 1990. The demand for money. In Benjamin M. Friedman and Frank H. Hahn, eds., *Handbook of Monetary Economics*, vol. I. Amsterdam: Elsevier, 299–356.

Hansen, Lars. 1982. Large sample properties of generalized method of moments. *Econometrica* 50 (4): 1029–54.

Helpman, Elhanan. 1981. An exploration in the theory of exchange-rate regimes. *Journal of Political Economy* 89 (5): 865–90.

Levy Yeyati, Eduardo, and Federico Sturzenegger. 2005. Classifying exchange rate regimes: Deeds vs. words. *European Economic Review* 49 (6): 1603–35.

Lucas, Robert E., Jr. 1982. Interest rates and currency prices in a two-country world. *Journal of Monetary Economics* 10 (3): 335–59.

Obstfeld, Maurice, 1986. Speculative attack and the external constraint in a maximizing model of the balance of payments. *Canadian Journal of Economics* 19 (1): 1–22.

Reinhart, Carmen M., and Kenneth Rogoff. 2004. The modern history of exchange rate arrangements: A reinterpretation. *Quarterly Journal of Economics* 119 (1): 1–48.

Reinhart, Carmen M., and Carlos A. Végh. 1995. Nominal interest rates, consumption booms, and lack of credibility: A quantitative examination. *Journal of Development Economics* 46 (2): 357–78.

Sargent, Thomas J., and Neil Wallace. 1981. Some unpleasant monetarist arithmetic. *Quarterly Review.* Federal Reserve Bank of Minneapolis (Fall): 1–17.

6 The Monetary Approach to the Balance of Payments

6.1 Introduction

We have seen that in our basic monetary model of chapter 5, both monetary policy (under flexible exchange rates) and exchange rate policy (under predetermined exchange rates) do not have real effects. We purposely chose such a setup to focus exclusively on some important monetary phenomena without having to worry about possible links between the real and the monetary sectors. While that model is an important conceptual benchmark, it certainly does not provide us with tools to understand the possible real effects of monetary/exchange rate policy in an open economy. At its core, the main task of open economy monetary economics is to study departures from the world of chapter 5.

The first such departure will be to abstract from interest bearing assets. In other words, we will modify the model of chapter 5 by assuming that money is the only asset available in the world economy. This will allow us to highlight a fundamental adjustment mechanism in economies operating under predetermined exchange rates: the so-called monetary approach to the balance of payments.[1] This approach emphasizes the idea that temporary "disequilibria" in the money market (in the sense of current money holdings that differ from the long-run demand for money) give rise to movements in international reserves (i.e., the balance of payments). More specifically, an excess demand for money will give rise to a trade surplus (and hence to a gain in international reserves) as the economy "imports" money from abroad to increase real money balances. Conversely, an excess supply of money will lead to a trade deficit (and thus to a loss of international reserves) as the economy gets rid of unwanted money balances. In this world, by increasing the price level, a devaluation reduces real money balances on impact and results in an excess money demand. This provokes a fall in consumption as households save in order to rebuild their cash balances. The resulting trade surplus leads to a gain in international reserves.[2] We can thus think of a

1. The expression "balance of payments"—which was the common parlance of the 1960s and 1970s—refers to changes in international reserves at the Central Bank.

2. In addition to being a fundamental adjustment mechanism in any open economy model, the monetary approach to the balance of payments has had a tremendous impact on policy. In fact it has been at the core of IMF's policy recommendations for more than half a century. Typically, low international reserves at the Central Bank would prompt the IMF to call for a devaluation, on the rationale that such a measure would increase international reserves.

devaluation as an *expenditure-reducing* mechanism. The reduction in expenditures translates into a trade surplus and reserve accumulation.

By introducing nontradable goods and endogenous production into the picture, this chapter's model will also allow us to get a fuller picture of the anatomy of a devaluation. Besides the expenditure-reducing effect isolated in the one-good model, we will encounter two additional effects: (1) an *expenditure-switching effect* whereby households switch consumption from tradable to nontradable goods and (2) a *production effect* whereby labor moves from the nontradable to the tradable goods sector, increasing production of tradables at the expense of nontradables. These two additional effects are induced by an increase in the relative price of tradable goods (i.e., a real depreciation of the currency). Intuitively, in response to a devaluation, households will want to reduce consumption of *both* tradable and nontradable goods (the expenditure-reducing effect). This causes—at the initial relative price of nontradable goods—an excess supply of nontradable goods. The resulting fall in the relative price of nontradable goods induces households to consume more nontradables (and fewer tradables) and firms to produce more tradables. This nicely illustrates the idea that a devaluation will improve the trade surplus by both reducing consumption and increasing production of tradable goods.

This two-good model will allow us to make two additional important points. First, contrary to many economists' best instincts, a large comovement between nominal and real exchange rates is not prima facie evidence of sticky prices. In fact—and despite no nominal rigidities of any kind—the nominal price of nontradable goods will respond very little to a devaluation if, as we expect in practice, there is not much substitution in production. Indeed, in the limiting case where there is no production substitution at all, a back-of-the-envelope calculation reveals that a 10 percent devaluation results in an increase of only 3.8 percent in the price of nontradable goods. Second, in this model a devaluation is *contractionary*, in the sense that it leads not only to a fall in consumption but also to a fall in total production (in terms of tradable goods). This prediction is thus consistent with the observation that particularly in developing countries, devaluations are often contractionary.[3]

Finally, we turn our attention to flexible exchange rates. We first show that unlike the case of fixed/predetermined exchange rates studied so far in the chapter, the economy adjusts instantaneously to a change in the level or rate of growth of the money supply. Interestingly, removing interest-bearing bonds from the picture does not alter the results obtained in our pure monetary model of chapter 5. The intuition is simply that the absence of interest-bearing assets does not affect the equilibrating mechanism under flexible exchange, which are changes in the nominal exchange rate. Hence a doubling of the money supply will lead to a doubling of the nominal exchange rate with no real effects. We then introduce a celebrated twist into the model by assuming that domestic agents use two monies (i.e., there is currency substitution). The point is to show that even under flexible exchange rates, the presence of currency substitution implies

3. See box 8.2 in chapter 8 for a review of the evidence on the output effects of devaluations.

that the economy will adjust in much the same way as that emphasized by the monetary approach. Intuitively, adjustments in the stock of foreign currency can only take place through trade imbalances. For instance, an increase in the rate of money growth, which induces households to increase their long-run holdings of foreign currency relative to domestic currency, will necessitate of a trade surplus to enable households to acquire more foreign currency.

The chapter proceeds as follows. Section 6.2 develops the main model of this chapter and analyzes several experiments that illustrate the adjustment mechanism highlighted by the monetary approach. Section 6.3 adds nontradable goods and endogenous production to the model of Section 6.2 and focuses on the effects of a devaluation. Section 6.4 analyzes the model of Section 6.2 under flexible exchange rates. Section 6.5 introduces currency substitution into the picture and analyzes the response of the economy to an increase in the rate of growth of the money supply. Section 6.6 offers concluding remarks.

6.2 The Monetary Approach to the Balance of Payments

Building on Calvo (1981), we modify the model of chapter 5 by assuming that money is the only asset available in the world economy. There is thus domestic money (used in the domestic economy for both transactions and store-of-value purposes) and foreign money (i.e., dollar bills) that is held as reserves by the Central Bank. There is a constant endowment of the only tradable (and nonstorable) good, denoted by y. The foreign price of the good is assumed to be constant and equal to one. Hence, by the law of one price, $P_t = E_t$, where P_t is the domestic price of the good and E_t is the nominal exchange rate (in domestic currency per unit of foreign currency).

6.2.1 Consumer's Problem

Let preferences be given by

$$\int_0^\infty [u(c_t) + v(m_t)] \exp(-\beta t) dt, \tag{6.1}$$

where $\beta(> 0)$ is the discount rate, c_t denotes consumption, and m_t are real money balances, defined as M_t/E_t, where M_t are nominal money balances.[4]

Since there are no bonds in this world, the consumer's flow constraint is given by

$$\dot{M}_t = E_t y + E_t \tau_t - E_t c_t, \tag{6.2}$$

where τ_t are lump-sum transfers from the government. From the definition of real money balances ($m_t = M_t/E_t$), it follows that

4. For notational clarity, we will use exp(.) to denote the exponential function in chapters in which e will be used to denote the real exchange rate.

$$\dot{m}_t = \frac{\dot{M}_t}{E_t} - \varepsilon_t m_t, \tag{6.3}$$

where ε_t is the rate of devaluation. Using (6.3), we can rewrite equation (6.2) as

$$\dot{m}_t = y + \tau_t - c_t - \varepsilon_t m_t. \tag{6.4}$$

The consumer maximizes (6.1) subject to the flow constraint (6.4). In terms of the current value Hamiltonian,[5]

$$H = u(c_t) + v(m_t) + \lambda_t \left(y + \tau_t - c_t - \varepsilon_t m_t\right), \tag{6.5}$$

where c_t is the control variable, m_t is the state variable, and λ_t is the associated co-state variable. The co-state variable, λ_t, can be interpreted as the shadow value of an additional unit of real money balances in terms of time t utility. At each point in time, the consumer chooses consumption. The choice of consumption yields direct utility (as captured by the term $u(c_t)$) but also affects the stock of real money balances for the next instant through the flow budget constraint. The value of such a change is captured by the third term on the RHS of (6.5). Hence, for a given value of λ_t, the Hamiltonian captures the total contribution to utility of the choice of consumption.

Optimal conditions are given by

$$\frac{\partial H}{\partial c_t} = u'(c_t) - \lambda_t = 0, \tag{6.6}$$

$$\dot{\lambda}_t = \beta\lambda_t - \frac{\partial H}{\partial m_t} = (\beta + \varepsilon_t)\lambda_t - v'(m_t). \tag{6.7}$$

We can rewrite these optimality conditions as

$$u'(c_t) = \lambda_t, \tag{6.8}$$

$$\underbrace{\frac{v'(m_t)}{\lambda_t} - \varepsilon_t}_{\text{“Net dividend”}} + \underbrace{\frac{\dot{\lambda}_t}{\lambda_t}}_{\text{Capital gain}} = \beta.$$

The first equation says that, at the margin, the consumer equates the benefits of an additional unit of consumption, $u'(c_t)$, to the shadow cost of that unit, λ_t. The second equation can be interpreted as an asset pricing equation. It equates the total return on real money balances—which consists of a “net dividend” and a capital gain—to the discount rate, β.

For further reference, notice that by differentiating (6.8) with respect to time and using (6.7) we obtain

5. Appendix 6.7.1 provides a basic introduction to optimal control techniques, which will be heavily used in the remainder of the book.

$$\dot{c}_t = -\frac{1}{u''(c_t)}[v'(m_t) - (\beta + \varepsilon_t)u'(c_t)]. \tag{6.9}$$

6.2.2 Government

The government holds foreign currency as international reserves (still denoted by h_t in real terms). Since foreign currency does not pay interest, the government's flow budget constraint takes the form

$$\dot{h}_t = \frac{\dot{M}_t}{P_t} - \tau_t. \tag{6.10}$$

The rate of growth of domestic credit is given by

$$\frac{\dot{D}_t}{D_t} = \theta_t. \tag{6.11}$$

Differentiating with respect to time the Central Bank's balance sheet ($h_t + d_t = m_t$) and using the fact that $\dot{d}_t/d_t = \theta_t - \varepsilon_t$, we obtain

$$\dot{h}_t = \dot{m}_t - d_t(\theta_t - \varepsilon_t).$$

As discussed in chapter 5—and to make the predetermined exchange rate system sustainable over time—we assume that $\theta_t = \varepsilon_t$. Hence

$$\dot{h}_t = \dot{m}_t. \tag{6.12}$$

Conceptually, this is an extremely important equilibrium condition. It says that under predetermined exchange rates, the change in international reserves will be determined by the change in real money demand. In other words, if, for some reason, real money demand is increasing (decreasing) over time, then the Central Bank will be gaining (losing) international reserves over time.

Finally, to find out the transfer policy implied by the domestic credit rule (6.11) and the assumption $\theta_t = \varepsilon_t$, solve for τ_t from (6.10) and use (6.12) to obtain

$$\tau_t = \varepsilon_t m_t. \tag{6.13}$$

6.2.3 Equilibrium Conditions

Combining the consumer's flow constraint (given by equation (6.4)) with the government's (given by equation 6.10), we obtain[6]

$$\dot{h}_t = y - c_t. \tag{6.14}$$

6. To be sure, equation (6.14) can also be obtained by substituting (6.13) into (6.4). But the derivation in the text makes the point that equation (6.14) does not depend on the assumption that $\varepsilon_t = \theta_t$.

Since there are no bonds in this world, the capital account is zero by construction. Hence, (6.14) says that the increase in international reserves equals the current account. Using (6.12), we can rewrite equation (6.14) as

$$\dot{m}_t = y - c_t. \tag{6.15}$$

6.2.4 Dynamic System

Equations (6.9) and (6.15) constitute a dynamic system in c_t and m_t for a constant value of ε_t, denoted by ε. To characterize the steady state of the system, set $\dot{c}_t = \dot{m}_t = 0$ to obtain

$$c_{ss} = y, \tag{6.16}$$

$$v'(m_{ss}) = u'(y)(\beta + \varepsilon), \tag{6.17}$$

where a subscript ss denotes steady-state values. Since there are no interest-bearing assets in this world, steady-state consumption will always be equal to the constant endowment, as indicated by equation (6.16). Equation (6.17) implicitly defines a steady-state real money demand with standard properties. Solving for m_{ss}, we obtain

$$m_{ss} = L(y, \beta + \varepsilon), \tag{6.18}$$

where

$$\frac{\partial L}{\partial y} = \frac{(\beta + \varepsilon)u''(y)}{v''(m_{ss})} > 0,$$

$$\frac{\partial L}{\partial(\beta + \varepsilon)} = \frac{u'(y)}{v''(m_{ss})} < 0.$$

We can think of $\beta + \varepsilon$ as a "shadow nominal interest rate" since it captures the steady-state opportunity cost of holding money.

We proceed by linearizing this dynamic system around the steady state. The linear approximation of the dynamic system around the steady state is given by

$$\begin{bmatrix} \dot{c}_t \\ \dot{m}_t \end{bmatrix} = \begin{bmatrix} \beta + \varepsilon & \frac{-v''(m_{ss})}{u''(y)} \\ -1 & 0 \end{bmatrix} \begin{bmatrix} c_t - y \\ m_t - m_{ss} \end{bmatrix}. \tag{6.19}$$

The determinant of the matrix associated with the linear approximation (denoted by Δ) is negative:

$$\Delta = \frac{-v''(m_{ss})}{u''(y)} < 0.$$

Since the determinant is the product of the two roots, a negative determinant implies that the system has one positive (i.e., unstable) and one negative (i.e., stable) root (see appendix 6.7.2 for details). Given that there is one predetermined variable (i.e., m_t), the system exhibits saddle-path stability: for a given value of m_0, c_t will adjust so as to position the system along the saddle path.[7]

We now proceed to fully characterize the qualitative behavior of the dynamic system in the (m_t, c_t) plane by resorting to the so-called phase diagram (figure 6.1). To construct the phase diagram, we first draw the $\dot{c}_t = 0$ and the $\dot{m}_t = 0$ curves. To obtain these curves, set $\dot{c}_t = 0$ in equation (6.9) to obtain

$$(\beta + \varepsilon)u'(c_t) = v'(m_t). \tag{6.20}$$

These are the loci of points along which consumption does not change. To figure out the slope of the $\dot{c}_t = 0$ locus, totally differentiate equation (6.20) to obtain

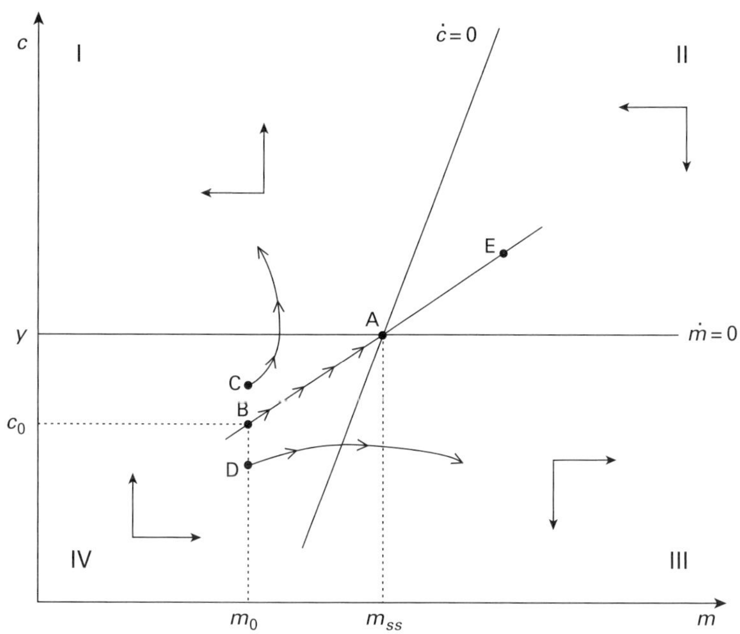

Figure 6.1
Phase diagram

7. Notice that this is the first time in the book that we are using a model with a stable root. Up to now, all the models have had a zero root (or unit root in discrete time). The presence of a stable root means that the system will converge to the steady state regardless of the initial conditions. (The reader is referred back to box 2.4 in chapter 2 for a discussion of roots in small open economy models.) Models with a stable root are often referred to as models with "intrinsic dynamics," as opposed to models with a zero root (or unit root) which only have "extrinsic" dynamics (i.e., they typically have dynamics only to the extent that exogenous processes follow nonconstant paths).

$$\left.\frac{dc_t}{dm_t}\right|_{\dot{c}_t=0} = \frac{v''(m_t)}{(\beta+\varepsilon)u''(c_t)} > 0.$$

Hence the $\dot{c}_t = 0$ curve will slope up, as depicted in figure 6.1.

To derive the $\dot{m}_t = 0$ locus, set $\dot{m}_t = 0$ in equation (6.15), to obtain

$$c_t = y.$$

The $\dot{m}_t = 0$ curve thus shows up in the phase diagram as a horizontal line.

The intersection of the $\dot{m}_t = 0$ and the $\dot{c}_t = 0$ curves (point A in figure 6.1) characterizes the system's steady state. If the system starts at that point, it will stay there. In addition the $\dot{m}_t = 0$ and $\dot{c}_t = 0$ curves define four different regions, labeled I through IV in figure 6.1. The next step is to determine in what direction the system will move in each of these four regions. To figure this out, we draw arrowheads in each of the four regions in the following way. Suppose that we are on a point along the $\dot{m}_t = 0$ curve in figure 6.1 and we increase c_t by a small amount. How will real money balances respond? To answer this question, differentiate equation (6.15) with respect to c_t to obtain

$$\left.\frac{\partial \dot{m}_t}{\partial c_t}\right|_{\dot{m}_t=0} = -1 < 0.$$

This says that if c_t is increased by a small amount, $\dot{m}_t$ becomes negative; that is, real money balances fall. Graphically, this means that we can draw arrowheads pointing west above the $\dot{m}_t = 0$ curve (i.e., in regions I and II) and, conversely, arrowheads pointing east below the $\dot{m}_t = 0$ curve (i.e., in regions III and IV).

Suppose now that we are on a point along the $\dot{c}_t = 0$ curve in figure 6.1 and we increase m_t by a small amount. How will consumption respond? This time differentiate the $\dot{c}_t = 0$ curve—given by (6.9)—with respect to m_t to obtain

$$\left.\frac{\partial \dot{c}_t}{\partial m_t}\right|_{\dot{c}_t=0} = \frac{-v''(m_{ss})}{u''(y)} < 0.$$

This implies that if m_t is raised by a small amount, consumption will fall. Conversely, if m_t is decreased a little bit, consumption will increase. Graphically, then, we can draw arrowheads pointing south to the right of the $\dot{c}_t = 0$ curve (i.e., in regions II and III) and pointing north to the left of $\dot{c}_t = 0$ curve (i.e., in regions I and IV).

The arrowheads that we have just drawn tell us in what direction the system will move in each of the four regions. Specifically, in region I the system will move in a northwestern direction, in region II in a southwestern direction, in region III in a southeastern direction, and in region IV in a northeastern direction.

How do we determine graphically the only convergent equilibrium path (i.e., the saddle path)?[8] It should be clear that if the system starts in either region I or III, it will diverge over time. Hence there are only two regions (regions II and IV) where the system will, in principle, move in a direction that is consistent with convergence to the steady state. Within these two regions, however, there is a unique path that will lead the system to the steady state. To illustrate this, suppose that the initial level of real money balances at $t = 0$ is given by m_0, which, as drawn in figure 6.1, is lower than m_{ss}. Since m_t is a predetermined variable but c_t is not, the system can position itself at any point along the vertical line corresponding to m_0. Suppose that c_0 is such that the system starts at point C. Then the system will travel in a northeastern direction, cross the $\dot{m}_t = 0$ locus with a vertical tangent, and then begin to travel in a northwestern direction. Such a path clearly diverges. By the same token, suppose that c_0 is such that the system starts at a point like D. The system then will travel in a northeastern direction, cross the $\dot{c}_t = 0$ locus with a horizontal tangent, and then head in a southeastern direction, clearly diverging. In fact it is only if c_0 is such that the system starts at point B (i.e., on a point along the saddle path) that it will converge over time to the steady state (i.e., point A).

6.2.5 Initial Steady State

Let us now fully characterize an initial steady state for a constant rate of devaluation, ε. The steady-state values of consumption and real money balances are given by equations (6.16) and (6.18), respectively. Clearly, the trade balance will be equal to zero:

$$TB_{ss} = y - c_{ss} = 0.$$

Since the rate of growth of domestic credit will be assumed constant (and given by θ) and equal to ε, the level of real domestic credit will be exogenously given at some value d. Given the stock of real domestic credit, the steady-state level of international reserves follows from the Central Bank's balance sheet ($h_t + d_t = m_t$):

$$h_{ss} = m_{ss} - d.$$

6.2.6 Effects of a Devaluation

Suppose that the economy is initially in the steady state given by point A in figure 6.1.[9] There is then an unanticipated and permanent increase in the level of the exchange rate (i.e., a permanent devaluation) (figure 6.2, panel a). How will the economy respond?

Let us use the phase diagram to find out the behavior of consumption and real money balances. The first question to ask is the following: Does this permanent devaluation change the steady

8. Appendix 6.7.2 provides an analytical derivation of the saddle path.

9. To fix ideas—and with no loss of generality—we assume $\varepsilon = \theta = 0$ so that the exchange rate is fixed.

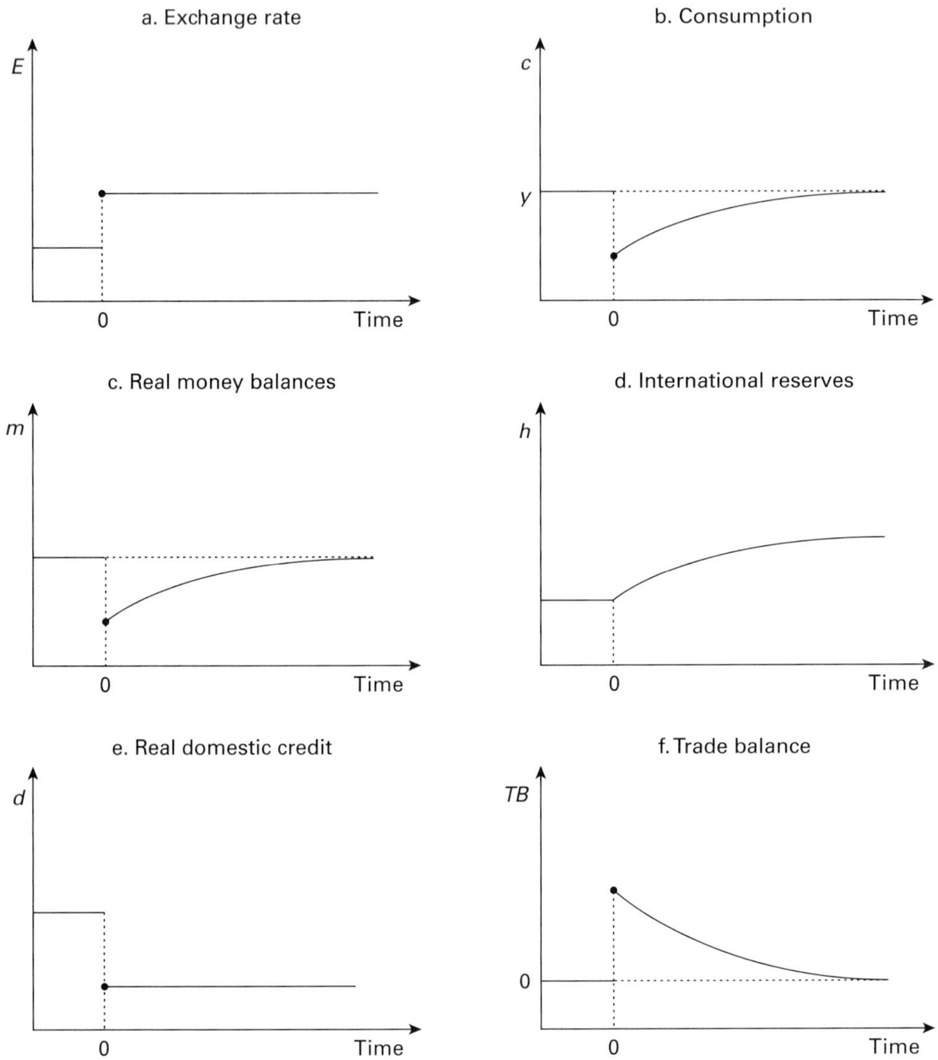

Figure 6.2
Permanent devaluation

state? The answer is clearly no. As equations (6.16) and (6.17) make clear, the steady-state values of consumption and real money balances do not depend on the nominal exchange rate.

How does the system respond on impact? On impact, real money balances must fall. To see this, write the Central Bank's balance sheet as

$$m_t = h_t + \frac{D_t}{E},$$

where E is the fixed exchange rate. International reserves cannot jump at time 0 and D_0 is a policy variable that, by assumption, does not change at time 0. Hence the increase in E at time 0 must lead to a fall in real money balances. In terms of the phase diagram depicted in figure 6.1, real money balances jump from m_{ss} to a point such as m_0. What happens to c_0? Based on our previous logic, c_0 will have to adjust so that the system lies along the saddle path. Hence, on impact, the system jumps for point A to point B in figure 6.1. The system then travels back to the unchanged steady state (point A). The corresponding time paths of consumption and real money balances are depicted in figure 6.2, panels b and c, respectively. Given that output is constant, the fall in consumption leads to a trade surplus at $t = 0$ (figure 6.2, panel f), which diminishes over time as consumption returns to its initial level.

How do international reserves respond? First, notice that real domestic credit falls at $t = 0$ and stays at that lower level thereafter (figure 6.2, panel e). It follows from the Central Bank's balance sheet ($h_{ss} = m_{ss} - d$) that international reserves will be higher in the new steady state because steady-state real money balances do not change but real domestic credit is lower. Hence, in the steady state, international reserves increase by precisely the amount that real domestic credit falls. On impact, international reserves do not change but then increase over time as equation (6.12) makes clear (see figure 6.2, panel d).

What is the intuition behind the adjustment of this economy to a devaluation? Since the devaluation reduces real money balances on impact but does *not* affect the desired long-run level of real money balances, the economy must rebuild real money balances over time. The only way for the economy to do so is to run a trade surplus (or, equivalently, a current account surplus), which increases international reserves over time and hence the nominal money supply. To run a trade surplus, the economy must reduce consumption in the short run (which we will refer to as the *expenditure reducing effect* of a devaluation). Put differently, the excess demand for real balances at time 0 (relative to the long-run real money demand) forces this economy to "import" the desired real money balances from the rest of the world. The fact that the balance of payments (i.e., the change in international reserves) responds to a "disequilibrium" in the money market explains why we refer to this kind of model as the "monetary approach to the balance of payments."

The key conclusion of this experiment is that *a devaluation will lead to a gain in international reserves*. This result provides a rationale for the typical IMF recommendation to countries that are losing international reserves.

Two final observations are in order. First, the result that a devaluation leads to an increase in international reserves is, of course, the same conclusion that we reached in chapter 5. The key difference is that in the model of chapter 5 the gain in international reserves occurred instantaneously and therefore involved no adjustment in the real sector. In contrast, in this chapter's model, the gain in international reserves occurs gradually over time through a trade surplus. Since the real world is surely somewhere in between chapter 5 (where there is perfect capital mobility) and chapter 6 (no capital mobility), this type of model would predict that a devaluation should lead to both an increase in international reserves and a trade surplus.[10]

The second observation is that, in this model, a devaluation is contractionary in the sense that it leads to a fall in consumption. Output is, of course, exogenous so it does not change. What would happen if we endogeneized production in this one-good world? Exercise 1 at the end of this chapter introduces a labor/leisure choice and linear production into the model and shows that a devaluation would still lead to a trade surplus in order to replenish real money balances. The trade surplus, however, would come about through two different channels: lower consumption and higher output. Intuitively, the fall in consumption needed to "import money" must be accompanied by a fall in leisure because the relative price of consumption in terms of leisure is not affected. The fall in leisure means more labor and higher production. The devaluation is thus expansionary in terms of output although it still leads to lower consumption. The conventional wisdom in this area (as we will review in box 8.2 in chapter 8) is that devaluations are expansionary. The empirical evidence, however, suggests that, in developing countries, devaluations are often contractionary (see Gupta, Mishra, and Sahay 2007).

6.2.7 Increase in Domestic Credit

Often times developing countries finance government spending with domestic credit (i.e., the fiscal authority "borrows" from the monetary authority). In our model such borrowing takes the form of the Central Bank printing money to buy (non-interest bearing) debt issued by the Finance Ministry.

Suppose, once again, that the economy is initially (i.e., just before $t = 0$) at the steady state given by point A in figure 6.1.[11] At $t = 0$ there is an unanticipated and permanent increase in the stock of domestic credit (figure 6.3, panel a). How does the economy respond?

In terms of figure 6.1, notice that a permanent increase in the stock of domestic credit does not change the economy's steady-state, as equations (6.16) and (6.17) make clear. From the Central Bank's balance sheet, we infer that on impact (i.e., at $t = 0$), real domestic credit increases and hence real money balances also increase. The system thus jumps from point A to a point like E

10. Incidentally, we should note that we would not want to use this model to draw normative implications. The reason is that unlike the model of chapter 5, the private sector is not "consuming" the international reserves at the Central Bank. In chapter 5 the consumer ends up consuming those reserves because the Central Bank transfers the interest on reserves at every instant, and hence the present discounted value of such transfers is equal to the initial stock of international reserves.

11. Again, suppose $\varepsilon = \theta = 0$.

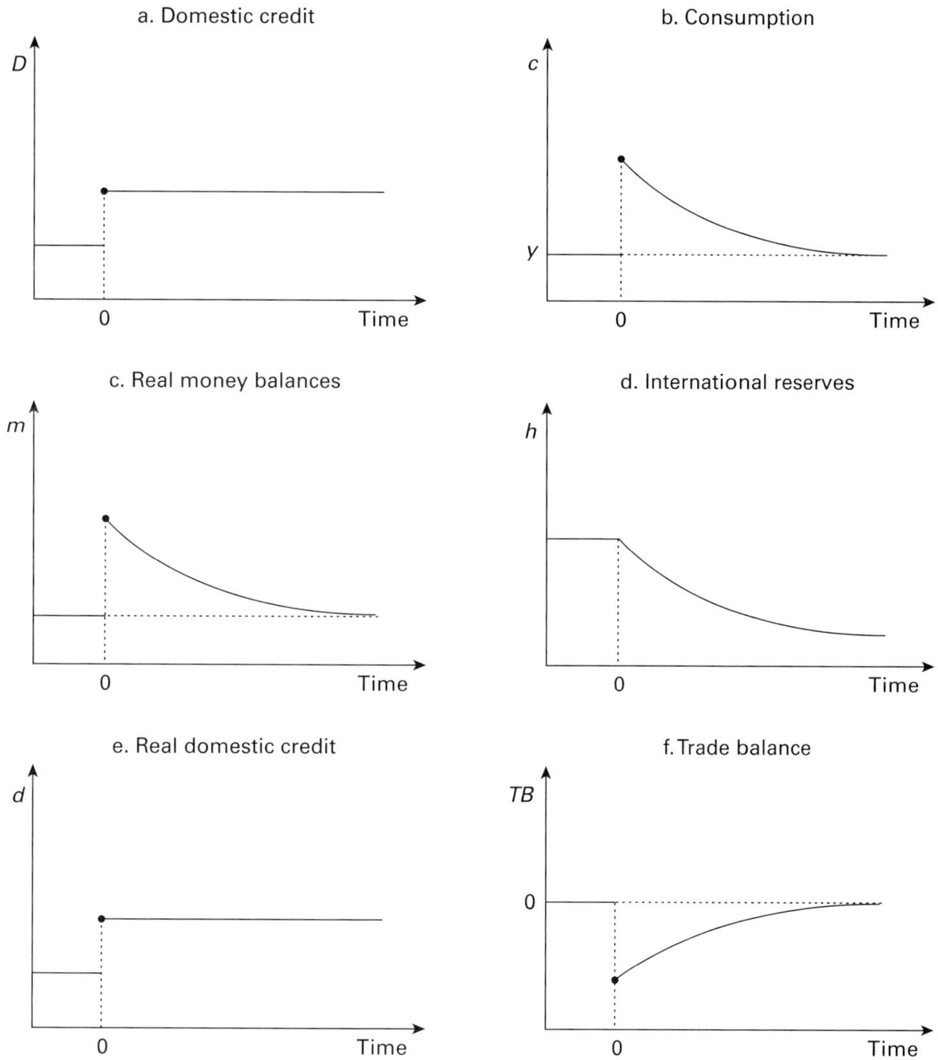

Figure 6.3
Permanent increase in domestic credit

in figure 6.1 and then travels back to point A over time. The corresponding paths of consumption and real money balances are illustrated in figure 6.3, panels b and c. The trade balance thus goes into deficit at time 0 and gradually recovers over time (panel f).

Since real domestic credit rises on impact and remains at that level thereafter (panel e) and steady-state real money demand does not change, we infer that steady-state international reserves will fall. Hence international reserves fall over time toward their lower steady-state value (panel d).

Intuitively, on impact the increase in domestic credit puts more real money balances in the hands of the public. The public, however, does not wish to hold more real money balances. To get rid of these unwanted real money balances, the economy runs a trade deficit. The trade (and current account) deficits lead to a persistent loss of international reserves that reduces the nominal money supply. In the new steady state, the *level* of the nominal money supply will be the same as before the shock, but the *composition* will be different (i.e., international reserves are lower and nominal domestic credit is higher).

In conclusion, the model's key prediction is that an increase in domestic credit will lead to a loss of international reserves of the same order of magnitude. Since, in practice, many developing countries use Central Bank credit to finance government spending, this result provides a key link between loose fiscal policy and loss of international reserves (see box 6.1). Based on this type of model, a typical component of an IMF policy package is to set a target for international reserves and, given an estimate of real money demand, set the growth of domestic credit in such a way as to meet that target (see box 6.2 on IMF financial programming).

6.2.8 Increase in the Rate of Devaluation

Suppose that the initial steady state (corresponding to the devaluation rate ε^L) is given by point A in figure 6.5. At $t = 0$ there is an unanticipated and permanent increase in the rate of devaluation from ε^L to ε^H (figure 6.6, panel a).[12]

How is the steady state affected by an increase in the rate of devaluation? From (6.16) and (6.17) it follows that while steady-state consumption does not change, steady-state real money balances fall. Intuitively, since the opportunity cost of holding real money balances is higher, consumers reduce their demand for money. The new steady-state will be thus at a point like B in figure 6.5.

How does the economy go from point A to point B? On impact, real money balances cannot jump. Hence the economy must jump on impact from point A to point C to position itself along the saddle path. It then travels over time from point C toward point B. The corresponding paths of consumption and real money balances are illustrated in figure 6.6, panels b and c. The behavior of

12. To ensure that the new predetermined exchange rate regime will be sustainable over time, we assume that the rate of growth of domestic credit, θ, is increased by the same amount as ε.

Box 6.1
The monetary approach Southern Cone style

The model of section 6.2 predicts that increases in Central Bank domestic credit should lead to losses in international reserves as the public gets rid of unwanted money balances. The final stages of the so-called Southern Cone "tablitas" provide an ideal testing ground for this key prediction of the monetary approach. The Southern Cone tablitas consisted of exchange rate based stabilization plans implemented in Argentina, Chile, and Uruguay in the late 1970s that were based on the pre-announcement of an exchange rate schedule (referred to as the "tablita" in Spanish), which would specify the daily exchange rate several months in advance (and typically implied a declining rate of

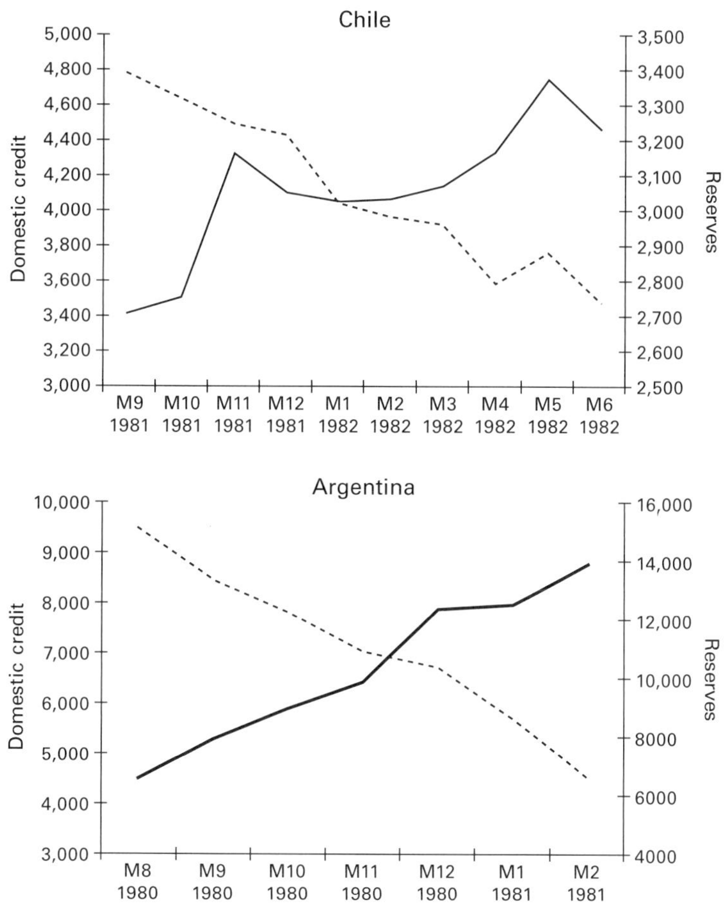

Figure 6.4
Domestic credit and reserves during the Southern Cone stabilizations

Box 6.1
(continued)

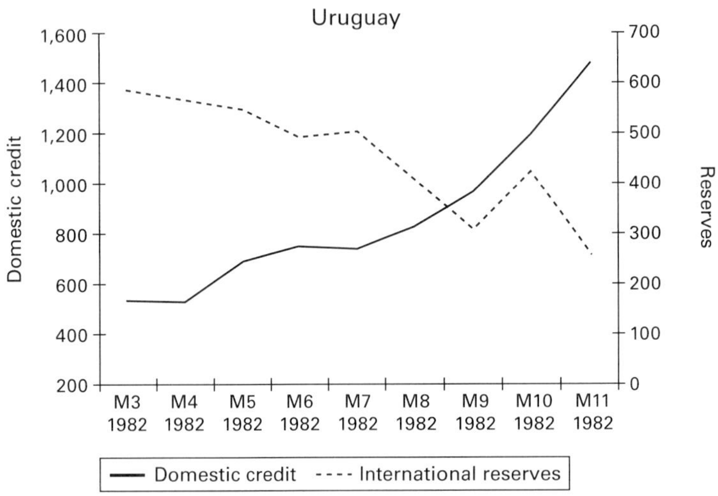

Figure 6.4
(continued)

devaluation).[a] The tablitas, however, were short-lived and the exchange rate pegs were abandoned in the midst of costly balance of payments and financial crises.

In all three cases a key factor contributing to the demise of the tablitas was a deteriorating fiscal situation in the months prior to the abandonment of the peg. As figure 6.4 shows, Central Bank domestic credit rose sharply in the final stages of the tablitas as Central Banks were forced to finance part of the fiscal deficits by printing money. In line with the predictions of the monetary approach, international reserves declined steadily reflecting the public's unwillingness to hold additional money balances. The steady loss of international reserves left Central Banks with no choice but to abandon the peg.[b]

a. The Argentinean, Chilean, and Uruguayan tablitas were implemented in December 1978, February 1978, and October 1978, and abandoned in February 1981, June 1981, and November 1982, respectively. See chapter 13 for more details.

b. We will study in detail balance of payments crises in chapter 16.

Box 6.2
IMF's financial programming

A key objective of the International Monetary Fund (IMF) is to provide financial assistance to member countries experiencing temporary balance of payments problems. Indeed the IMF's Articles of Agreement state that one of the purposes of the IMF is "[t]o give confidence to members by making the general resources of the institution available to them under adequate safeguards, thus providing them with opportunity to correct maladjustments in their balance of payments without resorting to measures destructive of national or international prosperity." The presumption is therefore that countries facing temporary financing problems would have no access to international credit (or that the costs of doing so would be prohibitively high) which—in the absence of IMF financing—would force them to costly adjustments (as analyzed in chapter 2).

The IMF lends subject to some conditionality. In other words, the IMF and the country in question agree on certain corrective measures and performance criteria that must be met in order for the Fund to continue disbursements.[a] Identifying measures to correct balance of payments problems requires an analytical framework linking policy instruments with the balance of payments. The framework developed in the Fund—known as "financial programming" and first published in Polak (1957)—is intimately linked to the monetary accounting discussed in this chapter. IMF financial programming focuses on domestic credit creation on the part of the Central Bank, which is the key policy variable in a predetermined exchange rate regime. Targets for domestic credit creation are therefore central to IMF's conditionality.

The most basic version of the model underlying the IMF's financial programming—which was built with a fixed exchange rate regime in mind though it has been applied much more generally—has three building blocks. The first one is the Central Bank's balance sheet:

$$\Delta M^s = \Delta H + \Delta D, \tag{6.2a}$$

where M^s is nominal money supply, H is the domestic currency value of international reserves at the Central Bank, D is net domestic credit, and Δ denotes discrete changes.[b]

The second building block is a flow equilibrium condition in the money market:

$$\Delta M^d = \Delta M^s. \tag{6.2b}$$

where M^d denotes nominal money demand. Combining (6.2a) with (6.2b), we obtain:

$$\Delta H = \Delta M^d - \Delta D. \tag{6.2c}$$

This equation says that the change in net foreign assets will be positive to the extent that the change in money demand exceeds the change in domestic credit. Since the demand for money is not affected by the level of domestic credit, any increases in domestic credit above the desired increase in money will be offset by decreases in international reserves on a one-for-one basis.

a. For a detailed analysis of IMF programs, see Mussa and Savastano (2000). (Michael Mussa, 1944–2012, a prominent academic economist from the University of Chicago, was the IMF's chief economist from 1991 to 2001.) See also Khan, Montiel, and Haque (1990) for an integration of the IMF and World Bank basic models and Easterly (2002) for a critique of IMF financial programming.

b. As discussed in chapter 5—and reflecting common practices in Central Banks—capital gains/losses on the stock of international reserves are not included as they are not typically "monetized."

Box 6.2
(continued)

The final building block is the demand for money, which can be specified in a variety of ways. For simplicity, we assume that the change in nominal money, ΔM^d, is a constant fraction of the change in nominal income, ΔY,

$$\Delta M^d = k\Delta Y, \tag{6.2d}$$

where k is the inverse of the income velocity of money.[c]

At its most basic core, the design of a financial program by the IMF in the context of this simple model requires three steps. First, it is necessary to set a target for the change in international reserves over some specified period, generally a year. Second, an estimate is made of the most likely path of the demand for money over the same period. Typically, velocity is assumed to remain constant over the relevant time period in which case—as equation (6.2d) makes clear—we only need a projection of nominal income to estimate the change in money demand. Finally, given the target for international reserves and the estimate in the change of money demand, the change in domestic credit needed to achieve the international reserves target can be computed as a residual using equation (6.2c).[d]

c. For operational purposes this simple model needs to be cast in a more general framework (as the IMF does). Typically, this entails decomposing the balance of payments into its individual components (and explaining these items separately) and linking the growth of domestic credit to the fiscal accounts. See Easterly (2002).
d. In countries with underdeveloped financial systems and/or in which the monetary authority resorts to direct controls to influence total credit, targets for domestic credit could be set for the banking system as a whole (see Mussa and Savastano 2000 for a discussion).

consumption implies that the economy runs a trade deficit over time (panel f). Since real domestic credit remains unchanged (panel e), we know from the Central Bank's balance sheet that in the new steady state, international reserves will be lower. Hence international reserves will fall over time (panel d).

Intuitively, the increase in the rate of devaluation induces a fall in the steady-state real money demand. To get rid of these unwanted real money balances, the economy must run a trade (current account) deficit. In other words, the economy "exports" its unwanted real money balances.

Finally, notice that for this experiment the interest rate elasticity of money demand plays a critical role. In other words, if real money demand were not interest rate elastic, consumers would not wish to reduce real money balances in the long run, and hence the monetary adjustment mechanism that we have just described would not take place. This is in sharp contrast to the previous two experiments—a permanent devaluation and a permanent increase in the stock of domestic credit—in which the interest rate elasticity of money demand played no critical role since the shocks affected real money *supply*. It should then be clear that if we introduced money into the model via a cash-in-advance constraint (which implies a non–interest rate elastic money demand), the results of the first two experiments would go through but the results of this third experiment would not. (Exercise 2 at the end of this chapter asks you to verify this.) We can conclude that

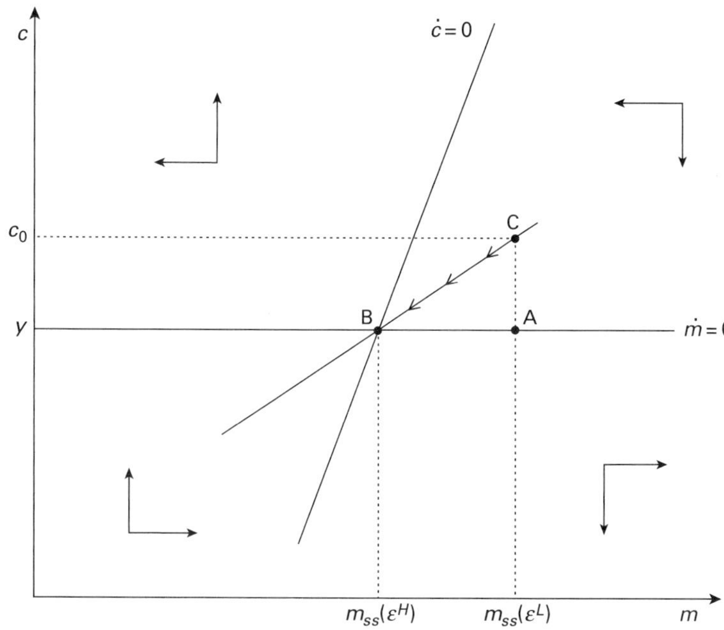

Figure 6.5
Permanent increase in devaluation rate: Phase diagram

as long as the interest rate elasticity of money demand is not critical for the experiment at hand, nothing is lost by adopting a cash-in-advance specification that will, in general, simplify the model. If the interest rate elasticity is critical, then one should adopt a money-in-the-utility function or transactions costs specification that gives rise to such a money demand since, in practice, money demand in developing countries is indeed interest rate elastic (recall appendix 5.8.6 in chapter 5).

6.3 Anatomy of a Devaluation: Devaluation in a Two-Good World

The one-good model in the previous section has illustrated a key mechanism associated with a devaluation: the *expenditure-reducing effect*. As the model makes clear, this expenditure-reducing effect results from the contraction in real money balances brought about by the increase in the price level (i.e., the increase in the exchange rate), which induces households to reduce consumption in order to replenish money balances. There are, however, two other important effects of a devaluation that the model has abstracted from: (1) an *expenditure-switching effect* and (2) a *production effect*. These effects are critical in obtaining a full understanding of the effects of a devaluation in this type of model.

To capture these effects, this section adds two features to the previous model: a nontradable good and endogenous production. Production will be endogeneized along the lines of section 4.5

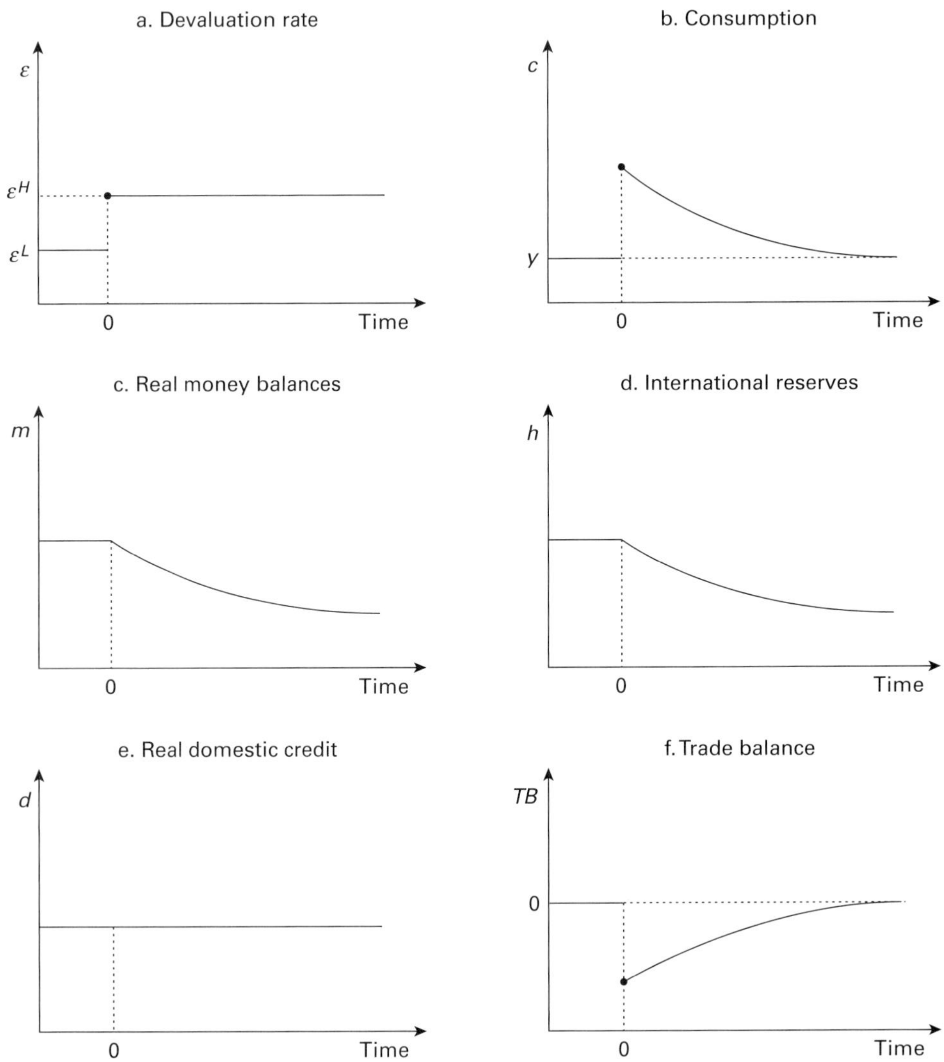

Figure 6.6
Permanent increase in devaluation rate

in chapter 4. Tradables and nontradables are produced with labor as the only input. Households are endowed with an exogenous amount of labor, which they supply inelastically to the labor market (i.e., there is no labor/leisure choice). For simplicity, we assume that households undertake the production themselves.

6.3.1 Household's Problem

Preferences are now given by

$$\int_0^{\infty} [\log(c_t^T) + \log(c_t^N) + \log(z_t)] \exp(-\beta t)dt, \tag{6.21}$$

where c_t^T and c_t^N denote consumption of tradable and nontradable goods, respectively, and $z_t(\equiv M_t/P_t)$ denotes real money balances in terms of the price index P_t, given by[13]

$$P_t \equiv \sqrt{P_t^T P_t^N}. \tag{6.22}$$

Since money balances enter the utility function to capture the liquidity services provided by money, it seems natural to deflate nominal balances by a price index because the household consumes both goods.[14] Since, as easily verified, $z_t = m_t\sqrt{e_t}$ (where e_t denotes the relative price of tradable goods in terms of nontradable goods), we can re-write the preferences above as

$$\int_0^{\infty} [\log(c_t^T) + \log(c_t^N) + \log(m_t) + \left(\frac{1}{2}\right) \log(e_t)] \exp(-\beta t)dt, \tag{6.23}$$

which makes clear that, in the logarithmic case, the price deflator is irrelevant. In other words, in terms of the dynamics of the model we will get exactly the same results as if we had assumed that m_t, instead of z_t, yields liquidity services.[15]

The flow budget constraint is given by

$$\dot{m}_t = y_t^T + \frac{y_t^N}{e_t} + \tau_t - c_t^T - \frac{c_t^N}{e_t} - \varepsilon_t m_t, \tag{6.24}$$

where y_t^T and y_t^N denote production of tradable and nontradable goods, respectively. Production is given by

13. To be consistent with our notation in this and the previous chapter, we use z_t to denote real money balances in terms of the price index and continue to use m_t to denote real money balances in terms of tradable goods. (We will continue to use tradable goods as the numéraire.)

14. This price index corresponds to the minimum nominal expenditure required to achieve a given level of utility (see appendix 6.7.3 for the derivation).

15. Of course, the welfare calculations would differ whenever there are changes in e_t.

$$y_t^T = Z^T \left(n_t^T\right)^\alpha, \tag{6.25}$$

$$y_t^N = Z^N n_t^N, \tag{6.26}$$

where Z^T and Z^N are the (constant) positive productivity parameters and $0 < \alpha < 1$.[16] As in chapter 4, the nontradable sector is assumed to be more labor intensive than the tradable sector.

The labor supply constraint is given by

$$n = n_t^T + n_t^N, \tag{6.27}$$

where n is the exogenous labor endowment.

Substituting (6.25), (6.26) and (6.27) into the flow constraint (6.24), we can set up the Hamiltonian:

$$H = \log(c_t^T) + \log(c_t^N) + \log(m_t\sqrt{e_t}) + \lambda_t \left[Z^T \left(n_t^T\right)^\alpha + \frac{Z^N\left(n - n_t^T\right)}{e_t} + \tau_t - c_t^T - \frac{c_t^N}{e_t} - \varepsilon_t m_t \right].$$

The control variables are c_t^T, c_t^N, and n_t^T, the state variable is m_t, and the co-state variable is λ_t. The first-order conditions are given by

$$\frac{1}{c_t^T} = \lambda_t, \tag{6.28}$$

$$\frac{1}{c_t^N} = \frac{\lambda_t}{e_t}, \tag{6.29}$$

$$\alpha Z^T \left(n_t^T\right)^{\alpha-1} = \frac{Z^N}{e_t}, \tag{6.30}$$

$$\dot{\lambda}_t = (\beta + \varepsilon_t)\lambda_t - \frac{1}{m_t}. \tag{6.31}$$

Relative to the previous model in this chapter, the only new optimality condition is equation (6.30) which, nonetheless, should be familiar from chapter 4. This condition, which captures efficiency in production, requires that the value of the marginal productivity of labor be equated across sectors. If that were not the case, total production could be increased by shifting labor away from the low marginal productivity sector to the high marginal productivity sector.

16. The case $\alpha = 1$ is also well defined and corresponds to linear production in both sectors (exercise 3 at the end of this chapter asks you to solve for this linear case). This extreme case proves quite useful as a benchmark for some questions posed below. The case $\alpha = 0$, however, is not formally well defined but, conceptually, corresponds to the endowment case discussed below.

Combining conditions (6.28) and (6.29), we get the familiar consumption-efficiency condition whereby the marginal rate of substitution between tradables and nontradables is equal to the relative price of tradables:

$$\frac{c_t^N}{c_t^T} = e_t. \tag{6.32}$$

Further, combining (6.30) and (6.32), we see that, at an optimum, the marginal rate of substitution in consumption and in production are equalized:

$$\frac{c_t^T}{c_t^N} = \frac{\alpha Z^T \left(n_t^T\right)^{\alpha-1}}{Z^N}. \tag{6.33}$$

6.3.2 Government

The government sector remains unchanged. Equations (6.10), (6.12), and (6.13) therefore remain valid.

6.3.3 Equilibrium Conditions

Equilibrium in the nontradable goods market requires that

$$c_t^N = y_t^N. \tag{6.34}$$

Substituting the government's flow constraint (6.10) into the household's flow constraint (6.24) and imposing equilibrium in the nontradable goods market, given by (6.34), yields

$$\dot{h}_t = y_t^T - c_t^T.$$

Substituting (6.12) into the last equation obtains

$$\dot{m}_t = y_t^T - c_t^T. \tag{6.35}$$

6.3.4 Dynamic System

As before, we set up a dynamic system in c_t^T and m_t. The first dynamic equation follows from time-differentiating (6.28) and using (6.31) to obtain

$$\dot{c}_t^T = c_t^T \left(\frac{c_t^T}{m_t} - \beta - \varepsilon_t \right). \tag{6.36}$$

To derive the second dynamic equation, substitute (6.25) into (6.35) to obtain

$$\dot{m}_t = Z^T \left(n_t^T\right)^\alpha - c_t^T. \tag{6.37}$$

We now express n_t^T as a function of c_t^T. From (6.26) through (6.30) and (6.34), it follows that

$$c_t^T = \frac{\alpha Z^T (n - n_t^T)}{\left(n_t^T\right)^{1-\alpha}}, \tag{6.38}$$

which implicitly defines n_t^T as a decreasing function of c_t^T:

$$n_t^T = \Psi(c_t^T), \tag{6.39}$$

where

$$\Psi'(c_t^T) = -\frac{1}{\alpha Z^T \left\{\left(n_t^T\right)^{\alpha-1} + [(1-\alpha)(n - n_t^T)/\left(n_t^T\right)^{2-\alpha}]\right\}} < 0$$

Substituting (6.39) into (6.37) yields our second differential equation:

$$\dot{m}_t = Z^T \left[\Psi(c_t^T)\right]^\alpha - c_t^T. \tag{6.40}$$

Equations (6.36) and (6.40) constitute a dynamic system in c_t^T and m_t, for a given and constant value of the rate of devaluation, ε.

The system's steady state is implicitly given by

$$m_{ss} = \frac{c_{ss}^T}{\beta + \varepsilon}, \tag{6.41}$$

$$c_{ss}^T = Z^T \left[\Psi(c_{ss}^T)\right]^\alpha. \tag{6.42}$$

Notice that equation (6.42) defines a unique value of c_{ss}^T because the LHS is an increasing function of c_{ss}^T whereas the RHS is a decreasing function of c_{ss}^T.

Linearizing the system and using (6.41) and (6.42), we obtain

$$\begin{bmatrix} \dot{c}_t^T \\ \dot{m}_t \end{bmatrix} = \begin{bmatrix} \beta + \varepsilon & -(\beta+\varepsilon)^2 \\ \alpha Z^T \left(n_{ss}^T\right)^{\alpha-1} \Psi' - 1 & 0 \end{bmatrix} \begin{bmatrix} c_t^T - c_{ss}^T \\ m_t - m_{ss} \end{bmatrix}.$$

The determinant of the matrix associated with the linear approximation is given by

$$\Delta = (\beta+\varepsilon)^2 \left[\alpha Z^T \left(n_{ss}^T\right)^{\alpha-1} \Psi' - 1\right] < 0,$$

which indicates that the system has one negative and one positive root and is thus saddle-path stable.

To construct the phase diagram, we proceed to find out the slope of the $\dot{c}_t^T = 0$ and $\dot{m}_t = 0$ loci. From (6.36) it follows that

$$\left.\frac{dc^T}{dm}\right|_{\dot{c}_t^T=0} = \beta + \varepsilon > 0.$$

Clearly, from (6.40) the $\dot{m}_t = 0$ schedule is a constant value of c^T. Qualitatively we therefore have the same phase diagram as before (figure 6.1).

6.3.5 Initial Steady State

Consider an initial steady state where the exchange rate is fixed (i.e., the rate of devaluation is zero). Then, from (6.41) it follows that

$$m_{ss} = \frac{c_{ss}^T}{\beta}.$$

The value of c_{ss}^T is still given by (6.42). Given c_{ss}^T, the steady-state value of n^T is implicitly determined by (recall equation 6.38)

$$c_{ss}^T = \frac{\alpha Z^T (n - n_{ss}^T)}{\left(n_{ss}^T\right)^{1-\alpha}}.$$

Given n_{ss}^T, the labor supply constraint (6.27) determines n_{ss}^N:

$$n_{ss}^N = n - n_{ss}^T.$$

Production of tradable and nontradable goods is then read off the production functions:

$$y_{ss}^T = Z^T \left(n_{ss}^T\right)^{\alpha},$$
$$y_{ss}^N = Z^N n_{ss}^N.$$

Equilibrium in the nontradable goods market determines consumption of nontradable goods:

$$c_{ss}^N = Z^N n_{ss}^N.$$

The real exchange rate follows from condition (6.32):

$$e_{ss} = \frac{c_{ss}^N}{c_{ss}^T}.$$

Finally, notice that the steady-state trade balance is zero:

$$TB_{ss} \equiv y_{ss}^T - c_{ss}^T = 0.$$

As should be clear, the steady-state conditions do not depend on the *level* of the nominal exchange rate. Hence, as in the one-good model, a devaluation is neutral in the long run.[17]

Figure 6.7 offers a graphical representation of the initial steady state. It depicts the production possibility frontier (henceforth PPF), which should be thought of as the locus of production points that are attainable by this economy (if, as is always the case in the model, the labor supply n is fully employed). To check that the PPF is negatively sloped, solve for n^T and n^N from (6.25) and (6.26), respectively, and substitute into the labor constraint (6.27) to obtain

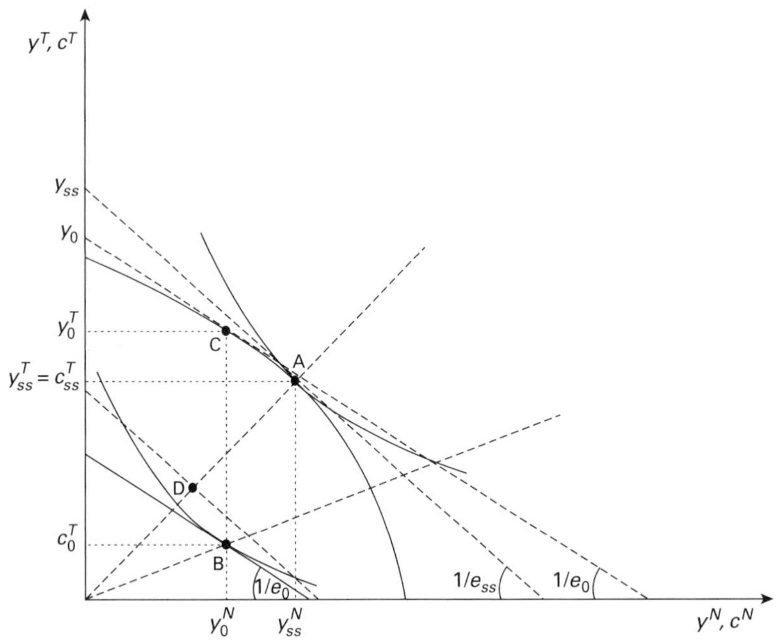

Figure 6.7
Expenditure reducing and expenditure switching

17. Only steady-state real money balances would be affected by a change in the rate of devaluation, so exchange rate policy is also superneutral in the long run.

$$n = \left(\frac{y_{ss}^T}{Z^T}\right)^{1/\alpha} + \frac{y_{ss}^N}{Z^N}.$$

Totally differentiate to obtain

$$\frac{dy_{ss}^T}{dy_{ss}^N} = -\alpha\frac{Z^T}{Z^N}\left(\frac{y_{ss}^T}{Z^T}\right)^{1-1/\alpha} < 0. \tag{6.43}$$

It is easy to check that $d^2y_{ss}^T/(dy_{ss}^N)^2 < 0$, which confirms that the PPF is concave.

At point A, the PPF and the indifference curve between tradables and nontradables are tangent to each other and to the relative price of nontradable goods, $1/e_{ss}$. Production of tradables, y_{ss}^T, can be read off the vertical axis while production of nontradable goods, y_{ss}^N, is read off the horizontal axis. Consumption of tradables equals production so that the trade balance is zero.

6.3.6 Devaluation

Suppose that the economy is initially in the steady-state equilibrium just described. At time 0 there is an unanticipated and permanent devaluation (figure 6.8, panel a). How does the economy react?

Dynamic Response

The increase in the nominal exchange rate reduces on impact real money balances, which takes the dynamic system from point A to a point such as B in figure 6.1. The dynamic system then travels back to the unchanged steady state along the saddle path. The path of c_t^T is depicted in figure 6.8, panel b.

Since c_t^T and n_t^T are negatively related at all points in time (recall equation 6.39), the path of n_t^T (and hence of production of tradable goods) will be the mirror image of that of c_t^T, as illustrated in figure 6.8, panel d. Production of tradable goods increases on impact and then falls gradually over time. Since, on impact, production of tradables increase while consumption of tradable falls, the trade balance improves on impact (figure 6.8, panel e). As time goes by, the increase in consumption of tradables and the fall in production of tradables implies that the trade balance falls over time.

Given the behavior of n_t^T, the path of n_t^N follows from the labor supply constraint (6.27). Production—and thus consumption—of nontradables falls on impact and then increases over time toward its unchanged steady state (figure 6.8, panel c). Through the production efficiency condition the path of n_t^T also allows us to infer the path of the real exchange rate. The real exchange rate increases on impact (real depreciation) and then falls over time (figure 6.8, panel f).

In sum, a devaluation leads to a fall in consumption of both goods, a switch in production from the nontradable sector to the tradable goods sector, a trade surplus, and real depreciation. What is

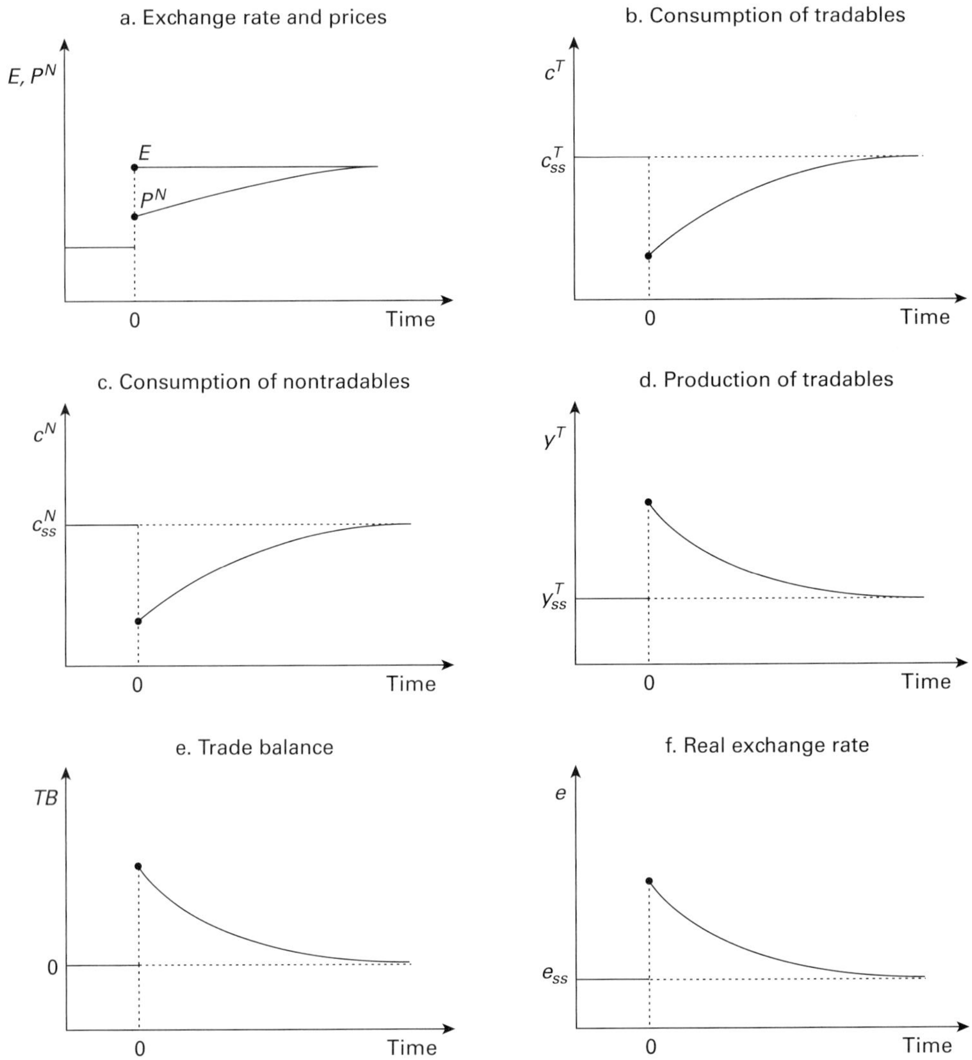

Figure 6.8
Permanent devaluation in two-good model

the intuition behind these results? While the devaluation does not affect steady-state real money demand, it reduces real money balances on impact by increasing the price level. To rebuild money balances over time—and for a given real exchange rate—households wish to reduce consumption of both goods. This results in excess supply of nontradable goods, which must cause a fall in their relative price (i.e., a rise in e_t). The fall in the relative price of nontradable goods reduces profitability in the nontradable goods sector and induces labor to shift from this sector to the tradable goods sector.

We now look in more detail at some key features related to the impact effect of a devaluation on expenditure, GDP, and prices.

Expenditure Reducing versus Expenditure Switching

Figure 6.7 will help us analyze the expenditure-reducing versus expenditure-switching effects. As described above, initial production and consumption are given by point A. Immediately after the devaluation (i.e., at time 0), consumption shifts to point B—where the indifference curve is tangent to $1/e_0$—and production to point C—where the PPF is tangent to $1/e_0$. The picture thus shows the fall in both consumption of tradable and nontradable goods and the increase in production of tradable goods at the expense of nontradable goods. On impact, the trade balance is given by the vertical distance between y_0^T and c_0^T.

While consumption jumps immediately from point A to point B, from a conceptual point of view we can decompose this adjustment in consumption into two effects:

- *An expenditure-reducing* effect (from point A to point D). This effect captures the fall in consumption that takes place for an unchanged relative price. This contraction in consumption is due to the household's desire to save in order to rebuild real money balances. This is, of course, the only effect present in the one-good model studied earlier in this chapter.[18]
- An *expenditure-switching* effect (from point D to point B). This effect captures the substitution in consumption that takes place as a result of the fall in the relative price of nontradable goods from $1/e_{ss}$ to $1/e_0$. As nontradable goods become relatively cheaper, the household consumes more nontradable goods and fewer tradable goods relative to point D. At point B the ratio c_t^N/c_t^T is therefore higher than at point D. In absolute terms, as well, consumption of tradables is lower and consumption of nontradables is higher.[19]

It is worth noting that when it comes to consumption of tradable goods, both effects reinforce each other. In contrast, for consumption of nontradable goods, the two effects go in opposite

18. It is also the only effect in the case where both production functions are linear, as exercise 3 at the end of this chapter makes clear. In this case the relative price of nontradable goods is completely determined by the technology.

19. Although not relevant for our argument, notice that consumption expenditure falls as we move from point D to point B due to the increase in e_t. To see this, use condition (6.32) to rewrite consumption expenditure $(c_t^T + c_t^N/e_t)$ as $2c_t^T$. Since c_t^T falls, consumption expenditure falls as well.

direction. We have already established, however, that the expenditure-reducing effect dominates and consumption of nontradable goods falls.

Finally, notice that the change in production from point A to point C captures the *production effect*. At the pre-shock labor allocation, the increase in the relative price of tradable goods increases the value of the marginal productivity of labor in the tradable goods sector relative to that in the nontradable goods sector. As a result labor switches from the nontradable to the tradable sector. Hence all three effects—expenditure reducing, expenditure switching, and production—reinforce each other in bringing about a trade surplus on impact: the first two by reducing consumption of tradable goods and the third one by increasing its production.

Impact Effect on GDP

We have shown that on impact—and as a result of the reallocation of labor across sectors—production of tradable goods increases while production of nontradable goods falls. But what happens to total production? In other words, does a devaluation lead to an overall reduction in GDP? To answer this question, define total production (in terms of tradable goods) as

$$y_t \equiv y_t^T + \frac{y_t^N}{e_t}. \tag{6.44}$$

This definition of total production corresponds to GDP (in terms of tradable goods).[20] In terms of figure 6.7 this corresponds to output measured along the vertical axis. Thus y_{ss} indicates the pre-shock level of output in terms of tradable goods. To find out how GDP responds to a (small) devaluation, differentiate (6.44) with respect to E_t, using (6.25) and (6.26), to obtain

$$\left.\frac{dy_t}{dE_t}\right|_{t=0} = \left[\frac{Z^T\alpha}{\left(n_t^T\right)^{1-\alpha}} - \frac{Z^N}{e_t}\right]\frac{dn_t^T}{dE_t} - \frac{Z^N n_t^N}{(e_t)^2}\frac{de_t}{dE_t}.$$

In light of the production efficiency condition (6.30), the term in square brackets on the RHS is zero. Hence the equation above reduces to

$$\left.\frac{dy_t}{dE_t}\right|_{t=0} = -\frac{Z^N n_t^N}{(e_t)^2}\frac{de_t}{dE_t} < 0,$$

since we know that, on impact, $de_t/dE_t > 0$ (figure 6.8, panel f). Intuitively, since production efficiency always holds at an optimum, the net effect of the labor reallocation on the value of production is zero. Hence the only effect on total production comes from a valuation effect: the initial production of nontradable goods (in terms of tradable goods) falls as a result of the increase

20. In this model it also corresponds to GNP because there is no debt service.

in the relative price of tradable goods. We can conclude that a devaluation will reduce GDP in terms of tradable goods.[21]

What would happen for a "larger" devaluation? To answer this question, it proves useful to write the change in output on impact as

$$y_0 - y_{ss} = \underbrace{y_{ss}^T + \frac{y_{ss}^N}{e_0} - \left(y_{ss}^T + \frac{y_{ss}^N}{e_{ss}}\right)}_{\text{Valuation effect (-)}} + \underbrace{\left(y_0^T + \frac{y_0^N}{e_0}\right) - \left(y_{ss}^T + \frac{y_{ss}^N}{e_0}\right)}_{\text{Reallocation effect (+)}}.$$

As indicated below the equation, we can decompose the change in output into two effects: a valuation effect and a reallocation effect. Figure 6.9 illustrates these two effects as well as the total effect. The valuation effect is the one that we just isolated when looking at a small devaluation, and is represented by the distance along the vertical axis between points y_{ss} and $(y_{ss})_{e_0}$. The valuation effect reduces GDP because the initial production (point A) evaluated at the new relative price $(1/e_0)$ is lower than evaluated at the initial relative price $(1/e_{ss})$. The second effect, the reallocation effect, is captured graphically by the distance between y_0 and $(y_{ss})_{e_0}$. This effect captures the labor reallocation from the nontradable goods sector to the tradable goods sector. This effect increases GDP because, at the new relative price, the marginal productivity in the tradable goods sector is larger than in the nontradable goods sector. Hence the output value of a unit of labor—except for the marginal one—will be higher in the tradable than in the nontradable goods sector. Since the reallocation effect is of second order, the valuation effect will dominate. This is clear from figure 6.9, where we see that $y_0 < y_{ss}$.

This initial fall in GDP is often mentioned as a "cost" of a devaluation. Indeed it is often argued that the price to be paid for the improvement in the trade balance is that the economy becomes "poorer." This model nicely illustrates this idea.

How Do Prices Respond to a Devaluation?

This section's model can also shed light on a highly relevant question: How do prices respond to a devaluation? In the context of our model, we take the question to be: what will be the impact effect of a rise in E_t on the price of nontradable goods, P_t^N? (Of course, the response of the price index, P_t, will simply be a geometric average of the rise in E_t and P_t^N.)

21. On the other hand, and as can be readily verified, GDP in terms of nontradable goods actually increases because, in terms of nontradable goods, production of tradable goods is higher. The more relevant measure of GDP, however, is in terms of tradables because this determines the country's flow resources relative to the rest of the world.

Notice that the theoretical concept of GDP in terms of tradable goods corresponds to what in practice is often referred to as "GDP in dollars." It is a well-known fact that in developing countries the GDP in dollars plummets in response to a devaluation. Just to give one example, in Uruguay, after an exchange rate band was abandoned in mid-2002 (as a result of the Argentinean crisis), the nominal exchange rate increased by roughly 94 percent (in calendar year 2002), the CPI by 26 percent (which yields a real depreciation of 54 percent) and GDP in dollars fell by 34 percent.

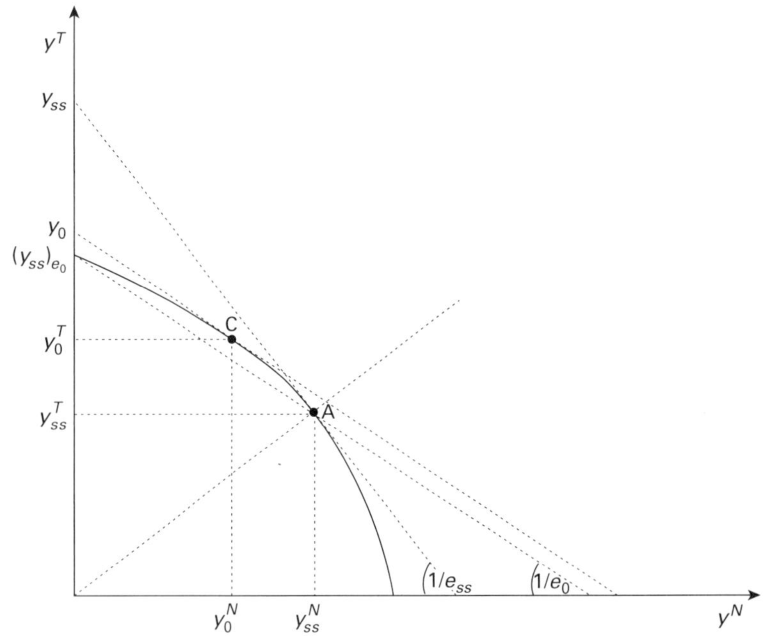

Figure 6.9
Output effect of a devaluation

When faced with an episode where a devaluation is followed by a less than proportional increase in P_t^N (and hence in P_t), economists often ask: Why? This is a good, but potentially misleading, question. It is potentially misleading because it seems to presume that even in the short run, a devaluation of x percent should be followed by an x percent rise in P_t^N. This presumption is often so entrenched in some economists' minds that when the data do not show an equi-proportional increase in P_t^N, they infer that it must be due to sticky prices! This inference is, however, incorrect. Of course, the less than proportional increase in prices *may* be due to sticky prices (as we will see in chapter 8), but that is not *necessarily* the case. This section's model will enable us to illustrate this point and thus dispel the notion that a less than proportional increase in P_t^N is somehow evidence of sticky prices.

Let us turn to the derivation of the path of P_t^N, illustrated in figure 6.8, panel a. In our model the path of P_t^N will be determined by the need to accommodate the path of the real exchange rate illustrated in figure 6.8, panel f. Recall that, by definition, $e_t = E_t/P_t^N$. Since the real exchange rate does not change across steady states, it follows that in the long run P_t^N will rise by the same proportion as E_t. Given that e_t increases on impact, we infer that P_t^N rises by less than the nominal exchange rate. Over time P_t^N rises. We can conclude that despite no nominal rigidities of any kind, the price of nontradable goods rises on impact by less than the nominal exchange rate.

Table 6.1
Impact response to a 10 percent devaluation (in percent)

α	e	P^N	P	y
1	0.0	10.0	10.0	0.0
0.8	0.9	9.0	9.5	−0.5
0.6	2.0	7.9	8.9	−1.0
0.4	3.1	6.7	8.3	−1.5
0.2	4.5	5.3	7.6	−2.1
Endowment	6.0	3.8	6.9	−2.8

Source: Author's computations based on model of section 6.3.

What determines in the model the magnitude of the impact response of P_t^N? The key parameter is α, which is a measure of the substitution in production between tradables and nontradables.[22] Table 6.1 shows the impact response of the real exchange (e_t), the price of nontradable goods (P_t^N), and the price index (P_t) to a devaluation of 10 percent for different values of α.[23] For instance, for $\alpha = 0.4$, a devaluation of 10 percent leads to an increase in the real exchange rate of 3.1 percent, a rise in P_t^N of 6.7 percent, and a rise in P_t of 8.3 percent. As the table makes clear, as α increases, the increase in the real exchange rate is smaller and hence the rise in P_t^N is larger. In particular, for $\alpha = 1$ the nominal price of nontradables increases by the same proportion as the nominal exchange rate, whereas in the endowment case (no substitution in production), the rise in P_t^N is only 3.8 percent.

To get intuition, let us go back to figure 6.7 and observe that at point D (which denotes consumption on impact evaluated at the pre-shock relative price) there is an incipient excess supply of nontradable goods. The adjustment to this incipient excess supply will take the form of some combination of lower production of nontradables (relative to point A) and higher consumption of nontradables (relative to point D). The parameter α controls how much of this adjustment will be reflected in lower production and how much will be reflected in higher consumption. To fix ideas, consider the two extreme cases: the linear case ($\alpha = 1$) and the endowment case (which corresponds, conceptually, to the $\alpha = 0$ case). The linear case is illustrated in figure 6.10, panel A. Recall from chapter 4 that in this case the real exchange rate is fully determined by the technology (i.e., $e_t = Z_t^N/Z_t^T$). Hence, as table 6.1 shows, P_t^N increases by the same proportion as the nominal exchange rate (10 percent). Since the relative price cannot adjust to clear the nontradable goods market, the entire adjustment must come through a shift in production. In figure 6.10, panel a, the incipient excess supply of nontradable goods at point B (given by $y_{ss}^N - y_0^N$) will be taken care of by a shift in production from point A to point C.

22. If we had CES preferences, substitution in consumption would also matter. The more substitutable are tradables and nontradables, the smaller is the required relative price adjustment and hence the larger is the initial increase in P_t^N. If both goods were perfect substitutes, then the relative price would not change and P_t^N would rise by the same proportion as E_t.

23. The computations underlying table 6.1 are presented in appendix 6.7.4.

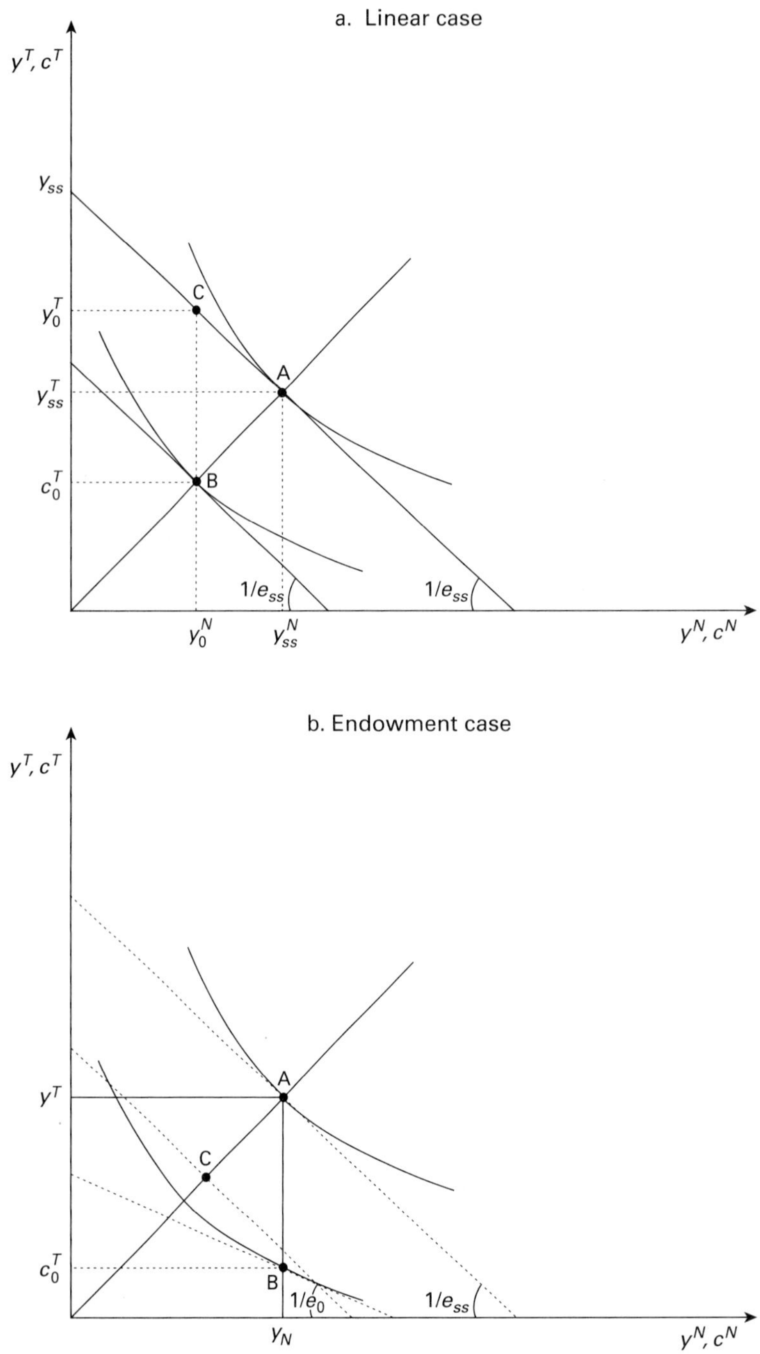

Figure 6.10
Impact effect of devaluation

Consider now the other extreme case where the supply of both goods is fixed (referred to as the endowment case in table 6.1), illustrated in figure 6.10, panel b. The fixed supply of goods is denoted by y^T and y^N, respectively. The initial steady state is at point A. After the devaluation—and if the relative price did not change—consumption would take place at a point like C, with an incipient excess supply of nontradable goods. Since the supply of nontradables is fixed and cannot adjust, all the burden of the adjustment must be borne by the relative price of nontradable goods, which must fall until households are willing to consume the available supply of nontradable goods (point B). This case captures the largest adjustment in the relative price and hence the smallest increase in P_t^N. As table 6.1 indicates, the real exchange rate increases by 6.0 percent, which implies that P_t^N goes up by only 3.8 percent.

All other cases (i.e., for $0 < \alpha < 1$) fall in between these two extreme cases just considered. In these intermediates cases—and as illustrated in figure 6.7—the adjustment takes the form of both a fall in the relative price of nontradable goods and a switch in resources from the nontradable to the tradable goods sector. The lower is α, the lower is the substitution between the two sectors and thus the larger's the increase in the real exchange rate.

We thus conclude that despite the absence of nominal rigidities, the price of nontradable goods will rise by less than the nominal exchange rate. Since, in practice, we expect substitutability between the two sectors of production to be rather low in the short run (which would correspond to a low value of α in table 6.1), this model actually predicts a small impact response in prices of nontradable goods. This prediction is in line with the stylized facts associated with large recent devaluations (see box 6.3).

6.4 Flexible Exchange Rates

We have just shown that under predetermined exchange rates, unanticipated and permanent changes in either the level of the nominal exchange rate or the rate of devaluation have real effects. In sharp contrast, we will now show that under flexible exchange rates, an unanticipated and permanent increase in either the level or the rate of growth of the money supply has no real effects. In other words, money is neutral and superneutral. To this effect, consider once again the monetary model with no bonds developed in section 6.2, but suppose now that the economy is operating under flexible exchange rates.

Let us first solve the model for a constant value of the money growth rate, μ. Under flexible exchange rates the change in international reserves is, by definition, zero. Hence equation (6.14) implies that $c_t = y$ for all t. As a result equation (6.9) reduces to

$$v'(m_t) = (\beta + \varepsilon_t)u'(y). \tag{6.45}$$

This is just an equilibrium condition because both m_t and ε_t are endogenous variables under flexible exchange rates. From the definition of real money balances,

$$\frac{\dot{m}_t}{m_t} = \mu - \varepsilon_t. \tag{6.46}$$

Box 6.3
How do prices respond to a large devaluation?

In section 6.3.6, we analyzed the impact of a devaluation on the real exchange rate, prices of nontradable goods, and the price level. We showed how, depending on the supply elasticity of tradable goods, prices of nontradable goods may respond little to the devaluation in the short run. For the extreme case of total inelastic supply, the price of nontradable goods in fact increases by only 3.8 percent in response to a 10 percent devaluation.

What do the data say? Burstein, Eichenbaum, and Rebelo (2005) document the response of prices after five large devaluations in developing countries: Argentina (December 2001), Brazil (December 1998), Korea (September 1997), Mexico (December 1994), and Thailand (June 1997). Table 6.2 reports the increases in the nominal exchange rate, the real exchange rate, price of tradable goods, price of nontradable goods, and a price index twelve months after the devaluation. The main findings are the following:

1. The increase in the price of tradable goods (proxied by import prices at the dock) generally matches the increase in the nominal exchange rate. This provides support for the assumption in our model—which is the standard assumption in small open economy models—that, to a first approximation, the law of one price holds for tradable goods.[a]

2. The price of nontradable goods rises by considerably less than the nominal exchange rate. The smallest increase (relative to the magnitude of the devaluation) was in Argentina, where prices of nontradables rose by only 10.5 percent of the nominal devaluation while the largest was in Mexico (40 percent).

3. A nominal devaluation leads to an increase in the real exchange rate (a real depreciation of the currency). The percentage of the nominal devaluation that gets reflected in the real exchange rate lies within a 50 to 80 percent range.

In sum, the large real depreciation and the small response of nontradable prices are consistent with our model and, as expected, would correspond to a case of low supply elasticity (i.e., a low α).[b]

Table 6.2
Price responses following large devaluations (logarithmic change after 12 months of devaluation)

Episode	E	e	P^T	P^N	P
Argentina (December 2001)	123.5	82.2	111.3	13.0	34.3
Brazil (December 1998)	42.4	32.7	43.1	5.1	8.6
Korea (September 1997)	41.2	30.4	21.5	5.1	6.6
Mexico (December 1994)	80.0	42.7	84.0	31.6	39.5
Thailand (June 1997)	49.7	26.2	40.4	n/a	10.1

Source: Burstein, Einchenbaum, and Rebelo (2005).
Note: Month and year of devaluation in parentheses. P^T denotes import prices at the dock, e is a CPI based measure of the real exchange rate, and P is the CPI.

a. As Burstein, Eichenbaum, and Rebelo (2005) persuasively argue, it would be misleading to look at retail prices of tradable goods (which rise by much less than the nominal exchange rate) and conclude that the law of one price does not hold. The problem is that retail prices of tradable goods include large distribution costs, which are nontradable in nature (see Burstein, Neves, and Rebelo 2003).
b. These findings, of course, might also be consistent with other paradigms such as the sticky prices model in chapter 8.

Solving for ε_t from (6.45) and substituting into (6.46), we obtain the following differential equation in m_t:

$$\dot{m}_t = m_t \left[\mu + \beta - \frac{v'(m_t)}{u'(y)} \right]. \tag{6.47}$$

It is easy to check that this is an unstable differential equation. Hence a convergent equilibrium path requires that m_t be constant over time at a level implicitly determined by

$$\frac{v'(m_t)}{u'(y)} = \mu + \beta, \tag{6.48}$$

which is, of course, a money demand-type equation.

Suppose now that there is an unanticipated and permanent increase in the level of the money supply. Clearly, the stationary value of m_t implicitly defined by condition (6.48) is not affected. We thus infer that the nominal exchange rate changes in the same proportion as M_t so as to leave real money balances unchanged. In other words, monetary policy is neutral.

Suppose instead that there is an unanticipated and permanent increase in the rate of growth of the money supply. From (6.48) we infer that real money balances must fall. Intuitively, since the opportunity cost of holding money has increased, money demand falls. But, since m_t is governed by the unstable differential equation (6.47), m_t needs to jump immediately to its new and lower value. This fall will be effected through a rise in the nominal exchange rate. There are thus no real effects: monetary policy is also superneutral.

Intuitively, the reason why money is neutral/superneutral is that the absence of capital mobility does not affect the economy's adjustment mechanism to changes in the money supply, which, as we saw in chapter 5, takes the form of changes in the exchange rate (price level). As a result the absence of interest-bearing bonds is inconsequential for the case of flexible exchange rates.

6.5 A Currency Substitution Model

Until August 15, 1971, when President Richard Nixon suspended convertibility of dollars into gold, most of the world operated under fixed exchange rates. Capital mobility was also limited by modern standards. It is then not surprising that most theoretical analyses in open economy macroeconomics were cast in a framework similar to the model studied above in section 6.2.[24] When the world began to switch to more flexible exchange rate arrangements, this paradigm became less relevant to explain the real world. Moreover—and as shown in section 6.4—the fact that under flexible exchange rates, money is neutral and superneutral prevented researchers

24. By providing explicit microfoundations and assuming rational expectations (i.e., perfect foresight in this case), we presented, of course, a modern version of this old paradigm.

from using it to explain real-world phenomena. For instance, suppose that we wanted to ask the question: what would be the real effects of an increase in the rate of money growth? "None" would be the answer of that model. Given this state of affairs, Calvo and Rodriguez (1977) came up with the idea of introducing currency substitution as a useful and certainly relevant friction in the model.[25] Interestingly, and as will become clear below, even though the model is one of flexible exchange rates, the adjustment mechanisms involved are very much reminiscent of the monetary approach.

6.5.1 The Model

We continue to consider a small open economy that consumes a single (tradable) good and operates under flexible exchange rates. Foreign inflation is assumed to be zero.

Preferences now take the form

$$\int_0^{\infty} [\log(c_t) + \log(x_t)] \exp(-\beta t) dt, \tag{6.49}$$

where c_t denotes consumption and x_t is a liquidity variable such that

$$qx_t = f_t, \tag{6.50}$$

$$(1 - q)x_t = m_t, \tag{6.51}$$

where q $(0 \leq q < 1)$ is a parameter, and m_t and f_t denote real domestic and foreign currency balances, respectively. One can therefore think of x_t as a composite of domestic and foreign currency. Notice that if $q = 0$, the model reduces to the one in section 6.2.

Let a_t denote real financial wealth, defined as

$$a_t \equiv m_t + f_t. \tag{6.52}$$

The consumer's flow constraint is now given by

$$\dot{a}_t = y + \tau_t - c_t - \varepsilon_t m_t, \tag{6.53}$$

where y denotes the constant endowment.

Before proceeding to the consumer's maximization, it will prove convenient to express the flow constraint in terms of x_t. To this end, use (6.50), (6.51), and (6.52) to rewrite the flow constraint (6.53) as

25. As discussed in Calvo and Végh (1992), Calvo and Rodriguez's motivation was the Argentinean experience during 1975 when a large increase in the rate of money growth led to a strong real depreciation of the currency. At the same time individuals in Argentina, as well as in many other chronic inflation countries, appeared to be holding large amounts of foreign currency (see chapter 15 for evidence on currency substitution and further theoretical analysis).

$$\dot{x}_t = y + \tau_t - c_t - (1-q)\varepsilon_t x_t. \tag{6.54}$$

The opportunity cost of holding the composite currency, x_t, is $(1-q)\varepsilon_t$, as we should have expected.

We can now write the current value Hamiltonian as

$$H \equiv \log(c_t) + \log(x_t) + \lambda_t \left[y + \tau_t - c_t - (1-q)\varepsilon_t x_t \right].$$

The optimality conditions are given by

$$\frac{1}{c_t} = \lambda_t, \tag{6.55}$$

$$\dot{\lambda}_t = \beta\lambda_t - \frac{\partial H}{\partial x_t} = \lambda_t \left[\beta + (1-q)\varepsilon_t \right] - \frac{1}{x_t}. \tag{6.56}$$

Government

We will assume, as usual, that the government holds no international reserves. The government's flow constraint thus becomes

$$\tau_t = \frac{\dot{M}_t}{E_t}. \tag{6.57}$$

Since the economy is operating under flexible exchange rates, the monetary authority will set the path of the nominal money supply. Let μ denote the constant rate of growth set by the monetary authority.

Equilibrium Conditions

Substituting the government's flow constraint (6.57) into the consumer's flow constraint (6.53), we obtain the economy's flow constraint:

$$\dot{f}_t = y - c_t. \tag{6.58}$$

This equation says that in order for the private sector to accumulate foreign currency, it must run a trade surplus.

Dynamic System

To solve the model, we will set up a dynamic system in c_t and x_t. To this end, differentiate first-order condition (6.55) and use (6.56) and (6.55) to obtain

$$\dot{c}_t = c_t \left[\frac{c_t}{x_t} - \beta - (1-q)\varepsilon_t \right]. \tag{6.59}$$

Since $(1-q)x_t = m_t$ and $\dot{m}_t/m_t = \mu - \varepsilon_t$, it follows that

$$\varepsilon_t = \mu - \frac{\dot{x}_t}{x_t}. \tag{6.60}$$

Using equation (6.58) and the fact that $qx_t = f_t$, we can rewrite this last equation as

$$\varepsilon_t = \mu - \frac{y - c_t}{qx_t}. \tag{6.61}$$

Substituting this equation into (6.59) and assuming that $q = 1/2$ to simplify the dynamic system, we obtain

$$\dot{c}_t = c_t\left[\frac{y}{x_t} - \beta - \frac{1}{2}\mu\right]. \tag{6.62}$$

Further, from (6.60) and (6.61),

$$\dot{x}_t = 2(y - c_t). \tag{6.63}$$

Equations (6.62) and (6.63) constitute a dynamic system in c_t and x_t, for a given value of μ. The steady state is given by

$$c_{ss} = y, \tag{6.64}$$

$$x_{ss} = \frac{y}{\beta + \frac{1}{2}\mu}. \tag{6.65}$$

The linear approximation of the dynamic system around the steady state is

$$\begin{bmatrix} \dot{c}_t \\ \dot{x}_t \end{bmatrix} = \begin{bmatrix} 0 & -\left(\beta + \frac{1}{2}\mu\right)^2 \\ -2 & 0 \end{bmatrix} \begin{bmatrix} c_t - y \\ x_t - x_{ss} \end{bmatrix}.$$

The determinant of the matrix associated with the linear approximation is thus

$$\Delta = -2\left(\beta + \frac{1}{2}\mu\right)^2 < 0,$$

which indicates that the system is saddle-path stable.

Graphically we can draw the phase diagram depicted in figure 6.11. To draw the $\dot{c}_t = 0$ and $\dot{x}_t = 0$ loci, set equations (6.62) and (6.63) to zero to obtain, respectively,

$$x_t = \frac{y}{\beta + \frac{1}{2}\mu},$$

$$c_t = y.$$

It follows that the $\dot{c}_t = 0$ locus is a vertical line while the $\dot{x}_t = 0$ locus is a horizontal line. These two loci define four regions. Proceeding as before, we can establish how the system will move in each of these regions by drawing the arrowheads as indicated. We thus conclude that as shown in figure 6.11, the saddle path is positively sloped.

Permanent Increase in Rate of Money Growth

Suppose that the economy is initially at the steady state given by point A in figure 6.11. At $t = 0$ there is an unanticipated and permanent increase in the rate of money growth from μ^L to μ^H (figure 6.12, panel a). How will the economy react?

In the new steady state—given by point B in figure 6.11—c_t is unchanged but x_t has fallen, as follows from (6.64) and (6.65). The system will therefore jump on impact from point A to point C and then proceed along the saddle path toward point B. The corresponding paths of c_t and x_t are depicted in figure 6.12, panel b and c, respectively. Naturally, since m_t and f_t are a fixed proportion of x_t, they will also follow a path qualitatively identical to that of x (as illustrated in panel d for foreign currency). Since consumption rises on impact, the economy runs a trade deficit throughout the transition (figure 6.12, panel f).

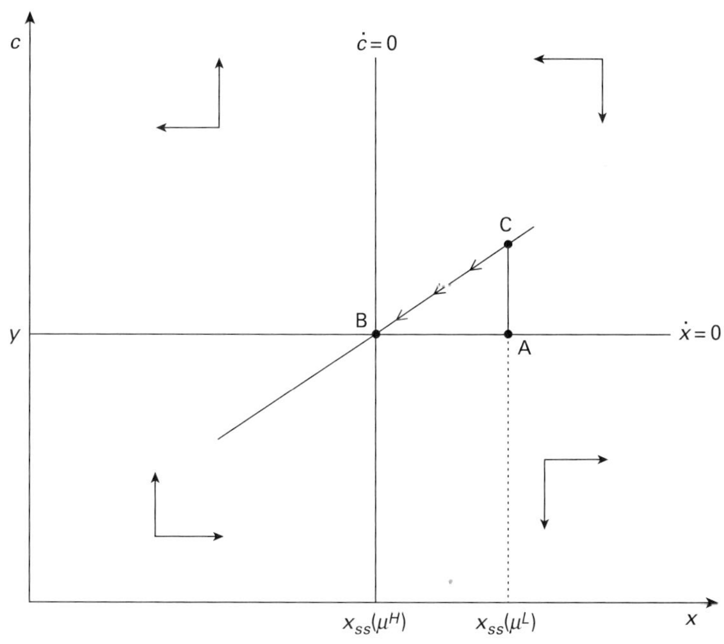

Figure 6.11
Currency substitution model: Phase diagram

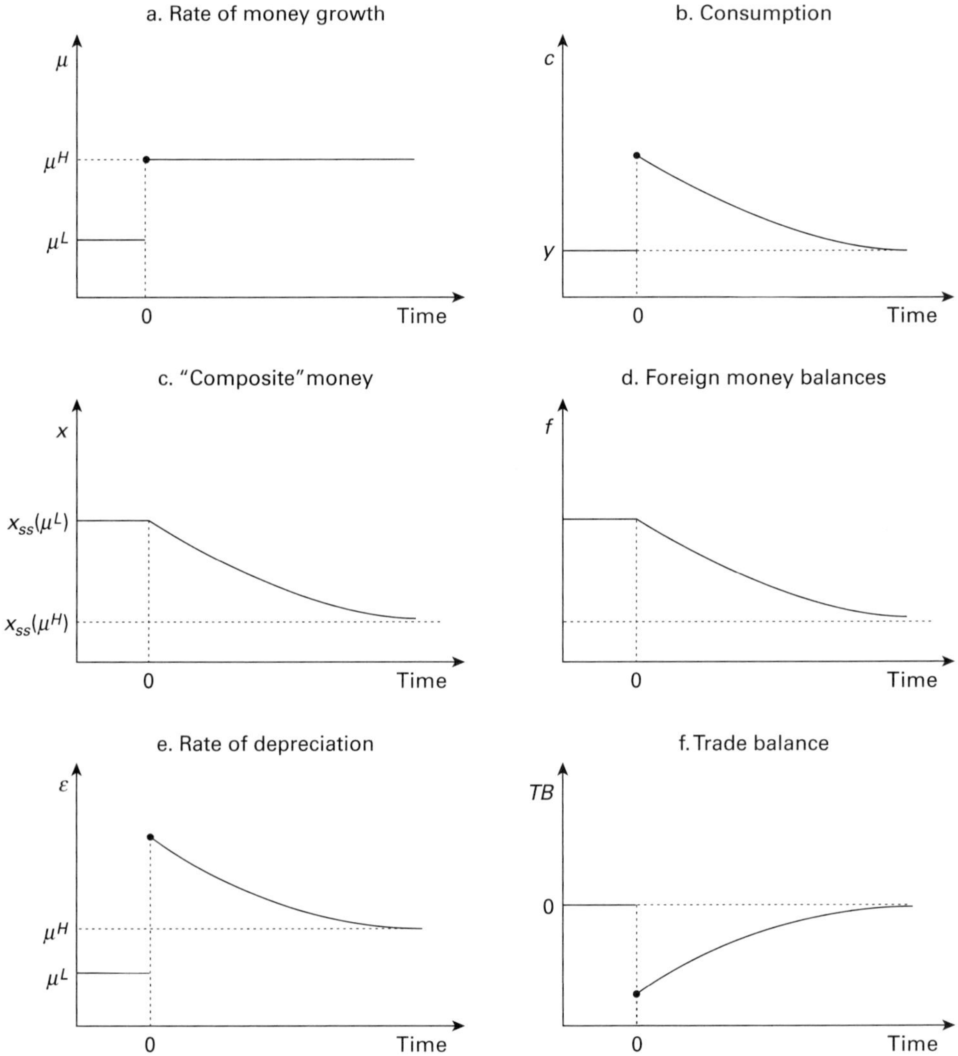

Figure 6.12
Permanent increase in rate of money growth

What will happen to the rate of depreciation? Notice that, from (6.60), we can write

$$\varepsilon_t = \mu^H - \frac{\dot{x}_t}{x_t} > \mu^H,$$

since $\dot{x}_t < 0$. Furthermore the rate of depreciation will be higher in the new steady state. Differentiating this last equation with respect to time (and noticing that from (6.63) and the fact that $\dot{c}_t < 0$, $\ddot{x}_t > 0$), we can check that $\dot{\varepsilon}_t < 0$. The rate of depreciation thus follows the path illustrated in figure 6.12, panel e. We also know that the nominal exchange rate will not jump on impact since x_t and hence m_t do not jump on impact.

What is the intuition behind our results? The increase in the rate of money growth implies a higher opportunity cost of the composite currency (x_t). As a result the public wishes to reduce its holdings of this composite money in the long run. Since this composite money consists of domestic and foreign currency in fixed proportions, foreign currency holdings must also fall in the long run. To achieve this goal, the economy must run a trade deficit, which requires an increase in consumption.

Interestingly, and even though the economy is operating under flexible exchange rates, the adjustment mechanism is analogous to that emphasized by the monetary approach to the balance of payments. While under flexible exchange rates the nominal exchange rate can adjust to bring about the desired real holdings of *domestic* currency, it is obviously powerless when it comes to changing holdings of *foreign* currency. Hence, changes in foreign currency holdings must take place through trade imbalances, as emphasized by the monetary approach.

6.6 Final Remarks

This chapter departed from the frictionless monetary world of chapter 5 by assuming away the existence of interest-bearing bonds. In such a world, which can be taken as a proxy for situations of low capital mobility, exchange rate policy ceases to be neutral or superneutral. A devaluation leads to a trade surplus and an increase in the Central Bank's international reserves, whereas an increase in the rate of devaluation results in a trade deficit and a loss of international reserves. These experiments illustrate the so-called monetary approach to the balance of payments, which emphasizes the idea that changes in international reserves are caused by "disequilibria" in the money markets (in the sense of the current stock of real money balances differing from its long-run equilibrium). In sharp contrast, monetary policy under flexible exchange rates continues to be neutral and superneutral because the absence of interest-bearing bonds does not affect the adjustment channel (i.e., changes in the nominal exchange rate) operating in the frictionless world of chapter 5.

The next two chapters will introduce alternative frictions in the world of chapter 5 that will also imply that monetary/exchange rate policy affect the real economy. Chapter 7 will introduce a link between changes in nominal interest rates and consumption, while chapter 8 will introduce sticky prices.

6.7 Appendixes

6.7.1 Dynamic Optimization in Continuous Time

For those readers not familiar with optimal control techniques, this appendix provides a "cookbook" for deriving optimality conditions in continuous-time dynamic problems and then illustrates this method with the familiar one-sector growth model.[26] This is all that you will need for the purposes of this book. For formal proofs of these techniques, see Kamien and Schwartz (1981) or Chiang (1992). The second part of either book deals with optimal control techniques and contains formal proofs and examples.

The General Problem

Consider the following standard problem in many areas of economics. Maximize

$$\int_0^\infty f(x_t, u_t)\exp(-\beta t)dt, \tag{6.66}$$

subject to

$$\dot{x}_t = g(x_t, u_t), \tag{6.67}$$

$$x_0 \text{ given.} \tag{6.68}$$

In optimal control problems, variables are divided into *state* variables and *control* variables. In the problem above, x_t is the state variable and u_t is the control variable. (The extension to several control and state variables is straightforward.) The movement of state variables is governed by first-order differential equations such as (6.67). Note that the state variable may or may not enter the objective function $f(.)$: it does not in the one-sector growth model below, but it does in the model in the text.

Faced with this maximization problem, the first step is to set up the *current value Hamiltonian*, denoted by $H(.)$:

$$H(x_t, u_t, \lambda_t) \equiv f(x_t, u_t) + \lambda_t g(x_t, u_t), \tag{6.69}$$

where λ_t is an auxiliary variable (analogous to a Lagrange multiplier) which is referred to as the *co-state* variable. This variable λ_t can be interpreted as the marginal valuation at time t of the associated state variable.

It can be shown (see Kamien and Schwartz 1981 or Chiang 1992) that, at an optimum, the following necessary conditions must be satisfied:

26. For extensive use of optimal control techniques in growth models, see Barro and Sala-i-Martin (1995).

$$\frac{\partial H}{\partial u_t} = f_u(x_t, u_t) + \lambda_t g_u(x_t, u_t) = 0, \tag{6.70}$$

$$\dot{\lambda}_t = \beta\lambda_t - \frac{\partial H}{\partial x_t} = \beta\lambda_t - f_x(x_t, u_t) - \lambda_t g_x(x_t, u_t). \tag{6.71}$$

Condition (6.71) gives the law of motion for the co-state variable. If $f(x_t, u_t)$ and $g(x_t, u_t)$ are concave in both arguments, the necessary conditions are also sufficient for an optimum.

In the typical optimal control problem, one would solve for u_t as a function of λ_t and x_t from (6.70) (i.e., $u_t = \tilde{u}(x_t, \lambda_t)$) and substitute this into (6.67) and (6.71) to obtain

$$\dot{x}_t = g[x_t, \tilde{u}(x_t, \lambda_t)],$$

$$\dot{\lambda}_t = \beta\lambda_t - f_x[x_t, \tilde{u}(x_t, \lambda_t)] - \lambda_t g_x[x_t, \tilde{u}(x_t, \lambda_t)].$$

This is a differential equation system in x_t and λ_t, which can be solved using standard phase-diagram techniques (an excellent discussion is contained in Kamien and Schwartz 1981 in the chapter "Equilibria in infinite horizon autonomous problems.")

An Example: The One-Sector Growth Model[27]

Consider the following one-sector growth model. Maximize

$$\int_0^{\infty} \log(c_t)\exp(-\beta t)dt, \tag{6.72}$$

subject to

$$\dot{k}_t = f(k_t) - c_t - \delta k_t, \tag{6.73}$$

$$k_0 \text{ given}, \tag{6.74}$$

where c_t is consumption, k_t is the capital stock, δ is the rate of depreciation, and $f(.)$ is a strictly increasing and strictly concave production function. In this case, c_t is the control variable and k_t is the state variable.

The current value Hamiltonian is given by

$$H(c_t, k_t, \lambda_t) \equiv \log(c_t) + \lambda_t[f(k_t) - c_t - \delta k_t]. \tag{6.75}$$

The variable λ_t can be interpreted as the price or value of an extra unit of capital at time t in terms of utility at time t. As emphasized by Barro and Sala-i-Martin (1995), the Hamiltonian can be interpreted as follows. At each instant in time the agent consumes c_t and owns a capital stock k_t.

27. Chiang (1992), chapter 9, and Barro and Sala-i-Martin (1995), chapter 2, contain a detailed discussion of the one-sector growth model.

These two variables impact utility through two channels. First, consumption has a direct effect on utility, as captured by the first term, $\log(c_t)$. Second, the choice of consumption affects the change in the capital stock through (6.73). The *value* of this change in the capital stock (in utility terms) is given by the second term on the RHS of (6.75). Hence, for a given value of the shadow price λ_t, the Hamiltonian captures the total contribution to utility of the choice of c_t.

Using (6.70) and (6.71), we can write the optimality conditions as

$$\frac{\partial H}{\partial c_t} = \frac{1}{c_t} - \lambda_t = 0, \tag{6.76}$$

$$\dot{\lambda}_t = \beta\lambda_t - \frac{\partial H}{\partial k_t} = \beta\lambda_t - \lambda_t[f'(k_t) - \delta] = \lambda_t[\beta + \delta - f'(k_t)]. \tag{6.77}$$

Notice that (6.77) can be expressed as

$$\underbrace{\frac{1}{\lambda_t}\frac{\partial H}{\partial k_t}}_{\text{“Dividend”}} + \underbrace{\frac{\dot{\lambda}_t}{\lambda_t}}_{\text{Capital gain}} = \beta,$$

and interpreted as an asset-pricing equation. As indicated, the first term on the LHS is the dividend rate received by the agent (i.e., the marginal contribution of capital to utility divided by the price of the asset), while the second term on the LHS is the rate of capital gain (i.e., the rate of change in the price of the asset). The total return on the asset is equated to the discount rate, β.

Solving for c_t from (6.76) and substituting it into (6.73) and (6.77) yields a dynamic system in k_t and λ_t:

$$\dot{k}_t = f(k_t) - \frac{1}{\lambda_t} - \delta k_t, \tag{6.78}$$

$$\dot{\lambda}_t = \lambda_t[\beta + \delta - f'(k_t)]. \tag{6.79}$$

The steady state is given by

$$f'(k_{ss}) = \beta + \delta,$$

$$\frac{1}{\lambda_{ss}} = f(k_{ss}) - \delta k_{ss}.$$

By linearizing the system around the steady state, it is easy to check that this dynamic system is saddle-path stable (see exercise 4 at the end of the chapter). Hence, for a given value of k_0, the value of λ_0 will be endogenously determined so as to place the dynamic system on the saddle path. (Alternatively, you could differentiate equation 6.76 with respect to time and use equation 6.77 to set up a dynamic system in k and c; this is what Chiang 1992 does.)

Finally, note that if the production function were linear (i.e., $f(k_t) = rk_t$, $r > 0$) and there were no depreciation (i.e., $\delta = 0$), then it is clear from (6.79) that we would need to assume that

$\beta = r$ for a stationary equilibrium to exist. This is exactly why we assume that $\beta = r$ in small open economy models.[28] In that case $\dot{\lambda}_t = 0$ for all t, and therefore λ would be constant along a perfect foresight equilibrium path.

6.7.2 Analytical Solution for the Saddle Path

In section 6.2 we resorted to the phase diagram to graphically derive the saddle path. It will prove useful to solve for the saddle path analytically.[29] In the process we will also review how to solve a two-equation differential equation system.

For convenience, we restate the linear version of the model, given by (6.19), as

$$\begin{bmatrix} \dot{c}_t \\ \dot{m}_t \end{bmatrix} = A \begin{bmatrix} c_t - y \\ m_t - m_{ss} \end{bmatrix}, \tag{6.80}$$

where

$$A \equiv \begin{bmatrix} \beta + \varepsilon & \frac{-v''(m_{ss})}{u''(y)} \\ -1 & 0 \end{bmatrix}$$

is the matrix associated with the linear approximation of the system.

To find the eigenvalues of the system, we need to solve for the characteristic polinomial of matrix A (recall that the eigenvalues are the roots of the characteristic polynomial of matrix A). Formally, we need to solve for

$$|A - \delta I| = 0,$$

where I is the identity matrix. In other words, we need to subtract δ from the diagonal elements of matrix A, set the determinant of this matrix equal to zero, and solve for δ. Proceeding in this way yields

$$\begin{vmatrix} \beta + \varepsilon - \delta & \frac{-v''(m_{ss})}{u''(y)} \\ -1 & -\delta \end{vmatrix} = \delta^2 - (\beta + \varepsilon)\delta - \frac{v''(m_{ss})}{u''(y)} = 0.$$

The characteristic polynomial is a quadratic equation in δ that can be solved to yield

$$\delta_{1,2} = \frac{\beta + \varepsilon \pm \sqrt{(\beta + \varepsilon)^2 + 4\frac{v''(m_{ss})}{u''(y)}}}{2}. \tag{6.81}$$

28. Intuitively, for a small open economy to have access to perfect international capital markets is like having access to a linear technology with marginal productivity of capital equal to r, with the added advantage that its "capital" (i.e., bonds) can be negative.

29. A classic reference on differential equation systems is Hirsch and Smale (1974).

Since $(\beta + \varepsilon)^2 + 4v''(m_{ss})/u''(y) > 0$, the two roots will be real and distinct. Hence the characteristic roots are given by

$$\delta_1 = \frac{\beta + \varepsilon - \sqrt{(\beta + \varepsilon)^2 + 4v''(m_{ss})/u''(y)}}{2} < 0, \tag{6.82}$$

$$\delta_2 = \frac{\beta + \varepsilon + \sqrt{(\beta + \varepsilon)^2 + 4v''(m_{ss})/u''(y)}}{2} > 0. \tag{6.83}$$

Using (6.82) and (6.83), we can verify that the product of the characteristic roots is given by the determinant of the matrix A:

$$\delta_1\delta_2 = -\frac{v''(m_{ss})}{u''(y)} = |A|.$$

For future reference, also note that the trace of matrix A (the trace is the sum of the diagonal elements of a square matrix) corresponds to the sum of the characteristic roots

$$\delta_1 + \delta_2 = \beta + \varepsilon = \text{Tr}(A).$$

It proves useful to notice that we can write (6.81) as a

$$\delta_{1,2} = \frac{\text{Tr}(A) \pm \sqrt{[\text{Tr}(A)]^2 - 4|A|}}{2}.$$

The roots are therefore real and distinct if $[\text{Tr}(A)]^2 - 4|A| > 0$, they are non–real complex conjugates if $[\text{Tr}(A)]^2 - 4|A| < 0$, and there is only one root—necessarily real—if $[\text{Tr}(A)]^2 = 4|A|$.

Since A is a 2×2 matrix with two distinct real eigenvalues, then every solution to the differential system (6.80) is of the form

$$c_t - y = \omega_1 h_{11} \exp(\delta_1 t) + \omega_2 h_{21} \exp(\delta_2 t),$$

$$m_t - m_{ss} = \omega_1 h_{12} \exp(\delta_1 t) + \omega_2 h_{22} \exp(\delta_2 t),$$

where ω_1 and ω_2 are arbitrary constants and h_{i1} and h_{i2} are the elements of the eigenvector h_i corresponding to the eigenvalues δ_i, $i = 1, 2$. Recall that there is a stable root ($\delta_1 < 0$) and an unstable root ($\delta_2 > 0$). Clearly, if $\omega_2 \neq 0$, as $t \to \infty$, the system will diverge (i.e., the limit of $c_t - y$ and $m_t - m_{ss}$ is $\pm\infty$). Therefore, to ensure convergence along a perfect foresight path, we set to zero the constant corresponding to the unstable root (i.e., we set $\omega_2 = 0$). By doing so, the system reduces to

$$c_t - y = \omega_1 h_{11} \exp(\delta_1 t),$$

$$m_t - m_{ss} = \omega_1 h_{12} \exp(\delta_1 t). \tag{6.84}$$

To find the eigenvector corresponding to the eigenvalue δ_1, we must solve the vector equation:

$$(A - \delta_1 I)h_1 = 0,$$

where h_1 is the eigenvector. Then

$$\begin{bmatrix} \beta + \varepsilon - \delta_1 & \frac{-v''(m_{ss})}{u''(y)} \\ -1 & -\delta_1 \end{bmatrix} \begin{bmatrix} h_{11} \\ h_{12} \end{bmatrix} = \begin{bmatrix} 0 \\ 0 \end{bmatrix}.$$

Since an eigenvector is determined up to a factor of proportionality, we need to solve only for the second equation:

$$-h_{11} = \delta_1 h_{12}.$$

As a normalization, set $h_{12} = 1$. (It is always convenient to normalize to one the element of the eigenvector corresponding to the predetermined variable.) Then

$$h_{11} = -\delta_1 > 0. \tag{6.85}$$

The last step in this derivation is to determine the constant ω_1. To do this, evaluate equation (6.84) at $t = 0$, to obtain

$$m_0 - m_{ss} = \omega_1. \tag{6.86}$$

Using (6.85) and (6.86), we can write the solution as

$$c_t - y = -(m_0 - m_{ss})\delta_1 \exp(\delta_1 t), \tag{6.87}$$

$$m_t - m_{ss} = (m_0 - m_{ss}) \exp(\delta_1 t). \tag{6.88}$$

As a check, we verify that both variables converge asymptotically to their steady-state values:

$$\lim_{t \to \infty} c_t = y,$$

$$\lim_{t \to \infty} m_t = m_{ss}.$$

To fix ideas, suppose that $m_0 < m_{ss}$. Then differentiating (6.87) and (6.88) with respect to time, we get

$$\dot{c}_t = -(m_0 - m_{ss})\delta_1^2 \exp(\delta_1 t) > 0,$$

$$\dot{m}_t = (m_0 - m_{ss})\delta_1 \exp(\delta_1 t) > 0,$$

which tells us that both c_t and m_t increase over time towards their steady-state values. Alternatively, we can derive the analytical expression for the saddle path of the system by simply dividing (6.87) by (6.88) to obtain

$$c_t - y = -\delta_1(m_t - m_{ss}).$$

Since $\delta_1 < 0$, the saddle path is positively sloped (i.e., the slope is equal to $-\delta_1$) which is, of course, consistent with the phase diagram in figure 6.1.

6.7.3 Derivation of Price Index

This appendix derives the price index used in the text, given by equation (6.22). Suppose that preferences are given by

$$u(c^T, c^N) = \log(c^T) + \log(c^N),$$

which correspond to the consumption component of the preferences given by (6.21). Denote by X the nominal expenditure associated with consumption:

$$X = P^T c^T + P^N c^N.$$

Then P, the price index, is defined as the minimum expenditure needed to achieve a given level of utility $\bar{u}$. In other words, P solves the problem

$$\min_{\{c^T, c^N\}} X = P^T c^T + P^N c^N$$

subject to

$$\log(c^T) + \log(c^N) = \bar{u}. \tag{6.89}$$

The price index P will therefore be given by X evaluated at the optimal choices of c^T and c^N.

In terms of the Lagrangian,

$$\mathcal{L} = P^T c^T + P^N c^N + \lambda\left[\bar{u} - \log(c^T) - \log(c^N)\right].$$

The first-order conditions with respect to c^T and c^N are given by, respectively,

$$P^T = \frac{\lambda}{c^T}, \tag{6.90}$$

$$P^N = \frac{\lambda}{c^N}. \tag{6.91}$$

Adding up these two expressions, we obtain

$$P = 2\lambda. \tag{6.92}$$

To find λ, we substitute (6.90) and (6.91) into (6.89) to obtain

$$\lambda = \sqrt{e^{\bar{u}}}\sqrt{P^T P^N}. \tag{6.93}$$

Substituting (6.93) into (6.92) we can write

$$P = 2\sqrt{e^{\bar{u}}}\sqrt{P^T P^N},$$

which is expression (6.22). (We ignore, for notational simplicity, constants that are inconsequential for our qualitative analysis.)

6.7.4 Computations Underlying Table 6.1

To construct table 6.1, we need to solve explicitly for the jump in c_t^T at $t = 0$. The general solution for the dynamic system is given by

$$\begin{aligned} c_t^T - c_{ss}^T &= \omega_1 h_{11} \exp(\delta_1 t), \\ m_t - m_{ss} &= \omega_1 h_{12} \exp(\delta_1 t), \end{aligned} \tag{6.94}$$

where δ_1 is the negative root of the system. To compute the negative root, we solve for the root polynomial:

$$\begin{vmatrix} \beta + \varepsilon - \delta_1 & -(\beta+\varepsilon)^2 \\ \alpha Z^T \left(n_{ss}^T\right)^{\alpha-1} \Psi' - 1 & -\delta_1 \end{vmatrix} = \delta_1^2 - (\beta+\varepsilon)\,\delta_1 + \left[\alpha Z^T \left(n_{ss}^T\right)^{\alpha-1} \Psi' - 1\right](\beta+\varepsilon)^2 .$$

The negative root is thus given by

$$\delta_1 = (\beta+\varepsilon)\,\frac{1 - \sqrt{1 - 4\left[\alpha Z^T \left(n_{ss}^T\right)^{\alpha-1} \Psi' - 1\right]}}{2}.$$

We now solve for the elements of the eigenvector:

$$\begin{pmatrix} \beta + \varepsilon - \delta_1 & -(\beta+\varepsilon)^2 \\ \alpha Z^T \left(n_{ss}^T\right)^{\alpha-1} \Psi' - 1 & -\delta_1 \end{pmatrix} \begin{pmatrix} h_{11} \\ h_{12} \end{pmatrix} = \begin{pmatrix} 0 \\ 0 \end{pmatrix}$$

Hence

$$\frac{h_{11}}{h_{12}} = \frac{\delta_1}{\alpha Z^T \left(n_{ss}^T\right)^{\alpha-1} \Psi' - 1} < 0.$$

In response to a devaluation, at time 0 (setting $h_{12} = 1$) we have

$$m_0 - m_{ss} = \omega_1.$$

Hence

$$c_0^T - c_{ss}^T = \frac{(\beta + \varepsilon)}{2}(m_0 - m_{ss})\frac{1 - \sqrt{1 - 4\left[\alpha Z^T\left(n_{ss}^T\right)^{\alpha-1}\Psi' - 1\right]}}{\alpha Z^T\left(n_{ss}^T\right)^{\alpha-1}\Psi' - 1}.$$

Dividing through by c_{ss}^T and taking into account that $m_{ss} = c_{ss}^T/(\beta + \varepsilon)$, we obtain

$$\frac{c_0^T - c_{ss}^T}{c_{ss}^T} = \frac{1}{2}\left(\frac{m_0 - m_{ss}}{m_{ss}}\right)\frac{1 - \sqrt{1 - 4\left[\alpha Z^T\left(n_{ss}^T\right)^{\alpha-1}\Psi' - 1\right]}}{\alpha Z^T\left(n_{ss}^T\right)^{\alpha-1}\Psi' - 1}, \tag{6.95}$$

where

$$\alpha Z^T\left(n_{ss}^T\right)^{\alpha-1}\Psi' = -\frac{1}{\left[1 + (1-\alpha)(n - n_{ss}^T)/n_{ss}^T\right]}.$$

Once we have computed the initial jump in consumption using equation (6.95), we can use equations (6.25), (6.26), (6.32), (6.34), (6.38), and (6.44) to compute the initial jumps in e_t and y_t and then use e_t and the price index (6.22) to compute the initial jumps in P_t^N and P_t.

Exercises

1. (The monetary approach model with a labor/leisure choice) Consider the model of section 6.2 with the following modifications. Preferences are now given by

$$\int_0^\infty [u(c_t) + z(\ell_t) + v(m_t)]\exp(-\beta t)dt,$$

where ℓ_t is leisure. Production takes the linear form

$$y_t = \alpha(1 - \ell_t),$$

where α is a positive parameter. The rest of the model is unchanged.

In this context:

a. Solve the model by proceeding as in the text.

b. Analyze the effects of an unanticipated and permanent devaluation. (In particular, show that, on impact, a devaluation increases output and reduces consumption.)

2. (The monetary approach model with a cash-in-advance) Consider the monetary model with no bonds developed in section 6.2 of this chapter with the following modification. Instead of introducing money into the utility function, suppose that preferences are given by

$$\int_0^\infty u(c_t)\exp(-\beta t)dt,$$

and that consumption is subject to a cash-in-advance constraint of the form[30]

$$m_t = \alpha c_t.$$

The rest of the model remains unchanged. In this context:

a. Analyze the effects of an unanticipated and permanent devaluation.

b. Analyze the effects of an unanticipated and permanent increase in the stock of domestic credit.

c. Analyze the effects of an unanticipated and permanent increase in the rate of devaluation.

In each case discuss whether the results differ from those in the text and explain why.

3. (The two-good model with linear production) Consider the model of section 6.3 with a linear production function for tradable goods. In other words, production of tradable goods is given by

$$y_t^T = Z^T n_t^T.$$

In the context of this model, analyze the economy's response to a permanent devaluation.

4. (The one-sector growth model) Linearize the dynamic system given by (6.78) and (6.79) around the steady state and show that it is saddle-path stable.

References

Barro, Robert J., and Xavier Sala-i-Martin. 1995. *Economic Growth.* New York: McGraw-Hill.

Burstein, Ariel, Martin Eichenbaum, and Sergio Rebelo. 2005. Large devaluations and the real exchange rate. *Journal of Political Economy* 113 (4): 742–84.

Burstein, Ariel, Joao C. Neves, and Sergio Rebelo. 2003. Distribution costs and real exchange rate dynamics during exchange-rate-based stabilizations. *Journal of Monetary Economics* 50 (6): 1189–1214.

Calvo, Guillermo A. 1981. Devaluation: Levels versus rates. *Journal of International Economics* 11 (2): 165–72.

Calvo, Guillermo A., and Carlos A. Rodriguez. 1977. A model of exchange rate determination under currency substitution and rational expectations. *Journal of Political Economy* 85 (3): 617–26.

Calvo, Guillermo A., and Carlos A. Végh. 1992. Currency substitution in developing countries: An introduction. *Revista de Analisis Economico* 7: 3–27.

Chiang, Alpha C.1992. *Elements of dynamic optimization.* New York: McGraw-Hill.

30. See appendix 7.7.1 in chapter 7 for the derivation of the cash-in-advance constraint in a continuous-time setting.

Easterly, William E. 2002. An identity crisis? Testing IMF financial programming. Working Paper 9. Center for Global Development. Washington, DC.

Gupta, Poonam, Deepak Mishra, and Ratna Sahay. 2007. Behavior of output during currency crises. *Journal of International Economics* 72 (2): 428–50.

Hirsch, Morris W., and Stephen Smale. 1974. *Differential Equations, Dynamical Systems, and Linear Algebra.* New York: Academic Press.

International Monetary Fund. 1987. Theoretical aspects of the design of fund-supported adjustment programs. IMF Occasional Paper 55. International Monetary Fund. Washington, DC.

International Monetary Fund. undated. *Articles of agreement.* International Monetary Fund. Washington, DC.

Kamien, Morton, and Nancy Schwartz. 1981. *Dynamic Optimization.* Amsterdam: North Holland.

Khan, Mohsin S., Peter Montiel, and Nadeem U. Haque. 1990. Adjustment with growth: Relating the analytical approaches of the IMF and the World Bank. *Journal of Development Economics* 32 (1): 155–79.

Mussa, Michael, and Miguel Savastano. 2000. The IMF approach to economic stabilization. *NBER Macroeconomics Annual* 14: 79–128.

Polak, Jacques. 1957. Monetary analysis of income formation and payments problems. *IMF Staff Papers* 5: 1–50.

7 Temporary Policy

7.1 Introduction

Chapter 5 introduced money as a veil in the endowment model of chapter 1. In the world of chapter 5, changes in monetary or exchange rate policy do not therefore affect the real economy. Chapter 6 removed the veil by abstracting from interest-bearing bonds and showing how, in that context, exchange rate policy has real effects by affecting the desired holdings of real money balances and thereby inducing consumers to run trade imbalances to alter the level of real money balances. Monetary policy, however, still did not have real effects because desired changes in real money balances could be accommodated through changes in the price level. This chapter introduces a different friction into the model of chapter 5, which will result in both exchange rate and monetary policy having real effects. Specifically, we will introduce a link between the nominal interest rate and consumption. With this channel present, we will be opening the door for *temporary* changes in monetary/exchange rate policy to affect consumption through changes in the nominal interest rate.

How can we model the link between nominal interest rates and consumption? The simplest way—but, as will become clear below, certainly not the only one—is to introduce money into the model via a cash-in-advance constraint. The cash-in-advance constraint, which goes back to Clower (1967), posits that goods must be bought with money (e.g., as opposed to credit) and requires that consumers be in possession of the required real money balances *before* they enter the goods market. As already touched upon in chapter 5, in discrete time there are two possible timings depending on whether asset markets open before or after goods markets. In the Lucas (1982) timing, asset markets open before goods markets (think of asset markets opening early in the morning and closing at noon, and goods markets opening at noon and closing at 5 pm). In this case consumers do not need to carry overnight the money needed to buy goods tomorrow because they can procure the needed cash in the morning. As a result the nominal interest rate does not affect consumption.[1]

1. Of course, households still carry money balances overnight (as a result of selling their endownment for cash in the goods market) but—and this is the critical point—these money balances are not related to tomorrow's consumption.

Imagine the opposite market timing: goods markets open and close in the morning while asset markets only open in the afternoon.[2] In such a case consumers will need to acquire during the previous afternoon the cash balances needed to buy goods the following morning. By carrying these money balances overnight, they will be subject to the inflation tax. The inflation tax thus becomes part of the effective cost of consuming goods. This is the channel whereby the nominal interest rate will affect consumption. In particular, by reducing the inflation tax, a fall in the nominal interest rate will reduce the *effective* price of consumption. A temporary fall in the nominal interest rate will thus alter the intertemporal profile of the effective price of consumption and induce consumers to substitute future for present consumption à la chapter 3. We will see that the continuous-time version of the cash-in-advance model—presented in section 2—is equivalent to assuming the Svensson timing. In this context a temporary reduction in the rate of devaluation—which, by interest parity, is equivalent to a temporary reduction in the nominal interest rate—leads to a temporary increase in consumption of tradable goods and a temporary increase in the relative price of nontradable goods. The temporary reduction in the nominal interest rate is welfare reducing because it induces a nonconstant path of consumption while not changing the present discounted value of resources.

In section 7.2 *permanent* changes in the rate of devaluation have no real effects because they do not affect the intertemporal profile of the effective price of consumption. In other words, starting with a stationary equilibrium, a permanent reduction in the rate of devaluation leads to a permanent reduction in the nominal interest rate but to no change in consumption because the path of the nominal interest rate remains flat over time. (There is no wealth effect either because proceeds from the inflation tax are rebated to the public in a lump-sum way.) This feature, however, critically depends on the absence of a labor/leisure choice. In the presence of a labor/leisure choice—as analyzed in section 7.3—a positive nominal interest rate constitutes an *intratemporal* distortion because it implies that the private relative price of consumption in terms of leisure is greater than its social cost. As a result, by reducing the relative price of consumption in terms of leisure, even a permanent reduction in the nominal interest rate will have real effects and lead to a substitution away from leisure (which increases labor supply and hence the present discounted value of output) and toward consumption. In this context temporary changes in the nominal interest rate will therefore have both intertemporal and intratemporal (i.e., static) effects. The welfare effects of a temporary fall in the nominal interest rate will thus depend on the relative strength of the intertemporal consumption substitution effect (which reduces welfare) and the wealth effect induced by higher labor supply (which increases welfare).

Aside from introducing a labor/leisure choice, there are other ways of incorporating wealth effects into this kind of model. Section 7.4 illustrates this idea by returning to the endowment economy of section 7.2 and introducing money via a transactions costs technology. The idea is that real money balances reduce transactions costs (which use up resources) associated with the purchase of goods. A fall in the nominal interest rate will thus have a wealth effect because it

2. This is often referred to as the Svensson (1985) timing, as opposed to the Lucas timing.

induces consumers to hold more real money balances, which reduces transactions costs. Hence a permanent reduction in the rate of devaluation—which, via interest parity, leads to a permanent fall in the nominal interest rate—leads to a permanently higher level of consumption due to a permanent reduction in transactions costs. In contrast, temporary reduction in the nominal interest rate will lead to a temporary increase in consumption (by reducing the implicit effective price of consumption). It follows that while a permanent reduction in the rate of devaluation is clearly welfare improving, the welfare effects of a temporary reduction in the nominal interest rate will depend on the relative strength of the intertemporal consumption substitution and wealth effects.

Finally, section 7.5 turns to the case of flexible exchange rates under a cash-in-advance constraint (i.e., the flexible exchange rates counterpart of the model of section 7.2) and shows how the same basic results go through in the sense that a temporary reduction in the rate of monetary growth also leads to a temporary consumption boom.

7.2 Basic Monetary Model with a Cash-in-Advance Constraint

This section considers the basic monetary model of chapter 5 but, following Calvo (1986), introduces money through a cash-in-advance constraint—rather than a money-in-the-utility-function formulation—and also adds nontradable goods. As in chapter 5, consider a small open economy that is perfectly integrated in both world goods and capital markets. The law of one price holds for the tradable good (i.e., $P_t^T = E_t P_t^{T*}$). Consumers derive utility from consuming both tradable (c_t^T) and nontradable (c_t^N) goods. The economy is endowed with a constant stream of tradable (y^T) and nontradable goods (y^N). The world real interest rate (r) is given and constant over time.

7.2.1 Consumer's Problem

Preferences are given by

$$\int_0^\infty [u(c_t^T) + v(c_t^N)] \exp(-\beta t) dt, \tag{7.1}$$

where $u(.)$ and $v(.)$ are strictly increasing and strictly concave and $\beta > 0$ is the discount rate. Let a_t denote real financial assets (in terms of tradable goods)

$$a_t \equiv m_t + b_t,$$

where $m_t (\equiv M_t / E_t P_t^{T*})$ denotes real money balances and b_t stands for net foreign bonds.

Proceeding as in chapter 5, we know that the flow constraint will be given by

$$\dot{a}_t = r a_t + y^T + \frac{y^N}{e_t} + \tau_t - c_t^T - \frac{c_t^N}{e_t} - i_t m_t, \tag{7.2}$$

where $e_t(\equiv P_t^T/P_t^N)$ is the real exchange rate (defined as the relative price of tradable goods in terms of nontradable goods), τ_t are lump-sum transfers from the government, and i_t is the nominal interest rate.

The cash-in-advance constraint requires that consumers hold a proportion α of real money balances to finance their consumption purchases in every period. Formally,[3]

$$m_t = \alpha\left(c_t^T + \frac{c_t^N}{e_t}\right). \tag{7.3}$$

It is convenient to get rid of m_t as a choice variable for the consumer by substituting the cash-in-advance constraint into the flow constraint (7.2) to obtain

$$\dot{a}_t = ra_t + y^T + \frac{y^N}{e_t} + \tau_t - \left(c_t^T + \frac{c_t^N}{e_t}\right)(1+\alpha i_t). \tag{7.4}$$

Integrating this flow constraint forward and imposing the appropriate transversality condition, we obtain

$$a_0 + \int_0^\infty \left(y^T + \frac{y^N}{e_t} + \tau_t\right)\exp(-rt)dt = \int_0^\infty \left(c_t^T + \frac{c_t^N}{e_t}\right)(1+\alpha i_t)\exp(-rt)dt. \tag{7.5}$$

Consumers then choose $\{c_t^T, c_t^N\}_{t=0}^\infty$ to maximize (7.1) subject to the intertemporal constraint (7.5). In terms of the Lagrangian,

$$\mathcal{L} = \int_0^\infty [u(c_t^T) + v(c_t^N)]\exp(-\beta t)dt$$
$$+ \lambda\left\{a_0 + \int_0^\infty \left[y^T + \frac{y^N}{e_t} + \tau_t - \left(c_t^T + \frac{c_t^N}{e_t}\right)(1+\alpha i_t)\right]\exp(-rt)dt\right\}.$$

In addition to (7.5), the first-order conditions are given by (assuming, as usual, $\beta = r$)

$$u'(c_t^T) = \lambda(1+\alpha i_t), \tag{7.6}$$

$$v'(c_t^N) = \lambda\frac{(1+\alpha i_t)}{e_t}. \tag{7.7}$$

First-order condition (7.6) says that, at the margin, the consumer equates the marginal utility from consuming tradable goods to the marginal utility of wealth times the *effective price* of tradable

3. This cash-in-advance constraint can be interpreted as a first-order approximation to the "true" cash-in-advance constraint (see appendix 7.7.1).

goods (given by $1 + \alpha i_t$). Notice that it follows from the cash-in-advance constraint (7.3) that to purchase one unit of tradable goods, consumers need to hold α units of real money balances. Hence the effective price of tradable goods comprises the real market price of the good (one) plus the opportunity cost of the α units of real money balances required to purchase one unit of the good (αi_t). In the same vein, the effective price of nontradable goods is given by $1/e_t + (\alpha/e_t)i_t$. In other words, the effective price of nontradable goods is equal to the market relative price $(1/e_t)$ plus the opportunity cost of holding the α/e_t units of real money balances required to purchase one unit of nontradables.

First-order condition (7.6) brings us back to the world of intertemporal distortions analyzed in chapter 3. Clearly, if the nominal interest rate is constant along a perfect foresight equilibrium path, the path of consumption of tradable goods will also be constant over time. However, if the nominal interest rate is not constant over time, the path of consumption will not be constant over time either since the consumer will prefer to substitute consumption away from high interest rate periods (when the effective price of consumption is relatively high) and toward low interest rate periods (when the effective price is relatively low). In other words, a nonconstant path of the nominal interest rate will introduce an intertemporal distortion in much the same way as a nonconstant tariff did in chapter 3. For a given path of the real exchange rate, this intertemporal distortion will also affect consumption of nontradable goods.

Combining first-order conditions (7.6) and (7.7) yields the condition (with which we are familiar from chapter 4):

$$\frac{u'(c_t^T)}{v'(c_t^N)} = e_t. \tag{7.8}$$

Since the path of the nominal interest rate affects both goods in the same way, it does not affect the marginal rate of substitution between the two goods.

7.2.2 Government

The government is the same as in chapter 5. Its flow constraint is thus given by

$$\dot{h}_t = rh_t + \frac{\dot{M}_t}{P_t^T} - \tau_t. \tag{7.9}$$

The corresponding intertemporal constraint is given by

$$h_0 + \int_0^\infty \frac{\dot{M}_t}{P_t^T} \exp(-rt)dt = \int_0^\infty \tau_t \exp(-rt)dt. \tag{7.10}$$

7.2.3 Equilibrium Conditions

Once again, perfect capital mobility implies that interest parity holds:

$$i_t = i_t^* + \varepsilon_t. \tag{7.11}$$

Equilibrium in the nontradable goods market requires that consumption of nontradables equal the constant endowment:

$$c_t^N = y^N. \tag{7.12}$$

Let $k_t(\equiv b_t + h_t)$ denote the economy's stock of net foreign assets. Combining the consumer's flow constraint (equation 7.2) with the government's (equation 7.9) yields the economy's flow constraint:

$$\dot{k}_t = rk_t + y^T - c_t^T. \tag{7.13}$$

Integrating forward the economy's flow constraint (equation 7.13) and imposing the corresponding transversality condition yields the economy's resource constraint:

$$k_0 + \frac{y^T}{r} = \int_0^\infty c_t^T \exp(-rt)dt. \tag{7.14}$$

Finally, notice for further reference that since, by definition, $e_t = P_t^T/P_t^N$, where $P_t^T = E_t P_t^{T*}$, it follows that

$$\frac{\dot{e}_t}{e_t} = \varepsilon_t + \pi_t^* - \pi_t, \tag{7.15}$$

where $\pi_t^*(\equiv \dot{P}_t^{T*}/P_t^{T*})$ and $\pi_t(\equiv \dot{P}_t^N/P_t^N)$ are, respectively, the foreign inflation rate and the rate of inflation of nontradable goods. In equilibrium the rate of change of the real exchange rate will therefore be given by the difference between tradable goods inflation (given by $\varepsilon_t + \pi_t^*$) and nontradable goods inflation (given by π_t).

7.2.4 Perfect Foresight Equilibrium

Suppose that the rate of foreign inflation is constant over time and equal to π^*.[4] We proceed to characterize a perfect foresight equilibrium path for a constant rate of devaluation, ε.

4. Since the world real interest rate, r, is also constant over time, the Fisher equation for the rest of the world implies that the foreign nominal interest rate (i^*) will also be constant over time.

Given the constant rate of devaluation, interest parity (given by equation 7.11) determines a constant nominal interest rate:

$$i = i^* + \varepsilon. \tag{7.16}$$

Since the nominal interest rate is constant over time, first-order condition (7.6) tells us that c_t^T will also be constant over time. It follows from the resource constraint (7.14) that

$$c^T = rk_0 + y^T. \tag{7.17}$$

Using (7.8), (7.12), and (7.17), we conclude that the real exchange rate will also be constant over time and given by

$$e = \frac{u'\left(rk_0 + y^T\right)}{v'(y^N)}. \tag{7.18}$$

Since $\dot{e}_t = 0$, it follows from (7.15) that

$$\pi = \pi^* + \varepsilon. \tag{7.19}$$

7.2.5 Permanent Changes in Exchange Rate Policy

Having set up the model, we now analyze two policy experiments: a permanent devaluation (i.e., a permanent increase in E_t) and a permanent increase in the rate of devaluation.

Permanent Devaluation

Suppose that just before $t = 0$ the economy is in the stationary perfect foresight equilibrium just described. At $t = 0$ there is an unanticipated and permanent devaluation. Since there has been an unexpected change in the exchange rate, the consumer reoptimizes. In the new perfect foresight path, consumption of tradable goods will still be constant. Furthermore, since the devaluation does not affect the resources available to this economy, c^T will still be given by (7.17). The real exchange rate will therefore still be given by (7.18). In sum—and despite the potential effect of the nominal interest rate on consumption—a devaluation is neutral, as was the case in chapter 5.

Permanent Reduction in the Rate of Devaluation

Suppose now that starting from the stationary equilibrium characterized above, there is an unanticipated and permanent reduction in the devaluation rate. Given the interest parity condition (7.16), the nominal interest rate will also fall permanently. After the consumer reoptimizes, the same first-order conditions will apply. Since it is still the case that the nominal interest rate is constant along the new perfect foresight equilibrium path (though at a lower level than before), consumption of tradable goods will be constant over time and, from (7.17), equal to $rk_0 + y^T$. Hence, from (7.18), the real exchange rate will also be constant over time. Since the real exchange rate is constant over time, equation (7.19) indicates that the rate of inflation of nontradable goods will fall instantaneously by the same amount as the rate of devaluation. In sum, a permanent change in the rate of devaluation reduces inflation with no real effects whatsoever.[5]

7.2.6 Temporary Stabilization

Once again, suppose that just before $t = 0$ the economy is in the stationary perfect foresight equilibrium characterized above. At $t = 0$ there is an unanticipated and temporary fall in the rate of devaluation from ε^H to ε^L, $\varepsilon^L < \varepsilon^H$ (figure 7.1, panel a). At time T, the rate of devaluation goes back to its initial level, ε^H. Formally,

$$\varepsilon_t = \begin{cases} \varepsilon^L, & 0 \leq t < T, \\ \varepsilon^H, & t \geq T, \end{cases}$$

for some $T > 0$.

Naturally, the interest parity condition implies that the nominal interest rate behaves analogously (figure 7.1, panel b):

$$i_t = \begin{cases} i^L = i^* + \varepsilon^L, & 0 \leq t < T, \\ i^H = i^* + \varepsilon^H, & t \geq T. \end{cases}$$

What will happen to the path of consumption of tradable goods? From the first-order condition (7.6), we know that consumption will be constant within each subperiod (denote those levels by $(c^T)^1$ and $(c^T)^2$), respectively:

$$\begin{aligned} u'((c^T)^1) &= \lambda(1 + \alpha i^L), \qquad 0 \leq t < T, \\ u'((c^T)^2) &= \lambda(1 + \alpha i^H), \qquad t \geq T. \end{aligned}$$

Clearly, by the strict concavity of $u(.)$, $(c^T)^1 > (c^T)^2$. Furthermore, since the temporary stabilization does not affect the economy's resources, it follows from the resource constraint (7.14) that $(c^T)^1$ will be higher than $rk_0 + y^T$ and $(c^T)^2$ will be lower (figure 7.1, panel c). Given this path of consumption, the trade balance will worsen at $t = 0$ and improve at time T (see figure 7.1, panel d, which assumes that $k_0 = 0$). The current account will therefore go into deficit at $t = 0$, worsen during the transition as the income balance falls over time, and jump back to zero at time T.

What happens with the real exchange rate? From (7.8) it follows that

$$e_t = \frac{u'\left(c_t^T\right)}{v'\left(y^N\right)}. \tag{7.20}$$

5. Notice, incidentally, that in this cash-in-advance setup, real money balances do not change either in response to the permanent fall in the rate of devaluation. The reason is that money demand is not interest rate elastic. In contrast, if we introduced money in the utility function, the fall in the nominal interest rate that results from a fall in the rate of devaluation would lead to an increase in real money balances along the lines of chapter 5.

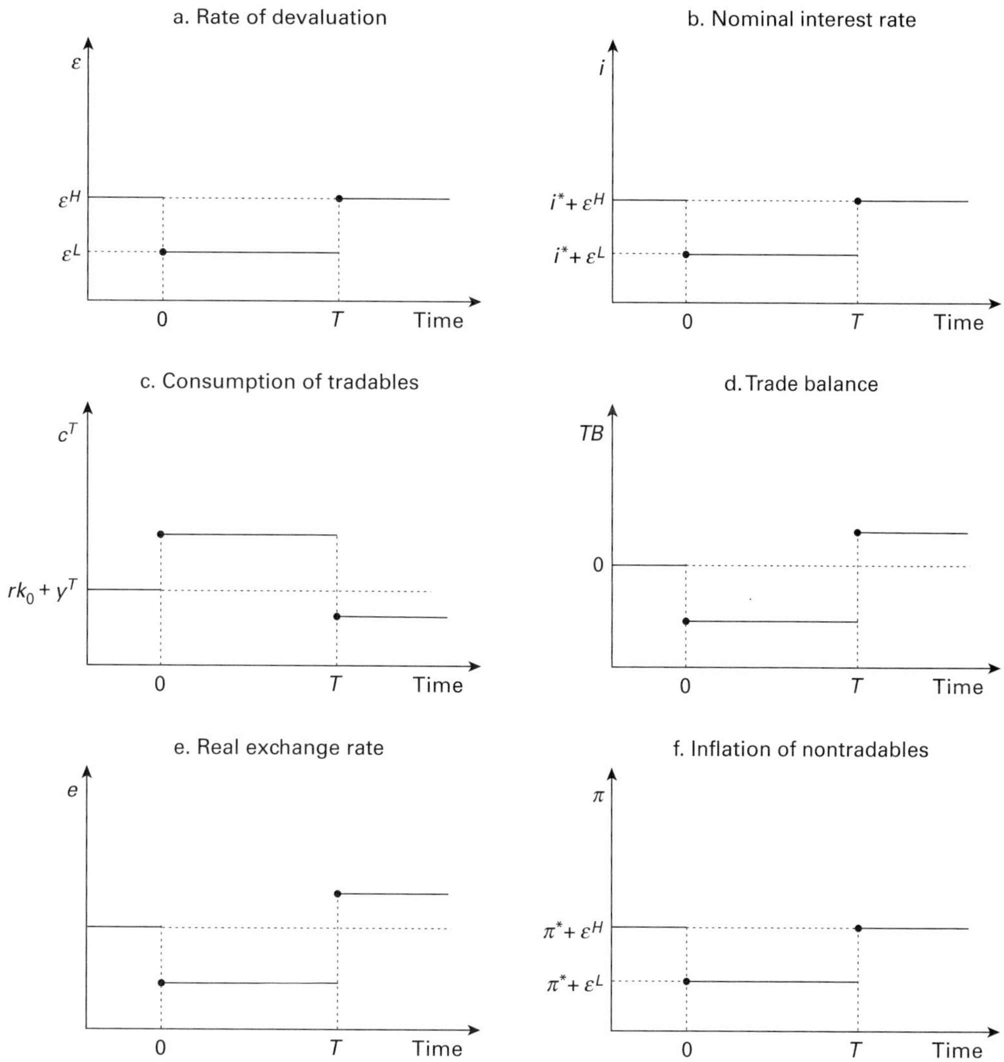

Figure 7.1
Temporary reduction in devaluation rate

Consequently e_t will fall on impact (real appreciation) and increase at T (real depreciation) (figure 7.1, panel e). Since c_t^T is below the pre-shock level after T, the real exchange rate will be above its pre-shock level.[6]

Since $\dot{e}_t = 0$ for $0 \leq t < T$ and $t \geq T$, it follows from (7.15) that the path of inflation of nontradable goods is given by

$$\pi_t = \pi^* + \varepsilon^L, \qquad 0 \leq t < T,$$
$$\pi_t = \pi^* + \varepsilon^H, \qquad t \geq T.$$

Inflation of nontradable goods thus falls on impact in line with the fall in the rate of devaluation and increases back to its pre-shock level at time T (figure 7.1, panel f).

In sum, a temporary exchange rate based stabilization leads to an initial consumption boom, real appreciation, and trade deficits followed at time T by a consumption bust, real depreciation, and trade surpluses.[7] What is the intuition behind the results? The fact that the nominal interest rate is lower during $[0, T)$ than afterward implies that the effective price of consumption is lower during $[0, T)$ than afterward. Hence—and for exactly the same reasons analyzed in chapter 3—consumers will engage in intertemporal consumption substitution by shifting consumption away from the relative expensive period (after T) toward the relatively cheap period, $[0, T)$. For the initial real exchange rate, nontradable goods also become relatively cheaper, and there is thus an excess demand for nontradable goods. Since the endowment of nontradables is fixed, however, the relative price (i.e., $1/e_t$) must increase to clear the market.

7.2.7 A Reinterpretation of the Results

As we did in chapter 3 for the case of a trade liberalization, we can reinterpret the results above for the permanent and temporary reduction in the rate of devaluation as applying to a situation in which the same policy announcement may have different degrees of credibility. As discussed in box 7.1, even though lack of credibility is hard to measure, it has undoubtedly been a perennial problem in developing countries.

Suppose that at time 0, policy makers announce a permanent reduction in the rate of devaluation. If the announcement is fully credible (i.e., if agents believe the government's announcement), then the economy will behave as in the permanent case analyzed above. Inflation will be stopped immediately with no output costs. As argued in chapter 13, this type of experiment can be taken to apply to the end of hyperinflations in which inflation has been reduced immediately with little or no real effects.

6. By "pre-shock," we mean just before $t = 0$.

7. Not surprisingly, the real effects of a temporary exchange rate based stabilization are the same that we encountered when we studied an anticipated fall in demand in chapter 4. We can in fact see this model as rationalizing changes in aggregate demand as a result of fluctuations in nominal interest rates. As exercise 1 at the end of this chapter shows, the same results obtain in a money-in-the-utility-function model if the cross derivative between consumption and real money balances is positive.

Box 7.1
How do we measure credibility in practice?

As discussed in section 7.2, the results of an unanticipated and temporary reduction in the rate of devaluation can be reinterpreted as arising from a policy announcement of a permanent stabilization that lacks credibility. Empirically the question is how to construct credibility measures and examine how they may have affected the behavior of various macroeconomic variables both on impact and as the program evolved. The task is rather difficult because expectations are not observable and therefore the credibility of a government plan needs to be quantified using some type of econometric technique.

Table 7.1 summarizes the results of three papers that analyze the role of expectations during specific inflation stabilization episodes. Baxter (1985) uses Bayesian econometric techniques applied to the Argentinean and Chilean exchange rate based stabilizations of the late 1970s and early 1980s.[a]

Table 7.1
Empirical work on the credibility of stabilization plans

Author(s)	Methodology	Episode(s)	Main results
Baxter (1985)	Bayesian estimation of bivariate system of domestic credit and government debt	Argentina and Chile exchange rate based stabilizations of the late 1970s and early 1980s	• Argentina: Credibility was 35 percent at the beginning of the reform program but fell dramatically 15 months later. • Chile: Credibility was initially low (around 20 percent) but drastically increased 3 years after the launching of the program. • Difference in outcomes of the two reforms may be explained by the fact that the Chilean reform was eventually credible, while the Argentinean reform was not.
Agenor and Taylor (1992)	VAR estimation of transitory component of parallel market premium. Kalman-filtering estimation of a time varying autoregressive process for inflation	Brazil's Cruzado stabilization plan, 1986	• Credibility was high at the beginning of the plan but fell rapidly in the following months. • Inflation inertia increased dramatically up until the collapse of the plan. • After the collapse of the plan, inflation inertia quickly reverted to its pre-program value, reflecting the explosive behavior of prices when credibility is low.
Ruge-Murcia (1995)	State space estimation of a trivariate system comprising inflation, interest rate, and government spending	Israel's stabilization plans of the mid-1980s	• Credibility was very low during the unsuccessful stabilization programs of 1982 and 1984. • Credibility increased almost to one following the implementation of the successful plan of July 1985. • Credibility significantly affected the short-run dynamics of inflation.

a. You may recall that we have already encountered these programs in chapter 4, box 4.2. See chapter 13 for further details on these programs and the Brazilian 1986 Cruzado plan and 1985 Israeli plan mentioned below.

Box 7.1
(continued)

Using a theoretical model, she finds two reform sustainability conditions associated to two key parameters of the model: (1) the "sustainable monetary policy condition" stating that the growth rate of domestic credit must be smaller than the international inflation rate and (2) the "sustainable fiscal policy condition" stating that the autoregressive coefficient of the equation governing the evolution of government debt must be smaller than one.[b] Since the policy regime—captured by the growth rate of domestic credit and the autoregressive component of government debt—is observable, credibility is defined as the probability assigned by agents to the event that the regime belongs to a "reform set" (i.e., the probability that monetary and fiscal policy will satisfy the sustainability conditions). Baxter estimates the likelihood functions of the two policy parameters and finds that in the Argentinean case the reform started out well, with a probability of sustainable reform of about 35 percent, but credibility sharply declined to a level close to zero about fifteen months after the beginning of the reform. In contrast, in the case of Chile the credibility measure remains low (around 20 percent) for the first three years of the reform but then climbs dramatically as the Central Bank cut lending to the government and caused a sharp decline in the money supply. The author also finds a correlation between the credibility measure and macroeconomic variables like inflation and interest rates, a finding that supports the hypothesis that agents look at both monetary and fiscal variables in assessing the likelihood that a "true" reform is taking place. Therefore the difference between the outcomes of the reforms (the Chilean one was more successful) may be explained, at least in part, by the fact that the Chilean reform was credible, while the Argentine reform was not.[c]

Agenor and Taylor (1992) explore an alternative procedure for estimating the size of credibility effects in the context of stabilization policies and apply their analysis to the Cruzado plan implemented in Brazil in 1986. Their approach is based on two assumptions. First, due to wage contracts and financial indexation, inflation follows a slow-moving process displaying considerable persistence. Second, the transitory component of the parallel market premium may be viewed as a proxy for the degree of credibility of a stabilization plan. The authors construct the transitory component of the parallel market premium as the residual of the first equation of a vector autoregression (VAR) of the parallel market premium and several macroeconomic variables included in the system with the purpose of capturing the behavior of macroeconomic fundamentals. Then they estimate an autoregressive process for inflation and let parameters vary with the credibility variable (the transitory component of the parallel market premium), the idea being that higher credibility should be associated with lower inflation inertia. The authors apply their methodology to the period covering the adoption and later abandonment of the Cruzado stabilization plan. They find that the credibility measure rose sharply at the beginning of the plan and fell rapidly in the following months. Inflation inertia, on the other hand, increased dramatically until the collapse of the plan after which it quickly returned to its preprogram value, reflecting the explosive behavior of prices when credibility is low.

Finally, Ruge-Murcia (1995) develops a rational expectations model of inflation where government expenditure follows an exogenous autoregressive process subject to discrete regime changes. The regimes are defined by whether the level of spending is or is not consistent with the rate of inflation

b. While a declining, but positive, rate of devaluation would allow for a higher rate of domestic credit growth, the idea behind the monetary policy condition is that agents would look at the condition required for long-run sustainability (when the rate of devaluation was supposed to be zero).

c. While the Chilean exchange rate based stabilization per se was abandoned in June 1982, the overall reform program—including the fiscal reforms—endures until today.

Box 7.1
(continued)

targeted by the government as part of a stabilization plan. In this context, credibility is measured by the agents' inferred probability that the joint observation of inflation, interest rates, and government spending is generated by the reformed expenditure regime. The approach is applied to the Israeli stabilization attempts of the mid-1980s. The author estimates the model using Hamilton's (1989) technique for regime switching models and reports a very low degree of credibility (captured by the estimated probability of reform) during the unsuccessful stabilization programs of 1982 and 1984. In contrast, for the successful program launched in July 1985, agents' inferred probability of reform increased almost to one between August and December 1985. The author also finds evidence that credibility significantly affects the short-run dynamics of inflation, explaining the speed of disinflation after July 1985.

Suppose instead that the public does not believe that the government will stick to the stabilization announcement. This lack of credibility is very likely to arise in countries with a history of failed stabilization attempts. When the latest finance minister goes on television and announces a major exchange rate based stabilization plan involving, say, a fixed exchange rate and swears that this parity will last for an eternity, the public—who has heard this before—will be rightly skeptical. To capture this lack of credibility in a simple way, suppose that the public expects that the government will abandon the stabilization plan at some time T in the future. Then all the real effects that we studied for the case of a temporary reduction in the devaluation rate would go through. We can thus reinterpret the exercise of a temporary reduction in the rate of devaluation as arising from a noncredible exchange rate based stabilization.[8] This case is particularly relevant for exchange rate based stabilization in chronic inflation countries, in which a history of failed stabilization attempts combined with the economy's ability to live with high inflation makes any attempt to stop inflation noncredible. In fact—and as we will see in detail in chapter 13—the model's predictions are fully consistent with the empirical regularities that have characterized exchange rate based stabilizations. In particular, exchange rate based stabilizations have resulted in pronounced booms in durable goods consumption, as documented in box 7.2.

7.2.8 Welfare Implications

What are the welfare implications of the above analysis? The analysis parallels that of a trade liberalization in chapter 3. A permanent exchange rate based stabilization has no welfare effects because the model does not incorporate any benefit of a lower *level* of inflation. Put differently, welfare in this model is the same for any constant level of the devaluation rate (and hence of the nominal interest rate). In contrast, a temporary exchange rate based stabilization is welfare

8. Proceeding as in chapter 3, it can be shown that the real effects at time T are independent of whether the government sticks to the plan (thus validating expectations) or discontinues it.

Box 7.2
Booms in durable goods consumption

We analyzed in section 7.2.6 how a temporary reduction in the rate of devaluation will lead to a consumption boom. The evidence on exchange rate based stabilization programs that we will review in chapter 13 is clearly consistent with such a theoretical prediction. In practice, the consumption boom observed in exchange rate based stabilizations has been particularly pronounced in durable goods consumption.[a] This is illustrated in figure 7.2 for five well-known stabilizations: the Southern

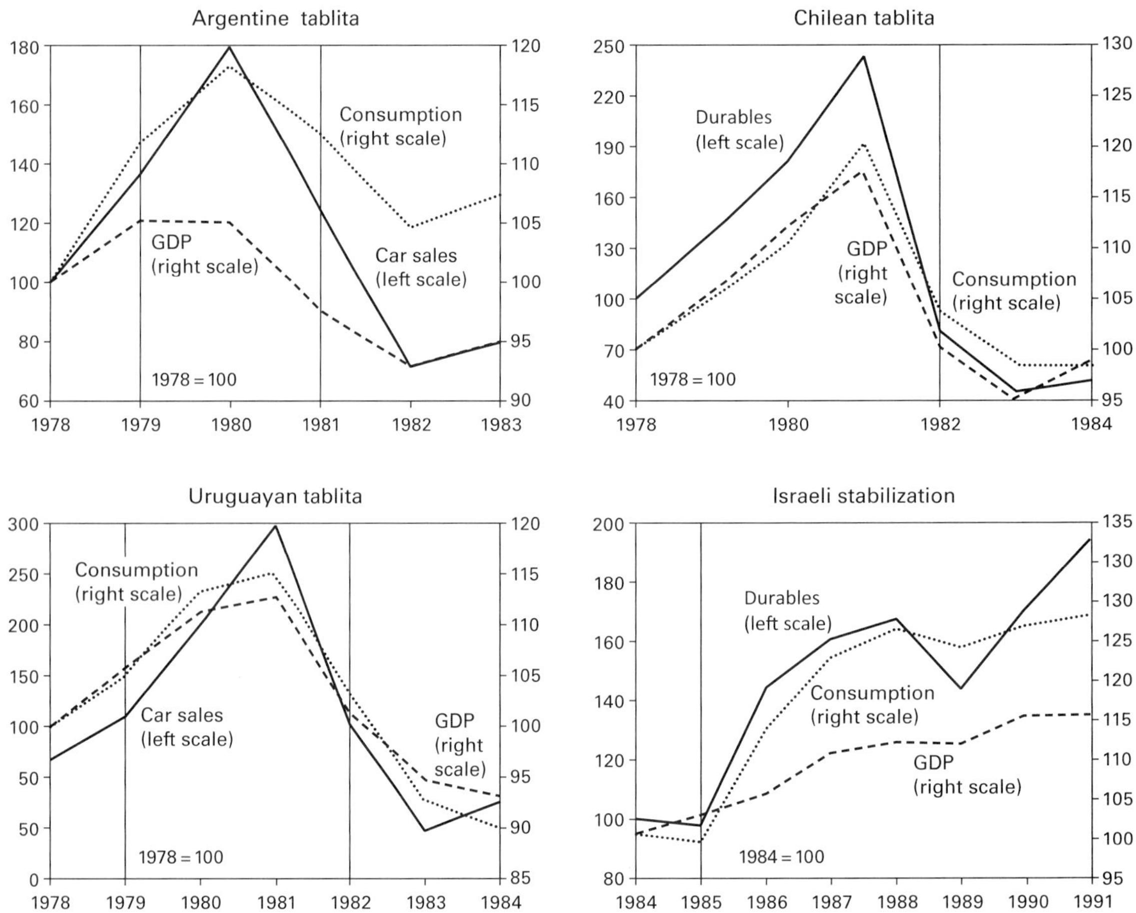

Figure 7.2
Consumption booms in exchange rate based stabilizations

a. See De Gregorio, Guidotti, and Végh (1998).

Box 7.2
(continued)

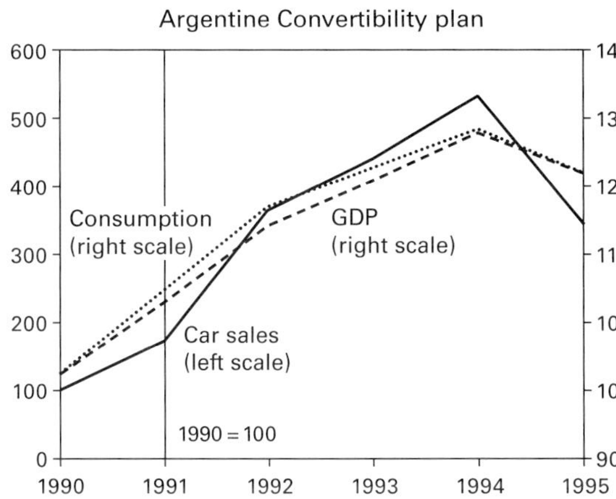

Source: De Gregorio, Guidotti, and Végh (1998)

Figure 7.2
(continued)

Cone tablitas of the late 1970s, the Israeli stabilization of 1985, and the Argentine Convertibility plan of 1991.[b] We can see that the boom in durable goods consumption was much more pronounced than in consumption in general. Car sales in Uruguay, for instance, tripled in just three years and increased fivefold in four years during the Argentine Convertibility plan.

While the theoretical model in this chapter has only included nondurable goods, we could easily generate a boom in durable goods following exercise 2 in chapter 3, which was based on Calvo (1988). If the purchase of durable goods were subject to a cash-in-advance constraint, then a boom in durable goods consumption would result from a temporary fall in the nominal interest rate due to intertemporal price speculation. An alternative interpretation of a possible effect of lower nominal interest rates on durable goods consumption is offered by Calvo and Végh (1999), based on the observation that, in many of these countries, purchases of durable goods were carried out by obtaining credit from the stores themselves in the form of constant monthly installments. In these circumstances it is easy to show that while the present discounted value of real installments does not depend on the level of the nominal interest rate, the path of real installments does. Specifically, the higher the nominal interest rate, the higher is the real value of the early installments. If consumers are liquidity-constrained, a reduction the nominal interest rate will thus lower the real value of the early installments triggering an increase in purchases of durable goods. This channel is certainly consistent with casual evidence that suggests a huge increase during these episodes in the sale of durable goods based on monthy installments. Yet another explanation is offered by De Gregorio, Guidotti, and Végh (1998) who show how a wealth effect associated with the implementation of an exchange rate based stabilization plan can lead consumers to anticipate purchases of durables goods and/or spend more in planned purchases, which results in a durables consumption boom.

b. For Argentina and Uruguay, durable goods consumption is proxied by car sales.

reducing because it introduces an intertemporal distortion. Hence, taken at face value, the model would have the uncomfortable implication that no stabilization attempt should ever be attempted!

Of course, the model ignores the fact that inflation stabilization plans are likely to bring about wealth effects through various channels (higher productivity, less time spent on financial engineering, and so forth). As shown in section 7.4, a simple way of incorporating a wealth effect of lower inflation and studying the resulting trade-off is by introducing money through a transactions costs technology. In that case a *permanent* exchange rate based stabilization will always be welfare improving. Whether a *temporary* program is welfare improving will depend on the relative strength of the intertemporal substitution effect and the wealth effect. The larger is the duration of the plan, the more likely it is that the wealth effect will dominate.

Another simple way of incorporating a wealth effect is to assume that the government uses the revenues from the inflation tax on unproductive government spending (think of the government simply throwing away into the sea the revenues from the inflation tax), a scenario analyzed in exercise 2 at the end of the chapter. Government spending is assumed to be endogenous and hence respond to available revenues. In this case a permanent exchange rate based stabilization will also be welfare improving because it leads to a permanently lower level of government spending. For the case of logarithmic preferences, a temporary exchange rate based stabilization will also raise welfare as the wealth effect dominates the intertemporal substitution effect.

7.3 Labor Supply

The model considered so far has assumed that there is a constant endowment path of both tradable and nontradable goods. The model therefore cannot explain a positive output response to an exchange rate based stabilization. We now consider an extension of the model which incorporates a consumption/leisure choice.[9] (For simplicity, the model now abstracts from nontradable goods.)

7.3.1 Household's Problem

Consider a one-good economy in which the representative household maximizes

$$\int_0^\infty u(c_t, \ell_t)\exp(-\beta t)dt, \tag{7.21}$$

where c_t and ℓ_t denotes consumption and leisure, respectively. The function $u(.)$ is assumed to be strictly increasing in both arguments and strictly concave:

$$u_c > 0, \quad u_\ell > 0, \quad u_{cc} < 0, \quad u_{cc}u_{\ell\ell} - u_{c\ell}^2 > 0.$$

9. See Roldos (1995, 1997) and Lahiri (2000) for further exploration of this channel.

We also assume that both goods are normal, which requires (as shown in chapter 4, appendix 4.8) that

$$u_\ell u_{c\ell} - u_c u_{\ell\ell} > 0, \tag{7.22}$$

$$u_c u_{\ell c} - u_\ell u_{cc} > 0. \tag{7.23}$$

Agents are endowed with one unit of time. Labor is thus $1 - \ell_t$. The production function is linear and given by

$$y_t = 1 - \ell_t. \tag{7.24}$$

The cash-in-advance constraint now takes the form

$$m_t = \alpha c_t. \tag{7.25}$$

The flow constraint is given by

$$\dot{a}_t = ra_t + y_t + \tau_t - c_t - i_t m_t. \tag{7.26}$$

Integrating forward and imposing the corresponding transversality condition, we obtain

$$a_0 + \int_0^\infty (y_t + \tau_t)\exp(-rt)dt = \int_0^\infty (c_t + i_t m_t)\exp(-rt)dt. \tag{7.27}$$

Substituting the production function (7.24) and the cash-in-advance constraint (7.25) into the intertemporal constraint (7.27), we obtain

$$a_0 + \int_0^\infty (1 - \ell_t + \tau_t)\exp(-rt)dt = \int_0^\infty (1 + \alpha i_t)c_t\exp(-rt)dt. \tag{7.28}$$

The representative consumer chooses $\{c_t, \ell_t\}_{t=0}^\infty$ to maximize (7.21) subject to the intertemporal constraint (7.28). In terms of the Lagrangian,

$$\begin{aligned}\mathcal{L} = &\int_0^\infty u(c_t, \ell_t)\exp(-\beta t)dt \\ &+ \lambda\left[a_0 + \int_0^\infty (1 - \ell_t + \tau_t)\exp(-rt)dt - \int_0^\infty (1 + \alpha i_t)c_t \exp(-rt)dt\right].\end{aligned}$$

First-order conditions imply that (assuming $\beta = r$):

$$u_c(c_t, \ell_t) = \lambda(1 + \alpha i_t), \tag{7.29}$$

$$u_\ell(c_t, \ell_t) = \lambda, \tag{7.30}$$

where λ is now the Lagrange multiplier associated with constraint (7.28).

Combining the two first-order conditions, we obtain

$$\frac{u_c(c_t, \ell_t)}{u_\ell(c_t, \ell_t)} = 1 + \alpha i_t. \tag{7.31}$$

The nominal interest rate now introduces an *intratemporal distortion* between consumption and leisure. It is a *distortion* because—as discussed in detail below—in an undistorted equilibrium, the relative price of consumption in terms of leisure should be equal to the marginal productivity of labor (which, in this model, is one). The distortion is *intratemporal* because it affects the contemporaneous choice between consumption and leisure.

7.3.2 Government

The government's constraint remains given by equations (7.9) and (7.10) with P_t in lieu of P_t^T.

7.3.3 Equilibrium Conditions

The interest parity condition, given by (7.11), continues to hold. Combining the consumer's and the government's flow constraints (given by equations 7.26 and 7.9, respectively), we obtain the economy's flow constraint:

$$\dot{k}_t = rk_t + 1 - \ell_t - c_t,$$

where $k_t (\equiv b_t + h_t)$ denotes the economy's total net foreign assets. The corresponding resource constraint is given by

$$k_0 + \int_0^\infty (1 - \ell_t)\exp(-rt)dt = \int_0^\infty c_t \exp(-rt)dt. \tag{7.32}$$

7.3.4 Perfect Foresight Equilibrium

Suppose that the foreign rate of inflation is constant. Let us characterize a perfect foresight equilibrium path for a constant path of the rate of devaluation, ε. From interest parity, the nominal interest rate will also be constant over time:

$$i = i^* + \varepsilon.$$

Due to the nonseparability of consumption and leisure, it is now a little bit more involved to show that consumption and leisure will also be constant over time. To this effect, totally differentiate first-order conditions (7.29) and (7.30) along a perfect foresight equilibrium path, taking into account that both i and λ are constant along such a path, to obtain[10]

$$u_{cc}dc_t + u_{c\ell}d\ell_t = 0,$$

$$u_{\ell c}dc_t + u_{\ell\ell}d\ell_t = 0.$$

Using the last equation to solve for $d\ell$ in terms of dc and substituting into the first equation, we obtain

$$dc_t\left(\frac{u_{cc}u_{\ell\ell} - u_{\ell c}^2}{u_{\ell\ell}}\right) = 0.$$

Since the term in parenthesis is negative (by strict concavity of the utility function, the numerator is positive and the denominator is negative), it must be the case that $dc_t = 0$ along a perfect foresight equilibrium path. Hence $d\ell_t = 0$.

The constant values of c_t and ℓ_t then satisfy condition (7.31):

$$\frac{u_c(c,\ell)}{u_\ell(c,\ell)} = 1 + \alpha i. \tag{7.33}$$

From the resource constraint (7.32), it follows that

$$c = rk_0 + 1 - \ell. \tag{7.34}$$

Equations (7.33) and (7.34) implicitly define c and ℓ as a function of rk_0 and i.

7.3.5 Permanent Reduction in Rate of Devaluation

Suppose that just before $t = 0$ the economy is in the stationary equilibrium described above. At $t = 0$, there is an unanticipated and permanent reduction in the devaluation rate from ε^H to ε^L (figure 7.3, panel a). In response, the nominal interest rate falls permanently as well (figure 7.3, panel b). Clearly, both consumption and leisure will be constant along the new perfect foresight equilibrium path as shown above for the initial perfect foresight path. To find out how the fall in the nominal interest rate affects consumption and leisure, totally differentiate equations (7.33) and (7.34) (rewritten as $1 - \ell - c = -rk_0$) with respect to c, ℓ, and i to obtain, in matrix form,

$$\begin{bmatrix} \frac{-(u_c u_{\ell c} - u_\ell u_{cc})}{u_\ell^2} & \frac{u_\ell u_{c\ell} \quad u_c u_{\ell\ell}}{u_\ell^2} \\ -1 & -1 \end{bmatrix}\begin{bmatrix} dc \\ d\ell \end{bmatrix} = \begin{bmatrix} \alpha \\ 0 \end{bmatrix} di.$$

10. To avoid notational clutter, we omit the arguments of $u(.)$.

Applying Cramer's rule, we obtain

$$\frac{dc}{di} = -\frac{\alpha}{\Delta} < 0, \tag{7.35}$$

$$\frac{d\ell}{di} = \frac{\alpha}{\Delta} > 0, \tag{7.36}$$

where

$$\Delta \equiv \frac{1}{u_\ell^2}\left(\underbrace{u_c u_{\ell c} - u_\ell u_{cc}}_{+} + \underbrace{u_\ell u_{c\ell} - u_c u_{\ell\ell}}_{+}\right) > 0.$$

The determinant Δ is positive—as indicated—due to the assumption of normality of c and ℓ (recall conditions 7.22 and 7.23). Hence, in response to a permanent reduction in the nominal interest rate, equations (7.35) and (7.36) tell us that consumption increases and leisure falls (i.e., output increases), as illustrated in figure 7.3, panels c and d, respectively. The trade balance and current account, of course, do not change (panels e and f).

In sum, a permanent reduction in the devaluation rate leads to a permanent increase in consumption and output. Intuitively, the corresponding fall in the nominal interest rate makes consumption more attractive in relation to leisure. Households thus consume more and work more.

7.3.6 Temporary Reduction in Rate of Devaluation

Suppose that just before $t = 0$ the economy is in the stationary equilibrium described above. Further suppose $u_{\ell c} < 0$.[11] At $t = 0$, there is an unanticipated and temporary reduction in the devaluation rate from ε^H to ε^L (figure 7.4, panel a). In light of the interest parity condition, the nominal interest rate follows the path depicted in figure 7.4, panel b.

We begin by characterizing the change in consumption and leisure at time T. To this effect, totally differentiate equations (7.29) and (7.30) at time T to obtain, in matrix form,

$$\begin{bmatrix} u_{cc} & u_{c\ell} \\ u_{\ell c} & u_{\ell\ell} \end{bmatrix}\begin{bmatrix} dc \\ d\ell \end{bmatrix} = \begin{bmatrix} \lambda\alpha \\ 0 \end{bmatrix} di.$$

Applying Cramer's rule, we obtain

$$\left.\frac{dc}{di}\right|_{t=T} = \frac{\lambda\alpha u_{\ell\ell}}{u_{cc}u_{\ell\ell} - u_{c\ell}^2} < 0, \tag{7.37}$$

$$\left.\frac{d\ell}{di}\right|_{t=T} = -\frac{\lambda\alpha u_{\ell c}}{u_{cc}u_{\ell\ell} - u_{c\ell}^2} > 0. \tag{7.38}$$

11. As will become clear below, the assumption that consumption and leisure are Edgeworth substitutes is critical to obtain a fall in ouput at time T. Exercise 3 at the end of this chapter examines the cases where $u_{\ell c} \geq 0$.

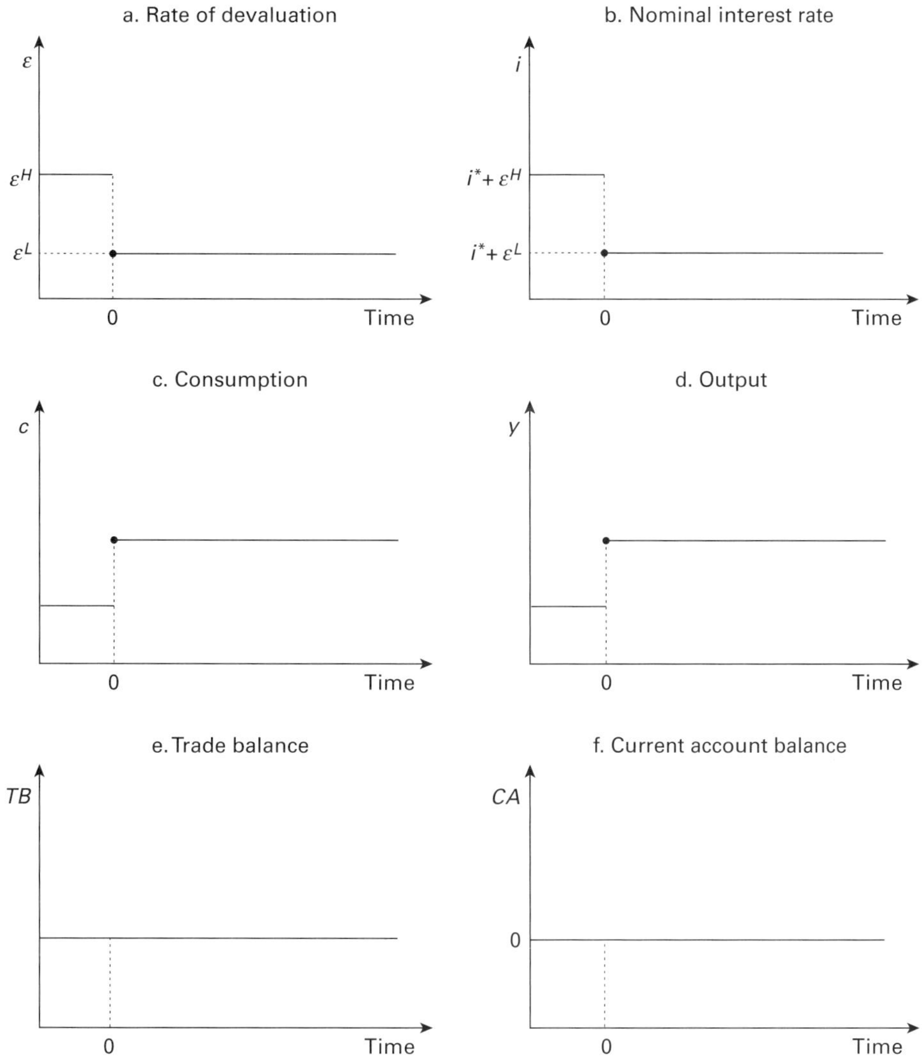

Figure 7.3
Permanent reduction in devaluation rate in model with labor supply

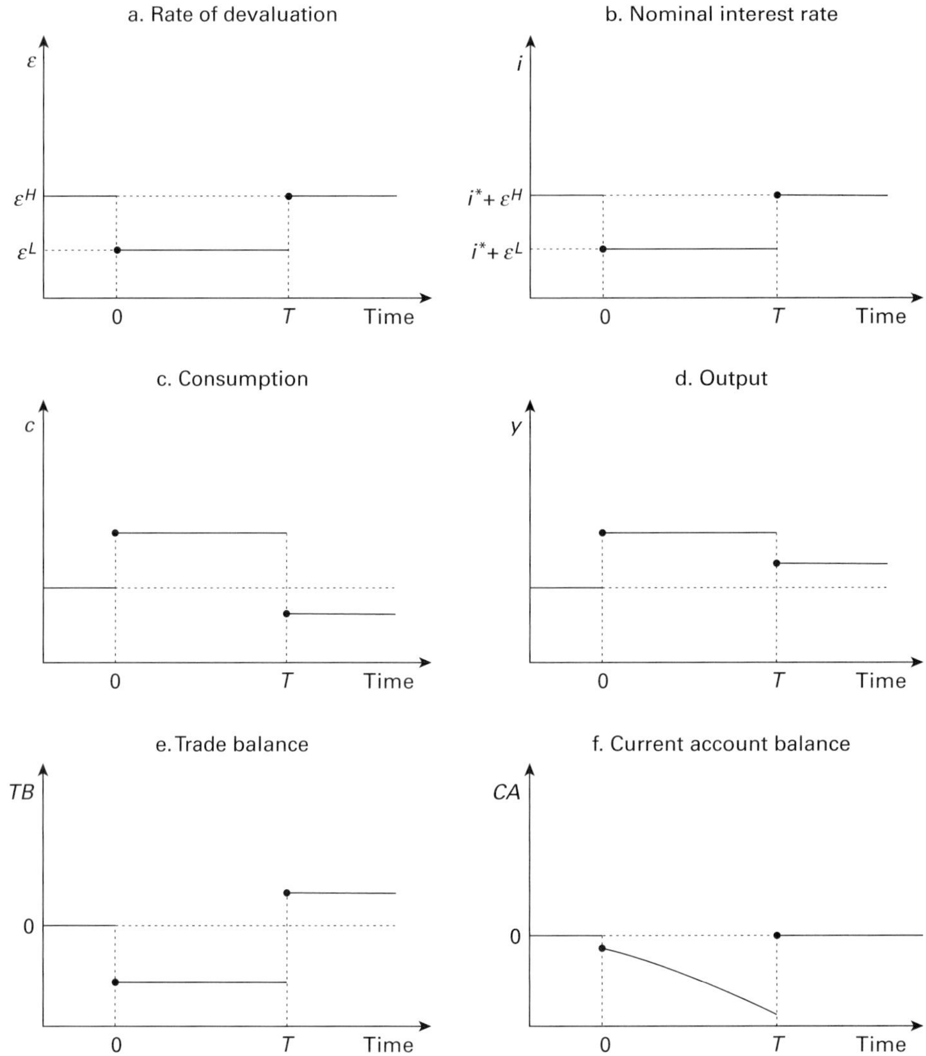

Figure 7.4
Temporary reduction in devaluation rate in model with labor supply

While consumption unambiguously falls at time T in response to the increase in the nominal interest rate, the change in leisure at time T depends on the sign of the cross-derivative between consumption and leisure. Under the assumption that $u_{\ell c} < 0$, the increase in the nominal interest rate at time T will lead to an increase in leisure (i.e., a reduction in labor). Hence at time T, both consumption and output fall.

As shown in appendix 7.7.2, the changes in consumption and leisure at time 0 can be found by contradiction. Consumption increases at time 0 while leisure falls (and hence output increases). Panels c and d in figure 7.4 illustrate the paths of consumption and output, respectively.[12]

What will happen to the trade balance? The behavior of the trade balance is, in principle, ambiguous. However, it is easy to establish that for the separable case (i.e., $u_{\ell c} = 0$), consumption increases by more than output on impact, which leads to a trade deficit.[13] Using a continuity argument, we infer that this will also be true for the case $u_{\ell c} < 0$, which is "close" to the separable case. For such cases the trade balance will go into deficit at time 0 (assuming initial net assets are zero), as illustrated in figure 7.4, panel e. The corresponding behavior of the current account is illustrated in figure 7.4, panel f.

In sum, under the assumption that $u_{\ell c} < 0$, a temporary reduction in the devaluation rate will lead to a boom–bust cycle in both consumption and output, which is consistent with the stylized facts associated with exchange rate based stabilization (see chapter 13).

7.3.7 Welfare Effects

The key idea is that unlike the model with no labor supply, a constant but positive nominal interest rate introduces a *static (i.e., intratemporal) distortion* in this model. To see this, notice that a planner would set the relative price between consumption and leisure equal to the marginal productivity of labor (which, given the linear production function 7.24, is one). In addition a nonconstant nominal interest rate would introduce the *intertemporal distortion* analyzed above. The first-best in this economy is therefore to have a constant nominal interest rate equal to zero.[14] This eliminates both the intratemporal and intertemporal distortions.

In light of this discussion, it should be clear that a permanent reduction in the rate of devaluation will always be welfare improving because it reduces the intratemporal distortion between consumption and leisure. A temporary stabilization, however, will have ambiguous welfare implications because the reduction in the intratemporal distortion during the period $[0, T)$—which is welfare improving—must be traded off against the intertemporal distortion introduced by a non constant path of the nominal interest rate (which is welfare reducing).

12. The magnitude of changes at T is also established in appendix 7.7.2.

13. Notice that in the separable case, labor goes up permanently at $t = 0$. To satisfy the intertemporal constraint, consumption must go up by more than output at $t = 0$ (for details, see exercise 3 at the end of this chapter).

14. In other words, the Friedman rule is optimal in this setting (see chapter 10 for further discussion on the optimality of the Friedman rule).

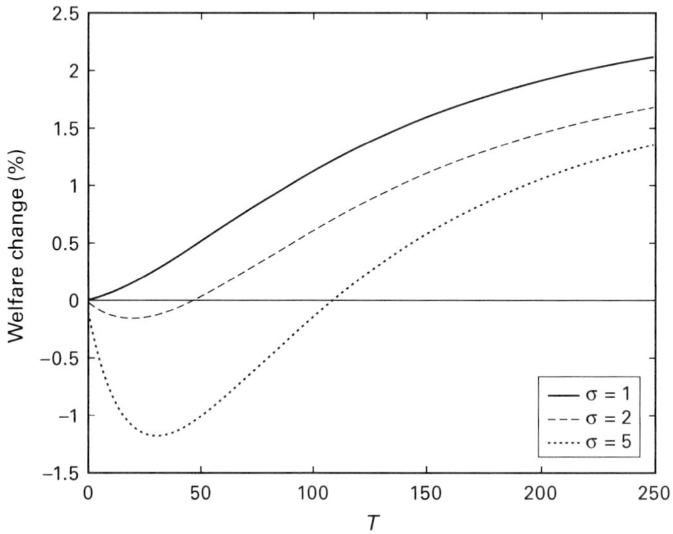

Figure 7.5
Welfare change as function of duration of stabilization

To illustrate these ambiguous welfare implications, consider the case in which preferences are given by the following CES specification:

$$u(c_t, \ell_t) = \frac{z_t^{1-1/\sigma} - 1}{1 - 1/\sigma}, \tag{7.39}$$

where z_t is a Cobb–Douglas composite given by

$$z_t = c_t^q \ell_t^{1-q}, \qquad 0 < q < 1, \tag{7.40}$$

and $\sigma (> 0)$ is the intertemporal elasticity of substitution.

Figure 7.5 plots the change in welfare (relative to an initial stationary equilibrium) resulting from a temporary stabilization as a function of T and for three different values of the intertemporal elasticity of substitution ($\sigma = 1$, 2, and 5).[15] The first observation is that, as we expected, the temporary stabilization is always welfare improving for large values of T. We knew this would be the case because, as analyzed above, a permanent stabilization is welfare improving due to the reduction in the intratemporal distortion. For small values of T, the welfare change depends on the value of σ. We can see that for the separable case (i.e., $\sigma = 1$), the temporary stabilization is always welfare improving as the wealth effect dominates the intertemporal substitution effect.[16]

15. The parameters underlying figure 7.5 are the following: $r = 0.01$, $\varepsilon^L = 0.01$, $\varepsilon = 0.9$, $\alpha = 0.5$, and $q = 0.5$.

16. Notice that, by L'Hôpital's rule (recall chapter 3, exercise 1), if $\sigma \to 1$, then $u(c_t, \ell_t) = q \log(c_t) + (1 - q) \log \ell_t$.

For $\sigma = 2$, however, the temporary stabilization is welfare reducing for low values of T, reflecting the larger intertemporal distortion. The negative welfare effects for small values of T are even larger for $\sigma = 5$, as the higher elasticity of substitution implies a larger intertemporal distortion.

In sum, when a labor/leisure choice is introduced into our model, the welfare implications of a temporary stabilization will depend on the relative strength of the intertemporal distortion effect and the wealth effect. For large values of T, however, the latter will always dominate.

7.4 A Transactions Costs Model

An alternative way of introducing money—which also generates a link between changes in the nominal interest rate and consumption—is the transactions costs model. Unlike the cash-in-advance model, the transactions costs model exhibits wealth effects resulting from changes in the nominal interest rate that have important implications from a welfare point of view.

7.4.1 Consumer's Problem

Let preferences be given by

$$\int_0^{\infty} \frac{c_t^{1-1/\sigma} - 1}{1 - 1/\sigma} \exp(-\beta t) dt, \tag{7.41}$$

where c_t is consumption of the only (tradable) good and $\sigma\,(> 0)$ denotes the intertemporal elasticity of substitution. Adopting these CES preferences will allow us to derive closed-form solutions that will nicely illustrate the strength of the intertemporal consumption substitution effects relative to the wealth effect.

Transacting is assumed to be a costly activity. Real money balances are assumed to reduce transactions costs, denoted by s_t, according to the following transactions technology:

$$s_t = c_t v\left(\frac{m_t}{c_t}\right), \qquad v'(.) \leq 0, v''(.) > 0. \tag{7.42}$$

The consumer's flow constraint is therefore given by

$$\dot{a}_t = r a_t + y + \tau_t - c_t - s_t - i_t m_t, \tag{7.43}$$

where y is the constant endowment of the good. After substituting (7.42) into (7.43), we can express the consumer's intertemporal constraint (imposing, of course, the standard transversality condition) as

$$a_0 + \frac{y}{r} + \int_0^{\infty} \tau_t \exp(-rt) dt = \int_0^{\infty} \left\{ c_t \left[1 + v\left(\frac{m_t}{c_t}\right) \right] + i_t m_t \right\} \exp(-rt) dt. \tag{7.44}$$

Consumers choose $\{c_t, m_t\}_{t=0}^{\infty}$ to maximize lifetime utility (7.41) subject to (7.44). The first-order conditions (assuming $\beta = r$) are given by

$$c_t^{-1/\sigma} = \lambda\left[1 + v\left(\frac{m_t}{c_t}\right) - \frac{m_t}{c_t} v'\left(\frac{m_t}{c_t}\right)\right], \tag{7.45}$$

$$-v'\left(\frac{m_t}{c_t}\right) = i_t.$$

The last equation implicitly defines a real money demand of the form

$$\frac{m_t}{c_t} = L(i_t), \qquad L'(i_t) < 0. \tag{7.46}$$

Substituting (7.46) into the RHS of (7.45), we can define the effective price of consumption as

$$p(i_t) \equiv 1 + v\left(L(i_t)\right) - L(i_t)v'\left(L(i_t)\right), \tag{7.47}$$

which is an increasing function of the nominal interest rate:

$$p'(i_t) = -L(i_t)v''\left(L(i_t)\right) L'(i_t) > 0.$$

Using (7.47), we can rewrite first-order condition (7.45) as

$$c_t^{-1/\sigma} = \lambda p(i_t), \tag{7.48}$$

which is, of course, reminiscent of first-order condition (7.6) in the cash-in-advance model.

7.4.2 Government

The government budget constraints continue to be given by equations (7.9) and (7.10) with P_t in lieu of P_t^T.

7.4.3 Equilibrium Conditions

Interest parity holds:

$$i_t = i_t^* + \varepsilon_t.$$

Combining the households' and the government's flow constraints—given by (7.43) and (7.9)—and using (7.42) and (7.46)—we obtain

$$\dot{k}_t = rk_t + y - c_t\left[1 + v(L(i_t))\right]. \tag{7.49}$$

As expected—since transactions costs constitute a social loss—they appear in the economy's flow constraint (i.e., the current account).

Combining the consumer's and the government's intertemporal constraints—given by equations (7.44) and (7.10), respectively—and using (7.42) and (7.46), we obtain

$$k_0 + \frac{y}{r} = \int_0^\infty \{c_t\,[1 + v(L(i_t))]\}\exp(-rt)dt. \tag{7.50}$$

7.4.4 Perfect Foresight Equilibrium

Let the foreign inflation rate, and hence the foreign nominal interest rate, be constant over time. Let us characterize the perfect foresight equilibrium path corresponding to a constant rate of devaluation, ε. By interest parity, the nominal interest rate will also be constant and equal to

$$i = i^* + \varepsilon.$$

The constancy of the nominal interest rate implies, by (7.47), that the effective price of consumption is also constant at a value given by $p(i)$. Then, by (7.48), consumption is also constant along a perfect foresight equilibrium path. Hence, taking into account the resource constraint (7.50), we have

$$c = \frac{rk_0 + y}{1 + v\,(L(i))}. \tag{7.51}$$

Finally, real money balances will be given by the money demand (7.46):

$$m = cL(i). \tag{7.52}$$

7.4.5 Permanent Reduction in the Devaluation Rate

Suppose that for $t < 0$ the economy is in the stationary equilibrium characterized above. At $t = 0$ there is an unanticipated and permanent reduction in the devaluation rate (figure 7.6, panel a). How will the economy respond?

By interest parity, the nominal interest rate falls permanently as well (panel b). As the consumer reoptimizes at $t = 0$, the expression for consumption given in (7.51) continues to be valid. Hence we infer that consumption will be higher in the new equilibrium path (panel c). By the same token, from (7.52), real money demand will be higher because of both higher consumption and a lower nominal interest rate (panel d).

Intuitively, the fall in the nominal interest rate reduces the opportunity cost of holding real money balances. Increased real money balances reduce transactions costs for any given level of consumption. The resulting wealth effect induces households to increase consumption.

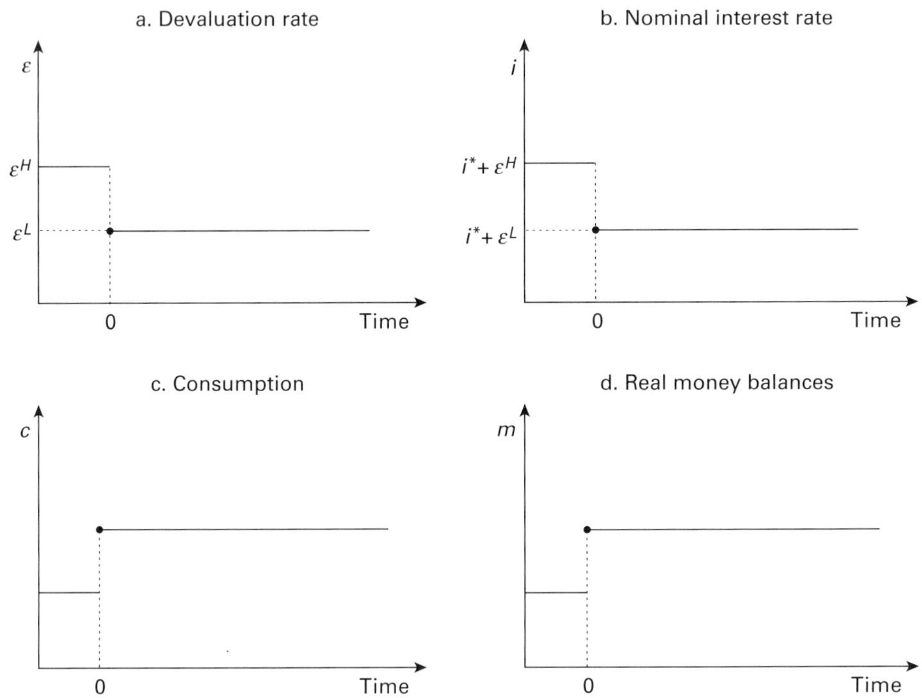

Figure 7.6
Transactions costs model: Permanent fall in devaluation rate

The higher path of consumption implies that lifetime utility is now higher. The economy's resources have increased because of the reduction in transactions costs. This benefit of lower inflation was not present in the cash-in-advance model.

7.4.6 Temporary Reduction in the Devaluation Rate

Suppose now that at $t = 0$ there is an unanticipated and temporary reduction in the devaluation rate from ε^H to ε^L (figure 7.7, panel a). By interest parity—and denoting by $i^1 (= i^* + \varepsilon^L)$ and $i^2 (= i^* + \varepsilon^H)$ the values of i between $[0, T)$ and $[T, \infty)$, respectively—the path of the nominal interest rate mimics the path of the devaluation rate (figure 7.7, panel b).

From the first-order condition (7.48), it follows that consumption between 0 and T (denoted by c^1) will be higher than after T (c^2). Notice, however, that the economy's resources are now higher since the temporary fall in the nominal interest rate will reduce transactions costs for a given level of consumption. Intuitively, we expect c^1 to be higher than consumption before the shock (c_{0^-}). We can in fact compute a reduced-form for c^1 to verify this conjecture. To this end, use (7.48) to solve for c_t and substitute in the resource constraint to solve for λ to obtain

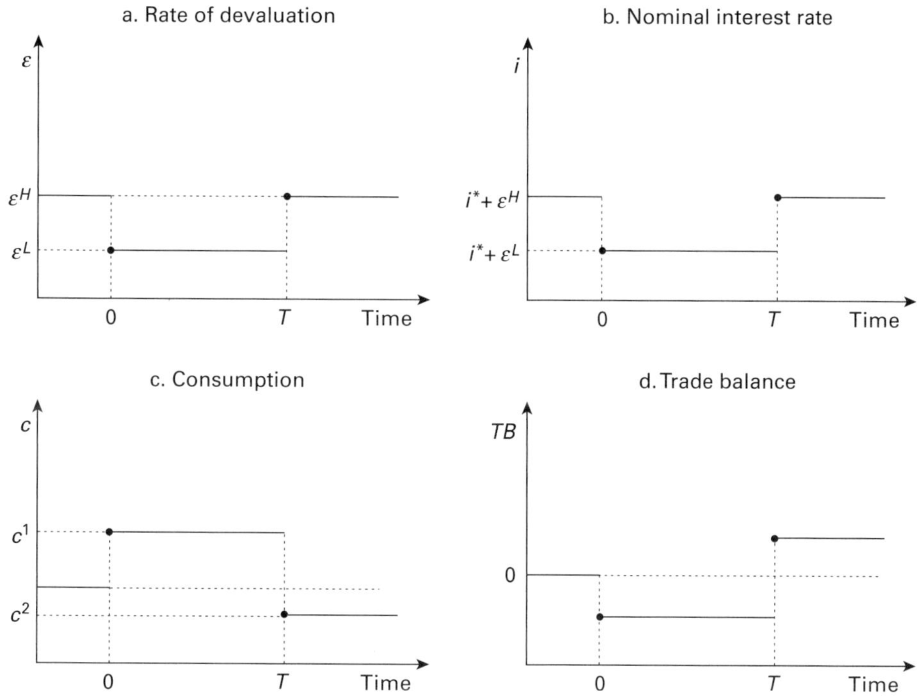

Figure 7.7
Transactions costs model: Temporary reduction in devaluation rate

$$\lambda^{\sigma} = \frac{\int_0^{\infty}\{1/[p(i_t)]^{\sigma}\}\{1 + v(L(i_t))\}\exp(-rt)dt}{k_0 + (y/r)}.$$

Now substitute back this expression into the first-order condition (7.48) to obtain

$$c_t = \frac{1}{[p(i_t)]^{\sigma}} \frac{k_0 + (y/r)}{\int_0^{\infty}\{1/[p(i_t)]^{\sigma}\}\{1 + v(L(i_t))\}\exp(-rt)dt}. \tag{7.53}$$

We can next use the path of the nominal interest rate depicted in figure 7.7, panel b, to compute c^1:

$$c^1 = \frac{c_{0^-}}{\left\{\left[1 + v(L(i^1))\right] / \left[1 + v(L(i^2))\right]\right\}(1 - e^{-rT}) + \left[p(i^1)/p(i^2)\right]^{\sigma} e^{-rT}} > c_{0^-},$$

where

$$c_{0^-} = \frac{rk_0 + y}{1 + v(L(i^2))}$$

is the value of consumption before the shock. As expected, $c^1 > c_{0^-}$ because both the intertemporal consumption substitution effect and the positive wealth effect call for higher consumption between 0 and T.

What about c^2? Using (7.53), we obtain

$$c^2 = \frac{c_{0^-}}{\{[1+v(L(i^1))]/[1+v(L(i^2))]\}[p(i^2)/p(i^1)]^{\sigma}(1-e^{-rT})+e^{-rT}} \gtreqless c_{0^-}. \tag{7.54}$$

As expected, the value of c^2 may be equal, higher, or lower than the pre-shock level of consumption, c_{0^-}. Intuitively, the two effects—intertemporal consumption substitution and wealth effect—affect c^2 in opposite directions. On the one hand, the intertemporal consumption substitution effect calls for a lower c^2 since c^2 has become more expensive relative to c^1. On the other hand, the positive wealth effect, stemming from reduced transactions costs, calls for a higher c^2. The relative strength of these two effects will determine the level of c^2 in comparison to c_{0^-}.

It is easy to see from (7.54) that a sufficient condition for $c^2 \geq c_{0^-}$ is that

$$\underbrace{\left[\frac{p(i^2)}{p(i^1)}\right]^{\sigma}}_{\text{Intertemporal substitution effect}} \leq \underbrace{\frac{1+v(L(i^2))}{1+v(L(i^1))}}_{\text{Wealth effect}},$$

where, as indicated, the LHS captures the intertemporal substitution effect while the RHS captures the wealth effect. (Notice that both sides of this inequality are greater than or equal to one.) As a particular case, if transactions costs were not a social cost (e.g., because these transactions costs were provided at no cost by some government agency), then the RHS would be equal to 1 and the inequality would never hold. In other words, there would be no wealth effect and we would be back to the cash-in-advance world in which a temporary fall in the nominal interest rate induces a pure intertemporal substitution effect. At the other extreme, if σ were close to zero (almost no intertemporal substitution), then the LHS would be close to one, which implies that the wealth effect would dominate and c^2 would be larger than c_{0^-}.

Figure 7.7, panel c, illustrates the path of consumption (assuming that the intertemporal substitution effect dominates). This implies that the trade balance follows the path illustrated in panel d (assuming initial net foreign assets equal to zero). To see this, refer to equation (7.50) and notice that if $c^2 < c_{0^-}$, then $c^2[1+v(L(i^2)] < (c_{0^-})[1+v(L(i^2)]$, and hence the trade balance is in surplus for $t \geq T$. Since the present value of output has not changed, the trade balance must be in deficit between time 0 and time T.

7.4.7 Welfare

Clearly, a permanent reduction in the devaluation rate increases welfare due to the wealth effect. What about a temporary fall in the devaluation rate? The welfare implications depend on the

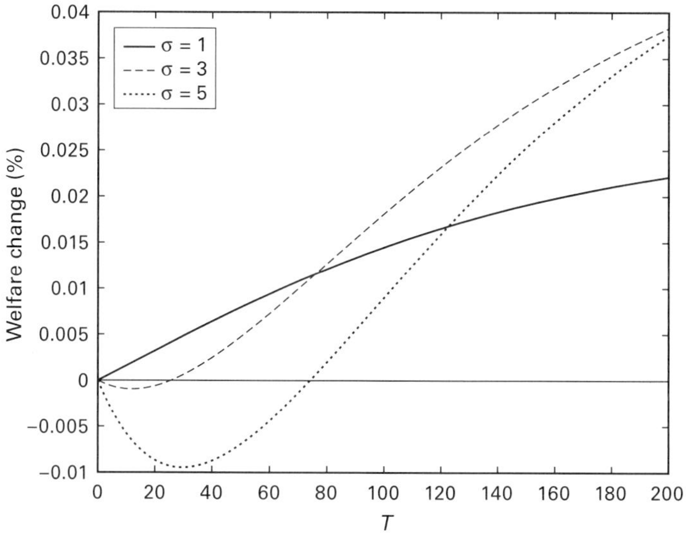

Figure 7.8
Welfare change as function of duration of stabilization

relative strength of the intertemporal consumption substitution effect and the wealth effect. To illustrate this, suppose that the transactions technology is given by

$$s_t = c_t\left[\left(\frac{m_t}{c_t}\right)^2 - \frac{m_t}{c_t} + \frac{1}{4}\right], \qquad \frac{m}{c} \le \frac{1}{2}. \tag{7.55}$$

Figure 7.8 depicts the change in welfare (relative to the initial stationary equilibrium) resulting from a temporary reduction in the devaluation rate as a function of T and for three different values of the intertemporal elasticity of substitution ($\sigma = 1$, 3, and 5).[17] As expected, for large values of T, the wealth effect dominates (in the limit, the reduction in the devaluation rate is permanent) and welfare increases regardless of the value of σ. For smaller values of T, however, whether or not the temporary stabilization is welfare improving depends on the value of σ. We can see in the figure that for $\sigma = 1$ (the logarithmic case), the temporary stabilization is always welfare improving. For $\sigma = 3$, the intertemporal distortion becomes larger and stabilization is welfare reducing for small values of T. For $\sigma = 5$, the fall in welfare for small values of T is, as expected, larger.

17. Parameter values are as follows: $k_0 = 0$, $r = 0.01$, $i^1 = 0.001$, $i^2 = 0.05$, and $y = 10$.

7.5 Monetary Policy under Flexible Exchange Rates

So far we have dealt with the case of predetermined exchange rates. We now study the same cash-in-advance model of section 7.2 for an economy operating under flexible exchange rates. We will see that a permanent change in the rate of monetary growth has no real effects but a temporary reduction will lead, as in the predetermined exchange rates case, to an initial consumption boom and real appreciation but with a different dynamic pattern.

To simplify the analysis, we consider a logarithmic version of the separable preferences given in (7.1):

$$\int_0^{\infty} [\log(c_t^T) + \log(c_t^N)]\exp(-\beta t)dt.$$

The rest of the model remains unchanged.

Under these logarithmic preferences, first-order conditions (7.6) and (7.7) reduce to

$$\frac{1}{c_t^T} = \lambda(1 + \alpha i_t), \tag{7.56}$$

$$\frac{1}{c_t^N} = \lambda\frac{(1 + \alpha i_t)}{e_t}. \tag{7.57}$$

Combining these two first-order conditions yields

$$\frac{c_t^N}{c_t^T} = e_t. \tag{7.58}$$

Substituting this expression into the cash-in-advance constraint (7.3), we obtain

$$m_t = 2\alpha c_t^T. \tag{7.59}$$

With these preliminary steps in place, we are ready to characterize a stationary perfect foresight equilibrium path.

7.5.1 Perfect Foresight Equilibrium Path

Let us characterize the perfect foresight equilibrium path for this economy for a constant rate of money growth, μ. We will first show that the nominal interest rate will be constant. To this effect, we will derive an unstable differential equation in the nominal interest rate.[18] Differentiating first-order condition (7.56) along a perfect foresight path (recall that λ is constant along such a path), we obtain

$$\frac{\dot{c}_t^T}{c_t^T} = -\frac{\alpha}{1+\alpha i_t}\dot{i}_t.$$

Since it follows from (7.59) that $\dot{m}_t/m_t = \dot{c}_t^T/c_t^T$, we can rewrite the last expression as

$$\frac{\dot{m}_t}{m_t} = -\frac{\alpha}{1+\alpha i_t}\dot{i}_t. \tag{7.60}$$

Recall that by definition, $m_t = M_t/E_t P_t^{T*}$. Hence

$$\frac{\dot{m}_t}{m_t} = \mu - \varepsilon_t - \pi^*. \tag{7.61}$$

Substituting (7.61) into (7.60) obtains

$$\dot{i}_t = \frac{1+\alpha i_t}{\alpha}(\varepsilon_t + \pi^* - \mu).$$

But, from the interest parity condition (equation 7.11) and the Fisher equation in the rest of the world ($i^* = r + \pi^*$), $\varepsilon_t + \pi^* = i_t - r$. Hence

$$\dot{i}_t = \frac{1+\alpha i_t}{\alpha}(i_t - r - \mu). \tag{7.62}$$

Linearizing this equation around the stationary value for the nominal interest rate (given by $r+\mu$), we can see that this an unstable differential equation. Formally,

$$\left.\frac{\partial \dot{i}_t}{\partial i_t}\right|_{i_t=r+\mu} = \frac{1+\alpha(r+\mu)}{\alpha} > 0$$

Hence, unless the nominal interest rate starts at the value $r+\mu$, it will diverge over time. We conclude that the only convergent perfect foresight equilibrium path is the one in which $i_t = r+\mu$ for all t. Then, from the interest parity condition (7.11), $\varepsilon = r + \mu - i^*$.

18. As exercise 4 at the end of the chapter shows, we could instead proceed as in chapter 5 and derive a differential equation in m_t, which would, of course, lead to the same results. In this case, however, deriving a differential equation in i_t is more convenient because it completely pins down the stationary value of the nominal interest rate. The differential equation in m_t would not, in and of itself, pin down the stationary value of m_t because the Lagrange multiplier, which in this case has not yet been determined, shows up.

Given that the nominal interest rate is constant along a perfect foresight equilibrium path—and so is, of course, λ—it follows from first-order condition (7.56) that consumption of tradables will also be constant along such a path. Hence, from the resource constraint (7.14),

$$c^T = rk_0 + y^T. \tag{7.63}$$

Since the endowment of nontradables is fixed, $c_t^N = y^N$ for all $t \geq 0$. From the static condition (7.58) and using (7.63), we infer that the real exchange rate will also be constant over time and given by

$$e = \frac{y^N}{rk_0 + y^T}.$$

Finally, from (7.15) and the fact that $\varepsilon = r + \mu - i^*$, we conclude that $\pi = \mu$. In other words, inflation of nontradable goods is completely pinned down by the rate of money growth.

7.5.2 Permanent Reduction in the Rate of Growth of Money Supply

Suppose that at time 0 there is an unanticipated and permanent reduction in the rate of money growth, μ. Clearly, differential equation (7.62) remains valid. The stationary value of the nominal interest rate falls. The nominal interest rate must adjust immediately to its lower stationary value for, if it did not, it would diverge over time. By interest parity, the rate of depreciation also falls immediately. Since i_t is still constant over time (though at a lower level), first-order condition (7.56) implies that c_t^T will be constant as well and given by (7.63). Clearly, consumption of nontradables and the real exchange rate are not affected either. In sum, a permanent reduction in the rate of monetary growth leads to an immediate fall in the nominal interest rate, the depreciation rate, and nontradable goods inflation without any real effects.

7.5.3 Temporary Reduction in Rate of Growth of Money Supply

Suppose now that starting from the stationary perfect foresight equilibrium characterized above, there is an unanticipated and temporary reduction in the rate of money growth from μ^H to μ^L (figure 7.9, panel a).

To figure out the path of the nominal interest rate, consider the differential equation for i_t given by (7.62). As always when dealing with a temporary change, we need to first check whether or not i_t will jump at time T. The first piece of information is that, from equation (7.59), we can infer that c_t^T will not jump at T (since M_t does not jump at T by assumption and E_t cannot jump at T because, if it did, it would give rise to infinite profit opportunities). Given that c_t^T does not jump at T, it follows from first-order condition (7.56) that i_t will not jump either at T. The second piece of information is that during $[0, T)$ the differential equation in i_t will be governed

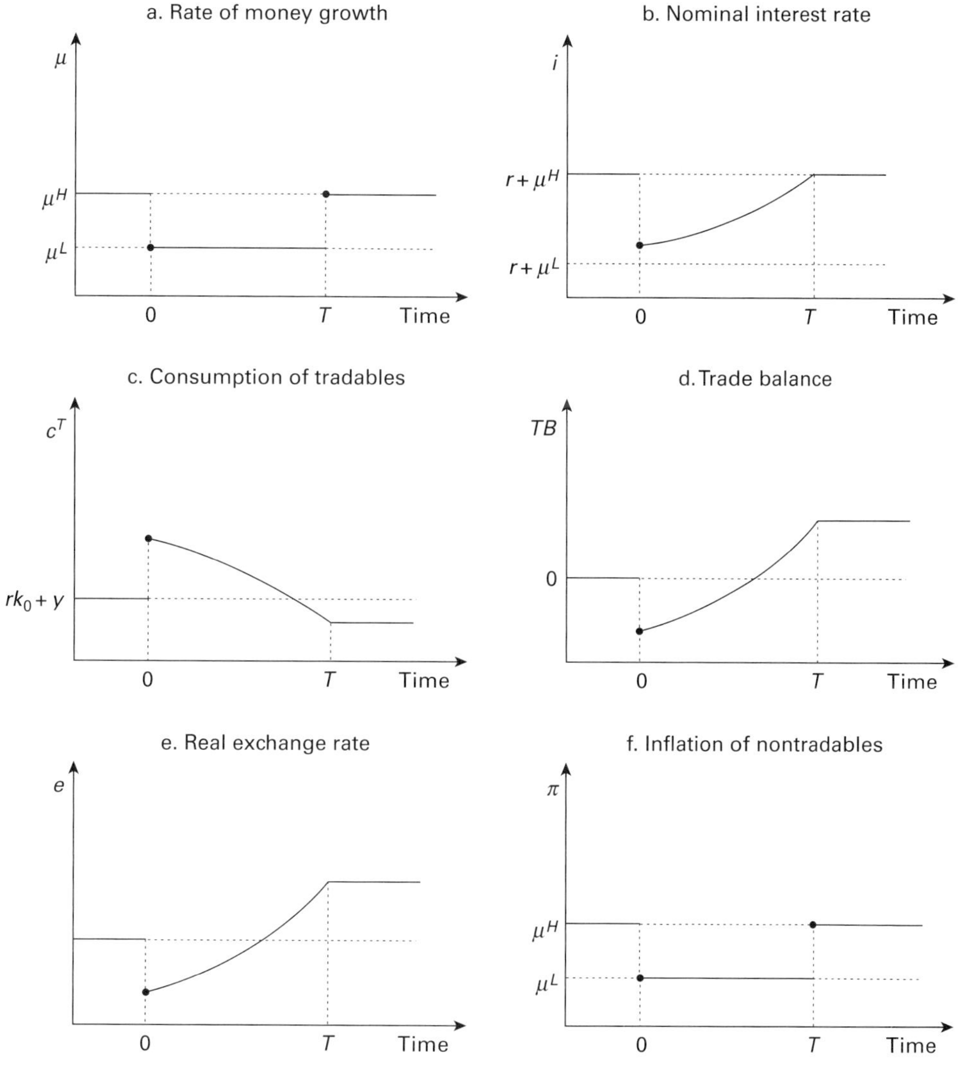

Figure 7.9
Temporary reduction in money growth rate

by the stationary state corresponding to $r + \mu^L$ in figure 7.9, panel b. Because this is an unstable differential equation, the nominal interest rate will be diverging from the value $r + \mu^L$. Given these two pieces of information, it follows that the only converging path is the one illustrated in figure 7.9, panel b. In other words, the nominal interest rate will be diverging from the value $r + \mu^L$ so as to hit the value $r + \mu^H$ precisely at time T.

From the path for the nominal interest rate and the first-order condition (7.56), we infer that consumption of tradables must be falling over time. Since the temporary reduction in μ_t does not affect the economy's resources, consumption of tradable goods must follow the path illustrated in figure 7.9, panel c. The corresponding path of the trade balance is shown in figure 7.9, panel d (assuming initial net foreign assets equal to zero). The path of the real exchange rate—illustrated in figure 7.9, panel e—then follows from equation (7.58) and the fact that consumption of nontradable goods is, of course, constant over time.

Finally, notice that the path of inflation of nontradable goods—illustrated in figure 7.9, panel f—follows the path of μ_t. To see this, rewrite (7.59) as (defining $n_t \equiv M_t/P_t^N$)

$$n_t = 2\alpha c_t^N,$$

which implies that since $c_t^N = y^N$ for all t, then $\dot{n}_t = 0$, and hence

$$\pi_t = \mu_t.$$

In sum, a temporary fall in money growth leads to a temporary consumption boom and a real appreciation as in the case of predetermined exchange rates.[19] The dynamics, however, are quite different, with consumption falling below its pre-shock level and the real exchange rate rising above its pre-shock level before T, in anticipation of the end of the stabilization. Exercise 5 at the end of this chapter shows that introducing a labor/leisure choice also leads to similar results as in the predetermined exchange rates case.[20]

7.6 Final Remarks

This chapter has analyzed models in which monetary and exchange rate policy have real effects because of the effects of the nominal interest rate on the path of consumption. This interaction has been modeled via a cash-in-advance constraint. In such a world the effective price of consumption includes the nominal interest rate because it represents the opportunity cost of holding the real money balances needed to purchase goods. A temporary reduction in the nominal interest rate

19. The same results would obtain if we introduced money in the utility function and assumed a positive cross-derivative; see exercise 6 at the end of this chapter.

20. In practice, many inflation stabilization programs reflect some fiscal reform that reduces the need for inflationary finance. Exercise 7 at the end of the chapter shows that if we view the fall in the rate of money growth as responding to a reduction in government spending, the same results would obtain.

thus makes today's consumption cheaper relative to tomorrow's and induces consumers to engage in intertemporal consumption substitution as in chapter 3. This is true regardless of the exchange rate regime under which the economy is operating.

In the absence of wealth effects, temporary changes in monetary or exchange rate policy will be welfare reducing because there is no intrinsic benefit of temporarily lower inflation. When labor supply is introduced into the picture, however, permanent reductions in either the rate of devaluation or the rate of money growth are welfare improving because they reduce the intratemporal distortion between consumption and leisure and lead to higher labor supply and thus output. Temporary reductions in the rate of devaluation or money supply growth can thus be welfare improving if the labor supply effect dominates the intertemporal distortion effect. In a similar vein, if money plays a productive role in the economy such as reducing transactions costs, then a temporary reduction in, say, the rate of devaluation may be welfare improving if the resulting wealth effect dominates the intertemporal distortion effect.

In the next chapter we will introduce yet another friction—sticky prices—that will cause monetary and exchange rate policy to have real effects.

7.7 Appendixes

7.7.1 The Cash-in-Advance Constraint in Continuous Time

This appendix—based on Feenstra (1985)—shows how the cash-in-advance constraint (7.3) can be viewed as a first-order approximation to the "true" cash-in-advance in continuous time.

For notational convenience, denote total consumption by c:

$$c \equiv c^T + \frac{c^N}{e}.$$

The counterpart in continuous time of a discrete-time cash-in-advance constraint would be

$$m_t = \int_t^{t+\alpha} c_s ds, \tag{7.64}$$

which says that at the beginning of the period $[t, t+\alpha]$, consumers are required to hold the real money balances necessary to purchase consumption during this period of length α.

Notice that the RHS of equation (7.64) is a function of the parameter α. Hence we can write

$$F(\alpha) \equiv \int_t^{t+\alpha} c_s ds. \tag{7.65}$$

Taking a first-order approximation of $F(\alpha)$ around $\alpha = 0$, we obtain

$$F(\alpha)|_{\alpha=0} \approx F(0) + F'(0)\alpha. \tag{7.66}$$

Clearly, $F(0) = 0$.

To find out $F'(0)$, we need to first differentiate the function $F(\alpha)$ with respect to α by applying Leibniz's rule.[21]

Applying Leibniz's rule to (7.65), we obtain (notice that the second and third terms of Leibniz's rule are equal to zero in this particular case)

$$F'(\alpha) = c_{t+\alpha}.$$

Evaluating this expression at $\alpha = 0$, we obtain

$$F'(0) = c_t.$$

Substituting this last expression into (7.66) and recalling that $F(0) = 0$, we get

$$F(\alpha)|_{\alpha=0} = \alpha c_t. \tag{7.67}$$

Hence, given (7.65) and (7.67), we can rewrite (7.64) as

$$m_t = \alpha c_t.$$

We conclude that the cash-in-advance constraint in the text (equation 7.3) can thus be viewed as a first-order approximation to the "true" cash-in-advance in continuous time given by (7.64).

7.7.2 Changes in Consumption and Leisure at $t = 0$

This appendix establishes the changes in consumption and leisure at time $t = 0$ that underlie figure 7.4, panels c and d. Recall that we have already established in the text that at time T leisure increases and consumption falls. Our intuition would tell us that, since the fall in i_t at time 0 makes consumption cheaper relative to leisure, we expect consumption to increase and leisure to fall at $t = 0$.

Our formal claim is therefore that leisure falls at $t = 0$. To prove it, we proceed by contradiction. In other words, we will assume that leisure either remains constant or increases and establish a contradiction.

1. Suppose that leisure does not change at $t = 0$. Since it goes up at time T, it follows that the present discounted value (PDV) of leisure increases or, which is the same, the PDV of output falls relative to its pre-shock value.

21. See appendix 1.7.1 for Leibniz's rule.

What about consumption? Consumption at T will be higher than before the shock. To show this, differentiate (7.31) with respect to c_t and ℓ_t, holding i_t constant to obtain

$$\left.\frac{dc_t}{d\ell_t}\right|_{\text{constant } i} = \frac{u_{c\ell}u_\ell - u_c u_{\ell\ell}}{u_c u_{\ell c} - u_{cc}u_\ell} > 0, \tag{7.68}$$

where the sign follows from the normality conditions, given by (7.22) and (7.23). Since ℓ_t for $t \geq T$ is higher than before the shock, so will c_t. This implies that consumption will go up at $t = 0$ and fall at time T to a value higher than before the shock. Hence the PDV value of consumption will be higher than before the shock, which is a contradiction since we have established that the PDV of output will be lower than before the shock.

2. Suppose now that leisure goes up at $t = 0$. Since it will also go up at time T, the PDV of leisure is higher, and then the PDV of output is lower than before the shock.

Since leisure from T onward is higher than before the shock, so will consumption, as follows from (7.68). This implies that consumption will go up at $t = 0$ and fall at time T to a value higher than before the shock. Hence the PDV value of consumption will be higher than before the shock, which is a contradiction since we have established that the PDV of output will be lower than before the shock. □

We have thus proved that consumption increases at $t = 0$ while leisure falls (i.e., output increases). As drawn in figure 7.4, panels c and d, from T onward, consumption is below its pre-shock value and output is above. This is not the only possible case, but consumption and leisure for T onward must satisfy condition (7.68) (which tells us that if, say, consumption is above its pre-shock value, leisure must also be above). Notice that by a continuity argument, the case depicted in figure 7.4 will be the one relevant for preferences with $u_{c\ell} < 0$, which are "close" to the separable case. We know this because we can easily show that for the separable case, labor goes up permanently at $t = 0$ and consumption increases at $t = 0$ and falls at time T *below* its pre-shock value.

Exercises

1. (Exchange rate based inflation stabilization with MIUF) This exercise shows that if money is introduced in the utility function and the cross-derivative between money and consumption is positive, the same results of a temporary exchange rate based stabilization with a cash-in-advance constraint derived in the text remain valid.

Consider the same economy analyzed in section 7.2 but with no nontradables and preferences given by

$$\int_0^\infty u(c_t, m_t)\exp(-\beta t)dt, \tag{7.69}$$

where c_t is consumption of a tradable good, m_t denotes real money balances, and $\beta(>0)$ is the rate of time preference. The utility function $u(c_t, m_t)$ is increasing in both arguments and strictly concave. Specifically, it satisfies

$$u_c > 0,\ u_m > 0,\ u_{cc} < 0,\ u_{mm} < 0,\ u_{cc}u_{mm} - u_{cm}^2 > 0. \tag{7.70}$$

(Notice that we have not assumed any particular sign for u_{cm}, so $u_{cm} \gtreqless 0$.) Naturally, the cash-in-advance constraint is dropped since we have introduced money in the utility function.

In addition, assume that both goods are normal, which implies that

$$u_m u_{cc} - u_c u_{mc} < 0,$$

$$u_c u_{mm} - u_m u_{cm} < 0.$$

The rest of the model (with no nontradables) remains unchanged.

In the context of this model:

a. Derive the first-order conditions. Show that they yield a standard money demand function.

b. Characterize a perfect foresight equilibrium path for a constant rate of devaluation.

c. Analyze the effects of an unanticipated and temporary exchange rate based stabilization. In particular, show how the results critically depend on the sign of u_{cm}.

d. Suppose that preferences are given by

$$u(c_t, m_t) = (c_t^{\alpha} + m_t^{\beta})^{1/\sigma}.$$

Show that u_{cm} is zero if $\sigma = 1$, positive if $\sigma < 1$ and negative if $\sigma > 1$.

2. (Exchange rate based inflation stabilization with fiscal implications) This exercise analyzes the case in which, instead of rebating the proceeds from the inflation tax and interest on reserves to the consumer, the government spends those proceeds (wasteful spending). We will see how in this case there is a wealth effect associated with either a permanent or temporary reduction in the devaluation rate.

The model is a one-good version of the cash-in-advance model of section 7.2. Unless otherwise noticed, the notation remains the same. Preferences are given by

$$\int_0^{\infty} \log(c_t)\exp(-\beta t)dt,$$

where c_t is consumption of the tradable good. Consumers' flow constraint takes the form

$$\dot{a}_t = ra_t + y - c_t - i_t m_t, \tag{7.71}$$

while the intertemporal constraint reads as

$$a_0 + \frac{y}{r} = \int_0^\infty (c_t + i_t m_t)\exp(-rt)dt.$$

The cash-in-advance constraint is given by

$$m_t = \alpha c_t.$$

The government's flow constraint is given by

$$\dot{h}_t = rh_t + \dot{m}_t + \varepsilon_t m_t - g_t,$$

where g denotes government spending. The economy's flow constraint is given by

$$\dot{k}_t = rk_t + y - c_t - g_t,$$

while the economy's resource constraint is given by

$$k_0 + \frac{y}{r} = \int_0^\infty (c_t + g_t)\exp(-rt)dt.$$

In the context of this model:

a. Characterize a perfect foresight equilibrium path for a constant path of the rate of devaluation.

b. Suppose that starting from the perfect foresight equilibrium path characterized above, there is an unanticipated and permanent reduction in the rate of devaluation. Derive the paths of all endogenous variables. What are the welfare implications?

c. Suppose that starting from the perfect foresight equilibrium path characterized above, there is an unanticipated and temporary reduction in the rate of devaluation. Derive the paths of all endogenous variables. What are the welfare implications?

3. (Temporary reduction in devaluation rate under alternative assumptions about the consumption–leisure cross-derivative) Consider the model with labor supply analyzed in section 7.3. In the case of a temporary reduction in the devaluation rate, we solved for the case in which $u_{c\ell} < 0$. You are asked to:

a. Solve for the separable case (i.e., $u_{c\ell} = 0$). In particular, show that labor rises permanently at $t = 0$ and that consumption rises at $t = 0$ and falls at time T below its pre-shock value. Discuss the intuition behind he results.

b. Solve for the case where $u_{c\ell} > 0$. In particular, show that consumption always rises at $t = 0$ whereas labor could either increase, remain the same, or fall.

4. (Alternative solution of flexible exchange rates model under a cash-in-advance constraint) Consider the flexible exchange rates model of section 7.5. Derive the perfect foresight path for a constant rate of money growth by deriving a differential equation in m_t, rather than in i_t as in the text.

5. (Flexible exchange rates model with labor/leisure choice) Consider the model of section 7.3 with preferences given by

$$\int_0^{\infty} [\log(c_t) + \log(\ell_t)] \exp(-\beta t) dt, \tag{7.72}$$

and operating under flexible exchange rates. In this context:

a. Analyze the effects of an unanticipated and permanent reduction in the rate of money growth.

b. Analyze the effects of an unanticipated and temporary reduction in the rate of money growth.

6. (Numerical solution of MIUF flexible exchange rates model). Consider the discrete-time, flexible exchange rates, MIUF model developed in an online appendix.[22] Perform the following numerical exercises using the corresponding MATLAB programs:

a. A temporary fall in the money growth rate for a value of $\sigma = 1$. (This is the separable case analyzed in chapter 5.)

b. A temporary fall in the money growth rate for a value of $\sigma = 0.5$.

c. Compute analytically U_{cz} and show how it depends on the value of σ. Explain intuitively why the sign of U_{cz} critically affects the response of c^T. What is the case that replicates the cash-in-advance results obtained in the text?

d. A temporary fall in y^T (for $\sigma = 1$).

e. A temporary fall in y^N (for $\sigma = 1$).

7. (Fiscal stabilization under flexible exchange rates) Consider the model of section 7.5 with only one (tradable) good. Suppose that there are no government transfers. The government must finance an exogenously given level of government spending, g_t, with inflationary finance (and the budget is balanced every period); formally,

$$g_t = \dot{m}_t + \varepsilon_t m_t.$$

(Note that while the rate of monetary growth will now be endogenous at any point in time and dictated by the need to finance g_t, the monetary authority still controls the *level* of the nominal money supply at each instant in time.)

22. Both this appendix and the MATLAB codes are available at the book's website.

In this context:

a. Analyze the effects of an unanticipated and permanent fall in g_t.

b. Analyze the effects of an unanticipated and temporary fall in g_t.

References

Agenor, Pierre Richard, and Mark Taylor. 1992. Testing for credibility effects. *IMF Staff Papers* 39 (3): 545–71.

Baxter, Marianne. 1985. The role of expectations in stabilization policy. *Journal of Monetary Economics* 15: 343–62.

Calvo, Guillermo A. 1986. Temporary stabilization: Predetermined exchange rates. *Journal of Political Economy* 94 (6): 1319–29.

Calvo, Guillermo A. 1988. Costly trade liberalizations: Durable goods and capital mobility. *IMF Staff Papers* 35 (3): 461–73.

Calvo, Guillermo A., and Carlos A. Végh. 1999. Inflation stabilization and BOP crises in developing countries. In John Taylor and Michael Woodford eds., *Handbook of Macroeconomics*, vol. c. Amsterdam: North-Holland, 1531–1614.

Clower, Robert W. 1967. A reconsideration of the microfoundations of monetary theory. *Western Economic Journal* 6 (1): 1–8.

De Gregorio, Jose, Pablo E. Guidotti, and Carlos A. Végh. 1998. Inflation stabilization and the consumption of durable goods. *Economic Journal* 108: 105–31.

Feenstra, Robert C. 1985. Anticipated devaluations, currency flight, and direct trade controls in a monetary economy. *American Economic Review* 75 (3): 386–401.

Lahiri, Amartya. 2000. Disinflation programs under policy uncertainty. *Journal of International Economics* 50 (2): 351–73.

Hamilton, James. 1989. A new approach to the economic analysis of nonstationary time series and the business cycle. *Econometrica* 57: 357–84.

Lucas, Robert E., Jr. 1982. Interest rates and currency prices in a two-country world. *Journal of Monetary Economics* 10 (3): 335–59.

Roldos, Jorge. 1995. Supply-side effects of disinflation programs. *IMF Staff Papers* 42 (1): 158–83.

Roldos, Jorge. 1997. On gradual disinflation, the real exchange rate, and the current account. *Journal of International Money and Finance* 16: 37–54.

Ruge-Murcia, Francisco. 1995. Credibility and changes in policy regime. *Journal of Political Economy* 103 (1): 176–208.

Svensson, Lars. 1985. Money and asset prices in a cash-in-advance economy. *Journal of Political Economy* 93 (5): 919–44.

8 Sticky Prices

8.1 Introduction

After studying the frictionless world of chapter 5 in which monetary and exchange rate policy had no effects on the real sector, chapters 6 and 7 introduced frictions into the model—no interest-bearing bonds in the case of chapter 6 and a link between nominal interest rates and consumption in the case of chapter 7—that allowed us to focus on some of the key channels whereby monetary and exchange rate policy affect the real economy in a small open economy. This chapter introduces the last—and perhaps best-known—friction in the model of chapter 5: sticky prices. This chapter's model can thus be viewed as an optimizing version of the Mundell–Fleming model.[1]

The main motivation for introducing sticky prices is that permanent changes in the level of the nominal money supply have no real effects in the context of the basic flexible-prices model introduced in chapter 5 and modified in chapters 6 and 7.[2] Once sticky prices come into the picture, however, monetary policy will have real effects and can thus potentially explain some key features of the real world. In particular, an expansion in the money supply will (1) lead to higher aggregate demand and hence output—since output is typically demand-determined in sticky-prices models, thus providing a possible explanation for business-cycle fluctuations; (2)

1. The Mundell–Fleming model is named after the contributions of Mundell (1963, 1964) and Fleming (1962). This was one of the two major contributions that earned Robert Mundell the 1999 Nobel Prize in Economics. The Mundell–Fleming model essentially refers to an open economy model with perfect capital mobility and sticky prices. Modern versions of the Mundell–Fleming model—couched in terms of Obstfeld and Rogoff's (1995) influential paper—have come to be known as "new open-economy macroeconomics." Since, conceptually, there is nothing "new" in these models, this label presumably refers to the fact that explicit microfoundations are introduced both on the demand and the supply side. In fact the title of Obtsfeld and Rogoff's paper ("Exchange rate dynamics redux")—"redux" meaning "redone" or "brought back"–pays homage to Dornbusch's 1976 paper titled "Expectations and exchange rate dynamics," his most famous paper and arguably the most influential paper in the Mundell–Fleming tradition (see Rogoff 2002). Rudi Dornbusch himself—a student of Robert Mundell at the University of Chicago—would have been a likely recipient of the Nobel Prize in Economics had it not been for his untimely death of cancer in 2002 at the age of 60.

2. There could be real effects, of course, if there is an endogenous labor/leisure choice or money were introduced through a transactions costs technology, but the adjustment would be instantaneous and there would be no dynamics.

generate a positive co-movement between nominal and real exchange rates, thus explaining a well-documented stylized fact in open economies (see Mussa 1986); and (3) possibly result in exchange rate overshooting, in the sense that the short-run increase in the nominal exchange rate is larger than in the long run, which could explain the high volatility of nominal exchange rates.

In contrast to flexible exchange rates, a permanent devaluation did have real effects in the world of chapter 6. Indeed, by reducing real money balances on impact, a devaluation led to a fall in consumption in order to generate the trade surpluses required to replenish real money balances over time. Under sticky prices, however, we will see that a devaluation leads to higher output and consumption. These contrasting results illustrate a long-standing debate in development macroeconomics regarding the real effects of a devaluation.

The chapter proceeds as follows. Section 8.2 lays out the groundwork by introducing sticky prices into the model of chapter 5. With the model in hand, section 8.3 analyzes the effects of monetary policy (i.e., permanent changes in the money supply and the rate of growth of the money supply). In particular, a permanent increase in the level of the money supply leads to an expansion in the nontradable goods sector, higher inflation, a real depreciation of the domestic currency, and a fall in the domestic real interest rate. Intuitively, the presence of sticky prices prevents the price index (which comprises the prices of both tradables and nontradable goods) to fully respond on impact to the increase in the money supply. As a result there is an incipient excess supply in the money market, which requires an increase in consumption of nontradable goods. This higher consumption is brought about by a fall in the relative price of nontradable goods (i.e., a real depreciation).

In section 8.4 we turn our attention to predetermined exchange rates. The main result is that under sticky prices, a devaluation is expansionary. Intuitively, sticky prices imply that on impact, a nominal devaluation leads to a real devaluation (i.e., a fall in the relative price of nontradable goods). As a result demand for nontradable goods increases, which results in an output expansion.

Finally, in section 8.5 we focus on one of the more influential results to come out of the Mundell–Fleming tradition: Dornbusch's (1976) exchange rate overshooting. In the model developed in section 8.3 the nominal exchange rate increases on impact by the same proportion as the money supply and hence by the same amount that it will increase in the long run. In other words, there is no overshooting in the sense of Dornbusch (1976). Section 8.5 studies a slightly more general version of the model of section 8.3, which, by generating a money demand with a consumption elasticity that is not necessarily equal to one, can yield both overshooting or undershooting of the nominal exchange rate. In fact, under the more relevant parameter configuration, the nominal exchange rate "overshoots" in the short run its long-run level. This is a remarkable result because it can explain short-run volatility in nominal exchange rates that goes beyond that of the "fundamentals" (in this case the money supply).

8.2 A Sticky-Prices Model

We now incorporate sticky prices into the model of chapter 5.[3] Sticky prices enter the picture through the supply side so there are no modifications of substance on the consumer side.

Consider a small open economy inhabited by a large number of identical, infinitely lived consumers, who are blessed with perfect foresight. The economy is perfectly integrated with the rest of the world in both goods and capital markets. There are two goods in this world (one tradable and the other nontradable, both nonstorable). The law of one price holds for the tradable good and the foreign price of the tradable good is assumed to be one; hence $P_t^T = E_t$, where P_t^T is the domestic nominal price of the tradable good and E_t is the nominal exchange rate (in domestic currency per unit of foreign currency). The economy can borrow/lend at a constant world real interest rate, r. As in chapter 5, money is introduced in the utility function.

8.2.1 Consumers

The only two minor modifications to the consumer side of chapter 5 are the adoption of logarithmic preferences and the introduction of a nontradable good. Preferences are thus given by

$$\int_0^\infty \left[\log(c_t^T) + \log(c_t^N) + \log(z_t)\right]\exp(-\beta t)dt, \tag{8.1}$$

where c_t^T and c_t^N denote consumption of tradable and nontradable goods, respectively, and z_t denotes real money balances in terms of the price index, defined as M_t/P_t, where M_t are nominal money balances and P_t is given by[4]

$$P_t \equiv \sqrt{P_t^T P_t^N}. \tag{8.2}$$

Let $a_t(\equiv m_t + b_t)$ denote real financial assets in terms of tradable goods, where b_t denotes net foreign bonds and $m_t(\equiv M_t/E_t)$ denotes real money balances in terms of tradable goods. The consumer's flow constraint is then given by

$$\dot{a}_t = ra_t + y_t^T + \frac{y_t^N}{e_t} + \tau_t - c_t^T - \frac{c_t^N}{e_t} - i_t\frac{z_t}{\sqrt{e_t}}, \tag{8.3}$$

3. Here we follow Calvo and Végh (1993). A similar model—but in discrete time and with a more refined supply side—can be found in the appendix of Obtsfeld and Rogoff's (1995) paper. The short-run dynamics behind the two models—including the conditions for overshooting/undershooting examined in section 8.5—are the same because both models assume that output is demand-determined.

4. This price index corresponds to the minimum nominal expenditure required to achieve a given level of utility; see appendix 6.7.3 in chapter 6 for the derivation.

where y_t^T and y_t^N denote output of tradable and nontradable goods, respectively, e_t ($\equiv P_t^T/P_t^N$) is the real exchange rate, i_t is the nominal interest rate, τ_t are lump-sum transfers from the government, and r is the constant world real interest rate. To understand the last term on the RHS of constraint (8.3), notice that since we continue to use tradable goods as the numéraire, the opportunity cost of holding real money balances, given by $i_t(M_t/E_t)$, can be expressed as $i_t(M_t/P_t)(P_t/E_t)$. After taking into account (8.2), the definition of the real exchange rate, and that $P_t^T = E_t$, we can rewrite this opportunity cost as $i_t z_t/\sqrt{e_t}$.

Integrating (8.3) and imposing the appropriate transversality condition, we obtain

$$a_0 + \int_0^\infty \left(y_t^T + \frac{y_t^N}{e_t} + \tau_t\right)\exp(-rt)dt = \int_0^\infty \left(c_t^T + \frac{c_t^N}{e_t} + i_t\frac{z_t}{\sqrt{e_t}}\right)\exp(-rt)dt. \tag{8.4}$$

The consumer chooses c_t^T, c_t^N, and z_t to maximize (8.1) subject to the intertemporal constraint (8.4). In terms of the Lagrangian,

$$\begin{aligned}\mathcal{L} = &\int_0^\infty [\log(c_t^T) + \log(c_t^N) + \log(z_t)]\exp(-\beta t)dt\\ &+ \lambda\left[a_0 + \int_0^\infty \left(y_t^T + \frac{y_t^N}{e_t} + \tau_t\right)\exp(-rt)dt - \int_0^\infty \left(c_t^T + \frac{c_t^N}{e_t} + i_t\frac{z_t}{\sqrt{e_t}}\right)\exp(-rt)dt\right].\end{aligned}$$

The first-order conditions with respect to c_t^T, c_t^N, and z_t are given, respectively, by (assuming, as usual, that $\beta = r$)

$$\frac{1}{c_t^T} = \lambda, \tag{8.5}$$

$$\frac{1}{c_t^N} = \frac{\lambda}{e_t}, \tag{8.6}$$

$$\frac{1}{z_t} = \lambda\frac{i_t}{\sqrt{e_t}}. \tag{8.7}$$

Combining (8.5) and (8.6), we obtain the condition

$$\frac{c_t^N}{c_t^T} = e_t. \tag{8.8}$$

This condition should, of course, be familiar from chapter 4 and says that at an optimum, the marginal rate of substitution between tradables and nontradables equals the relative price.

To obtain the money demand, combine (8.6) and (8.7) to obtain

$$z_t = \frac{c_t^N}{\sqrt{e_t}i_t}. \tag{8.9}$$

The demand for real money balances in terms of the price index, z_t, depends positively on nontradable goods expenditure expressed in terms of the price index, given by $c_t^N P_t^N / P_t = c_t^N / \sqrt{e_t}$, and negatively on the nominal interest rate.

For further reference, let us also derive the money demands in terms of tradable goods and nontradable goods. By combining (8.5) and (8.7), we obtain the demand for real money balances in terms of tradable goods:

$$m_t = \frac{c_t^T}{i_t}, \tag{8.10}$$

which is, of course, familiar from previous chapters.

Finally, to derive the money demand in terms of nontradable goods, notice that $z_t \sqrt{e_t} = M_t / P_t^N$ and rewrite (8.9) as

$$n_t = \frac{c_t^N}{i_t}, \tag{8.11}$$

where $n_t \equiv M_t / P_t^N$. The usefulness of defining a money demand in terms of nontradable goods will become apparent below.

8.2.2 Supply Side

The supply of tradable goods is assumed to be constant over time and equal to y^T. The major departure from the frictionless world of chapter 5 is that prices in the nontradable goods sector (P_t^N) are assumed to be sticky (i.e., they cannot change at any given point in time but can, of course, change over time).[5] Since prices are given at any point in time, they will not be able to adjust to clear the market in response to shocks that may lead to excess supply or demand of nontradable goods. Instead, we will assume that quantities adjust to clear the market for nontradable goods. More specifically, we will assume that output of nontradable goods is *demand-determined* and hence supply always adjusts to demand.

Formally, sticky prices are introduced into the model via Calvo's (1983) staggered prices formulation, which is a continuous-time version of overlapping contracts models à la Fischer (1977)–Taylor (1979, 1980). In this formulation the rate of change of the inflation rate of nontradable goods is a *negative* function of excess aggregate demand:

$$\dot{\pi}_t = -\theta(y_t^N - y_f^N), \qquad \theta > 0, \tag{8.12}$$

where $\pi_t (\equiv \dot{P}_t^N / P_t^N)$ is the inflation rate of nontradables, y_t^N is aggregate demand, y_f^N is the "full-employment" level of output, and θ is a positive parameter. In this formulation the price

5. How sticky are prices in practice? Box 8.1 reviews the available empirical evidence.

Box 8.1
How sticky are prices?

As mentioned in the introduction, price stickiness is by far the most common friction used in models that study the real effects of monetary and exchange rate policies. Many closed and open economy models assume the existence of a large number of differentiated goods and introduce price stickiness à la Calvo (1983) so that at every point in time there is a fraction of firms unable to change their price. But how sticky are prices in practice? Empirically, price stickiness is typically measured by analyzing time series for prices of different goods, estimating the frequency of price changes for each series, and aggregating the results by appropriately weighting each price in order to obtain an estimate of the average time between price changes for different categories of goods.

Early empirical work measuring the frequency of price changes in retail and wholesale prices established that many prices often go unchanged for many months. However, these estimates were usually based on a relatively narrow sample of goods (e.g., see Carlton 1986; Cecchetti 1986; Kashyap 1995; Levy et al. 1997; Blinder et al. 1999). In recent years the availability of richer datasets has allowed researchers to come up with a much clearer picture of the behavior of individual prices. In an influential paper Bils and Klenow (2004) examined the frequency of price changes for 350 categories of goods and services covering about 70 percent of the US Consumer Price Index (CPI). Surprisingly, they found a median time between price changes of 4.3 to 5.5 months, which is well below previous estimates. They also found a very large degree of heterogeneity in the behavior of price changes across goods.

More recently Nakamura and Steinsson (2008), Klenow and Kryvtsov (2008), and Klenow and Malin (2010) have also studied the CPI but using datasets that allowed them to differentiate between regular price changes and those related to temporary price sales, finding that the inclusion or exclusion of price sales has sizable effects on the estimated frequency of price changes. For example, Nakamura and Steinsson (2008) report a median duration of price changes between 4.4 and 4.6 months when sale-related prices are included in the data, and a median duration between 8 and 11 months when excluded. By now, many studies have applied approaches similar to Bils and Klenow's to the analysis of the frequency of price changes in other countries, as reported in table 8.1.

Table 8.1
Monthly mean duration of CPI price changes

		Mean duration*	
Country	Author(s)		Excluding sales
Austria	Baumgartner et al. (2005)	6.1	—
Belgium	Aucremanne and Dhyne (2004)	5.4	—
Brazil	Barros et al. (2009)	2.1	—
	Gouvea (2007)	2.2	—
Chile	Medina, Rappoport, and Soto (2007)	1.6	—
Denmark	Hansen and Hansen (2006)	5.3	—
Euro area	Dhyne et al. (2006)	6.1	—
Finland	Vilmunen and Laakkonen (2005)	5.5	—
France	Baudry et al. (2007)	4.8	—

Box 8.1
(continued)

Table 8.1
(continued)

Country	Author(s)	Mean duration*	
			Excluding sales
Germany	Hoffmann and Kurz-Kim (2006)	8.3	—
Hungary	Gabriel and Reiff (2010)	6.1	—
Israel	Baharad and Eden (2004)	3.6	—
Italy	Fabiani et al. (2006)	9.5	—
Japan	Saita et al. (2006)	3.8	—
Luxembourg	Lünnemann and Mathä (2005)	5.4	—
Mexico	Gagnon (2009)	2.9	—
Netherland	Jonker, Folkertsma, and Blijenberg (2004)	5.5	—
Norway	Wulfsberg (2009)	4.0	4.2
Portugal	Dias, Dias, and Neves (2004)	4.0	—
Sierra Leone	Kovanen (2006)	1.4	—
Slovakia	Coricelli and Horváth (2010)	2.4	—
South Africa	Creamer and Rankin (2008)	5.7	—
Spain	Álvarez and Hernando (2006)	6.2	—
United Kingdom	Bunn and Ellis (2009)	4.7	6.2
United States	Bils and Klenow (2004)	3.3	—
	Klenow and Kryvtsov (2008)	2.2	2.8
	Nakamura and Steinsson (2008)	3.2	4.2

Source: Klenow and Malin (2010).
* Klenow and Malin report the frequency of price changes. The duration is computed as $-1/\ln(1-x)$, where x $(0 < x < 1)$ is the frequency.

The availability of scanner data has enabled researchers to further probe into the issue of price stickiness. For example, on the one hand, using scanner data from a large grocery store chain in Chicago, Midrigan (2011) reports the presence of many small and short-lived price changes and uses this as a motivation to construct a menu cost model where firms face economies of scale when adjusting their prices. Eichenbaum, Jaimovich, and Rebelo (2011), on the other hand, use scanner data from a large US retailer and find that nominal rigidities take the form of inertia in reference prices, with weekly prices fluctuating around reference values that tend to remain constant over extended periods of time.[a] A newer and equally promising source of information on high-frequency price movements is scraped online data (data extracted from internet websites).[b]

a. A reference price is defined as the most common price in a given time window. Eichenbaum, Jaimovich, and Rebelo (2011) use a quarter.
b. Using scraped data for Argentina, Brazil, Chile, and Colombia, Cavallo (2010) finds that the distributions of the size of price changes in these countries are bimodal, that hazard functions are upward-sloping, and that there is strong daily price synchronization within narrow categories of goods, suggesting that strategic complementarities play an important role in price-setting decisions.

level is sticky (i.e., it is predetermined at each instant in time), but the inflation rate is fully flexible because it is a forward-looking variable.[6] As shown in appendix 8.8.1, equation (8.12) can be derived by assuming that firms set prices in a nonsynchronous manner taking into account the future path of aggregate demand and the average price level prevailing in the economy.

Intuitively, think of firms as being able to change their individual prices only if they receive some random signal. In this context suppose that there is an increase in aggregate demand. Then some firms—those that do receive the random signal—will be able to change their individual price (and hence inflation will rise). Most firms, however, will not be able to change prices, and hence the price level itself will not change. Next instant, there will be some firms that could not change their prices before that will be able to do so. But since the random signal follows an exponential distribution, the number of firms changing prices will be smaller than those that changed prices immediately after aggregate demand went up. Hence the inflation rate will rise by less (relative to the pre-shock situation) than before, which explains why the rate of change of inflation falls over time.

8.2.3 Government

The government is unchanged relative to chapter 5. Its flow constraint is therefore given by

$$\dot{h}_t = rh_t + \dot{m}_t + \varepsilon_t m_t - \tau_t, \tag{8.13}$$

where h_t denotes the level of international reserves and ε_t is the rate of depreciation/devaluation. The corresponding intertemporal constraint is

$$h_0 + \int_0^\infty (\dot{m}_t + \varepsilon_t m_t)\ \exp(-rt)dt = \int_0^\infty \tau_t \exp(-rt)dt. \tag{8.14}$$

8.2.4 Equilibrium Conditions

Since perfect capital mobility prevails, the interest parity condition holds:

$$i_t = r + \varepsilon_t. \tag{8.15}$$

Equilibrium in the nontradable goods market requires that

$$c_t^N = y_t^N. \tag{8.16}$$

6. If this is the first time that you encounter Calvo's (1983) staggered-prices formulation, you may be somewhat surprised to see that the change in the rate of inflation is a *negative* function of excess aggregate demand. This, however, makes perfect sense in light of the intuition given below. The key is that in this setup the inflation rate itself is fully flexible. If the inflation rate were sticky, then one would need to assume that the change in the inflation rate is a *positive* function of excess aggregate demand for the problem to be well-defined (see chapter 12, section 12.4).

Recall that, in the current setup, output of nontradable goods is demand-determined, so "equilibrium" in the nontradable goods market holds by construction.

By definition, $e_t = E_t/P_t^N$. Hence

$$\frac{\dot{e}_t}{e_t} = \varepsilon_t - \pi_t. \tag{8.17}$$

This dynamic equation simply states that if tradable goods inflation (given by ε_t) is, say, larger than nontradable goods inflation (π_t), then the relative price of tradable goods will be increasing over time (i.e., $\dot{e}_t > 0$).

As in chapter 4, let us now define the real interest rate in terms of nontradable goods, r_t^d, as

$$r_t^d \equiv r + \frac{\dot{e}_t}{e_t}. \tag{8.18}$$

We will refer to r_t^d as the "domestic real interest rate." If, say, the relative price of tradable goods is rising over time (i.e., $\dot{e}_t > 0$), then $r^d > r$. Intuitively, if you have invested in a tradable bond, your return in terms of nontradable goods will be higher if you are able to purchase more nontradable goods later on. For further reference, notice that using (8.15) and (8.17), we can rewrite (8.18) as $r_t^d = i_t - \pi_t$.

To derive the Euler equation for nontradable goods, totally differentiate (8.6) and use (8.18) to obtain

$$\frac{\dot{c}_t^N}{c_t^N} = r_t^d - r.$$

As discussed in chapter 4, if, say, $r_t^d > r$, today's consumption of nontradable goods is lower than "tomorrow's" because the return on postponing consumption (r_t^d) is higher than the utility cost of deferring consumption (β, which equals r).

Combining the consumers' flow constraint (given by equation 8.3) with the government's (given by equation 8.13) and imposing equilibrium in the nontradable goods market, we obtain

$$\dot{k}_t = rk_t + y^T - c_t^T, \tag{8.19}$$

where $k_t (\equiv b_t + h_t)$ denotes the economy's total net foreign assets.

Integrating forward (8.19) and imposing the appropriate transversality condition, we obtain

$$k_0 + \frac{y^T}{r} = \int_0^\infty c_t^T \exp(-rt)dt. \tag{8.20}$$

8.3 Flexible Rates

8.3.1 Perfect Foresight Equilibrium

Suppose that the economy is operating under flexible exchange rates. Hence we assume that $h_t = 0$ for all t. We will now solve for the perfect foresight equilibrium path for a constant rate of money growth, μ. To this effect, we proceed in three stages. In the first stage, we will show that consumption of tradables is constant (and in fact independent of monetary policy). In the second stage—and as we have done already in chapters 5 and 7—we will show that the path of m_t is governed by an unstable differential equation and argue that a convergent perfect foresight equilibrium path requires that m_t be constant over time. In the third and final stage, we will set up a dynamic system in n_t (real money balances in terms of nontradable goods) and π_t to solve for the rest of the model.

Consumption Path of Tradable Goods

First-order condition (8.5) makes clear that c_t^T will be constant over time. Using the resource constraint (8.20), this constant value will be given by

$$c^T = rk_0 + y^T. \tag{8.21}$$

For further reference, notice that the path of consumption of tradables will be given by (8.21) regardless of the path of the money supply and that consumption will not be affected by any (anticipated or unanticipated) change in monetary policy. Hence, from (8.5), the same is true of the multiplier λ.

Real Money Balances

By definition, $m_t = M_t/E_t$. Hence

$$\frac{\dot{m}_t}{m_t} = \mu - \varepsilon_t. \tag{8.22}$$

Solving for ε_t from the interest parity condition (8.15) and using (8.10)—taking also into account (8.21)—we obtain

$$\varepsilon_t = \frac{c^T}{m_t} - r.$$

Substituting this last expression into (8.22), we obtain a linear differential equation for m_t:

$$\dot{m}_t = (r + \mu)m_t - c^T, \tag{8.23}$$

where c^T is a constant given by (8.21). Given that

$$\frac{\partial \dot{m}_t}{\partial m_t} = r + \mu > 0,$$

the differential equation (8.23) is unstable. It follows that for m_t to follow a convergent path, $\dot{m}_t = 0$ for all $t \geq 0$. Hence, along a perfect foresight path with a constant μ, m_t will be constant and equal to

$$m = \frac{c^T}{r + \mu}. \tag{8.24}$$

An important implication is that in response to unanticipated and permanent changes in μ, real money balances in terms of tradable goods will need to adjust instantaneously to their new steady state. If they did not, they would diverge over time.

Finally, notice that since $\dot{m}_t = 0$ along a perfect foresight path with constant μ, it follows from (8.22) that ε_t will also be constant:

$$\varepsilon = \mu.$$

Hence the nominal interest rate is also constant and given by

$$i = r + \mu.$$

Dynamic System

To solve for the rest of the model, we will set up a dynamic system in n_t and π_t.[7] Recall that by definition, $n_t \equiv M_t/P_t^N$. Hence

$$\dot{n}_t = n_t(\mu - \pi_t). \tag{8.25}$$

The variable n_t is predetermined because M_t is exogenous (i.e., controlled by the monetary authority) and prices of nontradable goods are sticky (i.e., cannot jump at any point in time).

To derive our second dynamic equation, first use (8.16) to rewrite (8.12) as

$$\dot{\pi}_t = \theta \left(y_f^N - c_t^N \right). \tag{8.26}$$

Hence inflation of nontradables will be rising if consumption of nontradable goods is below its full-employment level, and vice versa.

7. The reader may wonder why we need to introduce a different measure of real money balances for the purposes of setting up the dynamic system. The answer is that when it comes to setting up a dynamic system, it is convenient to have a predetermined variable. In this case n_t is such a variable.

Taking into account (8.8) and noting that $e_t = n_t/m_t$, we can rewrite equation (8.26) as

$$\dot{\pi}_t = \theta\left(y_f^N - \frac{c^T}{m}n_t\right). \tag{8.27}$$

Equations (8.25) and (8.27) constitute a dynamic system in n_t and π_t, for given values of μ and m.[8]

To characterize the steady state of the dynamic system, set $\dot{n}_t = \dot{\pi}_t = 0$ in (8.25) and (8.27), respectively, to obtain

$$\pi_{ss} = \mu, \tag{8.28}$$

$$n_{ss} = \frac{y_f^N m}{c^T}. \tag{8.29}$$

Linearizing the system around the steady state, we obtain

$$\begin{bmatrix} \dot{n}_t \\ \dot{\pi}_t \end{bmatrix} = \begin{bmatrix} 0 & -n_{ss} \\ -\theta\frac{c^T}{m} & 0 \end{bmatrix} \begin{bmatrix} n_t - n_{ss} \\ \pi_t - \mu \end{bmatrix}.$$

The determinant of the matrix associated with the linear approximation is negative:

$$\Delta = -\theta\frac{n_{ss}c^T}{m} < 0.$$

The system has therefore one positive and one negative root and thus exhibits saddle-path stability.

As in chapter 6 we now proceed to characterize the qualitative behavior of this dynamic system by resorting to a phase diagram. To construct the phase diagram, we first draw the $\dot{n}_t = 0$ and $\dot{\pi}_t = 0$ loci. To obtain these curves, set $\dot{n}_t = 0$ in equation (8.25) and $\dot{\pi}_t = 0$ in (8.27) to obtain, respectively,

$$\pi_t = \mu,$$

$$n_t = \frac{y_f^N m}{c^T}.$$

Hence the $\dot{n}_t = 0$ locus shows up in the phase diagram (figure 8.1) as a horizontal line, whereas the $\dot{\pi}_t = 0$ locus shows as a vertical line. The intersection of both loci at point A determines the

8. Notice that as far as the dynamic system is concerned, m is like a parameter since it will adjust instantaneously in response to permanent changes in μ.

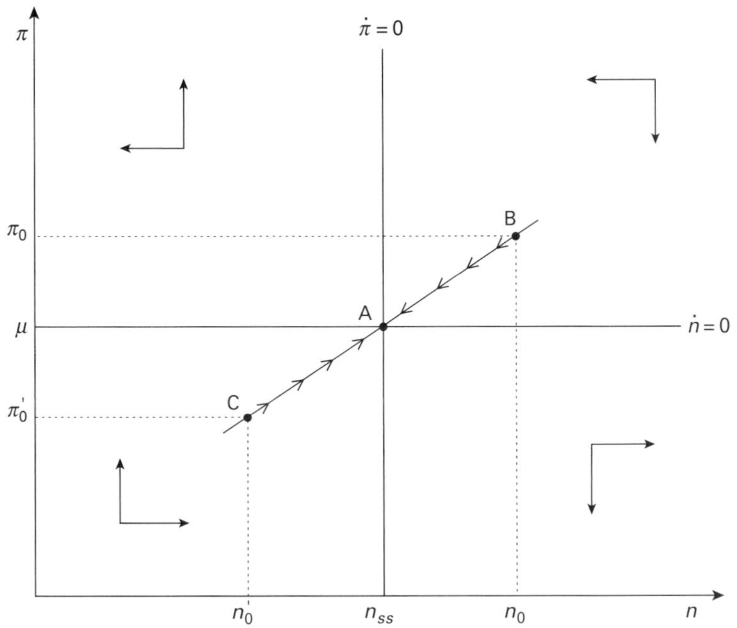

Figure 8.1
Phase diagram

steady state of the system. As we saw in chapter 6, the $\dot{n}_t = 0$ and $\dot{\pi}_t = 0$ curves define four regions. Proceeding in analogous fashion, we can draw the arrowheads shown in figure 8.1 and conclude that the saddle path will be positively sloped.

Recall that n_t is predetermined in the sense that it cannot jump in an endogenous way. Hence, if n_t at time 0 were above n_{ss} (denoted by n_0 in figure 8.1), then inflation at 0 would also be above μ (at a value given by π_0 in figure 8.1) so as to position the system along the saddle path at a point like B. Hence both π_t and n_t would fall during the adjustment process toward point A. Since $\dot{\pi} < 0$ during the adjustment, c_t^N would be above its full-employment level, as equation (8.26) makes clear. Conversely, if n_t at time 0 were below n_{ss}, (e.g., at a value given by n_0' in figure 8.1), then the rate of inflation would adjust endogenously to a value below μ (π_0' in figure 8.1) so as to position the system on the saddle path at a point like C. From then on, the system would travel along the saddle path toward point A. Both π_t and n_t would thus increase during this adjustment process. Since $\dot{\pi}_t > 0$ during the adjustment to the steady state, c_t^N would be below its full-employment level, as equation (8.26) makes clear.

We thus conclude that the model endogenously generates a Phillips-curve type relationship in the sense that when inflation is above μ, the economy is operating above its full-employment level (i.e., $c_t^N > y_f^N$) and when inflation is below μ, the economy is operating below its full-employment level (i.e., $c_t^N < y_f^N$). While traditional sticky-prices model postulate such a relationship, here it arises as an equilibrium phenomenon.[9]

8.3.2 Permanent Increase in the Money Supply

Suppose that just before $t = 0$, the economy is in the stationary equilibrium corresponding to $\mu = 0$ and point A in figure 8.1. At time 0, there is an unanticipated and permanent increase in the stock of money supply, M_t (figure 8.2, panel a). How does the economy react?

As we have already established, c_t^T will not change. It is also the case that an increase in M_t will not affect the steady-state value of m_t, as (8.24) makes clear. Hence the nominal exchange rate will increase by the same proportion as the nominal money supply so as to keep m_t constant.

In terms of the dynamic system, the increase in M_t will not affect the steady-state values of n_t and π_t, as follows from equations (8.28) and (8.29). Hence the steady state of the system will remain at point A in figure 8.1. On impact, however, n_t will increase to a value like n_0 in figure 8.1 because the nominal money supply goes up and the price of nontradables goods is sticky. Given n_0, the inflation rate will have to jump to π_0 so as to position the system on the saddle path (point B in figure 8.1). After this initial jump from point A to point B, the system travels back to point A along the saddle path. The corresponding paths of n_t and π_t as a function of time are depicted in figure 8.2, panels b and c, respectively.

To find out the path of the real exchange rate, recall that $e_t = n_t/m_t$. Since m_t does not change, e_t will behave in the same way as n_t, jumping up on impact (real depreciation) and then falling back to its initial steady state (figure 8.2, panel d).

Given condition (8.8) and the fact that c_t^T does not change, the behavior of c_t^N will mimic that of e_t, as illustrated in figure 8.2, panel e.

Finally, what will happen to the domestic real interest rate, r_t^d? Recall that $r_t^d = i_t - \pi_t$. Since the nominal interest rate remains constant, the behavior of r_t^d will be dictated by the behavior of inflation. Hence the domestic real interest rate falls on impact and then gradually reverts back to its unchanged steady state, r (figure 8.2, panel f).

In sum, a permanent increase in the level of the money supply leads to higher inflation, a real depreciation, an expansion in the nontradable goods sector, and a fall in the domestic real interest rate. This is, of course, in sharp contrast to the world of chapter 5 where a permanent increase in the money supply had no real effects.

What is the economic intuition behind these effects? For these purposes, and recalling (8.11), let us focus on the money market equilibrium for n_t at time 0:

9. This is true, of course, as long as the system is on the saddle path. Interestingly, if the economy is not on the saddle path (which can happen in response to a temporary shock), then this Phillips-curve relationship will not necessarily hold, which could explain, for example, periods of "stagflation" (i.e., high inflation and underutilization of resources) as illustrated by exercise 1 at the end of this chapter.

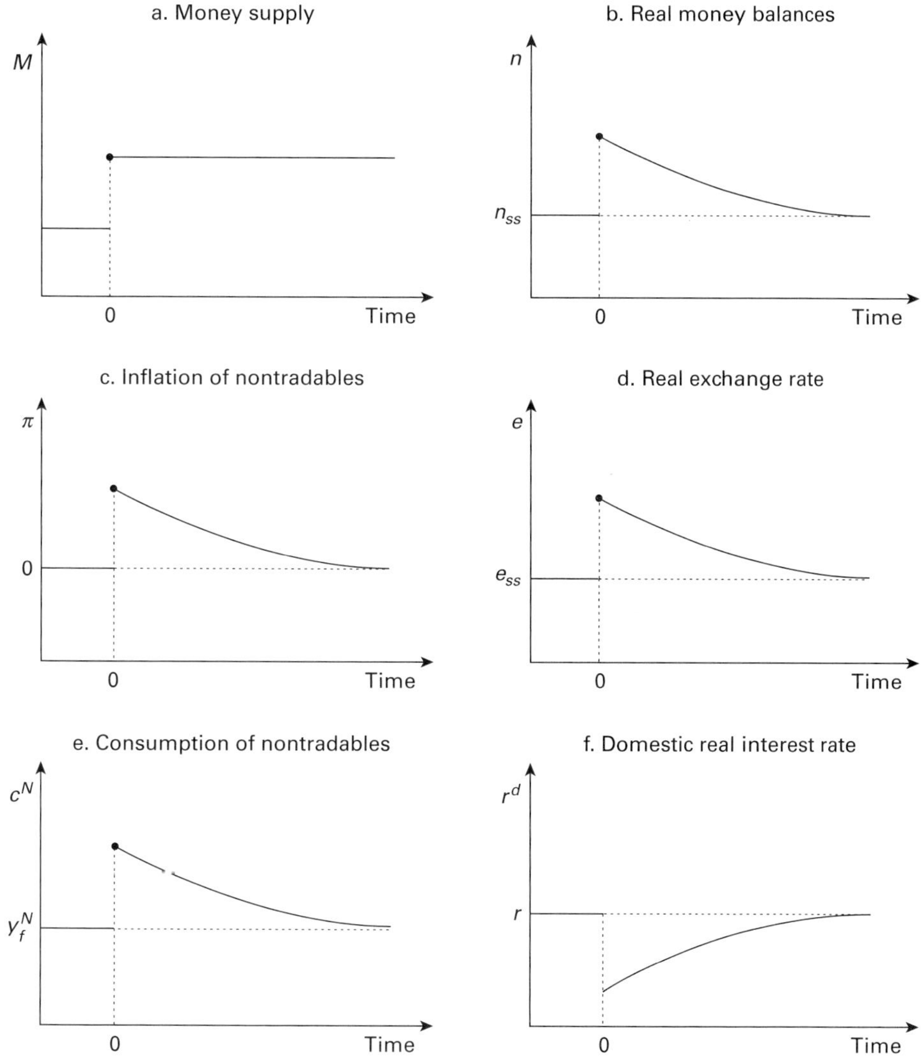

Figure 8.2
Permanent increase in money supply

$$\underbrace{\frac{M_0}{P_0^N}}_{\text{Real money supply}} = \underbrace{\frac{c_0^N}{i_0}}_{\text{Real money demand}}. \tag{8.30}$$

As indicated below the equation, think of the LHS as real money supply and the RHS as real money demand. The critical implication of price stickiness is that an increase in the *nominal* money supply translates into an increase in the *real* money supply. Hence, for unchanged real money demand, there would be an *incipient* excess supply of money. In their attempt to get rid of unwanted money balances by purchasing foreign bonds, households would bid up the domestic price of foreign bonds (E_t). Since P_t^N is sticky, this nominal depreciation translates into a real depreciation (i.e., a fall in the relative price of nontradable goods). As a result demand for nontradables increases which—given that output is demand-determined—leads to an output expansion in the nontradable sector. In other words, by increasing real money demand, the rise in c_t^N at $t = 0$ takes care of the incipient excess supply of money.

In the long run, however, real money demand will not change relative to its pre-shock value. Hence real money supply must fall over time to its pre-shock value. For this to happen, inflation of nontradable goods, π, must increase on impact above the (unchanged) rate of money growth, μ. This high inflation—coupled with no changes in the nominal exchange rate after the initial jump—explains the real appreciation that takes place over time.

Finally, notice that in this model the nominal exchange rate increases by the same proportion as the nominal money supply. There is thus no overshooting in the sense of Dornbusch (1976). Overshooting would occur if, on impact, the nominal exchange rate increased by more than the money supply does. Why does this model not generate overshooting? The answer to this question will become clear once we show in section 8.5 how a version of this model with more general preferences can indeed generate both overshooting and undershooting.

8.3.3 Permanent Reduction in the Rate of Money Growth

Suppose, once again, that an instant before time 0, the system is in the steady state characterized above (with the rate of money growth given by μ^H). At $t = 0$ there is an unanticipated and permanent reduction in the rate of money growth from μ^H to μ^L ($\mu^L < \mu^H$) (figure 8.3, panel a). Consumption of tradable goods—given by (8.21)—does not change because, as discussed above, its level is independent of monetary policy. From (8.24), we can see that real money balances in terms of tradable goods (m_t) will be higher in the new stationary state because the opportunity cost of holding money has fallen. Given the instability of the differential equation governing the behavior of real money balances, m_t must adjust instantaneously to its higher value. If it did not, it would diverge over time. The rate of depreciation will therefore also fall down immediately to its new steady-state value and so will the nominal interest rate.

In terms of the dynamic system, suppose that the system is initially at point A in figure 8.4. At point A the steady-state rate of inflation of nontradable goods is equal to μ^H, and the corresponding

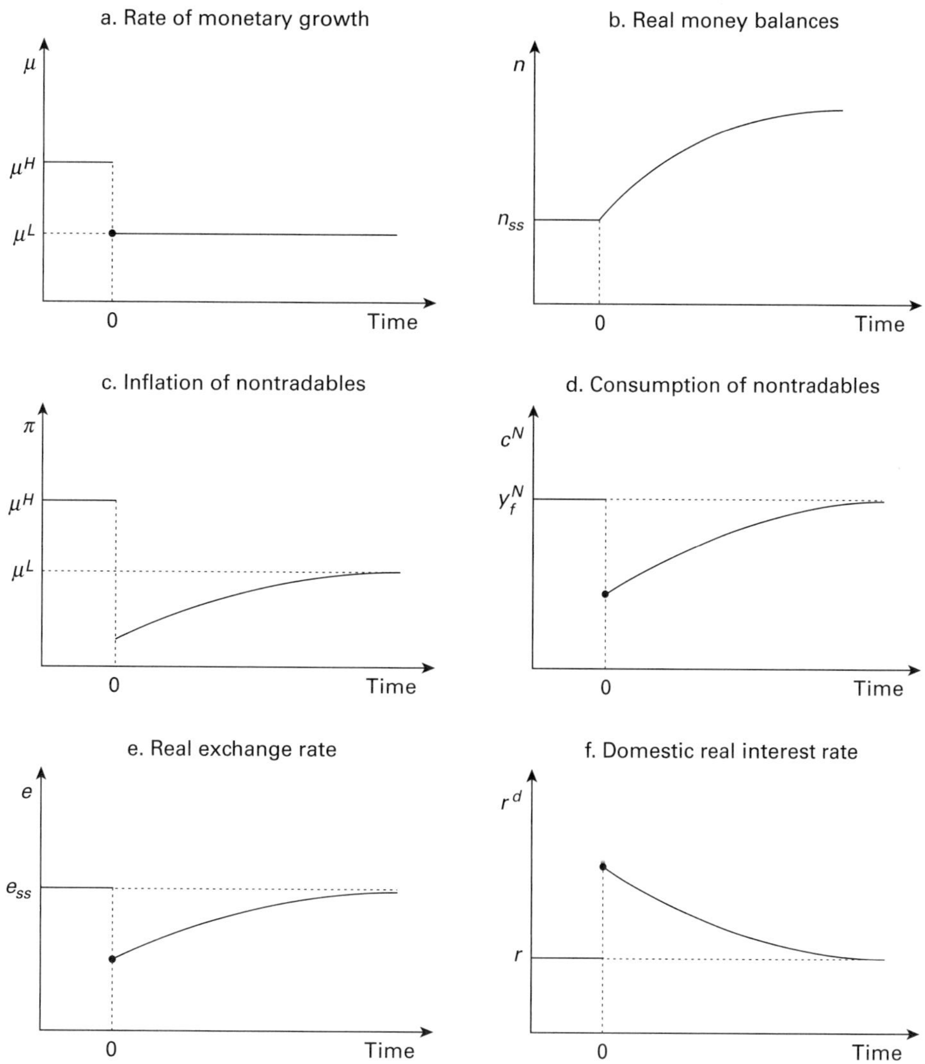

Figure 8.3
Permanent reduction in rate of money growth

real money balances are $n_{ss}(\mu^H)$. In the new steady state—and as (8.28) and (8.29) make clear—n_t will be higher and π_t will be lower (point B in figure 8.4). Hence, on impact, the system must jump from point A to point C and then travel along the saddle path toward point B. The corresponding paths of n_t and π_t are illustrated in figure 8.3, panels b and c, respectively. On impact, the inflation rate falls by more than it will in the long run.

To derive the path of the real exchange rate, recall that $e_t = n_t/m_t$. Since m_t increases at time 0, e_t will jump down at time 0 (real appreciation), as illustrated in figure 8.3, panel e. Given that the real exchange rate does not change across steady states, it will need to gradually rise back to its initial steady state. Given equation (8.8), consumption of nontradable goods follows the same path as the real exchange rate (figure 8.3, panel d). Finally, the domestic real interest rate will increase on impact because the fall in inflation is larger than the fall in the nominal interest rate (figure 8.3, panel f). It then falls gradually to its unchanged steady state.

Summing up, an unanticipated reduction in μ leads to a recession, real exchange rate appreciation, and higher domestic real interest rates. As documented in chapter 13, these are precisely the main stylized facts associated with money based stabilizations.

The economic intuition behind the results just discussed is as follows. Think again in terms of the money market equilibrium described by equation (8.30). The reduction in the money growth rate lowers the nominal interest rate and hence increases real money demand. Real money supply,

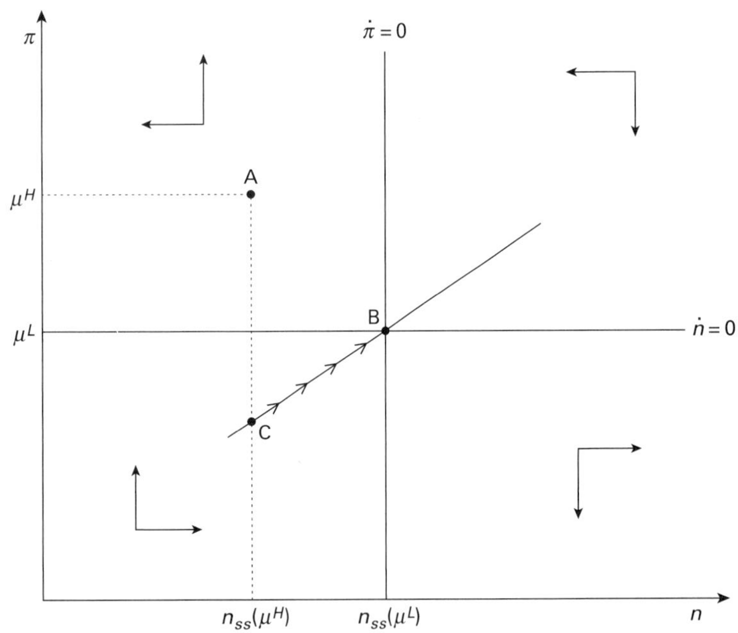

Figure 8.4
Permanent reduction in money growth rate: Phase diagram

however, does not change on impact. Hence, for the initial level of c_t^N, there is an excess demand for money. As a result the public will try to get rid of foreign bonds in order to acquire money, which pushes down the nominal domestic price of foreign bonds, E_t. Since the price of nontradable goods is sticky, the fall in E_t translates into a reduction in e_t. This increase in the relative price of nontradable goods reduces their demand, which leads to fall in output. In other words, the fall in c_t^N takes care of the incipient excess demand for money.

8.4 Predetermined Exchange Rates

We now solve the model for the case of predetermined exchange rates and use it to ask the question: How does the economy respond to a permanent devaluation? Contrary to our results in chapter 6—where a devaluation led to a reduction in consumption—in this sticky-prices model a devaluation will trigger an expansion in aggregate demand for nontradable goods and therefore output.

We begin by solving for the perfect foresight equilibrium corresponding to a constant rate of devaluation. We then turn our attention to a permanent devaluation and a permanent reduction in the rate of devaluation.

8.4.1 Perfect Foresight Equilibrium

Let us now characterize the perfect foresight equilibrium for a constant value of the rate of devaluation, ε. First notice that as in the flexible exchange rates case, consumption of tradables will be constant and given by (8.21). Furthermore consumption of tradables will not be affected by changes in the rate of devaluation.

From the interest parity condition (8.15), the nominal interest rate will be constant as well and given by

$$i = r + \varepsilon.$$

Given that both c_t^T and i_t are constant, the money demand equation (8.10) tells us that m_t will be constant as well.

To solve for the rest of the variables, we need to set up a different dynamic system from the one we used above for flexible exchange rates, given by (8.25) and (8.27), for the following reasons. For starters, that system has the variable μ, which is now an endogenous variable. Furthermore real money balances in terms of nontradable goods (n_t) are no longer a predetermined variable under predetermined exchange rates because the nominal money supply is an endogenous variable. As a methodological matter, it would not be wise to set up a dynamic system with two jumping variables because it would be harder to solve. We thus need to find a variable that will be predetermined under predetermined exchange rates and sticky prices. A moment's reflection should reveal that the obvious candidate is the real exchange rate, e_t. Since, by definition, $e_t = E_t/P_t^N$, the real exchange rate will be a predetermined variable in standard models of predetermined exchange rates under sticky prices.

We will therefore set up a dynamic system in e_t and π_t. The first dynamic equation is given by (8.17). To obtain the second dynamic equation, substitute (8.8) into (8.26) to obtain

$$\dot{\pi}_t = \theta\left(y_f^N - e_t c^T\right). \tag{8.31}$$

The system's steady state is given by

$$\pi_{ss} = \varepsilon, \tag{8.32}$$

$$e_{ss} = \frac{y_f^N}{c^T}. \tag{8.33}$$

Linearizing the system around the steady state, we obtain

$$\begin{bmatrix} \dot{e}_t \\ \dot{\pi}_t \end{bmatrix} = \begin{bmatrix} 0 & -e_{ss} \\ -\theta c^T & 0 \end{bmatrix} \begin{bmatrix} e_t - e_{ss} \\ \pi_t - \varepsilon \end{bmatrix}.$$

The determinant of the matrix associated with the linear approximation of the system is given by

$$\Delta = -\theta c^T e_{ss} < 0,$$

which implies that the system is saddle-path stable.

Proceeding as before, it is easy to construct the phase diagram illustrated in figure 8.5. As depicted, the saddle path is positively sloped.

The path of the remaining variables along a perfect foresight equilibrium will depend on the initial value of the real exchange rate. Suppose that the initial value of the real exchange rate were given by e_0 in figure 8.5. Then the inflation rate would need to be π_0 so as to position the system on the saddle path at point B. Both the real exchange rate and inflation would fall over time toward the steady state, given by point A. Given condition (8.8), consumption of nontradable goods would behave in the same way as the real exchange rate and hence fall over time.

8.4.2 Permanent Devaluation

Suppose that just before $t = 0$ the economy is in the steady state characterized above (with $\varepsilon = 0$). At $t = 0$ there is an unanticipated and permanent devaluation (figure 8.6, panel a). How does the economy react?

Clearly, c_t^T continues to be given by (8.21) and i_t does not change because the devaluation rate has not changed. In terms of the dynamic system, it is clear from equations (8.32) and (8.33) that the devaluation does not affect the steady-state values of the inflation rate of nontradable goods or the real exchange rate. On impact, however, the real exchange rate will increase. In other

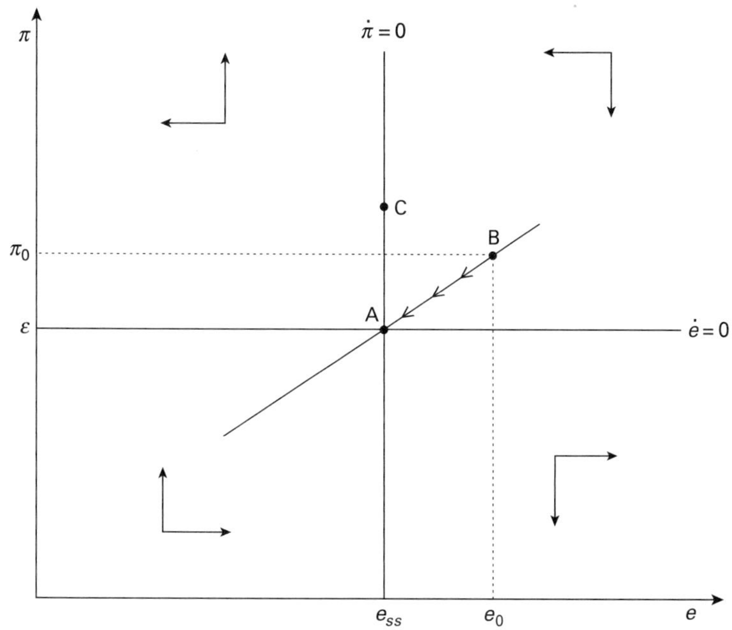

Figure 8.5
Phase diagram: Predetermined exchange rates

words, in this particular model, a nominal devaluation leads on impact to a real devaluation.[10] The real exchange rate thus jumps on impact to a value such as e_0 in figure 8.5. The inflation rate must then adjust so that the system positions itself along the saddle path (at point B in figure 8.5). The system then travels along the saddle path back to its initial steady state, point A. The corresponding path of π_t and e_t are illustrated in figure 8.6, panels c and d.

The path of consumption of nontradable goods follows from condition (8.8). Consumption of nontradable goods increases on impact and then falls back toward its full-employment level (figure 8.6, panel e). The domestic real interest rate falls on impact as a result of the increase in inflation and then gradually reverts back to its initial steady state (figure 8.6, panel f). The path of n_t—illustrated in figure 8.6, panel b—follows from the fact that $n_t = e_t m_t$ and that, from (8.10), m_t does not change.

We thus conclude that a devaluation is expansionary. Intuitively, the key is that due to sticky prices, a nominal devaluation translates into a real devaluation. The increase in the relative price of tradable goods induces consumers to switch expenditures toward nontradable goods. Since output is demand-determined, output of nontradable goods responds immediately.

10. The model is thus able to explain the high correlation between nominal and real exchange rates, as documented by Mussa (1986). See Chari, Kehoe, and McGrattan (2002) for a quantitative analysis. Remember, however, from chapter 6 that other frictions could generate the same outcome.

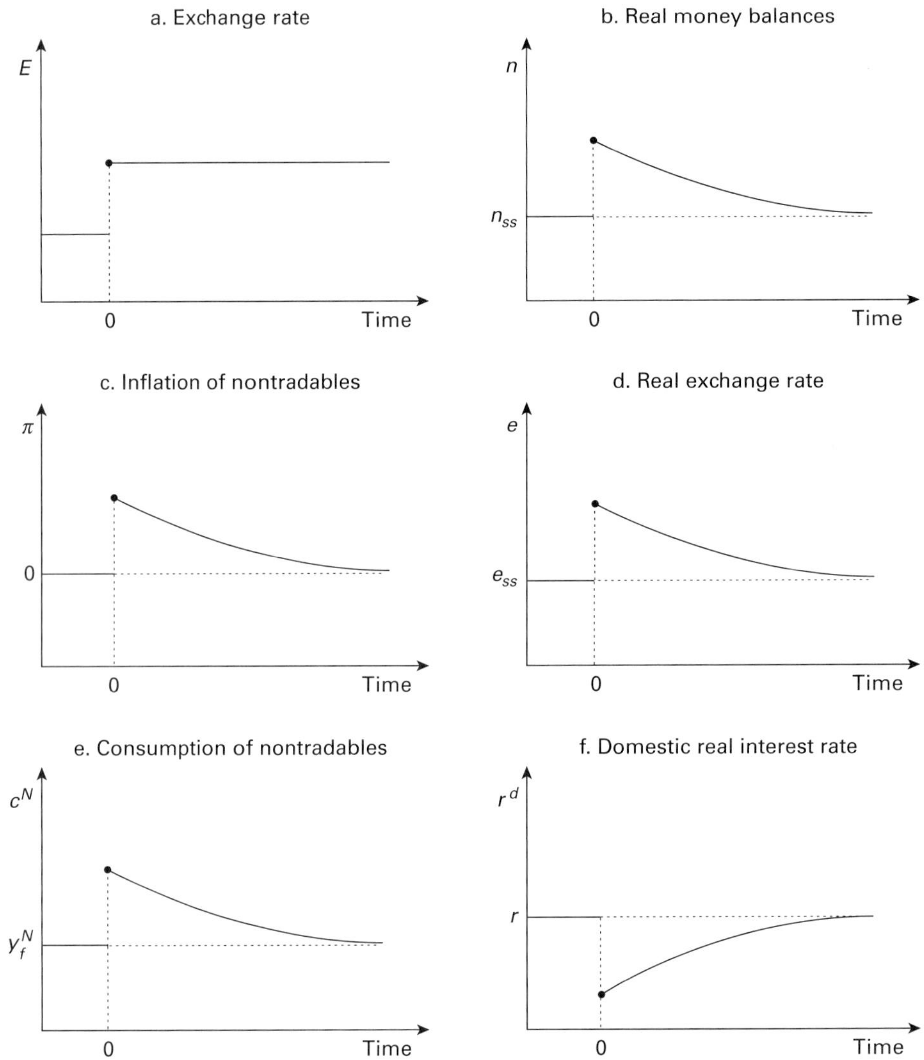

Figure 8.6
Permanent devaluation

The expansionary effects of a devaluation under sticky prices stand in sharp contrast to the results that we obtained in chapter 6 where a devaluation—by reducing real money balances and forcing consumers to reduce consumption to replenish real money balances—was actually contractionary. We have thus illustrated two possible channels through which a devaluation may impact the real economy. In fact—and as argued in box 8.2—there are other plausible channels, which makes the overall impact of a devaluation an empirical matter.

8.4.3 Permanent Reduction in Devaluation Rate

Suppose that the economy is initially in a situation of high inflation at a point like C in figure 8.5. At $t = 0$ there is an unanticipated and permanent reduction in the rate of devaluation. In the new steady state (point A in figure 8.5), the rate of inflation is lower and the real exchange rate remains unchanged. How will the economy adjust from point C to point A? A moment's reflection reveals that the economy must adjust instantaneously to its new steady state. Since e_t is a predetermined variable, the system must remain along the vertical line corresponding to e_{ss} at time 0. But if the system placed itself at any point other than A along that vertical line, it would diverge over

Box 8.2
Are devaluations expansionary or contractionary?

As argued in the text, the real effects of a currency devaluation are theoretically ambiguous. In the model laid out in chapter 6—with no interest-bearing bonds—a devaluation is contractionary, as private agents reduce consumption to rebuild their stock of real money balances. In this chapter's model with sticky prices, a devaluation is expansionary since it reduces on impact the relative price of nontradable goods, thus leading to an increase in aggregate demand and output. In addition to these two channels, the literature has explored other, mostly contractionary, channels. Among the most relevant ones:[a]

• *Effects on imported inputs/investment* In models with imported inputs, a devaluation will raise the domestic price of such inputs and thus be contractionary (e.g., see, Gylfason and Schmid 1983, van Wijnbergen 1986, and Edwards 1986). Similarly Buffie and Wong (2001) show how a devaluation is likely to reduce aggregate investment and output in a model in the spirit of chapter 6 (i.e., consumers hold no foreign bonds) but with capital accumulation.

• *Income redistribution* Profits will be boosted in export and import competing industries as devaluations lead to higher relative prices for tradable goods. When this increased price level leads to lower real wages, aggregate spending is likely to shrink since the marginal propensity to save from profits exceeds that from wages (e.g., see Díaz-Alejandro 1963, Cooper 1971, and Krugman and Taylor 1978).

• *Balance sheet effects* A devaluation reduces net worth if liabilities are more heavily dollarized than assets. Because of financial frictions, the reduction in net worth reduces investment and thus economic activity (e.g., Cespedes, Chang, and Velasco 2004).

a. The following list is far from exhaustive. The reader is referred to Lizondo and Montiel (1989) and Agenor and Montiel (1999, ch. 8) for a more detailed discussion.

Box 8.2
Are devaluations expansionary or contractionary?

Table 8.2
Empirical studies on output effects of devaluation

Author(s)	Dataset	Sign of effect	Methodology and controls
Gylfason and Schmid (1983)	1959–77 5 industrial and 5 developing countries	Positive in 8 out of the10 countries (after two to three years)	Parameter estimation based on dynamic single-equation models
Edwards (1986)	1965–80 12 developing countries	Negative in the short run (effect is offset in the second year)	Panel data (fixed effects) Government spending, money growth
Agenor (1991)	1978–87 23 developing countries	Negative (for anticipated movements of RER) Positive (for unanticipated movements of RER)	Panel data (pooled OLS) Government spending, money supply, foreign income
Morley (1992)	1974–84 28 developing countries	Negative (short run)	Cross section Terms of trade, import growth, money supply, and fiscal balance
Kamin and Klau (1998)	1970–96 27 countries	Very weakly negative (short run) Insignificant (long run)	Panel data Output gap, short-term interest rate, fiscal balance to GDP, terms of trade, capital account to GDP ratio, US interest rate. Two-stage least squares
Milesi-Ferretti and Razin (2000)	1970-1996 105 low –and middle –income countries	Negative (short run) Insignificant (long run)	Panel data Macroeconomic, external, debt, financial, foreign, and regional variables
Magendzo (2002)	1970–99 155 countries non–OECD countries	Insignificant	Matching estimators
Cavallo et al. (2004)	1992–2002 24 countries	Negative (2-year period); effect is stronger in presence of large foreign debt.	Cross-sectional analysis using OLS, IV and three-stage least squares.
Gupta, Mishra, and Sahay (2007)	1970–98 91 developing countries	57 percent of crises contractionary; 43 percent expansionary Outcome influenced by factors such as capital account liberalization and pre-crisis level of economic activity and capital flows	Frequency distribution and OLS Change in external long-term debt, cumulative flow of external private capital, capital controls, currency crises, business cycles, per capita GDP, banking crises, short-term debt to reserves, exchange rate overvaluation, proxies for monetary and fiscal policies, openness, competitive devaluations by others, economic size, external factors

Box 8.2
(continued)

The theory thus identifies several contractionary channels that could, in principle, more than outweigh the traditional expansionary effects emphasized by sticky-prices models. The overall effect thus becomes an empirical question.

What do the data say? Table 8.2 summarizes the results of some notable contributions on the subject. An early study by Gylfason and Schmid (1983) reported a mostly positive effect of a devaluation on output. Subsequent studies, however, tended to find a weak negative impact, if any, of devaluations on output. A recent study by Gupta, Mishra, and Sahay (2007), which relies on a large dataset comprising 91 developing countries and spanning almost 30 years, documents that on average, output has fallen when currency crises have taken place.[b] Still a significant number of episodes (43 percent) have been associated with output increases.

What could explain different responses of output to a devaluation? According to some authors, the output effects may be conditional on other relevant variables. Gupta, Mishra, and Sahay (2007), for instance, find that the output effect is positively associated with commercial integration with the rest of the world but negatively associated with financial integration and previous periods of capital inflows. They also report that large emerging economies are more likely to suffer contractionary devaluations than small ones. In contrast, Cavallo et al. (2004) stress the empirical importance of balance sheet mismatches. They claim that among developing economies, output contractions have been more pronounced in relatively large and more developed economies than in smaller and less developed economies.

In sum, the jury is still out on whether, in practice, devaluations are expansionary or contractionary. If anything, the often-mixed evidence suggests that the real effects of devaluation likely depend on the circumstances surrounding it. For instance, it stands to reason that a devaluation carried out in the middle of a full-fledged balance of payments and financial crisis and possibly accompanied by tighter fiscal and monetary policies is much more likely to be contractionary than a devaluation undertaken as part of an orderly adjustment to, say, a perceived exchange rate "misalignment." Unfortunately, controlling for these factors is not a trivial empirical task.

b. It should be noted that the focus of this paper is on currency crises (whose definition typically includes increases in the exchange rate and changes in reserves). Ideally one would like to see a similarly large dataset used to study the effects of devaluations only. The overlapping, of course, would be large.

time. Hence the only possible equilibrium is for the system to jump from point C to point A. The reduction in the devaluation rate is thus superneutral.

This is a remarkable result because it says that even if prices are sticky, a permanent reduction in the devaluation rate might reduce inflation at no real costs. This model may thus be used to think about the end of hyperinflations, which, by and large, have involved large and sudden reductions in inflation at little real costs (see chapter 13).[11]

11. We should notice the economy's very different response to a permanent reduction in the rate of devaluation compared to the response to a permanent reduction in the rate of money growth. Interestingly—and as shown in exercise 2 at the end of this chapter—under logarithmic preferences the response to a change in fiscal policy would be the same under either regime.

8.5 Overshooting

We mentioned earlier that our basic sticky-prices model does not generate over/undershooting. This section analyzes a more general version of the model in which both overshooting and undershooting are possible.

8.5.1 Consumers

The only change in the model is that the sub-utility for real money balances now takes a CES form:

$$\int_0^{\infty}\left[\log(c_t^T)+\log(c_t^N)+\frac{z_t^{1-1/\sigma}-1}{1-1/\sigma}\right]\exp(-\beta t)dt, \tag{8.34}$$

where σ is a positive parameter that, as will become clear below, will capture the consumption and interest rate elasticity of real money demand.

The intertemporal constraint remains given by (8.4). The first-order conditions for c_t^T and c_t^N continue to be given by (8.5) and (8.6). The first-order condition for z_t now reads as

$$z_t^{-1/\sigma}=\lambda\frac{i_t}{\sqrt{e_t}}. \tag{8.35}$$

Using this first-order condition to solve for z—taking into account (8.6)—we obtain the real money demand (in terms of the price index):

$$z_t=\left(\frac{c_t^N}{\sqrt{e_t}i_t}\right)^{\sigma}. \tag{8.36}$$

The parameter σ thus denotes the consumption and interest rate elasticity of money demand. When $\sigma=1$, the model reduces to the case analyzed in section 8.3 (recall equation 8.9).

For further reference, it is also convenient to obtain the real money demand in terms of tradable goods, m_t. Recalling that $m_t\equiv M_t/E_t$ and taking into account (8.2) and (8.8), we can rewrite equation (8.36) as

$$m_t=\left[\frac{e_t^{(1/2)(1-1/\sigma)}c_t^T}{i_t}\right]^{\sigma}. \tag{8.37}$$

Once again, notice that when $\sigma=1$, equation (8.37) reduces to (8.10).

8.5.2 Dynamic System

We now proceed to solve this model for the case of flexible exchange rates in the same way as we did before. A key difference, however, will be that, due to the CES preferences for money, the resulting dynamic system in m_t, n_t, and π_t will *not* be block recursive. In other words, with logarithmic preferences for z_t, the system breaks down into a single differential equation for m_t and a system of two differential equations for n_t and π_t. This will not be the case for CES preferences. As a result we will have no choice but to set up a system of three differential equations in m_t, n_t, and π_t.

For starters, solve for i_t from (8.35)—taking into account that $E_t/P_t = \sqrt{e_t}$—to obtain

$$i_t = \frac{e_t^{(1/2)(1-1/\sigma)}}{\lambda m_t^{1/\sigma}}.$$

Substituting this last equation into (8.22)—taking into account the interest parity condition—we obtain

$$\dot{m}_t = m_t \left[\mu + r - c^T \frac{n_t^{(1/2)(1-1/\sigma)}}{m_t^{1/\sigma+(1/2)(1-1/\sigma)}} \right], \tag{8.38}$$

where c^T is the constant value of consumption of tradable goods given by (8.21). This differential equation, together with (8.25) and (8.27) with m_t in lieu of m, constitute a dynamic system of three differential equations in n_t, π_t, and m_t.

To characterize the system's steady-state, set $\dot{m}_t = \dot{n}_t = \dot{\pi}_t = 0$ in (8.25), (8.27), and (8.38) to obtain

$$m_{ss} = \left[\frac{\left(c^T\right)^{1-\Phi} \left(y_f^N\right)^{\Phi}}{\mu + r} \right]^{\sigma}, \tag{8.39}$$

$$n_{ss} = \frac{y_f^N m_{ss}}{c^T}, \tag{8.40}$$

$$\pi_{ss} = \mu, \tag{8.41}$$

where

$$\Phi \equiv \frac{1}{2}\left(1 - \frac{1}{\sigma}\right) \tag{8.42}$$

is a parameter that will be critical for the dynamics of m_t.

Linearizing the system around the steady state, we obtain

$$\begin{pmatrix} \dot{m}_t \\ \dot{n}_t \\ \dot{\pi}_t \end{pmatrix} = \begin{pmatrix} \frac{1}{2}(1+1/\sigma)c^T \frac{n_{ss}^{\Phi}}{m_{ss}^{1/\sigma+\Phi}} & -c^T\Phi \frac{n_{ss}^{\Phi-1}}{m_{ss}^{1/\sigma+\Phi-1}} & 0 \\ 0 & 0 & -n_{ss} \\ \frac{\theta c^T n_{ss}}{m_{ss}^2} & -\theta \frac{c^T}{m_{ss}} & 0 \end{pmatrix} \begin{pmatrix} m_t - m_{ss} \\ n_t - n_{ss} \\ \pi_t - \mu \end{pmatrix}.$$

Taking into account (8.39) and (8.40), we can rewrite this dynamic system as

$$\begin{pmatrix} \dot{m}_t \\ \dot{n}_t \\ \dot{\pi}_t \end{pmatrix} = \begin{pmatrix} \frac{1}{2}(1+1/\sigma)(\mu+r) & -(\mu+r)\Phi\frac{m_{ss}}{n_{ss}} & 0 \\ 0 & 0 & -n_{ss} \\ \frac{\theta y_f^N}{m_{ss}} & -\frac{\theta y_f^N}{n_{ss}} & 0 \end{pmatrix} \begin{pmatrix} m_t - m_{ss} \\ n_t - n_{ss} \\ \pi_t - \mu \end{pmatrix}.$$

The trace and the determinant of the matrix associated with the linear approximation are given by, respectively,

$$Tr = \frac{1}{2}\left(1 + \frac{1}{\sigma}\right)(\mu+r) > 0,$$

$$\Delta = -(\mu+r)\frac{\theta}{\sigma}y_f^N < 0.$$

Since the determinant is negative (recall that the determinant is equal to the product of the roots), the system could have either three negative roots or one negative and two positive roots. The fact that the trace (which equals the sum of the roots) is positive, however, rules out the case of three negative roots. We thus conclude that the system has one negative and two positive roots.

Let δ denote the negative root associated with this system. Denoting by (h_1, h_2, h_3) the characteristic vector associated with the root δ, we can write

$$\begin{pmatrix} \frac{1}{2}(1+1/\sigma)(\mu+r)-\delta & -(\mu+r)\Phi\frac{m_{ss}}{n_{ss}} & 0 \\ 0 & -\delta & -n_{ss} \\ \frac{\theta y_f^N}{m_{ss}} & -\frac{\theta y_f^N}{n_{ss}} & -\delta \end{pmatrix} \begin{pmatrix} h_1 \\ h_2 \\ h_3 \end{pmatrix} = \begin{pmatrix} 0 \\ 0 \\ 0 \end{pmatrix}.$$

From the first and second rows, respectively, it follows that

$$\frac{h_1}{h_2} = \frac{(\mu+r)\Phi(m_{ss}/n_{ss})}{\frac{1}{2}(1+1/\sigma)(\mu+r)-\delta}, \tag{8.43}$$

$$\frac{h_2}{h_3} = -\frac{n_{ss}}{\delta} > 0.$$

As discussed below—and since the denonimator is positive—the sign of h_1/h_2 depends on the sign of Φ and hence on σ.

Setting to zero the constants corresponding to the positive roots, the solution to the dynamic system is given by

$$m_t - m_{ss} = \omega h_1 \exp(\delta t), \tag{8.44}$$

$$n_t - n_{ss} = \omega h_2 \exp(\delta t), \tag{8.45}$$

$$\pi_t - \mu = \omega h_3 \exp(\delta t). \tag{8.46}$$

where ω is an arbitrary constant. Combining (8.45) and (8.46), we get

$$\frac{n_t - n_{ss}}{\pi_t - \mu} = \frac{h_2}{h_3} > 0, \tag{8.47}$$

which tells us that along a perfect foresight path, n_t and π_t will move in the same direction. This should not come as a surprise since, in the logarithmic version of this model studied above, this was also the case.

Combining (8.44) and (8.45), we obtain

$$\frac{m_t - m_{ss}}{n_t - n_{ss}} = \frac{h_1}{h_2}.$$

Based on this expression, we can distinguish three possible cases:

1. $\boldsymbol{\sigma = 1}$ In this case, $\Phi = 0$, as follows from (8.42). From (8.43), $h_1/h_2 = 0$, which implies that m_t is always equal to its steady-state value. This is, of course, the case analyzed earlier in this chapter.

2. $\boldsymbol{\sigma < 1}$ In this case, $\Phi < 0$, as follows from (8.42). From (8.43), $h_1/h_2 < 0$. This implies that along a perfect foresight path, m_t and n_t will move in opposite directions. Together with (8.47), this implies that m_t and π_t also move in opposite directions.

3. $\boldsymbol{\sigma > 1}$ In this case, $\Phi > 0$, as follows from (8.42). From (8.43), $h_1/h_2 > 0$. This implies that along a perfect foresight path, m_t and n_t will move in the same direction. Together with (8.47), this implies that m_t and π_t also move in the same direction.

8.5.3 Permanent Increase in the Money Supply

Suppose that the economy is initially at the steady-state given by (8.39), (8.40), and (8.41), with $\mu = 0$. At $t = 0$ there is an unanticipated and permanent increase in the nominal money supply. To fix ideas, suppose that the money supply doubles from $\bar{M}$ to $2\bar{M}$. How will this economy react?

The first observation is that such a change does not alter the system's steady state. On impact, n_t will increase because P_t^N is a sticky variable. Further, since the system has only one negative root, it will adjust monotonically to its unchanged steady state. To show this formally, normalize h_2 to one, and evaluate (8.45) at $t = 0$ to obtain:

$$n_0 - n_{ss} = \omega > 0.$$

Differentiating (8.45) with respect to time and using this last piece of information, we obtain

$$\dot{n}_t = (n_0 - n_{ss})\delta \exp(\delta t) < 0.$$

Hence n_t will increase on impact and then fall gradually over time. And since we have already established that π_t and n_t will move in the same direction, π_t will increase on impact and fall gradually over time.

How will m_t behave? We need to consider three cases:

1. $\boldsymbol{\sigma = 1}$ In this case, $m_t = m_{ss}$ for all t. This case corresponds to the one analyzed in section 8.3.2. Since m_t does not change on impact, the nominal exchange rate increases by the same proportion as the nominal money supply. In terms of figure 8.7, the nominal exchange rate will double on impact from $\bar{E}$ to $2\bar{E}$ (point A) and stay there. Since the rate of devaluation is zero, there is no change in the nominal interest rate.

2. $\boldsymbol{\sigma < 1}$ In this case—and as established above—m_t and π_t move in opposite directions. It follows that m_t will fall on impact and then rise over time. The fall on impact in m_t implies that the nominal exchange rate rises by more than the nominal money supply. In the long run, however, the nominal exchange rate increases by the same proportion. Hence, on impact, the nominal exchange rate *overshoots* its long-run level. In terms of figure 8.7, the nominal exchange rate jumps on impact to a point such as B and then falls over time to its long-run level. Since the nominal exchange rate falls over time, $\varepsilon_t < 0$, which implies that the nominal interest rate falls on impact.

3. $\boldsymbol{\sigma > 1}$ In this case—and as established above—m_t and π_t move in the same direction. It follows that m_t will increase on impact and then fall over time. Hence, on impact, the nominal exchange rate increases by less than the nominal money supply. The exchange rate thus *undershoots* its long-run level. In terms of figure 8.7, the nominal exchange rate jumps to a point like C and then increases over time. Since the nominal exchange rate increases over time, $\varepsilon_t > 0$, which implies that the nominal interest rate increases on impact.

What is the intuition behind the over/undershooting results? Recall the real money demand equation given by (8.36)—rewritten below taking into account that $c_t^N/\sqrt{e_t} = P_t^N c_t^N/P_t$—and, once again, interpret it as the equilibrium condition in the money market with the LHS capturing real money supply and the RHS denoting real money demand:

$$\underbrace{\frac{M_t}{P_t}}_{\text{Real money supply}} = \underbrace{\left(\frac{P_t^N c_t^N/P_t}{i_t}\right)^{\sigma}}_{\text{Real money demand}}.$$

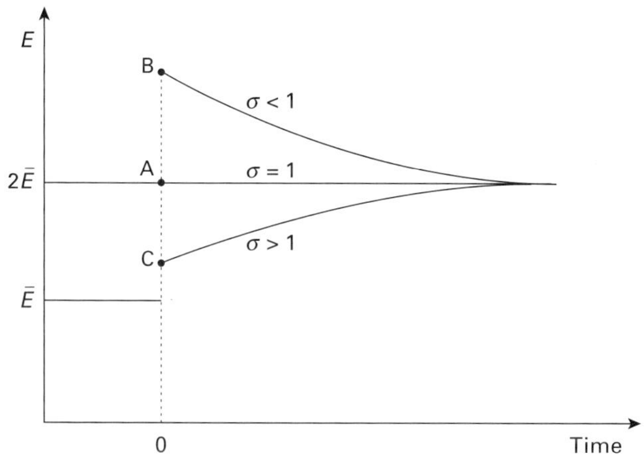

Figure 8.7
Overshooting

At $t = 0$ the nominal money supply doubles. Suppose that in response to this increase in the money supply, the nominal exchange rate also doubled (i.e., $\hat{E} = \hat{M}$), thereby adjusting instantaneously to its long-run equilibrium level.[12] This implies, of course, that the rate of depreciation would be zero and that the nominal interest rate would not change. Would the money market be in equilibrium? To answer this question, first notice that since $P = \sqrt{P^T P^N}$, P^N cannot jump, and $P^T = E$, the real money supply would increase by $\hat{M} - \hat{E}/2 = \hat{M}/2$. In other words, the real money supply would increase by 50 percent.

To find out the change in real money demand, we need to establish the change in the demand for nontradable goods. Since P^N does not change, the real exchange rate, $e(\equiv P^T/P^N)$, increases by the same proportion as the nominal money supply (i.e., it doubles). Given equation (8.8), the demand for nontradable goods also doubles (recall that c^T does not change). However, consumption of nontradables in terms of the price index (i.e., $c^N/\sqrt{e}$) increases by $\hat{M} - \hat{E}/2 = \hat{M}/2$. Since the consumption elasticity is σ (recall equation 8.36), the resulting increase in real money demand is therefore $\sigma \hat{M}/2$.

We can thus conclude that if the nominal exchange rate increased by the same proportion as the money supply, real money supply would increase by $\hat{M}/2$ and real money demand by $\sigma \hat{M}/2$. Hence the excess supply in the money market would be given by $\hat{M}/2 - \sigma \hat{M}/2$, which is simply $(1 - \sigma)\hat{M}/2$. Based on this expression, it follows immediately that:

- If $\sigma = 1$, both real money supply and real money demand increase by the same amount, and therefore the equiproportional increase in the nominal exchange rate (i.e., no overshooting or undershooting) is consistent with money market equilibrium.

12. A "hat" over a variable denotes proportional change; that is, $\hat{x} \equiv dx/x$. In the discussion that follows, all changes are being considered at $t = 0$.

- If $\sigma < 1$, real money supply would increase by more than real money demand, and there would be excess supply in the money market. This, of course, is not an equilibrium. The excess supply of money requires a fall in the nominal interest rate. For this to happen, the rate of depreciation must become negative (i.e., agents must expect a nominal *appreciation* of the currency over time). For the rate of depreciation to become negative, the nominal exchange rate must overshoot its long-run level and fall over time.
- If $\sigma > 1$, real money supply would increase by less than real money demand, and there would be excess demand for money. To equilibrate the money market, the nominal interest rate needs to increase. From the interest parity condition, this requires a depreciation of the currency over time. For this to happen, the nominal exchange rate must jump by less than its long-run level.

Finally, two observations are worth making. First, in general equilibrium, a sticky-prices model does not *necessarily* lead to a liquidity effect (i.e., an increase in M_t leading to a fall on impact of the nominal interest rate). In fact, as we have just seen, an increase in M_t is consistent with i_t falling, increasing, or remaining unchanged. Second, in the model the co-movement on impact between the nominal interest rate and the level of the exchange rate is also ambiguous. The model does not support the notion—typically found in the financial press and undergraduate textbooks—that a depreciation of the currency will be necessarily associated with a fall in nominal interest rates.

8.6 A Model of Sticky Wages

While the model with sticky prices developed above is extremely useful to ask a myriad of *positive* (as opposed to *normative*) questions—such as what happens when there is an increase in the money supply or a devaluation—it is not well suited to ask *normative* questions. The reason is that outside the steady state, output is demand-determined, and hence the present discounted value of output (which would determine the average level of consumption) does not obey any physical constraints. To address this shortcoming, this section develops a model with a fully specified supply side in which nominal wages—rather than prices—are sticky.[13] This will provide us with a model that, in addition to capturing the key dynamics of an economy with nominal rigidities, is perfectly suited to answer normative questions.

What are the kind of normative questions that we would like to ask? One of the most hotly debated by policy-oriented academic economists is under what circumstances a country would find it optimal to devalue its currency. In times of low growth and trade deficits, economists often call for a devaluation to address such imbalances. An excellent case in point is Rudiger Dornbusch's forceful advocacy of a devaluation in Mexico during 1994 (see box 8.3). The model

13. The model is a simpler version of Lahiri and Végh (2002). See Barro and Grossman (1971) for an early and highly influential contribution on disequilibrium models.

Box 8.3
To devalue or not to devalue? That is the question

In December 1987 annual inflation in Mexico had reached 160 percent. In response, the Mexican government implemented an exchange rate based stabilization program initially based on a fixed exchange rate and incomes and wages policies. As expected—and analyzed in detail in chapter 13—the exchange rate based stabilization program led to a significant real appreciation of the currency (figure 8.8). By April 1994 the continuing real appreciation accompanied by slow growth and a widening current account deficit had called into question the whole stabilization strategy. Further a speculative attack on the peso and a sharp upturn in interest rates were taken as an ominous sign of a future crisis.

At the time two sharply contrasting assessments of Mexico's situation became the subject of intense public debate. On the one hand, some observers, and in particular the authorities, put forth the view that the real appreciation simply reflected an equilibrium phenomenon resulting from the reforms that had been undertaken—both on the fiscal and trade fronts—and wealth effects stemming from the exchange rate based stabilization plan. The logical corollary of this view was that no policy remedies were needed. On the other hand, there was a disequilibrium view that, even if it accepted the potential benefits of reforms, liberalization, and the presence of NAFTA, argued that the overvaluation of the domestic currency was a policy mistake that could and should be remedied. Rudy Dornbusch, particularly in a joint 1994 paper with Alejandro Werner, was the most famous proponent of this view. Their idea was that the interaction of the exchange rate based stabilization and incomes policies had been responsible for the overvaluation. Using a model very similar to the sticky-inflation model to be used in chapter 12, they argued that fixing the nominal exchange rate would immediately reduce the nominal interest rate. Inertia in the inflation process, however, would imply that inflation would fall only slowly over time, leading to a real appreciation. Further the resulting fall in real interest rates

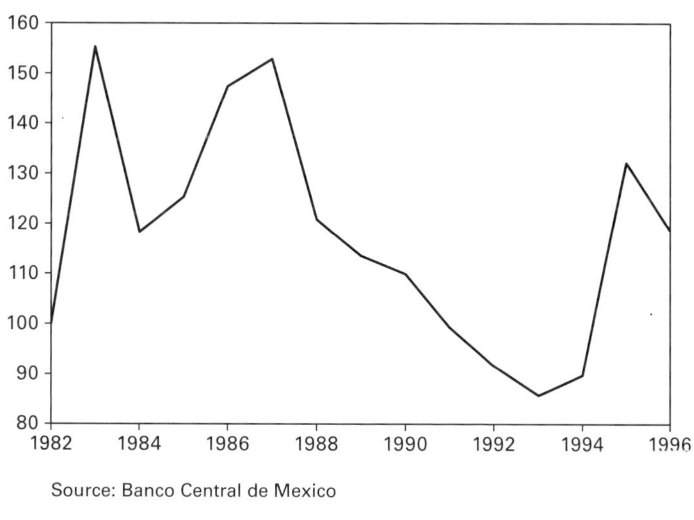

Figure 8.8
Real effective exchange rate (1982 = 100)

Box 8.3
(continued)

would push up aggregate demand and reinforce the process of real appreciation. In Dornbusch and Werner's view of the world, this real appreciation would slow growth and increase unemployment. In their minds the policy remedy was clear: a once-and-for-all devaluation of about 20 percent, which would take care of the real appreciation.

In his discussion of the Dornbusch–Werner piece, Guillermo Calvo (p. 303) vehemently disagreed. "In my opinion, this is not the time to implement a Dornbusch–Werner devaluation. The forces that have held together the "good" equilibrium may dissipate overnight." In Calvo's view, the biggest problem for Mexico was lack of credibility in government's policies, which would have led to a boom–bust cycle in consumption along the lines of chapter 7. In this scenario, real wages should have fallen and the currency should have depreciated in real terms in the bust phase. Downward price–wage rigidities, however, could have resulted in higher unemployment and excess capacity. A devaluation à la Dornbusch and Werner could solve the overappreciation problem in the short run, but it would also cause a more pronounced appreciation and inflation in the future. In Calvo's words (p. 301), "Authorities would have revealed their taste for discretionary policy, and people may come to believe that it could happen again. Therefore the same mechanism that provoked the present misalignment will be set in motion again."

In December 1994 Mexico devalued the peso by 15 percent. The devaluation set off a firestorm: since reserves were low before the devaluation, there was an immediate attack on the Mexican peso triggering a more substantial fall in reserves. Almost immediately the government was forced to allow the peso to float. From late 1994 to early 1995 the peso depreciated by almost 80 percent and the yield on CETES (Mexican T-bills) more than tripled (figure 8.9). The inescapable conclusion is that Calvo was right. Models such as the one in section 8.6 that ignore credibility problems may yield the wrong policy prescription!

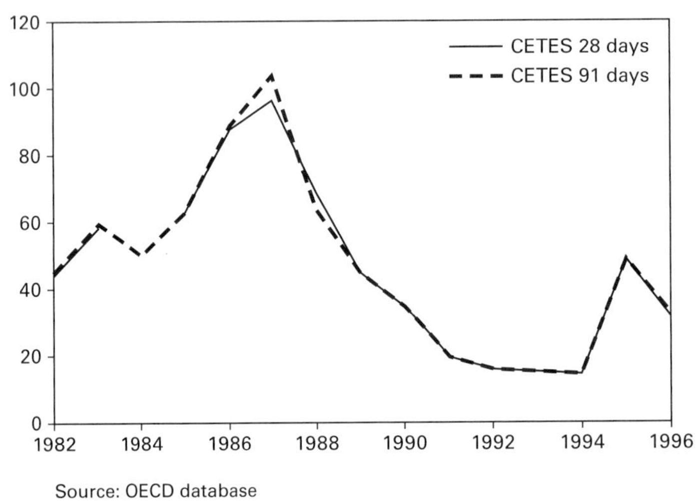

Figure 8.9
CETES yields (in percent)

developed in this section may in fact be viewed as the best-case scenario for a Dornbusch-type argument since, for conceptual clarity, the model focuses exclusively on nominal rigidities and ignores other potential problems that may be associated with a devaluation (like credibility problems). We will see that in this model it is optimal to devalue in response to a negative real shock.

To simplify the presentation, we will consider a one-good model and thus abstract from nontradable goods. We will, however, introduce a labor/leisure choice and hence endogenous production. The law of one price holds for the only good (i.e., $P_t = E_t P_t^*$). There is no foreign inflation, and to simplify notation, the foreign nominal price is taken to be unity (i.e., $P^* = 1$). Hence $P_t = E_t$. (Unless otherwise indicated, the notation is the same as above.) The economy operates under predetermined exchange rates, and for simplicity, the rate of devaluation is taken to be zero (i.e., the exchange rate is fixed).

8.6.1 Households

Preferences are now given by

$$\int_0^\infty \left\{\log[c_t - \phi(\ell_t^s)^\upsilon] + \log(m_t)\right\}\exp(-\beta t)dt, \qquad \phi > 0,\ \upsilon > 1, \tag{8.48}$$

where c_t is consumption of tradable goods (the only good in this world), ℓ_t^s denotes labor supply, m_t denotes real money balances ($m_t \equiv M_t/E_t$), and ϕ and ν are parameters.[14] These are the so-called GHH preferences—after Greenwood, Hercowitz, and Huffman (1988)—that generate a labor supply function that depends only on the real wage. In other words, there is no wealth effect on leisure, which greatly simplifies the solution of the model.[15]

The household's flow budget constraint is given by

$$\dot{a}_t = ra_t + w_t\ell_t^s + \tau_t + \Omega_t - c_t - i_t m_t, \tag{8.49}$$

where $a_t (\equiv m_t + b_t)$ denotes real financial wealth, $w_t (\equiv W_t/E_t)$ denotes the real wage, and Ω_t are dividends from firms (which are owned by households). The corresponding lifetime constraint reads as

$$a_0 + \int_0^\infty \left(w_t\ell_t^s + \Omega_t + \tau_t\right)\exp(-rt)dt = \int_0^\infty (c_t + i_t m_t)\exp(-rt)dt. \tag{8.50}$$

14. In this model it is critical to distinguish between labor supply and labor demand because, as discussed in detail below, the labor market may be in disequilibrium (i.e., labor supply may not be equal to labor demand at all points in time).

15. You may recall that we have already encountered these preferences in exercise 6 at the end of chapter 1.

The household chooses $\{c_t, \ell_t^s, m_t\}_{t=0}^{\infty}$ to maximize (8.48) subject to lifetime constraint (8.50). In terms of the Lagrangian,

$$\mathcal{L} = \int_0^{\infty} \{\log[c_t - \phi(\ell_t^s)^{\upsilon}] + \log(m_t)\}\exp(-\beta t)dt$$
$$+ \lambda \left[a_0 + \int_0^{\infty} (w_t \ell_t^s + \Omega_t + \tau_t)\exp(-rt)dt - \int_0^{\infty} (c_t + i_t m_t)\exp(-rt)dt \right].$$

The first-order conditions with respect to c_t, ℓ_t^s, and m_t are given by, respectively,

$$\frac{1}{c_t - \phi(\ell_t^s)^{\upsilon}} = \lambda, \tag{8.51}$$

$$\frac{\phi\upsilon(\ell_t^s)^{\upsilon-1}}{c_t - \phi(\ell_t^s)^{\upsilon}} = \lambda w_t, \tag{8.52}$$

$$\frac{1}{m_t} = \lambda i_t. \tag{8.53}$$

Condition (8.51) is a familiar condition in models with no intertemporal distortions; it says that along a perfect foresight path, the marginal utility of consumption will be constant. In this formulation, however, the marginal utility of consumption depends on labor supply. Hence consumption smoothing will not necessarily obtain.[16]

Substituting equation (8.51) into equation (8.52), we obtain [17]

$$\phi\upsilon(\ell_t^s)^{\upsilon-1} = w_t. \tag{8.54}$$

To obtain the labor supply schedule, solve for ℓ_t^s from this last equation:

$$\ell_t^s = \left(\frac{w_t}{\phi\upsilon}\right)^{1/\upsilon-1}. \tag{8.55}$$

As anticipated, labor supply depends solely on the real wage, w_t. Labor supply is an increasing function of the real wage, with the elasticity given by $1/(\upsilon - 1)$.

The money demand follows from combining (8.51) and (8.53):

$$m_t = \frac{c_t - \phi(\ell_t^s)^{\upsilon}}{i_t}. \tag{8.56}$$

16. As you may recall, this point was emphasized in exercise 6 in chapter 1.

17. In this disequilibrium model—and as discussed in detail below—actual employment may not coincide with labor supply, in which case first-order condition (8.52) and hence condition (8.54) will *not* hold.

GHH preferences thus generate a nonstandard money demand, in that the scale variable is consumption *net* of the disutility of labor.

8.6.2 Supply Side

Firms produce tradable goods according to the following technology:

$$y_t = \psi \left(\ell_t^d\right)^\alpha, \qquad \psi > 0, 0 < \alpha < 1, \tag{8.57}$$

where ℓ^d denotes labor demand and ψ and α are parameters.

The representative firm's profits are given by

$$\Omega_t = y_t - w_t \ell_t^d. \tag{8.58}$$

Substituting (8.57) into (8.58) yields

$$\Omega_t = \psi \left(\ell_t^d\right)^\alpha - w_t \ell_t^d. \tag{8.59}$$

Firms choose ℓ_t^d to maximize (8.59). The first-order condition is given by

$$\psi\alpha \left(\ell_t^d\right)^{\alpha-1} = w_t. \tag{8.60}$$

Production efficiency requires that the marginal productivity of labor be equated to the real wage. Solving for ℓ_t^d from equation (8.60) yields the labor demand equation:

$$\ell_t^d = \left(\frac{\alpha\psi}{w_t}\right)^{1/(1-\alpha)}. \tag{8.61}$$

Labor demand is a decreasing function of the real wage because a higher real wage induces firms to shed labor to increase its marginal productivity.

8.6.3 Labor Market

The key action in this model takes place in the labor market. To focus the discussion, figure 8.10 illustrates the labor market. Labor demand—given by equation (8.61)—is shown as a decreasing function of the real wage, whereas labor supply—given by equation (8.55)—is an increasing function of the real wage.[18] As a benchmark we will first discuss the flexible-wages case and then turn to the sticky-wages case.

18. For graphical exposition, both functions are shown as linear.

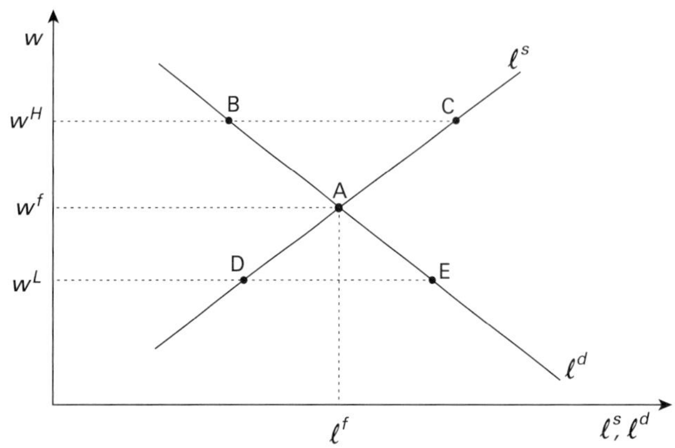

Figure 8.10
Labor market

Flexible Wages

In the flexible-wages version of this model, labor market equilibrium requires that

$$\ell_t^s = \ell_t^d.$$

Graphically, the economy is always at point A in figure 8.10. In other words, the economy always enjoys full employment in the sense that all workers that are willing to work at the prevailing real wage are employed. As indicated in figure 8.10, we will denote the flexible-wages equilibrium values of labor and the real wage by, respectively, ℓ_t^f and w_t^f. Formally, using (8.55) and (8.61), we have

$$\ell_t^f = \left(\frac{\psi\alpha}{\phi\upsilon}\right)^{1/(\upsilon-\alpha)}. \tag{8.62}$$

From (8.62) and (8.55), the equilibrium real wage can be expressed as:

$$w_t^f = (\alpha\psi)^{(\upsilon-1)/(\upsilon-\alpha)}\,(\phi\upsilon)^{(1-\alpha)/(\upsilon-\alpha)}. \tag{8.63}$$

Hence, in equilibrium, both the real wage and labor are an increasing function of the productivity parameter, ψ.

Sticky Wages

If the nominal wage is sticky (i.e., it is a predetermined variable), the labor market will not necessarily be in equilibrium.[19] The reason is that since the economy is operating under a fixed

19. To fix ideas, the discussion will assume that the nominal wage is sticky both upward and downward. An alternative assumption would be that the nominal wage is sticky downward but not upward. In that case sticky wages would not be a binding constraint for the economy's response to any shock that requires an *increase* in the equilibrium real wage.

exchange rate, a sticky *nominal* wage implies a sticky *real* wage. To illustrate the concept of labor market disequilibrium, suppose that the prevailing real wage is above the equilibrium real wage and given by w^H in figure 8.10. At the real wage w^H, labor supply (point C) exceeds labor demand (point B). Graphically, the excess supply of labor is given by the segment BC in figure 8.10. Conversely, suppose that the prevailing real wage is below the equilibrium real wage and given by w^L in figure 8.10. At this real wage, there is excess demand for labor—given by the segment DE.

If there is excess labor supply or demand, what will *actual* employment be? The more natural assumption—and the one commonly adopted in the literature—is that the *short end* of the market prevails. Specifically, if labor demand falls short of labor supply, actual employment is given by labor demand (point B in figure 8.10). If, however, labor supply falls short of labor demand, actual employment is given by labor supply (point D in figure 8.10). Formally, denoting actual labor by ℓ_t^a, we have

$$\ell_t^a = \begin{cases} \ell_t^f & \text{if } \ell_t^d = \ell_t^s, \\ \ell_t^d & \text{if } \ell_t^d < \ell_t^s, \\ \ell_t^s & \text{if } \ell_t^d > \ell_t^s. \end{cases}$$

As a result, if the real wage is w^H, there is involuntary unemployment in the sense that not all workers willing to work at the prevailing wage are employed (i.e., $\ell_t^a < \ell_t^s$). If the wage is w^L, firms would not be able to hire all the workers that they would like at the prevailing real wage (i.e., $\ell_t^a < \ell_t^d$). In either case the labor market is in *disequilibrium* because demand and supply are not the same. This is, of course, equivalent to saying that one of the two marginal conditions related to the labor market is not holding. If $\ell_t^a = \ell_t^d < \ell_t^s$, firms are operating on their demand curve (i.e., marginal condition 8.60 holds) but households are not on their labor supply curve (i.e., condition 8.54 does not hold because the marginal disutility of labor, evaluated at ℓ_t^a, falls short of the real wage). Conversely, if $\ell_t^a = \ell_t^s < \ell_t^d$, then households are on their labor supply curve, but firms are not on their demand curve (the marginal productivity of labor evaluated at ℓ_t^a in fact exceeds the real wage).

Finally, we need to ask: If the labor market is in disequilibrium, how will it adjust over time to reach equilibrium? A natural assumption regarding the adjustment in the labor market is to posit that the nominal wage evolves according to the deviation of the actual real wage from the full-employment real wage:

$$\dot{W}_t = \eta \left(w^f - \frac{W_t}{E_t} \right), \qquad \eta > 0, \ W_0 \text{ given.} \tag{8.64}$$

Hence, if the prevailing real wage is above the full-employment level (i.e., $W_t/E_t > w^f$), the nominal wage falls over time. The idea is that the excess labor supply leads to a gradual fall in nominal wages as unemployed workers become more willing over time to take jobs at lower nominal wages. In contrast, if the prevailing real wage is below the full-employment level (i.e., $W_t/E_t < w^f$) and there is thus excess demand for labor, the nominal wage increases over time reflecting the willingness of firms to pay higher nominal wages due to the tight labor market conditions.

8.6.4 Government

The government's budget constraints are unchanged relative to our previous model and continue to be given by equations (8.13) and (8.14).

8.6.5 Equilibrium Conditions

Given perfect capital mobility and a fixed exchange rate, it follows that

$$i_t = r. \tag{8.65}$$

Before aggregating the households' and firms' constraints, we need to take into account that when the labor market is in disequilibrium, the relevant labor variable for either households' wage income or firm's productive purposes is ℓ_t^a. Hence we can replace ℓ_t^s with ℓ_t^a in the households' budget constraint (8.49) and ℓ_t^d with ℓ_t^a in the firms' profits (8.59). We can then combine both to obtain

$$\dot{a}_t = ra_t + \psi \left(\ell_t^a\right)^\alpha + \tau_t - c_t - i_t m_t.$$

Combining this constraint with the government's flow constraint—given by (8.13)—yields

$$\dot{k}_t = rk_t + \psi \left(\ell_t^a\right)^\alpha - c_t,$$

where $k_t \equiv b_t + h_t$.

Integrating forward this last equation and imposing the appropriate transversality condition, we obtain the economy's resource constraint:

$$k_0 + \int_0^\infty \psi \left(\ell_t^a\right)^\alpha \exp(-rt)dt = \int_0^\infty c_t \exp(-rt)dt. \tag{8.66}$$

8.6.6 Initial Stationary Equilibrium

Consider an initial perfect foresight equilibrium path in which the economy is in a full-employment equilibrium. The equilibrium labor and real wage are constant over time and given by expressions (8.62) and (8.63), respectively. From (8.57) it follows that full-employment output is given by

$$y^f = \psi \left(\ell^f\right)^\alpha. \tag{8.67}$$

From the resource constraint (8.66), it follows that full-employment consumption is given by

$$c^f = rk_0 + \psi\left(\ell^f\right)^{\alpha}. \tag{8.68}$$

Finally, we can derive the real money demand from (8.56) and (8.65):

$$m^f = \frac{c^f - \phi(\ell^f)^{\upsilon}}{r}. \tag{8.69}$$

8.6.7 Permanent Fall in Productivity

Suppose that just before time $t = 0$ the economy is in the full-employment stationary equilibrium just described. At time 0, there is an unanticipated and permanent reduction in the productivity parameter ψ. As a benchmark, we will first analyze the adjustment that would take place under flexible wages and then focus on the sticky-wages case.

Flexible Wages

As (8.61) makes clear, the fall in ψ reduces labor demand for a given level of the real wage. In terms of figure 8.11, the initial equilibrium is given by point A. The fall in productivity shifts the labor demand to the left (from ℓ^d to $\left(\ell^d\right)'$). The labor market adjusts instantaneously from its initial equilibrium, point A, to the new equilibrium, point B, at which both the real wage $(w^f)'$ and employment $\left(\ell^f\right)'$ are lower. Since the exchange rate is fixed, the fall in the real wage is effected through a fall in the *nominal* wage, W. Both output and consumption fall, as follows from (8.67) and (8.68). (This adjustment is captured by the solid lines in figure 8.12.)

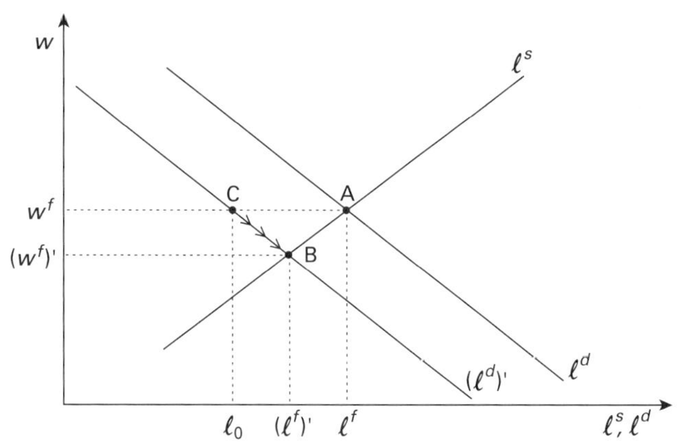

Figure 8.11
Labor market: Fall in productivity

Although it seems intuitive tha, in response to the fall in consumption, real money demand should fall, this is not formally obv, ›us from just glancing at equation (8.69). To formally show this, we compute the change in $c^f - \phi(\ell^f)^\upsilon$ in response to a small change in ψ which, using (8.68), leads to

$$\frac{d\left[c^f - \phi(\ell^f)^\upsilon\right]}{d\psi} = \left(\ell^f\right)^\alpha + \frac{d\ell^f}{d\psi}\left[\psi\alpha\left(\ell^f\right)^{\alpha-1} - \phi\upsilon(\ell^f)^{\upsilon-1}\right].$$

The term in square brackets on the RHS is simply the difference between the marginal productivity of labor and the marginal disutility of labor, which is always zero under flexible wages. Hence

$$\frac{d\left[c^f - \phi(\ell^f)^\upsilon\right]}{d\psi} = \left(\ell^f\right)^\alpha > 0. \tag{8.70}$$

Intuitively, this is an envelope condition that says that at an optimum, consumption net of the disutility of labor falls by the direct effect of the fall in productivity on output since, at the margin, production efficiency always implies that the marginal productivity of labor is equated to the marginal disutility of labor. In light of (8.70), it follows that real money demand falls.

Finally, we verify that, as one should expect, welfare falls. Given equation (8.69) and that the economy jumps from one stationary state to the next, we infer from (8.48) that the change in welfare depends on the change in $c^f - \phi(\ell^f)^\upsilon$. Since we have shown that $c^f - \phi(\ell^f)^\upsilon$ falls, welfare also falls.

Sticky Wages

Suppose now that the nominal wage is sticky. Since the economy is operating under a fixed exchange rate, the real wage cannot change on impact. Hence, on impact, the economy finds itself at point C in figure 8.11. At the prevailing wage, w^f, there is excess supply of labor and actual employment, ℓ^a, is given by labor demand at the level ℓ_0. We thus see how, in the presence of sticky nominal wages, this negative supply shock leads to involuntary unemployment, in the amount CA in figure 8.11.

How will the nominal wage evolve over time? At $t = 0$, we know, using (8.64), that

$$\dot{W}_0 = \eta\left[\left(w^f\right)' - \frac{W_0}{E}\right] < 0.$$

The nominal wage begins to fall at time 0 and then will continue falling over time. Since the exchange rate is fixed, the real wage, which does not change on impact, also falls over time towards its full-employment level (figure 8.12, panel b). As the real wage falls over time, actual employment will continue to be given by the short end of the market. In terms of figure 8.11, this means that actual employment will increase over time along the arrowed path from point C to point B as the nominal—and hence real—wage fall over time. Formally, it follows from (8.61) that

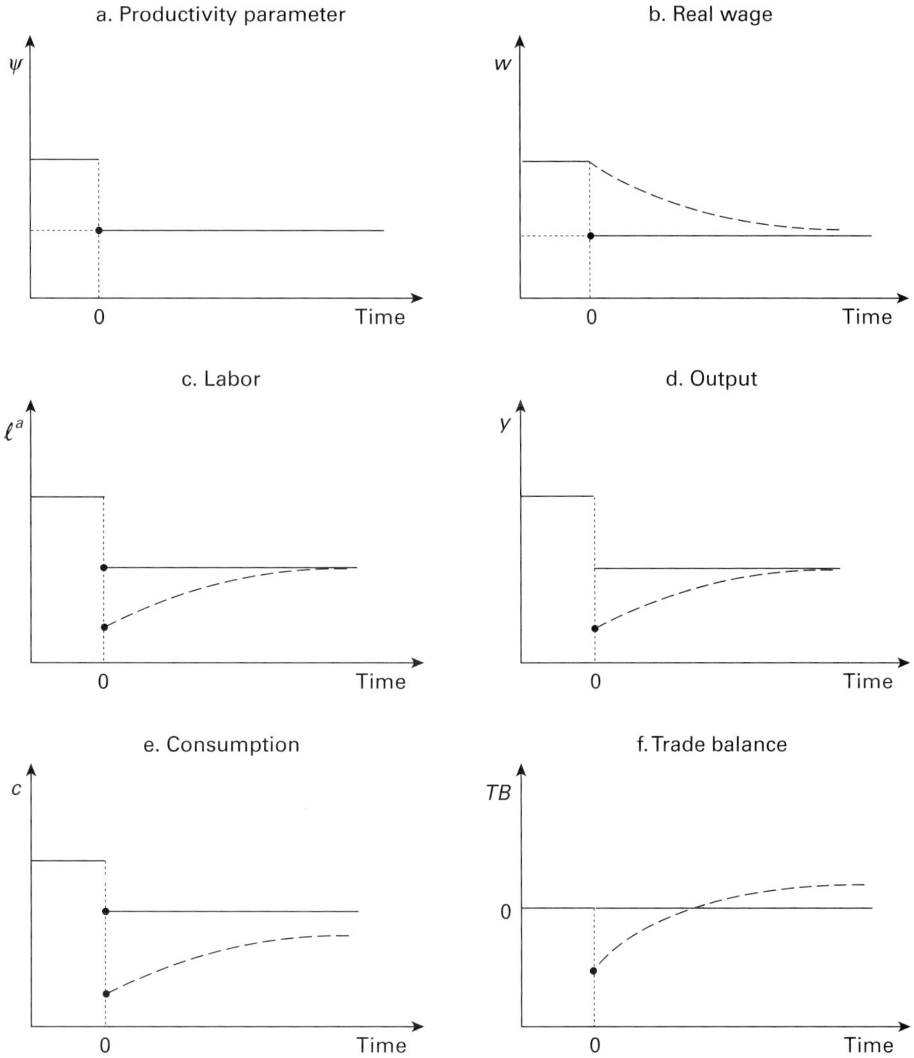

Note: A solid line indicates the adjustment under flexible wages; a dashed line under sticky wages.

Figure 8.12
Permanent fall in productivity

$$\dot{\ell}_t^a = \dot{\ell}_t^d = -\frac{\ell_t^d}{(1-\alpha)w_t}\dot{w}_t > 0.$$

The path of labor is given by figure 8.12, panel c. On impact the fall in employment is therefore larger than under flexible wages. Given the production function (8.57), the path of output follows that of labor (figure 8.12, panel d). The initial fall in output is thus also larger under sticky wages than under flexible wages.

Let us turn to the behavior of consumption.[20] From first-order condition (8.51) and the fact that labor increases over time, it follows that consumption also increases over time:

$$\dot{c}_t = \phi\upsilon\left(\ell_t^a\right)^{\upsilon-1}\dot{\ell}_t^a > 0. \tag{8.71}$$

To find out the change on impact, we need to look at the resource constraint. The output path illustrated in figure 8.12, panel d, indicates that the present discounted value of output falls. Hence consumption can neither increase nor stay the same for, if it did, the present discounted value of consumption would increase and thus violate the resource constraint. We thus conclude that consumption falls on impact. Figure 8.12, panel e, illustrates the path of consumption.[21]

What happens to the trade balance? By definition, $TB_t = y_t - c_t$. Hence, taking into account (8.57) and (8.71), we can write

$$\dot{TB}_t = \left[\psi\alpha\left(\ell_t^a\right)^{\alpha-1} - \phi\upsilon\left(\ell^a\right)^{\upsilon-1}\right]\dot{\ell}_t^a > 0, \tag{8.72}$$

where the sign follows from the fact that at point C in figure 8.11 (and any other point along the arrowed path CB), the marginal productivity of labor is greater than the marginal disutility of labor. The trade balance thus improves over time. On impact, the trade balance must therefore fall. If it did not change or increase on impact—and since it then increases over time—it would violate the resource constraint. The path of the trade balance is illustrated in figure 8.12, panel f (assuming $k_0 = 0$). It follows that there is some consumption smoothing taking place as the trade deficit is largest early on when the production is at its lowest point.

We now turn to the path of real money balances, which, from (8.56) and (8.65), is given by

$$m_t = \frac{c_t - \phi(\ell_t^a)^\upsilon}{r}. \tag{8.73}$$

20. Under sticky wages, one way to think about the household's optimization problem is that the household is now taking as given the path of labor illustrated in figure 12, panel c, and optimally choosing consumption and real money balances (see Barro and Grossman 1971 for a detailed discussion).

21. To show that consumption ends up below its full-employment level, notice that as shown in appendix 8.8.2, net consumption (i.e., $c_t - \phi(\ell_t^a)^\upsilon$), which is constant along a PFEP, is lower under sticky wages than under flexible wages. Since labor eventually converges to the same value in both cases, consumption must be lower in the long run under sticky wages than under flexible wages.

We know from first-order condition (8.51) that $c_t - \phi(\ell_t^a)^\upsilon$ will be constant along the new perfect foresight path. Further, as shown in appendix 8.8.2, $c_t - \phi(\ell_t^a)^\upsilon$ falls on impact. Hence real money demand will fall on impact as well and remain at that level thereafter.

Finally, we turn to the issue of welfare. It should be clear that the economy's adjustment under sticky wages is costlier than under flexible wages. In fact, since there are no distortions of any kind in the flexible wages case, the economy's adjustment constitutes the first-best response. In other words, given that the economy is poorer, it is optimal to adjust immediately to the new reality. It follows that the adjustment under sticky nominal wages—which deviates from the first-best adjustment—is costlier.

It is easy to formally verify that welfare falls by more in the sticky wage than in the flexible wage case. As shown in appendix 8.8.2, $c_t - \phi(\ell_t^a)^\upsilon$ falls by more in the sticky wage case than in the flexible wage case. Given (8.48) and (8.73), welfare depends directly on $c_t - \phi(\ell_t^a)^\upsilon$. Hence welfare will also be lower.

8.6.8 Optimal Devaluation

As illustrated in figure 8.12, we have concluded from our analysis that sticky nominal wages interfere with the optimal adjustment of the economy to a negative shock. Since the economy has become poorer as the result of a permanent fall in productivity, the optimal adjustment consists in an immediate reduction in the real wage (from point A to point B in figure 8.11), which ensures that full employment continues to prevail (albeit at a lower level given that the economy is now less productive). Under fixed exchange rates the adjustment in the real wage should take place through a fall in the nominal wage. By preventing the real wage from adjusting, wage stickiness causes the economy to undergo a costlier adjustment. Indeed the economy must go through a protracted period of unemployment before it finally reaches the long-run equilibrium. As a result welfare is lower than in the flexible wage equilibrium.

Is there anything policy makers can do to ease the economy's adjustment under sticky wages? They certainly can. By devaluing when the negative shock hits, policy makers can reduce the real wage from w^f to $(w^f)'$ in figure 8.11, and thus manage to take the economy from point A to point B despite sticky wages. The reduction in the real wage is achieved through a devaluation rather than through a fall in the nominal wage. Clearly, the devaluation is the first-best response to this negative shock as it replicates the outcome that would prevail under flexible wages.[22]

Even if policy makers do not devalue as soon as the negative shock hits, it would still be optimal to devalue at any point in time during the economy's adjustment from point C to point B

22. For the same reasons it is easy to see that under flexible exchange rates, the economy would adjust instantaneously from point A to point B *despite* sticky wages! This suggests that in a world with nominal rigidities—and in response to real shocks—flexible rates are better than fixed rates. The opposite, however, will be true for monetary shocks. We will study these issues in detail in chapter 11 on optimal exchange rate regimes. Notice nevertheless that a change in the nominal exchange rate (either a devaluation or a revaluation) starting from a steady state would always lead to a fall in labor and output, as analyzed in exercise 3 at the end of this chapter.

in figure 8.11 and to take the economy immediately to point B, rather than letting the adjustment take its natural course. The adjustment along the segment CB in figure 8.11 is characterized in fact by low output and (initial) trade deficits, symptoms that are often seen as requiring a discrete devaluation. Yet to make the best-case scenario for a devaluation, we have ignored many other important aspects of reality, such as credibility problems, that may play an important role in practice (see box 8.3).[23]

8.7 Final Remarks

This chapter has removed the veil from our monetary model in chapter 5 by incorporating sticky prices, by far the most popular friction in open economy models. In such an environment permanent increases in either the level or rate of growth of the money supply are expansionary as they lead to higher aggregate demand and output. Sticky prices also allowed us to rationalize the high volatility of nominal exchange rates (i.e., the overshooting phenomenon). In a similar vein, a devaluation leads to higher output and consumption, in contrast to the model of chapter 6 where a devaluation reduces consumption and total output. We have also studied a disequilibrium model of sticky wages, a slightly more complicated theoretical setup but arguably a more insightful representation of a world with nominal rigidities. In particular, we saw how such a model can rationalize the need for a devaluation of the domestic currency in response to a negative shock.

This chapter concludes our first incursion into monetary models. We studied the basic monetary model in chapter 5—in which money is a veil—and then removed the veil by abstracting from interest-bearing bonds (chapter 6), introducing a link between nominal interest rates and consumption (chapter 7) and sticky prices (chapter 8). We now move to part III of the book in which we will put all these tools to work in our quest for understanding important macroeconomic policy issues.

8.8 Appendixes

8.8.1 Calvo's (1983) Staggered Prices

Calvo (1983) developed an extremely useful continuous-time version of the staggered-prices models à la Taylor (1979, 1980) and Fischer (1977). Suppose that there is a large number (technically, a continuum) of firms in the [0, 1] interval. The total number of firms is therefore one. Each

23. This simple model would also capture the essence of Greece's policy dilemma in early 2012. We could think of Greece as being somewhere between points C and B. Its real wage is too high (Greece is "not competitive," as the financial press would put it), and barring exiting the eurozone and being able to devalue its currency, Greece will need to undergo a painful period of low output and unemployment before reaching full-employment equilibrium (point B). Leaving the euro area, however, could also bring unforeseen consequences due to credibility problems.

firm produces a nonstorable, nontradable good at zero variable cost whose quantity is demand-determined. Each firm may change its price only when it receives a random price signal. The probability of receiving a signal follows an exponential distribution. When a firm changes its price, it takes into account the expected average price and the level of excess aggregate demand expected to prevail in the future.

The probability of receiving a price signal j periods from now is $\delta e^{-\delta j}$, where $\delta > 0$. The firm's price setting rule is assumed to be given by

$$\log(V_t) = \delta \int_t^{\infty} [\log(P_s^N) + \omega A_s] \exp(-\delta(s-t)) ds, \qquad \omega > 0, \tag{8.74}$$

where V_t is the price quotation set at t, P_s^N is the price level of nontradables (to be defined below) A_s denotes excess aggregate demand and ω a parameter that captures the sensitivity of the price rule to aggregate demand. Note that V_t may jump if an unexpected change in, say, A takes place.

The (logarithm of) the price level of nontradables is defined as the weighted average of prices currently quoted. Hence

$$\log(P_t^N) = \delta \int_{-\infty}^{t} \log(V_s) \exp(-\delta(t-s)) ds. \tag{8.75}$$

An important observation is that unlike V_t, P_t^N is a *predetermined* variable because it is given by past price quotations. Along paths where P_t^N and A_t are uniquely determined, however, V_t is a continuous function of time. Differentiating equation (8.75) with respect to time yields (using Leibniz's rule)

$$\pi_t = \delta \left[\log(V_t) - \log(P_t^N)\right], \tag{8.76}$$

where $\pi_t \equiv \dot{P}_t^N / P_t^N$. Notice that anticipated changes in A_t will not affect π_t. In other words, along a perfect foresight path, π_t will be a continuous function of time.

At points in time at which A_t is continuous, we can differentiate equation (8.74) to obtain (again, using Leibniz's rule)

$$\frac{\dot{V}_t}{V_t} = \delta \left[\log(V_t) - \log(P_t^N) - \omega A_t\right]. \tag{8.77}$$

It follows from (8.76) and (8.77) that (at points in time at which A_t is continuous)

$$\dot{\pi}_t = -\theta A_t, \tag{8.78}$$

where $\theta \equiv \delta^2 \omega > 0$. Equation (8.78) is thus a "higher" order inverse Phillips curve, which indicates that the *change* in the inflation rate is *negatively* related to excess demand.

8.8.2 Sticky-Wage Model

This appendix analyzes the behavior of $c_t - \phi(\ell_t^a)^\upsilon$ in response to the permanent fall in the productivity parameter, ψ. First-order condition (8.51)—with ℓ_t^a in lieu of ℓ_t^s—indicates that $c_t - \phi(\ell_t^a)^\upsilon$ will be constant along the new perfect foresight path. To pin down the level, we need to compute the present discounted value of $c_t - \phi(\ell_t^a)^\upsilon$. Using the economy's resource constraint, we can write it as

$$PDV \equiv \int_0^\infty \left[c_t - \phi(\ell_t^a)^\upsilon\right]\exp(-rt)dt = k_0 + \int_0^\infty \left[\psi\left(\ell_t^a\right)^\alpha - \phi(\ell_t^a)^\upsilon\right]\exp(-rt)dt.$$

Let us focus then on the behavior of the expression $\psi\left(\ell_t^a\right)^\alpha - \phi(\ell_t^a)^\upsilon$. From (8.72), we know that in the case of sticky wages, this expression increases over time. Further we know that in the new stationary equilibrium, this expression will end up being the same under both flexible and sticky wages. Hence it must be the case that under sticky wages, this expression falls at time 0 and then increases over time. It follows that *PDV* above must be higher under flexible than sticky wages. This in turn implies that $c_t - \phi(\ell_t^a)^\upsilon$, which is constant over time in both the flexible and the sticky-wages cases, falls by more under sticky than flexible wages. From (8.73), it follows that m_t falls and, in fact, falls by more in the sticky than in the flexible-wages case.

Exercises

1. (Temporary reduction in money growth rate) The purpose of this exercise is to show that the sticky-prices model developed in the text is capable of explaining situations of "stagflation" (i.e., the coexistence of high inflation and output below the full-employment level).

In the context of the model developed in section 8.2, analyze the effects of a temporary reduction in the money growth rate.

2. (Fiscal policy in a sticky-prices model) This exercise incorporates fiscal policy into the sticky prices model analyzed in this chapter and studies the effects of a permanent increase in government spending on nontradable goods (denoted by g_t^N) under both flexible and predetermined exchange rates.

Specifically, suppose that preferences are given by

$$\int_0^\infty \left[\log(c_t^T) + \log(c_t^N) + \log(m_t)\right]\exp(-\beta t)dt,$$

The consumer's intertemporal constraint is given by

$$a_0 + \int_0^\infty \left(y_t^T + \frac{y_t^N}{e_t} + \tau_t\right)\exp(-rt)dt = \int_0^\infty \left(c_t^T + \frac{c_t^N}{e_t} + i_t m_t\right)\exp(-rt)dt.$$

The government's flow budget constraint is given by

$$\dot{h}_t = rh_t + \dot{m}_t + \varepsilon_t m_t - \tau_t - \frac{g_t^N}{e_t}.$$

The corresponding intertemporal constraint is given by

$$h_0 + \int_0^\infty (\dot{m}_t + \varepsilon_t m_t) \exp(-rt)dt = \int_0^\infty \left(\frac{g_t^N}{e_t} + \tau_t\right) \exp(-rt)dt.$$

Equilibrium in the nontradable goods market dictates that

$$y_t^N = c_t^N + g_t^N.$$

The rest of the model remains the same as in the text.

In the context of this model:

a. Analyze the effects of a permanent and unanticipated increase in government spending on nontradable goods under flexible exchange rates.

b. Analyze the effects of a permanent and unanticipated increase in government spending on nontradable goods under predetermined exchange rates.

c. Explain intuitively why the response is the same. Do you think that it would continue to be the same under non-logarithmic preferences? [24]

3. (Devaluation/revaluation in a sticky-wages model) In the context of the sticky-wages model of section 8.6, show that both a devaluation and a revaluation of the currency (i.e., an increase and a decrease in the nominal exchange rate) lead to a fall in actual labor and output. (Lahiri and Végh 2002 use this feature of the sticky-wages model to think about the costs of a fluctuating nominal exchange rate.)

References

Agenor, Pierre-Richard. 1991. Output, devaluation and the real exchange rate in developing countries. *Review of World Economics* 127 (1): 18–41.

Agenor, Pierre-Richard, and Peter J. Montiel. 1999. *Development macroeconomics*, 2nd ed. Princeton: Princeton University Press.

Alvarez, Luis J., and Ignacio Hernando. 2006. Price setting behaviour in Spain. Evidence from consumer price micro-data. *Economic Modelling* 23 (4): 699–716.

Aucremanne, Luc, and Emmanuel Dhyne. 2004. How frequently do prices change? Evidence based on the micro data underlying the Belgian CPI. ECB Working Paper 331. European Central Bank, Frankfurt.

24. The data in fact suggest that output responds differently under predetermined and flexible exchange rates (see Ilzetzki, Mendoza, and Végh 2010).

Baharad, Eyal, and Benjamin Eden. 2004. Price rigidity and price dispersion: Evidence from micro data. *Review of Economic Dynamics* 7 (3): 613–41.

Barro, Robert J,. and Herschel I. Grossman. 1971. A general disequilibrium model of income and employment. *American Economic Review* 61 (1): 82–93.

Barros, Rebecca, Marco Bonomo, Carlos Carvalho, and Silvia Matos. 2009. Price setting in a variable macroeconomic environment: Evidence from Brazilian CPI. Unpublished paper. Getulio Vargas Foundation and Federal Reserve Bank of New York.

Baudry, Laurent, Hervé Le Bihan, Patrick Sevestre and Sylvie Tarrieu. 2007. What do thirteen million price records have to say about consumer price rigidity? *Oxford Bulletin of Economics and Statistics* 69 (2): 139–83.

Baumgartner, Josef, Ernst Glatzer, Fabio Rumler, and Alfred Stiglbauer. 2005. How frequently do consumer prices change in Austria? Evidence from micro CPI Data. ECB Working Paper 523. European Central Bank, Frankfurt.

Bils, Mark, and Peter Klenow. 2004. Some evidence on the importance of sticky prices. *Journal of Political Economy* 112 (5): 947–85.

Blinder, Alan S., Elie R. D. Canetti, David F. Lebow, and Jeremy B. Rudd. 1999. Asking about prices: A new approach to understanding price stickiness. *Review of Industrial Organization* 15 (1): 97–101.

Bunn, Philip, and Colin Ellis. 2009. Price-setting behaviour in the United Kingdom: A microdata approach. *Bank of England Quarterly Bulletin* 2009 Q1.

Buffie, Edward, and Yongkul Won. 2001. Devaluation and investment in an optimizing model of the small open economy. *European Economic Review* 45 (8): 1461–99.

Calvo, Guillermo A. 1983. Staggered prices in a utility-maximizing framework. *Journal of Monetary Economics* 12 (3): 383–98.

Calvo, Guillermo A. and Carlos A. Végh. 1993. Exchange rate-based stabilisation under imperfect credibility. In Helmut Frisch and Andreas Worgotter, eds., *Open-Economy Macroeconomics*. London: Macmillan, 3–28.

Carlton, Dennis W. 1986. The Rigidity of Prices. *American Economic Review* 76 (4): 637–58.

Cavallo, Alberto. 2010. Scraped data and sticky prices: Frequency, hazards and synchronization. Mimeo. Harvard University.

Cavallo, Michele, Kate Kisselev, Fabrizio Perri, and Nouriel Roubini. 2004. Exchange rate overshooting and the costs of floating. Mimeo. New York University.

Cecchetti, Stephen. 1986. The frequency of price adjustment: A study of the newsstand prices of magazines. *Journal of Econometrics* 31 (3): 255–74.

Cespedes, Luis F., Roberto Chang, and Andres Velasco. 2004. Balance sheets and exchange rate policy. *American Economic Review* 94 (4): 1183–93.

Chari, V.V., Patrick K. Kehoe, and Ellen R. McGrattan. 2002. Can sticky price models generate volatile and persistent real exchange rates? *Review of Economic Studies* 69 (3): 533–63.

Cooper, Richard N. 1971. Currency Devaluation in Developing Countries. Princeton: (Princeton University) Press.

Coricelli, Fabrizio, and Roman Horváth, 2010. Price setting and market structure: An empirical analysis of micro data. *Managerial and Decision Economics* 31 (2–3): 209–33.

Creamer, Kenneth, and Neil A. Rankin. 2008. Price setting in South Africa 2001–2007: Stylised facts using consumer price micro data. *Journal of Development Perspectives* 1 (4): 93–118.

Dias, Daniel, Mónica Dias, and Pedro D. Neves. 2004. Stylised features of price setting behaviour in Portugal: 1992–2001. ECB Working Paper 332. European Central Bank, Frankfurt.

Díaz-Alejandro, Carlos F. 1963. A note on the impact of devaluation and the redistributive effect. *Journal of Political Economy* 71: 577–80.

Dhyne, E., L. J. Álvarez, H. Le Bihan, G. Veronese, D. Dias, J. Hoffmann, N. Jonker, P. Lünnemann, F. Rumler and J. Vilmunen. 2006. Price changes in the euro area and the United States: Some facts from individual consumer price data. *Journal of Economic Perspectives* 20 (2): 171–92.

Dornbusch, Rudiger. 1976. Expectations and exchange rate dynamics. *Journal of Political Economy* 84 (6): 1161–76.

Dornbusch, Rudiger, and Alejandro Werner. 1994. Mexico: Stabilization, reform, and no growth. *Brookings Papers on Economic Activity* 25 (1994–1): 253–316. (Includes discussions by Stanley Fisher and Guillermo Calvo.)

Edwards, Sebastian. 1986. Are devaluations contractionary? *Review of Economics and Statistics* 68 (3): 501–508.

Eichenbaum, Martin, Nir Jaimovich, and Sergio Rebelo. 2011. Reference prices, costs and nominal rigidities. *American Economic Review* 101 (1): 234–62.

Fabiani, Silvia, Angela Gattulli, Roberto Sabbatini and Giovanni Veronese. 2006. Consumer price setting in Italy. *Giornale degli Economisti e Annali di Economia* 65 (1): 31–74.

Fischer, Stanley. 1977. Long-term contracts, rational expectations,and the optimal money supply rule. *Journal of Political Economy* 85 (1): 191–205.

Fleming, Marcus J. 1962. Domestic financial policies under fixed and under floating exchange rates. *IMF Staff Papers* 9 (3): 369–79.

Gabriel, Peter, and Adam Reiff. 2010. Price setting in Hungary—a store-level analysis. *Managerial and Decision Economics* 31 (2–3): 161–76.

Gagnon, Etienne. 2009. Price setting during low and high inflation: Evidence from Mexico. *Quarterly Journal of Economics* 124: 1221–63.

Gouvea, Solange. 2007. Price rigidity in Brazil: Evidence from CPI micro data. Working Paper 143. Central Bank of Brazil, Brazilia.

Greenwood, Jeremy, Zvi Hercowitz and Gregory Huffman. 1988. Investment, capacity utilization, and the real business cycle. *American Economic Review* 78 (3): 402–17.

Gylfason, Thorvaldur and Michael Schmid. 1983. Does devaluation cause stagflation? *Canadian Journal of Economics* 16 (4): 641–54.

Gupta, Poonam, Deepak Mishra, and Ratna Sahay. 2007. Behavior of output during currency crises. *Journal of International Economics* 72 (2): 428–50.

Hansen, Bo William and Niels Lynggard Hansen. 2006. Price setting behavior in Denmark: A study of CPI micro data 1997–2005. Danmarks Nationalbank Working Paper 39. Copenhagen.

Hoffmann, Johannes and Jeong-Ryeol Kurz-Kim. 2006. Consumer price adjustment under the microscope: Germany in a period of low inflation. ECB Working Paper 652. European Central Bank, Frankfurt.

Ilzetzki, Ethan, Enrique Mendoza, and Carlos Végh. 2010. How big (small?) are fiscal multipliers? Working Paper 16479. National Bureau of Economic Research, Cambridge, MA.

Jonker, Nicole, Carsten Folkertsma, and Harry Blijenberg. 2004. Empirical analysis of price setting behaviour in the Netherlands in the period 1998–2003 using micro data. ECB Working Paper 413. European Central Bank, Frankfurt.

Kamin, Steven B., and Marc Klau. 1998. Some multi-country evidence on the effects of real exchange rates on output. Federal Reserve Board International Finance Discussion Paper 611. Washington, DC.

Kashyap, Anil. 1995. Sticky prices: New evidence from retail catalogs. *Quarterly Journal of Economics* 110 (1): 245–71.

Klenow, Peter, and Oleksiy Kryvtsov. 2008. State-dependent or time-dependent pricing: Does it matter for recent U.S. inflation? *Quarterly Journal of Economics* 123 (3): 863–904.

Klenow, Peter, and Benjamin Malin. 2010. Microeconomic evidence on price setting. In Benjamin Friedman and Michael Woodford, eds. *Handbook of Monetary Economics* vol. 313. Amsterdam: Elsevier North Holland, 231–181.

Kovanen, Arto. 2006. Why do prices in Sierra Leone change so often? A case study using micro-level price data. IMF Working Paper 06/53. International Monetary Fund. Washington D.C.

Krugman, Paul, and Lance Taylor. 1978. Contractionary effects of devaluation. *Journal of International Economics* 8 (3): 445–56.

Lahiri, Amartya, and Carlos A. Végh. 2002. Living with the fear of floating: An optimal policy perspective. In Sebastian Edwards and Jeffrey Frankel, eds., *Preventing Currency Crises in Emerging Markets*. Chicago: University of Chicago Press, 663–704.

Levy, Daniel, Mark Bergen, Shantanu Dutta, and Robert Venable. 1997. The magnitude of menu costs: Direct evidence from large U.S. supermarket chains. *Quarterly Journal of Economics* 112: 791–825.

Lizondo, J. Saul, and Peter J. Montiel. 1989. Contractionary devaluation: An analytical overview. *IMF Staff Papers* 36 (1): 182–227.

Lünnemann, Patrick, and Thomas Y. Mathä. 2005. Consumer price behaviour in Luxembourg: Evidence from micro CPI data. Working Paper 541. European Central Bank, Frankfurt.

Magendzo, Igal L. 2002. Are devaluation really contractionary? Working Paper 82. Central Bank of Chile, Santiago.

Medina, Juan Pablo, David Rappoport, and Claudio Soto. 2007. Dynamics of price adjustment: Evidence from micro level data for Chile. Working Paper 432. Central Bank of Chile, Santiago.

Midrigan, Virgiliu. 2011. Menu-costs, multi-product firms and aggregate fluctuations. *Econometrica* 79: 1139–80.

Milesi-Ferretti, Gian Maria, and Assaf Razin. 2000. Current account reversals and currency crises: Empirical regularities. In Paul Krugman, ed., *Currency Crises*. Chicago: University of Chicago Press, 285–326.

Morley, Samuel A. 1992. On the effect of devaluation during stabilization programs in LDCs. *Review of Economics and Statistics* 74 (1): 21–27.

Mundell, Robert A. 1963. Capital mobility and stabilization policy under fixed and flexible exchange rates. *Canadian Journal of Economic and Political Science* 29 (4): 475–85.

Mundell, Robert A. 1964. A reply: Capital mobility and size. *Canadian Journal of Economic and Political Science* 30: 421–31.

Mussa, Michael. 1986. Nominal exchange rate regimes and the behavior of real exchange rates: Evidence and implications. *Carnegie–Rochester Conference Series on Public Policy* 25 (1): 117–214.

Nakamura, Emi, and Jón Steinsson. 2008. Five facts about prices: A reevaluation of menu cost models. *Quarterly Journal of Economics* 123 (4): 1415–64.

Obstfeld, Maurice, and Kenneth Rogoff. 1995. Exchange rate dynamics redux. *Journal of Political Economy* 103 (3): 624–60.

Rogoff, Kenneth. 2002. Dornbusch's overshooting model after twenty-five years. Mundell-Fleming Lecture at the IMF's Second Annual Research Conference. Washington, DC.

Saita, Yumi, Izumi Takagawa, Kenji Nishizaki, and Masahiro Higo. 2006. Price setting in Japan: Evidence from individual retail price data. Working Paper Series 06-J-02. Bank of Japan, Tokyo (in Japanese).

Taylor, John B. 1979. Staggered wage setting in a macro model. *American Economic Review Papers and Proceedings* 69 (2): 108–13.

Taylor, John B. 1980. Aggregate dynamics and staggered contracts. *Journal of Political Economy* 88 (1): 1–23.

Van Wijnbergen, Sweder. 1986. Exchange rate management and stabilization policies in developing countries. *Journal of Development Economics* 23 (2): 227–247.

Vilmunen, Jouko, and Helinä Laakkonen. 2005. How often do prices change in Finland? Micro-level evidence from the CPI. Unpublished paper, Bank of Finland, Helsinki.

Wulfsberg, Fredrik. 2009. Price adjustments and inflation: Evidence from consumer price data in Norway 1975–2004. Norges Bank Working Paper 2009/11. Oslo.

9 Interest Rate Policy

9.1 Introduction

As discussed in detail in previous chapters, an open economy can choose either the nominal exchange rate or the money supply as its main nominal anchor. The analysis of monetary/exchange rate policy in small open economies has in fact traditionally been cast almost exclusively in those terms. There is, however, a third nominal variable that could act as a nominal anchor: the nominal interest rate. In the last fifteen years or so, this "third" nominal anchor has received increased attention in the academic literature, triggered particularly by the policy controversies surrounding IMF-sponsored high interest rates policies in Asian countries in the aftermath of the 1997 and 1998 crises and, more generally, by the ever-increasing literature on inflation targeting and Taylor rules.[1] This chapter will be entirely devoted to the analysis of the use of nominal interest rates as a nominal anchor in small open economies.

While analyzing the traditional nominal anchors (i.e., the exchange rate and the money supply) poses no particular challenges in terms of how to formulate such policies in a theoretical model, this is not the case when it comes to modeling interest rates as a nominal anchor. In this regard Sargent and Wallace (1975) were the first to point out that at an analytical level, "interest rate targeting" (as controlling nominal interest rates is often referred to) in a flexible prices model leads to a price level indeterminacy. Understanding such a theoretical problem should be the logical first step in any analysis of interest rates as a nominal anchor and is thus examined in detail in section 9.2. The main conclusion to come out of section 9.2, however, is that the Sargent–Wallace indeterminacy results from a theoretical failure to fully specify monetary policy. We will clearly see that the price level indeterminacy arises because targeting the nominal interest rate essentially amounts to setting the rate of growth of the nominal exchange rate but *not* its initial level (or setting the rate of growth of the money supply but not its initial level). It is thus hardly surprising that there is nothing in the model to tie down the initial price level.

1. See, for example, Svensson (2010) and Taylor and Williams (2010).

Having clarified the source of the price level indeterminacy, the chapter proceeds to discuss several ways in which the specification of monetary policy can be completed to generate a well-defined model. Section 9.3 discusses the so-called fiscal theory of the price level (as formulated by Auernheimer and Contreras 1992). The key assumptions behind this approach are that money must be introduced into the economy through open market operations (as opposed to "helicopter drops") and that government transfers are exogenously given. This has the implication that the price level, instead of being determined in the money market as in standard models, will be determined by the requirement that the fiscal constraint holds. While this approach offers an elegant solution to the problem of price-level indeterminacy and allows us to use the model to ask useful policy questions (i.e., how does an increase in interest rates affect the nominal exchange rate?), it has the problem that if we used this setup to analyze the two traditional anchors, the system would now be overdetermined. In any event, we show that under certain restrictions, an increase in interest rates leads to a nominal appreciation of the domestic currency.

Following Calvo and Végh (1995), section 9.4 pursues quite a different route in dealing with the Sargent–Wallace indeterminacy. This formulation essentially sidesteps the problem by assuming that the interest rate controlled by the monetary authority is the interest rate borne by some liquid asset. Thus, in this formulation, this policy-controlled nominal interest rate is an *additional* policy instrument. In other words, the monetary authority can control both this interest rate and either the money supply or the exchange rate. The model captures what is perhaps the most common channel alluded to by policy makers and practitioners alike: a rise in interest rates makes domestic-currency denominated assets more attractive to hold, thus leading to an appreciation of the domestic currency as investors dispose of foreign-currency denominated assets.

Finally, section 9.5 introduces sticky prices into the model. While one might think that this is perhaps the most obvious solution to the price-level indeterminacy (clearly, if prices are sticky, there cannot be price-level indeterminacy!), such is unfortunately not the case. This section shows that all that sticky prices accomplish is to push the indeterminacy problem to another area of the model. In particular, following Calvo (1983), we show that interest rate targeting in a sticky-prices model leads to a higher order indeterminacy (i.e., the rate of inflation is undetermined). We then solve this problem by introducing a Taylor-type rule whereby policy makers vary the nominal interest rate over time according to the difference between actual inflation and an inflation target. At least theoretically, such rules provide a perfectly sensible way of conducting monetary policy as long as the inflation target is fully credible.

9.2 Price-Level Indeterminacy

This section will illustrate how interest rate targeting leads to a price-level indeterminacy. We will show this in the context of the model studied in chapter 5.

Consider a small open economy inhabited by a large number of identical, infinitely lived consumers who are endowed with perfect foresight. The economy is perfectly integrated with the rest of the world in both goods and capital markets. There is only one (tradable and nonstorable) good, whose price is given by the law of one price. The foreign currency price of the good is taken to be unity (i.e., foreign inflation is zero). Hence the domestic price of the good is equal to the nominal exchange rate, E_t. The economy receives a constant endowment of the good (y). The international real interest rate (r) is constant over time.

9.2.1 Consumer's Problem

The consumer's lifetime utility is given by

$$\int_0^{\infty} [u(c_t) + v(m_t)]\exp(-\beta t)dt, \tag{9.1}$$

where c_t denotes consumption, m_t are real money balances (defined as M_t/E_t, where M_t are nominal money balances), $\beta(> 0)$ is the subjective discount rate, and the functions $u(.)$ and $v(.)$ are strictly increasing and strictly concave in their arguments.

Let b_t denote real foreign bonds and $a_t(\equiv b_t + m_t)$ denote real financial assets. The consumer's flow constraint takes the familiar form

$$\dot{a}_t = ra_t + y + \tau_t - c_t - i_t m_t, \tag{9.2}$$

where τ_t are lump-sum transfers from the government and i_t is the nominal interest rate. The corresponding intertemporal constraint is given by

$$a_0 + \frac{y}{r} + \int_0^{\infty} \tau_t \exp(-rt)dt = \int_0^{\infty} (c_t + i_t m_t)\exp(-rt)dt. \tag{9.3}$$

Assuming, as usual, that $\beta = r$, the first-order conditions imply that

$$u'(c_t) = \lambda, \tag{9.4}$$

$$v'(m_t) = \lambda i_t. \tag{9.5}$$

Equations (9.4) and (9.5) implicitly define a standard real money demand:

$$m_t = L(c_t, i_t). \tag{9.6}$$

9.2.2 Government

The government's budget constraint is given by

$$\dot{h}_t = rh_t + \dot{m}_t + \varepsilon_t m_t - \tau_t, \tag{9.7}$$

where h_t denotes international reserves and ε_t is the rate of depreciation/devaluation.

The corresponding intertemporal constraint takes the form

$$h_0 + \int_0^{\infty} (\dot{m}_t + \varepsilon_t m_t)\exp(-rt)dt = \int_0^{\infty} \tau_t \exp(-rt)dt. \tag{9.8}$$

9.2.3 Equilibrium Conditions

The assumption of perfect capital mobility implies that interest parity holds:

$$i_t = r + \varepsilon_t. \tag{9.9}$$

Let $k_t (\equiv b_t + h_t)$ denote the economy's stock of net foreign assets. Combining the consumer's flow constraint, equation (9.2), with the government's, equation (9.7), and using the interest parity condition (9.9), yields the economy's current account:

$$\dot{k}_t = rk_t + y - c_t. \tag{9.10}$$

Integrating forward this last equation and imposing the corresponding transversality condition yields the economy's resource constraint:

$$k_0 + \frac{y}{r} = \int_0^{\infty} c_t \exp(-rt)dt. \tag{9.11}$$

9.2.4 Perfect Foresight Equilibrium

Along a perfect foresight equilibrium path (PFEP), first-order condition (9.4) tells us that consumption will be constant. Hence, from the resource constraint,

$$c = rk_0 + y.$$

From (9.6), real money demand along a PFEP will be given by

$$m_t = L(c, i_t). \tag{9.12}$$

Hence real money demand will be constant if the nominal interest rate is constant over time.

9.2.5 Interest Rate Targeting

As analyzed in chapter 5, the determination of the nominal interest rate and the paths of both the nominal exchange rate and the nominal money supply depend on whether the economy is operating under predetermined or flexible exchange rates. Under predetermined exchange rates, the monetary authority sets the path of the nominal exchange rate and domestic credit, and allows the nominal money supply to adjust endogenously to changes in real money demand. The exogenously set rate of devaluation determines, through the interest parity condition, the nominal interest rate.

Under flexible exchange rates, the monetary authority sets the path of the nominal money supply and allows the nominal exchange rate to adjust endogenously to changes in real money demand. The endogenously determined rate of depreciation, together with the interest parity condition, pin down the nominal interest rate.

How are nominal variables pinned down under an interest rate targeting regime? Under interest rate targeting the monetary authority is assumed to set a constant level of the nominal interest rate, i. Given this value of the nominal interest rate, the interest parity condition (9.9) determines a constant rate of depreciation given by

$$\varepsilon = i - r.$$

From (9.12) the constant value of the nominal interest rate also determines a constant level of real money demand, given by

$$m = L(c, i). \tag{9.13}$$

Since real money balances are constant over time, the constant rate of growth of money is given by

$$\mu = \varepsilon.$$

Two nominal variables remain to be determined: M_0 and E_0. However, there is nothing in the model capable of tying down these variables. To see why, notice that, from (9.13),

$$\frac{M_0}{E_0} = m.$$

There are clearly infinitely many values of M_0 and E_0 that satisfy this equation. For example, if $\overline{M_0}$ and $\overline{E_0}$ satisfy this equation, so do $\alpha\overline{M_0}$ and $\alpha\overline{E_0}$ for any $\alpha > 0$. Hence the price level (i.e., the nominal exchange rate) is indeterminate. Interest rate targeting thus leads to a price level indeterminacy, which is Sargent and Wallace's (1975) celebrated result.

Of course, there is nothing surprising about this. To put it in the simplest possible way, think of the following two equations:

$$\frac{M_0}{E_0} = L(i),$$

$$i = r + \varepsilon.$$

There are four variables to be determined (M_0, E_0, i, and ε) but only two equations. Hence monetary policy needs to pin down two of the four variables for the equilibrium to be determined. Predetermined exchange rates pin down E_0 and ε; flexible exchange rates pin down M_0 and ε (since ε will be determined by μ). But interest rate targeting pins down only i. It should therefore come as no surprise that there is a nominal indeterminacy. We therefore conclude that the reason why there is a price-level indeterminacy under interest rate targeting is simply because monetary policy has not been completely specified in the model. It is a failure of theory, not of the real world!

9.2.6 Completing the Specification of Monetary Policy

Since our goal is to have an operational model of interest rate policy (i.e., a model in which we can ask policy questions), we need to complete the specification of monetary policy to have a fully determined model. How can we do this? The literature has come up with four (quite different) ways of dealing with this issue.

The first solution was proposed by McCallum (1981). He suggested perhaps the more obvious solution, which is (in terms of our formulation) to have the monetary authority also choose the initial level of the nominal money supply, M_0.[2] While this is certainly a perfectly fine solution, it is not particularly appealing because interest rate targeting becomes identical to flexible exchange rates (i.e., money supply targeting).

The second solution, originally proposed by Auernheimer and Contreras (1992) and Woodford (1994), amounts to the so-called fiscal theory of the price level.[3] The basic idea is to assume that the monetary authority cannot introduce money discretely into the economy via "helicopter drops" but instead can alter the nominal money supply only via open market operations. We will explore this setup in detail in section 9.3.

The third way of dealing with the price-level indeterminacy—proposed by Calvo and Végh (1995)—essentially sidesteps the problem by assuming that the interest rate controlled by the monetary authority is the interest rate borne by an interesting-bearing liquid asset (think of it as interest-bearing money). In this setup, this interest rate becomes an additional instrument of monetary policy. We analyze this setup in section 9.4.

Last, in a world of sticky prices, we can resort to specifying interest rules à la Taylor to solve the indeterminacy problem. This is dealt with in section 9.5.

9.3 The Fiscal Theory of the Price Level

This section shows how price level determinacy can be recovered by using the government's budget constraint and ruling out the possibility of endogenous transfers. Having obtained an operational model, we will study the effect of a higher nominal interest rate on the nominal exchange rate. We will follow Auernheimer and Contreras's (1992) model.

2. In McCallum's formulation, implementing this policy is more complicated due to the stochastic nature of the model, but the essence is the same: fix the nominal money supply at the beginning of each period.

3. See also Auernheimer (2008).

There are two important differences with respect to the standard monetary model that we used in the previous section: (1) the fiscal authority is no longer passive in the sense that government transfers are now exogenously set and (2) money is introduced through open market operations.

9.3.1 Consumer's Problem

Budget Constraints

As far as the consumer is concerned, the only change with respect to the model of section 9.2 is that the consumer can hold either foreign bonds or domestic bonds. The two assets, however, are perfect substitutes and will thus bear the same return in equilibrium. Real financial assets are given by

$$a_t = b_t + b_t^g + m_t, \tag{9.14}$$

where b_t^g denotes the consumer's real holdings of government bonds. With a_t so defined, the flow and intertemporal constraints remain the same as before (given by equations 9.2 and 9.3).

Utility Maximization

The consumer's lifetime utility is given by

$$\int_0^\infty \left[\log(c_t) + \frac{m_t^{1-1/\sigma}}{1-1/\sigma}\right]\exp(-\beta t)dt, \tag{9.15}$$

where $\beta(>0)$ is the subjective discount rate, and $\sigma < 1$.[4]

The consumer's problem is to choose $\{c_t, m_t\}$ for all $t \in [0, \infty)$ to maximize lifetime utility (9.15), subject to (9.3), given paths of τ_t and i_t and given values of y and a_0.

Assuming $\beta = r$, we can write the first-order conditions as

$$\frac{1}{c_t} = \lambda, \tag{9.16}$$

$$m_t^{-1/\sigma} = \lambda i_t. \tag{9.17}$$

It follows from (9.16) that consumption will be constant along a perfect foresight equilibrium path. Equations (9.16) and (9.17) implicitly define the real money demand:

$$m_t = \left(\frac{c_t}{i_t}\right)^\sigma. \tag{9.18}$$

4. We adopt a specific functional form for preferences just for algebraic convenience. The only critical assumption is that $\sigma < 1$, which (as we will see) ensures that we are always on the "correct" side of the Laffer curve. Exercise 1 at the end of this chapter asks you to solve the case where the utility function is nonseparable in consumption and real money balances. As long as the cross-derivative is positive, the same results obtain.

Notice, for further reference, that the interest rate elasticity of money demand is σ which, by assumption, is less than one.[5] This ensures that, for given consumption, the revenues from the inflation tax, $i_t m_t$, are an increasing function of i_t:

$$\frac{\partial i_t m_t}{\partial i_t} = (1-\sigma) i_t^{-\sigma} c_t^{\sigma} > 0. \tag{9.19}$$

As will become clear below, this implication will play a critical role in obtaining the result that a higher interest rate leads to a nominal appreciation of the domestic currency.

9.3.2 Government

The government holds no international reserves (i.e., no foreign assets).[6] The government issues a domestic bond, b_t^g. Its flow constraint (in real terms) is given by

$$\dot{b}_t^g = r b_t^g + \tau_t - \dot{m}_t - \varepsilon_t m_t. \tag{9.20}$$

Integrating forward constraint (9.20) and imposing the transversality condition $\lim_{t\to\infty} b_t^g \exp(-rt) = 0$, we obtain

$$b_0^g = \int_0^\infty \left(\dot{m}_t + \varepsilon_t m_t - \tau_t\right) \exp(-rt)dt. \tag{9.21}$$

Let $d_t (\equiv m_t + b_t^g)$ denote government's total liabilities. Using the interest parity condition (9.9), we can rewrite the government's flow constraint (9.20) as

$$\dot{d}_t = r d_t + \tau_t - i_t m_t. \tag{9.22}$$

Up to now (i.e., in chapters 5 through 8), we have assumed that money is introduced into the economy via "helicopter drops."[7] In other words, the Central Bank simply prints money and hands it out to the public. Since money (or, more precisely, the monetary base) is a government liability, the presence of "helicopters drops" implies that government's liabilities can change discretely at any instant in time. We will now assume instead that money may only be introduced into the economy through open market operations. In other words, when the government wishes to increase (reduce) the nominal money supply, it buys (sells) government bonds. Formally, we assume that

$$\Delta M_t = -\Delta B_t^g,$$

5. For the empirical plausibility of this assumption, see appendix 5.8.6 chapter 5.

6. Since the government allows the exchange rate to float freely, it does not need to hold international reserves for intervention purposes.

7. To withdraw money from circulation, imagine a "giant vacuum cleaner."

or, equivalently,

$$\Delta D_t = 0,$$

where $D_t = M_t + B_t^g$.[8] In other words, the government's liabilities, D_t, are a predetermined variable and cannot change discretely at any point in time.

In addition, we will assume that transfers are exogenously set at the constant level τ:

$$\tau_t = \tau.$$

This assumption implies that the monetary authority accommodates the fiscal authority and not viceversa. Up to this point in the book, we have always assumed the opposite (i.e., τ_t is endogenously determined), which implies that the fiscal authority accommodates the monetary authority.

9.3.3 Equilibrium Conditions

Interest parity, given by condition (9.9), continues to hold. As before, combining the consumer's and the government's flow constraints, given by equations (9.2) and (9.20), respectively, and using (9.9), we obtain the economy's flow constraint:

$$\dot{b}_t = rb_t + y - c_t. \tag{9.23}$$

Integrating forward and imposing the corresponding transversality condition, we obtain the economy's resource constraint:

$$b_0 + \frac{y}{r} = \int_0^\infty c_t \exp(-rt)dt. \tag{9.24}$$

9.3.4 Solution of the Model

Suppose that the monetary authority sets the nominal interest rate at a constant value given by i. We solve for the corresponding perfect foresight equilibrium path.

Given the interest parity condition (9.9), the rate of depreciation will be constant over time:

$$\varepsilon = i - r. \tag{9.25}$$

Along a PFEP, consumption is constant (by equation 9.16) and given by (from equation 9.24)

$$c = rb_0 + y. \tag{9.26}$$

8. Although we will focus on discrete changes in the money supply, open market operations would also cover situations where $\dot{M}_t = -\dot{B}_t^g$.

Since consumption and the nominal interest rate are constant over time, real money balances will also be constant along a PFEP and given by (from equation 9.18)

$$m = \left(\frac{c}{i}\right)^{\sigma}. \tag{9.27}$$

Since real money balances are constant along a PFEP, it follows that $\dot{m}_t/m_t = \mu_t - \varepsilon = 0$, which implies a constant rate of money growth:

$$\mu = \varepsilon.$$

We have arrived at a critical juncture. The rate of growth of both the nominal exchange rate and the nominal money supply has been determined. But how about the initial levels of nominal money balances and the nominal exchange rate? In other words, since the government is not setting the initial level of the nominal money supply, M_0, how will the initial exchange rate be determined?

Given the constant values of τ_t, i_t, and m_t, we can rewrite the government's flow constraint (9.22) as

$$\dot{d}_t = rd_t + \tau - im.$$

This is an unstable differential equation in d_t (i.e., the only root is $r > 0$). It follows that along a PFEP, $\dot{d}_t = 0$ and hence $d_t = d_0$ for all $t \geq 0$. Hence

$$d_0 = \frac{im - \tau}{r}. \tag{9.28}$$

Since $d_0 = D_0/E_0$, it follows that

$$E_0 = \frac{rD_0}{im - \tau}. \tag{9.29}$$

In other words, the initial level of the nominal exchange rate (i.e., of the price level) is such that the real value of government liabilities satisfies the government flow constraint. The fact that the initial price level is determined by the fiscal constraint explains why this type of model is referred to as "the fiscal theory of the price level."

9.3.5 Permanent Increase in the Interest Rate

Suppose that an instant before time 0, the economy is in the stationary equilibrium just characterized with the interest rate given by i^L. At time $t = 0$, there is an unanticipated and permanent increase in the nominal interest rate from i^L to i^H, where $i^L < i^H$ (see figure 9.1, panel a). The

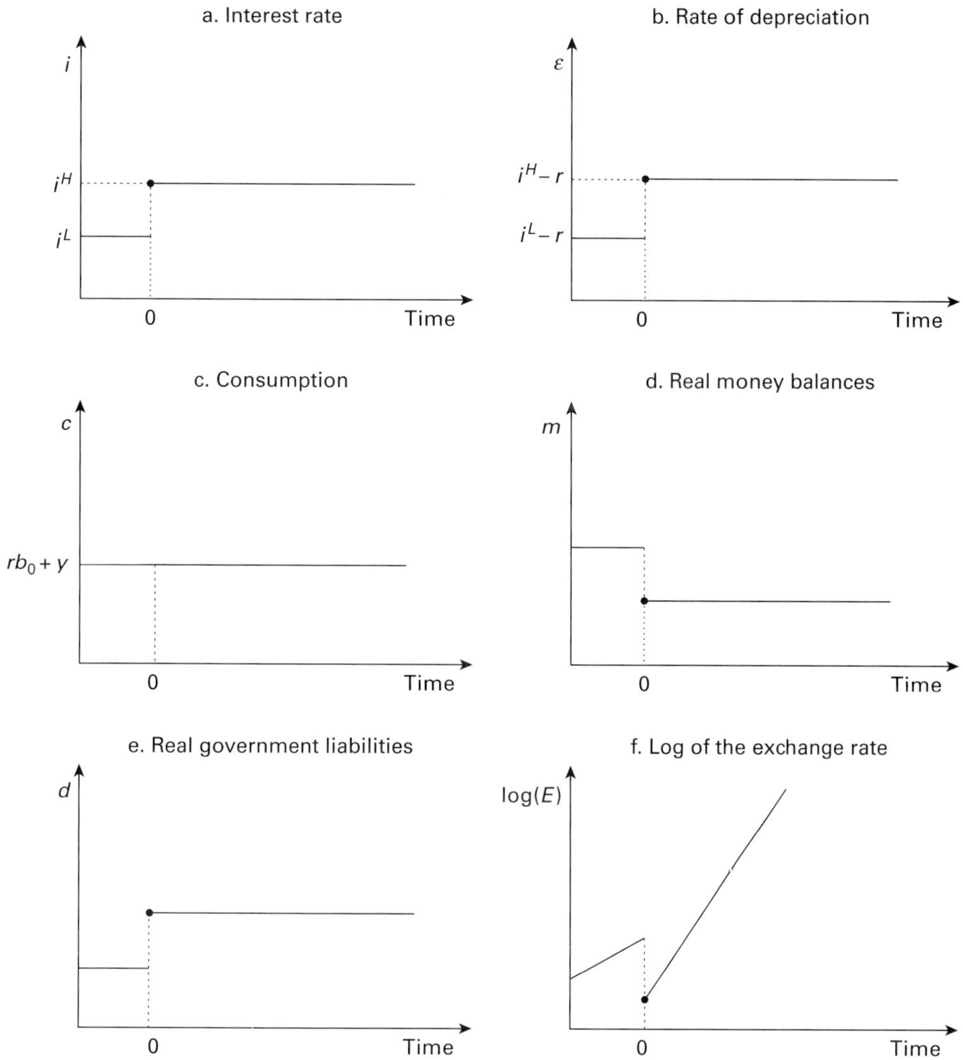

Figure 9.1
Permanent increase in the interest rate

consumer reoptimizes immediately. The economy will thus jump to a new PFEP characterized by the same equations as above, with the nominal interest rate given by i^H.

The rate of depreciation jumps up to a higher level (recall equation 9.25), as depicted in figure 9.1, panel b. Since the economy's resources have not changed, consumption remains unchanged and given by equation (9.26) (see figure 9.1, panel c).[9] From (9.27) we see that real money demand will fall because the opportunity cost of holding money has increased (see figure 9.1, panel d). Since, for a constant level of consumption, $i_t m_t$ is an increasing function of i_t (recall equation 9.19), equation (9.28) makes clear that real liabilities (d_0) will increase (see figure 9.1, panel e). Finally, notice from (9.29) that at $t = 0$ the nominal exchange rate must fall (figure 9.1, panel f) to generate the higher level of real liabilities.

The key result is thus that an increase in the nominal interest rate leads to a nominal appreciation of the domestic currency. Intuitively, an increase in the interest rate increases revenues from the inflation tax (given that the interest rate elasticity of money demand is less than one). This implies that government revenues increase. Therefore, at the pre-shock value of real government liabilities, there would be an operational surplus. The exchange rate (i.e., the price level) needs to fall to increase the government's real liabilities and restore fiscal balance.

9.3.6 A Final Comment

The fiscal theory of the price level offers an interesting and plausible way of recovering price level determinacy under interest rate targeting. Intuitively, however, the channel through which a higher interest rate leads to an appreciation of the domestic currency is not particularly appealing (coming, as it does, through the fiscal constraint as opposed to being a money market phenomenon).

Formally, a more important drawback of this specification is that if we analyze predetermined or flexible exchange rates, we will have an overdetermined system. Consider first the case of predetermined exchange rates, where the monetary authority sets the initial level and the rate of change of the exchange rate. Since the government's flow constraint would also determine an initial price level (i.e., an initial exchange rate), the system would be overdetermined. In the case of flexible exchange rates, the monetary authority sets the initial level of the money supply that determines an initial price level through the money market equilibrium. Again, this price level need not be consistent with the one determined by the fiscal constraint.

9.4 Interest Rates as an Additional Policy Instrument

The second way of dealing with the price level indeterminacy that arises under interest rate targeting—which follows Calvo and Végh (1995)—involves a sharp departure from the model

9. Given the assumption of separability between consumption and real money balances in the utility function, even a *temporary* increase in the interest rate would have no effect on consumption. Exercise 1 at the end of this chapter shows that if the utility function is nonseparable and the cross-derivative between consumption and real money balances is positive, then a temporary increase will lead to a temporary fall in consumption.

of section 9.2. The reason is that in this setup the monetary authority is assumed to control the interest rate on a liquid asset (which can be thought of as interest-bearing money).

The original motivation behind this way of thinking about interest rate policy was that in many high inflation countries (i.e., Argentina, Brazil, and Uruguay during the 1980s) commercial banks lent heavily to the government (compulsively and voluntarily) as high interest rates on public debt and scarce profitable opportunities in the private sector made this the best financial strategy. Commercial banks in turn issued time deposits of very short maturity (i.e., highly liquid deposits) to the public. The interest rate set by the government was thus indirectly determining the interest rate paid by banks to depositors. At some point in Brazil, the entire monetary base was in fact interest bearing. While perhaps in a less extreme form, this state of affairs is typical nowadays of many countries, both emerging and industrial, where commercial banks hold a large fraction of their assets in the form of public debt, as discussed in box 9.1.

9.4.1 Consumer's Problem

Budget Constraints

When it comes to the consumer's problem, the only difference from the case analyzed in section 9.2 is that money now bears interest.[10] Hence the consumer's flow constraint corresponding to (9.2) now reads as

$$\dot{a}_t = ra_t + y + \tau_t - c_t - (i_t - i_t^m)m_t, \tag{9.30}$$

where i_t^m denotes the interest rate borne by money. Notice that since money is interest-bearing, the opportunity cost of holding money is now given by $i_t - i_t^m$. As will become clear below, these two nominal interest rates will be related by an arbitrage condition that will incorporate the liquidity services provided by money. Hence, in equilibrium, $i_t > i_t^m$. The corresponding lifetime budget constraint is

$$a_0 + \frac{y}{r} + \int_0^\infty \tau_t \exp(-rt)dt = \int_0^\infty [c_t + (i_t - i_t^m)m_t]\exp(-rt)dt. \tag{9.31}$$

Utility Maximization

Let preferences take the logarithmic form[11]

$$\int_0^\infty [\log(c_t) + \log(m_t)]\exp(-\beta t)dt. \tag{9.32}$$

10. Alternatively, these may be thought of as interest-bearing demand deposits.

11. We adopt this log specification for simplicity. Any separable utility function would lead to the same results.

Box 9.1
How much government debt is held by banks?

Banks' holdings of government debt are generally large. Figure 9.2 shows, as of the end of 2009, the share of government debt in the hands of domestic financial institutions in the Euro area. In France, for example, 40 percent of the French public debt is held by French financial institutions. It is important to note that this measure does not incorporate the debt issued by foreign sovereigns that may be held by financial institutions.[a] As is evident from the figure, there is some variation in the share of government debt that financial institutions held, with Finland having the lowest share (14 percent) and Romania the largest (69 percent). On average, 43 percent of the public debt in the euro area is held by financial institutions.

Another way to understand the importance of public debt in the balance sheets of financial institutions is to look at how much public debt these institutions hold as a proportion of total assets. The top panel of figure 9.3 shows the share of government debt in the balance sheets of financial institutions, while the bottom panel presents data on financial institutions' net credit to the government as a share of their total assets.[b] As figure 9.3 shows, government debt represents a significant proportion of total assets, even reaching levels of 50 percent for some emerging markets.

Why do banks hold government debt? In order to answer this question, it is important to make a distinction between voluntary and involuntary holdings of government debt by banks.

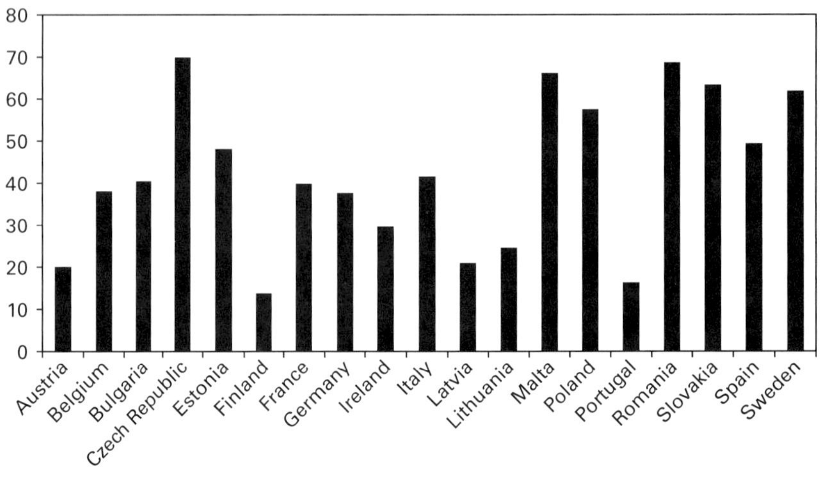

Source: Eurostat (for 2009)

Figure 9.2
Share of government debt held by financial institutions (in percent)

a. In fact, we know from the ongoing (as of early 2012) European crisis that such holdings (e.g., French banks holding Greek and Italian public debt) can be large as well.
b. Net credit to government includes nonmarketable government debt.

Box 9.1
(continued)

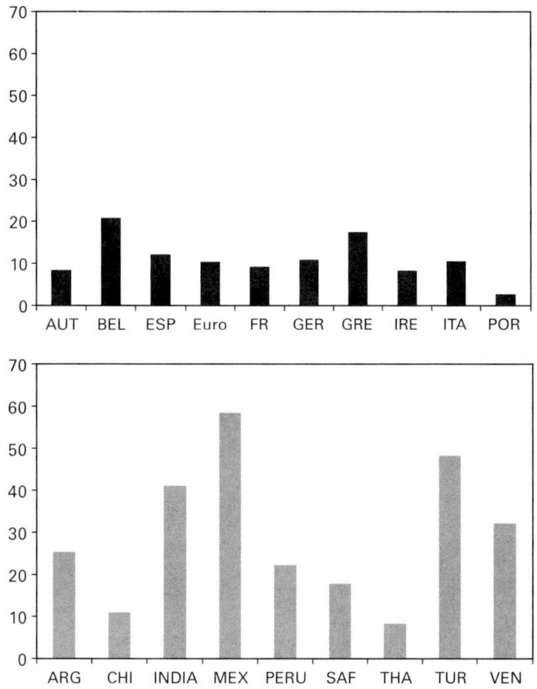

Source: Top panel: European Central Bank (data as of end of 2003); bottom panel: Kumhof and Tanner (2005)

Figure 9.3
Holdings of government debt as a proportion of total assets by financial institutions (in percent)

During the period of financial repression, which took place roughly between 1945 and 1980 in both developed and developing economies, governments adopted numerous measures that forced commercial banks to hold government debt in their portfolios. Such policies, combined with artificially low interest rates and relatively high inflation, provided the government with a source of cheap financing. The extent to which this was an effective measure varied across countries and over time, but it was nonetheless common practice in many countries. Even today, banks are forced to hold government debt in their portfolio as compulsory reserve and liquidity requirements.

But banks have also had reasons to choose to hold government debt voluntary. Rodriguez (1992) and Druck and Garibaldi (2000) point out that in periods of high inflation volatility, the default risk of firms increases making investing in the private sector more risky. As a result banks choose to lend more to the public sector in an attempt to reduce their exposure to the private sector's increased risk. In addition it is not uncommon for governments to resort to high interest rates to entice banks to hold their debt.

Box 9.1
(continued)

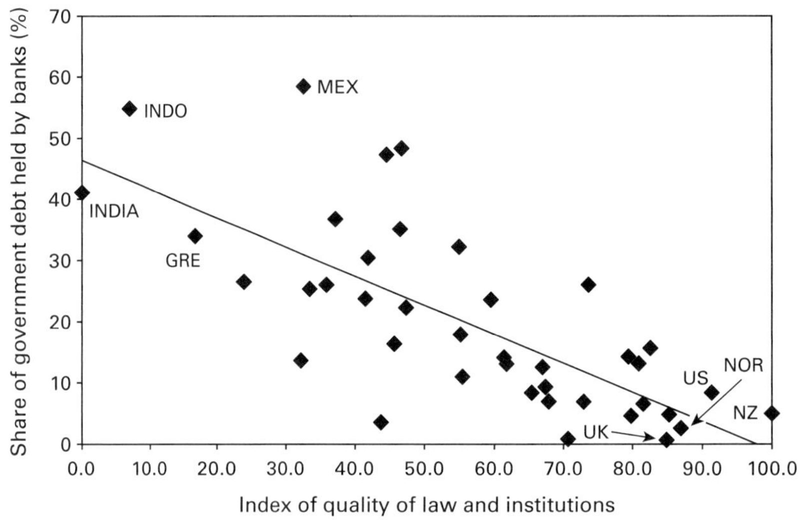

Source: Kumhof and Tanner (2005)

Figure 9.4
Institutional quality and the share of government debt held by banks

Kumhof and Tanner (2005) also point to legal and institutional imperfections as a determinant of how much government debt banks are willing to hold. The idea is that the degree of development determines the incentives of banks to lend to different players in the economy. They construct an index of quality of law and institutions by using data on access to credit, bankruptcy laws, degree of contract enforcement, and cost and time delays of transferring titles to real estate, among other factors. They then explore the connection between this index and the share of government debt held by banks. Figure 9.4 shows the very strong negative relationship, as captured by the depicted regression line, between the quality of law and institutions and the share of government debt held by banks. We can see, on the one hand, countries with high-quality institutions such as the United Kingdom, the United States, Norway, and New Zealand where banks hold little government debt and, on the other hand, emerging countries with historically more unstable institutions such as Indonesia, India, Mexico and Greece with banks holding a much larger share of government debt.

The consumer's problem thus consists in choosing c_t and m_t to maximize lifetime utility (9.32) subject to the lifetime budget constraint (9.31), for given paths of τ_t, i_t, and i_t^m and given values of y and a_0.

Assuming $\beta = r$, we can write the first-order conditions as

$$\frac{1}{c_t} = \lambda, \tag{9.33}$$

$$\frac{1}{m_t} = \lambda(i_t - i_t^m). \tag{9.34}$$

Equations (9.33) and (9.34) implicitly define the real demand for money:

$$m_t = \frac{c_t}{i_t - i_t^m}. \tag{9.35}$$

Notice that for a given value of i_t, an increase in i_t^m reduces the opportunity cost of holding money and leads to higher real money demand. This will be the key channel through which interest rate policy will operate in this model.

9.4.2 Government

Except for the fact that the government pays interest on money, the government's flow constraint remains the same as in section 9.2. Hence the constraint corresponding to (9.7) now reads

$$\dot{h}_t = rh_t + \dot{m}_t + (\varepsilon_t - i_t^m)m_t - \tau_t. \tag{9.36}$$

Integrating forward and imposing the usual transversality condition, we obtain the government's intertemporal constraint:

$$h_0 + \int_0^\infty [\dot{m}_t + (\varepsilon_t - i_t^m)m_t]\exp(-rt)dt = \int_0^\infty \tau_t \exp(-rt)dt \tag{9.37}$$

9.4.3 Equilibrium Conditions

As before, perfect capital mobility implies that the interest parity condition (9.9) holds. It is also easy to verify that combining the consumer's and the government's flow constraints (given by equations 9.30 and 9.36, respectively) yields the economy's current account, given by equation (9.10). By the same token, combining the consumer's and the government's intertemporal budget constraints (given by equations 9.31 and 9.37, respectively) yields the economy's resource constraint, given by equation (9.11).

9.4.4 Perfect Foresight Equilibrium

In this model the government can choose two policy instruments: the exchange rate or the money supply and i^m.[12] Let us assume that the government chooses the path of the money supply (i.e., its initial level, M_0, and the rate of money growth, μ) and the constant level of i^m.

Notice first that, from first-order condition (9.33), consumption will be constant along a PFEP. From (9.11) it follows that

$$c = rk_0 + y. \tag{9.38}$$

We now show that i_t is governed by an unstable differential equation and therefore will need to be constant along a PFEP. To see this, differentiate first-order condition (9.34), taking into account the interest parity condition (9.9) and the fact that $\dot{m}_t/m_t = \mu - \varepsilon_t$, to obtain

$$\dot{i}_t = (i_t - i^m)(i_t - r - \mu). \tag{9.39}$$

Since this is an unstable differential equation, i_t must be constant along a PFEP:

$$i = r + \mu.$$

Since both consumption and the nominal interest rate are constant along a PFEP, real money balances will be constant as well. From (9.35) it follows that

$$m = \frac{rk_0 + y}{r + \mu - i^m}. \tag{9.40}$$

Since real money balances are constant, then $\dot{m}_t = 0$, which implies that the rate of depreciation will also be constant:

$$\varepsilon = \mu.$$

Finally, the initial price level (i.e., the initial value of the exchange rate) will be determined by money market equilibrium at time 0:

$$E_0 = M_0\left(\frac{r + \mu - i^m}{rk_0 + y}\right). \tag{9.41}$$

12. Notice that the government could also set the path of the exchange rate and the initial level of the nominal money supply (or the path of the nominal money supply and the initial level of the exchange rate) and let i^m be determined endogenously. Exercise 2 at the end of this chapter asks you to show how all nominal variables are determined under these alternative policy scenarios.

9.4.5 Permanent Increase in Interest Rates

Suppose now that an instant before time 0, the economy is in the stationary equilibrium we have just characterized. At time 0, there is an unanticipated and permanent increase in the policy-controlled interest rate, i^m (figure 9.5, panel a).[13]

Since the shock is unanticipated, the consumer reoptimizes immediately and a new perfect foresight path as the one just described emerges, with the policy-controlled interest rate now at a higher level.

From (9.38), we see that consumption will not change (figure 9.5, panel b). From (9.39), it is clear that the nominal interest rate cannot jump because, if it did, it would follow a divergent path. Hence the nominal interest rate must remain put at its pre-shock level (as illustrated in panel c). Since i does not change at time 0 but i_t^m has gone up, the opportunity cost of holding real money balances falls (panel d). Hence real money demand goes up, as (9.40) makes clear (panel e). For real money balances to increase, the nominal exchange rate must fall, as follows from (9.41) (panel f).

The punchline of this exercise is thus that an increase in the policy-controlled interest rate leads to a nominal appreciation of the domestic currency. This is, of course, the same result that we obtained in the previous section. The intuition, however, is very different. In this case the higher interest rate on money reduces the opportunity cost of holding money, which increases real money demand and thus leads to a fall in the exchange rate.

9.4.6 Fiscal Effects of Higher Interest Rates

A common concern of policy makers when it comes to using higher interest rates to defend the currency is the negative effect on the fiscal accounts. Paying higher interest rates on the public debt will worsen the fiscal deficit. A case in point is Brazil during the Real Plan (the stabilization program implemented in July 1994). Commenting on Brazil (*Financial Times*, January 22, 1999), Jeffrey Sachs argued at the time that

> . . . at that point [when the Asian crises hit], an urgent re-assessment of monetary exchange rate policy was due. And yet the IMF defended the Brazilian decision in October 1997 to put up interest rates to 50 percent per year precisely in order to hold the currency. This decision was fateful. It cemented the end of Brazilian economic growth, and built in a fiscal time bomb. When the misguided defence of the currency began, the deficit was about 4 percent of GDP. A fiscal adjustment, supposedly of 2 percent of GDP was announced, and praised by the IMF. But instead of reducing the deficit to 2 percent of GDP, the 1998 budget deficit in fact jumped to 8 percent of GDP, in large part the result of the self-induced economic slowdown (which reduced tax collection) and the rapid build-up of interest payments on public debt.

13. Notice that there is no change in the path of the money supply.

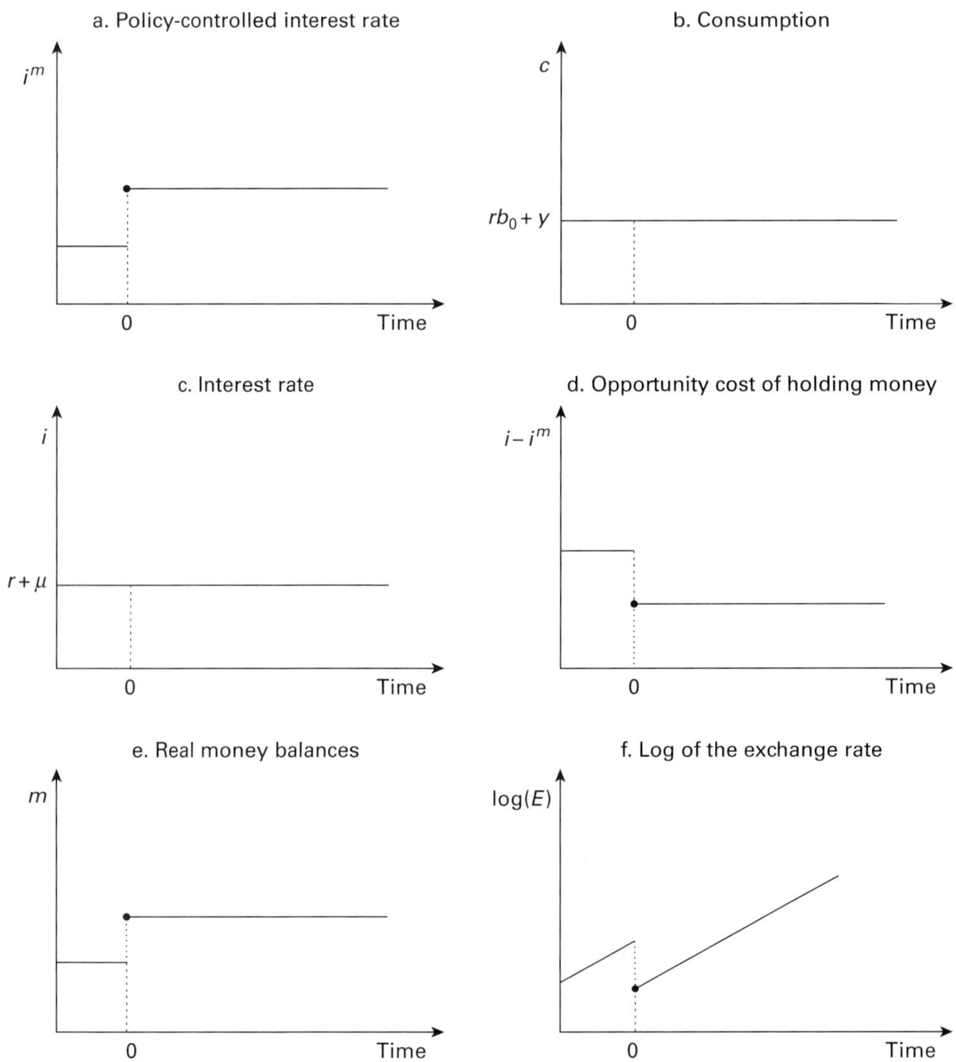

Figure 9.5
Permanent increase in the policy-controlled interest rate

How can we incorporate a fiscal effect in our model? This is easily done by assuming that government transfers are exogenously given at some level τ. Since the government needs to finance an exogenously given level of transfers, paying a higher interest rate on the Central Bank's liabilities will require an increase in the inflation rate (which will in turn increase the nominal interest rate). This inflationary effect of a higher interest rate will thus tend to undo some of the direct effect of a higher interest rate on money. Exercise 3 at the end of this chapter in fact shows a case where this fiscal effect exactly offsets the higher interest rate on money, leaving the opportunity cost of holding money $(i_t - i_t^m)$ unchanged. As a result the higher interest rate on money has no impact effect on the nominal exchange rate. This exercise thus illustrates the fiscal perils of higher interest rates.[14]

9.4.7 Output Effects of Higher Interest Rates

As the quote above by Jeffrey Sachs also illustrates, a second concern of policy makers on the use of higher interest rates to defend the currency is a potential negative output effect. This output effect can be introduced into our model by assuming a sticky-prices formulation in which output of nontradable goods is demand-determined, as in exercise 4 at the end of the chapter. In this setup an increase in i_t^m appreciates the domestic currency but at the cost of a fall in output of nontradable goods.[15]

9.4.8 A Final Comment

The approach to interest rate policy followed by Calvo and Végh (1995) has two advantages. First, it avoids indeterminacy problems. Second, it allows us to study interest rate policy independently of changes in money supply (or in the exchange rate). However, it should be emphasized that the results obtained in this framework are not directly comparable to those of the interest rate targeting literature because the interest rate controlled by policy makers is not the same.

9.5 Interest Rate Rules under Sticky Prices

This section deals with interest rate targeting in a model with sticky prices. At first glance it may seem that sticky prices will solve the indeterminacy problem. After all, if prices are sticky (i.e., they are a predetermined variable at each point in time), they surely cannot be undetermined! While this is certainly true, we will show that in the presence of sticky prices, interest rate targeting will lead to a "higher order indeterminacy." In other words, interest rate targeting will lead to a multiplicity of equilibrium paths for the inflation rate.

14. For a model of interest rate defense with fiscal costs in the context of balance of payments crisis models, see Lahiri and Végh (2003). See also chapter 16.

15. Alternatively, we could introduce an output cost by assuming that firms need to finance working capital with bank borrowing, as in Lahiri and Végh (2007).

Consider a small open economy inhabited by a large number of identical, infinitely lived consumers who are blessed with perfect foresight. The economy is perfectly integrated with the rest of the world in both goods and capital markets. There are two (nonstorable) goods: tradables and nontradables. The foreign currency price of the tradable good is assumed to be unity (i.e., foreign inflation is zero). The supply of the nontradable good is demand-determined. Unless otherwise noticed, the notation remains the same as above.

9.5.1 Consumer's Problem

Budget Constraints

As far as the consumer is concerned, the only difference with the model of section 9.2 is that there are now nontradable goods. The flow constraint corresponding to equation (9.2) is thus given by (using the tradable good as the numéraire):

$$\dot{a}_t = ra_t + y_t^T + \frac{y_t^N}{e_t} + \tau_t - c_t^T - \frac{c_t^N}{e_t} - i_t m_t, \tag{9.42}$$

where c_t^T and c_t^N denote consumption of tradables and nontradables, respectively, y_t^T and y_t^N denote output of tradables and nontradables, respectively, and e_t is the relative price of tradable goods in term of nontradable goods.

Integrating the flow constraint (9.42) forward and imposing the corresponding transversality condition, we obtain

$$a_0 + \int_0^\infty \left(y_t^T + \frac{y_t^N}{e_t} + \tau_t\right)\exp(-rt)dt = \int_0^\infty \left(c_t^T + \frac{c_t^N}{e_t} + i_t m_t\right)\exp(-rt)dt. \tag{9.43}$$

Utility Maximization

The consumer's lifetime utility takes the following logarithmic form:

$$\int_0^\infty \left[\log\left(c_t^T\right) + \log\left(c_t^N\right) + \log\left(m_t\right)\right]\exp(-\beta t)dt, \tag{9.44}$$

where $\beta(> 0)$ is the subjective discount rate. None of the results obtained below changes with general separable preferences.

The consumer's problem consists in choosing $\{c_t^T, c_t^N, m_t\}$ for all $t \in [0, \infty)$ to maximize lifetime utility (9.44), subject to (9.43), for given paths of τ_t, e_t, y_t^T, y_t^N, and i_t and a given value of a_0.

Assuming $\beta = r$, we can write the first-order conditions as

$$\frac{1}{c_t^T} = \lambda, \tag{9.45}$$

$$\frac{1}{c_t^N} = \frac{\lambda}{e_t}, \tag{9.46}$$

$$\frac{1}{m_t} = \lambda i_t. \tag{9.47}$$

First-order conditions (9.45) and (9.47) define a standard real money demand:

$$m_t = \frac{c_t^T}{i_t}. \tag{9.48}$$

9.5.2 Supply Side

We now turn to the supply side of the model, which follows chapter 8, section 8.2. The supply of the tradable good will be assumed to be constant over time and equal to y^T. The nontradables sector operates under staggered price setting and output is demand-determined. Following Calvo (1983), we postulate

$$\dot{\pi}_t = -\theta(y_t^N - y_f^N), \tag{9.49}$$

where π_t is the inflation rate of nontradable goods, θ is a positive parameter, and y_f^N is the "full-employment" level of output of nontradable goods. As shown in chapter 8, appendix 8.8.1, equation (9.49) can be derived from a setup where firms set prices in an asynchronous manner, taking into account the expected future path of the average price of nontradable goods and the path of excess demand in that market.

9.5.3 Government

The government's flow constraint is given by

$$\dot{h}_t = rh_t + \dot{m}_t + \varepsilon_t m_t - \tau_t. \tag{9.50}$$

Integrating forward and imposing the corresponding transversality condition, we obtain the government's intertemporal budget constraint:

$$\int_0^\infty \tau_t \exp(-rt)dt = h_0 + \int_0^\infty (\dot{m}_t + \varepsilon_t m_t)\exp(-rt)dt. \tag{9.51}$$

9.5.4 Equilibrium conditions

The assumption of perfect capital mobility (and no foreign inflation) implies that

$$i_t = r + \varepsilon_t. \tag{9.52}$$

Since the output of nontradable goods is demand-determined, it must be the case that

$$y_t^N = c_t^N. \tag{9.53}$$

Combining (9.42), (9.50), (9.52), and (9.53), we obtain the flow constraint of the economy (i.e., the current account):

$$\dot{k}_t = rk_t + y^T - c_t^T, \tag{9.54}$$

where $k_t \equiv h_t + b_t$.

Integrating forward and imposing the corresponding transversality condition, we obtain the economy's resource constraint:

$$k_0 + \frac{y^T}{r} = \int_0^\infty c_t^T \exp(-rt)dt. \tag{9.55}$$

9.5.5 Higher Order Indeterminacy

Suppose that the government sets the nominal interest rate at the level i. We will now solve for the corresponding PFEP and show how such a monetary rule leads to a multiplicity of equilibrium paths.

For starters, note that first-order condition (9.45) implies that consumption of tradables is constant along a PFEP. Hence, from the economy's resource constraint (9.55), it follows that

$$c^T = rk_0 + y^T. \tag{9.56}$$

Given the nominal interest rate set by the monetary authority and (9.56), real money demand will be constant:

$$m = \frac{rk_0 + y^T}{i}.$$

From the interest parity condition (9.52), it follows that the rate of depreciation is given by

$$\varepsilon = i - r.$$

To study the dynamic behavior of the rest of the endogenous variables of the model, we will construct a dynamic system of two differential equations in π_t and e_t. From (9.45) and (9.46) it follows that $c_t^N = e_t c_t^T$. Substituting this into (9.49) implies that

$$\dot{\pi}_t = \theta(y_f^N - e_t c_t^T). \tag{9.57}$$

Since, by definition, $e_t = E_t/P_t^N$ (recall that $P_t^* = 1$), using (9.52) yields

$$\dot{e}_t = e_t(i - r - \pi_t). \tag{9.58}$$

Since c^T is given to this system by (9.56) and i is the policy instrument, equations (9.57) and (9.58) constitute a dynamic system in π_t and e_t. The steady state of this dynamic system is given by (point A in figure 9.6)

$$e_{ss} = \frac{y_f^N}{c^T},$$

$$\pi_{ss} = i - r.$$

Linearizing the system around the steady state, we have

$$\begin{bmatrix} \dot{\pi}_t \\ \dot{e}_t \end{bmatrix} = \begin{bmatrix} 0 & -\theta c^T \\ -e_{ss} & 0 \end{bmatrix} \begin{bmatrix} \pi_t - \pi_{ss} \\ e_t - e_{ss} \end{bmatrix}. \tag{9.59}$$

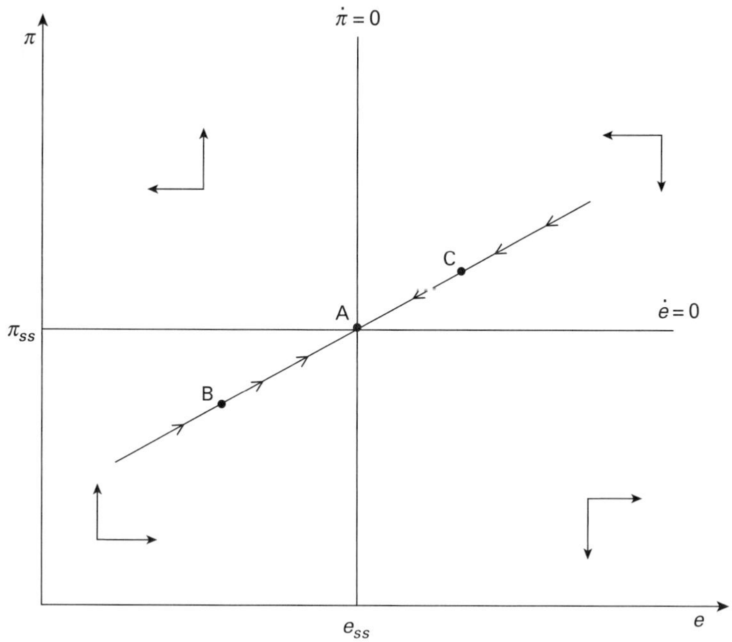

Figure 9.6
Multiple equilibrium paths

The determinant associated with the linear approximation is therefore

$$\Delta = -e_{ss}\theta c^{T} < 0.$$

Since there is one positive and one negative root, the system exhibits saddle path stability. There is thus a unique converging path (see figure 9.6). However, neither π_t nor e_t is a predetermined variable and is therefore free to take any value at time 0.[16] This implies that any initial pair (π_0, e_0) lying on the saddle path (including the steady state) will converge to the steady state. Figure 9.6 illustrates three such points: A, B, and C. There are thus a multiplicity of equilibrium paths. This is what we mean by a "higher order indeterminacy."

9.5.6 An Interest Rate Rule

We now show how a policy rule whereby the interest rate is varied according to some observable variable leads to a unique equilibrium path. Specifically, suppose that policy makers set an inflation target, $\bar{\pi}$, and vary the nominal interest rate according to the following rule:

$$\dot{i}_t = \alpha(\pi_t - \bar{\pi}), \tag{9.60}$$

where α is a positive parameter. Since the rule is specified in terms of rates of change, it also implies that the nominal interest rate is a predetermined variable at each point in time. In other words, by appropriately varying the nominal money supply, the monetary authority will not let the interest rate jump at any point in time. In practice, interest rate rules of this type have become the hallmark of "inflation targeting" regimes, as discussed in box 9.2.

We will solve the model by setting up a system of three differential equations. To this effect, differentiate first-order condition (9.46), taking into account that $\dot{e}_t = e_t(\varepsilon_t - \pi_t)$ and using (9.52), to obtain

$$\dot{c}_t^N = c_t^N(i_t - \pi_t - r). \tag{9.61}$$

Now substitute (9.53) in (9.49) to obtain

$$\dot{\pi}_t = \theta(y_f^N - c_t^N). \tag{9.62}$$

Equations (9.60), (9.61), and (9.62) constitute a system of three differential equations in i_t, c_t^N, and π_t.

The system's steady state is given by

$$\pi_{ss} = \bar{\pi}, \tag{9.63}$$

16. Recall the rule that the number of predetermined variables must be equal to the number of negative roots in order to have a unique solution. In this case there is one negative root and no predetermined variable and the system is thus undetermined (i.e., there are infinite solutions).

Box 9.2
Inflation targeting

Inflation targeting (IT) was first implemented in New Zealand in December 1989.[a] Since then, numerous advanced and emerging economies have followed suit. Most countries that have adopted inflation targeting as a monetary regime did so after many years (or even decades) of high and/or chronic inflation. In this sense—and as argued by Truman (2003)—inflation targeting may be viewed as an attempt to find a more effective nominal anchor (in the form of an inflation target) given the difficulties encountered with traditional nominal anchors (monetary aggregates and the nominal exchange rate).

There is no widespread agreement as to what defines a country as an inflation targeter. According to Truman (2003), a country is considered an inflation targeter if it has an explicit inflation target and has stated that it has adopted an IT regime. The International Monetary Fund (2010) uses a similar definition; namely a country is considered to be in the IT group if it has a "medium-term numerical target for inflation." As of 2010, the IMF lists 44 countries in the inflation targeting category.[b]

In general, an IT regime exhibits the following features. First, price stability is the main goal of monetary policy. Second, there is some numerical target or a sequence of numerical targets to be met (e.g., during a transition period). Third, countries stipulate a time horizon in which the target must be met. This allows for short-term deviations from the target without jeopardizing the credibility of the regime. Finally, the monetary authority is held accountable for meeting the target or, if it is not met, to give reasons why.

It should be noted that countries that have adopted an IT regime may not have price stability as the only goal of monetary policy. Truman (2003) looks at the Central Bank's mandate in 22 inflation targeting countries. In only 6 of those countries (or 27 percent) does the Central Bank pursue price stability as its only objective. In another 8 countries (36 percent), the Central Bank has other goals but there is a hierarchy in which price stability ranks first. In 2 countries (9 percent), currency stability is the main objective. In the remaining 6 countries, there are multiple objectives with no explicit hierarchy. In no country is there an explicit target for other variables (i.e., output). In principle, this distinguishes IT from other monetary regimes in which there may be an output target in addition to the inflation target (as in the typical Taylor rule).

Most of the empirical research compares the performance of adopters relative to non-adopters in terms of average inflation, inflation variability, output variability, and interest rates. The most common methodology is a difference-in-difference type of approach. Other studies use instrumental variables and propensity score matching techniques. Ball and Sheridan (2005) point out to an endogeneity problem that could arise because countries that have adopted IT regimes tended to have higher levels of inflation before implementing such a regime. To correct for this endogeneity, they suggest adding the prior level of inflation as a control variable. Table 9.1 summarizes the results of numerous studies reviewed in Ball (2010).

Two conclusions seem to emerge. First, IT appears to have reduced the mean and variance of inflation, especially in developing countries. Second, there is some evidence that IT may have reduced output variability in emerging economies.

a. See Svensson (2010) for a comprehensive review of inflation targeting.
b. The coutries are Albania, Armenia, Australia, Austria, Belgium, Brazil, Canada, Chile, Colombia, Cyprus, Czech Republic, Finland, France, Germany, Ghana, Greece, Guatemala, Hungary, Iceland, Indonesia, Ireland, Israel, Italy, Korea, Luxemburgo, Malta, Mexico, Netherlands, New Zealand, Norway, Peru, Philippines, Poland, Portugal, Romania, Serbia, Slovenia, South Africa, Spain, Sweden, Thailand, Turkey, United Kingdom, and Uruguay.

Box 9.2
(continued)

Table 9.1
Effects of inflation-targeting regimes on inflation and output

	No control for initial conditions	Control for initial conditions		
	Difference in difference	Difference in difference	Instrumental variables	Propensity score matching
Inflation: mean and variance	IT reduces both the mean and variance of inflation	Advanced economies: weak decrease in average inflation (0.6 percent)	Advanced economies: no effect	Advanced economies: no effect
		Emerging economies: large reduction in average inflation of 2.5 percent	Emerging economies: large effect in average inflation (7.5 percent in the long run)	Emerging economies: reduction in average inflation of 3 percent
Output: variance	Mixed results	Advanced economies: no effect		
		Emerging economies: decrease in 1.4 percent		

Source: Ball (2010).

Some studies have also looked at the effect of IT on inflation persistence and inflation expectations. On inflation persistence, the results parallel the findings above: no effect for advanced economies and lower persistence for emerging economies. However, Levin, Natalucci, and Pieger (2004) report large effects on inflation persistence for both groups of countries. On the effect of IT on inflation expectations, the results are mixed.

In sum, the empirical evidence seems to suggest that IT has been effective in developing countries but not necessarily in industrial countries.

$$i_{ss} = r + \bar{\pi}, \tag{9.64}$$

$$c_{ss}^N = y_f^N. \tag{9.65}$$

The linear approximation of the system around the steady state is given by

$$\begin{bmatrix} \dot{i}_t \\ \dot{c}_t^N \\ \dot{\pi}_t \end{bmatrix} = \begin{bmatrix} 0 & 0 & \alpha \\ y_f^N & 0 & -y_f^N \\ 0 & -\theta & 0 \end{bmatrix} \begin{bmatrix} i_t - i_{ss} \\ c_t^N - y_f^N \\ \pi_t - \bar{\pi} \end{bmatrix},$$

which implies that the trace and the determinant of the matrix associated with the linear approximation are given by, respectively,

$$\text{Tr} = 0,$$

$$\Delta = -\alpha\theta y_f^N < 0.$$

The fact that $\Delta < 0$ implies that there are either three negative roots or one negative and two positive roots. However, since the trace (which equals the sum of the roots) is zero, it must be the case that the system has one negative and two positive roots. The system is thus saddle path stable; that is, there is a single line converging to the steady state in R^3. Since there is only one predetermined variable (i_t), the system has a unique solution: for a given value of i_0, π_0 and c_0^N will adjust so as to position the system along the saddle path.

Let δ be the negative root. To obtain the eigenvector associated with this root, we should solve

$$\begin{bmatrix} -\delta & 0 & \alpha \\ y_f^N & -\delta & -y_f^N \\ 0 & -\theta & -\delta \end{bmatrix} \begin{bmatrix} h_1 \\ h_2 \\ h_3 \end{bmatrix} = \begin{bmatrix} 0 \\ 0 \\ 0 \end{bmatrix},$$

where (h_1, h_2, h_3) is the characteristic vector associated with root δ. Therefore

$$\frac{h_1}{h_3} = \frac{\alpha}{\delta} < 0,$$

$$\frac{h_2}{h_3} = -\frac{\delta}{\theta} > 0.$$

As will become clear below, this will provide a crucial piece of information when it comes to deriving the dynamic behavior of the system.

Setting to zero the constants corresponding to the unstable roots (i.e., the two positive roots), we can write the solution to the linear approximation of the dynamic system as

$$i_t - i_{ss} = \omega h_1 \exp(\delta t), \tag{9.66}$$

$$c_t^N - y_f^N = \omega h_2 \exp(\delta t),$$

$$\pi_t - \bar{\pi} = \omega h_3 \exp(\delta t),$$

where ω is an arbitrary constant.

It follows that

$$\frac{i_t - i_{ss}}{\pi_t - \bar{\pi}} = \frac{h_1}{h_3} < 0, \tag{9.67}$$

$$\frac{c_t^N - y_f^N}{\pi_t - \bar{\pi}} = \frac{h_2}{h_3} > 0. \tag{9.68}$$

Since there is only one negative root, the adjustment of all three variables towards the steady-state will be monotonic. Hence equation (9.67) indicates that i_t and π_t move in opposite directions, while equation (9.68) says that c_t^N and π_t move in the same direction.

To pin down the arbitrary constant ω, notice that i_t is a predetermined variable. Further, since the eigenvector is determined up to a scalar, we can set $h_1 = 1$. Hence evaluating (9.66) at $t = 0$ and solving for ω yields:

$$\omega = i_0 - i_{ss}. \tag{9.69}$$

9.5.7 Permanent Reduction in the Inflation Target

To understand the dynamic adjustment of this economy operating under a nominal interest rate rule, let us now analyze the response of the economy to an unanticipated and permanent reduction in the inflation target (see figure 9.7, panel a).

As is clear from (9.64), the nominal interest rate will be lower in the new steady state. Hence, from (9.69), $\omega > 0$. Differentiating (9.66) with respect to time (and recalling that $h_1 = 1$), it follows that i_t falls over time (figure 9.7, panel b). How does the inflation rate behave? From (9.63), inflation will be lower in the new steady state. Further, we know from (9.67) that π_t will move in the opposite direction as i_t. Hence π_t will increase over time. For this to happen, it must be the case that at $t = 0$ π_t falls below its new steady-state value and then gradually increase toward it (figure 9.7, panel c). Finally, from (9.65), consumption of nontradable goods does not change across steady states. Further, from (9.68), c_t^N and π_t move in the same direction. Hence c_t^N will be increasing over time. For this to be the case, c_t^N must fall on impact and increase gradually over time toward its unchanged steady state (figure 9.7, panel d). Given first-order condition (9.46), the real exchange rate will follow a path identical to c_t^N, falling on impact (real appreciation) and then gradually increasing over time toward its unchanged steady state (figure 9.7, panel e).

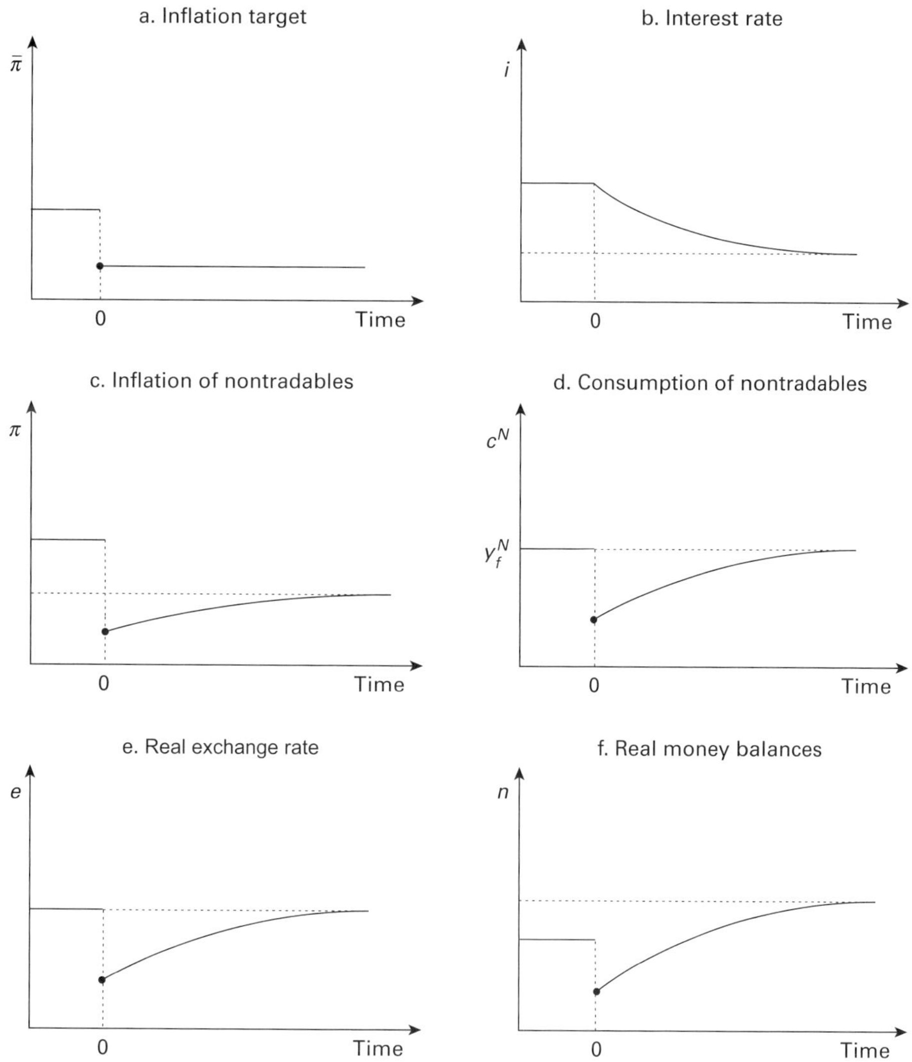

Figure 9.7
Permanent reduction in the inflation target

Finally, let us look at the behavior of real money balances in terms of nontradable goods. As in chapter 8, define real money balances in terms of nontradable goods as

$$n_t \equiv \frac{M_t}{P_t^N}. \tag{9.70}$$

Using (9.46) and (9.47), we obtain the demand for real money balances in terms of nontradable goods:

$$n_t = \frac{c_t^N}{i_t}. \tag{9.71}$$

In the new steady state, n_t will be higher reflecting the lower nominal interest rate. On impact, n_t falls since c_t^N falls and i_t remains unchanged. Hence n_t will increase over time towards its higher steady state, as illustrated in figure 9.7, panel f. Since P_t^N is sticky, it follows from (9.70) that the nominal money supply falls at time 0. It is precisely this reduction in the nominal money supply at time 0 that prevents the nominal interest rate from falling.

In sum, a reduction in the inflation target is successful in reducing inflation permanently, though at the cost of a recession as in the case of a reduction in the rate of growth of the money supply (chapter 8). Intuitively, the reduction in the inflation target implies that the nominal interest rate will be lower in the new steady state. Since the nominal interest rate is, by assumption, a predetermined variable, it needs to fall gradually over time toward its lower steady state value. For this to happen—and given the policy rule (9.60)—the inflation rate of nontradables needs to fall on impact *below* its new and lower steady-state value and then increase gradually over time. In other words, it is only if actual inflation is below its long-run value that the policy rule (9.60) calls for lowering the nominal interest rate over time. In turn, if inflation is increasing over time, c_t^N must be below full-employment output throughout the transition, as follows from (9.62). This increasing path of c_t^N calls for the relative price of tradable goods (e_t) to increase over time.

We conclude that the interest rate rule (9.60) thus offers a perfectly sensible way of conducting monetary policy as long as—and this is an important caveat—the inflation target is fully credible. If the public were to doubt the inflation target, the economy would lose its nominal anchor.

9.6 Real Interest Rate Rules

While interest rate rules based on a *nominal* interest rate are by far the most common in practice, some countries have occasionally experimented with *real* interest rate rules. Notably, Chile conducted monetary policy for more than a decade using as the main policy instrument a 90-day real interest rate on Central Bank liabilities (see box 12.3 in chapter 12). This, of course, raises the obvious question of whether nominal indeterminacies will arise under real interest rate targeting. Not surprisingly—and as illustrated in exercise 5 at the end of this chapter—a real interest rate targeting whereby the real interest rate (defined in terms of nontradable goods) is set at a constant level results in an undetermined inflation rate. The intuition is clear enough: since the monetary authority is not setting the rate of growth of any nominal magnitude, there is nothing tying down the rate of inflation. However, we also show that when combined with an inflation target (in the same vein as rule 9.60), a real interest rate rule leads to a well-behaved dynamic system.[17] The key is that the inflation target (which is assumed to be fully credible) provides the nominal anchor to the economy. In practice, of course, this should be viewed as a dangerous practice since any credibility problems on the part of the public regarding the announced inflation target will lead to a highly unstable system.

9.7 Final Remarks

This chapter has analyzed the use of interest rates as a policy instrument. We have seen how a pure nominal interest rate targeting leads to a price level indeterminacy because monetary policy has not been fully specified. We studied three different ways of completing monetary policy and used these models to understand the effects of changes in the nominal interest rate on the exchange rate. With flexible prices, higher nominal interest rates appreciate the domestic currency. This, however, may come at the cost of lower output and a higher public debt burden. The inflationary effects of a higher public debt service could in fact render interest rate policy ineffective. Hence, from a policy point of view, we conclude that there are perils associated with raising interest rates to defend the domestic currency which will need to be traded off against the benefits of a stronger currency.

Exercises

1. (Real effects of interest rates increases in the Auernheimer–Contreras model) Consider the same model as in section 9.3 with the following modification. Suppose that money now enters the utility function in a nonseparable way:

$$\int_0^\infty u(c_t, m_t)\exp(-\beta t)dt,$$

where $u(c_t, m_t)$ is increasing, strictly concave, and has positive cross derivative:

$$u_c > 0, u_m > 0, u_{cc} < 0, u_{mm} < 0, u_{cm} > 0, \; u_{cc}u_{mm} - u_{cm}^2 > 0.$$

a. Solve for the perfect foresight equilibrium path for a given value of the nominal interest rate.

17. Chapter 12 analyzes further this issue by studying a case where the supply side is characterized by sticky *inflation* (as opposed to sticky *prices*). A real interest rate rule that relies on an inflation target also leads to a well-behaved dynamic system.

b. Analyze the effects of an unanticipated and permanent increase in i_t at time 0.

c. Analyze the effects of an unanticipated and temporary increase in i_t at time 0 that lasts until T.

2. (Alternative policy specifications in the model of section 9.4) In section 9.4 we assumed that policy makers set the path of the money supply and choose i_t^m. Alternatively, policy makers could have chosen:

a. The path of the nominal exchange rate and i_t^m.

b. The path of the nominal exchange rate and M_0 (and let i_t^m be determined endogenously).

c. The path of the nominal money supply and E_0 (and let i_t^m be determined endogenously).
Show how nominal variables are determined in each of these alternative policy scenarios.

3. (Fiscal effects of higher interest rates) This exercise analyzes the fiscal effects of a higher interest rate on money in the context of the model of section 9.4. The only modification relative to the model of section 9.4 is that we now assume that lump-sum transfers from the government are set at a constant level τ. This has the important implication that the rate of money growth (μ_t) becomes an endogenous variable that will adjust so that the fiscal constraint is satisfied. In other words, policy makers now set i_t^m and the initial level of the nominal money supply (M_0) but not the rate of growth of the money supply (μ_t).

In this context:

a. Solve for the perfect foresight equilibrium path corresponding to a constant i_t^m and a given initial level of M_0.

b. Analyze the effects of an unanticipated and permanent increase in i_t^m at time 0. In particular, focus on what happens to the nominal exchange rate on impact.

4. (Interest rates as an additional instrument in a sticky-prices model) This exercise follows Calvo and Végh (1996). It deals with a two-good, sticky-prices version of the model of section 9.4. Let preferences be given by

$$\int_0^\infty \left[\log(c_t^T) + \log(c_t^N) + \log(m_t)\right]\exp(-\beta t)dt. \tag{9.72}$$

The consumer's intertemporal constraint is given by

$$a_0 + \int_0^\infty \left(y^T + \frac{y_t^N}{e_t} + \tau_t\right)\exp(-rt)dt$$
$$= \int_0^\infty \left[c_t^T + \frac{c_t^N}{e_t} + (i_t - i_t^m)m_t\right]\exp(-rt)dt, \tag{9.73}$$

where y^T is the constant endowment of tradable goods and y_t^N is the (demand-determined) level of output of nontradable goods. As in section 9.5, let the price of nontradable goods be sticky and the rate of change of inflation be given by (9.49).

In this context:

a. Suppose that, as in section 9.4, the monetary authority sets the path of the money supply and controls i_t^m. Solve for the perfect foresight equilibrium path for a given M_0 and constant μ_t and i_t^m. (Hint: Show first that i_t follows an unstable differential equation. Then set up a dynamic system in real money balances in terms of nontradable goods [i.e., $n_t \equiv M_t/P_t^N$] and π_t.)

b. Analyze the effects of an unanticipated and permanent increase in i_t^m.

5. (Real interest rate rules) This exercise furthers our understanding of interest rate rules by looking at real interest rate rules. Consider the model laid out in section 9.5. In this context:

a. As a benchmark for the rest of this exercise, solve the model for the case of predetermined exchange rates. In particular, analyze the effects on all endogenous variables of an unanticipated and permanent reduction in the rate of devaluation at time $t = 0$.

b. Consider now the case of real interest rate targeting. To this effect, define the domestic real interest rate as $r_t^d \equiv i_t - \pi_t$. (As discussed in chapter 8, r_t^d is the real interest rate relevant for the path of consumption of nontradable goods.) Suppose that policy makers set the domestic real interest rate at the constant level r^d (and set no other variable). Show formally that such a policy regime leads to an indeterminacy. (Hint: Notice that policy makers will have to set r^d equal to r, since this is the only value consistent with equilibrium).

c. Suppose that policy makers follow the real interest rate rule given by

$$\dot{r}_t^d = \alpha(\pi_t - \bar{\pi}),$$

where $\bar{\pi}$ is the inflation target chosen by the authorities and α is a positive constant. (Notice that under this policy regime, the domestic real interest rate is a predetermined variable.) Characterize an initial stationary equilibrium for a given and fully credible inflation target. Show what happens if policy makers announce at $t = 0$ an unanticipated and permanent reduction of the inflation target. Discuss the intuition behind the results (in particular, how do they compare with the results obtained for the predetermined exchange rates case and why?).

References

Auernheimer, Leonardo. 2008. Monetary policy rules, the fiscal theory of the price level, and (almost) all that jazz: In quest of simplicity, in Andres Velasco, Carmen M. Reinhart, and Carlos A. Végh, eds., *Money, Crises, and Transition: Essays in Honor of Guillermo Calvo.* Cambridge: MIT Press, 41–67.

Auernheimer, Leonardo, and Benjamin Contreras. 1992. A nominal interest rate rule in the open economy. Mimeo. Texas A&M University.

Ball, Laurence M. 2010. The performance of alternative monetary regimes. Working Paper 16124. National Bureau of Economic Research, Cambridge, MA.

Ball, Laurence M., and Niamh Sheridan. 2005. Does inflation targeting matter? in Ben S. Bernanke and Michael Woodford, eds., *The Inflation Targeting Debate*. Chicago: University of Chicago Press, 249–82.

Calvo, Guillermo A. 1983. Staggered prices in a utility-maximizing framework. *Journal of Monetary Economics* 12 (3): 383–98.

Calvo, Guillermo A., and Carlos A. Végh. 1995. Fighting inflation with high interest rates: The small open economy case under flexible prices. *Journal of Money, Credit and Banking* 27 (1): 49–66.

Calvo, Guillermo A., and Carlos A. Végh. 1996. Disinflation and interest-bearing money. *Economic Journal* 106 (439): 1546–63.

Druck, Pablo, and Pietro Garibaldi. 2000. Inflation risk and portfolio allocation in the banking system. University of CEMA Working Paper 181. Buenos Aires.

International Monetary Fund. 2010. *De facto Classification of Exchange Rate Regimes and Monetray Policy Frameworks*. Washington, DC: IMF.

Kumhof, Michael, and Evan Tanner. 2005. Government debt: A key role in financial intermediation. IMF Working Paper 05/57. Washington, DC.

Lahiri, Amartya, and Carlos A. Végh. 2003. Delaying the inevitable: Interest rate defense and BOP crises. *Journal of Political Economy* 111 (2): 404–24.

Lahiri, Amartya, and Carlos A. Végh. 2007. Output costs, BOP crises, and optimal interest rate policy. *Economic Journal* 117: 216–39.

Levin, Andrew T., Fabio M. Natalucci, and Jeremy M Pieger. 2004. The macroeconomic effects of inflation targeting. *Federal Reserve Bank of St. Louis Review* 86 (4): 51–80

McCallum, Bennett T. 1981. Price level determinacy with an interest rate policy rule and rational expectations. *Journal of Monetary Economics* 8 (3): 319–29.

Rodriguez, Carlos A. 1992. Financial reforms in Latin America: The cases of Argentina, Chile, and Uruguay. University of CEMA Working Paper 84. Buenos Aires.

Sargent, Thomas, and Neil Wallace. 1975. "Rational" expectations, the optimal monetary instrument, and the optimal money supply rule. *Journal of Political Economy* 83 (2): 241–54.

Svensson, Lars E. O. 2010. Inflation targeting. Working Paper 16654. National Bureau of Economic Research, Cambridge, MA.

Taylor, John B. and John C. Williams. 2010. Simple and robust rules for monetary policy. Working Paper 15908. National Bureau of Economic Research, Cambridge, MA.

Truman, Edwin M. 2003. *Inflation Targeting in the World Economy*. Washington, DC: Institute for International Economics.

Woodford, Michael. 1994. Monetary policy and price level determinacy in a cash-in-advance economy. *Economic Theory* 4 (3): 345–80.

10 Optimal Fiscal and Monetary Policy in the Open Economy

10.1 Introduction

Suppose that government spending rises temporarily, should the fiscal authority raise taxes, borrow, or both? In an uncertain world, how is this decision affected by the lack of complete asset markets? More generally, how should fiscal policy in a small open economy be conducted over the business cycle? These are clearly some of the most important public policy questions that we will encounter in this book. We will devote most of this chapter to analyzing the foundations of optimal fiscal policy in an open economy.

In a similar vein—and since inflation acts like a tax on real money balances—what should be the optimal rate of inflation? In other words, what is the optimal monetary policy in a world in which we take into account that inflation generates revenues for the government? This chapter will also answer this particular question.

We begin our journey into optimal fiscal policy in section 10.2 by analyzing the case of an endowment economy. In the absence of leisure, the only distortion that may arise is an *intertemporal* one (à la chapter 3). We will show that by setting a constant consumption tax rate over time, an optimal fiscal policy ensures that there will be no intertemporal distortion and, hence, that consumption will be fully smoothed over time. The resulting equilibrium in fact replicates the one that would obtain under lump-sum taxation. The government will borrow to finance temporarily high government spending and repay/save when government spending is temporarily low.

We then turn our attention to a production economy by introducing a labor/leisure choice in section 10.3. In such a case, imposing a consumption tax introduces an *intratemporal* distortion between consumption and leisure. The optimal fiscal policy will in fact entail setting a constant tax rate that avoids an intertemporal distortion but imposes an intratemporal distortion. In this case the optimal fiscal policy cannot therefore replicate the lump-sum tax equilibrium.

Up to this point, we will have assumed that the economy has perfect access to international capital markets. What would happen if that were not the case? To answer this question, in section 10.4 we consider the extreme case of financial autarky (i.e., the economy has no access to international capital markets). In such a situation temporarily high levels of government spending will have to be financed with a combination of higher tax rates and borrowing from the private sector.

To induce the private sector to lend to the public sector, the domestic real interest rate will have to rise above the world real rate of interest. Optimal fiscal policy thus introduces both intratemporal and intertemporal distortions relative to the lump-sum tax case.

Since, in practice, the degree of financial integration of developing countries with the rest of the world will lie somewhere between the two extremes cases of perfect integration and no integration analyzed in sections 10.3 and 10.4, respectively, our model would predict that periods of temporarily high government spending will be associated with some combination of higher tax rates, domestic and external borrowing, and increases in domestic real interest rates. In turn, periods of low government spending will be associated with lower tax rates, repayment of domestic and external borrowing, and low domestic real interest rates relative to world levels.

How does uncertainty in the level of government spending affect optimal fiscal policy? In the context of a two-period model, section 10.5 assumes that government spending in period 2 is stochastic. Under incomplete markets, the optimal fiscal policy will imply that tax rates will be high (low) when government spending is high (low). In other words, tax policy is procyclical.[1] Under complete markets, we recover the full tax smoothing results that we obtained for the perfect foresight case of section 10.3.

So far the chapter will have addressed the question: How *should* fiscal policy be conducted over the business cycle? But how is fiscal policy *actually* conducted in practice? The evidence seems to indicate that fiscal policy in developing countries is procyclical, in the sense that fiscal policy is expansionary in good times (i.e., government spending is high and tax rates are low) and contractionary in bad times (i.e., government spending is low and tax rates are high). This is in sharp contrast to industrial countries where fiscal policy is generally acyclical or countercyclical. To explain this phenomenon, in section 10.6 we endogeneize government spending to show how political pressures for more spending in good times can induce policy makers to act in a procyclical manner. Intuitively, if budget surpluses are "bad" in the sense that they lead to more unproductive government spending, then policy makers have an incentive to reduce fiscal surpluses in good times by lowering tax rates. The model can in fact rationalize the difference in fiscal policy between developing and industrial countries based on the volatility of tax revenues. Other things being equal, the larger is the volatility of tax revenues, the more procyclical is the optimal fiscal policy.

Finally, in section 10.7 we turn to the question of what is the optimal monetary policy. By introducing money into the model via a constant returns to scale transactions technology, we illustrate the idea that under certain restrictions on the transactions technology and/or preferences, the Friedman rule (i.e., a zero nominal interest rate) is optimal in a variety of monetary models (MIUF, CIA, or transactions costs models). In reality, of course, there is no obvious reason for these conditions to hold, and the key question becomes an empirical one: How large will the optimal nominal interest rate be when the Friedman rule is not optimal? Existing quantitative

1. As a matter of terminology, we will refer to a procyclical (countercyclical) tax *policy* as a situation where tax rates vary negatively (positively) with the cycle because lower (higher) tax rates should stimulate (depress) economic activity.

analysis suggest that it should be very small even when the inflation rate itself may fluctuate a lot. We then isolate tax collection costs as an empirically relevant friction for the optimal inflation tax to become positive and, if collection costs vary over time, as a rationale for time-varying inflation tax.

10.2 Optimal Fiscal Policy in an Endowment Economy

Consider a two-period model of a small open economy perfectly integrated with the rest of the world in both goods and capital markets.

10.2.1 Consumer's Problem

Let preferences be given by

$$W = \log(c_1) + \beta \log(c_2), \tag{10.1}$$

where c_t denotes consumption in period $t = 1, 2$ and $\beta < 1$ is the discount factor. Let initial net foreign assets be zero.

The flow budget constraints for periods 1 and 2 are then given by, respectively,

$$b_1 = y_1 - c_1(1+\theta_1), \tag{10.2}$$

$$0 = y_2 + (1+r)b_1 - c_2(1+\theta_2),$$

where b_1 denotes net foreign assets at the end of period 1, y_t is the endowment in period t ($t = 1, 2$), θ_t is the consumption tax in period t, and r is the world real interest rate. Combining the flow constraints, we obtain the consumer's intertemporal constraint:

$$y_1 + \frac{y_2}{1+r} = c_1(1+\theta_1) + \frac{c_2(1+\theta_2)}{1+r}. \tag{10.3}$$

The consumer chooses c_1 and c_2 to maximize lifetime utility, given by (10.1), subject to the intertemporal constraint (10.3). In terms of the Lagrangian,

$$\mathcal{L} = \log(c_1) + \beta \log(c_2) + \lambda \left\{ y_1 + \frac{y_2}{1+r} - c_1(1+\theta_1) - \frac{c_2(1+\theta_2)}{1+r} \right\},$$

where λ is the Lagrange multiplier associated with constraint (10.3). In addition to (10.3), the first order conditions are given by (assuming, as usual, that $\beta(1+r) = 1$)

$$\frac{1}{c_1} = \lambda(1+\theta_1),$$

$$\frac{1}{c_2} = \lambda(1+\theta_2).$$

Combining these two first-order conditions yields the Euler equation:

$$\frac{c_1}{c_2} = \frac{1+\theta_2}{1+\theta_1}. \tag{10.4}$$

This optimality condition takes us right back to the world of chapter 3 and the concept of intertemporal distortions. The (tax-inclusive) price of consumption faced by the consumer is $1+\theta_1$ in period 1 and $1+\theta_2$ in period 2. If $\theta_1 = \theta_2$, then there is no intertemporal distortion and consumption will be flat over time. If $\theta_1 \neq \theta_2$, there is an intertemporal distortion and consumption will not be flat over time. It should thus be already apparent that if feasible, an optimal fiscal policy will entail setting a constant consumption tax rate over time so as to avoid introducing an intertemporal distortion.

10.2.2 Government

The government faces an exogenous path of government consumption $\{g_1, g_2\}$ whose present discounted value must be financed by levying a consumption tax. In addition the government has perfect access to international capital markets and can therefore borrow/lend at the world interest rate, r. Assuming that initial net foreign assets are zero, the government's flow budget constraints are given by

$$b_1^g = \theta_1 c_1 - g_1, \tag{10.5}$$

$$0 = \theta_2 c_2 + (1+r)b_1^g - g_2, \tag{10.6}$$

where b_1^g denotes net government foreign assets. Define the *primary fiscal balance* (also referred to below as *public saving*) as the fiscal balance exclusive of interest payments:

$$PB_t \equiv \theta_t c_t - g_t. \tag{10.7}$$

If, for example, the government runs a primary deficit in period 1 (i.e., $PB_1 < 0$), it will need to finance it by borrowing. In the second period, it will need to run a primary surplus to repay the debt plus interests.

Combining the government's flow constraints (10.5) and (10.6), we obtain the government's intertemporal constraint:[2]

$$\theta_1 c_1 + \frac{\theta_2 c_2}{1+r} = g_1 + \frac{g_2}{1+r}. \tag{10.8}$$

Using the definition of primary balance given in expression (10.7), we can rewrite this expression as

2. To ensure positive consumption, we assume that the present discounted value of government spending is less than the present discounted value of ouput; that is, $g_1 + g_2/(1+r) < y_1 + y_2/(1+r)$.

$$PB_1 + \frac{PB_2}{1+r} = 0.$$

Intertemporal fiscal solvency thus requires that the present discounted value of primary balances add up to zero.[3]

10.2.3 Aggregate Constraints

Combining the period 1 consumer's and government's flow constraints—given by equations (10.2) and (10.5), respectively—we obtain the economy's flow constraint:

$$b_1^g + b_1 = y_1 - (c_1 + g_1).$$

By definition, the economy's accumulation of net foreign assets equals the current account balance. Hence

$$CA_1 = y_1 - (c_1 + g_1). \tag{10.9}$$

It will prove insightful to rewrite the current account balance as the sum of private and public saving. To do so, add and subtract $\theta_1 c_1$ to the RHS of equation (10.9) to obtain

$$CA_1 = \underbrace{y_1 - (1+\theta_1)c_1}_{\text{Private saving}} + \underbrace{\theta_1 c_1 - g_1}_{\text{Public saving}}. \tag{10.10}$$

The sum of private and public saving is, of course, the economy's total saving. Hence, as emphasized in chapter 1, in a world with no investment, the current account equals saving. This way of expressing the current account also calls attention to the possible link between primary fiscal deficits and current account deficits.[4] Clearly, if private saving is given, then a fall in public saving will increase the current account deficit. In equilibrium, however, this relationship between fiscal and current account deficits does not need to hold because private saving may also react to whatever shock is affecting public saving.

Combining the consumers' and government's intertemporal constraints (given by equations 10.3 and 10.8, respectively), we obtain the economy's resource constraint:

$$y_1 + \frac{y_2}{1+r} = c_1 + g_1 + \frac{c_2 + g_2}{1+r}. \tag{10.11}$$

As expected, the tax rates do not show up in the aggregate constraints because tax payments constitute a transfer between consumers and the government.

3. If initial net foreign assets were different from zero, the condition would be that the present discounted value of primary balances equal the initial debt.

4. This is, of course, the issue of the "twin deficits," which we already encountered in chapter 4, section 4.4.6.

10.2.4 Optimal Fiscal Policy

The government must finance the path of government spending by setting the tax rates θ_1 and θ_2. What are the optimal values of θ_1 and θ_2? The notion of optimality presupposes that one has some well-defined objective function. In an optimizing framework the natural objective function for the government is the consumer's lifetime utility. Hence optimal fiscal policy is defined as those values of θ_1 and θ_2 that will maximize consumer's welfare subject to the constraint that the present discounted value of tax revenues be enough to finance the present discounted value of government spending.

Methodologically, there are two ways of finding the optimal values of θ_1 and θ_2. The first—the more common approach in public finance—is the *dual approach to optimal taxation*. In this approach we first solve from the consumer's problem for c_1 and c_2 as functions of θ_1 and θ_2. We then substitute these functions into the utility function to obtain the indirect utility function (i.e., utility as a function of θ_1 and θ_2). The government chooses θ_1 and θ_2 to maximize this indirect utility function subject to its own intertemporal constraint. The problem with the dual approach is that it will not work in more complicated problems where it may be hard to obtain the indirect utility function.

The second approach is the *primal approach to optimal taxation* and is, by far, the more common approach in macroeconomics. The primal approach involves solving the *Ramsey planner*'s problem. The Ramsey planner is a constrained planner in the sense that he/she chooses quantities (as a planner would) but subject to the constraint that the chosen allocation be implementable as a competitive equilibrium (such constraints are known as *implementability conditions*).

In this section we will proceed by resorting to the dual approach to optimal taxation. We will introduce the primal or Ramsey approach when we deal with a production economy in section 10.3.

The Dual Approach to Optimal Taxation

The first step in the dual approach to optimal taxation is to solve for the consumer's demand functions. Substituting the Euler equation (10.4) into the intertemporal constraint (10.3), we obtain

$$c_1 = \widetilde{c_1}(\theta_1, Y) \equiv \frac{1}{1+\theta_1}\left(\frac{1+r}{2+r}\right)Y, \tag{10.12}$$

$$c_2 = \widetilde{c_2}(\theta_2, Y) \equiv \frac{1}{1+\theta_2}\left(\frac{1+r}{2+r}\right)Y. \tag{10.13}$$

where $\widetilde{c_1}(.)$ and $\widetilde{c_2}(.)$ denote functions and

$$Y \equiv y_1 + \frac{y_2}{1+r}$$

is the present discounted value of output. As expected, consumption demand depends positively on Y and negatively on the tax rate.

Substituting the consumption demands (10.12) and (10.13) into the consumer's lifetime utility (10.1), we obtain the consumer's welfare as a function of the tax rates θ_1 and θ_2:

$$W(\theta_1, \theta_2) = \log(\widetilde{c_1}(\theta_1, Y)) + \beta \log(\widetilde{c_2}(\theta_2, Y)). \tag{10.14}$$

The government chooses θ_1 and θ_2 to maximize the indirect utility function, given by (10.14), subject to the government's intertemporal constraint (10.8). The Lagrangian then takes the form

$$\mathcal{L} = \log(\widetilde{c_1}(\theta_1, Y)) + \beta \log(\widetilde{c_2}(\theta_2, Y)) + \Psi \left\{ \theta_1 \widetilde{c_1}(\theta_1, Y) + \frac{\theta_2 \widetilde{c_2}(\theta_2, Y)}{1+r} - g_1 - \frac{g_2}{1+r} \right\},$$

where Ψ is the multiplier associated with constraint (10.8).

Under the assumption that $\beta(1+r) = 1$, the first-order conditions with respect to θ_1 and θ_2 are given by, respectively,

$$\frac{1}{\widetilde{c_1}(\theta_1, Y)} \frac{\partial \widetilde{c_1}(\theta_1, Y)}{\partial \theta_1} = -\Psi \frac{\partial \left(\theta_1 \widetilde{c_1}(\theta_1, Y)\right)}{\partial \theta_1}, \tag{10.15}$$

$$\frac{1}{\widetilde{c_2}(\theta_2, Y)} \frac{\partial \widetilde{c_2}(\theta_2, Y)}{\partial \theta_2} = -\Psi \frac{\partial \left(\theta_2 \widetilde{c_2}(\theta_2, Y)\right)}{\partial \theta_2}. \tag{10.16}$$

But notice that from (10.12) and (10.13) it follows that

$$\frac{\partial \left(\theta_1 \widetilde{c_1}(\theta_1, Y)\right)}{\partial \theta_1} = -\frac{\partial \widetilde{c_1}(\theta_1, Y)}{\partial \theta_1},$$

$$\frac{\partial \left(\theta_2 \widetilde{c_2}(\theta_2, Y)\right)}{\partial \theta_2} = -\frac{\partial \widetilde{c_2}(\theta_2, Y)}{\partial \theta_2}$$

Taking into account the last two equations, we can reduce first-order conditions (10.15) and (10.16) to

$$\frac{1}{\widetilde{c_1}(\theta_1, Y)} = \Psi, \tag{10.17}$$

$$\frac{1}{\widetilde{c_2}(\theta_2, Y)} = \Psi. \tag{10.18}$$

From (10.17) and (10.18) we see that $\widetilde{c_1}(\theta_1, Y) = \widetilde{c_2}(\theta_2, Y)$ and hence from (10.12) and (10.13) that $\theta_1 = \theta_2 = \theta$. As expected, it is optimal for the government to keep the tax rate constant over time because, by so doing, there is no intertemporal distortion, which implies that consumption will be smoothed over time.

To obtain a reduced form for consumption, substitute $c_1 = c_2 = c$ into the economy's resource constraint (10.11) to obtain

$$c = \left(\frac{1+r}{2+r}\right)(Y - G), \tag{10.19}$$

where $G(\equiv g_1 + g_2/(1+r))$ is the present discounted value of government spending. Substituting (10.19) into the intertemporal government constraint (10.8) yields an expression for the constant tax rate:

$$\theta = \frac{G}{Y - G}. \tag{10.20}$$

The optimal tax rate is thus an increasing function of the PDV of government spending and does *not* depend on the particular path of government spending (g_1, g_2). Intuitively, much as the consumer in chapter 1, the government is able to smooth tax rates over time by borrowing when government spending is high and repaying when it is low.

An important observation is that the optimal fiscal policy replicates the lump-sum tax scenario. Put differently, the fact that the tax rate is constant over time implies that there is no *intertemporal* distortion, and the fact that there is no leisure implies that there is no *intratemporal* distortion. Clearly, this replicates the lump-sum tax case in which the consumer's intertemporal constraint would be given by

$$y_1 + \frac{y_2}{1+r} = c_1 + \frac{c_2}{1+r} - T, \tag{10.21}$$

where T denote lump-sum taxes. In this case the consumer would face no intertemporal distortions either.

Temporarily High Government Spending

To fix ideas, let us characterize a scenario in which period-1 government spending is high relative to period 2 (i.e., $g_1 > g_2$). To abstract from the saving motive analyzed in chapter 1, we assume that the endowment is constant over time ($y_1 = y_2 = y$).

We first check that—as we should expect—private saving will be zero. Since consumers are facing no intertemporal distortion (i.e., the tax rate is constant over time) and the endowment path is constant over time, there is no motive for them to save or dissave. Using (10.19) and (10.20), we can compute the constant level of private expenditure:

$$c(1+\theta) = \frac{1+r}{2+r}Y. \tag{10.22}$$

Recall that private saving is given by

$$S_1 = y_1 - c_1(1+\theta_1). \tag{10.23}$$

Since $y_1 = y$ and $c_1(1+\theta_1) = c(1+\theta)$, substituting (10.22) into (10.23) proves that $S_1 = 0$.

What about the primary balance (i.e., public saving)? Using (10.19) and (10.20) yields the constant level of tax revenues

$$\theta c = \left(\frac{1+r}{2+r}\right) G.$$

Substituting this equation into the definition of the primary fiscal balance—given by (10.7)—and recalling that $G \equiv g_1 + g_2/(1+r)$,

$$PB_1 = \frac{g_2 - g_1}{2+r} < 0,$$

$$PB_2 = \frac{1+r}{2+r}(g_1 - g_2) > 0.$$

Since $g_1 > g_2$, the government will run a primary deficit in the first period (i.e., $PB_1 < 0$) that is financed by borrowing from abroad. In the second period the government runs a primary surplus (i.e., $PB_2 > 0$) that enables it to repay the debt plus interest. It follows from (10.10) that the economy will run a current account deficit in period 1. We thus have a situation where the twin deficits (i.e., fiscal and current account deficits) emerge as the optimal response to a temporarily high level of government spending.[5]

Notice that it should be intuitively clear that the tax-smoothing result that we have obtained does not depend on the assumption of logarithmic preferences. Even under more general preferences, there is no reason for the government to impose a costly intertemporal distortion if it can avoid doing so. Exercise 1 at the end of this chapter asks you to verify that this is the case.

10.3 Optimal Fiscal Policy in a Production Economy

We now introduce leisure into the picture. We will see how it is still optimal to smooth tax rates over time. In this case, however, there will be an intratemporal distortion and hence the equilibrium cannot replicate the lump-sum tax case. (Unless otherwise noted, we continue to use the same notation.)

10.3.1 Household's Problem

Preferences are now given by

$$W = \log(c_1) + \log(h_1) + \beta[\log(c_2) + \log(h_2)], \tag{10.24}$$

5. But if, for example, $y_1 > y_2$ and the private sector saved in the first period, we could observe an equilibrium with fiscal deficit and current account surplus.

where h_t denotes leisure in period $t = 1, 2$. Households are endowed with one unit of time. Production (y_t) is given by

$$y_t = 1 - h_t, \qquad t = 1, 2.$$

The flow constraints take the form

$$b_1 = 1 - h_1 - c_1(1 + \theta_1), \tag{10.25}$$

$$0 = (1 + r)b_1 + 1 - h_2 - c_2(1 + \theta_2). \tag{10.26}$$

Combining the flow constraints yields the intertemporal constraint:

$$1 - h_1 + \frac{1 - h_2}{1 + r} = c_1(1 + \theta_1) + \frac{c_2(1 + \theta_2)}{1 + r}. \tag{10.27}$$

Consumers choose $\{c_1, h_1, c_2, h_2\}$ to maximize lifetime utility (10.24) subject to the intertemporal constraint (10.27). In terms of the Lagrangian,

$$\mathcal{L} = \log(c_1) + \log(h_1) + \beta[\log(c_2) + \log(h_2)]$$
$$+ \lambda\left\{1 - h_1 + \frac{1 - h_2}{1 + r} - c_1(1 + \theta_1) - \frac{c_2(1 + \theta_2)}{1 + r}\right\},$$

where λ is the multiplier associated with constraint (10.27). Assuming $\beta(1+r) = 1$, the first-order conditions with respect to c_1, h_1, c_2, and h_2 are given by, respectively,

$$\frac{1}{c_1} = \lambda(1 + \theta_1), \tag{10.28}$$

$$\frac{1}{h_1} = \lambda, \tag{10.29}$$

$$\frac{1}{c_2} = \lambda(1 + \theta_2), \tag{10.30}$$

$$\frac{1}{h_2} = \lambda. \tag{10.31}$$

The introduction of leisure into the picture implies that in addition to the intertemporal distortions examined in section 10.2, there may now be *intratemporal* distortions. To see this, combine (10.28) and (10.29), on the one hand, and (10.30) and (10.31), on the other, to obtain

$$\frac{h_1}{c_1} = 1 + \theta_1, \tag{10.32}$$

$$\frac{h_2}{c_2} = 1 + \theta_2. \tag{10.33}$$

If the consumption tax rate is positive, the relative price of leisure in terms of consumption—which would be unity in an undistorted equilibrium—will be larger than one, thus introducing an intratemporal distortion. We will see below that the optimal fiscal policy will in fact entail an intratemporal distortion.

To obtain the intertemporal conditions, combine first-order conditions (10.28) and (10.30), on the one hand, and (10.29) and (10.31) on the other, to obtain the Euler equations for consumption and leisure, respectively:

$$\frac{c_1}{c_2} = \frac{1+\theta_2}{1+\theta_1}, \tag{10.34}$$

$$h_1 = h_2. \tag{10.35}$$

The Euler equation for consumption—equation (10.34)—tells us once again that the consumption path will be constant over time as long as the tax rate is constant over time. On the other hand, the Euler equation for leisure—equation (10.35)—tells us that leisure will always be constant over time.

10.3.2 Government

As before, the government faces an exogenous path of government consumption that must be financed by imposing θ_1 and θ_2. The flow and intertemporal constraints continue to be given by equations (10.5), (10.6), and (10.8).

10.3.3 Aggregate Constraints

Combining the period 1 consumer's and government's flow constraints—given by equations (10.25) and (10.5), respectively—we obtain the economy's flow constraint:

$$b_1^g + b_1 = 1 - h_1 - c_1 - g_1. \tag{10.36}$$

Once again, by adding and subtracting $\theta_1 c_1$ on the RHS, we can write the current account balance as the sum of private and public saving:

$$CA_1 = \underbrace{1 - h_1 - (1+\theta_1)c_1}_{\text{Private saving}} + \underbrace{\theta_1 c_1 - g_1}_{\text{Public saving}}. \tag{10.37}$$

Combining the consumers' and government's intertemporal constraints (given by equations 10.27 and 10.8, respectively), we obtain the economy's resource constraint:

$$1 - h_1 + \frac{1-h_2}{1+r} = c_1 + g_1 + \frac{c_2 + g_2}{1+r}. \tag{10.38}$$

10.3.4 Optimal Fiscal Policy: The Ramsey Planner

We now ask the question: What is the optimal way of financing the exogenous path of government spending? As discussed above, the second—and most common—approach to fiscal policy is the *primal* approach. The primal approach consists of having a planner—the *Ramsey planner*—who, like the standard planner, will choose an *allocation* (as opposed to choosing tax rates as the government does in the dual approach to optimal taxation used in the previous section). In other words, the Ramsey planner will choose c_1, c_2, h_1, and h_2. However, unlike the typical planner—who would only be constrained by the overall resource constraint—the Ramsey planner will be restricted to choosing an allocation among those that can be implemented as a competitive equilibrium (which will be referred to as *Ramsey allocations*). The constraints that are imposed on the Ramsey planner that will force him/her to choose only among those allocations that can be implemented as a competitive equilibrium are referred to as the *implementability conditions*. By construction, the allocation chosen by the Ramsey planner (i.e., the optimal Ramsey allocation) will therefore be implementable as a competitive equilibrium with the optimal tax rates being those that induce households to choose such an allocation.

Implementability Conditions

The implementability conditions come from the household's first-order conditions and link static prices (i.e., tax rates) and intertemporal prices (i.e., the real interest rate) to quantities. In this case there are three implementability conditions: one intertemporal and two static. The first implementability condition is given by equation (10.35). This condition says that the Ramsey planner is restricted to choosing among allocations that imply constant leisure over time.[6] In other words, because consumers face a real interest rate that is equal to the discount rate, they choose a constant path of leisure. Hence a nonconstant path of leisure could not result from a competitive equilibrium and is therefore not in the set of allocations from which the Ramsey planner can choose.

The second and third implementability conditions follow immediately from the optimality conditions (10.32) and (10.33),

$$\theta_1 = \widetilde{\theta}_1(c_1, h_1) \equiv \frac{h_1}{c_1} - 1, \tag{10.39}$$

$$\theta_2 = \widetilde{\theta}_2(c_2, h_2) \equiv \frac{h_2}{c_2} - 1, \tag{10.40}$$

where $\widetilde{\theta}_1(.)$ and $\widetilde{\theta}_2(.)$ denote functions. These two static conditions express prices (i.e., tax rates) as a function of quantities.

6. Notice that this condition follows from the fact that $\beta(1 + r) = 1$. In a closed economy (or in the economy under financial autarky studied in section 10.4), r would be endogenous, and hence the Ramsey planner would not be restricted to choosing constant leisure.

For further reference (as we will need them when we solve the Ramsey problem), we compute the partial derivatives of $\widetilde{\theta}_1(.)$ and $\widetilde{\theta}_2(.)$ with respect to h_1 and h_2:

$$\frac{\partial \widetilde{\theta}_1(c_1, h_1)}{\partial h_1} = \frac{1}{c_1}, \tag{10.41}$$

$$\frac{\partial \widetilde{\theta}_2(c_2, h_2)}{\partial h_2} = \frac{1}{c_2}. \tag{10.42}$$

In the same vein, notice that multiplying (10.39) and (10.40) by c_1 and c_2, respectively, we can obtain the partial derivatives of tax revenues with respect to c_1 and c_2:

$$\frac{\partial (c_1 \widetilde{\theta}_1(c_1, h_1))}{\partial c_1} = -1, \tag{10.43}$$

$$\frac{\partial (c_2 \widetilde{\theta}_2(c_2, h_2))}{\partial c_2} = -1. \tag{10.44}$$

Ramsey Problem

We now proceed to solve the Ramsey problem. Typically we would need to impose all three implementability conditions as constraints on the Ramsey problem. In this particular case—and due to the assumption of logarithmic preferences—we will not need to impose the intertemporal condition (10.35) because, as will become clear below, the Ramsey solution will satisfy it anyway.

The Ramsey planner thus chooses c_1, c_2, h_1, and h_2 to maximize lifetime utility—given by (10.24)—subject to the economy's resource constraint (10.38), the government's intertemporal constraint (10.8), and implementability conditions (10.39) and (10.40). The Lagrangian then takes the form

$$\begin{aligned} \mathcal{L} &= \log(c_1) + \log(h_1) + \beta[\log(c_2) + \log(h_2)] \\ &\quad + \mu_1 \left(1 - h_1 + \frac{1 - h_2}{1 + r} - c_1 - g_1 - \frac{c_2 + g_2}{1 + r}\right) \\ &\quad + \mu_2 \left[\tilde{\theta}_1(c_1, h_1) c_1 + \frac{\tilde{\theta}_2(c_2, h_2) c_2}{1 + r} - g_1 - \frac{g_2}{1 + r}\right], \end{aligned}$$

where μ_1 and μ_2 denote the multipliers associated with constraints (10.38) and (10.8), respectively, and we have substituted the constraints (10.39) and (10.40) in the intertemporal constraint (10.8).

The first-order conditions for this Ramsey problem are given by

$$\frac{1}{c_1} = \mu_1 - \mu_2 \frac{\partial (\tilde{\theta}_1 c_1)}{\partial c_1},$$

$$\frac{1}{h_1} = \mu_1 - \mu_2 c_1 \frac{\partial \tilde{\theta}_1}{\partial h_1},$$

$$\frac{1}{c_2} = \mu_1 - \mu_2 \frac{\partial (\tilde{\theta}_2 c_2)}{\partial c_2},$$

$$\frac{1}{h_2} = \mu_1 - \mu_2 c_2 \frac{\partial \tilde{\theta}_2}{\partial h_2}.$$

Using the expressions for the various partial derivatives computed in (10.41) through (10.44), we can rewrite these first-order conditions as

$$\frac{1}{c_1} = \mu_1 + \mu_2, \tag{10.45}$$

$$\frac{1}{h_1} = \mu_1 - \mu_2, \tag{10.46}$$

$$\frac{1}{c_2} = \mu_1 + \mu_2, \tag{10.47}$$

$$\frac{1}{h_2} = \mu_1 - \mu_2. \tag{10.48}$$

Two important observations follow. First, equations (10.46) and (10.48) imply that $h_1 = h_2 = h$. Hence the Ramsey allocation satisfies implementability condition (10.35). Second, equations (10.45) and (10.47) imply that $c_1 = c_2 = c$. The optimal Ramsey allocation thus requires that consumption be constant over time.

Having characterized the optimal Ramsey allocation, we can now go back to the implementability conditions (10.39) and (10.40) and read off the optimal tax rates, which are given by

$$\theta_1 = \frac{h}{c} - 1, \tag{10.49}$$

$$\theta_2 = \frac{h}{c} - 1. \tag{10.50}$$

Hence $\theta_1 = \theta_2 = \theta$. The optimal tax rate is constant over time. In equilibrium therefore

$$\frac{h}{c} = 1 + \theta.$$

The constant tax rate (which, as shown below, will be positive if $G > 0$) thus imposes an *intratemporal* distortion. If the fiscal authority could resort to lump-sum taxes, the relative price of consumption in terms of leisure would be equal to unity and hence $h = c$. Due to the tax rate, this relative price is larger than one (i.e., it is equal to $1 + \theta$), which implies that households enjoy too little consumption relative to leisure. As a result welfare under distortionary taxation will be lower than it would be in the lump-sum tax case (exercise 2 at the end of this chapter asks you to work out the lump-sum tax case and verify all these claims).

Due to the logarithmic preferences, it is in fact easy to obtain closed form solutions for all endogenous variables. Substituting (10.32) and (10.33) into (10.27), it follows that[7]

$$h = \frac{1}{2}. \tag{10.51}$$

Taking into account that $h = \frac{1}{2}$ and that $c_1 = c_2 = c$, it follows from the economy's resource constraint (10.38) that

$$c = \frac{1}{2} - g^p, \tag{10.52}$$

where g^p denotes the *permanent* level of government spending, defined as

$$g^p \equiv \left(\frac{1+r}{2+r}\right)G.$$

Again, due to perfect capital mobility, the constant value of consumption depends only on the present discounted value of government spending and not on the specific path. Using (10.52) in the government's intertemporal constraint (10.8), we obtain a reduced form for the constant tax rate:

$$\theta = \frac{g^p}{\frac{1}{2} - g^p}.$$

Hence, if $g^p > 0$, $\theta > 0$.[8]

Finally, using (10.45), (10.46), (10.51), and (10.52), we can solve for the Lagrange multipliers:

$$\mu_1 = 1 + \frac{1}{1 - 2g^p},$$

$$\mu_2 = \frac{1}{1 - 2g^p} - 1.$$

Notice that if $g^p = 0$, then $\mu_1 = 2 > 0$ (indicating, as expected, that the resource constraint always binds), whereas $\mu_2 = 0$.

In sum, we have concluded that the optimal fiscal policy involves a constant consumption tax rate over time, which avoids imposing an intertemporal distortion on the path of consumption.

7. Notice that $h = \frac{1}{2}$ regardless of the path of the tax rates and follows directly from the household's problem. Hence we could have had the Ramsey planner take as given the condition $h = \frac{1}{2}$ and choose only c_1 and c_2 and obtain, of course, the same results.

8. Of course, we are imposing the restriction that $g^p < \frac{1}{2}$.

Such a tax, however, imposes an intratemporal distortion. This is a general result that does not depend on logarithmic preferences, as exercise 3 at the end of the chapter asks you to verify. Because of the intratemporal distortion, the optimal fiscal policy will not be able to replicate the equilibrium that would obtain under lump-sum taxation.[9]

10.4 Optimal Fiscal Policy under Financial Autarky

So far we have characterized optimal fiscal policy under conditions of perfect capital mobility. As a result it is possible—and indeed optimal—for the government to smooth tax rates over time, thus inducing households to smooth consumption over time. Any temporary shortfall in revenues due to temporarily high government spending is financed by borrowing in international capital markets. But what would happen if access to international capital markets were not perfect? Or, to consider an extreme case, what would happen if this small open economy had no access at all to international capital markets? How would this affect optimal fiscal policy?[10]

As we argued in chapter 2, the key characteristic of a small open economy under financial autarky is that the real interest rate becomes an *endogenous* variable, which we will denote by ρ to distinguish it from the world real interest rate, r. (Unless otherwise noticed, we continue to use the same notation.)

10.4.1 Households' Problem

As in chapter 2, households perceive themselves as being able to borrow as much as they want subject to their intertemporal constraint. The available bonds, however, are domestic (i.e., nontradable) bonds that bear the real interest rate ρ. The flow constraints are therefore given by

$$b_1 = 1 - h_1 - c_1(1+\theta_1), \tag{10.53}$$

$$0 = (1+\rho)b_1 + 1 - h_2 - c_2(1+\theta_2). \tag{10.54}$$

Combining the flow constraints yields the intertemporal constraint:

$$1 - h_1 + \frac{1-h_2}{1+\rho} = c_1(1+\theta_1) + \frac{c_2(1+\theta_2)}{1+\rho}. \tag{10.55}$$

9. We should note that while government spending is typically taken as exogenous in the optimal fiscal policy literature, we could well endogeneize the choice of g by, say, including it as an argument in the utility function. We could then analyze what would be the optimal choice of tax rate and government spending in the presence of some other, fluctuating, exogenous source of revenues. As exercise 4 at the end of the chapter asks you to verify, the optimal path of g and, of course, the tax rate would be constant.

10. This case with financial autarky corresponds to the closed economy case analyzed by Lucas and Stokey in their classic (1983) contribution.

Households choose $\{c_1, h_1, c_2, h_2\}$ to maximize lifetime utility (10.24) subject to the intertemporal constraint (10.55). In terms of the Lagrangian,

$$\mathcal{L} = \log(c_1) + \log(h_1) + \beta[\log(c_2) + \log(h_2)]$$
$$+ \lambda\left\{1 - h_1 + \frac{1-h_2}{1+\rho} - c_1(1+\theta_1) - \frac{c_2(1+\theta_2)}{1+\rho}\right\},$$

where λ is the multiplier associated with constraint (10.55). The first-order conditions with respect to c_1, h_1, c_2, and h_2 are given by

$$\frac{1}{c_1} = \lambda(1+\theta_1),$$

$$\frac{1}{h_1} = \lambda,$$

$$\frac{\beta}{c_2} = \lambda\left(\frac{1+\theta_2}{1+\rho}\right),$$

$$\frac{\beta}{h_2} = \frac{\lambda}{1+\rho}.$$

10.4.2 Government

As before, the government faces an exogenous path of government consumption that must be financed by levying consumption tax rates θ_1 and θ_2. The flow and intertemporal constraints remain unchanged relative to the cases examined above except for the fact that the government now faces the domestic real interest rate, ρ. The flow constraints are therefore given by

$$b_1^g = \theta_1 c_1 - g_1, \tag{10.56}$$

$$0 = \theta_2 c_2 + (1+\rho)b_1^g - g_2. \tag{10.57}$$

Combining these two flow constraints yields the government's intertemporal budget constraint:

$$\theta_1 c_1 + \frac{\theta_2 c_2}{1+\rho} = g_1 + \frac{g_2}{1+\rho}. \tag{10.58}$$

10.4.3 Aggregate Constraints

Since there is no external borrowing in this economy, net aggregate borrowing must equal zero:

$$b_1^g + b_1 = 0. \tag{10.59}$$

Combining the household's and government's period 1 flow budget constraints—given by equations (10.53) and (10.56), respectively—and imposing the bond market equilibrium condition (10.59), we obtain

$$1 - h_1 = c_1 + g_1. \tag{10.60}$$

Since the economy cannot borrow abroad, it can only consume whatever is produced. In the same vein, combining (10.54) and (10.57), we obtain

$$1 - h_2 = c_2 + g_2. \tag{10.61}$$

Combining the consumers' and government's intertemporal constraints (given by equations 10.55 and 10.58, respectively), we obtain the economy's resource constraint

$$1 - h_1 + \frac{1 - h_2}{1 + \rho} = c_1 + g_1 + \frac{c_2 + g_2}{1 + \rho}. \tag{10.62}$$

Implementability Conditions

Combining the household's first-order conditions leads to the following implementability conditions:

$$\theta_1 = \widetilde{\theta_1}(c_1, h_1) \equiv \frac{h_1}{c_1} - 1, \tag{10.63}$$

$$\theta_2 = \widetilde{\theta_2}(c_2, h_2) \equiv \frac{h_2}{c_2} - 1, \tag{10.64}$$

$$\rho = \tilde{\rho}(h_1, h_2) \equiv \frac{h_2}{\beta h_1} - 1, \tag{10.65}$$

where derivatives (10.41) through (10.44) continue to be valid. Notice that as we should have expected, the *static* implementability conditions (i.e., equations 10.63 and 10.64) are the same as in the perfect capital mobility case, given by (10.39) and (10.40). The critical difference is that the endogeneity of the real interest rate now implies that leisure need not be constant over time, as reflected in the third implementability condition, given by (10.65). In other words, the Ramsey planner can choose an allocation with h_1 different from h_2, which will require that in equilibrium, ρ be different from $1/\beta - 1$.

Ramsey Problem

The Ramsey planner must choose an allocation $\{c_1, c_2, h_1, h_2\}$ subject to the economy's constraints for periods 1 and 2—given by equations (10.60) and (10.61), respectively—the government's intertemporal constraint, given by equation (10.58), and the implementability conditions (10.63), (10.64), and (10.65). In terms of the Lagrangian,

$$\mathcal{L} = \log(c_1) + \log(h_1) + \beta[\log(c_2) + \log(h_2)] + \lambda_1(1 - h_1 - c_1 - g_1)$$
$$+ \lambda_2(1 - h_2 - c_2 - g_2)$$
$$+ \mu\left[\tilde{\theta}_1(c_1, h_1)c_1 + \frac{\tilde{\theta}_2(c_2, h_2)c_2}{1 + \tilde{\rho}(h_1, h_2)} - g_1 - \frac{g_2}{1 + \tilde{\rho}(h_1, h_2)}\right],$$

where λ_1, λ_2, and μ are the multipliers associated with constraints (10.60), (10.61), and (10.58), respectively, and the implementability conditions (10.63), (10.64), and (10.65) have been substituted into the government's intertemporal constraint.

The first-order conditions with respect to c_1, c_2, h_1, and h_2 are given by, respectively,

$$\frac{1}{c_1} = \lambda_1 - \mu\frac{\partial(\tilde{\theta}_1 c_1)}{\partial c_1},$$

$$\frac{\beta}{c_2} = \lambda_2 - \mu\frac{1}{1 + \tilde{\rho}}\frac{\partial(\tilde{\theta}_2 c_2)}{\partial c_2},$$

$$\frac{1}{h_1} = \lambda_1 - \mu\left[c_1\frac{\partial\tilde{\theta}_1}{\partial h_1} + (\tilde{\theta}_2 c_2 - g_2)\frac{\partial(1/(1 + \tilde{\rho}))}{\partial h_1}\right],$$

$$\frac{\beta}{h_2} = \lambda_2 - \mu\left[\frac{c_2}{1 + \tilde{\rho}}\frac{\partial\tilde{\theta}_2}{\partial h_2} + (\tilde{\theta}_2 c_2 - g_2)\frac{\partial(1/(1 + \tilde{\rho}))}{\partial h_2}\right].$$

Taking into account the derivatives that follow from (10.63), (10.64), and (10.65), we can rewrite these four optimality conditions as

$$\frac{1}{c_1} = \lambda_1 + \mu, \tag{10.66}$$

$$\frac{\beta}{c_2} = \lambda_2 + \frac{\mu}{1 + \tilde{\rho}}, \tag{10.67}$$

$$\frac{1}{h_1} = \lambda_1 - \mu\left[1 + (\tilde{\theta}_2 c_2 - g_2)\frac{\beta}{h_2}\right], \tag{10.68}$$

$$\frac{\beta}{h_2} = \lambda_2 - \mu\left[\frac{1}{1 + \tilde{\rho}} - (\tilde{\theta}_2 c_2 - g_2)\frac{\beta h_1}{(h_2)^2}\right]. \tag{10.69}$$

We now solve for the equilibrium corresponding to a flat path of government spending.

Claim 1: Suppose $g_1 = g_2 = g$. Then $\theta_1 = \theta_2 = \theta$ and $\rho = r$.

Proof: We verify that this solution satisfies the Ramsey optimality conditions by constructing the solution.

Since $\theta_1 = \theta_2 = \theta$ and $\rho = r$, it follows from the implementability conditions (10.63), (10.64), and (10.65) that

$$\frac{h_1}{c_1} = \frac{h_2}{c_2},$$

$$h_1 = h_2 = h.$$

These two equations imply, in turn, that

$$c_1 = c_2 = c.$$

Since $\theta_1 = \theta_2 = \theta$ and $c_1 = c_2 = c$, the government's intertemporal constraint (10.58) implies that

$$\theta c = g. \qquad (10.70)$$

We now show that $h = \frac{1}{2}$. From (10.70) and (10.63),

$$h = g + c.$$

Substituting this into (10.62) yields $h = \frac{1}{2}$.

It then follows from the economy's resource constraint (10.62) that

$$c = \frac{1}{2} - g$$

And hence from (10.70) that

$$\theta = \frac{g}{\frac{1}{2} - g}.$$

■

We have shown that when government spending is constant over time, it is optimal to smooth tax rates over time. This was to be expected because the government does not need to borrow/lend to finance a nonconstant path of spending, and therefore the solution coincides with the one that we obtain under perfect capital mobility.

The $g_1 \neq g_2$ Case: Numerical Examples

When $g_1 \neq g_2$, it becomes difficult to solve the model analytically. We therefore resort to providing some numerical examples. Numerically, we have a system of ten nonlinear equations in ten unknowns (c_1, c_2, h_1, h_2, θ_1, θ_2, ρ, λ_1, λ_2, and μ) for given values of g_1, g_2, and β that is easily solvable with any standard package like Mathematica or Matlab. The ten equations consist of the following:

- The four Ramsey optimality conditions (equations 10.66 through 10.69).
- The three implementability conditions (equations 10.63, 10.64, and 10.65).
- The government's intertemporal constraint, given by (10.58).
- The two-period constraints for the economy as a whole, given (10.60) and (10.61).

We set $\beta = 0.95$. As a benchmark, consider the case where $g_1 = g_2 = 0.1$ in table 10.1. Then, as shown in claim 1, $\theta_1 = \theta_2 = 0.25$ and $\rho = 1/\beta - 1 = 0.0526$. Suppose now that $g_1 = 0.15 > g_2 = 0.05$ (case 1 in table 10.1). We then see that $\theta_1 > \theta_2$ and $PB_1 < 0$. In other words, in the period of high government expenditures, the government increases the tax rate and borrows from households. To induce households to lend to the government, the real interest rate must be higher than the rate of time preference (16.5 percent as opposed to 5.26 percent). We then consider an even more extreme situation where $g_1 = 0.2$ and $g_2 = 0$ (case 2 in table 10.1). Then, as expected, θ_1 is even higher than before, and so is the primary deficit and hence the real interest rate because of the need to induce more lending from the private sector to the government.

Finally, case 3 in table 10.1 illustrates one of the examples provided in Lucas and Stokey (1983, p. 73), which they interpret as a perfectly anticipated war. In this case, $g_1 = 0$ and $g_2 = 0.05$. In anticipation of the expenditure in the second period, the government imposes a tax in period 1 to build a war chest, which is reflected in a primary surplus. These revenues are lent to the public, which is induced to borrow and consume more in the first period through a very low real interest rate. In the second period, the government uses its assets and additional tax revenue to finance the war.

We thus conclude that financial autarky will imply lower welfare relative to the case with perfect capital mobility since a temporarily high level of government spending, for example, will need to be financed by a combination of higher tax rates and borrowing, which will distort both the intratemporal and intertemporal margins. In contrast, with perfect capital mobility, tax rates would be constant over time and there would be no intertemporal distortion.

Since, in practice, the degree of financial integration of developing countries lies somewhere in between the extreme cases of perfect capital mobility in section 10.3 and financial autarky in this section, our model would predict that in times of relatively high government spending we should see a combination of higher tax rates, higher real interest rates, and current account deficits.

Table 10.1
Numerical examples for the $g_1 \neq g_2$ case

	g_1	g_2	θ_1	θ_2	ρ	c_1	c_2	$1-h_1$	$1-h_2$	PB_1	PB_2
Benchmark	0.1	0.1	0.25	0.25	0.0526	0.40	0.40	0.50	0.50	0	0
Case 1	0.15	0.05	0.275	0.248	0.165	0.37	0.42	0.52	0.47	−0.047	0.055
Case 2	0.20	0	0.320	0.261	0.290	0.34	0.44	0.54	0.44	−0.090	0.116
Case 3	0	0.05	0.051	0.054	0.001	0.49	0.46	0.49	0.51	0.025	−0.025

10.5 Optimal Fiscal Policy under Uncertainty

In the case analyzed in section 10.2, the path of government spending was known with certainty. What would happen if this was not the case? In other words, what would be the optimal fiscal policy if g_2 was uncertain? Based on our analysis of consumption decisions under uncertainty (chapter 2), we should already guess that the answer to this question will critically depend on whether this economy has access to state contingent claims or not.

Formally, consider the following modification of the model of section 10.3. (Unless otherwise noticed, we continue to use the same notation.) Government spending in the first period (g_1) is known with certainty. Government spending in the second period, however, is stochastic and follows a binomial distribution:

$$g_2 = \begin{cases} g_2^H & \text{with probability } p, \\ g_2^L & \text{with probability } 1-p, \end{cases}$$

where

$$g_2^H > g_2^L.$$

Further

$$E\{g_2\} = g_1.$$

Since g_2 is stochastic, so will, in principle, be the second-period consumption tax rate, θ_2. Therefore the consumer also faces uncertainty in terms of an uncertain tax rate in the second period.

10.5.1 Incomplete Markets

Suppose that asset markets are incomplete in the sense that the economy can freely borrow from/lend to the rest of the world at a given and constant world real interest rate, r, but has no access to state-contingent claims.

Households

Expected utility takes the form

$$W = \log(c_1) + \log(h_1) + \beta p[\log(c_2^H) + \log(h_2^H)] + \beta(1-p)[\log(c_2^L) + \log(h_2^L)], \tag{10.71}$$

where c_2^H and h_2^H denote consumption and leisure in the high-g state of the world, respectively, and c_2^L and h_2^L denote consumption and leisure in the low-g state of the world, respectively. Households' flow constraint for period 1 is given by

$$b_1 = 1 - h_1 - c_1(1+\theta_1). \tag{10.72}$$

In period 2, the relevant flow constraint will depend on the state of the world (recall from chapter 2 that the budget constraint must hold for *every* state of nature):

$$0 = (1+r)b_1 + 1 - h_2^H - c_2^H(1+\theta_2^H), \tag{10.73}$$

$$0 = (1+r)b_1 + 1 - h_2^L - c_2^L(1+\theta_2^L), \tag{10.74}$$

where θ_2^H and θ_2^L denote the consumption tax in the high-g and low-g states of the world, respectively.

Combining equations (10.72), (10.73) and (10.74), we obtain an intertemporal budget constraint for each state of the world:

$$1 - h_1 + \frac{1-h_2^H}{1+r} = (1+\theta_1)c_1 + \frac{(1+\theta_2^H)c_2^H}{1+r}, \tag{10.75}$$

$$1 - h_1 + \frac{1-h_2^L}{1+r} = (1+\theta_1)c_1 + \frac{(1+\theta_2^L)c_2^L}{1+r}. \tag{10.76}$$

Households choose $\{c_1, h_1, c_2^H, h_2^H, c_2^L, h_2^L\}$ to maximize lifetime utility (10.71) subject to the intertemporal constraints (10.75) and (10.76). The corresponding Lagrangian is given by

$$\begin{aligned}\mathcal{L} = {} & \log(c_1) + \log(h_1) + \beta p[\log(c_2^H) + \log(h_2^H)] \\ & + \beta(1-p)[\log(c_2^L) + \log(h_2^L)] \\ & + \lambda^H\left[1 - h_1 + \frac{1-h_2^H}{1+r} - (1+\theta_1)c_1 - \frac{(1+\theta_2^H)c_2^H}{1+r}\right] \\ & + \lambda^L\left[1 - h_1 + \frac{1-h_2^L}{1+r} - (1+\theta_1)c_1 - \frac{(1+\theta_2^L)c_2^L}{1+r}\right],\end{aligned}$$

where λ^H and λ^L are the Lagrange multipliers associated with constraints (10.75) and (10.76), respectively.

The first-order conditions with respect to $c_1, h_1, c_2^H, h_2^H, c_2^L$, and h_2^L are given, respectively, by

$$\frac{1}{c_1} = (1+\theta_1)(\lambda^H + \lambda^L), \tag{10.77}$$

$$\frac{1}{h_1} = \lambda^H + \lambda^L, \tag{10.78}$$

$$\frac{p}{c_2^H} = \lambda^H(1+\theta_2^H), \tag{10.79}$$

$$\frac{p}{h_2^H} = \lambda^H, \tag{10.80}$$

$$\frac{1-p}{c_2^L} = \lambda^L(1+\theta_2^L), \tag{10.81}$$

$$\frac{1-p}{h_2^L} = \lambda^L. \tag{10.82}$$

Government

The government's flow constraint for period 1 is given by

$$b_1^g = \theta_1 c_1 - g_1. \tag{10.83}$$

The period 2 flow budget constraints are given by

$$0 = (1+r)b_1^g + \theta_2^H c_2^H - g_2^H,$$

$$0 = (1+r)b_1^g + \theta_2^L c_2^L - g_2^L.$$

Combining the flow constraints, we obtain the government's intertemporal constraints for each history:

$$\theta_1 c_1 + \frac{\theta_2^H c_2^H}{1+r} = g_1 + \frac{g_2^H}{1+r}, \tag{10.84}$$

$$\theta_1 c_1 + \frac{\theta_2^L c_2^L}{1+r} = g_1 + \frac{g_2^L}{1+r}. \tag{10.85}$$

Aggregate Constraints

Combining the households' and government's period 1 flow budget constraint (given by equations 10.72 and 10.83, respectively), we obtain the current account balance:

$$b_1^g + b_1 = 1 - h_1 - c_1 - g_1.$$

Combining the households' and government's intertemporal constraints for each state of nature (equations 10.75 and 10.84, on the one hand, and equations 10.76 and 10.85, on the other), we obtain the economy's resource constraint for each history:

$$1+\frac{1}{1+r}=h_1+c_1+g_1+\frac{h_2^H+c_2^H+g_2^H}{1+r}, \tag{10.86}$$

$$1+\frac{1}{1+r}=h_1+c_1+g_1+\frac{h_2^L+c_2^L+g_2^L}{1+r}. \tag{10.87}$$

Optimal Fiscal Policy

Implementability Conditions Combining first-order conditions (10.77) through (10.82), we get the following implementability conditions:

$$\theta_1=\widetilde{\theta_1}(c_1,h_1)\equiv\frac{h_1}{c_1}-1, \tag{10.88}$$

$$\theta_2^H=\widetilde{\theta_2^H}(c_2^H,h_2^H)\equiv\frac{h_2^H}{c_2^H}-1, \tag{10.89}$$

$$\theta_2^L=\widetilde{\theta_2^L}(c_2^L,h_2^L)\equiv\frac{h_2^L}{c_2^L}-1, \tag{10.90}$$

$$\frac{1}{h_1}=\frac{p}{h_2^H}+\frac{1-p}{h_2^L}. \tag{10.91}$$

These four conditions will restrict the set of allocations that can be chosen by the Ramsey planner. The last condition imposes a constraint on the path of leisure.

For further reference, note that it follows from (10.88), (10.89), and (10.90) that

$$\frac{\partial(\widetilde{\theta_1}c_1)}{\partial c_1}=\frac{\partial(\widetilde{\theta_2^H}c_2^H)}{\partial c_2^H}=\frac{\partial(\widetilde{\theta_2^L}c_2^L)}{\partial c_2^L}=-1, \tag{10.92}$$

$$\frac{\partial(\widetilde{\theta_1}c_1)}{\partial h_1}=\frac{\partial(\widetilde{\theta_2^H}c_2^H)}{\partial h_2^H}=\frac{\partial(\widetilde{\theta_2^L}c_2^L)}{\partial h_2^L}=1. \tag{10.93}$$

Ramsey Planner The Ramsey planner chooses an allocation $\{c_1,h_1,c_2^H,h_2^H,c_2^L,h_2^L\}$ to maximize households' expected utility (10.71) subject to the resource constraints (10.86) and (10.87), the government's intertemporal constraints (10.84) and (10.85), and the implementability conditions (10.88), (10.89), and (10.90). We do not need to explicitly impose implementability condition (10.91) because in this logarithmic case—and as will become clear below—it would not be binding (i.e., the Ramsey planner's optimal allocation will satisfy this condition anyway).

In terms of the Lagrangian,

$$\begin{aligned}\mathcal{L} &= \log(c_1) + \log(h_1) + \beta p[\log(c_2^H) + \log(h_2^H)] \\ &\quad + \beta(1-p)[\log(c_2^L) + \log(h_2^L)] \\ &\quad + \lambda^H\left[1 + \frac{1}{1+r} - h_1 - c_1 - g_1 - \frac{h_2^H + c_2^H + g_2^H}{1+r}\right] \\ &\quad + \lambda^L\left[1 + \frac{1}{1+r} - h_1 - c_1 - g_1 - \frac{h_2^L + c_2^L + g_2^L}{1+r}\right] \\ &\quad + \mu^H\left[\widetilde{\theta}_1(c_1, h_1)c_1 + \frac{\widetilde{\theta_2^H}(c_2^H, h_2^H)c_2^H}{1+r} - g_1 - \frac{g_2^H}{1+r}\right] \\ &\quad + \mu^L\left[\widetilde{\theta}_1(c_1, h_1)c_1 + \frac{\widetilde{\theta_2^L}(c_2^L, h_2^L)c_2^L}{1+r} - g_1 - \frac{g_2^L}{1+r}\right],\end{aligned}$$

where λ^H, λ^L, μ^H, and μ^L are the multipliers corresponding to constraints (10.86), (10.87), (10.84), and (10.85), respectively, and $\widetilde{\theta}_1(.)$, $\widetilde{\theta_2^H}(.)$, and $\widetilde{\theta_2^L}(.)$ have been substituted in the government's intertemporal constraints.

The first-order conditions with respect to c_1, h_1, c_2^H, h_2^H, c_2^L, and h_2^L are given, respectively, by (assuming, as usual, that $\beta(1+r) = 1$)

$$\frac{1}{c_1} = \lambda^H + \lambda^L - (\mu^H + \mu^L)\frac{\partial(\widetilde{\theta}_1 c_1)}{\partial c_1},$$

$$\frac{1}{h_1} = \lambda^H + \lambda^L - (\mu^H + \mu^L)\frac{\partial(\widetilde{\theta}_1 c_1)}{\partial h_1},$$

$$\frac{p}{c_2^H} = \lambda^H - \mu^H\frac{\partial(\widetilde{\theta_2^H} c_2^H)}{\partial c_2^H},$$

$$\frac{p}{h_2^H} = \lambda^H - \mu^H\frac{\partial(\widetilde{\theta_2^H} c_2^H)}{\partial h_2^H},$$

$$\frac{1-p}{c_2^L} = \lambda^L - \mu^L\frac{\partial(\widetilde{\theta_2^L} c_2^L)}{\partial c_2^L},$$

$$\frac{1-p}{h_2^L} = \lambda^L - \mu^L\frac{\partial(\widetilde{\theta_2^L} c_2^L)}{\partial h_2^L}.$$

Taking into account the partial derivatives of the implementability conditions given by (10.92) and (10.93), we can rewrite these first-order conditions as

$$\frac{1}{c_1} = \lambda^H + \lambda^L + \mu^H + \mu^L, \tag{10.94}$$

$$\frac{1}{h_1} = \lambda^H + \lambda^L - \mu^H - \mu^L, \tag{10.95}$$

$$\frac{p}{c_2^H} = \lambda^H + \mu^H, \tag{10.96}$$

$$\frac{1-p}{c_2^L} = \lambda^L + \mu^L, \tag{10.97}$$

$$\frac{p}{h_2^H} = \lambda^H - \mu^H, \tag{10.98}$$

$$\frac{1-p}{h_2^L} = \lambda^L - \mu^L. \tag{10.99}$$

In order to characterize the optimal fiscal policy, we first get rid of the four multipliers ($\lambda^H, \lambda^L, \mu^H$, and μ^L) by combining, on the one hand, equations (10.94), (10.96), and (10.97) and, on the other hand, (10.95), (10.98), and (10.99) to obtain, respectively,

$$\frac{1}{c_1} = \frac{p}{c_2^H} + \frac{1-p}{c_2^L}, \tag{10.100}$$

$$\frac{1}{h_1} = \frac{p}{h_2^H} + \frac{1-p}{h_2^L}.$$

Note that the last equation is precisely implementability condition (10.91), which proves our contention above that we did not have to impose it explicitly since the Ramsey allocation would satisfy it anyway.

We now characterize the optimal fiscal policy implied by the Ramsey optimality conditions. To this end, we will first show that $h_1 = h_2^H = h_2^L = \frac{1}{2}$.[11] Substituting the implementability conditions (10.88) and (10.89) into the household's intertemporal constraint (10.75), we obtain

11. Again—and as the derivation below will make clear—this is a direct implication of the households' problem. Hence we could have imposed the condition $h_1 = h_2^H = h_2^L = \frac{1}{2}$ on the Ramsey problem and have the Ramsey planner choose only $\{c_1, c_2^H, c_2^L\}$. (The formulation that we chose has the advantage that it shows the general structure of this type of problem.)

$$h_1 + \frac{h_2^H}{1+r} = \frac{1}{2}\left(\frac{2+r}{1+r}\right), \tag{10.101}$$

By the same token, substituting the implementability conditions (10.88) and (10.90) into (10.76), we obtain

$$h_1 + \frac{h_2^L}{1+r} = \frac{1}{2}\left(\frac{2+r}{1+r}\right). \tag{10.102}$$

It immediately follows from (10.101) and (10.102) that $h_2^H = h_2^L$.

Since $h_2^H = h_2^L$, it follows from implementability condition (10.91) that $h_1 = h_2^H = h_2^L$. Hence, from (10.101) and (10.102), $h_1 = h_2^H = h_2^L = \frac{1}{2}$.

Since $h_1 = h_2^H = h_2^L = \frac{1}{2}$, it follows from the economy's intertemporal constraints (10.86) and (10.87) that

$$\frac{1}{2}\left(\frac{2+r}{1+r}\right) = c_1 + \frac{c_2^H}{1+r} + g_1 + \frac{g_2^H}{1+r},$$

$$\frac{1}{2}\left(\frac{2+r}{1+r}\right) = c_1 + \frac{c_2^L}{1+r} + g_1 + \frac{g_2^L}{1+r}.$$

Subtracting the second equation from the first one, we obtain

$$c_2^L - c_2^H = g_2^H - g_2^L.$$

Since $g_2^H > g_2^L$, it follows that $c_2^L > c_2^H$. In other words, consumption in the low-g state of the world is higher than in the high-g state of the world. This, together with the fact that $h_2^H = h_2^L$, implies from the implementability conditions (10.89) and (10.90) that $\theta_2^H > \theta_2^L$. The tax rate in the high-g state of the world will be higher than in the low-g state of the world. Further, since $c_2^L > c_2^H$, it follows from equation (10.100) that

$$c_2^H < c_1 < c_2^L.$$

How does the Ramsey case compare to the lump-sum tax case? The key difference is that once again, in the lump-sum tax case there would be no intratemporal distortion. In other words, $c_1 = h_1$, $c_2^H = h_2^H$, and $c_2^L = h_2^L$. (Exercise 5 at the end of the chapter asks you to work out the lump-sum case.) It would still be the case of course that $c_2^H < c_1 < c_2^L$, which would imply that $h_2^H < h_1 < h_2^L$. Interestingly, in the lump-sum case it would then be efficient for leisure to fluctuate alongside consumption, rather than being constant due to the intratemporal distortion as in the Ramsey case.

Table 10.2
Role of precautionary saving

	g_1	g_2^H	g_2^L	θ_1	θ_2^H	θ_2^L	c_2^H	c_2^L	PB_1	PB_1 as percent of GDP
Benchmark	0.1	0.1	0.1	0.25	0.25	0.25	0.4	0.4	0	0
Case 1	0.1	0.15	0.05	0.26	0.42	0.10	0.35	0.45	0.003	0.6
Case 2	0.1	0.18	0.02	0.275	0.52	0.02	0.33	0.49	0.007	1.4
Case 3	0.1	0.20	0.0	0.29	0.60	−0.02	0.31	0.51	0.012	2.4

The Role of Precautionary Saving

How important is self-insurance when markets are incomplete? In the presence of incomplete markets we expect the government to set tax rates in the first period so as to generate a primary surplus that can be used in the second period if government spending turns out to be high. Put differently, we expect the government to self-insure. Further, all else equal, we expect the amount of self-insurance to be larger, the larger the variability of government spending in the second period. We will now verify this conjecture in the context of a numerical example. Numerically—and taking into account that $h_1 = h_2^H = h_2^L = \frac{1}{2}$—we have a system of six nonlinear equations in six unknowns $(c_1, c_2^H, c_2^L, \theta_1, \theta_2^H, \theta_2^L)$ for given values of p, g_1, g_2^H, and g_2^L that consists of the following:

- The Ramsey first-order condition given by (10.100).
- The three implementability conditions given by equations (10.88), (10.89), and (10.90)
- The aggregate constraints (10.86) and (10.87)

We set $r = 0.03$ and $p = 0.5$. PB_1 follows from the definition given in (10.7). As a benchmark, table 10.2 shows the case where $g_1 = g_2^H = g_2^L$. Since there is no uncertainty, tax rates are equalized across time and states of nature. Government saving in period 1 is therefore zero. Consider now a mean-preserving spread for g_2 (case 1 in table 10.2). To this effect, we set $g_2^H = 0.15$ and $g_2^L = 0.05$, which implies that $E\{g_2\} = 0.10$ as in the benchmark case. We see how the tax rate in period 1 becomes higher (it increases from 0.25 to 0.26), which implies a primary surplus in the first period (equal to 0.6 percent of GDP).[12] The government thus acquires foreign assets from the rest of the world.[13] If the mean-preserving spread becomes $g_2^H = 0.18$ and $g_2^L = 0.02$ (case 2 in table 10.2), then the tax rate in the first period rises to 0.275, which implies a primary surplus of 1.4 percent of GDP. The primary surplus in period 1 implies that if the high-g state materializes in the second-period, the tax rate will be lower than it would be otherwise (i.e., if there were no precautionary saving in the first period). The counterpart of this is that the tax rate if the low-g

12. GDP in this economy is $1 - h_1 = \frac{1}{2}$.

13. It is easy to check that in this logarithmic case private saving are always zero, so the current account will be equal to public saving.

state materializes will be quite small (0.02) since the government has accumulated a lot of saving. In fact, if we make the mean-preserving spread as large as possible (case 3), the tax rate in the low-g state of nature would become negative! Due to the large amount of precautionary saving (2.4 percent of GDP), the government would have so many resources if the low-g state of nature materializes that it would need to return some of these resources to consumers.[14]

10.5.2 Complete Markets

In the previous subsection we analyzed the optimal fiscal policy problem with uncertain government spending when markets are incomplete. We saw how this forces the government to tax more heavily in those states where government spending is higher (implying that the intratemporal distortion is higher in those states). We will now analyze the case where asset markets are complete and see how the government recovers the ability to keep tax rates constant across time and across states of the world.

Households

Preferences continue to be given by (10.71). Denote by b_1^H and b_1^L the number of claims purchased by households in period 1 that promise to pay one unit of the good in the second period in state of nature H (i.e., high government spending) and L (i.e., low government spending), respectively. The price of such claims (in terms of period 2 output) is q^H and q^L, respectively. The flow constraint for period 1 is given by

$$\frac{q^H}{1+r}b_1^H + \frac{q^L}{1+r}b_1^L = 1 - h_1 - (1+\theta_1)c_1. \tag{10.103}$$

The flow constraints for period 2 are given by

$$0 = b_1^H + 1 - h_2^H - (1+\theta_2^H)c_2^H,$$

$$0 = b_1^L + 1 - h_2^L - (1+\theta_2^L)c_2^L.$$

Combining the flow budget constraints, we obtain the intertemporal constraint

$$\begin{aligned} 0 = 1 - h_1 - (1+\theta_1)c_1 + \frac{q^H}{1+r}\left[1 - h_2^H - (1+\theta_2^H)c_2^H\right] \\ + \frac{q^L}{1+r}\left[1 - h_2^L - (1+\theta_2^L)c_2^L\right]. \end{aligned} \tag{10.104}$$

The households' problem consists in choosing $\{c_1, h_1, c_2^H, h_2^H, c_2^L, h_2^L\}$ to maximize (10.71) subject to the intertemporal constraint (10.104). The Lagrangian takes the form

14. Of course, this assumes that we do not impose a nonnegativity constraint on θ_2^L.

$$\begin{aligned}\mathcal{L} = {} & \log(c_1) + \log(h_1) + \beta p[\log(c_2^H) + \log(h_2^H)] \\ & + \beta(1-p)[\log(c_2^L) + \log(h_2^L)] \\ & + \lambda\left\{1 - h_1 - (1+\theta_1)c_1 + \frac{q^H}{1+r}\left[1 - h_2^H - (1+\theta_2^H)c_2^H\right]\right. \\ & \left. + \frac{q^L}{1+r}\left[1 - h_2^L - (1+\theta_2^L)c_2^L\right]\right\},\end{aligned}$$

where λ is the multiplier corresponding to constraint (10.104). The first-order conditions with respect to c_1, h_1, c_2^H, h_2^H, c_2^L, and h_2^L are given by (assuming $\beta(1+r) = 1$)

$$\frac{1}{c_1} = \lambda(1+\theta_1), \tag{10.105}$$

$$\frac{1}{h_1} = \lambda, \tag{10.106}$$

$$\frac{p}{c_2^H} = \lambda q^H(1+\theta_2^H), \tag{10.107}$$

$$\frac{1-p}{c_2^L} = \lambda q^L(1+\theta_2^L), \tag{10.108}$$

$$\frac{p}{h_2^H} = \lambda q^H, \tag{10.109}$$

$$\frac{1-p}{h_2^L} = \lambda q^L. \tag{10.110}$$

Government

The government flow constraints are given by

$$\frac{q^H}{1+r}b_1^{gH} + \frac{q^L}{1+r}b_1^{gL} = \theta_1 c_1 - g_1, \tag{10.111}$$

$$0 = b_1^{gH} + \theta_2^H c_2^H - g_2^H,$$

$$0 = b_1^{gL} + \theta_2^L c_2^L - g_2^L.$$

Combining the flow constraints, we obtain the government intertemporal constraint

$$0 = \theta_1 c_1 - g_1 + \frac{q^H}{1+r}(\theta_2^H c_2^H - g_2^H) + \frac{q^L}{1+r}(\theta_2^L c_2^L - g_2^L). \tag{10.112}$$

As in the case of households, the government faces a single intertemporal constraint due to the presence of state-contingent claims.

Aggregate Constraints

Combining the household's and the government's flow budget constraints for period 1—given by (10.103) and (10.111), respectively—we obtain the economy's flow constraint for period 1:

$$\frac{q^H}{1+r}(b_1^H + b_1^{gH}) + \frac{q^L}{1+r}(b_1^L + b_1^{gL}) = 1 - h_1 - c_1 - g_1.$$

Combining the households' and the government's intertemporal constraints—given by (10.104) and (10.112), respectively—we obtain the economy's resource constraint:

$$0 = 1 - h_1 - c_1 - g_1 + \frac{q^H}{1+r}\left(1 - h_2^H - c_2^H - g_2^H\right) + \frac{q^L}{1+r}\left(1 - h_2^L - c_2^L - g_2^L\right). \tag{10.113}$$

Optimal Fiscal Policy

Implementability conditions Once again, we get the static implementability conditions (10.88), (10.89), and (10.90) from combining, respectively, (10.105) and (10.106), (10.107), and (10.109), and (10.108) and (10.110). These three implementability conditions are exactly the same that arose in the incomplete markets case because these static conditions are not affected by whether or not the household has access to state-contingent claims.

To obtain the fourth and final implementability condition, first combine (10.109) and (10.110) to obtain

$$\frac{q^H h_2^H}{p} = \frac{q^L h_2^L}{1-p}. \tag{10.114}$$

Recall from chapter 2 that if the prices of state-contingent claims are actuarially fair, then $q^H/q^L = p/(1-p)$. Hence equation (10.114) reduces to

$$h_2^H = h_2^L.$$

As expected, since households face actuarially fair prices, they will equate leisure across states of the world. Now combine (10.106), (10.109) and (10.110) to obtain the Euler equation for leisure:

$$\frac{1}{h_1} = \frac{p}{h_2^H} + \frac{1-p}{h_2^L}.$$

Since $h_2^H = h_2^L$, it follows that

$$h_1 = h_2^H = h_2^L, \tag{10.115}$$

which is the fourth implementability condition. For further reference, notice that expressions (10.92) and (10.93) continue to hold.

Ramsey Problem The Ramsey planner chooses an allocation $\{c_1, h_1, c_2^H, h_2^H, c_2^L, h_2^L\}$ to maximize households' utility (10.71) subject to the economy's resource constraint (10.113), the government's intertemporal constraint (10.112) and the implementability conditions (10.88), (10.89), and (10.90).[15] The Lagrangian takes the form

$$\begin{aligned}
\mathcal{L} = &\log(c_1) + \log(h_1) + \beta p[\log(c_2^H) + \log(h_2^H)] \\
&+ \beta(1-p)[\log(c_2^L) + \log(h_2^L)] \\
&+ \lambda \left\{ 1 - h_1 - c_1 - g_1 + \frac{q^H}{1+r}(1 - h_2^H - c_2^H - g_2^H) + \frac{q^L}{1+r}\left(1 - h_2^L - c_2^L - g_2^L\right) \right\} \\
&+ \mu \left\{ \widetilde{\theta}_1(c_1, h_1)c_1 - g_1 + \frac{q^H}{1+r}\left[\widetilde{\theta_2^H}(c_2^H, h_2^H)c_2^H - g_2^H\right] + \frac{q^L}{1+r}\left[\widetilde{\theta_2^L}(c_2^L, h_2^L)c_2^L - g_2^L\right] \right\},
\end{aligned}$$

where λ and μ are the multipliers associated with constraints (10.113) and (10.112), respectively, and we have substituted the implementability conditions into the government's intertemporal constraint.

Under the assumption that $\beta(1+r) = 1$, the first-order conditions with respect $c_1, h_1, c_2^H, h_2^H, c_2^L$, and h_2^L are given by, respectively,

$$\frac{1}{c_1} = \lambda - \mu \frac{\partial(\widetilde{\theta}_1 c_1)}{\partial c_1},$$

$$\frac{1}{h_1} = \lambda - \mu \frac{\partial(\widetilde{\theta}_1 c_1)}{\partial h_1},$$

$$\frac{p}{c_2^H} = \lambda q^H - \mu q^H \frac{\partial(\widetilde{\theta_2^H} c_2^H)}{\partial c_2^H},$$

$$\frac{1-p}{c_2^L} = \lambda q^L - \mu q^L \frac{\partial(\widetilde{\theta_2^L} c_2^L)}{\partial c_2^L},$$

$$\frac{p}{h_2^H} = \lambda q^H - \mu q^H \frac{\partial(\widetilde{\theta_2^H} c_2^H)}{\partial h_2^H},$$

15. Again, we do not impose (10.115) because, as we will check, the Ramsey allocation will satisfy it anyway.

$$\frac{1-p}{h_2^L} = \lambda q^L - \mu q^L \frac{\partial(\widetilde{\theta_2^L c_2^L})}{\partial h_2^L}.$$

Taking into account the partial derivatives in (10.92) and (10.93), we can rewrite these first-order conditions as

$$\frac{1}{c_1} = \lambda + \mu,$$

$$\frac{1}{h_1} = \lambda - \mu,$$

$$\frac{p}{c_2^H} = q^H(\lambda + \mu),$$

$$\frac{1-p}{c_2^L} = q^L(\lambda + \mu),$$

$$\frac{p}{h_2^H} = q^H(\lambda - \mu),$$

$$\frac{1-p}{h_2^L} = q^L(\lambda - \mu).$$

Getting rid of the multipliers, we can reduce this system to

$$\frac{1}{c_1} = \frac{1-p}{q^L c_2^L}, \tag{10.116}$$

$$\frac{1}{c_1} = \frac{p}{q^H c_2^H}, \tag{10.117}$$

$$\frac{1}{h_1} = \frac{1-p}{q^L h_2^L}, \tag{10.118}$$

$$\frac{1}{h_1} = \frac{p}{q^H h_2^H}, \tag{10.119}$$

$$\frac{q^H}{q^L}\frac{c_2^H}{c_2^L} = \frac{p}{1-p},$$

$$\frac{q^H}{q^L}\frac{h_2^H}{h_2^L} = \frac{p}{1-p}.$$

The last two conditions imply that, if prices are actuarially fair,

$$c_2^H = c_2^L, \tag{10.120}$$

$$h_2^H = h_2^L. \tag{10.121}$$

As expected, with actuarially fair prices, the optimal Ramsey allocation implies that both consumption and leisure will be constant across states of nature. It then follows from the implementability conditions (10.89), and (10.90) that

$$\theta_2^H = \theta_2^L.$$

Tax rates will be constant across states of the world. Further, given (10.120) and (10.121), equations (10.116) through (10.119) imply that

$$c_1 = c_2^H = c_2^L,$$

$$h_1 = h_2^H = h_2^L.$$

(Notice incidentally that implementability condition 10.115 is indeed satisfied.) Hence both consumption and leisure will be constant across time and states of nature. It follows from (10.88), (10.89), and (10.90) that

$$\theta_1 = \theta_2^H = \theta_2^L.$$

The tax rate is smoothed across both time and states of nature. Hence, with complete markets, we recover the optimal fiscal policy characterized in section 10.3 for the perfect foresight case.

10.6 Procyclical Fiscal Policy

Up to this point we have dealt with normative analysis; that is, we have asked the question: How *should* fiscal policy be conducted over the business cycle? But how is fiscal policy *actually* conducted in the real world? As discussed in box 10.1, fiscal policy in developing countries appears to be procyclical, whereas fiscal policy in industrial countries seems to be either acyclical or countercyclical. Since, as argued in box 10.1, normative models would call for either acyclical or countercyclical fiscal policy, the procyclicality of fiscal policy in developing countries constitutes a puzzle in search of an explanation.

Several explanations have been proposed in the literature to account for the procyclicality of fiscal policy in developing countries. Aizenman, Gavin, and Hausmann (2000) have argued that

Box 10.1
How is fiscal policy actually conducted?

Models of optimal fiscal policy tell us how fiscal policy *should* be conducted. In particular, the model of section 10.3 tells us that tax rates should be kept constant over time. If we endogeneized government spending along the lines of exercise 4 at the end of this chapter, we would conclude that government spending should also be kept constant over time. As shown in section 10.5.2, the constancy of tax rates and government spending is robust to introducing uncertainty as long as markets are complete. Even in more realistic models such as Chari, Christiano, and Kehoe (1994), optimal labor tax rates are basically constant. Hence neoclassical models of optimal fiscal policy call for an essentially acyclical fiscal policy. In contrast, models of optimal fiscal policy with sticky wages in the spirit of chapter 8 would call for a countercyclical fiscal policy. Intuitively, a negative shock to productivity, for example, would lead to involuntary unemployment as the real wage would not adjust downward as it would under flexible nominal wages. By temporarily increasing aggregate demand, a rise in government spending would increase production and employment, thus bringing the economy closer to its flexible wages equilibrium.

But how is fiscal policy *actually* conducted in practice? To answer this question, we should, of course, look at the cyclical behavior of the two main fiscal policy *instruments*: government spending and tax rates. Figure 10.1, which is an updated version of the one found in Kaminsky, Reinhart, and Végh (2005), depicts the average correlation between the cyclical components of government expenditure and GDP for both industrial countries (black bars) and developing countries (light bars). By and large, developing countries exhibit a positive correlation indicating that government spending increases in good times and decreases in bad times. This is in sharp contrast to the case of industrial countries, where government spending appears to be mostly countercyclical.[a]

What about tax rates? Figure 10.2, taken from Végh and Vuletin (2012), illustrates the correlation of an index of tax rates and GDP.[b] We can see that most light bars (developing countries) are negative, indicating that during good (bad) times, tax rates fall (increase), which constitutes procyclical tax rate policy. The dark bars (industrial countries) appear to be evenly distributed, suggesting an acyclical tax rate policy.

To corroborate the visual impression conveyed by figures 10.1 and 10.2, table 10.3 presents some simple OLS regressions of the cyclical components of government spending and the tax rate index on the cyclical component of output. For government spending, we can see that the regression coefficient is significantly positive for developing countries (indicating procyclical spending policy) and significantly negative for industrial countries (indicating countercyclical spending policy). For tax rates, the regression coefficient is significantly negative for developing countries (indicating procyclical tax rate policy) and not significantly different from zero for industrial countries. Needless to say, due to potential endogeneity problems (government spending might cause output), we should not read too much in terms of causality into the regressions of table 10.3. However, when output is properly instrumented, all the same results go through, indicating that there is indeed causality from the GDP cycle to government spending and tax rates (see Ilzetzki and Végh 2008 and Végh and Vuletin 2012).

a. It is worth noting that Chile is the only major emerging country that exhibits countercyclical fiscal policy, thanks to the fiscal rule based on a structural fiscal balance discussed in box 10.2.

b. See Végh and Vuletin (2012) for details on the construction of this tax rate index.

Box 10.1
(continued)

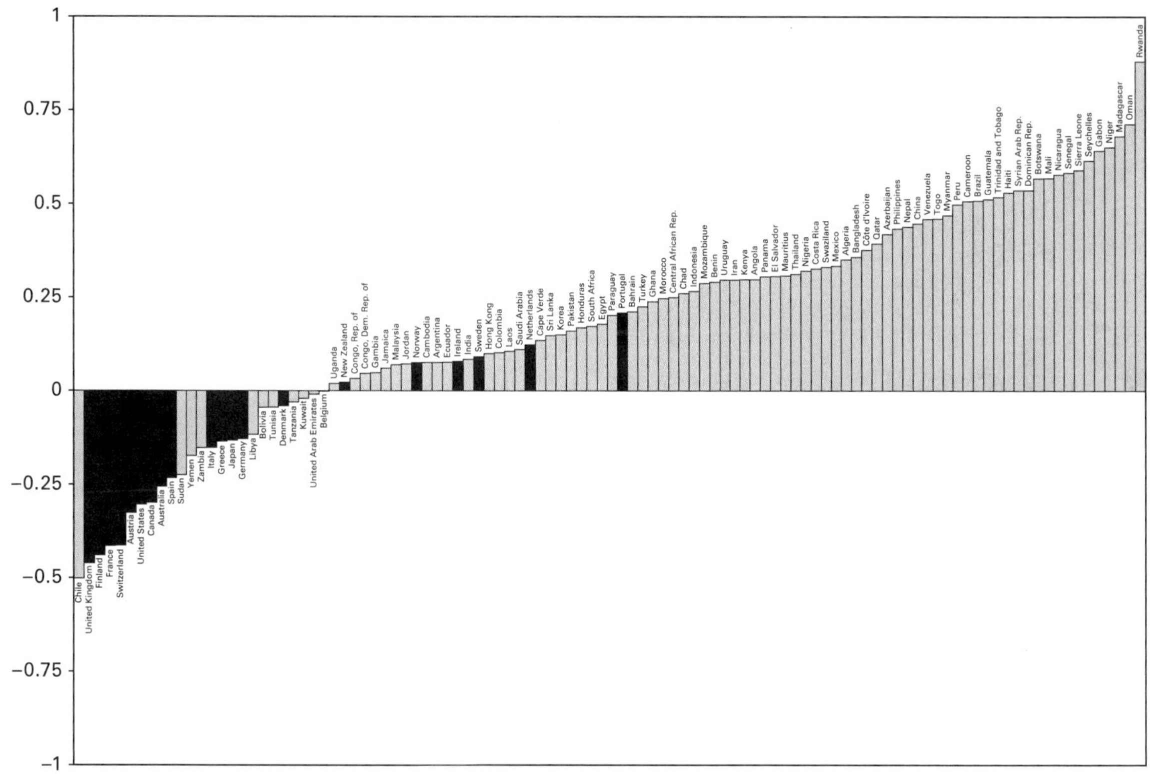

Notes: Dark bars are OECD countries and light ones are non–OECD countries. The cyclical components have been estimated using the Hodrick–Prescott filter. A positive (negative) correlation indicates procyclical (countercyclical) fiscal policy. Real government expenditure is defined as central government total expenditure and net lending deflated by the GDP deflator. Sample includes 105 countries.

Source: IMF, World Economic Outlook

Figure 10.1
Country correlations between the cyclical components of real government expenditure and real GDP, 1960 to 2009

Box 10.1
(continued)

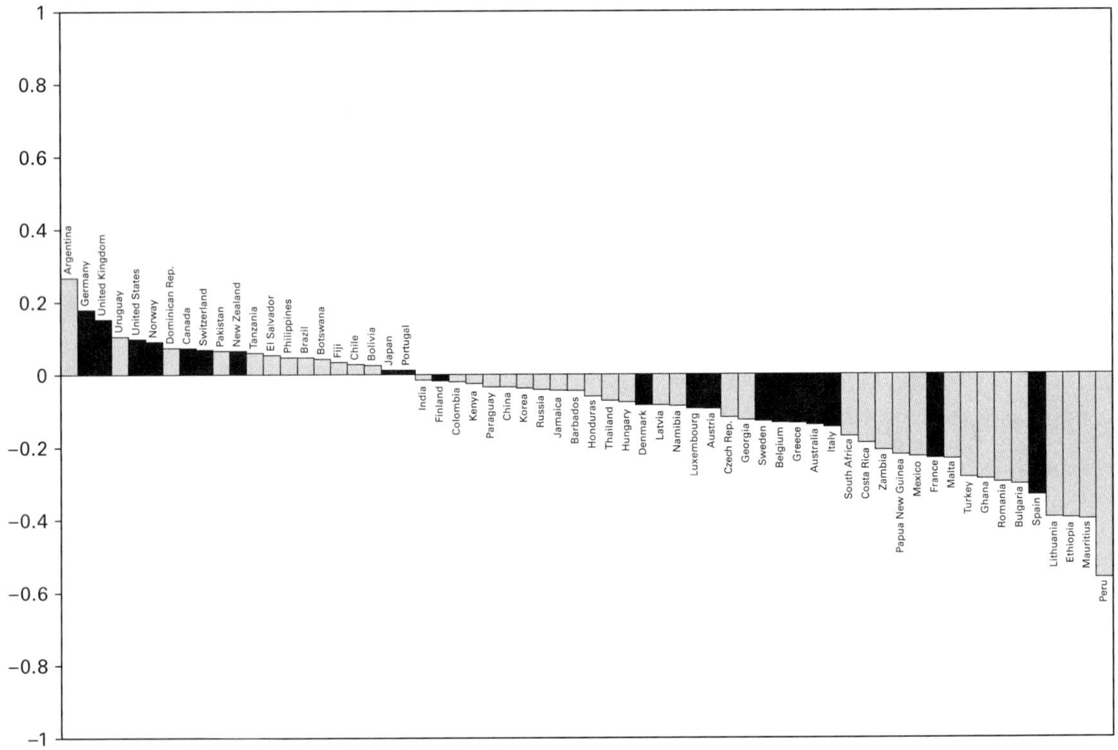

Notes: Dark bars are industrial countries and light ones are developing countries. The cyclical components have been estimated using the Hodrick–Prescott filter. A negative (positive) correlation indicates procyclical (countercyclical) tax policy. Sample includes 62 countries.

Source: Végh and Vuletin (2012)

Figure 10.2
Country correlations between the cyclical components of tax index and real GDP, 1960 to 2009

Box 10.1
(continued)

Table 10.3
Procyclicality regressions

	Expenditures	Tax index
OECD	−0.37***	−0.09
	(−2.9)	(−0.9)
Non-OECD	0.93***	−0.24***
	(4.3)	(−3.6)

Source: Data from Végh and Vuletin (2012).
Note: t-statistics in parentheses. *** denotes significance at the 1 percent level
Based on 88 (62) countries for expenditures (tax index), sample period 1960 to 2009, series detrended with HP filter. Panel data with country-fixed effects.

procyclical fiscal policy arises because developing countries are typically cut off from international markets in bad times, which forces them to reduce government spending and raise tax rates. A second, and related, explanation (see Riascos and Végh 2005) has to do with incomplete markets. The idea is that developing countries face credit markets that are more incomplete than those faced by industrial countries, which should lead to more procyclical tax rates. Again, this argument can be illustrated with the help of table 10.2 where we see a negative correlation between consumption and tax rates.[16]

This section presents a third explanation—due to Talvi and Végh (2005)—that unlike the first two is unrelated to frictions in international credit markets. The general idea is that weak domestic fiscal institutions make it difficult for the public sector in developing countries to save in good times. The other side of the coin is, of course, that the public sector will be unable to dissave in bad times. Weak fiscal institutions could naturally be modeled in a variety of ways. Here we capture the idea in a very simple way by assuming that spending pressures increase when there are fiscal surpluses. We will see how such a political distortion makes it optimal (as a second-best policy) for the government to reduce tax rates in good times as a way of decreasing the primary surplus and hence spending pressures.

10.6.1 Households

The households' problem is the same as in section 10.3 with the only difference that we will now have a shock to preferences. Let preferences be given by

$$W = \alpha_1 \log(c_1) + \log(h_1) + \beta[\alpha_2 \log(c_2) + \log(h_2)], \tag{10.122}$$

where α_t, $t = 1, 2$, is a positive parameter that will allow us to generate demand shocks.

16. We look at the relationship between consumption and tax rates because output is constant in this case.

The flow budget constraints continue to be given by (10.25) and (10.26) and the intertemporal constraint by (10.27).

Households choose $\{c_1, c_2, h_1, h_2\}$ to maximize (10.122) subject to constraint (10.27). In terms of the Lagrangian,

$$\mathcal{L} = \alpha_1 \log(c_1) + \log(h_1) + \beta[\alpha_2 \log(c_2) + \log(h_2)] + \lambda\left[1 - h_1 + \frac{1-h_2}{1+r} - c_1(1+\theta_1) - \frac{c_2(1+\theta_2)}{1+r}\right].$$

The first-order conditions are given by

$$\frac{\alpha_1}{c_1} = \lambda(1+\theta_1), \tag{10.123}$$

$$\frac{1}{h_1} = \lambda, \tag{10.124}$$

$$\frac{\alpha_2}{c_2} = \lambda(1+\theta_2), \tag{10.125}$$

$$\frac{1}{h_2} = \lambda. \tag{10.126}$$

10.6.2 Government

Budget Constraint

The government budget constraints continue to be given by (10.5), (10.6), and (10.8).

Political Distortion

To capture a political distortion in a simple way, we will assume that government spending is an increasing function of the primary surplus. The idea is that there are political pressures (not explicitly modeled) that put upward pressure on government spending when there is a primary surplus. In other words, it is more difficult for a finance minister to deny spending requests from different sectors of the economy when tax revenues are pouring into the treasury (as happens during good times) than in bad times.[17] Formally,

$$g_1 = \bar{g} + f(PB_1), \tag{10.127}$$

$$g_2 = \bar{g} + f(PB_2), \tag{10.128}$$

17. While we do not model this political distortion explicitly, the political economy literature offers various rationalizations; see, in particular, Tornell and Lane's (1999) "voracity effect." They show that as a result of a common pool problem, a positive terms of trade shock may lead to a more than proportional increase in fiscal spending.

where $\bar{g}$ denotes an exogenously given level of government spending and, as before,

$$PB_1 \equiv \theta_1 c_1 - g_1, \tag{10.129}$$

$$PB_2 \equiv \theta_2 c_2 - g_2, \tag{10.130}$$

denote the primary balance in periods 1 and 2, respectively, and $f(.)$ is an increasing and convex function

$$f'(.) > 0, \quad f''(.) > 0.$$

It is worth emphasizing that since PB_1 and PB_2 are endogenous variables, it is not necessarily the case that a positive shock to the tax base will increase spending. Whether or not it does will depend on the government's reaction to the shock, which will determine the primary balance.

10.6.3 Aggregate Constraints

The aggregate constraints continue to be given by (10.36) and (10.38).

10.6.4 Optimal Fiscal Policy

Implementability Conditions

Due to the logarithmic preferences, leisure will be constant across time and independent of the path of consumption tax rates. To show this, first combine (10.124) and (10.126), to obtain

$$h_1 = h_2 = h. \tag{10.131}$$

Then combine (10.123) and (10.124), on the one hand, and (10.125) and (10.126), on the other, to obtain

$$c_1(1+\theta_1) = \alpha_1 h, \tag{10.132}$$

$$c_2(1+\theta_2) = \alpha_2 h. \tag{10.133}$$

Substituting these last two equations into the consumer's intertemporal constraint (10.27) and solving for h yields

$$h = \frac{(2+r)/(1+r)}{(2+r)/(1+r) + \alpha_1 + \alpha_2/(1+r)}. \tag{10.134}$$

(Notice that if $\alpha_1 = \alpha_2 = 1$, then $h = \frac{1}{2}$, as in section 10.3.) Since equation (10.134) must hold in a competitive equilibrium, the Ramsey planner will take this value of h as given and not choose leisure as part of his/her maximization problem.

As usual, the static implementability conditions are obtained by combining (10.123) and (10.124), on the one hand, and (10.125) and (10.126), on the other,

$$\theta_1 = \tilde{\theta}_1(c_1, h) \equiv \alpha_1 \frac{h}{c_1} - 1, \tag{10.135}$$

$$\theta_2 = \tilde{\theta}_2(c_2, h) \equiv \alpha_2 \frac{h}{c_2} - 1, \tag{10.136}$$

where h is given by (10.134). For further reference, notice that

$$\frac{\partial \tilde{\theta}_1(c_1, h)c_1}{\partial c_1} = -1, \tag{10.137}$$

$$\frac{\partial \tilde{\theta}_2(c_2, h)c_2}{\partial c_2} = -1. \tag{10.138}$$

Ramsey Problem

The Ramsey planner chooses an allocation $\{c_1, c_2, g_1, \text{and } g_2\}$ to maximize lifetime utility (10.122) subject to the government's intertemporal constraint (10.8), the political distortions (10.127) and (10.128), and the implementability conditions (10.134), (10.135), and (10.136). We impose the implementability condition (10.134) by simply not allowing the Ramsey planner to choose h_1 and h_2 and take h as given by (10.134).[18] In terms of the Lagrangian, the Ramsey problem can therefore be expressed as

$$\begin{aligned}\mathcal{L} = {} & \alpha_1 \log(c_1) + \log(h) + \beta[\alpha_2 \log(c_2) + \log(h)] \\ & + \mu\left[\tilde{\theta}_1(c_1, h)c_1 + \frac{\tilde{\theta}_2(c_2, h)c_2}{1+r} - g_1 - \frac{g_2}{1+r}\right] \\ & + \Psi_1[g_1 - \bar{g} - f(\tilde{\theta}_1(c_1, h)c_1 - g_1)] \\ & + \frac{\Psi_2}{1+r}[g_2 - \bar{g} - f(\tilde{\theta}_2(c_2, h)c_2 - g_2)],\end{aligned}$$

where μ, Ψ_1, and Ψ_2 are the multipliers associated with constraints (10.8), (10.127), and (10.128), respectively, and we have substituted implementability conditions (10.135) and (10.136) into the government's intertemporal constraints and the expressions for government spending.

18. Note also that we do not need to impose the economy's resource constraint (10.38) because the household's intertemporal constraint—and hence, by Walras's law, the resource constraint—is always satisfied for the value of h given by (10.134), as already shown.

The first-order conditions are given by (assuming $\beta(1+r)=1$)

$$\frac{\alpha_1}{c_1} = -\mu \frac{\partial\left(\tilde{\theta}_1 c_1\right)}{\partial c_1} + \Psi_1 f'(PB_1) \frac{\partial\left(\tilde{\theta}_1 c_1\right)}{\partial c_1}, \tag{10.139}$$

$$\frac{\alpha_2}{c_2} = -\mu \frac{\partial\left(\tilde{\theta}_2 c_2\right)}{\partial c_2} + \Psi_2 f'(PB_2) \frac{\partial\left(\tilde{\theta}_2 c_2\right)}{\partial c_2}, \tag{10.140}$$

$$\Psi_1\left[1+f'(PB_1)\right] = \mu, \tag{10.141}$$

$$\Psi_2\left[1+f'(PB_2)\right] = \mu. \tag{10.142}$$

Taking into account the partial derivatives of the implementability conditions given by (10.137) and (10.138), we can rewrite (10.139) and (10.140) as

$$\frac{\alpha_1}{c_1} = \mu - \Psi_1 f'(PB_1), \tag{10.143}$$

$$\frac{\alpha_2}{c_2} = \mu - \Psi_2 f'(PB_2). \tag{10.144}$$

Solving for Ψ_1 from (10.141) and for Ψ_2 from (10.142) and substituting into (10.143) and (10.144), respectively, we obtain

$$\frac{\alpha_1}{c_1} = \frac{\mu}{1+f'(PB_1)}, \tag{10.145}$$

$$\frac{\alpha_2}{c_2} = \frac{\mu}{1+f'(PB_2)}. \tag{10.146}$$

Combining these two equations yields

$$\frac{\alpha_1}{c_1}\left[1+f'(PB_1)\right] = \frac{\alpha_2}{c_2}\left[1+f'(PB_2)\right]. \tag{10.147}$$

As a benchmark, we will first show that if there are no shocks to the tax base, then the political distortion is not binding and tax smoothing is optimal.

Claim 2: If $\alpha_1 = \alpha_2 = \alpha$, then it is optimal to smooth taxes over time (i.e., $\theta_1 = \theta_2 = \theta$).

***Proof*:** We verify that the solution $\theta_1 = \theta_2 = \theta$ satisfies the optimality conditions by constructing a solution. If $\theta_1 = \theta_2 = \theta$, then it follows from the implementability conditions (10.135) and (10.136) that $c_1 = c_2 = c$. It then follows from equation (10.147) that $PB_1 = PB_2$. Then, from equations (10.127) and (10.128), $g_1 = g_2$. ■

Intuitively, the fact that there are no shocks to the tax base implies that there is no need for the government to use primary imbalances to help keep tax rates constant. Since there are no primary imbalances, there are no political pressures for additional spending. Hence, the political distortions are nonbinding.

We now show that if $\alpha_1 > \alpha_2$, then $\theta_1 < \theta_2$.

Claim 3: If $\alpha_1 > \alpha_2$, then $\theta_1 < \theta_2$.

Proof: See the appendix. ■

We have thus established that $\theta_1 < \theta_2$. It then follows from (10.132) and (10.133) that

$$\frac{\alpha_1}{c_1} < \frac{\alpha_2}{c_2}. \tag{10.148}$$

Since $\alpha_1 > \alpha_2$, this last inequality implies that $c_1 > c_2$. Also inequality (10.148) implies, from (10.147), that $PB_1 > PB_2$. Hence, from (10.127) and (10.128), it follows that $g_1 > g_2$. Finally, since $PB_1 > PB_2$, it follows from (10.129) and (10.130) that $\theta_1 c_1 - g_1 > \theta_2 c_2 - g_2$. Since $g_1 > g_2$, then $\theta_1 c_1 > \theta_2 c_2$.

We have thus established that in this second-best world the optimal fiscal policy is procyclical. In other words, government spending will be high and tax rates low in good times (i.e., high consumption periods) and government spending will be low and tax rates high in bad times (i.e., low consumption periods). What is the intuition behind these results? Suppose that the government kept tax rates constant over time. Then there would be a primary surplus in the first period, which, due to the political distortion, would result in higher government spending. To avoid this waste of resources, the government finds it optimal to introduce an additional distortion (i.e., an intertemporal distortion) by lowering tax rates in the first period, thus reducing the primary surplus and hence government spending. Since it is not optimal to lower the tax rate by as much as it would be needed to complete eliminate the primary surplus, government spending will still increase but less than otherwise.[19]

10.7 Optimal Monetary Policy

We now turn to the analysis of optimal monetary policy. To illustrate some key points, we will introduce money via a transactions cost technology as in chapter 7.[20] Consider a small open economy, perfectly integrated with the rest of the world in both goods and assets markets, that operates under a predetermined exchange rate.[21]

19. The same results would obtain if $f(.)$ were a linear function but g entered in the utility fuction, as exercise 6 at the end of this chapter asks you to verify.

20. This section follows the presentation in Bordo and Végh (2002). See Walsh (2010) for a detailed analysis of optimal monetary policy in different types of monetary models.

21. The same analysis would go through under flexible exchange rates.

10.7.1 Household's Problem

There is only one (nonstorable) good, which is produced with labor (n_t) as the only input. Labor is taken to be the numéraire. Production (y_t) takes place under the linear technology given by $y_t = n_t$. Carrying out transactions is costly in that it requires the use of "shopping time," denoted by s_t. Since the representative household is endowed with one unit of time, its time constraint is given by $s_t + n_t + h_t = 1$, where h_t denotes leisure.

Households may hold two assets: domestic (non–interest-bearing) money and an internationally traded bond that bears a (constant) real rate of return, r. Households hold real money balances in order to reduce shopping time. Specifically, shopping time is given by

$$s_t = v\left[\frac{m_t}{c_t(1+\theta_t)}\right] c_t(1+\theta_t), \tag{10.149}$$

where $m_t (\equiv M_t/P_t)$ denotes real money balances, c_t stands for consumption, θ_t is the consumption tax, and $v(.)$, the transactions technology, which satisfies the following properties:

$$\begin{aligned} &v(.) \geq 0, \quad v'(.) \leq 0, \quad v''(.) > 0, \quad v'''(.) = 0, \\ &v'(X^s) = 0, \quad v(X^s) = 0, \quad 0 \leq X \leq X^s, \end{aligned} \tag{10.150}$$

where $X (\equiv m/[c(1+\theta)])$ denotes real money balances as a fraction of total expenditure. Additional units of X bring about positive but diminishing reductions in shopping time. There exists a level of X, X^s, such that the gains from holding additional liquidity are exhausted (i.e., $v'(X^s) = 0$). Transactions costs at that point are assumed to be zero (i.e., $v(X^s) = 0$).

The household's budget constraint is given by

$$f_t = (1+r)f_{t-1} + 1 - h_t - c_t(1+\theta_t) - s_t + \frac{m_{t-1}}{1+\pi_t} - m_t, \tag{10.151}$$

where f_t denotes real bond holdings, and π_t is the rate of inflation (and devaluation, given that the law of one price holds), defined as $P_t/P_{t-1} - 1$.

Letting $a_t (\equiv f_t + m_t/(1+i_t))$ denote real financial assets, we can rewrite the last expression as

$$a_t = (1+r)a_{t-1} + 1 - h_t - c_t(1+\theta_t) - s_t - I_t m_t, \tag{10.152}$$

where $1 + i_t \equiv (1+r)(1+\pi_{t+1})$ and $I_t (\equiv i_t/(1+i_t))$ is the opportunity cost of real money balances or inflation tax.[22] Iterating forward flow constraint (10.152), imposing the transversality condition $\lim_{t\to\infty} [1/(1+r)]^t a_t = 0$, and assuming, for simplicity, that $a_{-1} = 0$, we obtain

22. To understand why a_t is the economically relevant definition of real financial assets in this context, notice that $m_{t-1}/(1+\pi_t)$ is the real value of money brought into period t, which we can write as $(1+r)m_{t-1}/(1+i_{t-1})$. Hence, if all financial assets had a return of r, then real financial assets would be $f_{t-1} + m_{t-1}/(1+i_{t-1})$.

$$\sum_{t=0}^{\infty}\left(\frac{1}{1+r}\right)^t(1-h_t)=\sum_{t=0}^{\infty}\left(\frac{1}{1+r}\right)^t[c_t(1+\theta_t)+s_t+I_t m_t]. \tag{10.153}$$

Preferences are given by

$$\sum_{t=0}^{\infty}\beta^t[\log(c_t)+\log(h_t)]. \tag{10.154}$$

The household's maximization problem thus consists in choosing $\{c_t, h_t, m_t\}$ for $t = 0, 1, \ldots,$ to maximize (10.154) subject to the intertemporal constraint (10.153), with s_t given by (10.149). Write the Lagrangian as

$$\mathcal{L}=\sum_{t=0}^{\infty}\beta^t[\log(c_t)+\log(h_t)]$$
$$+\lambda\sum_{t=0}^{\infty}\left(\frac{1}{1+r}\right)^t[1-h_t-c_t(1+\theta_t)-s_t-I_t m_t],$$

where λ is the multiplier associated with constraint (10.153). Assuming, as usual, that $\beta(1+r)=1$, the first-order conditions with respect to $\{c_t, h_t, m_t\}$ are given by, respectively,

$$\frac{1}{c_t}=\lambda(1+\theta_t)[1+v(X_t)-v'(X_t)X_t], \tag{10.155}$$

$$\frac{1}{h_t}=\lambda, \tag{10.156}$$

$$-v'(X_t)=I_t. \tag{10.157}$$

Since $v''(.)>0$, condition (10.157) implicitly defines X_t as a decreasing function of the opportunity cost, I_t, which will be denoted by $\tilde{X}(I_t)$.

Equation (10.155) is the familiar condition whereby, at an optimum, consumers equate the marginal utility of consumption to the shadow value of wealth (λ) times the *effective* price of consumption.[23] The effective price of consumption is given by the real market price, $1+\theta_t$, plus the increase in shopping time associated with an additional unit of consumption, $(1+\theta_t)[v(X_t)-v'(X_t)X_t]$. Condition (10.156) implies that along a perfect foresight equilibrium path, leisure will be constant. Equation (10.157) states that at an optimum, consumers equate the marginal reduction in transactions costs derived from holding an additional unit of real money balances to its marginal cost, I_t.

23. Recall our discussion of a continuous version of this model in chapter 7, section 7.4.

For further reference, note that the effective price of consumption may also be viewed as the *effective tax rate* faced by the consumer. In effect, solving for X_t as a function of I_t from (10.157) and substituting into (10.155), we obtain

$$\frac{1}{c_t} = \lambda q(\theta_t, I_t), \tag{10.158}$$

where

$$q(\theta_t, I_t) \equiv (1+\theta_t)\{1 + v[\tilde{X}(I_t)] - v'[\tilde{X}(I_t)]\tilde{X}(I_t)\} \tag{10.159}$$

is the effective tax rate. The household will therefore care about the level of the effective tax rate and not about the particular levels of θ_t and I_t that bring it about. Further, from (10.156) and (10.158), it follows that

$$\frac{h_t}{c_t} = q(\theta_t, I_t). \tag{10.160}$$

In other words, $q(\theta_t, I_t)$ captures the *intratemporal* distortion between consumption and leisure.

Due to the logarithmic preferences—and as has been the case before in this chapter—a key characteristic of the consumer's program is that leisure will not be affected by government policy; that is, it does not depend on the path of either the consumption tax or the inflation tax. To see this, use (10.149), (10.157), and (10.159) to rewrite the consumer's intertemporal constraint (10.153) as

$$\sum_{t=0}^{\infty}\left(\frac{1}{1+r}\right)^t (1-h_t) = \sum_{t=0}^{\infty}\left(\frac{1}{1+r}\right)^t q(\theta_t, I_t)c_t. \tag{10.161}$$

Given (10.160), it then follows that

$$h_t = \frac{1}{2}. \tag{10.162}$$

Leisure will thus always be equal to one half regardless of government policy.

10.7.2 Government Budget Constraints

The government faces an exogenously given path of government spending, g_t, which it can finance by means of a consumption tax, θ_t, the inflation tax, I_t, or by borrowing in world financial markets.[24] The collection of the consumption tax is assumed to carry collection costs.

24. Note that since the consumption tax applies to a tradable good, it is essentially the same as a trade tax.

The government's budget constraint in each period is given by

$$z_t = (1+r)z_{t-1} + \theta_t c_t - T(\theta_t c_t) + m_t - \frac{m_{t-1}}{1+\pi_t} - g_t, \tag{10.163}$$

where z_t denotes the government's stock of internationally traded bonds at the end of period t, and $T(\theta_t c_t)$ represents the collection costs associated with the consumption tax. For simplicity, it will be assumed that $T(\theta_t c_t) = k_t(\theta_t c_t)^2$, where k_t is a nonnegative (and possibly time-varying) parameter. Taking this into account, as well as the definition of X_t, we can rewrite equation (10.163) as

$$b_t = (1+r)b_{t-1} + (1 - k_t\theta_t c_t)\theta_t c_t + I_t X_t c_t(1+\theta_t) - g_t, \tag{10.164}$$

where $b_t \equiv z_t - m_t/(1+i_t)$ denotes the government's net real financial assets. Furthermore the government's budget constraint can be expressed solely as a function of quantities, c_t and X_t, by substituting (10.168) and (10.169) into (10.164) to obtain

$$b_t = (1+r)b_{t-1} + \Gamma(c_t, X_t) - g_t, \tag{10.165}$$

where

$$\Gamma(c_t, X_t) \equiv [1 - k_t\tilde{\theta}(c_t, X_t)c_t]\tilde{\theta}(c_t, X_t)c_t + \tilde{I}(X_t)X_t c_t[1 + \tilde{\theta}(c_t, X_t)] \tag{10.166}$$

denotes total tax revenues.

Iterating forward flow constraint (10.165), imposing the transversality condition $\lim_{t\to\infty}[1/(1+r)]^t\, b_t = 0$, and assuming that $b_{-1} = 0$, we obtain

$$\sum_{t=0}^{\infty}\left(\frac{1}{1+r}\right)^t g_t = \sum_{t=0}^{\infty}\left(\frac{1}{1+r}\right)^t \Gamma(c_t, X_t). \tag{10.167}$$

10.7.3 Ramsey Problem

We will solve for the optimal policy by following the primal approach described in section 10.3.[25]

Implementability Conditions In this optimal taxation problem, there are three implementability conditions. The first is that $h_t = \frac{1}{2}$, as shown above. Given that in a competitive equilibrium, leisure will always be equal to one-half, the Ramsey planner cannot choose any other leisure allocation and will therefore take leisure as given. From (10.156), this implies that $\lambda = 2$. The other two implementability conditions, which follow from first-order conditions (10.155) and (10.157), are given by

25. We assume that there is full precommitment. This implies that by construction, policies are time-consistent. See Calvo (1978) for an analysis of optimal monetary policy under time-inconsistency.

$$\theta_t \equiv \tilde{\theta}(c_t, X_t) = \frac{1}{2c_t\,[1 + v(X_t) - v'(X_t)X_t]} - 1, \tag{10.168}$$

$$I_t \equiv \tilde{I}(X_t) = -v'(X_t). \tag{10.169}$$

Ramsey Allocations The Ramsey problem consists in choosing $\{c_t, X_t\}$ for $t = 0, 1, \ldots$, to maximize (10.154) with $h_t = \frac{1}{2}$ subject to the intertemporal constraint (10.167).[26] In terms of the Lagrangian,

$$\mathcal{L} = \sum_{t=0}^{\infty} \beta^t \left[\log(c_t) + \log\left(\frac{1}{2}\right)\right] + \gamma \left\{\sum_{t=0}^{\infty} \left(\frac{1}{1+r}\right)^t [\Gamma(c_t, X_t) - g_t]\right\},$$

where γ is the multiplier associated with constraint (10.167). Under the assumption that $\beta(1 + r) = 1$, the first-order conditions with respect to c_t and X_t are given by respectively,

$$\frac{1}{c_t} = -\gamma \Gamma_c(c_t, X_t), \tag{10.170}$$

$$\gamma \Gamma_X(c_t, X_t) = 0, \tag{10.171}$$

where

$$\Gamma_c(c_t, X_t) = -[1 - 2k_t\tilde{\theta}(c_t, X_t)c_t], \tag{10.172}$$

$$\Gamma_X(c_t, X_t) = -c_t[1 + \tilde{\theta}(c_t, X_t)] \times \left[v'(X_t) + \frac{v''(X_t)X_t[v(X_t) + 2k_t\tilde{\theta}(c_t, X_t)c_t]}{1 + v(X_t) - v'(X_t)X_t}\right]. \tag{10.173}$$

To solve the model, we would use (10.167), (10.170), and (10.171) to solve for c_t, X_t, and γ. For given values of c_t and X_t, (10.168) and (10.169) determine the optimal values of θ_t and I_t.

At an optimum, $\Gamma_c(c_t, X_t) < 0$.[27] In other words, at an optimum, an additional unit of consumption *lowers* revenues. Therefore equation (10.170) says that at an optimum, the Ramsey planner equates the marginal utility of consumption to the shadow value of government's wealth, γ, times the marginal loss in revenues from an additional unit of consumption. Also, at an optimum, $\Gamma_X(c_t, X_t) = 0$.[28] Since an additional unit of X_t has no direct effect on household's utility,

26. Note that as was the case in section 10.6, we do not need to impose the households' intertemporal contraint (or, which is the same, the aggregate constraint) in the Ramsey problem because the fact that $h_t = \frac{1}{2}$ implies that the households' intertemporal constraint holds for any allocation $\{c_t, X_t\}_{t=0}^{\infty}$ chosen by the Ramsey planner, as should be clear from the analysis above. This is, of course, particular to logarithmic preferences.

27. It can be checked that for the second-order conditions to hold, it must be the case that $\Gamma_c \Gamma_{XX} > 0$. Since, as follows from (10.173), $\Gamma_{XX} < 0$, then $\Gamma_c < 0$. By (10.170), it follows that, at an optimum, $\gamma > 0$, as expected.

28. Since, at an optimum, $\gamma > 0$, (10.171) implies that $\Gamma_X(c_t, X_t) = 0$.

first-order condition (10.171) says that at an optimum, the marginal increase in revenues from an additional unit of X_t should be zero.

10.7.4 Current Account

Combining equations (10.151) and (10.163), taking into account equation that $h_t = \frac{1}{2}$, yields the economy's flow resource constraint (i.e., the current account balance):

$$f_t + z_t = (1+r)(f_{t-1} + z_{t-1}) + \frac{1}{2} - c_t - g_t - s_t - k_t(\theta_t c_t)^2. \tag{10.174}$$

10.7.5 Full Tax Smoothing

The first two claims describe situations in which it is optimal to completely smooth out taxes over time.

Claim 4 (No collection costs): Suppose $k_t = 0$ for all t. Then the optimal tax policy consists of setting the inflation tax to zero and setting a constant consumption tax that finances permanent government spending in every period.

Proof: See the appendix. ■

Claim 4 is Barro's (1979) celebrated tax-smoothing result derived in a monetary, public finance model. In the absence of collection costs, it is also the case that it is optimal not to resort to the inflation tax.[29] Intuitively, recall from (10.158), that all that matters to the household is the effective tax on consumption. Households are thus indifferent between different combinations of taxes that yield the same effective tax. Socially, however, using the consumption tax entails no resource costs, while the inflation tax does. It is thus optimal to use only the consumption tax.

In this case any excess of actual government spending over its permanent value (due to wars, for example) will therefore be fully financed by public borrowing.[30] The current account thus deteriorates one to one with the temporary component of government spending. Under this optimal tax policy the intertemporal distortion is completely eliminated and only the intratemporal distortion remains; that is, $q(\theta, I) = 1 + \theta > 1$.

29. This is Kimbrough's (1986) result. The critical assumptions behind this result are the homogeneity of the transactions costs function and the assumption that $v(X^s) = 0$ (see Walsh's 2010 textbook on monetary economics for details and references). As further discussed in Walsh (2010), the Friedman rule is also optimal in MIUF and CIA models under certain restrictions on preferences. There is, of course, no reason to believe that any of these (rather strong) restrictions on the transactions technology or preferences will be satisfied in practice. Quantitatively, however, the optimal nominal interest rate appears to be small even when the Friedman rule is not optimal (e.g., see Chari and Kehoe 1999).

30. Permanent government spending, $\bar{g}$, is defined as that constant value of government spending whose present discounted value is the same as that of actual government spending. Formally, $\bar{g} = \frac{r}{(1+r)} \sum_{t=0}^{\infty} \left(\frac{1}{1+r}\right)^t g_t$.

Claim 5 (Positive collection costs): Suppose $k_t = k > 0$. Then both I and θ are positive and constant over time.

Proof: See the appendix. ■

Claim 5 shows that with positive but constant collection costs, full tax smoothing continues to be the optimal policy. The government, however, finds it now optimal to set positive values of both the consumption and the inflation tax. Intuitively, and unlike the previous case, both the consumption tax and the inflation tax carry resource costs. Hence, at an optimum, the government will be using both taxes. Once again—and as was the case for the real economy of section 10.3—no intertemporal distorsions are imposed, but intratemporal distortions are unavoidable because of the need to finance government spending.[31]

As shown in Végh (1989a), a higher level of permanent government spending or a higher k implies a higher (but still constant over time) inflation tax. As in the case described in claim 4, full tax smoothing implies that there is no intertemporal distortion. The intratemporal distortion, however, is higher than in claim 4 (and thus welfare is lower) because collecting the consumption tax is now socially costly, and the positive inflation tax generates positive transactions costs. Hence collecting the same amount of revenues will require a higher effective tax rate.

10.7.6 Time-Varying Collection Costs

In our analysis of optimal fiscal policy, we presented evidence in box 10.1 that suggests that in developing countries, tax rate policy appears to be procyclical (i.e., tax rates are negatively correlated with the business cycle), and we offered some possible explanations, such as incomplete markets and political distortions. In the same vein—and as shown, for example, by Talvi and Végh (2005)—the inflation tax appears to be negatively correlated with the business cycle in developing countries. Clearly, the cases described in claims 4 and 5 do not provide a rationale for the inflation tax to vary over time. A key assumption behind these results is that k_t does not change over time. This, however, may not always be a realistic assumption because bad times may be associated with an increase in the cost of collecting conventional taxes.[32] The following claim addresses this case.

Claim 6 (Time-varying *k*): Consider a perfect foresight equilibrium path for an arbitrary path of $\{k_t\}_{t=0}^{\infty}$. If, along such a path, $k_{t+1} > k_t$ for some t, then $I_{t+1} > I_t$ and $\theta_{t+1} < \theta_t$.

Proof: See the appendix. ■

31. Other frictions, particularly relevant for developing countries, that may rationalize a positive inflation tax are tax evasion (Nicolini 1998) and currency substitution (Végh 1989b).

32. As discussed in detail in Bordo and Végh (2002), Argentina in the first half of the nineteenth century offers a dramatic example of higher collection costs during times of war. Since Argentina's wars with foreign powers typically involved a blockade of Argentina's major port, revenues from trade taxes would fall dramatically reflecting higher collection costs.

Claim 6 says that in periods when collection costs are higher, then the inflation tax will be higher and the consumption tax will be lower. Intuitively, a higher k_t makes the consumption tax more costly to collect, which induces the government to switch from taxing consumption to taxing real money balances. Revenues from the consumption tax therefore fall during high-k_t periods. As shown in the appendix, total tax revenues also fall, reflecting the fact that it is relatively inefficient to raise revenues while k_t is high.

Notice that claim 6 could explain a situation where the rate of inflation is positive during wartime and negative (i.e., deflation) during peacetime in such a way that the average inflation rate is zero. To see this, recall that $I_t = i_t/(1 + i_t)$ and $1 + i_t = (1 + r)(1 + \pi_{t+1})$. Hence a zero inflation rate (i.e., $\pi_{t+1} = 0$) implies a positive inflation tax ($I = r/(1 + r)$). A low peacetime value of k_t could imply that the optimal peacetime inflation tax is less than $r/(1 + r)$, so that the optimal peacetime inflation rate is negative. During wars, the optimal inflation tax could be greater than $r/(1 + r)$, which implies a positive inflation rate.

10.7.7 Non-costly Unexpected Inflation

As discussed above, claim 6 could, in principle, explain a situation where the inflation rate is higher during wartime but is still zero on average, so that the price level exhibits mean reversion. This requires, of course, that collection costs increase during wars (claim 6).[33] We now consider yet another variation of the model intended to convey the basic intuition behind a result derived by Calvo and Guidotti (1993) in a stochastic setting, which suggests another scenario in which the inflation rate could rise during wars and still be zero on average. Although under perfect foresight the assumptions may seem somewhat extreme, this case provides the basic intuition for understanding the result in a stochastic environment.

Consider the case studied in claim 5 where collection costs are constant. Assume that the government must finance all current expenditures with current revenues (i.e., it does not have access to credit markets). Suppose that the government can also resort to a lump-sum tax, subject to the restriction that the present discounted value of the revenues collected with such a lump-sum tax be zero. Hence the government can resort, as before, to the consumption and inflation taxes and, in addition, to this lump-sum tax. Then we can show the following result:

Claim 7 (Zero-revenue, lump-sum tax available): Let $k_t = k > 0$. Suppose that the government must finance current spending with current revenues and has available a lump-sum tax that, on average, cannot generate any revenue (i.e., the present discounted value of the revenues derived from this lump-sum tax must be zero). The optimal policy then consists in financing permanent government spending with the consumption tax and the inflation tax, and finance all deviations of permanent spending from current spending by using the lump-sum tax.

Proof: See the appendix. ■

33. It could also be explained by imperfect access to capital markets (see Bordo and Végh 2002).

The intuition behind this result is simple enough. By definition, the deviations of current government spending from permanent government spending have a present discounted value of zero. By using the lump-sum tax to finance such deviations, the government replicates the solution under claim 5. The fact that it cannot borrow during bad times and lend during good times is not a binding constraint because by lump-sum taxing households in bad times and giving them subsidies in good times, it can achieve the same equilibrium.

Let us now consider the stochastic case (under precommitment) studied by Calvo and Guidotti (1993). Assume the following: (1) government spending is stochastic (i.i.d), (2) the government cannot issue state-contingent debt, and (3) households decide how much real money balances to hold *before* the state of nature is revealed. It is clear that unanticipated inflation will have no welfare costs, as it acts precisely as a lump-sum tax because it does not affect decisions. Of course, expected inflation has welfare costs. The optimal policy, as shown by Calvo and Guidotti (1993), is then to set conventional taxes so as to finance the expected value of government spending and use *unanticipated* inflation to finance all the unanticipated variability in government spending.

The logic behind this result follows from claim 7. In this case the government cannot issue state-contingent debt and hence is precluded from using debt to keep taxes constant when government spending rises unexpectedly. But it can resort to a lump-sum tax (unanticipated inflation)—which does not collect any revenue on average—to finance these unanticipated changes. By so doing, it reproduces the equilibrium that would obtain if it could issue state contingent debt.

10.8 Final Remarks

This chapter has looked at optimal fiscal and monetary policy in the context of models that were developed in the first part of the book. In the absence of uncertainty and restrictions to capital mobility, an optimal fiscal policy will entail fully smoothing tax rates over time in order to avoid introducing intertemporal distortions à la chapter 3. Intratemporal distortions between consumption and leisure cannot, however, be avoided. When restrictions to capital mobility are present, temporary increases in government spending will be optimally financed by a combination of higher taxes and more borrowing, which, in equilibrium, will be generated through higher real interest rates.

In practice, fiscal policy tends to be procyclical in developing countries—that is, fiscal policy is expansionary in good times and contractionary in bad times—whereas it is either acyclical or countercyclical in industrial countries. We analyzed two main competing explanations for this puzzle: (1) incomplete asset markets and (2) political distortions. Both incomplete markets and political distortions call for raising (reducing) government spending and lowering (raising) tax rates in good (bad) times. Some emerging countries, like Chile, have managed to escape the fiscal procyclicality trap by implementing fiscal rules based on a structural fiscal balance (box 10.2).

Box 10.2
How to deal with procyclicality the Chilean way?

As discussed in box 10.1, the evidence indicates that fiscal policy in developing countries is, by and large, procyclical. To the extent that procyclical fiscal policy reflects political/institutional distortions, it would be important to design more efficient fiscal arrangements (including redesigning existing revenue-sharing agreements between federal governments and provinces that tend to exacerbate procyclicality). Adopting fiscal rules based on structural (i.e., cyclically adjusted) fiscal balances should also help because, by design, such rules should allow automatic stabilizers to fulfill their role and delink government spending from actual tax revenues.

A case in point is Chile. In 2001 a fiscal rule was instituted whereby the central government's expenditures would be adjusted each year to the level needed to achieve a structural surplus of 1 percent of GDP.[a] Two cyclical adjustments are made to the actual fiscal balance. The first adjusts for the output gap and takes into account the tax revenues that would accrue to the government if GDP were at trend level. The second adjusts for deviations of the price of copper from its long-run value. These trend or long-run values are computed each year as the average of the individual forecasts produced by an independent group of experts, who are consulted by the Ministry of Finance before the budget is presented to the Congress.

Formally, the structural balance is computed as follows:

$$B_{s,t} = B_t + (T_{s,t} - T_t) + (CI_{s,t} - CI_t), \tag{10.2a}$$

where $B_{s,t}$ is the structural balance, B_t is the actual balance, T_t are actual tax revenues, CI_t are actual copper revenues, $T_{s,t}$ are tax revenues adjusted by the business cycle, and $CI_{s,t}$ are copper revenues adjusted for deviations from the current copper price from its long-run value, all in year t. Tax revenues adjusted for the business cycle, $T_{s,t}$, are computed as

$$T_{s,t} = T_t \left(\frac{y_t^*}{y_t}\right)^{\varepsilon},$$

where y_t^* is potential GDP in year t, y_t is actual GDP, and ε captures the responsiveness of tax revenues to GDP. If, for example, the economy is in a recession, then potential output would be above actual output (i.e., $y_t^* > y_t$), and hence adjusted tax revenues would be larger than actual revenues (i.e., $T_{s,t} > T_t$). The opposite is true during a boom; that is, adjusted revenues would be lower than actual revenues (i.e., $T_{s,t} < T_t$).

To calculate the term $CI_{s,t} - CI_t$ in equation (10.2a), government exports of copper, q_t, are multiplied by the difference between the long-run copper price, p_t^*, and the current price, p_t:

$$CI_{s,t} - CI_t = q_t(p_t^* - p_t).$$

During a period of high copper prices, for example, actual revenues ($q_t p_t$) will be higher than structural revenues ($q_t p_t^*$) and $CI_{s,t} < CI_t$. The opposite is true during periods of low copper prices.

In sum—and as equation (10.2a) makes clear—during good times (high GDP and high copper prices), the structural balance will be lower than the actual balance because $T_{s,t} < T_t$ and $CI_{s,t} < CI_t$. The opposite would be true during bad times (low GDP and low copper prices). Such a rule allows the government to run deficits in bad times as long as it runs surpluses in good times, which is exactly the policy prescription that would follow from our basic model in section 10.2. In contrast, a rule

a. The target of 1 percent mainly reflected the need to repay Central Bank debt associated with the bailout of private banks in the 1980s (see Frankel 2010 for details). As this debt was paid off over time, the targeted structural balance was reduced to 0.5 percent in 2008 and 0 percent in 2009.

Box 10.2
(continued)

based on the actual, as opposed to the structural, fiscal balance makes little sense because it may not allow a government to run large enough fiscal deficits in bad times.[b]

Figure 10.3 illustrates Chile's fiscal performance since 1990 and, in particular, how the fiscal rule has worked in practice since 2001. Between 1990 and 1997, as the economy grew at an average

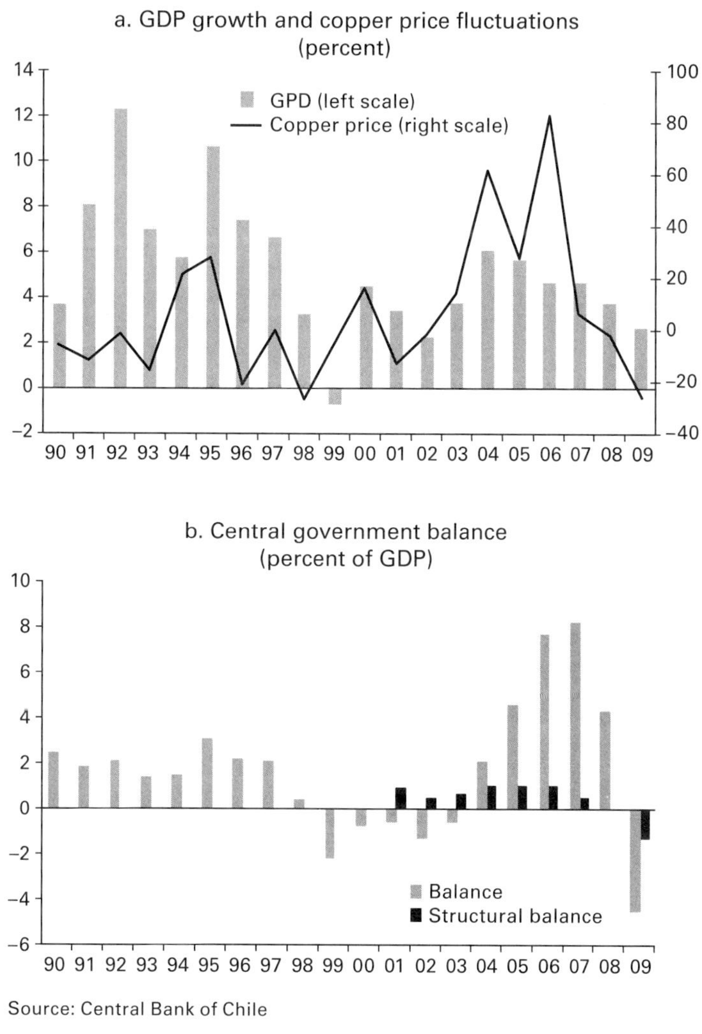

Source: Central Bank of Chile

Figure 10.3
Chile's fiscal rule in practice

b. In this context, the fiscal rule for the eurozone known as the Stability and Growth Pact, which was originally a simple ceiling on the budget deficit of 3 percent of GDP, makes little sense. It is thus not surprising that such a rule was consistently violated by both large and small euro countries and did not prevent large fiscal crises starting with Greece in 2010.

Box 10.2
(continued)

rate of 7.7 percent (panel a), the average fiscal surplus was around 2 percent of GDP, which already established a strong foundation for fiscal discipline (panel b). This solid fiscal performance took place despite high volatility in copper prices (panel a), which led to large fluctuations in government revenues, and contrasted sharply with a prior history of chronic fiscal deficits and high inflation. The fiscal balance then deteriorated in 1998 and reached a deficit of 2 percent of GDP in 1999, reflecting the government's countercyclical efforts in response to the Asian crisis and the effects of the 1999 recession. The government's need to run fiscal deficits in bad times was formalized in 2001 when the government adopted the fiscal rule discussed above, which allowed the government to run fiscal deficits in 2001, 2002, and 2003 as they actually reflected a structural fiscal surplus due to a sluggish recovery and low copper prices.

The Chilean economy recovered in earnest in 2004, reaching rates of growth of around 6 percent in 2004 and 2005. At the same time copper prices attained record levels in 2004 and hit even higher levels in 2006. Adhering to its fiscal rule, the government saved most the copper revenues and ran large actual surpluses starting in 2004 and throughout 2007, which corresponded to structural surpluses of around 1 percent as required by the fiscal rule. As mentioned above, the fiscal target was reduced to 0 percent by 2009. The major financial crisis of 2009, however, forced the government to temporarily abandon the fiscal rule in 2009, as it ran an actual deficit of 4.4 percent, which corresponded to a structural deficit of 1.2 percent. The earthquake that struck Chile in early 2010 led the government to disregard the fiscal target once again. The government plans to gradually return to the fiscal rule by 2014.

Despite having had to abandon the fiscal rule in recent years in light of some extreme events (global financial crisis and earthquake), it seems clear that the fiscal rule based on a structural fiscal balance has served Chile well, forcing both the government and the public in general to focus on the underlying structural fiscal balance rather than the actual balance, which will always be subject to the vagaries of the business cycle and copper prices.

Finally, we introduced money into the picture to address the issue of optimal monetary policy. We provided an example of the general idea that under certain restrictions on technology and/or preferences, the Friedman rule is optimal in a variety of monetary models. Such conditions, of course, need not hold in practice. But quantitative analyses suggest that even when the Friedman rule is not optimal, the optimal nominal interest rate is quite low. Hence our basic model calls for little or no use of the inflation tax.

10.9 Appendixes

10.9.1 Proof of Claim 3

We proceed by contradiction.

Suppose $\theta_1 = \theta_2$. Then from (10.132) and (10.133) it follows that

$$\frac{c_1}{\alpha_1} = \frac{c_2}{\alpha_2}. \tag{10.175}$$

Then from (10.147) it follows that $PB_1 = PB_2$. Hence from (10.127) and (10.128), $g_1 = g_2$. Since $\alpha_1 > \alpha_2$, equation (10.175) says that $c_1 > c_2$. Hence $\theta_1 c_1 > \theta_2 c_2$, which, since $g_1 = g_2$, implies from (10.129) and (10.130) that $PB_1 > PB_2$, a contradiction.

Suppose $\theta_1 > \theta_2$. Then from (10.132) and (10.133) it follows that

$$\frac{c_1}{\alpha_1} < \frac{c_2}{\alpha_2}. \tag{10.176}$$

From (10.147) it follows that $PB_1 < PB_2$. Hence from (10.127) and (10.128), $g_1 < g_2$. From the implementability conditions, it follows that

$$\frac{\theta_1 c_1}{\alpha_1} = h - \frac{c_1}{\alpha_1},$$

$$\frac{\theta_2 c_2}{\alpha_2} = h - \frac{c_2}{\alpha_2}.$$

Given (10.176), it follows that

$$\frac{\theta_1 c_1}{\alpha_1} > \frac{\theta_2 c_2}{\alpha_2}.$$

Further, since $\alpha_1 > \alpha_2$, then $\theta_1 c_1 > \theta_2 c_2$. Since $g_1 < g_2$, it follows from (10.129) and (10.130) that $PB_1 > PB_2$, which is a contradiction.

10.9.2 Proof of Claim 4

If $k_t = 0$, it follows from (10.171) that $-v'(X_t) - \frac{v''(X_t)X_t v(X_t)}{1+v(X_t)-v'(X_t)X_t} = 0$. Given (10.150), it follows that $X_t = X^s$ is the only value that satisfies this equation. Hence $I_t = 0$.[34] From (10.170) with $k_t = 0$, it follows that c_t is constant along a PFEP. Hence, from (10.155), so is θ_t. Assuming, for simplicity, that $b_{-1} = f_{-1} + z_{-1} = 0$, then from (10.168) and (10.167) we have $\theta = \bar{g}/(\frac{1}{2} - \bar{g})$.

10.9.3 Proof of Claim 5

We first show that if $k_t = k > 0$, then $1 - 2k\theta_t c_t$ is also constant over time.[35] The proof proceeds by contradiction. Suppose that for some t, $1 - 2k\theta_{t+1}c_{t+1} > 1 - 2k\theta_t c_t$. Hence $\theta_{t+1}c_{t+1} < \theta_t c_t$. The

34. In all cases it can be checked that second-order conditions are satisfied.

35. To prove this, we specialize the transactions technology to take the form $v(X) = X^2 - X + \frac{1}{4}$.

fact that $k\theta_{t+1}c_{t+1} < k\theta_t c_t$ also implies that $X_{t+1} > X_t$ since equation (10.171) implicitly defines a strictly inverse relationship between X_t and $k\theta_t c_t$. Hence, from (10.155), we have $c_{t+1}(1 + \theta_{t+1}) > c_t(1+\theta_t)$, and thus $c_{t+1} > c_t$. But this contradicts (10.170) since the LHS falls while the RHS increases. An analogous reasoning shows that assuming that $1 - 2k\theta_{t+1}c_{t+1} < 1 - 2k\theta_t c_t$ also leads to a contradiction.

Since $1 - 2k\theta_t c_t$ is constant over time, so is $\theta_t c_t$. Hence, from (10.171), X_t is constant over time, which implies from (10.155) that $c_t(1 + \theta_t)$, and hence c_t are constant over time. Hence both θ_t and I_t are constant over time. To establish that both taxes are positive, notice that θ cannot be zero. If it were, it would follow from (10.171) and (10.173) that $I = 0$. But since $\bar{g} > 0$, both taxes cannot be zero. Hence $\theta > 0$. Then from (10.171), $X < X^s$ and therefore, from (10.157), that $I > 0$.

10.9.4 Proof of Claim 6

We first show that if, for some t, $k_{t+1} > k_t$, then $1 - 2k_{t+1}\theta_{t+1}c_{t+1} < 1 - 2k_t\theta_t c_t$. The proof proceeds by contradiction. Suppose that $1 - 2k_{t+1}\theta_{t+1}c_{t+1} = 1 - 2k_t\theta_t c_t$. Hence $k_{t+1}\theta_{t+1}c_{t+1} = k_t\theta_t c_t$ and $\theta_{t+1}c_{t+1} < \theta_t c_t$. Since $k_{t+1}\theta_{t+1}c_{t+1} = k_t\theta_t c_t$, (10.171) implies that $X_{t+1} = X_t$. Hence from (10.155) we have $(1 + \theta_{t+1})c_{t+1} = (1 + \theta_t)c_t$. Since $\theta_{t+1}c_{t+1} < \theta_t c_t$, $c_{t+1} > c_t$. This is a contradiction since (10.170) is violated as the LHS falls but the RHS remains unchanged. An analogous reasoning shows that assuming that $1 - 2k_{t+1}\theta_{t+1}c_{t+1} > 1 - 2k_t\theta_t c_t$ also leads to a contradiction.

We have thus shown that if $k_{t+1} > k_t$, then $1 - 2k_{t+1}\theta_{t+1}c_{t+1} < 1 - 2k_t\theta_t c_t$. Hence $k_{t+1}\theta_{t+1}c_{t+1} > k_t\theta_t c_t$. By (10.171), $X_{t+1} < X_t$ and thus, by (10.157), $I_{t+1} > I_t$. Also, since $X_{t+1} < X_t$, by (10.155), $(1+\theta_{t+1})c_{t+1} < (1+\theta_t)c_t$. But, since $1 - 2k_{t+1}\theta_{t+1}c_{t+1} < 1 - 2k_t\theta_t c_t$, $c_{t+1} > c_t$ from (10.170). Then $\theta_{t+1}c_{t+1} < \theta_t c_t$ and thus $\theta_{t+1} < \theta_t$.

To find out the effect on total tax revenues, notice that using (10.166), we can compute the total differential change in total revenues (taking also into account the change in k) and evaluate it around an optimum to obtain

$$d\Gamma(c, X, k) = \Gamma_c(c, X, k)dc + \Gamma_X(c, X, k)dX + \Gamma_k(c, X, k)dk < 0, \tag{10.177}$$

since $dc > 0$ and $dk > 0$ and, around an optimum, $\Gamma_c(c, X, k) < 0$, $\Gamma_X(c, X, k) = 0$, and $\Gamma_k(c, X, k) < 0$. Hence $\Gamma(c_{t+1}, X_{t+1}, k_{t+1}) < \Gamma(c_t, X_t, k_t)$.

10.9.5 Proof of Claim 7

Since the government is constrained not to raise taxes on average with the lump-sum tax, it must finance $\bar{g}$ with distorting taxes. Given that $k_t = k > 0$, $\bar{g}$ is optimally financed with both the consumption tax and the inflation tax, for the same reasons as in claim 5. It is clearly not optimal to finance deviations of current spending from $\bar{g}$ with either the consumption or the inflation. If that were the case, the effective tax rate would vary over time and households' welfare would be lower. It follows that all fluctuations in spending should be financed with the lump-sum tax.

Exercises

1. (Non-leisure case with general preferences) Consider the non-leisure case analyzed for logarithmic preferences in section 10.2 for general preferences of the form

$$W = u(c_1) + \beta u(c_2).$$

Show that the optimal fiscal policy involves tax smoothing. (Hint: Verify that the solution $\theta_1 = \theta_2$ satisfies the Ramsey optimality conditions.)

2. (Leisure case with lump-sum taxation) Consider the production economy analyzed in section 10.3, but assume that the government can resort to lump-sum taxation. In this context:

a. Solve for the optimal fiscal policy. Obtain reduced forms for c_1, c_2, h_1, and h_2. Compare those expressions to the ones obtained in section 10.3 for distortionary taxation.

b. Verify that welfare under lump-sum taxation will be higher than under distortionary taxation (as long, of course, as the present discounted value of government expenditure is positive).

3. (Leisure case with general preferences) Consider the leisure case analyzed for logarithmic preferences in section 10.3 for general preferences of the form

$$W = u(c_1, h_1) + \beta u(c_2, h_2).$$

Show that the optimal fiscal policy involves tax smoothing. (Hint: Verify that the solution $\theta_1 = \theta_2$ satisfies the Ramsey optimality conditions.)

4. (Government consumption as a policy choice) Consider the production economy analyzed in section 10.3 but with the following two modifications. First, let preferences be given by

$$W = \log(c_1) + \log(h_1) + \log(g_1) + \beta[\log(c_2) + \log(h_2) + \log(g_2)].$$

Second, let the government have some exogenous source of revenues denoted by z_t. (Think of it as commodity revenues.) The government's flow constraints are therefore given by

$$b_1^g = z_1 + \theta_1 c_1 - g_1,$$

$$0 = z_2 + \theta_2 c_2 + (1+r)b_1^g - g_2.$$

In the context of this model:

a. Suppose that z_1 is different from z_2. Show that the optimal fiscal policy involves a constant tax rate and a constant level of government spending.

b. Assume nonseparable preferences of the form $u(c_1, h_1, g_1) + \beta u(c_2, h_2, g_2)$. Show that the same results hold.

5. (Incomplete markets case with lump-sum taxation) Consider the incomplete markets case analyzed in section 10.5.1, but assume that the government can resort to lump-sum taxation. Characterize the optimal fiscal policy and compare to the distortionary taxation case. In particular, show that there will be no intratemporal distortion.

6. (Procyclical fiscal policy with government spending in the utility function) Consider the following variation of the model of section 10.6 in which g_t enters the utility function and $f(.)$ is a linear function. Formally, preferences are now given by

$$W = \alpha_1 \log(c_1) + \log(h_1) + \log(g_1) + \beta[\alpha_2 \log(c_2) + \log(h_2) + \log(g_2)].$$

The political distortion becomes

$$g_1 = \bar{g} + \phi(\theta_1 c_1 - g_1), \tag{10.178}$$

$$g_2 = \bar{g} + \phi(\theta_2 c_2 - g_2), \tag{10.179}$$

where ϕ is a positive parameter. The rest of the model is unchanged. In this context:

a. Suppose $\alpha_1 = \alpha_2$. Show that the optimal fiscal policy involves tax smoothing over time.

b. Suppose $\alpha_1 > \alpha_2$. Show that the optimal fiscal policy involves $g_1 > g_2$ and $\theta_1 < \theta_2$. Why do the results coincide with those in section 10.6?

References

Aizenman, Joshua, Michael Gavin, and Ricardo Hausmann. 2000. Optimal tax and debt policy with endogenously imperfect creditworthiness. *Journal of International Trade and Economic Development* 9 (4): 367–95.

Barro, Robert J. 1979. On the determination of public debt. *Journal of Political Economy* 87 (5): 940–71.

Bordo, Michael D., and Carlos A. Végh. 2002. What if Alexander Hamilton had been Argentinean? A comparison of the early monetary experiences of Argentina and the United States. *Journal of Monetary Economics* 49: 459–94.

Calvo, Guillermo. 1978. On the time consistency of optimal policy in a monetary economy. *Econometrica* 46 (6): 1411–28.

Calvo, Guillermo A., and Pablo E. Guidotti. 1993. On the flexibility of monetary policy: The case of the inflation tax. *Review of Economic Studies* 60: 667–87.

Chari, V. V., and Patrick J. Kehoe. 1999. Optimal fiscal and monetary policy. Working Paper 6891. National Bureau of Economic Research, Cambridge, MA.

Chari, V.V., Lawrence J. Christiano, and Patrick J. Kehoe. 1994. Optimal fiscal policy in a business cycle model. *Journal of Political Economy* 102 (4): 617–52.

Frankel, Jeffrey. 2010. A solution to fiscal procyclicality: The structural budget institutions pioneered by Chile. Working Paper 604. Central Bank of Chile, Santiago.

Ilzetzki, Ethan, and Carlos A. Végh. 2008. Procyclical fiscal policy in developing countries: Truth or fiction? Working Paper 14191. National Bureau of Economic Research, Cambridge, MA.

Kaminsky, Graciela, Carmen M. Reinhart, and Carlos A. Végh. 2005. When it rains, it pours: Procyclical capital flows and macroeconomic policies. *NBER Macroeconomics Annual* 19: 11–82.

Kimbrough, Kent. 1986. The optimum quantity of money rule in the theory of public finance. *Journal of Monetary Economics* 18: 277–84.

Lucas, Robert E., and Nancy Stokey. 1983. Optimal fiscal and monetary policy in an economy without capital. *Journal of Monetary Economics* 12 (1): 55–93.

Nicolini, Juan Pablo. 1998. Tax evasion and the optimal inflation tax. *Journal of Development Economics* 55: 215–32.

Riascos, Alvaro, and Carlos A. Végh. 2005. Procyclical government spending in developing countries: The role of capital market imperfections. Mimeo. Banco de la Republica, Colombia, and UCLA.

Talvi, Ernesto, and Carlos A. Végh. 2005. Tax base variability and procyclical fiscal policy in developing countries. *Journal of Development Economics* 78 (1): 156–90.

Tornell, Aaron, and Philip Lane. 1999. The voracity effect. *American Economic Review* 89 (1): 22–46.

Végh, Carlos A. 1989a. Government spending and inflationary finance: A public finance framework. *IMF Staff Papers* 36 (3): 657–77.

Végh, Carlos A. 1989b. The optimal inflation tax in the presence of currency substitution. *Journal of Monetary Economics* 24: 139–46.

Végh, Carlos A., and Guillermo Vuletin. 2012. How is tax policy conducted over the business cycle? Working Paper 17753. National Bureau of Economic Research, Cambridge, MA.

Walsh, Carl E. 2010. *Monetary Theory and Policy*, 3rd ed. Cambridge: MIT Press.

11 Optimal Exchange Rate Regimes

11.1 Introduction

Should an open economy choose a predetermined exchange rate regime or a flexible one? This is one of the most important and hotly debated questions in open economy macroeconomics. Literally thousands of academic articles have been devoted to answering this question, and both academics and practitioners (and academics turned practitioners!) continue to debate the pros and cons of different exchange rate regimes.

The natural starting point in answering this question is the world of chapter 5. As section 11.2 makes clear, in such a world the exchange rate regime is immaterial. In other words, the real sector's response to different shocks will be the same regardless of the exchange rate regime in place. Of course, the response of the monetary sector may well depend on the exchange rate regime, but this will not affect the real sector. Hence, in the highly stylized world of chapter 5 in which money is a veil, exchange rate regimes do not matter. For example, a positive money demand shock leaves the real sector unaffected and leads to an increase in nominal money balances under predetermined exchange rates and a fall in the nominal exchange rate (i.e., a nominal appreciation of the currency) under flexible exchange rates. Instead, a shift in the demand from nontradables toward tradables calls for a fall in the relative price of nontradable goods (real depreciation). Under predetermined exchange rates, this increase in the real exchange rate comes about through a fall in the nominal price of nontradable goods. Under flexible exchange rates, the real depreciation is engineered through both an increase in the nominal exchange rate and a fall in the nominal price of nontradable goods.

When money ceases to be a veil, however, exchange rate regimes do matter. Section 11.3 reintroduces the cash-in-advance world of chapter 7 and illustrates the idea that flexible exchange rates are able to completely insulate the domestic economy from (temporary) shocks to foreign inflation. In contrast, under predetermined exchange rates, the domestic economy will import either foreign inflation or deflation, as the case may be. When it comes to real shocks, however, predetermined exchange rates have the upper hand and dominate flexible exchange rates. This latter result is rather remarkable because it contradicts the notion—found in the literature ever since the celebrated 1953 article by Milton Friedman—that under flexible prices the exchange rate regime should be immaterial for the response of the economy. Indeed Friedman (1953, p. 165) himself argued that "[i]f internal prices were as flexible as exchange rates, it would make little economic difference whether adjustments were brought about by changes in exchange rates of by equivalent changes in internal prices." He thus concludes that it is only under sticky prices that the exchange rate regime will matter.[1] This notion is, however, not true, and exchange rate regimes may matter even under fully flexible prices.

Section 11.4 then turns to sticky prices. The conventional wisdom in this area—which, again, dates back to Friedman (1953)—is that under sticky prices predetermined exchange rates provide a more efficient adjustment to monetary shocks while flexible exchange rates are better in dealing with real shocks. Intuitively, predetermined exchange rates allow for an instantaneous adjustment of real money balances to monetary shocks via the Central Bank window. In contrast, under sticky prices real money balances cannot adjust quickly under flexible exchange rates. In response to real shocks, however, flexible exchange rates allow for a quicker adjustment of relative prices. Intuitively, the real exchange rate needs to adjust in response to a real shock. Under predetermined exchange rates, this adjustment is hampered by the fact that nominal prices are sticky, which forces the economy to undergo a costly adjustment through a prolonged deflation. In contrast, under flexible exchange rates, this adjustment can be carried out much quicker and efficiently through a change in the nominal exchange rate.

In our benchmark sticky-prices model (with logarithmic preferences), and in response to monetary shocks, the economy does adjust instantaneously under predetermined exchange rates and only gradually over time under flexible exchange rates, reflecting the fact that in the latter case real money balances can only increase gradually over time. In response to real shocks (i.e., a demand shock), the economy will adjust gradually under both predetermined and flexible exchange rates. The adjustment under flexible exchange rates, however, will be welfare-superior to the one under predetermined exchange rates because the nominal depreciation of the currency—necessary to equilibrate the money market—helps in partially cushioning nontradables consumption. For this to be the case, the real shock must negatively affect the money market. If it does not, then flexible exchange rates will not provide a better adjustment to real shocks.

While sticky prices are the most popular friction in the academic literature, it is far from clear that they are the main friction in the real world, particularly when it comes to developing countries. It is arguably the case in fact that asset market frictions are as, if not more, important. In this vein, section 11.5 analyzes exchange rate optimality in the presence of asset market frictions, modeled as asset market segmentation. Under asset market segmentation only a fraction of households has access to asset markets. We will see that under this friction, the Mundell–Fleming results derived above are turned on their heads: predetermined exchange rates are now optimal under real shocks and flexible exchange rates are better under monetary shocks. Intuitively, asset market segmentation critically affects the adjustment mechanism under predetermined exchange rates, which involves exchanging money for bonds (and vice versa) at the Central Bank. In sharp contrast,

1. More than fifty years after Friedman's article, this notion is still very much cited as a truism (e.g., see Broda 2004).

Table 11.1
Optimal exchange rate regimes

Friction/shock	Goods market friction	Asset market friction
Real shock	Flexible	Fixed
Monetary shock	Fixed	Flexible

asset market segmentation does not affect the adjustment mechanism under flexible exchange rates (changes in the nominal exchange rate). As a result the economy adjusts most efficiently to monetary shocks under flexible exchange rates. In the case of real shocks, however, by keeping purchasing power constant across periods, predetermined exchange rates offer some risk diversification across time and are therefore preferable.

In sum—and combining the results of sections 11.4 and 11.5—whether predetermined or flexible exchange rates are preferable depends not only on the type of shock—as the conventional wisdom based on Mundell–Fleming holds—but also on the type of friction, as summarized in table 11.1.

The chapter proceeds as follows. Section 11.2 studies the world of chapter 5 in which money is a veil. Section 11.3 deals with the cash-in-advance model introduced in chapter 7. Section 11.4 considers the sticky-prices model of chapter 8. Section 11.5 introduces a new friction to our basic model in the form of asset market segmentation. Final remarks can be found in section 11.6.

11.2 Response to Shocks When Money Is a Veil

Consider the world of chapter 5 with nontradable goods. This is a small open economy perfectly integrated into world goods and capital markets. Let r denote the constant world real interest rate. Money enters into the model through the utility function. Let the foreign price level be constant and equal to one. The law of one price holds for the tradable good, so that $P_t^T = E_t$, where P_t^T denotes the domestic price of the tradable good and E_t is the nominal exchange rate (in units of domestic currency per unit of foreign currency).

11.2.1 Consumers' Problem

Preferences are given by

$$\int_0^\infty [\gamma \log(c_t^T) + (1-\gamma)\log(c_t^N) + \alpha \log(z_t)]\exp(-\beta t)dt, \tag{11.1}$$

where c_t^T and c_t^N denote consumption of tradable and nontradable goods, respectively, β is the discount rate, $\gamma \in (0,1)$ and $\alpha(> 0)$ are parameters that capture demand and money-demand shocks, respectively, and $z_t (\equiv M_t/P_t$, where M_t are nominal money balances) stands for real money balances in terms of the price index, P_t, defined as[2]

$$P_t = \left(P_t^T\right)^{\gamma} \left(P_t^N\right)^{1-\gamma}.$$

Let a_t denote real financial wealth:

$$a_t \equiv b_t + m_t,$$

where b_t denotes net foreign assets in the consumer's hands and $m_t (\equiv M_t/E_t)$ are real money balances in terms of tradable goods. The consumer's flow constraint is given by

$$\dot{a}_t = ra_t + y^T + \frac{y^N}{e_t} + \tau_t - c_t^T - \frac{c_t^N}{e_t} - i_t \frac{z_t}{e_t^{1-\gamma}}, \tag{11.2}$$

where y^T and y^N denote the constant endowments of tradable and nontradable goods, respectively; τ_t are lump-sum transfers from the government; i_t is the nominal interest rate; and e_t is the relative price of tradable goods, given by

$$e_t \equiv \frac{E_t}{P_t^N}. \tag{11.3}$$

The last term on the RHS of (11.2) is simply the opportunity cost of holding real money balances in terms of tradable goods, $i_t m_t$, which, in light of (11.3), can be rewritten as $i_t z_t / e_t^{1-\gamma}$.

Integrating (11.2) forward and imposing the transversality condition $\lim_{t\to\infty} a_t \exp(-rt) = 0$, we obtain

$$a_0 + \int_0^{\infty} \left(y^T + \frac{y^N}{e_t} + \tau_t\right) \exp(-rt)dt = \int_0^{\infty} \left(c_t^T + \frac{c_t^N}{e_t} + i_t \frac{z_t}{e_t^{1-\gamma}}\right) \exp(-rt)dt. \tag{11.4}$$

The consumer's problem consists in choosing $\{c_t^T, c_t^N, z_t\}$ for all $t \in [0, \infty)$ to maximize (11.1) subject to (11.4), for given paths of τ_t, i_t, and e_t, and given values of r, y^T, and y^N.

Under the assumption that $\beta = r$, the first-order conditions are given by

$$\frac{\gamma}{c_t^T} = \lambda, \tag{11.5}$$

$$\frac{1-\gamma}{c_t^N} = \frac{\lambda}{e_t}, \tag{11.6}$$

2. Following the same derivation as in chapter 6, appendix 6.7.3, one could show that this price index corresponds to the minimum nominal expenditure required to achieve a given level of utility.

$$\frac{\alpha}{z_t} = \lambda \frac{i_t}{e_t^{1-\gamma}}, \tag{11.7}$$

where λ is the multiplier associated with the intertemporal constraint (11.4).

Combining (11.5) and (11.6), we obtain a familiar expression for the equilibrium real exchange rate:

$$e_t = \frac{\gamma}{1-\gamma} \frac{c_t^N}{c_t^T}. \tag{11.8}$$

Combining (11.6) and (11.7), we obtain the real money demand in terms of the price index:

$$z_t = \frac{\alpha}{1-\gamma} \frac{c_t^N}{e_t^{\gamma} i_t}.$$

All else equal, an increase in α increases real money demand. Hence we will think of an increase in α as a positive money demand shock. Intuitively, a higher α increases the marginal utility provided by any given level of real money balances, which leads to higher demand.

It will prove more insightful, however, to focus the discussion on the demand for real money balances in terms of tradable goods, m_t. Combining equations (11.5) and (11.7) and recalling that $z_t = m_t e_t^{1-\gamma}$, it follows that

$$m_t = \frac{\alpha}{\gamma} \frac{c_t^T}{i_t}. \tag{11.9}$$

An increase in α increases the demand for m_t. An increase in γ will reduce real money demand. Intuitively, a higher γ increases the marginal utility of tradable goods consumption. To keep the marginal utility of m_t equal to that of consumption of tradables, real money balances need to fall.[3]

As we have done before, it will also prove useful to derive the demand for real money balances in terms of nontradable goods, $n_t (\equiv M_t/P_t^N)$. To this effect, recall that $m_t = M_t/P_t^T$ and multiply and divide the left-hand side of equation (11.9) by P_t^N and use (11.8) to obtain

$$n_t = \left(\frac{\alpha}{1-\gamma}\right) \frac{c_t^N}{i_t}. \tag{11.10}$$

As in the case of m_t, a higher α leads to a higher demand for n_t. In contrast to the case of m_t, however, a higher γ leads to an increase in the demand for n_t (the opposite effect that it has on m_t). Intuitively, a higher γ decreases the marginal utility of nontradable goods and hence requires an increase in n_t to keep the equality of marginal utilities.

3. The marginal utility of m_t is α/m_t, as follows from (11.7) and the fact that $z_t = m_t e_t^{1-\gamma}$.

11.2.2 Government

The government's budget constraint is given by (recall that foreign inflation is zero)

$$\dot{h}_t = rh_t + \dot{m}_t + \varepsilon_t m_t - \tau_t, \tag{11.11}$$

where h_t denotes international reserves and ε is the rate of depreciation/devaluation.

Integrating forward equation (11.11) and imposing the corresponding transversality condition, we obtain the government's intertemporal constraint:

$$h_0 + \int_0^\infty (\dot{m}_t + \varepsilon_t m_t)\exp(-rt)dt = \int_0^\infty \tau_t \exp(-rt)dt. \tag{11.12}$$

11.2.3 Equilibrium Conditions

The assumption of perfect capital mobility implies that interest parity holds:

$$i_t = r + \varepsilon_t. \tag{11.13}$$

Equilibrium in the nontradable goods market requires that

$$y^N = c_t^N. \tag{11.14}$$

Combining the consumer's and the government's flow budget constraints—given by (11.2) and (11.11), respectively—and taking into account the definition of z_t, the interest parity condition (11.13), and nontradable goods market equilibrium (11.14), we obtain the flow constraint for the economy as a whole:

$$\dot{k}_t = rk_t + y^T - c_t^T, \tag{11.15}$$

where $k_t (\equiv b_t + h_t)$ denotes the economy's holdings of net foreign assets.

Finally, integrating forward (11.15) and imposing the corresponding transversality condition, we obtain the resource constraint:

$$k_0 + \frac{y^T}{r} = \int_0^\infty c_t^T \exp(-rt)dt. \tag{11.16}$$

11.2.4 Real Equilibrium

We now solve for the perfect foresight equilibrium path corresponding to a constant path of γ and α. Since money is a veil in this economy, we can proceed as in chapter 5 and first solve for the real equilibrium and only then solve for the monetary equilibrium.

As usual, first-order condition (11.5) indicates that consumption of tradables will be constant along a perfect foresight equilibrium path (PFEP). Given the resource constraint (11.16), the constant level of c_t^T is

$$c^T = rk_0 + y^T. \tag{11.17}$$

Given nontradable goods market equilibrium (11.14), consumption of nontradables is, of course, also constant over time and equal to y^N.

From (11.8), (11.14), and (11.17) it follows that the equilibrium real exchange rate is constant over time and given by

$$e = \left(\frac{\gamma}{1-\gamma}\right)\frac{y^N}{rk_0 + y^T}. \tag{11.18}$$

11.2.5 Predetermined Exchange Rates

We now solve for the monetary sector of the economy under the assumption that, along a perfect foresight equilibrium path, the exchange rate is fixed at the value E and hence $\varepsilon_t = 0$. The interest parity condition implies that the nominal interest rate is constant over time and given by

$$i = r. \tag{11.19}$$

From (11.9) and (11.19) it follows that real money balances (in terms of tradable goods) are therefore constant over time and given by

$$m = \frac{\alpha}{\gamma}\left(\frac{rk_0 + y^T}{r}\right). \tag{11.20}$$

Given real money demand, nominal money balances will also be constant:

$$M = Em. \tag{11.21}$$

The domestic price of tradable goods follows from the law of one price. For given nominal and real exchange rate, the price of nontradable goods can be derived from the definition of the real exchange rate, given by (11.3),

$$P^N \equiv \frac{E}{e}. \tag{11.22}$$

11.2.6 Flexible Exchange Rates

Suppose that the economy is operating under flexible exchange rates and that the nominal money supply is constant and equal to M (i.e., $\mu_t = 0$). As in chapter 5 we solve for the case of flexible exchange rates by deriving an unstable differential equation for real money balances.

By definition, $m_t = M_t/E_t$ (recall that we are assuming that $P_t^* = 1$). Since the money supply is constant over time, it follows that

$$\frac{\dot{m}_t}{m_t} = -\varepsilon_t. \tag{11.23}$$

Taking into account the interest parity condition (11.13), equation (11.9), and the fact that c^T is constant, we can rewrite this equation as

$$\dot{m}_t = m_t\left(r - \frac{\alpha c^T}{\gamma m_t}\right). \tag{11.24}$$

Since this is an unstable differential equation, the only convergent equilibrium path is the one in which m_t is constant over time and equal to (using equation 11.17)

$$m = \frac{\alpha}{\gamma}\left(\frac{rk_0 + y^T}{r}\right). \tag{11.25}$$

The fact that m_t is constant over time implies, from (11.23), that $\varepsilon_t = 0$ for all t. Hence, from (11.13), the nominal interest rate will be constant over time and given by

$$i = r.$$

The equilibrium and constant value of the nominal exchange rate is determined by the money market equilibrium condition:

$$\frac{M}{E} = \frac{\alpha}{\gamma}\left(\frac{rk_0 + y^T}{r}\right). \tag{11.26}$$

Hence

$$E = \frac{\gamma}{\alpha}\left(\frac{r}{rk_0 + y^T}\right)M. \tag{11.27}$$

Given the nominal exchange rate, the law of one price determines the domestic price of tradable goods. To find out the price of nontradable goods, recall that by definition, $e = P^T/P^N$. Hence $P^N = P^T/e$. Using the law of one price and equation (11.18), we can express P^N as

$$P^N = \frac{1-\gamma}{\alpha}\left(\frac{r}{y^N}\right)M. \tag{11.28}$$

11.2.7 Money Demand Shocks

Let us analyze how the economy responds to a permanent and positive money demand shock under both predetermined and flexible exchange rates. To this effect, suppose that the economy is initially in the stationary perfect foresight equilibrium path characterized above with the parameter α given by α^L. At time 0 there is an unanticipated and permanent increase in α from α^L to α^H. How does the economy respond?

Predetermined Exchange Rates

Clearly, the real equilibrium is not affected and continues to be given by (11.14), (11.17), and (11.18). The same is true of the nominal interest rate, which remains given by (11.19). Real money demand, however, will increase, as follows from (11.20). This increase in real money balances will be effected through an increase in nominal money balances, as follows from (11.21). Prices of nontradable goods, P_t^N, remain constant, as follows from (11.22).

Flexible Exchange Rates

The new perfect foresight equilibrium path remains characterized by the unstable differential equation (11.24). Using the same logic as before, we conclude that in the new perfect foresight equilibrium path, real money balances will be higher and given by

$$m = \frac{\alpha^H}{\gamma}\left(\frac{rk_0 + y^T}{r}\right).$$

As equation (11.27) indicates, the nominal exchange rate falls. The price of nontradable goods also falls, as follows from (11.28). Since, from (11.18), the real exchange rate does not change, we infer that the nominal exchange rate and the price of nontradable goods fall by the same proportion.[4]

We conclude that the economy adjusts instantaneously under both exchange rate regimes, and therefore that the exchange rate regime is irrelevant. Under predetermined exchange rates, the higher level of real money balances will be effected through an increase in nominal money balances, while under flexible exchange rates it will be effected through a fall in the nominal exchange rate and in the price of nontradable goods.

11.2.8 Real Shocks

We now consider the economy's response to real shocks. Specifically, suppose that at time 0 there is an unanticipated and permanent increase in γ. This amounts to a demand shock that shifts demand from nontradables to tradables. How does the economy respond?

Since money is a veil in this economy, we know that the response of the real sector will be the same regardless of the exchange rate regime. In fact from (11.18) it follows that e will increase (i.e., there is a real depreciation) Specifically—and as indicated in table 11.2—if γ increases by a proportion $\hat{\gamma}$, the real exchange rate will increase by $[1/(1-\gamma)]\,\hat{\gamma}$. Intuitively, the shift

4. This implies, of course, that the price index, P_t, also falls by the same proportion, which leads to an increase in z_t.

Table 11.2
Response to an increase in γ

Regime/variable	e	M	E	P^N
Fixed	$\frac{1}{1-\gamma}\hat{\gamma}$	$-\hat{\gamma}$	0	$-\frac{1}{1-\gamma}\hat{\gamma}$
Flexible	$\frac{1}{1-\gamma}\hat{\gamma}$	0	$\hat{\gamma}$	$-\frac{\gamma}{1-\gamma}\hat{\gamma}$

in demand away from nontradable goods and toward tradable goods means that at the initial real exchange rate, there is an excess supply of nontradable goods. Hence the relative price of nontradable goods needs to fall. The difference between the two exchange rate regimes will be the way in which the increase in the real exchange rate takes effect.

Predetermined Exchange Rates

Under predetermined exchange rates—and as indicated in table 11.2—the increase in the real exchange rate takes place through a fall in the price of nontradables, P_t^N, as equation (11.3) makes clear. Since, from (11.9), the demand for m_t falls, the nominal money supply needs to fall, as follows from (11.21).

Flexible Exchange Rates

In the case of flexible exchange rates the adjustment in the real exchange rate will occur through a combination of a rise in the nominal exchange rate and a fall in P_t^N. To see this, notice that equation (11.27) indicates that the nominal exchange rate will increase in the same proportion as γ, while equation (11.28) tells us that the price of nontradable goods will fall.

It is important to note, though, that the extent to which, under flexible exchange rates, the nominal exchange rate "helps" in the adjustment of the real exchange rate depends on how the demand shock is modeled (i.e., it depends on preferences). As exercise 1 at the end of this chapter makes clear, the real depreciation (i.e., increase in e_t) required by a change in the demand of nontradable relative to tradable goods may be effected solely through an increase in the nominal exchange rate or solely through a fall in the price of nontradable goods.

11.3 A Cash-in-Advance Economy

Consider now the world of chapter 7 in which money is introduced via a cash-in-advance constraint. To simplify the presentation, we will abstract from nontradable goods and consider an economy that consumes only importable goods but is endowed with exportable goods.[5] The relative price of importables in terms of exportables, p_t, is exogenously given to this economy.[6]

5. This is, of course, the same setup of chapter 3 with the important difference that we will focus on the terms of trade rather than on imports tariffs as in chapter 3.

6. The variable p_t will only be allowed to change discretely, if at all. At all other points in time, $\dot{p}_t = 0$.

(The terms of trade are thus $1/p_t$.) This setup will allow us to study the effects of both external *nominal* shocks (changes in the foreign inflation rate) and external *real* shocks (shocks to the terms of trade). Unless otherwise noted, the notation remains the same as above.

11.3.1 Consumer's Problem

Preferences are now given by

$$\int_0^\infty \frac{c_t^{1-1/\sigma}}{1-1/\sigma}\exp(-\beta t)dt, \tag{11.29}$$

where c_t denotes consumption of the importable good and $\sigma > 0$ denotes the intertemporal elasticity of substitution. The cash-in-advance constraint takes the form

$$m_t = \alpha p_t c_t, \qquad \alpha > 0, \tag{11.30}$$

where we have used the exportable good as the numéraire and α is a positive parameter. The consumer's flow constraint is given by

$$\dot{a}_t = ra_t + y + \tau_t - p_t c_t - i_t m_t, \tag{11.31}$$

where y is the constant endowment of the exportable good. Integrating forward the flow constraint and imposing the relevant transversality condition, we obtain the consumer's intertemporal constraint:

$$a_0 + \frac{y}{r} + \int_0^\infty \tau_t \exp(-rt)dt = \int_0^\infty (p_t c_t + i_t m_t)\exp(-rt)dt. \tag{11.32}$$

Substituting the cash-in-advance constraint (11.30) into the intertemporal constraint, we obtain

$$a_0 + \frac{y}{r} + \int_0^\infty \tau_t \exp(-rt)dt = \int_0^\infty p_t c_t(1+\alpha i_t)\exp(-rt)dt. \tag{11.33}$$

Consumers choose $\{c_t\}$ to maximize (11.29) subject to (11.33). The first-order condition is given by (assuming $\beta = r$)

$$c_t^{-1/\sigma} = \lambda p_t(1+\alpha i_t), \tag{11.34}$$

where λ is the multiplier associated with constraint (11.33).

11.3.2 Government

The government's flow constraint remains given by (11.11) and (11.12) with the only difference that the term ε_t should be replaced by the term $\varepsilon_t + \pi_t^*$ since foreign inflation may now be positive.

11.3.3 Equilibrium Conditions

Since we are allowing for a positive foreign inflation rate, the interest parity condition becomes

$$i_t = i_t^* + \varepsilon_t, \tag{11.35}$$

where i_t^* is the foreign nominal interest rate. For further reference, notice that assuming that the Fisher equation holds in the rest of the world (i.e., $i_t^* = r + \pi_t^*$), we can rewrite (11.35) as

$$i_t = r + \pi_t^* + \varepsilon_t. \tag{11.36}$$

Combining the consumer's and the government's flow constraints—given by (11.31) and (11.11), respectively—we obtain the economy's flow constraint:

$$\dot{k}_t = rk_t + y - p_t c_t, \tag{11.37}$$

where $k_t (\equiv b_t + h_t)$ denotes the economy's total stock of net foreign assets. For further reference, notice that the trade balance is given by

$$TB_t = y - p_t c_t. \tag{11.38}$$

Integrating forward (11.37) and imposing the corresponding transversality condition, we obtain the economy's resource constraint:

$$k_0 + \frac{y}{r} = \int_0^\infty p_t c_t \exp(-rt)dt.$$

11.3.4 Predetermined Exchange Rates

Under predetermined exchange rates, policy makers set a constant rate of devaluation, ε. From (11.36) the interest parity condition thus becomes

$$i_t = r + \pi_t^* + \varepsilon. \tag{11.39}$$

11.3.5 Flexible Exchange Rates

Under flexible exchange rates, policy makers set a constant rate of money growth, μ. To solve the model under flexible exchange rates, we will proceed as in chapter 7 and derive an unstable differential equation in i_t. To this end, totally differentiate first-order condition (11.34) and the cash-in-advance constraint (11.30)—taking into account that along a PFEP λ is constant and, by assumption, $\dot{p}_t = 0$—and combine them to obtain

$$\frac{\dot{m}_t}{m_t} = -\frac{\sigma\alpha}{1+\alpha i_t}\dot{i}_t. \tag{11.40}$$

By definition, $\dot{m}_t/m_t = \mu - \varepsilon_t - \pi_t^*$. Hence, using the interest parity condition (11.36), we can write

$$\frac{\dot{m}_t}{m_t} = \mu + r - i_t. \tag{11.41}$$

Substituting (11.41) into (11.40) and rearranging terms, we obtain

$$\dot{i}_t = \frac{1+\alpha i_t}{\sigma\alpha}(i_t - r - \mu). \tag{11.42}$$

This is an unstable differential equation in i_t. Hence the only converging perfect equilibrium path is $i_t = r + \mu$.

11.3.6 Nonconstant Foreign Inflation Path

Consider a PFEP along which p_t is constant over time and the path of the foreign inflation rate is given by

$$\pi_t^* = \begin{cases} \pi^{*L}, & t \in [0, T), \\ \pi^{*H}, & t \geq T. \end{cases} \tag{11.43}$$

The foreign inflation rate is thus low until time T and high afterwards (see figure 11.1, panel a). We will now solve for the corresponding PFEP under both predetermined and flexible exchange rates.

Predetermined Exchange Rates

Under predetermined exchange rates, the path of the nominal interest rate follows from the interest parity condition (11.39) and the path of the foreign inflation rate, given by (11.43):

$$i_t = \begin{cases} r + \pi^{*L} + \varepsilon, & t \in [0, T), \\ r + \pi^{*H} + \varepsilon, & t \geq T. \end{cases} \tag{11.44}$$

The path of the nominal interest rate is illustrated in figure 11.1, panel b. The nominal interest rate fully reflects the changes in foreign inflation. In particular, the inflation rate of exportable

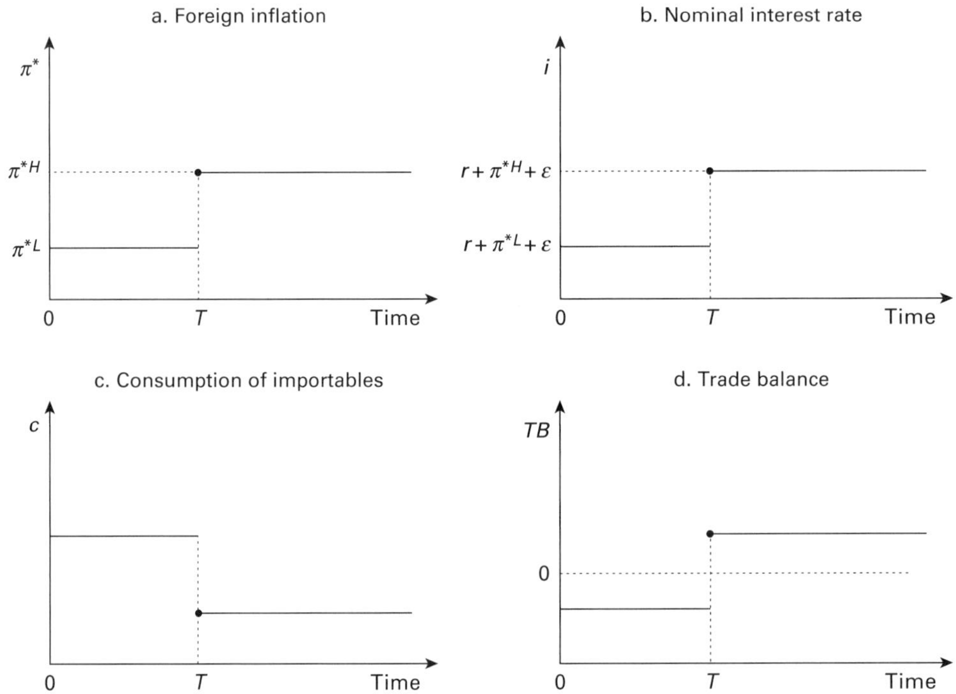

Figure 11.1
Foreign inflation shock under predetermined exchange rates

goods, given by $\pi^* + \varepsilon$, increases one to one with the foreign inflation rate at time T. In other words, the economy fully "imports" foreign inflation.

Given the path of the nominal interest rate, first-order condition (11.34) indicates that consumption of importable goods will be higher between time 0 and T than afterward (as illustrated in figure 11.1, panel c). The corresponding path of the trade balance (assuming $k_0 = 0$) is depicted in panel d.

Flexible Exchange Rates

The first step under flexible exchange rates is to determine whether endogenous variables will jump at T or not. We know that E_t cannot jump at T because, if it did, there would be infinite arbitrage opportunities. Hence, since M_t does not change at time T either, m_t cannot change. From the cash-in-advance constraint (11.30) and the fact that p_t is constant, it follows that c_t does not jump at T. In turn the fact that c_t does not jump at time T implies, through first-order condition (11.34), that the nominal interest rate does not jump at time T either.

Having established that the nominal interest rate will not jump at time T, we can now solve for the path of i_t. Given that the path of i_t is governed by the unstable differential equation (11.42), it follows that i_t must be constant over time and equal to $r + \mu$ (figure 11.2, panel b). If i_t were not equal to $r + \mu$ at time 0, then it would diverge over time and, since it does not jump at time T, would continue to diverge after time T. Since the nominal interest rate is flat over time, first-order condition (11.34) indicates that consumption will also be flat over time (panel c). As a result, provided that $k_0 = 0$, the trade balance is always zero (panel d).

Given that $i_t = r + \mu$ for all t, the interest parity condition implies that

$$\mu = \pi_t^* + \varepsilon_t.$$

Hence the rise in the foreign inflation rate at time T is exactly offset by a fall in the rate of depreciation and does not affect domestic inflation.

We thus conclude that flexible exchange rate rates completely insulate the economy from changes in foreign inflation. By anchoring the nominal interest rate, monetary policy prevents domestic inflation from being affected by foreign inflation.

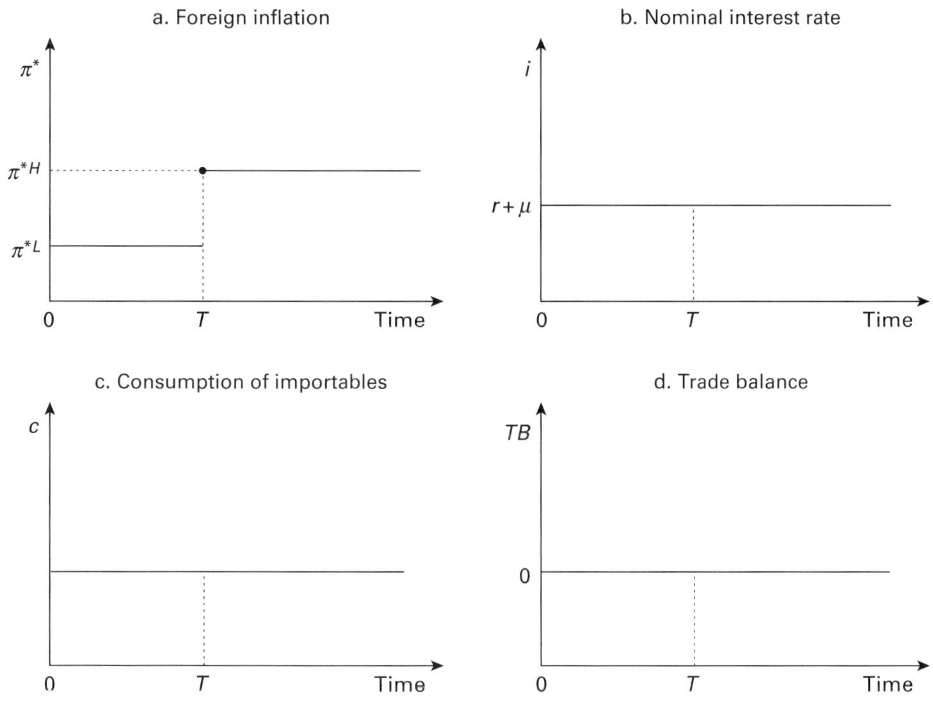

Figure 11.2
Foreign inflation shock under flexible exchange rates

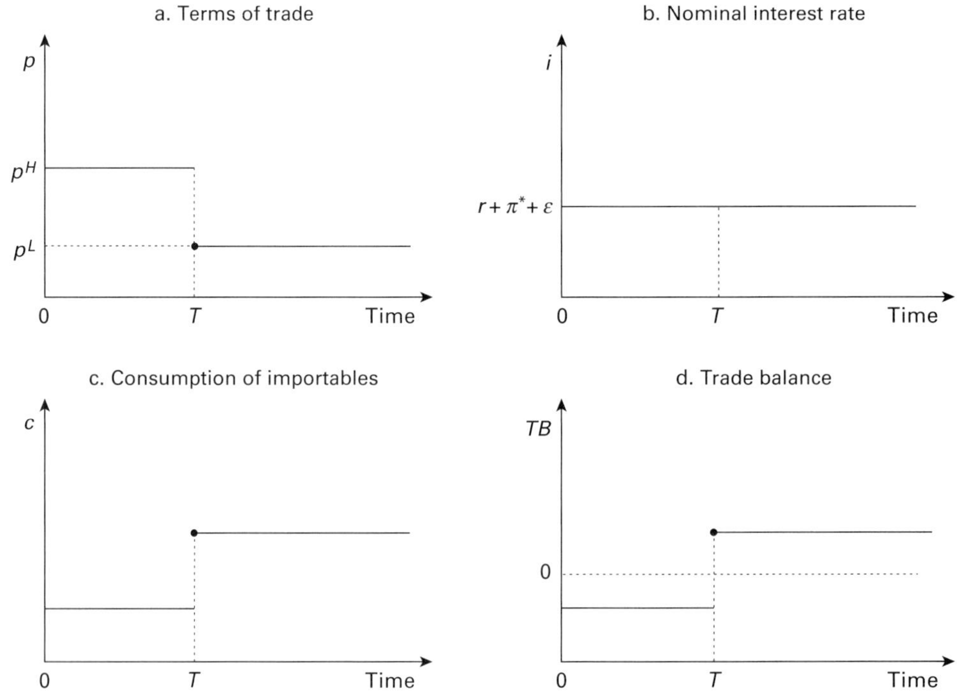

Figure 11.3
Terms of trade shock under predetermined exchange rates ($\sigma < 1$)

11.3.7 Terms of Trade Shocks

Consider now a PFEP along which the foreign inflation rate is constant at the level π^* but the path of p_t is given by (figure 11.3, panel a)

$$p_t = \begin{cases} p^H, & t \in [0, T), \\ p^L, & t \geq T. \end{cases} \tag{11.45}$$

In this case—and as will become clear below—the results depend on whether σ is greater than, equal to, or smaller than 1. We will solve for the empirically relevant case of $\sigma < 1$.[7]

Predetermined Exchange Rates

Since both the foreign inflation rate and the devaluation rate are constant over time, the interest parity condition (11.39) indicates that the nominal interest rate is constant at the level $r + \pi^* + \varepsilon$

7. Recall from box 3.1 in chapter 3 that most estimates of σ fall in the range 0.2 to 0.5. Exercise 2 at the end of the chapter asks you to solve for the case where $\sigma \geq 1$.

(figure 11.3, panel b). Given the path of p_t, first-order condition (11.34) therefore says that consumption will be low between time 0 and time T and high afterward (panel c).

The path of the trade balance depends on the value of σ. To see this, multiply both sides of equation (11.34) by c_t to obtain

$$\frac{1}{c_t^{1/\sigma-1}} = \lambda p_t c_t(1+\alpha i_t). \tag{11.46}$$

If $\sigma < 1$, the rise in c_t at time T implies that $c_t^{1/\sigma-1}$ also increases. It then follows from equation (11.46) that $p_t c_t$ falls at time T (remember i_t is constant and does not change at time T). From (11.38) this implies that the trade balance jumps up at time T and thus follows the path illustrated in panel d (for $k_0 = 0$). There is a trade deficit between time 0 and time T and a surplus thereafter. Intuitively, $\sigma < 1$ implies that consumption is relatively inelastic with respect to its price, p_t. Hence, when p_t is high (low), consumption expenditure ($p_t c_t$) is high (low) and the trade balance will be in deficit (surplus).

Finally, notice that the fact that $p_t c_t$ falls at time T implies, from the cash-in-advance constraint (11.30), that real money balances will jump down at time T. This fall in real money balances is accommodated through a fall in nominal money balances as households get rid of unwanted money balances by exchanging them for foreign bonds at the Central Bank's window.

Flexible Exchange Rates

As usual, we first need to determine whether endogenous variables jump at time T or not. Since m_t cannot jump at time T, the cash-in-advance constraint (11.30) indicates that $p_t c_t$ does not jump either. Since $p_t c_t$ does not change at time T and p_t jumps down, it follows that c_t jumps up at that time.

To find out the jump in i_t at time T, we resort to equation (11.46). Since $p_t c_t$ does not jump at time T and $c_t^{1/\sigma-1}$ increases at time T (because $\sigma < 1$), it follows that i_t falls at time T.

We now have the information that we need to derive the time path of the nominal interest rate. Since i_t jumps down at time T and i_t is governed by the unstable differential equation (11.42), it follows that i_t must be above the value $r+\mu$ at $t=0$, increase over time, and then jump down at time T (figure 11.4, panel b).

What about consumption? From first-order condition (11.34), it follows that since i_t is increasing over time, c_t will be falling over time. Since we have already established that c_t jumps up at time T, the path of consumption must look like the one depicted in panel c.

To find out the path of the trade balance, first note that from (11.40) and the fact that i_t will be increasing between 0 and T, it follows that m_t will be falling over time. From the cash-in-advance constraint (11.30), this implies that $p_t c_t$ will also be falling over time. Hence TB_t will be increasing between 0 and T. Further the cash-in-advance constraint (11.30) implies that

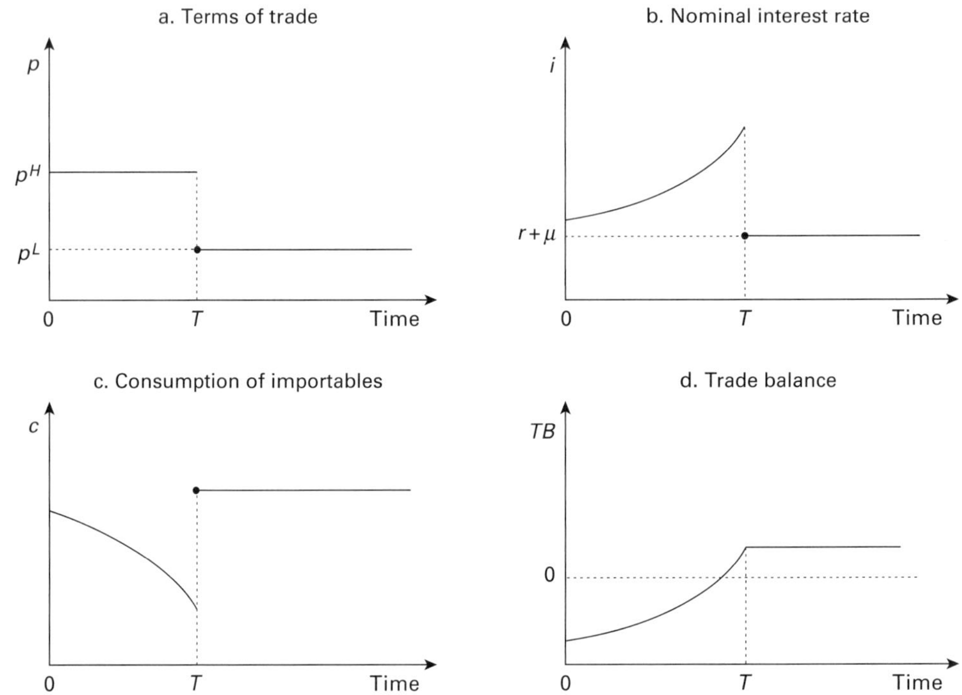

Figure 11.4
Terms of trade shock under flexible exchange rates ($\sigma < 1$)

TB_t cannot change at time T. The trade balance then follows the path illustrated in panel d (for $k_0 = 0$).[8]

Comparison

We can conclude that the behavior of the economy in response to a nonconstant path of the terms of trade depends on the exchange rate regime. The question then becomes: Which regime provides the higher welfare? The answer is that predetermined exchange rates do. To see this, think of what would happen in the real version of this economy (i.e., an economy with no money). In that case the path of consumption would correspond exactly to the one that results in the predetermined exchange rates case. Hence the outcome under predetermined exchange rates replicates the first-best equilibrium and dominates the outcome under flexible exchange rates. Intuitively,

8. Notice that TB_t must cross the zero axis before time T. If it did not, then it would stay below zero (since it cannot jump at time T), which would violate the resource constraint.

the fact that the nominal money supply is fixed under flexible exchange rates and hence cannot respond to changes in real money demand implies that the nominal interest rate must change, thus introducing an intertemporal distortion that is not present under predetermined exchange rates.[9]

Interestingly enough—and as remarked in the introduction—this result shows that the almost universal assertion in the literature that, under flexible prices, the exchange rate regime does not matter is incorrect.

11.4 Sticky Prices

We now turn to sticky prices and resort to the model developed in chapter 8. In the context of this model, we will derive the well-known Mundell–Fleming result that predetermined exchange rates are better in dealing with monetary shocks while flexible exchange rates are to be preferred in response to real shocks. We will assume that $P_t^* = 1$ for all t.

11.4.1 Consumer's Problem

The consumer's problem remains unchanged. Preferences remain given by (11.1) and the intertemporal budget constraint by (11.4) with now a possible time-varying path of y_t^N. First-order conditions are therefore given by (11.5), (11.6), and (11.7).

11.4.2 Supply Side

The supply side follows section 8.2.2 in chapter 8. There is a constant endowment of the tradable good, y^T. In the nontradable sector, prices are assumed to be sticky and output demand-determined. Price-setting is assumed to follow Calvo's (1983) staggered-prices formulation. As shown in chapter 8, appendix 8.8.1, this formulation results in a negative relationship between the *change* in the inflation rate of nontradable goods and excess aggregate demand:

$$\dot{\pi}_t = -\theta(y_t^N - y_f^N), \qquad \theta > 0, \tag{11.47}$$

where y_t^N is aggregate demand and y_f^N is the "full-employment" level of output.

11.4.3 Government

The government's budget constraints remain given by (11.11) and (11.12).

9. In the $\sigma = 1$ case, welfare would be the same because real money demand does not need to change (see exercise 2 at the end of the chapter).

11.4.4 Equilibrium Conditions

With foreign inflation equal to zero, the interest parity condition is given by

$$i_t = r + \varepsilon_t. \tag{11.48}$$

Equilibrium in the nontradable goods market is given by

$$c_t^N = y^N. \tag{11.49}$$

Recall that in this model, this equilibrium condition holds by construction since output of nontradable goods is assumed to be demand-determined. The economy's constraints (11.15) and (11.16) continue to hold.

Finally—and for further reference—notice that since $e_t = E_t/P_t^N$, then

$$\frac{\dot{e}_t}{e_t} = \varepsilon_t - \pi_t. \tag{11.50}$$

11.4.5 Consumption of Tradables

First-order condition (11.5) indicates that consumption of tradables will be constant along a PFEP. Hence, taking into account the resource constraint (11.16), we can write

$$c^T = rk_0 + y^T. \tag{11.51}$$

For further reference, notice that the path of consumption of tradables will be given by (11.51) regardless of the path of the money supply and, furthermore, will not affected by any (anticipated or unanticipated) change in monetary policy. Hence from (11.5) the same is true of the multiplier λ.

11.4.6 Predetermined Exchange Rates

Suppose that the economy is operating under a predetermined exchange rate regime with a constant rate of devaluation, given by ε. By the interest parity condition, the nominal interest rate is also constant over time:

$$i = r + \varepsilon.$$

Hence from (11.9) money demand will also be constant along a PFEP and given by

$$m = \frac{\alpha}{\gamma}\frac{c^T}{i}. \tag{11.52}$$

Since $\dot{m}_t = 0$ along a PFEP and $\dot{m}_t/m_t = \mu_t - \varepsilon$, it follows that money growth will be constant and given by

$$\mu = \varepsilon.$$

To solve for the rest of the economy, we proceed as in chapter 8 (section 8.4) and set up a dynamic system in π_t and e_t. Substituting the nontradable goods market equilibrium condition into (11.47) and using (11.8), we obtain

$$\dot{\pi}_t = \theta\left[y_f^N - \left(\frac{1-\gamma}{\gamma}\right)e_t c^T\right]. \tag{11.53}$$

From (11.50) it follows that

$$\dot{e}_t = e_t(\varepsilon - \pi_t). \tag{11.54}$$

Equations (11.53) and (11.54) constitute our dynamic system. The system's steady state is given by

$$\pi_{ss} = \varepsilon, \tag{11.55}$$

$$e_{ss} = \left(\frac{\gamma}{1-\gamma}\right)\frac{y_f^N}{c^T}. \tag{11.56}$$

As can be easily checked (see chapter 8, section 8.4 for details), this dynamic system has one positive and one negative root and is therefore saddle-path stable.

11.4.7 Flexible Exchange Rates

Suppose that the economy is operating under a flexible exchange rates regime with a constant rate of money growth, μ. To solve the corresponding PFEP, we first derive an unstable differential equation in m_t. To this effect, notice that since $m_t = M_t/E_t$,

$$\frac{\dot{m}_t}{m_t} = \mu - \varepsilon_t. \tag{11.57}$$

Using the interest parity condition to substitute for ε_t, taking into account equation (11.9), we obtain

$$\dot{m}_t = m_t(\mu + r) - \frac{\alpha c^T}{\gamma}. \tag{11.58}$$

Since this is an unstable differential equation, the only convergent PFEP is the one along which m_t is constant over time and equal to $\alpha c^T/[\gamma\,(\mu + r)]$. Given that $\dot{m}_t = 0$ along a PFEP, then from (11.57),

$$\varepsilon_t = \mu. \tag{11.59}$$

From the interest parity condition (11.48) and (11.59) it follows that

$$i_t = r + \mu.$$

To solve for the rest of the economy, we need to set up a dynamic system in n_t and π_t. Define $n_t \equiv M_t/P_t^N$. Then

$$\dot{n}_t = n_t(\mu - \pi_t). \tag{11.60}$$

To obtain our second differential equation, use the fact that $e_t = n_t/m$ to write equation (11.53) as

$$\dot{\pi}_t = \theta\left[y_f^N - \left(\frac{1-\gamma}{\gamma}\right)\frac{c^T n_t}{m}\right]. \tag{11.61}$$

Equations (11.60) and (11.61) constitute a dynamic system in n_t and π_t. The system's steady state is given by

$$\pi_{ss} = \mu, \tag{11.62}$$

$$n_{ss} = \left(\frac{\gamma}{1-\gamma}\right)\frac{y_f^N m}{c^T}. \tag{11.63}$$

It is easy to check (see chapter 8, section 8.3) that this system exhibits saddle-path stability.

Finally, the steady-state value of the real exchange rate follows from equation (11.8):

$$e_{ss} = \left(\frac{\gamma}{1-\gamma}\right)\frac{y_f^N}{c^T}. \tag{11.64}$$

11.4.8 Money-Demand Shock

Suppose that the economy is initially in a steady state. How does the economy respond to a positive money demand shock (i.e., an unanticipated and permanent increase in α)? As shown below, the adjustment will be instantaneous under predetermined exchange rates but only gradual over time under flexible exchange rates.

Predetermined Exchange Rates

In the new PFEP, tradable consumption is, of course, still constant over time and hence remains given by (11.51) (figure 11.5, panel b). From (11.52), it follows that real money demand increases on impact and remains constant thereafter (panel c). The increase in real money balances is carried out by an increase in the stock of nominal money balances, as a result of consumers exchanging bonds for money at the Central Bank's window (panel d). Clearly—from (11.55) and (11.56)—the money shock does not affect the steady-state values of inflation of nontradable goods and the

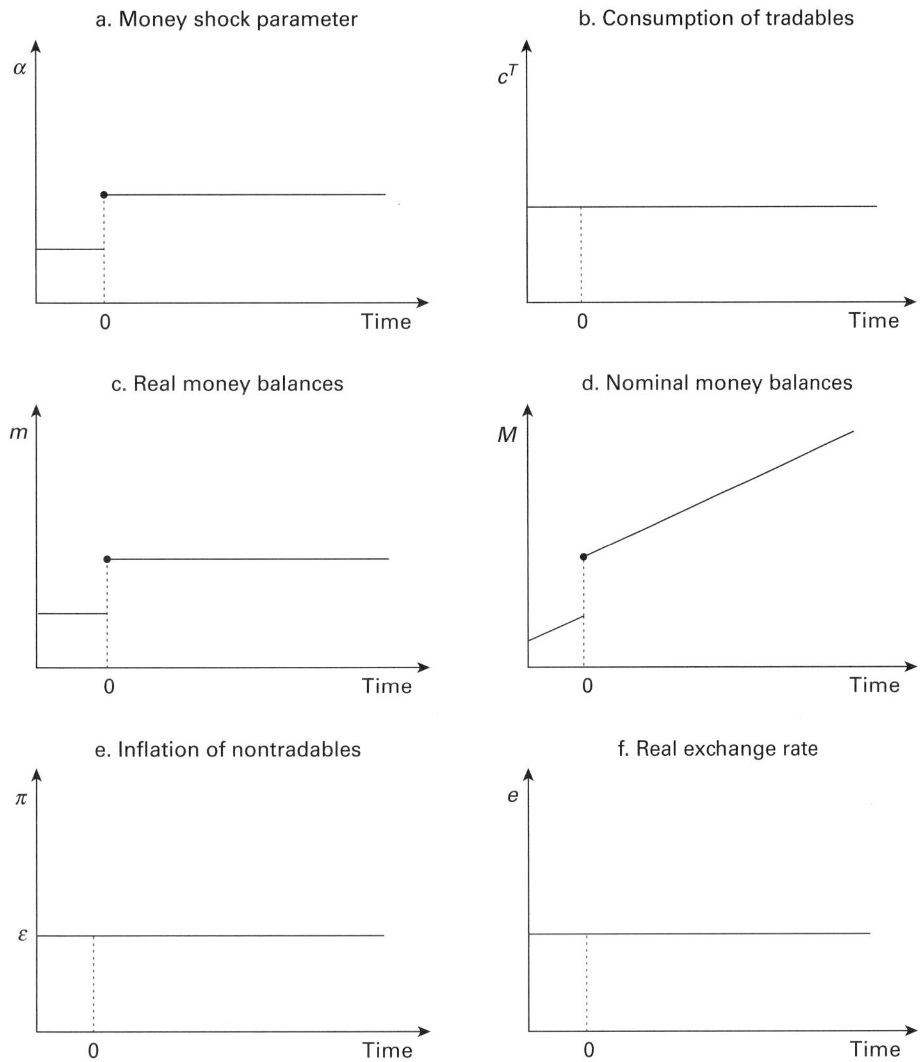

Figure 11.5
Money demand shock under predetermined exchange rates

real exchange rate, and hence neither variable reacts to the shock (panels e and f). Since the real exchange rate does not change, neither does consumption of nontradable goods, as follows from equation (11.8).

Flexible Exchange Rates

In the new PFEP, real money balances will also be constant but at a higher level (figure 11.6, panel c), as follows from (11.58). The increase in real money balances is effected through a fall in the nominal exchange rate at time 0 (panel d).

Turning to the dynamic system, we can see from (11.63) that the rise in m increases n_{ss}. In terms of figure 11.7, the steady state shifts from point A to point C. On impact, the system jumps from point A to point B and then travels along the saddle path toward point C. Figure 11.6, panel e, illustrates the path of inflation.

To derive the path of the real exchange rate, first notice that the steady-state real exchange rate does not change, as (11.64) makes clear. The dynamic behavior of e_t can be inferred from the fact that $e_t = n_t/m_t$. Since n_t is a predetermined variable and hence does not jump at $t = 0$, the upward jump in m_t on impact implies that e_t will jump down on impact and then gradually rise back to its unchanged steady state (figure 11.6, panel f). Consumption of nontradable goods mimics the path of e_t (falling on impact and then gradually rising back to its unchanged steady state), as follows from equation (11.8).

Comparison

In response to a positive money demand shock, it is clear that predetermined exchange rates dominate because they allow for an instantaneous adjustment of real money balances through an adjustment in nominal money balances. The shock has therefore no real effects. Under flexible exchange rates, however, real money balances in terms of nontradables can only increase over time because the nominal money supply is given at any point in time. On impact, the incipient excess demand for real money balances therefore leads to a fall in the consumption of nontradables. As follows from (11.1), welfare is higher under predetermined than under flexible exchange rates.[10]

11.4.9 Real Shock

Consider an unanticipated and permanent increase in γ; that is, a demand shock that shifts demand away from nontradable goods and towards tradable goods.

10. Welfare is lower under flexible exchange rates because the path of both c_t^N and z_t are lower at any point in time during the transition. The path of z_t is lower because $\log(z_t) = \log(m_t) + (1-\gamma)\log e_t$ and, under flexible exchange rates, the path of e_t is always below the corresponding path under predetermined exchange rates.

Note that this model is suitable for welfare analysis as long as we examine shocks that imply a fall in output of nontradables below its full-employment level. In the opposite case (shocks that imply a rise in output above its full-employment level) the welfare analysis is meaningless because there is no physical constraint on productive resources.

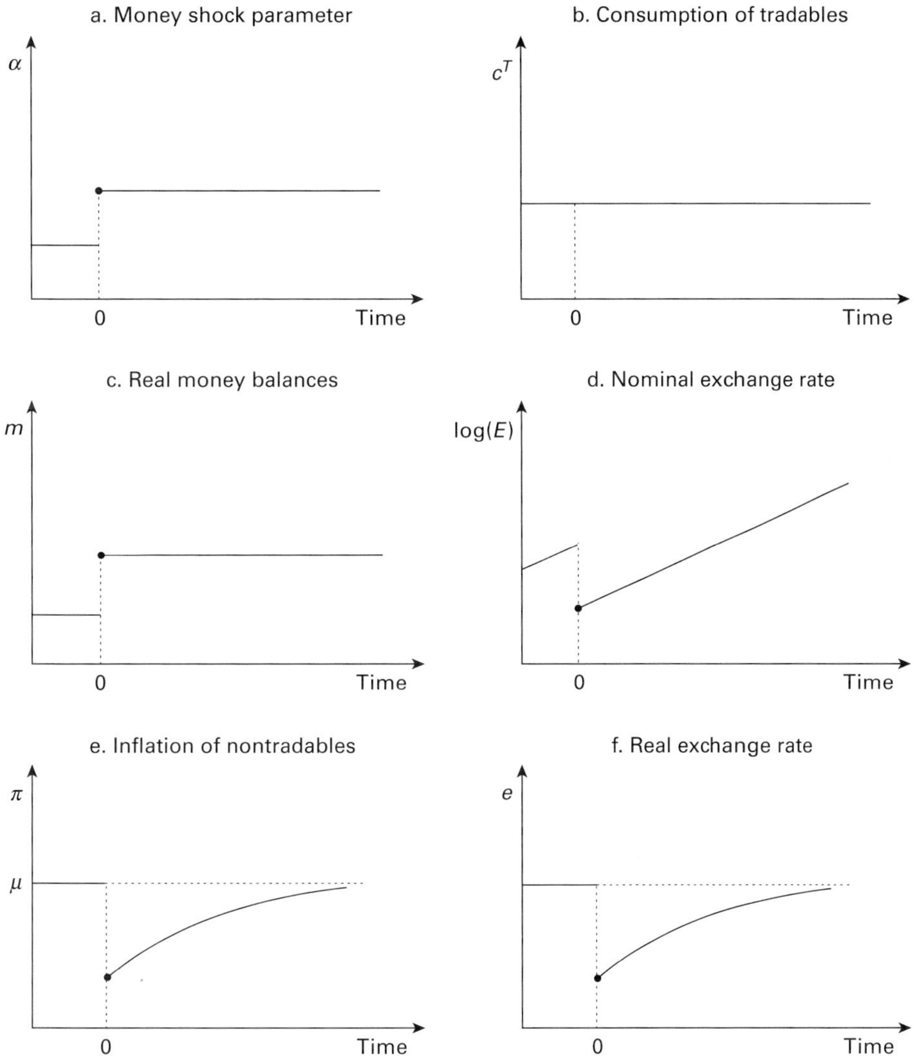

Figure 11.6
Money demand shock under flexible exchange rates

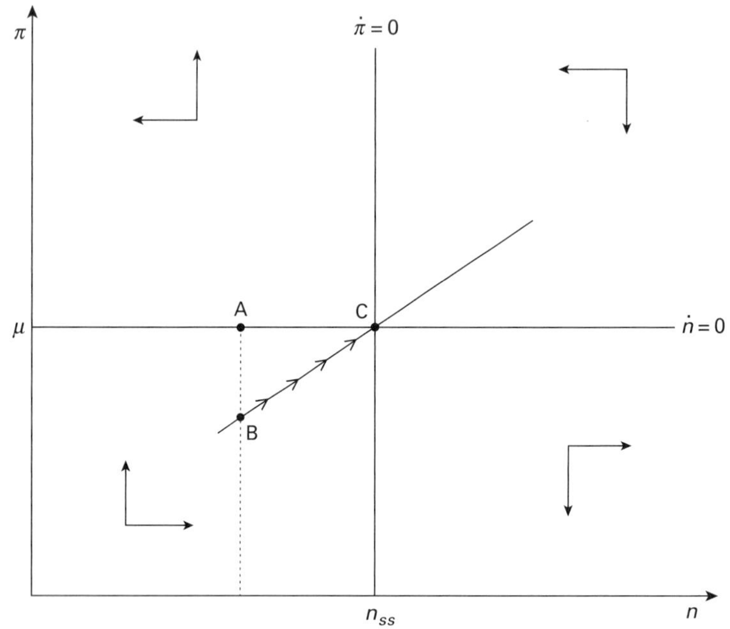

Figure 11.7
Phase diagram: Money demand shock under flexible exchange rates

Predetermined Exchange Rates

Once again, consumption of tradable goods does not change (figure 11.8, panel b). From (11.52) the increase in γ reduces real money demand (panel c). Intuitively, notice that at an optimum, consumers are equating the marginal utility from consumption of tradable goods and real money balances. An increase in γ is tantamount to an increase in the marginal utility of consumption of tradable goods. Hence, for a given level of consumption of tradable goods, real money balances need to be reduced to increase the marginal utility of real money balances and keep marginal utilities equalized. The fall in real money demand is carried out through a fall in nominal money balances (panel d).

How will π_t and e_t respond? From (11.55) and (11.56) we see that while steady-state inflation does not change, the steady-state real exchange rate increases (real depreciation). In terms of figure 11.9, the new steady state becomes point C (with the initial steady state being at point A). On impact, the system jumps from point A to point B and then travels over time along the saddle path toward point C. The corresponding time paths for inflation and the real exchange rate are depicted in figure 11.8, panels e and f, respectively.

What about consumption of nontradable goods? From (11.8), taking into account that consumption of tradables is unchanged, we have

$$c_t^N = \left(\frac{1-\gamma}{\gamma}\right) e_t c^T. \qquad (11.65)$$

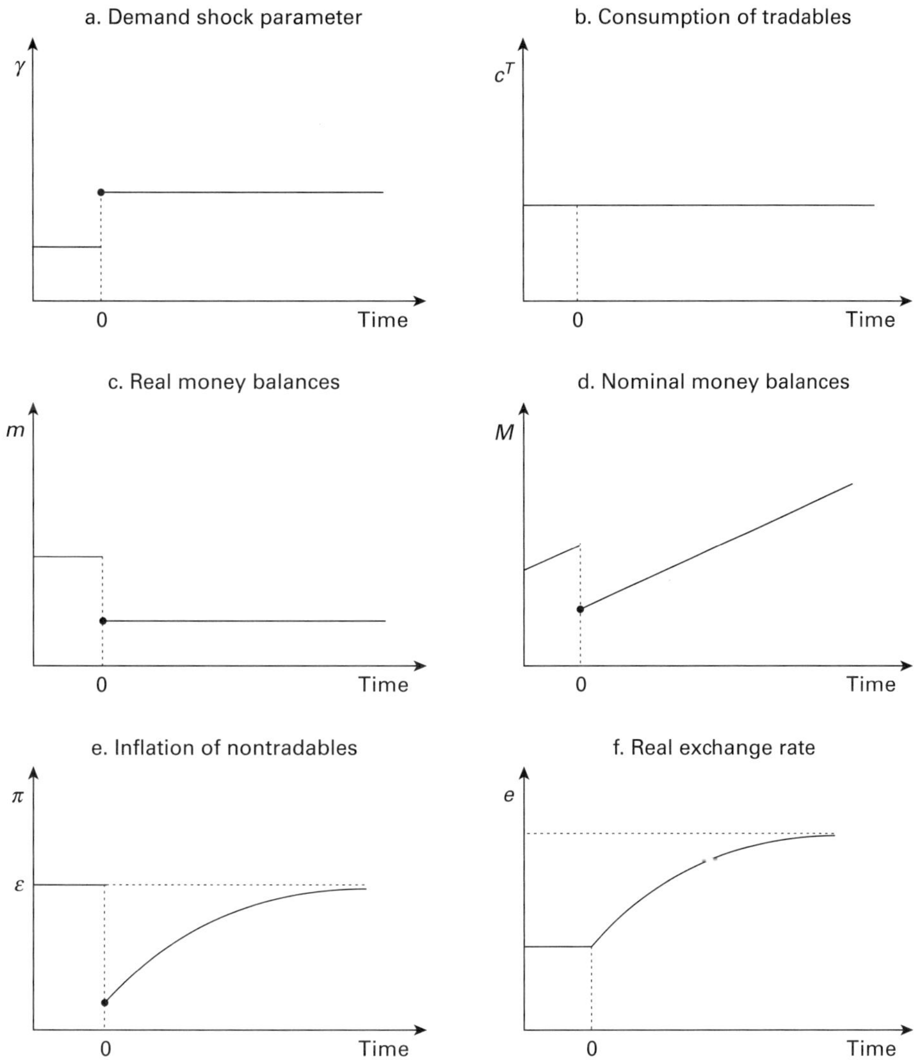

Figure 11.8
Demand shock under predetermined exchange rates

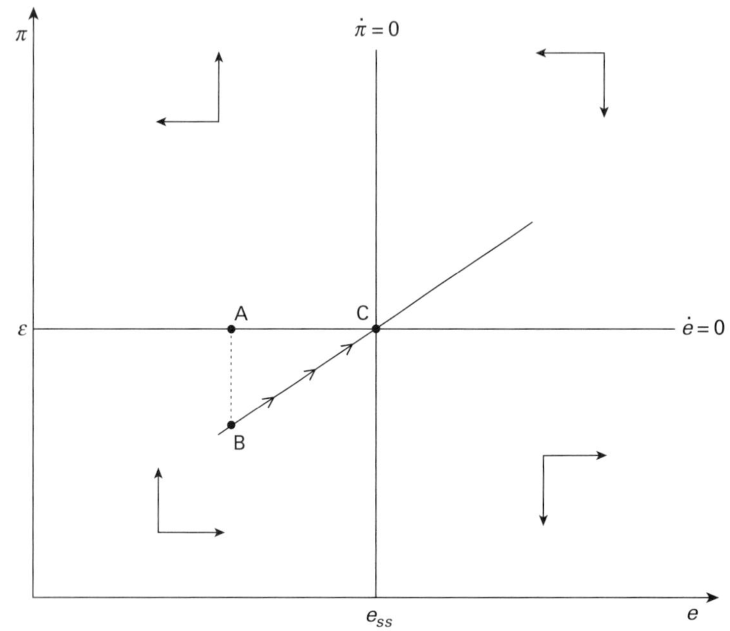

Figure 11.9
Phase diagram: Demand shock under predetermined exchange rates

It follows that c_t^N falls on impact (since γ increases) and then increases over time toward its unchanged steady state.

The key aspect of the economy's adjustment is the fact that for the real exchange rate to increase in the long run, the economy must undergo a prolonged period of deflation, as reflected in inflation being below its steady-state value during the transition to the new steady state (figure 11.8, panel e).

Flexible Exchange Rates

Consumption of tradable goods remains unchanged (figure 11.10, panel b). In the new stationary equilibrium, m_t will still be flat over time (otherwise, it would diverge) but at a lower level (panel c). The fall in m is engineered through a rise in the nominal exchange rate at time 0 (panel d).

How do π_t and n_t respond? From (11.62) and (11.63) we see that while π_{ss} does not change, n_{ss} increases. The dynamic response is therefore the same as that illustrated for the case of the money shock in figure 11.7. The inflation rate falls on impact and then rises gradually toward its unchanged steady state (panel e). In contrast, n_t does not change on impact and gradually rises over time, as follows from figure 11.7.

What is the response of the real exchange rate? First, notice from (11.64), that e_{ss} increases. What about the impact effect? Since, by definition, $e_t = E_t/P_t^N$ and P_t^N is a predetermined variable, the increase in the nominal exchange rate established above will also imply an increase

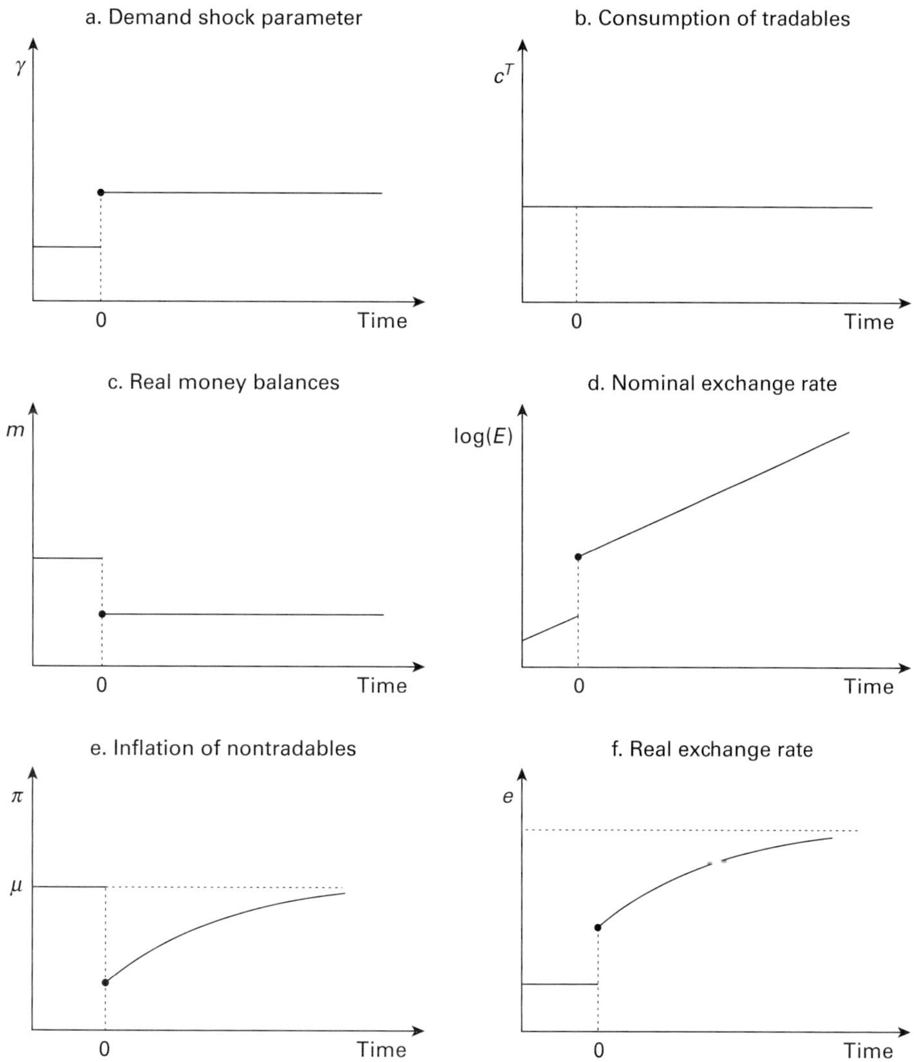

Figure 11.10
Demand shock under flexible exchange rates

on impact of the real exchange rate. From the fact that $e_t = n_t/m_t$, we infer that e_t will be rising over time. Hence the real exchange rate follows the path illustrated in panel f.

What about consumption of nontradable goods? Since c_{ss}^N clearly remains unchanged and, from (11.65), we know that c_t^N will be rising over time, we infer that it must fall on impact. Notice, however, that the initial fall in c_t^N will be *smaller* than under predetermined exchange rates because—as equation (11.65) makes clear—the rise in e_t partially offsets the increase in γ.

Welfare Comparison

Figure 11.11 compares the path of the real exchange rate and consumption of nontradable goods under predetermined and flexible exchange rates. As shown above—and illustrated in panel a—the real exchange rate increases on impact under flexible exchange rates and hence the path of the real exchange rate will always lie above the corresponding path under predetermined exchange rates. The counterpart of the upward jump of the real exchange rate under flexible exchange rates is that—as illustrated in panel b—consumption of nontradable goods will fall by less under flexible exchange rates than under predetermined exchange rates. In other words, the path of c_t^N under flexible exchange rates always lies above the corresponding path under predetermined exchange rates. Since the behavior of c_t^T and m_t is identical under the two regimes, it follows from (11.1) that welfare will be higher under flexible exchange rates than under predetermined exchange rates.[11] We therefore conclude—at least based on this example—that flexible exchange rates are more efficient than predetermined exchange rates when it comes to responding to real shocks.

What is the intuition behind this result? The key is that the real shock is also affecting the money market (i.e., the market for m_t). Because the demand for m_t falls as a result of the shock, under flexible exchange rates the nominal exchange rate needs to increase (nominal depreciation) to adjust the money market. Since prices are sticky, this nominal depreciation implies a real depreciation, which helps in cushioning the negative impact of the shock on consumption of nontradables (and hence on output of nontradables).

The intuition above clearly suggests that the more money demand responds to the shock (i.e., the more elastic is money demand), the higher will be the nominal, and hence real, depreciation and the more the consumption of nontradables will be cushioned. Of course, we cannot check this intuition in this version of the model since we have assumed a logarithmic subutility for z_t, which implies a unitary elasticity. To check our intuition, let us suppose that preferences are given instead by

$$\int_0^\infty \left[\gamma \log(c_t^T) + (1-\gamma)\log(c_t^N) + \alpha \frac{z_t^{1-1/\sigma} - 1}{1-1/\sigma}\right] \exp(-\beta t)dt, \tag{11.66}$$

11. Once again, recall that $\log(z_t) = \log(m_t) + (1-\gamma)\log(e_t)$. Hence the fact that the path of both c_t^N and e_t is higher during the transition under flexible exchange rates ensures that welfare will be higher.

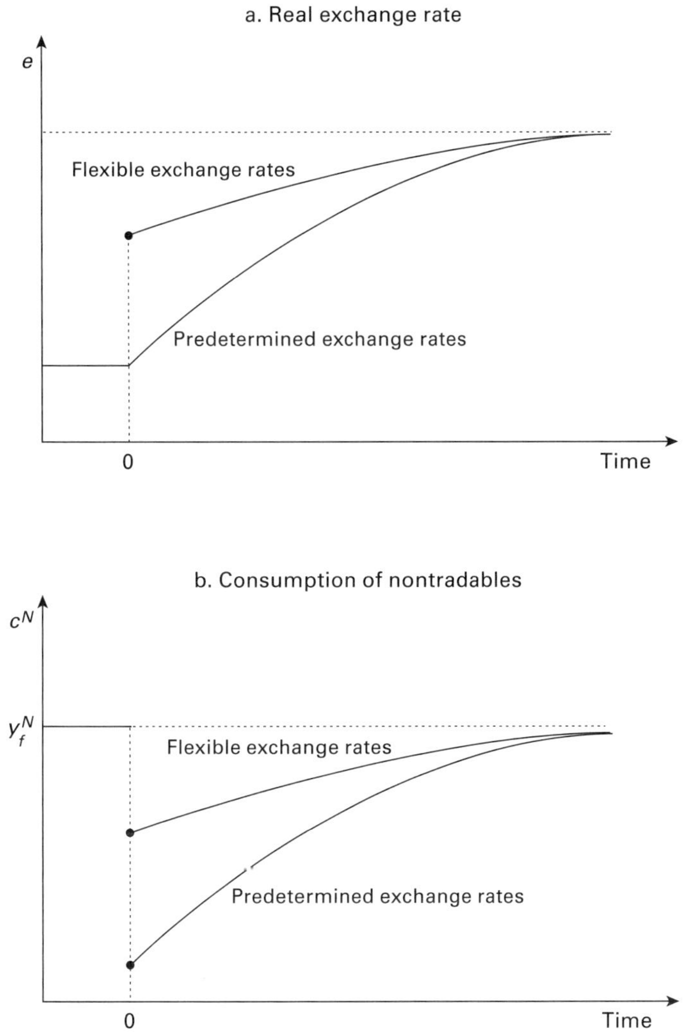

Figure 11.11
Comparison between predetermined and flexible exchange rates

where $z_t (\equiv M_t/P_t)$ denotes real money balances in terms of the price index P_t, given by[12]

$$P_t \equiv (P_t^T)^{\gamma}(P_t^N)^{1-\gamma}. \tag{11.67}$$

Combining the first-order conditions, we can show that the demand for m_t is given by

$$m_t = \left[\frac{\alpha e_t^{(1-\gamma)(1-1/\sigma)} c_t^T}{\gamma i_t}\right]^{\sigma},$$

which makes clear that σ measures the money-demand elasticity to shocks in γ. Under flexible exchange rates this model is more complicated to solve than the one above because it is not block recursive, and we thus need to solve a three differential equation system in m_t, n_t, and π_t (as we did in chapter 8 to study the overshooting phenomenon). For the purposes at hand, we solve the model numerically (see appendix 11.7.1). Figure 11.12 shows the behavior of the real exchange rate and consumption of nontradable goods for different values of σ. The case of $\sigma = 1$ corresponds to the logarithmic case analyzed above. We see in panel a that the higher the value of σ, the more the real exchange rate jumps up on impact, and hence the smaller is the fall in consumption of nontradable goods (panel b). In other words, the higher is σ, the higher will be welfare. A higher elasticity helps because it entails a larger increase in the nominal exchange rate, and hence a larger real depreciation.

A Caveat

While we have replicated above the conventional results arising from the Mundell–Fleming model regarding the advantages of flexible exchange rates in dealing with real shocks, the discussion should have made clear that the theoretical robustness of such results is open to question. In essence, if the real shock does not directly affect the money market, then flexible exchange rates will not offer any advantage over predetermined exchange rates. A case in point would be the model discussed above with preferences given by

$$\int_0^{\infty} [\log(c_t^T) + \phi \log(c_t^N) + \alpha \log(z_t)] \exp(-\beta t)\, dt, \tag{11.68}$$

instead of (11.1), where ϕ is a positive parameter. As exercise 3 at the end of this chapter asks you to verify, a fall in ϕ will lead to the same adjustment under predetermined and flexible exchange rates. The reason is that under flexible exchange rates, the money market is

12. If $\sigma = 1$, then preferences (11.66) reduce to the logarithmic specification studied above.

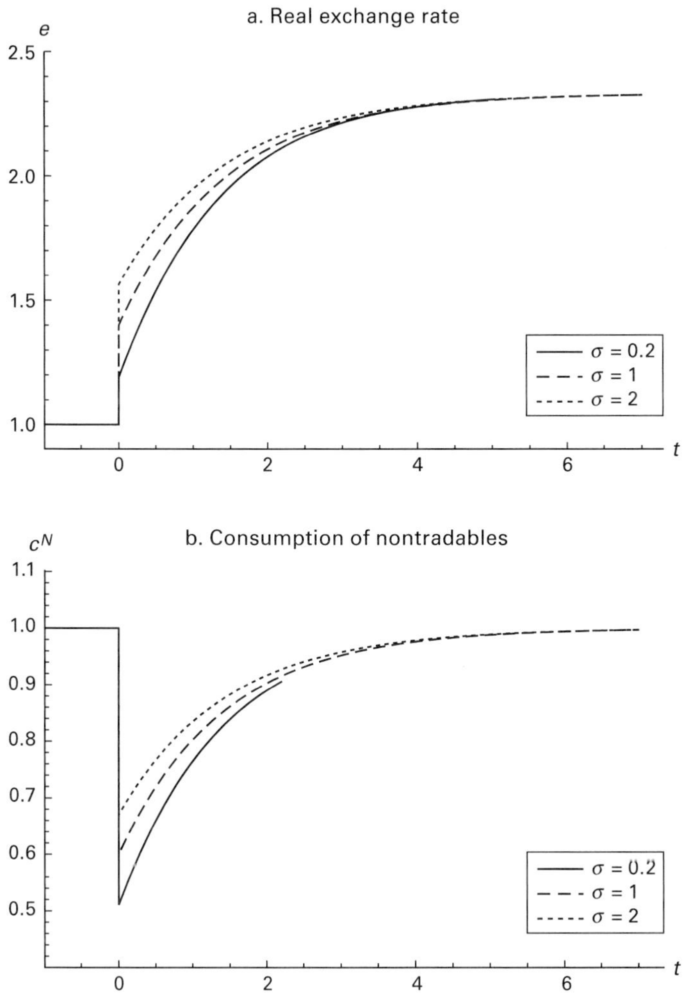

Figure 11.12
Response of real exchange rate and consumption of nontradable goods to demand shock

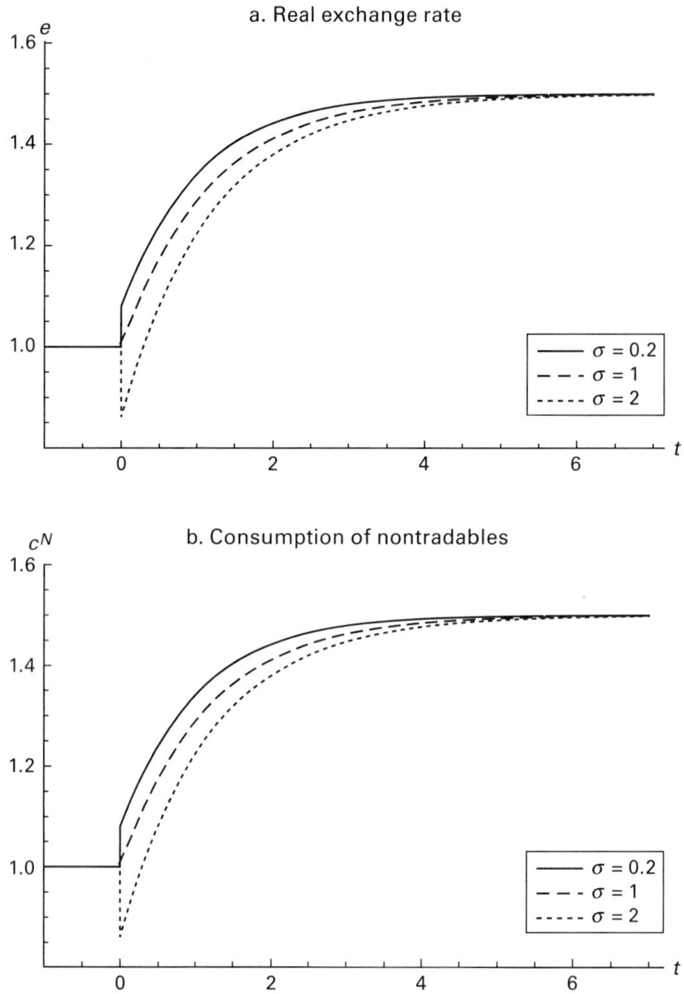

Figure 11.13
Response of real exchange rate and consumption of nontradable goods to supply shock

not affected by the shock. Hence the nominal exchange rate will not change in response to the fall in ϕ, providing no cushioning in the goods market.

Another example would be a fall in y_f^N in the model studied above (see exercise 4 at the end of this chapter). In the case of logarithmic preferences (given by equation 11.1), the nominal exchange rate will not change, and hence the adjustment will be the same under both exchange rate regimes. However, if the subutility for money is modeled as a CES (i.e., preferences are given by equation 11.66) and the system becomes nonrecursive, then the results will depend on the value of σ. As figure 11.13 shows, for $\sigma = 1$ (the logarithmic case) the economy adjusts as it would under predetermined exchange rates. For $\sigma < 1$, however, a nominal depreciation of the currency causes a real depreciation and facilitates the adjustment. The opposite is true for $\sigma > 1$.

In sum, while the theoretical robustness of these results can be called into question, in practice we certainly expect negative real shocks to impact money demand adversely, and hence lead to a nominal depreciation, which will help the real adjustment.[13] In fact—and as detailed in box 11.1—econometric estimations of Mundell–Fleming models support the notion that flexible exchange rates are more efficient in responding to real shocks.

11.5 Asset Market Segmentation

We have argued above that, in the presence of sticky prices, flexible exchange rates are optimal if real shocks dominate, whereas predetermined exchange rates are optimal if monetary shocks dominate. As discussed in box 11.2, however, frictions in asset markets are extremely common as well. In particular, asset markets are typically segmented in the sense that only a fraction of the population has access to asset markets. We will now see that—as shown by Lahiri, Singh, and Végh (2008)—in the presence of asset market frictions the traditional results obtained under sticky prices are turned on their heads.

Consider a discrete-time model of a small open economy perfectly integrated with the rest of the world in goods markets.[14] There are two types of agents: traders (who have access to capital markets) and nontraders (who do *not* have access to capital markets). The fraction of traders is ψ while that of nontraders is $1 - \psi$. There is no uncertainty in the model and agents are blessed with perfect foresight. The law of one price holds for the only good; hence $P_t = E_t P_t^*$. Foreign inflation is assumed to be zero, and for simplicity, P_t^* is taken to be unity, so $P_t = E_t$.

13. Another important assumption—which underlies all traditional formulations of the Mundell–Fleming models—is that prices of tradable goods are flexible (which can be thought of as the price of tradable goods being set in the currency of the producer). This implies that changes in the nominal exchange rate affect relative prices. An alternative formulation—more natural in a two country setting—is to assume that goods are priced in the consumer's currency, as analyzed by Devereux and Engel (1998). This alternative price-setting formulation affects the insulation properties of fixed versus flexible exchange rates because changes in the nominal exchange rate do not directly affect relative prices.

14. Similar results obtain in an economy with uncertainty and incomplete markets (see Lahiri, Singh, and Végh 2007).

Box 11.1
Do flexible exchange rates cushion the economy against real shocks?

Section 11.4 examines the insulation properties of alternative exchange rate arrangements under sticky prices. When it comes to monetary shocks, the economy adjusts instantaneously under predetermined exchange rates but only gradually under flexible exchange rates. In contrast, while a real shock affects the real sector under both predetermined and flexible exchange rates, the adjustment is less costly under flexible exchange rates (provided that the shock has negative effects on the money market). This is because the nominal depreciation of the domestic currency translates into a real depreciation, which partly cushions against the shock.

From an empirical point of view, identifying the source of the shock is clearly a critical step in testing this theoretical prediction. Early empirical studies (e.g., Baxter and Stockman 1989 and Ghosh et al. 1997) looked at the volatility of output under alternative exchange rate regimes but without identifying the nature of the shock. More recent econometric studies, summarized in table 11.3, have looked at the short-run volatility of output in response to terms-of-trade shocks, which are easily observable and quantifiable. By and large, the empirical evidence is consistent with the theoretical predictions and suggests that flexible exchange regimes perform better in accommodating real shocks than do predetermined exchange rate regimes.

Table 11.3
Econometric studies on insulation properties

Author(s)	Dataset	Methodology and type of shocks	Main results
Edwards and Levy Yeyati (2003)	183 Countries Annual data for 1974-2000	• Two-step FGLS • Terms of trade shocks	• 10 Percent fall in terms of trade associated with a (contemporaneous) average fall in real GDP per capita growth of 0.80 and 0.43 percentage points for fix and flex, respectively • Output response larger for negative shocks (asymmetric response to shocks)
Broda (2004)	75 Developing countries Annual data for 1973–1996	• Panel VAR • Terms of trade shocks	• Smaller short-run response of real GDP for countries with flexible rates • Real depreciation takes time in pegs, but is immediate in flex after a negative terms of trade shock • Long-run differences are absent across regimes (neutrality) • Overall, common wisdom holds: flexible rates are better real shock absorbers
Aghion et al. (2006)	83 Countries Annual data, 1960–2000	• GMM dynamic panel data with robust two-step standard errors • Terms of trade growth and volatility	• Although exchange rate flexibility mitigates the impact of terms of trade shocks, it reduces growth for countries with low financial development • Flexible exchange rates dampen volatility from terms of trade shocks, except for the less financially developed countries

Box 11.1
(continued)

Table 11.3
(continued)

Author(s)	Dataset	Methodology and type of shocks	Main results
Magud (2006)	32 Countries with foreign-currency debt Annual data, 1980–2001	• Near VAR • Terms-of-trade shocks	In the presence of balance sheet effects: • For relatively open economies, flexible rates are better real shock absorbers • For relatively closed economies, fixed rates are better real shock absorbers because they insulate the economy from net worth fluctuations • Openness threshold is 40 percent (size of tradable production relative to total output) • Pooled sample: flexible regimes are better real shock absorbers
Dai and Chia (2008)	9 East-Asian countries Annual data 1980–2007	• Panel VAR • Terms-of-trade shocks	In response to terms of trade shocks: • Real output volatility does not depend on exchange rate regime • For very open economies, however, flexible rates provide more insulation

In the presence of liability dollarization, however, the size of the tradable sector could play an important role for the choice of the exchange rate regime: a larger degree of currency mismatch can have negative effects on firms' net worth due to exchange rate fluctuations, and hence, make a fixed exchange rate more attractive even for real shocks. The degree of financial development could also matter. Specifically, flexible exchange rates seem to provide more insulation as long as the domestic financial system is well developed.

Both traders and nontraders are subject to a cash-in-advance constraint. For the case of traders—and as in chapter 5—we adopt the specification that asset markets open first followed by goods markets. By assumption, of course, nontraders do not have access to asset markets, and hence they only visit goods markets.[15]

There are two types of shocks: real and monetary shocks. Real shocks are captured by fluctuations in the endowment of the only good. Monetary—or velocity—shocks are captured by allowing both traders and nontraders to access a fraction v_t of current period sales ($v_t E_t y_t$).

To fix ideas, recall the story that we told in chapter 5 about the physical environment underlying cash-in-advance models à la Lucas (1982). Households consist of two individuals: a shopper

15. Asset market segmentation could be endogeneized by assuming that there is a fixed cost of accessing asset markets. If agents have different endowments, then some of them will choose not to enter asset markets in any given period; see Alvarez and Atkeson (1997).

Box 11.2
How segmented are asset markets in practice?

The model of section 11.5 treats asset market segmentation as an asset market friction based on the idea that a fraction of households do not have access to interest-bearing assets. In practice, this lack of access is typically due to limited financial development caused by both supply factors (e.g., lack of competition in the financial sector and high operating costs, particularly in rural areas) and demand factors (e.g., low income and education levels that make households unaware of financial opportunities or unwilling to take advantage of them).

But how segmented are asset markets in practice? Table 11.4 summarizes some relevant studies. A common definition of asset market segmentation has been access to interest-bearing assets that are not liquid enough to be included in the monetary aggregate M1. By this definition, asset market segmentation was still quite widespread in the United States by the end of the 1980s with close to 60 percent of households not holding any interest-bearing financial assets (Mulligan and Sala-i-Martin 2000). But in 2001 this figure had already fallen substantially with 80 percent of households in the bottom 10th percentile of the wealth distribution holding some form of interest-bearing assets (Campbell 2006).

Table 11.4
Empirical studies on asset market segmentation

Author(s)	Dataset	Source	Main results
Mulligan and Sala-i-Martin (2000)	US household level data, 1989	Survey of Consumer Finance	• 59 Percent of households hold interest-bearing financial assets • 75 Percent of households hold deposit accounts
Campbell (2006)	US household level data, 2001	Survey of Consumer Finance	• 80 Percent of households in 10th bottom percentile of wealth distribution hold safe financial assets; for higher percentiles this figure converges to 100 percent
Claessens (2006)	Household level data, includes 48 economies, date of survey varies (1988–2004)	Main source: Living Standards Measurement Study (World Bank)	• Average usage of checking or savings bank accounts in OECD countries close to 90 percent, compared to 26 percent in developing countries.
Beck, Demirguc-Kunt, and Martinez Peria (2007)	Cross-country data, includes 99 economies, 2003–2004	Surveys of bank regulatory agencies on number of bank branches, number of ATMs, and number and value of bank loans and deposits	• Deposits per capita and branches per square kilometer are good predictors of household share with bank accounts • Cross-country median value of 53 percent of deposit accounts per capita

Box 11.2
(continued)

Not surprisingly, the empirical evidence points to much higher asset market segmentation in developing than in developed economies. Taking deposits per capita as an indicator, Beck, Demirguc-Kunt, and Martinez Peria (2007) report an overall cross-country median value of 0.53 deposit accounts per capita (e.g., Guyana and Venezuela) compared to both the bottom 5th percentile median value of 0.06 deposit accounts per capita (e.g., Bolivia, Madagascar, and Uganda), and the top 5th percentile median value of 2.57 deposit accounts per capita (e.g., Austria, Belgium, and Denmark).

and a seller. As the goods markets are about to open, the seller and the shopper part and, in the standard model studied in chapter 5, do not see each other until the end of the day. In other words, the seller stays in the store selling the endowment to other households' shoppers and the shopper goes to other stores to purchase goods. Hence, in the standard story, the shopper does *not* return to the store until after goods markets close and therefore has no access to the money balances accrued to the seller from the sale of the current-period endowment ($E_t y_t$). In the current model it is as though we are allowing the shopper to come back to the store once during the goods market session, empty the cash register, and go back shopping. The amount of money in the register is $v_t E_t y_t$.

11.5.1 Nontraders

Nontraders (NT) do not have access to asset markets. Hence they only hold money (like the households of chapter 6). Preferences of nontraders are given by

$$U^{NT} = \sum_{t=0}^{\infty} \beta^t u(c_t^{NT}), \tag{11.69}$$

where c_t^{NT} denotes consumption of nontraders and β now denotes the discount factor.

Since nontraders only hold money, their flow budget constraint is given by

$$M_{t+1}^{NT} = M_t^{NT} + E_t y_t - E_t c_t^{NT}, \tag{11.70}$$

where M_t^{NT} denotes end-of-period $t-1$ (and hence beginning of period t) nominal money balances in the hands of nontraders. The initial level of nominal money balances, M_0, is given. Nontraders are subject to a cash-in-advance constraint (CIA) of the form

$$M_t^{NT} + v_t E_t y_t \geq E_t c_t^{NT}. \tag{11.71}$$

The nominal money balances that nontraders can use to purchase goods consist of the nominal money balances that they brought into period t, M_t^{NT}, and a fraction v_t of current-period sales.

We will only consider equilibrium paths along which the cash-in-advance constraint binds.[16] Contrary to what our intuition would first tell us—that the CIA would rarely bind because NT would like to save some money for low endowment periods—the cash-in-advance constraint may bind under weak conditions. Intuitively, periods of high endowment—which induce saving for consumption smoothing purposes—also imply a negative return on money—which induces dissaving.

If the cash-in-advance constraint binds, then we can solve for c_t^{NT} from equation (11.71) to obtain

$$c_t^{NT} = \frac{M_t^{NT} + v_t E_t y_t}{E_t}, \qquad t \geq 0. \tag{11.72}$$

To find out how much money balances nontraders will carry on to the next period, substitute (11.72) into (11.70) to obtain

$$M_{t+1}^{NT} = (1 - v_t)E_t y_t. \tag{11.73}$$

When the cash-in-advance constraint binds, the problem of the nontraders becomes completely mechanical. In other words, their opportunity set consists of only one point in every period—given by (11.72)—and there is thus no need to carry out any maximization. Intuitively, nontraders begin their life with a given level of nominal money balances, M_0^{NT}. They augment these cash balances with a fraction v_0 of period 0 sales, $v_0 E_0 y_0$. Since the cash-in-advance constraint binds, they spend all of their money balances, $M_0^{NT} + v_0 E_0 y_0$, on consumption in period 0. Their end-of-period cash balances consist of the cash proceeds from selling their endowment, $E_0 y_0$, minus the amount of period 0 sales spent in period 0, $v_0 E_0 y_0$. They thus enter period 1 with $M_1^{NT} (= (1 - v_0)E_0 y_0)$, and the process begins anew.

11.5.2 Traders

Traders have access to asset markets and thus behave like the consumers in any of our models with perfect capital mobility. In particular, they behave in exactly the same manner as in our discrete-time, cash-in-advance model of chapter 5, section 5.6. The only difference is that like nontraders, they have access to a fraction v_t of current-period sales.

Let us first look at the flow constraint for the asset market. Traders enter the asset market with a certain amount of nominal money balances, M_t^T, and a certain amount of bonds, b_t. Once in

16. Appendix 11.7.2 derives the restrictions on the output and velocity processes needed to ensure that the cash-in-advance constraint for nontraders binds. We assume that these conditions are satisfied.

the asset market they receive/pay interest on the bonds they carried into the asset markets, $E_t r b_t$, receive transfers from the government, Γ_t, and buy/sell bonds in exchange for money.[17] Traders exit the asset market with a quantity $\hat{M}_t^T$ of nominal money balances and b_{t+1} of bonds. The flow constraint for the asset market is thus

$$E_t b_{t+1} + \hat{M}_t^T = M_t^T + E_t(1+r)b_t + \frac{\Gamma_t}{\psi}. \tag{11.74}$$

Traders are subject to a cash-in-advance constraint:

$$\hat{M}_t^T + v_t E_t y_t \geq E_t c_t^T. \tag{11.75}$$

What will be traders' nominal money balances at the end of period t? Traders will have the money brought from the asset market plus the proceeds from the sale of their endowment ($E_t y_t$) minus the money balances used to purchase goods ($E_t c_t^T$):

$$M_{t+1}^T = \hat{M}_t^T + E_t y_t - E_t c_t^T. \tag{11.76}$$

By substituting (11.76) into (11.74), we obtain the traders' flow constraint for period t as a whole:

$$E_t b_{t+1} + M_{t+1}^T = M_t^T + E_t(1+r)b_t + E_t y_t + \frac{\Gamma_t}{\psi} - E_t c_t^T. \tag{11.77}$$

Utility Maximization

For the purposes of the maximization—and by substituting (11.74) into (11.75)—we rewrite the cash-in-advance constraint as

$$M_t^T + E_t(1+r)b_t + \frac{\Gamma_t}{\psi} - E_t b_{t+1} + v_t E_t y_t \geq E_t c_t^T. \tag{11.78}$$

We will assume that the cash-in-advance constraint binds.[18]

Traders thus choose $\{c_t^T, M_{t+1}^T, b_{t+1}\}_{t=0}^{\infty}$ to maximize lifetime utility subject to the flow constraint (11.77) and the CIA constraint (11.78). In terms of the Lagrangian,

17. We assume that transfers are made in the asset market, where only the traders are present. Note that since Γ_t denotes aggegate transfers per capita, the corresponding per trader value is Γ_t/ψ since traders comprise a fraction ψ of the population.

18. Appendix 11.7.2 derives the restrictions on the driving processes for output and velocity needed for the CIA constraint for traders to bind.

$$\mathcal{L} = \sum_{t=0}^{\infty} \beta^t u(c_t^T)$$
$$+ \sum_{t=0}^{\infty} \beta^t \eta_t \left[M_t^T + E_t(1+r)b_t + \frac{\Gamma_t}{\psi} + E_t y_t - E_t c_t^T - E_t b_{t+1} - M_{t+1}^T \right]$$
$$+ \sum_{t=0}^{\infty} \beta^t \Psi_t \left[M_t^T + E_t(1+r)b_t + \frac{\Gamma_t}{\psi} - E_t b_{t+1} + v_t E_t y_t - E_t c_t^T \right],$$

where η_t and Ψ_t are the multipliers associated with constraints (11.77) and (11.78), respectively.

The first-order conditions for c_t^T, M_{t+1}^T, and b_{t+1} are given, respectively, by (assuming $\beta(1+r) = 1$)

$$u'(c_t^T) = E_t(\eta_t + \Psi_t),$$

$$\eta_t = \beta(\eta_{t+1} + \Psi_{t+1}),$$

$$E_{t+1}(\eta_{t+1} + \Psi_{t+1}) = E_t(\eta_t + \Psi_t).$$

From the first and third first-order conditions, it follows that

$$u'(c_t^T) = u'(c_{t+1}^T).$$

As in the discrete-time cash-in-advance model of chapter 5, section 5.6, traders will fully smooth consumption over time.

Combining the first-order conditions also yields

$$\eta_t \left(\frac{E_{t+1}}{\beta E_t} - 1 \right) = \Psi_t,$$

$$\eta_t i_t = \Psi_t,$$

where the last equation follows from the definition of the nominal interest rate, i_t, in (11.80) below. If $i_t > 0$, then $\Psi_t > 0$, which implies that the cash-in-advance constraint indeed binds.

11.5.3 Government

The government's flow constraint is given by

$$E_t h_{t+1} = (1+r)E_t h_t + M_{t+1} - M_t - \Gamma_t, \tag{11.79}$$

where h_t denotes international reserves.

11.5.4 Equilibrium Conditions

Perfect capital mobility (for traders) implies that the nominal interest rate is given by the interest parity condition (recall that $P_t^* = 1$):

$$1 + i_t = (1 + r)\frac{E_{t+1}}{E_t}. \tag{11.80}$$

Money market equilibrium implies that

$$M_t = \psi M_t^T + (1 - \psi)M_t^{NT}. \tag{11.81}$$

To obtain the economy's flow constraint, multiply the nontraders' flow constraint (given by equation 11.70) by $1 - \psi$ and the traders' flow constraint (given by equation 11.77) by ψ. Then add them up, taking into account the government's flow constraint (11.79) and the money market equilibrium condition (11.81):

$$k_{t+1} - k_t = rk_t + y_t - [\psi c_t^T + (1 - \psi)c_t^{NT}], \tag{11.82}$$

where $k_t \equiv h_t + \psi b_t$ are the per-capita net foreign assets of the economy as a whole.

Iterating forward (recalling that $\beta(1 + r) = 1$) and imposing the transversality condition $\lim[k_t/(1 + r)^{t-1}] = 0$ as $t \to \infty$, we obtain the resource constraint

$$(1 + r)k_0 + \sum_{t=0}^{\infty} \beta^t y_t = \sum_{t=0}^{\infty} \beta^t [\psi c_t^T + (1 - \psi)c_t^{NT}]. \tag{11.83}$$

In what follows, we will assume that $k_0 = 0$.[19] Substituting equations (11.73), (11.75), and (11.76) into the money market equilibrium condition (11.81) yields a quantity theory equation:

$$M_{t+1} = (1 - v_t)E_t y_t, \qquad t \geq 0. \tag{11.84}$$

To make it directly comparable to the quantity theory equation derived in chapter 5, and typically found in textbooks (usually written as $M_t V_t = P_t y_t$, where V_t denotes velocity), we can rewrite this last equation as

$$\frac{M_{t+1}}{1 - v_t} = E_t y_t, \qquad t \geq 0. \tag{11.85}$$

19. This assumption just ensures that the present discounted value of income is identical across traders and nontraders when the money supply or the exchange rate is fixed.

Velocity is thus given by $1/(1-v_t)$. Hence a higher v_t captures an increase in the velocity of circulation, which rationalizes our terminology of "velocity shocks" when referring to changes in v_t.

For further reference, notice that equations (11.73) and (11.84) imply that $M_{t+1}^{NT} = M_{t+1}$. Together with the money market equilibrium condition, this implies that

$$M_t = M_t^{NT} = M_t^T.$$

Since there are no differences across agents in terms of the endowment, all agents hold the same amount of money (on a per capita basis).

11.5.5 Equilibrium Consumption

We will now derive expressions for consumption of both traders and nontraders. To obtain nontraders' consumption, substitute the quantity theory equation (11.84) into (11.72) to obtain (recall that $M_t = M_t^{NT}$)

$$c_t^{NT} = \begin{cases} \frac{M_0}{E_0} + v_0 y_0, & t = 0, \\ \frac{(1-v_{t-1})E_{t-1}y_{t-1} + v_t E_t y_t}{E_t}, & t \geq 1. \end{cases} \tag{11.86}$$

This expression will prove useful when dealing with predetermined exchange rates. When dealing with flexible exchange rates, however, it will prove useful to use (11.84) to rewrite (11.86) as

$$c_t^{NT} = y_t - \frac{(M_{t+1} - M_t)}{E_t}, \quad t \geq 0. \tag{11.87}$$

To obtain traders' consumption, substitute (11.86) into (11.83) and solve for the constant level of c_t^T, denoted by c^T, to obtain

$$c^T = y^p + \frac{1-\psi}{\psi}\left[y^p - \frac{r}{1+r}\left(\frac{M_0}{E_0} + v_0 y_0 + \sum_{t=1}^{\infty}\beta^t \frac{(1-v_{t-1})E_{t-1}y_{t-1} + v_t E_t y_t}{E_t}\right)\right], \tag{11.88}$$

where

$$y^p \equiv \frac{r}{1+r}\sum_{t=0}^{\infty}\beta^t y_t$$

denotes permanent income. Alternatively, substitute (11.87) into (11.83) to obtain

$$c^T = y^p + \frac{r}{1+r}\frac{1-\psi}{\psi}\sum_{t=0}^{\infty}\beta^t\left(\frac{M_{t+1} - M_t}{E_t}\right). \tag{11.89}$$

11.5.6 Flexible Exchange Rates

Consider a flexible exchange rate regime in which the monetary authority sets a constant path of the nominal money supply:[20]

$$M_t = M, \qquad t \geq 0. \tag{11.90}$$

Substituting (11.90) into (11.87), we obtain nontraders' consumption:

$$c_t^{NT} = y_t, \qquad t \geq 0. \tag{11.91}$$

Two observations are worth making. First, consumption of nontraders will fluctuate one to one with fluctuations in the endowment. Flexible exchange rates provide no insulation whatsoever for nontraders from output fluctuations. Second, consumption of nontraders is not affected by velocity shocks.

Substituting (11.90) into (11.89), we obtain traders' consumption:

$$c^T = y^p. \tag{11.92}$$

Let us now derive the path of the nominal exchange rate. From the quantity theory equation (11.84), we obtain

$$E_t = \frac{M}{(1 - v_t)y_t}, \qquad t \geq 0. \tag{11.93}$$

It follows that

$$\frac{E_{t+1}}{E_t} = \frac{(1 - v_t)}{(1 - v_{t+1})} \frac{y_t}{y_{t+1}}.$$

When output increases (i.e., $y_{t+1} > y_t$) – and for constant velocity—the nominal exchange rate will fall (i.e., the domestic currency appreciates). Intuitively, higher output increases real money demand and hence leads to a fall in the price level (i.e., the nominal exchange rate). In contrast, when there is an increase in velocity (i.e., $v_{t+1} > v_t$)—and for constant output—the nominal exchange rate will increase (i.e., the domestic currency depreciates). Intuitively, an increase in velocity implies that more money is available to purchase the same level of output, which will lead to a higher price level.

20. We will consider only the extreme cases of a constant money supply (under flexible exchange rates) or a fixed exchange rate (under predetermined exchange rates). Exercise 5 at the end of the chapter shows that in the absence of output shocks and with logaritmic preferences, $\mu = 0$ is the optimal policy. For an extension of the analysis to more general policies, see Lahiri, Singh, and Végh (2006).

11.5.7 Fixed Exchange Rates

Consider now a fixed exchange rate regime where the monetary authority sets a constant value of the nominal exchange rate:

$$E_t = E.$$

Under a fixed exchange rate, we can use (11.86) to obtain consumption of nontraders:

$$c_t^{NT} = \begin{cases} \frac{M_0}{E} + v_0 y_0, & t = 0, \\ (1 - v_{t-1}) y_{t-1} + v_t y_t, & t \geq 1, \end{cases} \tag{11.94}$$

where M_0 is given. Since the exchange rate is fixed, initial real money balances are also given and equal to M_0/E. For the sake of comparison with the flexible exchange rate case, we will set initial real money balances equal to the value they take in the flexible exchange rates case. From equation (11.93), it follows that initial real money balances in the flexible exchange rates case are given by $M/E_0 = (1 - v_0)y_0$. We will therefore assume that in the fixed rates case, $M_0/E = (1 - v_0)y_0$. With this assumption, it follows that $c_0^{NT} = y_0$.

By the same token, using (11.88), consumption of traders is given by

$$c^T = y^p + \frac{1 - \psi}{\psi} \left\{ y^p - \frac{r}{1 + r} \left(y_0 + \sum_{t=1}^{\infty} \beta^t [(1 - v_{t-1}) y_{t-1} + v_t y_t] \right) \right\}. \tag{11.95}$$

Let us now derive the path of the nominal money supply, which is endogenous under fixed exchange rates. M_0 is given, as remarked earlier. The path of M_t, for $t \geq 1$, then follows from the quantity theory equation (11.84):

$$M_{t+1} = (1 - v_t) E y_t, \qquad t \geq 0.$$

11.5.8 Comparing Flexible versus Fixed Exchange Rates

We are now ready to ask the question: which exchange rate regime is better?

Velocity Shocks Only

Suppose that there are only velocity shocks (i.e., set $y_t = y^p$). Then, under flexible exchange rates, consumption of nontraders is completely flat and equal to y^p (as follows from equation 11.91). Further, as equation (11.92) indicates, traders' consumption is also equal to permanent income. Clearly, this equilibrium corresponds to the first-best. Both traders and nontraders perfectly smooth consumption over time.

Under fixed rates it follows from equation (11.94) that consumption of nontraders is given by

$$c_t^{NT} = \begin{cases} y^p, & t = 0, \\ y^p(1 + v_t - v_{t-1}), & t \geq 1. \end{cases} \tag{11.96}$$

Consumption of traders is in turn given by (from equation 11.95)

$$c^T = y^p\left[1 - \frac{r}{1+r}\frac{1-\psi}{\psi}\sum_{t=1}^{\infty}\beta^t(v_t - v_{t-1})\right]. \tag{11.97}$$

In what follows, it will prove useful to define a "permanent" velocity shock, v^p, as

$$v^p \equiv (1-\beta)\sum_{t=0}^{\infty}\beta^t v_t.$$

Under the assumption that $v_0 = v^p$, it follows that (see appendix 11.7.3)[21]

$$\sum_{t=1}^{\infty}\beta^t(v_t - v_{t-1}) = 0. \tag{11.98}$$

Substituting (11.98) into (11.97), we obtain traders' consumption:

$$c^T = y^p.$$

Traders' consumption is therefore the same under flexible and fixed exchange rates, and traders are thus indifferent between the two regimes. As for nontraders, it follows from (11.96) and (11.98) that the present discounted value of nontraders' consumption under fixed rates is the same as under flexible exchange rates. As a result nontraders are clearly better off under flexible exchange rates, in which case they have a flat path of consumption. Since traders are indifferent, we conclude that flexible exchange rates dominate.

What is the underlying intuition? The key lies in the role of the exchange rate as a shock absorber in the presence of velocity shocks. If velocity increases, the nominal exchange rate also increases (a nominal depreciation of the domestic currency), thus offsetting the shock. Under fixed exchange rates, the natural adjustment mechanism (i.e., the agents' ability to recompose their nominal money balances through the Central Bank) is not fully operative because nontraders cannot access asset markets. Hence fluctuations in velocity lead to fluctuations in consumption. Specifically, an increase in velocity (i.e., $v_t > v_{t-1}$) implies that more money balances are available for consumption; a decrease in velocity (i.e., $v_t < v_{t-1}$) implies that fewer money balances are available for consumption.

21. In a stochastic version of the model, the equivalent assumption would be that velocity shocks are white noise.

Output Shocks Only

Suppose that there are only output shocks (i.e., set $v_t = v > 0$). Then, under flexible exchange rates, consumption of nontraders and traders continues to be given by (11.91) and (11.92). Nontraders absorb the full variability of the endowment path.

Under fixed exchange rates, consumption of nontraders follows from (11.94):

$$c_t^{NT} = \begin{cases} y_0, & t = 0, \\ y_t + (1-v)(y_{t-1} - y_t), & t \geq 1. \end{cases} \tag{11.99}$$

Under the assumption that $y_0 = y^p$, it follows that (see appendix 11.7.4)

$$\sum_{t=1}^{\infty} \beta^t (y_{t-1} - y_t) = 0. \tag{11.100}$$

From (11.99) and (11.100) the present discounted value of c_t^{NT} under fixed rates will then be the same as under flexible exchange rates.

Consumption of traders follows from (11.95) and (11.100):

$$c^T = y^p. \tag{11.101}$$

As is the case under velocity shocks, traders' consumption is the same under flexible and fixed exchange rates. Traders are therefore indifferent between the two regimes.

For expositional clarity, it is useful to rewrite nontraders' consumption under fixed exchange rates, given by (11.99), as

$$c_t^{NT} = \begin{cases} y_0, & t = 0, \\ vy_t + (1-v)y_{t-1}, & t \geq 1, \end{cases} \tag{11.102}$$

which makes clear that from $t = 1$ onward, nontraders' consumption is an average of this period's and last period's output. Clearly, consumption of nontraders will fluctuate under both flexible and fixed exchange rates but will fluctuate less under fixed rates. Since, as shown above, the present discounted value of c_t^{NT} is the same under both regimes, nontraders' welfare will be higher under fixed exchange rates.

Intuitively, (11.102) states that today's consumption is a weighted average of last period's and this period's real sales revenues. Fixed exchange rates allow purchasing power to be transferred across periods, which, as equation (11.102) makes clear, results in some consumption smoothing over time. In contrast, under flexible exchange rates, a constant money supply implies that the real value of last period's sales is equal to current output. As a result current consumption depends solely on current output.

We conclude that since traders are indifferent between the two regimes and nontraders are better off under a fixed exchange rate, social welfare will be maximized if, in the presence of output shocks, a fixed exchange rate is adopted.

11.6 Final Remarks

This chapter has looked at how a small open economy responds to various shocks under different exchange rate regimes. We have seen that, as summarized in table 11.1, the optimal exchange rate regime will depend on both the type of friction and the type of shock. In particular, under sticky prices, if monetary shocks are predominant, then predetermined exchange rates will be optimal. In contrast, if real shocks dominate, flexible exchange rates become optimal. If, however, the economy is mainly characterized by asset market frictions, then the opposite is true: flexible exchange rates are optimal under monetary shocks and predetermined exchange rates are optimal under real shocks. In practice, which regime is optimal may therefore well vary from country to country and even over time.

In addition to the type of friction and type of shock, there are surely other important factors in practice that we have ignored. In particular, we have not focused on the properties of the instrument themselves. For example, as argued by Calvo and Végh (1999), by the mere virtue of being a price rather than a quantity, the nominal exchange rate conveys a much clearer signal to the markets of the Central Bank's policy than a money supply target. In other words, the nominal exchange rate is a more "transparent" instrument than the money supply. Atkeson, Chari, and Kehoe (2007) formalize this argument—while also taking into account the "tightness" of different instruments in terms of how close they are to the variable they are meant to influence—and conclude that the nominal exchange rate dominates the money supply as a policy instrument.

11.7 Appendixes

11.7.1 Mathematica Program on Demand Shocks in Sticky-Prices Model

The economy of section 11.4.9 can be reduced to the following dynamic system in m_t, n_t, and π_t:

$$\dot{m}_t = m_t\left[\mu + r - \frac{c^T}{\gamma}\frac{\alpha n_t^{(1-\gamma)(1-1/\sigma)}}{m_t^{1/\sigma+(1-\gamma)(1-1/\sigma)}}\right],$$

$$\dot{n}_t = n_t(\mu - \pi_t),$$

$$\dot{\pi}_t = \theta\left(y_f^N - \frac{1-\gamma}{\gamma}\frac{c^T}{m_t}n_t\right).$$

This program was solved numerically using Mathematica for the following parameter values: $c^T = 1$; $y_f^N = 1, \alpha = 1, \gamma = 0.5, \mu = 0.5, \theta = 0.5$, and $\sigma = 0.5$.

11.7.2 Conditions for a Binding Cash-in-Advance Constraint in the Asset Market Segmentation Model

This appendix derives the conditions needed for the cash-in-advance constraint to bind for both nontraders and traders in the model of section 11.5 and then provides an example of the restrictions that need to be imposed on the output and velocity processes.

When Does the Cash-in-Advance Constraint Bind for Nontraders?

Nontraders choose $\{c_t^N, M_{t+1}^N\}_{t=0}^{\infty}$ to maximize lifetime utility (11.69) subject to the sequence of flow constraints given by (11.70) and the sequence of cash-in-advance constraints given by (11.71) for a given M_0. In terms of the Lagrangian, we have

$$\mathcal{L} = \sum_{t=0}^{\infty} \beta^t u(c_t^{NT}) + \sum_{t=0}^{\infty} \beta^t \lambda_t (M_t^{NT} + E_t y_t - E_t c_t^{NT} - M_{t+1}^{NT})$$

$$+ \sum_{t=0}^{\infty} \beta^t \Psi_t \left(M_t^{NT} + v_t E_t y_t - E_t c_t^{NT}\right),$$

where λ_t and Ψ_t are the multipliers associated with constraints (11.70) and (11.71), respectively. The first-order conditions for c_t^{NT} and M_{t+1}^{NT} are given by

$$u'(c_t^{NT}) = E_t(\lambda_t + \Psi_t), \tag{11.103}$$

$$\beta(\lambda_{t+1} + \Psi_{t+1}) = \lambda_t. \tag{11.104}$$

The Kuhn–Tucker condition for Ψ_t is given by

$$M_t^{NT} + v_t E_t y_t \geq E_t c_t^{NT}, \qquad \Psi_t \geq 0,$$

$$\left(M_t^{NT} + v_t E_t y_t - E_t c_t^{NT}\right) \Psi_t = 0.$$

Suppose that $\Psi_t > 0$; that is, the cash-in-advance constraint binds. Then using (11.103) and (11.104), we can write

$$\frac{u'(c_{t+1}^{NT})}{u'(c_t^{NT})} = \frac{1}{\beta} \frac{E_{t+1}}{E_t} \frac{\lambda_t}{\lambda_t + \Psi_t}.$$

Hence, for the cash-in-advance constraint to bind, it must be the case that

$$u'(c_t^{NT}) > \beta \frac{E_t}{E_{t+1}} u'(c_{t+1}^{NT}). \tag{11.105}$$

If the cash-in-advance constraint binds, it means that nontraders prefer not to carry over nominal money balances from one period to the next even though doing so would provide more consumption tomorrow. In other words, money balances are not used for saving purposes. In this case—and as condition (11.105) indicates—the consumer is unwilling to save and therefore today's marginal utility will be higher than tomorrow's adjusted by the discount factor and the return on money.

To fix ideas, consider the case of logarithmic preferences. Condition (11.105) then reduces to

$$c_t^{NT} < c_{t+1}^{NT} \frac{1}{\beta} \frac{E_{t+1}}{E_t}. \tag{11.106}$$

Using the quantity theory (equation 11.84), we can rewrite this equation (defining $1 + \mu_{t+1} \equiv M_{t+2}/M_{t+1}$):

$$\frac{c_t^{NT}}{c_{t+1}^{NT}} < \frac{1}{\beta}(1 + \mu_{t+1}) \left(\frac{1 - v_t}{1 - v_{t+1}} \right) \left(\frac{y_t}{y_{t+1}} \right). \tag{11.107}$$

Flexible Exchange Rates Consider the case of flexible exchange rates with a constant money supply. In this case, $c_t^{NT} = y_t$ and $\mu_{t+1} = 0$. Equation (11.107) then reduces to

$$\beta < \frac{1 - v_t}{1 - v_{t+1}}. \tag{11.108}$$

As long as this condition holds (which implies a restriction on the variability of the velocity shocks), the cash-in-advance constraint will bind. Clearly, since this condition involves exogenous variables, one can always choose parameters such that it will hold.

Fixed Exchange Rates Consider the case of fixed exchange rates. In this case, $E_{t+1} = E_t = E$. Therefore use condition (11.106), taking into account (11.94), to obtain

$$\beta < \frac{(1 - v_t)y_t + v_{t+1}y_{t+1}}{(1 - v_{t-1})y_{t-1} + v_t y_t}. \tag{11.109}$$

Again, since this condition involves only exogenous variables, one can always choose β and output and velocity processes such that it holds.

Intuition To understand the intuition as to why the cash-in-advance constraint may bind for nontraders, consider the case of flexible exchange rates and no velocity shocks (i.e., output shocks only). In that case, condition (11.108) will always hold because, by assumption, $\beta < 1$. Intuitively, suppose that $y_t > y_{t+1}$ and consider the nontrader's choice at time t. Based on the consumption-smoothing motive, nontraders would want to save in order to consume more next period when output will be low. However, given that $\mu_t = 0$, periods of high output will coincide with periods in which the real return on nominal money balances is low. To see this, notice that using the cash-in-advance constraint the gross real return on holding money is given by

$$\frac{E_t}{E_{t+1}} = \frac{y_{t+1}}{y_t}.$$

Since $y_t > y_{t+1}$, then $E_t/E_{t+1} < 1$, which means a negative real return on money. Hence, with logarithmic preferences, the nontrader's desire to dissave based on the negative real return on money more than offsets the desire to save based on consumption-smoothing motives.

When Does the Cash-in-Advance Constraint Bind for Traders?

For the cash-in-advance constraint to bind for traders, we just need to ensure that the nominal interest rate is positive. The restrictions needed for this depend on the exchange rate regime.

Flexible Exchange Rates From the interest parity condition (11.80), a positive nominal interest rate requires that

$$\frac{E_{t+1}}{E_t} > \frac{1}{1+r}.$$

Using the quantity theory equation (11.84), it follows that

$$\frac{E_{t+1}}{E_t} = \left(\frac{1-v_t}{1-v_{t+1}}\right)\frac{y_t}{y_{t+1}}.$$

Combining the last two equations—and recalling that $\beta(1+r) = 1$—it follows that if

$$\beta < \left(\frac{1-v_t}{1-v_{t+1}}\right)\frac{y_t}{y_{t+1}}, \tag{11.110}$$

then the nominal interest rate will always be positive and the cash-in-advance constraint will always bind for traders as well.

Fixed Exchange Rates Under fixed exchange rates, the interest parity condition (11.80) indicates that the nominal interest rate will always be positive since $1 + i_t = 1 + r$.

An Example

Let us illustrate the restrictions necessary to ensure a binding cash-in-advance constraint for the cases of only one shock at a time (the case studied in the text). Suppose that $\beta = 0.96$.

Output Shocks Only Suppose that $v_t = v = 0.2 > 0$ and that y_t alternates between 1.04 and 1. For nontraders, (11.108) holds since $\beta < 1$ and condition (11.109) becomes (assuming the most restrictive case which is $y_{t-1} = 1.04$, $y_t = 1$, and $y_{t+1} = 1.04$)

$$\beta < \frac{(1-v)y_t + vy_{t+1}}{(1-v)y_{t-1} + vy_t},$$

which reduces to $\beta < 0.977$ and hence holds. For traders, (11.110) is satisfied since $\beta < y_t/y_{t+1} = 0.962$, and hence the cash-in-advance constraint binds under both flexible and fixed exchange rates.

Velocity Shocks Suppose that $y_t = y_{t+1} = y^p$. The velocity variable alternates between two values: 0.20 and 0.22. Assume first that $v_{t-1} = 0.2$, $v_t = 0.22$, and $v_{t+1} = 0.2$. Then, for nontraders under flexible exchange rates, it must be the case that

$$\beta < \frac{1-v_t}{1-v_{t+1}}, \tag{11.111}$$

which holds since $\beta < 0.975$. Under fixed rates, it must the case that

$$\beta < \frac{1-v_t+v_{t+1}}{1-v_{t-1}+v_t}, \tag{11.112}$$

which holds—since under the most restrictive case where $v_{t-1} = 0.2$, $v_t = 0.22$, and $v_{t+1} = 0.2$—then $\beta < 0.961$.

For traders, the cash-in-advance constraint always binds under fixed exchange rates.

11.7.3 Proof That $\sum_{t=1}^{\infty} \beta^t (v_t - v_{t-1}) = 0$ If $v_0 = v^p$

Rewrite $\sum_{t=1}^{\infty} \beta^t (v_t - v_{t-1})$ as

$$\sum_{t=1}^{\infty} \beta^t (v_t - v_{t-1}) = -\beta v_0 + (1-\beta) \sum_{t=1}^{\infty} \beta^t v_t.$$

But, by definition of v^p and given that $v_0 = v^p$, $\sum_{t=1}^{\infty} \beta^t v_t = [v^p/(1-\beta)] - v^p = [\beta/(1-\beta)]v^p$. Hence

$$\sum_{t=1}^{\infty} \beta^t (v_t - v_{t-1}) = \beta(v^p - v_0) = 0,$$

as $v_0 = v^p$.

11.7.4 Proof That $\sum_{t=1}^{\infty} \beta^t (y_{t-1} - y_t) = 0$ If $y_0 = y^p$

Replace v_t by y_t in section 11.7.3 above.

Exercises

1. (Role of the nominal exchange rate in the adjustment to a real shock) This exercise shows that the extent of the adjustment in the nominal exchange rate in the world of section 11.2 depends on how preferences are specified (i.e., on how the demand shock is modeled). To this effect, consider the model of section 11.2 and, in this context,[22]

a. Suppose that preferences are given by

$$\int_0^{\infty} [\log(c_t^T) + \gamma \log(c_t^N) + \alpha \log(z_t)] \exp(-\beta t) dt, \tag{11.113}$$

where γ and α are positive parameters. Suppose, as in the text, that there is a reduction in the demand for nontradables (a fall in γ in this case). Show that under flexible exchange rates, the corresponding increase in the real exchange rate will be effected solely through a fall in the nominal price of nontradable goods.

b. Suppose that preferences are given by

$$\int_0^{\infty} [\gamma \log(c_t^T) + \log(c_t^N) + \alpha \log(z_t)] \exp(-\beta t) dt, \tag{11.114}$$

and suppose that that there is an increase in γ. Show that under flexible exchange rates, the corresponding increase in the real exchange rate will be effected through an increase in the nominal exchange rate.

2. (Terms of trade shocks for different values of σ) Repeat the analysis of section 11.3.7 for the cases of $\sigma = 1$ and $\sigma > 1$. In particular, show that for the case of $\sigma > 1$, the trade balance will be initially in surplus.

3. (Demand shocks under alternative preferences specification) Solve the model of section 11.4 with preferences given by (11.68). Analyze the economy's response to a permanent reduction in ϕ under both predetermined and flexible exchange rates and show that the adjustment is the same.

4. (Shocks to full employment output of nontradable goods in sticky-prices model) Consider the model of section 11.4 with preferences given by (11.66). Solve the model numerically for an

22. Technically, the price index used to deflate nominal money balances would change depending on the weights attached to c_t^T and c_t^N in the preferences below, but that is really irrelevant for our purposes.

unanticipated and permanent fall in y_f^N. In particular, make sure that you can replicate figure 11.13. (To carry out this exercise, you may want to modify the Mathematica program available online, which solves for the case of a rise in γ.)

5. (Optimality of constant money supply in segmented markets economy) Consider the model with segmented asset markets developed in section 11.5. Assume logarithmic preferences. Suppose that the policy maker maximizes the following objective function:

$$\sum_{t=0}^{\infty} \beta^t \left[\psi \log(c_t^T) + (1 - \psi) \log(c_t^{NT}) \right], \tag{11.115}$$

where $\psi \in (0, 1)$ is a parameter. Show that, in the absence of output shocks, the policy maker finds it optimal to set the rate of money growth to zero.

References

Aghion, Philippe, Philippe Bacchetta, Romain Ranciere, and Kenneth Rogoff. 2006. Exchange rate volatility and productivity growth: The role of financial development. Working Paper 12117. National Bureau of Economic Research, Cambridge, MA.

Alvarez, Fernando and Andrew Atkeson. 1997. Money and exchange rates in the Grossman–Weiss–Rotemberg model. *Journal of Monetary Economics* 40: 619–40.

Atkeson, Andrew, V.V. Chari, and Patrick J. Kehoe. 2007. On the optimal choice of a monetary policy instrument. Working Paper 13398. National Bureau of Economic Research, Cambridge, MA.

Baxter, Marianne and Alan C. Stockman. 1989. Business cycles and the exchange-rate regime: Some international evidence. *Journal of Monetary Economics* 23: 377–400.

Beck, Thorsten, Asli Demirguc-Kunt, and Maria Soledad Martinez Peria. 2007. Reaching out: Access to and use of banking services across countries. *Journal of Financial Economics* 85 (1): 234–66.

Broda, Christian. 2004. Terms of trade and exchange rate regimes in developing countries. *Journal of International Economics* 63 (1): 31–58.

Calvo, Guillermo A. 1983. Staggered prices in a utility-maximizing framework. *Journal of Monetary Economics* 12 (3): 383–98.

Calvo, Guillermo A., and Carlos A. Végh. 1999. Inflation stabilization and BOP crises in developing countries. In John B. Taylor and Michael Woodford eds., *Handbook of Macroeconomics*. Amsterdam: North Holland, 1551–1614.

Campbell, John Y. 2006. Household Finance. *Journal of Finance* 61 (4): 1553–1604.

Claessens, Stijn. 2006. Access to financial services: A review of the issues and public policy objectives. *World Bank Research Observer* 21 (2): 207–40.

Dai, Chenyuan, and Wai-Mun Chia. 2008. Terms of trade shocks and exchange rate regimes in East Asian countries. Unpublished. Singapore: Nanyang Technological University.

Devereux, Michael B., and Charles Engel. 1998. Fixed vs. floating exchange rates: How price setting affects the optimal choice of exchange-rate regime. Working Paper 6867. National Bureau of Economic Research, Cambridge, MA.

Edwards, Sebastian, and Eduardo Levy Yeyati. 2003. Flexible exchange rates as shock absorbers. Working Paper 9867. National Bureau of Economic Research, Cambridge, MA.

Friedman, Milton. 1953. The case for flexible exchange rates. In *Essays on Positive Economics*. Chicago: University of Chicago Press, 157–203.

Ghosh, Atish, Anne-Marie Gulde, Jonathan Ostry, and Holger Wolf. 1997. Does the nominal exchange rate regime matter? Working Paper 5874. National Bureau of Economic Research, Cambridge, MA.

Lahiri, Amartya, Rajesh Singh, and Carlos A. Végh. 2006. Optimal monetary policy under asset market segmentation. Unpublished manuscript. University of British Columbia.

Lahiri, Amartya, Rajesh Singh, and Carlos A. Végh. 2007. Segmented asset markets and optimal exchange rate regimes. *Journal of International Economics* 72 (1): 1–21.

Lahiri, Amartya, Rajesh Singh, and Carlos A. Végh. 2008. Optimal exchange rate regimes: Turning Mundell–Fleming's dictum on its head. In Carmen M. Reinhart, Carlos A. Végh, and Andres Velasco, eds., *Money, Crises, and Transition: Essays in Honor of Guillermo A. Calvo*. Cambridge: MIT Press, 21–40.

Lucas, Robert E., Jr. 1982. Interest rates and currency prices in a two-country world. *Journal of Monetary Economics* 10 (3): 335–59.

Magud, Nicolas. 2006. Exchange rate regime choice and country characteristics: An empirical investigation into the role of openness. Unpublished Manuscript. University of Oregon.

Mulligan, Casey B., and Xavier Sala-i-Martin. 2000. Extensive margins and the demand for money at low interest rates. *Journal of Political Economy* 108 (5): 961–91.

12 Real Anchors

12.1 Introduction

As discussed in chapter 5, the "traditional" nominal anchors for an open economy are either the nominal money supply or the nominal exchange rate. We refer to them as "anchors" because the rate of growth of either the money supply or the nominal exchange rate will determine (i.e., anchor) the long-run inflation rate. While, in the short or medium run, the inflation rate may deviate from the rate of money growth or the rate of devaluation, it will eventually converge to those values in the long run. A newer nominal anchor—and clearly the most widely used in recent times—is the nominal interest rate, as covered in chapter 9. While a policy based on controlling the level of the nominal interest rate may lead to indeterminacies, we have seen that under certain conditions, such a policy can lead to a well-defined long-run inflation rate. Long-run inflation targets—as long as they are fully credible—may also provide a nominal anchor in the context of inflation-targeting rules.

In this context, it seems clear that policy makers need to set *some* nominal anchor (i.e., the money supply, the exchange rate, the nominal interest rate, or an inflation target) to anchor long-run inflation. Economic agents' expectations will adjust accordingly. In the absence of a nominal anchor, there would be nothing in the model to tie down long-run inflation. In practice, we take this to mean that inflation would be determined just by expectations (which in turn would have no fundamentals to be based on) and hence would be highly unstable.

Despite such strong theoretical prescriptions, policy makers around the world have often resorted to real, as opposed to nominal, anchors. After all, the reasoning goes, if one is interested in real variables (e.g., the real exchange rate or the real interest rate) that have a direct bearing on growth and consumption, why not try to bypass nominal variables altogether and set the value of these real variables? Hence, and despite dire warnings from neoclassically inclined economists about the perils of forgoing a nominal anchor, policy makers have time and time again tried to conduct monetary policy by attempting to control real variables such as the real exchange rate or the real interest rate.

Being a key relative price in any open economy, the real exchange rate is arguably the most popular real target among policy makers. A policy of "real exchange rate targeting" typically aims at controlling (at least in the short and medium term) the level of the real exchange rate in an effort to keep it roughly constant in the face of external or domestic shocks and/or engineering a higher level of the real exchange rate (i.e., a more depreciated currency in real terms) to keep exports competitive and achieve a smaller deficit/larger surplus in the trade balance. A particular case of real exchange rate targeting are the so-called purchasing power parity (PPP) rules that typically adjust the nominal exchange rate by past inflation in an effort to keep the real exchange rate roughly constant. As discussed in box 12.1, these PPP rules were highly popular in Latin America, starting with Chile in 1965 and Brazil in 1968.

Box 12.1
PPP rules in practice: How did it all begin?

Purchasing power parity rules refer to monetary policy rules that set the rate of devaluation as a function of some measure of the differential between domestic and foreign inflation with the aim of keeping a relatively stable real exchange rate. As such, they are a particular case of "crawling pegs," a term coined by John Williamson in a 1965 article to refer to predetermined exchange rate regimes where the peg is adjusted in small or gradual steps, as opposed to the so-called adjustable pegs that prevailed under the Bretton Woods regime, in which currencies would be devalued only occasionally but by a large magnitude (and, if some capital mobility was allowed, in conjunction with a loss of international reserves and/or capital outflows). The key qualifier of PPP rules as crawling pegs is that they are *passive* crawling pegs because the rate of devaluation is set in reaction to past inflation differentials, in sharp contrast to *active* crawling pegs of the type described in chapter 13 in which the rate of devaluation is set with the objective of influencing future expectations of inflation.

The first country to adopt a formal PPP rule appears to have been Chile in April 1965. The idea—as related in personal communication with the author by Carlos Massad—was to abandon the existing regime whereby the exchange rate would only be adjusted when exchange rate pressures had become unbearable and replace it by a system of frequent and small adjustments, in such a way as to discourage speculative attacks and keep a relatively stable real exchange rate.[a] Table 12.1 provides details on the number, frequency, and rates of adjustment. This PPP rule was implemented in the context of unified exchange rate markets and other market-oriented measures. The rule ended in November 1970 when President Salvador Allende took power and returned to exchange rate controls and widespread regulation of the economy.[b] The idea of frequent but small devaluations—in contrast to periods of fixed exchange rates followed by large devaluations—comes across clearly in figure 12.1, which plots the nominal exchange rate in Chile during the period 1960 to 1971.

In August 1968—and partly influenced by the Chilean experience—Brazil adopted a PPP rule as well, officially described as a regime of "mini-desvalorizacoes," the Portuguese expression for "mini-devaluations."[c] Up to that point Brazil used to devalue once a year, with devaluations exceeding 15 percent. The devaluation would typically be the result of domestic inflation exceeding world inflation

a. Carlos Massad (born in 1932), a Chilean economist, was president of the Central Bank of Chile from 1967 to 1970 and from 1996 to 2003. In 1964–1965, when the Chilean PPP rule was born, he was vice president of the Central Bank (a position he held from 1964 to 1967) and part of President Eduardo Frei's economic team.
b. For a detailed account of this period, see Ffrench-Davis (1981). Chile returned to a PPP rule in the period 1985 to 1992, as discussed in box 12.2.
c. See Fendt (1981) for an account of the Brazilian experience.

Box 12.1
(continued)

Table 12.1
Chile: Adjustments of the nominal exchange rate, 1965 to 1970

	Number of adjustments	Average number of days between adjustments	Rates of adjustment (%)		
			Maximum	Average	Minimum
1965 (May–December)	8	30.0	2.9	1.5	0.1
1966	12	30.4	2.3	1.8	1.2
1967	16	22.8	2.4	1.8	0.7
1968	24	15.3	1.9	1.2	0.8
1969	19	19.2	1.7	1.4	0.8
1970 (January–July)	12	17.6	1.9	1.7	1.4

Source: Ffrench-Davis (1981).

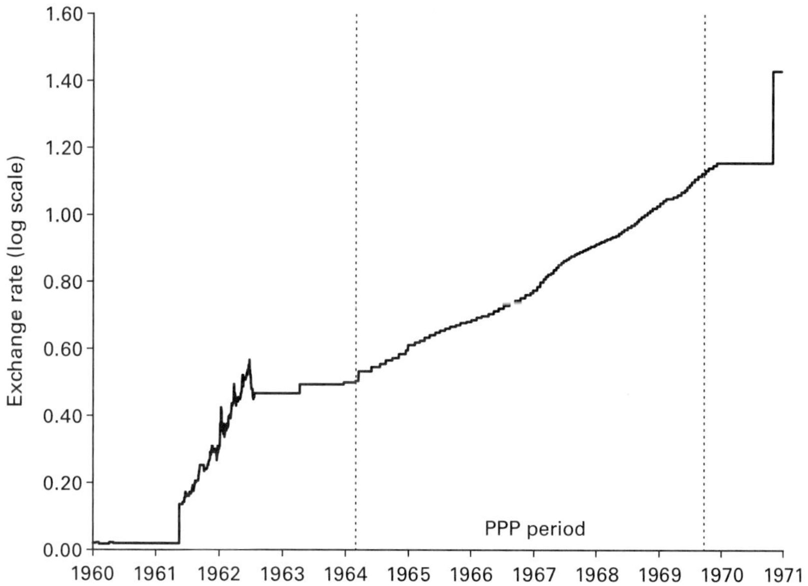

Years on horizontal axis denote data as of December.

Figure 12.1
Chile: Nominal exchange rate, 1960 to 1971.

Box 12.1
(continued)

and the pressure on international reserves brought about by the anticipation of yet another large devaluation. According to Bacha (1979), from the inception of the system until December 1976, the currency was devalued 81 times, or about once every 38 days. The mean devaluation was 1.5 percent. Unlike the Chilean case, the adoption of a PPP rule in Brazil went hand in hand with rather stringent exchange rate controls. With occasional deviations (due to terms of trade shocks or short-lived inflation stabilization programs), Brazil followed PPP rules—even if those rules were not made explicit—until the implementation of the Real Plan in July 1994.

In a similar vein, and after a very serious exchange rate crisis in 1967, Colombia implicitly adopted a PPP rule whereby the currency was devalued once or twice a week in response to the differential between domestic inflation and that of its major trading partners. Such a regime continued essentially in place until 1991 (see Cardenas 2007, ch. 6). As recounted by Urrutia (1981), Colombia's PPP rule was never made explicit when originally implemented and for many years the government maintained the fiction that the mini-devaluations reflected supply and demand considerations. Like Brazil, Colombia's implicit PPP rule was implemented in the midst of severe exchange rate controls.

In sum, the birth of PPP rules can be traced back to Latin America (in particular, Chile, Brazil, and Colombia) in the mid- to late 1960s. The motivation for the adoption of a regime of mini-devaluations was to escape the vicious cycle (theoretically described in chapter 16) in which a high rate of domestic inflation—inconsistent with a fixed exchange rate—would lead eventually to a costly exchange rate crisis and a large devaluation. Policy makers thought of avoiding these recurrent crises by devaluing frequently and by small amounts. At least from a conceptual point of view, this policy change was arguably for the better. If one takes as given that domestic inflation will be higher than foreign inflation due to monetary financing of underlying fiscal deficits, then setting a rate of devaluation consistent with that rate of inflation (and have a "sustainable" regime, to use the language of chapter 5) is clearly better than the alternative of living in a world in which, with daunting regularity, the economy goes through a full-fledge exchange rate crisis.[d] The perils—as stressed in the text—is that the economy may lose its nominal anchor and/or that shocks that require a real depreciation will be more inflationary than would otherwise be the case.

d. Theoretically, in terms of our cash-in-advance model, a constant rate of devaluation is better in terms of welfare than a zero rate of devaluation followed at time T by a discrete jump.

From a macroeconomic point of view, two main questions arise regarding real exchange rate targeting. First, is it effective? In other words, can policy makers "control" the level of the real exchange rate, at least temporarily? Second—and in light of the discussion above on nominal anchors—does real interest rate targeting lead to higher (and possibly more variable) inflation?

As always, our first instinct is to go back to the simplest model and see what we can learn from it. To this effect, section 12.2 focuses on real exchange rate targeting in the simple cash-in-advance model with flexible prices introduced in chapter 7. As two useful conceptual extremes, we first focus on perfect capital mobility and then on financial autarky. Under perfect capital mobility, we first show that in a stationary equilibrium, the real exchange rate is fully determined by consumption of tradable and nontradable goods and cannot be affected by (permanent) changes in policy. Policy makers can, however, affect the level of the real exchange rate temporarily. A (temporarily) higher real exchange rate (i.e., a more depreciated level of the domestic currency in real terms) can be achieved by a temporarily higher rate of devaluation (inflation) that makes tradable consumption more expensive. Under no capital mobility, we show that a temporarily higher level of the real exchange rate can also be achieved. Remarkably, while this does not require higher inflation, it does call for ever-increasing domestic real interest rates, which are engineered by a tight monetary policy. Since, in practice, most economies fall somewhere in between the extremes of perfect capital mobility and no capital mobility, this section's overall message is that, while policy makers can succeed in setting a temporarily higher level of the real exchange rate (i.e., a more depreciated level of the currency in real terms), it will come at the cost of some combination of higher inflation and higher domestic real interest rates.

Before leaving the world of flexible prices, section 12.3 illustrates the perils of PPP-type rules in the context of our basic model. Suppose that policy makers set the (future) rate of devaluation as a function of some future target for the real exchange rate relative to today's level. If today's real exchange rate is, say, low (i.e., the currency is relatively appreciated in real terms) relative to the future target, policy makers will set a high rate of devaluation. We show that this economy completely loses its nominal anchor in the sense that the rate of devaluation is undetermined. Whatever is the path of the real exchange rate expected by the private sector, there will exist a rate of devaluation that is consistent with such a path. There is nothing in the model to tie down the future rate of devaluation.

Section 12.4 focuses on a sticky-inflation economy. Policy makers follow a PPP-type rule whereby the rate of devaluation is set taking into account the current inflation rate of nontradable goods. In this context think of a shock—such as an increase in the supply of tradable goods—that requires a fall in the relative price of tradable goods (i.e., a real appreciation). In the absence of a PPP rule, this real appreciation would take place over time, with the nontradable goods inflation being above the (constant) rate of devaluation. With a PPP rule in place, a higher rate of devaluation delays this process in the short term but, of course, cannot prevent the required real appreciation in the long run. The higher rate of devaluation requires, however, an even higher rate of inflation to effect the required real appreciation. Hence the presence of the PPP rule is clearly inflationary.

We then switch our attention to real interest rate targeting. A prime example of using a real interest rate as the main policy instrument is Chile during the period 1985 to 2001. Section 12.5 makes use of the sticky-inflation economy developed in section 12.4 to shed light on this issue. Our first result is that a pure real interest rate targeting whereby policy makers set a given level of the real interest rate leads to an undetermined inflation rate. There is nothing in the model to tie down the level of inflation. We then study a Taylor-type rule whereby the real interest rate is changed according to the deviation of inflation from an inflation target. If credible, the inflation target anchors long-term inflation expectations and thus provides a nominal anchor to the economy.

Finally, Section 12.6 illustrates the perils of the so-called threshold rules whereby policy makers pre-announce policy measures conditional on some target. For instance, policy makers could announce that if the current account deficit reaches a certain threshold, then a tariff will be imposed. We show how this type of rules may lead to multiple equilibria situations in which the mere announcement of such a rule precipitates the precise scenario that policy makers are trying to avoid.

12.2 Real Exchange Rate Targeting in a Flexible Prices Model

We begin our journey by looking at real exchange rate targeting in the context of a world with flexible prices. Specifically, consider the cash-in-advance, two-good model (tradables and nontradables) analyzed in chapter 7. Unlike in chapter 7, however, we will also consider the case of no capital mobility. We will therefore set up the model in such a way that we can then specialize it to the cases of perfect capital mobility or no capital mobility.[1] We will assume that the economy is operating under predetermined exchange rates and that the foreign inflation rate is zero.

12.2.1 Consumers

Let preferences be given by

$$\int_0^\infty [u(c_t^T) + v(c_t^N)] \exp(-\beta t) dt, \tag{12.1}$$

where c_t^T and c_t^N denote consumption of tradable and nontradable goods, respectively, $\beta(> 0)$ is the discount rate, and $u(.)$ and $v(.)$ are strictly increasing and strictly concave functions. The country faces a given world real interest rate, r. The domestic real interest rate in terms of tradable goods, ρ, may differ from r due to imperfect capital mobility.[2] The domestic discount factor (in terms of tradable goods) is then given by

$$D_t = \exp\left(-\int_0^t \rho_s ds\right). \tag{12.2}$$

Notice that in the particular case in which $\rho_s = r$, then $D_t = \exp(-rt)$.

The intertemporal constraint is given by (see appendix 12.8.1)[3]

$$\int_0^\infty \left(y^T + \frac{y^N}{e_t} + \tau_t\right) D_t dt = \int_0^\infty \left(c_t^T + \frac{c_t^N}{e_t} + i_t m_t\right) D_t dt, \tag{12.3}$$

1. We follow Calvo, Reinhart, and Végh (1995).

2. Note that ρ is not to be confused with r^d, introduced later in the chapter, which denotes the domestic real interest rate in terms of *nontradable* goods.

3. For simplicity, and with no loss of generality, we assume initial real financial assets equal to zero.

where y^T and y^N are the constant levels of the endowment of tradable and nontradable goods, respectively, e_t is the real exchange rate, defined as the relative price of tradables in terms of nontradables, τ_t are lump-sum transfers from the government, i_t is the nominal interest rate, and m_t are real money balances in terms of the numéraire (tradable goods). Money is introduced through a cash-in-advance constraint:

$$m_t = \alpha\left(c_t^T + \frac{c_t^N}{e_t}\right), \tag{12.4}$$

where α is a positive parameter. Substituting the cash-in-advance constraint (12.4) into the intertemporal budget constraint, we obtain

$$\int_0^\infty \left(y^T + \frac{y^N}{e_t} + \tau_t\right) D_t dt = \int_0^\infty \left(c_t^T + \frac{c_t^N}{e_t}\right)(1+\alpha i_t) D_t dt. \tag{12.5}$$

The consumer chooses $\{c_t^T, c_t^N\}_{t=0}^\infty$ to maximize (12.1) subject to (12.5). In terms of the Lagrangian,

$$\begin{aligned}\mathcal{L} = &\int_0^\infty [u(c_t^T) + v(c_t^N)] \exp(-\beta t) dt \\ &+ \bar{\lambda}\left[\int_0^\infty \left(y^T + \frac{y^N}{e_t} + \tau_t\right) D_t dt - \int_0^\infty \left(c_t^T + \frac{c_t^N}{e_t}\right)(1+\alpha i_t) D_t dt\right],\end{aligned}$$

where we have denoted by $\bar{\lambda}$ the multiplier associated with constraint (12.5).

The first-order conditions are given by

$$u'(c_t^T) \exp(-\beta t) = \bar{\lambda}(1+\alpha i_t) D_t, \tag{12.6}$$

$$v'(c_t^N) \exp(-\beta t) = \frac{\bar{\lambda}}{e_t}(1+\alpha i_t) D_t. \tag{12.7}$$

These are, of course, the familiar first-order conditions from chapter 7. The only difference is that, because of the possible endogeneity of the real interest rate under capital controls, the term $\exp(-\beta t)$ is not necessarily equal to D_t. Naturally, under perfect capital mobility, these two terms would cancel out (see below).

12.2.2 Government

The government's budget constraint takes its usual form:

$$\dot{h}_t = r h_t + \dot{m}_t + \varepsilon_t m_t - \tau_t, \tag{12.8}$$

where h_t denote the government's net foreign assets and ε_t is the rate of devaluation.

12.2.3 Equilibrium Conditions

Under perfect capital mobility, $\rho_t = r$ and interest parity holds (recall that foreign inflation is zero):

$$i_t = r + \varepsilon_t. \tag{12.9}$$

For the case of capital controls, we will define the nominal interest rate as

$$i_t = \rho_t + \varepsilon_t. \tag{12.10}$$

Equilibrium in the nontradable goods market requires that

$$c_t^N = y^N. \tag{12.11}$$

As shown in appendix 12.8.1, the economy's resource constraint is given by (assuming the economy's initial net foreign assets are zero)

$$\frac{y^T}{r} = \int_0^\infty c_t^T \exp(-rt)dt. \tag{12.12}$$

12.2.4 Perfect Capital Mobility

Under perfect capital mobility, $\rho_t = r$ for all t and the model reduces to our standard cash-in-advance model introduced in chapter 7. Assuming $\beta = r$ and using equation (12.11), first-order conditions (12.6) and (12.7) can be expressed as

$$u'(c_t^T) = \bar{\lambda}(1 + \alpha i_t), \tag{12.13}$$

$$e_t = \frac{u'(c_t^T)}{v'(y^N)}. \tag{12.14}$$

Consider first a perfect foresight equilibrium path (PFEP) with a constant real exchange rate; that is, $e_t = e$. Condition (12.14) makes clear that for e_t to be constant over time, c_t^T must be constant. From the resource constraint (12.12), this constant value of c_t^T would be given by

$$c^T = y^T.$$

From equation (12.14), the constant value of the real exchange rate would thus be given by

$$e = \frac{u'(y^T)}{v'(y^N)}.$$

From (12.13), the constancy of c_t^T requires a constant nominal interest rate, which, by the interest parity condition (12.9), necessitates a constant rate of devaluation. Notice that as long as the rate of devaluation is constant, its level is in fact irrelevant. Hence, a constant real exchange rate is independent of the level of the devaluation rate. In other words, policy makers cannot influence the real exchange rate by permanent changes in the rate of devaluation.

Suppose now that policy makers want to implement a temporarily higher (i.e., more depreciated) level of the real exchange rate, perhaps to accumulate reserves through a surplus in the current account. Specifically, assume that policy makers aim at setting a level $e^1 (> e)$ of the real exchange rate for $t \in [0, T)$ (panel a in figure 12.2). To achieve this, the level of consumption of tradable goods, denoted by $(c^T)^1$, would need to be given by

$$e^1 = \frac{u'((c^T)^1)}{v'(y^N)}. \tag{12.15}$$

Clearly, $(c^T)^1 < c^T$. For given values of $(c^T)^1$ and T, the economy's resource constraint will determine a unique value of $(c^T)^2$ (see panel b). The corresponding path of the trade balance is illustrated in panel c. The value of the nominal interest rate for $t \in [0, T)$ necessary to implement the level $(c^T)^1$ follows from using expression (12.13) to derive the Euler equation:

$$\frac{u'((c^T)^1)}{u'((c^T)^2)} = \frac{1 + \alpha i^1}{1 + \alpha i^2}. \tag{12.16}$$

For a given i^2—chosen by policy makers—equation (12.16) determines the value of i^1 required to set a given level of $(c^T)^1$ and hence, through equation (12.15), of e^1. Figure 12.2, panel d, illustrates the path of i_t. By interest parity, the rate of devaluation will also be higher between 0 and T.[4]

We conclude that it is possible to target a temporarily higher real exchange rate at the cost of higher inflation. From a welfare point of view, however, it should be clear that this policy is suboptimal since the first-best involves a flat consumption path.[5] As discussed in box 12.2, empirical evidence suggests that episodes of real exchange rate targeting—typically involving an attempt on the part of policy makers to engineer a higher level of the real exchange rate (i.e., a more depreciated currency in real terms)—have indeed led to temporarily higher inflation.

4. The rate of inflation of nontradable goods, π_t, will also be higher between 0 and T because $\dot{e}_t = 0$ implies that $\pi_t = \varepsilon_t$.

5. Interestingly, however, one can construct examples in which a policy of real exchange rate targeting is actually optimal. One such example can be found in exercise 1 at the end of the chapter. If foreign inflation is positive, a non-flat path of i_t^* introduces an intertemporal distortion, à la chapter 3. By setting a non-flat path of ε_t, policy makers can offset this distortion and restore the first-best equilibrium.

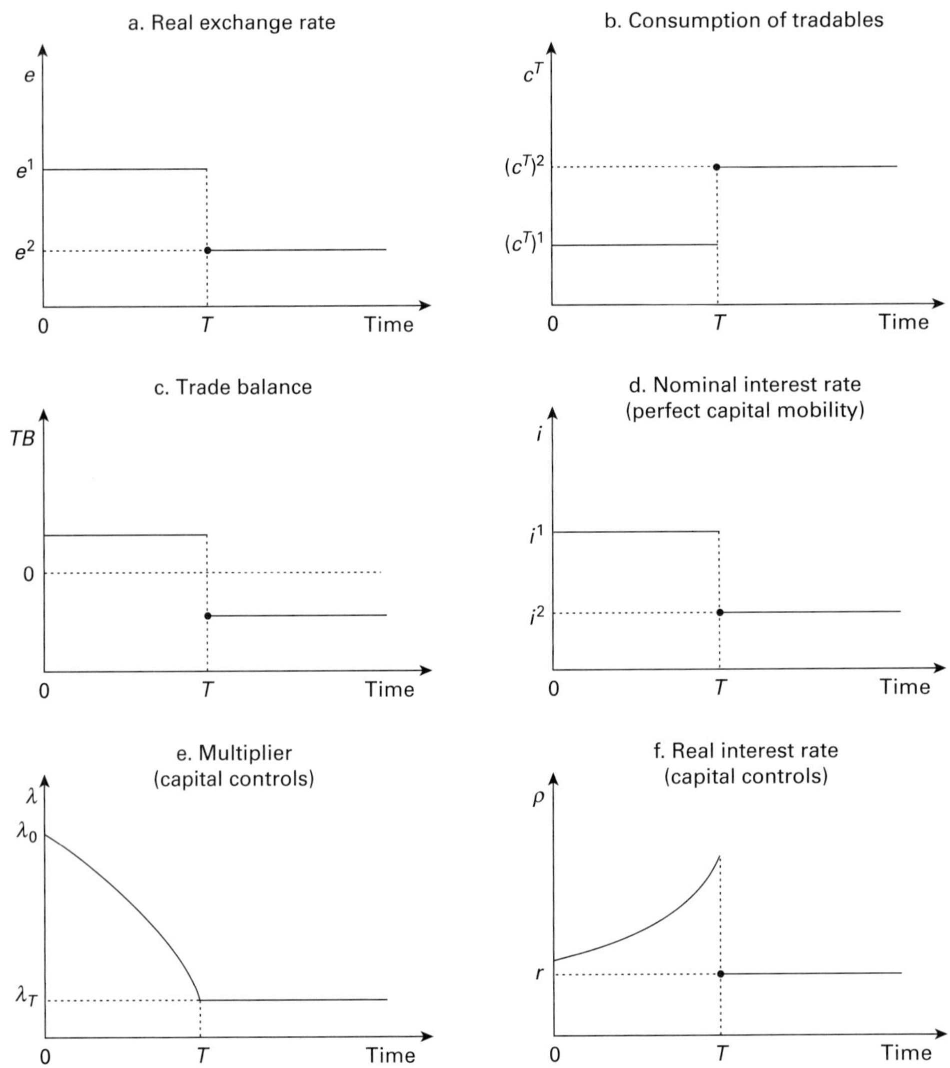

Figure 12.2
Real exchange rate targeting under flexible prices

Box 12.2
Is real exchange rate targeting inflationary?

Sections 12.2 through 12.4 emphasized the potential inflationary consequences of targeting the real exchange rate. But what does the empirical evidence say? Brazil, Chile, and Colombia have had a long history of real exchange rate targeting and PPP rules (see box 12.1). Figure 12.3 provides some relevant data for analyzing the experiences of these three countries.[a] The left panels show the evolution of both the logarithm of the nominal exchange rate and the logarithm of the PPP exchange rate.[b] Vertical bars indicate periods during which either explicit or implicit PPP rules were in effect. The idea is that if a PPP rule was being pursued, the actual exchange rate should be close to its PPP value. The right panels show the evolution of the real exchange rate and the inflation rate for each country.[c]

In July 1985 Chile established an exchange rate band whose central parity was adjusted at daily intervals according to the differential between domestic and foreign inflation. Remarkably, there were no deviations from this rule until January 1992, when strong capital inflows led to a revaluation of 5 percent (see left-hand panel in figure 12.3, row A). In the right-hand side panel we can see that inflation remains relative high and variable during the PPP period and begins to fall systematically only after Chile gives up the PPP rule in 1992.[d] Earlier, Chile also provides an excellent example of policies aimed at achieving a higher level (i.e., more depreciated) level of the real exchange rate. Indeed, in the period 1982 to 1985, Chile pursued an aggressive policy of nominal devaluation in order to engineer a real depreciation. This episode is clear from the left-hand panel in row A.

As discussed in box 12.1, Brazil implemented a PPP rule in August 1968 and with, occasional interruptions, essentially maintained this policy until the Real Plan in July 1994. The left-hand side panel in figure 12.3, row B, which shows the actual nominal exchange rate tracking very closely the PPP exchange rate, is clearly consistent with this interpretation. The right-hand side panel shows how inflation became high and variable in response to various external shocks, starting with the oil price shock of 1979. The lack of a nominal anchor allowed inflation to take a life of its own.

As also mentioned in box 12.1, Colombia first implemented a PPP rule in 1967 and essentially kept such a regime in place until 1991. Once again, the left-hand side panel in row C of figure 12.3 is consistent with this view. Notice also an attempt in 1985 to engineer a real depreciation by rapidly depreciating the currency. The right-hand side panel suggests that inflation remained high and variable until the PPP rule regime was abandoned in 1991.

Calvo, Reinhart, and Végh (1995) then proceed to test for these three countries the idea that there should be a positive correlation between the temporary components of inflation and the real exchange rate. To this effect, they decompose the real exchange rate, which is nonstationary in all three countries, into its permanent and temporary component using the Beveridge–Nelson decomposition. In all three cases the correlation has the expected sign and is statistically different from zero, with values ranging from 0.26 to 0.42. The formal evidence thus supports the idea that targeting a more depreciated currency in real terms or preventing the currency from appreciating in real terms in response to a positive shock is inflationary.

a. Data are from the IMF's International Financial Statistics (IFS) and Global Financial Data (GFD).
b. Following Calvo, Reinhart, and Végh (1995), the PPP exchange rate was computed as the ratio of the domestic CPI to that of the United States, and set equal to the actual value of the exchange rate in 78.01 for Brazil, 85.07 for Chile, and 86.01 for Colombia. In the case of Brazil, the base date coincides with the beginning of the sample; in the case of Chile and Colombia, the base date marks the beginning of a period during which a PPP rule was in effect.
c. The real exchange rate is defined as EP^*/P, where E is the nominal exchange rate, P^* is the CPI of the United States and P is the CPI of the domestic country.
d. Since we are not controlling for a myriad of factors, these figures should be seen only as suggestive.

Box 12.2
(continued)

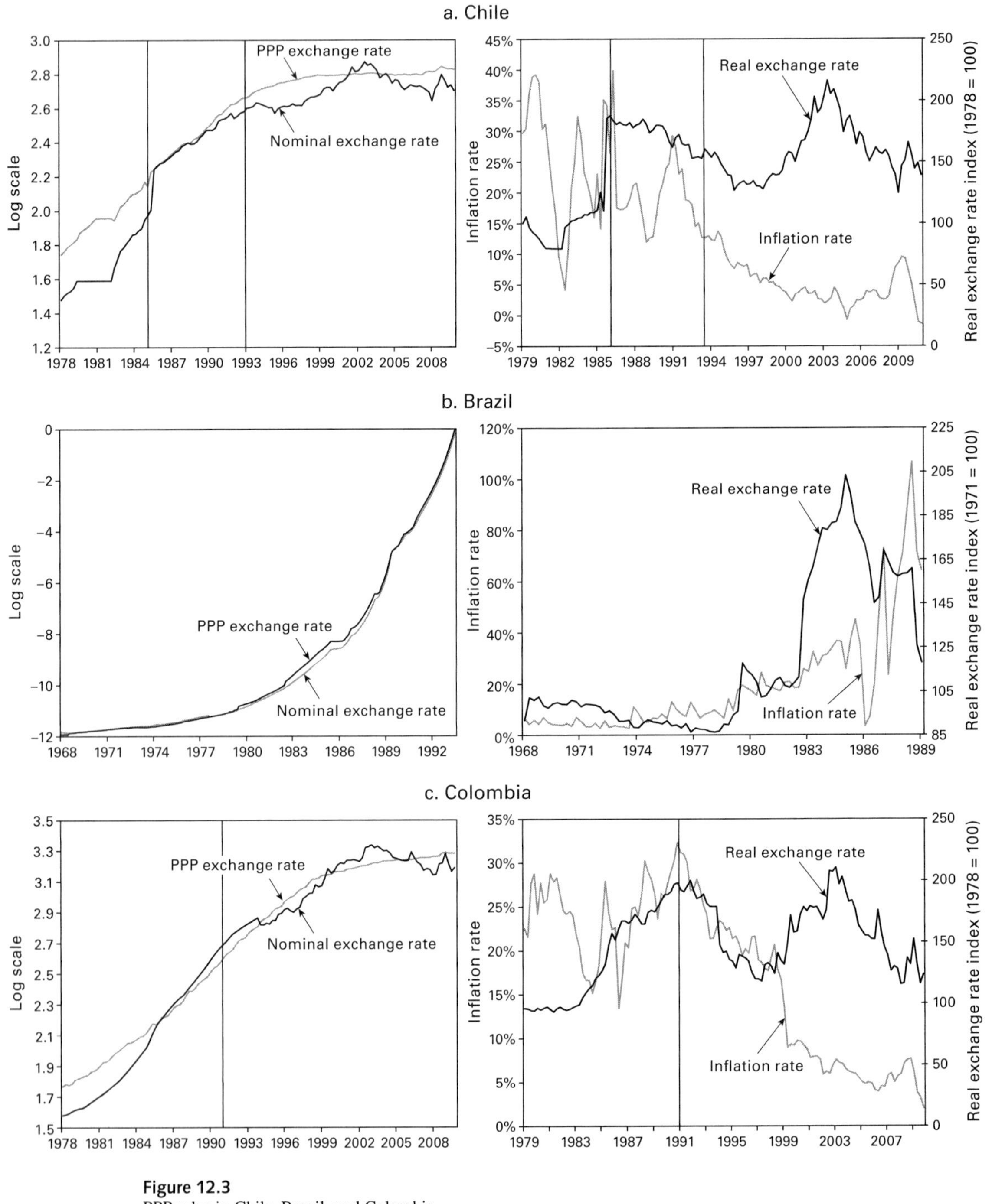

Figure 12.3
PPP rules in Chile, Brazil, and Colombia

12.2.5 Capital Controls

To illustrate the case of imperfect capital mobility, let us focus on the extreme case of no capital mobility (financial autarky), as in chapter 2. With no loss of generality, we assume that the rate of devaluation set by policy makers is zero. Again, let us assume that policy makers wish to set a level e^1 for the real exchange rate for $t \in [0, T)$. As before, this requires the level of consumption of tradable goods given by (12.15). We will now show that policy makers can manipulate the money supply so as to induce that path.

It is easy to show that since the economy will be stationary from T onwards, $\rho_t = r$ for all $t \geq T$. Hence from equation (12.6),

$$u'((c^T)^1) = \lambda_t(1 + \alpha i_t), \qquad 0 \leq t < T, \tag{12.17}$$

$$u'((c^T)^2) = \lambda_t(1 + \alpha r), \qquad t \geq T. \tag{12.18}$$

where

$$\lambda_t \equiv \begin{cases} \bar{\lambda} D_t \exp(\beta t), & 0 \leq t < T, \\ \lambda_T, & t \geq T. \end{cases} \tag{12.19}$$

Differentiating (12.19) with respect to time (taking into account that, since $\varepsilon_t = 0$, $i_t = \rho_t$, as follows from equation 12.10) yields

$$\dot{\lambda}_t = \lambda_t(\beta - i_t), \qquad 0 \leq t < T. \tag{12.20}$$

Using (12.17) to solve for i_t and substituting into (12.20), we obtain

$$\dot{\lambda}_t = \left(\frac{1}{\alpha} + \beta\right)\lambda_t - \frac{u'((c^T)^1)}{\alpha}, \qquad 0 \leq t < T. \tag{12.21}$$

By definition—recall (12.19) and (12.2)—λ_t is continuous at time T. Hence the equilibrium path of λ_t solves differential equation (12.21) with a terminal condition for $t = T$ given by (12.18). Appendix 12.8.2 shows that the path of λ_t that satisfies these conditions is the one depicted in figure 12.2, panel e.

Let us now derive the path of ρ_t $(= i_t)$. The fact that λ_t decreases over time implies, from (12.17), that ρ_t increases over time. Furthermore, since λ_t is continuous at time T, equations (12.17) and (12.18) imply that ρ_t must fall at time T. Further we can show that $\rho_0 > \beta$. To this effect, notice that since $\dot{\lambda}_0 < 0$, it follows from (12.21) that

$$(1 + \alpha\beta)\,\lambda_0 < u'((c^T)^1).$$

Given (12.17), this implies that $\rho_0 > \beta$ (recall that $\beta = r$). Figure 12.2, panel f, illustrates the path of the real interest rate.

How do policy makers engineer this path of the domestic real interest rate? By tight money. To see this, use the nontradable goods market equilibrium (12.11) to rewrite the cash-in-advance constraint (12.4) as

$$m_t = \alpha \left(c_t^T + \frac{y^N}{e_t} \right).$$

Since during $t \in [0, T)$, c_t^T is constant and relatively low and e_t is constant and relatively high, m_t will be constant as well and relatively low. This implies that the nominal money supply is lower during $[0, T)$ than afterward. At time T, the nominal money supply goes up to support higher consumption of tradables and a lower e_t. Given that the exchange rate is fixed, the path of m_t dictates the path of M_t. The nominal money stock is thus relatively low during $t \in [0, T)$ and rises at time T. The tight money policy in place during $t \in [0, T)$ restricts the amount of liquidity available in the economy and forces low consumption of tradable goods and low demand for nontradables, which translates into a relatively low price of nontradables (i.e., high e_t).

12.3 Real Exchange Rate Rules in a Flexible-Prices Model

This section shows an example, inspired by Uribe (2003), where a real exchange rate rule leads to multiple equilibria.[6] The model remains the same as in section 12.2.4 (i.e., the case with perfect capital mobility) with the only modification that to simplify the exposition, we will assume logarithmic preferences. We continue to use the superscript 1 to denote values for $t \in [0, T)$ and superscript 2 for values of $t \geq T$.

Suppose that policy makers set $\varepsilon^1 = 0$ but that they will set ε^2 according to the following real exchange rate rule:

$$\varepsilon^2 = \frac{1 + \alpha r}{\alpha} \left(\frac{e^2}{e^1} - 1 \right). \tag{12.22}$$

To interpret this rule, think of policy makers as having some "long-run" target, e^2, for the real exchange rate. If the current real exchange rate differs from that target, they will adjust ε^2. For instance, if $e^1 < e^2$, then they will set a positive rate of devaluation (i.e., $\varepsilon^2 > 0$).

With the logarithmic specification, and taking into account conditions (12.12), (12.14), and (12.16), the equilibrium paths are determined by

6. See Uribe (2003) for a fuller analysis. In a similar model Lahiri (2001) analyzes the use of taxes on foreign bonds to target the real exchange rate (or, equivalently, the trade balance) and shows that such a policy leads to unstable dynamics. Though in a rather different model, this section's message is reminiscent of Dornbusch's (1982) early contribution, where he argues that PPP rules may lead to increased instability of prices and output. In a broader context Bruno (1993, ch. 3) analyzes how the lack of a nominal anchor may lead to a process of "shocks and accommodation" whereby inflation acquires a life of its own (i.e., unrelated to the underlying fiscal deficit).

$$\frac{(c^T)^1}{(c^T)^2} = \frac{1+\alpha(r+\varepsilon^2)}{1+\alpha r}, \tag{12.23}$$

$$e^1(c^T)^1 = y^N, \tag{12.24}$$

$$e^2(c^T)^2 = y^N, \tag{12.25}$$

$$y^T = (c^T)^1\,[1-\exp(-rT)] + (c^T)^2\exp(-rT). \tag{12.26}$$

We will show that if the Central Bank follows rule (12.22), then ε^2 is undetermined. In other words, any path of the real exchange rate that satisfies (12.24), (12.25), and (12.26) is a perfect foresight equilibrium path.

To show this, pick a given e^1. Then condition (12.24) determines a given value of $(c^T)^1$. This value of $(c^T)^1$ determines, through the resource constraint (12.26), a value of $(c^T)^2$. This value in turn determines, through (12.25), a value of e^2. Then equation (12.23) will give us the value of ε^2 that is consistent with the ratio $(c^T)^1/(c^T)^2$. This value of ε^2 is validated by policy rule (12.22). Hence any value of e^1 expected by the public is validated by some corresponding ε^2.[7]

Intuitively, if the consumer expects for today a relative low real exchange rate (i.e., a low e^1 relative to e^2), then, following rule (12.22), policy makers will react by setting a positive ε^2. This introduces an intertemporal distortion (recall that $\varepsilon^1 = 0$) by making today's consumption cheaper than future consumption. As a result consumers substitute consumption away from the future and toward the present period. The higher demand for nontradables today relative to the future leads to a low e^1 relative to e^2, thus validating initial expectations.

We have thus shown that the adoption of rule (12.22) implies that the future rate of devaluation is undetermined. The economy has no nominal anchor.[8]

12.4 RER Targeting in a Sticky-Inflation Model

In the last two sections we have looked at real exchange rate targeting under flexible prices. While such a framework provided us with some useful insights, it does not lend itself to studying real exchange rate rules of the type often encountered in practice. To this end, this section focuses on real exchange rate rules in the context of a model where both the price level and the inflation rate of nontradables are sticky.

Consider a small open economy perfectly integrated into world goods and capital markets. Foreign inflation is taken to be zero (and we normalize the foreign nominal price to one). Unless otherwise noticed, we continue to use the same notation as above.

7. Mechanically, notice that since expression (12.22) follows from combining (12.23), (12.24), and (12.25), we have a system of four equations, (12.23) through (12.26), in five unknows (e^1, e^2, $(c^T)^1$, $(c^T)^2$, and ε^2). The system is therefore undetermined.

8. With endogenous production and a productive role for inflation (e.g., because of real money balances entering the production function), this indeterminacy would extend itself to the real sector of the economy.

12.4.1 Consumers

Let preferences be given by

$$\int_0^\infty [\log(c_t^T) + \log(c_t^N) + \log(m_t)] \exp(-\beta t) dt. \tag{12.27}$$

The flow constraint reads as

$$\dot{a}_t = ra_t + y_t^T + \frac{y_t^N}{e_t} + \tau_t - c_t^T - \frac{c_t^N}{e_t} - i_t m_t. \tag{12.28}$$

The corresponding intertemporal constraint is given by

$$a_0 + \int_0^\infty \left(y_t^T + \frac{y_t^N}{e_t} + \tau_t \right) \exp(-rt) dt = \int_0^\infty \left(c_t^T + \frac{c_t^N}{e_t} + i_t m_t \right) \exp(-rt) dt. \tag{12.29}$$

The first-order conditions take the familiar form (assuming $\beta = r$)

$$\frac{1}{c_t^T} = \lambda, \tag{12.30}$$

$$\frac{1}{c_t^N} = \frac{\lambda}{e_t}, \tag{12.31}$$

$$\frac{1}{m_t} = \lambda i_t. \tag{12.32}$$

Combining (12.30) and (12.31), we obtain the standard intratemporal condition:

$$c_t^T = \frac{c_t^N}{e_t}. \tag{12.33}$$

Our standard money demand follows (12.30) and (12.32):

$$m_t = \frac{c_t^T}{i_t}. \tag{12.34}$$

For further reference, recall from chapter 8 that we can define real money balances in terms of nontradable goods (n_t) as

$$n_t \equiv \frac{M_t}{P_t^N}.$$

Since, as can be easily checked, $n_t = e_t m_t$, we can combine first-order conditions (12.31) and (12.32) to yield

$$n_t = \frac{c_t^N}{i_t}. \tag{12.35}$$

12.4.2 Supply Side

The supply of tradables is assumed to be exogenous and constant over time, and denoted by y^T. The output of nontradable goods, however, is demand-determined. Both the price level and the rate of inflation of nontradables are assumed to be sticky. The inflation rate of nontradables is assumed to be governed by the following differential equation:

$$\dot{\pi}_t = \theta(c_t^N - y_f^N) + \gamma(\varepsilon_t - \pi_t), \tag{12.36}$$

where θ and γ are positive parameters and y_f^N is the full-employment level of output of nontradable goods. The inflation rate of nontradables increases when aggregate demand is above its full-employment level (first term on the RHS of equation 12.36) and when the current inflation rate is below the rate of devaluation (second term on the RHS).

12.4.3 Government

The government's accounting is standard. The government's flow constraint is given by

$$\dot{h}_t = rh_t + \dot{m}_t + \varepsilon_t m_t - \tau_t. \tag{12.37}$$

12.4.4 Policy Rule

As an example of a policy rule that reflects policy makers' concerns with the real exchange rate, suppose that the actual rate of devaluation is set according to the following rule:

$$\varepsilon_t = \eta\bar{\varepsilon} + (1-\eta)\pi_t, \qquad 0 < \eta \leq 1, \tag{12.38}$$

where $\bar{\varepsilon}$ may be viewed as the long-run devaluation rate (i.e., the steady-state rate of devaluation and inflation). The rate of devaluation is now an endogenous variable. If $\eta = 1$, the rate of devaluation acts as a "pure" nominal anchor in the sense that it does not respond to the current state of the economy. If $\eta < 1$, then the rate of devaluation responds to the current inflation rate. The lower η is, the more the current devaluation rate responds to current inflation, reflecting policy makers' attempt to prevent the real exchange rate from falling too rapidly (i.e., to prevent the domestic currency from appreciating too rapidly in real terms).

12.4.5 Equilibrium Conditions

Given that perfect capital mobility prevails, the interest parity condition holds:

$$i_t = r + \varepsilon_t. \tag{12.39}$$

Equilibrium in the nontradable goods market requires that

$$c_t^N = y_t^N. \tag{12.40}$$

By definition, $e_t = E_t/P_t^N$. Hence

$$\frac{\dot{e}_t}{e_t} = \varepsilon_t - \pi_t. \tag{12.41}$$

Combining the consumers' flow constraint (given by equation 12.28) with the government's (given by equation 12.37) and using (12.39) and (12.40), we obtain

$$\dot{k}_t = rk_t + y^T - c_t^T, \tag{12.42}$$

where $k_t (\equiv b_t + h_t)$ denotes the economy's total net foreign assets. Integrating forward (12.42) and imposing the corresponding transversality condition, we obtain

$$k_0 + \frac{y^T}{r} = \int_0^\infty c_t^T \exp(-rt)dt. \tag{12.43}$$

For further reference, notice that, from (12.30) and (12.43), c_t^T will be constant along a PFEP and given by

$$c^T = rk_0 + y^T. \tag{12.44}$$

12.4.6 Dynamic System

We will set up a two differential equation system in π_t and e_t. To this effect, substitute policy rule (12.38) into equations (12.36) and (12.41) and use (12.33) to obtain, respectively,

$$\dot{\pi}_t = \theta(e_t c^T - y_f^N) + \gamma\eta(\bar{\varepsilon} - \pi_t), \tag{12.45}$$

$$\dot{e}_t = e_t\eta(\bar{\varepsilon} - \pi_t), \tag{12.46}$$

where c^T is given by (12.44). To establish the system's steady state, set $\dot{\pi}_t = \dot{e}_t = 0$ in equations (12.45) and (12.46) to obtain

$$\pi_{ss} = \bar{\varepsilon}, \tag{12.47}$$

$$e_{ss} = \frac{y_f^N}{c^T}. \tag{12.48}$$

Linearizing the system around the steady state, we obtain

$$\begin{bmatrix} \dot{\pi}_t \\ \dot{e}_t \end{bmatrix} = \begin{bmatrix} -\gamma\eta & \theta c^T \\ -e_{ss}\eta & 0 \end{bmatrix} \begin{bmatrix} \pi_t - \pi_{ss} \\ e_t - e_{ss} \end{bmatrix}. \tag{12.49}$$

The trace and the determinant of the matrix associated with the linear approximation are, respectively,

$$\text{Tr} = -\gamma\eta < 0,$$

$$\Delta = e_{ss}\eta\theta c^T > 0.$$

A negative trace indicates that at least one of the roots is negative. A positive determinant then implies that both roots have the same sign. We can conclude that both roots are negative (or have a real negative part) and, hence, that the dynamic system is globally stable.

As shown in appendix 12.8.3, roots will be real if

$$\eta \geq \frac{4\theta y_f^N}{\gamma^2}. \tag{12.50}$$

All else equal, roots are more likely to be complex the lower η is. This is intuitive because, from policy rule (12.38), a lower η implies that policy makers put a larger weight on current inflation in setting the devaluation rate.[9]

As usual, we proceed to characterize the qualitative behavior of this dynamic system by constructing a phase diagram. We first draw the $\dot{\pi}_t = 0$ and $\dot{e}_t = 0$ loci. To this end, set $\dot{\pi}_t = 0$ in equation (12.45) and $\dot{e}_t = 0$ in equation (12.46) to obtain, respectively,

$$\theta(e_t c^T - y_f^N) = -\gamma\eta(\bar{\varepsilon} - \pi_t), \tag{12.51}$$

$$\pi_t = \bar{\varepsilon}. \tag{12.52}$$

The last equation implies that the $\dot{e}_t = 0$ locus is a horizontal line, as depicted in figure 12.4. From (12.51) it follows that the slope of the $\dot{\pi}_t = 0$ locus, which is given by

$$\left.\frac{d\pi_t}{de_t}\right|_{\dot{\pi}_t=0} = \frac{\theta c^T}{\gamma\eta} > 0,$$

9. For the purposes of the theoretical analysis that follows, we will assume that both roots are real.

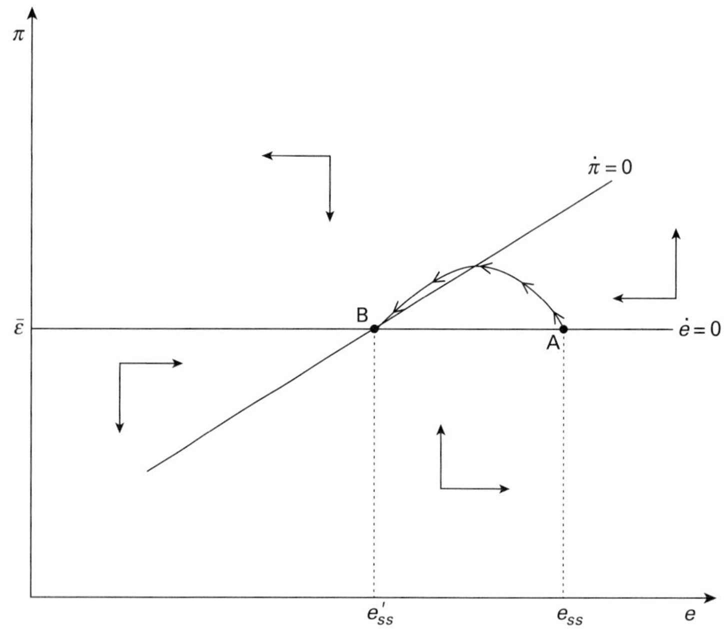

Figure 12.4
Real exchange rate targeting in a sticky inflation model: Phase diagram

is positive (see figure 12.4). Proceeding as in previous chapters, we can draw the laws of motion depicted in figure 12.4. Since the system is globally stable, whatever the initial conditions, it will converge to the steady state.[10]

12.4.7 Permanent Increase in Supply of Tradable Goods

Suppose that, just before time $t = 0$, the economy is in the steady state given by point A in figure 12.4. At $t = 0$, there is an unanticipated and permanent increase in the endowment of tradable goods, y^T (figure 12.5, panel a). From (12.44) it follows that consumption of tradable goods adjusts instantaneously to its new steady state (panel b).

In terms of the dynamic system, and as (12.48) makes clear, e_{ss} falls as a result of the increase in c^T. Let point B in figure 12.4 denote the new steady state (and $e_{ss}^{'}$ denote the new steady state value of the real exchange rate). Since both π_t and e_t are predetermined variables, the transition begins at point A. The system then travels along the arrowed path until it finally converges to point B. The corresponding paths of the real exchange rate and inflation of nontradable goods are depicted in figure 12.5, panels c and d, respectively.

10. Graphically, the role of condition (12.50) in determining whether or not roots are real can be seen in figure 12.4 by noting that the lower η is, the more vertical will be the $\dot{\pi}_t = 0$ locus, which makes it less likely that the system will converge without fluctuating.

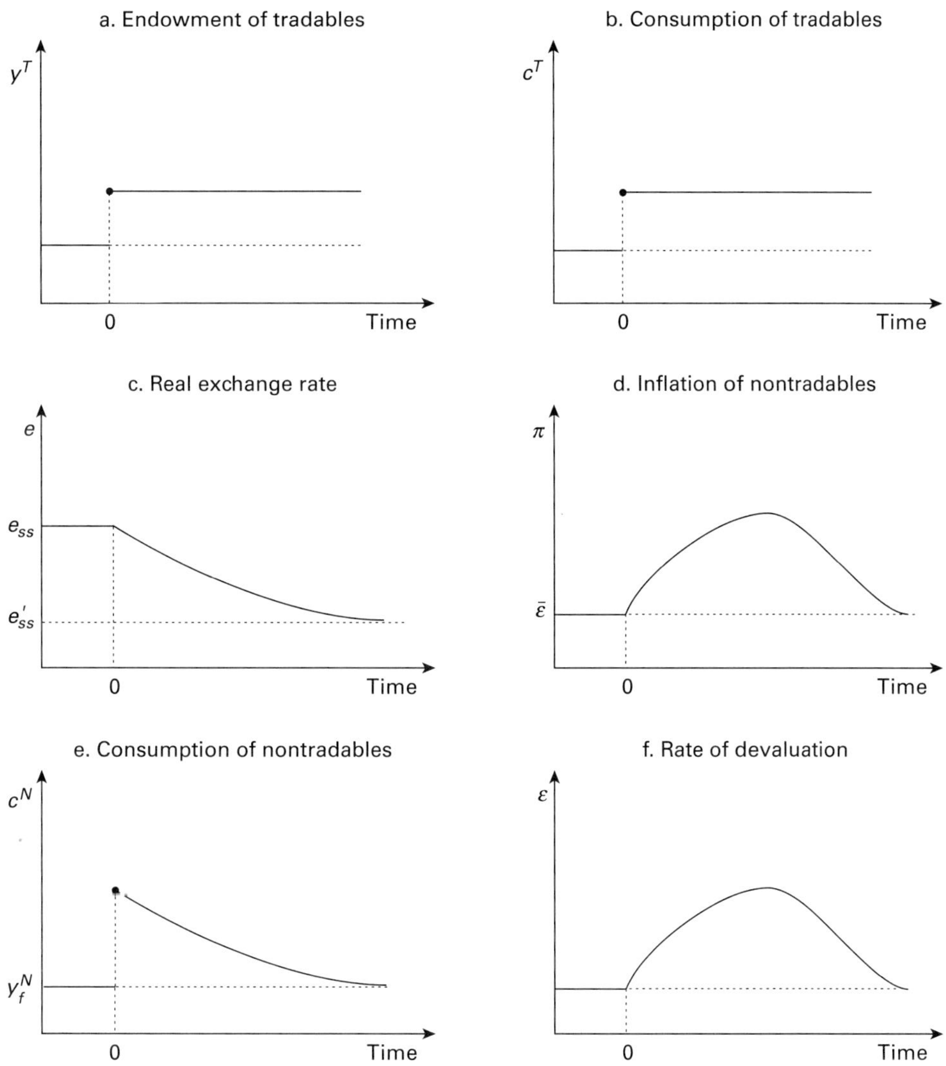

Figure 12.5
Permanent increase in endowment of tradables

The path of c_t^N (figure 12.5, panel e) follows from equation (12.33). Since e_t does not jump at $t = 0$ while c_t^T jumps up, c_t^N also increases up on impact. Then c_t^N falls over time toward its unchanged steady-state value, y_f^N.

The path of ε_t follows from equation (12.38). Differentiating with respect to time yields

$$\dot{\varepsilon}_t = (1 - \eta)\,\dot{\pi}_t.$$

The path of ε_t is depicted in panel f.

Intuitively, the increase in y^T requires a fall in the steady-state relative price of tradables in terms of nontradables (i.e., a real appreciation). Since the economy is operating under predetermined exchange rates (and hence the nominal exchange rate cannot adjust), the required real appreciation can only occur gradually over time through a rate of inflation that is higher than the rate of devaluation.

12.4.8 Inflationary Consequences of Real Exchange Rate Targeting

A PPP rule such as (12.38) that attempts to smooth out the real appreciation will inevitably lead to higher inflation. How much inflation is generated critically depends on the value of η, which captures the policy maker's attempt to maintain a certain level of the real exchange rate. To illustrate this idea, figure 12.6 illustrates the paths of the inflation rate and the real exchange in response to a permanent increase in y^T from 1 to 2 for three different values of η (1, 0.5, and 0.2).[11]

In response to the increase in tradable goods, the real exchange rate must fall across steady states from an initial value of 1 to a value of 0.5. How it gets there, of course, depends on the particular value of η. The lower η is, the more inflation is needed for the real exchange rate to fall to its new steady-state value. We thus see inflation reaching its highest level for $\eta = 0.2$ and its lowest value for $\eta = 1$. The counterpart is that early on (i.e., until about period 10), the level of the real exchange rate is highest for $\eta = 0.2$ and the lowest for $\eta = 1$. Policy makers are thus able to have a less appreciated level of the domestic currency in real terms but at the cost of higher inflation.

12.5 Real Interest Rate Targeting

A real interest rate has often served as a real anchor as well. The best-known example is the case of Chile where, from August 1985 to July 2001, the main instrument of monetary policy was an interest rate on an indexed bond (see box 12.3).

This section looks at real interest rate targeting in the context of the sticky-inflation model of section 12.4. Recall that we have already seen an example of real interest rate targeting under

11. Parameters are as follows: $\theta = 0.2$, $\gamma = 1$, $y^T = y_f^N = 1$, and $\bar{\varepsilon} = 0.5$. Refer to appendix 12.8.3 where the condition for roots to be real is $\eta \geq 4\theta y_f^N/\gamma^2$. For the parameters above, $4\theta y_f^N/\gamma^2 = 0.8$. Hence roots are real for $\eta = 1$ and complex for $\eta = 0.5$ and 0.2.

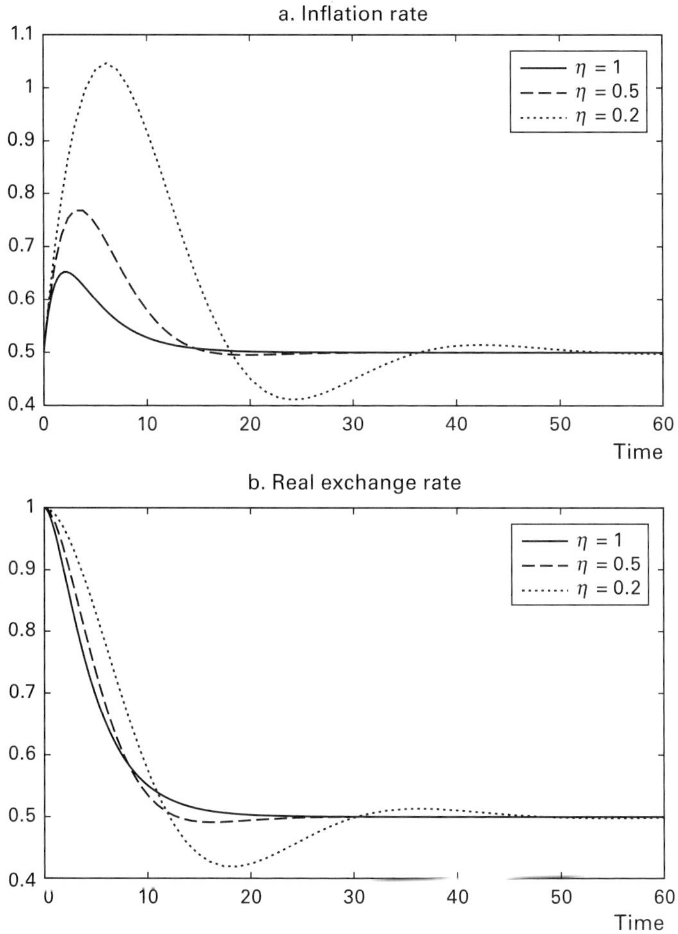

Figure 12.6
Real exchange rate targeting in a sticky-inflation model

sticky prices in chapter 9, exercise 5. The only change is that since the economy will be operating under flexible exchange rates, the law of motion for the inflation rate now takes the form

$$\dot{\pi}_t = \theta(c_t^N - y_f^N) + \gamma(\mu_t - \pi_t). \tag{12.53}$$

In other words, and compared to equation (12.36), μ_t has taken the place of ε_t.[12]

12. We should note that although the nominal exchange rate will be flexible in this model, the monetary authority will not be setting the path of the nominal money supply. While expression (12.53) still seems the more natural choice in this context, exercise 2 at the end of the chapter shows that the indeterminacy of the inflation rate under pure real interest rate targeting remains valid, of course, under equation (12.36).

Box 12.3
Real interest rate targeting: A look at the Chilean experience

In August 1985 Chile adopted as its main policy instrument the interest rate on bonds issued by the Central Bank of Chile and denominated in UFs, an indexed unit of account.[a] By all accounts, the peculiar choice of what was effectively a real interest rate as the main instrument of monetary policy was simply a recognition of the importance that the UF had acquired as the unit of account for most financial instruments. During the first two years, bonds of different maturities were offered at a fixed interest rate by the Central Bank. By 1987 the main instrument had become the 90-day PRBC.[b] As indicated in table 12.2, in 1995 the Central Bank of Chile switched from the 90-day PRBC to targeting an overnight interest rate denominated in UFs. This real interest rate target policy was in effect until August 2001, when the Central Bank switched to an overnight nominal interest rate as its main policy instrument.

How did this policy fare in practice? Figure 12.7 shows the evolution over time of the reference interest rate and the inflation rate. Inflation remained high until the early 1990s and then fell steadily over time. Importantly, the Central Bank of Chile became autonomous in 1989 and in 1990 proceeded to announce inflation targets. Our theoretical discussion of section 12.5 suggests that while a pure real interest rate target would leave the inflation rate undetermined, a real interest rate rule based on a *credible* inflation target would provide a perfectly sensible way of conducting monetary policy. The evidence offered in Valdés (1997) is fully consistent with this interpretation. Valdés estimates a vector-autoregression model to empirically account for the monetary transmission mechanisms

Table 12.2
Chile: Monetary policy instrument and inflation rate, 1985 to 2002

		Rate of monetary policy in UF (%)		Inflation rate (%)	
Period	Instrument	Average	Standard deviation	Average	Standard deviation
August 1985–April 1995	PRBC-90	5.7	1.4	16.9	5.4
May 1995–December 2000	Interbank rate–1 day in UF	6.7	1.5	5.5	1.8
January 2001–July 2001	Interbank rate–1 day in UF	4.0	0.5	3.7	0.5
August 2001–March 2003	Interbank rate–1 day in pesos	1.4	1.6	2.9	0.7

Note: UF: Unidad de fomento. The rate for the monetary policy instrument corresponds to the effective rate expressed in UF for the first three periods. The rate shown for the last period (August 2001–March 2003) corresponds to an ex ante real interest rate, defined as the effective rate for monetary policy in nominal terms minus the center of the target inflation band (3%).

a. In January 1967—and in the midst of high and chronic inflation—Chile introduced the UF ("unidad de fomento"), a unit of account constructed using CPI values for the previous months. It was originally intended to be used to index the price of houses, but soon became a popular way of protecting savings from inflation. By the early 1980s, the UF had become a cornerstone of the financial sector, with most loans and deposits denominated in UFs.
b. PRBC is the Spanish acronym for "Pagarés Reajustables del Banco Central," which stands for "Central Bank readjustable obligations."

Box 12.3
(continued)

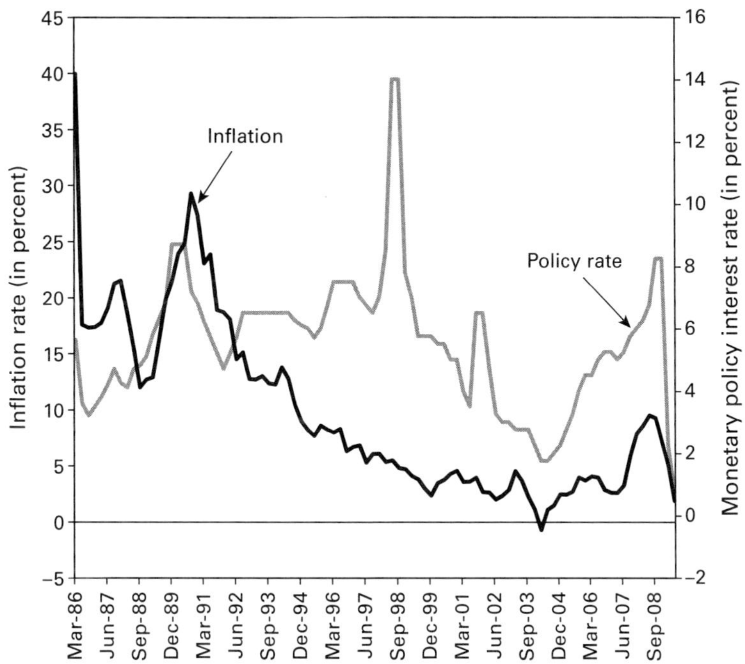

Figure 12.7
Chile: Policy interest rate and inflation

operating in Chile during this period. He concludes that while changes in the 90-day PRBC affect the output path, they only influence inflation indirectly. Specifically, changes in the 90-day PRBC affect the differential between the inflation target and the actual inflation rate but not the level of the inflation rate itself. This suggests that the key nominal anchor in Chile during the disinflation period of the 1990s illustrated in figure 12.7 was a credible inflation target.

The decision to "nominalize" the system in August 2001 did not come without much debate on the pros and cons of doing so (see Morandé 2002b; Fuentes et al. 2003). There were concerns, on the one hand, about whether the new policy would be as effective as the old one in affecting the target real variables (output and inflation) and whether it would increase the variability of interest rates on UF-denominated assets (which, presumably, would increase the variability of the real interest rate relevant for economic decisions). On the other hand, nominalizing the system would likely get rid of inflation inertia due to backward-looking indexation mechanisms embedded in the calculation of the UF. As it turns out, even though the variability of UF interest rates does appear to have increased after the policy change, Fuentes et al. (2003) argue that no major changes occurred in the transmission mechanism because of arbitrage between indexed and nominal rates.[c] Theoretically, one would not expect a large difference in transmission mechanisms between a nominal interest rate rule or a real interest rate rule, as long as they are combined with a credible inflation target (Végh 2002).

c. See also Chumacero (2002).

12.5.1 Pure Real Interest Rate Targeting

We will first show that if policy makers target a given level of the domestic real interest rate, the inflation rate is undetermined. Recall from chapter 8 that the domestic real interest rate (i.e., the real interest rate in terms of nontradable goods) is defined as

$$r_t^d = i_t - \pi_t. \tag{12.54}$$

Differentiating (12.31) with respect to time, using (12.41), and noting that, in light of (12.39), $r_t^d = r + \varepsilon_t - \pi_t$, we obtain

$$\frac{\dot{c}_t^N}{c_t^N} = r_t^d - r. \tag{12.55}$$

Clearly, for a steady state to exist, policy makers need to target the level r for the real interest rate (denote by $\overline{r^d}$ the target):

$$\overline{r^d} = r. \tag{12.56}$$

It then follows from the Euler equation (12.55) that $\dot{c}_t^N = 0$ for all $t \geq 0$. Then from (12.53) we have

$$\dot{\pi}_t = \gamma(\mu_t - \pi_t). \tag{12.57}$$

By definition, real money balances in terms of nontradable goods (n_t) are given by $n_t \equiv M_t/P_t^N$. Then

$$\frac{\dot{n}_t}{n_t} = \mu_t - \pi_t. \tag{12.58}$$

Using (12.35)—and taking into account that (12.54) and (12.56) imply $\dot{i}_t = \dot{\pi}_t$—we can rewrite this last equation as

$$\mu_t - \pi_t = -\frac{\dot{\pi}_t}{i_t}.$$

Substituting this last equation into (12.57), we have

$$\dot{\pi}_t \left(1 + \frac{\gamma}{i_t}\right) = 0.$$

Along a PFEP, $\dot{\pi}_t = 0$. Denote the constant level of inflation of nontradable goods by $\tilde{\pi}$. Hence $\mu_t = \tilde{\pi}$, $i_t = r + \tilde{\pi}$, and $c_t^N = y_f^N$. But what ties down $\tilde{\pi}$? The answer is nothing. To see this, suppose that for whatever reason, the public came to expect that the inflation rate will be $2\tilde{\pi}$. Then $\mu_t = 2\tilde{\pi}$ and $i_t = r + 2\tilde{\pi}$. The demand for n_t would go down, of course, but this would be accommodated by a fall in the nominal stock of money.[13] Any other value of constant inflation would be similarly accommodated by policy makers. There is absolutely nothing tying down $\tilde{\pi}$.

12.5.2 A Real Interest Rate Rule

We will now show that if the real interest rate targeting is complemented with an inflation target, the indeterminacy discussed above disappears.

Suppose that policy makers set an inflation target, $\bar{\pi}$, and follow the rule

$$\dot{r}_t^d = \psi(\pi_t - \bar{\pi}), \tag{12.59}$$

where ψ is a positive parameter. The domestic real interest rate is thus raised (lowered) whenever actual inflation is above (below) the inflation target.

To solve the model, we will set up a system of three differential equations in r_t^d, c_t^N, and π_t. To this effect, differentiate equation (12.34) with respect to time, taking into account that $\dot{m}_t/m_t = \mu_t - \varepsilon_t$, the interest parity condition, and (12.54) to obtain

$$\mu_t = i_t - r - \left(\frac{\dot{r}_t^d + \dot{\pi}_t}{i_t}\right).$$

Substituting this equation into (12.53) and rearranging terms, we obtain

$$\dot{\pi}_t = \frac{\theta}{1 + (\gamma/i_t)}(c_t^N - y_f^N) + \frac{\gamma}{1 + \gamma/i_t}\left(r_t^d - r\right) - \frac{(\gamma/i_t)\psi}{1 + \gamma/i_t}(\pi_t - \bar{\pi}). \tag{12.60}$$

Equations (12.59), (12.55), and (12.60) constitute a three differential equation system in r^d, c_t^N, and π_t.[14] In the steady state,

$$r_{ss}^d = r,$$

$$c_{ss}^N = y_f^N,$$

$$\pi_{ss} = \bar{\pi}.$$

13. Notice, of course, that the nominal money supply is endogenous even though we are operating under flexible exchange rates because the monetary authority is not setting the path of the money supply.

14. Note that even though equation (12.60) contains terms in i_t, these terms will not be part of the linear approximation because they are multiplied by terms which, in the steady state, will be equal to zero.

Linearizing this system around the steady state, we obtain

$$\begin{bmatrix} \dot{r}_t^d \\ \dot{c}_t^N \\ \dot{\pi}_t \end{bmatrix} = \begin{bmatrix} 0 & 0 & \psi \\ y_f^N & 0 & 0 \\ \frac{\gamma}{1+\gamma/i_{ss}} & \frac{\theta}{1+\gamma/i_{ss}} & -\frac{(\gamma/i_{ss})\psi}{1+\gamma/i_{ss}} \end{bmatrix} \begin{bmatrix} r_t^d - r \\ c_t^N - y_f^N \\ \pi_t - \bar{\pi} \end{bmatrix},$$

where $i_{ss} = r+\bar{\pi}$. The trace and determinant of the matrix associated with the linear approximation are given by

$$\text{Tr} = -\frac{(\gamma/i_{ss})\psi}{1+\gamma/i_{ss}} < 0,$$

$$\Delta = \psi\frac{\theta}{1+\gamma/i_{ss}}y_f^N > 0.$$

Since the trace is the sum of the roots, a negative trace indicates that at least one of the three roots is negative. A positive determinant in turn implies that the system has either three positive roots or one positive and two negative roots. We can conclude that the system has one positive and two negative roots. Since there are two nonjumping variables (r_t^d and π_t), the system exhibits saddle-path stability. For given initial values of r_t^d and π_t, the value of c_t^N will be such so as to position the system along its unique perfect foresight equilibrium path.

Let δ_i, $i = 1, 2$, denote the two negative roots with $\delta_1 < \delta_2$. Let h_{ij}, $j = 1, 2, 3$, denote the elements of the eigenvector associated with root δ_i. For $i = 1, 2$, it follows that

$$\begin{bmatrix} -\delta_i & 0 & \psi \\ y_f^N & -\delta_i & 0 \\ \frac{\gamma}{1+\gamma/i_{ss}} & \frac{\theta}{1+\gamma/i_{ss}} & -\frac{(\gamma/i_{ss})\psi}{1+\gamma/i_{ss}} - \delta_i \end{bmatrix} \begin{bmatrix} h_{i1} \\ h_{i2} \\ h_{i3} \end{bmatrix} = \begin{bmatrix} 0 \\ 0 \\ 0 \end{bmatrix}.$$

Hence

$$\frac{h_{i3}}{h_{i1}} = \frac{\delta_i}{\psi} < 0. \tag{12.61}$$

As will become clear below, this expression will provide a critical piece of information when it comes to solving the dynamic behavior of this system.

Setting to zero the constant corresponding to the unstable root, we can write the solution to this dynamic system as

$$r_t^d - r = \omega_1 h_{11}\exp(\delta_1 t) + \omega_2 h_{21}\exp(\delta_2 t),$$

$$c_t^N - y_f^N = \omega_1 h_{12}\exp(\delta_1 t) + \omega_2 h_{22}\exp(\delta_2 t),$$

$$\pi_t - \bar{\pi} = \omega_1 h_{13}\exp(\delta_1 t) + \omega_2 h_{23}\exp(\delta_2 t).$$

Hence

$$\lim_{t\to\infty}\frac{r_t^d - r}{\pi_t - \bar{\pi}} = \lim_{t\to\infty}\frac{\omega_1 h_{11}\exp[(\delta_1-\delta_2)t] + \omega_2 h_{21}}{\omega_1 h_{13}\exp[(\delta_1-\delta_2)t] + \omega_2 h_{23}}.$$

Since, by assumption, $\delta_1 - \delta_2 < 0$,

$$\lim_{t\to\infty}\frac{r_t^d - r}{\pi_t - \bar{\pi}} = \frac{h_{21}}{h_{23}} < 0,$$

where the sign follows from (12.61). This implies that as t becomes large, the domestic real interest rate and the inflation rate of nontradables will converge to their steady-state values from opposite directions. Put differently, the "dominant eigenvector ray," which is illustrated in figure 12.8, is negatively sloped (see Calvo 1987). Graphically, the system must converge asymptotically to the dominant eigenvector ray. From (12.59) we know that when $\pi_t > \bar{\pi}$, $\dot{r}_t^d > 0$ and when $\pi_t < \bar{\pi}$, $\dot{r}_t^d < 0$. The corresponding directional arrows are drawn in figure 12.8.

Let us now study how the economy responds to a reduction in the inflation target. Suppose that the initial steady state is given by point A in figure 12.8, where $\pi_{ss} = \bar{\pi}^H$ and $r_{ss}^d = r$. At time 0

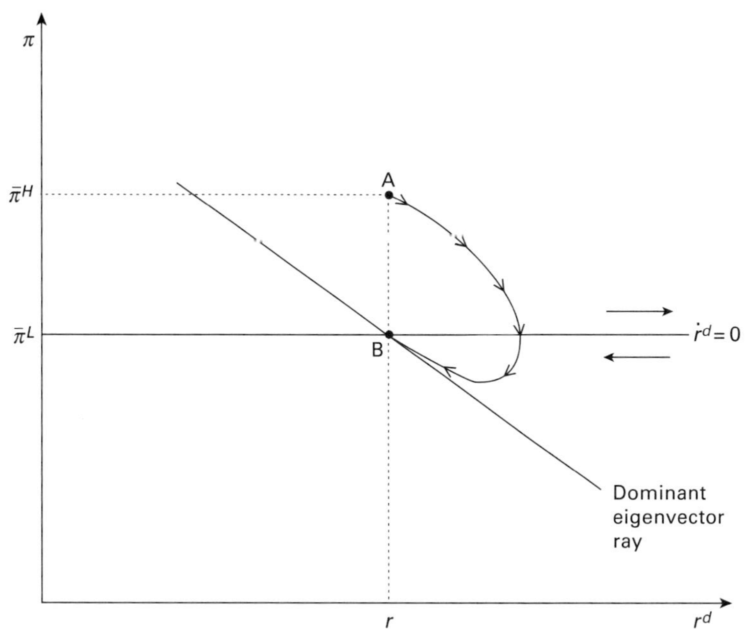

Figure 12.8
Dynamics in the (r^d, π) plane

there is an unanticipated and permanent reduction in the inflation target from $\bar{\pi}^H$ to $\bar{\pi}^L$. The new steady state is denoted by point B in figure 12.8.

How does the economy adjust to the new equilibrium? The arrowed path in figure 12.8 indicates the transition from point A to point B.[15] Figure 12.9, panels b and c, illustrates the corresponding paths of inflation and the domestic real interest rate, respectively.[16]

To derive the path of c_t^N, notice that since r_t^d is always greater than r during the transition, it follows from equation (12.55) that $\dot{c}_t^N > 0$ for all $t \geq 0$. Since c_t^N does not change across steady states, it must fall on impact and then rise gradually toward its unchanged steady state (figure 12.9, panel d).

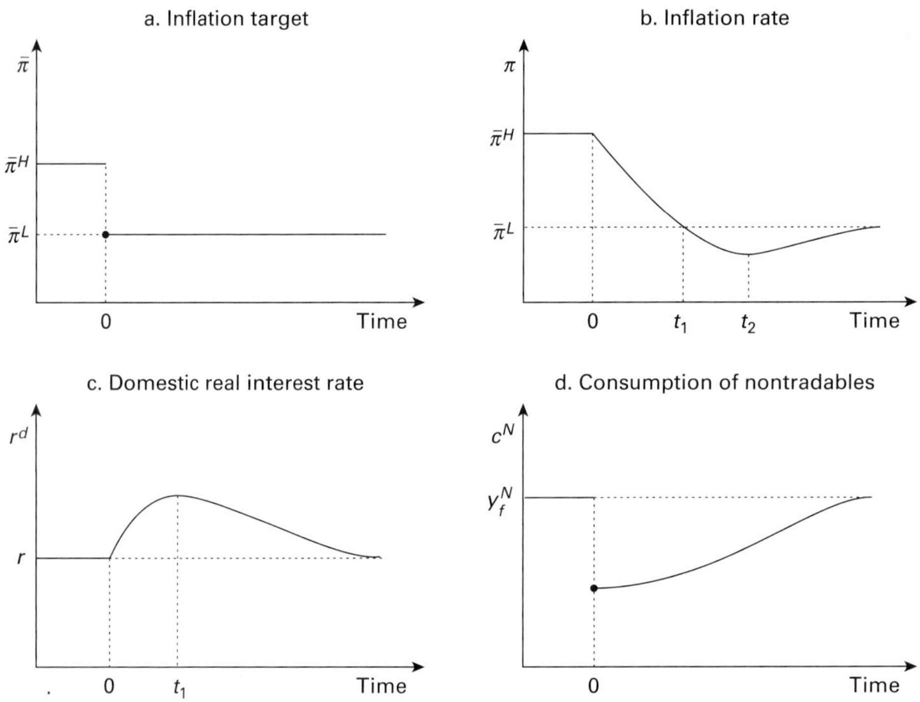

Figure 12.9
Reduction in inflation target

15. Since, as we will show below, c_t^N falls on impact, it follows from (12.60) that $\dot{\pi}_0 < 0$. The system must head in a southeastern direction as indicated in figure 12.8. Note that we are assuming that roots are real, and therefore that the adjustment is noncyclical.

16. We are denoting by t_1 the point in time at which r_t^d reaches a maximum in figure 12.8 and t_2 the point in time at which π_t reaches a minimum.

Regarding the nominal interest rate, note from (12.54) that it will fall across steady states. Further, since neither r_t^d nor π_t jump on impact, i_t will not change on impact. Hence, on average, i_t will fall during the transition.

What about real money balances, n_t? From (12.35) we infer that (1) n_t increases across steady states because the nominal interest rate is lower in the new steady state and consumption of nontradable goods is the same, and (2) n_t jumps down on impact because i_t does not change while c_t^N falls. We also know that $\dot{n}_t > 0$ from t_1 onward because $\pi_t < \mu_t$ (recall equation 12.58). Hence n_t will increase, on average, during the transition.

We conclude that a real interest rate rule like (12.59) does provide a nominal anchor to the economy. Of course, for this to be true, the inflation target must be fully credible on the part of the public. If that is the case, our model suggests that a real interest rate could be used effectively as a policy instrument.[17]

12.6 Real Targeting and Multiple Equilibria

As mentioned at the start of the chapter, countries have often followed threshold rules whereby some policy measure will be enacted if some macroeconomic variable reaches a certain threshold. The Central Bank of Chile, for instance, has traditionally had the mandate of maintaining a "sustainable" current account deficit, which has been taken to mean a deficit no larger than 4 to 5 percent of GDP, at trend terms of trade.[18] One of the major perils associated with threshold rules that target real variables is the possibility of multiple equilibria.

We will illustrate this idea in a simple two-period model. Consider an economy with constant endowments of tradable (y^T) and nontradable goods (y^N). The economy is small and perfectly integrated into world goods and capital markets.

The representative consumer's preferences are given by

$$U = \log(c_1^T) + \log(c_1^N) + \beta\left[\log(c_2^T) + \log(c_2^N)\right],$$

where c_t^T and c_t^N, $t = 1, 2$, denote consumption of tradable and nontradable goods, respectively, and β is the discount factor.

The intertemporal constraint takes the form

$$y^T + p_1 y^N + \frac{y^T + p_2 y^N + \tau}{1+r} = c_1^T + p_1 c_1^N + \frac{(1+\theta)(c_2^T + p_2 c_2^N)}{1+r}, \tag{12.62}$$

17. As shown in exercise 3 at the end of the chapter, we can in fact find some basic equivalences between real interest rules, nominal interest rules, and controlling the money supply. The rules, however, become more complex as we move from traditional instruments (the money supply) to less conventional ones (e.g., the real interest rate).

18. See Medina and Valdés (2002) and Morandé (2002a).

where p_t, $t = 1, 2$, is the relative price of nontradable goods in terms of tradable goods, r is the world real interest rate, θ is a consumption tax that may be imposed in the second period, and τ are lump-sum transfers that may occur in the second period.

Suppose that for reasons not modeled explicitly, the government is concerned about trade deficits. As a result it announces that if the trade deficit is greater than a certain level, a consumption tax $\bar{\theta}$ (> 0) will be imposed on second-period consumption:

$$\theta = \begin{cases} 0, & \text{if } TB_1 \geq \overline{TB}, \\ \bar{\theta}, & \text{if } TB_1 < \overline{TB}. \end{cases} \tag{12.63}$$

Formally, we proceed in the following way. We will first solve for the case where households do not expect the rule above to bind (i.e., they expect that no tariff will be imposed in the second period). We will then establish the range of parameter values for which the rule does not indeed bind. We will then solve for the case where households expect the rule to bind (i.e., they expect that a tariff will be imposed in the second period). We finally establish the range of parameter values for which the rule will indeed bind.

12.6.1 Households Do Not Expect the Threshold Rule to Bind

If households do not expect that a tariff will be imposed, the Lagrangian is given by

$$\mathcal{L} = \log(c_1^T) + \log(c_1^N) + \beta\left[\log(c_2^T) + \log(c_2^N)\right]$$
$$+ \lambda\left[y^T + p_1 y^N + \frac{y^T}{1+r} + \frac{p_2 y^N}{1+r} - c_1^T - p_1 c_1^N - \frac{c_2^T}{1+r} - \frac{p_2 c_2^N}{1+r}\right].$$

Since the government will not levy a tariff in the second period, lump-sum transfers will be zero.

The first-order conditions are given by

$$\frac{1}{c_1^T} = \lambda, \tag{12.64}$$

$$\frac{1}{c_1^N} = \lambda p_1, \tag{12.65}$$

$$\frac{\beta}{c_2^T} = \frac{\lambda}{1+r}, \tag{12.66}$$

$$\frac{\beta}{c_2^N} = \frac{\lambda p_2}{1+r}. \tag{12.67}$$

Combining first-order conditions (12.64) and (12.66) yields

$$\frac{1}{c_1^T} = \frac{\beta(1+r)}{c_2^T}. \tag{12.68}$$

To generate a trade deficit in the first period, we will assume that $\beta(1+r) < 1$. It follows from (12.68) that

$$c_1^T > c_2^T.$$

Imposing equilibrium in the nontradable goods markets, the intertemporal constraint (12.62) reduces to

$$\left(\frac{2+r}{1+r}\right) y^T = c_1^T + \frac{c_2^T}{1+r}. \tag{12.69}$$

Combining (12.68) and (12.69), we can solve for first-period consumption:

$$c_1^T = y^T \frac{2+r}{(1+r)(1+\beta)}. \tag{12.70}$$

By definition, the trade balance is given by

$$TB_1 = y^T - c_1^T. \tag{12.71}$$

Substituting (12.70) into the last equation, we obtain

$$TB_1 = y^T \left[1 - \frac{2+r}{(1+r)(1+\beta)}\right] < 0,$$

since $\{(2+r)\,/\,[(1+r)(1+\beta)]\} > 1$.

From threshold rule (12.63) we know that the government will not impose a tariff as long as the trade balance is above $\overline{TB}$. Hence the condition

$$y^T \left[1 - \frac{2+r}{(1+r)(1+\beta)}\right] \geq \overline{TB} \tag{12.72}$$

ensures that this case is a rational expectations equilibrium. In other words, if parameter values satisfy condition (12.72), then it is rational for consumers to expect that the government will not impose a tariff.

12.6.2 Households Expect the Threshold Rule to Bind

If households expect that a tariff will be imposed, the Lagrangian is given by

$$\mathcal{L} = \log(c_1^T) + \log(c_1^N) + \beta\left[\log(c_2^T) + \log(c_2^N)\right] + \lambda\left[y^T + p_1 y^N + \frac{y^T + p_2 y^N + \tau}{1+r} - c_1^T - p_1 c_1^N - \frac{(1+\bar{\theta})(c_2^T + p_2 c_2^N)}{1+r}\right].$$

First-order conditions are given by

$$\frac{1}{c_1^T} = \lambda,$$

$$\frac{1}{c_1^N} = \lambda p_1,$$

$$\frac{\beta}{c_2^T} = \frac{\lambda(1+\bar{\theta})}{1+r},$$

$$\frac{\beta}{c_2^N} = \frac{\lambda p_2(1+\bar{\theta})}{1+r}.$$

From the first and third first-order conditions, it follows that

$$c_2^T = c_1^T \frac{\beta(1+r)}{1+\bar{\theta}}.$$

In this case the government's budget constraint is given by

$$\tau = \bar{\theta}(c_2^T + p_2 c_2^N).$$

Using the last equation and the equilibrium in the nontradable goods market ($c_1^N = c_2^N = y^N$), we can solve for c_1^T from the intertemporal budget constraint (12.62):

$$\widetilde{c_1^T} = y^T\left(\frac{2+r}{1+r}\right)\frac{1}{1+\beta/(1+\bar{\theta})}, \tag{12.73}$$

where we are using a tilda superscript to denote equilibrium values in the consumption tax case. Comparing (12.70) and (12.73), we conclude that as expected,

$$\widetilde{c_1^T} > c_1^T$$

for $\bar{\theta} > 0$. Intuitively, if the consumption tax is positive in period 2, intertemporal substitution leads to higher consumption in period 1.

Given (12.73), the trade balance is given by

$$\widetilde{TB}_1 = y^T \left[1 - \left(\frac{2+r}{1+r} \right) \frac{1}{1+\beta/(1+\bar{\theta})} \right].$$

Given the threshold rule (12.63), the following must hold for this to be a rational expectations equilibrium:

$$y^T \left[1 - \left(\frac{2+r}{1+r} \right) \frac{1}{1+\beta/(1+\bar{\theta})} \right] < \overline{TB}. \tag{12.74}$$

To summarize, we have derived the conditions that ensure that a tax will not be imposed (given by equation 12.72) and that a tax will be imposed (given by condition 12.74). We can rewrite these two conditions as

$$y^T - \widetilde{c}_1^T - \overline{TB} < 0,$$

$$y^T - c_1^T - \overline{TB} \geq 0.$$

Figure 12.10 plots these two expressions as a function of the threshold $\overline{TB}$. Consider first the line $y^T - \widetilde{c}_1^T - \overline{TB}$, which intersects the horizontal axis at point A (where $\overline{TB} = y^T - \widetilde{c}_1^T$). For any point to the right of point A, a tax would always be imposed because the trade balance would be below the threshold. Consider then the line $y^T - c_1^T - \overline{TB}$, which intersects the horizontal axis at point B. For any point to the left of point B, no tax would ever be imposed because the trade balance would always be above the threshold. Three regions are then defined, labeled I (to the left of point A), II (between points A and B), and III (to the right of point B). For large values of $\overline{TB}$ (i.e., above point B), a tax will always be imposed. For low values of $\overline{TB}$ (i.e., to the left of point A), a tax will never be imposed. For intermediate values of $\overline{TB}$ (i.e., between points A and B), there is multiple equilibria. If agents expect a consumption tax rate to be imposed in the second period, their consumption will be such that the threshold will be hit and the tax rate will indeed be imposed. If agents do not expect a consumption tax rate to be imposed, they will consume less today and the threshold will not be hit, which implies that a tax rate will not be imposed. Ironically, the mere existence of threshold rule (12.63) may then trigger the precise scenario that policy makers are trying to avoid to begin with!

Finally, notice that we could express the threshold rule as a function of the real exchange rate (i.e., the inverse of p_t) because for each value of TB_1 there is a corresponding value of p_1. Formally, from (12.64) and (12.65), and imposing nontradable goods market equilibrium, we obtain

$$c_1^T = p_1 y^N.$$

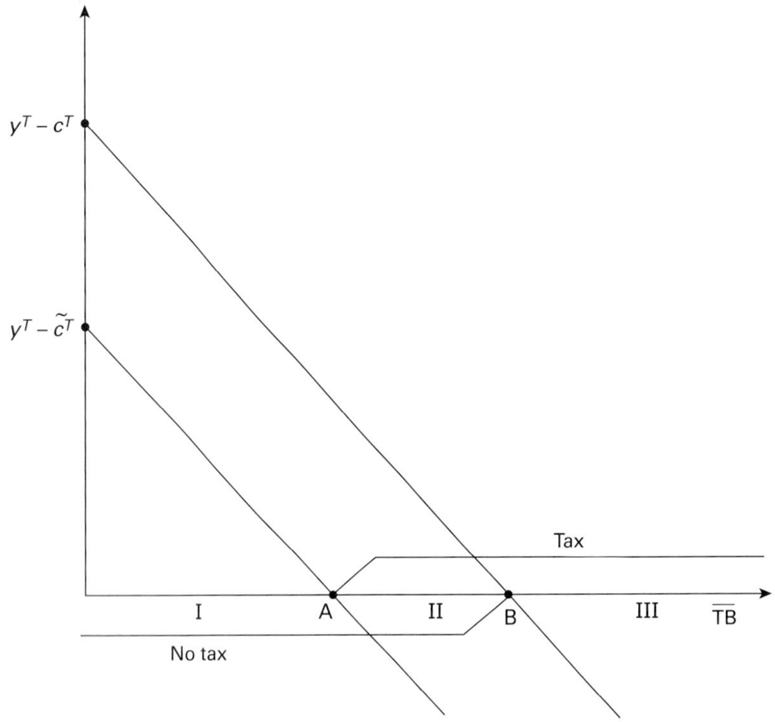

Figure 12.10
Multiple equilibria

Substituting this expression into the definition of the trade balance (equation 12.71) and solving for p_1 obtains

$$p_1 = \frac{y^T - TB_1}{y^N}.$$

The rule could then be expressed as

$$\theta = \begin{cases} 0 & \text{if } p_1 \leq \overline{p}, \\ \bar{\theta} & \text{if } p_1 > \overline{p}. \end{cases} \tag{12.75}$$

In this case the announcement of this rule could trigger the precise real appreciation that the rule is presumably intended to avoid.

12.7 Final Remarks

Policy makers often use real variables either as policy targets or policy instruments. An example of a real policy target would be a so-called PPP rule whereby the rate of devaluation is set as a function of the past differential between domestic and foreign inflation. An example of a real policy instrument would be the use of an interest rate on an indexed bond as the main monetary policy instrument. In principle, under either scenario the economy risks losing its nominal anchor, which could lead to high and/or volatile inflation. This chapter has analyzed whether those fears are warranted.

By and large, our theoretical results suggest that such fears are indeed justified. While the details differ depending on the model and the type of experiment, the main message that emerges from our analysis is that depriving an economy of a "traditional" nominal anchor (in the form of the money supply, the exchange rate, or a nominal interest rate) will sow the seeds of nominal instability and/or leave the economy at the hands of private sector's expectations. When such policies do work, it is typically due to some implicit nominal anchor like a fully credible inflation target. In practice, however, such targets are unlikely to carry the level of credibility needed to function as a nominal anchor.

12.8 Appendixes

12.8.1 Derivations of Constraint in the Model of Section 12.2[19]

Under capital controls (modeled as a dual exchange rate regime), the consumer's flow constraint is given by

$$\dot{a}_t = \rho_t s_t b_t + y^T + \frac{y^N}{e_t} + \tau_t - c_t^T - \frac{c_t^N}{e_t} - \varepsilon_t m_t, \tag{12.76}$$

where b_t is the stock of net foreign bonds; s_t is the domestic price of real bonds; $a_t (\equiv m_t + s_t b_t)$ denotes real financial assets; and τ_t are real transfers from the government.[20] The intertemporal constraint (12.3) in the text follows from multiplying (12.76) by D_t, integrating forward, imposing the standard transversality condition, and assuming that $a_0 = 0$ (note that $i_t = \rho_t + \varepsilon_t$).

To derive the resource constraint (12.12), combine the government's flow constraint (equation 12.8 in the text) with the consumer's flow constraint (12.76) to obtain (after imposing condition 12.11 and taking into account that arbitrage implies that $\rho_t = r/s_t + \dot{s}_t/s_t$):

$$\dot{h}_t + s_t \dot{b}_t = y^T - c_t^T + r(h_t + b_t). \tag{12.77}$$

19. This appendix follows Guidotti and Végh (1992).

20. Notice that in a regime of capital controls, the domestic real price of bonds, s_t, may differ from the international price (one). Further the stock of net foreign bonds will be constant since the private sector cannot acquire bonds from either abroad or the Central Bank.

Under perfect capital mobility, $s_t \equiv 1$. Under capital controls, $b_t = b_0$ for all t so that $\dot{b}_t = 0$. In either case, equation (12.12) in the text follows from integrating forward (12.77), imposing the appropriate transversality condition, and assuming that $h_0 + b_0 = 0$.

12.8.2 Path of λ_t

We first show that λ decreases over time. We proceed by contradiction.

1. Suppose that λ_t were constant over time; that is, $\lambda_t = \lambda_0$ for all $t \in [0, T)$. Since $\dot{\lambda}_t = 0$, it follows from (12.21) that

$$\lambda_0 = \frac{u'((c^T)^1)}{(1+\alpha\beta)}.$$

From (12.18), however, $\lambda_T \neq \lambda_0$, which is a contradiction.

2. Suppose that λ_t increased over time. Given that $\dot{\lambda}_0 > 0$, it follows from (12.21) that

$$(1+\alpha\beta)\,\lambda_0 > u'((c^T)^1).$$

Since $\lambda_T > \lambda_0$, it follows that

$$(1+\alpha\beta)\,\lambda_T > u'((c^T)^1).$$

And since $(c^T)^1 < (c^T)^2$,

$$(1+\alpha\beta)\,\lambda_T > u'((c^T)^2).$$

The last expression, however, contradicts (12.18).

We conclude that λ_t decreases over time.

12.8.3 Roots of System for Real Exchange Targeting under Sticky Prices

Let δ_i, $i = 1, 2$, denote the roots of the differential equation system given by (12.49) in the text. To derive the characteristic equation, we need to solve for

$$\begin{vmatrix} -\gamma\eta - \delta_i & \theta c^T \\ -e_{ss}\eta & -\delta_i \end{vmatrix} = 0.$$

This can be rewritten as

$$\delta_i^2 + \gamma\eta\delta_i + e_{ss}\eta\theta c^T = 0.$$

Roots are thus given by

$$\delta_i = \frac{-\gamma\eta \pm \sqrt{(\gamma\eta)^2 - 4e_{ss}\eta\theta c^T}}{2}.$$

Roots are real if

$$\eta \geq \frac{4\theta y_f^N}{\gamma^2},$$

where we have used the fact that $e_{ss}c^T = y_f^N$.

Exercises

1. (Shocks to the foreign nominal interest rate) Consider the model of section 12.2 under perfect capital mobility and with a positive foreign inflation rate. In this context:

a. Solve the model for a PFEP along which i_t^* is first low and then high.

b. Show that by an appropriate choice of the path of ε_t, policy makers can restore the first-best equilibrium.

2. (Pure real interest rate targeting under alternative law of motion for inflation) Suppose that the law of motion for inflation of nontradable goods is given by (12.36), rather than (12.53). Show that pure real interest rate targeting still leads to inflation indeterminacy as in section 12.5.1.

3. (An equivalence proposition) This exercise follows Végh (2002). Consider a one-good closed economy with preferences given by

$$\int_0^\infty u(c_t)\exp(-\beta t)dt,$$

where c_t denotes consumption. Consumers hold two assets: a bond (indexed to the price level and in zero net supply) and money. Let a_t denote the household's real financial wealth:

$$a_t = b_t + m_t,$$

where b_t and m_t denote the real stocks of bonds and money, respectively. The nominal interest rate on the bond is denoted by i_t. As in chapter 7, money is introduced into the model through a transactions costs technology $v(m_t)$, where $v'(m_t) < 0$ and $v''(m_t) > 0$.[21] The consumer's flow constraint is given by

21. For simplicity, and unlike chapter 7, we assume that the transactions technology does not depend on consumption, which implies that the corresponding real money demand will only depend on the nominal interest rate.

$$\dot{a}_t = r_t a_t + y_t + \tau_t - c_t - i_t m_t - v(m_t),$$

where y_t denotes output of the good and τ_t are lump-sum transfers from the government. Further assume that the transactions costs technology takes the form

$$v(m_t) = m_t \left[\frac{1}{\sigma} \log(m_t) - \chi \right],$$

where χ is a positive parameter. The government plays no active role. It gives back to consumers as lump-sum transfers the proceeds from money creation and transactions costs. The government's constraint is thus[22]

$$\tau_t = \mu_t m_t + v(m_t).$$

Output is endogenous and assumed to be demand-determined; that is, $y_t = c_t$. As in section 12.4, the inflation rate is assumed to be predetermined at each point in time. The change in the inflation rate is given by

$$\dot{\pi}_t = \gamma(\mu_t - \pi_t) + \alpha(c_t - y_f), \tag{12.78}$$

where y_f denotes the "full-employment" level of output.

In the context of this model, show that the following three monetary policy rules are exactly equivalent:

a. Policy makers set a fixed-money growth rule:

$$\mu_t = \bar{\mu}.$$

b. Policy makers announce an inflation target, $\bar{\pi}$ (equal to $\bar{\mu}$), and follow the nominal interest rate rule

$$\dot{i}_t = \theta(\pi_t - \bar{\mu}), \qquad \theta = \frac{1}{\sigma}.$$

c. Policy makers announce an inflation target, $\bar{\pi}$ (equal to $\bar{\mu}$), and follow the real interest rate rule:

$$\dot{r}_t = \theta^1(\pi_t - \bar{\mu}) + \theta^2(c_t - y^f), \qquad \theta^1 = \gamma + \frac{1}{\sigma},\ \theta^2 = -\alpha.$$

22. The fact that $v(m_t)$ appears in the government's flow constraint reflects the assumption that $v(m_t)$ is a private cost for consumers but not a social cost. Formally, one could think of some federal agency providing (at zero cost) the transactions costs needed by consumers. The profits of this federal agency are returned to households as lump-sum transfers. This assumption is made to eliminate wealth effects associated with changes in inflation, which would unnecessarily complicate the analysis.

References

Bacha, Edmar L. 1979. Notes on the Brazilian experience with minidevaluations, 1968–1976. *Journal of Development Economics* 6 (4): 463–81.

Bruno, Michael. 1993. *Crisis, Stabilization and Economic Reform: Therapy by Consensus.* Oxford, Clarendon Press.

Calvo, Guillermo A. 1987. Real exchange rate dynamics with nominal parities: Structural change and overshooting. *Journal of International Economics* 22 (1–2): 141–55.

Calvo, Guillermo A., Carmen M. Reinhart, and Carlos A. Végh. 1995. Targeting the real exchange rate: Theory and evidence. *Journal of Development Economics* 47 (1): 97–133.

Cardenas, Mauricio. 2007. *Introducción a la economía colombiana.* Colombia: Editorial Alfaomega.

Chumacero, Rómulo A. 2002. Arbitraje de tasas de interés en Chile. Unpublished manuscript. Central Bank of Chile.

Dornbusch, Rudiger. 1982. PPP exchange-rate rules and macroeconomic stability. *Journal of Political Economy* 90 (1): 158–165.

Fendt, Robert. 1981. The Brazilian experience with the crawling peg. In John Williamson, ed., *Exchange Rate Rules: The Theory, Performance, and Prospects of the Crawling Peg*. New York: St. Martin's Press, 140–51.

Ffrench-Davis, Ricardo. 1981. Exchange rate policies in Chile: The experience with the crawling peg. In John Williamson, ed., *Exchange Rate Rules: The Theory, Performance, and Prospects of the Crawling Peg*. New York: St. Martin's Press, 152–74.

Fuentes, Rodrigo S., Alejandro Jara, Klaus Schmidt-Hebbel, and Matias Tapia. 2003. La nominalizacion de la politica monetaria en Chile: Una evaluacion. *Revista Economia Chilena* 6 (2): 5–27.

Guidotti, Pablo E., and Carlos A. Végh. 1992. Macroeconomic interdependence under capital controls: A two-country model of dual exchange rates. *Journal of International Economics* 32: 353–67.

Lahiri, Amartya. 2001. Controlling capital flows: Targeting stocks versus flows. Unpublished manuscript. University of British Columbia.

Morandé, Felipe L. 2002a. A decade of inflation targeting in Chile: Developments, lessons, and challenges. In Norman Loayza and Raimundo Soto, eds., *Inflation Targeting: Design, Performance, Challenges*. Santiago: Central Bank of Chile, 583–626.

Morandé, Felipe L. 2002b. Nominalización de la tasa de política monetaria: Debate y consecuencias. *Cuadernos de Economia* 39 (117): 239–52.

Medina, Juan Pablo, and Rodrigo O. Valdés. 2002. Optimal monetary policy when the current account matters. In Norman Loayza and Klaus Schmidt Hebbel, eds., *Monetary Policy: Rules and Transmission Mechanisms*. Santiago: Central Bank of Chile, 65–94.

Uribe, Martin. 2003. Real exchange rate targeting and macroeconomic instability. *Journal of International Economics* 59 (1): 137–59.

Urrutia, Miguel. 1981. Experience with the crawling peg in Colombia. In John Williamson, ed., *Exchange Rate Rules: The Theory, Performance, and Prospects of the Crawling Peg*. New York: St. Martin's Press, 207–20.

Valdés, Rodrigo O. 1997. Transmisión de política monetary en Chile. Working Paper 16. Cental Bank of Chile, Santiago.

Végh, Carlos A. 2002. Monetary policy, interest rate rules, and inflation targeting: Some basic equivalences. In Fernando Lefort and Klaus Schmidt-Hebbel, eds., *Indexation, Inflation, and Monetary Policy*. Santiago: Central Bank of Chile, 151–83

Williamson, John. 1965. *The Crawling Peg*. Princeton: Princeton University Press.

13 Stopping High Inflation

13.1 Introduction

High and chronic inflation has been one of the most pressing macroeconomic problems of developing countries for more than fifty years. Already in the 1950s—and as indicated in table 13.1—countries such as Argentina, Bolivia, Brazil, Chile, Uruguay, and Turkey had annual inflation rates of above 10 percent.[1] Inflation reached its heyday during the 1980s when all the developing countries in table 13.1 endured inflation rates of above 15 percent. Annual compounded rates of inflation for the last sixty years are all above 15 percent compared to 3.7 percent for the United States. After decades of failed stabilization attempts, some major inflation stabilization programs during the 1980s and 1990s finally succeeded in taming the inflation beast. During the first decade of the new century—and with the exception of Turkey—annual inflation in the traditionally high inflation countries of table 13.1 was below 10 percent, with countries such as Chile and Israel having achieved US inflation levels. Like a recovering alcoholic, however, emerging countries remain keenly aware of the need to remain vigilant and avoid falling into the high-inflation trap once again by strengthening Central Bank independence and building stronger fiscal institutions. Current inflation in Venezuela (above 25 percent for 2011) and Argentina (believed to be running at an annual rate of 25 to 30 percent, even though official inflation is "just" 10 percent) are vivid reminders of how easy it is for emerging countries to succumb once more to the inflationary scourge.

Even before the academic profession had reached a consensus on the benefits of keeping inflation low and stable (see chapter 10), policy makers in emerging countries had spent several decades trying to achieve such an elusive objective. This long history of inflation stabilization programs in chronic inflation countries offers a rich and fascinating laboratory to understand the macroeconomic dynamics associated with disinflation attempts. This chapter studies in detail

1. In the case of Brazil, we use the Sao Paolo price index to ensure consistency over time because national figures are only available since the 1970s. The correlation, however, between the national and the Sao Paolo price indexes since the 1970s is 99 percent.

Table 13.1
Inflation in selected countries (annual compounded rate; percent)

	United States	Argentina	Bolivia	Brazil*	Chile**	Mexico	Uruguay	Israel***	Turkey****
1950–2010	3.7	67.2	38.8	75.3	32.4	17.2	35.8	23.1	29.8
1950–1959	1.9	24.8	58.4	18.0	34.6	6.9	13.0	7.7	14.4
1960–1969	2.2	19.7	5.1	41.6	23.1	2.2	41.8	4.9	3.3
1970–1979	6.5	104.7	14.3	26.7	123.5	13.9	54.9	30.2	21.6
1980–1989	4.2	291.0	217.7	193.3	17.6	61.3	48.9	88.2	38.9
1990–1999	2.5	15.0	8.6	197.0	9.0	17.3	34.5	9.4	68.6
2000–2009	2.2	8.5	4.5	5.3	3.1	4.3	8.0	1.9	17.0

Source: International Financial Statistics (International Monetary Fund) and Central Bank of Brazil.
Note: * Index for Sao Paulo; ** data end in 2009; *** data start in 1952; **** data start in 1953.

the stylized facts associated with stopping high inflation and the main models that have been developed to understand these facts.

The central theme of the large literature on stopping high inflation has been the strikingly different real effects observed in these episodes compared to the real effects that had been observed in industrial countries. In industrial countries, bringing down inflation has always come at the cost of a contraction in economic activity. In fact the question has not been *if* there would be a contraction but *how large* this contraction would be (e.g., see Ball 1994). The term "sacrifice ratio" was coined to indicate how much output would need to fall to bring down inflation by a certain amount. This long-standing conventional wisdom on the recessionary effects of disinflationary policies was badly shaken by two key findings of the new literature on stopping high inflation. First, in a celebrated 1982 article, Thomas Sargent argued that hyperinflations have been brought to an end with virtually no output costs. Sargent contrasted this finding with the received wisdom on the contractionary effects of disinflations in industrial countries and argued that a credible change in regime was responsible for the different real effects. A decade later Kiguel and Liviatan (1992) were the first to convincingly argue that exchange rate based stabilizations in developing countries actually lead to an output *expansion* rather than a contraction. While this fact had already been pointed out by several authors—most notable Rodriguez (1982)—inspired by the Southern Cone stabilization programs of the late 1970s (the so-called tablitas), no systematic evidence based on a large sample of programs dating back to the 1960s had been put together until Kiguel and Liviatan's influential contribution. In light of the closed economy literature, these empirical findings came as a major puzzle and led to a large theoretical literature and further empirical work.

The chapter's departing point in section 13.2 is the distinction, first pointed out by Pazos (1972), between chronic inflation and hyperinflation. Up to that time—and following Cagan's (1956) celebrated study of the hyperinflations after the two world wars—high inflation had been essentially synonymous with hyperinflation. Pazos's (1972) key insight was to identify a new breed of high inflation—for which he coined the term "chronic inflation"—that had markedly different characteristics from Cagan's classical hyperinflations. In contrast to hyperinflations—which are of short duration and explosive in nature—chronic inflation may last several decades and is highly persistent due to indexation and expectational rigidities that develop as economies adapt to living with high inflation. As a result the dynamics associated with stopping hyperinflation and chronic inflation are radically different.

After contrasting hyperinflation and chronic inflation in section 13.2, section 13.3 illustrates the main stylized facts associated with stopping hyperinflation and chronic inflation. We argue that by fixing the nominal exchange rate, hyperinflations have been stopped virtually overnight with little real dislocations associated with the stabilization per se. The real effects stemming from stopping chronic inflation seem to depend instead on the nominal anchor that is used (i.e., the exchange rate versus the money supply). In exchange rate based stabilizations, there seems to be an initial boom in economic activity (particularly in GDP and consumption), followed by a later recession. In sharp contrast, in money based stabilizations, the recession occurs early in the programs, as is typically the case in industrial countries. Given the different timing of the real costs, it has been argued that the choice of the nominal anchor in developing countries amounts to a choice between recession now (money based) or recession later (exchange rate based).

With these stylized facts in mind, we present in section 13.4 a familiar model—the staggered prices model of chapter 8—to understand the dynamics associated with stopping hyperinflation. The model's main prediction is that a fully credible exchange rate based stabilization should stop inflation in its tracks with no real costs, which is consistent with the stylized facts reviewed in section 13.3.

Section 13.5 then turns to the dynamics associated with stopping chronic inflation using the exchange rate as the nominal anchor. Since the boom–recession cycle associated with exchange rate based stabilization has proved to be a major puzzle in search of an explanation, a large theoretical literature developed over the last thirty years aiming to provide an answer. The earliest explanation—first developed by Rodriguez (1982)—relied on a sticky-inflation *rate* (as opposed to a sticky-price *level* only) that resulted in his case from the assumption of adaptive inflationary expectations. We develop a perfect foresight version of this kind of model that delivers similar results. We then analyze lack of credibility—modeled as temporary policy—as an alternative explanation for the stylized facts associated with exchange rate based stabilization. We then turn to supply side effects as a possible source of the initial boom.

Section 13.6 focuses on money based stabilization (i.e., inflation stabilization programs that rely on the money supply as the main nominal anchor). We revisit the sticky-prices model of chapter 8 but now assume that preferences are nonseparable in tradables and nontradables to generate a dynamic response of the trade balance and current account. We develop this model in discrete time and solve it numerically. While the economy initially contracts regardless of preferences, the response of the trade balance depends on the magnitude of the intertemporal elasticity of substitution. We close this section by looking at the dynamics of money based stabilization in the model with inflation inertia first developed in section 13.5. Inflation responds gradually to the fall in the rate of money growth and needs to fall below it for real money balances to reach their higher steady-state value.

The chapter closes in section 13.7 with some concluding remarks. Two online appendixes detail the linearization of two of the chapter's models together with the coefficients that need to be inputted in the corresponding MATLAB programs.[2]

13.2 Chronic Inflation versus Hyperinflation[3]

In order to understand the stylized facts associated with stopping high inflation, we first need to focus on the main characteristics of inflationary processes in high-inflation countries. While high inflation comes in many guises, there is a key distinction—which goes back to Pazos (1972)—that will prove critical for the purposes of understanding inflation stabilization plans: hyperinflation and chronic inflation.

When Pazos (1972) wrote his influential book, high inflation was almost synonymous with hyperinflation, mostly due to Cagan's (1956) path-breaking study of the hyperinflations that occurred in the aftermath of the two world wars. Cagan used 50 percent per month as the threshold needed for an episode to qualify as a hyperinflation.[4] Table 13.2 lists eight hyperinflationary episodes that fit Cagan's definition. Hyperinflations are short episodes—typically lasting less than a year—that exhibit an explosive behavior of monthly inflation.

Pazos's key insight was that the inflationary processes then underway in several Latin American countries—which he labeled "chronic inflation"—differed from Cagan's hyperinflations in three key respects:

- Chronic inflation may last for prolonged periods of times: it is not measured in terms of months—as is the case of hyperinflations—but rather in terms of years and even decades. Countries such as Argentina, Brazil, Chile, Israel, Mexico, and Uruguay have experienced chronic inflation processes that have lasted several decades (table 13.1).[5] Figure 13.1 depicts the 12-month inflation rate for perhaps the quintessential chronic inflation country in the world: Uruguay. Over the last sixty years, Uruguay's average annual inflation rate has been 35 percent. In fact, until August 1997 when the 12-month inflation rate finally fell below 20 percent per annum for good—with a temporary blip in late 2002 and early 2003 due to the Argentinean December 2001 crisis—inflation in Uruguay had dropped below 20 percent only sporadically, typically as a result of major stabilization plans (the June 1968 plan and the October 1978 "tablita").

2. Both the appendixes and the MATLAB programs are available on the book's website.

3. This section draws heavily on Calvo and Végh (1999) and Végh (1992).

4. More precisely, Cagan (1956, p. 25) defines a hyperinflation episode "as beginning in the month the rise in prices exceeds 50 percent and as ending in the month before the monthly rise in prices drops below that amount and stays below for at least a year."

5. Long periods of chronic inflation may eventually lead to hyperinflation (defined, following Cagan, as monthly inflation rates of over 50 percent a month). The monthly inflation rate reached 76 percent in Argentina in May 1989 and 51 percent in Brazil in December 1989. These hyperinflationary outbursts, which represent an explosive stage of a long period of chronic inflation, have, however, very different characteristics from the classical hyperinflations (see Kiguel and Liviatan 1995).

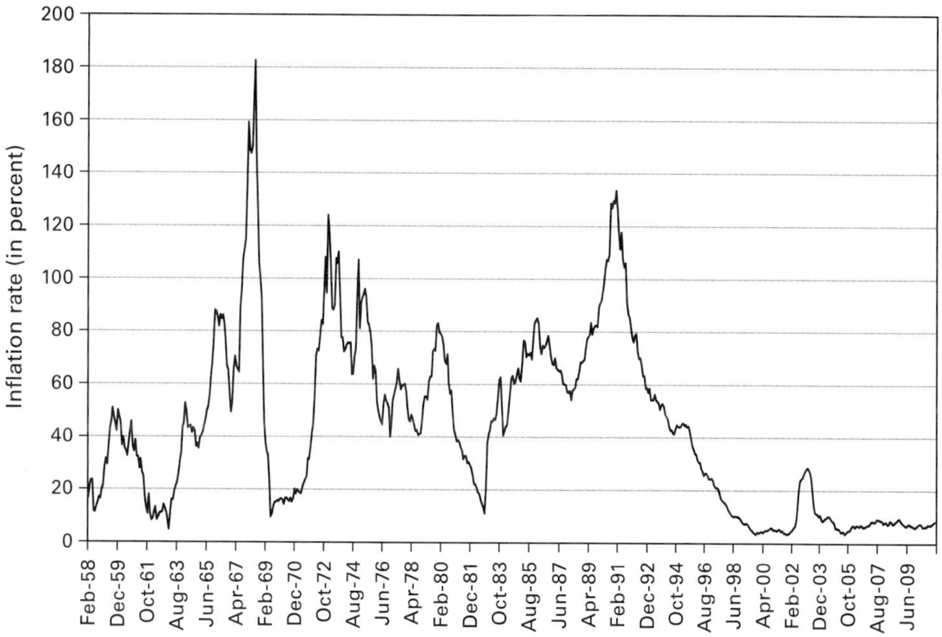

Source: International Financial Statistics (IMF)

Figure 13.1
Uruguay, 1957 to 2011: Twelve-month inflation rate (in percent)

• Chronic inflation exhibits a high degree of persistence, as countries learn how to live with high inflation by creating formal and informal indexation mechanisms that tend to perpetuate the inflationary process. Inflation does not exhibit an inherent propensity to accelerate and, if it does, soon reaches a new plateau.

In sharp contrast, during hyperinflations—and to quote Pazos's (1972, p. 19) masterful description of the German hyperinflation—"oscillations [in the inflation rate] were so large and erratic that the chart seems to register the movements of an object that has been let loose in a frictionless environment and is reacting, without offering resistance, to the external forces being applied to it." Figure 13.2 illustrates these wild oscillations in the inflation rate for four of the eight hyperinflations listed in table 13.2.

• Unlike hyperinflations, whose fiscal origin is clear and unmistakable (see Cagan 1956), the ultimate fiscal cause of chronic inflation is much less obvious due to the much more subtle contemporaneous relationship between fiscal deficits and inflation.[6] This makes any attempt at eliminating

6. As discussed in box 13.1, the short-run link between fiscal deficits and inflation is more difficult to discern than in the long run.

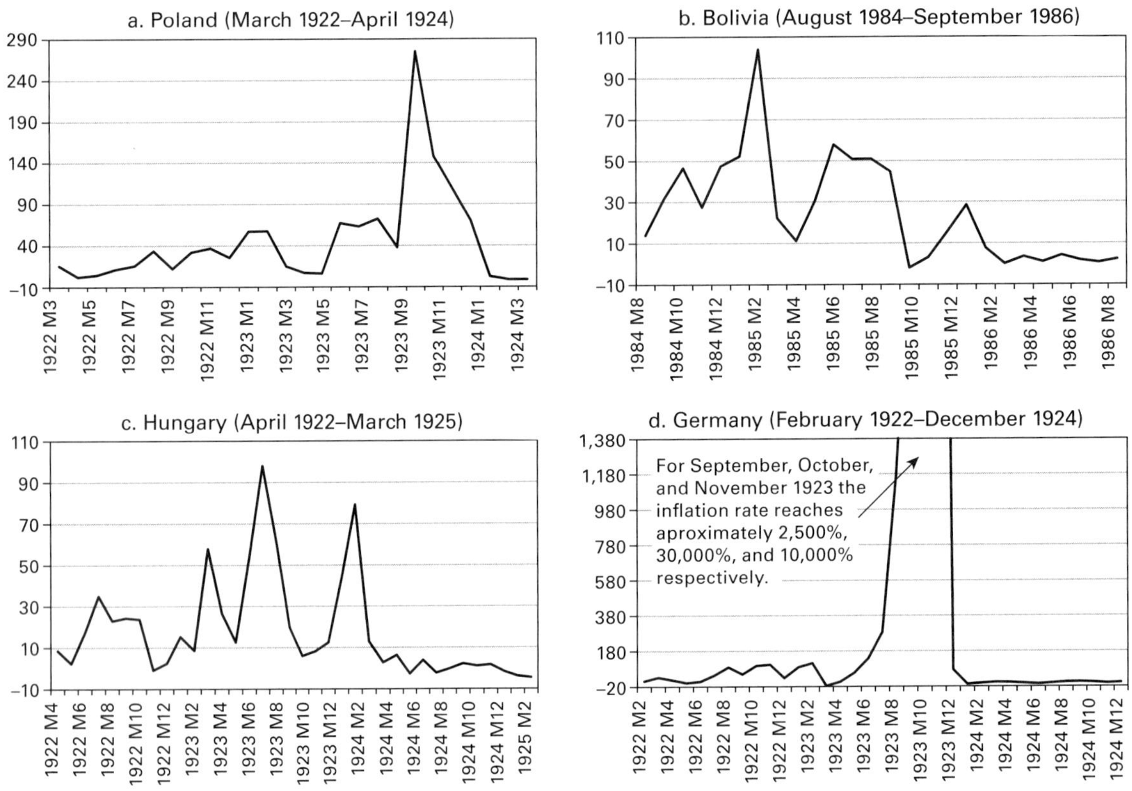

Source: Végh (1992)

Figure 13.2
Monthly inflation rates in four hyperinflations (in percent)

chronic inflation much more difficult because a fiscal reform may not have an immediate and drastic effect on inflation, which will quickly erode the credibility of the stabilization attempt itself.

Beyond the general notion of high and persistent inflation, there is no generally accepted definition of chronic inflation. Moreover any definition would probably not withstand the test of time since the notion of what constitutes high inflation changes over time.[7] While a widely accepted definition has proved elusive, it is easy to recognize a chronic inflation process once one has taken hold.[8]

7. Most telling in this respect is the fact that in the US inflation rates of around 5 percent, which would be viewed as quasi-price stability today, prompted the Nixon administration to impose price controls in August 1971!

8. Rudi Dornbusch used to refer to this as the "duck test": if it walks like a duck and quacks like a duck, you can be reasonably sure that it is a duck.

Table 13.2
Devaluation, inflation, and money growth in hyperinflations (geometric averages, percent per month)

Country	Devaluation rate	Inflation rate	Money growth
Austria (October 1922)			
October 1921–September 1922	32.6	46	35.7
October 1922–September 1923	−0.4	0.4	8.7
Poland (February 1924)			
February 1923–January 1924	63.7	66.2	62.7
February 1924–November 1924	0.8	1.2	11.1
Greece (February 1946)			
February 1945–January 1946	—	27	31.6
February 1946–December 1946	—	−0.8	13.4
Taiwan (June 1949)			
January 1948–May 1949	—	30.7	23.7
June 1949–December 1950	—	6.7	11.4
Germany (January 1924)			
January 1923–December 1923	409.8	455.1	419.7
January 1924–December 1924	−3.9	0.3	12
Hungary (April 1924)			
April 1923–March 1924	28	33.3	28.1
April 1924–March 1925	0	0.2	8.5
Hungary (August 1946)			
August 1945–July 1946	—	19,800	12,200
August 1946–July 1947	—	1.3	14.2
Bolivia (October 1985)			
October 1984–September 1985	44	57.9	48.5
October 1985–September 1986	4.9	5.7	8.3

Source: Végh (1992).
Note: The dates in parentheses following the country name indicate the month in which the exchange rate stabilized. Money refers to notes in circulation, except in Bolivia and Taiwan where it indicates M1.

13.3 Stopping High Inflation: Stylized Facts

13.3.1 Stopping Hyperinflation

The two main stylized facts regarding hyperinflation stabilization that we wish to emphasize are as follows:

• Inflation is stopped immediately. In most episodes involving hyperinflation stabilization, price stability has been achieved virtually overnight following the fixing of the nominal exchange rate.[9] To illustrate this point, table 13.2 shows monthly averages for the rates of devaluation and inflation

9. With the exception of Bolivia (where, although the system is best characterized as a dirty floating, the nominal exchange rate still provided a de facto nominal anchor), the exchange rate was generally stabilized by fixing the value of the domestic currency in terms of gold or foreign currency.

Box 13.1
What is the link between fiscal deficits and inflation?

While the fiscal origin of hyperinflations is clear, the link between fiscal deficits and inflation in chronic-inflation countries is more difficult to discern. This is to be expected because in the short-run fiscal deficits can be financed not only by printing money but also by issuing domestic and/or external debt. Over the long run, however, the link between fiscal deficits and inflation should be much more evident. Broadly speaking, this is precisely what the data show. While cross-country panel regressions based on annual observations already show a negative relationship between fiscal balance and inflation, the estimated coefficients are larger (in absolute terms) when the data is averaged over a five-year interval. In other words, the negative relationship between inflation and the fiscal balance seems to be stronger when short-run transitory fluctuations are smoothed out from the data.

Following Fischer, Sahay, and Végh (2002), we look at the short-run relation between fiscal balances and inflation by running a panel regression of the fiscal balance against inflation using a sample of annual observations for 77 countries covering the 1950 to 2010 period. The dependent variable is defined as the log of gross inflation, while the independent variable corresponds to the fiscal balance as a percent of GDP. The top panel of table 13.3 shows the result of OLS and fixed effects specifications for both the original sample and a subsample of 20 high-inflation countries. The fiscal balance coefficient is negative and significant in all cases and, as expected, larger (in absolute value) for high-inflation countries.

To illustrate the long-run relation between inflation and fiscal balance, a similar panel is constructed but defining each time period as a nonoverlapping five-year interval. That is, each observation corresponds to the five-year average of the original variable. This formulation helps filter out transitory short-term fluctuations. The results are presented in the bottom panel of table 13.3. All coefficients are larger in absolute value than those estimated using annual observations, and the difference is particularly large in the case of high-inflation countries.

Table 13.3
Fiscal balance and inflation

	Dependent variable: ln(1 + inf/100)			
	Regular panel			
	OLS		Fixed effects	
Independent variables	All countries (1)	High-inflation countries[b] (2)	All countries (3)	High-inflation countries (4)
Constant	0.1009 (0.000)	0.1766 (0.000)		
Fiscal balance[a]	−0.0090*** (0.006)	−0.0402*** (0.001)	−0.0106* (0.097)	−0.0478*** (0.003)
R^2	0.027	0.011	0.033	0.144

Box 13.1
(continued)

Table 13.3
(continued)

Independent variables	Panel of five-year averages			
	OLS		Fixed effects	
	All countries (1)	High-inflation countries (2)	All countries (3)	High-inflation countries (4)
Constant	0.1100 (0.000)	0.1744 (0.005)		
Fiscal balance[a]	−0.0115** (0.032)	−0.0621** (0.018)	−0.0139* (0.071)	−0.0825*** (0.000)
R^2	0.027	0.1273	0.032	0.176

Data: IFS (IMF), 77 countries, 1950 to 2010.
Note: The fiscal balance corresponds to the cash surplus/deficit. Country selection was based on having at least ten joint observations for inflation and fiscal balance. *p*-Values (based on robust standard errors) in parenthesis. A coefficient of −0.04, for example, means that a reduction in the fiscal balance of 1 percent of GDP increases the inflation rate by approximately 4 percentage points (e.g., from 10 to 14 percent). *** Significant at the 1% level; ** significant at the 5% level; * significant at the 10% level.
a. Percent of GDP.
b. Countries with an inflation average in the top 25th percentile.

In sum, the data support the idea that the relationship between inflation and fiscal balance is negative, and that this relationship appears to be stronger for high-inflation countries and when short-run fluctuations are filtered out from the data.

12 months before and 12 months after the exchange rate was stabilized in eight hyperinflations (Austria, Poland, Germany, Greece, Hungary after both world wars, Bolivia, and Taiwan).[10] The figures clearly illustrate how anchoring the nominal exchange rate can ensure a swift return to price stability. The most dramatic examples are Hungary in 1946 and Germany, when the monthly inflation rate in the 12 months before stabilization averaged 19,800 and 455.1 percent, respectively. After stabilization the monthly average dropped to 1.3 percent and 0.3 percent, respectively. In more moderate hyperinflations, such as in Hungary after World War I where monthly inflation averaged 33.3 percent before stabilization, the same phenomenon of overnight price stability took place. Even when price stability was not fully achieved, as in Bolivia and Taiwan, the drop

10. For the Polish, Greek, and Taiwanese stabilizations, slightly different periods had to be considered because of insufficient data.

in inflation was substantial. Not surprisingly, in Bolivia and Taiwan, the exchange rate did not stabilize completely.[11]

This drastic and immediate fall in inflation is perhaps not surprising if we keep in mind that during hyperinflations nominal frictions tend to disappear. In other words, when such astronomical rates of inflation are reached, nominal contracts virtually disappear and all prices (including wages) typically become indexed to the exchange rate. Since all prices are indexed to the exchange rate, stabilizing the exchange rate is tantamount to stabilizing the price level.

• Output costs are relatively small. While this stylized fact is less clearcut than the first one, the available evidence seems to indicate that hyperinflations have been stopped at little or no real cost (see Sargent 1982 and Végh 1992). It should be noted that the output response in the aftermath of hyperinflation stabilization is particularly difficult to assess for three reasons. First, available data are often sparse and unclear. Second, the real effects of the stabilization per se are difficult to disentangle from the real dislocations that characterize the transition from hyperinflation to price stability. Finally, in the case of the European hyperinflations following the two world wars, the effects of the war and the burden of heavy reparations payments have tended to blur the picture even further. With all these caveats in mind—and as reported in Végh (1992)—of the seven episodes listed in table 13.2 for which data are available, economic activity appears to have increased following stabilization in three cases (Germany, Greece, and Poland) and shown little change in two other cases (Taiwan and Bolivia). In yet two other cases (Austria and Hungary 1946) there is conflicting evidence.

13.3.2 Stopping Chronic Inflation

Stylized Facts Associated with ERBS

Table 13.4 lists 13 major exchange rate based stabilizations (ERBS) in emerging markets over the last fifty years. These are the episodes that have been at the heart of the large literature on the empirical regularities associated with ERBS.

Based on the last ten programs listed in table 13.4, figure 13.3 shows the typical time profile of an exchange rate based stabilization:[12]

1. Slow convergence of the inflation rate to the devaluation rate. Although panel a seems to show a faster convergence, the average figures mask some important heterogeneity. The typical situation for the celebrated Southern Cone tablitas of the late 1970s was a very slow convergence of inflation to the devaluation rate. It was in fact this lack of convergence—typically attributed to

11. In the Taiwanese stabilization, the black market rate stood 60 percent above the official rate six months after devaluation (Makinen and Woodward 1989).

12. The choice of programs was dictated by data availability. In both figures 13.3 and 13.4, the different panels show simple averages for all the programs. T denotes the year in which the stabilization plan was implemented; vertical lines indicate the year before stabilization (i.e., $T-1$).

Table 13.4
Major exchange rate based inflation stabilization plans

Programs	Beginning and ending dates	Exchange rate arrangement	Inflation rate: Initial	Inflation rate: Lowest	Inflation rate: Date achieved	How did the program end?
Brazil 1964	March 1964–August 1968	Fixed exchange rate with periodic devaluations	93.6	18.9	May 1968	Despite switching to a regime of minidevaluations after August 1968 devaluation, inflation remained stable around 20 percent per year until 1974.
Argentina 1967	March 1967–May 1970	Fixed exchange rate	26.4	5.7	Feb. 1969	Initial 14 percent devaluation was followed by further devaluations and an 82 percent decline in reserves.
Uruguay 1968	June 1968–December 1971	Fixed exchange rate	182.9	9.5	June 1969	Initial 48 percent devaluation was followed by successive devaluations and an 81 percent decline in reserves.
Chilean tablita	February 1978–June 1982	February 1978–June 1979: pre-announced crawling peg; June 1979–June 1982: fixed exchange rate	52.1	3.7	May 1982	About 65 percent of reserves were lost, and by February 1983 the currency had depreciated by 55 percent.
Uruguayan tablita	October 1978–November 1982	Pre-announced crawling	41.2	11.0	Nov. 1982	By March 1983, the Central Bank had lost 90 percent of its reserves and the peso had depreciated by 70 percent.
Argentine tablita	December 1978–February 1981	Pre-announced crawling	169.9	81.6	Feb. 1981	By April 1982, the currency had depreciated by 410 percent and reserves fallen by 71 percent.
Israel 1985	July 1985–present	Initial peg against the dollar; starting in August 1986 against a basket of currencies	445.4	−2.6	Jan. 2004	Inflation has continued to decline gradually and is below 5 percent per year as of end of 2012.
Austral (Argentina)	June 1985–September 1986	June 1985–March 1986: fixed exchange rate. March 1986–September 1986: crawling peg	1,128.9	50.1	June 1986	By September 1987, reserves had fallen by 75 percent and monthly inflation was above 10 percent.
Cruzado (Brazil)	February 1986–November 1986	Fixed exchange rate	286.0	76.2	Nov. 1986	By March 1987, reserves had fallen 58 percent and by December 1987, monthly inflation had reached 21 percent.

Table 13.4
(continued)

Programs	Beginning and ending dates	Exchange rate arrangement	Inflation rate: Initial	Inflation rate: Lowest	Inflation rate: Date achieved	How did the program end?
Mexico 1987	December 1987–December 1994	February 1988–December 1988: fixed exchange rate; January 1989–November 1991: pre-announced crawling peg; November 1991–December 1994: exchange rate band	159.0	6.7	Sep. 1994	Between February 1994 and January 1995, reserves fell by 85 percent, and following the December 1994 devaluation, the peso depreciated by about 100 percent in four months.
Uruguay 1990	December 1990–present	Exchange rate band with a declining rate of devaluation	133.7	3.1	June 2005	Uruguay was not much affected by the Mexican crisis, and despite a temporary outburst following the December 2001 Argentinean crisis, inflation has continued to decline gradually.
Convertibility (Argentina)	April 1991–December 2001	Currency board with a one-to-one parity to the US dollar	267.0	−2.3	Nov. 1999	Between January and July of 2002, reserves fell by 39 percent and there was a sharp depreciation of about 260 percent during the first half of 2002.
Real plan (Brazil)	July 1994–January 1999	In the months preceding the plan, an indexed unit was created, with a stable value in terms of dollars. In July 1994, the indexed unit was converted into a new currency and an exchange rate anchor instituted.	4,005.0	1.6	Jan. 1999	In the midst of a heavy loss of international reserves (a fall of 40.8 percent in the second half of 1998), the authorities decided to abandon the exchange rate anchor and let the real depreciate. The exchange rate increased by 52.8 percent in 1999.

Note: Unless otherwise noticed, all pegs are against the US dollar. Inflation measured as the 12-month change (in percent). Fall in reserves is measured relative to peak during program.
Source: Reinhart and Végh (1996), updated as of 2012 with IFS (IMF) data

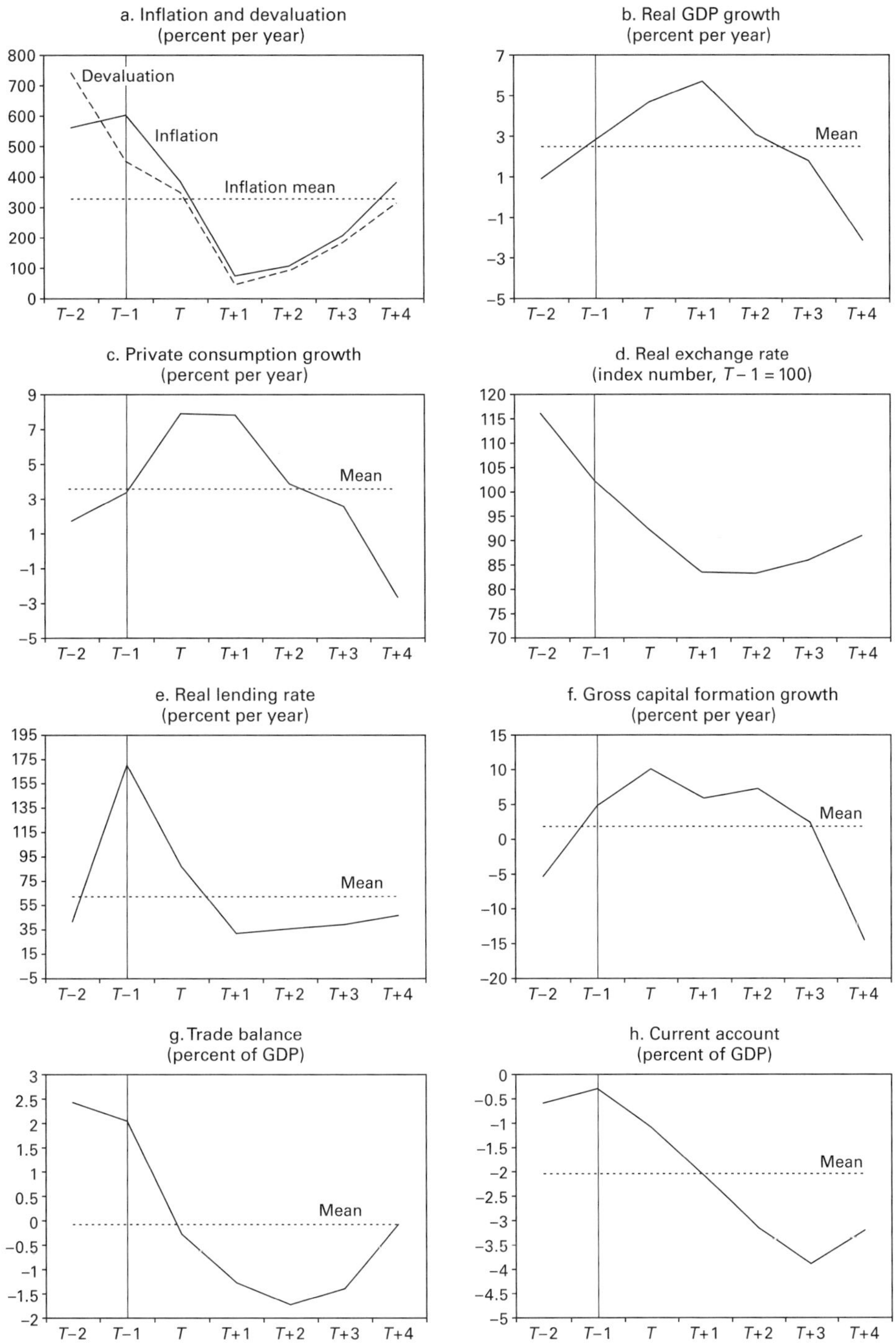

Source: Calvo and Végh (1999)

Figure 13.3
Exchange rate based stabilization

expectational and/or nominal rigidities—that prompted Argentina, Brazil, and Israel to implement the so-called heterodox programs in the mid-1980s, which included price and wage controls. Not surprisingly, inflation converged faster in such programs, though it was only in the Israeli case that the inflation gains proved to be permanent.

2. GDP and private consumption expand at the beginning of the program and later contract (panels b and c). This boom–recession cycle associated with exchange rate based stabilization has characterized most of the programs listed in table 13.4.

3. Sustained real appreciation. The U-pattern shown in panel d is typical of exchange rate based stabilizations. The relative price of nontradable goods rises sharply at the beginning of the programs and falls later on.

4. On average, real interest rates have fallen (panel e). However, there is considerable variation across programs. Real rates tended to fall in the tablitas but increased in heterodox programs.

5. Investment increases (panel f). Most programs saw a rise in investment in the early stages.

6. Deterioration of both trade balance and current account. As shown in panels g and h, both the trade balance and the current account deteriorate quite sharply in the initial years of exchange rate based stabilizations.

Stylized Facts Associated with MBS

Table 13.5 lists major money based stabilization programs (MBS) over the last 40 years. The small sample reflects the fact that, by and large, the nominal exchange rate has been a much more popular anchor in emerging markets.

Based on the five programs listed in table 13.5, the main empirical regularities associated with money based stabilization are as follows (figure 13.4):

1. Inflation converges slowly to the rate of money growth (panel a). Again, panel a masks some heterogeneity, with several programs showing extremely slow convergence of the inflation rate to the rate of money growth. Indeed it was precisely this problem that led policy makers in both Chile and Uruguay to replace a money anchor by an exchange rate anchor in the late 1970s.

2. GDP and private consumption contract in the early stages of the program (panels b and c). This is in fact the behavior of output and consumption observed during disinflation in industrial countries; see Ball (1994).

3. Initial real appreciation at the beginning of the programs (panel d). Contrary to what is often claimed to the effect that money based stabilization may prevent the real appreciation observed in exchange rate based programs, the evidence indicates that the relative price of nontradable goods has also increased during money based stabilizations.

4. Real interest rates increase (panel e).

5. Investment falls at the beginning of the program (panel f)

Table 13.5
Major money based inflation stabilization plans

Programs	Beginning and ending dates	Monetary/exchange rate policy	Inflation rate: Initial	Inflation rate: Lowest	Inflation rate: Date achieved	How did the program end?
Chile 1975	April 1975–December 1977	Control of monetary aggregates was cornerstone; exchange rate adjusted by past inflation	394.3	63.4	December 1977	Since inflation was falling at very slow pace, Chile switched to an exchange rate anchor in February 1978.
Bonex (Argentina)	December 1989–February 1991	Drastic cut in liquidity through forced rescheduling of domestic debt; dirty floating	4,923.3	287.3	February 1991	Due to the plan's lack of success (during the first quarter of 1991, reserves fell by 37 percent and depreciation and inflation were around 40 percent), authorities switched to an exchange rate anchor in April 1991 (Convertibility plan).
Collor (Brazil)	March 1990–January 1991	Sharp liquidity squeeze through freeze of 70% of financial assets; tight monetary policy. Exchange rate had a passive role and simply accommodated inflation.	5,747.3	1,119.5	January 1991	After Collor's allies were defeated in the November 1990 mid-term elections, the government began to flounder amid rising inflation: between December and March of 1991, inflation increased 93 percent and the exchange rate increased by 48 percent
Dominican Republic 1990	August 1990–August 2002	August 1990–December 1990: exchange controls/black markets; January 1991–July 1991: dual exchange rates; July 1991: exchange rate unification and floating	60.0	2.5	November 1993	Starting in September 2002, a bank run and an eventual bungled bank bailout triggered a major crisis: by August 2003, the 12-month increase in prices and the exchange rate had reached 33 percent and 84 percent, respectively.
Peru 1990	August 1990–present	Control of monetary aggregates; dirty floating.	12,377.8	−1.6	February 2002	Inflation remains below 5 percent per year as of end of 2012.

Source: Calvo and Végh (1999), updated as of 2012 with IFS (IMF) data.
Note: Inflation measured as the 12-month change (in percent).

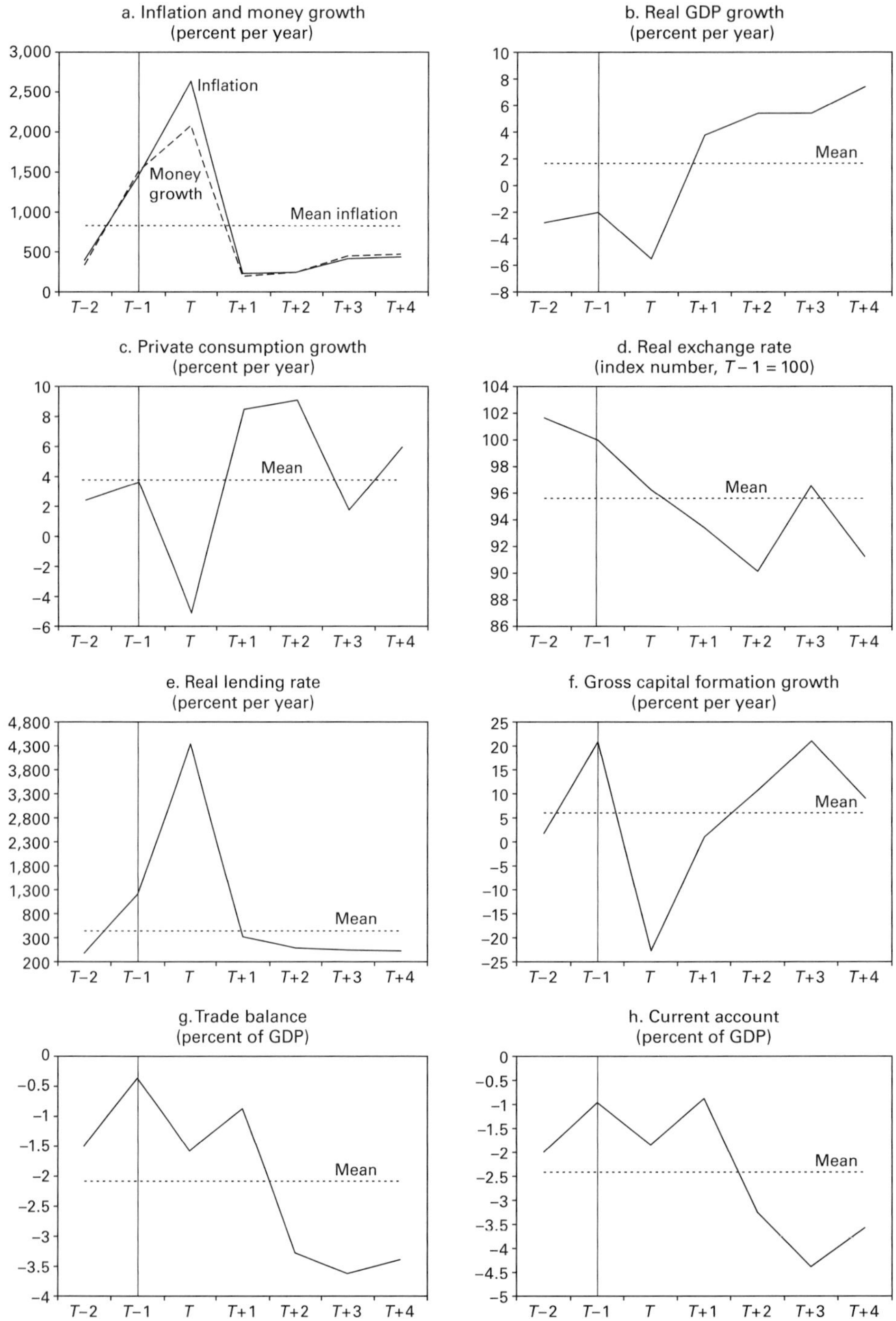

Source: Calvo and Végh

Figure 13.4
Money based stabilization

6. The behavior of the external accounts is unclear (panels g and h). If anything, we seem to observe no major effects over the first two years of the programs followed by a deterioration as GDP recovers.

13.4 Stopping Hyperinflation

We have seen above that the main stylized facts associated with stopping hyperinflation are that inflation stops abruptly once a fixed exchange rate is implemented and that this drastic reduction in inflation comes essentially at no output cost. This section develops a money-in-the-utility-function (MIUF) model with sticky prices that will explain these stylized facts.

Consider a small open economy perfectly integrated into world goods and capital markets. There are two goods: tradables and nontradables. The law of one price holds for the tradable good and the foreign price is constant and equal to one. Hence the domestic price of the tradable good is equal to the nominal exchange rate, E_t.

13.4.1 Households

Preferences are given by

$$\int_0^\infty [\log(c_t^T) + \log(c_t^N) + \log(m_t)] \exp(-\beta t) dt, \tag{13.1}$$

where c_t^T and c_t^N denote consumption of tradable and nontradable goods, respectively; m_t ($\equiv M_t/E_t$, where M_t are nominal money balances) denotes real money balances in terms of tradable goods; and β (> 0) is the discount rate.[13]

The households' flow constraint is given by

$$\dot{a}_t = ra_t + y_t^T + \frac{y_t^N}{e_t} + \tau_t - c_t^T - \frac{c_t^N}{e_t} - i_t m_t, \tag{13.2}$$

where $a_t (\equiv b_t + m_t)$ denotes real financial assets; r is the constant world real interest rate; y_t^T and y_t^N denote output of tradables and nontradables, respectively; e_t denotes the real exchange rate (i.e., the relative price of tradable goods in terms of nontradable goods); i_t is the nominal interest rate; and τ_t are government lump-sum transfers. Integrating forward and imposing the appropriate transversality condition, we obtain

$$a_0 + \int_0^\infty \left(y_t^T + \frac{y_t^N}{e_t} + \tau_t \right) \exp(-rt) dt = \int_0^\infty \left(c_t^T + \frac{c_t^N}{e_t} + i_t m_t \right) \exp(-rt) dt. \tag{13.3}$$

13. For analytical simplicity, we assume that households derive utility from m_t rather than from real money balances in terms of a price index. With logaritmic preferences—and as shown in chapter 8—this does not affect the dynamics of the model (other than for welfare computations, which will not concern us here).

The consumer chooses $\{c_t^T, c_t^N, m_t\}_{t=0}^{\infty}$ to maximize (13.1) subject to the intertemporal constraint (13.3). The first-order conditions are given by (assuming $\beta = r$)

$$\frac{1}{c_t^T} = \lambda, \tag{13.4}$$

$$\frac{1}{c_t^N} = \frac{\lambda}{e_t}, \tag{13.5}$$

$$\frac{1}{m_t} = \lambda i_t, \tag{13.6}$$

where λ is the multiplier associated with constraint (13.3). Combining first-order conditions (13.4) and (13.5), we obtain the familiar condition

$$c_t^N = e_t c_t^T. \tag{13.7}$$

Combining first-order conditions (13.4) and (13.6), we obtain the real money demand equation:

$$m_t = \frac{c_t^T}{i_t}. \tag{13.8}$$

13.4.2 Supply Side

The supply side follows chapter 8. The supply of tradable goods is assumed to be exogenous and constant over time (i.e., $y_t^T = y^T$). Sticky prices for nontradable goods are introduced into the model following Calvo's (1983) staggered prices formulation. In such a setup the rate of change of the inflation rate of nontradable goods (π_t) is a *negative* function of excess aggregate demand:

$$\dot{\pi}_t = -\theta(y_t^N - y_f^N), \qquad \theta > 0, \tag{13.9}$$

where y_t^N is aggregate demand for nontradables and y_f^N is the "full-employment" level of output of nontradables. In this formulation, the price level of nontradables is sticky (i.e., it is predetermined at each instant in time), but the inflation rate is fully flexible because it is a forward-looking variable. Equation (13.9) can be derived by assuming that firms set prices in a nonsynchronous manner taking into account the future path of aggregate demand and the average price level prevailing in the economy (see appendix 8.8.1 in chapter 8 for the formal derivation of equation 13.9).

13.4.3 Government

The government's flow constraint is given by

$$\dot{h}_t = rh_t + \dot{m}_t + \varepsilon_t m_t - \tau_t, \tag{13.10}$$

where h_t denotes the government's stock of net foreign assets and ε_t is the rate of devaluation.

13.4.4 Equilibrium Conditions

Perfect capital mobility implies that the interest parity condition holds:

$$i_t = r + \varepsilon_t. \tag{13.11}$$

Equilibrium in the nontradable goods market requires that

$$c_t^N = y_t^N. \tag{13.12}$$

Recall that in the current setup, output of nontradable goods is demand-determined, so "equilibrium" in the nontradable goods market holds by construction.

By definition, $e_t = E_t/P_t^N$. Hence

$$\frac{\dot{e}_t}{e_t} = \varepsilon_t - \pi_t. \tag{13.13}$$

This dynamic equation simply states that if, say, nontradable goods inflation is larger than tradable goods inflation (given by ε_t), the relative price of tradable goods will be falling over time.

Combining the consumers' flow constraint (given by equation 13.2) with the government's (given by equation 13.10) and imposing the interest parity condition (13.11) and equilibrium in the nontradable goods market, given by (13.12), we obtain

$$\dot{k}_t = rk_t + y^T - c_t^T, \tag{13.14}$$

where $k_t (\equiv b_t + h_t)$ denotes the economy's net foreign assets. Integrating forward (13.14) and imposing the corresponding transversality condition, we obtain

$$k_0 + \frac{y^T}{r} = \int_0^\infty c_t^T \exp(-rt)dt. \tag{13.15}$$

13.4.5 Perfect Foresight Equilibrium

Let us now characterize the perfect foresight equilibrium path for a constant value of the rate of devaluation, ε. From the interest parity condition (13.11), the nominal interest rate will be constant and given by

$$i = r + \varepsilon. \tag{13.16}$$

First-order condition (13.4) indicates that c_t^T will be constant over time. From the resource constraint (13.15), it then follows that

$$c^T = rk_0 + y^T. \tag{13.17}$$

Given that both the nominal interest rate and consumption of tradable goods are constant along a perfect foresight equilibrium path, so is the real money demand (from equation 13.8):

$$m = \frac{rk_0 + y^T}{r + \varepsilon}. \tag{13.18}$$

To solve for the rest of the model, we proceed as in chapter 8 and set up a dynamic system in π_t and e_t. Recall that since, by definition, $e_t = E_t/P_t^N$, the real exchange rate is a predetermined variable. To obtain the first dynamic equation, substitute (13.7) into (13.9), taking into account (13.17), to obtain

$$\dot{\pi}_t = \theta\left(y_f^N - e_t c^T\right).$$

The second dynamic equation is given by (13.13).

The system's steady state is given by

$$\pi_{ss} = \varepsilon, \tag{13.19}$$

$$e_{ss} = \frac{y_f^N}{c^T}. \tag{13.20}$$

Linearizing the system around the steady state, we obtain

$$\begin{bmatrix} \dot{e}_t \\ \dot{\pi}_t \end{bmatrix} = \begin{bmatrix} 0 & -e_{ss} \\ -\theta c^T & 0 \end{bmatrix} \begin{bmatrix} e_t - e_{ss} \\ \pi_t - \varepsilon \end{bmatrix}.$$

The determinant of the matrix associated with the linear approximation of the system is given by

$$\Delta = -\theta c^T e_{ss} < 0,$$

which implies that the system is saddle-path stable. Proceeding as usual, it is easy to construct the phase diagram illustrated in figure 13.5. For a given initial value of the real exchange rate, e_0,

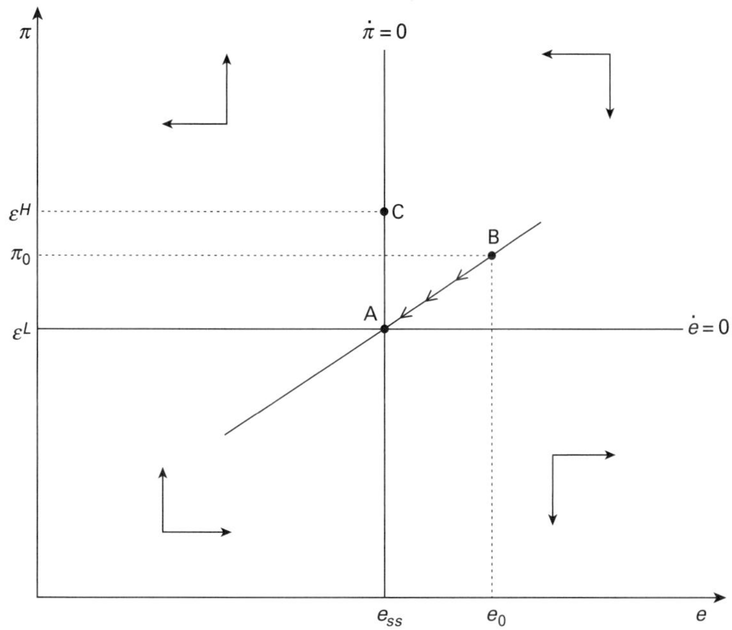

Figure 13.5
Stopping hyperinflation: Phase diagram

the inflation rate of nontradables will be such that the system positions itself at point B and then travels along the saddle path toward the steady state given by point A.

13.4.6 Permanent Stabilization

Suppose that the economy is initially in the equilibrium just described for a high rate of devaluation, ε^H. At time 0 there is an unanticipated and permanent reduction in the devaluation rate from ε^H to ε^L (figure 13.6, panel a).[14]

Since, in the new perfect foresight equilibrium path, the devaluation rate is constant (though at a lower level), the nominal interest rate, consumption of tradables, and real money balances will be constant as well as analyzed above. By the interest parity condition (13.16), the nominal interest rate falls one-to-one with the rate of devaluation (figure 13.6, panel b). Consumption of tradable goods remains given by (13.17) because the fall in the nominal interest rate does not affect existing resources (panel c). Finally, from (13.18), real money demand increases (panel d), through an increase in the stock of nominal money balances (panel e).

14. Of course, ε^L could be zero (i.e., the exchange rate is fixed, the most common scenario in practice when stabilizing from hyperinflation).

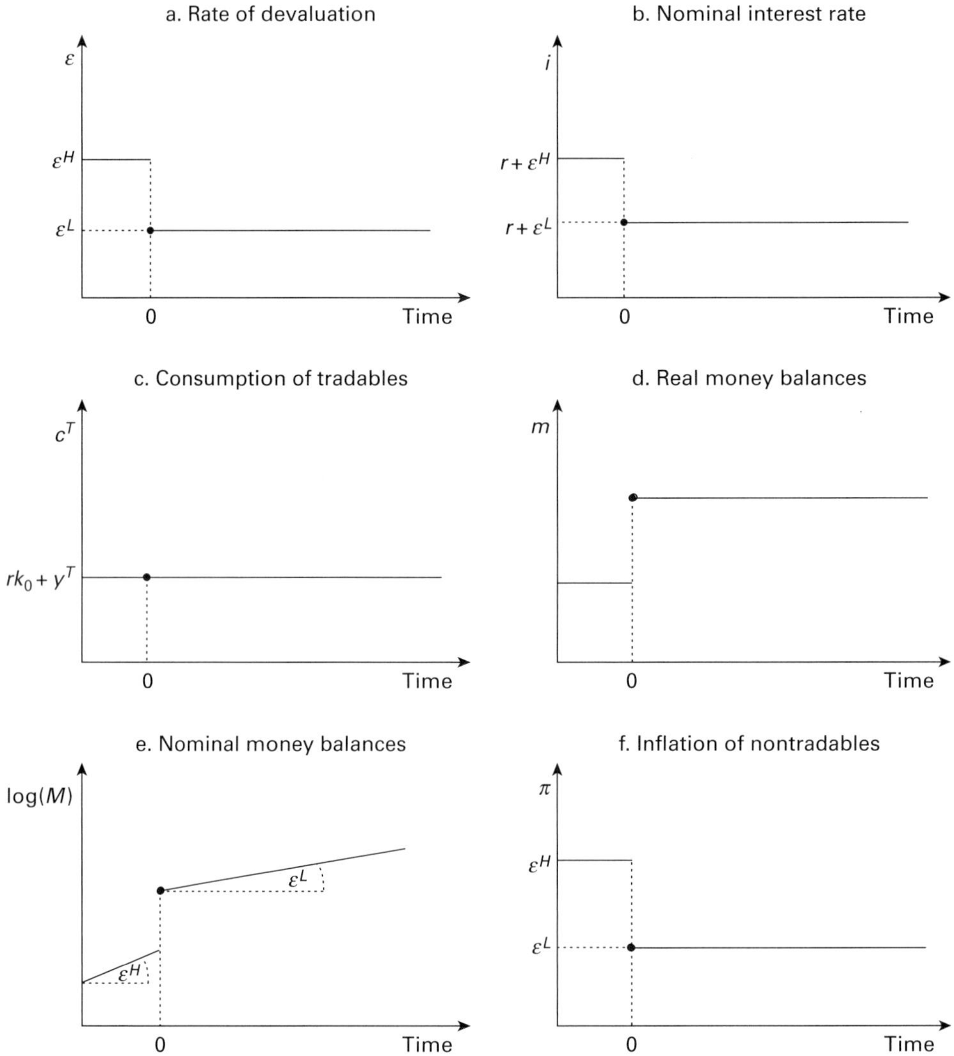

Figure 13.6
Stopping hyperinflation: Time paths

We now turn to the behavior of inflation and the real exchange rate. In terms of the phase diagram (figure 13.5), suppose that the initial equilibrium is given by point C. In the new steady state (point A in figure 13.5), the rate of inflation is lower and the real exchange rate remains unchanged. How will the economy adjust from point C to point A? A moment's reflection reveals that the economy must adjust instantaneously to its new steady state. Since e_t is a predetermined variable, the system must remain along the vertical line corresponding to e_{ss} at time 0. But, if the system jumped to any point other than point A along that vertical line, it would diverge over time. Hence the only possible equilibrium is for the system to jump from point C to point A. The inflation rate of nontradable goods thus falls immediately to its lower steady-state value (figure 13.6, panel f).

13.4.7 Matching Theory with Evidence

We have seen that the model predicts that a permanent reduction in the devaluation rate should lead to an immediate fall in the inflation rate, a rise in real money balances, and no real effects. These facts are consistent with the stylized facts associated with stopping hyperinflation reviewed above.

We will now argue that the main assumptions underlying this experiment—the reduction in the devaluation rate is permanent and the inflation rate is forward looking—capture some critical features of the real world associated with hyperinflation stabilization. First, notice that we can reinterpret this permanent exchange rate based stabilization as a fully credible exchange rate based stabilization. In other words, think of policy makers announcing a reduction in the devaluation rate (which, as a particular case, would include fixing the nominal exchange rate) and the public believing that this policy will be permanent. As argued above, the fact that the fiscal root of hyperinflation is clear and well known by the public and the country's economic and social fabric is disintegrating rapidly typically lends a great deal of credibility to any serious attempt to stop it. Hence, reinterpreted as capturing a situation of credible policy, the experiment of a permanent exchange rate based stabilization captures an essential element of actual hyperinflation stabilizations.

Second—and as also argued above—any vestiges of nominal rigidities in prices and/or wages disappear in the midst of a hyperinflation. Typically all prices become indexed—on a daily or even hourly basis—to the easily observable nominal exchange rate. As a result there is no backward-looking component to the inflation rate. In this light Calvo's (1983) staggered prices formulation—which implies a fully flexible inflation rate—seems to accord well with a key reality of hyperinflation.

We thus conclude that while highly stylized, the experiment illustrated in figure 13.6 captures the main elements of hyperinflation stabilizations and matches the actual data.

13.5 Stopping Chronic Inflation: Exchange Rate Based Stabilization

This section will consider several models that can account for the stylized facts reviewed in section 13.3.2 regarding exchange rate based stabilizations. We will first analyze a model with inflation inertia (i.e., sticky inflation), then turn to a model of temporary policy (reinterpreted as lack of credibility), and finally focus on supply-side models.

13.5.1 Inflation Inertia

Rodriguez (1982) was the first to point out that under perfect capital mobility, a permanent decline in the rate of devaluation may provoke an initial expansion in economic activity. The main motivation behind his model was the fall in real interest rates observed in the initial stages of the 1978 Argentinean tablita. In Rodriguez's reduced-form model, inflationary expectations are sticky (i.e., adaptive) and aggregate demand is assumed to depend negatively on the real interest rate. A permanent reduction in the devaluation rate leads, through the interest parity condition, to a fall in the nominal interest rate. If expected inflation is somehow sticky, the domestic real interest rate falls, inducing an expansion in aggregate demand and output. The initial expansion, however, eventually gives way to a recession as inflation inertia leads to a sustained real appreciation of the domestic currency.

To capture these dynamics in an optimizing model, consider a small open economy perfectly integrated with the rest of the world in both goods and capital markets. The law of one price holds for the tradable good and, for simplicity, the foreign nominal price of the tradable good is assumed to be one. On the supply side we will assume that the inflation rate of nontradable goods is sticky and that output of nontradable goods is demand-determined. Unless otherwise noticed, we continue to use the same notation as above.

Consumers' Problem

The consumer's problem remains identical to that in section 13.4.1.

Supply Side

The supply side is identical to that introduced in chapter 12, section 12.4. Output of tradable goods is assumed to be exogenous and constant over time, $y_t^T = y^T$ for all t. Output of nontradables, y_t^N, is demand-determined. Both the price of nontradable goods and the rate of inflation are assumed to be sticky (i.e., they are predetermined variables which cannot jump at any instant in time). The rate of change of the inflation rate of nontradables, π_t, is given by

$$\dot{\pi}_t = \theta(c_t^N - y_f^N) + \gamma(\varepsilon_t - \pi_t), \tag{13.21}$$

where θ and γ are positive parameters and y_f^N is the full-employment level of output of nontradable goods. In this context, equation (13.21) is meant to capture an economy where backward-looking indexation of nominal wages generates a substantial degree of inflation inertia (see Dornbusch and Simonsen 1987). The rate of inflation will thus respond only slowly over time to changes in aggregate demand and to reductions in the rate of growth of the nominal anchor (in this case, the rate of devaluation).

Government

The government's flow constraint continues to be given by (13.10).

Equilibrium Conditions

The equilibrium conditions (13.11), (13.12), and (13.13) remain valid. For further reference, it will prove useful at this point to define the domestic real interest rate as

$$r_t^d \equiv i_t - \pi_t. \tag{13.22}$$

The economy's constraints continue to be given by (13.14) and (13.15).

Consumption of Tradable Goods

First-order condition (13.4) tells us that, along a perfect foresight equilibrium path (PFEP), consumption of tradables goods will be constant. Taking into account the resource constraint (13.15), we obtain

$$c^T = rk_0 + y^T. \tag{13.23}$$

Dynamic System

To solve for the rest of the model, we need to set up a dynamic system in π_t and e_t, for a given and constant rate of devaluation, ε. To this effect, substitute (13.7) into (13.21) and take into account (13.23) to obtain

$$\dot{\pi}_t = \theta(e_t c^T - y_f^N) + \gamma(\varepsilon - \pi_t), \tag{13.24}$$

Taking into account that $\varepsilon_t = \varepsilon$, we can rewrite (13.13) as

$$\dot{e}_t = e_t(\varepsilon - \pi_t). \tag{13.25}$$

Equations (13.24) and (13.25) constitute a dynamic system in π_t and e_t, with c^T given by (13.23). The system's steady state is given by

$$\pi_{ss} = \varepsilon,$$

$$e_{ss} = \frac{y_f^N}{c^T}.$$

Linearizing the system around this steady state, we obtain

$$\begin{bmatrix} \dot{\pi}_t \\ \dot{e}_t \end{bmatrix} = \begin{bmatrix} -\gamma & \theta c^T \\ -e_{ss} & 0 \end{bmatrix} \begin{bmatrix} \pi_t - \pi_{ss} \\ e_t - e_{ss} \end{bmatrix}.$$

The trace and the determinant of the matrix associated with the linear approximation are given by, respectively,

$$\mathrm{Tr} = -\gamma < 0,$$

$$\Delta = e_{ss}\theta c^T > 0.$$

Since the determinant is the product of the roots and the trace is negative (indicating that there is at least one negative root), we infer that there are two negative roots (or complex roots with negative real part). The system is thus globally stable as it should be given that both variables are predetermined.[15]

As usual, we proceed to characterize the qualitative behavior of this dynamic system by constructing the phase-diagram in the (e, π) plane. We first draw the $\dot{\pi}_t = 0$ and $\dot{e}_t = 0$ loci. To this effect, set $\dot{\pi}_t = 0$ in equation (13.24) and totally differentiate with respect to e_t and π_t to obtain

$$\left.\frac{d\pi_t}{de_t}\right|_{\dot{\pi}_t=0} = \frac{\theta c^T}{\gamma}.$$

The $\dot{\pi}_t = 0$-locus thus shows as an upward-sloping schedule in figure 13.7. Then set $\dot{e}_t = 0$ in (13.25) to obtain

$$\pi_t = \varepsilon.$$

The $\dot{e}_t = 0$ locus is thus a horizontal line in figure 13.7. The intersection of both loci at point B determines the system's steady state. The $\dot{\pi}_t = 0$ and $\dot{e}_t = 0$ loci define four regions. Proceeding as we have before, we can draw the law of motions in each of the regions, which, as expected, indicate that the system is globally stable. Hence, for any given initial values of e_t and π_t, the system will converge to point B.

Permanent Reduction in Devaluation Rate

Suppose that just before time 0, the economy is in a steady state characterized by a constant and high devaluation rate, ε^H. At time 0 there is an unanticipated and permanent reduction in the devaluation rate from ε^H to ε^L, with $\varepsilon^L < \varepsilon^H$ (figure 13.8, panel a). Clearly, consumption of tradable goods is not affected and remains given by equation (13.23), as illustrated in panel b.

15. In what follows, we assume that $\gamma^2 \geq 4e_{ss}\theta c^T$, which ensures that roots are real.

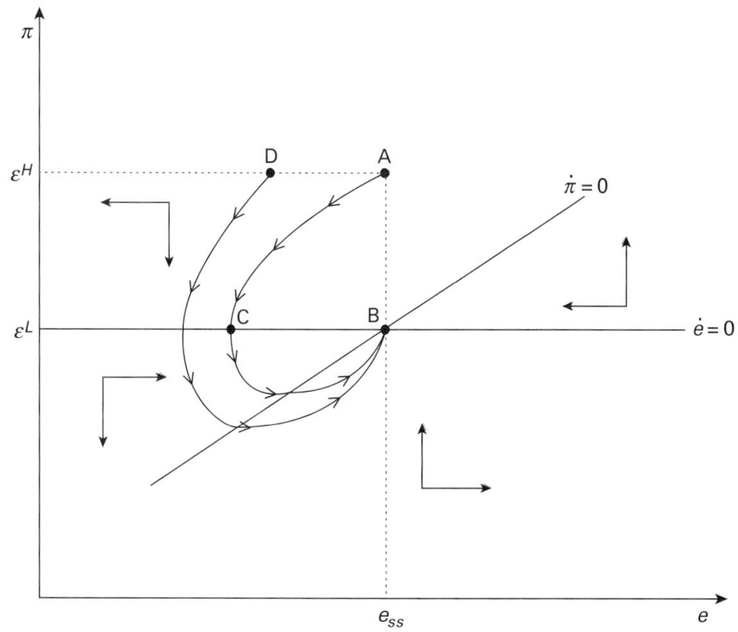

Figure 13.7
Exchange rate based stabilization under sticky inflation: Phase diagram

In terms of the phase diagram depicted in figure 13.7, suppose that the steady state prior to the reduction in the devaluation rate is given by point A. The new steady state (i.e., the one corresponding to ε^L) is at point B in figure 13.7. The dynamic system follows the arrowed path ACB indicated in figure 13.7. The corresponding time paths for π_t and e_t are illustrated in figure 13.8, panels c and d, respectively. As panel c makes clear, the inflation rate falls *below* its new steady-state value at time t_1 (which corresponds to point C in figure 13.7; i.e., the point in time at which the dynamic system crosses the $\dot{e} = 0$ locus) and then converges from below. Figure 13.8, panel d, shows that while the real exchange rate does not change across steady states, it falls until time t_1 and then gradually returns to its initial value. Intuitively, the fall in steady-state inflation requires that inflation fall gradually over time. The fall in the inflation rate, however, leads to a gradual real appreciation of the currency. For the real exchange rate to come back to its pre-shock value, the inflation rate needs to fall below the rate of devaluation.[16]

The path of consumption of nontradable goods (panel e) follows from expression (13.7) and the path of the real exchange rate. Finally, panel f shows the path of the domestic real interest

16. If the exchange rate is fixed, this adjustment requires an actual deflation (i.e., negative inflation of nontradable goods). In practice—and as the discussion of the Convertibility plan in box 13.2 illustrates—such deflationary adjustment has proved extremely difficult to achieve.

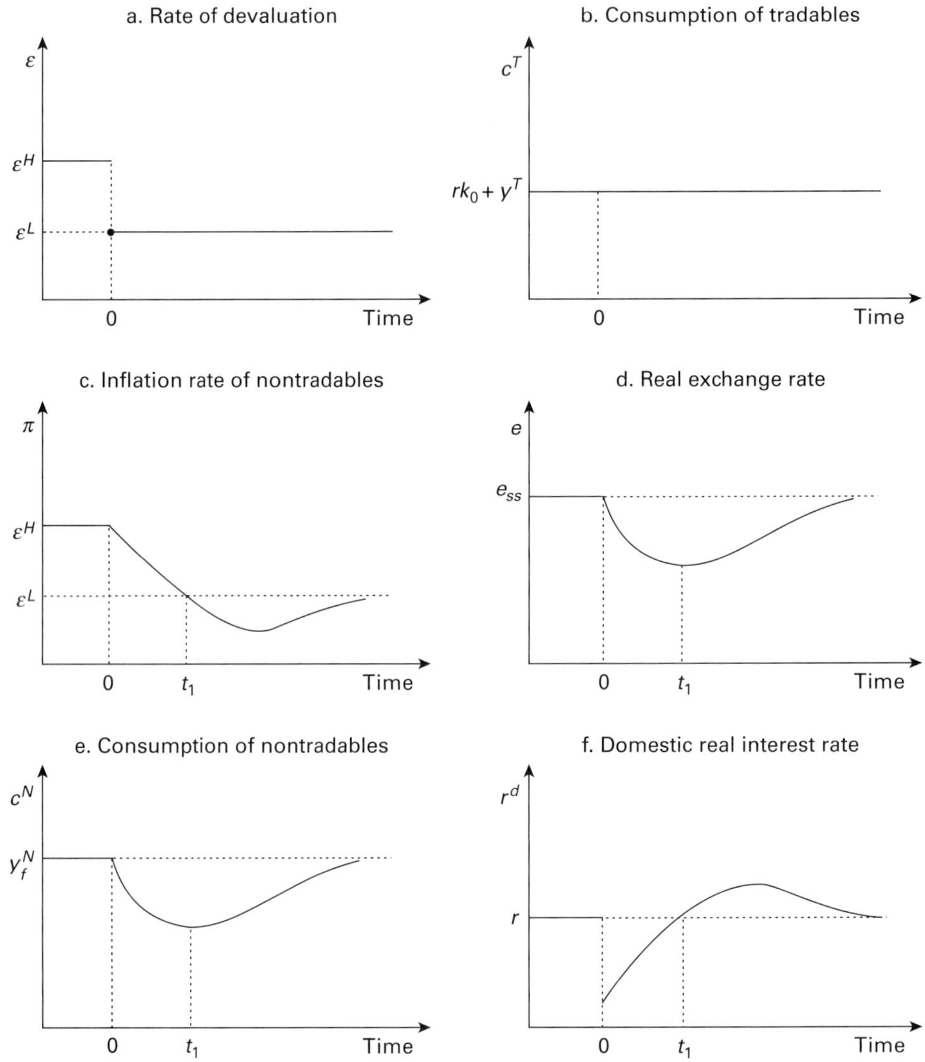

Figure 13.8
Exchange rate based stabilization under sticky inflation: Time paths

rate, r_t^d, which follows from the definition, given by (13.22), and the path of inflation illustrated in panel c.

A key observation is that consumption of nontradables falls in the early stages of the program despite the fact that the domestic real interest rate falls on impact. The reason is that in utility-maximization models, the real interest rate determines the *slope* of the consumption path but not the *level* of consumption. Hence the initial fall in r_t^d implies that as long as $r^d < r$, consumption of nontradable goods will follow a declining path. We thus conclude that, even though the real interest rate falls on impact (as in Rodriguez's 1982 model), our model cannot replicate the initial boom in consumption.

Extending the Model

Calvo and Végh (1994) extend this analysis to the case where instantaneous utility is represented by a constant-elasticity-of-substitution utility function. They show that the results obtained in the context of Rodriguez's model hold true only if the intertemporal elasticity of substitution exceeds the elasticity of substitution between tradables and nontradables. In that case, consumption of both tradable and nontradable goods increases on impact, which implies that the current account goes into deficit. The relative magnitude of these parameters is, of course, an empirical issue. Estimates provided by Ostry and Reinhart (1992), however, cast some doubts on the relevance of backward-looking models. They show that for a number of developing countries, the intertemporal elasticity of substitution is typically smaller than that between tradables and nontradables (see chapter 4, exercise 2).[17]

An important feature of Calvo and Végh's (1994) formulation is that the stabilization does not bring about a wealth effect, in the sense that wealth in terms of tradable goods remains unchanged. This appears as the natural assumption to make when the purpose of the exercise is to isolate the effects of inflation inertia on the outcome of an exchange rate based stabilization. However, in a more general model with capital accumulation and endogenous labor supply, the wealth effect associated with a permanent reduction in the rate of devaluation will cause an increase in consumption of tradable goods and, given that the real exchange rate cannot change on impact, a corresponding increase in consumption of nontradable goods (see Rebelo and Végh 1995, fig. 11). Hence wealth effects associated with supply-side effects (analyzed in more detail below) could help explain the initial boom under backward-looking indexation even under the more plausible parameter configuration in which the intertemporal elasticity of substitution is smaller than the elasticity of substitution between tradable and nontradable goods.

17. The more common criticism of Rodriguez (1982) is the assumption of adaptive expectations—an assumption that has fallen out of favor within the profession. This criticism is, however, misplaced since Rodriguez's (1982) results still hold under rational expectations, as shown in Calvo and Végh (1994). In other words, the key assumption in Rodriguez (1982) is *not* adaptive expectations but rather that aggregate demand depends *negatively* on the real interest rate (provided, of course, that there is some other source of inflation inertia).

When to Devalue?

A recurrent and highly controversial policy debate centers on whether, in the aftermath of an exchange rate based stabilization, policy makers should devalue the currency at some point to help correct a perceived "real overvaluation" of the domestic currency. As analyzed in chapter 8, box 8.3, a case in point was the Mexican stabilization program initiated in December 1987. In a oft-cited paper, Dornbusch and Werner (1994) argued that a devaluation of around 20 percent was needed to correct the existing real overvaluation that, in their view, was fueling a growing trade deficit. Rather than representing a response to reforms and capital inflows—they argued—the real appreciation that had taken place in Mexico since 1987 was the result of an exchange rate based disinflation strategy coupled with inflation inertia. Dornsbusch and Werner (1994) in fact used a model similar to the one in this section to make their case. Argentina's Convertibility plan, discussed in box 13.2, ignited a similar debate on whether to devalue at some point during the program even though the program's main architect, Domingo Cavallo, always ruled it out as an option.

Models such as this one that exhibit inflation inertia provide the best-case scenario for a "corrective" devaluation that would ease the adjustment process. Specifically, in this model it would be optimal to devalue at time t_1 by the amount needed to take the economy from point C to point B in figure 13.7. Such a devaluation would spare the economy the deflationary adjustment that takes place after t_1 (recall figure 13.8, panel c), which is needed for the real exchange rate to gradually increase back to its pre-stabilization value. As discussed in chapter 8, box 8.3, however, it is essential to keep in mind that this type of model completely abstracts from credibility problems. If, in practice, credibility is an issue, then one should be careful in using this type of model to draw policy recommendations.

13.5.2 Lack of Credibility

We now illustrate an alternative explanation for the stylized facts associated with exchange rate stabilization: lack of credibility. To this effect, we will make use of the sticky-prices model developed in section 13.4, with the only modification that money will be introduced via a cash-in-advance constraint (as in chapter 7) rather than through money in the utility function. As in chapter 7, we will study a temporary exchange rate based stabilization and reinterpret it as a permanent stabilization that suffers from lack of credibility. Unless otherwise noticed, we continue to use the same notation.

Households

Preferences are now given by

$$\int_0^{\infty} [\log(c_t^T) + \log(c_t^N)] \exp(-\beta t) dt. \tag{13.26}$$

Box 13.2
Why did Argentina's Convertibility plan fail?

The 1980s was a decade of low growth and very high inflation in Argentina. Between 1981 and 1990 real GDP contracted at an average rate of 1 percent per year and inflation actually reached 5,000 percent in 1989. Against this background, in April 1991 Argentina introduced an exchange rate based stabilization program usually referred to as the Convertibility plan. The defining features of the program were (1) one peso would be convertible into one dollar at any time, (2) the Central Bank would hold one dollar for each peso in circulation (i.e., the money supply would be fully backed), and (3) the Central Bank would become an independent body and would be forbidden from issuing money to finance the government's deficit.

The economy's response to the Convertibility plan, which was fully consistent with the stylized facts discussed in the text, is illustrated in figure 13.9. Inflation fell fairly quickly but only converged to the rate of devaluation (zero) around 1995 (panel a). Real GDP and consumption increased sharply in the early stages of the program (panels b and c, respectively). There was a sustained real appreciation (panel d) and the current account deteriorated steadily in the first four years of the program. Leaving aside a short recession in 1995—triggered by Mexico's Tequila crisis—the economy expanded fairly consistently throughout the 1990s, inflation remained stable and very low, and capital flew in. In 1998, however, the economy entered into a recession that, together with large fiscal deficits, led to increasing levels of sovereign debt. In late 2001, the debt ratio reached 50 percent with 30 billion dollars due in 2002. Faced with increasingly shorter maturities, difficulties with rolling over maturing debt, and plunging international reserves (panel f), the Argentine government put an end to the Convertibility plan and defaulted in what was, at the time, the largest sovereign default in history.

What went wrong with the Convertibility plan? Analysts have focused on two main explanations: (1) the large real appreciation and (2) unsustainable fiscal deficits. Proponents of the first explanation—for instance, Eichengreen (2001) and Feldstein (2002)—argue that the loss of competitiveness in international goods markets led to sustained current account deficits (panel e). Argentina was not getting enough foreign exchange to pay for its growing debt and relied heavily on (volatile) capital inflows to service interest payments. The Brazilian crisis of 1999 worsened even further the terms of trade of the country whose only alternative to regain international competitiveness was through deflation (since a devaluation was not regarded as an option).[a] This turned out not to be a viable alternative either, as unions were not willing to accept cuts in wages despite the unemployment rate reaching more than 18 percent (panel h). Domingo Cavallo, the architect of the Convertibility plan and Finance Minister at the time, was fully aware of this risk but was of the idea that the economy could recover some competitiveness through increases in productivity. While true in theory, this turned out not to be enough in practice.

The second explanation—forcefully put forward by Mussa (2002)—stresses the government's inability to save during good times as the key factor leading to the crisis.[b] As panel g illustrates, even

a. This is in line with the sticky inflation model of section 13.5.1, as illustrated in figure 13.8. Inflation needs to fall below its long-run value (which would have been world inflation for Argentina, given its fixed exchange rate) for the real exchange rate to go back to its original level.

b. This is, of course, the problem of procyclical fiscal policy in emerging markets stressed in chapter 10 (see, in particular, box 10.1). The inability to save in good times precludes emerging markets from borrowing as much as they would need in bad times.

Box 13.2
(continued)

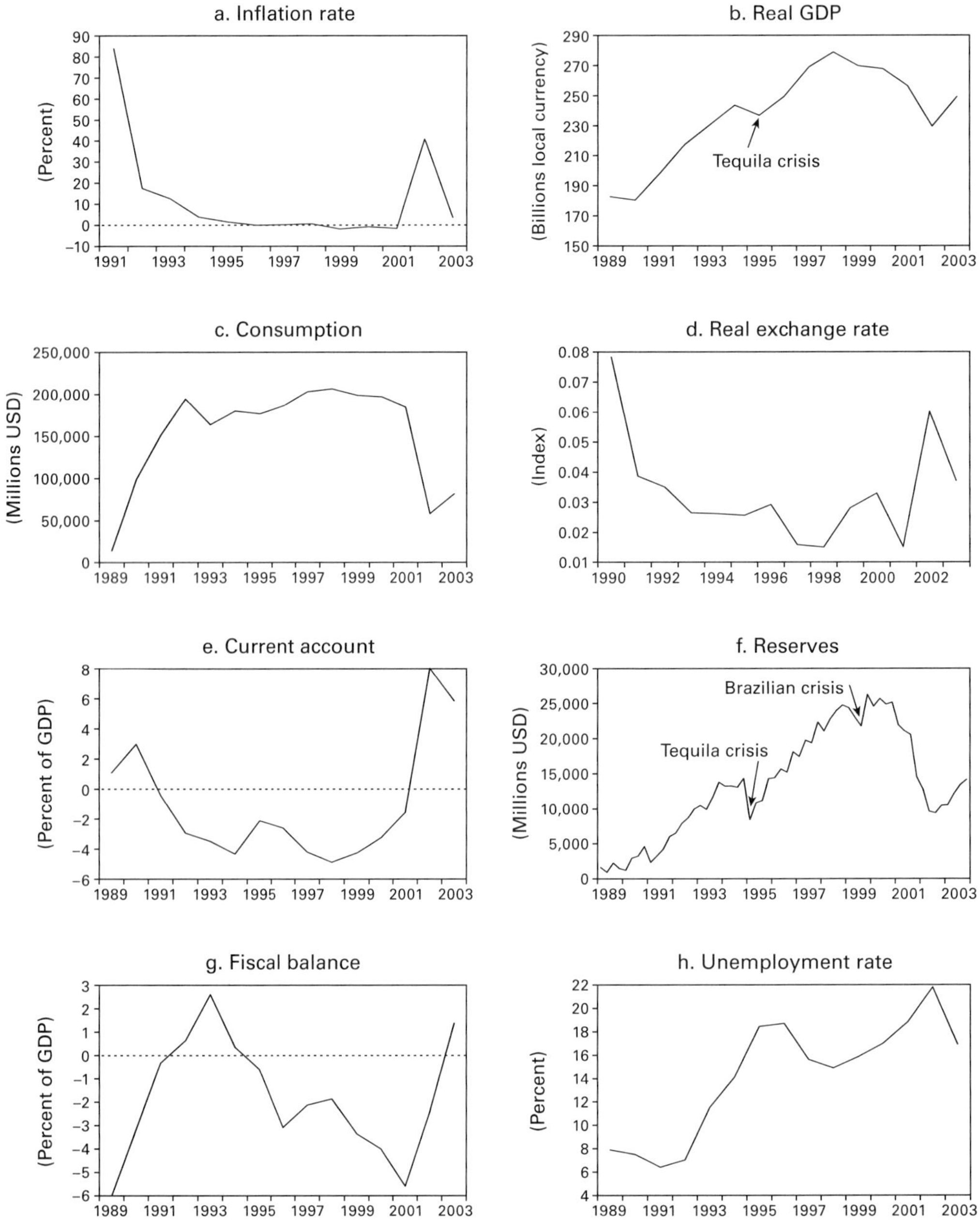

Sources: IFS and national agencies

Figure 13.9
Argentina's Convertibility plan

Box 13.2
(continued)

in the boom years of the early 1990s, fiscal surpluses were rather small, becoming deficits in 1995 and growing increasingly large toward the end of the decade. This deterioration in the public finances occurred despite not only buoyant tax revenues but also substantial proceeds from privatization of state-owned enterprises and delayed interest payments stemming from the Brady Plan. In addition provincial governments were engaging in loose fiscal policy, as spending decisions are made at the provincial level but an important share of provinces' revenues comes from the federal government through a revenue-sharing arrangement.[c] At the same time the private sector was becoming highly indebted in foreign currency. A devaluation or an attempt to exit the currency peg could have led to the collapse of the economy as debtors turned insolvent. And even though the Central Bank would have had enough reserves to back the money in circulation, it did not have enough to guarantee the deposits in the banking system. In sum, loose fiscal policy contributed to a massive increase in debt and made the economy extremely vulnerable to external shocks. When the Brazilian crisis of January 1999 triggered a recession in Argentina, even larger fiscal deficits ensued, which led to a further weakening of Argentina's external position, making a financial crisis all but inevitable.[d] Mussa is also of the view that the IMF should share some of the blame for not pushing Argentina to save more while the economy was growing.

In the final analysis, while Mussa's fiscal explanation is probably closer to the truth and reminds us that fiscal discipline is particularly critical in fixed exchange rate regimes where, by construction, the government has forgone the printing press as a source of fiscal revenues, the downward flexibility in prices and wages required for the realignment of relative prices in fixed exchange rate regimes was simply not there, particularly in light of highly rigid labor markets. Instead, the deflationary forces led to rising unemployment (panel h), increasing social pressures for the government to put an end to the Convertibility plan.

c. It can be shown that this revenue-sharing agreement may actually exacerbate procyclical fiscal policy at the provincial level; see Végh and Vuletin (2011).
d. Recall from table 13.4 that January 1999 marked the end of the Real plan in Brazil, which had been put into place in July 1994.

Money is needed to satisfy the following cash-in-advance constraint:

$$m_t = \alpha\left(c_t^T + \frac{c_t^N}{e_t}\right).$$

Under this formulation the first-order conditions will now read (assuming $\beta = r$)

$$\frac{1}{c_t^T} = \lambda(1 + \alpha i_t), \tag{13.27}$$

$$\frac{1}{c_t^N} = \frac{\lambda}{e_t}(1 + \alpha i_t). \tag{13.28}$$

These two first-order conditions are already familiar to us from chapter 7, where we first saw cash-in-advance models in continuous time. In cash-in-advance models the effective price of consumption is $1 + \alpha i_t$ for tradables goods and $(1 + \alpha i_t)/e_t$ for nontradable goods because the opportunity cost of the cash balances needed for consumption adds to the real market price of the goods (unity for tradable goods and $1/e_t$ for nontradable goods). Hence first-order conditions (13.27) and (13.28) simply capture the standard condition that at an optimum, the marginal utility of consuming must be equal to the shadow value of wealth times the effective price of consumption. Combining these two conditions, we obtain (13.7) once again.

The rest of the model remains unchanged relative to section 13.4.

Temporary Stabilization

Suppose that just before $t = 0$, the economy is in a stationary equilibrium with a rate of devaluation of ε^H. At $t = 0$ there is a unanticipated and temporary reduction in the rate of devaluation from ε^H to ε^L, where $\varepsilon^L < \varepsilon^H$ (figure 13.10, panel a).

By interest parity, the nominal interest rate also falls at time 0 and returns to its original level at time T. The effective price of consumption, $1+\alpha i_t$, is thus low between time 0 and T and high afterward. As first-order condition (13.27) indicates, this implies that c_t^T will be high between time 0 and time T (denote that level by $(c^T)^H$) and low afterward ($(c^T)^L$). For this time profile to be consistent with the economy's resources—given by (13.15)—c_t^T must jump up at time 0 and then fall at time T below its pre-shock level (panel b). The initial increase in c_t^T leads to a deterioration in the trade balance and the current account. Over time the current account continues to deteriorate (not shown).

Figure 13.11—which reproduces the phase diagram of figure 13.5—can be used to derive the time paths of inflation of nontradable goods and the real exchange rate. The initial steady state is at point A. The new steady state is given by point C where—as follows from (13.19) and (13.20)—the inflation rate is the same but the real exchange rate is higher in light of the lower level of c_t^T. The system must therefore hit C′C′—the saddle path corresponding to point C—at time T. Otherwise, the system would diverge.[18] During the transition the dynamic system is governed by the laws of motion corresponding to point B, which represents the stationary point of the dynamic system during the transition (where $e = y_f^N/(c^T)^H$ and $\pi = \varepsilon^L$). There are three qualitatively different responses of the dynamic system:

- For large values of T, the system jumps on impact from point A to a point such as G, travels over time along the arrowed path toward point H, and then travels along the saddle path C′C′ toward point C. The corresponding paths of π_t and e_t are illustrated in figure 13.10, panels c and d, respectively. After jumping down on impact, the inflation rate falls over time but begins to increase back to its initial level even before time T.

18. Notice that neither π_t nor e_t can jump at time T. The continuity of π_t at time T follows from the derivation of the $\dot{\pi}$-equation (see chapter 8, appendix 8.8.1).

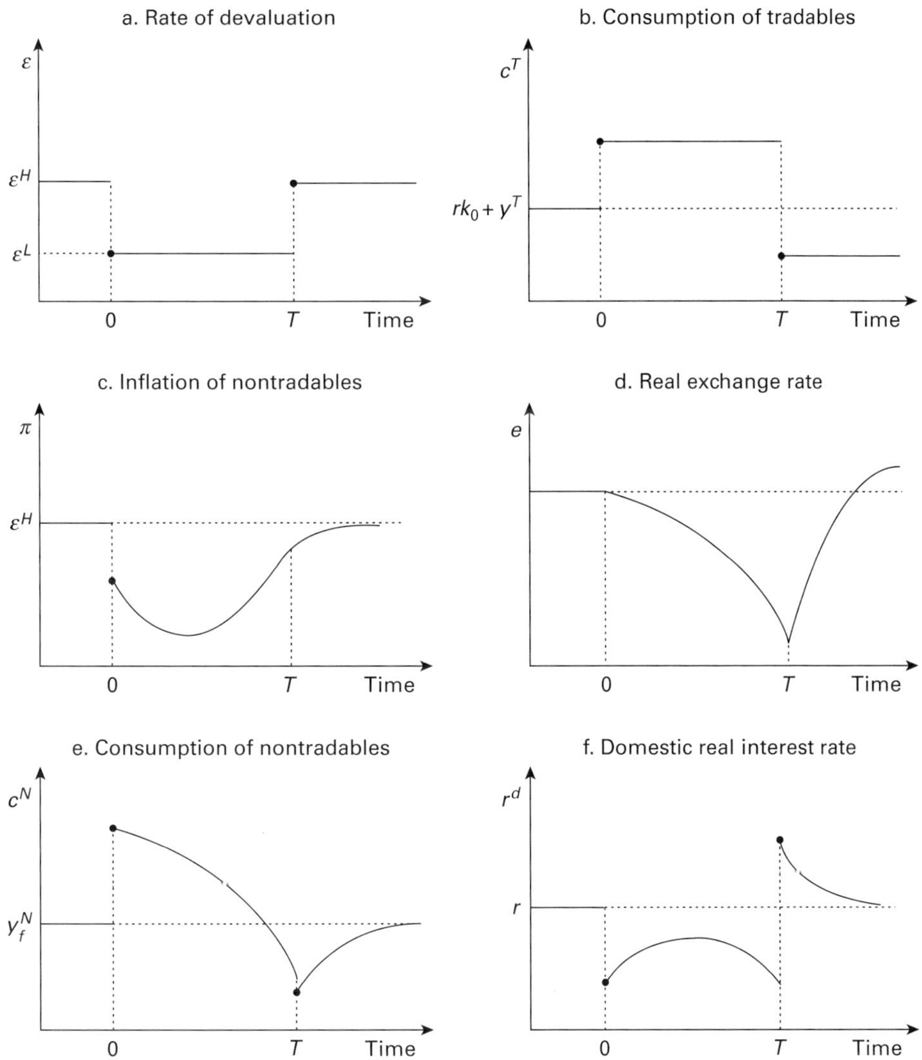

Figure 13.10
Temporary exchange rate based stabilization under sticky prices

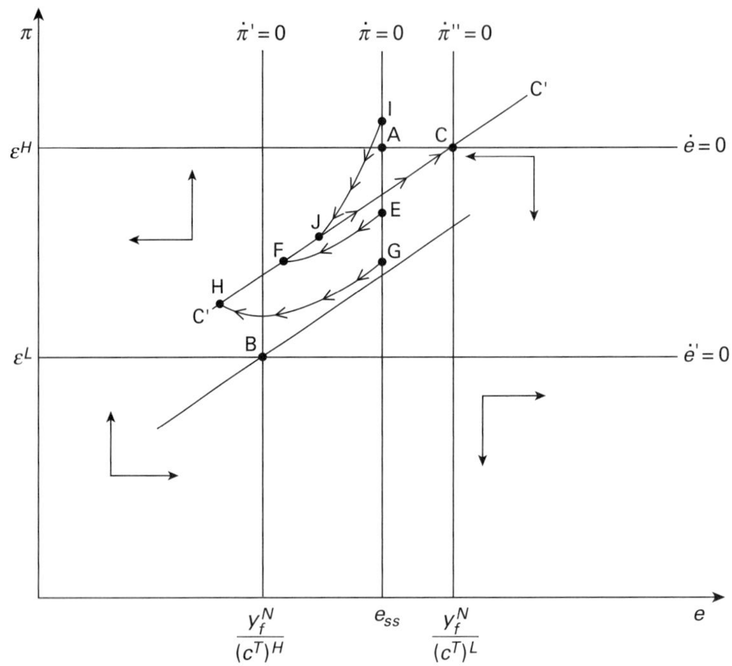

Figure 13.11
Temporary ERBS: Phase diagram

- For smaller values of T, the system may jump on impact from point A to a point such as E, then travel toward point F, and then along the saddle path toward point C. In this case, inflation falls until T and only then begins to return back to its original level.
- For small values of T and large values of ε, the system may follow a path like AIJC. In other words, the inflation rate may actually *increase* on impact.[19]

Intuitively, there are two forces determining the impact effect on π_t. The first, which tends to reduce π_t, is the direct effect of the fall in the devaluation rate. All else equal, a larger reduction in ε_t will lead to a larger reduction in π_t. For a given reduction in ε_t, the fall in π_t will be larger the larger is T. Conversely, for very small T, this effect is very small. The second effect, which tends to increase π_t, is the consumption boom in nontradables. Other things being equal, a rise in c_t^N will tend to increase π_t. To see this, notice from (13.9) that an increase in c_t^N will lead to $\dot{\pi}_t < 0$. For this to happen, π_t must increase so as to fall over time to its unchanged steady state.

19. The existence of these different paths could be proved formally by solving the model analytically and computing the impact effect as a function of the different parameters. This, however, involves quite a bit of painstaking algebra. For our purposes, we will prove existence of these cases numerically below.

Since the consumption boom becomes larger as T becomes smaller, an increase in inflation on impact is more likely.

In this light, as T becomes larger, the first effect becomes larger while the second effect becomes smaller and hence the initial fall in π_t is the largest (from point A to point G in figure 13.11). For intermediate values of T, the consumption boom becomes larger and hence partly offsets the fall in inflation. Inflation thus jumps on impact to a point such as E. For very small values of T, the first effect tends to vanish and the second effect becomes even larger. Hence π_t may increase on impact to a point such as I. In this model "inflation stickiness" may therefore arise entirely due to credibility problems.

To derive the path of c_t^N, combine (13.27) and (13.28) to obtain $c_t^T = c_t^N/e_t$, and differentiate with respect to time to obtain

$$\frac{\dot{c}_t^N}{c_t^N} = \frac{\dot{e}_t}{e_t}.$$

Since e_t falls during the transition, so will c_t^N. Further, since c_t^T jumps up on impact and e_t does not change, c_t^N must also increase on impact. (The path of c_t^N is illustrated in figure 13.10, panel e.) For large values of T, c_t^N will fall below its full-employment level before time T arrives, as illustrated in panel e. (For smaller values of T, c_t^N will remain above its full-employment level until time T.) At time T the fall in c_t^T implies that c_t^N also falls.

Finally, the path of r_t^d—illustrated in panel f—follows from the definition $r_t^d = i_t - \pi_t$. On impact, r_t^d falls because inflation of nontradable goods declines by less (if at all) than the nominal interest rate. Between time 0 and time T, the behavior of r_t^d follows from that of π_t: the real interest rate increases first and then falls. At time T, r_t^d jumps up, reflecting the increase in the nominal interest rate. It then falls over time.

To show existence of the inflation paths mentioned above, we have set up a discrete time version of this model and computed the response to a reduction of 10 percent in the rate of devaluation for three different values of T.[20] Figure 13.12 shows the time path of inflation of nontradable goods for three different values of T ($T = 2$, 5, and 10). We can see that the largest initial fall in inflation corresponds to the largest value of T ($T = 10$), in which case inflation falls almost 7 percent on impact. For $T = 5$, the initial fall is less than 4 percent, and for $T = 2$, inflation actually rises on impact.[21] The counterpart of this is that the boom in c_t^N is bigger the smaller T is: on impact, c_t^N rises by 3.3, 3.1, and 2.9 percent for $T = 2, 5$, and 10, respectively. This behavior of inflation is quite remarkable because, to an outside observer, it could appear that there is some

20. The parameterization is as follows: $r = 0.01$, $k_0 = 0.6283$, $\theta = 0.1$, $y_f^N = y^T = 1$, and $\varepsilon^H = 0.5$. The model, log-linearization, and MATLAB coding may be found in an online appendix. The figure shows percentage deviations from the initial steady state.

21. Using the same parameterization and setting $T = 3$ or 4, one can show existence of the case where inflation falls until T and only then begins to increase (which corresponds to the second case mentioned above).

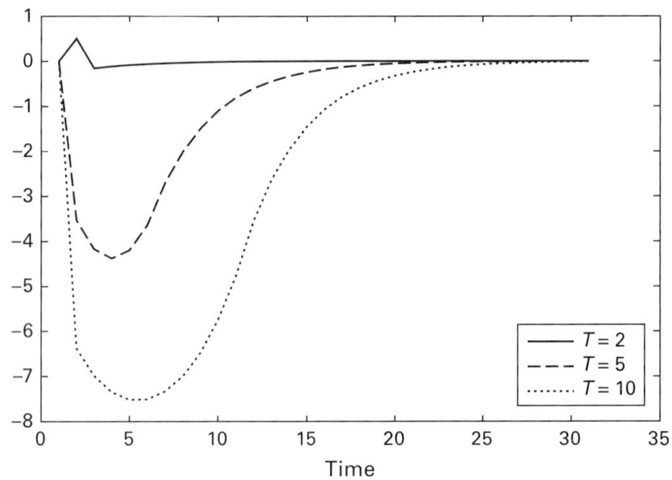

Figure 13.12
Inflation of nontradables for different values of T

inertial component in inflation when, in reality, the "stickiness" in inflation is due only to the fact that the program is temporary!

Finally, we should note that, as figure 13.10 makes clear and Uribe (2002) discusses in detail, this type of model tends to generate a positive comovement along the new PFEP between consumption and the real exchange rate. In figure 13.10 this is true of the comovement between c_t^N and e_t and would also be true of a consumption composite and e_t. In numerous episodes, however, the data tend to show the opposite: consumption and the real exchange rate tend to comove negatively; that is, as consumption increases over time, the real exchange rate falls over time.[22] One way of addressing this issue is to introduce habit formation, as in Uribe (2002). Habit formation makes it optimal for consumption to increase slowly over time. Alternatively, and as analyzed in exercise 1 at the end of this chapter, assuming a declining rate of devaluation over time would generate a negative comovement along the new PFEP between consumption and the real exchange. The problem is that in and of itself, this experiment would induce, on impact, a fall in consumption and an increase in the real exchange rate (i.e., a real depreciation), which is counterfactual.

Reinterpretation as Lack of Credibility

As in chapter 7, we can now reinterpret the outcome of the temporary exchange rate based stabilization just analyzed (and illustrated in figure 13.10) as arising from the public's lack of credibility in the stabilization effort. To this effect, suppose that at $t = 0$ policy makers announce a *permanent* stabilization. In other words, policy makers announce that starting from time 0, the

22. Interestingly this is not true in figure 13.3. If we think of the change in consumption from $T - 1$ to T as the impact effect, consumption begins to fall afterward. But in many individual episodes, consumption continues to increase for several periods.

rate of devaluation will be lower forever (at the level ε^L). The public, however, disbelieves the announcement, due perhaps to a history of failed stabilizations. In particular, suppose that the public expects that at some point in the future (i.e., time T), the rate of devaluation will be back to its initial level. In this scenario the impact effect will be exactly the same as that analyzed for the case of a temporary stabilization. In fact the whole path of the real variables will be the same. To see this, notice that if when time T arrives, policy makers abandon the program—as expected by the public—then clearly the dynamics will be identical to the case of the temporary stabilization. If, however, at time T policy makers stick to the announced plan, from the point of view of the public, this amounts to an unanticipated and permanent reduction in the devaluation rate from ε^H to ε^L at time T. Since, in this model, permanent changes in the rate of devaluation are superneutral, the path of the real variables will be identical. The path of inflation of nontradables, of course, will be different, reflecting the fact that the reduction in inflation has become permanent.

13.5.3 Supply-Side Effects: Investment Channel

Up to this point, we have looked at explanations based on demand-side considerations. This is perhaps only natural given that much of this literature was originally inspired by the Southern Cone tablitas of the late 1970s where, to most casual observers, the most striking fact was the rise in consumers' demand for goods, particularly durable goods (see De Gregorio, Guidotti, and Végh 1998). As other programs came along, however, particularly the Argentinean 1991 Convertibility plan, some authors advanced the idea that supply-side effects might be an important channel behind the initial economic expansion (see Lahiri 2000, Roldos 1995, 1997; Uribe 1997). In chapter 7, we explored the labor supply channel; we will now look at the investment channel.

A simple way of generating an investment and output boom as a result of a reduction in the rate of devaluation is to assume that investment is a "cash" good. Specifically, we will assume that cash is needed not only for consumption purposes—as in the standard CIA model—but also for investment. When the rate of devaluation and hence the nominal interest rate fall, investment becomes cheaper, which leads to an investment boom.

To illustrate this channel, consider a small open economy perfectly integrated into the world economy. Production of tradable goods is endogenous and carried out with capital as the only input. Capital accumulation (i.e., investment) is subject to adjustment costs. Production of nontradables is assumed to be exogenous. Unless otherwise noticed, we keep the same notation as above.

Production

Tradable Goods Production of tradable goods takes place with capital as the only input through a standard production function:

$$y_t^T = f(k_t), \tag{13.29}$$

where $f'(.) > 0$ and $f''(.) < 0$.

Capital accumulation is subject to adjustment costs. Specifically, assume that to invest an amount I_t, the economy needs to spend $\psi(I_t) \geq 0$, which satisfies[23]

$$\psi(0) = 0, \psi'(I_t) > 0, \psi'(0) = 0, \psi''(I_t) > 0.$$

Hence total expenditure associated with investing I_t ("gross investment"), denoted by $\phi(I_t)$, is given by

$$\phi(I_t) \equiv I_t + \psi(I_t) \geq 0, \tag{13.30}$$

$$\phi(0) = 0,$$

$$\phi'(I_t) = 1 + \psi'(I_t) > 0,$$

$$\phi'(0) = 1,$$

$$\phi''(I_t) = \psi''(I_t) > 0.$$

Capital accumulation is given by

$$\dot{k}_t \equiv I_t, \tag{13.31}$$

where, for simplicity (and with no loss of generality), we have set the rate of depreciation to zero.

Nontradable Goods Production of nontradable goods is exogenous and given by a constant endowment:

$$y_t^N = y^N. \tag{13.32}$$

Households

Households consume and carry out production activities.[24] Preferences are given by

$$\int_0^\infty [u(c_t^T) + v(c_t^N)]\exp(-\beta t)dt, \tag{13.33}$$

where $u(.)$ and $v(.)$ are strictly increasing and strictly concave functions. The household's flow budget constraint is given by

$$\dot{a}_t = ra_t + y_t^T + \frac{y^N}{e_t} + \tau_t - c_t^T - \frac{c_t^N}{e_t} - \phi(I_t) - i_t m_t. \tag{13.34}$$

23. An example would be $\psi(I_t) = ZI_t^2/2$ for any $Z > 0$.

24. It would be straightforward to decentralize this economy.

Since investment is a cash good, the cash-in-advance constraint takes the form[25]

$$m_t = \alpha\left(c_t^T + \frac{c_t^N}{e_t} + I_t\right). \tag{13.35}$$

Substituting (13.29), (13.32), and (13.35) into the flow constraint (13.34), we can rewrite it as

$$\dot{a}_t = ra_t + f(k_t) + \frac{y^N}{e_t} + \tau_t - \left(c_t^T + \frac{c_t^N}{e_t}\right)(1+\alpha i_t) - \phi(I_t) - \alpha i_t I_t. \tag{13.36}$$

Households choose $\{c_t^T, c_t^N, I_t\}_{t=0}^{\infty}$ to maximize (13.33) subject to (13.31) and (13.36). The current-value Hamiltonian is given by[26]

$$H = u(c_t^T) + v(c_t^N) + \lambda_t\left[ra_t + f(k_t) + \frac{y^N}{e_t} + \tau_t - \left(c_t^T + \frac{c_t^N}{e_t}\right)(1+\alpha i_t) - \phi(I_t) - \alpha i_t I_t\right] + \theta_t I_t,$$

where θ_t and λ_t are the multipliers associated with constraints (13.31) and (13.36), respectively. The first-order conditions are given by

$$u'(c_t^T) = \lambda_t(1+\alpha i_t), \tag{13.37}$$

$$v'(c_t^N) = \frac{\lambda_t}{e_t}(1+\alpha i_t), \tag{13.38}$$

$$\theta_t = \lambda_t\left[\phi'(I_t) + \alpha i_t\right], \tag{13.39}$$

$$\dot{\lambda}_t = \lambda_t(\beta - r), \tag{13.40}$$

$$\dot{\theta}_t = \theta_t\beta - \lambda_t f'(k_t), \tag{13.41}$$

where the last two expressions capture the laws of motion for the two co-state variables, λ_t and θ_t, respectively.

The first-order conditions (13.37) and (13.38) are already well familiar to us and arose earlier in this chapter (recall equations 13.27 and 13.28). By combining these two first-order conditions, we obtain the familiar condition

25. The reader should verify that if the cash-in-advance did not include investment, then permanent (or temporary) changes in the rate of devaluation would not affect investment. In other words, investment being a "cash good" is essential for the channel illustrated in this section. This would not be the case, however, if preferences included a consumption/leisure choice, as shown by Lahiri (2001). Still, from a quantitative point of view, investment being a cash good is needed for this type of model to generate sizable effects, as shown by Rebelo and Végh (1995).

26. The reader is referred to chapter 6, appendix 6.7.1, for a review of optimal control techniques.

$$e_t = \frac{u'(c_t^T)}{v'(c_t^N)}. \tag{13.42}$$

First-order condition (13.39) captures the optimal choice of investment. To see this, notice that $\phi'(I_t)+\alpha i_t$ captures the "marginal effective cost of investing": $\phi'(I_t)$ is the marginal physical cost of an additional unit of investment, while αi_t captures the opportunity cost of the cash balances needed to carry out an additional unit of investment. In this light, first-order condition (13.39) equates the shadow benefit of an additional unit of investment, θ_t, to the marginal cost in terms of consumption, given by $\lambda_t \left[\phi'(I_t) + \alpha i_t\right]$.

Finally, condition (13.40) is the familiar condition describing the evolution of the shadow value of wealth. Given our usual assumption that $\beta = r$, equation (13.40) says that λ_t will be constant along a PFEP. We will denote this constant value by λ. Condition (13.41) describes the evolution of the shadow value of investing.

To gain further insight into these optimality conditions, define a new variable, q_t, as

$$q_t \equiv \frac{\theta_t}{\lambda}, \tag{13.43}$$

which can be interpreted as the shadow price of a unit of investment (i.e., of installed capital) in terms of tradable goods.[27] Using (13.43), rewrite the first-order condition (13.39) as

$$q_t = \phi'(I_t) + \alpha i_t. \tag{13.44}$$

This condition says that at an optimum, households equate the marginal benefit of investing, given by q_t, to its marginal cost, given by $\phi'(I_t) + \alpha i_t$. Further equation (13.44) implicitly defines

$$I_t = \tilde{I}(\underset{+}{q_t}, \underset{-}{i_t}), \tag{13.45}$$

where a sign under a variable denotes the sign of the corresponding partial derivative. As we should have expected, investment is an increasing function of the shadow value of capital, q_t, and a decreasing function of the nominal interest rate (which increases the effective cost of investing).

Government

The government's flow budget constraint continues to be given by (13.10).

Equilibrium Conditions

Interest parity holds (recall foreign inflation is zero):

$$i_t = r + \varepsilon_t.$$

27. This is often referred to as Tobin's q; see Blanchard and Fischer (1989, ch. 2) for a more detailed discussion.

Equilibrium in the nontradable goods market takes the form

$$c_t^N = y^N. \tag{13.46}$$

Given (13.46), we can rewrite (13.42) as

$$e_t = \frac{u'(c_t^T)}{v'(y^N)}. \tag{13.47}$$

For a given path of c_t^T, equation (13.47) will determine the path of e_t.

Combining the households' and the government's flow constraints, given by (13.34) and (13.10), respectively, and imposing interest parity and equilibrium in the nontradable goods market, we obtain

$$\dot{b}_t + \dot{h}_t = r(b_t + h_t) + TB_t, \tag{13.48}$$

where the trade balance is defined as

$$TB_t \equiv f(k_t) - c_t^T - \phi(I_t). \tag{13.49}$$

Integrating forward (13.48) and imposing the corresponding transversality condition, we obtain the economy's resource constraint:

$$b_0 + h_0 + \int_0^{\infty} [f(k_t) - \phi(I_t)] \exp(-rt)dt = \int_0^{\infty} c_t^T \exp(-rt)dt. \tag{13.50}$$

Perfect Foresight Equilibrium Path

We now solve for the perfect foresight equilibrium path corresponding to a constant rate of devaluation, ε. By interest parity, the nominal interest rate will also be constant over time, and given by

$$i = r + \varepsilon.$$

Since λ_t is constant over time, first-order condition (13.37) indicates that consumption of tradables will also be constant along a PFEP. In light of the resource constraint (13.50), this constant level will be given by

$$c^T = r\left[b_0 + h_0 + \int_0^{\infty} [f(k_t) - \phi(I_t)]\exp(-rt)dt\right]. \tag{13.51}$$

Substituting (13.46) and (13.51) into (13.42), we obtain the constant level of the real exchange rate along a PFEP:

$$e_t = \frac{u'(c^T)}{v'(y^N)}. \tag{13.52}$$

To solve for the rest of the system, we need to set up a dynamic system in q_t and k_t. Differentiating (13.43) with respect to time and using (13.41), we obtain

$$\dot{q}_t = \beta q_t - f'(k_t). \tag{13.53}$$

For our second dynamic equation, substitute (13.45) into (13.31) to obtain

$$\dot{k}_t = \tilde{I}(q_t, i). \tag{13.54}$$

Equations (13.53) and (13.54) constitute a two differential equation system in k_t and q_t for a given value of i_t, i. By setting $\dot{q}_t = \dot{k}_t = 0$ in equations (13.53) and (13.54), respectively, we can see that the steady state is characterized by (recall that $\phi'(I = 0) = 1$):

$$f'(k_{ss}) = \beta(1 + \alpha i), \tag{13.55}$$

$$q_{ss} = 1 + \alpha i. \tag{13.56}$$

In the steady state, investment is zero. If investment were not included in the CIA constraint, this would require that q_{ss} be equal to one. In this model in which investment is a cash good, however, zero investment requires that q_{ss} be equal to $1 + \alpha i$ so that households do not have any incentive to invest or disinvest.

The linear approximation of the system around the steady state is given by

$$\begin{bmatrix} \dot{q}_t \\ \dot{k}_t \end{bmatrix} = \begin{bmatrix} \beta & -f''(k_{ss}) \\ \tilde{I}_q & 0 \end{bmatrix} \begin{bmatrix} q_t - (1 + \alpha i) \\ k_t - k_{ss} \end{bmatrix}. \tag{13.57}$$

The determinant associated with the matrix of the linear approximation is given by

$$\Delta = \tilde{I}_q f''(k_{ss}) < 0,$$

which implies that there is a negative and a positive root, indicating that the system is saddle-path stable.

We now construct the phase diagram in the (k, q) plane (figure 13.13). From (13.53) and (13.54), it follows that

$$\left.\frac{dq_t}{dk_t}\right|_{\dot{k}_t=0} = 0,$$

$$\left.\frac{dq_t}{dk_t}\right|_{\dot{q}_t=0} = \frac{f''(k_t)}{\beta} < 0,$$

which indicates that the $\dot{k}_t = 0$-locus is a horizontal line whereas the $\dot{q}_t = 0$-locus is downward-sloping. The intersection of the two loci at point A determines the system's steady state. The saddle path is negatively sloped, as shown in figure 13.13. Hence, if, say, k_0 were below its steady-state value, q_0 would be such so as to place the system at a point like C in figure 13.13. Over time the system would travel along the saddle-path toward point A.

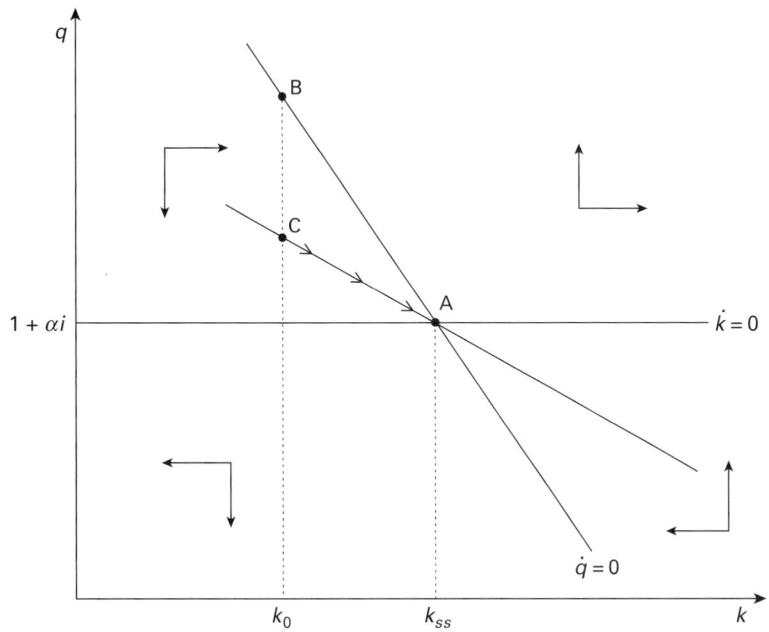

Figure 13.13
Investment as a cash good: Phase diagram

What is the path of the trade balance along a PFEP? To find this out, differentiate (13.49) with respect to time (recall that c_t^T is constant along a PFEP) to obtain

$$\dot{TB}_t = f'(k_t)\dot{k}_t - \phi'(I_t)\dot{I}_t.$$

Using (13.31) to substitute out for $\dot{I}_t$ and rearranging terms, we obtain

$$\dot{TB}_t = \underbrace{f'(k_t)}_{+}\dot{k}_t \underbrace{- \phi'(I_t)\ddot{k}_t}_{+}, > 0. \tag{13.58}$$

The trade balance will thus be increasing over time. In light of the economy's resource constraint (and assuming, for the sake of argument, that $h_0 + b_0 = 0$), this implies that the economy will be running a trade deficit followed by a trade surplus.

Permanent Exchange Rate Based Stabilization

Suppose that the economy is initially (i.e., before time 0) in the stationary equilibrium characterized by point B in figure 13.13. At time 0 there is an unanticipated and permanent reduction in the rate of devaluation from ε^H to ε^L(figure 13.14, panel a).

How will the steady-state values of q_t and k_t be affected by the reduction in the rate of devaluation? The corresponding fall in i_t implies, from (13.55) and (13.56), that k_{ss} increases while q_{ss}

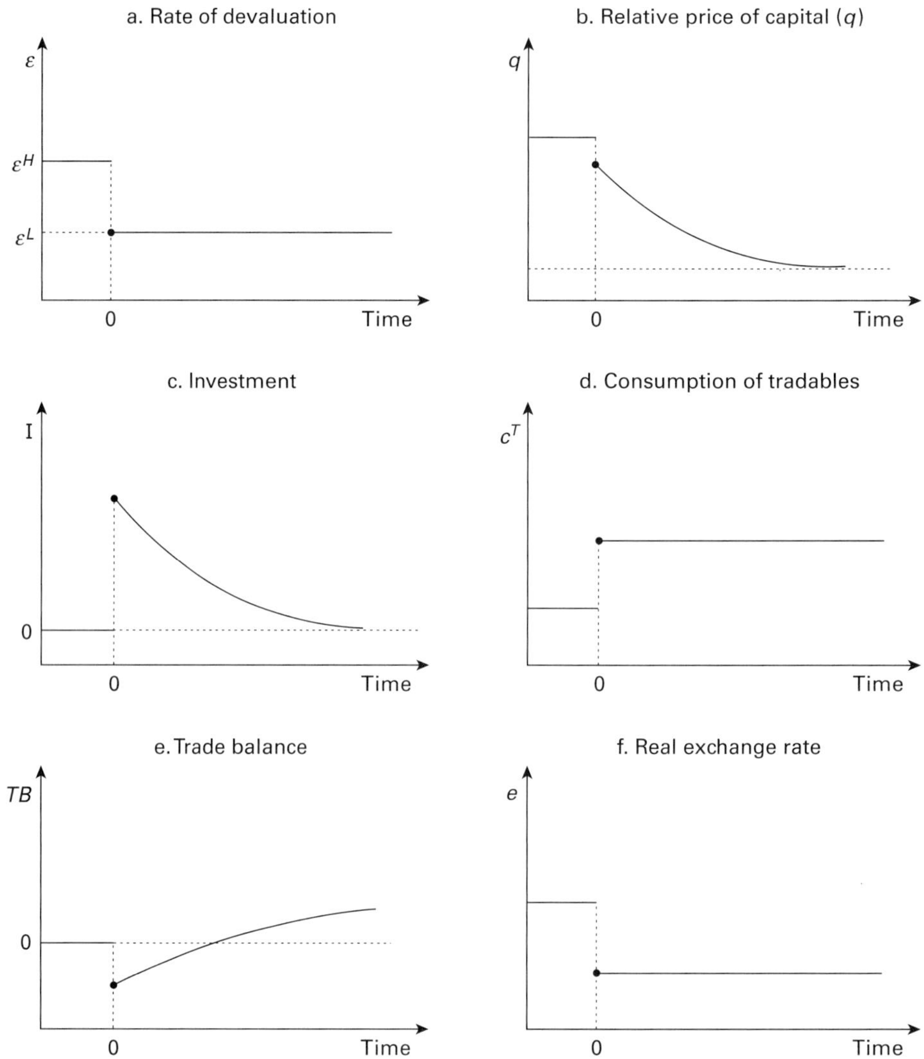

Figure 13.14
Permanent stabilization in investment model

falls. Intuitively, the fall in the nominal interest rate reduces the effective cost of investing, which makes it optimal to invest more. As a result the shadow value of capital will be lower in the new steady state. The new steady state is thus at point A in figure 13.13.[28]

In terms of the dynamic adjustment, the system jumps on impact from point B to point C and then travels along the saddle path in a southeastern direction toward the steady state (point A). In particular, q_t jumps down on impact and then falls gradually over time toward its lower steady state (figure 13.14, panel b). The capital stock rises gradually over time toward its higher steady state, which implies, through the production function (13.29), that output will also be rising over time. The path of investment is illustrated in panel c: investment jumps up on impact and then falls over time toward its unchanged steady state. The impact effect follows from equation (13.31) and the fact that $\dot{k}_0 > 0$, whereas the fall over time follows from equation (13.45).

How does consumption of tradable goods respond? From first-order condition (13.37), we know that in the new PFEP c^T will be flat over time. Since the present discounted value of net output increases, consumption will jump up on impact and remain at that level thereafter (panel d).[29] The corresponding path of the trade balance is shown in panel e: the economy will run a trade deficit early on (assuming a pre-shock trade balance of zero) and a trade surplus later on to repay the debt.

Finally, from (13.47) and the path of c^T depicted in panel d, we infer that the real exchange rate falls on impact (real appreciation) and remains at that level thereafter (panel f).

We thus conclude that the model is able to generate an initial increase in consumption of tradable goods, a gradual increase in output of tradable goods, and a real appreciation of the domestic currency. The initial increase in investment matches the stylized facts reviewed above. While the model cannot explain a late recession, when we combine supply-side effects with the lack of credibility hypothesis, the quantitative effects are reasonably in accordance with the empirical evidence (Rebelo and Végh 1995).[30]

13.6 Stopping Chronic Inflation: Money Based Stabilization

We have seen that the stylized facts associated with money based stabilization involve an initial contraction in economic activity, an increase in real interest rates, and a real appreciation of the currency. This section develops two models to explain these stylized facts.

The first model will be a discrete-time version of the MIUF, sticky-prices model developed in chapter 8 and used in this chapter in section 13.4. The only new twist will be that preferences

28. Note that the reduction in i_t shifts the $\dot{k}_t = 0$ locus down but leaves unchanged the $\dot{q}_t = 0$ locus. This explains the shift in the steady state in figure 13.13 from point B to point A.

29. To see that the present discounted value (PDV) of net output increases, notice that the initial change has measure zero and subsequently the PDV of net output depends on the change in $f(k_t) - \phi(I_t)\dot{k}_t$, which is positive (recall expression 13.58).

30. The model, however, generates a real appreciation that is quantitatively small compared to the data. As illustrated in exercise 2 at the end of the chapter, the introduction of distribution costs can amplify the response of the real exchange rate to more realistic levels; for a full analysis, see Burstein, Neves, and Rebelo (2003).

will not be separable in c_t^T and c_t^N, which will imply that unlike chapter 8, the trade balance will respond to a permanent reduction in μ_t. We will solve this model numerically using the King–Plosser–Rebelo (1998, 2001) linearization method.

We will then study the sticky inflation model developed above in section 13.5.1 for the case of a money based stabilization.

13.6.1 Sticky Prices

The basic setup from section 13.4 remains unchanged: this is a small open economy perfectly integrated into world goods and capital markets. The law of one price holds for the tradable good so that $P_t^T = E_t$ (the nominal foreign price of the tradable good is set to one). Unless otherwise noticed, the notation remains the same as in section 13.4.

Consumers

Preferences are given by

$$\sum_{t=0}^{\infty} \beta^t \left\{ \frac{\left[\left(c_t^T\right)^{\gamma} \left(c_t^N\right)^{1-\gamma} \right]^{1-1/\sigma} - 1}{1 - 1/\sigma} + \log(z_t) \right\}, \tag{13.59}$$

where $z_t (\equiv M_t/P_t)$ denotes real money balances in terms of the price index, P_t, given by

$$P_t \equiv \left(P_t^T\right)^{\gamma} \left(P_t^N\right)^{1-\gamma}, \tag{13.60}$$

β is the discount factor $(0 < \beta < 1)$ and $\sigma (> 0)$ is the intertemporal elasticity of substitution.

Proceeding as in chapter 5, section 5.6, and using tradable goods as the numéraire, we can show that the consumer's flow constraint is given by

$$a_t = (1+r)a_{t-1} + y_t^T + \frac{y_t^N}{e_t} + \tau_t - \left(c_t^T + \frac{c_t^N}{e_t}\right) - \frac{i_{t-1}}{1+\varepsilon_{t-1}} m_{t-1}, \tag{13.61}$$

where ε_{t-1} is the rate of depreciation, defined as

$$1 + \varepsilon_{t-1} \equiv \frac{E_t}{E_{t-1}},$$

and i_t, the nominal interest rate, is given by the interest parity condition (recall that foreign inflation is zero)[31]

$$1 + i_t = (1+r)(1+\varepsilon_t). \tag{13.62}$$

31. Notice that for the purposes of MATLAB coding, we have changed the definition of ε_t relative to chapter 5.

Taking into account that by definition, $e_t = P_t^T / P_t^N$, we can rewrite m_{t-1} as

$$m_{t-1} = \frac{z_{t-1}}{e_{t-1}^{1-\gamma}}. \tag{13.63}$$

Substituting (13.63) into the consumer's flow constraint (13.61), we can rewrite the latter as

$$a_t = (1+r)a_{t-1} + y_t^T + \frac{y_t^N}{e_t} + \tau_t - \left(c_t^T + \frac{c_t^N}{e_t}\right) - \frac{i_{t-1}}{1+\varepsilon_{t-1}} \frac{z_{t-1}}{e_{t-1}^{1-\gamma}}. \tag{13.64}$$

The representative consumer chooses c_t^T, c_t^N, z_t, and a_t to maximize (13.59) subject to (13.64). In terms of the Lagrangian,

$$\mathcal{L} = \sum_{t=0}^{\infty} \beta^t \left\{ \frac{\left[\left(c_t^T\right)^{\gamma} \left(c_t^N\right)^{1-\gamma} \right]^{1-1/\sigma} - 1}{1 - 1/\sigma} + \log(z_t) \right\}$$
$$+ \sum_{t=0}^{\infty} \beta^t \lambda_t \left[(1+r)a_{t-1} + y_t^T + \frac{y_t^N}{e_t} + \tau_t - \left(c_t^T + \frac{c_t^N}{e_t}\right) - \frac{i_{t-1}}{1+\varepsilon_{t-1}} \frac{z_{t-1}}{e_{t-1}^{1-\gamma}} - a_t \right].$$

The first-order conditions are given by

$$\gamma c_t^{-1/\sigma} \left(\frac{c_t^N}{c_t^T}\right)^{1-\gamma} = \lambda_t, \tag{13.65}$$

$$(1-\gamma) c_t^{-1/\sigma} \left(\frac{c_t^T}{c_t^N}\right)^{\gamma} = \frac{\lambda_t}{e_t}, \tag{13.66}$$

$$\frac{\beta^t}{z_t} = \beta^{t+1} \lambda_{t+1} \frac{i_t}{1+\varepsilon_t} \frac{1}{e_t^{1-\gamma}}, \tag{13.67}$$

$$\beta^t \lambda_t = \beta^{t+1} \lambda_{t+1} (1+r), \tag{13.68}$$

where $c_t (\equiv \left(c_t^T\right)^{\gamma} \left(c_t^N\right)^{1-\gamma})$ is a consumption aggregator.

Combining first-order conditions (13.65) and (13.66), we obtain the familiar condition

$$\frac{\gamma}{1-\gamma} \frac{c_t^N}{c_t^T} = e_t. \tag{13.69}$$

Under our usual assumption that $\beta(1+r)=1$, condition (13.68) reduces to

$$\lambda_t = \lambda_{t+1}. \tag{13.70}$$

Using conditions (13.62) and (13.70), and the fact that $\beta(1+r)=1$, we can rewrite first-order condition (13.67) as

$$z_t = \frac{e_t^{1-\gamma}}{\lambda_t} \frac{1}{i_t/(1+i_t)},$$

which, using (13.63) for time t, reduces to a standard money demand,

$$m_t = \frac{1}{\lambda_t \left[i_t/(1+i_t)\right]}. \tag{13.71}$$

In the separable case (as in chapter 8), λ_t would equal γ/c_t^T, the marginal utility of consumption of tradable goods. In this more general case, the marginal utility of consumption of tradable goods is given by the LHS of first-order condition (13.65).

For further reference, notice that we can multiply both sides of (13.71) by e_t and define real money balances in terms of nontradable goods as $n_t \equiv M_t/P_t^N$ to obtain

$$n_t = \frac{e_t}{\lambda_t \left[i_t/(1+i_t)\right]}. \tag{13.72}$$

For intuitive purposes, it proves useful to log differentiate first-order condition (13.65), taking into account (13.70), to obtain

$$\widehat{c_t^T} = \frac{(1-\gamma)(\sigma-1)}{\gamma+\sigma(1-\gamma)}\widehat{c_t^N}, \tag{13.73}$$

where a hat over a variable denotes proportional change.

Equation (13.73) makes clear that if $\sigma = 1$, the model reduces to that of chapter 8, section 8.2: the path of c_t^T is flat over time along any PFEP. If $\sigma > 1$, consumption of tradables and nontradables comoves positively. If $\sigma < 1$, they comove negatively. As shown in exercise 2 at the end of chapter 4, the intuition is that since we have assumed a Cobb–Douglas formulation for the instantaneous utility, the case $\sigma > 1$ ($\sigma < 1$) corresponds to tradables and nontradables being Edgeworth complements (substitutes), which implies that they move together (in opposite direction) along a PFEP.

Supply Side

The supply side is the same as in chapter 8 but specified in discrete time. The supply of tradable goods is exogenously given at the constant level y^T. The domestic price of tradable goods is fully flexible and given by the law of one price. In contrast, the nominal price of nontradable goods is sticky and output of nontradables is demand-determined. As in chapter 8, sticky prices are introduced following a discrete-time version of Calvo's (1983) staggered prices. Formally, the change in the future inflation rate is *negatively* related to excess aggregate demand:

$$\pi_{t+1} - \pi_t = -\theta(c_t^N - y_f^N), \tag{13.74}$$

where $\pi_t (\equiv P_{t+1}^N / P_t^N - 1)$ is the inflation rate of nontradable goods and y_f^N is the full-employment level of nontradable output.

Government

Under flexible exchange rates, the level of international reserves is constant and, for simplicity, assumed to be zero. The government's flow constraint is thus given by

$$\frac{M_t - M_{t-1}}{P_t^T} = \tau_t.$$

For further reference, notice that we can rewrite this equation as

$$m_t - m_{t-1} + \frac{\varepsilon_{t-1}}{1 + \varepsilon_{t-1}} m_{t-1} = \tau_t. \tag{13.75}$$

Equilibrium Conditions

Since perfect capital mobility prevails, the interest parity condition (13.62) holds. Equilibrium in the nontradable goods market implies that

$$c_t^N = y_t^N.$$

Since, by definition, $m_t = M_t / P_t^T$, the corresponding law of motion is given by

$$\frac{m_{t+1}}{m_t} = \frac{M_{t+1}}{P_{t+1}^T} \frac{P_t^T}{M_t} = \frac{1 + \mu_t}{1 + \varepsilon_t}, \tag{13.76}$$

where, by definition,

$$\mu_t \equiv \frac{M_{t+1}}{M_t} - 1.$$

By the same token, the law of motion for n_t, is given by

$$\frac{n_{t+1}}{n_t} = \frac{1 + \mu_t}{1 + \pi_t}. \tag{13.77}$$

By definition, $e_t = P_t^T / P_t^N$. It follows that

$$\frac{e_{t+1}}{e_t} = \frac{1+\varepsilon_t}{1+\pi_t}. \tag{13.78}$$

The domestic real interest rate (i.e., the real interest rate in terms of nontradable goods) is defined as

$$r_t^d = \frac{1+i_t}{1+\pi_t} - 1. \tag{13.79}$$

Combining the consumer's flow constraint (13.61) with the government's (13.75), we obtain the economy's flow constraint (i.e., the current account):

$$b_t = (1+r)b_{t-1} + y^T - c_t^T, \tag{13.80}$$

where the trade balance is given by

$$TB_t = y^T - c_t^T. \tag{13.81}$$

Numerical Solution

Since real money balances enter separably into the utility function, the system is recursive in m_t, i_t, and ε_t, on the one hand, and c_t^T, c_t^N, π_t, on the other. In fact—and as shown in exercise 3 at the end of the chapter—it is easy to show, along the lines of chapter 5, appendix 5.8.4, that m_t is governed by an unstable differential equation and that therefore m_t will adjust instantaneously in response to an unanticipated and permanent change in μ_t. Since m_t adjusts instantaneously, the same would be true of the nominal interest rate, i_t, and through the interest parity condition, of ε_t. Having solved this part of the model, one would then set up a dynamic system in c_t^T, c_t^N, and π_t. This dynamic system, however, would be hard to solve analytically because it would have an integral constraint for the path of c_t^T. In other words, the path of c_t^T would need to meet the condition that its present discounted value be equal to the present discounted value of tradable resources. In light of this, we will solve this model numerically using the linearization method popularized by King, Plosser, and Rebelo (1988, 2001).

We already know from (13.73) that the comovement of c_t^T and c_t^N depends on whether σ is greater, equal, or smaller than one. To illustrate these different cases, figure 13.15 shows the numerical solution for the case of $\sigma = 0.5$. As expected from equation (13.73), c_t^T and c_t^N comove negatively.[32] While there is a contraction in consumption of nontradables (panel d), there is a boom in consumption of tradables (panel b). As a result the trade balance falls on impact (panel c).

32. The parameterization underlying figures 13.15 and 13.16 is as follows: $r = 0.04$, $\mu^H = 0.5$ $\gamma = 0.5$, $\theta = 0.1$, $y^T = y_f^N = 1$, and initial foreign assets equal to 0.6283. Plots show percentage deviations from the initial steady state. The log-linearization of the model and MATLAB coding may be found in an online appendix.

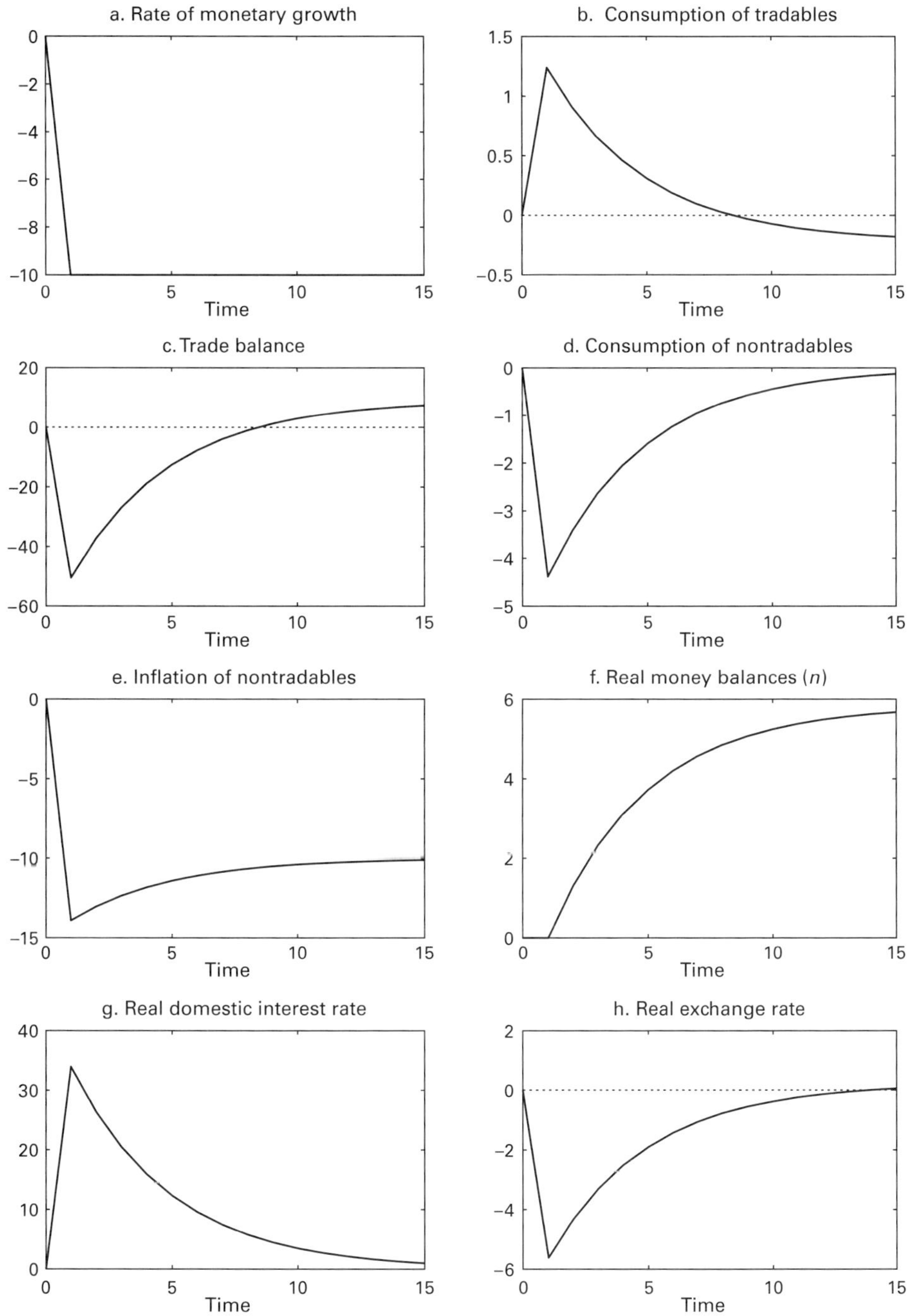

Figure 13.15
Permanent 10 percent reduction in money growth ($\sigma = 0.5$)

The behavior of the remaining variables coincides with the separable case analyzed in chapter 8, section 8.3: inflation of nontradables (panel e) falls below its new and lower long-run value; real money balances in terms of nontradables increase gradually toward their higher steady-state value (panel f); the real domestic interest rate rises on impact and falls thereafter (panel g); and the real exchange falls on impact (i.e., real appreciation) and returns gradually to its unchanged steady state (panel h).

Figure 13.16 shows the case of $\sigma = 1.5$. In this case, c_t^T and c_t^N comove positively: both fall on impact and gradually recover over time (panels b and d, respectively). Aside from the trade balance, the behavior of the remaining variables parallels that of figure 13.15.

We can conclude that as expected, the value of σ is critical for the behavior of c_t^T, and hence the external accounts. The behavior of the rest of the system is the same. Since the data seem to show little change in the external accounts during the first two years (recall figure 13.4, panels g and h), it would seem that the case of $\sigma = 1$ is not a bad first approximation to reality. Still, we suspect that if we had data on consumption of tradable goods, it would show a fall (overall consumption, after all, does fall in the data). If that were the case, we would need $\sigma > 1$ to replicate the facts. However, this is arguably not the more relevant case from an empirical point of view since, in practice, $\sigma < 1$ (recall box 3.1 in chapter 3). Further frictions may thus be needed to replicate the stylized facts illustrated in figure 13.4 for realistic values of σ.

13.6.2 Sticky Inflation

We will now examine the dynamics of money based stabilization under sticky inflation. The model will be the same that we used in section 13.5.1 to analyze the dynamics of exchange rate based stabilization under sticky inflation.

Consumers' Problem

The consumers' problem remains the same and hence the first-order conditions are still given by (13.4), (13.5), and (13.6). The intratemporal consumption efficiency condition (equation 13.7) and money demand (equation 13.8) remain valid as well.

Supply Side

The supply side also remains essentially unchanged. Output of tradable goods is exogenously given and constant over time. Output of nontradable goods is demand-determined. Its price and rate of change are sticky. Inflation of nontradable goods is assumed to be given by

$$\dot{\pi}_t = \theta(c_t^N - y_f^N) + \gamma(\mu_t - \pi_t). \tag{13.82}$$

Notice that the second term on the RHS is different than that in equation (13.21), reflecting the fact that this economy will be operating under flexible exchange rates, and hence the nominal anchor will be the money supply rather than the exchange rate.

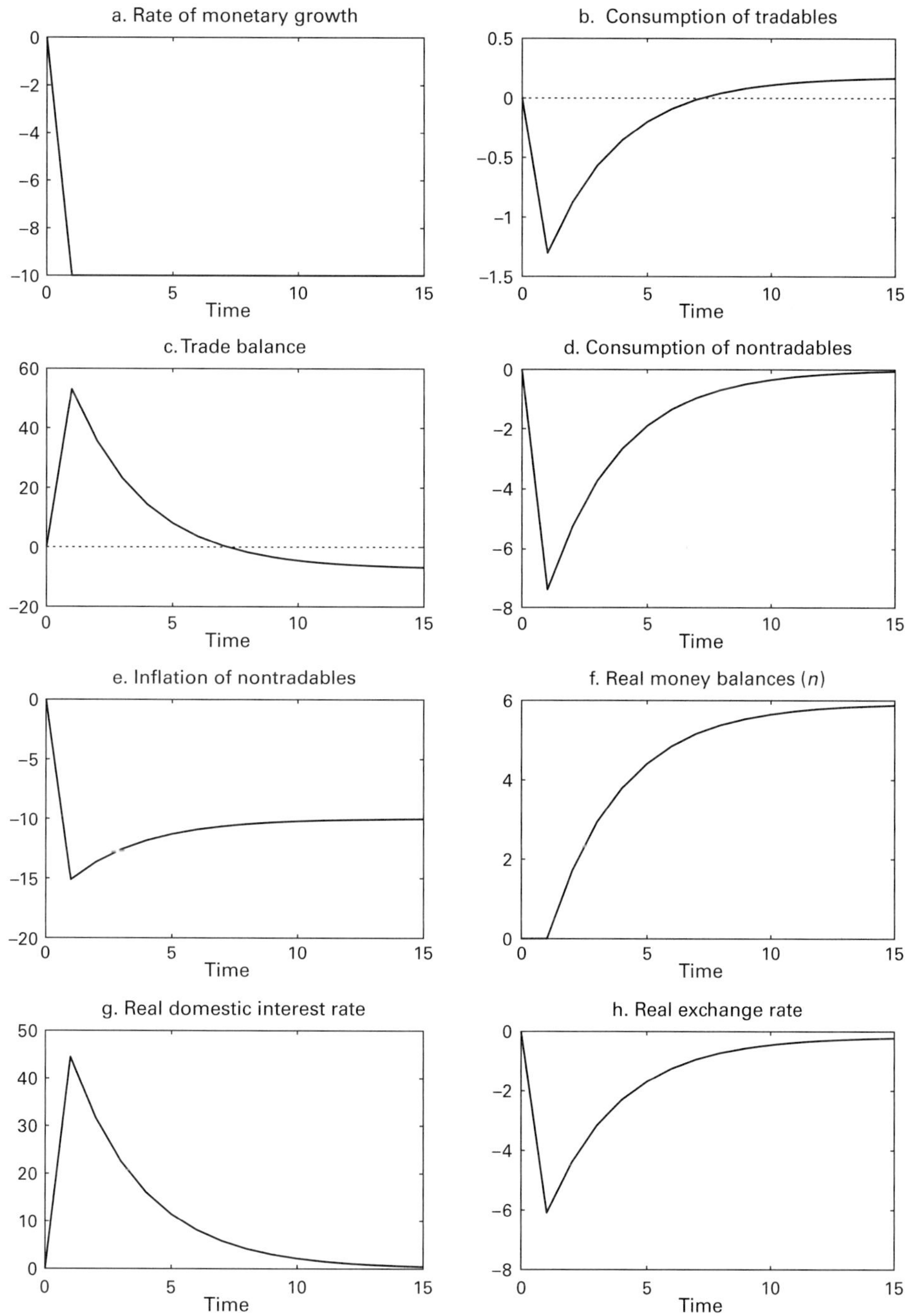

Figure 13.16
Permanent 10 percent reduction in money growth ($\sigma = 1.5$)

Government

The government's flow constraint remains given by (13.10).

Equilibrium Conditions

Equilibrium conditions remain given by equations (13.11) through (13.15).

Consumption of Tradable Goods

Along a PFEP, consumption of tradables is still given by (13.23). Furthermore this consumption level does not depend on the particular value of μ_t.

Solving the Model

Differential Equation in m_t The first step in solving the model—and as we have done many times before—is to derive an unstable differential in m_t. Since $m_t = M_t/E_t$,

$$\frac{\dot{m}_t}{m_t} = \mu - \varepsilon_t, \tag{13.83}$$

where μ denotes the constant value of the rate of money growth. From the interest parity condition, $\varepsilon_t = i_t - r$. Using this and first-order condition (13.6), we obtain

$$\dot{m}_t = m_t\left(\mu + r - \frac{c_t^T}{m_t}\right). \tag{13.84}$$

This is an unstable differential equation in m_t. Hence m_t needs to be constant along a PFEP with a constant μ_t. Since $\dot{m}_t = 0$ along a PFEP, it follows from (13.83) that

$$\varepsilon_t = \mu. \tag{13.85}$$

In other words, along a PFEP, the rate of depreciation is constant and equal to the rate of money growth. The nominal interest rate will thus also be constant and equal to $r + \mu$.

Dynamic System The second step is to construct a dynamic system in π_t and e_t. The first equation is given by (13.82). The second follows from substituting (13.85) into (13.13) to obtain

$$\dot{e}_t = e_t(\mu - \pi_t). \tag{13.86}$$

Equations (13.82) and (13.86) constitute a two differential equation system in π_t and e_t. The system is in fact identical to the one analyzed in section 13.5.1, and the phase diagram depicted in figure 13.7 thus remains valid. The system has two negative roots and is therefore globally stable. As before, we assume that roots are real.

Permanent Stabilization

Suppose that the economy is initially in a steady state with the rate of monetary growth given by μ^H. At time 0 there is an unanticipated and permanent fall in the rate of money growth from μ^H to μ^L (figure 13.17, panel a). How does the economy adjust?

Since m_t will still be governed by differential equation (13.84) (with the rate of monetary growth given by μ^L), real money balances will adjust instantaneously to their higher steady-state level. This increase in m_t comes about through a fall in the nominal exchange rate, E_t. Since prices are sticky, the fall in the nominal exchange rate also implies a fall in the real exchange rate, e_t. This piece of information will prove important when it comes to analyzing the response of the dynamic system to the reduction in μ_t. Finally, both ε_t and i_t will fall instantaneously to their lower steady-state values, given by μ^L and $r + \mu^L$, respectively.

In terms of the dynamic system, the initial fall in e_t will be reflected in a jump at $t = 0$ from point A to point D in figure 13.7. The system then follows the arrowed path until it reaches point B. The corresponding paths of the inflation rate and the real exchange rate are depicted in figure 13.17, panels b and c, respectively.

To derive the path of consumption of nontradable goods, recall that $c_t^N = e_t c^T$. Hence consumption of nontradable goods falls on impact and then follows the same time pattern as the real exchange rate (panel d).

What is the adjustment path of real money balances (in terms of nontradables goods)? Taking into account that (1) n_t is a predetermined variable, (2) $n_t = m_t e_t$, and (3) $\dot{m}_t = 0$, the path of n_t follows that of e_t. Hence n_t first falls and then increases to reach its new and higher steady state (panel e). The path of the domestic real interest rate follows from the definition, $r_t^d = i_t - \pi_t$, and the paths of i_t and π_t (panel f).

We conclude that while this experiment generates some of the stylized facts associated with money based stabilization—in particular, the initial contraction and the initial real appreciation—it is not consistent with others such as the initial rise in real interest rates. It does offer an explanation, of course, for those cases where the convergence of the inflation rate to the rate of monetary growth has taken place only slowly over time.

13.7 Final Remarks

This chapter has analyzed the macroeconomic dynamics associated with inflation stabilization in developing countries. A key distinction was drawn between hyperinflation and chronic inflation. Hyperinflations are relatively short and explosive inflationary processes with a clear fiscal origin and inflation rates surpassing 50 percent per month. In sharp contrast, chronic inflation processes exhibit much lower inflation rates—though still high by industrial country standards—and may last for decades as inflation tends to become self-sustaining through widespread indexation of nominal wages and prices to past inflation. While clearly present, the fiscal origin of chronic inflation is harder to establish essentially because inflation takes a life of its own. By fixing the

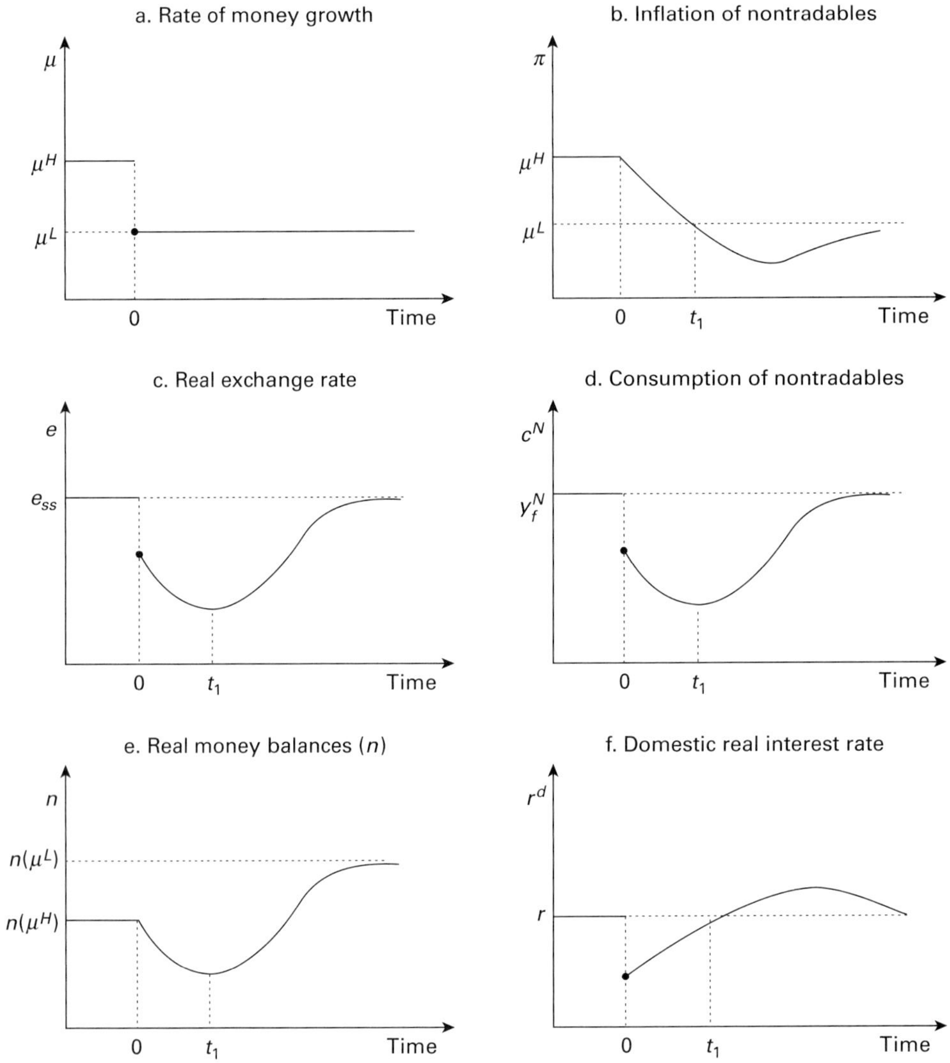

Figure 13.17
Money based stabilization under sticky inflation

exchange rate, hyperinflations have often been stopped overnight with little output costs. This is possible because, by its very nature, hyperinflation eliminates any inertia in prices, which essentially become quoted in some foreign currency. In contrast, stopping chronic inflation has proved much more difficult and many countries have gone through repeated attempts before finally succeeding in eliminating it.

A second key distinction is related to the nominal anchor used to stop chronic inflation (the exchange rate or the money supply). We have seen that on the one hand, exchange rate based stabilizations have typically been associated with an initial boom in output and consumption followed by a later recession. Money based stabilizations, on the other hand, seem to lead to an initial recession. This choice of nominal anchor has been cast in terms of having to choose between "recession now versus recession later." We examined several theoretical models that could explain the stylized facts associated with exchange rate based stabilization. Sticky inflation leads to a fall in real interest rates, which under certain conditions, is accompanied by an initial boom. Lack of credibility—modeled as temporary stabilization—provides an alternative explanation for the stylized facts. The possible role of supply-side channels, such as investment, was also explored. The initial recession under money based stabilization can be explained with a fairly standard sticky prices or sticky-inflation model.

Exercises

1. (ERBS with a declining rate of devaluation) Consider the cash-in-advance model of section 13.5.2 but in the context of an endowment economy (as in chapter 7). Suppose that the rate of devaluation just before time zero is ε^H. At time 0 an unanticipated disinflation program is implemented with the rate of devaluation given by

$$\varepsilon_t = \varepsilon^H e^{-\psi t}.$$

In other words, the rate of devaluation is reduced gradually over time at the rate ψ.[33] In the context of this model:

a. Show that consumption of tradables and the real exchange rate comove negatively along the new PFEP.

b. Show that consumption of tradables falls and the real exchange rate increases on impact.

2. (Distribution costs and the effect on the real exchange rate) Consider a real model of a small open economy perfectly integrated into world goods and capital markets. The endowments of tradable and nontradable goods are constant and given by y^T and y^N, respectively. Suppose that

33. The declining rate of devaluation is in the spirit of the Southern Cone tablitas of the 1970s; see Obstfled (1985) and Roldos (1997) for models of gradual disinflation.

it takes ϕ units of nontradables to consume one unit of tradables. In other words, the total cost of consuming one unit of tradables is $1 + \phi p_t$. The intertemporal budget constraint is thus given by

$$b_0 + \int_0^\infty (y^T + p_t y^N)\exp(-rt)dt = \int_0^\infty \left[c_t^T(1 + \phi p_t) + p_t c_t^N\right]\exp(-rt)dt,$$

where b_0 are the household's initial net foreign assets, p_t is the relative price of nontradable goods, and c_t^T and c_t^N denote consumption of tradables and nontradables, respectively.

Let preferences be given by

$$\int_0^\infty \left[\log(c_t^T) + \log(c_t^N)\right]\exp(-\beta t)dt.$$

Equilibrium in the nontradables goods market requires that

$$y^N = c_t^N + \phi c_t^T.$$

In the context of this model,

a. Derive the first-order conditions (assume, as usual, that $\beta = r$).

b. Show that c_t^T, c_t^N, and p_t will be constant along a PFEP.

c. Derive reduced forms for c_t^T and p_t along a PFEP.

d. Analyze the effects of an unanticipated and permanent increase in initial net foreign assets. Explain the role of ϕ.

3. (Behavior of real money balances) Show, in the context of the model of section 13.6, that m_t (real money balances in terms of tradable goods) follows an unstable difference equation.

References

Ball, Laurence. 1994. What determines the sacrifice ratio? In N. Gregory Mankiw, ed., *Monetary Policy*. Chicago: University of Chicago Press, 155–93.

Blanchard, Olivier, and Stanley Fischer. 1989. *Lectures on Macroeconomics*. Cambridge: MIT Press.

Burstein, Ariel T., Joao C. Neves, and Sergio Rebelo. 2003. Distribution costs and real exchange rate dynamics during exchange-rate-based stabilizations. *Journal of Monetary Economics* 50 (6): 1189–1214.

Cagan, Phillip. 1956. The monetary dynamics of hyperinflation. In Milton Friedman, ed., *Studies in the Quantity Theory of Money*. Chicago: University of Chicago Press, 25–117.

Calvo, Guillermo A. 1983. Staggered prices in a utility-maximizing framework. *Journal of Monetary Economics* 12 (31): 383–98.

Calvo, Guillermo A., and Carlos A. Végh. 1994. Stabilization dynamics and backward-looking contracts. *Journal of Development Economics* 43 (1): 59–84.

Calvo, Guillermo A., and Carlos A. Végh. 1999. Inflation stabilization and BOP crises in developing countries. In John Taylor and Michael Woodford, eds., *Handbook of Macroeconomics*, vol. C. Amsterdam: North Holland, 1531–1614.

De Gregorio, Jose, Pablo E. Guidotti, and Carlos A. Végh. 1998. Inflation stabilization and the consumption of durable goods. *Economic Journal* 108: 105–31.

Dornbusch, Rudiger, and Mario H. Simonsen. 1987. *Inflation Stabilization with Incomes Policy Support: A Review of Recent Experience in Argentina, Brazil, and Israel.* New York: Group of Thirty.

Dornbusch, Rudiger, and Alejandro Werner. 1994. Mexico: Stabilization, reform, and no growth. *Brookings Papers on Economic Activity* 25 (1): 253–316. (Includes discussions by Stanley Fischer and Guillermo Calvo.)

Eichengreen, Barry. 2001. Crisis prevention and management: Any new lessons from Argentina and Turkey? Background paper written for the World Bank's *Global Development Finance 2002.*

Feldstein, Martin. 2002. Argentina's Fall: Lesson from the latest financial crisis. *Foreign Affairs* 81 (2): 7–14.

Fischer, Stanley, Ratna Sahay, and Carlos A. Végh. 2002. Modern hyper- and high inflation. *Journal of Economic Literature* 40 (3): 837–80.

Kiguel, Miguel, and Nissan Liviatan. 1992. The business cycle associated with exchange rate-based stabilizations. *World Bank Economic Review* 6: 279–305.

Kiguel, Miguel, and Nissan Liviatan. 1995. Stopping three big inflations: Argentina, Brazil, and Peru. In Rudiger Dornbusch and Sebastian Edwards, ed., *Reform, Recovery, and Growth: Latin America and the Middle East.* Chicago: University of Chicago Press, 369–414

King, Robert, Charles Plosser, and Sergio Rebelo. 1988. Production, growth, and business cycles: I. The basic neoclassical model. *Journal of Monetary Economics* 21 (2–3): 195–232.

King, Robert, Charles Plosser, and Sergio Rebelo. 2001. Production, growth, and business cycles: Technical appendix. *Computational Economics* 20 (1–2): 87–116.

Lahiri, Amartya. 2000. Disinflation programs under policy uncertainty. *Journal of International Economics* 50 (2): 351–73.

Lahiri, Amartya. 2001. Exchange rate based stabilizations under real frictions: The role of endogenous labor supply. *Journal of Economic Dynamics and Control* 25 (8): 1157–77.

Makinen, Gail E. and G. Thomas Woodward. 1989. The Taiwanese hyperinflation and stabilization of 1945–52. *Journal of Money, Credit and Banking* 21: 90–105.

Mussa, Michael. 2002. Argentina and the Fund: From triumph to tragedy. *Policy Analyses in International Economics* 67. Institute for International Economics. Washington, DC.

Obstfeld, Maurice. 1985. The capital inflows problem revisited: A stylized model of Southern-Cone disinflation. *Review of Economic Studies* 52 (4): 605–25.

Ostry, Jonathan and Carmen M. Reinhart. 1992. Private saving and terms of trade shocks. *IMF Staff Papers* 39 (3): 495–517.

Pazos, Felipe. 1972. *Chronic Inflation in Latin America*. New York: Prager.

Rebelo, Sergio, and Carlos A. Végh. 1995. Real effects of exchange rate-based stabilizations: An analysis of competing theories. *NBER Macroeconomics Annual* 10: 125–74.

Reinhart, Carmen M., and Carlos A. Végh. 1996. Do exchange rate based stabilizations carry the seeds of their own destruction? Mimeo. IMF, Washington, DC.

Rodriguez, Carlos A. 1982. The Argentina stabilization plan of December 20th. *World Development* 10 (9): 801-811.

Roldos, Jorge. 1995. Supply-side effects of disinflation programs. *IMF Staff Papers* 42 (1): 158–83.

Roldos, Jorge. 1997. On gradual disinflation, the real exchange rate, and the current account. *Journal of International Money and Finance* 16 (1): 37–54.

Sargent, Thomas. 1982. The ends of four big inflations. In Robert E. Hall, ed., *Inflation: Causes and effects*. Chicago: University of Chicago Press, 41–97.

Uribe, Martin. 1997. Exchange-rate-based inflation stabilization: The initial real effects of credible plans. *Journal of Monetary Economics* 39 (2): 197–221.

Uribe, Martin. 2002. The price-consumption puzzle of currency pegs. *Journal of Monetary Economics* 49 (3): 533–69.

Végh, Carlos A. 1992. Stopping high inflation: An analytical overview. *IMF Staff Papers* 39 (3): 626–95.

Végh, Carlos A., and Guillermo Vuletin. 2011. How do federal transfers systems affect fiscal cyclicality at the sub-national level? Unpublished manuscript. University of Maryland and Colby College.

14 Capital Inflows

14.1 Introduction

The flow of capital to developing countries follows a marked cyclical pattern. Figure 14.1 depicts total private capital flows to developing economies since 1980. We can observe four cycles, with peaks in 1981, 1993, 1995, and 2007. The year following the peak is typically a year of financial crises: the 1982 debt crisis, the 1994 Tequila crisis, the East Asian crises in 1997, and the American financial crisis in 2008. This chapter will deal with the macroeconomic causes, consequences, and policy implications of capital flows cycles.

Section 14.2 sets the stage for the rest of the chapter by laying out the main stylized facts associated with capital inflows. Typically, capital inflows episodes are associated with higher aggregate demand and output, real appreciation of the domestic currency, and trade and current account deficits. As we will see, this "overheating" of the economy—which often includes higher inflation as well—is a cause of concern for policy makers and leads to various policy responses.

A very basic conceptual issue that arises regarding capital flows is whether they are endogenous or exogenous. In all the models that we have seen so far in this book, capital inflows have been an *endogenous* response to some shock. In the endowment economy of chapter 1, for instance, a temporary negative shock to the endowment leads to a temporary current account deficit that is financed with a capital inflow (i.e., a surplus in the capital account). In the same vein, in the monetary world of chapter 7, a temporary fall in the world nominal interest rate induces a consumption boom and current account deficit which, again, is financed by a capital inflow. The capital inflow is thus a response to the consumption boom. This way of thinking, however, is at odds with a frequent interpretation of capital flows in policy circles as being *exogenous* to the economy. Clearly, when observers talk about a "sudden stop" (a term coined by Calvo 1998), they are referring to an exogenous stop in the flow of capital into a country. In other words, the idea is that small emerging economies may be subject to the vagaries of international capital flows, which may stop and restart at the whim of international investors.

Two important conceptual questions then arise. First, how can we think of an "exogenous" capital inflow in our models? Second, will the effects of exogenous capital flows differ from those stemming from endogenous capital flows? Section 14.3 addresses these questions. It develops

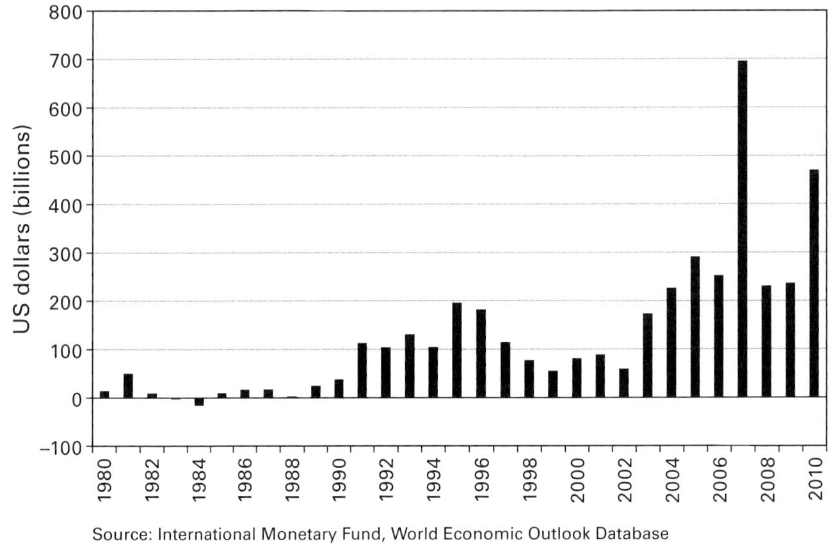

Figure 14.1
Emerging and developing economies: Private capital flows

a simple two-period real model (à la chapter 2) and analyzes the economy's response to three different shocks: a domestic demand shock, a fall in the world real interest rate, and an exogenous capital inflow (modeled as an exogenous change in the capital account balance). We show that—in terms of consumption (and hence welfare) and the current and capital accounts—the economy's response to all three shocks is identical. Hence an outside observer who can only see consumption and the external accounts would not be able to tell what is the underlying shock. While this strict equivalence may not hold exactly in more complicated models, it serves to make the point that the macroeconomic effects of capital flows are likely to be similar *regardless* of the specific trigger.[1]

As already mentioned, the term "sudden stops" is used to refer to episodes where capital inflows into a country come to a screeching halt. What will be the macroeconomic effects of sudden stops? Section 14.4 answers this question in the context of a three-period endowment economy. The endowment is assumed to grow over time (capturing a "growing" economy). In an unconstrained world (i.e., a world without sudden stops), consumption would be flat over time and the economy would borrow in the first two periods and repay in the last one. If we now impose the constraint of a sudden stop in period two (i.e., the current account must be nonnegative from period 2 onward), then consumption will be higher in period one, fall precipitously in period 2, and recover in period 3. The fall in consumption in period 2 will be accompanied by a sharp real depreciation. Intuitively, the sudden stop acts like an intertemporal distortion (à la chapter 3), making period-2

1. In monetary models, however, the behavior of inflation may depend on the source of the shock, as analyzed below.

consumption more expensive relative to period-1 consumption and inducing the boom–bust cycle just described.

Section 14.5 then presents a cash-in-advance version of the sticky-prices model introduced in chapter 8 to rationalize the stylized facts discussed in section 14.2. We solve the model under both predetermined and flexible exchange rates and show the economy's response to aggregate demand shocks and reductions in world real interest rates. While a real appreciation occurs regardless of the shock and the exchange rate regime, the bulk of the initial real appreciation takes place through higher inflation of nontradable goods under predetermined exchange rates compared to a fall in the nominal exchange rate under flexible exchange rates. Hence, while policy makers may be unable to prevent a real appreciation accompanying a capital inflows episode, they may be able to choose how this real appreciation is effected.

In the context of the model of section 14.5, section 14.6 analyzes some of the most common policy responses to episodes of capital inflows: foreign exchange market intervention and fiscal tightening. While these policies go some way toward lessening the initial real appreciation, they come at the cost of higher inflation in the case of foreign exchange market intervention and an output contraction in the case of fiscal tightening. We also discuss policy responses involving macroprudential regulation.

Section 14.7 closes the chapter with some concluding remarks.

14.2 Capital Inflows: Stylized Facts

The macroeconomic effects of capital inflows to developing countries were thoroughly reviewed in the 2007 *World Economic Outlook* (WEO). To identify episodes of large capital inflows, the WEO used both a country and a region based criterion:

- *Country based criterion* If the ratio of net capital inflows to GDP for a given country is one standard deviation larger than this country's trend, then the episode is identified as a capital inflows episode.
- *Region based criterion* If capital inflows are significantly larger than an arbitrary regional threshold (the 75th percentile of the regional distribution of the ratio of net capital inflows to GDP), then the episode is flagged as a capital inflows episode.

If either of these criteria is met, the event is classified as a capital inflows episode. The WEO chapter identifies 73 recently completed episodes in emerging countries for the period 1987 to 2006. Figure 14.2 shows the impact of these inflows on the main macroeconomic variables of interest. In each panel, "before" denotes the average of the variable in the two years prior to the episode, "during" is the average of the variable during the inflow episode, and "after" is the average of the variable in the two years that follow the final year of the event. The scale represents the median of each variable across all episodes.

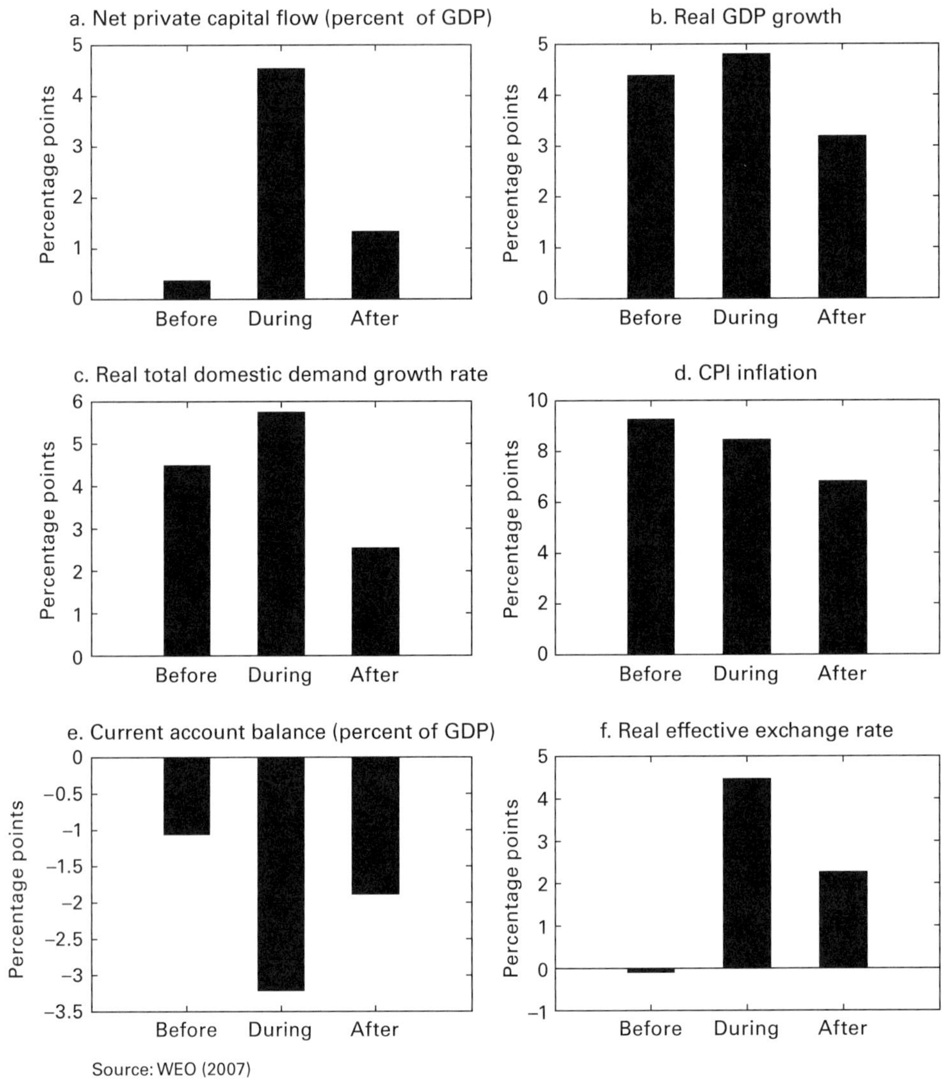

Figure 14.2
Capital inflows: Stylized facts

Let us look at the impact on different variables:

- By construction, of course, panel a shows that net capital flows peak at around 4.5 percent of GDP during the episodes.
- Panels b and c show the effect on GDP growth and aggregate demand. Both peak during the capital inflows episode and fall sharply thereafter.
- Panel d illustrates the behavior of inflation. The graph suggests that there is in fact a slight fall in inflation during the capital inflows episode.

This evidence, however, is somewhat misleading as it includes many inflation stabilization programs where the fall in inflation was accompanied by capital inflows (as documented in chapter 13). As the theoretical model in section 14.5 will make clear, capital inflows episodes that are triggered by higher domestic demand or a fall in international real interest rates (as opposed to a reduction in the rate of depreciation or the rate of money growth) will be accompanied by an *increase* in the inflation rate. Ideally, then, to analyze empirically the behavior of inflation during capital inflows episodes, one would like to distinguish between the various possible sources of capital inflows, an inherently difficult task.

- Panel e shows that capital inflows episodes are associated with current account deficits. The current account deficit increases sharply during the episodes and falls afterward.
- Panel f shows that capital inflows go hand in hand with a real appreciation of the domestic currency.[2]

In addition we should point out that capital inflows episodes are accompanied by a substantial increase in international reserves (see section 14.6). These stylized facts will guide our theoretical journey below.

14.3 A Simple Model

This section develops a simple two period model (as in chapter 2) to illustrate the idea that, while the trigger of a capital inflow may vary from case to case (see box 14.1), the macroeconomic consequences will be very similar. In particular, we will illustrate how three different shocks—a domestic demand shock, a fall in international real interest rates, and an exogenous capital flow—will all give rise to the same outcome: higher consumption, a trade deficit that is financed by a capital inflow, and an increase in the relative price of nontradable goods.

Formally, consider a two period, real model of a small open economy. Consumers derive utility from consuming both tradable (c_t^T) and nontradable (c_t^N) goods. The economy is endowed with a constant stream of tradable (y^T) and nontradable goods (y^N).

2. Here the definition of the real exchange rate follows the IMF's practice of computing it as P^N/EP^*. Hence a rise in this measure entails a real appreciation.

Box 14.1
Capital inflows: Push or pull?

What triggers capital inflows? The literature has broken down possible explanations into two main categories:

- *External or "push" factors* Factors associated with a common set of favorable external factors, such as low interest rates in industrial countries and/or an upswing in the world business cycle.
- *Domestic or "pull" factors* Country-specific factors, such as demand shocks, inflation stabilization programs, capital account liberalization, debt reduction agreements, and improvements in the institutional environment (e.g., enforcement of property rights).

While, as the text makes clear, the macroeconomic effects of capital inflows are essentially the same regardless of their origin, the distinction between push and pull factors is still important for policy considerations. Clearly, capital inflows that are due to push factors are outside the policy maker's reach and their frequency and intensity will be dictated by industrial countries' business cycles and international credit conditions.[a] In contrast, when pull factors are at play, policy makers may have the possibility of enacting policies that will smooth the capital flows cycle. Hence whether capital inflows are due to domestic shocks in developing countries or to a common set of external factors remains an important empirical question. Table 14.1 summarizes several econometric studies that intend to shed light on this matter.

Table 14.1
Capital inflows: push or pull?

Author(s)	Dataset	Methodology	Main results
Calvo, Leiderman, and Reinhart (1993)	Monthly data for 10 Latin American countries, 1988–1992	Principal components analysis, structural VAR	• External factors account for around 50 percent of the monthly forecast error variance of the real exchange rate. • External factors seem to be main driving force behind capital inflows to developing countries.
Fernandez-Arias (1996)	Quarterly data for 13 middle-income developing countries, 1989–1992	OLS estimation	• External factors (international interest rates) are main driving force behind capital flows, minor role for domestic factors. • Domestic and external factors played an equally important role for larger countries (Argentina, Korea, and Mexico). • Country creditworthiness seems to play an important role, but this variable is mainly driven by external factors.
Taylor and Sarno (1997)	Monthly US capital flow data from 9 Latin American and 9 Asian countries, 1988–1992	Cointegration techniques and seemingly unrelated error correction system	• Domestic and external factors found to be important in explaining long-run bond and equity flows to developing countries. • External factors (mainly changes in US interest rates) more important in explaining short-run dynamics of bond flows to developing countries. • Push and pull factors equally important in determining short-run equity flows for Asian and Latin American economies.

a. Though policy makers can certainly try to influence how much actually comes into the country by imposing capital controls (see below).

Box 14.1
(continued)

Table 14.1
(continued)

Author(s)	Dataset	Methodology	Main results
Chuhan, Claessens, and Mamingi (1998)	Monthly US capital flow data from 9 Latin American and 9 Asian countries, 1988–1992	Panel data, fixed effects	• Both external factors (changes in US interest rates and US industrial activity) and country-specific factors found to be relevant in explaining capital inflows. • Equity flows found to be more sensitive than bond flows to external factors. • Bond flows more sensitive than equity flows to credit ratings and secondary market debt prices.
Kim (2000)	Quarterly data for Mexico (1958–1995), Chile (1981–1995), Korea (1977–1995), and Malaysia (1972–1995)	Structural VAR	• Capital movements over last 10 years of the sample mainly due to external factors (changes in the world interest rate or recession in industrial countries). • Domestic factors relatively less important. • Relative importance of external factors has increased over time.
Ying and Kim (2001)	Quarterly data for Korea and Mexico, 1960–1996	Structural VAR	• US business cycles found to be a dominant factor in capital inflows to Mexico and Korea. • Changes in foreign interest rates an important factor for capital inflows from 1980 to 1996. • External factors more important than domestic factors in explaining capital flows to both countries.
Edison and Warnock (2003)	Monthly US capital flow to 4 Latin American and 5 emerging Asian countries, 1989–1999	Panel data, fixed effects	• In both Latin America and emerging Asia, US interest rates and economic activity matter for capital inflows. • A reduction in capital controls results in higher equity flows to emerging Asia, but not to Latin America. • A cross-border listing has a positive long-term effect on equity flows to Latin America but not emerging Asia.
Baek (2006)	Quarterly data for 5 Latin American countries and 4 Asian countries, 1989–2002	Panel data, fixed effects	• For Latin American countries, domestic economic growth, US interest rates, and world stock market performance play a significant role in capital inflows. But market appetite for risk has no impact. • For Asian countries, domestic economic fundamentals have little impact while all external factors (US interest rates, appetite for risk, world income growth, and world stock market performance) have a significant impact.
Alfaro, Kalemli-Ozcan, and Volosovych (2007)	Annual capital flow data for 47 countries, 1970–2000	Cross-country regressions	• Institutional quality and macroeconomic policy play an important role for capital inflows in terms of both level and volatility. • Better institutions, higher growth, and relaxation of capital controls attract more capital inflows.

Box 14.1
(continued)

Calvo, Leiderman, and Reinhart's (1993) study was one of the first formal analyses of this issue. They found that external factors were mainly responsible for the capital inflows to Latin American countries from 1988 to 1992. In a similar vein, Fernandez-Arias (1996) assessed the relative importance of push and pull factors for a sample of emerging economies from 1989 to 1992 and also concluded that once the effect of external factors on country creditworthiness is taken into account, external factors were mainly responsible for the surge of capital inflows to developing countries. Kim's (2000) findings were consistent with the importance of global factors.

However, two other studies—Taylor and Sarno (1997) and Chuhan, Claessens, and Mamingi (1998)—concluded that both push and pull factors were relevant and that different types of flows (short- or long-term flows, bond or equity flows) responded differently to various factors. For example, Taylor and Sarno (1997) reported that short-term bond flows were mainly affected by changes in US interest rates, whereas Chuhan, Claessens, and Mamingi (1998) found that equity flows, rather than bond flows, were more sensitive to push factors.

The relative importance of push and pull factors appears to differ across regions. Baek (2006) found that capital inflows into Asia were primarily due to push factors, including investors' appetite for risk, and that domestic economic conditions had a negligible role. Capital inflows into Latin America were somewhat "pulled" by strong domestic growth, and pushed into the region by global financial factors but not by shifts in the market mood. The role of capital controls also seems to have differed between Latin America and Asia: Edison and Warnock (2003) found that a reduction in capital controls results in higher equity flows to emerging Asia but not to Latin America. Institutions also appear to play an important role in capital flows. Alfaro, Kalemli-Ozcan, and Volosovych (2007) found that institutional quality and historical legal origins had a direct effect on capital inflow mobility during the period 1970 to 2000.

Finally, the financial crisis that started in the United States in 2008 and led to an extremely loose monetary policy on the part of the Federal Reserve (with the Federal Funds rate close to zero) has resulted in a tremendous incentive for speculative money to flow into emerging markets through the so-called carry trade, which involves borrowing at very low interest rates in the United States and investing in emerging markets (e.g., see Burnside, Kleshchelski, and Rebelo 2011).

14.3.1 Consumer's Problem

Lifetime utility of the representative household (W) is given by

$$W = \alpha\left[u(c_1^T) + v(c_1^N)\right] + \beta[u(c_2^T) + v(c_2^N)], \tag{14.1}$$

where $\alpha \geq 1$ is a preference parameter that will be used to capture demand shocks in period 1, $\beta > 0$ is the discount factor, and $u(.)$ and $v(.)$ are strictly increasing and strictly concave functions.

Assume, for simplicity, that initial net foreign assets are zero. The first period budget constraint then takes the form

$$b_1 = y^T + p_1 y^N - c_1^T - p_1 c_1^N, \tag{14.2}$$

where $p_t, t = 1, 2$, denotes the relative price of nontradable goods in terms of the numéraire (tradable goods) and b_1 denotes net foreign assets at the end of period 1. Since the transversality condition requires that $b_2 = 0$, we can write period 2's budget constraint as

$$0 = y^T + p_2 y^N + (1+r)b_1 - c_2^T - p_2 c_2^N. \tag{14.3}$$

Combining constraints (14.2) and (14.3), we can derive the intertemporal budget constraint:

$$\frac{2+r}{1+r} y^T + p_1 y^N + \frac{p_2 y^N}{1+r} = c_1^T + p_1 c_1^N + \frac{c_2^T + p_2 c_2^N}{1+r}. \tag{14.4}$$

The consumer chooses $\{c_1^T, c_1^N, c_2^T, c_2^N\}$ to maximize lifetime utility—given by (14.1)—subject to constraint (14.4). In terms of the Lagrangian,

$$\begin{aligned}\mathcal{L} = {} & \alpha\left[u(c_1^T) + v(c_1^N)\right] + \beta[u(c_2^T) + v(c_2^N)] \\ & + \lambda\left[\frac{2+r}{1+r} y^T + p_1 y^N + \frac{p_2 y^N}{1+r} - c_1^T - p_1 c_1^N - \frac{(c_2^T + p_2 c_2^N)}{1+r}\right].\end{aligned}$$

The first-order conditions are given by

$$\alpha u'(c_1^T) = \lambda, \tag{14.5}$$

$$\alpha v'(c_1^N) = \lambda p_1, \tag{14.6}$$

$$\beta u'(c_2^T) = \frac{\lambda}{1+r}, \tag{14.7}$$

$$\beta v'(c_2^N) = \frac{\lambda p_2}{1+r}. \tag{14.8}$$

Combining first-order conditions (14.5) and (14.7), on the one hand, and (14.6) and (14.8), on the other, we obtain

$$\frac{\alpha u'(c_1^T)}{u'(c_2^T)} = \beta(1+r), \tag{14.9}$$

$$\alpha \frac{v'(c_1^N)}{v'(c_2^N)} = \beta(1+r)\frac{p_1}{p_2}. \tag{14.10}$$

14.3.2 Equilibrium Conditions

Equilibrium in the nontradable goods market requires that

$$c_1^N = c_2^N = y^N.$$

Imposing equilibrium in the nontradable goods markets, we can rewrite (14.10) as

$$\alpha = \beta(1+r)\frac{p_1}{p_2}. \tag{14.11}$$

For further reference, notice that by imposing nontradable goods market equilibrium in (14.2) and (14.3), we get

$$b_1 = y^T - c_1^T, \tag{14.12}$$

$$-b_1 = rb_1 + y^T - c_2^T. \tag{14.13}$$

Equation (14.12) is the trade balance (and current account) for period 1, while equation (14.13) is the current account for period 2. Combining these two expressions yields the economy's resource constraint:

$$\frac{2+r}{1+r}y^T = c_1^T + \frac{c_2^T}{1+r}. \tag{14.14}$$

We now solve the model under three different scenarios.

14.3.3 Scenario 1: Demand Shock

Suppose $\beta(1+r) = 1$ and $\alpha > 1$. This captures a situation in which a domestic shock (in the form of higher demand) will cause a temporary boom in consumption. From (14.9), it follows that

$$\alpha u'(c_1^T) = u'(c_2^T),$$

which, since $\alpha > 1$, implies that $c_1^T > c_2^T$. Then from (14.14), $c_1^T > y^T$. The economy thus runs a trade deficit in period 1. It follows, from (14.11), that $p_1 > p_2$.

In sum, in period 1—and relative to period 2—the economy experiences high tradables consumption, high relative price of nontradable goods, and a trade deficit. Intuitively, the higher demand for consumption in period 1 relative to period 2 leads to a trade deficit and, given that the supply of nontradable goods is completely inelastic, to a higher relative price of nontradable goods.

14.3.4 Scenario 2: Lower World Real Interest Rate

Suppose now that $\alpha = 1$ but

$$\frac{1}{1+r} > \beta.$$

In other words, the real interest rate is lower than the rate of time preference (recall that, by definition, $\beta = 1/(1+\delta)$, where δ is the rate of time preference). Then from (14.9), $c_1^T > c_2^T$. Hence, from (14.14), $c_1^T > y^T$ and the economy runs a trade deficit in period 1. And from (14.11), $p_1 > p_2$. The low real interest rate (relative to the rate of time preference) thus leads to higher consumption, a trade deficit, and a higher relative price of nontradable goods. The results are identical to the case of the demand shock analyzed above.

14.3.5 Scenario 3: Exogenous Capital Inflow

Continue to assume that $\alpha = 1$. To think of an exogenous capital inflow, suppose that b_1 is exogenously given to this economy at a level $\overline{b_1} < 0$. As a result r will now be endogenously determined. From (14.12) it follows that $c_1^T > y^T$. Hence, from (14.14), $c_2^T < y^T$. Since $c_1^T > c_2^T$, first-order condition (14.9) implies that $\beta(1+r) < 1$. Equation (14.11) then implies that $p_1 > p_2$.

Intuitively, by increasing available resources in period 1, the exogenous capital inflow "forces" the economy to consume more tradable goods in period 1. For this to be an equilibrium, the real interest rate must fall below the rate of time preference. This in turn generates an excess demand for nontradable goods in period 1 (relative to period 2), which leads to an increase in their relative price.

In sum, we have seen that the three different scenarios—a shock to aggregate demand, a fall in the international real interest rate, and an exogenous capital flow—lead to the same outcome: higher consumption, a trade deficit, and an increase in the relative price of nontradable goods. Hence, while the origin of capital inflows ("push or pull," in the language of box 14.1) may vary from case to case, the macroeconomic consequences are likely to be very much the same.

14.4 The Simple Economics of Sudden Stops

As figure 14.1 illustrates, capital flows into developing countries go through marked cyclical patterns and may fall precipitously from one year to the next. For instance, capital inflows fell by about 60 percent in 1982, 66 percent in 1998, and 45 percent in 2008.[3] These sudden stop

3. The WEO chapter reports that of the 87 episodes of capital inflows that it identified (73 in emerging countries and 14 in advanced open economies), 34 ended in a sudden stop and 13 with a currency crisis. In seven cases a sudden stop coincided with a currency crisis. (A sudden stop is defined as a fall in capital inflows of more than 5 percentage points of GDP when the episode ends.)

episodes are typically characterized by sharp drops in consumption and reversals in trade deficits. This section uses a simple model to think about the consequences of a sudden stop.

Consider a three-period endowment economy perfectly integrated into world goods and capital markets. The endowment of tradable and nontradable goods are denoted by y_i^T and y_i^N, $i = 1, 2,$ and 3, respectively. To capture a growing economy, we will assume that the endowment path of tradable goods is rising over time; that is, $y_1^T < y_2^T < y_3^T$. In contrast, we will assume that the path of the endowment of nontradable goods is constant over time; that is, $y_1^N = y_2^N = y_3^N = y^N$. Consumers will, of course, smooth consumption of tradables over time.

14.4.1 Consumers

For simplicity, assume logarithmic preferences given by

$$\log(c_1^T) + \log(c_1^N) + \beta[\log(c_2^T) + \log(c_2^N)] + \beta^2[\log(c_3^T) + \log(c_3^N)]. \tag{14.15}$$

The corresponding flow constraints take the form (notice that we are assuming initial net foreign assets equal to zero and imposing the condition that consumers "die" with no assets)

$$b_1 = y_1^T + p_1 y_1^N - c_1^T - p_1 c_1^N, \tag{14.16}$$

$$b_2 = (1+r)b_1 + y_2^T + p_2 y_2^N - c_2^T - p_2 c_2^N, \tag{14.17}$$

$$0 = (1+r)b_2 + y_3^T + p_3 y_3^N - c_3^T - p_3 c_3^N. \tag{14.18}$$

Combining these last three expressions yields the intertemporal constraint:

$$y_1^T + p_1 y_1^N + \frac{y_2^T + p_2 y_2^N}{1+r} + \frac{y_3^T + p_3 y_3^N}{(1+r)^2} = c_1^T + p_1 c_1^N + \frac{c_2^T + p_2 c_2^N}{1+r} + \frac{c_3^T + p_3 c_3^N}{(1+r)^2}. \tag{14.19}$$

The representative consumer chooses $\{c_1^T, c_1^N, c_2^T, c_2^N, c_3^T, c_3^N\}$ to maximize lifetime utility (14.15) subject to (14.19). The corresponding first-order conditions (under our usual assumption that $\beta(1+r) = 1$) imply that

$$c_1^T = c_2^T = c_3^T, \tag{14.20}$$

$$p_i c_i^N = c_i^T, \qquad i = 1, 2, 3. \tag{14.21}$$

14.4.2 Equilibrium Conditions

Equilibrium in the nontradable goods market implies that

$$c_1^N = c_2^N = c_3^N = y^N.$$

Taking into account these equilibrium conditions, we can rewrite constraints (14.16), (14.17), and (14.18) as

$$CA_1 \equiv b_1 = y_1^T - c_1^T, \tag{14.22}$$

$$CA_2 \equiv b_2 - b_1 = rb_1 + y_2^T - c_2^T, \tag{14.23}$$

$$CA_3 \equiv -b_2 = rb_2 + y_3^T - c_3^T, \tag{14.24}$$

which, as indicated, correspond to the economy's current account.

By the same token, using the above equilibrium conditions, we can derive the economy's resource constraint:

$$Y^T = c_1^T + \frac{c_2^T}{1+r} + \frac{c_3^T}{(1+r)^2}, \tag{14.25}$$

where

$$Y^T \equiv y_1^T + \frac{y_2^T}{1+r} + \frac{y_3^T}{(1+r)^2}$$

denotes the present discounted value of the endowment of tradable goods.

14.4.3 Solution

Denote by c^T the constant level of consumption of tradable goods characterized by condition (14.20). Then, using (14.25), we obtain

$$c^T = \frac{Y^T}{1+\beta+\beta^2}. \tag{14.26}$$

We now compute the path of the trade balance. Recalling that, by definition, $TB_i \equiv y_i^T - c_i^T$, $i = 1, 2, 3$ and using (14.26), we obtain

$$TB_1 = \frac{1}{1+\beta+\beta^2}\left[\beta\underbrace{\left(y_1^T - y_2^T\right)}_{-} + \beta^2\underbrace{\left(y_1^T - y_3^T\right)}_{-}\right] < 0,$$

$$TB_2 = \frac{1}{1+\beta+\beta^2}\left[\underbrace{\left(y_2^T - y_1^T\right)}_{+} + \beta^2\underbrace{\left(y_2^T - y_3^T\right)}_{-}\right],$$

$$TB_3 = \frac{1}{1+\beta+\beta^2}\left[\underbrace{(y_3^T - y_1^T)}_{+} + \beta\underbrace{(y_3^T - y_2^T)}_{+}\right] > 0.$$

Since the constant level of consumption will fall somewhere between y_1^T and y_3^T, it comes as no surprise that $TB_1 < 0$ and $TB_3 > 0$. Hence $CA_1 < 0$. The sign of TB_2 is, in principle, ambiguous, but we will assume that parameters are such that TB_2 is negative (i.e., $c^T > y_2^T$). Therefore, since both $TB_2 < 0$ and $b_1 < 0$, it follows from (14.23) that $CA_2 < 0$. This in turn implies that $b_2 < 0$ and hence, from (14.24), that $CA_3 > 0$.

The path of the relative price of nontradable goods follows from (14.21) and the equilibrium in the nontradable goods market:

$$p_1 = p_2 = p_3 = \frac{c^T}{y^N}.$$

14.4.4 Constrained Equilibrium

Let us now solve the model under the assumption that the economy experiences a sudden stop in period 2, in the sense that—for some reason that we take as given—starting in period 2 foreigners decide not to lend to this economy any longer. Formally, we impose the constraints that $CA_2 \geq 0$ and $CA_3 \geq 0$.

To simplify, we will solve the planner's problem. (We will later derive the intertemporal prices that would sustain the competitive equilibrium.) The planner thus chooses $\{c_1^T, c_1^N, c_2^T, c_2^N, c_3^T, c_3^N, b_1, b_2\}$ to maximize the consumer's lifetime utility (14.15) subject to the flow constraints (14.16), (14.17), and (14.18) and the constraints $b_2 - b_1 \geq 0$ and $-b_2 \geq 0$. Clearly, one or both of the constraints will be binding because the unconstrained path that we derived above violates the constraint that $CA_2 \geq 0$.

To solve this constrained problem, we can write the following Lagrangian:

$$\begin{aligned}
\mathcal{L} = {} & \log(c_1^T) + \log(c_1^N) + \beta[\log(c_2^T) + \log(c_2^N)] + \beta^2[\log(c_3^T) + \log(c_3^N)] \\
& + \lambda_1\left(y_1^T + p_1 y_1^N - c_1^T - p_1 c_1^N - b_1\right) \\
& + \lambda_2\left[(1+r)b_1 + y_2^T + p_2 y_2^N - c_2^T - p_2 c_2^N - b_2\right] \\
& + \lambda_3\left[(1+r)b_2 + y_3^T + p_3 y_3^N - c_3^T - p_3 c_3^N\right] \\
& + \psi(b_2 - b_1).
\end{aligned}$$

To simplify the maximization, we have conjectured that the constraint $-b_2 \geq 0$ will not bind in equilibrium and, hence, have omitted it from the problem. Once we derive the optimal solution, we will, of course, verify that this is indeed the case in equilibrium.

First-order conditions are given by

$$\frac{1}{c_1^T} = \lambda_1, \tag{14.27}$$

$$\frac{\beta}{c_2^T} = \lambda_2, \tag{14.28}$$

$$\frac{\beta^2}{c_3^T} = \lambda_3, \tag{14.29}$$

$$\frac{1}{c_1^N} = p_1\lambda_1,$$

$$\frac{\beta}{c_2^N} = p_2\lambda_2,$$

$$\frac{\beta^2}{c_3^N} = p_3\lambda_3,$$

$$\lambda_2(1+r) = \lambda_1 + \psi, \tag{14.30}$$

$$\lambda_3(1+r) = \lambda_2 - \psi, \tag{14.31}$$

$$b_2 - b_1 \geq 0, \qquad \psi\,(b_2 - b_1) = 0. \tag{14.32}$$

Clearly, $\psi = 0$ cannot be a solution because we would obtain the unconstrained solution derived above, which violates the constraint $CA_2 \geq 0$. Hence $\psi > 0$ and $b_2 = b_1$. To solve the model for $\psi > 0$, combine first-order conditions (14.27) through (14.31) to obtain

$$\frac{c_1^T}{c_2^T} = \frac{\lambda_1 + \psi}{\lambda_1}, \tag{14.33}$$

$$\frac{c_3^T}{c_1^T} = \frac{\lambda_1}{\lambda_1 - r\psi}. \tag{14.34}$$

Since $\psi > 0$, conditions (14.33) and (14.34) imply, respectively, that $c_1^T > c_2^T$ and $c_3^T > c_1^T$. In other words,

$$c_3^T > c_1^T > c_2^T.$$

Further, notice that it must be the case that $c_2^T < c^T$, where c^T is the value given by (14.26). If this were not the case, the present discounted value of the path of consumption would be higher

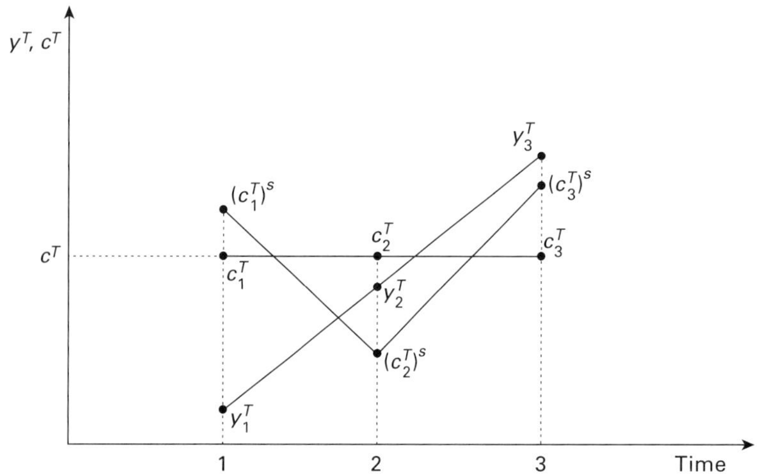

Figure 14.3
Sudden stop: Consumption of tradables

than the present discounted value of the endowments. Finally, we can show (see claims 1 and 2 in appendix 14.8) that $c_2^T < y_2^T$ and $c_3^T < y_3^T$.

Figure 14.3 illustrates the path of consumption of tradables in the unconstrained and constrained cases.[4] In the unconstrained case, c^T is flat over time (so that $c_1^T = c_2^T = c_3^T = c^T$ in the figure). In the constrained case, first-period consumption is higher ($\left(c_1^T\right)^s > c_1^T$), second-period consumption is lower ($\left(c_2^T\right)^s < c_2^T$) and third-period consumption is higher ($\left(c_3^T\right)^s > c_3^T$).[5]

Intuitively, the constraint requiring that $CA_2 \geq 0$ is binding and therefore implies that the shadow value of second-period consumption is higher—as captured by the fact that $\psi > 0$ in equations (14.33) and (14.34). The shadow value is higher because, in addition to its direct cost, an additional unit of consumption contributes to making the constraint binding. This introduces an intertemporal distortion in consumption, as in chapter 3. The shadow price of period 2 consumption is correspondingly higher, which prompts consumers to reduce second-period consumption relative to both first and third-period consumption.

What about the behavior of p_t? From (14.21),

$$p_t = \frac{c_t^T}{y^N}, \qquad t = 1, 2, 3.$$

Hence, compared to the unconstrained equilibrium, p_1^s is higher, p_2^s is lower, and p_3^s is higher, as illustrated in figure 14.4.

4. In the constrained case we have denoted equilibrium values with a superscript "s" for "sudden stop."

5. We have established numerically that a solution exists in which $(c_1^T)^s > c^T$ as depicted in figure 14.3.

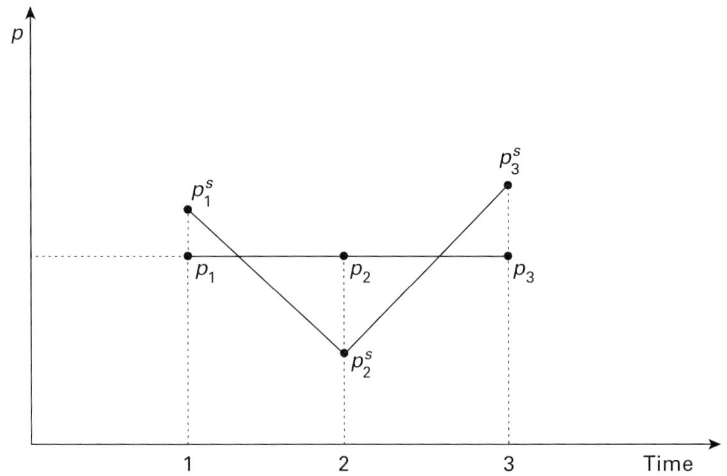

Figure 14.4
Sudden stop: Relative price of nontradables

The effects of a sudden stop are thus to provoke a consumption boom and real appreciation in the period preceding the sudden stop followed by a drastic fall in consumption of tradables and a real depreciation in the sudden stop period.[6]

14.5 Sticky-Prices Model

Section 14.2 above reviewed the main stylized facts associated with capital inflows. This section will develop a sticky-prices model—along the lines of chapter 8—that will be able to account for, and shed light on, these stylized facts. Instead of introducing real money balances in the utility function as in chapter 8, however, we will postulate a cash-in-advance constraint in the spirit of the models of chapter 7. We do so because we would like to incorporate potential interactions between the monetary and real side of the model stemming from changes in the effective price of consumption.

We will develop this model in discrete time because our aim is to solve it numerically with the help of the computer.[7] We will assume that goods markets open first followed by asset markets which, as discussed in chapter 7, introduces an intertemporal distortion in consumption. The law of one price holds and the foreign nominal price is assumed to be unity; hence $P_t^T = E_t$, where P_t^T is the domestic price of the tradable good and E_t is the nominal exchange rate.

6. As exercise 1 at the end of the chapter analyzes, if the sudden stop in period 2 were unanticipated, then the period 2 implications would be the same (fall in consumption and real depreciation) but the consumption boom in period 1 would naturally not take place.

7. While we could solve the model analytically along the lines of the temporary stabilization analyzed in chapter 13, section 13.5.2, the main economic insights will be readily apparent from the numerical solution.

14.5.1 Consumers

Let preferences be given by

$$\sum_{t=0}^{\infty} \beta^t \alpha_t \{\log(c_t^T) + \log(c_t^N)\}, \tag{14.35}$$

where β is the discount factor, α_t is a preference shock, and c_t^T and c_t^N denote consumption of tradable and nontradable goods, respectively.

The consumer's flow constraint is given by

$$b_t + \frac{M_t}{E_t} = (1 + r_{t-1})b_{t-1} + \frac{M_{t-1}}{E_t} + \tau_t + y_t^T + \frac{y_t^N}{e_t} - c_t^T - \frac{c_t^N}{e_t}, \tag{14.36}$$

where b_t denotes holding of net foreign assets by the private sector (denominated in units of the tradable good, the numéraire), M_t are nominal money balances, r_{t-1} is the world real interest rate, τ_t are lump-sum transfers from the government, y_t^T and y_t^N stand for output of tradable and nontradable goods, respectively, and e_t is the relative price of tradable goods.

The cash-in-advance constraint requires that today's consumption bundle be purchased with nominal money balances acquired yesterday:[8]

$$M_{t-1} = E_t\left(c_t^T + \frac{c_t^N}{e_t}\right). \tag{14.37}$$

Since the nominal money balances relevant for period t are chosen in period $t-1$ (i.e., M_{t-1}), it will prove convenient to define real money balances as follows:

$$m_t \equiv \frac{M_{t-1}}{E_t}. \tag{14.38}$$

Using equation (14.38), we can rewrite the cash-in-advance constraint as

$$m_t = c_t^T + \frac{c_t^N}{e_t}. \tag{14.39}$$

In the same vein, we can use equation (14.38) to rewrite the flow constraint (14.36) as

$$b_t + m_{t+1}(1 + \varepsilon_t) = (1 + r_{t-1})b_{t-1} + m_t + \tau_t + y_t^T + \frac{y_t^N}{e_t} - c_t^T - \frac{c_t^N}{e_t}, \tag{14.40}$$

8. Since the nominal interest rate will be positive along all the equilibrium paths that we will consider, we impose the condition that the cash-in-advance constraint holds with strict equality.

where

$$\varepsilon_t \equiv \frac{E_{t+1}}{E_t} - 1,$$

denotes the rate of depreciation/devaluation between periods t and $t+1$.

Consumers choose $\{c_t^T, c_t^N, m_{t+1}, b_t\}_{t=0}^{\infty}$ to maximize lifetime utility, given by (14.35), subject to a sequence of flow constraints, given by (14.40), and the cash-in-advance constraint (14.39). In terms of the Lagrangian,

$$\begin{aligned}\mathcal{L} = & \sum_{t=0}^{\infty} \beta^t \alpha_t \{\log(c_t^T) + \log(c_t^N)\} \\ & + \sum_{t=0}^{\infty} \beta^t \lambda_t \left[(1 + r_{t-1})b_{t-1} + m_t + \tau_t + y_t^T + \frac{y_t^N}{e_t} - c_t^T - \frac{c_t^N}{e_t} - b_t - m_{t+1}(1 + \varepsilon_t)\right] \\ & + \sum_{t=0}^{\infty} \beta^t \Psi_t \left[m_t - \left(c_t^T + \frac{c_t^N}{e_t}\right)\right],\end{aligned}$$

where λ_t and Ψ_t are the Lagrange multipliers associated with constraints (14.40) and (14.39), respectively. The first-order conditions are given by

$$\frac{\alpha_t}{c_t^T} = \lambda_t + \Psi_t, \tag{14.41}$$

$$\frac{\alpha_t}{c_t^N} = \frac{\lambda_t}{e_t} + \frac{\Psi_t}{e_t}, \tag{14.42}$$

$$\beta\left(\lambda_{t+1} + \Psi_{t+1}\right) = \lambda_t\left(1 + \varepsilon_t\right), \tag{14.43}$$

$$\lambda_{t+1}\beta\left(1 + r_t\right) = \lambda_t. \tag{14.44}$$

To rewrite the first-order conditions in more familiar terms, notice that perfect capital mobility implies that interest parity holds:

$$1 + i_t = (1 + r_t)(1 + \varepsilon_t). \tag{14.45}$$

Lagging expression (14.43), substituting it into equation (14.41), and using (14.44) lagged, and (14.45), we obtain

$$\frac{\alpha_t}{c_t^T} = \lambda_t(1 + i_{t-1}). \tag{14.46}$$

This expression should remind the reader of the continuous time cash-in-advance model of chapter 7. At an optimum, the marginal utility of consuming tradables is equated to the Lagrange multiplier times the effective price of consumption, $1+i_{t-1}$.

Leading equation (14.46) and taking the ratio in two consecutive periods enables us to write the Euler equation as

$$\frac{c_{t+1}^T}{c_t^T}=\left(\frac{\alpha_{t+1}}{\alpha_t}\right)\left(\frac{1+i_{t-1}}{1+i_t}\right)\beta(1+r_t). \tag{14.47}$$

This expression makes clear the three channels that will govern the dynamics of tradable goods consumption. The first one α_{t+1}/α_t, captures changes in preferences (i.e., temporary demand shocks). The second one, $(1+i_{t-1})\,/\,(1+i_t)$, reflects variations over time in the effective price of consumption. The third one, $\beta(1+r_t)$, captures intertemporal substitution in consumption stemming from differences between the discount rate and the world real interest rate.[9]

Finally, combining (14.41) and (14.42), we obtain the familiar intratemporal condition:

$$c_t^T=\frac{c_t^N}{e_t}. \tag{14.48}$$

For further reference, notice that by substituting this last equation into the cash-in-advance constraint (14.39), we can rewrite the latter as

$$m_t=2c_t^T. \tag{14.49}$$

As in chapter 8, let n_t denote real money balances in terms of nontradable goods (i.e., $n_t\equiv M_{t-1}/P_t^N$). It follows that

$$e_t m_t=n_t. \tag{14.50}$$

Hence we can rewrite (14.49) as

$$n_t=2c_t^N. \tag{14.51}$$

14.5.2 Supply Side

The supply side follows our standard setup for sticky prices introduced in chapter 8 and used already, in a discrete-time setup, in chapter 13. There is an exogenous (and constant) endowment of tradable goods:

9. This channel was not present in the continuous-time model of chapter 7. In the present case we will allow for temporary deviations of $1+r$ from $1/\beta$.

$$y_t^T = y^T.$$

In contrast, nontradable goods output is demand-determined. The nominal price of the nontradable good is sticky (i.e., predetermined at each point in time) and follows the discrete-time version of Calvo's (1983) staggered prices (see chapter 8, appendix 8.8.1)

$$\pi_{t+1} - \pi_t = \theta(y_f^N - c_t^N),$$

where π_t is the inflation rate of nontradables, y_f^N is the full-employment level of output of nontradable goods, and θ is a positive parameter.

14.5.3 Government

The government's budget constraint is given by

$$h_t = (1 + r_{t-1})h_{t-1} + \frac{M_t - M_{t-1}}{E_t} - \tau_t,$$

where h_t denotes international reserves. Taking into account (14.38), we can rewrite this constraint as

$$h_t = (1 + r_{t-1})h_{t-1} + m_{t+1}(1 + \varepsilon_t) - m_t - \tau_t. \tag{14.52}$$

14.5.4 Equilibrium Conditions

Equilibrium in the nontradable goods market requires that

$$c_t^N = y_t^N. \tag{14.53}$$

As already mentioned, perfect capital mobility implies that the interest parity condition, given by (14.45), holds.

By definition, $e_t = E_t / P_t^N$. Hence

$$\frac{e_{t+1}}{e_t} = \frac{1 + \varepsilon_t}{1 + \pi_t}.$$

Let k_t denote the economy's net stock of foreign assets (i.e., $k_t \equiv h_t + b_t$). Solving for τ_t from (14.52), substituting it into the household's flow constraint (14.40), and using (14.45) and (14.53), we obtain the economy's flow constraint:

$$k_t = (1 + r_{t-1})k_{t-1} + y_t^T - c_t^T.$$

For further reference, let us rewrite this last equation as

$$\underbrace{h_t - h_{t-1}}_{\Delta IR} = \underbrace{-(b_t - b_{t-1})}_{KA} + \underbrace{r_{t-1}(h_{t-1} + b_{t-1}) + y_t^T - c_t^T}_{CA}, \tag{14.54}$$

where ΔIR, KA, and CA denote the increase in international reserves, the capital account, and the current account, respectively. Hence expression (14.54) states the familiar identity that the increase in international reserves is equal to the sum of the capital and current accounts.

14.5.5 Predetermined Exchange Rates

We first solve the model under predetermined exchange rates (for a constant devaluation rate). As in chapter 13, we linearize the model around a steady state using the King–Plosser–Rebelo method.[10] We then analyze the economy's response to two temporary shocks: a positive demand shock and a fall in world real interest rates.

Temporary Demand Shock

Figure 14.5 illustrates the economy's response to a temporary and positive demand shock; that is, an increase in the parameter α_t at time $t = 1$ that lasts until period $t = 10$ (panel a).[11] As the Euler equation (14.47) makes clear for the case of tradable goods, the temporary increase in α_t raises the demand for both goods at $t = 1$ and reduces it at $t = 10$. The higher demand for both goods is reflected in higher consumption of both tradables and nontradables until the shock is reversed (figure 14.5, panels b and d).

How is the rise in the demand for both goods accommodated? As always, the economy procures the additional tradable goods from the rest of the world by running a trade deficit (panel c). What about nontradable goods? In an endowment economy the higher demand for nontradable goods would get fully reflected on impact in an increase in the relative price of nontradable goods (i.e., a fall in e_t). The exact opposite is true in this case: since e_t cannot change on impact under predetermined exchange rates (because the nominal exchange rate is controlled by policymakers and P_t^N is sticky), the higher demand for nontradable goods is fully reflected in an increase in output of nontradable goods.[12] Starting in period 2, however, the real exchange rate begins to fall (panel g) and thus partly accommodates the higher demand for nontradable goods. Given that the economy is operating under predetermined exchange rates, this real appreciation must be effected through higher inflation of nontradable goods (panel f).[13] The higher consumption of

10. See chapter 13, online appendix, for the log-linearization and MATLAB coding for this model.

11. The parameterization is as follows: $r = 0.015$, $k = 5$, $\theta = 0.5$, $y_f^N = 1$, $y^T = 1$, $\varepsilon = 0.1$, and $\pi^* = 0.1$. In this figure, as well as in figures 14.6–14.13 and 14.15–14.17, plots show percentage deviations from the initial steady state.

12. Since output of nontradables is demand-determined, panel d can also be read as depicting the path of nontradable output.

13. Recall from figure 14.2 that the data indicate that inflation falls slightly but, as already mentioned, this reflects the presence in the sample of many inflations stabilization programs. As made clear in chapter 13, an exchange rate based inflation stabilization program will lead to the same dynamics (consumption boom, trade and current account deficits, real appreciation) except for the behavior of inflation.

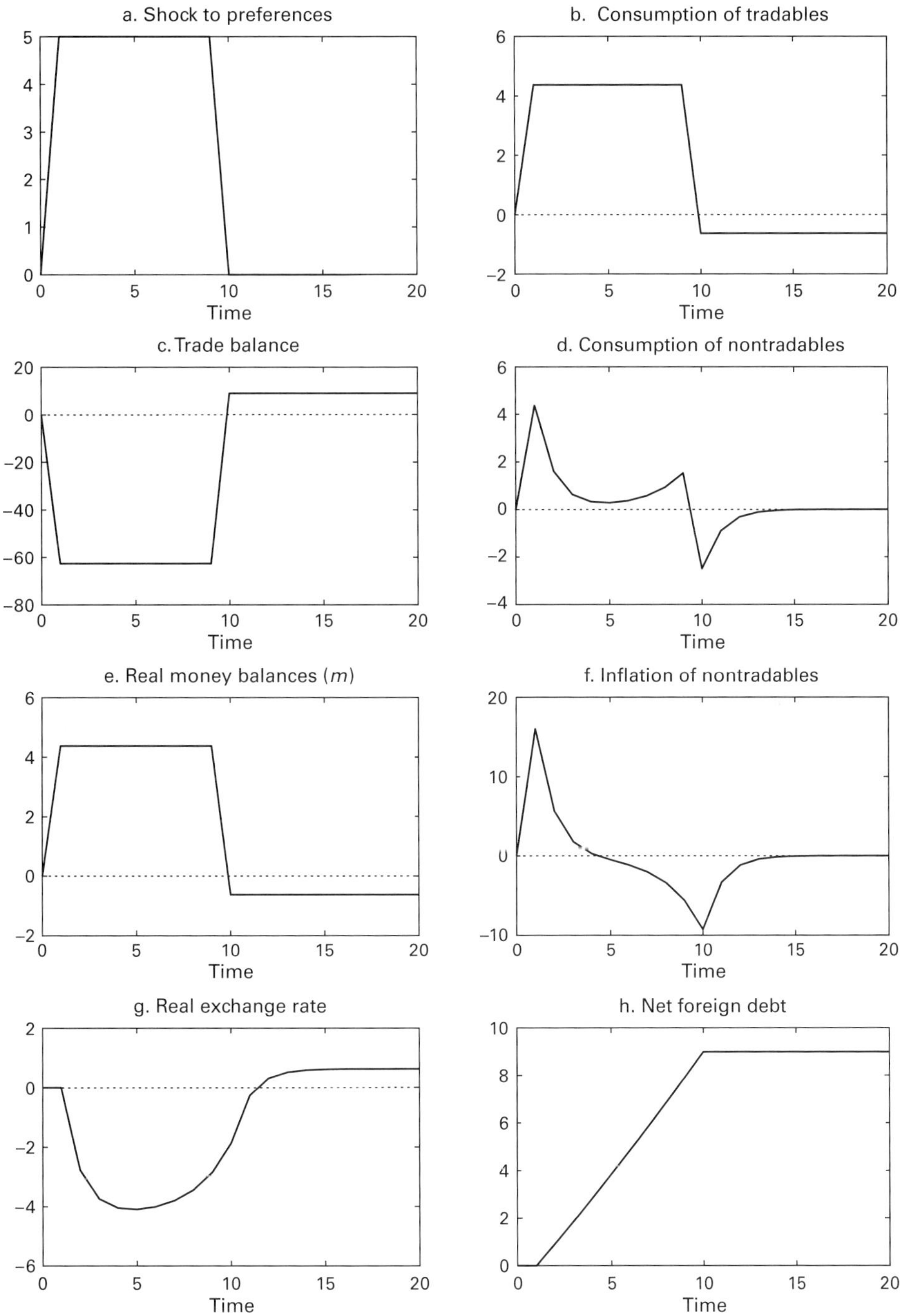

Figure 14.5
Temporary positive demand shock under predetermined exchange rates (separable case)

both goods increases real money demand (recall equation (14.49)) which, under predetermined exchange rates, is passively accommodated by the Central Bank (panel e).

As expected, panel h indicates that the economy's aggregate debt increases steadily until the shock is reversed, which implies that the current account is in deficit throughout. Further, from the Central Bank's balance sheet ($h_t + d_t = m_t$) and the fact that, as usual under predetermined exchange rates, we assume that real domestic credit is constant, it follows that

$$h_1 - h_0 = m_1 - m_0.$$

Hence the increase in real money balances at time $t = 1$ implies that the Central Bank gains international reserves.

Finally, we can use the balance of payments identity (14.54) to infer that in period 1 the capital account shows a surplus because there is an increase in international reserves and the current account is in deficit. Further the capital account continues to show a surplus until the shock is reversed because, even though international reserves are constant, the current account is in deficit throughout. In other words, the economy is financing the current account deficit by a capital inflow (i.e., by the private sector getting indebted abroad).

Temporary Fall in World Real Interest Rate

Figure 14.6 shows how very similar dynamics arise when the economy responds to a temporary fall in the world real interest rate (panel a). Since today's consumption becomes cheaper relative to tomorrow's due to the fall in the world real interest rate (recall equation 14.47), consumption of both tradables and nontradables increases (panels b and d, respectively). Qualitatively speaking, the way in which this increased demand for both goods is accommodated is the same as above. This qualitatively identical response of the economy to either a demand shock or to a fall in world real interest rates is thus fully consistent with the theoretical example provided in section 14.3.

Temporary Fall in Devaluation Rate

To illustrate the idea that the behavior of inflation will depend on the source of the shock, figure 14.7 illustrates the case of a temporary reduction in the rate of devaluation.[14] Remarkably, the behavior of all variables with the exception of inflation is qualitatively the same as in figure 14.5 (positive demand shock) and figure 14.6 (temporary fall in world real interest rate). Inflation, however, increases in figures 14.5 and 14.6 but falls in this case (panel f).

We thus conclude that depending on the source of the shock, we may see episodes of capital inflows accompanied by either lower or higher inflation.

14. This experiment corresponds, of course, to the temporary exchange rate based stabilization analyzed in chapter 13 and depicted in figure 13.10 of the same chapter.

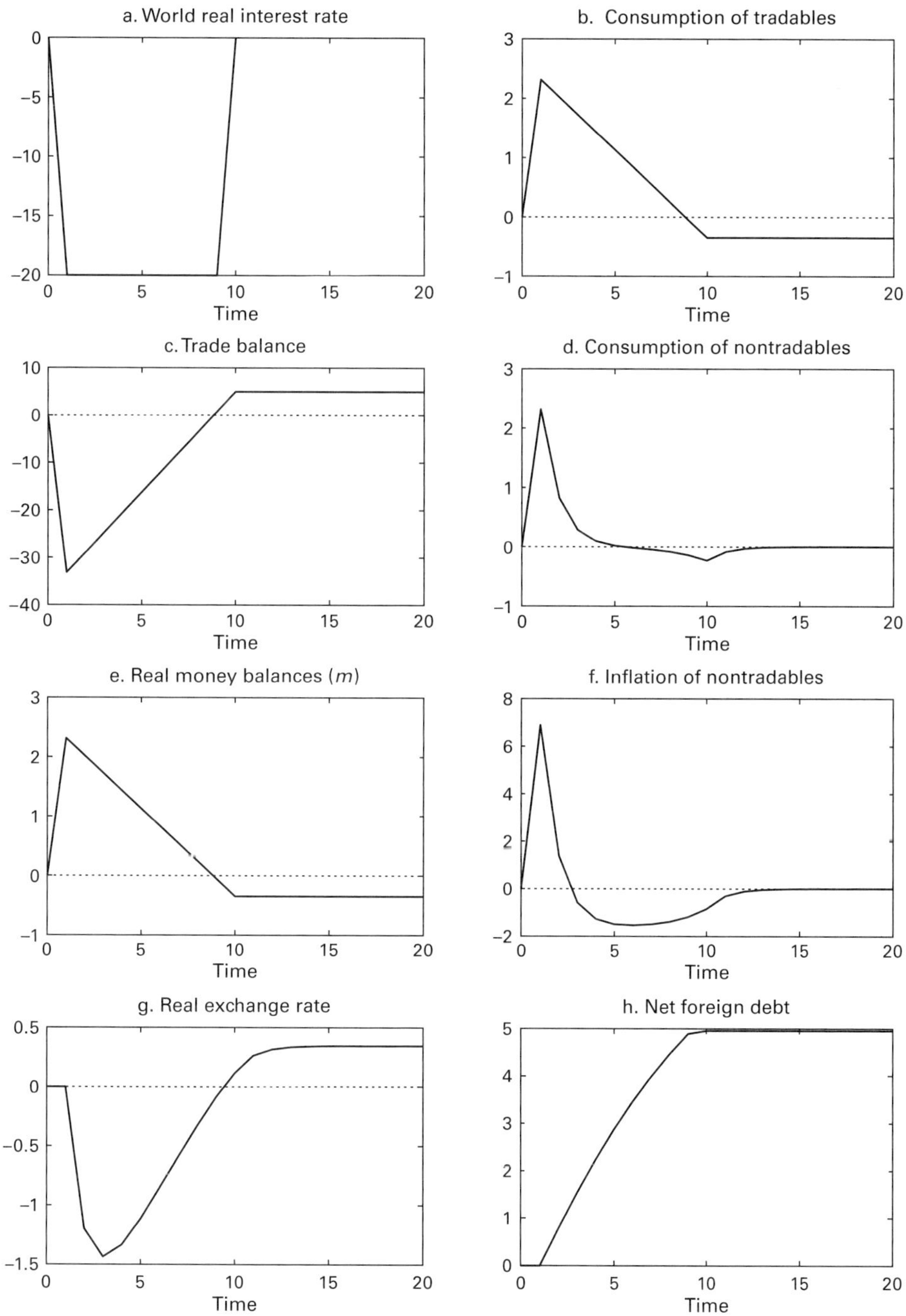

Figure 14.6
Temporary fall in world real interest rate under predetermined exchange rates (separable case)

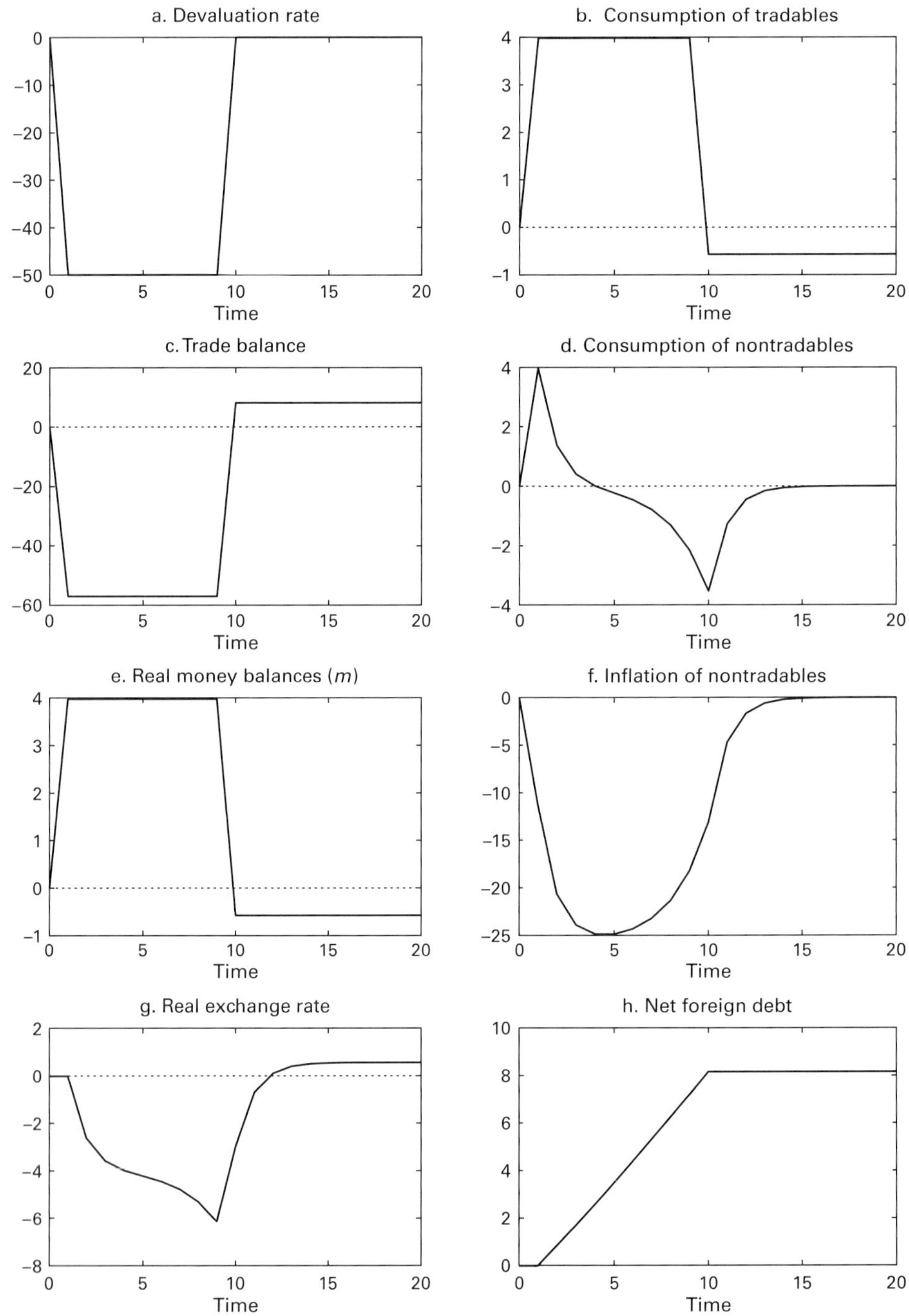

Figure 14.7
Temporary fall in devaluation rate under predetermined exchange rates (separable case)

14.5.6 Flexible Exchange Rates

We now turn to how the economy responds to the same two shocks (a temporary positive demand shock and a temporary fall in the world real interest rate) under flexible exchange rates.

Temporary Demand Shock

Figure 14.8 illustrates the case of a temporary positive demand shock. Remarkably, while consumption of tradable goods increases (panel b), consumption of nontradable goods does not respond at all (panel d). In other words, the increase in the demand for nontradable goods is fully absorbed by an increase in the relative price of nontradable goods (i.e., a fall in e_t; panel g). To understand this, think of equation (14.51) as capturing money market equilibrium. Since real money supply, given by n_t, does not change on impact, consumption of nontradable goods cannot change either. To induce households to keep consumption of nontradables constant, the relative price of nontradables must increase (i.e., e_t must fall) equiproportionately with c_t^T (recall equation 14.48). Since prices of nontradable goods are sticky, this initial real appreciation takes place through a fall in the nominal exchange rate. Inflation of nontradables remains constant throughout (panel f). While the behavior of nontradable consumption and the inflation rate depends critically on the assumption that preferences are separable in tradable and nontradable consumption and the presence of a cash-in-advance constraint, it illustrates the notion that under flexible exchange rates, monetary policy is a powerful nominal anchor. While consumption of nontradable goods will no longer be constant under nonseparable preferences, it will change by a relatively small amount compared to tradable consumption.[15]

Temporary Fall in World Real Interest Rate

Figure 14.9 depicts the case of a temporary fall in the world real interest rate. Once again, the nontradable goods sector is insulated from the shock by the increase in the relative price of nontradable goods.[16]

14.5.7 Comparison

While somewhat extreme in its implications for flexible exchange rates, the separable case enables us to isolate the critical difference between a capital inflows episode under predetermined exchange rates and one under flexible exchange rates. In both cases the increase in aggregate demand that results from either a preference shock or a fall in the world real interest rate leads in the short term to an increase in the relative price of nontradable goods. The key difference,

15. To gain further insights into this experiment and next, exercise 2 asks you to solve analytically the continuous-time version of this model.

16. Exercise 3 at the end of the chapter asks you to illustrate the economy's response to a reduction in the rate of monetary growth. Note that, as expected, inflation behaves differently.

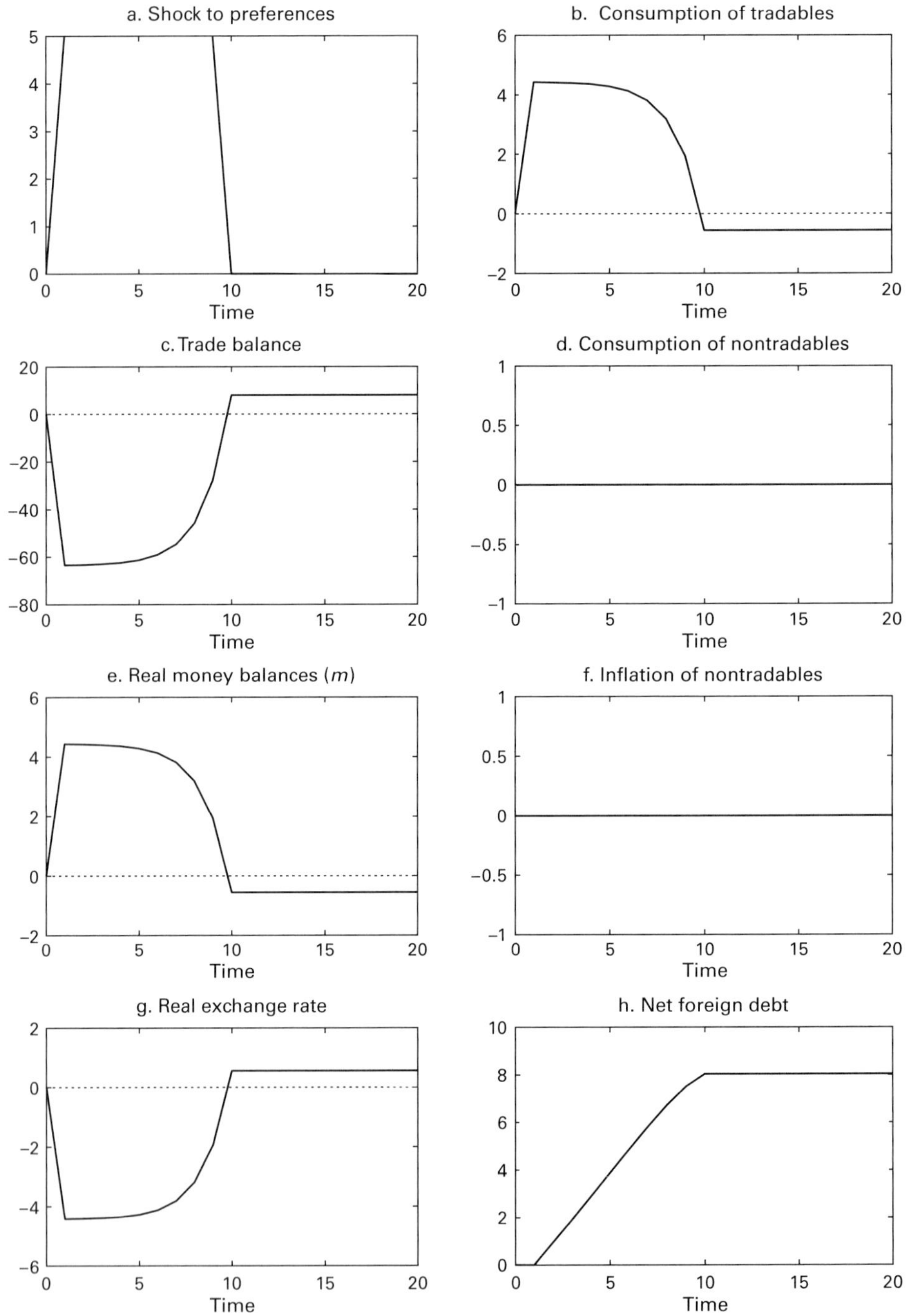

Figure 14.8
Temporary positive demand shock under flexible exchange rates (separable case)

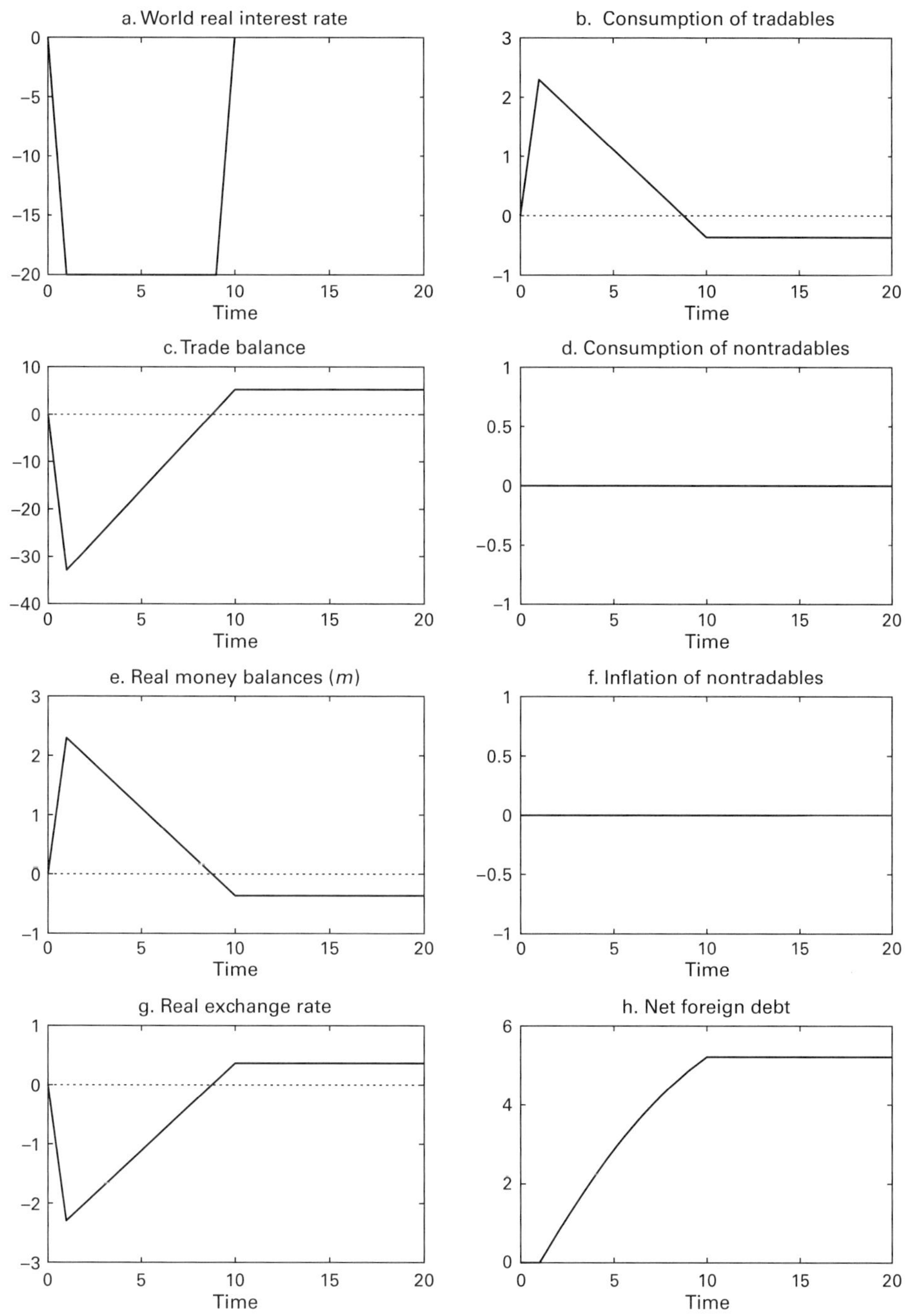

Figure 14.9
Temporary fall in world real interest rate under flexible exchange rates (separable case)

however, is how this real appreciation is effected. Under predetermined exchange rates, the real appreciation must come about through higher inflation of nontradable goods. In contrast, under flexible exchange rates, it comes about through a fall in the nominal exchange rate. In other words, flexible exchange rates allow policy makers to keep domestic inflation under control whereas predetermined exchange rates do not.

14.5.8 Nonseparable Case

Suppose now that preferences are given by

$$\sum_{t=0}^{\infty} \beta^t \alpha_t \left[\frac{c_t^{1-1/\sigma} - 1}{1 - 1/\sigma} \right], \tag{14.55}$$

where

$$c_t = \left[\gamma \left(c_t^T\right)^{(\rho-1)/\rho} + (1-\gamma) \left(c_t^N\right)^{(\rho-1)/\rho} \right]^{\rho/(\rho-1)}.$$

The rest of the model remains the same as above. As before, we proceed to solve it using the linearization method of King–Plosser–Rebelo.

We then repeat the two experiments carried out above.[17] Figures 14.10 and 14.11 illustrate the effects of a temporary demand shock and a temporary fall in the world real interest rate, respectively, under predetermined exchange rates. As is clear, the results are essentially the same as those obtained in figures 14.5 and 14.6 for the separable case.[18]

Figures 14.12 and 14.13 illustrate the results for the same two experiments under flexible exchange rates. The key difference relative to the separable case illustrated in figures 14.8 and 14.9 lies in the fact that the nontradable goods sector is no longer insulated. In other words, the increase in the demand for nontradable goods is now reflected in both an increase in the relative price of nontradable goods and an increase in output of nontradable goods. Notice, however, that for the temporary positive demand shock (figure 14.12), the increase in output (and consumption) of nontradable goods (0.3 percent) is about ten times smaller than the increase in consumption of tradable goods (2.7 percent). The same is true in the case of a fall in the world real interest rate (figure 14.13). Quantitatively, it is still true therefore that the nontradable goods sector is little affected by these shocks.

17. The parameters for the nonseparable case are the same as for the separable case and, in addition, $\rho = 0.8$ and $\sigma = 0.5$. These are "realistic" values of these parameters (see chapter 3, box 3.1, and chapter 4, exercise 2).

18. In comparing, say, figures 14.5 and 14.10, the different orders of magnitude regarding the response of consumption of both tradables and nontradables are due to the fact that in figure 14.5 the implicit value of σ is one, whereas in figure 14.10 the value is 0.5. Since the intertemporal elasticity of substitution is lower in figure 14.10, the response of consumption is smaller.

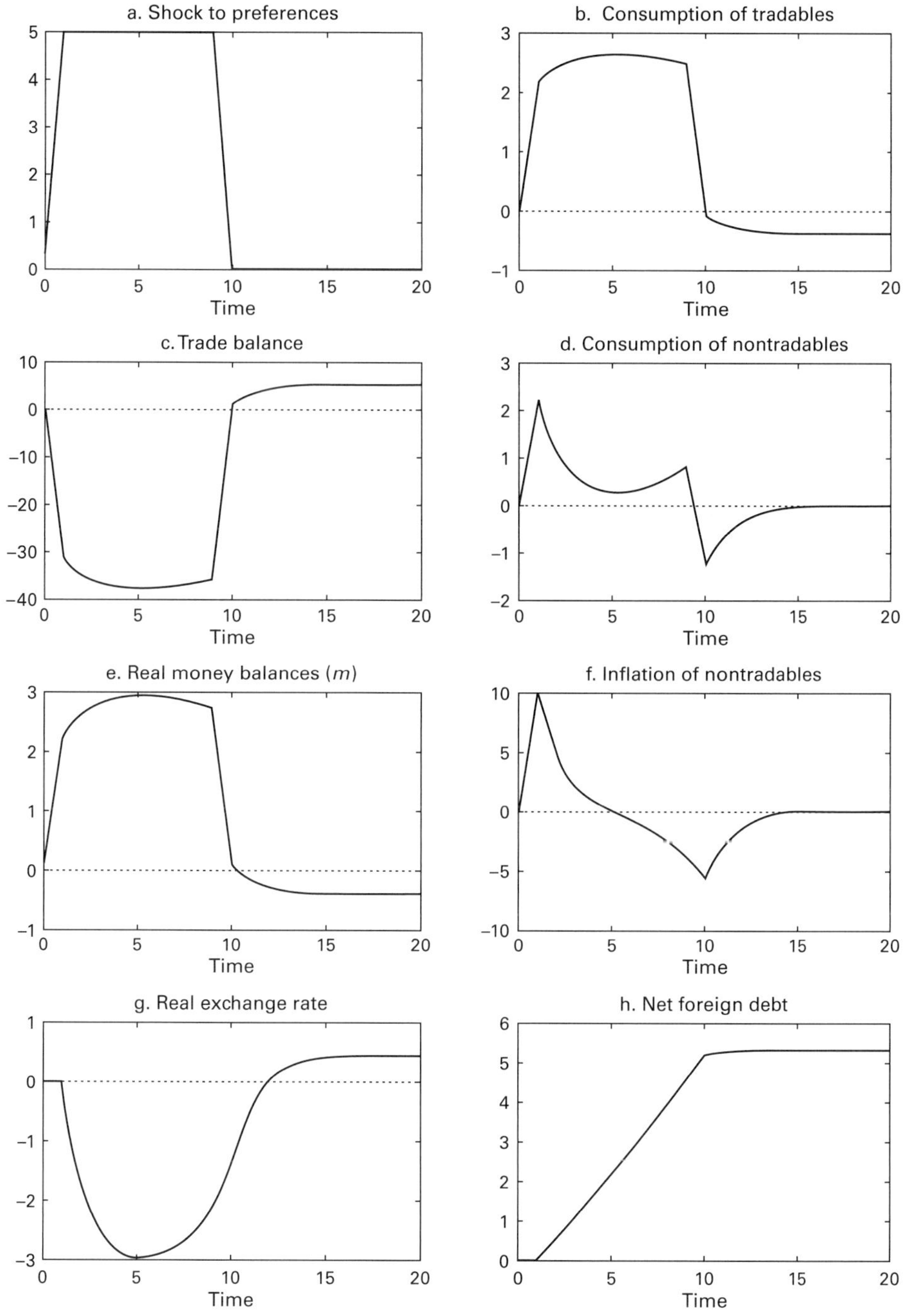

Figure 14.10
Temporary positive demand shock under predetermined exchange rates (nonseparable case)

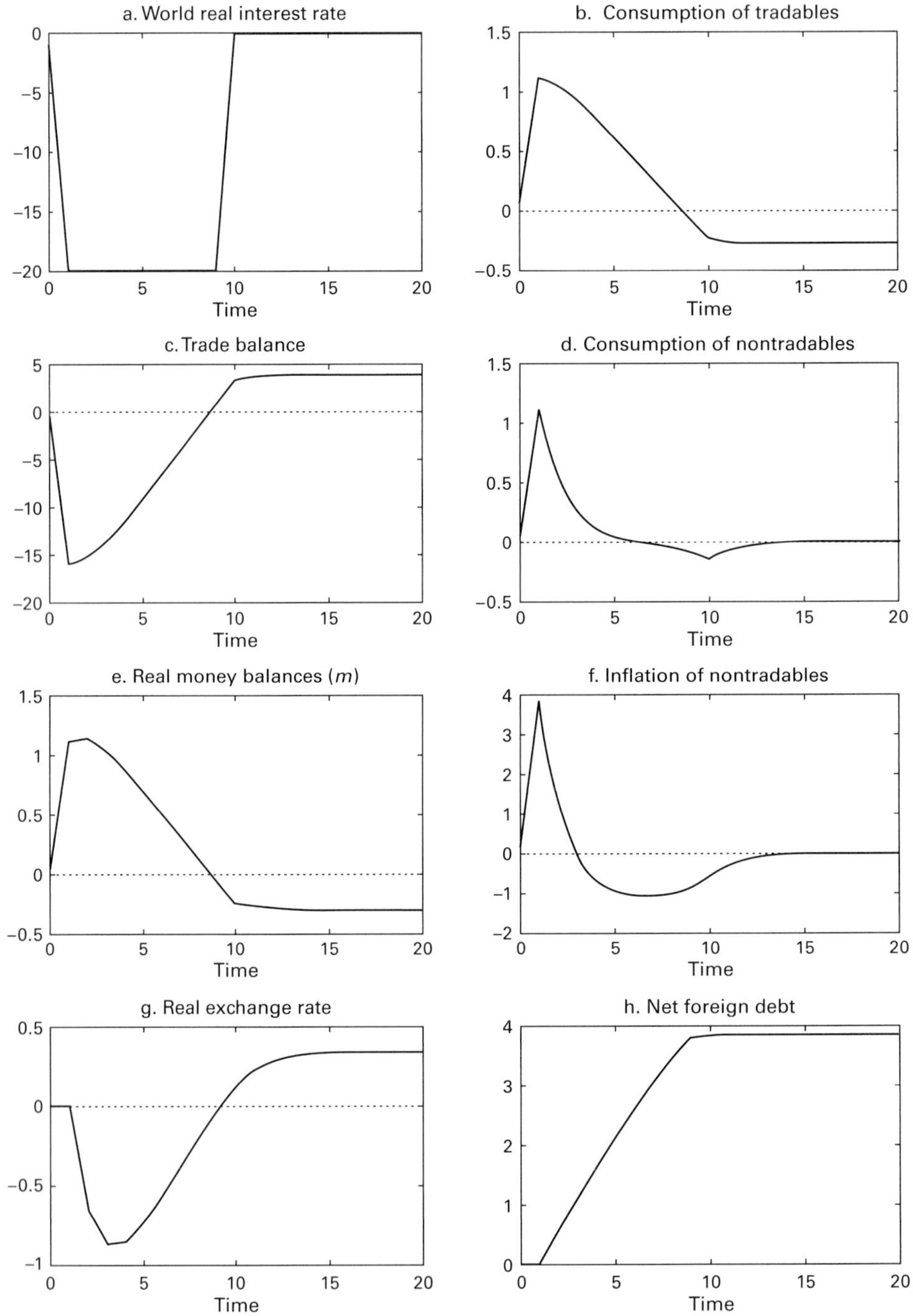

Figure 14.11
Temporary fall in world real interest rate under predetermined exchange rates (nonseparable case)

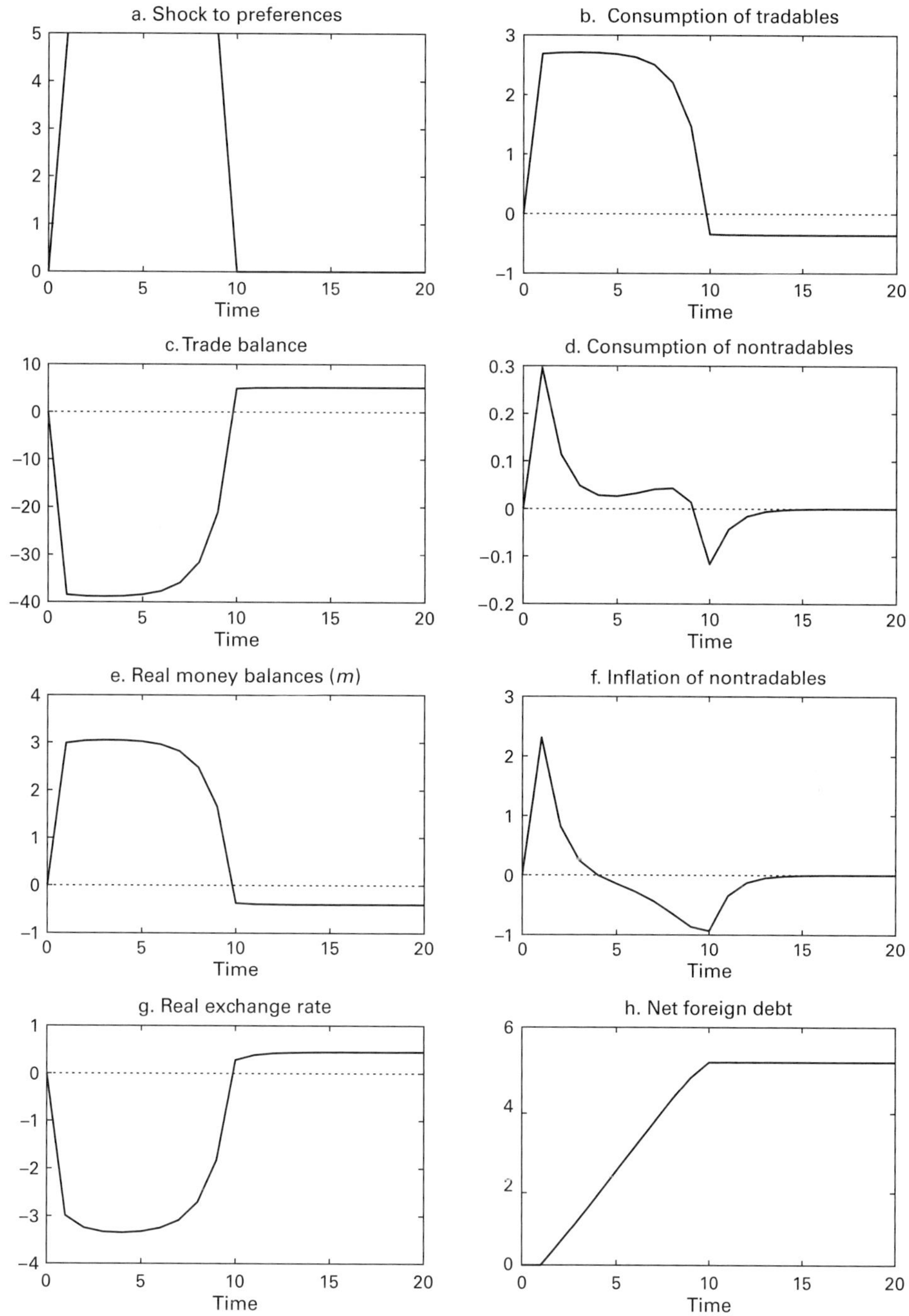

Figure 14.12
Temporary positive demand shock under flexible exchange rates (nonseparable case)

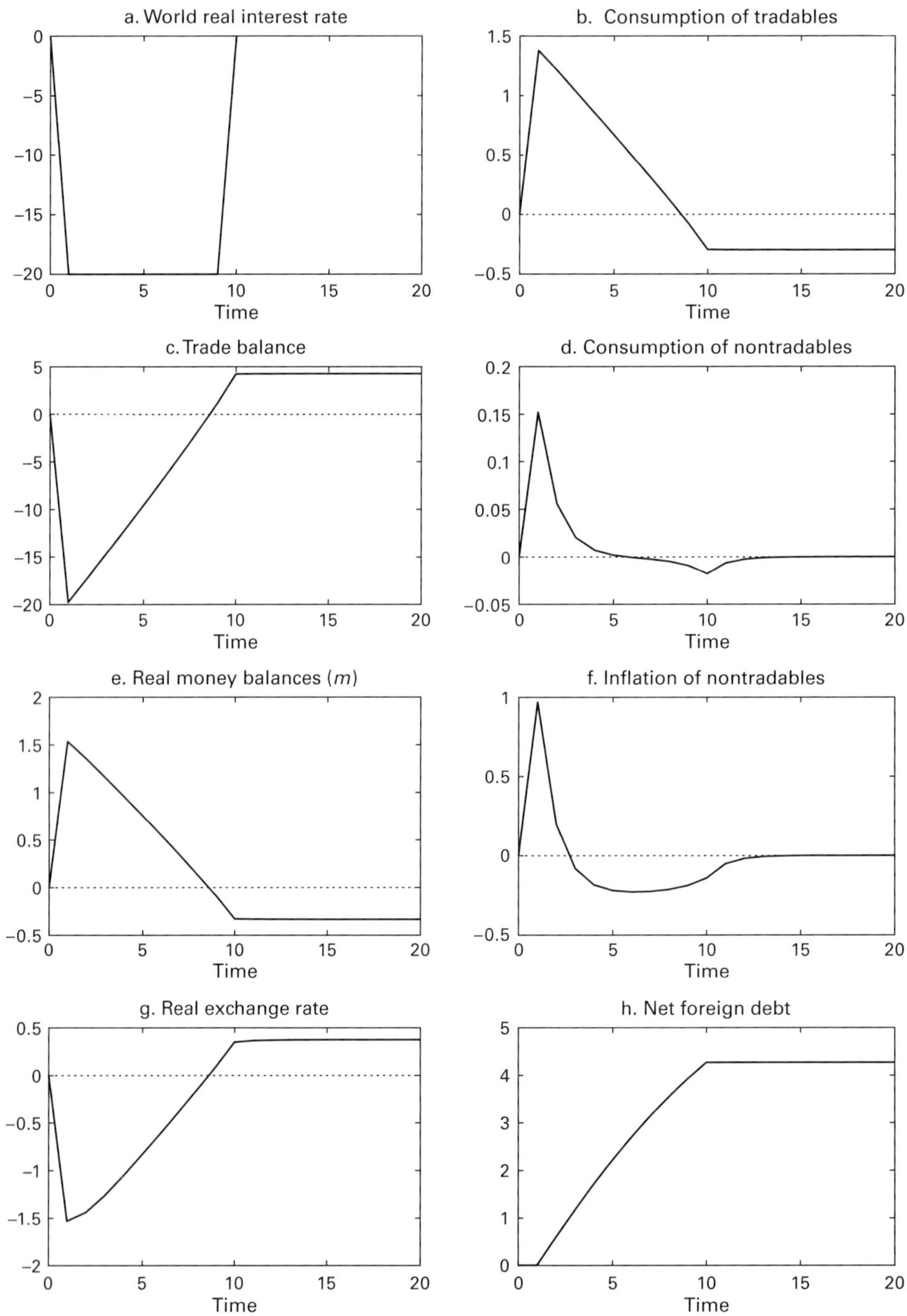

Figure 14.13
Temporary fall in world real interest rate under flexible exchange rates (nonseparable case)

In terms of comparing the outcomes under flexible and predetermined exchange rates, the key observation made above regarding the different inflationary effects remains valid. Comparing figures 14.10 and 14.12, on the one hand, and figures 14.11 and 14.13, on the other, we can see that the same shock leads to an increase in the inflation rate of nontradable goods that is roughly four times higher under predetermined exchange rates than under flexible exchange rates.[19]

14.6 Policy Responses to Capital Inflows

The empirical evidence of section 14.2 clearly shows that capital inflows episodes are associated with an overheating of the economy (higher aggregate demand and output), current account deficits, and real appreciation. While the effects on inflation are less clear-cut, abundant anecdotal evidence suggests that many episodes are also associated with higher inflation. Furthermore all these stylized facts are broadly consistent with the predictions of our sticky-prices model in section 14.5. While policy makers typically welcome capital inflows as beneficial for the economy's medium and long-run growth prospects, they are weary of such adverse macroeconomic consequences and attempt to fight them off by means of various policy measures. The most common policy responses are the following:

- Foreign exchange market intervention (nonsterilized and sterilized)
- Fiscal contraction
- Capital controls

We analyze each of these policies in turn.[20]

14.6.1 Foreign Exchange Rate Market Intervention

Nonsterilized Intervention

We have seen analytically that, under flexible exchange rates, a given shock will cause the real exchange rate to fall faster (i.e., will cause the currency to appreciate faster in real terms) than under predetermined exchange rates. Consider, for instance, the case of a temporary positive demand shock. Comparing panel g in figure 14.10 and figure 14.12, we can see that the real exchange rate falls by 3 percent in the first period already under flexible exchange rates whereas it remains put in the predetermined exchange rate case. It takes in fact five periods for the real exchange rate to fall by 3 percent under predetermined exchange rates. Panel c in figures 14.10 and 14.12 reveals that this larger real appreciation is associated with a larger trade deficit under

19. Inflation even falls under flexible exchange rates for some parameterizations (e.g., try $\sigma = 1.5$ and $\rho = 1.5$). (Programs are posted on the book's website.) Exercise 3 at the end of the chapter asks you to illustrate the economy's response to a fall in the rate of money growth and a fall in the devaluation rate. Notice that except for the behavior of inflation, the response is similar to the cases illustrated in the text.

20. Other, but less common, policy responses include trade policy (e.g., subsidizing exports) and marginal reserve requirements on bank deposits; see Calvo (2010), Calvo, Leiderman, and Reinhart (1993), and De La Torre, Ize, and Schmukler (2012, ch. 11).

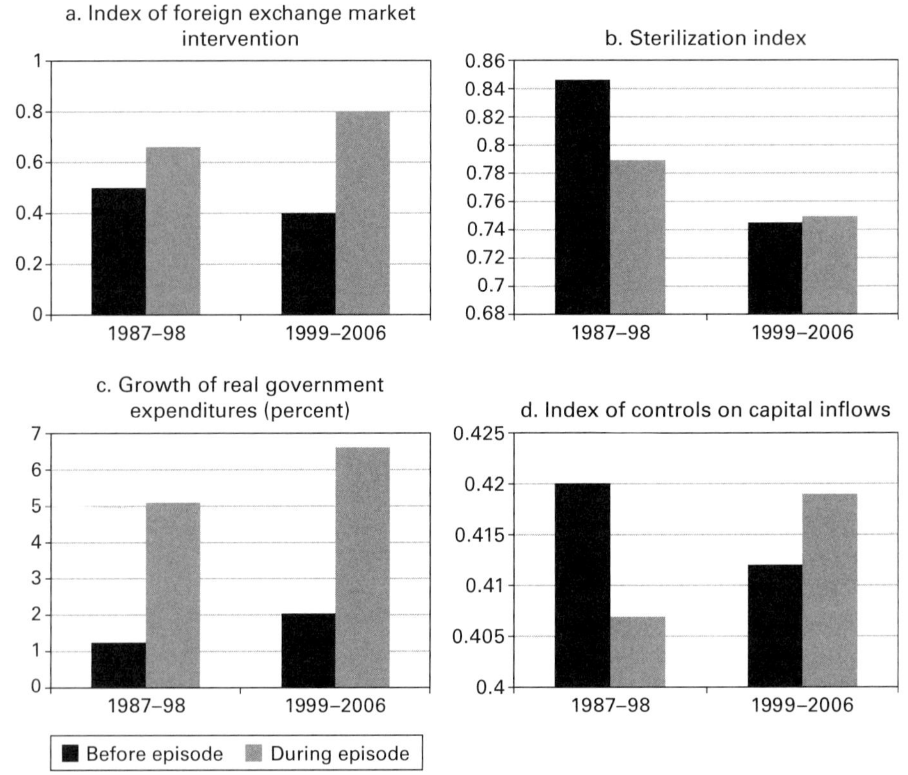

Note: Based on 73 episodes of capital inflows episodes in developing countries
Source: WEO (2007)

Figure 14.14
Policy responses to capital inflows episodes

flexible exchange rates than under predetermined (a fall in the trade balance of 38.5 percent under flexible rates compared to 31.5 percent under predetermined exchange rates).

To prevent nominal—and hence, real—appreciation, the Central Bank often buys foreign exchange (typically dollars) to increase the nominal price of a dollar (i.e., the nominal exchange rate), which results in the accumulation of international reserves. Figure 14.14, panel a, depicts an index of foreign exchange market intervention, which varies between 0 and 1 (0 representing no intervention and 1 representing full intervention), for capital inflows episodes in two different periods.[21] We can clearly see that foreign exchange market intervention increases suggesting

21. The foreign exchange market intervention index is computed by dividing the change in international reserves by an index of "exchange rate market pressures" (a combination of movements in the nominal exchange rate and international reserves). Thus the foreign exchange market intervention index would take a value of 0 for a clean float and of 1 for a fixed exchange rate. Figure 14.14 is based on the 73 episodes mentioned above for figure 14.2, which have been divided into two nonoverlapping periods.

that Central Banks have been actively trying to prevent nominal appreciation of the domestic currency.

To capture this idea in the simplest possible way, let us focus on the nonseparable and flexible exchange rate case analyzed above. Specifically, let us assume that in response to a temporary fall in the world real interest rate, the monetary authority increases the nominal money supply as much as needed to prevent the nominal exchange rate from changing on impact.[22] While, strictly speaking, the nominal money supply increase does not entail foreign exchange market intervention (the counterpart of this increase is an increase in domestic credit and not international reserves), it captures the effect of monetary policy on the level of the nominal exchange rate. The impact of this type of intervention is illustrated in figure 14.15 where, as a reference point, the full line depicts the case of nonintervention while the circled line indicates the case of intervention. Panel g indicates that the intervention policy indeed achieves its objective of lessening the initial real appreciation. Specifically, while in the nonintervention case the initial fall in e_t is 1.5 percent, in the intervention case the real exchange stays put in $t = 1$ and reaches a maximum fall of 1 percent in $t = 3$. As panel c makes clear, this is associated with a smaller trade deficit. Policy makers achieve the objective of a smaller real appreciation, however, at the cost of more overheating (panel d) and higher inflation (panel f). Intuitively, since the real exchange rate is kept constant on impact, then all the increase in aggregate demand gets reflected in higher output, which leads to higher inflation.

Sterilized Intervention

Our discussion so far has assumed that the foreign exchange market intervention is *nonsterilized* in the sense that the increase in international reserves is fully reflected in a corresponding increase in the monetary base. In practice, however, policy makers often fear the consequences of additional liquidity in the economy since, as we have seen, it will tend to be associated with higher inflation and overheating of the economy. One way of attempting to deal with these undesirable consequences is to sell government (or Central Bank) bonds to absorb this additional liquidity. This is referred to as *sterilized intervention*. Full sterilization amounts to the Central Bank reducing domestic credit so as to leave the monetary base unchanged. This is tantamount to the Central Bank acquiring foreign bonds (i.e., international reserves) in exchange for domestic bonds. The higher supply of domestic bonds will tend to reduce their price and hence increase interest rates. This in turn will contribute to Central Bank losses (commonly referred to as a "quasi-fiscal" cost) because foreign bonds typically carry a lower interest rate than domestic bonds (after adjusting for the change in the exchange rate).

22. To see that this is always possible, think of solving the model for a value of e_1 (i.e., the value of the real exchange rate in the period that the shock occurs) equal to e_0 (the value just before the shock occurs) and then backing out the value of the nominal money supply consistent with such an equilibrium.

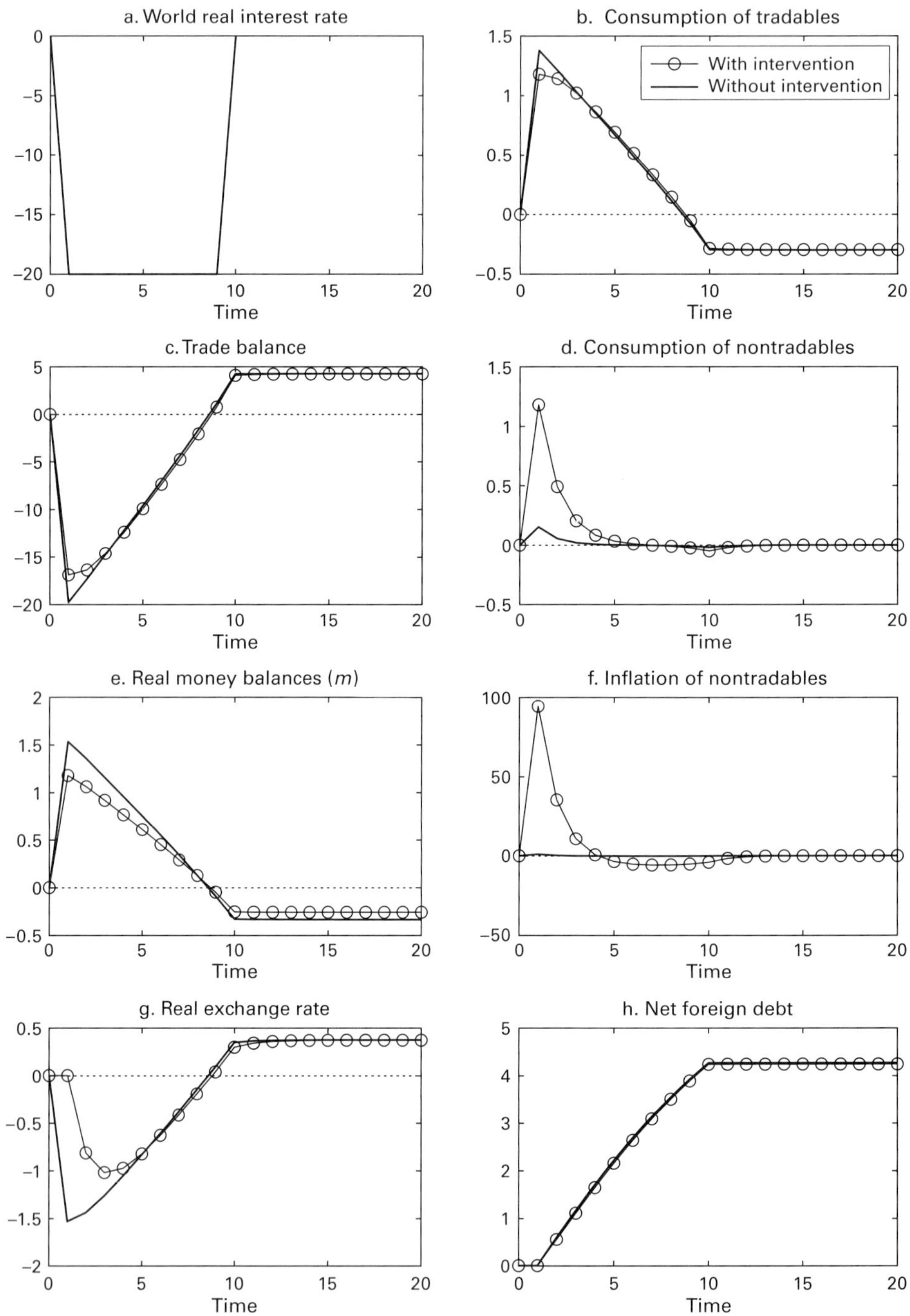

Figure 14.15
Temporary fall in world real interest rate under flexible rates with intervention (nonseparable case)

Figure 14.14, panel b shows a sterilization index before and during the two sets of capital inflows episodes mentioned above.[23] The picture makes clear that, on average, sterilization has not increased during capital inflows episodes. Based on anecdotal evidence, the reason is probably that sterilization efforts are typically short-lived due to the fact that (1) they tend to actually encourage further capital flows by increasing domestic interest rates and (2) imply substantial quasi-fiscal costs.

To capture sterilized intervention in terms of our model, we would need to introduce imperfect asset substitutability between domestic and foreign bonds.[24] The effectiveness of sterilized intervention will critically depend on the degree of substitution between domestic and foreign bonds. If the degree of substitution is low, then the higher supply of domestic bonds will lead to an increase in the nominal interest rate, which will reduce real money demand and thus tend to depreciate the domestic currency. The higher the degree of substitution, the less effective the policy will be.[25] Empirically, the evidence on the effectiveness of sterilized intervention in affecting nominal exchange rates is mixed at best (e.g., see Craig and Humpage 2001).

14.6.2 Fiscal Contraction

Another common policy measure in response to a capital inflows episode is to tighten fiscal policy. In particular, policy makers often reduce government spending (which is typically biased toward spending on nontradable goods) in order to induce a real depreciation that would at least partly offset the real appreciation associated with the capital inflows episode. Indeed—and as discussed in chapter 4—the direct effect of a reduction in government spending on nontradable goods in an endowment economy would be to reduce the relative price of nontradable goods (i.e., a real depreciation).

Figure 14.14, panel c shows the growth in real government expenditure before and during each set of episodes. The evidence clearly shows that government expenditure goes up during episodes of capital inflows. This is hardly surprising given that fiscal policy in developing countries is strongly procyclical (see chapter 10, box 10.1). The procyclicality of government spending is likely to more than offset individual cases where a contractionary fiscal response has been observed.

The simplest model to illustrate the effectiveness of contracting government spending in order to fight real appreciation would be a flexible prices, cash-in-advance model à la chapter 7. In fact exercise 4 at the end of this chapter shows that a reduction in g_t^N could completely offset the real appreciation induced by a capital inflows episode. While extreme, this example shows the power of fiscal policy in this context.

23. This sterilization index indicates the extent to which the monetary authority contracted domestic credit to offset the increase in the monetary base associated with foreign exchange market intervention (see IMF 2007 for details). A value of one (or higher) indicates full sterilization, whereas a value of 0 (or negative) implies no sterilization.

24. For models of imperfect asset substitutability, see Flood and Jeanne (2005) and Lahiri and Végh (2003).

25. In the extreme case of perfect substitution, the effect is nil because the nominal interest rate is not affected at all.

To address this issue in the context of the sticky prices model used in this chapter, suppose that policy makers follow the fiscal policy rule given by

$$g_t^N = \overline{g^N} + \phi(e_t - e_{ss}), \tag{14.56}$$

where $\overline{g^N}$ is the exogenously given component of government spending on nontradable goods, g_t^N is total government spending on nontradable goods, and ϕ is a positive parameter that captures the degree of "leaning against the wind" embedded in the fiscal policy rule. Equation (14.56) calls for policy makers to reduce government spending on nontradable goods whenever the current real exchange rate, e_t, is below its steady-state level, e_{ss}. The opposite is true when the current real exchange rate is above its steady-state level.

Figure 14.16 illustrates the effects of putting into effect the fiscal policy rule (14.56) when there is a temporary fall in the world real interest rate for the nonseparable case analyzed above under predetermined exchange rates.[26] As a benchmark, the full line denotes the no fiscal intervention case depicted in figure 14.11. The circled path corresponds to the case of $\phi = 10$. In response to the initial real appreciation, g_t^N is reduced following policy rule (14.56) (panel i). This in turn reduces the fall in e_t in $t = 2$ by around 35 percent (from 0.74 percent under nonintervention to 0.48 percent), as illustrated in panel g. The contraction in government spending reaches its peak in $t = 4$ at 5 percent.[27] The smaller real appreciation, however, comes at the cost of a substantial contraction in output starting in $t = 2$ (panel j).[28]

Figure 14.17 illustrates the effectiveness of a fiscal contraction in lessening the initial real appreciation under flexible exchange rates.[29] On impact, the fall in e_t is reduced by around 7 percent and in $t = 2$ by about 60 percent (panel g). As under predetermined exchange rates, this comes at the cost of a substantial contraction in output in $t = 1$ (panel j) and, in this case, of deflation (panel f).

14.6.3 Capital Controls

Yet another way of dealing with the unwanted consequences of capital inflows (including the possibility of financial crises once the direction of capital flows reverses) is to impose controls on short-term capital inflows, as discussed in box 14.2. This idea goes back to Tobin's (1978) celebrated suggestion of throwing some sand in the wheels of well-oiled global capital markets. The best-known example of this type of policy is the case of Chile during the period 1991 to 1998 where controls took the form of unremunerated reserve requirements on short-term capital

26. We keep the same parameterization as above and set $\overline{g^N} = 0.5$.

27. If government spending were 20 percent of GDP, this would correspond to a peak contraction of around 1 percent of GDP.

28. We know from exercise 2 in chapter 8 that in a sticky-prices model, a reduction in g_t^N is contractionary.

29. Here we set $\phi = 0.9$.

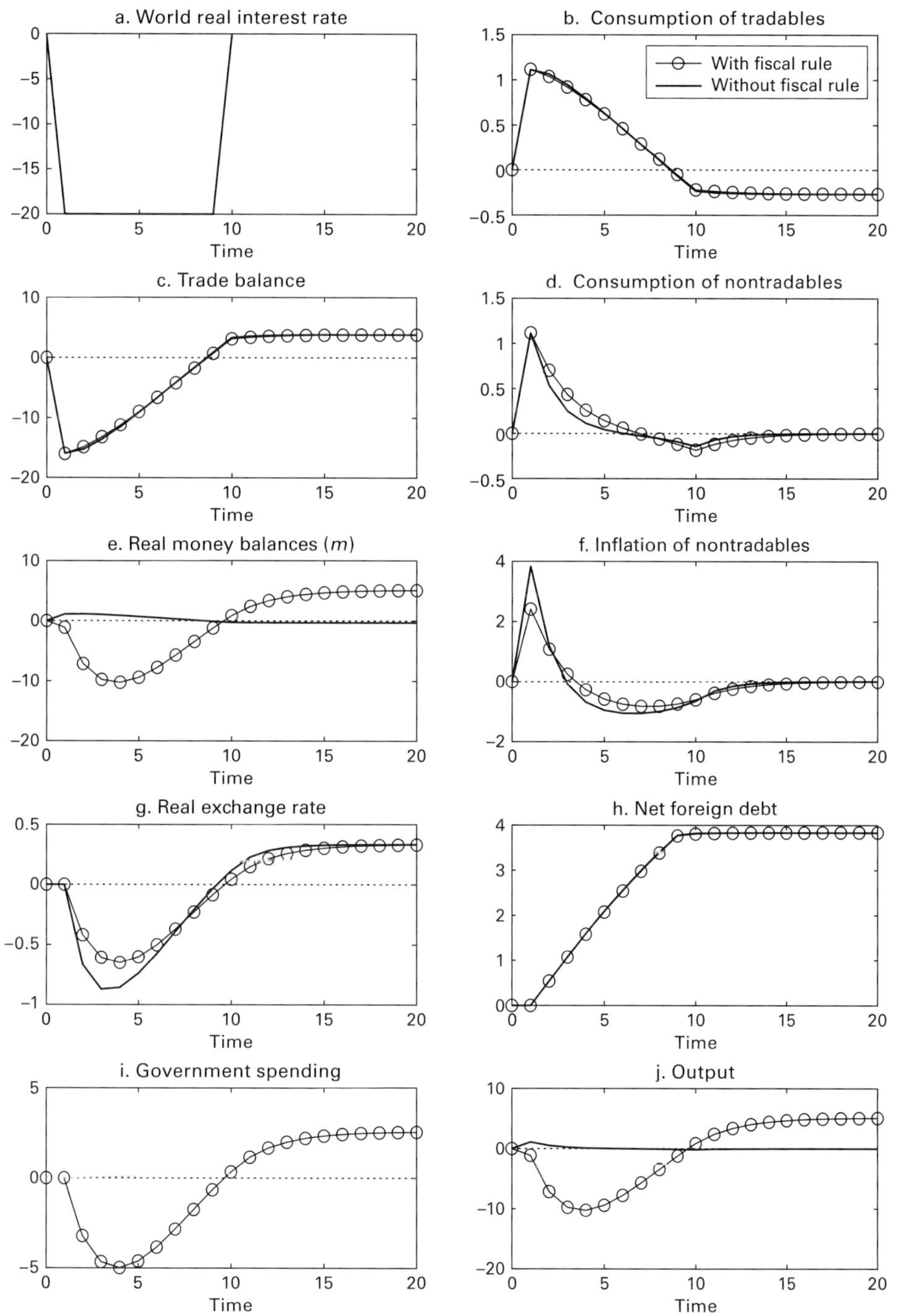

Figure 14.16
Temporary fall in world real interest rate under predetermined exchange rates and fiscal rule (nonseparable case)

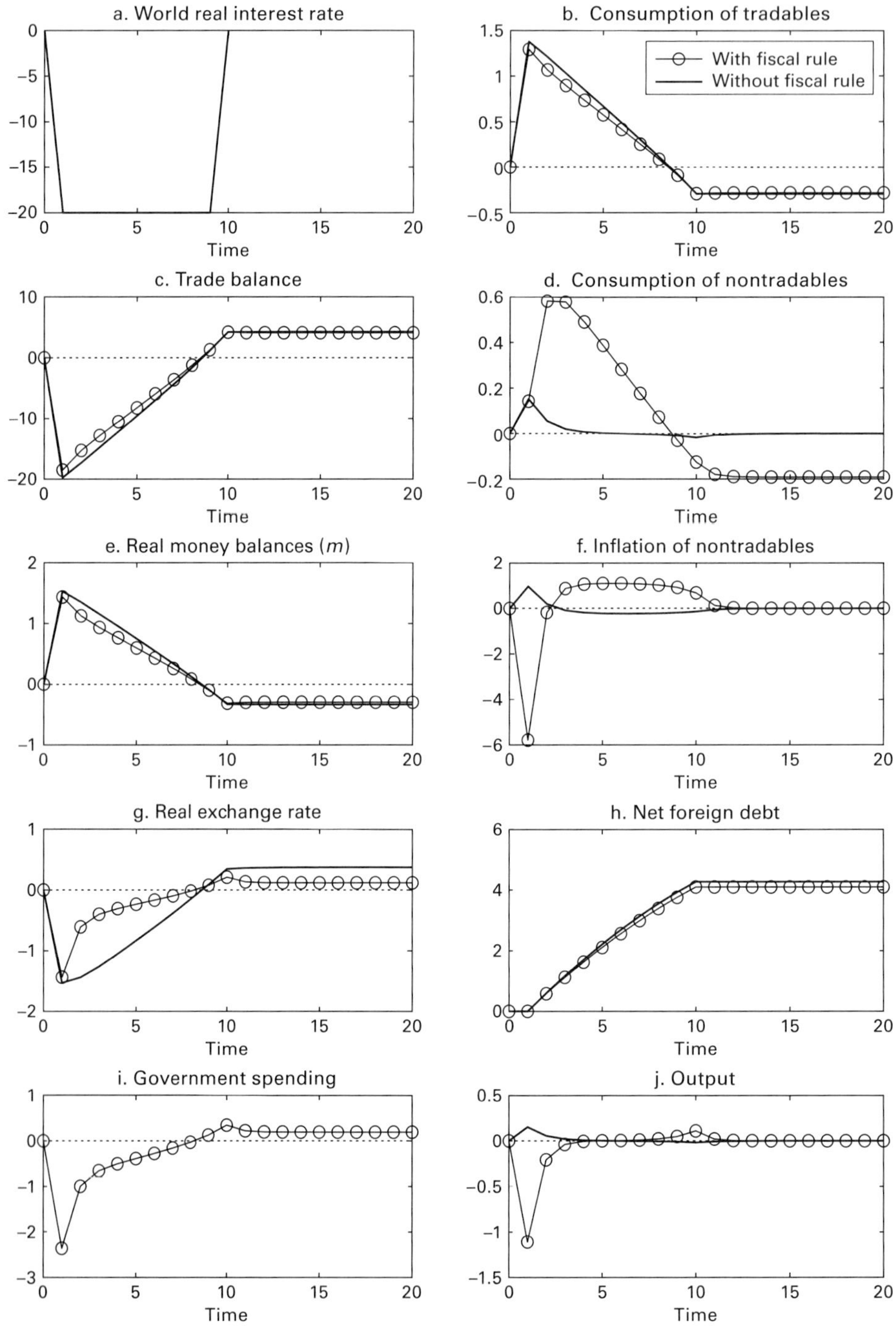

Figure 14.17
Temporary fall in world real interest rate under flexible rates and fiscal rule (nonseparable case)

Box 14.2
Throwing sand in the wheels

Many emerging economies have resorted to capital controls in response to large and temporary surges in capital inflows. Broadly speaking, the idea behind the implementation of capital controls is to slow down the inflow of short-term capital and hence prevent a large real appreciation of the domestic currency and overheating of the economy (i.e., higher inflation and current account deficits). In principle, capital controls would also enhance the monetary authority's ability to conduct an independent monetary policy in the presence of fixed or predetermined exchange rates. An additional goal that is often mentioned is to decrease the vulnerability of the domestic banking system to a sudden outflow of capital (i.e., a sudden stop).

While controls on capital inflows can take numerous forms, the most common are the following:

- Unremunerated reserve requirements on both bank and portfolio flows.
- Direct tax on portfolio inflows and nonresidents' deposits on banks.
- Restrictions on foreign liability positions of banks.

How effective have capital controls been? As suggested by Magud and Reinhart (2007), the effectiveness of capital controls can be assessed based on their ability to

- limit capital inflows,
- shift the composition of flows toward long-term flows,
- alleviate real exchange rate pressures, and
- preserve some monetary policy autonomy by severing the link between domestic and international interest rates.

Table 14.2 presents a summary of findings in the literature, which has employed a variety of empirical techniques (ranging from sophisticated econometric models to descriptive and comparative analysis of time series) to test the effectiveness of controls on capital inflows. The general conclusion seems to be that capital controls have been most successful in achieving the second and fourth goals above, while evidence on the first and third is decidedly mixed.

It should be noted that most of the tools summarized in table 14.2 were designed to act as a much stronger deterrent to short-term rather than long-term capital inflows. In the case of the tax on portfolio investment, the tax is typically a one-time tax charged upon entrance, thus penalizing relatively more short-term inflows (for a given interest rate differential). In the case of unremunerated reserve requirements, the Central Bank keeps the unremunerated reserves usually for a year, regardless of the time horizon of the capital inflow, which, again, implies that the effect is larger on short-term inflows while barely affecting incentives regarding long-term inflows. In fact the idea of penalizing short-term inflows has been taken to an extreme in the cases of taxes on financial transactions that have applied only to inflows that leave the country within less than a year, having no effect at all on long-term inflows.

While the traditional consensus was against the use of capital controls, this received wisdom has been challenged recently as financial crises have become commonplace and policy makers and international organizations such as the IMF struggle to come up with effective policy tools. As of 2011, Brazil is the latest example of a major emerging country that has not only imposed capital controls (see table 14.2) but also enacted measures to directly restrict domestic borrowing such as raising

Box 14.2
(continued)

Table 14.2
Country experiences with capital controls

Country	Period	Tool	Goal achieved? Reduce the volume of net inflows	Shift the composition of inflow toward longer term	Reduce real exchange rate pressures	More independent monetary policy
Chile	1991–1998	• Unremunerated reserve requirements on bank and portfolio flows	No	Yes	No	Yes
Brazil	1993	• Extended minimun term of external borrowing • Restricted portfolio investment by foreign investors • Financial transaction tax	No	No	No	No
Malaysia	1994	• Prohibition against residents selling money market funds to nonresidents • Limits on banks' external liability position with nonresidents • Unremunerated reserve requirements on bank flows	Yes	Yes	Yes	Yes
Colombia	2007	• Unremunerated reserve requirements on bank flows • Restriction on derivative position of banks	No	Yes	No	No
Brazil	2009–2011	• Tax on portfolio investment by foreign investors • Unremunerated reserve requirements on bank flows	?	?	?	?

Sources: Cardoso and Goldfajn (1997), Ariyoshi et al. (2000), De Gregorio, Edwards, and Valdes (2000), Magud and Reinhart (2007), Clements and Kamil (2009), Ostry et al. (2010), and Gallagher (2011).

Box 14.2
(continued)

the tax on consumer credit from 1.5 to 3 percent. Even the IMF has argued that in circumstances where the usual macroeconomic policy remedies are not appropriate (because of inflation concerns, an overvalued currency, or a more than adequate level of reserves) or when it might not be possible to quickly address financial fragility concerns through the domestic prudential framework, capital controls may be a legitimate component of the policy response to surges in capital inflows (see Ostry et al. 2010).

In a lucid critique of the IMF position, however, Calvo (2010) has argued that even as a last resort, countercyclical reserve requirements are bound to be more effective than capital controls in smoothing out the credit cycle and hence the undesirable macroeconomic consequences of capital inflows. An additional argument against capital controls, which should receive more attention, is the numerous rent-seeking activities that they are likely to generate, fostering an environment of potential corruption and crony capitalism, which leads to substantive, if hard to measure, efficiency costs.

inflows. Capital controls, however, may take various other forms as discussed in box 14.2. The effectiveness of capital controls is, at best, mixed. While capital controls seem to have altered the composition of flows toward longer horizons and give policy makers some monetary autonomy, it can be argued that the costs of such controls—particularly when it comes to generating socially-inefficient rent-seeking activities and making credit more expensive to small and medium-size firms that are less able to circumvent these controls—have typically outweighed the benefits.[30]

14.7 Final Remarks

Emerging markets go through recurrent cycles of capital inflows and subsequent outflows. Capital outflows—particularly if sudden—are typically associated with balance of payments and financial crises, which we will cover in chapters 16 and 17. Capital inflows, in contrast, are clearly beneficial from a long-term perspective as they provide much needed finance for projects that might not be otherwise undertaken. However, when they are short term and/or take the form of portfolio investment, capital inflows present a host of short-term macroeconomic problems that pose serious dilemmas for policy makers.

This chapter has both characterized the macroeconomic consequences of capital inflows and analyzed some of the possible policy responses. We first showed that the macroeconomic scenario typically associated with capital inflows—consumption booms, trade and current account deficits, and real appreciation of the domestic currency—is likely to arise regardless of whether capital inflows are triggered by domestic or external factors. This is conceptually important because while in most models capital inflows are an endogenous response to some shock, in policy circles

30. See Forbes (2007) for a detailed analysis of the microeconomic costs of capital controls.

capital inflows are often implicitly or explicitly thought of as exogenous and reflecting the vagaries of international capital markets. Our analysis thus suggests that to a first approximation, the source of the capital inflows is not relevant when it comes to understanding their macroeconomic implications.

If one views capital flows cycles as driven mainly by external factors, then one can ask the question: What are the macroeconomic effects of a sudden stop (defined as an exogenous end to capital inflows)? We saw how the anticipation of a sudden stop may be interpreted as introducing an intertemporal distortion, à la chapter 3, and thus lead to a consumption boom and real appreciation followed by a consumption bust and real depreciation cycle.

We then compared the economy's response to a capital inflow depending on whether the economy is operating under predetermined or flexible exchange rates. We saw that even though a real appreciation of the currency will occur regardless of the exchange rate regime, policy makers do have a choice as to how this real appreciation will come about. Under predetermined exchange rates, the real appreciation will occur mainly through higher inflation of nontradables, whereas under flexible exchange rates, it will occur mainly through a fall in the nominal exchange rate.

Finally, we analyzed two key policy responses aimed at alleviating the initial real appreciation: foreign exchange intervention and fiscal tightening. Both may lessen the initial real appreciation, but at the cost of higher inflation in the case of foreign exchange intervention and an output contraction in the case of fiscal tightening.

14.8 Appendix: Proofs of Claims in Section 14.4

Claim 1: $y_2^T - c_2^T > 0$. We proceed by contradiction.

Suppose $y_2^T - c_2^T = 0$. Then, since $b_2 - b_1 = 0$, it follows from (14.23) that $b_1 = 0$. Hence, from (14.22), $y_1^T - c_1^T = 0$. Further, since $b_1 = 0$, it follows that $b_2 = 0$. Hence from (14.24), $y_3^T - c_3^T = 0$. This implies that consumption is always equal to the endowment and hence $c_3^T > c_2^T > c_1^T$, which is a contradiction since we have established that $c_1^T > c_2^T$.

Suppose $y_2^T - c_2^T < 0$. Then, since $b_2 - b_1 = 0$, it follows from (14.23) that $b_1 > 0$. Hence from (14.22), $y_1^T > c_1^T$. Since $y_2^T > y_1^T$, this implies that $c_2^T > c_1^T$, which is a contradiction.

Since $TB_2 > 0$ and $b_1 = b_2$, then by (14.23), $b_1 < 0$. Then by (14.22), $y_1^T < c_1^T$ and hence $TB_1 < 0$.

Claim 2: $c_3^T < y_3^T$. We proceed by contradiction.

Suppose $c_3^T = y_3^T$. Since $y_3^T - c_3^T = -(1+r)b_2$, this implies that $b_2 = 0$. But, since $y_2^T - c_2^T = -rb_1$, $b_1 = 0$ implies that $c_2^T = y_2^T$, which is a contradiction because we have shown that $c_2^T < y_2^T$.

Suppose $c_3^T > y_3^T$. Since $y_3^T - c_3^T = -(1+r)b_2$, this implies that $b_2 > 0$. Since $y_2^T - c_2^T = -rb_1$, $b_1 > 0$ implies that $c_2^T > y_2^T$, which is a contradiction.

Claim 3: $c_3^T > c^T$. Recall from the text that $c_3^T > c_1^T > c_2^T$. We have also established that $c_2^T < c^T$. Suppose that $c_1^T \geq c^T$, then clearly $c_3^T > c^T$. Suppose $c_1^T < c^T$. Then it must also be the case that $c_3^T > c^T$ because otherwise the present discounted value of the path of consumption would be lower than the present discounted value of the endowments.

Exercises

1. (Unanticipated sudden stop) Consider the three-period model of section 14.4. Initially, the economy is characterized by the unconstrained solution discussed in the text. When period 2 comes along, however, there is an unanticipated sudden stop that requires that the current account in periods 2 and 3 be nonnegative. In this context:

a. Solve for consumption of tradables, the real exchange rate, the trade balance, and the current account in periods 2 and 3.

b. How does this solution compare to the solution for an anticipated sudden stop discussed in the text? Explain the differences, if any.

2. (Shocks under flexible exchange rates) To gain intuition behind the results illustrated in figures 14.8 and 14.9, this exercise asks you to solve the continuous-time version of the model of section 14.5. (The same notation is used.)

Let preferences be given by

$$\int_0^\infty \alpha_t\left[\log(c_t^T) + \log(c_t^N)\right]\exp(-\beta t)dt. \tag{14.57}$$

The intertemporal budget constraint takes the form

$$a_0 + \int_0^\infty \left(y_t^T + \frac{y_t^N}{e_t} + \tau_t\right)\exp(-rt)dt = \int_0^\infty \left(c_t^T + \frac{c_t^N}{e_t} + i_t m_t\right)\exp(-rt)dt. \tag{14.58}$$

The cash-in-advance constraint is given by

$$m_t = c_t^T + \frac{c_t^N}{e_t},$$

where, for notational simplicity, we have set to one the parameter associated with the continuous-time cash-in-advance constraint. The supply side of the model follows chapter 8 with Calvo pricing. In this context:

a. Derive the first-order conditions and set up a dynamic system in n_t and π_t.

b. Analyze the effects of an unanticipated and temporary increase in α_t.

c. Analyze the effects of an unanticipated and temporary fall in r_t.

3. (Inflation dynamics and capital inflows) Using the MATLAB programs posted on the book website, perform the following experiments:

a. Temporary reduction in rate of money growth under flexible exchange rates for the separable case.

b. Temporary reduction in rate of money growth under flexible exchange rates for the nonseparable case.

c. Temporary reduction in rate of devaluation rate under predetermined exchange rates for the nonseparable case.

4. (Contractionary fiscal policy as a policy response to capital inflows) This exercise illustrates the use of contractionary fiscal policy as a way of alleviating the real exchange rate appreciation that accompanies episodes of capital inflows. Consider a small open economy operating under predetermined exchange rates with fixed endowment of tradables (y^T) and nontradables (y^N) and perfectly integrated into world goods and capital markets. Preferences are given by

$$\int_0^\infty [\log(c_t^T) + \log(c_t^N)]\exp(-\beta t)dt,$$

where c_t^T and c_t^N denote consumption of tradables and nontradables, respectively, and β is the discount rate. The intertemporal constraint takes the form

$$a_0 + \int_0^\infty \left(y^T + \frac{y^N}{e_t} - \psi_t\right)\exp(-rt)dt = \int_0^\infty \left(c_t^T + \frac{c_t^N}{e_t} + i_t m_t\right)\exp(-rt)dt,$$

where a_0 are initial real financial assets, $r(=\beta)$ is the world real interest rate, e_t is the real exchange rate (i.e., the relative price of tradables in terms of nontradables), ψ_t denotes lump-sum taxes, i_t is the nominal interest rate, and m_t are real money balances in terms of tradable goods.

The cash-in-advance constraint is given by

$$m_t = \alpha\left(c_t^T + \frac{c_t^N}{e_t}\right),$$

where α is a positive parameter. The government's flow budget constraint is given by

$$\dot{h}_t = rh_t + \dot{m}_t + (\varepsilon_t + \pi_t^*)m_t + \psi_t - \frac{g_t^N}{e_t}, \tag{14.59}$$

where g_t^N is government spending on nontradables (which we take as the policy instrument), ε_t is the rate of devaluation, and π_t^* is the foreign inflation rate. The government sets a constant rate of devaluation, ε. Lump-sum taxes adjust endogenously to ensure that the government's budget constraint holds.

Equilibrium in the nontradable goods market requires that

$$y^N = c_t^N + g_t^N.$$

Interest parity holds:

$$i_t = i_t^* + \varepsilon.$$

In the context of this model:

a. Suppose that starting from an initial stationary equilibrium, there is an unanticipated and temporary reduction in i_t^* between time 0 and time T. (Assume that g_t^N is constant.) Show that this will lead to a consumption boom in the tradable sector and to real appreciation.

b. Suppose now that in response to the temporary reduction in i_t^*, the government reduces g_t^N temporarily by as much as needed to keep the real exchange rate between time 0 and time T at its pre-shock level. Compute a reduced form solution for the level of g_t^N that will keep e_t constant.

References

Alfaro, Laura, Sebnem Kalemli-Ozcan, and Vadym Volosovych. 2007. Capital flows in a globalized world: The role of policies and institutions. In Sebastian Edwards, ed., *Capital Controls and Capital Flows in Emerging Economies: Policies, Practices, and Consequences*. Chicago: University of Chicago Press, 19–72.

Ariyoshi, Akira, Karl Habermeier, Bernard Laurens, Inci Otker-Robe, Jorge Iván Canales-Kriljenko, and Andrei Kirilenko. 2000. Capital controls: Country experiences with their use and liberalization. IMF Ocassional Paper 190. International Monetary Fund, Washington, DC.

Baek, In-Mee. 2006. Portfolio investment flows to Asia and Latin America: Pull, push or market sentiment? *Journal of Asian Economics* 17 (2). 363–73.

Burnside, Craig, Isaac Kleshchelski, and Sergio Rebelo. 2011. Do peso problems explain the returns to the carry trade? *Review of Financial Studies* 24 (3): 853–91

Calvo, Guillermo A. 1983. Staggered prices in a utility-maximizing framework. *Journal of Monetary Economics* 12 (3): 383–98.

Calvo, Guillermo A. 1998. Capital flows and capital-market crises: The simple economics of sudden stops. *Journal of Applied Economics* 1: 35–54.

Calvo, Guillermo A. 2010. Controls on cyclical capital inflows: Some skeptical notes. Unpublished manuscript. Columbia University.

Calvo, Guillermo, Leonardo Leiderman, and Carmen Reinhart. 1993. Capital inflows to Latin America: The role of external factors. *IMF Staff Papers* 40 (1): 108–51.

Cardoso, Eliana, and Ilan Goldfajn. 1997. Capital flows to Brazil: The endogeneity of capital controls. IMF Working Paper 97/115. International Monetary Fund, Washington, DC.

Chuhan, Punam, Stijn Claessens, and Nlandu Mamingi. 1998. Equity and bond flows to Latin America and Asia: The role of global and country factors. *Journal of Development Economics* 55 (2): 439–63.

Clements, Benedict, and Herman Kamil. 2009. Are capital controls effective in the 21st century? The recent experience of Colombia. IMF Working Paper 09/30. International Monetary Fund, Washington, DC.

Craig, Ben, and Owen Humpage. 2001. Sterilized intervention, non-sterilized intervention, and monetary policy. Working Paper 01/10. Federal Reserve Bank of Cleveland.

De Gregorio, Jose, Sebastian Edwards, and Rodrigo Valdes. 2000. Controls on capital inflows: Do they work? *Journal of Development Economics* 63 (1): 59–83.

De La Torre, Augusto, Alain Ize, and Sergio Schmukler, 2012. *Financial development in Latin American and the Caribbean: The Road Ahead.* Washington, DC: World Bank.

Edison, Hali, and Francis E. Warnock. 2003. Cross-border listings, capital controls, and equity flows to emerging markets. IMF Working Paper 03/236. International Monetary Fund, Washington, DC.

Edwards, Sebastian. 1999. How effective are capital controls? *Journal of Economic Perspectives* 13 (4): 65–84.

Fernandez-Arias, Eduardo. 1996. The new wave of private capital inflows: Push or pull? *Journal of Development Economics* 48 (2): 389–418.

Flood, Robert P., and Olivier Jeanne. 2005. An interest rate defense of a fixed exchange rate? *Journal of International Economics* 66 (2): 471–84.

Forbes, Kristin J. 2007. The microeconomic evidence on capital controls: No free lunch. In Sebastian Edwards, ed., *Capital Controls and Capital Flows in Emerging Economies: Policies, Practices, and Consequences*. Chicago: University of Chicago Press, 171–202.

Gallagher, Kevin. 2011. Regaining control? Capital controls and the global financial crisis. Working Paper 250. Political Economy Research Institute. University of Massachusetts, Amherst.

International Monetary Fund. 2007. *World Economic Outlook*. Washington DC: International Monetary Fund.

Kim, Yoonbai. 2000. Causes of capital flows in developing countries. *Journal of International Money and Finance* 19 (2): 235–53.

Lahiri, Amartya, and Carlos A. Végh. 2003. Delaying the inevitable: Interest rate defense and BOP crises. *Journal of Political Economy* 111 (2): 404–24.

Magud, Nicolas, and Carmen M. Reinhart. 2007. Capital controls: An evaluation. In Sebastian Edwards, ed., *Capital Controls and Capital Flows in Emerging Economies: Policies, Practices, and Consequences*. Chicago: University of Chicago Press, 645–74.

Ostry, Jonathan D., Atish R. Ghosh, Karl Habermeier, Marcos Chamon, Mahvash S. Qureshi, and Dennis B. S. Reinhardt. 2010. Capital inflows: The role of controls. IMF Staff Position Note 10/04. International Monetary Fund, Washington, DC.

Taylor, Mark, and Lucio Sarno. 1997. Capital flows to developing countries: Long- and short-term determinants. *World Bank Economic Review* 11 (5): 451–70.

Tobin, James. 1978. A proposal for international monetary reform. *Eastern Economic Journal* 4: 154–59.

Ying, Yung-Hsiang, and Yoonbai Kim. 2001. An empirical analysis on capital flows: The case of Korea and Mexico. *Southern Economic Journal* 67 (4): 954–68.

15 Dollarization

15.1 Introduction

Domestic currencies have often fallen victim to high and variable inflation. Not surprisingly, households are reluctant to rely on a currency whose value tends to fall over time and fluctuate wildly. Domestic currencies are probably the most vulnerable as a store of value, as real returns on domestic deposits often turn negative. The public reacts by taking refuge in foreign currency deposits at domestic banks. The unit of account function follows soon, particularly when it comes to big-ticket items, such as real estate and cars. Rather than trying to keep up with huge and ever-rising figures in domestic currency, households get used to quoting prices in terms of a stable currency. Soon after, big-ticket transactions often begin to be executed in terms of foreign currency. Domestic money, however, typically holds on to its role as medium of exchange for small transactions.[1]

Unfortunately, the literature has not used a uniform terminology to describe the process whereby a foreign currency gradually displaces the domestic currency as store of value, unit of account, and medium of exchange. For the purposes of this chapter, we will follow the terminology suggested in Calvo and Végh (1996). The term *currency substitution* will refer to the use of a foreign currency as a *medium of exchange*, while the term *dollarization* may refer to the use of a foreign currency in any of the three traditional functions of money: store of value, unit of account, and medium of exchange.[2] We will typically, however, reserve the use of the term dollarization to mean *asset substitution*, that is, the use of a foreign currency as store of value. An important theme of this chapter will in fact be the different conceptual implications of *currency* substitution versus *asset* substitution.

By the very nature of cash, the amount of foreign currencies circulating in countries around the world is hard to measure. A few estimates, however, are available. For instance, Porter and Judson

1. The reader is referred to Calvo and Végh (1992, 1996) and Reinhart, Rogoff, and Savastano (2003) for a detailed discussion of many of these issues.

2. The term "dollarization," of course, reflects the fact that US dollars are the most commonly held foreign currency in developing countries, but the term is used generally to denote holdings of any foreign currency.

(1996) estimate that, in the mid-1990s, around 50 to 70 percent of the US currency stock was held outside the United States while, as shown in figure 15.1, Doyle (2000) puts this number at 30 percent for 1996. As also illustrated in figure 15.1, Doyle (2000) estimated the amount of German and Swiss currency circulating outside the national borders at around 70 and 76 percent respectively in 1996. While these measures overestimate the amount of currency substitution—since it is likely that large amounts of foreign currency are kept under the mattress as store of value and not used for transactions—they underestimate the extent of dollarization since they do not include other foreign-currency denominated assets. Figure 15.1 also illustrates the dramatic increase in dollarization starting around the mid-1970s. This is not surprising given that many developing countries started to open up financial markets at around that time.

Due to its ready availability the most common empirical measure of dollarization is the share of foreign currency deposits in the domestic banking system as a proportion of M2 (inclusive of foreign currency deposits). Figure 15.2 shows the evolution of this indicator over time for ten selected emerging countries. While often associated with Latin American countries, dollarization is a widespread phenomenon around the world, as evidenced by the presence of Egypt, Israel,

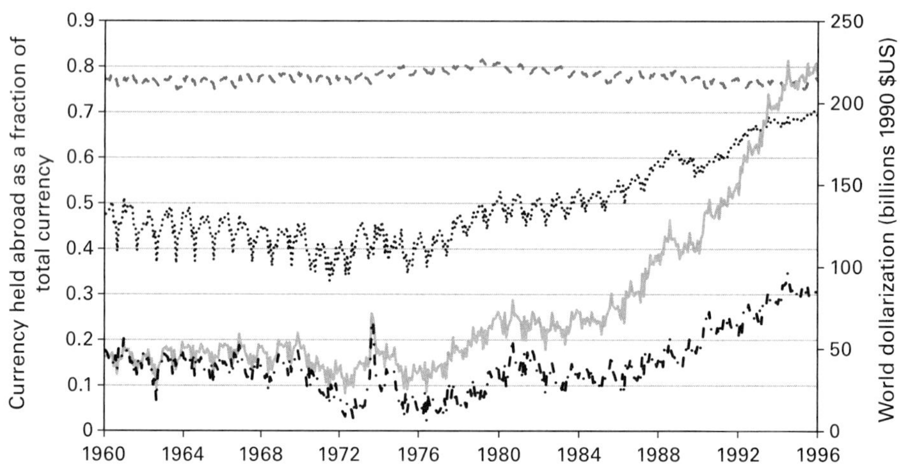

- · · Currency held abroad as a percentage of total currency outstanding for the United States
······ Currency held abroad as a percentage of total currency outstanding for Germany
– – Currency held abroad as a percentage of total currency outstanding for Switzerland
—— World dollarization (in billions 1990 US dollars)

Source: Doyle (2000)

Figure 15.1
World dollarization and currency held abroad for the United States, Germany, and Switzerland

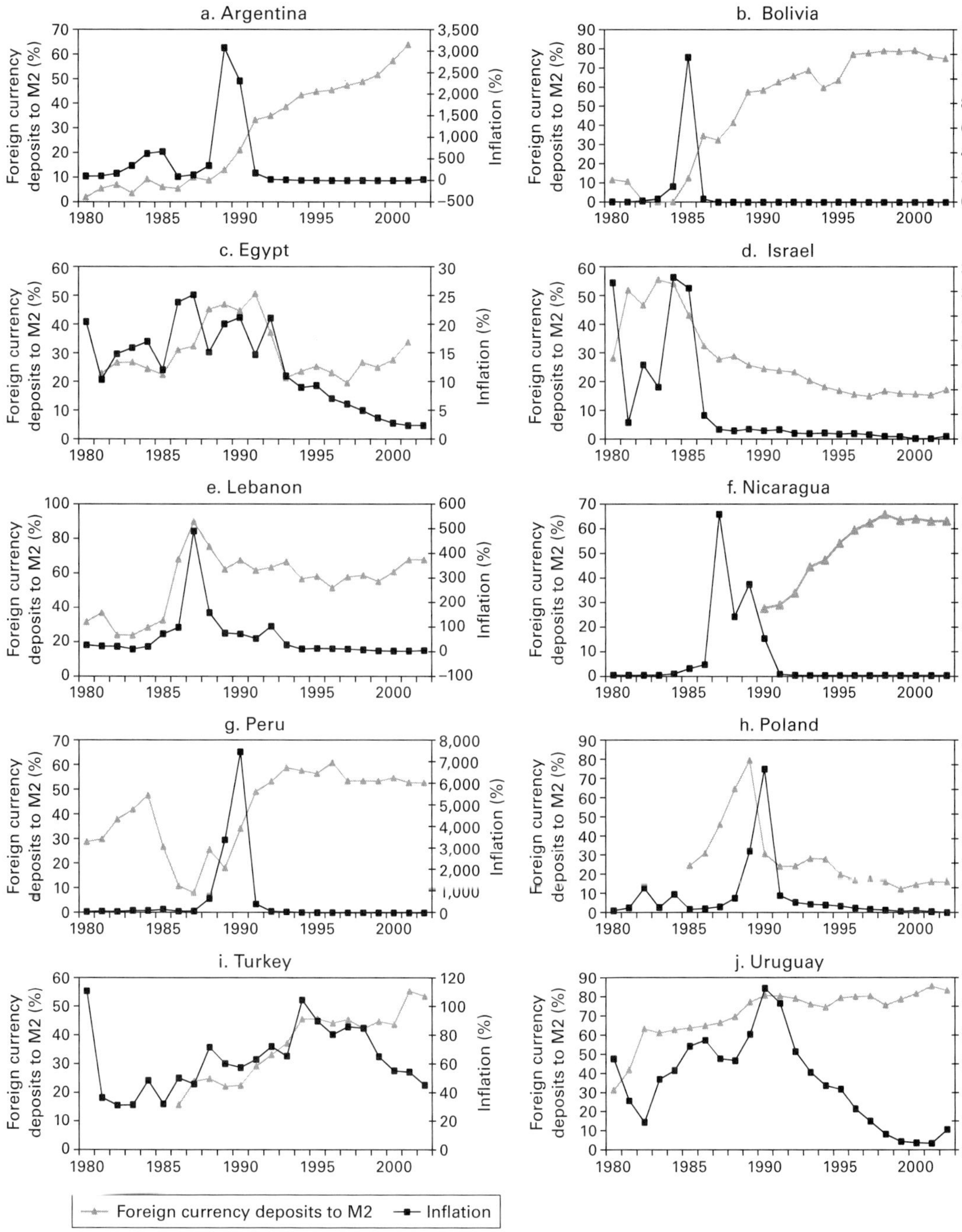

Sources: Reinhart, Rogoff, and Savastano (2003) and World Economic Outlook Database (October 2009), IMF

Figure 15.2
Foreign currency deposits and inflation

Lebanon, Poland, and Turkey in figure 15.2.[3] In addition to reflecting market forces (i.e., the flight from a weak domestic currency mentioned above), the dollarization process also responds to institutional features that are peculiar to each country. The most obvious one is whether or not foreign currency deposits are allowed. Uruguay, for instance, allowed foreign currency deposits as part of a 1974 financial sector liberalization, which quickly led to an almost complete dollarization of the financial system. In other cases, notably Bolivia in 1982 and Peru in 1985, governments decreed the conversion of foreign currency deposits into domestic currency only to re-allow them as macroeconomic instability became rampant.

The phenomenon of currency substitution and, more generally, dollarization brings about a host of fascinating issues in open economy macroeconomics. As a natural starting point, section 15.2 introduces foreign currency into our simplest monetary model (chapter 5). In such a world a demand for foreign currency arises that, like domestic currency, depends positively on consumption and negatively on its opportunity cost (the foreign nominal interest rate). If, along a perfect foresight equilibrium path (PFEP), there is a positive liquidity shock to foreign currency, consumers exchange foreign bonds for foreign currency in international money markets and the adjustment occurs instantaneously under either predetermined or flexible exchange rates.

In contrast, if there is a positive liquidity shock to *both* domestic and foreign currency, the adjustment is different under predetermined or flexible exchange rates for precisely the reasons discussed in chapter 5. Under predetermined exchange rates, households can increase their holdings of domestic money instantaneously at the Central Bank's window, whereas under flexible exchange rates, real domestic money balances can only increase slowly over time. As a result the ratio of foreign to domestic money will behave quite differently under predetermined and flexible exchange rates. The punchline is that even in a world with no frictions, shocks to overall liquidity will lead to rather different dynamics in the presence of currency substitution.

Until August 15, 1971, when President Nixon suspended convertibility of dollars into gold, most of the world operated under fixed exchange rates. At that point the world began to switch to flexible exchange rate regimes. Capital mobility, however, was rather limited by modern standards. A suitable model to capture this state of affairs is the no-bond model of chapter 6 under flexible exchange rates. As shown in chapter 6, however, a "problem" with that model was that changes in either the level or the rate of growth of money did not have any real effects. Consequently the model would be of little use to explain the observation that an increase in money growth would lead to a real depreciation of the domestic currency, as was occurring in Argentina in 1975. A natural missing ingredient—as proposed by Calvo and Rodriguez (1977) and Kouri (1976)—was currency substitution. This assumption was consistent with the fact that particularly in high-inflation countries, consumers were holding large amounts of foreign currency. Such a

3. See Savastano (1992), Reinhart, Rogoff, and Savastano (2003), and the references therein for detailed empirical evidence. In particular, Reinhart, Rogoff, and Savastano (2003) cover a much broader definition of dollarization (e.g., including government debt issued in a foreign currency).

framework would provide a nontrivial answer to the question: What is the effect of an increase in the rate of monetary expansion on the real exchange rate?

Section 15.3 seeks to answer this classic question by first adding nontradable goods to the model with no interest-bearing bonds of chapter 6. In this setup, domestic and foreign currency are held in fixed proportions. An increase in the rate of money growth leads to an increase in the relative price of nontradable goods (a real appreciation), as in Liviatan (1981). Intuitively, the rise in money growth, and hence inflation, reduces the steady-state demand for this "composite" money. The only way for the economy to get rid of foreign money balances is to run a trade deficit, which requires a rise in the consumption of tradable goods. At an unchanged real exchange rate, this provokes an excess demand for nontradable goods, which leads to a real appreciation.

We then set up a version of the model with a liquidity-in-advance constraint where there is substitution between the two monies but no substitution between consumption and liquidity services. We show that in this case we obtain the opposite result (which we associate with Calvo and Rodriguez 1977): an increase in the rate of money growth leads to a real depreciation. Intuitively, the increase in the rate of money growth implies that in the steady state, consumers wish to increase the ratio of foreign to domestic currency. Since "liquidity services" do not change across steady states, this requires an increase in steady-state foreign money balances and a fall in domestic money balances. To increase its holdings of foreign currency, the economy must run a trade surplus. Hence consumption of tradables must fall on impact, which, by causing an excess supply of nontradable goods, leads to a real depreciation.

We conclude this section by setting up a general model of currency substitution to illustrate the principle that whether an increase in the rate of money growth leads to a real appreciation or depreciation depends on the relative magnitude of the elasticity of substitution between the two monies (ρ) and the elasticity of substitution between consumption and liquidity services (σ). If $\rho < \sigma$, then an increase in money growth leads to a real appreciation. If $\rho > \sigma$, the converse is true. Available estimates based on Israeli data provided by Bufman and Leiderman (1993) suggest that in practice, the elasticity of substitution between domestic and foreign money is greater than the elasticity of substitution between liquidity services and consumption, providing support to the idea that a monetary expansion should lead to a real depreciation of the domestic money.

According to the traditional model of currency substitution, a fall in the inflation rate (and hence in the nominal interest rate) should lead to a fall in the ratio of foreign to domestic currency. A puzzling phenomenon, however, is that the currency substitution ratio has not always come down in countries where inflation, and hence nominal interest rates, have fallen drastically. This phenomenon is typically referred as "hysteresis." Indeed, as figure 15.2 illustrates, a good example of hysteresis is the case of Uruguay where inflation has fallen gradually but persistently since 1990 while the dollarization ratio has remained at around 80 percent. Section 15.4 presents a simple version of Guidotti and Rodriguez's (1992) model, which offers an explanation for hysteresis. The idea is that there is a fixed cost of switching the currency of denomination of transactions. As a result, once the economy has reached an equilibrium where foreign currency is used for many transactions, it would be costly to revert back to an equilibrium where only domestic money is used. In other words, there is an "inaction band" within which the currency substitution ratio will not change even if domestic inflation falls.

In terms of the conduct of monetary policy, the typical concern raised in policy discussions found in the literature is that in an economy subject to a high degree of currency substitution (and flexible exchange rates), the monetary authority loses the ability to anchor the price level (or the nominal exchange rate in a one-good world) by setting the nominal money supply. In a nutshell, think of $M + EF$ (where E is the nominal exchange rate and M and F denote domestic and foreign nominal money balances, respectively) as being the relevant measure of the money supply in an economy with a high degree of currency substitution. While the price level will be determined by $M + EF$, policy makers only control M and hence will have no control over the determination of the price level.

The more extreme version of this idea is found in a celebrated article by Kareken and Wallace (1981). Section 15.5 illustrates this idea in the context of the simplest cash-in-advance model by assuming that domestic and foreign money are perfect substitutes for transactions purposes. We show that in this context, the nominal exchange rate is undetermined. Put differently, there are infinite values of the nominal exchange rate that are consistent with an exogenously set level of the domestic money supply. While the case of perfect substitutability is an extreme one, the model nicely illustrates the idea that if substitution between domestic and foreign currency is high, flexible exchange rates are likely to become highly unstable. In such a world, fixed exchange rates may therefore be a more suitable choice.

To close the chapter, we come back to the hysteresis puzzle. A critical point is that hysteresis is indeed a puzzle to the extent that we think of dollarization as currency substitution. Indeed, it is only if a foreign currency is held as a medium of exchange that we should expect the ratio of foreign to domestic currency to fall as domestic inflation falls. If we think of dollarization as asset substitution, however, the ratio of foreign-currency denominated to domestic-currency denominated assets will depend on real, as opposed to nominal returns, and therefore hysteresis ceases to be a puzzle. To illustrate this point, section 15.6 develops a model due to Thomas (1985), where domestic and foreign inflation are uncertain. The inflation uncertainty renders real returns on domestic-currency and foreign-currency denominated bonds uncertain as well. In such a model the share of foreign-currency denominated assets depends on real, as opposed to nominal, returns. A reduction in the domestic nominal interest rate does not affect the dollarization ratio. We would argue that this is the most relevant model to think about the phenomenon of dollarization, which, after all, mainly captures asset as opposed to currency substitution.

The chapter proceeds as follows. Section 15.2 introduces foreign currency into our basic monetary model of chapter 5. Section 15.3 adds nontradable goods to our no-bonds model of chapter 6 to analyze the effects of changes in the rate of monetary growth on the real exchange rate. Section 15.4 presents a model in which it is costly to change the currency of denomination of transactions to explain the phenomenon of hysteresis. Section 15.5 focuses on a model where domestic and foreign currency are perfect substitutes to illustrate how monetary policy loses control over the determination of the nominal exchange rate. Finally, section 15.6 develops a model that highlights the critical distinction between the determinants of currency and asset substitution.

15.2 A Basic Model of Currency Substitution

Consider a small open economy perfectly integrated into world goods and capital markets. There is only one tradable (and nondurable) good. The law of one price applies; that is, $P_t = E_t P_t^*$, where P_t is the domestic price of the good, P_t^* is the foreign price of the good, and E_t is the nominal exchange rate (in terms of domestic currency per unit of foreign currency). Consumers may hold three financial assets: foreign bonds, foreign currency, and domestic currency.

15.2.1 Consumer's Problem

Total financial assets in nominal terms (A_t) are given by

$$A_t \equiv E_t B_t^* + M_t + E_t F_t,$$

where B_t^* are net foreign bonds denominated in the foreign currency, M_t are nominal money balances, and F_t are foreign currency balances. Dividing by P_t and using the law of one price, we obtain

$$a_t \equiv b_t + m_t + f_t, \tag{15.1}$$

where $a_t(\equiv A_t/P_t)$, $m_t(\equiv M_t/P_t)$, $b_t(\equiv B_t^*/P_t^*)$, and $f_t(\equiv F_t/P_t^*)$ denote real financial assets, real money balances, real foreign bonds, and real foreign currency balances, respectively.

The consumer's flow constraint is given by

$$\dot{a}_t = ra_t + y + \tau_t - c_t - i_t^* f_t - i_t m_t, \tag{15.2}$$

where c_t is consumption, r is the constant world real interest rate, i_t^* is the world nominal interest rate, i_t is the domestic nominal interest rate, y is the constant endowment of the good, and τ_t are lump-sum transfers from the government.

After imposing the standard transversality condition, we obtain the corresponding intertemporal constraint:

$$a_0 + \frac{y}{r} + \int_0^\infty \tau_t \exp(-rt)dt = \int_0^\infty \left(c_t + i_t m_t + i_t^* f_t\right)\exp(-rt)dt. \tag{15.3}$$

Preferences are given by

$$\int_0^\infty \{\log(c_t) + \alpha_t\left[\log(m_t) + \log(f_t)\right]\}\exp(-\beta t)dt, \tag{15.4}$$

where the parameter α_t, which is strictly positive, stands for liquidity shocks.

Consumers choose $\{c_t, m_t, f_t\}_{t=0}^{\infty}$ to maximize lifetime utility (15.4), subject to the intertemporal constraint (15.3). In terms of the Lagrangian,

$$\mathcal{L} = \int_0^{\infty} \{\log(c_t) + \alpha_t [\log(m_t) + \log(f_t)]\}\exp(-\beta t)dt$$
$$+ \lambda \left[a_0 + \frac{y}{r} + \int_0^{\infty} \tau_t \exp(-rt)dt - \int_0^{\infty} \left(c_t + i_t m_t + i_t^* f_t\right) \exp(-rt)dt \right].$$

The first-order conditions are given by (assuming, as usual, that $\beta = r$)

$$\frac{1}{c_t} = \lambda, \tag{15.5}$$

$$\frac{\alpha_t}{m_t} = \lambda i_t, \tag{15.6}$$

$$\frac{\alpha_t}{f_t} = \lambda i_t^*. \tag{15.7}$$

Combining the first two optimality conditions yields a standard money demand equation

$$m_t = \frac{\alpha_t c_t}{i_t}. \tag{15.8}$$

An analogous condition obtains for foreign currency by combining (15.5) and (15.7):

$$f_t = \frac{\alpha_t c_t}{i_t^*}. \tag{15.9}$$

In a world where a foreign currency is used for liquidity purposes, its demand will depend positively on consumption and negatively on the opportunity cost of holding foreign currency, i_t^*.

Finally, combining (15.6) and (15.7), we obtain a portfolio equation for liquidity demand:

$$\frac{f_t}{m_t} = \frac{i_t}{i_t^*}. \tag{15.10}$$

Equation (15.10) is a typical equation of currency substitution models. It says that at an optimum, the ratio of foreign to domestic currency depends on the ratio of the opportunity costs. For a given i_t^*, an increase in the opportunity cost of holding domestic currency (i_t) increases the ratio of foreign to domestic currency. This captures the idea that all else equal, high-inflation countries (i.e., countries with high i_t) should have a higher ratio of foreign to domestic currency.

15.2.2 Government

The government's budget constraint is standard and given by

$$\dot{h}_t = rh_t + \dot{m}_t + (\varepsilon_t + \pi_t^*)m_t - \tau_t, \tag{15.11}$$

where h_t denotes the government's stock of net foreign assets (i.e., international reserves), ε_t is the rate of depreciation/devaluation, and π_t^* is the foreign inflation rate.

15.2.3 Equilibrium Conditions

Since perfect capital mobility prevails, the interest parity condition holds:

$$i_t = i_t^* + \varepsilon_t. \tag{15.12}$$

Let

$$k_t \equiv b_t + f_t + h_t$$

denote the economy's stock of net foreign assets. Combining the consumer's flow constraint with the government's—given by equations (15.2) and (15.11), respectively—and imposing the interest parity condition (15.12), we obtain the economy's flow constraint (i.e., the current account)

$$\dot{k}_t = rk_t + y - c_t - i_t^* f_t.$$

The last term, $i_t^* f_t$, is typical of currency substitution models and captures the inflation tax revenues that this small open economy pays to the rest of the world (the issuers of the foreign currency) for the privilege of using the foreign currency. In other words, the opportunity cost of holding foreign currency worth f_t is $i_t^* f_t$.[4]

The corresponding resource constraint is given by

$$k_0 + \frac{y}{r} = \int_0^\infty (c_t + i_t^* f_t)\exp(-rt)dt. \tag{15.13}$$

15.2.4 Perfect Foresight Equilibrium Path

Let us solve the model for a perfect foresight equilibrium path along which α_t may not be constant.

4. How important is this term in practice? Box 15.1 discusses empirical estimates based on the extreme case of full dollarization where the economy uses only a foreign currency.

Box 15.1
How costly is it to give up the national currency?

An explicit decision by a country to give up its own currency and fully dollarize its economy is highly unusual. The largest economies to have done so are Panama in 1904, Ecuador in 2000, and El Salvador in 2001. In cases like Panama, the decision was primarily based on political and historical considerations rather than a cost–benefit analysis (see Goldfajn and Olivares 2000). However, when the decision to dollarize is made based on purely economic considerations, what are the main benefits and costs that should be taken into account?[a]

In terms of benefits, dollarization is typically viewed as an extreme but highly effective way of eliminating inflation. By giving up the domestic currency, the country will essentially inherit the inflation rate of the United States.[b] In theory, dollarization should also impose stricter fiscal discipline because the country gives up inflationary finance.[c] In the particular case of Ecuador, the country was undergoing a severe financial crisis when the decision to dollarize was adopted. Analysts believed that the need to undertake a structural reform, combined with a high degree of informal dollarization in the economy, would make full dollarization a plausible and credible reform strategy.

The costs associated with full dollarization can be significant as well. By dollarizing, the country gives up monetary policy, which can make future crises even worse. The country also loses its lender of last resort as the Central Bank cannot print money to help domestic banks weather a financial crisis. The country also gives up seignorage revenues. In addition, there is a one-time cost associated with dollarization as the Central Bank needs to acquire the high-powered foreign currency needed to replace the stock of domestic currency in circulation.

Fischer (1982) puts particular emphasis on the loss of seigniorage as a reason why many countries would be deterred from dollarizing. He presents estimates of the two costs that would be borne by an economy that decides to dollarize: the one-time cost mentioned above and the flow of seignorage revenues. He argues that the annual flow cost is typically 1 percent of GNP while the stock cost is around 10 percent of GNP.

Could one estimate these costs for economies that have actually dollarized? Part of the challenge of doing so is the lack of data on the relevant monetary aggregates. By opting to dollarize, there is no monetary authority that controls the money supply. The effective currency in circulation will not only comprise the initial dollars supplied by the Central Bank but also those entering the economy through remittances, tourism, and illicit activities. For the case of Ecuador, Vera (2007) proposes an indirect way to calculate both M1 and M2. The method has two steps: first calculate the stock of currency in circulation at the end of 1999 (i.e., just before dollarization) and then calculate the stock in the subsequent periods. In the first step, Vera (2007) uses the money multiplier together with other basic monetary relationships to estimate the stock of currency in December 1999. Then, using data on remittances and holdings of dollars by the Central Bank and monetary institutions, he calculates the variation for each period and hence the outstanding amounts at the end of each year.

a. See Fischer (1982) for a detailed analysis.
b. Of course, idiosyncratic shocks that require a change in relative prices could still cause domestic inflation to deviate from world inflation, but we would expect such differentials to be temporary and small.
c. This argument, of course, is rather doubtful given the experiences of states like California in the United States or countries like Greece in the euro area. Not having their own currency clearly did not impose much fiscal discipline in either case!

Box 15.1
(continued)

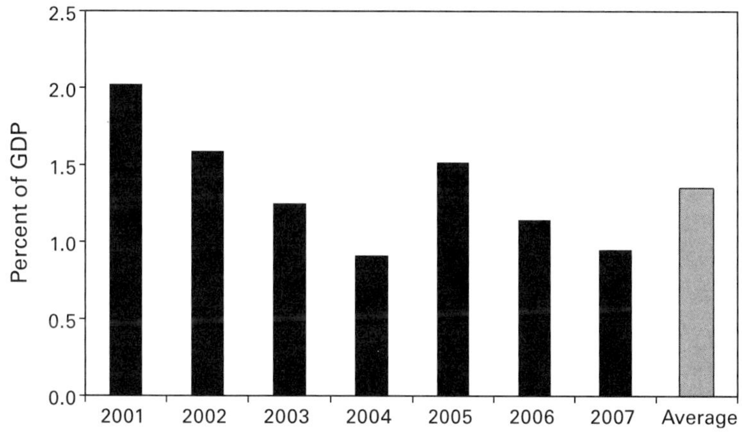

Figure 15.3
Seigniorage loss in Ecuador

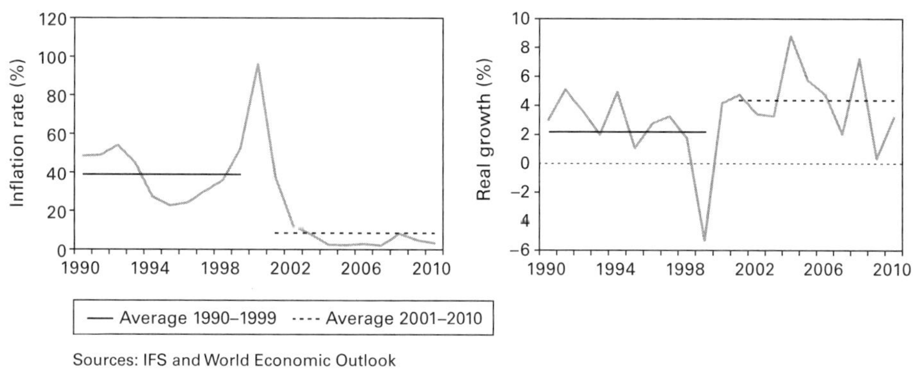

Figure 15.4
Ecuador: Inflation and GDP growth

Based on Vera's (2007) estimates of the monetary base, figure 15.3 depicts the seigniorage loss as the change in the monetary base relative to GDP. Between 2001 and 2007 (last year in Vera's sample) Ecuador lost on average 1.3 percent of GDP that would have been collected as seigniorage. Using Vera's estimate for currency in circulation as of December 1999, the estimate for the cost of exchanging sucres for dollars is about 3.3 percent of GDP.

Fischer (1982) had estimated an initial cost of exchanging local currency for dollars ranging from 3.6 percent of GDP for Australia, New Zealand, and South Africa, to 19.8 percent of GDP for Middle East countries. His estimate for "other Western countries" was of 5.6 percent of GDP, almost

Box 15.1
(continued)

two percentage points higher than the estimates provided here for Ecuador. Compared to Fischer's estimates of seigniorage lost every period, the numbers for Ecuador are larger. Fischer's estimates of the flow cost are 0.5 percent of GDP for "other Western countries" whereas the average seigniorage loss is 1.3 percent of GDP in the case of Ecuador.

There are several studies that have looked at the benefits from full dollarization in Ecuador (Quispe-Agnoli and Whisler 2006 and Banco Central del Ecuador 2001, 2010). As illustrated in figure 15.4, dollarization seems to have been effective in bringing down inflation and increasing real growth in the economy. Specifically, average inflation fell from an average of 39 percent during 1990 to 1999 to 9 percent in the decade after dollarization while growth increased from 2.2 percent to 4.4 percent over the same periods of time.

Consumption Path

Given our assumption of separable preferences, we can easily solve for consumption along a PFEP independently of the exchange rate regime.

First-order condition (15.5) says that consumption will be constant along a PFEP; that is, $c_t = c$ for all $t \in [0, \infty)$. From the resource constraint (15.13), it follows that

$$c = rk_0 + y - r\int_0^{\infty} i_t^* f_t \exp(-rt)dt. \tag{15.14}$$

But we know from the portfolio condition (15.10) that $i_t^* f_t = i_t m_t$. From the money demand condition (15.8) it follows that $i_t^* f_t = \alpha_t c$. Substituting this into expression (15.14), we obtain

$$c = \frac{rk_0 + y}{1 + r\displaystyle\int_0^{\infty} \alpha_t \exp(-rt)dt}.$$

In particular, notice that if $\alpha_t = \alpha$ for all $t \in [0, \infty)$, then this expression simplifies to

$$c = \frac{rk_0 + y}{1 + \alpha}. \tag{15.15}$$

Intuitively, the fact that it is costly for the economy to hold foreign currency implies that in a stationary PFEP, consumption is lower than permanent income, $rk_0 + y$. It is worth noting as well that (15.15) does not depend on i_t^*. The reason is that, because of the logarithmic specification of preferences, an increase in i_t^* reduces f_t by the same proportion leaving $i_t^* f_t$ unchanged. As shown in exercise 1 at the end of the chapter, this would not be so under more general preferences, in which case an increase in i_t^* may increase or reduce consumption depending on the interest rate elasticity. (In what follows, and with no loss of generality, we assume that π_t^*, and hence i_t^*, are constant at π^* and i^*, respectively.)

Predetermined Exchange Rates

Assume that policy makers set a constant rate of devaluation, ε. Then, by interest parity (15.12), the nominal interest rate is also constant over time at i. From (15.8) real money demand is given by

$$m_t = \frac{\alpha_t c}{i}. \tag{15.16}$$

If α_t is not constant over time, m_t will change accordingly. The changes in m_t will be accommodated by the Central Bank.

Similarly from (15.9) it follows that

$$f_t = \frac{\alpha_t c}{i^*}. \tag{15.17}$$

Again, if α_t is not constant over time, f_t will evolve accordingly. How are these changes in f_t accommodated? When α_t increases along a PFEP, consumers will sell some of their foreign bonds in exchange for foreign currency. The opposite is true when α_t falls.

Along a PFEP, the ratio of foreign to domestic money is constant and given by

$$\frac{f_t}{m_t} = \frac{i}{i^*}. \tag{15.18}$$

As a concrete example of changes in α_t along a PFEP, figure 15.5 depicts the case of an increase in α_t at $t = T$ from α^L to α^H, $\alpha^L < \alpha^H$ (panel a). As already established, consumption is flat along a PFEP (panel b).[5] The same is true of the nominal interest rate (panel c) and of the ratio of foreign to domestic money (panel d). From (15.16) and (15.17) we know that both m_t and f_t will increase at time T, as depicted in panels e and f, respectively. Since consumer's real financial wealth, given by (15.1), is constant along this PFEP, we infer that m_t and f_t increase at the expense of b_t. In other words, at time T consumers sell foreign bonds to the Central Bank to obtain domestic money balances and sell foreign bonds in international money markets to avail themselves of foreign currency.

Flexible Exchange Rates

Assume now that policy makers set a constant rate of money growth, μ. As usual, we will derive a differential equation in m_t. Since, by definition,

$$m_t \equiv \frac{M_t}{E_t P_t^*},$$

it follows that

5. Of course—and as can be easily verified—the *level* of consumption will be lower than if $\alpha_t = \alpha^L$ for all $t \geq 0$.

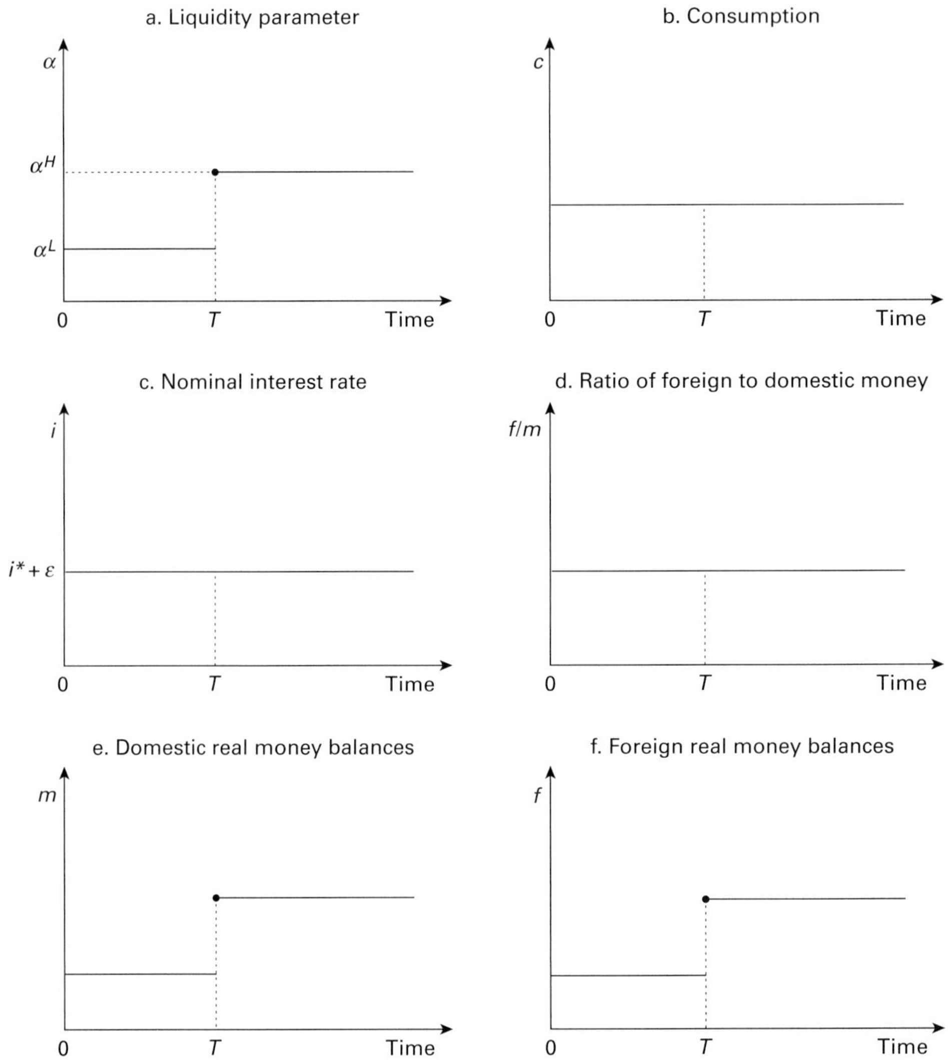

Figure 15.5
Positive money demand shock under predetermined exchange rates

$$\frac{\dot{m}_t}{m_t} = \mu - \varepsilon_t - \pi^*.$$

Using the money demand equation, given by (15.8), the interest parity condition, given by (15.12), and taking into account that $i^* = r + \pi^*$, we can rewrite this expression as

$$\dot{m}_t = m_t \left(\mu + r - \frac{\alpha_t c}{m_t} \right). \tag{15.19}$$

The stationary value of m_t, m, is given by

$$m = \frac{\alpha_t c}{\mu + r}.$$

The differential equation (15.19), together with the behavior of m_t at time T, will determine the time path of m_t.

Foreign currency balances continue to be given by expression (15.17). The ratio of foreign to domestic currency will be governed by

$$\frac{f_t}{m_t} = \frac{i_t}{i^*}. \tag{15.20}$$

Since i_t will not necessarily be constant along a PFEP when α_t fluctuates over time (as the example below makes clear), the ratio f_t/m_t may vary over time.

To fix ideas, figure 15.6 illustrates the case of an increase in α_t at $t = T$ for the case of flexible exchange rates. To solve for the corresponding PFEP, we need to first establish the jumps that may occur at time T. At time T, m_t cannot jump because M_t is a policy variable and the nominal exchange rate cannot jump along a PFEP for it would give rise to unbounded arbitrage opportunities. It follows from (15.8) that i_t needs to increase at time T. Equation (15.20) then tells us that f_t jumps up at time T.

Given that m_t does not jump at time T and is governed by the unstable differential equation (15.19), we infer that m_t must follow the path illustrated in panel e.[6] From (15.17) it follows that f_t is flat during $[0, T)$ and $[T, \infty)$, and hence follows the path illustrated in panel f. Intuitively, the adjustment of foreign money balances is the same as under predetermined exchange rates because it involves swapping foreign bonds for foreign currency, an operation that does not depend on the prevalent exchange rate regime. The path of i_t, illustrated in panel c, follows from (15.8) and the fact that, as already established, i_t jumps up at time T. From (15.8) we infer that since $\dot{m}_t > 0$ during $[0, T)$, $\dot{i} < 0$ during the same time frame. The path of f_t/m_t, depicted in panel d, follows from equation (15.20) and the path of i_t illustrated in panel c.

6. Notice that the stationary value of m_t goes up at time T, so that between 0 and T the differential equation is governed by the law of motion corresponding to $m(\alpha^L)$, while for T onward it is governed by the law of motion corresponding to $m(\alpha^H)$.

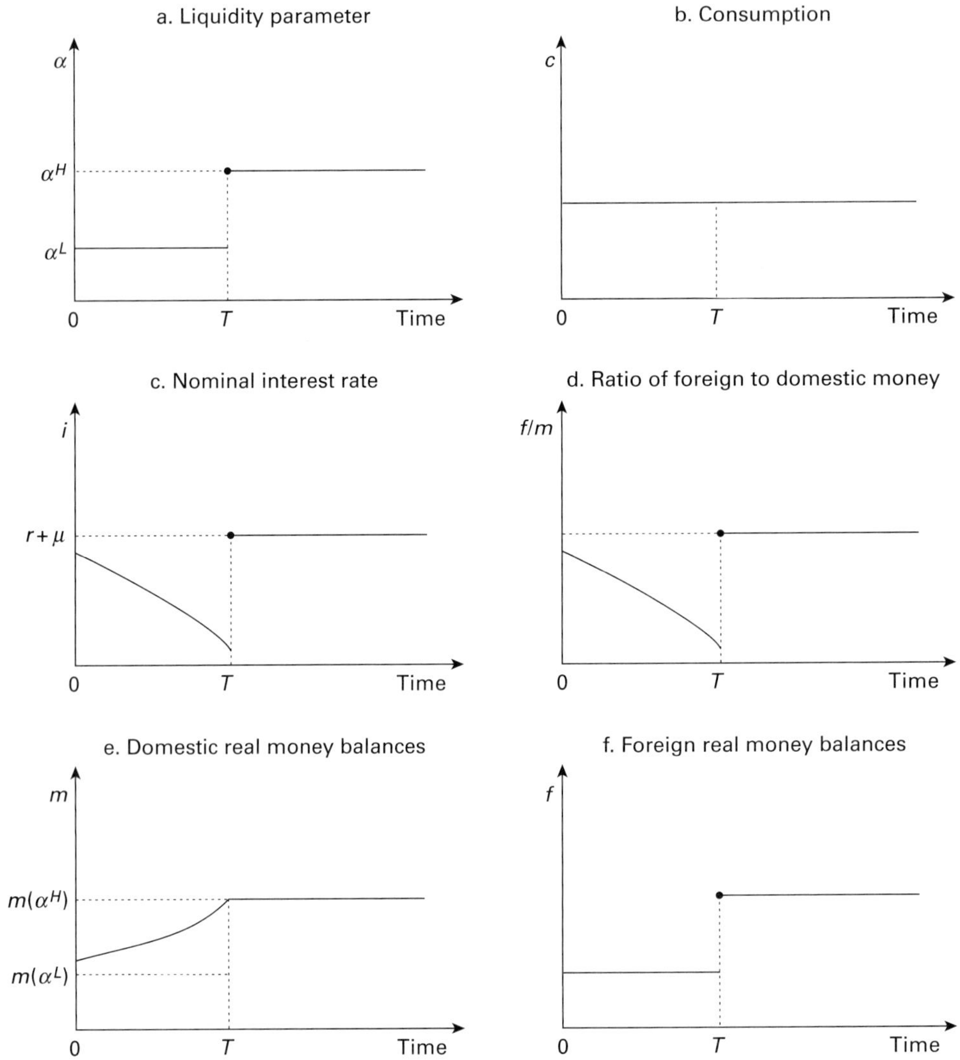

Figure 15.6
Positive money demand shock under flexible exchange rates

Comparison

A comparison of figures 15.5 and 15.6 makes clear how differently the monetary variables adjust under predetermined and flexible exchange rates. Under flexible exchange rates the nominal interest rate falls in anticipation of the liquidity shock at time T, which reduces the economy's dollarization before time T. At time T both the nominal interest rate and hence foreign real balances jump up. In sharp contrast, the ratio of foreign to domestic money is completely flat under predetermined exchange rates. Hence, based on this model and in response to liquidity shocks, we would expect more fluctuations in the currency substitution ratio under flexible than under predetermined exchange rates.

As exercise 2 at the end of the chapter illustrates, the same results hold even if the shock has real effects. In fact, while the mechanics are identical (i.e., the response of m_t and f_t is identical to the case just analyzed), we can reinterpret this case as follows. Suppose that a preference shock at time T increases consumption along a PFEP. This increases demand for both domestic and foreign money. Under predetermined exchange rates, consumers are indeed able to increase their holdings of both currencies at time T without a change in the f_t/m_t ratio. Under flexible exchange rates, however, the increase in demand for m_t at time T leads to an increase in the nominal interest rate because m_t cannot change. Real domestic balances will in fact have to rise gradually before time T, which implies that the currency substitution ratio, f_t/m_t, will fall between time 0 and time T and then jump up at time T.

In sum, our simple model suggests that in response to both liquidity and real shocks, we expect the currency substitution ratio to vary more under flexible exchange rates than under predetermined exchange rates.

15.3 Monetary Expansion and the Real Exchange Rate

As mentioned in the introduction, a classic question in the currency substitution literature (and the issue that put the currency substitution literature on the map) is: How does a monetary expansion affect the real exchange rate under flexible exchange rates? There has in fact been some controversy surrounding the answer to this question in the literature. To illustrate the controversy, we present a model with no bonds (à la chapter 6) that delivers the Liviatan result (a monetary expansion leads to a real appreciation) and then a slightly different version of the model that delivers the Calvo–Rodriguez result (a monetary expansion leads to a real depreciation). We will follow with a general model that clarifies the "deep" parameters that affect this channel.

15.3.1 A Liviatan-Type Model

We add nontradable goods to the currency substitution model developed in chapter 6, section 6.5, in which domestic and foreign currency are demanded in fixed proportions. (We will assume that $P_t^* = 1$ and hence that foreign inflation is zero.) Preferences now take the form

$$\int_0^{\infty} [\log(c_t^T) + \log(c_t^N) + \log(x_t)] \exp(-\beta t) dt, \tag{15.21}$$

where c_t^T and c_t^N denote consumption of tradable and nontradable goods, respectively, and x_t is a liquidity variable such that

$$qx_t = f_t, \tag{15.22}$$

$$(1-q)x_t = m_t, \tag{15.23}$$

where $0 \leq q < 1$ and m_t and f_t denote real domestic and foreign currency, respectively. (All real variables are defined in terms of tradable goods.) One could therefore think of x_t as a composite of domestic and foreign currency. Notice that if $q = 0$, the model reduces to the one in chapter 6, section 6.2 (with nontradable goods, of course).

Let a_t denote real financial wealth, defined as

$$a_t \equiv m_t + f_t. \tag{15.24}$$

The consumer's flow constraint is now given by

$$\dot{a}_t = y^T + \frac{y^N}{e_t} + \tau_t - c_t^T - \frac{c_t^N}{e_t} - \varepsilon_t m_t, \tag{15.25}$$

where y^T and y^N denote the constant endowments of tradables and nontradables, respectively, and e_t denotes the real exchange rate (defined as the relative price of tradable goods in terms of nontradable goods).[7]

Before proceeding to the consumer's maximization, it will prove convenient to express the flow constraint in terms of x_t. To this end, use (15.22), (15.23), and (15.24) to rewrite the flow constraint (15.25) as

$$\dot{x}_t = y^T + \frac{y^N}{e_t} + \tau_t - c_t^T - \frac{c_t^N}{e_t} - (1-q)\varepsilon_t x_t. \tag{15.26}$$

Intuitively, notice that the opportunity cost of holding the composite currency, x_t, is $(1-q)\varepsilon_t$ as we should have expected.

We can now write the current value Hamiltonian as

$$H \equiv \log(c_t^T) + \log(c_t^N) + \log(x_t) + \lambda_t \left[y^T + \frac{y^N}{e_t} + \tau_t - c_t^T - \frac{c_t^N}{e_t} - (1-q)\varepsilon_t x_t \right].$$

7. If foreign inflation were not zero, there would be a term $-\pi_t^* f_t$ on the RHS of equation (15.25).

The optimality conditions are given by

$$\frac{1}{c_t^T} = \lambda_t, \tag{15.27}$$

$$\frac{1}{c_t^N} = \frac{\lambda_t}{e_t}, \tag{15.28}$$

$$\dot{\lambda}_t = \beta\lambda_t - \frac{\partial H}{\partial x_t} = \lambda_t\left[\beta + (1-q)\varepsilon_t\right] - \frac{1}{x_t}. \tag{15.29}$$

For further reference, notice that by combining (15.27) and (15.28), we obtain

$$e_t = \frac{c_t^N}{c_t^T}. \tag{15.30}$$

Government

Since the economy is operating under flexible exchange rates, we will assume that the government holds no international reserves. The government's flow constraint thus becomes

$$\tau_t = \frac{\dot{M}_t}{E_t}. \tag{15.31}$$

As usual, under flexible exchange rates the monetary authority will set the path of the nominal money supply.

Equilibrium Conditions

Equilibrium in the nontradable goods market requires that

$$c_t^N = y^N. \tag{15.32}$$

Substituting the government's flow constraint (15.31) into the consumer's flow constraint (15.25)—and taking into account (15.32)—we obtain the economy's flow constraint:

$$\dot{f}_t = y^T - c_t^T. \tag{15.33}$$

This equation says that in order for the private sector to accumulate foreign currency, it must run a trade surplus.

Dynamic System

To solve the model, we will set up a dynamic system in c_t^T and x_t for a constant value of money growth, μ. To this end, differentiate first-order condition (15.27) and use (15.29) and (15.27) to obtain

$$\dot{c}_t^T = c_t^T \left[\frac{c_t^T}{x_t} - \beta - (1-q)\varepsilon_t \right]. \tag{15.34}$$

Since $(1-q)x_t = m_t$ and $\dot{m}_t/m_t = \mu - \varepsilon_t$, it follows that

$$\varepsilon_t = \mu - \frac{\dot{x}_t}{x_t}. \tag{15.35}$$

Using equation (15.33) and the fact that $qx_t = f_t$ we can rewrite this last equation as

$$\varepsilon_t = \mu - \frac{y^T - c_t^T}{qx_t}.$$

Substituting this equation into (15.34) and assuming—to simplify the dynamic system—that $q = 1/2$, we obtain

$$\dot{c}_t^T = c_t^T \left(\frac{y^T}{x_t} - \beta - \frac{\mu}{2} \right), \tag{15.36}$$

where μ denotes the constant money growth rate set by the monetary authority. Using (15.22), we can rewrite (15.33) as

$$\dot{x}_t = 2(y^T - c_t^T). \tag{15.37}$$

Equations (15.36) and (15.37) constitute a dynamic system in c_t^T and x_t, for a given value of μ. The steady state is given by

$$c_{ss}^T = y^T, \tag{15.38}$$

$$x_{ss} = \frac{y^T}{\beta + \mu/2}. \tag{15.39}$$

The linear approximation of the dynamic system around the steady state is

$$\begin{bmatrix} \dot{c}_t^T \\ \dot{x}_t \end{bmatrix} = \begin{bmatrix} 0 & -\frac{c_{ss}^T y^T}{x_{ss}^2} \\ -2 & 0 \end{bmatrix} \begin{bmatrix} c_t^T - y^T \\ x_t - x_{ss} \end{bmatrix},$$

which implies that since the determinant of the matrix associated with the linear approximation is

$$\Delta = -\frac{2c_{ss}^T y^T}{x_{ss}^2} < 0,$$

the system is saddle-path stable.

We can now draw the phase diagram depicted in figure 15.7. To draw the $\dot{c}_t^T = 0$ and $\dot{x}_t = 0$ loci, set equations (15.36) and (15.37) to zero to obtain, respectively,

$$x_t = \frac{y^T}{\beta + \mu/2},$$

$$c_t^T = y^T.$$

It follows that the $\dot{c}_t^T = 0$ locus is a vertical line while the $\dot{x}_t = 0$ locus is a horizontal line. These two loci define four regions. Proceeding as before, we can establish how the system will move in each of these regions by drawing the arrowheads as indicated. We conclude that as shown in figure 15.7, the saddle path is positively sloped.

Permanent Increase in Rate of Money Growth

Suppose that the economy is initially at the steady state given by point A in figure 15.7. At $t = 0$ there is an unanticipated and permanent increase in the rate of money growth from μ^L to μ^H (figure 15.8, panel a). How will the economy react?

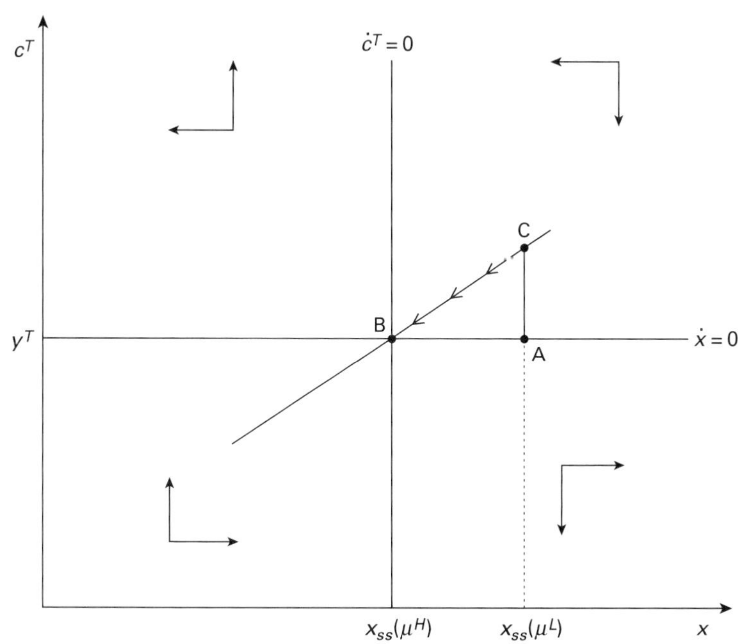

Figure 15.7
Currency substitution model: Phase diagram

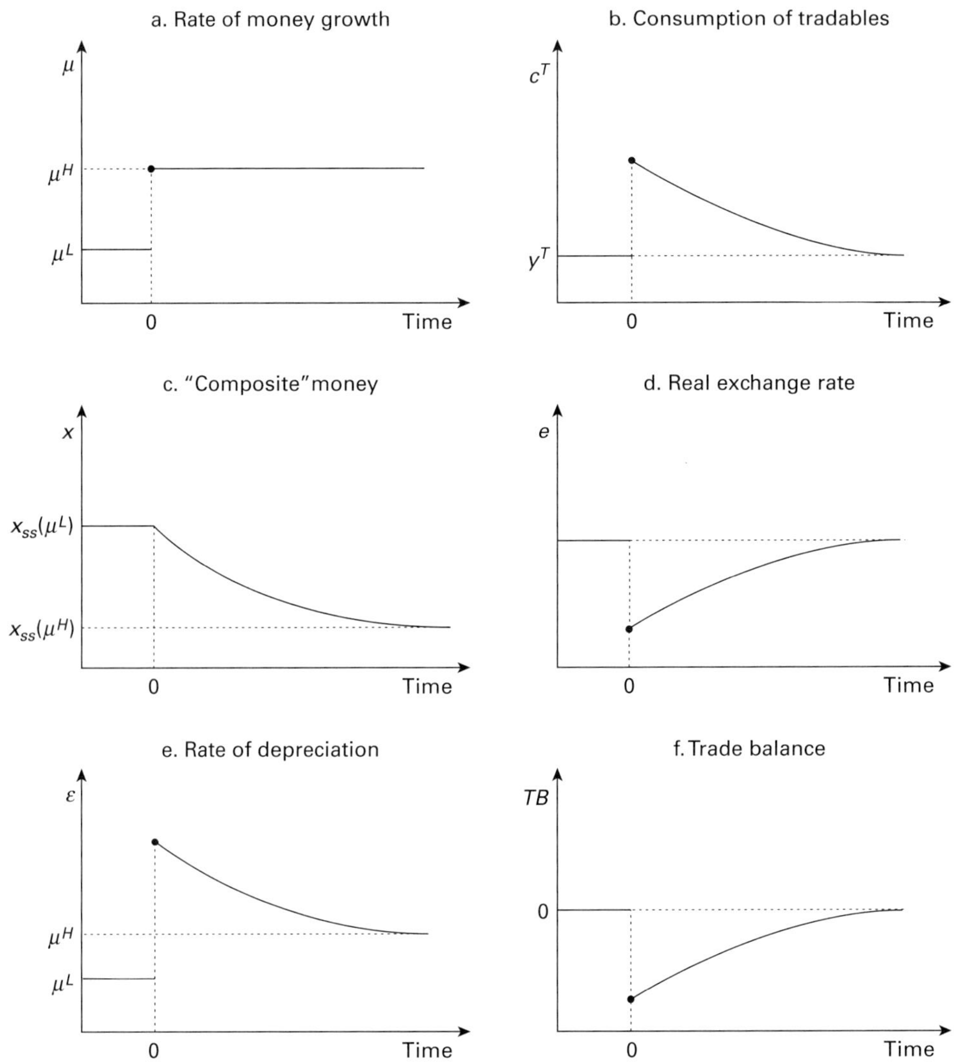

Figure 15.8
Permanent increase in rate of money growth (Liviatan case)

In the new steady state—given by point B in figure 15.7—c_{ss}^T is unchanged but x_{ss} has fallen, as follows from (15.38) and (15.39). The system will therefore jump on impact from point A to point C and then proceed along the saddle path toward point B. The corresponding paths of c_t^T and x_t are depicted in figure 15.8, panels b and c, respectively. Naturally, since m_t and f_t are a fixed proportion of x_t, they will also follow a path qualitatively identical to that of x_t. Since consumption of tradable goods rises on impact, the economy runs a trade deficit throughout the transition (figure 15.8 panel f).

Naturally, consumption of nontradable goods does not change since the endowment of nontradable goods is constant. What will happen to the real exchange rate? From (15.30) and (15.32) it follows that

$$e_t = \frac{y^N}{c_t^T}. \tag{15.40}$$

Hence the real exchange rate mirrors the behavior of c_t^T. It will fall on impact (real appreciation) and then rise over time toward its unchanged steady state (figure 15.8, panel d).

What will happen to the rate of depreciation? Given (15.35), we can write

$$\varepsilon_t = \mu^H - \frac{\dot{x}_t}{x_t} > \mu^H,$$

where the inequality follows from the fact that $\dot{x}_t < 0$ during the transition. Furthermore we know that at the steady state, the rate of devaluation is equal to μ^H. Since the adjustment of all variables is monotonic (because there is only one negative root), we can infer that the rate of depreciation follows the path illustrated in figure 15.8, panel e. We also know that the nominal exchange rate will not jump on impact since x_t and hence m_t do not jump on impact.

What is the intuition behind our results? The increase in the rate of money growth implies a higher opportunity cost of the composite currency (x_t). As a result the public wishes to reduce its holdings of this composite money in the long run. Since this composite money consists of domestic and foreign currency held in fixed proportions, foreign currency holdings must also fall in the long run. To achieve this goal, the economy must run a trade deficit, which requires an increase in the consumption of tradable goods. Given the rise in consumption of tradable goods, at the pre-shock real exchange rate, consumers would wish to increase consumption of nontradable goods as well. The excess demand for nontradable goods leads on impact to a rise in their relative price (i.e., a real appreciation).

Finally, notice that the adjustment mechanism is analogous to that emphasized by the monetary approach to the balance of payments in chapter 6. While under flexible exchange rates the nominal exchange rate can adjust to bring about the desired real holdings of *domestic* currency, it is obviously powerless when it comes to changing holdings of *foreign* currency. Hence changes in foreign currency holdings must take place through trade imbalances, as emphasized by the monetary approach.

15.3.2 A Calvo–Rodriguez Type Model

We now develop a model in which due to the presence of a liquidity-in-advance constraint, there is no substitution between consumption and liquidity services. We will see that under this specification an increase in the rate of monetary expansion will lead to a real depreciation of the domestic currency. (As before, we will assume that the monetary authority sets a constant rate of money growth, μ.) Unless otherwise noted, we continue to use the same notation.

Consumers

Suppose that preferences are given by

$$\int_0^{\infty} [\log(c_t^T) + \log(c_t^N)]\exp(-\beta t)dt. \tag{15.41}$$

Consumers are subject to a liquidity-in-advance constraint whereby consumption must be financed with liquidity services produced by a liquidity function that has as inputs real domestic and foreign money balances:

$$c_t^T + \frac{c_t^N}{e_t} = \alpha v(m_t, f_t). \tag{15.42}$$

The function $v(.)$ is assumed to be increasing in both arguments, concave, and homogeneous of degree one. The flow constraint remains given by (15.25).

In order to set up the current value Hamiltonian, it proves helpful to use $a_t = m_t + f_t$ to get rid of f_t in the liquidity-in-advance constraint. As a result the control variables will be c_t^T, c_t^N, and m_t, while the state variable is a_t. The current value Hamiltonian is thus given by

$$H = \log(c_t^T) + \log(c_t^N) + \lambda_t \left(y^T + \frac{y^N}{e_t} + \tau_t - c_t^T - \frac{c_t^N}{e_t} - \varepsilon_t m_t \right) + \psi_t \left[\alpha v(m_t, a_t - m_t) - \left(c_t^T + \frac{c_t^N}{e_t} \right) \right],$$

where λ_t and ψ_t are the multipliers associated with constraints (15.25) and (15.42), respectively. The first-order conditions are given by

$$\frac{1}{c_t^T} = \lambda_t + \psi_t, \tag{15.43}$$

$$\frac{1}{c_t^N} = \frac{\lambda_t + \psi_t}{e_t}, \tag{15.44}$$

$$-\lambda_t \varepsilon_t + \psi_t \alpha (v_m - v_f) = 0, \tag{15.45}$$

$$\dot{\lambda}_t = \beta \lambda_t - \psi_t \alpha v_f. \tag{15.46}$$

By combining (15.43) and (15.44), we obtain the familiar condition:

$$c_t^T = \frac{c_t^N}{e_t}. \tag{15.47}$$

Since the rest of the model remains unchanged, the government flow constraint (15.31) and the economy's flow constraint (15.33) remain unchanged.

For further reference, notice that we can use (15.47) to rewrite the liquidity-in-advance constraint (15.42) as

$$2c_t^T = \alpha v(m_t, f_t). \tag{15.48}$$

Solution of the Model

This model is not simple to solve because it cannot be reduced to a two differential equation system as above. Fortunately, for the purpose of showing that, on impact, an increase in the rate of monetary expansion leads to a real depreciation of the currency, we can take a short-cut. We will first derive a steady-state relationship involving m_t, f_t, and μ and show that, in the steady state, an increase in μ leads to an increase in f_t and a reduction in m_t. We will then show that to achieve a higher steady-state value of f_t, the economy needs to run a trade surplus, which requires a real depreciation on impact.

To simplify the presentation—and with no loss of generality—assume that $v(m_t, f_t)$ takes the form

$$v(m_t, f_t) = m_t^{\gamma} f_t^{1-\gamma}, \qquad 0 < \gamma < 1. \tag{15.49}$$

If $\dot{\lambda}_t = 0$, then from (15.46) $\beta \lambda_t = \psi_t \alpha v_f$. Substituting this into equation (15.45) and rearranging, we obtain

$$\frac{f_{ss}}{m_{ss}} = \frac{1-\gamma}{\gamma}\left(\frac{\beta + \mu}{\beta}\right), \tag{15.50}$$

where we have used the fact that in the steady state, $\varepsilon_t = \mu$. As expected, the ratio f_{ss}/m_{ss} depends positively on the opportunity cost of holding domestic money (μ).

Using equations (15.42), (15.49), and (15.50), and taking into account that $c_{ss}^T = y^T$, we can derive the steady-state demands for m_t and f_t:

$$m_{ss} = A \frac{y^T}{[(\beta + \mu)/\beta]^{1-\gamma}}, \tag{15.51}$$

$$f_{ss} = By^T\left(\frac{\beta+\mu}{\beta}\right)^{\gamma}, \tag{15.52}$$

where A and B are positive constants given by

$$A \equiv \frac{2}{\alpha[(1-\gamma)/\gamma]^{1-\gamma}} > 0,$$

$$B \equiv \frac{2}{\alpha}\left(\frac{1-\gamma}{\gamma}\right)^{\gamma} > 0.$$

Equations (15.51) and (15.52) thus say that an increase in μ lowers m_{ss} and increases f_{ss}. Intuitively, the higher rate of money growth increases the ratio f_{ss}/m_{ss}. Given that, as follows from (15.48), total liquidity—as measured by $v(m_{ss}, f_{ss})$—will be constant across steady states because c_t^T is constant across steady states, an increase in the ratio f_{ss}/m_{ss} must imply that f_{ss} increases and m_{ss} falls.

Increase in Money Growth Rate

Consider now an unanticipated and permanent increase in the rate of monetary growth, μ. Since the dynamic system has just one state variable, f_t, there will be only one stable root. This implies that after the initial jump, the system will adjust monotonically to its new steady state. Furthermore we know that f_{ss} increases. Hence $\dot{f}_t > 0$ along the transition path (see figure 15.9, panel d). From equation (15.33) it follows that on impact, c_t^T must fall for $\dot{f}_t$ to become positive. It will then gradually rise back to its unchanged steady state (panel b). Since $c_t^N = y^N$ for all t, we infer from the intratemporal condition (15.47) that e_t needs to jump on impact (i.e., a real depreciation of the currency). It will then fall gradually toward its unchanged steady state (panel c).

What happens to m_t? In light of (15.48), and since we have already established that c_t^T falls on impact while f_t does not change, we infer that m_t must fall on impact.[8]

We conclude that an increase in the rate of monetary growth leads to a real depreciation. Intuitively, since total liquidity services are constant across steady states, the increase in money growth leads to a fall in steady-state real domestic money balances and an increase in foreign money balances. To accumulate foreign money balances during the transition, the economy needs to run a trade surplus to "import" this money from abroad, which requires a reduction in the consumption of tradable goods on impact. At the initial real exchange rate, there is thus an excess supply of nontradable goods which calls for a fall in their relative price (a real depreciation).

8. To find out how m_t moves over time, we would need to dig deeper into the solution of the model. But this is not relevant to our main point.

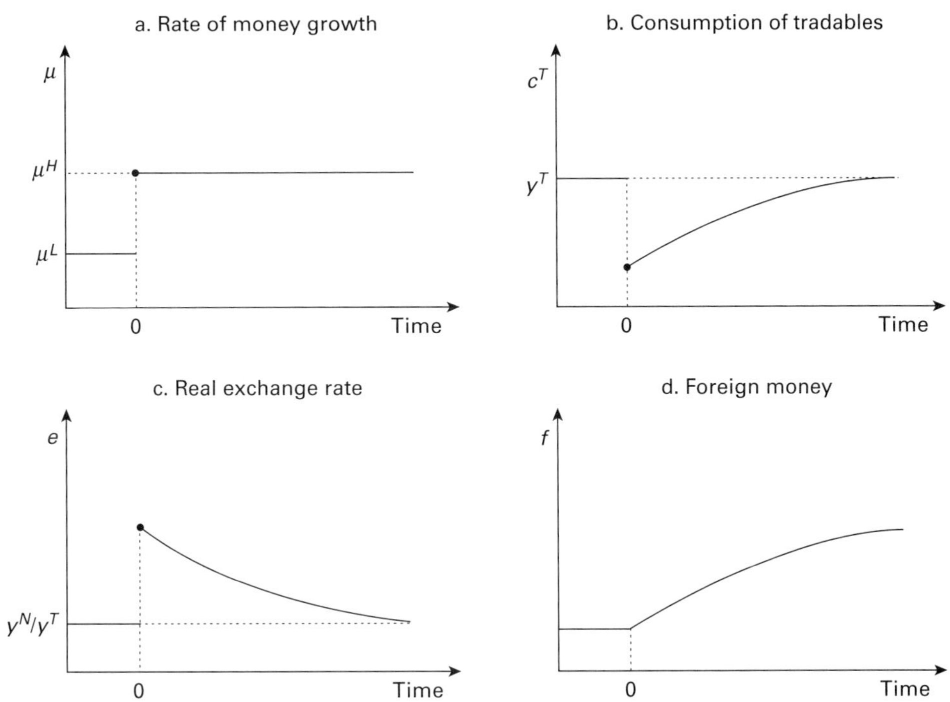

Figure 15.9
Permanent increase in rate of money growth (Calvo–Rodriguez case)

15.3.3 A General Model

Having solved analytically two extreme cases, we will now set up a general model of currency substitution in discrete time that will allow us to focus on the role of the elasticity of substitution between domestic and foreign currency and the elasticity of substitution between consumption and liquidity services. (Unless otherwise noted, we continue to use the same notation.) Since an analytical solution is rather involved, we will solve the model numerically.[9]

Consumers

Let preferences be given by

$$\sum_{t=0}^{\infty} \beta^t \log z(c_t, \ell_t), \tag{15.53}$$

9. See Calvo (1985) for an analytical proof of the main result.

where

$$c \equiv \left(c^T\right)^\alpha \left(c^N\right)^{1-\alpha},$$

$$\ell(m,f) = \left[\gamma\,(m)^{(\rho-1)/\rho} + (1-\gamma)\,(f)^{(\rho-1)/\rho}\right]^{\rho/(\rho-1)},$$

$$z(c,\ell) = \left[\eta\,(c)^{(\sigma-1)/\sigma} + (1-\eta)\,(\ell)^{(\sigma-1)/\sigma}\right]^{\sigma/(\sigma-1)}.$$

Preferences are defined over a consumption composite, c_t, which takes a Cobb–Douglas form, and a liquidity composite, ℓ_t, which takes a CES specification. The parameter $\rho(>0)$ captures the elasticity of substitution between domestic (m_t) and foreign currency balances (f_t). The parameter $\sigma(>0)$ denotes the elasticity of substitution between the consumption composite and liquidity services. To simplify—and since it is of no relevance for our purposes—we have implicitly assumed that the intertemporal elasticity of substitution is one by positing logarithmic preferences over time.

Conceptually, the two models studied in sections 15.3.1 and 15.3.2 may be thought of as particular cases of this general model: in the Liviatan model there is no substitution between domestic and foreign currency (i.e., $\rho = 0$) and in the Calvo–Rodriguez model—due to the liquidity-in-advance specification—the elasticity of substitution between consumption and liquidity services is zero (i.e., $\sigma = 0$).

The flow constraint in nominal terms is given by

$$M_t + E_tF_t = M_{t-1} + E_tF_{t-1} + E_ty^T + P_t^Ny^N - E_tc_t^T - P_t^Nc_t^N + E_t\tau_t. \tag{15.54}$$

Assume that $P_t^* = 1$ for all t and define $f_t \equiv F_t/P_t^* = F_t$ and $m_t \equiv M_t/E_t$. In real terms, the constraint (15.54) then becomes

$$m_t + f_t = \frac{m_{t-1}}{1+\varepsilon_{t-1}} + f_{t-1} + y^T + \frac{y^N}{e_t} - c_t^T - \frac{c_t^N}{e_t} + \tau_t, \tag{15.55}$$

where

$$\varepsilon_{t-1} \equiv \frac{E_t}{E_{t-1}} - 1.$$

Denote by λ_t the multiplier associated with constraint (15.55). The first-order conditions imply that

$$\frac{\alpha}{1-\alpha}\frac{c_t^N}{c_t^T} = e_t, \tag{15.56}$$

$$\frac{1}{z_t} z_\ell \ell_t^{1/\rho} \gamma m_t^{-1/\rho} = \lambda_t - \beta \lambda_{t+1} \frac{1}{1+\varepsilon_t}, \tag{15.57}$$

$$\frac{1}{z_t} z_\ell \ell_t^{1/\rho} (1-\gamma) f_t^{-1/\rho} = \lambda_t - \beta \lambda_{t+1}. \tag{15.58}$$

Let us focus on the steady state. Using (15.57) and (15.58), we obtain

$$\frac{\gamma}{1-\gamma} \left(\frac{f_{ss}}{m_{ss}} \right)^{1/\rho} = \frac{1 - \beta/(1+\varepsilon_{ss})}{1-\beta},$$

which is the typical portfolio equation in currency substitution models. This expression tells us that, in response to an increase in the rate of money growth (which increases ε_{ss}), the steady-state ratio f/m will increase.

We will now look at three different cases:

1. Benchmark case: $\sigma = \rho$.
2. Liviatan case: $\sigma > \rho$.
3. Calvo–Rodriguez case: $\sigma < \rho$.

Benchmark Case Suppose $\sigma = \rho$.[10] Consider an unanticipated and permanent increase in μ_t. Figure 15.10 illustrates the economy's adjustment.[11] Since steady-state foreign money balances do not change, there is no need for the economy to run a trade imbalance. The economy can therefore adjust instantaneously. To satisfy the higher f_{ss}/m_{ss} ratio (panel b), m_{ss} falls instantaneously through an increase in the nominal exchange rate (panel d).[12]

Liviatan Case Suppose $\sigma > \rho$.[13] In other words, the elasticity of substitution between consumption and liquidity services is higher than the elasticity of substitution between domestic and foreign currency. In this case, as illustrated in figure 15.11, steady-state demand for foreign money balances falls (panel c) in response to the increase in the opportunity cost of holding domestic money. Put differently, the liquidity effect (which calls for lower f_{ss}) dominates the currency substitution effect (which calls for higher f_{ss}). To lower foreign money balances over time, the economy needs to run a trade deficit. Consumption of tradables thus jumps on impact (panel e). At the pre-shock level of the real exchange rate, there is thus an excess demand for nontradable

10. We set $\sigma = \rho = 0.5$.

11. The parameterization is as follows: $r = 0.1$, $\alpha = \eta = \gamma = 0.5$, $y^T = y^N = 1$, $\mu = 0.1$. As in chapters 13 and 14, we solve the model by using the King–Plosser–Rebelo linearization method. Plots in figures 15.10 to 15.12 show percentage deviations from the initial steady state.

12. Exercise 3 at the end of the chapter asks you to show analytically that the economy will adjust instantaneously and that, in the case $\sigma = \rho = 1$, preferences simplify to the separable case.

13. We set $\sigma = 0.9$ and $\rho = 0.5$.

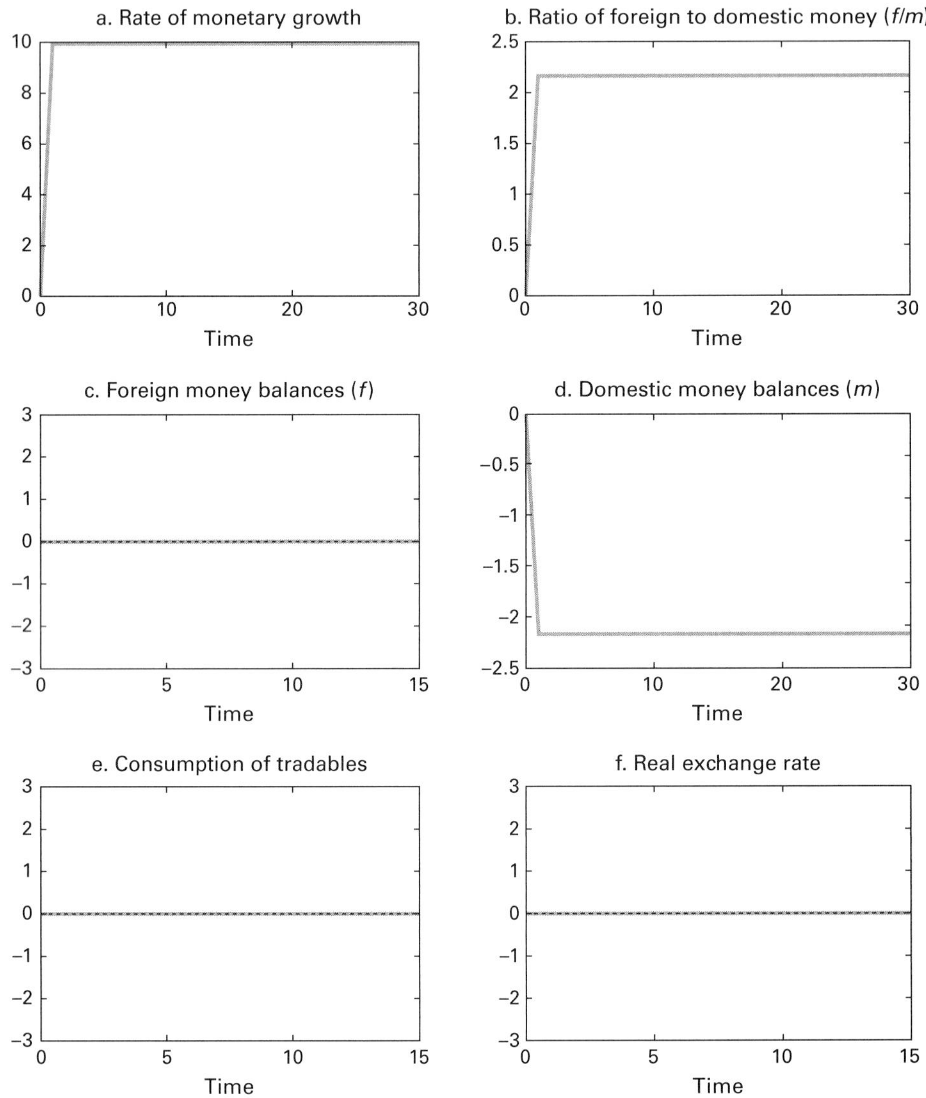

Figure 15.10
Increase in rate of monetary growth in currency substitution model (benchmark)

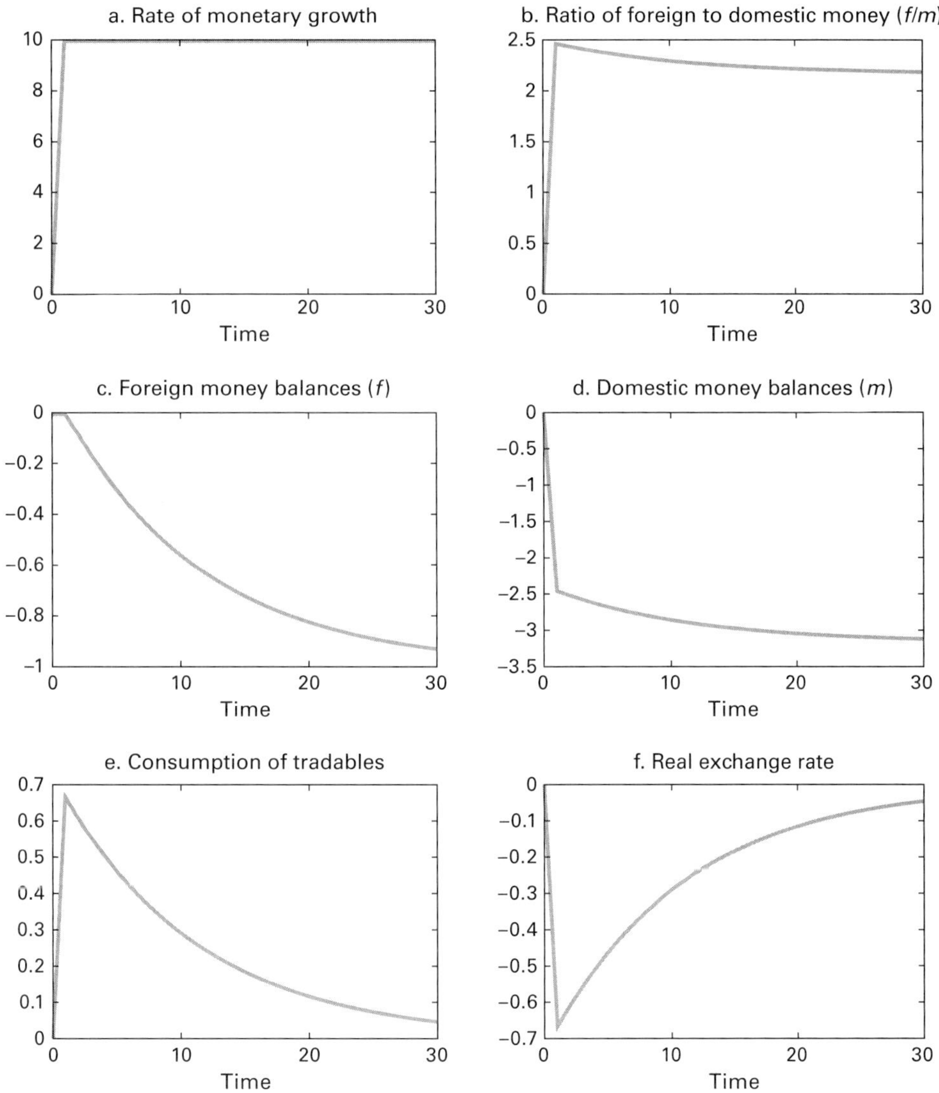

Figure 15.11
Increase in rate of monetary growth in currency substitution model (Liviatan case)

goods. This calls for an increase in the relative price of nontradable goods (real appreciation), as illustrated in panel f.

Calvo–Rodriguez Case Suppose $\sigma < \rho$.[14] In this case, as illustrated in figure 15.12, steady-state demand for foreign money balances increases in response to the increase in μ_t (panel c). Consumption of tradable goods must therefore fall in order for the economy to accumulate foreign money balances over time (panel e). At the pre-shock level of the real exchange rate, there would be an excess supply of nontradable goods. Hence the relative price must fall (real depreciation), as illustrated in panel f.

The estimates provided by Bufman and Leiderman (1993) for the case of Israel suggest that the parameter σ is in the range 0.1 to 0.3 while the parameter ρ is in the range 1.3 to 3.6. In fact for every estimation, $\rho > \sigma$. Hence the available evidence suggests that the Calvo–Rodriguez case is the relevant one in practice.

15.4 Hysteresis

Traditional models of currency substitution, such as those reviewed up to this point, would predict that the ratio of foreign to domestic money should fall in the aftermath of a successful disinflation. In principle—and leaving aside for the moment measurement problems—this is not what the data seem to suggest. We have already observed in figure 15.2 that foreign currency deposits as a proportion of broad money—the traditional measure of dollarization—have not fallen substantially in many countries in response to a drastic reduction in inflation. A more encompassing measure of dollarization, computed in Reinhart, Rogoff, and Savastano (2003), conveys a similar message. Indeed, as illustrated in figure 15.13, we see that the dollarization indexes before and after disinflation roughly lie along the 45 degree line.[15] This so-called "hysteresis" has been viewed as a puzzle in search of an explanation. We present here a simplified version of a model due to Guidotti and Rodriguez (1992) that provides an explanation for this puzzle.[16]

15.4.1 A Simple Model

Consider a small open economy perfectly integrated in world goods and capital markets. There is a single (tradable) good. The endowment of the good is constant and equal to y. We assume that the economy is operating under a predetermined exchange rate regime with a constant rate of devaluation, ε. The foreign nominal interest rate is also assumed to be constant over time at i^*. (Unless otherwise noted, we continue to use the same notation.)

14. We set $\sigma = 0.5$ and $\rho = 0.9$.

15. This composite dollarization index comprises (1) foreign currency deposits as a proportion of broad money, (2) total external debt in foreign currency as a share of GNP, and (3) domestic government debt denominated in (or linked to) a foreign currency as a share of total government debt. Figure 15.13 shows data for 17 emerging countries (see Reinhart, Rogoff, and Savastano 2003 for details.)

16. Uribe (1997) provides a related explanation.

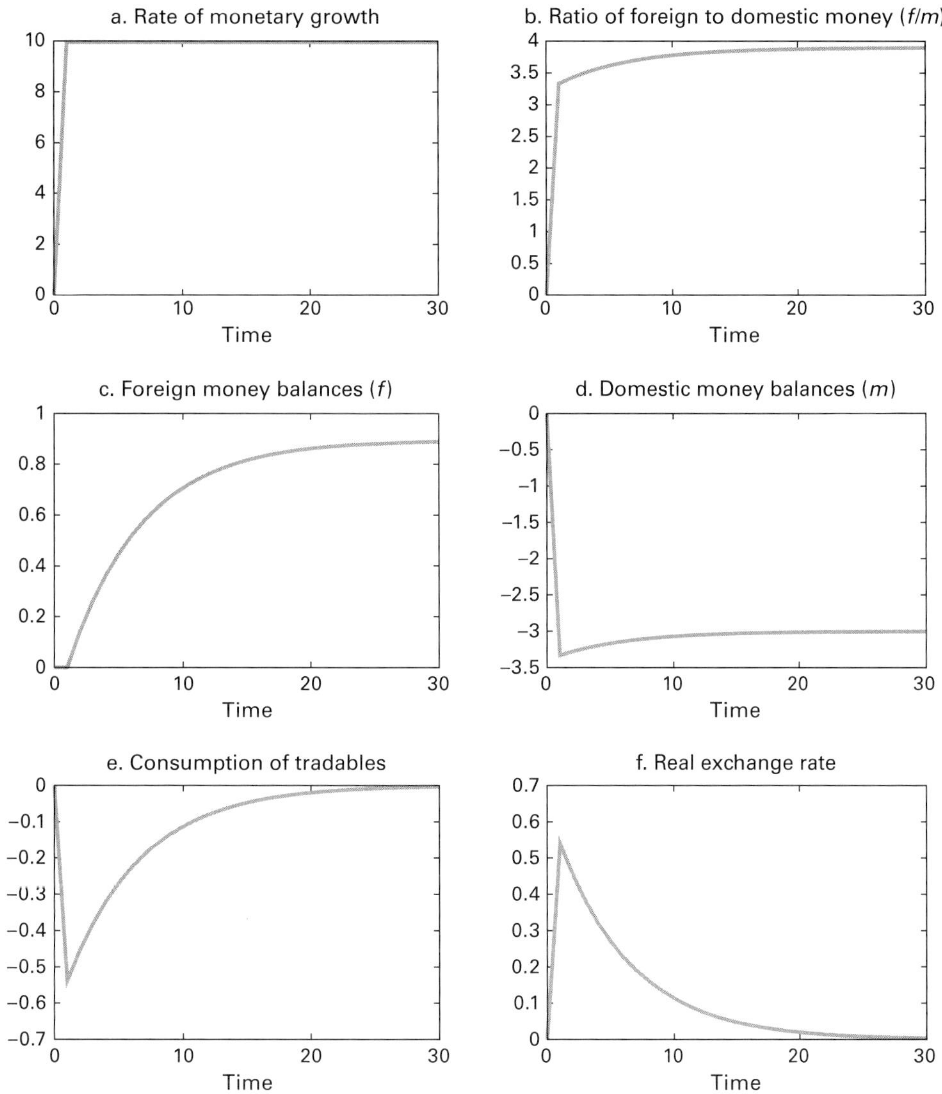

Figure 15.12
Increase in rate of monetary growth in currency substitution model (Calvo–Rodriguez case)

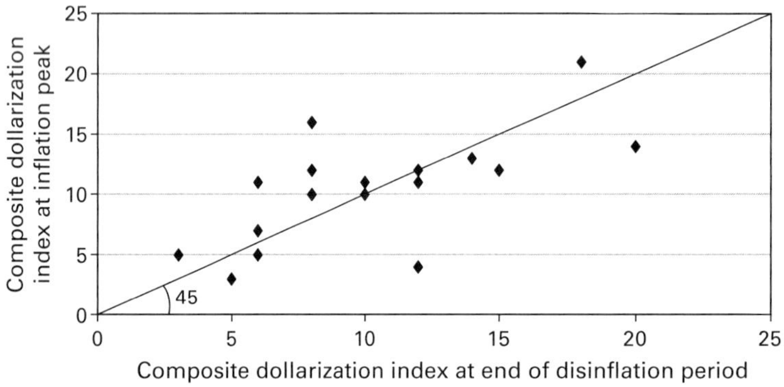

Figure 15.13
Hysteresis in dollarization

Preferences are given by

$$\int_0^\infty u(c_t)\exp(-\beta t)dt, \tag{15.59}$$

where c_t denotes consumption. We will assume that a fraction of total consumption (c_t^m) is subject to a domestic cash-in-advance constraint while the remaining portion (c_t^f), which can be zero, is subject to a foreign cash-in-advance constraint:

$$m_t = \alpha c_t^m, \tag{15.60}$$

$$f_t = \alpha c_t^f, \tag{15.61}$$

$$c_t = c_t^m + c_t^f,$$

where α is a positive parameter. The key feature of the model is that consumers may choose the currency in which purchases are denominated. For simplicity, we will assume that c_t^f can take only two values:

$$c_t^f = \begin{cases} 0, \\ \gamma c_t. \end{cases} \tag{15.62}$$

In other words, consumers must choose between (1) not using foreign currency at all, or (2) using the amount that finances a fraction γ of total consumption.[17] We will assume that, at $t = 0$, con-

17. This choice can be made continuous along the lines of Guidotti and Rodriguez (1992), but at the cost of increased technical difficulty. The model's punchline remains exactly the same.

sumers must decide whether to "dollarize" (which, in this model, will be defined as switching the currency of denomination of a fraction γ of their consumption) or not. If they choose to dollarize, they must pay a cost ϕ per unit of consumption whose currency of denomination they choose to change.

To solve this problem, we will proceed by having the consumer choose optimal consumption in the nondollarized case and the dollarized case and then compare which one gives him/her the higher level of utility. Let c^{nd} and c^{d} denote total consumption for the nondollarized and dollarized cases, respectively. Total cost of dollarizing is thus[18]

$$\Phi = \phi\gamma c^{nd}. \tag{15.63}$$

Nondollarized Case

If they choose not to dollarize (i.e., $c_t^f = 0$), consumers face the following intertemporal constraint (where we have already imposed our usual assumption $r = \beta$):

$$\frac{y}{r} + \int_0^\infty \tau_t \exp(-\beta t)dt = \int_0^\infty \left(c_t^m + i_t m_t\right)\exp(-\beta t)dt,$$

which, using (15.60) and noting that $c_t^{nd} = c_t^m$, can be rewritten as

$$\frac{y}{r} + \int_0^\infty \tau_t \exp(-\beta t)dt = \int_0^\infty c_t^{nd}(1 + \alpha i_t)\exp(-\beta t)dt. \tag{15.64}$$

The consumer chooses c_t^{nd} to maximize (15.59) subject to (15.64). In terms of the Lagrangian,

$$\mathcal{L} = \int_0^\infty u(c_t^{nd}) \exp(-\beta t)dt + \lambda \left\{ \frac{y}{r} + \int_0^\infty \tau_t \exp(-\beta t)dt - \int_0^\infty c_t^{nd}(1 + \alpha i_t)\exp(-\beta t)dt \right\}.$$

This problem yields the familiar first-order condition:

$$u'(c_t^{nd}) = \lambda(1 + \alpha i_t).$$

Since, in equilibrium, the nominal interest rate will be constant by interest parity ($i = i^* + \varepsilon$), consumption will be constant time over time at a level c^{nd}. From (15.64) it then follows that

$$c^{nd} = \frac{y + r\int_0^\infty \tau_t \exp(-\beta t)dt}{1 + \alpha i}. \tag{15.65}$$

18. We could have assumed that $\Phi = \phi\gamma c^{d}$. This would have complicated the presentation without adding new insights. We will also assume that the rest of the world rebates back to this economy the inflation tax paid on the holdings of foreign currency, which implies that transfers from the government to consumers will be the same in either case.

Dollarized Case

The intertemporal constraint faced by consumers if they decide to dollarize is given by

$$\frac{y}{r}+\int_0^{\infty}\tau_t\exp(-\beta t)dt-\Phi=\int_0^{\infty}\left(c_t^m+c_t^f+i_tm_t+i^*f_t\right)\exp(-\beta t)dt, \tag{15.66}$$

where Φ, given by (15.63), is the fixed cost of dollarizing. Using (15.60) and (15.61), we can rewrite (15.66) as

$$\frac{y}{r}+\int_0^{\infty}\tau_t\exp(-\beta t)dt-\Phi=\int_0^{\infty}\left[c_t^m(1+\alpha i_t)+c_t^f(1+\alpha i^*)\right]\exp(-\beta t)dt.$$

This expression can be further simplified by using the fact that $c_t^d=c_t^m+c_t^f$ to obtain

$$\frac{y}{r}+\int_0^{\infty}\tau_t\exp(-\beta t)dt-\Phi=\int_0^{\infty}c_t^d\left\{1+\alpha[(1-\gamma)i_t+\gamma i^*]\right\}\exp(-\beta t)dt. \tag{15.67}$$

Intuitively, since the consumer uses a fraction $1-\gamma$ of domestic money and γ of foreign money, the effective price of a unit of consumption is $1+\alpha[(1-\gamma)i_t+\gamma i^*]$

The consumer chooses $\{c_t^d\}$ to maximize (15.59) subject to (15.67). In terms of the Lagrangian,

$$\begin{aligned}\mathcal{L}=&\int_0^{\infty}u(c_t^d)\exp(-\beta t)dt\\&+\lambda\left\{\frac{y}{r}+\int_0^{\infty}\tau_t\exp(-\beta t)dt-\Phi-\int_0^{\infty}c_t^d\left\{1+\alpha[(1-\gamma)i_t+\gamma i^*]\right\}\exp(-\beta t)dt\right\},\end{aligned}$$

where $c_t^d=c_t^m+c_t^f$. The first-order condition for c_t^d is given by

$$u'(c_t^d)=\lambda\left\{1+\alpha[(1-\gamma)i_t+\gamma i^*]\right\}.$$

Since, by interest parity the effective price of consumption is constant over time at the level $1+\alpha[(1-\gamma)i+\gamma i^*]$, consumption will also be constant over time at the level c^d. Hence it follows from (15.67) that

$$c^d=\frac{y+r\int_0^{\infty}\tau_t\exp(-\beta t)dt-r\Phi}{1+\alpha[(1-\gamma)i+\gamma i^*]}. \tag{15.68}$$

To Dollarize or Not to Dollarize?

The consumer will choose to dollarize if the constant level of consumption in the dollarized case is higher than in the nondollarized case:

$$c^d\geq c^{nd}.$$

Using (15.65) and (15.68), we can rewrite this condition as

$$\frac{y + r\int_0^\infty \tau_t \exp(-\beta t)dt - r\Phi}{1 + \alpha[(1-\gamma)i + \gamma i^*]} \geq \frac{y + r\int_0^\infty \tau_t \exp(-\beta t)dt}{1 + \alpha i}.$$

From (15.63) this condition reduces to

$$\frac{\alpha(i - i^*)}{r} \geq \phi. \tag{15.69}$$

Intuitively, consider the case where $i - i^* > 0$ and think about the decision of whether to dollarize. For each unit of consumption for which foreign currency is used, the flow saving amounts to $\alpha(i - i^*)$, which has a present discounted value of $\alpha(i - i^*)/r$. The cost per unit of consumption is ϕ. Hence consumers will choose to dollarize if the present discounted value of the per-unit saving is greater than the per-unit cost of doing so. All else equal, the higher is $i - i^*$, the more likely that condition (15.69) will hold and that the consumer will choose to dollarize.

A critical feature of condition (15.69) is that $i - i^*$ being positive is a *necessary* but not *sufficient* condition for dollarization to occur. As illustrated in figure 15.14, the nominal interest rate differential needs to be large enough to offset the cost of dollarization. To fix ideas, consider values of $i - i^* \geq 0$. For all values of $i - i^*$ lower than $r\phi/\alpha$, the economy remains nondollarized.

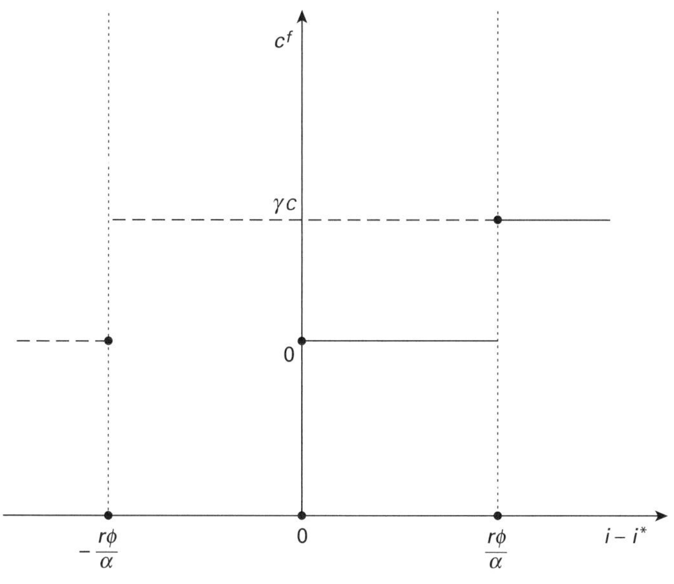

Figure 15.14
Hysteresis model: Inaction band

It is only if $i - i^*$ reaches the value $r\phi/\alpha$ that the economy becomes dollarized (i.e., a fraction γ of total consumption is carried out in dollars).

15.4.2 De-dollarization and Hysteresis

Suppose that just before time 0 the economy is in the dollarized equilibrium described above. At $t = 0$ there is an unanticipated and permanent reduction in ε. By interest parity, the nominal interest rate falls as well. Will consumers choose to de-dollarize? To answer this question, we need to go through the same analysis as above with the only difference that now the fixed cost applies to the de-dollarization process and is given by

$$\Phi = \phi\gamma c^d. \tag{15.70}$$

Proceeding in such a way, it is easy to show that consumers will choose to de-dollarize if

$$\frac{y + r\int_0^\infty \tau_t \exp(-\beta t)dt - r\Phi}{1 + \alpha i} \geq \frac{y + r\int_0^\infty \tau_t \exp(-\beta t)dt}{1 + \alpha[(1-\gamma)i + \gamma i^*]}.$$

Using (15.70), we can simplify this condition to

$$\frac{\alpha(i^* - i)}{r} \geq \phi.$$

This is saying that for de-dollarization to take place, the domestic nominal interest rate would need not only to decrease but to actually fall *below* the foreign nominal interest rate by a margin large enough that it compensates consumers for the fixed cost of de-dollarizing the economy. In terms of figure 15.14, the dashed line indicates that the economy would remain dollarized even if i falls below i^* and would only de-dollarize if the interest rate differential, $i - i^*$, turned negative and in fact reached $-r\phi/\alpha$. This model would thus predict hysteresis in the sense that the economy would remain dollarized even if domestic inflation and hence domestic nominal interest rates fall.

15.5 Monetary Policy and Currency Substitution

It is often argued that monetary policy loses some of its ability to anchor nominal variables in a highly dollarized economy. To illustrate this point theoretically, we develop a version of Kareken and Wallace's (1981) celebrated article on exchange rate indeterminacy. We will resort to the simple cash-in-advance model developed in chapter 7 and assume that domestic and foreign money are perfect substitutes in satisfying some of the required liquidity services.

Consider then a small open economy perfectly integrated into world goods and capital markets. There is only one (nonstorable and tradable) good. The foreign nominal interest rate is assumed to be constant at the level i^*. The economy operates under flexible exchange rates. Unless otherwise noted, the notation remains the same.

15.5.1 Consumers

Let preferences be given by

$$\int_0^\infty u(c_t)\exp(-\beta t)dt. \tag{15.71}$$

In the spirit of our previous model, we will require that a fraction $1-\gamma$ of consumption be purchased with domestic money. The remaining consumption (i.e, a fraction γ) can be purchased with either domestic or foreign money:[19]

$$m_t^e = \alpha\,(1-\gamma)\,c_t, \tag{15.72}$$

$$m_t^n + f_t = \alpha\gamma c_t, \tag{15.73}$$

$$m_t^e + m_t^n = m_t, \tag{15.74}$$

where m_t^e denotes "essential" real money balances and m_t^n nonessential ones. Notice that unlike our previous model, there are no costs associated with switching from domestic to foreign money or viceversa. In other words, both monies are fully substitutable when it comes to spending on a fraction γ of total consumption. Since, in principle, consumers could choose not to use any foreign currency or set $m_t^n = 0$, we need to impose the following nonnegativity constraints:

$$m_t^n \geq 0, \tag{15.75}$$

$$f_t \geq 0. \tag{15.76}$$

Let total real financial assets be given by

$$a_t \equiv b_t + m_t + f_t,$$

where b_t denotes net foreign assets.

The consumer's intertemporal constraint remains given by (15.3). Using (15.74), we can write it as

19. As usual, we assume that because of positive nominal interest rates, the cash-in-advance constraints will hold with equality at an optimum.

$$a_0 + \frac{y}{r} + \int_0^\infty \tau_t \exp(-rt)dt = \int_0^\infty \left[c_t + i_t\left(m_t^e + m_t^n\right) + i^* f_t\right]\exp(-rt)dt. \tag{15.77}$$

The representative consumer chooses $\{c_t, m_t^e, m_t^n, f_t\}$ to maximize (15.71) subject to (15.72), (15.73), (15.75), (15.76) and (15.77). In terms of the Lagrangian,

$$\begin{aligned}\mathcal{L} = &\int_0^\infty u(c_t)\exp(-\beta t)dt \\ &+ \lambda\left[a_0 + \frac{y}{r} + \int_0^\infty \tau_t \exp(-rt)dt - \int_0^\infty \left[c_t + i_t\left(m_t^e + m_t^n\right) + i^* f_t\right]\exp(-rt)dt\right] \\ &+ \int_0^\infty \phi_t\left[m_t^e - \alpha(1-\gamma)c_t\right]\exp(-rt)dt + \int_0^\infty \theta_t(m_t^n + f_t - \alpha\gamma c_t)\exp(-rt)dt.\end{aligned}$$

The first-order conditions are given by (assuming $\beta = r$)

$$u'(c_t) = \lambda + \phi_t\alpha(1-\gamma) + \theta_t\alpha\gamma, \tag{15.78}$$

$$-\lambda i_t + \phi_t = 0, \tag{15.79}$$

$$-\lambda i_t + \theta_t \leq 0, \qquad m_t^n \geq 0, \qquad m_t^n(\theta_t - \lambda i_t) = 0, \tag{15.80}$$

$$-\lambda i^* + \theta_t \leq 0, \qquad f_t \geq 0, \qquad f_t\left(\theta_t - \lambda i^*\right) = 0.$$

For further reference, notice that it is not possible for both $-\lambda i_t + \theta_t < 0$ and $-\lambda i^* + \theta_t < 0$ to hold at the same time. If this were the case, it would imply that $m_t^n = f_t = 0$, which would violate the cash-in-advance constraint (15.73). Hence at least one of the two must hold as an equality.

We now discuss the three cases that may arise. Since the economy is operating under flexible exchange rates, the domestic nominal interest rate is an endogenous variable. We will proceed by assuming a value of i_t relative to i^*, solve for the consumer's problem, and then verify that our initial assumption for i_t is consistent with equilibrium.

15.5.2 Equilibrium with Domestic Currency Only

Suppose that $i_t < i^*$. Since either $(\theta_t - \lambda i_t)$ or $(\theta_t - \lambda i^*)$ must be zero, the fact that $i_t < i^*$ implies that $\theta_t - \lambda i_t = 0$ and $\theta_t - \lambda i^* < 0$. Hence $m_t^n > 0$ and $f_t = 0$. Further $m_t^n = \alpha\gamma c_t$. Using (15.72) and (15.74), we obtain

$$m_t = \alpha c_t. \tag{15.81}$$

Further, since $\phi_t = \theta_t = \lambda i_t$, we can rewrite (15.78) as

$$u'(c_t) = \lambda(1 + \alpha i_t). \tag{15.82}$$

We are thus back to the world of chapter 7. We would then set up a differential equation in i_t that is unstable. Hence $i_t = r + \mu$ for all t, where μ is the constant rate of monetary growth set by the monetary authority.[20] From (15.82), it follows that consumption is constant over time and determined, in equilibrium, by the economy's resource constraint. This constant level of consumption determines, in equilibrium, real money balances through equation (15.81). For a given M_0, this would determine the initial level of the nominal exchange rate, E_0.

15.5.3 Dollarized Equilibrium

Suppose that $i_t > i^*$. Again, since either $\theta_t - \lambda i_t = 0$ or $\theta_t - \lambda i^* = 0$, it must be the case that $\theta_t - \lambda i^* = 0$ and then $\theta_t - \lambda i_t < 0$. Hence $f_t > 0$ and $m_t^n = 0$. The cash-in-advance constraint (15.73) now takes the form

$$f_t = \alpha \gamma c_t.$$

Further, since $\phi_t = \lambda i_t$ and $\theta_t = \lambda i^*$, we can rewrite (15.78) as

$$u'(c_t) = \lambda \left\{1 + \alpha \left[(1-\gamma)\, i_t + \gamma i^*\right]\right\}. \tag{15.83}$$

Since domestic money is used for a fraction $1-\gamma$ of consumption and foreign money for a fraction γ, the opportunity cost associated with consuming is $(1-\gamma)\, i_t + \gamma i^*$. Again, to determine i_t, we would set up our standard differential equation and conclude that $i_t = r + \mu$.[21] Consumption is thus constant over time and determined by the economy's resource constraint. Finally, we would use the cash-in-advance constraint (15.72) to determine the initial nominal exchange rate.

In this equilibrium consumers therefore use as little domestic currency as possible given that its opportunity cost is higher than that of foreign currency.

15.5.4 Equilibrium with Indeterminacy

Suppose that $i_t = i^*$. Since either $\theta_t - \lambda i_t = 0$ or $\theta_t - \lambda i^* = 0$, both must be zero in this case. We can thus rewrite first-order condition (15.78) as

$$u'(c_t) = \lambda(1 + \alpha i_t). \tag{15.84}$$

Hence consumption is constant over time at a level c determined by the resource constraint.[22] Using (15.72), (15.73), and (15.74), we can write

$$m_t + f_t - \alpha c.$$

20. Notice that as long as $\mu < i^* - r$, the assumption $i_t < i^*$ is satisfied.

21. We can always choose μ so that $i_t > i^*$.

22. Again, by deriving the differential equation in i_t, we can verify that $\mu = 0$ would deliver $i = i^*$.

Notice that there are infinite combinations of $m_t \geq m_t^e$ and $f_t \geq 0$ that can satisfy this equation. There is nothing in the model to pin down these values. We will express this basic indeterminacy in terms of the initial nominal exchange rate. To do so, rewrite this last equation as

$$\frac{M_t}{E_t} + f_t = \alpha c.$$

Consider this condition at time $t = 0$:

$$\frac{\overline{M_0}}{E_0} + f_0 = \alpha c, \tag{15.85}$$

where $\overline{M_0}$ denotes the value of M_0 set by the monetary authority. By definition, at $t = 0$,

$$a_0 = b_0 + f_0 + \frac{\overline{M_0}}{E_0}. \tag{15.86}$$

These two last equations determine E_0, f_0, and b_0. The system is undetermined. For each value of E_0, there is a unique value of f_0 that satisfies equation (15.85). This value of f_0 then determines, through equation (15.86), a unique value of b_0. In other words, a higher value of E_0 implies lower domestic real money balances, which requires more foreign real money balances to satisfy the cash-in-advance constraint. This higher f_0 is achieved by selling foreign bonds (i.e., a lower b_0). There are infinite triplets (E_0, f_0, b_0) that satisfy equations (15.85) and (15.86). The exchange rate is therefore undetermined. A given value of $\overline{M_0}$ would be consistent with any E_0. This shows how monetary policy fails to tie down the value of the nominal exchange rate in an economy subject to currency substitution.

Adding just a tiny bit of imperfect substitution is enough to render the nominal exchange rate determinate. But in that case small changes in monetary policy would lead to large fluctuations in the nominal exchange rate. In particular, a small increase in the rate of money growth could lead to a very large nominal depreciation of the currency. This model's message is thus that in a world where domestic and foreign money are highly substitutable, we would expect to see large fluctuations in nominal exchange rates that are unrelated to fundamentals. More generally, the model illustrates the idea that monetary policy is likely to become ineffective in a world with high currency substitution. As discussed in box 15.2, the idea that currency substitution would render monetary policy ineffective under flexible exchange rate has been one of the main driving forces behind many of the empirical studies of currency substitution.

15.6 An Asset Substitution Model

As discussed in section 15.4, the empirical phenomenon of hysteresis has been viewed as a puzzle because the traditional model of currency substitution would predict that the ratio of foreign to domestic currency should fall as a response to a fall in the level of inflation (or nominal interest

Box 15.2
Does currency substitution undermine monetary independence?

One of the main motivations for early empirical studies on currency substitution was that a high degree of currency substitution would affect monetary policy independence through two main channels. First, a high degree of currency substitution would make the nominal exchange rate react strongly to even small changes in monetary policy, as analyzed in section 15.5. Second, the presence of currency substitution would undermine the effectiveness of monetary policy under flexible exchange rates. In terms of our basic model, this point can be seen most clearly in the context of the no-bonds model developed in chapter 6. Under flexible exchange rates a reduction, for example, in the rate of monetary growth would lead to an immediate reduction in the inflation rate without any real effects. In the presence of currency substitution, however, the same reduction in money growth would lead, in the short run, to a fall in consumption and a trade surplus, which is needed for the private sector to readjust foreign money balances. The adjustment to lower inflation thus requires a costly transition. In that sense, monetary policy becomes less effective. Hence, determining the degree of currency substitution was deemed important for assessing monetary policy independence.

Early studies estimated simple regression equations consisting of demands for domestic and foreign money as functions of the yields on both of these monies (see table 15.1 for a summary of selected studies on currency substitution).[a] The degree of currency substitution was determined by the coefficients on these yield variables. Miles (1978) found significant currency substitution between the US and Canadian dollars during the floating exchange rate period. Bordo and Choudhri (1982),

Table 15.1
Studies on currency substitution

Author(s)	Dataset	Methodology	Main results
Miles (1978)	Canada; quarterly data; 1960–1975	OLS estimation with Cochrane-Orcutt procedure	• US and Canadian dollars are not perfect substitutes. • The large significant elasticity of substitution (5.8 for the entire period) between US and Canadian dollars seems to be the result of the floating rate subperiod (1970.III–1975.IV) instead of fixed rate subperiod (1962.III–1970.II).
Bordo and Choudhri (1982)	Canada; quarterly data; 1970–1979	OLS estimation with Cocharane-Orcutt procedure	• The influence of the (expected) return on foreign money on the demand for domestic money in Canada during the flexible exchange rate period is found to be negligible.
Savastano (1992)	Bolivia, Mexico, Peru and Uruguay; quarterly data; 1970–1987 (dollarization episodes)	OLS estimation with Hafer-Hein and Miller procedures	• The presence of foreign currency deposits had adverse effect on the stability of these countries' demands for domestic money. • With the liberalization of foreign currency deposits in the domestic banking system, there was a gradual substitution of domestic currency balances for foreign currency deposits. However, lack of fiscal discipline eventually led to reintroduction of controls in Bolivia, Mexico, and Peru.

a. The empirical literature on currency substitution is voluminous and the reader is referred to Calvo and Végh (1992, 1996) for detailed references.

Box 15.2
(continued)

Table 15.1
(continued)

Author(s)	Dataset	Methodology	Main results
Bufman and Leiderman (1993)	Israel; quarterly data; 1978–1988	GMM procedure in a nonexpected utility model	• The estimated elasticity of currency substitution between domestic currency and Patam (deposits indexed to the exchange rate) ranges from 0.8 to 3.6. • The estimated elasticity of substitution between consumption and liquidity services ranges from 0.1 to 0.3. • Domestic money is more effective in generating liquidity services than a comparable unit of Patam.
Imrohoroglu (1994)	Canada; monthly and quarterly data; 1974–1990	GMM procedure in a money-in-the-utility-function model	• The estimated elasticity of currency substitution between US and Canadian dollars ranges from 0.29 to 0.43, suggesting that US dollar is a weak substitute for the domestic currency. • However, US dollar has a statistically significant role in reducing the transactions costs associated with carrying out domestic Canadian consumption plans.
Reinhart, Rogoff and Savastano (2003)	Annual data. Long sample: 48 countries, 1980–2001: short sample: 90 countries, 1996–2001	Using a composite index, four types of dollarization are defined	• Increase in the degree and incidence of dollarization in developing countries between the early 1980s and the late 1990s. • Large regional variation in terms of dollarization. Africa has been the least dollarized region in the world, followed by Asia and the Middle East, and with South America being the most dollarized.
Serletis and Feng (2010)	Canada; quarterly data; 1982–2006	Semi-nonparametric approach—AIM (asymptotically ideal model)	• Based on the Mundlak elasticities of substitution, they find low substitutability between monetary assets. • Based on the Marshallian demand elasticities, they find US dollar deposits are complements to domestic monetary assets.

however, reached the opposite conclusion—currency substitution was negligile in Canada—and argue that Miles's model was mis-specified. Savastano (1992) studied the dollarization episodes of four Latin American countries and found that the presence of foreign currency deposits had an adverse effect on the stability of these countries' demand for domestic money. This would, of course, affect the effectiveness of monetary policy.

A potential problem with this early empirical approach was that the estimated equations are (implicitly or explicitely) based on static models that abstract from potentially important intertemporal channels of transmission. As discussed in section 15.3.3 and emphasized by Calvo (1985), the effects of a change in monetary policy depend not only on the degree of currency substitution but also on the degree of substitution between consumption and liquidity services. Bufman and Leiderman (1993) followed this approach and used GMM procedures to estimate currency substitution in Israel. They found that the estimated elasticity of currency substitution is greater than one and larger than

Box 15.2
(continued)

the intratemporal elasticity between consumption and liquidity services. Applying these parameter values to a hypothetical steady state, they find that relatively small changes in the degree of currency substitution can have a marked impact on seigniorage, thus undermining monetary policy independence. Imrohoroglu (1994), however, used a similar method and found that the elasticity of currency substitution between US and Canadian dollars ranges from 0.29 to 0.43, indicating relatively weak currency substitution.

Reinhart, Rogoff, and Savastano (2003) broaden the traditional empirical definition of currency substitution (usually proportion of M2 denominated in foreign currency) to include foreign-currency denominated debt, both private and public. They show that the incidence of dollarization increased in developing countries between 1980 and 2000 and that there is a large regional variation in terms of dollarization. However, they also argue that dollarization did not hinder the effectiveness of monetary policy, especially in terms of inflation control.

A recent paper by Serletis and Feng (2010) challenges the GMM approach. They also study the Canadian case by first estimating the demand for liquid assets using a semiparametric approach and then estimating substitution elasticities between domestic and foreign currency deposits. They find low substitutability between monetary assets, which should make monetary policy effective. Furthermore they find that US dollar deposits are complements to domestic monetary assets and therefore conclude that flexible exchange rates are optimal for Canada.

In sum, it appears that currency substitution has not been a major factor in industrial countries and hence should have little impact on the effectiveness of monetary policy. In contrast, currency substitution appears to have been important in many developing countries, though its impact on the effectiveness of monetary policy remains an open question. We should also keep in mind that the whole empirical literature is plagued by the problem of distinguishing between currency and asset substitution. This is clearly important because, in theory at least, asset substitution would have no effect on monetary policy independence under flexible exchange rates. Recall that our basic monetary models introduced in chapter 5 assume perfect substitution between domestic and foreign bonds and yet monetary policy retains all of the effectiveness that it would have in a closed economy. It is only under currency substitution that the effectiveness of monetary policy is called into question, as in section 15.5.

rate). The problem, however, is that what the data measures (mainly asset substitution) is not what the theory talks about (currency substitution). There is a thus mismatch between theory and empirics.

To remedy this, we now develop a model of asset substitution due to Thomas (1985). In this model, consumers have a nontrivial portfolio decision because real returns on different assets are uncertain. Uncertainty is critical to the model because the main idea is that consumers will diversify risk by holding assets denominated in both domestic and foreign currency. We will see that dollarization (measured as the share of the asset portfolio denominated in foreign currency) does not depend on the level of inflation (or the nominal interest rate) but rather on real returns and measures of risk. In this world, we would not expect a fall in the domestic nominal interest rate to have any effect on the degree of dollarization.[23]

15.6.1 Households

Household's preferences are given by

$$E_0\left\{\int_0^\infty u(c_t)\exp(-\beta t)dt\right\},$$

where $E_0\{.\}$ denote expectations as of time 0, $u(.)$ is strictly increasing and strictly concave, c_t is consumption, and β is the positive discount rate. As in chapter 7, section 7.4, we will introduce money through a transactions costs technology and assume that both domestic and foreign currency reduce transactions costs:

$$s_t = c_t v\left(\frac{m_t}{c_t}, \frac{f_t}{c_t}\right), \tag{15.87}$$

where m_t and f_t denote domestic and foreign money balances, respectively, and $v(.,.)$ satisfies $v \geq 0$, $v_1 \leq 0$, $v_2 \leq 0$, $v_{11} > 0$, $v_{22} > 0$, $v_{12} > 0$, and $v_{11}v_{22} - v_{12}^2 > 0$. In other words, additional real money balances reduce transactions costs at a decreasing rate (i.e., the transactions technology is convex).

The domestic (P_t) and foreign (P_t^*) price levels are assumed to evolve according to the following Ito's processes:

$$\frac{dP_t}{P_t} = \pi dt + SdZ,$$

$$\frac{dP_t^*}{P_t^*} = \pi^* dt + S^* dZ^*,$$

where π and π^*, the (constant) drift of the processes, denote the expected rate of inflation per unit of time; S^2 and S^{*2} are the variances of the processes per unit of time; and dZ and dZ^* are the increments of a Wiener process. (S^{c2} will denote the covariance of these two processes.) By construction, dZ and dZ^* are independent over time (think of a Weiner process as the continuous-time analogue of a random walk).

Denote by B_t and B_t^* the holdings of nominal domestic and foreign bonds, respectively, and i and i^* the (constant) domestic and foreign nominal interest rates, respectively. Real holdings will be denoted by b_t and b_t^*. As shown in appendix 15.8.2, b_t and b_t^* follow the processes:

23. Technically, we will need to introduce a new tool: stochastic calculus. Continuous-time stochastic models are a convenient and widely used tool in finance and macroeconomics (particularly investment theory). See, for instance, Malliaris and Brock (1982) and Dixit and Pindyck (1994).

$$\frac{db_t}{b_t} = rdt - SdZ,$$

$$\frac{db_t^*}{b_t^*} = r^* dt - S^* dZ^*,$$

where

$$r \equiv i - \pi + S^2,$$

$$r^* \equiv i^* - \pi^* + S^{*2},$$

denote the (constant) expected real returns on domestic and foreign bonds, respectively.

By the same token, the expected real returns on domestic and foreign currency will be given by, respectively,

$$\left(-\pi + S^2\right)dt - SdZ = (r - i)dt - SdZ,$$
$$\left(-\pi^* + S^{*2}\right)dt - S^* dZ^* = (r^* - i^*)dt - S^* dZ^*.$$

Real financial wealth, a_t, is thus given by

$$a_t \equiv m_t + f_t + b_t^* + b_t.$$

Let θ_t^m, θ_t^f, θ_t^b, and $\theta_t^{b^*}$ denote the shares of domestic currency, foreign currency, domestic bonds, and foreign bonds in consumers' financial portfolio. Of course, $\theta_t^m + \theta_t^f + \theta_t^b + \theta_t^{b^*} = 1$. Define by Γ_t^f the share of dollar denominated assets; that is,

$$\Gamma_t^f \equiv \theta_t^f + \theta_t^{b^*}. \tag{15.88}$$

If $\Gamma_t^f = 0$, for example, the consumer's holdings of foreign currency have been financed in their entirety by dollar borrowing. If $\Gamma_t^f < 0$, dollar borrowing exceeds foreign currency holdings.

Real financial wealth evolves according to

$$da_t = \theta_t^m a_t \underbrace{[(r - i)\,dt - SdZ]}_{\text{Flow return on domestic currency}} + \theta_t^f a_t \underbrace{\left[(r^* - i^*)\,dt - S^* dZ^*\right]}_{\text{Flow return on foreign currency}}$$
$$+ \theta_t^b a_t \underbrace{(rdt - SdZ)}_{\text{Flow return on domestic bonds}} + \theta_t^{b^*} a_t \underbrace{\left(r^* dt - S^* dZ^*\right)}_{\text{Flow return on foreign bonds}}$$
$$+ \left[y - c_t - c_t v\left(\frac{\theta_t^m a_t}{c_t}, \frac{\theta_t^f a_t}{c_t}\right)\right] dt. \tag{15.89}$$

Using (15.88), equation (15.89) can be rewritten as

$$da_t = \left\{ \left[\Gamma_t^f r^* + (1 - \Gamma_t^f) r - \theta_t^m i - \theta_t^f i^* \right] a_t + \left[y - c_t - c_t v \left(\frac{\theta_t^m a_t}{c_t}, \frac{\theta_t^f a_t}{c_t} \right) \right] \right\} dt$$
$$- \Gamma_t^f a_t S^* dZ^* - (1 - \Gamma_t^f) a_t S dZ. \tag{15.90}$$

The evolution of real financial wealth has a nonstochastic component (the first term on the RHS) and a stochastic component (the last two terms on the RHS).

Following appendix 15.8.3, we can formulate this stochastic dynamic programming problem as

$$\beta J(a_t) = \max_{\left\{c_t, \theta_t^m, \theta_t^f, \Gamma_t^f\right\}} \left[u(c_t) \right.$$
$$+ \left\{ \left[\Gamma_t^f r^* + (1 - \Gamma_t^f) r - \theta_t^m i - \theta_t^f i^* \right] a_t + \left[y - c_t - c_t v \left(\frac{\theta_t^m a_t}{c_t}, \frac{\theta_t^f a_t}{c_t} \right) \right] \right\} J'(a_t)$$
$$\left. + \frac{1}{2} \left[\left(\Gamma_t^f \right)^2 S^{*2} + \left(1 - \Gamma_t^f \right)^2 S^2 + 2\Gamma_t^f \left(1 - \Gamma_t^f \right) S^{c2} \right] a_t^2 J''(a_t) \right]. \tag{15.91}$$

The first-order conditions with respect to c_t, θ_t^m, θ_t^f, and Γ_t^f yield

$$u'(c_t) = \left[1 + v \left(\frac{m_t}{c_t}, \frac{f_t}{c_t} \right) - v_1 \left(\frac{m_t}{c_t}, \frac{f_t}{c_t} \right) \frac{m_t}{c_t} - v_2 \left(\frac{m_t}{c_t}, \frac{f_t}{c_t} \right) \frac{f_t}{c_t} \right] J'(a_t), \tag{15.92}$$

$$- v_1 \left(\frac{m_t}{c_t}, \frac{f_t}{c_t} \right) = i, \tag{15.93}$$

$$- v_2 \left(\frac{m_t}{c_t}, \frac{f_t}{c_t} \right) = i^*, \tag{15.94}$$

$$\left(r^* - r \right) a_t J'(a_t) + \frac{1}{2} \left[2\Gamma_t^f S^{*2} - 2 \left(1 - \Gamma_t^f \right) S^2 \right.$$
$$\left. + 2S^{c2}(1 - 2\Gamma_t^f) \right] a_t^2 J''(a_t) = 0. \tag{15.95}$$

15.6.2 Currency Holdings

Currency holdings will be determined as in any standard currency substitution model. Equations (15.93) and (15.94) implicitly define the following money demand functions:

$$m_t = c_t\tilde{m}(i, i^*), \quad \tilde{m}_i < 0, \quad \tilde{m}_{i^*} > 0,$$

$$f_t = c_t\tilde{f}(i, i^*), \quad \tilde{f}_i > 0, \quad \tilde{f}_{i^*} < 0.$$

Combining these two equations yields

$$\frac{m_t}{f_t} = \Psi(i, i^*), \quad \Psi_i < 0, \quad \Psi_{i^*} > 0. \tag{15.96}$$

Thus, for given i and i^*, currency holdings are proportional to household consumption, which, in light of (15.87), implies that transactions costs s_t are also proportional to c_t.

15.6.3 Asset Holdings

To simplify the analysis further, assume that $u(c) = c^{1-\sigma}/(1-\sigma)$, where $\sigma > 0$ is the constant coefficient of relative risk aversion. Since mean and variances of asset returns are time-invariant and transactions costs are proportional to household consumption, it can be verified that $J(a) = \kappa a^{1-\sigma}/(1-\sigma)$, $c_t = \omega a_t$, and θ_t^m, θ_t^f, and Γ_t^f are time-invariant. κ and ω are constants that, along with portfolio shares, can be determined by solving (15.92) through (15.95) together with (15.91).

Since $-aJ''(a)/J'(a) = \sigma$, expression (15.95) can be rearranged as

$$\Gamma^f = \underbrace{\frac{S^2 - S^{c2}}{S^{*2} + S^2 - 2S^{c2}}}_{\text{Hedging}} + \underbrace{\frac{r^* - r}{\sigma(S^{*2} + S^2 - 2S^{c2})}}_{\text{Speculative}}. \tag{15.97}$$

This expression tells us that the degree of dollarization (i.e., the share of assets denominated in foreign currency) has two components. The first is a hedging term and the second is a speculative component.

The speculative component is easy to understand. The higher the real return on foreign-currency denominated bonds, the larger should be the share of dollar-denominated assets. The smaller is the coefficient of relative risk aversion, the larger will be the effect.

To develop intuition about the hedging component, consider the following particular cases:

- Real rates of return and variances are the same (i.e., $r^* = r$ and $S^2 = S^{*2}$). Then $\Gamma^f = \frac{1}{2}$ regardless of the covariance. Since risk and return are the same, the covariance is immaterial. Consumers will choose to hold half of their financial portfolio in foreign currency.
- Real rates of return are the same and covariance is zero (i.e., $r^* = r$ and $S^{c2} = 0$). Then the portfolio choice reduces to

$$\Gamma^f = \frac{S^2}{S^{*2} + S^2}.$$

If both variances are the same, then $\Gamma^f = \frac{1}{2}$, as in the previous example. If $S^2 > S^{*2}$, then $\Gamma^f > \frac{1}{2}$. Domestic assets are more risky and thus the portfolio is biased toward foreign assets.

- Real rates of return are the same, variance of domestic inflation is higher, and the covariance is positive (i.e., $r^* = r$, $S^2 > S^{*2}$, and $S^{c2} > 0$). In this case, and for given variances, the larger the covariance, the larger is Γ^f. Formally, impose $r^* = r$ in equation (15.97) and differentiate with respect to S^{c2} to obtain

$$\frac{d\Gamma^f}{dS^{c2}} = \frac{\left(S^2 - S^{*2}\right)}{\left(S^{*2} + S^2 - 2S^{c2}\right)^2} > 0$$

since $S^2 > S^{*2}$. This makes sense because, as the covariance increases, domestic-currency assets are still more risky but offer less diversification. The portfolio should then be biased toward foreign-currency assets.

15.6.4 Implications

This simple model makes transparent the important distinction between *currency* and *asset* substitution. Currency substitution, on the one hand, is captured by (15.96). This is the traditional definition of currency substitution popularized by Calvo and Rodriguez (1977) and Kouri (1976). Asset substitution (i.e., dollarization), on the other hand, is captured by (15.97).

A key point is that the degree of asset substitution (dollarization) does *not* depend on nominal returns. It depends only on real returns (in addition to variability of inflation). In this light, the phenomenon of hysteresis is not a puzzle because the model predicts that a reduction in i should not have any effect on the degree of dollarization. In this model a reduction in i will, as in traditional currency substitution models, lead to a increase in holding of real domestic money balances and a reduction in the holdings of foreign currency and hence to an increase in the ratio m/f. The degree of currency substitution will therefore fall. But the degree of dollarization will not change. In other words, the consumer wishes to decrease its holdings of foreign currency for transactions motives but does not wish to change its overall asset holdings of foreign denominated assets. To achieve this, the consumer will simply use foreign currency to buy a foreign-currency denominated bond. His exposure to foreign currency does not change.

Of course, if the fall in i is accompanied by a fall in the variance of domestic inflation, then dollarization will fall because domestic currency assets have become less risky.

15.7 Final Remarks

This chapter has studied the implications of currency substitution (defined as the use of both domestic and foreign currency for transactions motives) for various important issues in open economy macroeconomics. First, we looked at how the economy responds to shocks under predetermined and flexible exchange rates and concluded that the ratio of foreign to domestic currency will be more variable under flexible exchange rates than under predetermined exchange rates. Second, we analyzed how the real exchange rate responds to an expansion in money growth and concluded that the response depends on the relative magnitude of the elasticity of substitution between domestic and foreign currency, on the one hand, and the elasticity of substitution between consumption and liquidity services, on the other. According to existing estimates of these two elasticities, an increase in monetary growth should lead to a real depreciation of the currency. Third, we showed that the presence of hysteresis (the observation that, in practice, the ratio of foreign to domestic money does not fall in response to a fall in the inflation rate) can be explained by adding a cost of switching between currencies to an otherwise standard model. Finally, we illustrated the idea that very high degrees of substitution between the two monies are likely to lead to exchange rate instability.

In terms of how to think about dollarization, we have argued that what the data are capturing is *asset* substitution (i.e., the use of a foreign currency as a store of value) rather than *currency* substitution. We developed a model that nicely illustrates this critical distinction by showing that asset substitution depends on *real* rates of returns rather than *nominal* rates of return (i.e., nominal interest rates) as is the case with currency substitution. In this world—which we would argue is the relevant paradigm—hysteresis is not a puzzle since a fall in the domestic nominal interest rate does not necessarily imply a change in real returns. There is thus no theoretical presumption that an economy will de-dollarize as inflation falls.

15.8 Appendixes

15.8.1 Ito's Lemma

Ito's lemma is the foundation of continuous-time stochastic calculus. We state it here in a general form.[24]

Suppose that we have a number of stochastic processes described by

$$\frac{dP_i}{P_i} = \sigma_i dt + s_i dz_i, \qquad i = 1, \ldots, n. \tag{15.98}$$

The increments of any Wiener process, dz_i, are independently and normally distributed with mean 0 and variance dt. Intuitively, think of a Wiener process as the continuous-time analogue of a random walk. After t steps, the random walk is normally distributed with mean 0 and variance t.

24. For a brief introducion to stochastic calculus, see Kamien and Schwartz (1991, ch. 22). For a fuller treatment and numerous examples in economics and finance, see Dixit and Pindyck (1994) and Malliaris and Brock (1982). Following common practice in this area, this appendix and next drop time subscripts.

The differential elements dz_i and dz_j satisfy:

$$E\{(dz_i)^2\} = dt; \tag{15.99}$$

$$E\{dz_i dz_j\} = \rho_{ij} dt. \tag{15.100}$$

Let $F(P_1, \ldots, P_n, t)$ be a function that depends on the stochastic processes and is at least twice differentiable. According to Ito's lemma, the stochastic differential of F includes up to second-order terms and is given by

$$dF = \sum_i^n \frac{\partial F}{\partial P_i} dP_i + \frac{\partial F}{\partial t} dt + \frac{1}{2} \sum_i \sum_j \frac{\partial^2 F}{\partial P_i \partial P_j} dP_i dP_j, \tag{15.101}$$

where the products $dP_i dP_j$ are computed using (15.98), multiplication rules (15.99)–(15.100), and higher order terms of dt are ignored.

As an example, consider a single process

$$\frac{dP}{P} = \sigma\, dt + s dz, \tag{15.102}$$

and the function $F(P)$. Then a second-order Taylor series expansion obtains

$$dF = F' dP + \frac{1}{2} F'' \, (dP)^2 \,. \tag{15.103}$$

Using (15.102), recalling that $(dz)^2$ is proportional to dt while other terms in $(dP)^2$ are of the order of dt^2 and $dt^{3/2}$, Ito's lemma, by ignoring the higher order terms of dt, allows (15.103) to be rewritten as

$$dF = F' \sigma P dt + F' P s dz + \frac{1}{2} F'' s^2 P^2 dt.$$

The next appendix applies Ito's lemma to a system of two Ito's processes.[25]

15.8.2 Computing Real Rates of Return

This appendix computes the real rates of return for the stochastic problem analyzed in section 15.6.[26] We will compute the real return for a bond denominated in domestic currency. An analogous derivation holds for the foreign nominal bond.

25. Exercise 4 at the end of the chapter provides an illustration of how the solution to stochastic differential equations differs from ordinary differential equations.

26. This appendix follows Malliaris and Brock (1982, ch. 4). For an application in the context of indexed bonds, see Fischer (1975).

We have two Ito's processes given by

$$\frac{dP}{P} = \pi dt + SdZ, \tag{15.104}$$

$$\frac{dQ}{Q} = idt. \tag{15.105}$$

The first process describes the price level, while the second describes the nominal return of the bond.

We now use Ito's lemma to compute the stochastic process for the variable $q = \tilde{q}(P, Q) = Q/P$, that is, the real value of the bond. Following (15.101), we have the differential of q and include second-order terms

$$dq = \frac{\partial q}{\partial t}dt + \frac{\partial q}{\partial P}dP + \frac{\partial q}{\partial Q}dQ + \frac{1}{2}\left(\frac{\partial^2 q}{\partial P^2}dP^2 + 2\frac{\partial^2 q}{\partial P \partial Q}dPdQ + \frac{\partial^2 q}{\partial Q^2}dQ^2\right). \tag{15.106}$$

Let us compute the different terms involved:

$$\frac{\partial q}{\partial t} = 0,$$

$$\frac{\partial q}{\partial P} = -\frac{Q}{P^2},$$

$$\frac{\partial q}{\partial Q} = \frac{1}{P},$$

$$\frac{\partial^2 q}{\partial P^2} = \frac{2Q}{P^3},$$

$$\frac{\partial^2 q}{\partial Q^2} = 0,$$

$$\frac{\partial^2 q}{\partial P \partial Q} = -\frac{1}{P^2}.$$

Substituting these terms into (15.106), we obtain

$$dq = -\frac{Q}{P}\frac{dP}{P} + \frac{1}{P}dQ + \frac{1}{2}\left(\frac{2Q}{P^3}dP^2 - 2\frac{1}{P^2}dPdQ\right). \tag{15.107}$$

Ignoring higher order terms of dt drops the term $dPdQ$ and implies $dP^2 = S^2P^2dt$. Then, by Ito's lemma,

$$dq = \frac{1}{P}dQ - \frac{Q}{P}\frac{dP}{P} + \frac{Q}{P}S^2 dt.$$

Using (15.104) and (15.105), rewrite this last expression as

$$\frac{dq}{q} = \left(i - \pi + S^2\right) dt - SdZ.$$

The term $i - \pi + S^2$ captures the expected real rate of return on the bond. In the absence of uncertainty, the real return would simply be $i - \pi$. This somewhat surprising feature is the result of Jensen's inequality (e.g., see Eden 1976).

15.8.3 Dynamic Optimization in Continuous-Time Stochastic Models

For those of you who are not familiar with optimal control techniques in a stochastic setting, this appendix provides a "cookbook" for deriving optimality conditions in such a setting.[27]

Standard Case

First consider the standard case. The problem consists in maximizing

$$J(x_0) = E_0 \left\{ \int_0^{\infty} f(x_t, u_t) \exp(-\beta t) dt \right\}, \tag{15.108}$$

subject to

$$dx_t = \alpha dt + \gamma dW, \quad x_0 \text{ given}, \tag{15.109}$$

where x_t is the state variable and u_t is the control variable. This is simply a stochastic version of the continuous-time problem analyzed in appendix 6.7.1 in Chapter 6.

The first step is to write down the Bellman equation:

$$\beta J(x_t) dt = \max[f(x_t, u_t) dt + E\{dJ(x_t)\}]. \tag{15.110}$$

The next is to apply Ito's lemma to get dJ as a second-order expansion:

$$dJ(x_t) = J'(x_t) dx_t + \frac{1}{2} J''(x_t) (dx_t)^2.$$

Then take expectations to get $E\{dJ(x_t)\}$:

$$E\{dJ(x_t)\} = J'(x_t) E\{dx_t\} + \frac{1}{2} J''(x_t) E\{(dx_t)^2\} \tag{15.111}$$

27. This appendix largely follows Driscoll (2001, ch. 4). See also Kamien and Schwartz (1991, ch. 22), and Dixit and Pindyck (1994).

Use (15.109), and recall that $E\{dW\} = E\{dtdW\} = 0$ and $E\left\{(dW)^2\right\} = dt$, to write (15.111) as (ignoring higher order terms of dt)

$$E\{dJ(x_t)\} = \alpha J'(x_t)dt + \frac{1}{2}\gamma^2 J''(x_t)dt.$$

Now substitute this expression into the Bellman equation, (15.110) to obtain

$$\beta J(x_t)dt = \max\left[f(x_t, u_t)dt + \alpha J'(x_t)dt + \frac{1}{2}\gamma^2 J''(x_t)dt\right].$$

Last, take derivatives with respect to the control variable u, which will yield $u = g(x)$. Substituting this back into the Bellman equation yields a second-order differential equation in J, which can often be solved.

Thomas's Case

The asset substitution model of section 15.6 requires a minor modification to the standard case just described. In this case the Ito process that acts as the constraint takes the form

$$da_t = \alpha dt - \Gamma^f a_t S^* dZ^* - (1 - \Gamma^f)a_t S dZ, \tag{15.112}$$

where α is the coefficient of dt in expression (15.90). Unlike constraint (15.109), this constraint depends on two Wiener processes (dZ and dZ^*). Compared to the standard case reviewed above, the expression for $E\left\{(da_t)^2\right\}$ changes as follows. From (15.112) obtain

$$E\{(da_t)^2\} = \left[(1 - \Gamma^f)^2 a_t^2 S^2 + \left(\Gamma^f\right)^2 a_t^2 S^{*2}\right]dt + 2\Gamma^f(1 - \Gamma^f)a_t^2 S^{c2}dt, \tag{15.113}$$

using the fact that $E\{dtdZ\} = E\{dtdZ^*\} = 0$, $E\{dZdZ^*\} = \rho dt$, and $S^{c2} = \rho SS^*$, and ignoring higher order terms of dt.

Substitute $E\{da_t\} = \alpha dt$ and (15.113) into (15.111) to obtain

$$\begin{aligned} E\{dJ(a_t)\} &= \alpha J'(a_t)dt \\ &\quad + \frac{1}{2}J''(a_t)a_t^2\left\{\left[(1 - \Gamma^f)^2 S^2 + \left(\Gamma^f\right)^2 S^{*2}\right]dt + 2\Gamma^f(1 - \Gamma^f)S^{c2}dt\right\}. \end{aligned}$$

Finally, substitute this last expression into the Bellman equation (15.110) to obtain

$$\begin{aligned} \beta J(a_t) = \max\Bigg\{& f(a_t, u_t) + \alpha J'(a_t) \\ &+ \frac{1}{2}J''(a_t)a_t^2\left[(1 - \Gamma^f)^2 S^2 + \left(\Gamma^f\right)^2 S^{*2} + 2\Gamma^f(1 - \Gamma^f)S^{c2}\right]\Bigg\}, \end{aligned}$$

which corresponds to equation (15.91) in the text.

Exercises

1. (Shocks to the foreign nominal interest rate) Solve the basic currency substitution model of section 15.2 under the following preferences:

$$\int_0^\infty \left\{ \log(c_t) + \alpha_t \left[\log(m_t) + \frac{f_t^{1-1/\sigma} - 1}{1 - 1/\sigma} \right] \right\} \exp(-\beta t) dt.$$

In this context:

a. Solve for a PFEP with a constant i_t^*.

b. Analyze the effects of an unanticipated and permanent increase in i_t^*. Show how the results depends on whether $\sigma \lesseqgtr 1$ and explain the intuition behind the results.

2. (Behavior of currency substitution ratio under real shocks) Consider the model of section 15.2 for the following preferences:

$$\int_0^\infty \alpha_t [\log(c_t) + \log(m_t) + \log(f_t)] \exp(-\beta t) dt.$$

Solve for a PFEP along which α_t increases at time T under both predetermined and flexible exchange rates.

3. (General model of currency substitution) Consider the general model of currency substitution of section 15.3.3. In this context:

a. For the case $\sigma = \rho$, use the first-order conditions to argue that the economy will adjust instantaneously to a change in the rate of monetary growth.

b. For the case $\sigma = \rho = 1$, show that the general preferences specified in (15.53) simplify to the separable case.

4. (Ordinary calculus versus stochastic calculus[28]) To illustrate how the rules of integration for a stochastic differential equation differ from those from ordinary calculus, consider the differential equation

$$dy = y dz.$$

a. Suppose that dz is nonstochastic. Show that the solution is $y = \exp(z)$.

b. Suppose that dz is a Wiener process. Show that the solution is $y = \exp[z - (t/2)]$.

28. From Kamien and Schartz (1991, ch. 22).

References

Banco Central de Ecuador. 2001. La Dolarización en Ecuador. Un año después.

Banco Central de Ecuador. 2010. La Economía Ecuatoriana Luego de 10 Años de Dolarización. Dirección General de Estudios.

Bordo, Michael D., and Ehsan U. Choudhri. 1982. Currency substitution and the demand for money: Some evidence for Canada. *Journal of Money, Credit and Banking* 14 (1): 48–57.

Bufman, Gil, and Leonardo Leiderman. 1993. Currency substitution under non-expected utility: Some empirical evidence. *Journal of Money, Credit and Banking* 25 (3): 320–35.

Calvo, Guillermo A. 1985. Currency substitution and the real exchange rate: The utility maximization approach. *Journal of International Money and Finance* 4 (2): 175–88.

Calvo, Guillermo A., and Carlos A. Rodriguez. 1977. A model of exchange rate determination under currency substitution and rational expectations. *Journal of Political Economy* 85 (3): 617–26.

Calvo, Guillermo A., and Carlos A. Végh. 1992. Currency substitution in developing countries: An introduction. *Revista de Analisis Economico* 7: 3–27.

Calvo, Guillermo A., and Carlos A. Végh. 1996. From currency substitution to dollarization and beyond: Analytical and policy issues. In Guillermo Calvo, *Money, Exchange Rates, and Output*. Cambridge: MIT Press, 153–75.

Dixit, Avinash, and Robert S. Pindyck. 1994. *Investment under Uncertainty*. Princeton: Princeton University Press.

Doyle, Brian M. 2000. Here, dollars, dollars ... Estimating currency demand and worldwide currency substitution. International Finance Discussion Papers 657. Board of Governors of the Federal Reserve System, Washington DC.

Driscoll, John C. 2001. Lectures notes in macroeconomics. Mimeo. Brown University.

Eden, Benjamin. 1976. On the specification of the demand for money: The real rate of return versus the rate of inflation. *Journal of Political Economy* 84 (6): 1353–59.

Fischer, Stanley. 1975. The demand for index bonds. *Journal of Political Economy* 83 (3): 509–34.

Fischer, Stanley. 1982. Seigniorage and the case for a national money. *Journal of Political Economy* 90 (2): 295–313.

Goldfajn, Ilan, and Gino Olivares. 2000. Full dollarization: The case of Panama. Mimeo. Pontificia Universidade Catolica (Rio de Janeiro, Brazil).

Guidotti, Pablo E., and Carlos A. Rodriguez. 1992. Dollarization in Latin America: Gresham's law in reverse? *IMF Staff Papers* 39 (3): 518–44.

Imrohoroglu, Selahattin. 1994. GMM estimates of currency substitution between the Canadian dollar and the U.S. dollar. *Journal of Money, Credit and Banking* 26 (4): 792–807.

Kamien, Morton I., and Nancy L. Schwartz. 1991. *Dynamic Optimization*. Amsterdam: North Holland.

Kareken, John, and Neil Wallace. 1981. On the indeterminacy of equilibrium exchange rates. *Quarterly Journal of Economics* 96 (2): 207–22.

Kouri, Pentti. 1976. The exchange rate and the balance of payments in the short run and in the long run: A monetary approach. *Scandinavian Journal of Economics* 78 (2): 280–304

Liviatan, Nissan. 1981. Monetary expansion and real exchange rate dynamics. *Journal of Political Economy* 89 (6): 1218–27.

Malliaris, A. G., and W. A. Brock. 1982. *Stochastic Methods in Economics and Finance*. Amsterdam: North Holland.

Miles, Marc A. 1978. Currency substitution, flexible exchange rates, and monetary independence. *American Economic Review* 68 (3): 428–36.

Porter, Richard D., and Ruth A. Judson. 1996. *The Location of U.S. Currency: How Much is Abroad*? Federal Reserve Bulletin. Washington DC: Board of Governors of the Federal Reserve System.

Quispe-Agnoli, Miriam, and Elena Whisler. 2006. Official dollarization and the banking system in Ecuador and El Salvador. *Federal Reserve Bank of Atlanta Economic Review* (third quarter): 55–71.

Reinhart, Carmen M., Kenneth S. Rogoff, and Miguel A. Savastano. 2003. Addicted to dollars. Working Paper 10015. National Bureau of Economic Research, Cambridge, MA.

Rodriguez, Carlos A. 1993. Money and credit under currency substitution. *IMF Staff Papers* 40 (2): 414–26.

Savastano, Miguel A. 1992. The pattern of currency substitution in Latin America: An overview. *Revista de Analisis Economico* 7 (1): 29–72.

Serletis, Apostolos, and Guohua Feng. 2010. Semi-nonparametric estimates of currency substitution between the Canadian dollar and the U.S. dollar. *Macroeconomic Dynamics* 14 (1): 29–55.

Thomas, Lee R. 1985. Portfolio theory and currency substitution. *Journal of Money, Credit and Banking* 17 (3): 347–57.

Uribe, Martin. 1997. Hysteresis in a simple model of currency substitution. *Journal of Monetary Economics* 40 (1): 185–202.

Vera, Wilson. 2007. Medición del circulante en circulación. *Cuestiones Económicas* 23 (2): 2–3.

16 Balance-of-Payments Crises

16.1 Introduction

Developing countries frequently face notorious difficulties in sustaining fixed (or predetermined) exchange rate regimes. More often than not, countries are forced to abandon such regimes in response to a gradual but sustained loss of international reserves that typically culminates in a full-blown speculative attack that depletes the Central Bank's coffers. The frequency and severity of balance-of-payments crises all over the developing world raise several fascinating and highly relevant questions regarding their causes and dynamics and the appropriate policy responses.

By and large, the most common cause of balance-of-payments crises is weak fiscal fundamentals. This "traditional view" of balance-of-payments crises—pioneered by Krugman (1979) and Flood and Garber (1984)—remains the pillar of our understanding of balance-of-payments crises and is at the core of theoretical models examined in this chapter.[1] Section 16.2 sets the stage by developing an optimizing version of Krugman's (1979) seminal paper. This model illustrates how, in the presence of a fiscal deficit, a fixed exchange rate will lead to a continuous loss of international reserves, eventually forcing the monetary authority to give up the peg. But perhaps the most remarkable feature of the Krugman–Flood–Garber (hereafter KFG) model is that the abandonment of the peg is precipitated by a discrete fall in international reserves (a "speculative attack") that occurs even though all events in this economy are perfectly anticipated. That such a "speculative attack" (clearly, the most spectacular feature of balance-of-payments crises in practice) can be generated in the context of a simple perfect foresight model certainly makes the KFG model one of the most intellectually satisfying in modern international finance. The rest of the chapter examines several important extensions and modifications of the KFG model.

1. In a well-known paper by Burnside, Eichenbaum, and Rebelo (2001)—inspired by the Asian crises of 1997—the focus is on future (or "prospective") fiscal deficits but the fiscal origin remains at the core of the analysis.

From a policy perspective, a glaring omission of the KFG model is the implicit assumption that the Central Bank watches its reserves dwindle without trying to "defend" the fixed exchange rate by actively raising interest rates to make domestic-currency assets more attractive, as is typical in practice. Following Lahiri and Végh (2003), section 16.3 modifies the basic model to allow for a role for interest rate defense and shows the basic mechanism through which an active interest rate defense enables the Central Bank to delay the crisis and thus buy precious time (which, in practice, may give the fiscal authority the opportunity to solve the underlying fiscal problems).

Mostly for analytical simplicity, the basic KFG model assumes that there is an exogenous rate of domestic credit creation that is inconsistent with the existing predetermined exchange rates regime. Presumably this reflects the need to print money to finance an underlying fiscal deficit. Section 16.4 makes explicit this idea by assuming that there is an exogenous fiscal deficit that must be financed by the monetary authority. In other words, the rate of domestic credit creation is now endogenously determined. We show that the results are the same as those derived in section 16.2.

In practice, balance-of-payments crises are preceded by consumption booms, real appreciation of the domestic currency, and large trade deficits. In the aftermath of the crisis, consumption plummets, the currency depreciates in real terms, and the trade deficit falls dramatically. Section 16.5 shows how the basic KFG model can easily account for all these stylized facts if we simply allow consumption to be affected by changes in nominal interest rates, along the lines of Chapter 7.

A peculiar aspect of the Mexican balance-of-payments crisis of December 1994 is that it did not seem to be preceded by a large fiscal deficit. The absence of a fiscal deficit in fact led many observers to argue that if a large current account deficit was due to private decisions (as opposed to reflecting fiscal imbalances), there should be no cause for concern. This position came to be known as the Lawson doctrine (named after the then Chancellor of the Exchequer, Nigel Lawson). Section 16.6 develops a remarkable twist of the KFG model—due to Talvi (1997)—in which, owing to the presence of a consumption tax, fiscal revenues are endogenous as the consumption boom that precedes the crisis increases consumption tax revenues. We show an example in which, even though by construction the crisis has a fiscal origin as in the standard KFG model, the primary deficit that precedes the crisis is zero and international reserves in fact rise in the run-up to the crisis. This example serves as a stern warning of the dangers of relying on fiscal figures that are not cyclically adjusted to judge the sustainability of a fixed (or predetermined) exchange rate.

Finally, section 16.7 tackles an important methodological shortcoming of the KFG model (which also has a bearing on the model's predictions). As already mentioned, the fiscal unsustainability of the fixed exchange rate is the proximate cause of the crisis in the KFG model. But what determines *when* the fixed exchange rate is abandoned? The way KFG close the model is by postulating an arbitrary threshold rule that requires that the government abandon the fixed exchange if and only if international reserves reach a certain critical threshold. Clearly, this rule suggests that policy makers are acting irrationally (as opposed to the private sector that acts optimally). After all, if the regime is unsustainable, why not abandon the fixed exchange rate immediately (i.e., before reserves reach some arbitrary threshold) and avoid a potentially costly delay? Following Rebelo and Végh (2008), section 16.7 assumes away the KFG abandonment rule and instead allows policy makers to choose the time of abandonment optimally (in a Ramsey sense). In other words, policy makers will choose to abandon the fixed exchange rate whenever it is most convenient to do so from a social point of view. In this context we show that it is optimal to abandon the fixed exchange rate as soon as the regime becomes unsustainable, *regardless of the level of international reserves*. The intuition is clear: since the regime will have to be abandoned at some point, any delay will impose a socially costly distortion by introducing a boom–bust cycle in consumption. Abandoning it right away avoids this costly cycle. We conclude that the KFG abandonment rule is, in general, not optimal and that, to make sense out of it in a world of rational policy makers, one needs to introduce some cost of abandoning the peg.

16.2 The Basic Model

Consider a small open economy inhabited by a large number of identical, infinitely lived consumers who are blessed with perfect foresight. There is one physical (tradable and nonstorable) good. The domestic price of the good is given by the law of one price. The foreign price of the good is assumed to be one. The economy is endowed with a constant flow of the good, y. There is perfect capital mobility in the sense that agents can borrow or lend at a given (and, by assumption, constant) international real interest rate, r.

16.2.1 Consumer's Problem

Let real financial assets, a_t, be given by

$$a_t \equiv m_t + b_t,$$

where m_t are real money balances (i.e., nominal money balances, M_t, deflated by the domestic price of the good, E_t) and b_t are holdings of net foreign assets.

The consumer's flow constraint is given by

$$b_T - b_{T^-} = -\frac{M_T - M_{T^-}}{E_T},$$

$$\dot{b}_t = rb_t + y + \tau_t - c_t - \dot{m}_t - \varepsilon_t m_t, \qquad \text{if } t \neq T, \tag{16.1}$$

where c_t is consumption, ε_t is the rate of devaluation, τ_t are transfers from the government and, for full expositional clarity and following appendix 5.8.2 in chapter 5, we are allowing for a possible discrete changes in b_t and M_t at time $t = T$.[2] Integrating forward and imposing the condition $\lim_{t\to\infty} e^{-rt} b_t = 0$, we obtain the consumer's lifetime budget constraint:

2. By definition, T is the time at which the balance-of-payments crisis will happen and will be determined endogenously later. In the perfect foresight world analyzed in this section, T is the only time at which there may be a discrete change in m_t and b_t. In section 16.7 where we study an unanticipated change in government spending at time 0, there will also be a discrete change in m_t and b_t at time 0.

$$b_0 + \frac{y}{r} + \int_0^\infty \tau_t e^{-rt} dt = \int_0^\infty (c_t + \dot{m}_t + \varepsilon_t m_t) e^{-rt} dt + \frac{M_T - M_{T-}}{E_T} e^{-rT}, \tag{16.2}$$

where b_0 denotes initial net foreign assets.[3]

This intertemporal constraint can be further simplified if we impose the condition that $\lim_{t\to\infty} e^{-rt} m_t = 0$ and use the interest parity condition ($i_t = r + \varepsilon_t$) to obtain[4]

$$a_0 + \frac{y}{r} + \int_0^\infty \tau_t e^{-rt} dt = \int_0^\infty (c_t + i_t m_t) e^{-rt} dt. \tag{16.3}$$

The lifetime utility of the representative consumer is given by

$$\int_0^\infty [u(c_t) + v(m_t)] e^{-\beta t} dt, \tag{16.4}$$

where $\beta (> 0)$ is the subjective discount rate, and the functions $u(.)$ and $v(.)$ are strictly increasing and strictly concave in their arguments.

The consumer's problem consists in choosing $\{c_t, m_t\}$ for all $t \in [0, \infty)$ to maximize lifetime utility (16.4), subject to (16.3), for a given path of τ_t and i_t and given values of y and a_0.

Under the standard assumption that $\beta = r$, the first order conditions imply that

$$u'(c_t) = \lambda, \tag{16.5}$$

$$v'(m_t) = \lambda i_t, \tag{16.6}$$

where λ is the Lagrange multiplier associated with constraint (16.3). From (16.5) it follows that consumption will be constant along a perfect foresight equilibrium path. Using equation (16.5) to eliminate λ from equation (16.6) implicitly yields a real money demand function with standard properties

$$m_t = L(\underset{+}{c_t}, \underset{-}{i_t}), \tag{16.7}$$

where a sign under a variable denotes the sign of the corresponding partial derivative.

16.2.2 Government

Let h_t denote the government's stock of net foreign assets (i.e., international reserves). The flow constraint of the government as a whole is given by:

3. When we study unanticipated shocks at $t = 0$ later in the chapter, then these are stocks in the instant before the shock (and would, strictly speaking, be denoted with a subscript 0^- as in chapter 5, appendix 5.8.2).

4. This condition will hold in equilibrium because, at an optimum, the choice of m_t will be finite.

$$h_T - h_{T^-} = \frac{M_T - M_{T^-}}{E_T},$$
$$\dot{h}_t = rh_t + \dot{m}_t + \varepsilon_t m_t - \tau_t, \qquad \text{if } t \neq T, \tag{16.8}$$

where, as in the case of the consumer, we are allowing for discrete changes in h_t and M_t at time T.

If we integrate forward equation (16.8), imposing the condition that $\lim_{t\to\infty} e^{-rt} h_t = 0$, we obtain the following intertemporal constraint for the government:

$$\int_0^\infty \tau_t e^{-rt} dt = h_0 + \int_0^\infty (\dot{m}_t + \varepsilon_t m_t) e^{-rt} dt + \frac{M_T - M_{T^-}}{E_T} e^{-rT}, \tag{16.9}$$

where h_0 denotes the initial level of international reserves. Notice that a discrete fall in real money balances, for example, implies a loss of revenues for the government. This intertemporal constraint simply says that the present discounted value of transfers must be financed with the initial stock of international reserves plus the present discounted value of revenues from money creation (including discrete jumps).

Let us now turn our attention to the monetary authority (i.e., the Central Bank). Assume, as is standard, that the Central Bank's net worth is zero. The Central Bank's balance sheet then indicates that

$$m_t = d_t + h_t, \tag{16.10}$$

where d_t denotes the stock of real domestic credit (i.e., $d_t = D_t/E_t$). Let the rate of growth of nominal domestic credit be given by θ_t, namely

$$\frac{\dot{D}_t}{D_t} = \theta_t. \tag{16.11}$$

Differentiating (16.10) with respect to time and taking into account (16.11), it follows that

$$\dot{h}_t = \dot{m}_t - d_t(\theta_t - \varepsilon_t). \tag{16.12}$$

This equation will determine the path of international reserves.

Finally, on the fiscal side, define the fiscal balance, s_t^g, as

$$s_t^g \equiv rh_t - \tau_t. \tag{16.13}$$

Using (16.8), we can rewrite the last equation as

$$-s_t^g = \dot{m}_t + \varepsilon_t m_t - \dot{h}_t, \tag{16.14}$$

which says that the fiscal *deficit* (i.e., $-s_t^g$) must be financed by either printing money or running down international reserves.

16.2.3 Equilibrium Conditions

The assumption of perfect capital mobility (coupled with the assumption that foreign inflation is zero) implies that

$$i_t = r + \varepsilon_t. \tag{16.15}$$

Let k_t denote the economy's total stock of net foreign assets (i.e., $k_t \equiv b_t + h_t$). Combining the consumer's and the government's flow constraint, given by equations (16.1) and (16.8), respectively, we obtain the flow constraint for the economy as a whole (i.e., the current account):

$$\dot{k}_t = rk_t + y - c_t.$$

Integrating forward this last expression and imposing the appropriate transversality condition, we obtain the economy's resource constraint:

$$k_0 + \frac{y}{r} = \int_0^{\infty} c_t e^{-rt} dt. \tag{16.16}$$

16.2.4 Real Equilibrium

As follows from (16.5), consumption will be constant along any perfect foresight path (at a level denoted by c). From (16.16),

$$c = rk_0 + y. \tag{16.17}$$

The fact that consumption will be constant and equal to permanent income *regardless* of the monetary and fiscal policy followed by the government greatly simplifies the solution of the model.

Substituting (16.17) into (16.7), we obtain real money demand along a perfect foresight equilibrium path (PFEP):

$$m_t = L(c, i_t). \tag{16.18}$$

Real money demand depends on the path of the nominal interest rate, i_t, and thus on the path of the rate of devaluation.

16.2.5 Exchange Rate and Domestic Credit Policy

So far we have made no behavioral assumptions regarding fiscal and monetary policy. We now specify such policies.

Monetary Authority

The monetary authority is assumed to set the path of nominal domestic credit (D_t) and the path of the nominal exchange rate (E_t). In other words, the monetary authority sets the initial level of domestic credit (D_0) and a constant rate of growth ($\theta \equiv \dot{D}_t/D_t$). Similarly it sets the initial exchange rate ($E_0 = \bar{E}$) and sets the rate of devaluation (ε_t) equal to zero. Hence the interest parity condition (16.15) simplifies to

$$i_t = r. \tag{16.19}$$

Notice that setting D_0 and $\bar{E}$ determines the initial level of real domestic credit $d_0 (= D_0/\bar{E})$.

How is the initial level of reserves, h_0, determined? From the Central Bank's balance sheet, given by (16.10), evaluated at $t = 0$, we have

$$h_0 = m_0 - d_0 = L(c, r) - \frac{D_0}{\bar{E}} > 0. \tag{16.20}$$

The initial level of reserves is thus determined by the difference between real money demand and real domestic credit at $t = 0$. We will assume that the parameter configuration is such that initial reserves are positive (i.e., $h_0 > 0$).

Finally, to complete the specification of monetary policy, we assume that the monetary authority announces as of $t = 0$ that if the stock of international reserves ever hits a critical threshold (assumed, for simplicity, to be zero), then the fixed exchange rate will be abandoned in favor of a flexible exchange rate.[5]

Fiscal Authority

The fiscal authority is assumed to passively accommodate the monetary authority. In other words, from (16.8), transfers, τ_t, will be given by[6]

$$\tau_t = rh_t + \dot{m}_t + \varepsilon_t m_t - \dot{h}_t. \tag{16.21}$$

16.2.6 Sustainability of a Fixed Exchange Rate Regime

The first question we want to ask is: Given the exogenous abandonment rule specified above, is the fixed exchange rate sustainable over time? As already touched upon in chapter 5, the answer to this question depends on the value of the rate of growth of domestic credit, θ. If $\theta = 0$, the fixed exchange rate is sustainable indefinitely. But if $\theta > 0$, then the fixed exchange rate is

5. We will refer to this policy as the "exogenous abandonment rule" to stress its ad hoc (i.e., arbitrary) nature. As section 16.7 will make clear, if the government acts optimally (in a Ramsey sense), then such a rule is not necessarily optimal.

6. Assuming that fiscal spending is an endogenous variable that adjusts to the exogenous level of domestic credit creation enables us to solve this model in a very simple and illuminating fashion. The more realistic case, in which fiscal spending is exogenous and domestic credit endogenously adjusts to finance it, will be dealt with in section 16.4.

unsustainable in the sense that international reserves will hit the critical threshold at some point in time (call it T) and the fixed exchange rate will have to be abandoned. In this latter case, we want to examine what determines T and characterize the perfect foresight paths of international reserves and real money balances.

Sustainable Peg

Suppose that $\theta = 0$. Since $\varepsilon_t = 0$, it follows from (16.12) that

$$\dot{h}_t = \dot{m}_t. \tag{16.22}$$

In other words, changes in international reserves will reflect only changes in real money demand. But, from (16.7) and (16.19), it follows that real money demand is constant along a PFEP:

$$m_t = L(c, r). \tag{16.23}$$

Hence $\dot{m}_t = 0$ for all $t \geq 0$. This implies that $\dot{h}_t = 0$ for all $t \geq 0$. Thus

$$h_t = h_0,$$

where h_0 is given by (16.20). International reserves will therefore be constant over time and equal to their initial value.

The endogenous value of transfers follows from (16.21), taking into account that $\dot{m}_t = \varepsilon_t = 0$:

$$\tau_t = rh_0. \tag{16.24}$$

Since $h_0 > 0$, the fiscal authority is just giving the interest on reserves back to consumers. Finally, notice that, given (16.24), (16.13) implies that the fiscal balance is constant over time and equal to zero:

$$s_t^g = rh_0 - rh_0 = 0.$$

In sum, a sustainable fixed exchange rate is characterized by constant levels of consumption and real money balances and a zero fiscal balance.

Unsustainable Peg

Suppose now that $\theta > 0$. Notice first that real money demand continues to be given by (16.23) and hence $\dot{m}_t = 0$. It follows from (16.12) that

$$\dot{h}_t = -\theta d_t < 0.$$

International reserves will be falling over time. In addition, since during the fixed exchange rate regime, $d_t = d_0 e^{\theta t}$, reserves fall at an *increasing* rate (i.e., the path of h_t is a strictly decreasing and strictly concave function of time):

$$\ddot{h}_t = -\theta^2 d_t < 0.$$

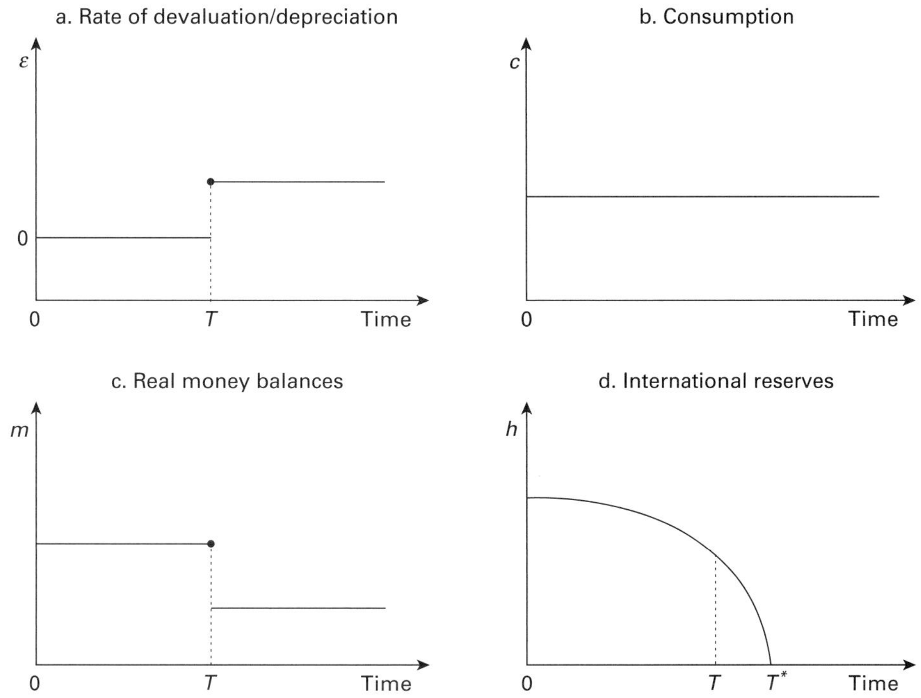

Figure 16.1
Balance-of-payments crisis

It follows that international reserves will hit the critical threshold (zero) in finite time. At some point the Central Bank will then abandon the fixed exchange rate and let the exchange rate float.

Let T denote the point in time at which the fixed exchange rate is abandoned (which we will also refer to as the "crisis"). A quick (but mistaken!) reaction would be to think that T will be the point in time at which the path of international reserves would hit zero in a continuous fashion (i.e., point T^* in figure 16.1, panel d). We will in fact show that the crisis occurs *before* this point.

Since for $t \geq T$ the economy will be in a stationary equilibrium under flexible exchange rates, we know from chapter 5 that $\varepsilon_t = \theta$.[7] The path of the rate of devaluation/depreciation is thus given by (see figure 16.1, panel a):

$$\varepsilon_t = \begin{cases} 0, & 0 \leq t < T, \\ \theta, & t \geq T. \end{cases} \tag{16.25}$$

7. To show this, just notice that real money balances for $t \geq T$ will be governed by an unstable diferential equation. Hence $\dot{m}_t = 0$ for $t \geq T$, which implies that $\varepsilon_t = \theta$.

Given the interest parity condition (16.15), the path of the nominal interest rate will be given by

$$i_t = \begin{cases} r, & 0 \leq t < T, \\ r + \theta, & t \geq T. \end{cases} \tag{16.26}$$

Taking into account (16.26), we can write the path of real money balances (see figure 16.1, panel c) as

$$m_t = \begin{cases} L(c, r), & 0 \leq t < T, \\ L(c, r + \theta), & t \geq T. \end{cases}$$

This tells us that at time T there will be a discrete fall in real money demand in response to the rise in the nominal interest rate. Since real domestic credit is given at any instant in time, this discrete fall in real money demand will translate into an equivalent loss of international reserves. Formally, the loss in reserves at time T is given by

$$\Delta h = L(c, r + \theta) - L(c, r) < 0.$$

It is worth noticing that the loss in reserves depends only on θ and is independent of the time at which it occurs (i.e., independent of T).

How is T determined? A key piece of information for determining T is that the nominal exchange rate cannot jump along a perfect foresight equilibrium path (i.e., the path of the exchange rate cannot be discontinuous). If it did, there would be infinite arbitrage opportunities that would be inconsistent with an equilibrium. Specifically, an instant before the nominal exchange rate is expected to, say, increase, the public's demand for money would be driven down to zero in anticipation of an infinite capital loss, which is inconsistent with equilibrium.

Since the nominal exchange rate cannot jump at T, money market equilibrium at T requires that[8]

$$L(c, r + \theta) = \frac{M_T}{\bar{E}}. \tag{16.27}$$

Since, by construction, international reserves are zero at T (otherwise the fixed exchange rate would not have been abandoned), we know from the Central Bank's balance sheet that $M_T = D_T$. Furthermore, since nominal domestic credit grows at the rate θ, $D_T = D_0 e^{\theta T}$. Hence $M_T = D_0 e^{\theta T}$. Substituting this into (16.27), we obtain

$$L(c, r + \theta) = \frac{D_0 e^{\theta T}}{\bar{E}}. \tag{16.28}$$

8. An alternative way of deriving this condition is presented in appendix 16.9.

This equilibrium condition implicitly defines T as a function of c, θ, and D_0:

$$T = f(c, \theta, D_0).$$

Figure 16.2 illustrates the determination of T by plotting the LHS and RHS of (16.28) as a function of T. The LHS (real money demand) is a horizontal line since real money demand at T does not depend on T. In contrast, the RHS (real money supply) is an increasing function of T. The intersection of the two curves at point A determines the equilibrium value of T. As illustrated in figure 16.1, panel d, time T is the point in time at which the speculative attack occurs.

What is the path of the fiscal balance and how is it financed? From (16.14), it follows that

$$s_t^g = \begin{cases} \dot{h}_t < 0, & 0 \leq t < T, \\ -\theta L(c, r + \theta) < 0, & t \geq T. \end{cases}$$

The fiscal authority is thus always running a fiscal deficit (forced, of course, by the assumption that it accommodates the actions of the monetary authority). Before the crisis, the fiscal deficit is financed by running down reserves, whereas after the crisis the deficit is financed with the inflation tax.

We have thus completely characterized the perfect foresight equilibrium path associated with an unsustainable fixed exchange rate (see figure 16.1). The more remarkable result of the Krugman–Flood–Garber model is the existence of a discrete speculative attack at T even though everything is, by construction, perfectly anticipated and hence nobody is taken by surprise. Intuitively, the key to understanding this result is that the size of the attack (which is given by the change in real money demand) depends only on θ and not on when the attack occurs. In this light, it should be

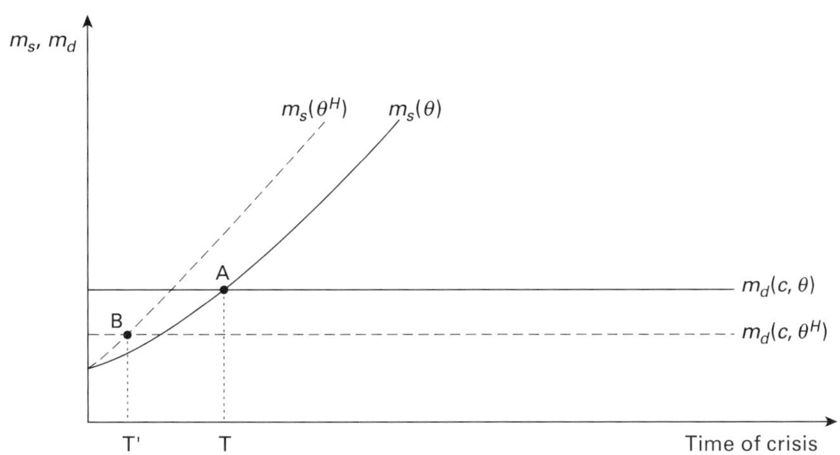

Figure 16.2
Time of crisis

clear why this final attack must occur precisely at the point in time at which the attack exactly depletes the Central Bank's international reserves. If it occurred an instant later, not all agents would be able to get rid of their unwanted money balances. If it occurred an instant before, the loss of international reserves would not reduce the stock to zero, and therefore the Central Bank would not abandon the fixed exchange rate (which would make the run inconsistent with equilibrium).[9]

Finally, how does a higher θ (which would reflect a larger underlying fiscal deficit) affect the perfect foresight equilibrium path? As can be seen in figure 16.2, a higher θ, denoted by θ^H, implies a leftward shift of the upward-sloping curve and a downward shift of the money demand curve, with both effects inducing a lower T (point B). Hence the crisis will occur sooner and the size of the run will be bigger as well.

16.3 Interest Rate Defense

The model just described assumes that the Central Bank sits passively as it watches its stock of reserves fall steadily over time until they are wiped out completely by a final speculative attack. In practice, however, Central Banks hardly ever play such a passive role. Quite to the contrary, Central Banks typically fight long and hard before giving up a peg. The main weapon in a Central Bank's arsenal is some short-term interest rate. Short-term interest rates are often raised to extraordinary levels in an attempt to induce the public to hold domestic-currency assets

Box 16.1
Behavior of nominal exchange rate and international reserves in major currency crises

The basic model of section 16.2 predicts that a traditional balance-of-payments crisis is characterized by a steady fall in international reserves followed by a sharp drop at the time of the crisis. Due to the lack of uncertainty, our model predicts no jump in the nominal exchange rate at the time of the crisis. If we assumed, however, that domestic credit growth is stochastic, then the nominal exchange rate would jump at the time of the crisis (see Flood and Garber 1984 and Dornbusch 1987). Intuitively, the nominal exchange rate can jump because the presence of uncertainty rules out infinite arbitrage opportunities as agents do not know for certain whether the peg will be abandoned for sure next period or not. This will be reflected in a positive expected depreciation as long as there is some probability that the zero threshold of reserves may be hit next period. Hence, in the presence of uncertainty, the basic Krugman–Flood–Garber model would predict that reserves should fall and the nominal exchange rate should increase at the time of the crisis.

9. In practice—and as documented in box 16.1—we see indeed a sharp fall in international reserves at the time of the crisis. Yet we also see a sudden increase in the nominal exchange rate which, in our model, cannot occur because of the assumption of perfect foresight. As discussed in the box, adding uncertainty would generate this feature as well.

Box 16.1
(continued)

Do we observe this pattern in the data? Table 16.1 lists six well-known balance-of-payments crises—Uruguay (November 1982), Mexico (December 1994), Thailand (1997), Russia (August 1998), Brazil (January 1999), and Argentina (January 2002)—and quantifies the changes in the nominal exchange rate and international reserves around the time of the crisis.[a] With the exception of Thailand, the nominal exchange rate was pegged against the dollar (following arrangements varying from a fixed exchange rate in Argentina to exchange rate bands in Mexico and Russia). Figure 16.3 plots the behavior of international reserves and the nominal exchange rate 36 months before and 36 months after the crises.[b] A vertical line indicates the month of the crisis. By and large—and as predicted by the theoretical model—we see a sharp increase in the nominal exchange rate and a fall in international reserves around the time of the crisis. The sharp fall in international reserves is preceded by a gradual but steady fall.

Table 16.1
Major balance-of-payments crises

		Devaluation		12-Month change in international reserves				Exchange rate regime	
Country	T	Monthly rate at T	12-Month rate at $T+11$	One year before T	Six months before T	Three months before T	At T	Until crisis	After crisis
Uruguay	Nov-82	39%	178%	−2%	−73%	−61%	−72%	Pre-announced crawling peg	Flexible
Mexico	Dec-94	54%	122%	33%	−28%	−29%	−75%	Exchange rate band	Flexible
Thailand	Jul-97	24%	64%	15%	4%	−4%	−23%	Pegged to a basket of currencies	Flexible
Russia	Aug-98	27%	288%	62%	−8%	−39%	−58%	Exchange rate band	Flexible
Brazil	Jan-99	64%	48%	−9%	16%	−22%	−35%	Exchange rate band since 1995	Flexible
Argentina	Jan-02	40%	232%	5%	−36%	−22%	−46%	Fixed with respect to the US dollar since April 1991	Managed float

Note: T corresponds to the date at which the fixed/managed exchange rate regime was abandoned.

a. Box 13.2 in chapter 13 analyzes in detail Argentina's 1991 Convertibility plan.
b. Data from IFS. Reserves are in millions of US dollars.

Box 16.1
(continued)

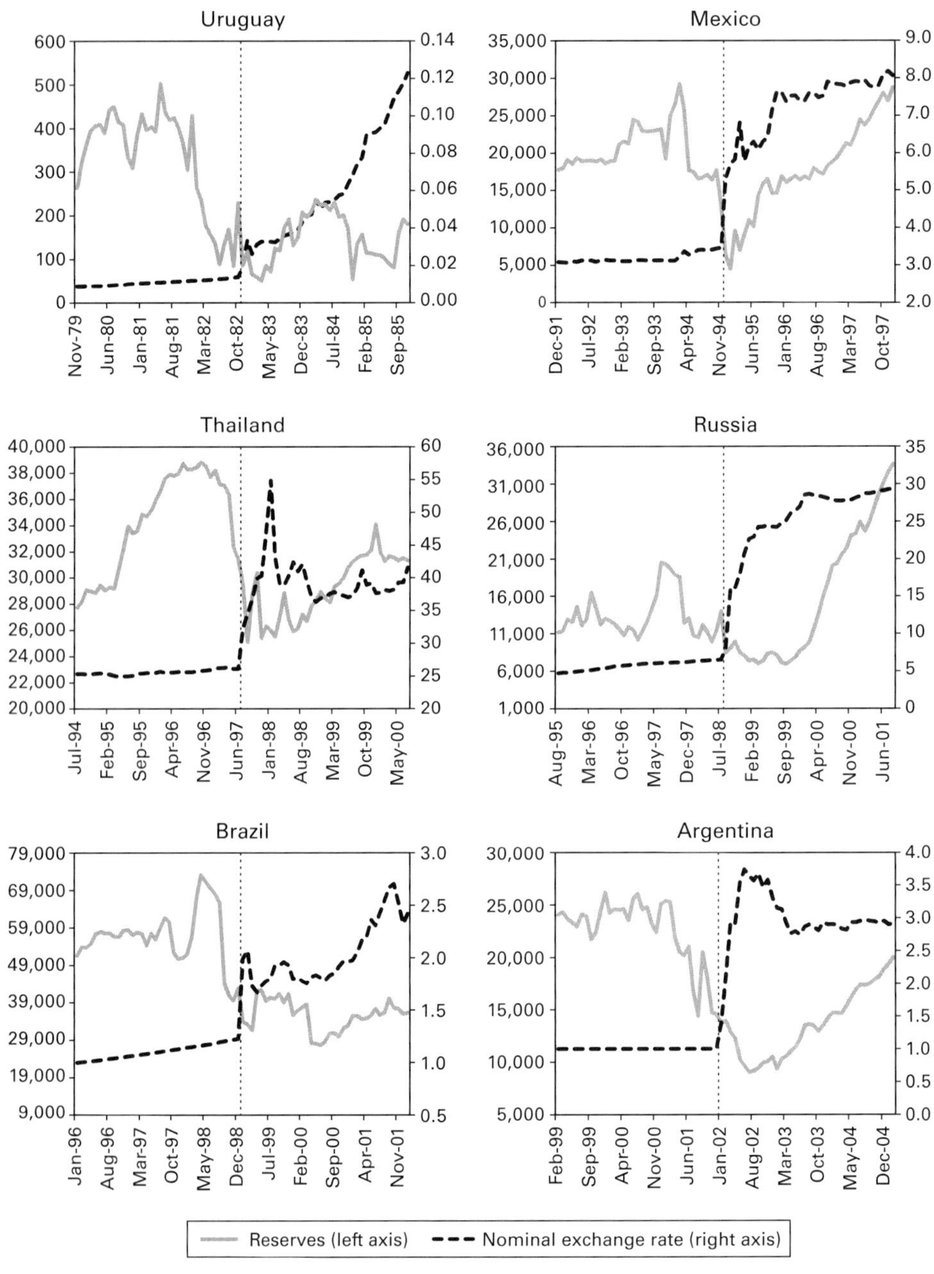

Figure 16.3
Exchange rate and reserves in major balance-of-payments crises

and thus buy time for the fiscal authority to address the fundamental fiscal imbalances.[10] Using high interest rates to defend the currency is hence a key policy issue that has been ignored by the literature until very recently.

To speak of interest rate defense, we need to introduce some friction into the model above. As it stands, the model is clearly not equipped to deal with this issue since, given a fixed exchange rate, the nominal interest rate is fully determined by the interest parity condition (16.15). To introduce a role for interest rate policy, we follow the approach introduced in chapter 9, section 9.4, and developed in the context of balance-of-payments crises by Lahiri and Végh (2003). Specifically, we make a minor modification to the above model by assuming that the monetary authority pays an interest rate i_t^m on money.[11] By assumption, $i_t^m < i_t$; in other words, money always pays below-market interest rates. Other than this, the model remains unchanged. The previous model can in fact be viewed as a particular case of this one with $i_t^m = 0$.

16.3.1 Consumer's Problem

Since money is now interest bearing, the consumer's intertemporal budget constraint—previously given by (16.3)—will be given by

$$a_0 + \frac{y}{r} + \int_0^\infty \tau_t e^{-rt} dt = \int_0^\infty [c_t + (i_t - i_t^m) m_t] e^{-rt} dt. \tag{16.29}$$

The consumer's problem consists in choosing $\{c_t, m_t\}$ for all $t \in [0, \infty)$ to maximize lifetime utility (16.4), subject to (16.29) for a given path of τ_t, i_t, i_t^m, and given values of y and a_0.

Under the standard assumption that $\beta = r$, the first-order conditions imply that

$$u'(c_t) = \lambda, \tag{16.30}$$

$$v'(m_t) = \lambda(i_t - i_t^m). \tag{16.31}$$

10. Higher interest rates to defend the currency (under either a fixed or flexible exchange rate) have been a standard component of IMF-led rescue packages. In this regard, it is worth quoting from Stanley Fischer's (1998) remarks, at the time the IMF's First Deputy Managing Director and main policy architect:

> Are the programs [in Asia in the aftermath of the July 1997 Thai crisis] too tough? In weighing this question, it is important to recall that when they approached the IMF, the reserves of Thailand and Korea were perilously low, and the Indonesian rupiah was excessively depreciated. Thus, the first order of business was, and still is, to restore confidence in the currency. To achieve this, countries have to make it more attractive to hold domestic currency, which, in turn, requires increasing interest rates temporarily, even if higher interest costs complicate the situation of weak banks and corporations. This is a key lesson of the tequila crisis in Latin America 1994–95, as well as from the more recent experience of Brazil, the Czech Republic, Hong Kong, and Russia, all of which have fended off attacks on their currencies in recent months with a timely and forceful tightening of interest rates along with other supporting policy measures. Once confidence is restored, interest rates can return to more normal levels.

11. This setup can be interpreted as consumers holding interest-bearing demand deposits for transactions purposes issued by banks holding 100 percent cash reserves remunerated at the rate i_t^m. For an alternative formulation that also allows for an interest rate defense, see Flood and Jeanne (2005).

Once again, condition (16.30) implies that consumption will be constant along a perfect foresight equilibrium path. Together, equations (16.30) and (16.31) implicitly define the following real money demand:

$$m_t = L(c_t, i_t - i_t^m). \tag{16.32}$$

Notice that for a given i_t, a rise in i_t^m *reduces* the opportunity cost of holding money and will therefore increase real money demand. This is the key channel through which interest rate policy operates in this model.

16.3.2 Government

Taking into account that money is now interest-bearing, the government's flow constraint – previously given by (16.8) – now becomes:

$$\begin{aligned} h_T - h_{T^-} &= \tfrac{M_T - M_{T^-}}{E_T}, \\ \dot{h}_t &= rh_t + \dot{m}_t + (\varepsilon_t - i_t^m)m_t - \tau_t \quad \text{if } t \neq T. \end{aligned} \tag{16.33}$$

The new feature is that now the monetary authority has three policy instruments: the exchange rate, the stock of domestic credit, and the interest rate on money.[12] With respect to exchange rate policy, we assume that the monetary authority initially sets a fixed exchange rate and announces the same abandonment rule: if reserves ever reach zero, the fixed exchange rate is abandoned. We will analyze the unsustainable peg case and thus assume that $\theta > 0$.

What about the path of i_t^m? We will assume that this policy interest rate is set to zero before the crisis (i.e., $i_t^m = 0$ for $t \in [0, T)$) and that if the market interest rate changes at some point in time, the policy interest rate will be changed according to the following rule (which is announced as of time 0):

$$\Delta i_t^m = \gamma \Delta i_t, \qquad \gamma \in [0, 1], \tag{16.34}$$

where γ is a policy parameter. In particular, if $\gamma = 0$, the model reduces to the standard KFG model analyzed above in which the government does not engage in an active interest rate defense. When $0 < \gamma < 1$, the Central Bank is announcing its intention of defending the currency by raising the policy interest rate and thus partly counteracting the increase in market interest rates. When $\gamma = 1$, the monetary authority is exactly matching the rise in market interest rates.

12. See the discussion in chapter 9, section 9.4 and exercise 2.

16.3.3 Defending the Currency

We now show how an active interest rate defense (by which we mean setting $\gamma > 0$) can delay the crisis relative to the KFG case analyzed before.[13]

As before, it is easy to check that the constant level of consumption is still given by (16.17) (see figure 16.4, panel b). Also, as before, the initial fixed exchange rate is unsustainable because the monetary authority is losing international reserves at an increasing rate. Let T denote the time at which the fixed exchange rate is abandoned. The paths of ε_t and i_t are thus given, as before, by (16.25) and (16.26), respectively. The relevant variable for determining money demand, however, is the opportunity cost given by $i_t - i_t^m$. The path of this variable is given by

$$i_t - i_t^m = \begin{cases} r, & 0 \leq t < T, \\ r + (1-\gamma)\theta, & t \geq T. \end{cases} \tag{16.35}$$

Given (16.35), the path of real money balances will be given by

$$m_t = \begin{cases} L(c, r), & 0 \leq t < T, \\ L(c, r + (1-\gamma)\theta), & t \geq T. \end{cases}$$

Hence the jump in real money demand at time T is given by

$$\Delta m = L(c, r + (1-\gamma)\theta) - L(c, r) \leq 0.$$

Notice that the fall in real money demand at T is a decreasing function of γ. In other words, the more aggressive the interest rate defense, as captured by a higher γ, the smaller the fall in real money demand. If $\gamma = 1$, there will in fact be no fall in real money demand at T (figure 16.4, panel c). In this case there will be a crisis but no run!

Again, T is determined by the money market equilibrium at T, given by

$$L[c, r + (1-\gamma)\theta] = \frac{D_0 e^{\theta T}}{\bar{E}}. \tag{16.36}$$

It follows that T is an increasing function of γ. In other words, the more aggressive the interest rate defense is, the more the time of the crisis can be delayed. In the case of $\gamma = 1$ the delay is maximized. It is thus remarkable that even though the monetary authority is actually not doing anything before the crisis actually occurs, the mere announcement of policy rule (16.34) is enough to delay the crisis even to the point where there will be no run when the fixed exchange rate is abandoned (figure 16.4, panel d).

It is easy to see that in this simple version of the model in which there are no fiscal or output costs of delaying the crisis, the optimal interest rate defense would be to set $\gamma = 1$ and delay the

13. While not explicitly modeled, the idea is that the delay may help the government in addressing the underlying fiscal problems and hopefully averting a crisis altogether.

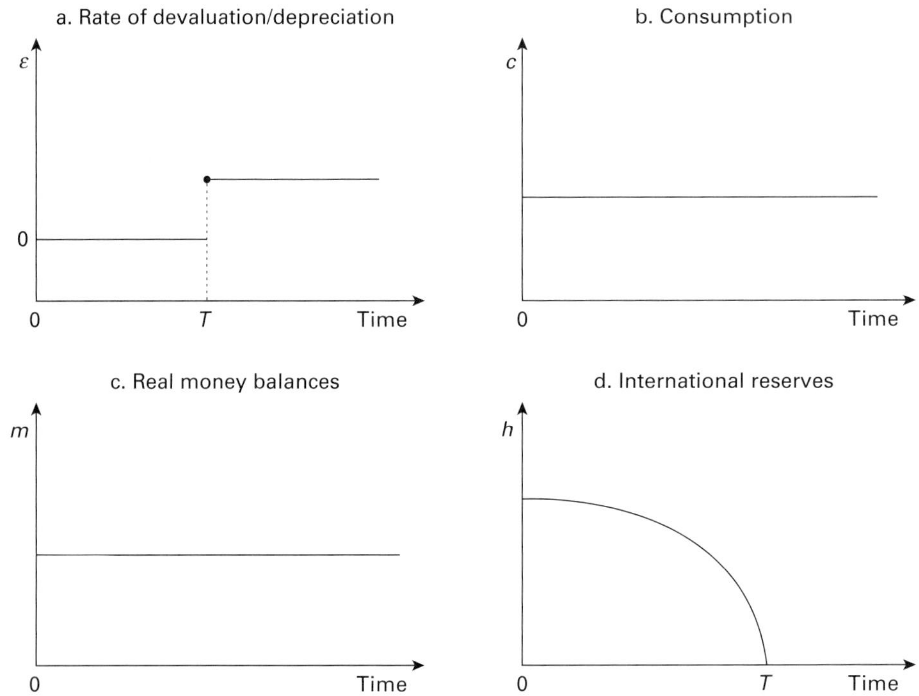

Figure 16.4
Crisis with no run

crisis as much as possible. In practice, of course, delaying a crisis comes at some economic cost. Two main costs come to mind. First, higher interest rates increase the burden of the public debt service thus requiring higher future inflation. Second, higher interest rates will tend to cause an output contraction, which not only will be costly in its own right but will in fact worsen the fiscal problems by reducing conventional tax revenues. From a positive point of view—and as shown by Lahiri and Végh (2003, 2007)—the presence of fiscal and/or output costs implies that there is some increase in interest rates that maximizes the delay and raising interest rates beyond that point may have "perverse effects" and actually bring forward the crisis. From a normative point of view, they show that there is a whole range of interest rate increases for which it is *feasible* to further delay the crisis but *not optimal* to do so. The policy lesson is therefore that while the conventional response of raising interest rates (espoused by the IMF) is appropriate, raising interest rates too much may lead to perverse effects, which validates some of the criticisms raised by prominent analysts such as Jeffrey Sachs and Joseph Stiglitz.[14]

14. See, for instance, Furman and Stiglitz (1998) and Radelet and Sachs (2000).

16.4 Exogenous Fiscal Spending

To keep things as simple as possible, we have assumed so far that fiscal spending was endogenous and passively accommodated the rate of domestic credit growth set by the monetary authority. We now analyze the opposite case (which is clearly the more relevant case in practice): fiscal spending is exogenous and must be financed endogenously by the monetary authority.

Since the consumer's problem is unaffected, consumption and real money demand along a PFEP continue to be given by equations (16.17) and (16.18), respectively. Let us now turn our attention to the government.

16.4.1 Government

Naturally, the flow constraint given by (16.8) remains valid, with transfers now exogenously given at the constant level τ. Taking into account that, along the perfect foresight path to be examined in this section, there may only be a jump in real money balances at T, we can rewrite the intertemporal fiscal constraint (16.9) as

$$\frac{\tau}{r} = h_0 + \int_0^\infty (\dot{m}_t + \varepsilon_t m_t) e^{-rt} dt + (m_T - m_{T^-}) e^{-rT}. \qquad (16.37)$$

Since the level of transfers is exogenously given, the path of domestic credit will now be endogenously determined. The monetary authority still sets the initial exchange rate at $\bar{E}$ and announces the same abandonment rule. The stock of international reserves at time 0, h_0, is now taken as given.[15] Further we will assume that there is a fiscal deficit as of time 0; namely $rh_0 - \tau < 0$.

16.4.2 Unsustainable Peg

We begin by showing that the fixed exchange rate will indeed be unsustainable. To show this, notice that in taking into account that in $\tau_t = \tau$, $\varepsilon_t = 0$, and that real money balances are constant, the government flow constraint (16.8) becomes

$$\dot{h}_t = rh_t - \tau. \qquad (16.38)$$

Solving this (unstable) differential equation, we get

$$h_t = \frac{\tau}{r} + e^{rt}\left(h_0 - \frac{\tau}{r}\right). \qquad (16.39)$$

15. Notice that in the previous case (endogenous transfers), h_0 was endogenous while d_0 was exogenous. The opposite is true now.

Since, by assumption $h_0 - \tau/r < 0$, h_t will hit the zero threshold in finite time.

As before, denote the time of abandonment by T. At time T the government will have to set a positive (and, by assumption, constant) rate of devaluation, ε. How is ε determined? It will be the rate of depreciation (inflation) needed to finance the fiscal deficit for $t \geq T$. Since, by construction, $h_t = 0$ for $t \geq T$, then it follows from (16.8) that the fiscal constraint for $t \geq T$ is given by

$$\tau = \varepsilon L(c, r + \varepsilon), \tag{16.40}$$

where $L(c, r+\varepsilon)$ is the post-crisis real money demand. Depending on the specific money demand, equation (16.40) may have more than one solution. We will assume that real money demand is inelastic with respect to ε and hence that the solution is unique.[16]

Having determined ε, we now determine T. Intuitively, since the path of the inflation rate (i.e., the path of the rate of devaluation/depreciation) has been determined, T will be such that the government's intertemporal constraint holds. To this effect, notice that the government's intertemporal budget constraint (16.37) can be rewritten as

$$\frac{\tau}{r} = h_0 + \frac{e^{-rT}}{r}\left[\varepsilon m_T - r(m_0 - m_T)\right].$$

Intuitively, this equation captures the fact that in addition to the initial stock of international reserves, the only other source of revenues for the government is the collection of inflation tax revenues as of time T, net of the fall in real money balances at T (which implies a loss of revenues). We can then solve for T (taking into account equation 16.40):

$$T = \frac{1}{r}\log\left[\frac{\tau - r(m_0 - m_T)}{\tau - rh_0}\right] > 0,$$

assuming that $r(m_0 - m_T) < rh_0$. We have thus shown that the insights derived in the endogenous-τ case continue to hold. The crisis will be accompanied by a speculative attack and a switch to a flexible exchange rate regime in which the rate of inflation (depreciation) will be such that it finances government spending.

16.5 The Dynamics of Balance-of-Payments Crises

In practice, balance-of-payments crises are generally preceded by consumption booms, current account deficits, and real appreciation of the domestic currency. It is in fact often argued in policy circles that these dynamics "cause" the ensuing balance-of-payments crisis. To shed light on these

16. This will be the case, for example, if $v(m) = (m^{1-1/\sigma} - 1)/(1 - 1/\sigma)$ and $\sigma < 1$. In this case real money demand is given by $m = [1/u'(c)i]^{\sigma}$, as follows from first-order conditions (16.5) and (16.6). The elasticity of this money demand with respect to ε is given by $\sigma\varepsilon/i$, which is less than σ and hence less than one.

issues, we now modify the model of section 16.4 by introducing a link between consumption and the nominal interest rate, along the lines of chapter 7. To this end, we will reformulate the model of section 16.4 in a cash-in-advance setting.[17] In addition, exercise 1 at the end of this chapter adds nontradable goods to this model and shows how the consumption boom and trade deficit before the crisis will also be accompanied by a real appreciation. To simplify the solution of the model, we will assume logarithmic preferences and that fiscal spending is a social waste.

16.5.1 Consumer's Problem

Let preferences be given by

$$\int_0^{\infty} \log(c_t)e^{-\beta t}dt, \tag{16.41}$$

where c_t denotes consumption of the only (tradable) good.

The cash-in-advance constraint requires that

$$m_t = \alpha c_t, \tag{16.42}$$

where α is a positive parameter.

The consumer's intertemporal constraint is now given by

$$a_0 + \frac{y}{r} = \int_0^{\infty} (c_t + i_t m_t)\, e^{-rt}dt, \tag{16.43}$$

where y is the (constant) endowment. Notice that government transfers are no longer part of the consumer's income (due to the assumption that fiscal spending is a social waste). Substituting the cash-in-advance constraint (16.42) into (16.43), we can get rid of real money balances as a choice variable:

$$a_0 + \frac{y}{r} = \int_0^{\infty} c_t(1 + \alpha i_t)e^{-rt}dt. \tag{16.44}$$

The consumer chooses c_t to maximize (16.41) subject to (16.44), for a given path of i_t and given values of y and a_0. The first-order condition is given by (assuming $\beta = r$)

$$\frac{1}{c_t} = \lambda(1 + \alpha i_t). \tag{16.45}$$

17. As should be clear from chapter 7, exercise 1, the same results could be obtained in a MIUF setting with nonseparability between consumption and real money balances as long as the cross-derivative between consumption and real money balances is positive.

16.5.2 Government

The government's constraints do not change relative to the exogenous fiscal spending case examined above. We will, however, make a slight notation change to stress the fact that government spending is now a social waste and denote its constant level by g. With this change in notation, the flow and intertemporal fiscal constraints are now given by

$$\begin{aligned} h_T - h_{T^-} &= \frac{M_T - M_{T^-}}{E_T}, \\ \dot{h}_t &= rh_t + \dot{m}_t + \varepsilon_t m_t - g, \qquad \text{if } t \neq T, \end{aligned} \tag{16.46}$$

$$\frac{g}{r} = h_0 + \int_0^\infty (\dot{m}_t + \varepsilon_t m_t) e^{-rt} dt + (m_T - m_{T^-}) e^{-rT}. \tag{16.47}$$

The policy assumptions are also the same as in the exogenous fiscal spending case examined above. The monetary authority sets a fixed exchange rate and announces that if international reserves ever reach zero, the peg will be abandoned.

16.5.3 Solution of the Model

Given (16.38), with g in lieu of τ, and the assumption that $h_0 - g/r < 0$, the fixed exchange rate is unsustainable. As before, denote by T the time of abandonment and by ε the rate of depreciation for $t \geq T$ (both of which will be determined endogenously). The path of the nominal interest rate will thus be given by

$$i_t = \begin{cases} r, & 0 \leq t < T, \\ r + \varepsilon, & t \geq T. \end{cases} \tag{16.48}$$

Since, as shown below, ε will have to be positive to finance the fiscal deficit, the effective price of consumption (given by $1 + \alpha i_t$) will not be constant over time and the consumer will thus be facing an intertemporal distortion (as in chapters 3 and 7). Hence it should be intuitively clear that consumption of tradable goods will be high during the fixed exchange rate period and low afterwards (see figure 16.5, panel b). Formally, taking into account (16.48), we can rewrite the first order condition (16.45) as

$$\frac{1}{c^1} = \lambda(1 + \alpha r), \tag{16.49}$$

$$\frac{1}{c^2} = \lambda[1 + \alpha(r + \varepsilon)], \tag{16.50}$$

where c^1 denotes the constant level of consumption for $0 \leq t < T$ and c^2 the constant level for $t \geq T$. Clearly, $c^1 > c^2$. It follows that there will be a trade deficit (assuming $k_0 - g/r = 0$) before

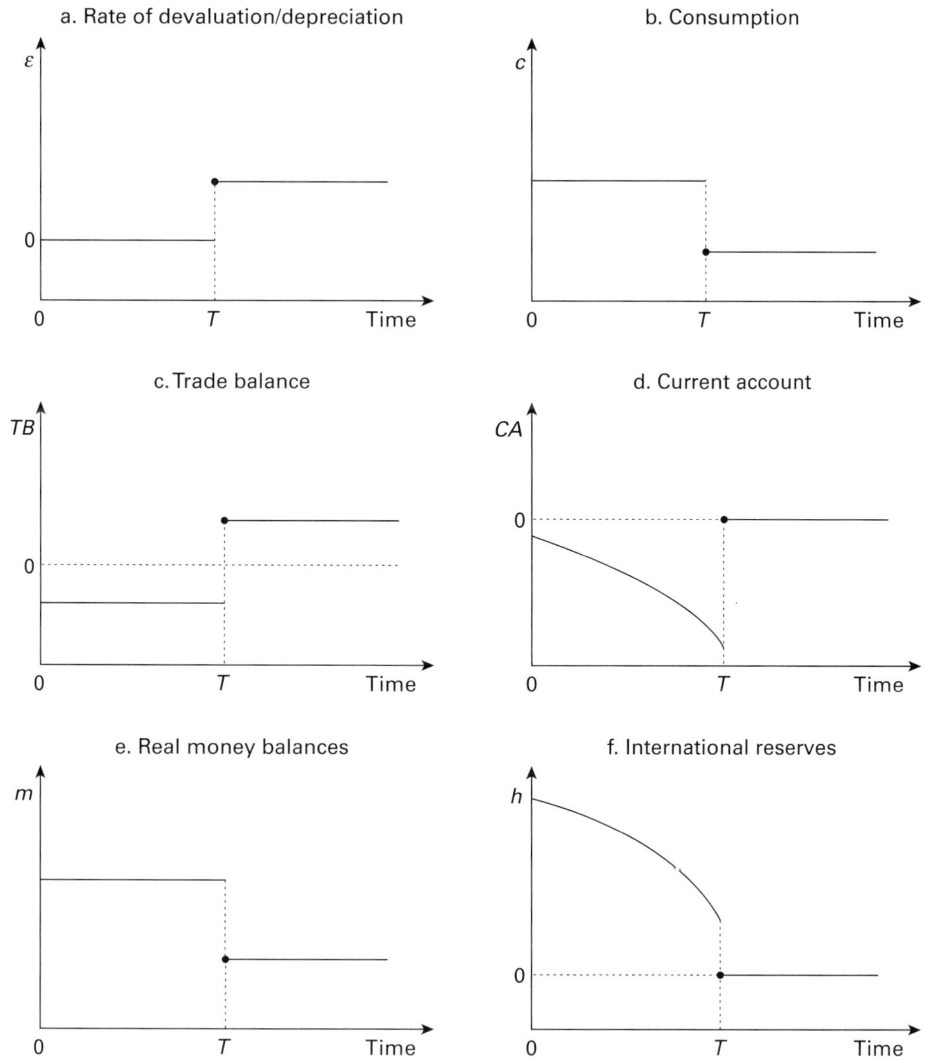

Figure 16.5
Balance-of-payments crisis with consumption dynamics

time T (panel c) as well as a current account deficit (panel d). Given the path of consumption illustrated in panel b, the path of real money balances (panel e) follows from the cash-in-advance constraint (16.42).

Using (16.44), (16.49), and (16.50), we can derive a reduced form for c^1 and c^2:

$$c^1 = \frac{ra_0 + y}{1 + \alpha r}, \tag{16.51}$$

$$c^2 = \frac{ra_0 + y}{1 + \alpha(r + \varepsilon)}. \tag{16.52}$$

We can now derive ε from the fiscal constraint. The derivation of ε is analogous to the exogenous-τ case analyzed above. From (16.46) the flow fiscal constraint for $t \geq T$ is now given by

$$g = \varepsilon m^2, \tag{16.53}$$

where m^2 denotes real money demand for $t \geq T$. Using (16.42) and (16.52), we can solve for ε:

$$\varepsilon = \frac{1 + \alpha r}{\alpha} \left(\frac{A}{1 - A} \right), \tag{16.54}$$

where $A \equiv g/(ra_0 + y)$ can be interpreted as government spending as a proportion of GDP. As expected, ε is a strictly increasing function of g and would be zero if $g = 0$.

We now turn to the determination of T. Again, we proceed in the same way as in the exogenous-τ case and use the intertemporal fiscal constraint to determine T. From (16.47), and using (16.42) and (16.53), it follows that

$$T = \frac{1}{r} \log \left\{ \frac{g - r\alpha \left(c^1 - c^2\right)}{g - rh_0} \right\} > 0.$$

Notice that under the assumption that $\alpha \left(c^1 - c^2\right) < h_0$ (i.e., the fall in real money demand at T is smaller than initial reserves), T is positive as indicated. The path of international reserves is illustrated in panel f.

In sum, before the crisis consumption is high and the trade balance is in deficit. At time T consumption falls and the trade balance shifts into surplus. If we add nontradable goods to the model—as in exercise 1 at the end of the chapter—we can show that the initial consumption boom is accompanied by a relatively low real exchange rate (i.e., an appreciated currency in real terms) and that the crisis at time T entails a sharp rise in the real exchange rate (i.e., a real depreciation). The model's predictions are thus consistent with the evidence for nine major balance-of-payments crises reviewed in chapter 4, box 4.2.

16.6 A Crisis with No Contemporaneous Fiscal Deficit

As just illustrated, balance-of-payments crises are often preceded by a consumption boom. In practice, this surge in consumption leads to a dramatic increase in tax revenues—particularly in developing countries where tax systems are heavily biased in favor of consumption taxes. As tax revenues increase during the boom, the primary deficit falls dramatically, which often leads policy makers and observers alike to argue that there is no underlying fiscal problem and that the boom in economic activity and the real appreciation of the currency really reflect the effects of successful "structural reforms." Of course, while the boom is taking place, it is hard to tell which interpretation is correct.[18] Following Talvi (1997), we now provide an example that nicely illustrates the perils of relying on contemporaneous fiscal indicators to judge the sustainability of a fixed exchange rate.

Formally, our starting point is the cash-in-advance model developed in section 16.5 where government spending is exogenous (and a social waste). We will make the following modifications to that setup: (1) in addition to inflation tax revenues, the government also collects revenues from a consumption tax and (2) preferences are CES with an intertemporal elasticity of substitution greater than one.[19]

16.6.1 Consumer's Problem

Let preferences be given by

$$\int_0^\infty \frac{c_t^{1-1/\sigma} - 1}{1 - 1/\sigma} e^{-\beta t} dt, \qquad \sigma > 1, \tag{16.55}$$

where c_t denotes consumption of the only good. Denote the (constant) consumption tax by θ. The consumer's intertemporal budget constraint thus becomes

$$a_0 + \frac{y}{r} = \int_0^\infty [c_t(1+\theta) + i_t m_t] e^{-rt} dt. \tag{16.56}$$

The cash-in-advance constraint continues to be given by (16.42). Substituting (16.42) into (16.56), we can rewrite the intertemporal budget constraint as

$$a_0 + \frac{y}{r} = \int_0^\infty c_t(1 + \theta + \alpha i_t) e^{-rt} dt. \tag{16.57}$$

18. While use of cyclically adjusted fiscal indicators would provide contemporaneous evidence on this issue, cyclical adjustments in highly volatile developing countries are fraught with methodological problems of their own.

19. The critical role of the second assumption will be discussed below.

The consumer chooses c_t to maximize (16.55) subject to (16.57), for a given path of i_t and given values of y, θ, and a_0. The first-order condition is given by (assuming $\beta = r$)

$$c_t^{-1/\sigma} = \lambda(1 + \theta + \alpha i_t), \tag{16.58}$$

where the effective price of consumption now includes the consumption tax and is thus given by $1 + \theta + \alpha i_t$. However, since θ is assumed to be flat over time, it will play no role in inducing a nonconstant consumption path over time.

For further reference, note that from (16.57) and (16.58), it follows that for a permanently fixed exchange rate (so that $i_t = r$), the constant consumption level, denoted by $\tilde{c}$, would be given by

$$\tilde{c} = \frac{ra_0 + y}{1 + \theta + \alpha r}. \tag{16.59}$$

16.6.2 Government

As in section 16.5, the government faces an exogenous level of government spending, g. In addition to revenues from the inflation tax, however, it now collects revenues from the (exogenously given) consumption tax, θ. With this modification, the government's flow and intertemporal budget constraints become

$$h_T - h_{T^-} = \frac{M_T - M_{T^-}}{E_T},$$

$$\dot{h}_t = rh_t + \theta c_t + \dot{m}_t + \varepsilon_t m_t - g, \qquad \text{if } t \neq T, \tag{16.60}$$

$$\frac{g}{r} = h_0 + \int_0^\infty (\theta c_t + \dot{m}_t + \varepsilon_t m_t)e^{-rt}dt + (m_T - m_{T^-})e^{-rT}. \tag{16.61}$$

Define the fiscal balance as

$$s_t^g \equiv rh_t + \theta c_t - g. \tag{16.62}$$

Further, since there are now revenues from conventional taxes, it is useful to define the *primary* fiscal balance (which excludes interest on reserves) as

$$s_t^{pg} \equiv \theta c_t - g. \tag{16.63}$$

To generate an unsustainable peg, it will be assumed that, for the consumption level associated with a sustainable fixed exchange rate (which is given by equation 16.59) and the initial level of reserves, there is a fiscal deficit. In other words, we assume that $rh_0 + \theta\tilde{c} - g < 0$.

The policy assumptions remain unchanged: the monetary authority sets a fixed exchange rate and announces that if international reserves ever reach zero, the peg will be abandoned.

16.6.3 An Example with No Fiscal Deficit

Instead of providing a general solution of the model, we will construct a particular example that will illustrate the dramatic consequences of having endogenous fiscal revenues.[20] In this example, the primary fiscal deficit will be zero during the period leading up to the crisis and international reserves will be actually rising.

For starters, it should be clear that a fixed exchange rate regime is unsustainable. If the rate of devaluation is expected to be zero indefinitely, consumption will be given by (16.59) and real money balances will be constant as well. Hence the flow fiscal constraint (16.60) becomes

$$\dot{h}_t = rh_t + \theta\tilde{c} - g,$$

which, as before, is an unstable differential equation. Hence reserves would hit the critical threshold in finite time. The government will thus have to abandon the peg at some point in time, T, and switch to a positive rate of depreciation to cover the fiscal deficit with inflation tax revenues. Let us denote by ε the rate of depreciation for $t \geq T$. Since ε will have to be positive, it follows from (16.58) that consumption will be high before T (denoted by c^1) and low afterward (denoted by c^2):

$$(c^1)^{-1/\sigma} = \lambda(1 + \theta + \alpha r), \tag{16.64}$$

$$(c^2)^{-1/\sigma} = \lambda[1 + \theta + \alpha(r + \varepsilon)]. \tag{16.65}$$

By construction, we want the primary deficit before the crisis to be zero. From (16.63), this requires c^1 to be

$$c^1 = \frac{g}{\theta}. \tag{16.66}$$

For simplicity, define a new variable, $x \equiv c^1/c^2$. It then follows from (16.64) and (16.65) that

$$x^{1/\sigma} = \frac{1 + \theta + \alpha(r + \varepsilon)}{1 + \theta + \alpha r}. \tag{16.67}$$

For time T onward, international reserves will be zero. Hence from (16.60) it follows that

$$g - \theta c^2 = \varepsilon m^2.$$

20. Exercise 2 at the end of the chapter asks you to work out a general solution for this model for the case of logarithmic preferences.

Using the cash-in-advance constraint (16.42), along with (16.66), and recalling that, by definition, $x \equiv c^1/c^2$, we can solve for ε from the last equation to obtain

$$\varepsilon = \frac{\theta}{\alpha}(x - 1). \tag{16.68}$$

Substituting (16.68) into (16.67), we obtain

$$x^{1/\sigma} = 1 + \frac{\theta}{1 + \theta + \alpha r}(x - 1), \tag{16.69}$$

which will determine the equilibrium value of x. Figure 16.6 illustrates the determination of x by plotting the LHS (denoted by $f(x)$ in the figure) and the RHS (denoted by $g(x)$ in the figure) of equation (16.69) as a function of x. Under the assumption that $\theta/(1 + \theta + \alpha r) < 1/\sigma$ and recalling that $\sigma > 1$, we see that the LHS of the equation will intersect the RHS for some $x > 1$, denoted x^* in figure 16.6.[21] Since the equilibrium value of x is greater than unity, it follows from (16.68) that $\varepsilon > 0$.

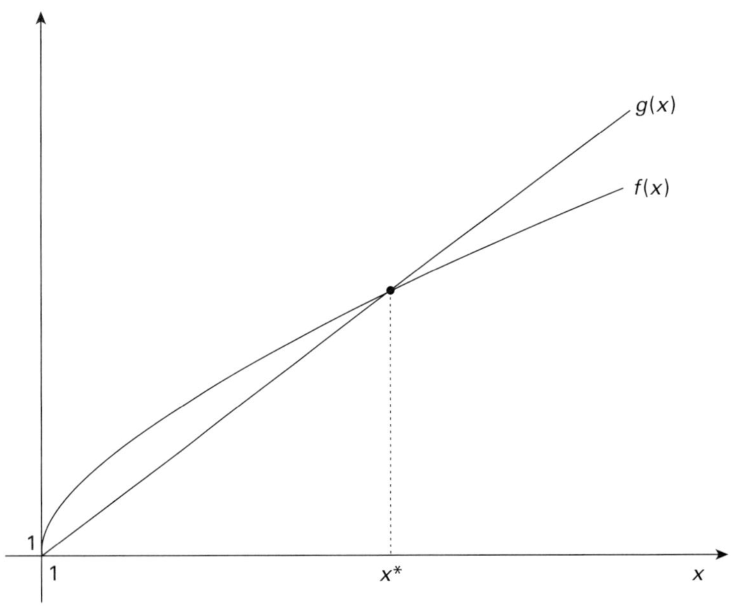

Figure 16.6
Determination of x

21. Note that the assumption that $\theta/(1+\theta+\alpha r) < 1/\sigma$ ensures that at $x = 1$ the slope of the LHS is greater than that of the RHS. The assumption that $\sigma > 1$ (and hence $1/\sigma < 1$) ensures that the LHS will intersect the RHS for some $x > 1$. Note that $x = 1$ cannot be an equilibrium because it would imply that $c^2 = c^1 = g/\theta$, which would violate the resource constraint.

What will be the path of international reserves? From (16.60) and taking into account that $\varepsilon_t = \dot{m}_t = 0$ and the primary deficit is, by construction, also zero, it follows that

$$\dot{h}_t = rh_t.$$

Hence international reserves increase over time. Intuitively, since the primary fiscal balance is zero, there is a fiscal surplus as the fiscal authority accumulates (and reinvests) interest on reserves.

How is T determined? It is determined in the same way as before. Namely T will the be value needed for the intertemporal fiscal constraint to hold. Hence from (16.61), (16.66), and (16.68) it follows that

$$T = \frac{1}{r}\log\left(\frac{m_{T^-} - m_T}{h_0}\right) > 0,$$

since the fall in real money balances will be higher than initial reserves (as reserves have accumulated over time).

Figure 16.7 illustrates the time path of the main variables. Notice how, during $[0, T)$, inflation (i.e., the rate of devaluation) is zero, the primary deficit is zero, and international reserves are increasing. Such an outcome could, quite naturally, be interpreted as a clear signal of a successful program. In reality, however, it reflects the underlying fiscal unsustainability of the program.

16.7 Optimal Abandonment Rule

For all its remarkable insights, the Krugman–Flood–Garber model has a somewhat disturbing feature: even though households act optimally, the government follows a completely arbitrary abandonment rule (i.e., give up the peg if and only if reserves reach certain threshold). In other words, if the fixed exchange rate is unsustainable and will have to be abandoned at some point, why not abandon it right away (i.e., at time 0) and avoid a discrete loss in international reserves and a boom–bust cycle in economic activity? This section relaxes the ad hoc abandonment rule of the classical KFG model and examines what happens when policy makers act optimally.[22]

A key advantage of optimizing models is that they offer the possibility of evaluating the welfare consequences of alternative policies and establishing the optimal one. The optimal policy is thus the one that maximizes consumers' welfare subject to the constraint that such a policy be implementable as a competitive equilibrium. We thus have all the ingredients necessary to answer the following question. Suppose that there is initially (i.e., before time 0) a sustainable fixed exchange rate. At time 0 there is an unanticipated shock that renders the fixed exchange rate unsustainable (i.e., the intertemporal fiscal constraint cannot be satisfied for a zero devaluation rate). When is it optimal to abandon the fixed exchange rate?

22. A more radical departure of the KFG model is captured by the so-called second- and third-generation models of BOP crises discussed in box 16.2.

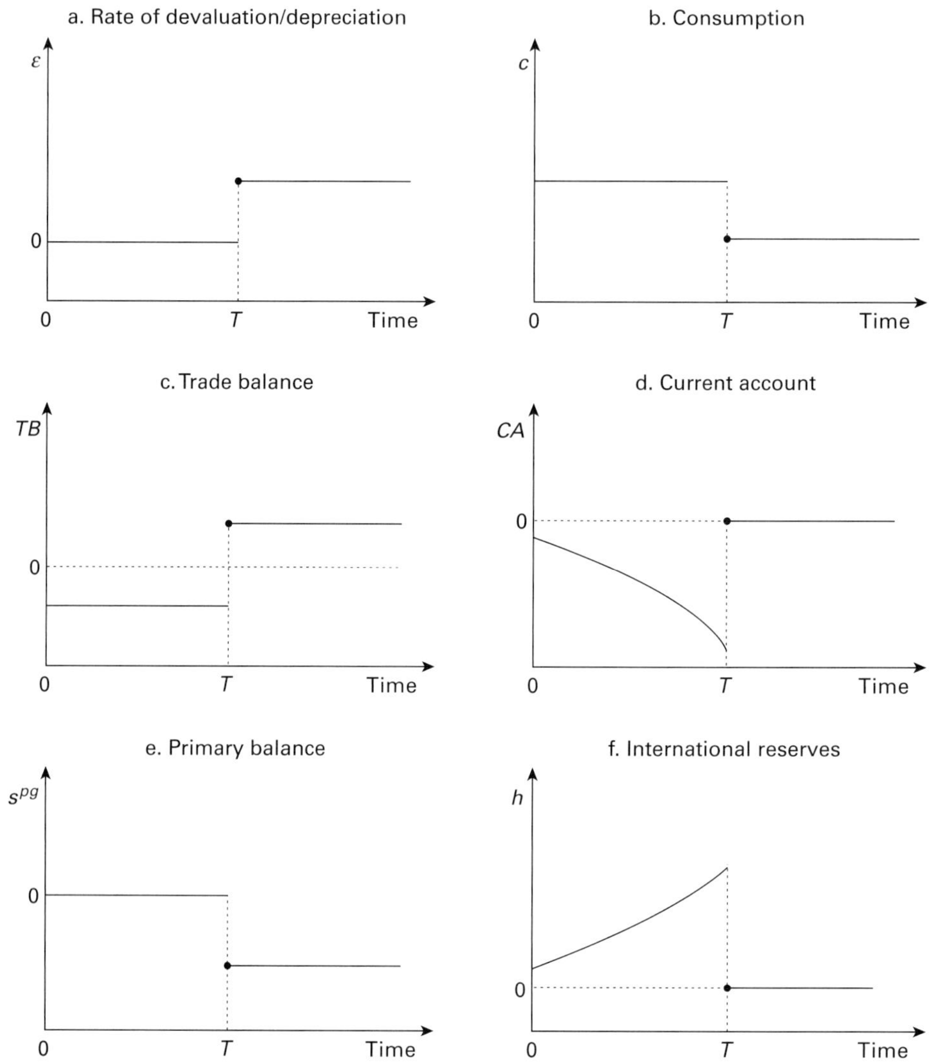

Figure 16.7
Crisis with no primary deficit

Box 16.2
Second- and third-generation models of balance-of-payments crises

Second- and third-generation models of currency crises were developed to explain a number of crises in the 1990s and 2000s that did not fit the framework of first-generation models described in this chapter.

Second-generation models of currency crises were born after the European exchange rate mechanism crisis that culminated in August 1993. It was argued that at the time of the speculative attacks, none of the exchange rates in question were obviously unsustainable, which is the critical assumption behind first-generation models. As a result researchers developed frameworks in which speculative attacks occur because of self-fulfilling expectations that the fixed exchange rate regime is unsustainable (thus a fundamental characteristic of the second-generation models is that they exhibit multiple equilibria). Two classic papers on second-generation models are Obstfeld (1994, 1996).

In Obstfeld's models the Central Bank is an optimizing agent that minimizes a loss function that depends on inflation and on the deviation of output from its potential. The level of output is determined by a Phillips curve, creating a tradeoff between output and inflation, and the Central Bank decides whether to maintain the fixed exchange rate regime or to float. In the case where agents expect the government to devalue, and to produce inflation as a consequence, there will be an unexpected low level of inflation if the Central Bank does not devalue, with output falling below potential. This feature makes it costly to defend the currency. If the costs associated with devaluing (lost reputation or inflation volatility) are sufficiently low, the government will devalue, validating agents' expectations. In contrast, if agents expect the exchange rate to remain fixed, it can be optimal for the government to validate agents' expectations if the output gains from an unexpected devaluation are not too large. Depending on the costs and benefits of the government's actions and on agents' expectations, there can be more than one equilibrium.[a]

As will be analyzed in chapter 17, box 17.4, many currency crises coincide with crises in the financial sector. This observation has motivated researchers to emphasize the role of banks in causing and amplifying currency crises, which constitutes the basis of third-generation models. The key mechanism of this type of models relies on the role of balance sheet effects. In some of these models, balance sheet problems arise when banks (and firms) have explicit currency mismatches. Typically, banks and firms face currency risk because revenues are denominated in terms of nontradable goods while liabilities are specified in tradable goods. This mismatch makes devaluations, which increase the relative price of tradables in terms of nontradables, an unattractive option. In other models the balance sheet problems arise when banks and firms are exposed to liquidity shocks because they finance long-term projects with short-term borrowing. Both sources of risks expose emerging markets to currency crises through balance sheet effects.

Velasco (1987) is perhaps the first example of this type of model.[b] The author extends the first-generation models to a situation in which the private banking system is explicitly modeled. In this model the excessive rate of domestic credit creation is not the result of an exogenously determined fiscal deficit but arises as the result of the government's commitment to guarantee the liabilities of the banking system once it collapses. The size of this burden is determined by the behavior of the banks prior to the collapse. In particular, banks undertake foreign borrowing to cover losses triggered by negative real shocks, postponing and enlarging the burden passed on to the government. After the government inherits a sufficiently large stock of liabilities, the mechanisms that lead to a balance-of-payments crisis in first-generation models follow. McKinnon and Pill (1996), Burnside, Eichenbaum, and Rebelo (2004), Chang and Velasco (2001), and Caballero and Krishnamurthy (2001) are other important contributions to this literature.

a. See Jeanne (2000) for a survey of second-generation models and Morris and Shin (1998) for a critique of such models.

b. Section 17.7 in chapter 17 presents a version of Velasco's (1987) model.

We will show that it is optimal to abandon the fixed exchange rate immediately (i.e., at $t = 0$) *regardless of the level of international reserves*. Hence, without costs of abandoning the peg, the exogenous abandonment rule assumed in the KFG model will, in general, not be optimal.[23]

16.7.1 Consumer's Problem

The consumer's problem remains the same as in section 16.5, with preferences and cash-in-advance constraint given by (16.41) and (16.42), respectively.

The consumer's lifetime constraint corresponding to equation (16.2) is now given by (notice that there are no government transfers)

$$b_{0^-} + \frac{y}{r} = \int_0^\infty (c_t + \dot{m}_t + \varepsilon_t m_t) e^{-rt} dt + \frac{M_0 - M_{0^-}}{E_0} + \frac{M_T - M_{T^-}}{E_T} e^{-rT}, \tag{16.70}$$

which takes into account possible discrete changes in real money balances at time 0 and T.[24] The stock of net foreign bonds just before time 0 (i.e., just before possible jumps in b_t and m_t at 0) is denoted by b_{0^-}.

Imposing the condition that $\lim_{t\to\infty} e^{-rt} m_t = 0$ and taking into account the cash-in-advance constraint (16.42), equation (16.70) can be rewritten as

$$b_{0^-} + \frac{M_{0^-}}{E_0} + \frac{y}{r} = \int_0^\infty c_t (1 + \alpha i_t) e^{-rt} dt. \tag{16.71}$$

The consumer chooses c_t to maximize (16.41) subject to (16.71). Assuming, as usual, that $\beta = r$, the first-order condition is given by

$$\frac{1}{c_t} = \lambda(1 + \alpha i_t). \tag{16.72}$$

16.7.2 Government

As in section 16.5, the government carries out expenditures (g_t) and collects seigniorage revenues. The government's intertemporal budget constraint is now given by

$$\Gamma_{0^-} = h_{0^-} + \int_0^\infty (\dot{m}_t + \varepsilon_t m_t) e^{-rt} dt + \frac{M_0 - M_{0^-}}{E_0} + \frac{M_T - M_{T^-}}{E_T} e^{-rT}, \tag{16.73}$$

23. We say "in general" because even in the presense of the ad hoc KFG abandonment rule, it might be optimal to abandon the peg right away if the fiscal deficit is large enough relative to the size of the existing stock of international reserves.

24. As it turns out, in equilibrium there will only be a discrete change in b_t and m_t at time 0 and not at time T. However, when we add a cost of abandoning the peg as in exercise 3 at the end of the chapter, there may also be a discrete change at time T.

where, by definition, Γ_{0^-} is the present discounted value of government spending just before time 0:

$$\Gamma_{0^-} \equiv \int_0^\infty g_t e^{-rt} dt.$$

The formulation in (16.73) thus allows for the possibility of discrete changes in the nominal money supply at time 0 and time T.

16.7.3 Initial Equilibrium

First, notice that combining (16.70) and (16.73), we obtain the economy's resource constraint:

$$b_{0^-} + h_{0^-} + \frac{y}{r} = \int_0^\infty c_t e^{-rt} dt + \Gamma_{0^-}. \tag{16.74}$$

We assume that before $t = 0$ the economy is operating under a sustainable fixed exchange rate. In other words, the government is able to finance the present discounted value of expenditures with its initial net foreign assets and hence does not need to resort to revenues from money creation. To ensure this, assume that

$$\Gamma_{0^-} = h_{0^-}.$$

This condition implies that we can rewrite the economy's resource constraint (16.74) as

$$b_{0^-} + \frac{y}{r} = \int_0^\infty c_t e^{-rt} dt. \tag{16.75}$$

We now verify that the initial fixed exchange rate regime is indeed sustainable. Notice that if $\varepsilon_t = 0$, then $i_t = r$, which combined with first-order condition (16.72), the cash-in-advance constraint (16.42), and the economy's resource constraint (16.75) imply that consumption and real money balances are constant over time and given by

$$c_{0^-} = rb_{0^-} + y, \tag{16.76}$$

$$m_{0^-} = \alpha c_{0^-}.$$

Since real money balances are constant over time and $\varepsilon_t = 0$, the intertemporal fiscal constraint (16.73) reduces to $\Gamma_{0^-} = h_{0^-}$. Hence the initial level of net foreign assets is exactly enough to finance government expenditures.

16.7.4 Unanticipated Fiscal Shock: When to Abandon the Peg?

Suppose that at time 0 there is an unanticipated and permanent increase in the present discounted value of government expenditures from Γ_{0^-} to Γ_0, where $\Gamma_{0^-} < \Gamma_0$. Clearly, given this fiscal shock, the fixed exchange rate cannot be maintained because, if it were, equation (16.73) would imply that

$$\Gamma_0 > h_{0^-}.$$

Hence, to satisfy the intertemporal fiscal constraint, the government will need to abandon the fixed exchange rate and set a positive rate of devaluation (i.e., a positive rate of inflation) to finance the higher expenditures. The question is thus: When is it optimal to abandon the fixed exchange rate?

We now show that it is optimal to abandon the fixed exchange rate immediately (i.e., at $t = 0$). Notice that after the shock, the new resource constraint corresponding to (16.75) becomes

$$b_{0^-} + \frac{y}{r} - \Delta\Gamma = \int_0^\infty c_t e^{-rt} dt, \tag{16.77}$$

where $\Delta\Gamma \equiv \Gamma_0 - \Gamma_{0^-}$ denotes the present discounted value of the *additional* fiscal expenditures.

Clearly, the present discounted value of resources available for private consumption—given by the LHS of equation (16.77)—does not depend on when the fixed exchange rate regime is abandoned. Further we know from chapter 3 that, for a given social wealth, a flat path of consumption is always welfare-superior to a non-flat path of consumption. It thus follows immediately that it would never be optimal for a Ramsey planner to abandon the peg at $T > 0$ because doing so would imply setting a positive rate of devaluation (dictated by the intertemporal fiscal constraint) which would impose an intertemporal distortion in consumption.[25] Hence the optimal policy is clearly to abandon the fixed exchange rate immediately (i.e., to choose $T = 0$).

Since the abandonment of the peg at time 0 will involve a constant rate of devaluation from time 0 on (as discussed below), the new level of consumption will be constant and, from (16.77), equal to

$$c_0 = rb_{0^-} + y - r\Delta\Gamma. \tag{16.78}$$

The behavior of the nominal exchange rate and the rate of devaluation at $t = 0$ depends on the specific monetary policy chosen by the government. After the fiscal shock at $t = 0$, the intertemporal fiscal constraint becomes (taking into account that consumption, and hence real money balances, will be constant over time)

25. Notice that since in a perfect foresight model an anticipated increase in the exchange rate is inconsistent with equilibrium, abandoning the peg for some positive T necessarily implies that a change in the rate of devaluation is needed to intertemporally balance the budget.

$$\Delta\Gamma = \int_0^{\infty} \varepsilon_t m_t e^{-rt} dt + \frac{M_0 - M_{0^-}}{E_0}. \tag{16.79}$$

The government has two choices (or combinations thereof), both of which are consistent with a flat path of consumption. The first consists in keeping the money supply unchanged at $t = 0$ (i.e., $M_0 = M_{0^-}$) and set a constant rate of money growth (i.e., rate of depreciation) dictated by the need to satisfy the intertemporal fiscal constraint (16.79). Solving for ε from (16.79), taking into account the cash-in-advance constraint (16.42), yields

$$\varepsilon = \frac{r}{\alpha c_0} \Delta\Gamma.$$

Using (16.42), (16.76), and (16.78), we see that this policy would be accompanied by a discrete change in the exchange rate at time 0 given by

$$\frac{E_0 - E_{0^-}}{E_{0^-}} = \frac{r\Delta\Gamma}{c_{0^-} - r\Delta\Gamma}.$$

The second choice is to finance the increased expenditures solely by printing more money at $t = 0$. This implies that the additional government expenditures are financed by taxing away existing real money balances (which is equivalent to a lump-sum tax). From (16.79) this implies that

$$\Delta\Gamma = \frac{M_0 - M_{0^-}}{E_0}. \tag{16.80}$$

Using (16.42), (16.76), (16.78), and (16.80), we see that the devaluation at time 0 is given by

$$\frac{E_0 - E_{0^-}}{E_{0^-}} = \frac{(1 + \alpha r)\,\Delta\Gamma}{\alpha c_{0^-} - (1 + \alpha r)\,\Delta\Gamma}.$$

In this case a larger devaluation occurs at $t = 0$ but the rate of devaluation remains zero.

Of course, any combination of these two policies is also an optimal policy. Whatever the specific policy at time 0, however, any policy implies abandoning the fixed exchange rate at $t = 0$.

We have just concluded that in the absence of any costs of abandoning the peg, it would be optimal to give up the fixed exchange rate as soon as it becomes unsustainable. Furthermore the decision to abandon the peg is totally independent of the stock of reserves and/or the size of the fiscal shock. We thus conclude that it is not easy to rationalize the ad hoc KFG abandonment rule when policy makers act rationally.

To rationalize some delay in abandoning a fixed exchange rate once it has become unsustainable, we need in fact to introduce some cost of abandoning the peg. The simplest case would be to assume that there is an exogenous cost ϕ of abandoning the peg, which is both a fiscal and a social cost (see exercise 3 at the end of this chapter). This cost could represent an output loss and/or the cost of bailing out the banking system in the event of a crisis. It could also capture the option value of remaining in the peg if there is some probability that a fiscal reform that would make the regime sustainable again may take place as long as the fixed exchange rate is in place (see Rebelo and Végh 2008 for details). The punchline of exercise 3 is that even if there is a fixed cost of abandoning the peg, it will be optimal to abandon it for any fiscal shock above a certain threshold. Hence rationalizing the KFG abandonment rule requires *both* some cost of abandoning the peg *and* a "small" fiscal shock.

16.8 Final Remarks

This chapter has examined in detail balance-of-payments crises models where the abandonment of a predetermined exchange rate regime is due to inconsistent fiscal and monetary policies. The basic model yields the remarkable result that there is a discrete loss of reserves at the time of the crisis even though all events are perfectly anticipated. The chapter then analyzed several extensions of the basic model with important policy implications. First, we saw that an active interest rate defense can delay the crisis and thus buy time to address the underlying fiscal problems. Such an interest rate defense, however, can be costly both in terms of output losses and a higher public debt burden. Second, if the pre-crisis consumption boom fuels tax revenues, we could have a balance-of-payments crisis that is not preceded by a contemporaneous fiscal deficit. An outside observer could mistakenly conclude that there is no cause for concern. Hence judging the sustainability of a fixed exchange rate regime by looking at contemporaneous fiscal deficits could result in costly policy mistakes. Finally, when the abandonment rule is endogeneized, we saw that it could be optimal to abandon the fixed exchange rate regime as soon as it becomes unsustainable, regardless of the level of international reserves.

16.9 Appendix: Alternative Derivation of T

This appendix shows how the condition determining T could be derived in an alternative way by solving the differential equation that governs the path of international reserves and finding out the point in time at which the level of reserves will be exactly equal to the required jump in real money demand. Specifically, taking into account that $\dot{m}_t = \varepsilon_t = 0$, solve differential equation (16.12) by integrating between 0 and t to obtain

$$h_t = h_0 - d_0(e^{\theta t} - 1). \tag{16.81}$$

Since the nominal exchange rate cannot jump at T, the level of international reserves an instant before T must be equal to the change in real money demand:

$$h_{T^-} = L(c, r) - L(c, r + \theta).$$

Using (16.81), we can rewrite the last equation as

$$h_0 - d_0(e^{\theta T^-} - 1) = L(c, r) - L(c, r + \theta),$$

which, given that $h_0 + d_0 = L(c, r)$, simplifies to

$$d_0 e^{\theta T^-} = L(c, r + \theta).$$

This is, of course, the same condition as (16.28).

Exercises

1. (Dynamics of BOP crisis with nontradable goods) This exercise follows Calvo (1987) and adds nontradable goods to the model of section 16.5. Specifically, suppose that households consume only nontradable goods and that nontradable goods are produced using tradable goods as the only input with the use of the following technology:

$$c_t^N = f(c_t^T), \quad f'(.) > 0, \quad f''(.) < 0.$$

In this context of this model:

a. Show that a balance-of-payments crisis at time T will be accompanied by a fall in the relative price of nontradable goods (i.e., a real depreciation).

b. Suppose that the government spends only on tradable goods. Derive a reduced form for ε and T.

2. (Talvi 1997 model with logarithmic preferences) This problem asks you to provide a general solution for the model of section 16.6 for the case of logarithmic preferences. The punchline will be that while the primary deficit is lower than it would be in a sustainable fixed exchange rate, it is still positive and hence international reserves are falling over time (in contrast to the example illustrated in figure 16.7).

a. Consider the model of section 16.6 with logarithmic preferences. Solve for an unanticipated and temporary exchange rate based stabilization at $t = 0$.

b. Show that there is an initial fall in international reserves.

3. (Optimal abandonment with a fixed cost of abandoning) This exercise follows Rebelo and Végh (2008). Consider the model presented in section 16.7 with the following modification. Assume that there is an exogenous and fixed cost ϕ of abandoning the peg. This is both a fiscal and social cost and therefore should enter both the fiscal constraint and the resource constraint. (To ensure positive consumption, you will need to restrict the admissible values of ϕ.) In this context:

a. Derive the consumer's indirect lifetime utility (i.e., express the consumer's lifetime utility as a function of parameters and $p(\equiv (1+r+\varepsilon)/(1+r))$, which is the relative effective price of consumption across regimes).

b. Rewrite the intertemporal fiscal constraint as a function of parameters and p.

c. Using the intertemporal fiscal constraint that you just derived, solve for p as a function of T, ϕ, and $\Delta\Gamma$.

d. Taking into account the expression for p that you just derived, solve for the optimal T. (Hint: Choose the T that maximizes the consumer's indirect utility function.) Show that for any ϕ (in the admissible range), there is a certain value of the fiscal shock (i.e., $\Delta\Gamma$) above which it is always optimal to set T equal to zero (i.e., it is optimal to abandon the peg right away).

References

Burnside, Craig, Martin Eichenbaum, and Sergio Rebelo. 2001. Prospective deficits and the Asian currency crisis. *Journal of Political Economy* 109 (6): 1155–97.

Burnside, Craig, Martin Eichenbaum, and Sergio Rebelo. 2004. Government guarantees and self-fulfilling speculative attacks. *Journal of Economic Theory* 119 (1): 31–63.

Caballero, Ricardo, and Arvind Krishnamurthy. 2001. International and domestic collateral constraints in a model of emerging market crises. *Journal of Monetary Economics* 48 (3): 513–48.

Calvo, Guillermo A. 1987. Balance of payments crises in a cash-in-advance economy. *Journal of Money, Credit and Banking* 19 (1): 19–32.

Chang, Roberto, and Andres Velasco. 2001. A model of financial crises in emerging markets. *Quarterly Journal of Economics* 116 (2): 489–517.

Dornbusch, Rudiger. 1987. Collapsing exchange rate regimes. *Journal of Development Economics* 27(1–2): 71–83.

Fischer, Stanley. 1998. The IMF and the Asian crisis. Forum Funds Lecture. University of California, Los Angeles.

Flood, Robert P., and Peter M. Garber. 1984. Collapsing exchange-rate regimes: Some linear examples. *Journal of International Economics* 17 (1–2): 1–13.

Flood, Robert P., and Olivier Jeanne. 2005. An interest rate defense of a fixed exchange rate? *Journal of International Economics* 66 (2): 471–84.

Furman, Jason and Joseph E. Stiglitz. 1998. Economic crises: Evidence and insights from East Asia. *Brooking Papers on Economic Activity* 29 (2): 1–136.

Jeanne, Olivier. 2000. Currency crises: A perspective on recent theoretical developments. Special Papers in International Economics 20. International Finance Section, Princeton University.

Krugman, Paul. 1979. A model of balance-of-payments crises. *Journal of Money, Credit and Banking* 11 (3): 311–25.

Lahiri, Amartya, and Carlos A. Végh. 2003. Delaying the inevitable: Interest rate defense and BOP crises. *Journal of Political Economy* 111 (2): 404-424.

Lahiri, Amartya, and Carlos A. Végh. 2007. Output costs, BOP crises, and optimal interest rate policy. *Economic Journal* 117: 216–239.

McKinnon, Ronald, and Huw Pill. 1996. Credible liberalizations and international capital flows: the overborrowing syndrome. In Takatoshi Ito and Anne Krueger, eds., *Financial Deregulation and Integration in East Asia*. Chicago: University of Chicago Press, 7–50.

Morris, Stephen, and Hyun Song Shin. 1998. Unique equilibrium in a model of self-fulfilling currency attacks. *American Economic Review* 88 (3): 587–97.

Obstfeld, Maurice. 1994. The logic of currency crises. *Cahiers Economiques et Monétaires* 43: 189–213.

Obstfeld, Maurice. 1996. Models of currency crises with self-fulfilling features. *European Economic Review* 40 (3–5): 1037–47.

Radelet, Steven, and Jeffrey Sachs. 2000. The onset of the East Asian financial crisis. In Paul Krugman, ed., *Currency Crises*. Chicago: University of Chicago Press: 105–53.

Rebelo, Sergio and Carlos A. Végh. 2008. When is it optimal to abandon a fixed exchange rate? *Review of Economic Studies* 75: 929–55.

Talvi, Ernesto. 1997. Exchange rate-based stabilization with endogenous fiscal response. *Journal of Development Economics* 54 (1): 59–75.

Velasco, Andres. 1987. Financial crises and balance of payments crises: A simple model of the southern cone experience. *Journal of Development Economics* 27 (1–2): 263–83.

17 Financial Crises

17.1 Introduction

The recent global financial crisis took the world by storm. Before the fall of 2008 it would have been hard to predict that a seemingly minor crisis in a submarket in the United States (the subprime mortgage market) would eventually lead to a financial crisis that literally spread around the world like wildfire. Many economic analysts were quick to point out to the presumably terrible failure of macroeconomics in analyzing and hopefully warning the world about the macrofinancial linkages responsible for the crisis.[1] Be that as it may, there is a growing body of work that attempts to shed light on the causes of the crisis and on the frictions that may need to be added to standard models to understand the links between the macroeconomy and financial institutions. While covering all the relevant aspects of the recent crisis would be an impossible task—and certainly out of the scope of a textbook focused on building blocks—this chapter attempts to gain some important insights into key aspects of financial crises in general, some of which were inspired, of course, by the recent crisis.

If anything, the recent financial crisis in the United States brought to the fore the idiosyncratic and systemic risks posed by highly leveraged financial institutions. Although there are several related measures of leverage, we will think of leverage as the ratio of assets to net worth. As discussed in box 17.1, large financial institutions drastically increased their leverage ratios in the run-up to the crisis. Lehman Brothers' leverage ratios, for instance, were below 10 in the late 1990s and early 2000s but drastically increased to above 30 by 2007. A similar pattern holds for the other three large financial institutions depicted in figure 17.1. This phenomenon raises, of course, many questions that will not be addressed here (e.g., How do firms get to take such enormous risks? What are the associated systemic risks?). Rather, and always in the spirit of going back to basics, section 17.2 makes a deceptively simple, but critical, point about the arithmetics of leverage: an institution that has, say, a leverage ratio of 30 will see its net worth wiped out if the price of

1. See Krugman (2009) for a frontal attack on the so-called freshwater macroeconomics of the last forty years and Cochrane (2009) for an equally spirited defense.

Box 17.1
How leveraged were financial institutions in the run-up to the financial crisis?

As discussed in the text, "leveraging" captures the idea of borrowing in order to acquire assets. There are different ways to measure leverage. The two most common are (1) debt over equity (i.e., net worth) or (2) assets over equity. We will follow here the second definition.

Figure 17.1 shows the leverage ratios for what were four of the main investment banks before the crisis unfolded. The four panels tell a consistent story. Leverage ratios were low (i.e., below 10) in the late 1990s and early 2000s (Morgan Stanley being an exception). By 2003 and 2004, however, leverage ratios were clearly on the uprise and by 2007 had reached 30. As shown in the text, with a leverage of 30, and if we think of all assets as mortgage-backed securities, just for the sake of argument, it would have taken a fall of just 3.33 percent in the price of these securities for equity to be wiped out! In retrospect, the level of risk taken by these large firms certainly looks like a recipe for disaster.

Out of these four banks, only two survived the financial crisis—Goldman Sachs and Morgan Stanley—though they converted to commercial banks. Lehman Brothers filed for bankruptcy and Merrill Lynch was bought by Bank of America. Bear Stearns—not shown in the picture—was acquired by J.P. Morgan Chase after a failed rescue attempt by the New York Federal Reserve.

The factors that led financial institutions to take such inordinate amount of risk will be studied and debated for years to come. Clearly, exceptionally low interest rates combined with the ability to pool risk by securitizing mortgages and the perception that housing prices would keep rising—or at least not fall, on average, at a national level—gave financial institutions strong incentives to make profits on borrowed money. It has also been argued that the fact that executives' compensation depended on stock prices, regardless of the amount of debt, provided incentives to becoming more leveraged. Finally, it is clear in retrospect that large firms were not internalizing any systemic risk derived from their own actions.

Not surprisingly, there is a heated debate—both among economists and in legislatures across the industrial world—on how to prevent a similar crisis from repeating itself. Of particular concern is how to prevent financial institutions from becoming so highly leveraged. Though this debate will go on for the foreseeable future, there are some key elements that are likely to be present in any future regulatory framework. First, some legal limit to banks' leverage ratios (a cap on leverage ratios at 25 has been suggested in Europe). Second, provisions that would effectively increase funding costs by forcing financial institutions to keep 5 percent of loans bundled into securities so as to retain some of the risk involved. Third, to somehow force lenders to keep higher standards when offering loans. Finally, to make executives' remuneration contingent also on the firm's debt level to prevent them from taking excessive leverage aimed at boosting share prices.

the underlying assets falls by a mere 3.33 percent. This illustrates the tremendous vulnerability of a variety of assets that were built around real estate mortgages and were priced by models that essentially ruled out any fall in housing prices at the national level.

Needless to say, taking such a great deal of risk was "justified" in the eyes of (presumably!) financial wizards by the enormous returns associated with leveraging. The ability to borrow at a given rate and invest that money at a higher rate implies that a financial institution that is operating with a leverage ratio of, say, 30 will make an excess return of 29 times the spread between the rate of return on the asset and the borrowing rate! The losses, of course, are magnified accordingly.

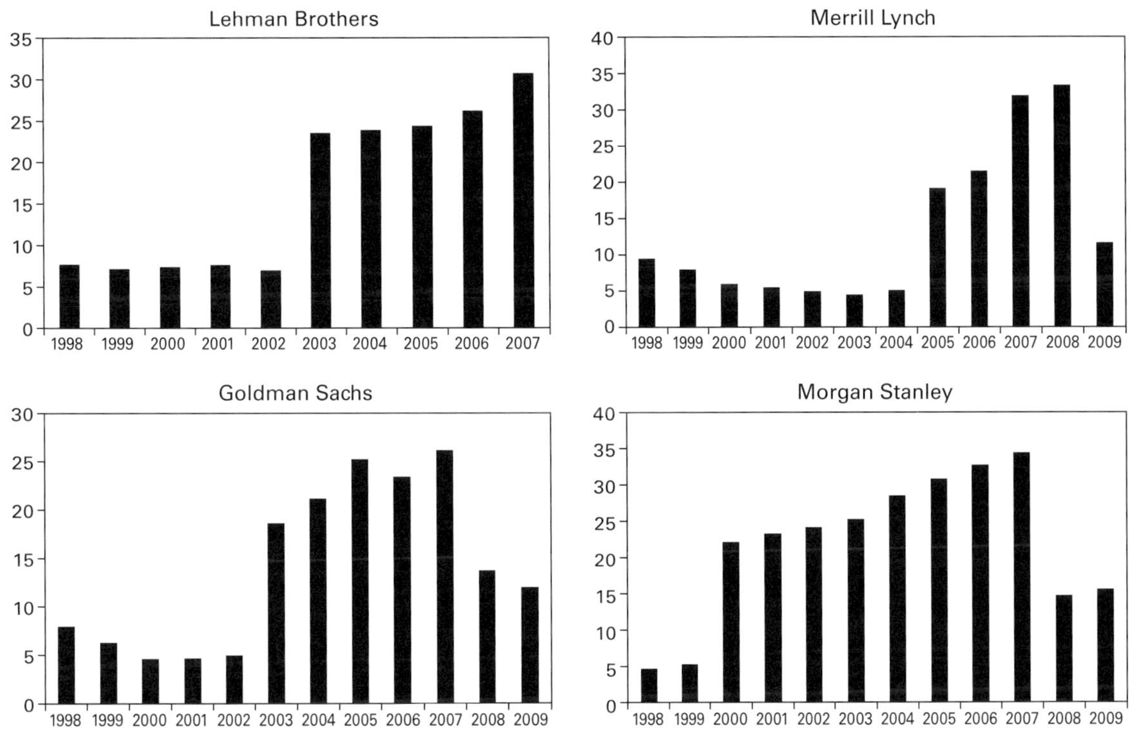

Source: SEC Annual Report (Form10-K) filed by each company each year

Figure 17.1
Leverage ratios

Section 17.3 introduces some basic content into the macroeconomics of leverage by analyzing its determinants in the simplest possible model. While the model cannot account for "excess" leverage (defined as leverage taken beyond that justified by fundamentals or not socially optimal due to systemic risk), it illustrates the idea that rational financial agents will increase leverage in response to more productive investment opportunities, higher tolerance for risk, and less uncertainty. Our model would thus suggest that to the extent that the early 2000s were a period of reduced uncertainty and higher tolerance for risk, we should have expected firms to become more leveraged.

Having dealt with the basic macroeconomics of leverage in section 17.3, in section 17.4 we turn to the potential amplification of shocks due to financial frictions. To this effect, we develop a model due to Jeanne and Korinek (2010) that illustrates some of the issues involved. In the model an agent can borrow from abroad but subject to limited commitment, which generates a financial friction due to the agent's incentive to renegotiate existing obligations. To remedy this, lenders require some collateral to be willing to make a loan. The value of the collateral in turn depends on asset prices. In response to a negative shock, the fall in asset prices reduces the value of the collateral, which reduces borrowing, which further reduces consumption, and so forth. This Fisherian debt deflation mechanism amplifies the consequences of the original shock.

According to some observers (see Calvo 2009), a key ingredient of the recent financial crisis in the United States was the development of a "shadow" banking system that grew very large and without supervision and, more important, without a lender of last resort. Moreover this shadow banking system succeeded in "printing money" through financial innovations such as collateralized debt obligations (CDOs).[2] This process greatly increased the degree of liquidity or "moneyness" associated with the underlying asset. Figure 17.2 plots global CDO issuance in billions of dollars for the period 2000 to 2009. CDO issuance peaked in 2006 at around 520 billion dollars. It plummeted in 2008 to around 62 billion dollars. To capture the effects of such a process, section 17.5 develops a model—due to Calvo (2009)—that captures the "liquidity" associated with the underlying asset by including land in the utility function as a source of liquidity services. The price of land will, of course, reflect this liquidity component. The model illustrates how an increase in the liquidity of land raises the relative price of land. We also model the role of monetary policy by assuming that policy makers control the interest rate paid on cash, as in chapter 9. Our main experiment consists in analyzing a perfect foresight equilibrium path along which the parameter that reflects the liquidity value of land is first high and then low. This would correspond to the boom–bust housing market cycle in the United States. Interestingly, asset prices begin to fall even before the exogenous fall in liquidity takes place. Our experiment also highlights the potential role for monetary policy. By announcing that it would reduce the policy interest rate in the event of an exogenous fall in liquidity, the monetary authority would be able to completely eliminate the asset price cycle! While this is an extreme example, it does offer a rationale for the very loose monetary policy implemented by the Federal Reserve since the fall of Lehman.

In terms of propagation, a puzzling feature of the crisis that began in the US subprime sector was that, at first, emerging markets were not only immune but continued to perform strongly, aided by large capital inflows. The financial press rapidly coined the term "decoupling" to refer to this phenomenon. Emerging markets' leaders would brag about it.[3] Sometime in the fall of 2008, however, the decoupling period came to a screeching halt and emerging markets imported the global crisis, with steep falls in stock and currency values. Section 17.6 develops a simple

2. CDOs are a certain type of asset-backed security whose value and payments are derived from a portfolio of fixed income underlying assets. They are typically sliced into different "tranches," depending on the level of risk. CDOs were first created in 1987 by Drexel Burnham Lambert, a defunct dealer in junk bonds.

3. In mid-September 2008, Brazil's president, Lula da Silva, in response to a question about a possible contagion of the crisis to Brazil, was quoted as saying "What crisis? Go ask Bush." A few weeks later, Brazil's stock market and currency plummeted by 20 and 13 percent, respectively (Bloomberg.com, December 3, 2008, "Lula, like Bush, gives bad shopping advice").

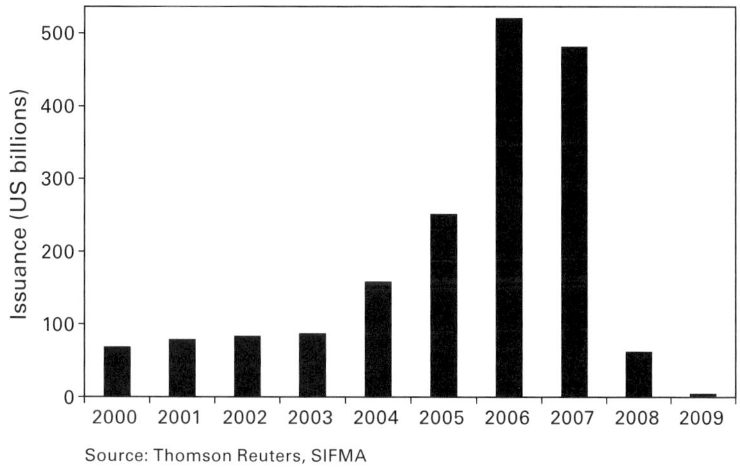

Figure 17.2
Global CDO issuance

model—due to Korinek, Roitman, and Végh (2010)—that provides a theoretical rationale for the observed decoupling–recoupling cycle. The model has a household sector that saves and thus provides financing to two countries (or firms). Both countries potentially face a leverage constraint but it only binds in, say, country B. A negative shock in country B will, at first, be transmitted negatively because the shock decreases the borrowing needs of country B and thus leads to a fall in the world real interest rate. If the shock becomes bigger, however, the country defaults and cannot repay the households, which decreases the amount of savings for any given interest rate. As a result country A also suffers. This leads to recoupling.

Last, but certainly not least, we focus on the so-called "twin crises." This term, popularized by Kaminsky and Reinhart's (1999) pathbreaking empirical study, refers to the simultaneous occurrence of banking and balance-of-payments crises. According to their study, banking crises typically precede balance-of-payments crises which, of course, does not necessarily indicate causality since these twin crises are most likely caused by common (bad) fundamentals. Section 17.7 develops an optimizing version of Velasco's (1987) model, which generates the twin crises. In the model, banks hold households' deposits backed by a stream of future output. The return on deposits is guaranteed. When a negative shock reduces banks' assets, banks resort to debt accumulation to keep paying depositors the contractual return. Once banks' debt hits a certain level, the government takes over their foreign debt (which, by definition, constitutes a banking crisis). The government's obligation to service the banks' debt puts in motion a Krugman-type balance-of-payments crisis, as in chapter 16. The model thus provides a plausible description of the mechanics behind the twin crises phenomenon.

17.2 Basic Arithmetics of Leverage

Many observers have argued that high levels of leverage (defined, for our purposes, as the ratio of total assets to net worth) were at the core of the recent financial crisis in the United States. The idea is that a highly leveraged institution is extremely vulnerable to fluctuations in the price of its assets. To understand this point, we now illustrate how, in the presence of high leverage ratios, a small fall in asset prices could completely wipe out a financial institution's net worth.

17.2.1 Arithmetics

Let the balance sheet of a financial institution be given by

Balance sheet	
qk	d
	n

where k is the stock of a certain asset, q is the price of the asset, d is debt, and n is net worth, defined as

$$n \equiv qk - d.$$

The leverage ratio is defined as

$$\theta = \frac{qk}{n}. \tag{17.1}$$

We will now show that if leverage is x, a fall of $100/x$ percent wipes out the net worth. For example, if the leverage ratio is 40, then a fall of 2.5 percent in the price of the asset would reduce net worth to zero.

Let n_0 denote initial net worth (i.e., $n_0 = q_0 k_0 - d_0$). Suppose that the asset price falls by $100/x$ percent. In other words, the new asset price, q_1, is given by

$$q_1 = q_0 \left(1 - \frac{1}{x}\right). \tag{17.2}$$

The new level of net worth, n_1, is given by

$$n_1 = q_1 k_1 - d_1. \tag{17.3}$$

Substituting (17.2) into (17.3) and noticing that $k_1 = k_0$ and $d_1 = d_0$, we obtain

$$n_1 = q_0 \left(1 - \frac{1}{x}\right) k_0 - d_0.$$

Rearranging and using the fact that $n_0 = q_0k_0 - d_0$, we get

$$n_1 = n_0 - \frac{q_0k_0}{x}.$$

For $n_1 = 0$ (i.e., for net worth to be wiped out completely), x needs to be

$$x = \frac{q_0k_0}{n_0}.$$

This says that if, for example, leverage is 40 (i.e., $x = 40$), a fall in asset prices of just 2.5 percent (i.e., a fall of $100/40$ percent) would completely wipe out net worth. Given the enormous leverage levels documented in box 17.1, it is not surprising (at least ex post!) that since large financial institutions had been buying mortgage-backed securities with borrowed money, a crisis was triggered by a steep fall in housing prices.

17.2.2 Returns with and without Leverage

The main incentive for financial institutions to become leveraged is to chase higher returns. We now show that leverage amplifies returns (both in the upswing and the downswing).

Suppose that the rate of return on assets is r^* and that you can borrow at r. The (gross) return on investing with borrowed funds is

$$\text{Return} = \frac{(n+d)(1+r^*) - d(1+r)}{n}.$$

This expression can be rearranged to yield

$$\text{Return} = (1+r^*) + \frac{d}{n}\left(r^* - r\right).$$

Since $d/n = \theta - 1$, we can write this expression as

$$\text{Return} = (1+r^*) + (\theta - 1)\left(r^* - r\right).$$

Since the return on investing with own funds is $1 + r^*$, we can summarize the returns as

$$\text{Return with own funds} = 1 + r^*,$$

$$\text{Return with borrowed funds} = (1+r^*) + (\theta - 1)\left(r^* - r\right).$$

Hence, if $r^* - r > 0$, a financial institution with a leverage ratio of, say, 30, will make an excess return of 29 times the spread between the rate of return on the asset and the borrowing rate! The opposite, however, is also true. If $r^* - r < 0$, leverage magnifies the loss.

17.3 Determinants of Leverage in a Simple Model

Thus far we have been dealing with financial accounting. While insightful, it certainly does not provide us with a "theory of leverage." To this effect, this section develops a simple two-period model with uncertainty in the second period (in the spirit of Chapter 2) to analyze the main determinants of leverage.

17.3.1 The Model

Consider a small open economy perfectly integrated into world goods and capital markets. There is only one (tradable) good that can be consumed or used as a capital good. Households are the only agents in this economy; they consume and carry out productive activities. There are only non–state contingent assets (i.e., financial markets are incomplete).

Preferences are given by

$$U = \frac{c_1^{1-\sigma}}{1-\sigma} + \beta E\left\{\frac{c_2^{1-\sigma}}{1-\sigma}\right\}, \tag{17.4}$$

where c_1 and c_2 denote consumption, σ is the coefficient of relative risk aversion, and β ($0 < \beta < 1$) is the discount factor.

Production in the first period, y_1, is given by

$$y_1 = A_1 k_1, \tag{17.5}$$

where A_1 is a productivity parameter and k_1 is the exogenously given initial capital stock.

Production in the second period is stochastic and given by

$$y_2 = \begin{cases} y_2^H = A_2^H k_2 & \text{with probability } p, \\ y_2^L = A_2^L k_2 & \text{with probability } 1-p, \end{cases} \tag{17.6}$$

where $A_2^H > 1 + r > A_2^L$.[4] The flow budget constraint for period 1 is given by

$$b_2 = (1+r)\, b_1 + y_1 - c_1 - k_2, \tag{17.7}$$

where b_i, $i = 1, 2$, denotes net foreign assets and b_1 is exogenously given. For simplicity, we are assuming that capital depreciates fully at the end of the period.[5] The flow budget constraint in the second period depends on the realization of the productivity shock:

4. This condition, together with the assumption that $E\{A_2\} > 1 + r$, ensures that we will have an interior solution for b_2 and k_2. If, for example, $A_2^L = 1 + r$, then capital would dominate bonds in terms of return. If $A_2^H = 1 + r$, then bonds would dominate capital.

5. This ensures investment in the first period (e.g., as opposed to disinvestment).

$$0 = (1+r)\,b_2 + y_2^H - c_2^H, \tag{17.8}$$

$$0 = (1+r)\,b_2 + y_2^L - c_2^L, \tag{17.9}$$

where c_2^H and c_2^L denote consumption in the good and bad state of nature, respectively.

Households choose $\{c_1, c_2^H, c_2^L, k_2, b_2\}$ to maximize lifetime utility, given by (17.4), subject to (17.7), (17.8), and (17.9), with output given by (17.5), and (17.6), for given initial values of k_1 and b_1. In terms of the Lagrangian,

$$\mathcal{L} = \frac{c_1^{1-\sigma}}{1-\sigma} + \beta\left[p\frac{\left(c_2^H\right)^{1-\sigma}}{1-\sigma} + (1-p)\frac{\left(c_2^L\right)^{1-\sigma}}{1-\sigma}\right] + \lambda_1\left[(1+r)\,b_1 + A_1k_1 - c_1 - k_2 - b_2\right]$$
$$+ \lambda_2^H\left[(1+r)\,b_2 + A_2^Hk_2 - c_2^H\right] + \lambda_2^L\left[(1+r)\,b_2 + A_2^Lk_2 - c_2^L\right]$$

Assume that $\beta(1+r) = 1$. First-order conditions with respect to $\{c_1, c_2^H, c_2^L, k_2, b_2\}$ are given by, respectively,

$$c_1^{-\sigma} = \lambda_1, \tag{17.10}$$

$$\beta p\left(c_2^H\right)^{-\sigma} = \lambda_2^H, \tag{17.11}$$

$$\beta(1-p)\left(c_2^L\right)^{-\sigma} = \lambda_2^L, \tag{17.12}$$

$$\lambda_1 = \lambda_2^H A_2^H + \lambda_2^L A_2^L, \tag{17.13}$$

$$\lambda_1 = (1+r)\left(\lambda_2^H + \lambda_2^L\right). \tag{17.14}$$

Combining first-order conditions (17.10), (17.11), (17.12), and (17.14), we can derive the stochastic Euler equation:

$$c_1^{-\sigma} = p\left(c_2^H\right)^{-\sigma} + (1-p)\left(c_2^L\right)^{-\sigma}, \tag{17.15}$$

which can be rewritten, of course, as

$$u'(c_1) = E\left\{u'(c_2)\right\}. \tag{17.16}$$

As discussed in chapter 2, the stochastic Euler equation equates today's marginal utility with tomorrow's expected marginal utility.

Substituting first-order conditions (17.10), (17.11), and (17.12) into (17.13), we obtain an arbitrage condition for the investment decision:

$$c_1^{-\sigma} = \beta\left[p\left(c_2^H\right)^{-\sigma} A_2^H + (1-p)\left(c_2^L\right)^{-\sigma} A_2^L\right], \tag{17.17}$$

which can be rewritten as

$$u'(c_1) = \beta E\left\{A_2 u'(c_2)\right\}. \tag{17.18}$$

The choice is between consuming one unit today or buying capital and consuming tomorrow. The left-hand side (i.e., the marginal utility of c_1) captures the opportunity cost of forgoing one unit of consumption today to buy capital. The right-hand side represents the discounted value (in terms of utility) of tomorrow's expected marginal utility. The unit of capital will return A_2^H in the good state of nature, which yields a marginal utility of $A_2^H u'(c_2^H)$, and A_2^L in the bad state of nature, which yields a marginal utility of $A_2^L u'(c_2^L)$. Expected marginal utility is thus $E\left\{A_2 u'(c_2)\right\} = pA_2^H u'(c_2^H) + (1-p)A_2^L u'(c_2^L)$.

An alternative interpretation, which emphasizes asset pricing considerations, is as follows. Rewrite equation (17.18) as[6]

$$u'(c_1) = \beta E\{A_2\} E\left\{u'(c_2)\right\} + \beta \operatorname{Cov}\left\{A_2, u'(c_2)\right\}.$$

Using (17.16) and taking into account that $\beta = 1/(1+r)$, we can rearrange this expression to read as[7]

$$E\{A_2\} - (1+r) = \frac{\operatorname{Cov}\left\{A_2, -u'(c_2)\right\}}{E\left\{u'(c_2)\right\}}.$$

Notice that since $-u''(c_2) > 0$, a positive covariance indicates a positive comovement between A_2 and c_2. This expression is thus saying that the higher the expected excess return of the risky asset (LHS), the more covariance (i.e., the more risk) the agent is willing to bear (RHS). In the spirit of standard asset-pricing models, risk is measured by the covariance between the return and second-period consumption.

Before proceeding to solve the model, let us define the leverage ratio in the context of this model. The household's balance sheet takes the form

Balance sheet	
k_2	$-b_2$
	n_2

6. Recall that for two stochastic variables, X and Y, $E\{XY\} = E\{X\}E\{Y\} + \operatorname{Cov}\{XY\}$.

7. We have also used the fact that $a \operatorname{Cov}\{X, Y\} = \operatorname{Cov}\{X, aY\}$.

where n_2 denotes net worth. Following the definition in (17.1), we define the leverage ratio as the ratio of assets to net worth:

$$\theta = \frac{k_2}{k_2 + b_2}.$$

Notice that higher investment financed exclusively with debt would leave net worth unchanged and therefore increase leverage. By the same token, lower investment that gets fully reflected in lower debt would leave net worth unchanged and hence decrease leverage. In the experiments below, first-period consumption will change and hence changes in investment will not get reflected one to one in changes in debt, but the basic idea that more (less) investment will increase (decrease) leverage will still hold.

17.3.2 Solving the Model

To solve the model, we can substitute equations (17.7), (17.8), and (17.9) into (17.15) and (17.17), which results in a system of two nonlinear equations in two unknowns: b_2 and k_2. The parameters of interest in this system are A_2^H, A_2^L, and σ. We solved the model numerically by solving this system for b_2 and k_2 and then using (17.7), (17.8), and (17.9) to obtain c_1, c_2^H, and c_2^L.

We will conduct three experiments.[8] The first answers the question: How does the economy's equilibrium change as the mean return on investment increases for a given variance? Figure 17.3 illustrates this case.[9] As expected, k_2 increases (panel a) because, on average, capital will be more productive tomorrow. This higher capital stock is financed by higher debt (panel b). First-period consumption (panel c) increases as households are, on average, richer. The leverage ratio also increases as the mean return goes up (panel d), reflecting the fact that households borrow more to finance the increase in investment. So, not surprisingly, an economy that becomes more productive will, all else equal, become more leveraged.

The second question is: How does the equilibrium change as a function of a mean preserving spread (i.e., when volatility increases)?[10] As illustrated in figure 17.4, panel a, k_2 falls because the added uncertainty makes it less attractive for households to invest. As a result borrowing falls (panel b). First-period consumption decreases reflecting the higher uncertainty (panel c). The fall in investment leads to a fall in the leverage ratio (panel d). Hence more uncertainty reduces leverage.

The third question is: How does the equilibrium change as the coefficient of risk aversion increases? As illustrated in figure 17.5, panel a, investment (k_2) falls as the degree of risk aversion

8. We choose the following parameter values: $A_1 = 1, p = 0.5, b_1 = 0, k_1 = 1, r = 0.05$, and $\beta = 1/(1+r)$.

9. Figure 17.3 assumes that $\sigma = 2$ and, starting from $A_2^H = 1.2$ and $A_2^L = 1$, increases A_2^H and A_2^L while keeping the difference, $A_2^H - A_2^L$, constant. Since, as can be easily shown, $\text{Var}(A) = (A_2^H - A_2^L)^2 p(1-p)$, this experiment keeps the variance constant.

10. Figure 17.4 assumes that $\sigma = 2$ and, starting from $A_2^H = 1.21$ and $A_2^L = 0.99$, increases A_2^H and reduces A_2^L, keeping the mean constant.

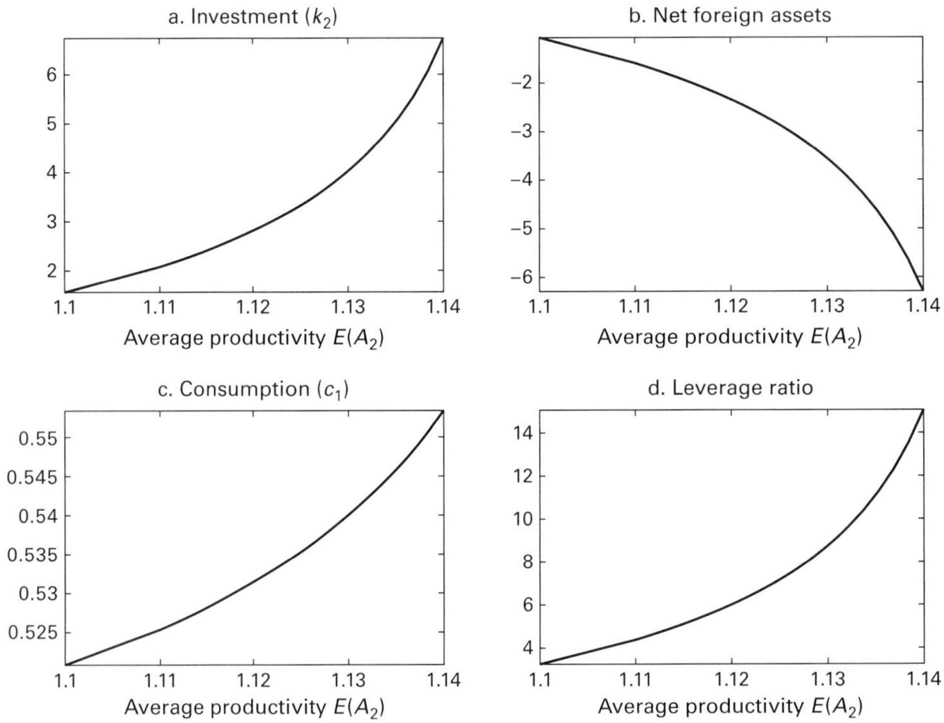

Figure 17.3
Variance preserving increase in average productivity $E(A_2)$

increases, which gets reflected in lower debt (panel b).[11] This is to be expected because a higher degree of risk aversion makes the households less willing to take on the risk associated with investing. As a result leverage also decreases as the degree of risk aversion increases (panel d). It is interesting to note that although k_2 becomes larger as the degree of risk aversion decreases, it remains finite. Why? The reason is that the Inada condition implies that c_2^L cannot become zero, so this effectively imposes an upper limit on the amount of borrowing carried out by the household.[12] As shown for our benchmark parameterization in exercise 1 at the end of the chapter, the limit of the leverage ratio as the degree of risk aversion tends to zero is $(1+r)/(1+r-A_2^L)$.[13]

In sum, we have shown that the leverage ratio is higher, the higher is average productivity, the lower is uncertainty, and the lower is the degree of risk aversion. It is not unreasonable to think

11. Figure 17.5 assumes that $A_2^H = 1.2$ and $A_2^L = 1$.

12. Notice that $c_2^L = (1+r)b_2 + A_2^L k_2$ and $A_2^L < 1+r$. Hence, for a given c_1, a fall in b_2 (higher debt) needed to finance a higher k_2 will drive c_2^L to zero.

13. Since $A_2^L = 1$ in our parameterization, the maximum leverage becomes $(1+r)/r$. For $r = 0.05$, this number is 21, which is the limit in panel d as the coefficient of risk aversion approaches zero.

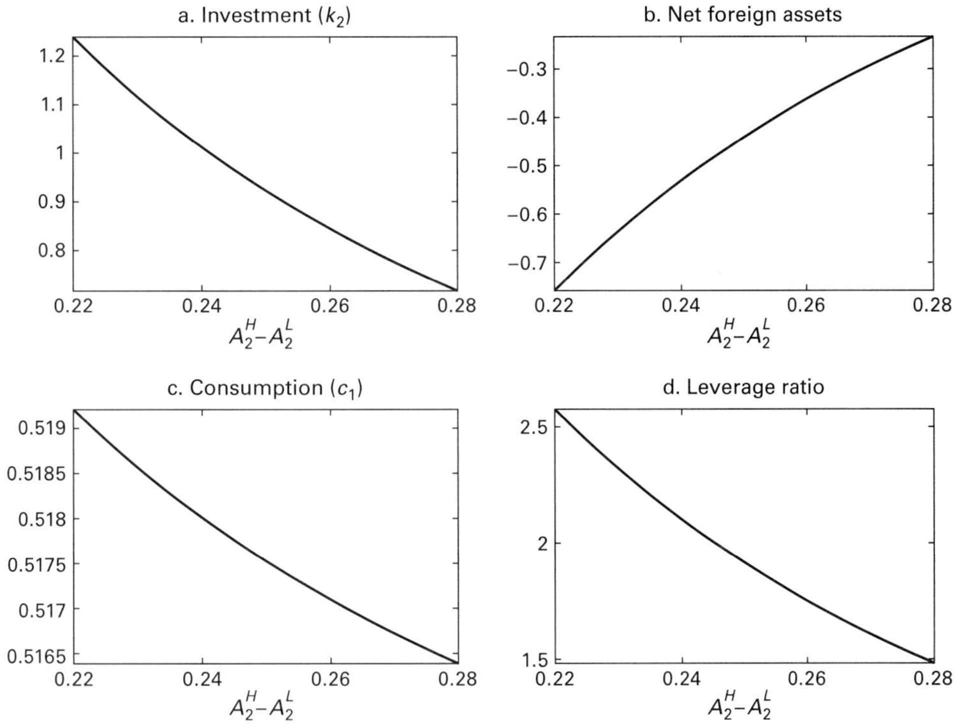

Figure 17.4
Mean preserving spread

that all three factors characterized the years leading up to the financial crisis in the fall of 2008. In that case, our simple model would correctly predict the increase in leverage observed in practice (see box 17.1).[14] Of course, the increase in the leverage ratio in the model is socially optimal. We are thus not taking into account distortions that may lead an economy to take an inefficiently high level of leverage.

17.4 Leverage as Amplification Mechanism

To illustrate the idea that leverage amplifies shocks, we develop a version of Jeanne and Korinek (2010). Consider a small open economy in a one-good world with two time periods $t = 1, 2$. The economy is populated by a continuum of atomistic identical consumers, with a mass normalized to one. The consumer issues debt d in period 1 and repays it in period 2. The utility of the representative consumer is given by

14. According to the Bureau of Labor Statistics figures, the average annual productivity growth during the boom of 2002 to 2007 was 4.1 percent. Productivity growth fell to 1.1 and 1.8 percent in 2008 and 2009, respectively.

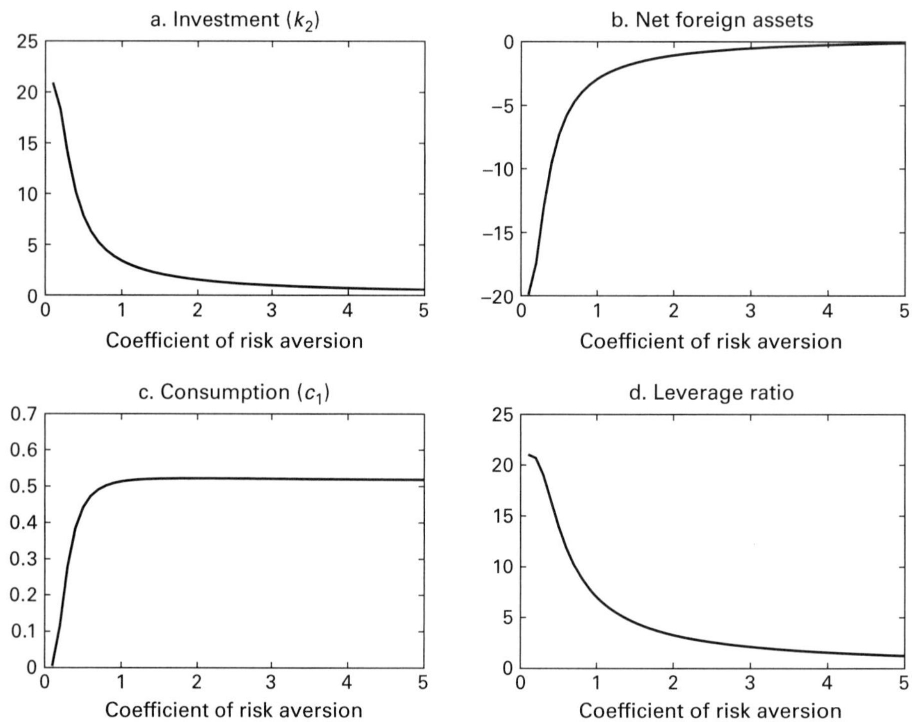

Figure 17.5
Risk aversion

$$u(c_1) + c_2. \tag{17.19}$$

The riskless world interest rate is normalized to zero. Because of the linearity of preferences in the second period—and as will become clear below—the first-best level of consumption in period 1, denoted by c^*, will satisfy $u'(c^*) = 1$.

The consumer is endowed with $\ell_1 = 1$ unit of land that yields a harvest y_1 and y_2 in periods 1 and 2, respectively. Land can be traded among domestic consumers at a price p in period 1. Land completely depreciates in period 2. The consumer's flow budget constraints are thus given by

$$c_1 = y_1\ell_1 + d + (\ell_1 - \ell_2)\,p, \tag{17.20}$$

$$c_2 = y_2\ell_2 - d. \tag{17.21}$$

We introduce a financial friction based on limited commitment by assuming that borrowers could default on their debts at the end of period 1. To protect their interests, international lenders demand land as collateral. If domestic consumers attempt to renegotiate, lenders can threaten to seize up to $\phi \leq 1$ units of land from them. However, domestic consumers have a strong comparative advantage in cultivating land. For simplicity, we assume that land would not deliver a harvest at all if foreign investors held on to it between periods 1 and 2—therefore foreign investors who seize land will immediately re-sell it on the domestic market for land at the prevailing market price p. To make sure domestic consumers abstain from renegotiating at the end of period 1, international lenders limit their lending such that[15]

$$d \leq \phi p. \tag{17.22}$$

Consumers thus choose $\{c_1, c_2, \ell_2, d\}$ to maximize (17.19) subject to the flow constraints (17.20) and (17.21) and the collateral constraint (17.22). In terms of the Lagrangian,

$$\mathcal{L} = u(c_1) + c_2 + \lambda_1 [y_1\ell_1 + d + (\ell_1 - \ell_2)p - c_1] + \lambda_2 [y_2\ell_2 - d - c_2] + \psi (\phi p - d).$$

The first-order conditions with respect to $\{c_1, c_2, \ell_2, d\}$ are given by, respectively,

$$u'(c_1) = \lambda_1, \tag{17.23}$$

$$1 = \lambda_2, \tag{17.24}$$

$$-\lambda_1 p + \lambda_2 y_2 = 0, \tag{17.25}$$

$$\lambda_1 - \lambda_2 = \psi. \tag{17.26}$$

Combining (17.23), (17.24), and (17.26), we get

$$u'(c_1) = 1 + \psi. \tag{17.27}$$

This optimality condition can be thought of as the standard Euler equation given linear utility in period 2 and the possibility of a binding borrowing constraint.

Combining (17.23) through (17.25), we obtain

$$p = \frac{y_2}{u'(c_1)}. \tag{17.28}$$

This condition states that the price of land is equal to its period-2 return times the marginal utility of period-2 consumption (which is 1) divided by the marginal utility of period-1 consumption.

We focus first on the unconstrained equilibrium. If the borrowing constraint does not bind, then $\psi = 0$. From condition (17.27), it follows that $c_1 = c^*$ and $p = y_2$. This solution is feasible if and only if the value of collateral is sufficiently high to cover the debt; that is, $d = c^* - y_1 \leq \phi y_2$ (notice that market clearing for land implies that $\ell_1 = \ell_2 = 1$), which requires that period-1 output be higher than a certain threshold:

15. Nothing changes, of course, if the constraint is written as $d \leq \phi \ell_1 p$ since ℓ_1 is given. Exercise 2 at the end of the chapter analyzes the case where the collateral constraint takes the form $d \leq \phi \ell_2 p$ and concludes that the thrust of the results remains unchanged.

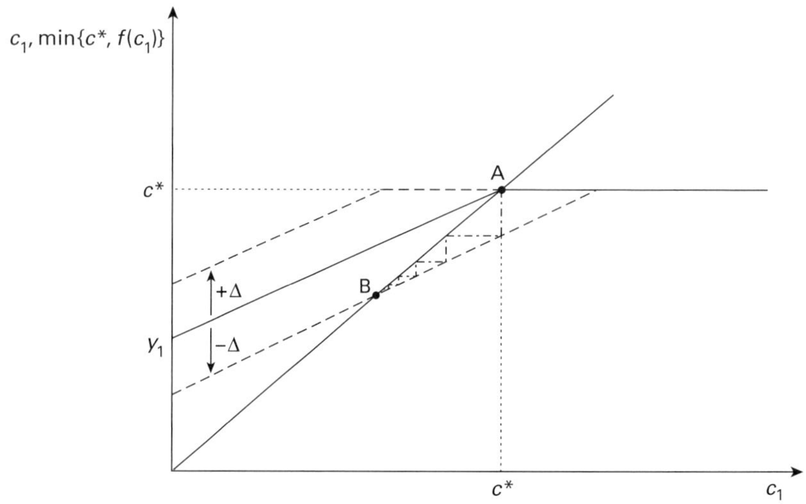

Figure 17.6
Amplification model

$$y_1 \geq c^* - \phi y_2. \tag{17.29}$$

For a given c^* we can, of course, always choose parameters such that (17.29) holds.

If condition (17.29) were violated, however, then the equilibrium is constrained and characterized by

$$c_1 = y_1 + \frac{\phi y_2}{u'(c_1)}. \tag{17.30}$$

Both sides of equation (17.30) are increasing with c_1, as plotted in figure 17.6.[16] Specifically, the LHS of equation (17.30) is plotted as a 45-degree line, whereas the RHS is plotted as such until c_1 reaches c^* at point A. Beyond c^*, the figure plots c^*, which is the unconstrained solution.[17] Point A therefore captures the unconstrained solution.

In the constrained region (i.e., for $c_1 < c^*$), both lines are upward-sloping and hence even small shocks to period 1 harvest will lead to large movements in consumption and land prices.

16. We impose the restriction $\phi y_2 \partial(1/u'(c_1))/\partial c_1 < 1$, for $c_1 \leq c^*$, to ensure that the model has a unique solution. This guarantees that the derivative of the RHS of equation (17.30) with respect to c_1 is strictly smaller than 1; that is, the RHS is flatter than the LHS. If this condition is not satisfied—and as analyzed further in exercise 3 at the end of the chapter—multiple equilibria may arise, where a fall in land prices becomes self-fulfilling because it depresses domestic consumption c_1. The condition is always satisfied for sufficiently low ϕ and y_2.

17. In other words, figure 17.6 is a plot of the RHS of equation (17.30) as $\min\{c^*, f(c_1)\}$, where $f(c_1) \equiv y_1 + \phi y_2/u'(c_1)$. For graphical convenience, we plot the RHS as linear even though this may not be the case (if preferences are logarithmic, however, it will be a line with slope ϕy_2 that will intersect the y-axis at y_1, as depicted).

To see this, imagine how the economy would react to a shock to the harvest y_1 by $-\Delta$, indicated by the downward shift in the dashed line.[18] As a benchmark, first notice that in the absence of the collateral constraint, this shock would have no effect on c_1, which would remain at c^*. The economy would simply borrow more to keep the same level of consumption in the first period. In our constrained model, however, at the original level of consumption, the borrowing constraint would be violated and the new equilibrium would in fact be at point B in figure 17.6.

In the model, of course, the equilibrium would "jump" from point A to point B. But, to convey ideas, we can imagine a "dynamic" adjustment following the dash-dotted zigzag line in the figure. The initial fall in c_1 lowers the price of land, given by (17.28), and thus tightens the collateral constraint, leading to a downward spiral of declining consumption and dropping asset prices. This is the the general mechanism behind models of financial amplification.[19] By contrast, an increase in y_1, as illustrated by the upper dashed line, would have no effect on c_1 because we would be in the unconstrained region.

Notice that in the unconstrained regime as determined by equation (17.29), capital inflows are decreasing in y_1 as a greater harvest reduces the need for consumers to borrow from abroad (as in our basic model of chapter 1). Conversely, if the economy is credit-constrained (in the "sudden stop regime"), capital flows become procyclical. Indeed, by decreasing the price of land and hence of the collateral, a lower y_1 leads to a reduction in foreign borrowing (i.e., capital outflow) and thus amplifies the effects of a shock on consumption.[20] From (17.30), we can express the factor of amplification as the change in consumption for a given change in the harvest:

$$\frac{dc_1}{dy_1} = \frac{1}{1 + \phi y_2 u''(c_1) / [u'(c_1)]^2} > 1.$$

17.5 Role of Liquidity in Asset Markets

We argued in the introduction that the development of a shadow banking system and financial instruments such as CDOs increased the degree of liquidity of the underlying (sometimes physical) assets. To capture the effects of such a process on asset prices and the possible role of monetary policy, we develop a model due to Calvo (2009).

Consider a small open economy perfectly integrated into world goods and capital markets and operating under predetermined exchange rates. There is only one (nonstorable and tradable)

18. Formally, we are really comparing two economies with different values of y_1, but in an abuse of language, we will talk as though we are performing a comparative statics exercise.

19. Frequently the phenomenon of financial amplification is also referred to as "financial accelerator." We prefer the term "amplification" since "acceleration" in physics refers to an increase in the second derivative of a variable, which is not taking place in models of the "financial accelerator." The phenomenon is also closely linked to what Irving Fisher (1933) described as "debt deflation" during the Great Depression, when nominal incomes and prices fell because of a general decline in the price level whereas long-term nominal debt contracts were fixed.

20. This is consistent with the procyclicality of capital inflows documented in Kaminsky, Reinhart, and Végh (2003). Chapter 7 offered an alternative explanation based on consumption boom–busts cycles.

good. The foreign nominal price of the good is assumed to be one. Money is modeled as yielding liquidity services that provide utility.

17.5.1 Consumers

Preferences are given by

$$\int_0^\infty [u(c_t) + v(m_t + \eta_t p_t \ell_t)] e^{-\beta t} dt, \tag{17.31}$$

where c_t is consumption of the only (tradable and nonstorable) good, which acts as the numéraire; β is the discount rate; m_t are interest-bearing real money balances; ℓ_t is land; p_t is the relative price of land in terms of the consumption good; and $\eta_t (\geq 0)$ captures the degree of liquidity or "moneyness" of land.[21] In principle, η_t can be time-varying. Our main experiment will in fact consist in characterizing a perfect foresight path where η_t is first high and then low.

Let total real assets (a_t) be given by

$$a_t \equiv b_t + p_t \ell_t + m_t,$$

where b_t stands for net foreign bonds. Production (y_t) takes the linear form

$$y_t = \rho \ell_t,$$

where ρ is a positive parameter. The consumer's flow budget constraint reads as

$$\dot{a}_t = r b_t + (\rho + \dot{p}_t) \ell_t + \tau_t - c_t - (\varepsilon_t - i_t^m) m_t, \tag{17.32}$$

where τ_t are lump-sum transfers from the government, ε_t is the rate of devaluation, and i_t^m is interest paid on money. The pecuniary return of land is composed of the return on production (ρ) plus the change in the price of the land $(\dot{p}_t)$. Rearranging this expression, integrating forward, and imposing the appropriate transversality condition, we obtain the consumer's lifetime constraint:

$$a_0 + \int_0^\infty [(\rho + \dot{p}_t - r p_t) \ell_t + \tau_t] e^{-rt} dt = \int_0^\infty \left[c_t + (i_t - i_t^m) m_t\right] e^{-rt} dt. \tag{17.33}$$

The representative consumer chooses $\{c_t, m_t, \ell_t\}$ to maximize lifetime utility, given by (17.31), subject to the intertemporal budget constraint (17.33). In terms of the Lagrangian,

$$\begin{aligned} \mathcal{L} = & \int_0^\infty [u(c_t) + v(m_t + \eta_t p_t \ell_t)] e^{-\beta t} dt \\ & + \lambda \left\{ a_0 + \int_0^\infty \left[(\rho + \dot{p}_t - r p_t) \ell_t - c_t - (i_t - i_t^m) m_t + \tau_t\right] e^{-rt} dt \right\}. \end{aligned}$$

21. We will impose an upper bound on η below to ensure that land is dominated by money in producing liquidity services, which will ensure a well-defined relative price for land.

Assuming, as usual, that $\beta = r$, the first-order conditions are given by

$$u'(c_t) = \lambda, \tag{17.34}$$

$$v'(m_t + \eta_t p_t \ell_t) = \lambda(i_t - i_t^m), \tag{17.35}$$

$$v'(m_t + \eta_t p_t \ell_t)\eta_t p_t + \lambda\left(\rho + \dot{p}_t - r p_t\right) = 0. \tag{17.36}$$

First-order condition (17.34) is a familiar one. First-order condition (17.35) implicitly defines liquidity $(m_t + \eta_t p_t \ell_t)$ as a function of λ (and hence c_t) and $i_t - i_t^m$:

$$m_t + \eta_t p_t \ell_t = L\left(\lambda(i_t - i_t^m)\right), \tag{17.37}$$

where L is the inverse function of $v'(.)$. The demand for real money balances is therefore given by[22]

$$m_t = L\left(\lambda(i_t - i_t^m)\right) - \eta_t p_t \ell_t. \tag{17.38}$$

Real money demand thus depends negatively on the liquidity value of land $(\eta_t p_t \ell_t)$. An increase in the liquidity value of land (i.e., a rise in η_t or p_t) will decrease money demand.

To understand the intuition behind equation (17.36), it proves convenient to rewrite it as

$$\frac{v'(m_t + \eta_t p_t \ell_t)\eta_t p_t}{\lambda} + \rho + \dot{p}_t = r p_t. \tag{17.39}$$

The LHS captures the marginal benefit of holding land, which has two components: the first term represents the direct marginal return in terms of consumption, while the second term $(\rho + \dot{p}_t)$ is the pecuniary return to land. The RHS captures the opportunity cost of acquiring land (the consumer could have used p_t units of the good to buy a bond instead of land, and obtain a flow return of r).

17.5.2 Government

The government's flow budget constraint is given by

$$\dot{h}_t = r h_t + \dot{m}_t + (\varepsilon_t - i_t^m) m_t - \tau_t, \tag{17.40}$$

where h_t are the government's net foreign assets.

22. Notice that given $u(.)$, $v(.)$, η_t, and $i_t - i_t^m$, we will always be able to choose initial assets to ensure that consumption and hence λ are such that $m_t > 0$.

17.5.3 Equilibrium Conditions

Since foreign inflation is zero, interest parity dictates that

$$i_t = r + \varepsilon_t. \tag{17.41}$$

The overall stock of land is fixed at $\bar{\ell}$, so equilibrium in the land market requires that

$$\ell_t = \bar{\ell}. \tag{17.42}$$

Combining the consumer's and government's flow constraints, given by (17.32) and (17.40), respectively, and using (17.42), we obtain the economy's flow constraint:

$$\dot{b}_t + \dot{h}_t = r\,(b_t + h_t) + \rho\bar{\ell} - c_t.$$

Integrating forward and imposing the appropriate transversality condition, we obtain the economy's resource constraint:

$$b_0 + h_0 + \frac{\rho\bar{\ell}}{r} = \int_0^\infty c_t e^{-rt} dt. \tag{17.43}$$

17.5.4 Perfect Foresight Equilibrium Path

The monetary authority sets the path for the exchange rate and the value of i_t^m.[23] Suppose that both the rate of devaluation and the policy interest rate are constant over time and equal to ε and i^m, respectively. Then, by interest parity, $i = r + \varepsilon$. This implies that $i_t - i_t^m$ will also be constant over time, at a value given by $i - i^m$. Substituting (17.35) into (17.36), we can derive the following differential equation in p_t:

$$\dot{p}_t = p_t\left[r - \eta_t(i - i^m)\right] - \rho. \tag{17.44}$$

This is an unstable differential equation in p_t.[24] Assume that η_t is constant over time (i.e., $\eta_t = \eta$ for $t \geq 0$). In a stationary equilibrium, the value of p_t is given by

$$p = \frac{\rho}{r - \eta(i - i^m)}.$$

23. This setup can be interpreted as consumers holding interest-bearing demand deposits for transactions purposes issued by banks holding one hundred percent cash reserves remunerated at the rate i^m. See chapter 9, section 9.4, and chapter 16, section 16.3, for previous analyses that rely on this formulation of interest rate policy.

24. We impose the condition that $r - \eta_t(i - i^m) > 0$. This would, of course, always hold in the standard case where $\eta_t = 0$.

Assuming, for simplicity, that $\rho = r$, we have

$$p = \frac{1}{1 - \frac{\eta}{r}(i - i^m)}. \tag{17.45}$$

To ensure that the economy travels along a convergent equilibrium path, p_0 must be at its stationary value. Hence, along a perfect foresight equilibrium path (PFEP),[25]

$$p_t = \frac{1}{1 - \frac{\eta}{r}(i - i^m)} \qquad \text{for all } t \geq 0. \tag{17.46}$$

First-order condition (17.34) indicates that consumption is constant along a PFEP at the level c. From (17.43) it follows that

$$c = r\,(b_0 + h_0) + \rho\bar{\ell} \qquad \text{for all } t \geq 0. \tag{17.47}$$

From (17.35) we infer that $m_t + \eta p_t \ell_t$ will be constant along a PFEP, at a level that we will denote by x. Given (17.42) and the constant value of p_t derived in (17.46), m_t will also be constant along a PFEP and, from (17.38), given by

$$m = L\left(\lambda(i - i^m)\right) - \eta p\bar{\ell}. \tag{17.48}$$

We will conduct three experiments in the context of this model.

17.5.5 Increase in η

Suppose that starting from the stationary equilibrium just described, there is an unanticipated and permanent increase in η. The economy will, of course, adjust instantaneously to the new stationary equilibrium. We infer from equation (17.46) that p will increase. The level of consumption does not change, as follows from equation (17.47). Since both η and p increase, it follows from equation (17.48) that real money balances will be lower in the new stationary equilibrium.

What is the intuition behind the rise in p? A rise in η increases the liquidity associated with land, which makes land more valuable. The resulting higher demand for land leads to a rise in its relative price. As emphasized by Calvo (2009), this very simple experiment arguably captures an essential element of the rise in housing prices before the fall of Lehman in September 2008. The creation of new instruments (e.g., collateralized debt obligations or CDOs) increased the liquidity associated with land or derivatives of land.

25. Notice that the condition $r - \eta(i - i^m) > 0$ ensures that p is finite. If $i^m = 0$ and $i = r$, this simplifies to $\eta < 1$. If, in this case, $\eta = 1$, then land would dominate money (same liquidity services plus a real return) and the relative price of land would be "infinite."

17.5.6 Policy Reductions in i^m

Let us now analyze a permanent change in the policy interest rate, i^m. Consider an unanticipated and permanent fall in i^m. Once again, the economy would adjust instantaneously to its new stationary equilibrium. It follows from equation (17.46) that p will increase. Real money balances would fall, as indicated by equation (17.48). Intuitively, the reduction in i^m implies that the opportunity cost of holding real money balances $(i - i^m)$ increases. As a result households shift away from money and toward land. This increases the price of land. This simple exercise thus illustrates the idea that easy monetary policy on the part of the Federal Reserve might have contributed to rising housing prices, as argued by critics (see box 17.2).

Box 17.2
Is the Federal Reserve to blame for the housing price bubble? The Taylor–Greenspan debate

In a 2009 book John Taylor essentially blames lax monetary policy on the part of the Federal Reserve for causing the housing price bubble that eventually led to the financial crisis of 2008.[a] Taylor uses figure 17.7 to argue that had the Federal Reserve continued to use the Taylor rule, policy rates should not have been kept so low for a such prolonged period of time. Taylor argues that keeping the interest rate so low contributed to increasing housing prices. Had the Federal Reserve set the interest rate according to the one prescribed by the Taylor rule—the path labeled counterfactual in figure 17.7—the boom and consequent bust could have been avoided.

Taylor uses as evidence the results from his 2007 article on housing and monetary policy. In Taylor's view, the boom in the housing sector was mainly supply driven. He estimates a model of the relation between interest rates (i.e., the federal funds rate) and housing starts and then uses the coefficients to simulate what would have happened had the interest rate been set in accordance to the Taylor's rule. The results can be seen in figure 17.8. Basically there would have been no large increase in the number of houses being built and the decline would have been much smoother. In order to explain the boom in housing prices across countries, Taylor argues that Central Banks in other countries essentially followed the Federal Reserve in setting the interest rate in their corresponding countries. Therefore the low interest rate policy followed by the Federal Reserve had an impact also on housing prices in other countries.

Greenspan vehemently disagrees with Taylor's view.[b] In an article written for the *Brookings Papers on Economic Activity*, Greenspan argues that housing prices depend mainly on long-term interest rates, which cannot be influenced by monetary policy. His argument—not devoid of logic—is that housing prices are determined by long-term interest rates and that the relationship between the federal funds rate and long-term market interest rates was tenuous at best during 2002 to 2005 when the increase in housing prices was the largest. Table 17.1 supports this contention by showing that, while

a. John B. Taylor (born in 1946) is an American academic economist, currently at Stanford University. The "Taylor rule" is named after him. He has also been active in public policy, having served as the Under Secretary of the Treasury for International Affairs during the first term of the George W. Bush administration.
b. Alan Greenspan (born in 1926) is an American economist who served as Chairman of the Federal Reserve from 1987 to 2006.

Box 17.2
(continued)

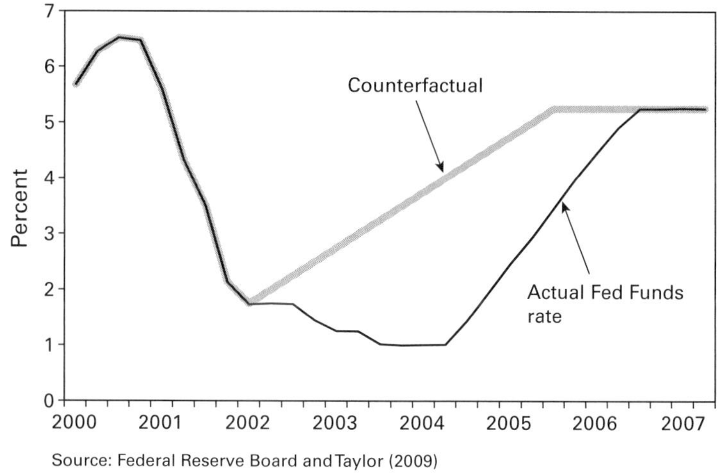

Figure 17.7
Federal Funds rate: Actual and counterfactual

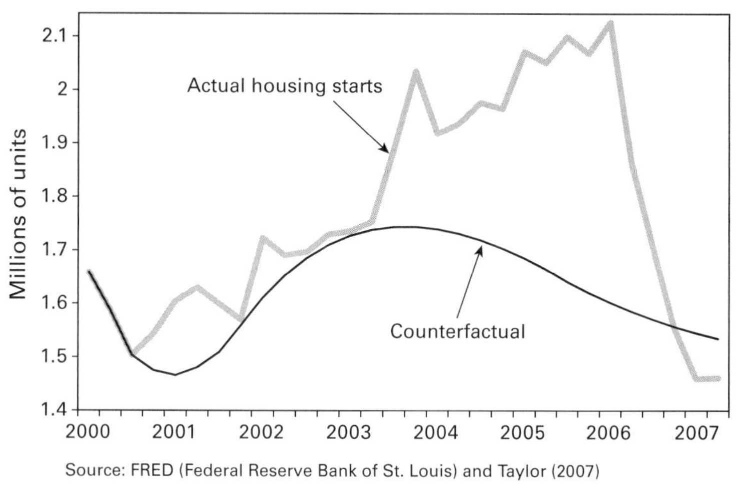

Figure 17.8
Housing starts: Actual versus counterfactual

Box 17.2
(continued)

Table 17.1
Correlation between the Federal Funds rate and mortgage rates

1964/01–2010/06	0.86
1964/01–1999/12	0.84
2000/01–2010/06	0.76
2002/01–2005/12	0.02

Source: Author's calculations based on data from Federal Reserve Board and FRED (Federal Reserve Bank of St. Louis).

over the long-term the correlation between the federal funds rate and mortgage rates has been high, it was rather low for the 2002 to 2005 period.

Greenspan also argues that since the Taylor rule was designed to determine the appropriate federal funds rate to balance the trade-off between inflation and unemployment, it cannot be applied to asset prices (i.e. housing prices). He also explains that the reason why the Taylor rule's prescribed interest rate was higher than the one set by the Federal Reserve is that product price inflation was a threat. However, inflation remained low over the 2002 to 2005 period. Hence the Taylor rule also failed to provide correct policy signals.

A point on which probably both Taylor and Greenspan would agree is that low interest rates were a main determinant of the crisis. Greenspan, however, would argue that while long-term interest rates were low, the federal funds rate was not. In Greenspan's view, the decline in long-term interest rates was due to an increase in saving in the developing world and, particularly, to a decline in investment in the developed world. Low interest rates led to excessive leverage, which proved to be unsustainable.

The Taylor–Greenspan debate has important implications for whether or not the crisis could have been avoided. In Taylor's view, had the federal funds rate been higher, the bubble would not have occurred and the crisis would have been avoided. In Greenspan's view, policy makers could, in theory, always set a rate high enough to eliminate an asset price bubble but the costs of doing so would be simply too high. Hence Greenspan believes that preventing bubbles is unfeasible and that the best policy would be to learn how to, once they burst, lessen their deflationary impact.

In a recent paper Glaeser, Gottlieb, and Gyourko (2010) build a model to study to what extent lower real interest rates and easier credit can explain the recent housing boom. They find that interest rates can only account for one-fifth of the rise in housing prices over the period 1996 to 2010. Moreover the authors find that neither data on approval rates nor on down payment requirements can explain much of the housing boom either. They conclude that there may be some truth to Case and Shiller's (2003) claim that what drove the boom was overoptimism by buyers about future housing prices. They argue, however, that unless we can understand the process by which irrational beliefs are created and propagated, we cannot discuss whether different monetary policies would have led to different outcomes.

In sum, the jury is certainly still out on both the causes and policy implications of the 2008 financial crisis. One thing is for sure though: hundreds of papers will be written on this topic over the next five to ten years, which will hopefully lead to a much better understanding of both the causes of the crisis and the lessons to be learned.

The experiment of a reduction in i^m can also be used to think about the Federal Reserve's response of lowering the federal funds rate to essentially zero starting in December 2008. In the context of our model, we could capture the drop in housing prices as the result of a fall in η. The Fed's reaction—lowering i^m—would have as its main purpose preventing a precipitous fall in housing prices.

17.5.7 Boom–Bust Cycle in Asset Prices

Our last experiment consists in computing a PFEP along which η_t is first high and then low (figure 17.9, panel a). (Policy makers keep i_t^m constant at i^m.) From first-order condition (17.34), we know that consumption is flat along such a PFEP (panel b). To rule out infinite arbitrage opportunities, we cannot allow discrete jumps in p_t at time T. Otherwise, in anticipation of, say, a discrete upward jump in p_t at time T, the demand for land would be infinite.

Based on (17.45), we infer that the locus corresponding to $\dot{p}_t = 0$ will fall at time T. Since p_t cannot jump at T, this implies that p_t must start falling at time 0, as illustrated in figure 17.9, panel c. Interestingly, land prices begin to fall *before* the actual fall in η_t.

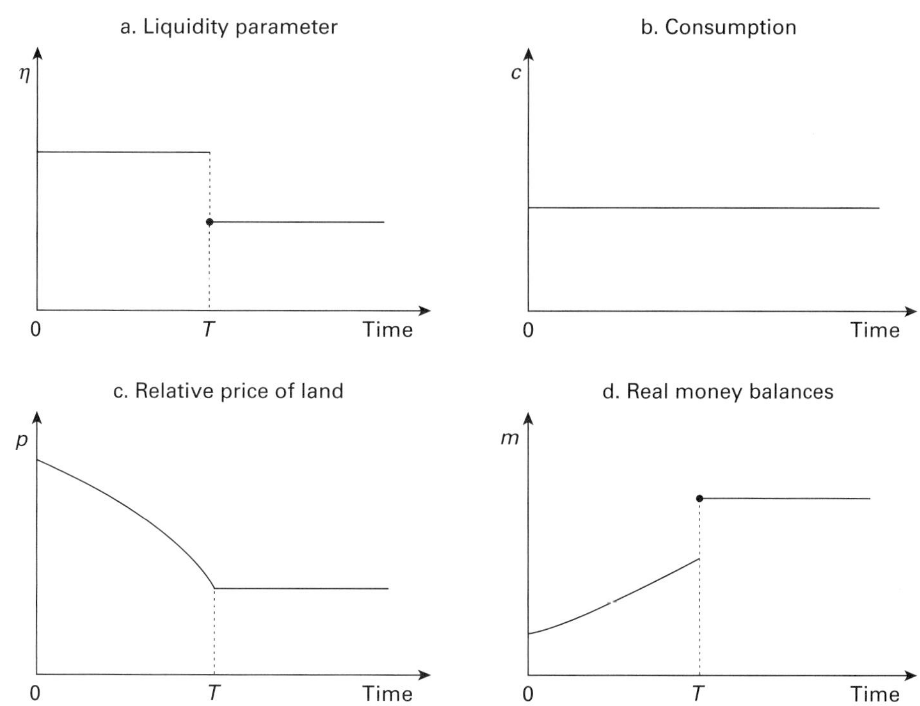

Figure 17.9
Boom–bust cycle in asset prices

The time path of real money balances follows from equation (17.38), which, using equilibrium condition (17.42), can be rewritten as

$$m_t = L\left(\lambda(i_t - i^m)\right) - \eta_t p_t \bar{\ell}. \tag{17.49}$$

Two pieces of information follow from this equation. First, at time $t = T$, m_t will jump up in response to the fall in η_t. Second, since $\dot{p}_t < 0$ for $t \in [0, T)$, $\dot{m}_t > 0$. It follows that real money balances follow the path illustrated in figure 17.9, panel d.

Of course, we have assumed that policymakers keep the policy rate i_t^m unchanged. But, interestingly, policy makers could lower i_t^m so as to maintain the $\dot{p}_t = 0$ locus constant. This would completely eliminate the asset price cycle! The reduction in i_t^m, which in and of itself would lead to higher demand for land, exactly matches the reduction in land demand caused by the fall in η_t. Figure 17.10 illustrates this case.

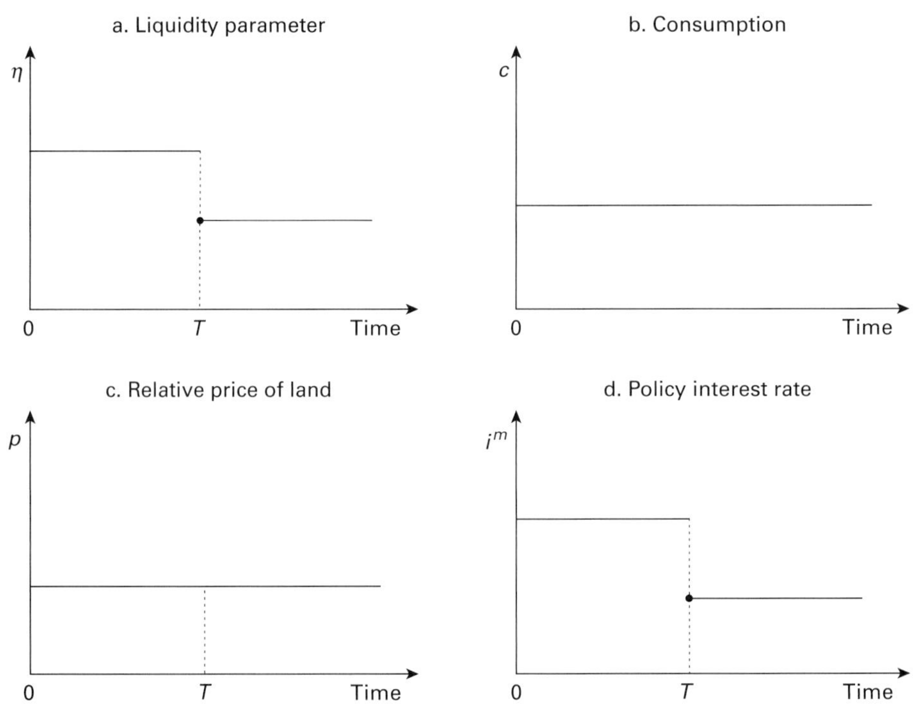

Figure 17.10
Countercyclical monetary policy

17.6 A Decoupling–Recoupling Model

As discussed in box 17.3, there is evidence that the financial crisis was associated with a decoupling–recoupling cycle. This section develops a model—due to Korinek, Roitman, and Végh (2010)—that can explain this phenomenon.

Consider a two-period model of an economy with a household that values consumption and supplies funds for production and two entrepreneurial sectors, labeled X and Z, that borrow from households and produce. Households receive a constant endowment y. This set–up can be interpreted as (1) a closed economy with two different sectors of production or (2) an open economy in which the world's households provide finance to two different countries or group of countries, X and Z. As will become clear below, a negative shock in sector X may be transmitted, positively or negatively, to sector Z. Hence, in the closed economy interpretation, we can think of the United States and sectors X and Z as the real estate and manufacturing sectors, respectively. In the open economy interpretation, we can think of the world's households as a common lender that provides finance to the United States (sector X) and emerging markets as a whole (sector Z).[25]

17.6.1 Households

Preferences are given by

$$U(c_1, c_2) = \log(c_1) + \beta \log(c_2), \tag{17.50}$$

where c_i, $i = 1, 2$, denotes consumption in period i and $\beta(> 0)$ is the discount factor.

The household's flow budget constraints for periods 1 and 2 are given by, respectively,

$$b_2 = (1 + r_1)b_1 + y - c_1, \tag{17.51}$$

$$0 = (1 + r_2)b_2 + y - c_2, \tag{17.52}$$

where b_i and r_i, $i = 1, 2$, are assets (i.e., loans) from households to entrepreneurs and an average real interest rate (more on this below), respectively. The term $(1 + r_1)b_1$ denotes repayments from entrepreneurs to households at the beginning of the first period.

Households choose $\{c_1, c_2, b_2\}$ so as to maximize lifetime utility—given by (17.50)—subject to constraints (17.51) and (17.52), taking as given r_1, r_2, and b_1. In terms of the Lagrangian,

$$\mathcal{L} = \log(c_1) + \beta \log(c_2) + \lambda_1 \left[(1 + r_1)b_1 + y - c_1 - b_2\right] + \lambda_2 \left[(1 + r_2)b_2 + y - c_2\right].$$

25. See Kaminsky, Reinhart, and Végh (2003) for evidence that episodes of contagion typically involve a common lender.

Box 17.3
The decoupling–recoupling phenomenon[a]

The trigger for the global financial meltdown of 2008 and 2009 was the crisis in the US subprime real estate sector.[b] The rise in US interest rates from about 1 to 5 percent between mid-2004 and 2006 combined with lax lending standards led to a wave of defaults on mortgages, particularly in the subprime sector, which resulted in a severe slowdown in the housing market. As illustrated in figure 17.11, panel a, housing starts peaked in early 2006 and fell dramatically thereafter.

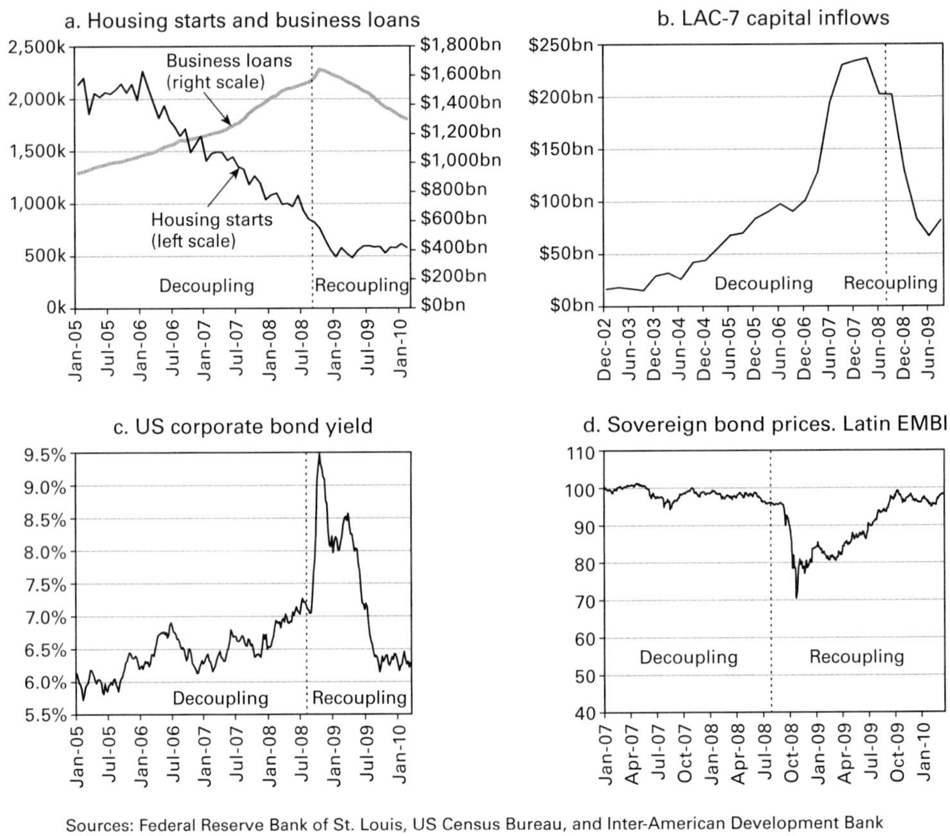

Figure 17.11
Decoupling–recoupling phenomenon

a. This box relies heavily on Korinek, Roitman, and Végh (2010). See also Izquierdo and Talvi (2009) and Dooley and Hutchison (2009).
b. The expression "subprime" loans (as opposed to prime loans) refers to those morgages that carried a high probability of default. Most of these loans were adjustable-rate mortgages and were often bundled together (i.e., securitized) with the purpose of diversifying risk.

Box 17.3
(continued)

At first (until around May 2008) the crisis unfolding in the subprime sector did not affect either the rest of the US economy or foreign countries, including emerging markets. Indeed, as indicated in figure 17.11, panel a, business loans in the United States continued to grow strongly throughout this period and, if anything, capital inflows to LAC-7 (the biggest economies in Latin America) increased more rapidly (panel b). Corporate yields and sovereign bond prices also remained relatively stable during this period (panels c and d). This "decoupling" period was viewed at the time as a validation of sound macroeconomic policies pursued by emerging countries during the 2000s. It was even argued that the world economy would weather any significant slowdown in the United States because emerging markets would become the world's "growth locomotive." Unfortunately, this "Panglossian" view of the world—to borrow the term from Izquierdo and Talvi (2009)—came to a screeching halt around May 2008 and particularly after "Lehman day" (September 15, 2008).[c] At that point, the crisis engulfed not only the US economy as a whole but spread around the world like wildfire. Corporate bond yields in the United States skyrocketed (panel c) and sovereign bond prices plummeted (panel d). In emerging countries the value of currencies and stock markets fell dramatically as well.

c. Panglossian view, after the eternally optimistic Dr. Pangloss in Voltaire's famous novel *Candide*.

First-order conditions are given by

$$\frac{1}{c_1} = \lambda_1,$$

$$\frac{\beta}{c_2} = \lambda_2,$$

$$\lambda_1 = \lambda_2(1 + r_2).$$

Combining the three first-order conditions, we obtain the Euler equation

$$\frac{c_2}{c_1} = \beta(1 + r_2). \tag{17.53}$$

Let us derive some partial equilibrium reduced forms that will be helpful for the subsequent analysis. Combining constraints (17.51) and (17.52), we obtain the household's lifetime budget constraint:

$$c_1 + \frac{c_2}{1 + r_2} = (1 + r_1)b_1 + y + \frac{y}{1 + r_2}. \tag{17.54}$$

Using (17.53) to solve for c_2 and substituting into (17.54), we obtain a partial-equilibrium reduced form for c_1:[26]

$$c_1 = \frac{1}{1+\beta}\left[(1+r_1)b_1 + y + \frac{y}{1+r_2}\right].$$

First-period consumption is thus a negative function of r_2. Hence from (17.51) it follows that b_2 (i.e., loans to entrepreneurs) are an increasing function of r_2, as one would expect. Formally,

$$b_2 = \underset{+}{\widetilde{b_2}(r_2)}. \tag{17.55}$$

Keep in mind that this upward-sloping supply of funds takes as given first-period repayments.

17.6.2 Entrepreneurs

Each entrepreneurial sector consists of a continuum of identical and risk-neutral entrepreneurs of mass 1. Each sector values their profits π^i, which they consume at the end of period 2, according to the linear utility function:[27]

$$U^i = \beta\pi^i, \qquad i = X, Z. \tag{17.56}$$

Let d_1^i be the initial debt obligation of a representative entrepreneur in sector i and r_1^i the corresponding real interest rate.[28] Each entrepreneur enters period 1 with a predetermined debt obligation of $(1+r_1^i)d_1^i$. Output in each of the two periods is given by

$$y_1^i = A_1^i F\left(k_1^i\right),$$

$$y_2^i = AF\left(k_2^i\right),$$

where A_1^i is a productivity parameter that can take values in $\left[0, \bar{A}\right]$, k_1^i is a predetermined level of capital that fully depreciates at the end of period 1, and $F(\cdot)$ is a decreasing returns-to-scale production function. Notice that we have assumed that in the second period the productivity parameter is the same across sectors.

Two scenarios arise here. If production is enough to repay the households, the entrepreneur does so and operates the firm in the second period as well. If production is not enough to repay

26. In general equilibrium, r_2 will be determined endogenously.

27. Note that each sector will consume its own production because there is only trade in risk-free bonds.

28. We index r_1^i by i because, even though this falls outside the scope of the model, different sectors could have faced different gross real interest rates in light of the possibility of default. In contrast, we assume no default in period 2, and hence there is a single real interest rate.

the households, the entrepreneur goes bankrupt and lenders (i.e., households) take possession of the entire output. Formally, then, the entrepreneur's repayment is given by

$$x_1^i = \min\left\{(1+r_1^i)d_1^i,\quad A_1^i F\left(k_1^i\right)\right\}.$$

If the entrepreneur continues to operate, his/her second-period profits are given by

$$\pi^i = AF\left(k_2^i\right) - (1+r_2)d_2^i, \tag{17.57}$$

where d_2^i is the entrepreneur's borrowing in the second period.

The entrepreneur's net worth at the end of period 1 (n_1^i) is given by

$$n_1^i = \max\left\{A_1^i F\left(k_1^i\right) - (1+r_1^i)d_1^i, 0\right\}.$$

Period-2 investment can be financed from either net worth or by borrowing

$$k_2^i = n_1^i + d_2^i. \tag{17.58}$$

Last, we assume that there is a moral hazard problem that limits borrowing on the part of entrepreneurs. After borrowing in period 1, entrepreneurs have a chance to run a scam that allows them to hide their period 2 income. Creditors have a legal recourse against this but can only recover at most a fraction $[\alpha/(1+\alpha)] \in (0,1)$ of the entrepreneur's total assets because of imperfect enforcement. As a result creditors (i.e., households) limit their lending to entrepreneurs to

$$d_2^i \leq \frac{\alpha}{1+\alpha} k_2^i.$$

Using (17.58), we can rewrite the last constraint as

$$d_2^i \leq \alpha n_1^i. \tag{17.59}$$

We are now ready to formulate the entrepreneur's maximization problem. Given the linear preferences (17.56), the entrepreneur chooses k_2^i and d_2^i to maximize profits, given by (17.57), subject to (17.58) and the borrowing constraint (17.59), for a given value of n_1^i. By solving for k_2^i from (17.58) and substituting it in (17.57), we can formulate the problem as choosing d_2^i to maximize

$$\mathcal{L} = \beta\left[AF\left(n_1^i + d_2^i\right) - (1+r_2)d_2^i\right] - \phi^i\left(d_2^i - \alpha n_1^i\right),$$

where ϕ^i is the multiplier associated with constraint (17.59). The first-order condition is given by

$$\beta AF'\left(n_1^i + d_2^i\right) = \beta(1+r_2) + \phi^i. \tag{17.60}$$

If the borrowing constraint is not binding (i.e., $\phi^i = 0$), then

$$AF'\left(k_2^i\right) = 1 + r_2.$$

This familiar condition defines k_2^i as a function solely of the economy wide real interest rate, r_2:

$$k_2^i = \widetilde{k_2}(\underset{-}{r_2}), \tag{17.61}$$

where $\widetilde{k_2}(.)$ is the inverse of the function $F'(.)$. The demand for loans in this case follows from (17.58) and (17.61):

$$d_2^i = \widetilde{k_2}(r_2) - n_1^i. \tag{17.62}$$

For further reference, notice that, for a given r_2, a reduction in net worth increases the demand for loans.

In this case profits are given by

$$\pi^i_{\text{unc}} = AF\left(\widetilde{k_2}(r_2)\right) - (1 + r_2)\left[\widetilde{k_2}(r_2) - n_1^i\right].$$

It follows that

$$\frac{\partial \pi^i_{\text{unc}}}{\partial n_1^i} = 1 + r_2 > 0,$$

$$\frac{\partial \pi^i_{\text{unc}}}{\partial r_2} = -\left[\widetilde{k_2}(r_2) - n_1^i\right] < 0,$$

where the last expression follows from the envelope theorem. Profits are increasing in net worth and decreasing in the real interest rate (as long as the entrepreneur is a net borrower). Intuitively, higher net worth reduces the borrowing needs and thus increases profits. A higher real interest rate increases second-period repayments thus reducing profits.

If the borrowing constraint binds (i.e., if $\phi^i > 0$), then it follows from (17.60) that $AF'\left(n_1^i + d_2^i\right) > 1 + r_2$. In other words, the marginal productivity of capital exceeds the market real interest rate because the entrepreneur cannot borrow as much as he/she would like. Since the borrowing constraint binds, borrowing is given by (from equation 17.59)

$$d_2^i = \alpha n_1^i. \tag{17.63}$$

The level of capital then follows from (17.58) and (17.63):

$$k_2^i = (1 + \alpha)\, n_1^i. \tag{17.64}$$

The capital stock is now independent of the real interest rate and depends only on entrepreneurial net worth. Substituting (17.63) and (17.64) into (17.57) yields

$$\pi^i_{\text{cons}} = AF\left((1 + \alpha)\, n_1^i\right) - \alpha(1 + r_2)n_1^i.$$

It follows that as in the unconstrained case,

$$\frac{\partial \pi^i_{\text{cons}}}{\partial n^i_1} = AF'\left((1+\alpha)\, n^i_1\right)(1+\alpha) - \alpha(1+r_2) > 0,$$

$$\frac{\partial \pi^i_{\text{cons}}}{\partial r_2} = -\alpha n^i_1 < 0,$$

where the sign of the first expression follows from the fact that $AF'\left((1+\alpha)\, n^i_1\right) > 1 + r_2$. Intuitively, if the entrepreneur is constrained, then an increase in net worth allows him/her to borrow more and make more profits because, at the margin, the marginal productivity of capital is higher than the cost of funds.

17.6.3 Equilibrium Conditions

Equilibrium in the loan market requires that the loans offered by the household equal the borrowing carried out by entrepreneurs:

$$b_2 = d^X_2 + d^Z_2.$$

17.6.4 Unconstrained Equilibrium

We will now characterize the economy's equilibrium as a function of A^X_1, which can vary in the range $[0, \bar{A}]$. We will assume that sector Z is always unconstrained. If productivity in sector X is sufficiently high—that is, $A^X_1 \geq A^X_{\text{unc}}$—then sector X is also unconstrained and the economy is governed by neo-classical considerations. The threshold A^X_{unc} is determined by the level of A^X_1 such that net worth, n^X_1, is just enough for the borrowing constraint (17.59) to hold as an equality for the first-best level of capital:

$$(1+\alpha)\, n^X_1 = \widetilde{k_2}(r_2).$$

Even a slightly lower value of A^X_1 would not allow the entrepreneur to borrow the amount needed to invest the first-best level of capital.

How does r_2 get determined? Figure 17.12 illustrates the market for loans. The supply of loans, which comes from the households and is given by (17.55), is an increasing function of r_2. The demand for loans from each sector, given by (17.62), and hence the aggregate demand for loans, is a decreasing function of r_2. The demand for loans takes n_1 as given. The intersection of supply and demand (point A in figure 17.12) depicts the equilibrium value of r_2.

Within this region, what happens if there is a fall in A^X_1? A lower A^X_1 reduces net worth, n^X_1, which in turn shifts the demand for loans to the right (see figure 17.12). The new equilibrium is

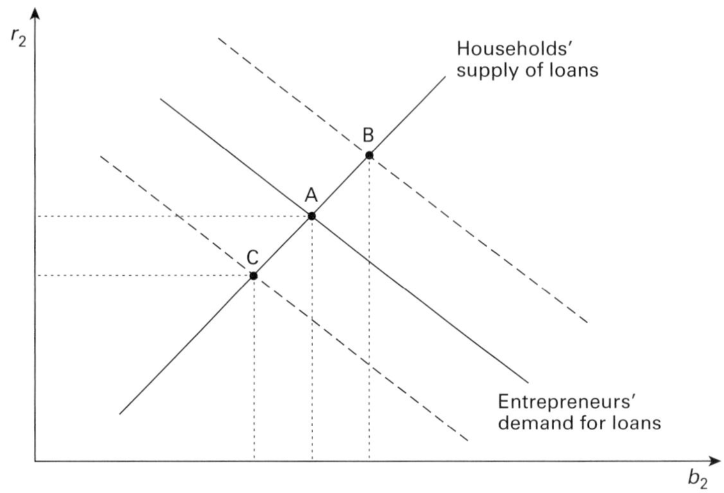

Figure 17.12
Decoupling

at point B, where r_2 is higher. A higher r_2 reduces profits in sector Z. Profits in sector X fall both because of the increase in r_2 and because of the fall in n_1^X. In other words, within this region the shock is transmitted positively (i.e., a negative shock to sector X implies a negative outcome for sector Z).

17.6.5 Decoupling

Suppose that A_1^X falls below A_{unc}^X but is above the level of A_1^X, denoted by A_{fail}^X, below which sector X's entrepreneur goes bankrupt.

Within this region, a fall in A_1^X reduces, as before, net worth (n_1^X). The fall in net worth implies that sector X's demand for loans falls for a given r_2 (recall equation 17.63). Since sector Z's demand for loans, however, continues to be given by (17.62) and is therefore a decreasing function of r_2, the aggregate demand for loans from entrepreneurs is still a decreasing function of r_2 and moves to the left in figure 17.12. In the new equilibrium, at point C, r_2 is lower. This helps sector Z whose profits increase as a result of the fall in r_2. Sector X will eventually hurt.[29] The shock is therefore transmitted negatively (i.e., there is decoupling).

29. There are two effects on the welfare of sector X (on the one hand, it is hurt by the binding constraint but, on the other hand, it benefits from the lower interest rate). As argued in Korinek, Roitman, and Végh (2010), however, the negative effect will always dominate eventually.

17.6.6 Recoupling

If A_1^X falls below A_{fail}^X, sector X goes bankrupt. Households receive a total repayment of $(1+r_1)d_1 = (1+r_1^Z)d_1^Z + A_1^X F\left(k_1^X\right)$. As A_1^X falls, this repayment falls, which makes households poorer. The supply of loans shifts to the left (figure 17.13), which increases the equilibrium value of r_2 (point B). This hurts sector Z. The shock is therefore transmitted positively (i.e., there is recoupling).

17.6.7 Illustration

Figure 17.14 provides a numerical illustration of the decoupling–recoupling cycle.[30] As we move from right to left, the value of A_1^X falls. In the right-most region (unconstrained), the shock is transmitted positively. The real interest rate increases, which also reduces profits in sector Z. As we enter the second region (decoupling), a fall in A_1^X leads to a lower real interest rate, which increases sector Z's profit. Sector X's profits eventually reach zero. In the last region (recoupling) the shock is transmitted positively: the real interest rate increases which reduces sector Z's profits. The model thus provides a plausible story for the recoupling–decoupling phenomenon discussed in box 17.3.[31]

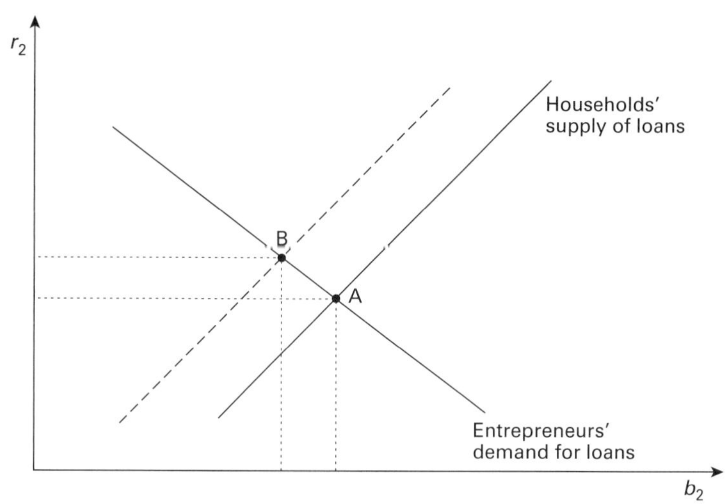

Figure 17.13
Recoupling

30. We use $F(k) = \sqrt{k}$ and the following parameter values: $\alpha = 0.5$, $y = 0$, $A = 1.2$, $A_1^Z = 1$, $k_1^i = 1$, and $(1+r_1)b_1 = 0.5$.

31. Strictly speaking, we have, of course, conducted comparative statics exercises. In reality, the decoupling–recoupling phenomenon is dynamic in nature. To truly capture this dynamic aspect, we would need to develop a multi-period version of this economy where a series of shocks to A_1^X progressively deplete sector X's net worth and pushes it into bankruptcy. This would greatly complicate the presentation without adding to the basic insights.

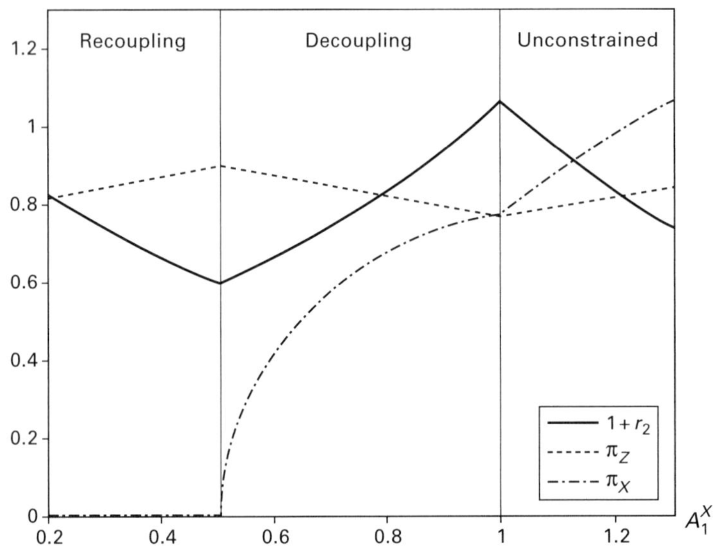

Figure 17.14
Decoupling and recoupling

17.7 A Twin-Crises Model

As box 17.4 discusses, the so-called twin crises (i.e., the simultaneous occurrence of both balance-of-payments and banking crises) have been an important theme in the empirical literature since Kaminsky and Reinhart's (1999) contribution. This section develops a micro-founded version of Velasco's (1987) early analysis, which provides a theoretical story consistent with the twin-crises phenomenon.[32] Formally, we can think of this model as endogenizing the exogenously given level of fiscal spending in chapter 16, section 16.4. A banking crisis will force the government to take over the private banks' foreign debt and service it. This debt service is financed with reserve losses and will eventually lead to a balance-of-payments (BOP) crisis.

Consider a small open economy. There are three agents in the economy: consumers, banks, and the government. The economy is perfectly integrated into world goods and capital markets (with an exception noted below involving an upper bound on banks' debt). The law of one price holds and the foreign price of the good is normalized to one.

As a guide to the presentation of the model, figure 17.15 presents a timeline of the main events that will take place, which will become clear as we proceed to analyze the different agents in this economy. At this point, however, it may help the reader to keep in mind that there will be three

32. See also Singh (2009) who links twin crises through asset prices and shows that in the presence of government bailouts and inflationary finance, the crises may be self-fulfilling.

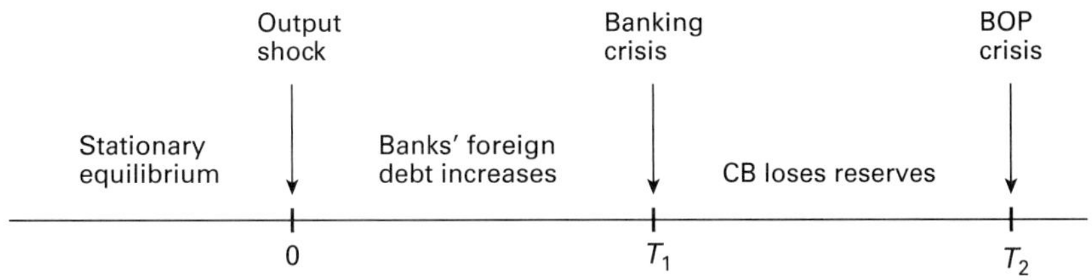

Figure 17.15
Timeline

critical junctures in the story: (1) an output shock at time 0, which will lead the banks to increase their foreign debt over time; (2) a banking crisis at T_1 (defined as banks reaching a debt limit), which forces the government to take over the banks' foreign debt and use international reserves to service it; and (3) a balance-of-payments crisis à la chapter 16 at T_2, as the government runs out of international reserves.

17.7.1 Consumers

The consumer's preferences are given by

$$\int_0^\infty [u(c_t) + v(m_t)]e^{-\beta t}dt, \tag{17.65}$$

where c_t denotes consumption of the only (tradable good) and m_t denotes real money balances in terms of tradable goods. Real financial assets, a_t, comprise net foreign bonds (b_t), domestic bank deposits (b_t^d), and real money balances:

$$a_t = b_t + b_t^d + m_t. \tag{17.66}$$

Consumers were originally endowed with a constant output stream, y. We assume that just before $t = 0$ consumers sold to the bank their claims to this endowment stream and got y/r worth of real domestic deposits in return. Hence

$$b_0^d = y/r.$$

Further the bank has committed to paying an interest rate of r on these deposits. Foreign bonds and domestic bonds are thus perfect substitutes in the consumer's portfolio.

The consumer's flow constraint reads as

$$\dot{a}_t = ra_t + \psi_t - c_t - i_t m_t + \tau_t^h, \tag{17.67}$$

where ψ_t are dividends from the bank (which is owned by households), i_t is the nominal interest rate, and τ_t^h are lump-sum transfers from the government.[33] Further, at time $T_1 > 0$, the household may receive a transfer from a foreign source (e.g., the World Bank, to fix ideas) with a present discounted value as of time 0 of Ω^h (more on this below). Integrating forward the flow constraint (17.67) and imposing the appropriate transversality condition, we obtain the consumer's lifetime constraint:

$$a_0 + \Omega^h + \int_0^\infty \left(\psi_t + \tau_t^h\right) e^{-rt} dt = \int_0^\infty (c_t + i_t m_t) e^{-rt} dt. \tag{17.68}$$

Consumers choose $\{c_t, m_t\}$ to maximize (17.65) subject to (17.68) for a given a_0.

The familiar first-order conditions are given by

$$u'(c_t) = \lambda, \tag{17.69}$$

$$v'(m_t) = \lambda i_t.$$

Combining these two first-order conditions yields a real money demand function with standard properties:

$$m_t = L(c_t, i_t). \tag{17.70}$$

17.7.2 Banks

Banks hold as assets the claims on the output flow (y/r) and net foreign bonds (f_t). As liabilities, they hold deposits. The representative bank's net worth (n_t) is therefore given by

$$n_t \equiv \frac{y}{r} + f_t - b_t^d. \tag{17.71}$$

The bank's flow budget constraint is given by

$$\dot{n}_t = rf_t + y - rb_t^d - \psi_t + \tau_t^b, \tag{17.72}$$

where ψ_t are dividends paid to the consumer and τ_t^b are transfers from the government.[34]

We will assume banks face a debt limit given by

$$f_t \geq -\Psi,$$

33. As we will show later, dividends will be zero in equilibrium. The transfers from the governments will be positive until time T_1 and zero afterward (see the discussion below).

34. As will become clear below, the transfers from the government will be positive in the event that a banking crisis occurs and the government needs to take over the servicing of banks' debt.

where $\Psi > 0$. By definition, we will speak of a "banking crisis" when the bank's debt $(-f_t)$ reaches the debt limit Ψ. The underlying idea is that creditors are willing to lend to domestic banks because there are implicit/explicit guarantees but, when the debt reaches a certain level, they become unwilling to do so as they fear that guarantees will not extend beyond that level. (As shown below and illustrated in figure 17.15, a banking crisis will occur in equilibrium at time T_1.)

Just before $t = 0$, $\tau_t^b = 0$ because no banking crisis is expected. We can then integrate flow constraint (17.72) for $t < 0$ to obtain

$$n_{0^-} = \int_0^\infty \psi_t e^{-rt} dt.$$

Since $n_{0^-} = y/r + f_0 - b_0^d$ and $y/r = b_0^d$ then (assuming, for simplicity, that $f_0 = 0$)

$$\int_0^\infty \psi_t e^{-rt} dt = 0.$$

Hence the PDV of banks' dividends is zero.

At $t = 0$ two unanticipated events take place that have an impact on the bank's budget constraint. First, the stream of output that the banks purchased from consumers falls from y to y^L, with $y > y^L$. Second, the bank becomes eligible to receive a contingent bailout from, say, the IMF, which can only be tapped in the event of a banking crisis. Since, as shown below, a banking crisis will occur at time $T_1 > 0$, this will be the date when the bailout resources become available. The value of the fund as of time T_1 is $\left(y - y^L\right)/r$.[35] The present discounted value as of time 0, denoted by Ω^b, is therefore

$$\Omega^b \equiv \left(\frac{y - y^L}{r}\right) e^{-rT_1}. \tag{17.73}$$

To derive the bank's lifetime constraint for $t \geq 0$, we integrate flow constraint (17.72)—taking into account that at $t = T_1$ the bank receives the contingent bailout from the IMF—to obtain

$$\int_0^\infty \psi_t e^{-rt} dt = n_0 + \Omega^b + \int_0^\infty \tau_t^b e^{-rt} dt, \qquad t \geq 0, \tag{17.74}$$

where (recall that $f_0 = 0$)

$$n_0 = \frac{y^L}{r} - b_0^d.$$

35. The reason for this particular value will become clear below.

The present discounted value as of time 0 of transfers from the government (see appendix 17.9) is assumed to be

$$\int_0^\infty \tau_t^b e^{-rt} dt = \left(\frac{y - y^L}{r}\right)(1 - e^{-rT_1}). \tag{17.75}$$

Intuitively, when the banking crisis occurs at time T_1 and the bank cannot service its debt any longer, the government takes over the bank's debt service. The expression above is simply the present discounted value (as of time 0) of the stream of interest payments on the bank debt that starts at time T_1.

Taking into account (17.75) and that $\Omega^b = \left[\left(y - y^L\right)/r\right] e^{-rT_1}$ and $y/r = b_0^d$, note that expression (17.74) reduces to

$$\int_0^\infty \psi_t e^{-rt} dt = 0.$$

Two remarks are called for. First, the bank's setup determines only the present discounted value of dividends, but the particular time path of dividends is undetermined. We will thus assume that banks pay constant and hence zero dividends over time, that is,

$$\psi_t = 0. \tag{17.76}$$

Second, given the dividend policy just assumed, the bank's behavior is completely mechanical in the sense that the bank has no choice variable to play with. Given its initial foreign assets, f_0, its contractual obligations, rb_t^d, and its dividend policy, the bank's flow constraint determines the change in net assets.

17.7.3 Government

The government's flow budget constraint takes the usual form:

$$\dot{h}_t = rh_t + \dot{m}_t + \varepsilon_t m_t - \tau_t^h - \tau_t^b \tag{17.77}$$

where h_t denotes international reserves, ε_t is the rate of devaluation, and $h_0 > 0$ is given.

The economy is initially operating under a fixed exchange rate regime. The regime will be sustainable until time T_1 when the banking crisis occurs. Up until T_1, the government's rate of domestic credit creation is zero (i.e., consistent with a fixed exchange rate). The fixed exchange rate and constant real money demand imply that $\dot{m}_t = \varepsilon_t m_t = 0$. Transfers to the bank, τ_t^b, will be zero for $0 \leq t < T_1$ (but positive for $t \geq T_1$ as explained below). Hence, for $0 \leq t < T_1$, the government's flow budget constraint (17.77) reduces to

$$\dot{h}_t = rh_t - \tau_t^h, \qquad 0 \leq t < T_1. \tag{17.78}$$

And since reserves will be constant and equal to h_0, we have that

$$\tau_t^h = rh_0, \qquad 0 \le t < T_1.$$

For $t \ge T_1$, transfers to households are assumed to be exogenous and equal to zero.

At time T_1, a banking crisis will occur and τ_t^b will become positive (at a level determined below) because the government takes over the bank and starts servicing its foreign debt. At time T_2, a balance-of-payments crisis will occur (recall figure 17.15) and reserves become depleted. Hence, starting at $t = T_2$, the government's flow budget constraint (17.77) becomes

$$\tau_t^b = \varepsilon_t m_t, \qquad t \ge T_2.$$

In other words, the government will be collecting the inflation tax from households and transferring these resources to the banks to service their debt.

17.7.4 Equilibrium Conditions

Perfect capital mobility implies that

$$i_t = r + \varepsilon_t.$$

We now derive the economywide constraints. Combining the flow constraints of the consumers, banks, and government—given, respectively, by (17.67), (17.72), and (17.77)—and taking into account (17.66) and (17.71), we obtain

$$\dot{b}_t + \dot{f}_t + \dot{h}_t = r(b_t + f_t + h_t) + y - c_t. \tag{17.79}$$

At time T_1 the economy receives one bailout from the IMF and another from the World Bank. The IMF gives Ω^b (expressed in time 0 terms) to the banks, given by (17.73). The World Bank gives Ω^h (expressed in time 0 terms) to the households, which, by assumption, is given by[36]

$$\Omega^h \equiv \left(\frac{y - y^L}{r}\right)(1 - e^{-rT_1}). \tag{17.80}$$

Since the economy receives these bailouts, we need to derive the resource constraint for both $t < 0$ and $t \ge 0$. Integrating (17.79) for $t < 0$ and imposing the appropriate transversality condition, we obtain

$$b_0 + h_0 + \frac{y}{r} = \int_0^\infty c_t e^{-rt} dt. \tag{17.81}$$

36. The reason for this assumption is technical as it allows private consumption to remain constant at time 0 and is not essential for the underlying story. In the absence of this grant, the same story would go through but the model would be more difficult to solve because private consumption would fall at time 0.

Integrating (17.79) for $t \geq 0$ and taking into account that at $t = T_1$ the economy receives (expressed in time 0 terms) Ω^b and Ω^h, we obtain

$$b_0 + h_0 + \frac{y^L}{r} + \Omega^b + \Omega^h = \int_0^\infty c_t e^{-rt} dt. \tag{17.82}$$

Substituting (17.73) and (17.80) into the last expression, we obtain

$$b_0 + h_0 + \frac{y}{r} = \int_0^\infty c_t e^{-rt} dt. \tag{17.83}$$

As a comparison of expressions (17.81) and (17.83) reveals, the economy's resource constraint does not change at $t = 0$. Intuitively, the bailouts received by the banks and households exactly compensate the economy for the loss in the PDV of output from y/r to y^L/r. The World Bank transfer to households compensates the economy for the output loss between 0 and T_1 and the IMF transfer to banks compensates the economy for the loss of output starting at T_1.

Within the economy there are transfers from both the government (i.e., the Central Bank) and households to banks. Specifically, the government takes over the banks at T_1 and services their debt thereafter, first by using international reserves and then, starting at T_2, by using the inflation tax. The inflation tax, of course, is paid by the households so this amounts to a transfer from households to banks.

17.7.5 Stationary Equilibrium

Let us characterize a PFEP for a constant value of ε_t. In particular, we will be thinking of this economy as having a fixed exchange rate (i.e., $\varepsilon_t = 0$). First-order condition (17.69) tells us that c_t will be constant along a PFEP. As usual, the resource constraint (17.81) allows us to pin down the level of consumption:

$$c = rb_0 + rh_0 + y. \tag{17.84}$$

Since $i_t = r$, real money demand—given by (17.70)—is also constant over time.

17.7.6 Permanent Fall in Output

Suppose that just before $t = 0$ the economy is in the stationary equilibrium described above (see figure 17.15 for an illustration of the model's timeline). At $t = 0$ there is an unanticipated and permanent reduction in the endowment (from y to y^L, $y > y^L$), as depicted in figure 17.16, panel a. Consumption will remain constant in the new PFEP and since the economy's resource constraint—now given by (17.83)—remains unchanged, the level of consumption continues to be given by (17.84), as illustrated in figure 17.16, panel b.

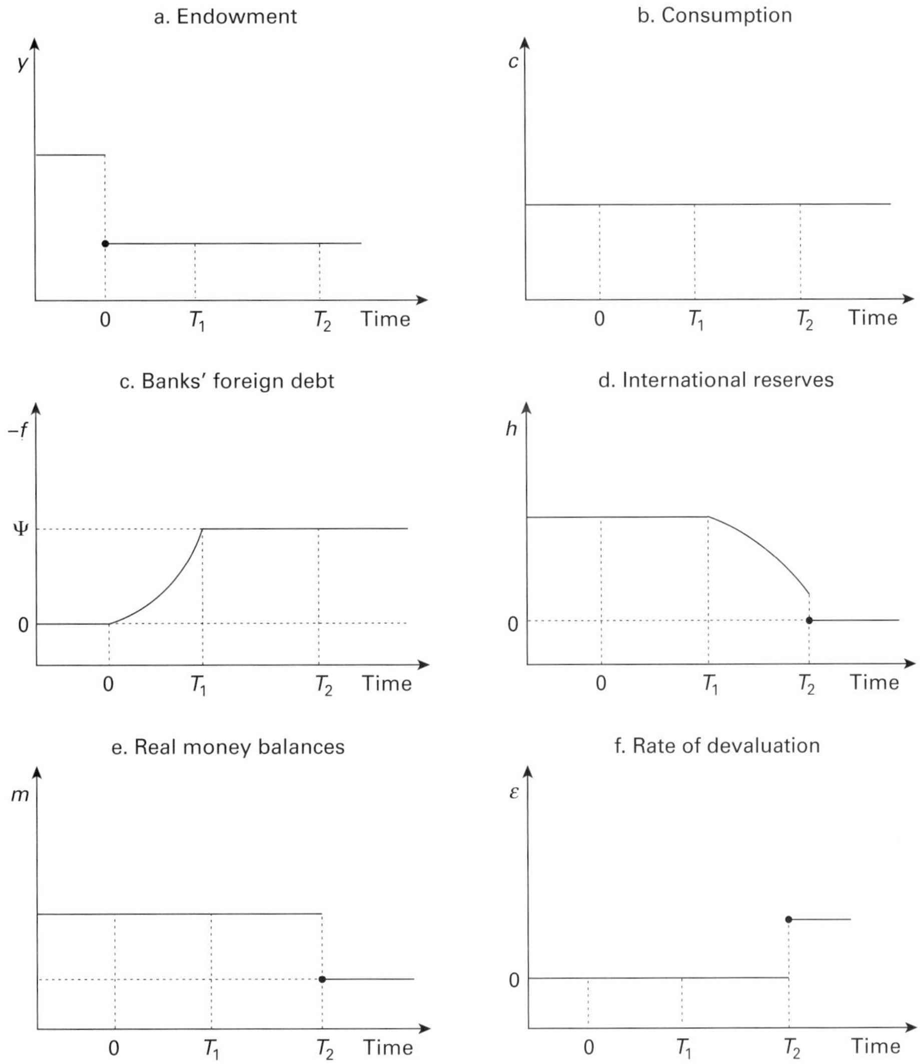

Figure 17.16
Twin crises in Velasco model

Banks have a contractual obligation to pay interest on their deposits, $rb_0^d (= y)$, even though the value of their assets has fallen to y^L/r. As a result banks begin to accumulate debt. To see this, and taking into account (17.71), the dividend policy (17.76), and the fact that $b_t^d = b_0^d$, rewrite (17.72) for $0 \leq t < T_1$ as

$$\dot{f}_t = rf_t + y^L - rb_0^d < 0. \tag{17.85}$$

This is an unstable differential equation. Further, at $t = 0$, equation (17.85) becomes

$$\dot{f}_0 = y^L - rb_0^d < 0. \tag{17.86}$$

Banks' net foreign assets thus begin to fall at $t = 0$ (i.e., debt begins to increase), as illustrated in figure 17.16, panel c. Since debt increases at an increasing rate, it will hit the debt limit, Ψ, in finite time. Let us denote by T_1 the point in time at which the banks' debt hits the debt limit. By definition, we will refer to this as a banking crisis, as indicated in the timeline illustrated in figure 17.15.

What is happening to international reserves between $t = 0$ and $t = T_1$? They remain constant, of course. Real money demand continues at the same level as before $t = 0$ because both consumption and the nominal interest rate are the same.

17.7.7 Banking Crisis

As established above, the bank's debt hits the debt ceiling at $t = T_1$, which, by definition, constitutes a banking crisis. We assume that the government takes over the bank, whose balance sheet at time T_1 looks like

$\frac{y^L}{r}$	b_0^d
$\Omega^b e^{rT_1}$	$-f_{T_1}$
	n_{T_1}

where Ω^b is given by (17.73). Since a crisis has occurred, the contingent bailout fund can now be tapped. This bailout fund will cover the gap between the bank's assets, y^L/r, and the present discounted value of its obligation to the depositors, $b_0^d = y/r$. In other words, $y^L/r + \Omega^b e^{rT_1} = b_0^d$. Taking this into account, we can rewrite the bank's balance sheet as

0	$-f_{T_1}$
	n_{T_1}

In other words, the banks' net worth is negative and equal to f_{T_1}. Hence, by taking over the bank, the government's net obligations become

$$-n_{T_1} = -f_{T_1} > 0.$$

The government thus takes over all of the bank's foreign debt. We will assume that the Central Bank's international reserves are not sufficient to cover this debt:

$$0 < h_0 < -f_{T_1}. \tag{17.87}$$

This leaves the government with no choice but to resort to money printing. Starting at time T_1, the government begins to transfer to the bank the resources necessary to service its debt. Formally, this constant level of transfers is given by

$$\tau^b = -rf_{T_1}, \qquad t \geq T_1. \tag{17.88}$$

17.7.8 Balance-of-Payments Crisis

Starting at $t = T_1$, we are back to the world of balance-of-payments crises analyzed in chapter 16. Since both consumption and the nominal interest rate are constant, real money demand is constant as well. Hence $\dot{m}_t = 0$ and, of course, $\varepsilon_t = 0$. The government's flow constraint (17.77) thus reduces to (recall that $\tau_t^h = 0$ for all $t \geq T_1$)

$$\dot{h}_t = rh_t - \tau^b. \tag{17.89}$$

Given that, by (17.87), reserves are not enough to cover the service of the debt, $rh_{T_1} - \tau^b < 0$. Hence $\dot{h}_{T_1} < 0$. Further, since (17.89) is an unstable differential equation, it follows that the level of reserves will hit the lower bound of zero in finite time. Denote this point in time by T_2 (see the timeline in figure 17.15). At time T_2 the government runs out of international reserves and needs to abandon the peg.

Starting at $t = T_2$, the government will need to finance the deficit with the inflation tax. Let ε_{T_2} denote this constant rate of devaluation. From the government's budget constraint (17.77) and (17.88), it follows that

$$\varepsilon_{T_2} m_{T_2} = -rf_{T_1}, \tag{17.90}$$

where m_{T_2} is given by

$$m_{T_2} = L(c, r + \varepsilon_{T_2}). \tag{17.91}$$

If the real money demand is inelastic, equation (17.90) has a unique solution, as discussed in section 16.4 of chapter 16. We can then solve for T_2 using the government's intertemporal budget constraint. Specifically, integrate forward the government's budget constraint (17.77) for $t \geq T_1$ to obtain

$$\frac{\tau^b}{r} = h_0 + \frac{e^{-r(T_2-T_1)}}{r}\left[\varepsilon_{T_2} m_{T_2} - r(m_{T_1} - m_{T_2})\right]. \tag{17.92}$$

The LHS of this expression says that, starting at $t = T_1$, the PDV of government spending is τ^b/r. The RHS indicates the sources of financing: the stock of international reserves at time T_1, given by h_0, plus the PDV of inflation tax revenues that begin to accrue at time $t = T_2$ minus the discrete loss in international reserves that will take place at $t = T_2$.[37]

Solving for T_2 from (17.92), we obtain

$$T_2 = T_1 + \frac{1}{r} \log \left[\frac{\varepsilon_{T_2} m_{T_2} - r(m_{T_1} - m_{T_2})}{\tau^b - rh_0} \right].$$

In sum, this model offers a plausible story for the twin crises phenomenon. In the model—as in the data (see box 17.4)—the banking crisis precedes the balance-of-payments crisis. The source of the crisis, however, goes back to the negative output shock at $t = 0$. Ideally, consumers should reduce consumption permanently in response to this shock. But, due to the deposit guarantee, consumers do not internalize this social loss and continue to consume at the pre-shock level. The fall in banks' assets, coupled with unchanged liabilities, forces banks to become indebted and eventually hit the debt ceiling. The government's takeover of banks in turn sows the seeds for an eventual balance-of-payments crisis.

17.8 Final Remarks

This chapter has analyzed various aspects of financial crises, many inspired by the recent global financial crisis. Just by looking at the very simple arithmetics of leverage, we saw that if, say, the leverage ratio is 40, a fall in the price of the underlying asset of only 2.5 (100/40) percent is enough to completely wipe out the financial institution's net worth. The incentive to invest with borrowed money, however, is very large because the higher the leverage, the higher is the return on equity. We then analyzed the fundamental determinants of leverage in a simple model and concluded that all else equal, leverage will be higher, the higher the expected productivity is, the lower uncertainty is, and the lower risk aversion is. To the extent that these three factors were present during the 2000s, we should have expected a more leveraged economy. Needless to say, it is likely that leverage ratios had already reached levels beyond what could be explained by fundamentals, particularly due to borrowing externalities and other systemic risk frictions that are not internalized by economic agents, so corrective policy actions might have been called for.[38] In addition we saw how the presence of leverage constraints, which may depend on the price of the assets themselves, can amplify the effects of negative shocks.

We then analyzed how the increased "liquidity" associated with real assets (e.g., through CDOs and other asset-backed securities) could have contributed to higher asset prices and, consequently,

37. Notice that since $\dot{h}_t = 0$ for $0 \leq t < T_1$, we have $h_{T_1} = h_0$.

38. See, for example, Caballero and Krishnamurthy (2003), Lorenzoni (2008), Korinek (2009), Bianchi (2011), and Jeanne and Korinek (2010).

Box 17.4
The twin crises

In a highly influential contribution, Kaminsky and Reinhart (1999) studied the interaction between banking and currency crises. The authors conducted an empirical analysis covering episodes in both advanced and developing countries for the period 1970 to 1995 (in addition to the Asian crises of 1997).[a] Their goal was to (1) draw inferences about any possible causal patterns and (2) identify common macroeconomic patterns around the financial crises to understand up to which point they were predictable. Table 17.2 shows the frequency distribution of currency and banking crises.

In order to study the extent to which banking and currency crises are linked, the authors first calculated the unconditional probability of either of these crises taking place in their sample. They then calculated different conditional probabilities. The idea is that if, for example, knowing that a banking crisis took place within the past 24 months helps predict a currency crisis, then the probability of a currency crisis conditional on a banking crisis should be greater than the unconditional probability of a currency crisis.

Table 17.3 shows that knowing that a banking crisis took place increases the probability that a currency crisis will unfold: the unconditional probability of a currency crisis is 29 percent, whereas the probability conditional on the beginning of a banking crisis is 46 percent. Moreover a banking crisis is more likely to take place after financial liberalization and the peak of a banking crisis usually follows a BOP crisis.

In terms of the main findings of the paper, Kaminsky and Reinhart show that the twin crises are a phenomenon of the 1980s and 1990s, but not of the 1970s when financial markets were repressed. The general timing of the crises that they are able to identify is as follows: the beginning of a banking crisis

Table 17.2
Number of crises

	Number of crises					
	1970–1995		1970–1979		1980–1995	
Type of crisis	Total	Average per year	Total	Average per year	Total	Average per year
Balance of payments	76	2.92	26	2.6	50	3.13
Twin	19	0.73	1	0.1	18	1.13
Single	57	2.19	25	2.5	32	2.00
Banking	26	1.00	3	0.3	23	1.44

Source: Kaminsky and Reinhart (1999).
Note: Episodes in which the beginning of a banking crisis is followed by a BOP crisis within 48 months are classified as twin crises.

a. Currency crises are identified using an index of currency market turbulence, which consists of a weighted average of exchange rate changes and reserve changes. The beginning of a banking crisis is defined to take place if either there are "bank runs that lead to the closure, merging, or takeover by the public sector of one or more financial institutions (as in Venezuela 1993)" or, absent runs, in the presence of "the closure, merging, takeover, or large-scale government assistance of an important financial institution (or group of institutions) that marks the start of a string of similar outcomes for other financial institutions (as in Thailand 1996–1997)." (The reader is referred to the Kaminsky–Reinhart paper for more details.)

Box 17.4
(continued)

Table 17.3
Probabilities of balance-of-payments and banking crises

Probabilities of balance-of-payments crises		Probabilities of banking crises	
Type	Probability (%)	Type	Probability (%)
Unconditional	29	Unconditional	10
Conditional on the beginning of a banking crisis	46	Beginning of a banking crisis conditional on a BOP crisis	8
Conditional on the peak of a banking crisis	22	Beginning of a banking crisis conditional on financial liberalization	14
		Peak of a banking crisis conditional on a BOP crisis	16

Source: Kaminsky and Reinhart (1999).

precedes the currency crisis which, in turn, precedes the peak of the banking crisis. There is a vicious circle: problems in the financial sector weaken the currency and devaluations, in turn, aggravate the existing problems in the banking sector. However, the authors are careful to point out that banking crises cannot be taken as the immediate cause of currency crises. There are common macroeconomic fundamentals deteriorating, which implies to some extent that which crisis takes place first is a matter of circumstance.

This paper has not only led to a vast literature (both theoretical and empirical) that further studies the interactions between different types of crises (e.g., Chang and Velasco 2001, and Demirgüç-Kunt and Detragiache 1998, 1999) but has also spanned the "early warning literature," which attempts to identify variables that exhibit an unusual behavior before a crisis (e.g., see Kaminsky, Lizondo, and Reinhart 1998).

to the crisis itself. This model also gave a role to monetary policy. In our simple world a reduction in the policy interest rate at the time of the potential bust can in fact prevent the boom–bust cycle in asset prices altogether.

Another fascinating stylized fact that emerged out of the recent financial crisis was the decoupling–recoupling phenomenon. When the subprime mortgage crisis first surfaced, other sectors in the United States and certainly emerging countries continued to perform strongly. It was only after Lehman's fall in September 2008 that the crisis became widespread. We developed a model that can explain this phenomenon. At first, a negative shock to the sector (country) in question leads to a fall in the demand for credit and hence a fall in real interest rates, which benefits other sectors (countries). A larger shock, however, may bankrupt the affected sector, negatively affecting the owners' (households') wealth and reducing the supply of credit, leading to an increase in real interest rates.

Finally, we presented a model that can account for the dynamics behind the so-called twin crises (i.e., the simultaneous occurrence of both banking and balance-of-payments crises). In a world where deposits are guaranteed, a negative shock to the banks' assets forces them to borrow externally to service their domestic deposits. Once they hit a debt limit, the government takes over and needs to service the external debt. It can only do so by resorting to printing money, which sows the seeds for a balance-of-payments crisis.

17.9 Appendix: Transfers from Government to Banks in Twin-Crises Model

In the model of section 17.7, the PDV of interest payments as of time T_1 is assumed to be equal to the bank's debt as of time T_1. The source of the bank debt between time 0 and time T_1 lies in the fact that the bank is required to pay y to depositors while receiving a resource flow of only y^L, $y^L < y$. Formally, the bank's debt as of time T_1 is given by

$$f_{T_1} = e^{rT_1} \int_0^{T_1} \left(y - y^L\right) e^{-rt} dt,$$

which can be expressed as

$$f_{T_1} = \left(\frac{y - y^L}{r}\right) (e^{rT_1} - 1).$$

The PDV as of time 0 of the bank's debt is thus obtained by multiplying both sides of this expression by e^{-rT_1}. The resulting right-hand side is the PDV as of time 0 of government's transfers to banks, as expressed in equation (17.75).

Exercises

1. (Maximum leverage ratio in model of section 17.3) Consider the model of section 17.3. Assume that $b_1 = 0$ and $A_1 = A_2^L = 1$. Show that leverage ratio tends to $(1 + r)/(1 + r - A_2^L)$ as the degree of risk aversion tends to zero.

2. (Alternative collateral constraint in the model of section 17.4) Consider the model of section 17.4. Solve the model for the case where the collateral constraint takes the form

$$d \leq \phi \ell_2 p.$$

How do results change?

3. (Multiplicity of equilibria in the model of section 17.4) Consider the model of section 17.4. Assume that period 1 utility is logarithmic and that the economy is operating in the constrained equilibrium. Determine under what conditions multiplicity of equilibria arises.

References

Bianchi, Javier. 2011. Overborrowing and systemic externalities in the business cycle. *American Economic Review* 101(7): 3400–26.

Caballero, Ricardo, and Arvind Krishnamurthy. 2003. Excessive dollar debt: Financial development and underinsurance. *Journal of Finance* 58 (2): 867–94.

Calvo, Guillermo A. 2009. Financial crises and liquidity shocks: A bank-run perspective. Working Paper 15425. National Bureau of Economic Research, Cambridge, MA.

Case, Karl E., and Robert J. Shiller. 2003. Is there a bubble in the housing market? *Brookings Papers on Economic Activity* (Fall): 299–342.

Chang, Roberto, and Andrés Velasco. 2001. A model of financial crises in emerging markets. *Quarterly Journal of Economics* 116 (2): 489–517.

Cochrane, John. 2009. Why did Paul Krugman get it so wrong? Unpublished manuscript. Chicago Business School.

Demirgüç-Kunt, Asli, and Enrica Detragiache. 1998. The determinants of banking crises in developing and developed countries. *IMF Staff Papers* 45 (1): 81–109.

Demirgüç-Kunt, Asli, and Enrica Detragiache. 1999. Financial liberalization and financial fragility. In Boris Pleskovic and Joseph Stiglitz, eds., *Annual World Bank Conference on Development Economics* 1998. Washington DC: World Bank. 303–31.

Dooley, Michael P., and Michael M. Hutchison. 2009. Transmission of the U.S. subprime crisis to emerging markets: Evidence on the decoupling–recoupling hypothesis. Working Paper 15120. National Bureau of Economic Research, Cambridge, MA.

Fisher, Irving. 1933. The debt-deflation theory of great depressions. *Econometrica* 1 (4): 337–57.

Glaeser, Edward L., Joshua D. Gottlieb, and Joseph Gyourko. 2010. Can cheap credit explain the housing boom? Working Paper 16230. National Bureau of Economic Research, Cambridge, MA.

Greenspan, Alan. 2010. The crisis. *Brookings Papers on Economic Activity* (Spring): 201–46.

Izquierdo, Alejandro, and Ernesto Talvi. 2009. *Policy Trade-offs for Unprecedented Times.* Washington, DC: Inter-American Development Bank.

Jeanne, Olivier, and Anton Korinek. 2010. Excessive volatility in capital flows: A Pigouvian taxation perspective. *American Economic Review, Papers and Proceedings* 100 (2): 403–70.

Kaminsky, Graciela L., and Carmen M. Reinhart. 1999. The twin crises: The causes of banking and balance-of-payments problems. *American Economic Review* 89 (3): 473–500.

Kaminsky, Graciela L., Carmen M. Reinhart, and Carlos A. Végh. 2003. The unholy trinity of financial contagion. *Journal of Economic Perspectives* 17 (4): 51–74.

Kaminsky, Graciela, Saul Lizondo, and Carmen M. Reinhart. 1998. Leading indicators of currency crises. *IMF Staff Papers* 45 (1): 1–48.

Korinek, Anton. 2009. Excessive dollar borrowing in emerging markets: Amplification effects and macroeconomic externalities. Manuscript. University of Maryland.

Korinek, Anton, Agustin Roitman, and Carlos A. Végh. 2010. Decoupling and Recoupling. *American Economic Review, Papers and Proceedings* 100 (2): 393–97.

Krugman, Paul. 2009. How did economists get it so wrong? *New York Times Magazine.* September 2, 2009.

Lorenzoni, Guido. 2008. Inefficient credit booms. *Review of Economic Studies* 75 (3): 809–33.

Singh, Rajesh. 2009. Asset prices and twin crises. *Journal of International Money and Finance* 28: 26–55.

Taylor, John. 2007. Housing and monetary policy. Working Paper 13682. National Bureau of Economic Research, Cambridge, MA.

Taylor, John. 2009. *Getting off Track: How Government Actions and Interventions Caused, Prolonged, and Worsened the Financial Crisis.* Hoover Institution Press Publication 570. Stanford, CA: Hoover Institution Press. Stanford University. California.

Velasco, Andrés. 1987. Financial crises and balance of payments crises. *Journal of Development Economics* 27 (1–2): 263–83.

Index